Praise for
The Bloomsbury Anthology of Transcendental Thought

"In this unique and timely collection, David LaRocca offers us a thoughtful reminder that the very possibility and urgent task of thinking, of our acting and judging, ethics and politics, rests upon a willing exposure to an aspect of our everyday and ordinary experience that is hard to grasp and eludes most, perhaps all, epistemic criteria. Metaphysicians, mystics, and moral perfectionists of all stripes have called this 'the transcendental,' thus risking the fatal misunderstanding that this means only 'the transcendent,' leading to the dualist assumption that we are citizens of two separate (earthly and heavenly) cities or (phenomenal and noumenal) worlds. Yet the truth is far more simple, if much harder to accept and then also live by. We are what we are, here and now. Yet we're not, therefore, irrevocably bound by what thus is said 'to be'—much less by the proverbial powers that will always be—in what we can still further imagine and aim or hope for, against the odds, as it were. In this brilliantly edited and introduced anthology, LaRocca presents us with the broadest selection of authors, philosophers, visionaries, and artists, who have expressed this simple, difficult truth and freedom in the most profound and varied of ways."

—HENT DE VRIES, *Russ Family Professor in the Humanities*
and Philosophy, Johns Hopkins University, USA,
and Director of The School of Criticism and Theory,
Cornell University, USA

"*The Bloomsbury Anthology of Transcendental Thought* brings together an excellent selection of texts from several philosophical perspectives on the question of the transcendental, demonstrating the complexity of the concept's meaning, its rich and often contradictory histories. Edited with great erudition and care by David LaRocca, the collection will be an indispensable handbook for anybody researching the heritage of that tradition."

—BRANKA ARSIĆ, *Professor of English and Comparative Literature,*
Columbia University, USA

"The concept of the transcendental is often invoked in philosophy and literature, but until now its history has been neglected. This volume, bringing together a variety of writings from different disciplines and different traditions, allows us to begin to reflect on the character of this elusive concept. In that sense, this volume is more than an overview of a field of study—it is participating in the creation of one."

—TODD MAY, *Class of 1941 Memorial Professor of the Humanities, Clemson University, USA*

"In the editor's own words, this anthology is at once 'essential' and 'impossible,' since it portends to give textual shape to a topic that has defied the entire tradition of Western philosophy, which concerns the very question from which all philosophizing begins, i.e., the transcendental. In taking up this task, LaRocca assumes more the guise of a curator than an editor, and provides us with a veritable *Kunstkammer*, that is, a cabinet of curiosities, a theater of memory, a world theater of philosophers, artists, and writers from all ages who have addressed the transcendental as a constant and elemental aspect of philosophy and life."

—GREGG LAMBERT, *Dean's Professor of Humanities, Syracuse University, USA*

"A splendid collection of some of the deepest thoughts of which humans are capable. The book is full of insights and surprises."

—JOHN LACHS, *Centennial Professor of Philosophy, Vanderbilt University, USA*

The Bloomsbury Anthology of Transcendental Thought

AUTHORED, EDITED, AND COEDITED BOOKS BY DAVID LaROCCA

On Emerson

Emerson's Transcendental Etudes by Stanley Cavell

The Philosophy of Charlie Kaufman

Estimating Emerson: An Anthology of Criticism from Carlyle to Cavell

Emerson's English Traits and the Natural History of Metaphor

The Philosophy of War Films

A Power to Translate the World: New Essays on Emerson and International Culture

The Philosophy of Documentary Film: Image, Sound, Fiction, Truth

The Bloomsbury Anthology of Transcendental Thought

From Antiquity to the Anthropocene

Edited by David LaRocca

Bloomsbury Academic

An imprint of Bloomsbury Publishing Inc

B L O O M S B U R Y

NEW YORK · LONDON · OXFORD · NEW DELHI · SYDNEY

Bloomsbury Academic

An imprint of Bloomsbury Publishing Inc

1385 Broadway	50 Bedford Square
New York	London
NY 10018	WC1B 3DP
USA	UK

www.bloomsbury.com

BLOOMSBURY and the Diana logo are trademarks of Bloomsbury Publishing Plc

First published 2017

Introductory material and compilation © David LaRocca, 2017

Library of Congress Cataloging-in-Publication Data

A catalog record for this book is available from the Library of Congress.

ISBN: HB: 978-1-5013-0556-6
PB: 978-1-5013-0555-9
ePub: 978-1-5013-0557-3
ePDF: 978-1-5013-0558-0

Cover design: Catherine Wood

Typeset by Deanta Global Publishing Services, Chennai, India
Printed and bound in the United States of America

Dedicated, with love, to my mother,
da dove provengo
Frances LaRocca
in sintonia con le leggi mistica dell'universo

Contents

Introduction

David LaRocca

Defying Definition: Opening Remarks on the Transcendental

THE BLOOMSBURY ANTHOLOGY OF TRANSCENDENTAL THOUGHT aspires to provide a luminous, coruscating assembly of representative excerpts—from antiquity to the anthropocene—that explore the varied meanings and manifold forms of the "transcendental." Ideally, the reader will find a book in hand that serves many needs at once: a convenient and reliable academic resource, a repository of philosophical and literary marvels, and an edifying and indelible spiritual companion. Here, then, is a library-as-conversation addressing *what we mean when we say (or allude to the) transcendental*—a perennial, shared preoccupation of widespread human significance.

The word "transcendental," though it enjoys prominent and prevalent use, is also as ambiguously and contentiously defined as the name "philosophy" itself. There are as many instances, invocations, and intimations of the concept as there are definitions on offer for it. Every generation of thinkers evinces an attempt to clarify, apply, and lay claim to an interpretation of transcendental thought—beginning in earnest in the antiquity of Greece but discernible in other traditions elsewhere and elsewhen (such as in Africa, Arabia, Scandinavia, India, the Trans-Himalayas, China, Japan, Aboriginal Australia, pre-colonial New Zealand and Oceania, and the pre-Columbian Americas, and including myriad tribes and collectives representing less dominant, more regionally circumscribed intellectual histories[1]), and continuing through to our own time of widespread, instantaneous global connectivity paired with uncanny, simulated simultaneity. The volume in hand is a collection meant to reflect something of the diverse ways the category and concept have been characterized over the course of two-and-a-half millennia. In the chronological presentation of these works, there is a hope to lend some perspective to the abiding importance of the transcendental for philosophical, religious, and literary thinking and also some sense of the complexity, richness, and continued relevance of the contested term.

What *is* transcendental thought, you ask? If I had a ready-to-hand definition, as I might for some empirically oriented question (what is the distance between x and y, what happens when chemical compounds p and q interact), I would gladly relay it on the occasion of introducing a volume aimed at anthologizing evocative and emblematic remarks on or about or approaching the transcendental. As things stand, as the reasoning for which, in what follows, will hopefully make clear, asking this question is a significant part of articulating any reply. Transcendental thought, that is to say, is decidedly reflexive for it demands that we think about something that may not be thinkable; it is among our most hearty and enduring metaphilosophies. To forestall the worry that "transcendental thought" is, in practice, or even in fact, an oxymoron, we must, it seems, acknowledge reflexivity as one of its inherently useful and meaningful attributes.

Friedrich Schiller crystalized an expression, poetic and rhyming no less, that explaining (or trying to define) is often a fruitless task ("a lot of talking doesn't do it"), but finding a satisfying *example* may "bring things—or you—to the light" [*Nur ein Beispiel fuehrt zum Licht / Vieles Reden tut est nicht*].[2] At first blush Schiller's bifurcation may seem a tad anti-intellectual, but one must keep in mind that the ordering is important: first an example, *then* an account of the example. We can do a lot of talking, but having an example beforehand—and before us—will make all the difference. Likewise, and very fitting for his temperament, we find Aristotle many centuries earlier saying: "For to gain light on things imperceptible we must use the evidence of sensible things."[3] Since the stated object of the current collection is, we might say, one of these "things imperceptible," I have adopted a methodology in editing this volume that turns to the "evidence of sensible things"—to texts of a certain sense and sensibility that are, in Schiller's poetic invocation, "examples"—or what Carlyle or Emerson or Nietzsche might call textual "exemplars." In taking up the role of curator, I have aimed to select some of the most representative specimens from some of the most relevant species. For if the term "transcendental" will be defined less by explanation and more by example (or "description" in Wittgenstein's terminology), then selection *is*, in large measure, the explanation. And so an introduction, such as this, will become less a terminological disquisition or defense (*apologia*) and more a curator's excursus on *the why of what* is included.

The claim that "transcendental thought" cannot be quickly defined is not, I assure you, a bid for cleverness (much less a bit of it!), but an admission that the phrase itself is a created one—not a denotation of categorical or canonical precedent, but a way of describing what appears to be a matter of proclivity, tradition, habit, a set of preoccupying concerns, even an outlook—or in a superannuated term—temperament. As such, the title is observational (that is, taking note of a common feature of intellectual concern), but also suggestive, allusive, and perhaps for those reasons also illusive. For the purposes of this book, and beyond it—for a general readership as well as one already familiar with the terms and the debates it implies—this is potentially a good thing, so it reminds everyone that we are *participating* in the development of a canon, not merely reacting to one we have passively inherited (or one that we feel compelled to accept, defend, or resist). Unlike subjects such as ethics or aesthetics, classics of rhetoric from pagan antiquity, or contemporary works of conceptual art, all of which have received broad inter- and trans-disciplinary attention, and as a result enjoy well-defined canons of texts, field-defining questions, governing parameters, and the like (if not also uncontested), transcendental thought, such as we are using the term here, has not shared that attention and thus lacks a comparatively clear and established canon, set of questions, and parameters.

* * * *

The terms "transcendental" and "transcendentalism" enjoy a certain degree of cultural prominence in Western thought owing to variegated trends that nevertheless share a root term: from Immanuel Kant's transcendental idealism to Ralph Waldo Emerson's contribution to New England (or American) Transcendentalism, and more recently, techniques such as transcendental meditation (albeit drawn from ancient ritual practices and presuppositions). Frederic Chopin modified the title of his compositional "studies" so that they are understood to be transcendental *études*. Later, Stanley Cavell found reason to draw from the virtuosity of Chopin's achievement—and its connotations—to describe his own studies of Emerson in a fitting double entendre.[4] Film scholar and director Paul Schrader proposed a reading of the "transcendental style" of cinema directors Yasujirô Ozu, Robert Bresson, and Carl Dreyer.[5] And I could go on with further variations and permutations, yet even this cursory list reminds us, more accurately admonishes us, to temper any eager desire to consolidate a fixed, uniform, limited, or monolithic meaning for the word "transcendental." Instead, a more productive and ultimately more rewarding approach (the one hopefully in evidence in the selections that follow) will involve a certain amount of movement and flexibility with the term—a willingness to shift from excerpt to excerpt, text to text, time to time, author to author, and see the same word (or its synonyms, cognates, and euphemisms) employed in ways that illuminate shared features as well as distinct traits. We would not, then, read the present anthology to know what one thing or definition the transcendental refers to, but, instead, to what *constellation* of thought we find ourselves within.

Given limitations of space, we will not have occasion to include writing on transcendental meditation or transcendental filmmaking, and other inflections, but instead will focus on the domain of "transcendental thought" in so far as it finds expression in a certain cluster of work drawn from the sprawling, multiform incarnations we encounter in the humanities, though mainly emerging from texts populating the history of philosophy, religion, literature, and poetry—as well as private expressions of the same (as in journal entries and autobiographical remarks) and more public declarations (such as in lectures and sermons).

Despite the durability, and in some cases popularity and influence, enjoyed by many of the pieces adduced in the table of contents, this volume is, based on my research, a first-of-its-kind and thus also a one of a kind. No book like this exists on the market, nor has there ever been such a book. I mention this not as a boast (for in making the claim I must fear there *is* such a book I have missed or failed to find), but as a point informing the methodology and modus operandi behind assembling the collection. In editing other books, for instance, on Emerson or transnational studies or war films or documentary film, I had the benefit of many fine volumes created by others, all aiming at the same or similar objects; the goal for my interventions (as I was endeavoring to contribute to a region of inquiry) was to distinguish the selections (e.g., by means of the newness and vitality of the research, or by way of helpful critical apparatus) from what was already available. But in the present case, there is a clear sense that a canon had to be formed, as if from the ground up, as if from *a* to *z*, from Aristotle to Žižek.

Allow me, then, to clarify what I mean by there being no such book as this. Despite the existence of volumes that take up a narrower focus on transcendental ideas, say, in relation to a specific thinker or writer (e.g., Plato, Kant, Hegel, or Heidegger—as with *Transcendental Heidegger*), or a period or domain (e.g., as in *Transcendental Philosophy and Naturalism*, or *Transcendental Ontology*), no single resource exists of formally diverse, chronologically expansive, geographically wide-ranging selections of prominent remarks on the broad scope of the transcendental as we encounter it in philosophy, religion, and literature.[6] By this concatenation, I mean to mark out (1) not only a temporally significant range, albeit for many readers in Western culture, an admittedly familiar way of marking out an intellectual tradition (viz., "Greeks to the present day" is not an original formula); (2) but also a conceptually disparate field, so that transcendental thought, in so far as space allows in a single volume, can include different and divergent ways of thinking about what we might call "transcendentalisms"; and (3) complementing temporal and conceptual breadth, I aimed too for sensitivity to a geographically latitudinous spectrum of possibilities—if hardly exhausted, then at least pushing beyond the usual precincts of canonical, mainstream, "retail brand" European philosophy to find and include those who write from ancient Persia and the Middle East, from India, and in this long history, from relatively new outposts, such as America. The West, broadly construed, does not have a monopoly on expressions of transcendental thought, yet there is a need to take stock of it in a direct way even while acknowledging the existence of complementary works that lay beyond the temporal and geographical purview of this specific edition.

One of the apparent and appealing aspects of the book's contents is the way it weaves spacio-temporally—and intellectually—from ancient Greece, Persia, and Indo-Asia to the European middle ages, then through the Enlightenment and into German Romanticism before skipping across the Channel to dwell with the English before setting out across the Atlantic to hear from Americans before, at last, alternating back and forth across the ocean in the twentieth century and into the twenty-first—in the last frenzy, setting a course directly for the tumultuous headwinds of the contending theories and contested movements that have come to define our contemporary age. The list shows that transcendental philosophy was "there from the beginning" and has been a steady current, with many indelible and influential crests, reaching all the way into present day undulations of the intellectual topography.

One of the anonymous readers of this collection remarked that it could be understood "as setting the agenda of a new subfield of intellectual exploration." The reader is making two points: first, that the volume is involved in proposing the shape and content of a canon, and secondly, that, perhaps surprisingly, that canon will represent a "new subfield." Suppose one were charged with the task of creating an anthology of aesthetics. Bloomsbury, in fact, has a conspicuously successful instance of just such a collection.[7] When a general reader—or for that matter, a professional academic, such as a philosopher—picks up the volume of collected excerpts meant to represent the field of aesthetics, there is an expectation that certain players and specific texts will be included (e.g., Longinus, Burke, and Lyotard on the sublime; Hume on taste; Kant from the *Critique of Judgment*, etc.). Who is to say what the *minimal* extent of such a canon would (or should) include? Even so, we are sure that to be serviceable the volume needs to cover and incorporate prominent, indelible remarks on aesthetics. Determining what is included in that minimal library, and deciding what can be added to it, is no enviable undertaking. But the work here is different.

Unlike an anthology of aesthetics, where an existing canon calls out for recognition (perhaps to acknowledge it, to reinforce its authority, or to contend with it by means of exclusion or counter-instance), the present anthology involves an effort to *constitute* a canon—and thus not to reproduce or to adjust an existing one. There are no other anthologies of transcendental thought that we must defer to, or put differently, have the pleasure of relying on, for orientation (or as if in response to). But if a canon must be made in order to set out some terms and parameters of "a new subfield," then let me note my awareness of my limitations to do just that—as well as my cognizance and acknowledgment of the contestation involved in canon formulation, including, among other usual points of contention, the politics of selection.[8] Consequently, admitting my appreciation for the often vexed nature of choosing (who is choosing? what is being chosen? why this and not that? and the like), the selection of pieces here in hand is offered humbly to the reader as the *beginning of a conversation*—not as the definitive or last word on the subject. If anything, the presumption to fill out the contours of a new subfield will mutatis mutandis be little more than a first word—an invitation for others to speak, to add, to subtract, to adjust and augment. The spirit of the collection, then, is one of "exploration" (as the anonymous reader said), and hypothesizing, of postulation and provocation, not announcement of discovery or declaration of final achievement—not an imposition (as if) from on high.

For anthologies that do sustain an established canon (again, for example, as with aesthetics), it is a common ambition to seek *definitiveness*—to include just the right things, in the right amounts, and to displace any volumes that are not similarly calibrated. A definitive edition would hope, in some sense, to inoculate itself from the threat of lacunae, to entrench itself against the possibility of new additions (and even editions!). "Definitiveness" becomes a veiled claim that the volume has, in its very manner and content, *defined* the term or the field. Perhaps uncannily befitting our subject, in this volume we seek the *indefinite*: a collection addressing the indefinite that is itself "indefinitive." Still, the editor is called to choose, the curator summoned to assemble.

If well-chosen, the pieces here should by their own merits justify their admission, though they may (and many times must)—at the same time—be, in terms of the scope of selection, insufficiently represented. The point is not to offer a comprehensive set of works by one author, or even a tradition or school, but rather to present a generous spectrum of *brief* encounters that is nevertheless full of crucial and substantive extracts in what could be deemed the philosophy or theology or history or literature or poetry or poetics of transcendental thought. A useful analog here may be a gallery of portraits of the same person: each picture is said to be "of" the known subject, but since each painting is made by a different painter (working across as a span of time, with different styles of application, using a range of materials, some artists knowing the person himself, others working from written descriptions of his physiognomy, etc.), we would not say these are identical works. There is a painting of Montaigne, there an etching, there a terracotta bust, and so on; each new form yields its own qualities and also its own glimpse of its subject. Likewise here, again keeping to the analogy, we do not go deep into the corpus of any given painter (or sculptor or master of chiaroscuro) but rather stand back to see how these diverse works on a purportedly shared subject look on their own terms (as individual works of art) *and* how those individual works refract when placed in each other's company. What effects do *we*, the onlookers, the readers, register for their proximity and arrangement? The heuristic value, then, comes, if it does, partly from the significance of the individual contribution on its own terms (despite its modest extent), but *mostly* from the *interactivity* of the selections. (Admittedly, there are writers who—keeping to the trope—suggest we have been paying attention to the wrong subject! We need to create a portrait of some other figure.)

As with so many galleries or curated cabinets—in this case, "of thought"—this volume is an illustration of Ralph Waldo Emerson's praiseful assessment of "how much finer things are in composition than alone. 'Tis wise in man to make Cabinets."[9] When Emerson toured the cabinets of natural history in Paris in the 1830s, while Charles Darwin was still aboard the *Beagle*, he (Emerson) could already discern the virtues of making such collections. The talents of curator George Cuvier and other natural scientists were detected by Emerson: we learn a lot by arrangement, juxtaposition, ordering, proximity, naming, noticing traits (that are similar *and* different), etc. A specimen speaks for itself until it is placed beside another, and then a dialogue begins; of course, it is we "readers" of these specimens that must provide that conversation, undertake that translation.[10] Consider, then, how this volume is a literary-philosophical "cabinet" of specimens, a notion that finds etymological significance in a word featured in its title: anthology.

When thinking of the root elements of the word "anthology," we observe that it is the concatenation of *anthos* and *logos*, and as such might be defined in quick paraphrase as "the study or logic of flowers."[11] These are no ordinary flowers, but rather fine emblems of their kinds and classes—at once remarkable instances from the genus *and* the species. Likewise, this anthology employs a logic that would govern the plucking of the finest flowers (as the vernacular tells us, from "fields" of inquiry). As it is an anthology, so it is also a florilegium (a gathering or collection of floral types) and, to an important extent, a commonplace book (where one's favorite and most abiding exhibits and case studies are set down for future reference and reflection).[12] Among many effects a reader can expect from these models is an appreciation for the way the display of those special specimens—those flowers (*anthos, flos*) of thought (*logos*), which have been collected, gathered (*legere*)—appear to demonstrate an apparently familiar preoccupation with transcendental themes among authors, however diverse and disparate their approaches to the subject.

Each contribution in this collection can *seem*, in its own right, on its own terms, definitive, that is, until another is read—either as a complement or as an act of revision, perhaps even a displacement. If that volatility makes it difficult to choose what to include (and it does), it also makes reading in this volume—either consecutively/chronologically or randomly—remarkably stimulating to any settled notion of transcendental thought. Despite more than two-and-a-half millennia of achieved debate, discovery, eloquence, and persuasion, the grandness and diversity of the expressions only provide the context for *further* thinking on the subject.

This anthology—if in some measure an admittedly Borgesian project—might (or could) include ten thousand volumes of prose and poesy, argument and analysis, all of them fit and bona fide representatives of the art of thinking through transcendental thought. As it stands, if only for the limitations of a book-in-hand, 800 or so pages must suffice. The eighty-five authors drawn together for this occasion of collaborative investigation therefore tacitly imply an invitation to the broader, longer sources (or deeper soils) from which these works are plucked—and to be sure, the many excellent specimens that exceeded or eluded the volume altogether.

Admittedly, this collection is shaped by my own idiosyncrasies of reading and sense of relatedness or relevance; it is therefore *partial* in a double sense. To offset the negative impacts of such selecting—for example, that the volume might miss essential pieces, or even quote the wrong passages from the right figures—I have consulted widely among leading experts and trusted readers from a diverse range of fields in the humanities, literary arts, and religion, to help constitute, in effect, a reader-reading list that aims to manifest signature instances of transcendental thought across the ages (through time, tradition, terrain, type, tone, and temperament). To make this undertaking at least plausible for me, I have relied on the informed input of many scholars, who, in turn, out of the generosity of their erudition—and their sense that this is a "new subfield" worth cultivating—have helped shape its content. They may be better able to make such calls (that is, to be sure, why I asked), but, for the present occasion, I have accepted the labor, and thus cannot blame them for my lapses; as this book finds its readers, I hope to be forgiven for my own. Still, we must start somewhere.

As a hedge on even the well-informed suggestions of the well-read, however, we may turn to a current instantiation of the digital humanities: the Open Syllabus Project.[13] At the time of this writing, the OSP has gathered one million university syllabi, an aggregation that among other things, allows a glimpse into rankings of an exceptionally broad range of student curricula. For instance, what is the most assigned text—across one million syllabi—after Strunk and White's *Elements of Style*? —Plato's *Republic*. Along these lines, we might conclude that part of the work involved in the present anthology is to create a dialogue with canon-formation and canon-maintenance (and occasionally canon-revision or -repudiation), such as that practice is revealed in the OSP. In the table of contents of the present volume, for example, one can find dozens of authors that appear in the top one-hundred most assigned texts. Even if the present collection does not reproduce those specific texts (e.g., the *Republic* is not excerpted here but other works by Plato are), it does draw from those authors who remain—as this initiative of the digital humanities purports to show us—at the center of contemporary debates and pedagogy. Yet, as if in response to the making and keeping of a canon, perhaps, for some, the extent to which the present anthology *deviates* from this crowd-sourced list will reveal the volume's charms and virtues—including its ideological and pedagogical usefulness.

Though I have reached out to scholars to discuss what is most worth gathering between two covers, relied on the written researches of others, and explored the challenges and invitations of canonicity-as-activity (glancing both its static and its dynamic elements), there are other limitations any anthologist or florilegist must contend with, such as practical, empirical impediments: (1) the number of a pages in a book (even a hefty one such as this!); (2) the availability of elegant and reliable translations; (3) the willingness of rights-holders to share their intellectual property; and (4) the costs associated with securing the rights to reprint. I will resist the temptation to adduce the many excellent pieces that had to be left out, for it seems begrudging to dwell on losses and absences—as if I had invited a host of scintillating intellects to supper, but bemoaned all of those who could not attend; it seems especially wise to deflect any perceived injury for, to be sure, none of the "regrets" were personal. We may instead appreciate those who made the time to call on us. If writing and editing is an intellectual undertaking, publishing is a business endeavor: an obvious observation, but here, a relevant one.

On these last two points (viz., 3 and 4), is it not intriguing, captivating even, to think about how the economics of property rights comes to (in)form the aggregation of this prospective canon? As editor, I have as often as not wanted what I could not have; and so, once again, I learned of the instructiveness of obstacles—the way they turn us back to search, mine, discover, and even invent.[14] On more than a few occasions, I have found myself feeling (almost) grateful for the rejection of rights or the imposition of exorbitant fees, for the piece that is now collected seems so much finer, fitting, and fecund. I do not want to think that such an emotional response is a case of sour grapes, but instead a reminder that such books are shaped not solely by (an editor's) intention, but also by many extra-authorial factors. In short, and in summary of items 1 through 4, this library of transcendental thought—as expansive as it hopes to be—at once enjoys the liberty to form a canon (and thereby stir conversations about its very definition, category, and criteria) and is simultaneously limited by external factors beyond mere editorial wish and whim.

So it is in this way—by the liberties of choice and the constraints that bear down on each instance of choice (again, items 1 through 4)—that the volume progresses to suggest a nascent canon in what may, according to outside readers, amount to a new or evolving subfield of investigation. Of course, I realize how much is left out. What hopefully will prove true is a new list of four items that countermand the constraints listed above, namely: (1¹) that these selected, representative works will interact with one another in productive ways; (2¹) that such company enclosed in a "cabinet," or plucked to form an alluring "bouquet," will reveal new connections and affiliations (and even propitious conflicts) otherwise and as yet unseen; (3¹) that the selections may draw us deeper into a given author's work, to appreciate anew the radiating significance of this shorter excerpt; and (4¹) that what remains to be included—as part of this burgeoning project—will make itself known.

That's a lot of apology and conciliation—and I am well aware how it skirts the edge of presumptuousness and vanity (for me, a very painful risk)—but the foregoing is *also* meant in a spirit of heuristic clarification: that is, as a way of making the scaffolding of the enterprise a little more visible (as if building a work of illuminating ferrovitreous architecture instead of a claustrophobic crypt or a marble mausoleum). Seeing is believing, or at least seeing is seeing what is at stake. I would not say these admissions and behind-the-scenes pointers are meant to reveal a politics of selection (much less a discernible philosophical or religious outlook of one vintage or another), but instead perhaps something like an acknowledgment that such collections are created (and do not merely appear ex nihilo, as if of their own accord). In place of a politics, then, I would say (at least in so far as I can be aware of such things) that this collection is informed by a twofold priority: (a) to siphon out, whenever possible, some of the richest, most vital moments of direct literary-philosophical engagement with the concept, theme, or problem of the transcendental; and (b) to celebrate the variety of ways such engagements take form—from the epistolary to the poetic; in dialogues, essays, epigrams, critiques, confessions, sermons, lectures, inquiries, interviews, propositions, schematisms, meditations, treatises and tractates, novels, autobiographies, and journals—and thereby, as part of that appreciation, echo our awareness of the *rhetorical* dimensions of a work's constitution. Attunement to the metaphilosophical and the methodological, therefore, become part of the broader investigation into the subject. Taken together, (a) and (b) invite us to consider—and also challenge—the extent to which it is true to say that the collected prose and opinions here gathered have shaped what we mean by the transcendental. And so, as Schiller said, by an example we come to the light.

* * * *

If the antecedent notes have explored how the domain of this collection took form in terms of editorial *methodology*, something also can be said about how the *traits* of a given piece of work recommended it for inclusion in that domain.

We began by wondering after the syntagma "transcendental thought," so let us continue to address what, in this context, we mean by "thought." Perhaps "criticism" is the best analog for the allusions and associations of "thought" on this occasion. The book might have been modified differently as an anthology of transcendental *philosophy* or *literature* or *religion*, etc. "Thought," then, becomes a surrogate intervening amidst the widespread use of such disciplinary titles, a term meant to limn the customary and canonical boundaries that have come to define (and often divide) one "field" from another—as if the realm of religious inquiry, for example, were not *also* philosophical and literary and rhetorical and political and linguistic and more broadly cultural (that is, historically situated). (Note too, if an anthology is aimed at becoming a bouquet of beauty and representative merit, we ought to pluck from *many* fields.)

As a point of reference, consider how Jacques Derrida suggests that "thought" is "a dimension that is not reducible to technique, nor to science, nor to philosophy."[15] We could take up this negative definition by saying that if "thought" is not reducible to each of them individually, it may yet incorporate *all* of them; *thinking*, can we say, is something we do *through* the expressions that we come to call technique and science and philosophy? Criticism is a medium. For Derrida, at least, "thought" can contain or name more than those realms, go beyond them to also include "basic" research: "The *value and meaning* of the basic, the fundamental, on its opposition to goal-orientation, on the ruses of orientation in all its domains."[16] To illustrate his point, Derrida reminds us of Nietzsche's *Lectures on the Future of our Educational Establishments*, where Nietzsche exclaims "one must not have viewpoints alone, but also thoughts!"[17] (Nietzsche here offers a devastating gloss on perspectivism and its limits—a marvel of his capacity to push beyond the complacency of merely destroying what came before him.) And as Nietzsche was a close, careful, and admiring reader of Emerson, we may yet sense echoes of the American's address to the Phi Beta Kappa Society at Harvard, "The American Scholar," in which he contends that "as Man Thinking, the theory of his office is contained."[18]

Though a quick scan of the table of contents will reveal a diverse crowd of writers—from philosophy, religion, and poetry, and those dedicated to autobiographical projects, letters, and fiction—one way to figure all the work, especially in terms of its attitude of approach, is to think of it as *criticism*, in particular, criticism of the idea (or ideal or persistence or aspiration or problem) of the transcendental. The volume, then, might be a reply to the question, asked only in retrospect, after everything had been written: "How would you address the nature, meaning, and purpose of the transcendental in human life?" (Equivocation on offering a precise definition of the "transcendental" is intentional, since I do not wish to forestall legitimate experiments that, owing to my errors or ignorance, do not line up; again, "indefinitiveness" on this occasion is meant to be a virtue.) There is some reverse engineering going on: writers have understood, in some cases defined, what they mean by the transcendental, and in their responses—and the fitness of those remarks—we, as readers, will come to some clarity about what *they* mean by the transcendental. Perhaps, as readers, we will agree, or perhaps we will object, or perhaps we will not understand—and thus look on with curiosity or frustration, as the case may be. But, at least, we will have replies to grapple with.

Still, even as soberly as I have tried to engineer my way out of the proceedings, aimed to dislocate myself as a kind of mediator or gatekeeper of "what counts," I realize there are several instances when my selection may strike a reader as queer (in the Wittgensteinian sense): in a word, it will not seem like it belongs. If such instances of criteriological befuddlement exist, I presume they may be different to different readers, and so I cannot give any examples of such apparent aberrations. My hope, however, is that these oddities do not become grounds for dismissal but, instead, the pretext for further investigation and questioning. Not just "Why did he include this work?" but "What *qualities* of this work—which claims, what style—make it seem out of keeping with the rest?" The latter question befits anyone conducting a kind of "natural history" of the transcendental, such as I think we are implicitly undertaking here. As they are in nature, the inclusion of mutations is instructive either to mark out the features of the standard-bearers, or, perhaps to announce the arrival of a new status quo—the origin of a new line. Nature thrives by deviations.

One trait that might be common to the selections here gathered is that they "share an object," in the sense in which Matthew Arnold used the phrase.[19] That shared object is nothing else (and indeed, given the expansiveness of the term, we should hope, nothing more) than the transcendental. Criticism, as I am using the term here, likewise might be understood in its Arnoldian enunciation, since the project or practice of seeking an object of thought is synonymous with criticism—its very definition. And this is as much the case for the critic as the reader of that criticism: both are asking, "What is the author's object?" As Arnold writes, the critic should focus on her own qualities of intellectual "curiosity" and "disinterestedness," and in this coupling may yield some service through her criticism.[20] Such a disinterested curiosity would aim "to see the object as in itself it really is," which in this volume, invites a useful double entendre: (1) for the shared object of these inquiries is, so we think, certain reflections on or appeals to the transcendental, but also (2) because there is much debate—for and against, and perhaps ambivalence about—whether the transcendental "in itself . . . really is." If I were editing a volume about, say, a film genre, I could list examples of films that illustrate and embody the genre; but here what counts are not examples of the "transcendental," so much as literary instances in which writers take it up, in some form or fashion, as their object. One of the most appealing effects an anthology such as this might inspire in its readers is a consideration of the static and dynamic elements that define transcendental philosophy. After Wittgenstein, we can speak of the "grammar and criteria" of transcendental thought: that it has these specific traits that recur from work to work, and then a likely larger set of variable traits (that help us identify and distinguish individual efforts).[21]

Though it may seem peculiar, for some, to see Plato in the same table of contents as Proust, and Duns Scotus as Emily Dickinson, and Edmund Burke as Alain Badiou, the Arnoldian approach to criticism may offer some clarification of—and validation for—such connubial relations, namely, that all these writers, despite their dissipation across time and place (from

Greek antiquity to sylvan Massachusetts in the nineteenth century), share a locus of inquiry: the transcendental. As if a substance—salt (NaCl) or sugar ($C_{12}H_{22}O_{11}$)—were an object of investigation from antiquity to the present. What is salt? What is sugar? Though they resemble one another, why—how—are they different, and put to such disparate uses with such varied effects? Instead of some history of remarks on the nature of salt and sugar—what they are and what they mean for us—we have, in this volume, a forensic inquiry into the transcendental. Whether it is salty or sweet, tangible or ineffable, remains one of the promising virtues of such a study: two-and-half-millennia of criticism on the transcendental (what it is, what it is not; for, against, and in between). In a double sense, we are testing our taste for the transcendental.

Despite these efforts to articulate what the author's share, there is a latent paradox that should be admitted, or least, noted: namely, that the "object" of the volume is, in a word, a non-object. For, as will be clear in what follows, the transcendental often keeps company with such philosophical cognates as the noumenal, divine, ethereal, heavenly, sacred, celestial, holy, ideal, unseen, unutterable, sublime, indescribable, indefinable, inexpressible, the incommensurable, the *in*-credible, and the like. Consequently, the title, as if translated into the register of everyday speech might have been the philosophy ". . . of what is not there," ". . . of the beyond," ". . . of what lies apart from sensory confirmation," "of that which cannot be named," and so on. On this last token, one thinks of Thomas Carlyle's invocation of the "Professors in the Nameless."[22] Or how Emerson, as if in response to Carlyle, heralds the job of the poet as "the Namer," and tells us that "the poet names the thing because he sees it, or comes one step nearer to it than any other."[23] Carlyle was, to be sure, mocking those professors at the same time that he was underscoring the crucial task of naming and having names: "For indeed as Walter Shandy often insisted, there is much, nay almost all, in Names. . . . What mystic influences does it not send inwards. . . ."[24] Carlyle, still in the voice of Diogenes Teufelsdröckh writes: "Of the Poet's and Prophet's inspired Message, and how it makes and unmakes whole worlds, I shall forbear mention." Yet earlier we know he said many verities on the very topic:

> Not only all common Speech, but Science, Poetry itself is no other, if thou consider it, than a right *Naming*. Adam's first task was giving names to natural Appearances: what is ours still but a combination of the same; be the Appearances exotic-vegetable, organic, mechanic, stars, or starry movements (as in Science); or (as in Poetry) passions, virtues, calamities, God-attributes, Gods?[25]

Not incidentally, all of this making and unmaking—often by means of naming—seems but an effect of the "grand thaumaturgical art of Thought!"—that is, thinking itself is an art that invokes superpowers, the supernatural—for the process itself is a conjuring. How precisely are we to think about thought? If John Searle is right, "consciousness is a biological process"—so it is *also* a supervenient phenomenon that will not admit of reduction.[26] We cannot get a thought from an is. And as Martin Heidegger said of death—that it is for humans our "ownmost possibility" and yet it is not something we can experience *in* life—so the transcendental would appear to be, after Plato, after Kant, the *condition of the possibility* (*Bedingungen der Möglichkeit*) of experience, of thought, of truth. The inquiries here gathered would seem to be as necessary for thinking about the transcendental as they are at odds with any empirical ratification of it. What we have instead, then, are two-and-a-half millennia of efforts to speak directly—or, as the case may be, at odd angles, with various concessions made—to this abiding, yet invisible condition, and always, or as yet, without proof or evidence.

The "transcendental" holds another paradox: that by appealing to it we may perceive truth, reality, and the like, without personal foibles and idiosyncrasies. In short, truth and reality that is impersonal, "scientific," objective. How many philosophers from Pythagoras to Plato to Descartes to Leibniz have entreated mathematics (and its luminous, seemingly unmatched capacity for impersonality, universality, and necessity) as a fitting means—and instantiation—of the Forms, or Ideal, or God? One thinks of the hope and longing contained in the phrase "perfect number." These petitions to and from mathematics, early and late, admit of a nascent, emerging scientific method, for if the medicine of sixth century BCE fails us today, the Pythagorean theorem does not. Given the efficacy of such formulas, why not be moved to think that mathematics is a part of the mind of God—an activity whose being exceeds the modest extent of the human altogether? Mathematics, like physics, seems to trade in realities that yet find their truths beyond sensory proofs; they recommend themselves as transcendental arts.

Still, even if we characterize today's natural science as empirical—and thus devoted to studying (and knowing) things as they appear to us (*phenomena*), natural science still pushes the limits at both the micro (quantum) level and the macro (cosmic) level to explore what transcends human corporeal perception (including the scale of the human), and perhaps even the laws that govern our planet or galaxy. Thus, in another way, the *theoretical* elements of natural science—what remains in a state of postulation and is thus provisional, experimental—bears the mark, or has the spirit of transcendental investigation. Some say the edges of physics resemble poetry.[27] A scientist once wrote: "The most beautiful and most profound emotion we can experience is the sensation of the mystical. It is the power of all true science. He to whom this emotion is a stranger, who can no longer stand, rapt in awe, is as good as dead."[28] The scientist who authored these lines? Albert Einstein.

When René Descartes told Marin Mersenne he had "found a way of proving metaphysical truths that is more evident than the truths of geometry," he captured an inversion of worldviews, and of domains (e.g., the phenomenal and the noumenal).[29] Descartes, like Galileo and Newton, set natural science and mathematics on course to address transcendental issues—until that project faded in the nineteenth century, taking blows from Darwin, then Nietzsche, and in the twentieth century, from Russell and Sartre, and later Dawkins and Dennett. In fact, Descartes admonished that others "should not devote so much attention to the *Meditations* and to metaphysical questions [since they] draw the mind too far away from physical and observable things, and make it unfit to study them."[30] The supernatural was, in effect, in the natural. Centuries later, the celebrated, controversial Einstein (a scientist iconic to the point of cliché) echoed Descartes: "Enough for me, the mystery of the eternity of life, and the inkling of the marvelous structure of reality, together with the single-hearted endeavor to comprehend a portion, be it ever so tiny, of the reason that manifests itself in nature."[31] Gustav Flaubert, in a letter to Louise Colet, inscribed a complex variation on this theme:

> Devil take me if I don't feel just as kindly toward the lice biting a beggar as a I do toward the beggar. I am certain moreover that men are no more brothers to each other than the leaves in the woods are alike: they worry together, that's all. Aren't we made with the emanations of the universe? . . . Sometimes after looking at a pebble, an animal, a painting, I feel I have entered it. Communications between humans are no more intense.[32]

Emerson, of course, soberly lamented that we no longer behold God "face to face," as preceding generations did, but instead "through their eyes."[33] Yet, when Emerson stood face to face with animal life—even when it was inanimate, taxidermied, labeled, and arranged—in Paris, before the Cabinets of Natural History, he noted "strange sympathies" and surmised an "occult relation between the very scorpions and man. I feel the centipede in me."[34] And why shouldn't he! The impression of inherency is entirely fitting given the cladogram of evolutionary science; since we evolved from earlier vertebrates, amphibians, and reptiles—not to mention the four-billion-year-old "Luca" (Last Universal Common Ancestor)—the continuity is at once evident and astonishing.[35] "Just six million years ago, a single female ape had two daughters. One became the ancestor of all chimpanzees, the other is our own grandmother."[36] The occult relations might go further, for the water we drink—and to a significant extent, the water that composes our own bodies—is said to have preexisted the formation of the earth and the sun.[37] So why not reach all the way back to galactic history and trace the line from stardust to human consciousness?

If we live in an age enthralled by the achievements of natural science, the topic of transcendental thought may seem anachronistic at best and wrongheaded at worst. Though we can appreciate the pronounced successes of medical vaccines, space exploration, genetics, mobile telecommunications, and nanotechnology, and therefore, how the limits of human knowledge and experience may be transgressed by means of science, we also marvel at what we do not know, cannot experience—what lies beyond our comprehension (and control). Looking back at these empirical instances of boundary-crossing, we can also look ahead to see how, for example, the speculations of the "singularity" have about them the transcending of our condition. Before the singularity comes to pass, however, we are already very much in the age of "transgenics"—that point in the 4.5 billion years of natural selection when human intentionality coupled with human ingenuity can begin making decisions about what traits we wish to select for: as if literalizing Nietzsche's "overman," the species is beginning to transcend itself.

The implied premise of both the cutting edge of transgenics (an instantiation of the proposed and increasingly evident post-human) and the nineteenth-century figure who philosophizes with a hammer (and not to build so much as to dismantle) is precisely to overcome the human as we have known it (or *not* known it!). More recently, Stanley Cavell has remarked on several occasions that "nothing could be more human" than "the power of the motive to reject the human."[38] We hear a useful rehearsal and focalization of this point when Cavell observes that there is "inherent in philosophy a certain drive to the inhuman," and that we find in this propulsive movement "the most inescapably human of motivations."[39] Whether we look to the ascetics and early Christians, those whom Nietzsche called the "despisers of the body," to Simone de Beauvoir (who spoke of how a person's need to "justify his existence . . . involves an undefined need to transcend himself"), or to the twenty-first-century technological elite— namely, the augmenters and experimenters who wish to "hack" the human, or, to our appointed topic, transcendental thought, we may come away with the impression that the "motive" or "drive" to posit the transcendental is, in fair measure, but a euphemism for the overcoming of the human, whether that wish is understood, at the extremes, as a desire to shrink from it (as with the ascetic) or to surpass it (as with the invitations of the bionic human).[40] And still steadily abiding, there are the solicitations of the afterlife—the ultimate transcendental promise. In another one of these uncanny doublings, we can see clearly how the sentiments of the deeply religious and those of the post-religious are, in fact, agreed: both aim to deny or exceed the bounds of the human form—seeking reality beyond it.

And so the further we push the scope of the human, the more we seem to return to Parmenides, Heraclitus, and Plotinus; we arrive, despite science's apparent allergy to mysticism in the realm of Carlyle's "natural supernaturalism," or later in Giorgio Agamben and Slavoj Žižek, to a regard for transcendence as immanence.[41] As M. H. Abrams inquired, to what extent are the theological and spiritual tendencies of any age found translated into secular expressions (poetically, metaphorically, even, on occasion, via natural scientific models and theorems)? Abrams sees, for example, the Romantic movement—which is ever so much a coupling of Kantian and post-Kantian thought with classical Greek and Roman metaphysics—as an attempt to "reformulate [traditional concepts, schemes, and values] within the prevailing two-term system of subject and object, ego and non-ego, the human mind or consciousness and its transactions with nature."[42] The Romantic movement is not old news even today since we *still* inhabit a "two-term system," one that includes Abrams' list as well as the other binaries that animate our current conversation, as they did Plato's: phenomena/noumena, transcendental/immanent, among others.

Some cultural historians, such as Yuval Noah Harari, have suggested that it was precisely the human capacity to agree on and debate—and thus believe in—"fictional realities" (e.g., ideas, imagined concepts, variations on the transcendental) that proved to be the decisive factor in the advancement of *Homo sapiens* above competing animals, including primates and other now-extinct members of the genus *Homo*.[43] Faith in the unseen—in *ideas*—manifested immediate, proximate, and practical effects (at the very minimum, survival), and in time it also conferred the luxuries and surpluses of human experience that we might call culture. At the dawn of this abstraction, even the smallest gestures—a wave of the hand, a nod of the head, a glance of acknowledgment—can seem like the birth of concepts: the transcendentalizing of everyday life; indeed, this process could mark the transition from nature to culture. Because empirical, material effects are more conspicuous, it may be easy to overlook the extent to which human life is underwritten by a pervasive trust in the nonempirical—what persists from moment-to-moment in one's thoughts, memories, and conceptual inventions, and in the wider society wherein one finds oneself. In present day America, for example, contending with its own secular/sacred tensions (perhaps so intractable because they are antinomies), it is hard to tell whether the "In God We Trust" that adorns the nation's currency is meant to appeal to a beneficent super-being, or rather to the need for trust in something that is itself fiat and ephemeral, namely, in late-stage capitalism, in late-stage democracy, the seemingly redundant appeal to "the almighty dollar." With "fictional realities" such as currency, property rights, governmental laws, language, history, religion or, for that matter, the nature and definition of the transcendental realm, we—as a species—might never have been able to organize ourselves into (relatively) peaceable conspirators. As if the concept "peace" were inherent in those first moments of person-to-person acknowledgment—a wave of the hand instead of the descent of the fist.

Conspicuously, though, we could also cite innumerable "holy wars" as evidence of violent dissension over the shape and meaning of the transcendental. As much as, say, money has been a common, global currency of abstract (transcendental) value, perhaps we may also lament the degree to which we, as humans—all members of the same genus—still entertain bloody, death-littered confrontations in the name(s) of our gods (fights that recurrently contest their types, their qualities, their powers); wars are predicated on philology—on the authority of sources and translations; somehow, politics comes too late to mediate. Transcendental thought may today seem esoteric, a remnant of ancient, tribal primitives, but it is, in fact, at least on this reading, at the core of the kind of imaginative conjectures that define our species—for better and worse, one of the attributes that made it "rise" into the form we know today. What, in this context, is the difference between transgressing the border of the planet's atmosphere or valences at the subatomic level and generating human rights or moral laws, to say nothing of creating (and destroying!) god(s)? Some are empirical, some are invented—but all are movements beyond the prehistorical known and the prescientific given.

Scientific successes, as well as the hypotheses for future developments, designs, and discoveries, return us anew to the long history of rumination on the transcendental. Look at who is writing (in the works collected here) and how *what* is said remains (largely) pertinent. There is still much we do not know—or know what to do with. As the prehistorian Jean Clottes remarks: "*Homo sapiens*—the man who knows. I don't think it's a good definition at all. We *don't* know;

we don't know much. I would think *Homo spiritulis*."[44] Hence, at minimum, we can acknowledge the heuristic value of these exercises in transcendental thought, many of which consist in a kind of spiritual exploration. That the world continues to convulse over not just the competing political economies of capitalism and communism but also about a medieval religious fervor *and* a just as vigorously held atheism (with these disparate "faiths" vying against one another) suggests that appeals to the empirical (to sensory proof, the norms of logic, and the standards of scientifically verified evidence) do not contain the whole scope of human experience. Once again, or we might say *still*, there is much that exceeds the world as it appears (that is, as we find it described by empirical realists).

That "excess"—what lies beyond—is present in at least four domains of contemporary intellectual experience: (1) secular science (including what may be described as anti- or post-transcendental sentiment); (2) humanistic philosophy (as we have known it since the Renaissance) (3) the humanities (including humanistic, post-humanistic, transhumanistic, and post-secular thought); and (4) various instantiations of the religious temperament. How and whether these four domains interact (or do not) reveals a great deal about who we are as individuals, as societies, and as a species.

Given the range and diversity of the included roster, it may be useful to think of the volume itself as a prismatic attempt to orient ourselves to the transcendental. If peering from one direction does not compel, and observing from another confuses, perhaps a third will enlighten. If not Plotinus, if not Aquinas, then Melville. If not Hegel, if not Russell, then Schopenhauer. Though the volume is arranged chronologically, one can imagine many profitable hours spent in darting movements across time, place, and person—each new session of reading, each new coupling or tripling of selections, yielding new and different insights.

Since the entire collection is presented in English, though many of the pieces did not originate in English, the influence of linguistic translation affords a way, among others, for thinking about not just the term "transcendental," but also the variegated effects of having many theories of it, many names for it. For instance, how we *say* something informs how we *think* something. "Language is fossil poetry."[45] And so it will make a difference to the reader in English if one translator renders a word equivalent as "transcendental" or "supernatural," "divine" or "sublime," "God" or "Nature." While one translation may push a text in a mystical direction, another translation of the same text may aim to naturalize it. The work of the translator, thus involves (1) whatever authority the translator wishes to grant—or project upon—the author; (2) the context of the text's creation; (3) a sense of what the text-in-itself (in an ahistorical way) appears to say, in so far as it is possible to descry such things; (4) the problem of finding appropriate matching terms from one language to the next (especially when no satisfying cognates and parallels may exist—consider how difficult it is to find a fitting synonym for Aristotle's nuanced understanding of *eudaimonia* or, more broadly, the Greek notion of *parrhesia*); (5) the anticipated needs and capacities of the reading audience; (6) the push toward a poetic rendering as it is ever in tension with staunch literalism; and we could add more factors. One not insignificant question to ask of the translations here gathered is the extent to which the translators "transcendentalize" the text.

* * * *

Arguably, there are two seminal instigators—and progenitors—of transcendental thought in Western civilization: Plato and Immanuel Kant. No matter how brief or diffuse the selections from these authors may be (as they must be in this volume), one can easily discern the extent to which Plato and Kant contribute approaches to transcendental thought that subsequently initiate cascades of responses over many centuries. We, of course, at the outset of the twenty-first century, stand in the wake of both radiating forces. And as ripples are wont to do, they sometimes complement, cancel, or otherwise crash into one another—all such movements unleash distinctive forms of energy and influence. Knowingly or not (and in large measure knowingly) most of the writers here are responding to Plato and Kant, and the legacies of their effects on our conceptualization of reality.

Though we could begin our survey before the beginning of this book, say, with Confucius and Lao Tzu, who predate Plato, we picked up the plot of the transcendental in the pagan antiquity of Greece. Still, and for that reason, we might have commenced instead with Heraclitus or Thales or Parmenides, who also predate Plato. But having to start this story somewhere, we settle on Plato, and not entirely for arbitrary reasons, since, in the fourth century BCE, Plato coalesces many of the key topics and questions of the transcendental as he inherited them from the presocratics. Thus, Heraclitus' attention to the flux of time, Thales' notion that "all things are one," and Parmenides' preoccupation with Being find their registration in Plato's incantation stated and stylized in a host of Socratic dialogues. The famous allegory of the cave, in the *Republic*, has become almost a metonym for asking questions such as: What is real? What is the relationship between mental ideas and objects in the world? Does human perception create reality or does reality exist apart from cognitive conceptual construction? How does mental experience coordinate, if at all, with natural laws and material phenomena? Are there really two worlds, or just one?—These are questions that radiate through Plato's many works, but they are also, or by virtue of his legacy, some of the many questions that philosophers, theologians, poets, and writers across time and tradition have been asking since the allegory and its allied arguments were formulated.

Plato's metaphysics has been told and retold many times, and this is not the time to explore it in much detail, but it is worthy of a sketch in part because of its representativeness and in part because of the lengthy shadow of its influence. For a start, we could note that Plato believed human perceptual experience yielded a superficial grasp of reality: that we live, in a word, in a world of appearances (*phainomena*). Notice the implied hierarchy of the spiritual over the physical: the human body is, in a commonly invoked phrase, "the prison house of the soul"—Plato here finding reason to preserve the Pythagorian metaphor.[46] Millennia later, Carlyle's trope—where the body is a "garment" we wear—endorses the same sort of picture.[47] The Platonic hierarchy imposes a division between soul and body, and thereby anticipates Cavell's mapping of our alternatives: "either I am inside my body or I am my body."[48] Since it is settled for Plato that body and soul are distinct, and asymmetrically related, he pushes on.

In the *Phaedo*, Socrates asks Simmias rhetorically: "Is it not in the course of reflection, if at all, that the soul gets a clear view of facts?" In the soul's "search for reality," we must "ignor[e] the body."[49] On this score, we can quickly apprehend how thoroughly Christianity is Platonized, and how, millennia later, even the minister who gave up his pulpit, Emerson, sustains the presumed bifurcation: "We were put into our bodies."[50] Emerson's much-admired Carlyle relates similar sentiments: "So spiritual (*geistig*) is our whole daily Life: all that we do springs out of Mystery, Spirit, invisible Force; only like a little Cloud-image, or Armida's Palace, air-built, does the Actual body itself forth from the great mystic Deep."[51] Novalis, speaking a kindred tongue, believed "Only one thing matters, and that is the search for our transcendental self."[52] Maurice Maeterlinck's contribution to the conversation becomes a gloss on Plato, Emerson, Carlyle, and Novalis: "We live only by virtue of our transcendental being, whose actions and thoughts momentarily pierce the envelope which surrounds us."[53]

For Plato, as so many before him and since, what lies beyond the body, on the other side of the "envelope," is the *real* world: the world of Forms or Ideas. From this conceit, many sorts of robust faiths in the afterlife are supported as are myriad ascetic practices. Reality, for Plato, involves access to this realm of Forms or Ideas—a realm that *transcends* the everyday world of appearances (and errors of judgment about those appearances—as Carlyle put it: "This poor, miserable, hampered, despicable Actual"[54]). For Plato, we are said not so much to discover the truths of the Forms as remember them (via *anemnesis*), and in this mode of engagement are understood to be addressing what is real. Real reality is, as it were, otherworldly.

The trouble (and we might even say trauma) of this predication of hierarchy and difference is registered in the confusing ways in which Plato's outlook is described by historians of philosophy and critics of his thought, namely, as Idealism *and* as Realism. If the only real domain (say, for truth) is in the Forms or *Ideas*, then we should call this view Idealism; but, if the Forms and Ideas are the only real things, then we should call this view Realism. The debate between what to title Plato's philosophical commitments—how to characterize them—has not yet been resolved. Perhaps it is most useful to think of Plato as a *classical* realist. And so, as a reader in this volume may begin her inquiries by reading Plato's *Parmenides*, she joins a tradition of interpreting the meaning of the transcendental, and that undertaking may also resolve itself into a question, such as: "Is the transcendental the name we give to the things that are the most real, or is it the name we assign to those that are the least real?"

The hierarchy has evolved, especially in recent centuries, with the emergence of secularism, where aspects of the religious, mystical, and transcendental were displaced, denied, or otherwise denigrated in favor of atheism, scientism, naturalism, and forms of logical positivism. Or, put more tersely, where secularism and scientism became the new faith, the only defensible faith for reasoning beings. Even Aristotle, long ago, complained that "such an inquiry" as his, into the universal good, "is made an uphill one by the fact that the Forms have been introduced by friends of our own." And yet, he concludes, "piety requires us to honor truth above our friends."[55] Characterized by a radical empiricism—and a privileging of sense experience—we can trace Aristotle's view as a precursor of *contemporary* realism (and thus mark it as defiantly anti-Platonic). Under the sway of this trend, we are encouraged to dispense with all "magical thinking," any affirmation of the transcendental (cf. the confident pronouncements offered by "new atheists" such as Richard Dawkins, Daniel Dennett, Sam Harris, Christopher Hitchens, et al.).[56]

Yet, as pendulums (and trends of extreme thought) are inclined to do, a new moderation may be emerging. Given the range of voices in the present volume, some may regard it as a contribution to the broader study and practice known, if somewhat inchoately, as post-secularism—variously articulated with anything by inchoateness by Jürgen Habermas, Charles Taylor, Hent de Vries, and Gregg Lambert among others—where the asymmetries of the secular society (in relation to, or in antagonism with, the religious society) may be reformulated to allow for productive co-existence and mutual enrichment.[57] In this latest dispatch from the ideological clashes of religion and science, there may be reason to believe that the transcendental is already, or may soon become, a newly revitalized term.

Nearly twenty-two centuries after Plato gave shape—and metaphor—to the transcendental, Kant devised what he called "transcendental idealism." After Plato, after Plotinus, Kant's critical project seems like a fitting heir to the Greek vision of reality as bifurcated between perceptible entities (*phenomena*) and imperceptible ones (*noumena*). Yet, unlike a demotic (or Aristotelian, or even a contemporary scientific) reading of this split—where phenomena are believed to be real and noumena, which are said to lay beyond perception, are not real—Kant, *inverts* the Platonic ascriptions. While the divide between worlds remains intact, for Kant, phenomena contain the only reality while noumena are defined by artifice and illusion. Somewhat confusingly, though, Kant describes phenomena as *things-as-they-appear* while noumena are *things-in-themselves*; a quick reading would assume that the Platonic legacy (and hierarchy) remain, but Kant demurs.

One glimpse of how Kant departs from Plato comes in the so-called "transcendental deduction," which Kant glosses in the *Critique of Pure Reason* as follows:

> There are two conditions under which alone the knowledge of an object is possible, first, *intuition*, through which it is given, though only as appearance; secondly, *concept*, through which an object is thought corresponding to this intuition. . . . Concepts of objects in general underlie all empirical knowledge as its *a priori* conditions. The objective validity of the categories as *a priori* concepts rests, therefore, on the fact that, so far as the form of thought is concerned, through them alone does experience become possible.[58]

Kant defined the "general problem of transcendental philosophy" as finding its resolution in reply to the question "how are synthetic *a priori* judgments possible?,"[59] which is coupled with the question "what and how much can the understanding and reason know apart from all experience?"[60] In Kant's summative response:

> When in *a priori* judgment we seek to go out beyond the given concept, we come in the *a priori* intuitions upon that which cannot be discovered in the concept but which is certainly found *a priori* in the intuition corresponding to the concept, and can be connected with it synthetically. Such judgments, however, thus based on intuition, can never extend beyond objects of the senses; they are valid only for objects of possible experience.[61]

Kant concludes: "We then assert that the conditions of the *possibility of experience* in general are likewise conditions of the *possibility of the objects of experience*, and that for this reason they have objective validity in a synthetic *a priori* judgment."[62] Such an account, as technically difficult as it is, should nevertheless provide some orientation to the diverging interpretations of "the transcendental" found in Plato's classical realism and Kant's transcendental idealism. The divide between these positions, though, returns us anew to Plato's student, and how he was already assessing the implications of his master's teachings on the two worlds known colloquially as phenomena and the Forms.

Aristotle, again for his part in resisting (metaphysical) assertions made by "friends of our own," (viz., Plato and the like) declared allegiance to the *reality* of phenomena, or as Martha Nussbaum ably interprets it: "Aristotle's *phainomena* must be understood to be our beliefs and interpretations, often as revealed in linguistic usage. To set down the *phainomena* is not to look for belief-free fact, but to record our usage and the structure of thought and belief which usage displays."[63] For Nussbaum, Aristotle "describe[es] the world *as it appears to*, as it is experienced by, observers who are members of our kind." It was Aristotle, after all, who exclaimed "And one might ask the question, what in the world they mean by 'thing in itself'. . . ."[64] To be sure it is useful to acknowledge the dissenters, Aristotle prominently among them—and his Peripatetic inheritors, such as Theophrastus, even as we parse the variations of the opposing (until recently, dominant) Christo-Platonic tradition. Aristotle's skepticism of such philosophical system-building by means of non-empirical conjecture finds later expression in Carlyle's description of the activity as akin to the making of a "dream theorem: a net quotient, confidently given out, where divisor and dividend are both unknown," and Wittgenstein's dismissal of "advancing theses."[65] Nietzsche, characteristically, draws down all the bold options—Plato's classical realism, Kant's transcendental idealism, Christianity, *and* contemporary (scientific) realism by noting that "natural scientists do no better when they say 'force moves, force causes,' and so on,—our entire science, despite all its coolness, its freedom from affect, still stands under the seduction of language and has not gotten rid of the changelings slipped over on it, the 'subjects' (the atom, for example, is such a changeling, likewise the Kantian 'thing-in-itself')."[66] The transcendental, in Donald Pease's phraseology from another context, may be regarded as a "volatile transfer point," a "mobile category," and a "promiscuous signifier" of meaning.[67] The volatility, mobility, and promiscuity needless to say continue into the present era.

As we move from Plato's (classical) "realism" to Kant's (transcendental) "idealism," we should also shift sideways to Christianity, which can seem a post-Platonic rendering of Platonism by way of Plotinus. Among the "fathers" of the Western church, Augustine sought to reconcile Christian practice and faith with the Neoplatonism made available by Plotinus; for instance, as he observed and cultivated affinities between Christian and Plotinian outlooks, we can glean, among other attributes, a central emphasis on a trinity (Father, Son, Holy Ghost; the One, the Intellect, the Soul). Though we have, for the moment, transitioned from the binaries of real/ ideal or phenomena/noumena (to these inventive triads), it is not readily apparent how a trinity might achieve reconciliation as a triune (viz., three-in-one)—for aren't all properties of *both* trinities legitimate versions of the divine or ideal? When Augustine came to write about the bishop of Milan, he "noticed frequently in the sermons of our priest [Ambrose], and sometimes in yours [Manlius Theodorus], that, when speaking of God, no one should think of Him as something corporeal; nor yet of the soul, for of all things the soul is nearest to God."[68] Disparaging "something corporeal" not only gives credence to ascetic practices (again, by those "despisers of the body"), but also to the presumption that material existence is not in fact reality at all—and certainly not coextensive with *divine* reality.[69] We are back to, or never left, it seems, the Platonic contention that the most real—and indeed only real—is that which is ideal.

The historian of philosophy, as much as the historian of science, might wonder if such descriptions are themselves not inventions—even perturbations—of the mind that declares them. For his part, Kant believed that it was the structure of the mind (and its faculties) that gave shape to reality; time and space were not "out there" but "in here." The capacity to conceive of the transcendental, it would seem, lay within. Yet the formality and inherency of this arrangement does not set up the conditions for totalizing metaphysical revelation, if anything, just the opposite. When Kant commenced the *Critique of Pure Reason*, he wrote: "Human reason has this peculiar fate that in one species of its knowledge it is burdened by questions which, as prescribed by the very nature of reason itself, it is not able to ignore, but which, as transcending all its powers, it is also not able to answer."[70] The sorts of questions we ask (and seek answers for)—does God exist? is the soul immortal? do humans have free will?—exceed our power to reply. Why is this so? Because, as Kant says, "For since the principles of which [reason] is making use transcend the limits of experience, they are no longer subject to any empirical test."[71] By the standards of modern natural science, reason affords no quarter on the perennial questions for which we most desire answers, or at the very least, plausible indications of truth.

The human condition—"burdened by questions" we are "not able to answer"—is, therefore, arguably, worse with Kant (than Plato) because in *his* two world theory we cannot know noumena: there is no coming to the light, emerging unchained from the cave—not even a vestigial theory of *anamnesis*. We are free to postulate, but never to prove. "Practical reason," as Kant called it, would therefore arrive as an afterthought. When Heinrich Heine depicted the scenario, in a mode of excoriating satire, he noted that Kant

> deliberated and said, half good-naturedly and half ironically, "Old Lampe [Kant's loyal manservant] must have a God, otherwise the poor fellow can't be happy. But man ought to be happy in this world—practical reason says so—that's certainly all right with me—then let practical reason also guarantee the existence of God." As a result of this argument Kant distinguished between theoretical [viz., pure] reason and practical reason, and by means of the latter, as with a magician's wand, he revived the corpse of Deism, which theoretical reason had killed.[72]

When Kant tells the story, he is not half so troubled as Heine, or even "old Lampe," "a mournful spectator, . . . cold sweat and tears pouring from his face."[73]

> The dictum of all genuine idealists from the Eleatic school to Bishop Berkeley, is contained in this formula: "All cognition through the senses and experience is nothing but sheer illusion, and only, in the ideas of the pure understanding and reason there is truth."
>
> The principle that throughout dominates and determines my Idealism, is on the contrary: "All cognition of things merely from pure understanding or pure reason is nothing but sheer illusion, and only in experience is there truth."[74]

Given that Kant says his view—so-called "critical" idealism—is "directly contrary to idealism proper," that is, in the tradition running from the Eleatics to Berkeley (and *including* Plato's classical realism), we should be glad then for Paul Carus to help decode what Kant means when he says "thoughts without content are empty, intuitions without concepts are blind":[75]

> In place of the old metaphysics which used to derive from pure concepts a considerable amount of pretended knowledge concerning God, the world, and man, concerning substance, . . . the soul, . . . and immortality, Kant drew up an inventory of the possessions of Pure Reason and came to the conclusion that all knowledge of purely formal thought is in itself empty and that sense-experience in itself is blind; the two combined form the warp and woof of experience, which alone can afford positive information concerning the nature of objects. Empirical knowledge of the senses furnishes the material, while formal thought supplies the method by which perceptions can be organised and systematised into knowledge.[76]

Recall that Kant wanted to explore the limits of knowledge [*Wissen*] in order to "make room for faith [*Glaube*]," that is, provide a defensible space for religion *within* the expanding scope of Enlightenment science (including the specter of a skepticism that would yield only atheism);[77] earlier, in the previous century, Descartes—who was a contemporary of Galileo—had to make room for *science* (e.g., mathematics) in the midst of a dominant religious orthodoxy. The scandals of these two ages (Descartes' early seventeenth century and Kant's late eighteenth century) are, therefore, inverted. But what can we say about our *contemporary* relation to work in transcendental thought—work that evidently draws its pedigree from the deep time and entrenched habits of civilization? Does the hegemony of (contemporary, natural) science allow for "mystical" investigations—or are the latter mocked as pseudo-science or non-science or nonsense? The contours of post-secular thinking may inform our best current reply. Not incidentally, Wittgenstein, whose work was heralded by logical positivists and atheists alike, himself said: "I am not a religious man but I cannot help seeing every problem from a religious point of view."[78]

But, of course, Kant is just one take on the realist/idealist debate, though an iconic and indelible one. (And as Emerson reminds us: "There are degrees in idealism."[79]) Given the lengthy list of contributors here gathered, one must presume that not all of them are Kantians after-the-fact, much less avant la lettre. So, there is tremendous reason to believe that the approaches to "the transcendental" on offer are anything but uniform, cohesive, or monolithic (even if the heft of the volume might let it serve as a standing stone!). Transcendental thought is not one thing. And it is not a synonym for idealism, since, as Plato and Kant make evident, even idealism is sometimes not idealism! Here we have many varied texts for sorting and sifting the diversity of opinion on the transcendental, again if not definitively (for that would court hubris and anti-intellectualism), then for the worthy ambition of getting clearer about what has been said on the matter.

A century after Kant died, and thus a century after the descendants of Kant's "transcendental idealism" tried to codify and clarify how pure reason is related to sense experience (and the functions of practical reason), Henry Adams found himself in Paris amidst the Great Exposition of 1900 wondering aloud about the collision of forces embodied by "The Dynamo and the Virgin." In this new century, in this new science of steam and mechanism, x-ray and atom, "man had translated himself into a new universe which had no common scale of measurement with the old. He had entered a supersensual world . . ."—a term meant to connote the transcendental at the atomic level; in effect puzzling out the transcendental *within* the immanent: unknowable scales and spaces of which we are said to be composed but concomitantly ignorant of, "movements imperceptible to his senses, perhaps even imperceptible to his instruments" and thus, not even capable of being known by proxy (say, through a lens)—or, for us, some computer-generated *virtual* representation.[80] As Emerson might say, the infinite now lies within: and increasingly, his intuitions appear authenticated by the interstellar spaces discovered betwixt electrons; contemporary neuroscience has traded scalpels for electrochemistry, shifted from the haptic queries of gross anatomy to those made "beyond reach" at the level of molecule and cell. And so, as we move onward from Kant, who in the contours of his own intellectual autobiography traded physics for metaphysics, so in Adams, the direction is reversed as we find "physics stark mad in metaphysics."

The nearest approach to the revolution of 1900 was that of 310, when Constantine set up the Cross. The rays that [Samuel Pierpont] Langley disowned, as well as those which he fathered, were occult, supersensual, irrational; they were a revelation of mysterious energy like that of the Cross; they were what, in terms of mediæval science, were called immediate modes of the divine substance.[81]

While Adams concluded that "the force of the Virgin was still felt at Lourdes, and seemed to be as potent as X-rays," its power was never felt in America.[82] The separation of geographical location may not be as important as the gap in time and technology—from 310 to 1900, from the force of a metaphor to the force of a mechanism. But here we are again, in a new register of thought, finding our way to another innovation of a divided world—this time written up by a self-described historian, someone who "insisted on a relation of sequence," but would have to admit that "the sequence of time was artificial, and the sequence of thought was chaos."[83] All that remained for Adams was "the sequence of force": how do we get from the (force of the) Virgin to (force of) the Dynamo? In this year of Nietzsche's death, his critique, noted above—about scientists who speak of "force moves, force causes," and so on—achieves a new layer of significance.[84] "The *causa sui* is the best self-contradiction that has been conceived thus far," wrote Nietzsche; "it is a sort of rape and perversion of logic."[85] Today we still live in the time of the Dynamo, though it goes by more names than steam: neural network, electro biochemistry, nanotechnology, semiconductors, the Internet, genetics, transgenics, and the like.

From the cutting edge precision of the present-day back again to the parched intonations of desert sects, the idea of making progress on the meaning of the transcendental seems endlessly illusive. So though we have sentiments from Genesis ("for dust thou art, and unto dust shalt thou return."), Ecclesiastes ("Then shall the dust return to the earth as it was: and the spirit shall return unto God who gave it."), and 1 Corinthians ("The first man *is* of the earth, earthy: the second man *is* the Lord from heaven."), we remain beholden to the mysteries of the flesh *and* consciousness.[86] At such times when, again, physics courts metaphysics, or better, poetry, we ought to turn to the poets themselves. Emily Dickinson wrote: "Death is a dialogue between / The spirit and the dust"; and another poet, Herman Melville inscribed, a decade before Dickinson's own death—"The sign o' the cross—*the spirit above the dust!*"[87] In *Moby-Dick*, we can trace the lineaments of Plato's *Phaedrus* (the body as fettered like an oyster to its shell) and *Phaedo* (that man is like a fish), when Ishmael confides an inflection of the Cartesian cogito in a whaler's diction:

Methinks that what they call my shadow here on earth is my true substance. Methinks that in looking at things spiritual, we are too much like oysters observing the sun through the water, and thinking that thick water the thinnest of air. Methinks my body is but the less of my better being. In fact take my body who will, take it I say, it is not me.[88]

How often the transcendental (by whatever name it appears) is contrasted with the concrete, the material, the flesh (be it whale blubber or human body) and yet what a weighty term it is: "Methinks we have hugely mistaken this matter of Life and Death." Touché Ishmael: *matter* indeed. In a nonfictional space, when Melville wrote about authorship—how we write, how we create by means of words—he continues to query aloud, like his brave narrator aboard the Pequod: "But that dust of which our bodies are composed, how can it fitly express the nobler intelligences among us?"[89] In short, how does material come to speak of the immaterial? These are, to be sure, old, old questions.

In the dialogue between the Neoplatonic and Christian inheritance of the Platonic tradition, there is continual slippage between binaries and trinities (both so often distilled to unities!), but the differences between the schemas (is it two or is it three? . . . or it is one!) seem less conspicuous than the shared value both maintain for the spirit—for that which transcends the material, the body, the dust. As Ambrose intoned and Augustine inscribed, "our thoughts should not dwell on any material reality whatsoever" because it is not a *reality* after all. In our age, we have been encouraged to think that material reality is the *only* reality: that, among other things, "consciousness is a biological process."[90] Or as Galen Strawson puts it more colloquially: "Conscious experience is itself a form of physical stuff."[91] And the deduction made possible by this reductiveness is meant to assures us, according to Strawson, that "having conscious experience is knowing what it is." Our negotiations are therefore hardly ossified, and, it would seem barely clarified. Ask ancient ascetic or modern cognitive scientist, ask medieval mystic or contemporary clergy, ask philosopher, physicist, or poet, and the nature of transcendental thought will be translated again and anew.

The foregoing (admittedly cursorily drawn) sketch of Plato and Kant may lead us to wonder if the transcendental itself is not a kind of ideology taken up from one generation to the next, worked over, and then re-set along the terms, values, and preoccupations of one's present age. If this is so, then, the transcendental "refuses," as Emerson noted, "to be recorded in propositions," is not something that will ever achieve a satisfying, terminal definition, but, by design (or by nature), will remain an abstraction used to express the sense (or promote the agenda) of a given writer, tradition, power structure, or critical outlook.[92] The transcendental is a discourse, or an evolving set of competing discourses.

Though Karl Marx is minimally included in these proceedings, and Sigmund Freud is likewise only lent a phrase from his epoch-shaping outlook, one has to wonder if their interpretations (respectively) of history and consciousness are not themselves readings of the transcendental (by other names). Thinking of Freud, then, we would not say merely that we have noticed in humans a propensity to figure or project or invent a totemic realm for absolute value, but that the very nature of consciousness is a transcendental affair; the perennial query "Am I awake or dreaming?" hints at the dramas nested in our pictures of reality; Pascal and Descartes, as we find here, were already on the case centuries earlier. A useful text for thinking through the ideological underpinnings of the transcendental—perhaps especially as they emerge in Marx and Freud—can be found in a late-nineteenth-century letter from Friedrich Engels to Franz

Mehring in which "false consciousness" is synonymous with the human failure to see things as they really are. With italics added, Engels writes:

> Ideology is a process accomplished by the so-called thinker consciously, indeed, but with a false consciousness. The real motives impelling him remain unknown to him, otherwise it would not be an ideological process at all. Hence he imagines false or apparent motives. Because it is a process of thought he derives both its form and its content from pure thought, either his own or that of his predecessors. He works with mere thought material which he accepts without examination as the product of thought, he does not investigate further for *a more remote process independent of thought*; indeed its origin seems obvious to him, because as all action is produced through the medium of thought it also appears to him to be ultimately based upon thought. The ideologist who deals with history (history is here simply meant to comprise all the spheres—political, juridical, philosophical, theological—belonging to society and not only to nature), the ideologist dealing with history then, possesses in every sphere of science material which has formed itself independently out of the thought of previous generations and has gone through an independent series of developments in the brains of these successive generations. True, external facts belonging to its own or other spheres may have exercised a co-determining influence on this development, but the tacit pre-supposition is that these facts themselves are also only the fruits of a process of thought, and so *we still remain within that realm of pure thought* which has successfully digested the hardest facts.[93]

The lengthy quotation is meant to show that the legacies of Plato and Kant can reveal themselves in perhaps unexpected places—and simultaneously. What else is Engels' appeal to "a more remote process independent of thought" other than a gesture toward the real that is *not* a mental construct? (as we locate the kindred notion of Platonic Ideas set apart from the empirical world—beyond historically situated thinkers). And what else is Engels' contention that "we still remain within that realm of pure thought" but a question about whether mental forms are real, inherent—as in Kantian "categories" and "faculties"? Consequently, should the "reality" of mental constructs, at last, be divorced from the real altogether, since what we call "thought," as Engels implies, seems to be a feature of history—and thus caught up in the accidents of personalities and their idiosyncratic states of consciousness? Such questions, somewhat oddly, appear to be asking about the fate of the transcendental in the midst of a contest about the meaning of materialism (e.g., the legacy of Hegelian dialectics as it comes to inform Marxian dialectical materialism). Once again, the real and the ideal are conspicuously engaged, admit shared features, and sometimes even trade places.

The bifurcations, analogies, and overlaps that have been adduced offer signs that the "transcendental" may be invoked by parties and principals that are (often understood to be) at odds with one another. As Stanley Fish has astutely noted, "all ideology is narrow," so we, as readers in this collection might relax into that condition as a partial explanation both for the scope of a given project (its terms, techniques, time period, etc.) and how that scope generates a distinctively ideological portrait.[94] As discourses regularly contest one another, why not also appreciate that there exist multiple discourses of the transcendental? No wonder there is debate, diversity, dissent. Take your pick—Stoics, Platonists, Epicureans, Christians, Scholastics, Kantians, Hegelians, Marxians, Romantics, realists, idealists, ascetics, atheists, nominalists, naturalists, humanists, psychoanalysts, structuralists, deconstructionists, post-secularists, materialists, atomists, vitalists, object-oriented ontologists, ordinary language philosophers, and so on—all share an interest, in some cases a primary one, in the value of the "transcendental" (whatever name it might go by), and yet, for that inflection of a common object, there is a scattered, contested series of reports on it. So, as we acknowledge variability in readings, we can also marvel at the shared root of so much ratiocination. In fact, adapting Žižek's notion of "the sublime object of ideology" for present purposes, we could conjecture that it is not *ideology* that is the sublime object, but the transcendental itself.[95] Time and again, text after text, from antiquity to the anthropocene, the transcendental—by this or that name—looms as the telos, implied or explicit, of a given argument or observation. Why might this be the case? How could so many disparate, competing agendas find common ground? Perhaps because it is not a ground at all.

We can suss a first clue to the evacuation of content or reference by thinking etymologically. At its base, and beginning, the transcendental invokes the power of the *trans*: the crossing or the going across.[96] So we ask, reasonably: from what to what? What precisely is in transit—and where is it from (viz., what is its source?) and where is it going (viz., what is its destination?)? The transcendental, in this bare bones definition-by-description, can be identified in any number of shapes and schemas, metaphors and metonyms: from the vertical of the Christological ascension to the implied (teleological) progression of Hegelian dialectics (where "synthesis" is a further position *beyond* the present contest of thesis/anti-thesis). I will not belabor these notions with a compendium of similar examples, but hope that in pointing out the "transcendentalized" structure of many philosophical, religious, literary, and historical accounts, we find repeated appeals to a realm "beyond" or "over" or "across" some such threshold, membrane, body, or "envelope." Moreover, as Heidegger noted in his reading of Plato and Parmenides, the achievement of such a "crossing" is nothing less than the "disclosure" of a "world"—where *aletheia* (ἀλήθεια) is made equivalent to light—a trope familiar to Plato's allegory (and to Schiller's verse, and much in between).[97] The status of the transcendental-as-metaphor (in whatever form it takes) is more than a curiosity, since we are returned (anew) to the suggestion that metaphors are not real things, but surrogates for them—stand-ins. Does the transcendental name the (real) thing we think it names, or, more likely, does it allude to it by oblique glances, indirect blows, sputtering chances, and larks?

With regular appeals to spatial location or types of movement (e.g., directions, passageways, liminal spaces, etc.) the transcendental suggests itself, at more times than others, as a euphemism—a cipher-like category that serves the interests of those who invoke it, but may confound those who are forced to contend with its (purported) content and value. The diversity of accounts on offer here reinforces the impression that categories are not straightforward (either in proposal or comprehension), for since we have, in nature, a fish that can fly, a bird that can swim, a monkey that uses rocks for tools, and a carnivorous plant, we might find that the "transcendental" transcends itself. Perhaps the transcendental is immanent after all. What sorts of (useful) questions a reader might ask about the transcendental—what is its object? what is it for? how does the term find purchase in our contemporary intellectual landscape?—will, hopefully, emerge naturally from encounters with its variety of invocations in this collection. Borrowing John Rawls' phrase (from another realm of inquiry), what precisely—or what at all—could we say is the "overlapping consensus" from Plato and Aristotle to Spivak and Rancière? And if something shared is revealed, that would be worth of our efforts; and if nothing, that too would be clarifying.

If we accept that Plato and Kant offer two dominant, and mostly contrasting, nay inverted, options for thinking through the transcendental (and thereby supply a useful, if still negotiable frame), we can also pause to dwell on (what appears to be) Nietzsche's wholesale dismissal of the transcendental—and in particular, his trouncing of Plato and Kant, coupled with his beckoning, taunting, mocking invitation that philosophers give up on the transcendental altogether. He asks: "Suppose such an incarnate will to contradiction and antinaturalness [as we find it in the 'ascetic priest'] is induced to *philosophize*: upon what will it vent its innermost contrariness?"[98] Herewith a ready reply: "Upon what is felt most certainly to be real and actual."

> To renounce belief in one's ego, to deny one's own "reality"—what a triumph! not merely over the senses, over appearance, but a much higher kind of triumph, a violation and cruelty against *reason*—a voluptuous pleasure that reaches its height when the ascetic self-contempt and self-mockery of reason declares: "*there is* a realm of truth and being, but reason is *excluded* from it!"[99]

And Nietzsche takes Kant head-on: "Things are so constituted that the intellect comprehends just enough of them to know that for the intellect they are—*utterly incomprehensible*."[100] With his characteristic use of exclamations and italics, Nietzsche's position is manifest—and yet, what should we call his summons? Anti-transcendental? Or, perhaps, post-transcendental? In our own day—a century beyond the freshly made censure of Nietzsche's critique, does talk of the post-secular provide a way, as noted above (with reference to Habermas, et al.) to re-think and return to (as part of the "turn" toward) the transcendental? Or does Nietzsche's assault linger, haunting any recovery or recasting of this tradition? Not surprisingly, Nietzsche speaks to us, his future audience, with some blend of playfulness and pity, yet ever with hope that we might hear him:

> Henceforth, my dear philosophers, let us be on guard against the dangerous old conceptual fiction that posited a "pure, will-less, painless, timeless knowing subject"; let us guard against the snares of such contradictory concepts as "pure reason," "absolute spirituality," "knowledge in itself": these always demand that we should think of an eye that is completely unthinkable, an eye turned in no particular direction, in which the active and interpreting forces, through which alone seeing becomes seeing *something*, are supposed to be lacking; these always demand of the eye an absurdity and a nonsense.[101]

If Nietzsche's special pleading is warranted, we may ask if post-secularism is providing a way forward with transcendental thought (either as a form of recovery or reconceptualization) that honors his admonition by not repeating history. Thus far, we have seen how modern secularism, for example, in the form of a so-called "new atheism," has aimed to eviscerate the credentials of the other-than-empirical. Yet, for the all the diversity of styles and appeals, such anti- or post-transcendental voices often convey a passionate agreement; the new atheism is nothing if not full of spiritual intensity—perhaps traveling under the auspices of a trenchant hyper-rationality.[102]

At present, there are critics who, like Nietzsche, would appear convicted by the need to sustain the de-authorization of any such transcendental—or more broadly, metaphysical—project. When, for example, Alex Rosenberg tells us "Why I Am a Naturalist," he offers no quarter for the genuineness, virtue, and relevance of contemporary thinking on the subject:

> If semiotics, existentialism, hermeneutics, formalism, structuralism, post-structuralism, deconstruction and post-modernism transparently flout science's standards of objectivity, or if they seek arbitrarily to limit the reach of scientific methods, then naturalism can't take them seriously as knowledge. That doesn't mean anyone should stop doing literary criticism any more than forgoing fiction. Naturalism treats both as fun, but neither as knowledge.[103]

The condescension is not subtle, but spelled out. (Nietzsche, to be sure, would lean forward to whisper that science *too* is perspectival, including its purported "standards of objectivity."[104]) Taking Nietzsche's critique even further, however, when Rosenberg addresses Galen Strawson's remarks (noted above), he says there is good reason to believe—in the light of evolving, emerging cognitive scientific researches—that "there is no first-person point of view."[105] Perspectivism is a myth as much as the self and the soul. Here is a representative report on the state of affairs that we are now encouraged to believe as true, as real, and as constitutive of experience:

> Our access to our own thoughts is just as indirect and fallible as our access to the thoughts of other people. We have no privileged access to our own minds. If our thoughts give the real meaning of our actions, our words, our lives, then we can't ever be sure what we say or do, or for that matter, what we think or why we think it.

Philosophers' claims that by reflecting on itself thought reliably reveals our nature, grounds knowledge, gives us free will, endows our behavior with moral value, are all challenged. And the threat doesn't stem from some tendentious scientistic worldview. It emerges from the detailed understanding of the mind that cognitive science and neuroscience are providing.

Despite these assurances from philosophy, empirical science has continued to build up an impressive body of evidence showing that introspection and consciousness are not reliable bases for self-knowledge. As sources of knowledge even about themselves, let alone anything else human, both are frequently and profoundly mistaken.[106]

Our situation, according to Rosenberg, is worse than even Descartes's skepticism-cum-solipsism would suggest, for we cannot so much as regard as given the condition that one's thinking is *one's own*; the cogito is suddenly a bit of poetry, a fiction, "fun," and no longer in the knowledge business. How, then, the logic follows, can an individual posit the transcendental if—on Rosenberg's cognitive/neuro/empirical scientific tack—there is no self (or individuated mind) to fathom it or give it shape and articulation in language, in thought? Where it seemed Nietzsche had little patience for the Platonic and Kantian legacies of the transcendental, Rosenberg, and the conversation that dismisses philosophical thought in favor of explanations from cognitive/neuro/empirical science, dissolves Nietzsche's hard-won insights as well. The self, and thus self-knowledge, it would seem, is as "completely unthinkable" as the transcendental—as *utterly incomprehensible*.

How does one give textual shape or definition to a phenomenon that defies or exceeds the expanse of Western philosophical thought? An anthology of transcendental philosophy can seem at once essential (why don't we have several such volumes to choose from? at present, there are none!) and impossible—for the ideas that animate this robust, eclectic, millennia-old tradition *saturate* human experience. Yet, somehow, perhaps for that very pervasiveness, the ideas—and their source texts—elude us, make it hard for us to discuss, much less define or defend. So, herewith is a forthright attempt to present a wide chronological sweep, a representative range, of writers who have identified, embodied, and otherwise enriched the tradition—or habit—of addressing the transcendental as a feature of life and thereafter (and seemingly always) as an elemental part of philosophy—or thought, generally. Despite intervals when the transcendental may have seemed an empty, eviscerated, and irrelevant notion—a palaver long-since retired, or marked for evisceration—select contributions provide ample evidence of its once and ongoing pertinence, the continuation of a long, uninterrupted tradition of inquiry. The transcendental, as the foregoing should attest and the contents to follow should convincingly suggest, is not an epiphenomenon of some other, more central philosophical inquiry, but the meat and marrow— and even bone—of the enterprise that we find composing the body of metaphysical thought throughout the ages. And yet, as the contents should also reveal, the substantiveness of the subject, and the trials of time have not resolved or settled opinions but rather have deepened, disturbed, and distributed them. Even in the present day, as we appear to preside over the longest period of sustained secular and atheistic thinking in human history—a modern tradition no doubt bolstered by the remarkable, undeniable achievements of the natural sciences—novel and compelling remarks on transcendental philosophy nevertheless continue to appear. As such, transcendental thought itself seems to have become a transcendental notion!

Transcendental thought is not solely the province of Judaism or Christianity—or for that matter, any "religious tradition"—much less the general, extra-traditional name of mysticism or the vagaries implicit in defining spirituality; nor is the term a signifier of, on the one hand, strict ascetic/monastic thinking or, on the other hand, syncretist lines of thought; and it does not have propriety claims from any specific philosophical outlook to the exclusion of others. Rather, transcendental thought can be said to share in *all* these traditions (and vice versa) and range over the instincts and expressions of their creators. As such, the present collection cannot be identified by one tradition, trope, or type of thinking, but rather—and quite contrary to any effort to harmonize disparate notions into a unified formula or definition or canon—the volume traces (and embraces) the long arc of varied and multiform engagement with the human relation to a transcendent idea, being, or realm (e.g., Forms, God, the One, the Absolute, mind, soul, spirit, truth, law, noumena, ideas, the ideal, etc.); attempts to argue or articulate a reading of the mind's relation to matter; assembles artful, perceptive efforts to come to terms with skepticism— along with knowledge of one's self, others, and the wider world; and congregates contentious but illuminating debates about the meaning and implications of idealism *and* realism (and related legacies of entrenched conceptual binaries).

Transcendental philosophy is not one thing, and yet, as this collection may reveal, it is— perhaps for its open-endedness and indeterminacy—a perpetual part of the intellectual landscape from ancient Greece to the present day, from Plato and Aristotle to Agamben, Badiou, Cavell, and Deleuze. And even in coming to the "end" of the pieces collected here, we find ourselves returned to the beginning—or at least one of the originators of this thinking—since Badiou, for instance, writes partly in recovery of Plato. Internally, within smaller time segments, we discover emanations of influence and serial engagement between thinkers and texts—for example, not just in the wake of Plato, but also, especially after Kant, and again after Nietzsche. And for each commentator who says that "our modern times have seen Truth relativized, allotted with value and distanced from the Absolute,"[107] there is another who claims a new or *revitalized* relation to both. The worthy debate abides.

* * * *

At the very end of his *Enquiry Concerning Human Understanding*, David Hume undertook to complete the following eliminative questionnaire for himself—by which, of course, he meant to implicate us, his readers:

> When we run over libraries, persuaded of these principles, what havoc must we make? If we take in our hand any volume; of divinity or school metaphysics, for instance; let us ask, *Does it contain any abstract reasoning concerning quantity or number?* No. *Does it contain*

any experimental reasoning concerning matter of fact or existence? No. Commit it then to the flames: for it can be nothing but sophistry and illusion.[108]

Kant was famously unsettled by Hume's outlook, and labored to counter it, and yet Kant's illustrious and hard-won synthetic *a priori* would seem to be among the first to be tossed on the pyre. Yet, for every Hume, ready to dismiss what Emerson called "that gleam of light which flashes across his mind from within," we find a Robinson Crusoe who pulls us close for his counsel:

> Let no man despise the secret hints and notices of danger, which sometimes are given him, when he may think there is no possibility of its being real. That such hints and notices are given us, I believe few that have made any observations of things, can deny; that they are certain discoveries of an invisible world, and a converse of spirits, we cannot doubt.[109]

Daniel Defoe must have read his Descartes for he adds the reassuring coda: "And if the tendency of them seems to be to warn us of danger, why should we not suppose they are from some friendly agent, whether supreme, or inferior, and subordinate, is not the question; and that they are given for our good?"[110] Emerson, centuries later, still finds the need to countermand the Cartesian fear of a deceiving, evil genius, and does not worry over the origins or intentions of such a "tendency," but instead offers a boast underwritten by self-trust: "If I am the Devil's child, I will live then from the Devil."[111] Such spirited replies correspond adroitly with Carlyle's willing admission of a "Descendentalism"![112] Herewith, we are given purchase on the fact that we are not merely addressing ourselves to the transcendental, but are doing so through thought—and it may take us places, and call us from positions, we could not fathom in advance. How we *think* about the transcendental remains as elemental to our critical enquiry as it was for Hume, et al. Where we stand in relation to the "flames" or the "gleam" becomes part of any reading in this contentious, wide-ranging, quintessentially human investigation.

If the writing collected in this volume fails to meet Hume's scorching criteria, let us perhaps pause and pushback, and save the work inherent in his challenge for the day's reflections—and perhaps tomorrow's too. There are those for whom whatever has been written on such matters as metaphysics threatens to squander our time, and there are Hamlets who aver that "There are more things in heaven and earth, Horatio / Than are dreamt of in your philosophy." So, we, as readers-in-transcendental-thought sit between the Scylla and Charybdis of Hume and Hamlet. If this book, or some part of it, could survive the skeptical Scot, or convince the depressive Dane that philosophy—in its myriad transcendental instantiations—has imagined many wonderful things *worthy* of our attention, then the volume could be esteemed more than kindling and not less than kind. It will be an aid to further thinking and thinking further.

Partly, a reader may be served to distinguish (1) the instances in this collection that are offered as systematic and doctrinaire, part of an "architectonic" (in Kant's term of praise), or otherwise promoting "theses" (in Wittgenstein's pejorative sense) from (2) the occasions when the works take on a different course and cast, that is, when they are allusive, poetic, and comfortable in the conceptual spaces afforded by language itself (beyond its service to system-building). In this latter case, the writing is its own milieu (instead of a paltry proxy for some better, clearer, more defensible mode of communication); this latter kind of work, therefore, invites us to read it as if entering an atmosphere, not to read past it or through it to achieve some anticipated effect or specified conclusion. Depending on whence one reads—for example, from a training and interest and practice of philosophy, or from literature; from poetics or cognitive science; from a ministry or from mysticism—and depending on what one extols or exalts to be the "proper work" of such domains, one will likely find the criteria that solicit and reinforce the division as articulated in (1) and (2). Yet, since these two "types" (and even then, in a capacious sense of both) appear within the space of a single volume, the question remains for the reader to determine the extent to which this is not one book but two. Stanley Cavell concluded *The Claim of Reason* with the question "Can philosophy become literature and still know itself?"[113] Decades later, in the wake of the "linguistic turn," in the midst of the "cognitive turn" and the "post-secular turn" (and any number of other turns—"cultural," "deconstructive," "multimodal," "neo-materialist," "objective," "pictorial," "speculative," "technological," "translational," "transnational," . . . "dorsal"!), and still processing the impact of ordinary language philosophy, the question of what philosophy, for the present-day reader, knows as its own, as itself, haunts these pages.[114] If philosophy has become literature, without loss and without remainder, then the book is one. And if divided (or at least, on occasion, overlapping), then, perhaps we are, despite our efforts to the contrary, or our positions as inheritors of these texts, and after millennia of debate, still living in two worlds—among others, and at the very least, the literary and the philosophical, the ideal and the real, the transcendent and the immanent, a world of value and a world of chance.

Notes

1   Anthropological and ethnographic researches are especially attuned to the breadth of engagement with the transcendental across time and peoples. Of signature merit in this regard, see James G. Frazer, *The Golden Bough: The Roots of Religion and Folklore* (New York: Gramercy Books, 1981; originally published as *The Golden Bough: A Study in Comparative Religion*, 1890); and Paul Radin, *Primitive Man as Philosopher* (Mineola, NY: Dover Publications, Inc., second rev. ed., 1957; originally published by D. Appleton and Co., 1927).

2   I am grateful to Herwig Friedl and Reiner Wild for their help tracking down the origins of this verse by Friedrich Schiller, and also for their input translating it from the German. The late Newton Garver first brought this exemplary, illuminating verse to my attention.

3   Aristotle, *Nicomachean Ethics*, trans. W. D. Ross (Oxford: Oxford University Press, rev. ed., 2009), Book II, Sec. 2.

4   Stanley Cavell, *Emerson's Transcendental Etudes*, ed. David Justin Hodge (Stanford: Stanford University Press, 2003).

5 Paul Schrader, *Transcendental Style in Film: Ozu, Bresson, Dreyer* (New York: Da Capo, 1972).

6 *Transcendental Heidegger*, ed. Steven Crowell and Jeff Malpas (Stanford: Stanford University Press, 2007); *Transcendental Philosophy and Naturalism*, ed. Joel Smith and Peter Sullivan (Oxford: Oxford University Press, 2011); *Transcendental Ontology: Essays in German Idealism*, ed. Markus Gabriel (New York: Continuum, 2011).

7 *The Bloomsbury Anthology of Aesthetics*, ed. Joseph Tanke and Colin McQuillan (New York: Bloomsbury, 2012).

8 Perhaps we stand in need of an anthology on the "culture wars," especially in so far as they find expression in the "anthology wars." See, among others, Allan Bloom, *The Closing of the American Mind: How Higher Education Has Failed Democracy and Impoverished the Souls of Today's Students* (New York: Simon & Schuster, 1987); James Davison Hunter, *Culture Wars: The Struggle to Define America* (New York: Basic Books, 1992); Henry Louis Gates, Jr., *Loose Canons: Notes on the Culture Wars* (New York: Oxford University Press, 1992); David Denby, *Great Books* (New York: Simon & Schuster, 1996); Gregory S. Jay, *American Literature and the Culture Wars* (Ithaca: Cornell University Press, 1997); *Culture Wars: An Encyclopedia of Issues, Viewpoints, and Voices*, ed. Roger Chapman (London: M. E. Sharpe, Inc., 2010); Andrew Hartman, *A War for the Soul of America: A History of the Culture Wars* (Chicago: University of Chicago Press, 2015). My allusion here, then, is to that subset of the culture wars that involves how canons are formed (and contested), and relatedly how anthologies (of those canonical works) get made— presuming the often fraught social and political context of their creation and reception.

9 Ralph Waldo Emerson, *The Journals and Miscellaneous Notebooks of Ralph Waldo Emerson*, ed. Alfred R. Ferguson (July 13, 1833), IV.198. See also David LaRocca, *Emerson's English Traits and the Natural History of Metaphor* (New York: Bloomsbury, 2013), 74.

10 See David LaRocca, "Performative Inferentialism: A Semiotic Ethics," *Liminalities: A Journal of Performance Studies* 9, no. 1 (February 2013).

11 See LaRocca, *Emerson's English Traits and the Natural History of Metaphor*, 141.

12 Ibid., 147–51.

13 Opensyllabusproject.org

14 See David LaRocca, "The Limits of Instruction: Pedagogical Remarks on Lars von Trier's *The Five Obstructions*," *Film and Philosophy* 13 (2009): 35–50.

15 Jacques Derrida, "The Principle of Reason: The University in the Eyes of Its Pupils," *Diacritics* 13, no. 3 (Autumn 1983): 16.

16 Ibid.; italics in original.

17 Ibid., 18.

18 Ralph Waldo Emerson, "The American Scholar," in *The Complete Works of Ralph Waldo Emerson*, ed. Edward Emerson (Boston: Houghton, Mifflin, and Company, 1903), Concord Edition, Vol. I, 84. See also, Cavell, *Emerson's Transcendental Etudes*, 14–16, 31, 142, 149–52, 194.

19 Matthew Arnold, "The Function of Criticism at the Present Time," in *Culture and Anarchy*, ed. Stefan Collini (Cambridge: Cambridge University Press, 1993), 26 and passim.

20 Arnold, "The Function of Criticism at the Present Time," 35–37.

21 See Newton Garver's dissertation *Grammar and Criteria* (Cornell University, Department of Philosophy, 1965); see also his *This Complicated Form of Life: Essays on Wittgenstein* (Chicago: Open Court, 1994), esp. ch. 11, 177–96.

22   Thomas Carlyle, *Sartor Resartus: The Life and Opinions of Diogenes Teufelsdröckh* (Oxford: Oxford University Press, 1987/2008), 87.

23   Ralph Waldo Emerson, "The Poet," in *The Complete Works of Ralph Waldo Emerson*, ed. Edward Emerson (Boston: Houghton, Mifflin, and Company, 1903), Concord Edition, Vol. III, 22.

24   Carlyle, *Sartor Resartus*, 67.

25   Ibid., 68.

26   John Searle, *Mind, Language, and Society: Philosophy in the Real World* (New York: Basic Books, 2008), 53.

27   See Robert K. Logan, *The Poetry of Physics and the Physics of Poetry* (Hackensack, NJ: World Scientific Publishing Co., 2010).

28   Albert Einstein, *The World as I See It* (1949). An alternate translation: "The fairest thing we can experience is the mysterious. It is the fundamental emotion which stands at the cradle of true art and true science. He who knows it not and can no longer wonder, no longer feel amazement, is as good as dead, a snuffed-out candle." Trans. Alan Harris (Philosophical Library, 2011).

29   René Descartes to Marin Mersenne, April 15, 1630, *Works of Descartes*, ed. Charles Adam and Paul Tannery (Paris: Vrin/CNRS, 1964–76), Vol. I, 144; Descartes, *Philosophical Writings*, trans. John Cottingham, et al. (New York: Cambridge University Press, 1984–91), Vol. III, 22.

30   René Descartes to Frans Burman, April 16, 1648, *Works of Descartes*, Vol. V, 165; *Philosophical Writings*, Vol. III, 346.

31   Einstein, *The World as I See It*.

32   Letter from Gustav Flaubert to Louise Colet (May 26, 1853), quoted in Jacques Rancière, *The Flesh of Words: The Politics of Writing* (Stanford: Stanford University Press, 2004), 157–58.

33   Emerson, *Nature* in *Complete Works*, Vol. I, 3.

34   Emerson, *Journals* (July 13, 1833), Vol. IV, 200; LaRocca, *Emerson's English Traits and the Natural History of Metaphor*, 122.

35   See LaRocca, *Emerson's English Traits and the Natural History of Metaphor*, 205–13. See also, Nicolas Wade, "Meet Luca, the Ancestor of All Living Things," *The New York Times* (July 25, 2016), nytimes.com.

36   See Yuval Noah Harari, *Sapiens: A Brief History of Humankind* (New York: Harper Collings, 2015), 5.

37   Nicholas St. Fleur, "The Water in Your Glass May Be Older than the Sun," *The New York Times* (April 15, 2016), nytimes.com.

38   Stanley Cavell, *The Claim of Reason: Wittgenstein, Skepticism, Morality, Tragedy* (Oxford: Oxford University Press, 1979/99), 207.

39   Stanley Cavell, "An Interview with Stanley Cavell," James Conant, in *The Senses of Stanley Cavell*, ed. Richard Fleming and Michael Payne, *Bucknell Review* 32, no. 1 (1989) and (Cranbury, NJ: Associated University Presses, 1989), 50. See also Richard Eldridge, "Between Acknowledgment and Avoidance," in *Stanley Cavell* (Cambridge: Cambridge University Press, 2003), 4. See also David LaRocca, "The Education of Grown-ups: An Aesthetics of Reading Cavell," *The Journal of Aesthetic Education* 47, no. 2 (Summer 2013): 109–31; and "Reading Cavell Reading," in *Stanley Cavell, Literature, and Film: The Idea of America*, ed. Andrew Taylor and Áine Kelly (London: Routledge, 2013), 26–41.

40   Friedrich Nietzsche, *Thus Spoke Zarathustra: A Book for None and All*, trans. Walter Kaufmann (New York: Penguin, 1954), see ch. 4; Simone de Beauvoir, *The Second Sex*, trans. H. M. Parshley (New York: Alfred A. Knopf, 1952), xxxiii. See also Plato, *Phaedo*, in *The Collected Dialogues of Plato*, ed. Edith Hamilton and Huntington Cairns (Princeton: Princeton University Press, 1961), 65d.

41 See Carlyle, *Sartor Resartus* and G. B. Tennyson, *Sartor Called Resartus: The Genesis, Structure, and Style of Thomas Carlyle's First Major Work* (Princeton: Princeton University Press, 1965); Giorgio Agamben, "Absolute Immanence," in *Potentialities: Collected Essays in Philosophy* (Madison: University of Wisconsin Press, 1999), 220–39; and Slavoj Žižek, "The Descent of Transcendence into Immanence, or Deleuze as a Hegelian," in *Transcendence: Philosophy, Literature, and Theology Approach the Beyond*, ed. Regina Schwartz (London: Routledge, 2004), 235–48.

42 M. H. Abrams, *Natural Supernaturalism: Tradition and Revolution in Romantic Literature* (New York: W. W. Norton & Company, 1971), 13.

43 Yuval Noah Harari, "What Explains the Rise of the Humans?" (July 2015). Transcript at ted.com. See also Harari's *Sapiens* (2015).

44 Werner Herzog, *Cave of Forgotten Dreams* (New York: Creative Differences Productions, 2010), 01:09:19.

45 Emerson, "The Poet," *Complete Works*, Vol. III, 22.

46 See Diogenes Allen, *Philosophy for Understanding Theology* (Louisville: John Knox Press, 1985), 55.

47 Carlyle, *Sartor Resartus*, ch. 8 passim.

48 Cavell, *The Claim of Reason*, 397.

49 Plato, *Phaedo*, in *The Collected Dialogues of Plato*, 65c.

50 Emerson, "The Poet," *Complete Works*, Vol. III, 3; see also David LaRocca, "'Eternal Allusion': Maeterlinck's Readings of Emerson," in *A Power to Translate the World: New Essays on Emerson and International Culture*, ed. David LaRocca and Ricardo Miguel-Alfonso (Hanover: Dartmouth College Press, 2015), 124.

51 Carlyle, *Sartor Resartus*, 131–32.

52 Maurice Maeterlinck, "Emerson," in *Estimating Emerson: An Anthology of Criticism from Carlyle to Cavell*, ed. David LaRocca (New York: Bloomsbury, 2013), 361.

53 Ibid., 363.

54 Carlyle, *Sartor Resartus*, 149.

55 Aristotle, *Nicomachean Ethics*, Book I, Sec. 6.

56 If the new atheists have their accomplices, they also have their adversaries: see, for instance, Terry Eagleton, *Reason, Faith, and Revolution: Reflections on the God Debate* (The Terry Lectures Series, New Haven: Yale University Press, 2009) and *Culture and the Death of God* (New Haven: Yale University Press, 2014); Gary Gutting, *Talking God: Philosophers on Belief* (New York: W. W. Norton & Company, 2017); David Bentley Hart, *Atheist Delusions: The Christian Revolution and its Fashionable Enemies* (New Haven: Yale University Press, 2009); and Marilynne Robinson, *Absence of Mind: The Dispelling of Inwardness from the Modern Myth of the Self* (New Haven: Yale University Press, 2010).

57 See Jürgen Habermas, "Secularism's Crisis of Faith: Notes on Post-Secular Society," *New Perspectives Quarterly* 25 (2008): 17–29; Charles Taylor, *A Secular Age* (Cambridge: Harvard University Press, 2007); and Gregg Lambert, *Return Statements: The Return of Religion in Contemporary Philosophy* (Edinburgh: Edinburgh University Press, 2016). Work by Hent de Vries includes *Philosophy and the Turn to Religion* (Baltimore: The Johns Hopkins University Press, 1999); *Religion and Violence: Philosophical Perspectives from Kant to Derrida* (Baltimore: The Johns Hopkins University Press, 2002); *Minimal Theologies: Critiques of Secular Reason in Adorno and Levinas* (Baltimore: The Johns Hopkins University Press, 2005); *Political Theologies: Public Religions in a Post-Secular Age*, edited with Lawrence E. Sullivan (New York: Fordham University Press, 2006). See also Gregor McLennan, "The Postsecular Turn," *Theory, Culture & Society* 27, no. 4 (2010): 3–20.

58 Immanuel Kant, *Critique of Pure Reason*, trans. Norman Kemp Smith (New York: St. Martin's Press, 1965), A93–94, 126.

59 Ibid., B73, 90–91.

60 Ibid., Preface to the First Edition, Axvii, 12.

61 Ibid., B73, 91.

62 Ibid., A158, 194.

63 Martha C. Nussbaum, *The Fragility of Goodness: Luck and Ethics in Greek Tragedy and Philosophy* (Cambridge: Cambridge University Press, 1986, rev. ed., 2001), 245.

64 Aristotle, *Nicomachean Ethics*, Book I, Sec. 6.

65 Carlyle, *Sartor Resartus*, 43.

66 Friedrich Nietzsche, *On Genealogy of Morality: A Polemic*, trans. Maudemarie Clark and Alan J. Swensen (Indianapolis: Hackett Publishing Company, 1998), Sec. 13 of "Good and Evil, Good and Bad," 25.

67 Donald Pease as quoted in David LaRocca and Ricardo Miguel-Alfonso, "Thinking Through International Influence," in *A Power to Translate the World*, 4.

68 Augustine, *De Beata Vita*, trans. Ludwig Schopp, in *The Fathers of the Church: The Writings of Saint Augustine* (New York: CIMA Publishing, Inc., 1948), Vol. V, Ch. 1, 47–48. See also, Chad Tyler Gerber, *The Spirit of Augustine's Early Theology: Contextualizing Augustine's Pneumatology* (Burlington: Ashgate, 2012), 22n66, 81–82.

69 See esp. the third treatise "What Do Ascetic Ideals Means?" in Friedrich Nietzsche, *On the Genealogy of Morals: A Polemic*, ed. and trans. Maudemarie Clark and Alan J. Swensen (Indianapolis: Hackett Publishing Company, Inc., 1998), 67–118.

70 Kant, *Critique of Pure Reason*, 7.

71 Ibid.

72 Heinrich Heine, "Concerning the History of Religion and Philosophy in Germany," in *The Romantic School and Other Essays*, ed. Jost Herman and Robert C. Holub (New York: Continuum, 1985/2002), 212.

73 Ibid.

74 Immanuel Kant, *Prolegomena to Any Future Metaphysics Than Can Qualify as a Science*, trans. Paul Carus (Chicago: Open Court Publishing Company, 1902), 151.

75 Ibid., 153.

76 Paul Carus, "Kant's Philosophy," in Kant, *Prolegomena*, 172.

77 See Kant, *Critique of Pure Reason*, B-Preface, Bxxx.

78 Ray Monk, *Wittgenstein: The Duty of Genius* (New York: Penguin, 1990), 464.

79 Emerson, "Circles," *Complete Works*, Vol. II, 309.

80 Henry Adams, "The Dynamo and the Virgin (1900)," in *The Education of Henry Adams* (New York: Library of America, 1983), 1068.

81 Ibid., 1069.

82 Ibid., 1070.

83   Ibid., 1069.

84   Friedrich Nietzsche, *On Genealogy of Morality: A Polemic*, trans. Maudemarie Clark and Alan J. Swensen (Indianapolis: Hackett Publishing Company, 1998), Sec. 13 of "Good and Evil, Good and Bad," 25.

85   Friedrich Nietzsche, *Beyond Good and Evil: Prelude to a Philosophy of the Future*, trans. Walter Kaufmann (New York: Vintage, 1966, §21, 28).

86   King James Bible, Gen. 3:19; Eccl. 12:7; and 1 Cor. 15:47.

87   See Dickinson in this volume, 478. Herman Melville, Epilogue to *Clarel: A Poem and Pilgrimage in the Holy Land* (1876), as part of *The Writings of Herman Melville*, ed. Harrison Hayford, et al. (Evanston: Northwestern University Press and The Newberry Library, 1991), 498; italics and exclamation point in the original.

88   Herman Melville, "The Chapel" (ch. 7), *Moby-Dick; or, The Whale* (New York: Penguin, 2001), 42. See also Branka Arsić, "Oyster Metaphysics: Melville and the Ethics of Matter," a lecture delivered on June 27, 2016 at The School of Criticism and Theory, Cornell University.

89   Herman Melville, "Hawthorne and His Mosses," in *Pierre; or, The Ambiguities* (and other works), ed. Harrison Hayford, et al. (New York: The Library of America, 1984), 1154.

90   See note 26 above.

91   Galen Strawson, "Consciousness Isn't a Mystery. It's Matter," *The New York Times*, May 16, 2016, nytimes. com.

92   Emerson, "Spirit" in *Nature*, *Complete Works*, Ch. VII, Vol. I, 62.

93   Friedrich Engels letter to Franz Mehring, July 14, 1893, in *Marx and Engels Correspondence*, trans. Donna Torr (New York: International Publishers, 1968).

94   Stanley Fish, "Freedom of Speech is Not an Academic Value," a lecture delivered on June 20, 2016 at The School of Criticism and Theory, Cornell University.

95   See Slavoj Žižek, *The Sublime Object of Ideology* (New York: Verso, 1989).

96   See LaRocca and Miguel-Alfonso, *A Power to Translate the World*, 3–4.

97   See, for example, Martin Heidegger, *The Essence of Truth: On Plato's Cave Allegory and Theaetetus*, trans. Ted Sadler (New York: Continuum, 2002), esp. §§6–9. For decades, Heidegger had argued for an equivalency between *aletheia* and truth, but amended this view—offering at once a recantation and a clarification—in the lecture "The End of Philosophy and the Task of Thinking": "To raise the question of *aletheia*, of unconcealment [viz., disclosure] as such, is not the same as raising the question of truth. For this reason, it was inadequate and misleading to call *aletheia* in the sense of opening, truth." *On Time and Being*, trans. Joan Stambaugh (Chicago: The University of Chicago Press, 1972), 70.

98   Friedrich Nietzsche, *On the Genealogy of Morals*, in *Basic Writings of Friedrich Nietzsche*, trans. Walter Kaufmann (New York: The Modern Library, 1968), 554; italics in original.

99   Ibid.; italics in original.

100 Ibid., 555; italics in original.

101 Ibid., 555.

102 See above, note 56.

103 Alex Rosenberg, "Why I Am a Naturalist," *The New York Times* (September 17, 2011), nytimes.com.

104   See above, note 66.

105   Alex Rosenberg, "Why You Don't Know Your Own Mind," *The New York Times* (July 18, 2016), nytimes. com.

106   Ibid.

107   Introduction by Norman Madarasz to Alain Badiou, *Manifesto for Philosophy* (Albany: State University of New York Press, 1999), 3.

108   David Hume, *An Enquiry Concerning Human Understanding* (1748), ed. Peter Millican (Oxford: Oxford University Press, 2007), Sec. XII, No. 34, 120; italics in original.

109   Daniel Defoe, *The Life and Strange Surprising Adventures of Robinson Crusoe of York, Mariner* (New York: Harper & Brothers, 1900), 303.

110   Ibid. Crusoe continues: "So little do we see before us in the world, and so much reason have we to depend cheerfully upon the great Maker of the world, that He does not leave His creatures so absolutely destitute, but that in the worst circumstances they have always something to be thankful for, and sometimes are nearer their deliverance than they imagine; nay, are even brought to their deliverance by the means by which they seem to be brought to their destruction," 305.

111   Emerson, "Self-Reliance," *Complete Works*, Vol. II, 50.

112   Carlyle, *Sartor Resartus*, 51.

113   Cavell, *The Claim of Reason*, 496.

114   As a representative sample, see *The Linguistic Turn: Essays in Philosophical Method*, ed. Richard M. Rorty (Chicago: The University of Chicago Press, 1967/92); Charlotte Ann Frick, *The Cognitive Turn: The Interdisciplinary Story of Thought in Western Culture* (Lanham: Rowman & Littlefield, 1994); Gregor McLennan, "The Postsecular Turn," *Theory, Culture & Society* 27, no. 4 (2010), 3–20; *Global Secularisms in a Post-Secular Age*, ed. Michael Rectenwald and Rochelle Almeida (Berlin: Walter de Gruyter, 2015); Frederic Jameson, *The Cultural Turn: Selected Writings on the Postmodern, 1983-1998* (New York: Verso, 1998); Christopher Norris, *The Deconstructive Turn: Essays in the Rhetoric of Philosophy* (New York: Routledge, 1983/2003); Jason Palmeri, *Remixing Composition: A History of Multimodal Writing Pedagogy* (Carbondale: Southern Illinois University Press, 2012); Selmin Kara, "Redefining Documentary Materialism: From Actuality to Virtuality in Víctor Erice's *Dream of Light*," in *The Philosophy of Documentary Film: Image, Sound, Fiction, Truth*, ed. David LaRocca (Lanham: Rowman & Littlefield, 2017), 343–60; Graham Harman, *Guerilla Metaphysics: Phenomenology and the Carpentry of Things* (Chicago: Open Court, 2005); W. J. T. Mitchell, "The Pictorial Turn," in *Picture Theory* (Chicago: University of Chicago Press, 1994), 11–34; *The Speculative Turn: Continental Materialism and Realism*, ed. Levi Bryant, Nick Srnicek, and Graham Harman (Melbourne: Re.Press, 2011); Alfred Nordmann, "Changing Perspectives: The Technological Turn in the Philosophies of Science and Technology," in *Philosophy of Technology After the Empirical Turn*, ed. Maarten Franssen, Pieter E. Vermaas, Peter Kroes, and Anthonie W. M. Meijers (New York: Springer, 2016), 107–25; Doris Bachmann-Medick, "The Translational Turn," *Translation Studies*, 2, no. 1 (2009): 2–16; Donald E. Pease, "The Anti-Slave from Emerson to Obama," in *A Power to Translate the World: New Essays on Emerson and International Culture*, ed. David LaRocca and Ricardo Miguel-Alfonso (Hanover: Dartmouth College Press, 2015), 31–42; and David Wills, *Dorsality: Thinking Back Through Technology and Politics* (Minneapolis: University of Minnesota Press, 2008).

1

Plato

Phaedrus

Phaedrus SPEAK, AND FEAR NOT.

Socrates But where is the fair youth whom I was addressing before, and who ought to listen now; lest, if he hear me not, he should accept a non-lover before he knows what he is doing?

Phaedr. He is close at hand, and always at your service.

Soc. Know then, fair youth, that the former discourse was the word of Phaedrus, the son of Vain Man, who dwells in the city of Myrrhina (Myrrhinusius). And this which I am about to utter is the recantation of Stesichorus the son of Godly Man (Euphemus), who comes from the town of Desire (Himera), and is to the following effect: "I told a lie when I said" that the beloved ought to accept the non-lover when he might have the lover, because the one is sane, and the other mad. It might be so if madness were simply an evil; but there is also a madness which is a divine gift, and the source of the chiefest blessings granted to men. For prophecy is a madness, and the prophetess at Delphi and the priestesses at Dodona when out of their senses have conferred great benefits on Hellas, both in public and private life, but when in their senses few or none. And I might also tell you how the Sibyl and other inspired persons have given to many an one many an intimation of the future which has saved them from falling. But it would be tedious to speak of what every one knows.

There will be more reason in appealing to the ancient inventors of names, who would never have connected prophecy (μαντιχή), which foretells the future and is the noblest of arts, with madness (μανιχὴ), or called them both by the same name, if they had deemed madness to be a disgrace or dishonour;—they must have thought that there was an inspired madness which was a noble thing; for the two words, μαντιχή and μανιχὴ), are really the same, and the letter τ is only a modern and tasteless insertion. And this is confirmed by the name which was given by them to the rational investigation of futurity, whether made by the help of birds or of other signs—this, for as much as it is an art which supplies from the reasoning faculty mind (νοῦς) and information (ἱστορία) to human thought (οἴησις), they orignally termed οἰονοϊστική, but the word has been lately altered and made sonorous by the modern introduction of the letter Omega (οἰονοϊστι χὴ) and οἰωνιστιχὴ), and in proportion as prophecy (μαντιχὴ) is more perfect and august than augury, both in name and fact, in the same proportion, as the ancients testify, is madness superior to a sane mind (σωφροσύνη), for the one is only of human, but the other of divine origin. Again, where plagues and mightiest woes have bred in certain families, owing to some ancient blood-guiltiness, there madness has entered with holy prayers and rites, and by inspired utterances found a way of deliverance for those who are in need; and he who has part in this gift, and is truly possessed and duly out of his mind, is by the use of purifications and mysteries made whole and exempt from evil, future as well as present, and has a release from the calamity which was afflicting him, The third kind is the madness of those who are possessed by the Muses; which taking hold of a delicate and virgin soul, and there inspiring frenzy, awakens lyrical and all other numbers; with these adorning the myriad actions of ancient heroes for the instruction of posterity. But he who, having no touch of the Muses' madness in his soul, comes to the door and thinks that he will get into the temple by the help of art—he, I say, and his poetry are not admitted; the sane man disappears and is nowhere when he enters into rivalry with the madman.

I might tell of many other noble deeds which have sprung from inspired madness. And therefore, let no one frighten or flutter us by saying that the temperate friend is to be chosen rather than the inspired, but let him further show that love is not sent by the gods for any good to lover or beloved; if he can do so we will allow him to carry off the palm. And we, on our part, will prove in answer to him that the madness of love is the greatest of heaven's blessings, and the proof shall be one which the wise will receive, and the witling disbelieve. But first of all, let us view the affections and actions of the soul divine and human, and try to ascertain the truth about them. The beginning of our proof is as follows:—

The soul through all her being is immortal, for that which is ever in motion is immortal; but that which moves another and is moved by another, in ceasing to move ceases also to live. Only the self-moving, never leaving self, never ceases to move, and is the fountain and beginning of motion to all that moves besides. Now, the beginning is unbegotten, for that which is begotten has a beginning; but the beginning is begotten of nothing, for if it were begotten of something, then the begotten would not come from a beginning. But if unbegotten, it must also be indestructible; for if beginning were destroyed, there could be no beginning out of anything, nor anything out of a beginning; and all things must have a beginning. And therefore the self-moving is the beginning of motion; and this can neither be destroyed nor begotten, else the whole heavens and all creation would collapse and stand still, and never again have motion or birth. But if the self-moving is proved to be immortal, he who affirms that self-motion is the very idea and essence of the soul will not be put to confusion. For the body which is moved from without is soulless; but that which is moved from within has a soul, for such is the nature of the soul. But if this be true, must not the soul be the self-moving, and therefore of necessity unbegotten and immortal? Enough of the soul's immortality.

Of the nature of the soul, though her true form be ever a theme of large and more than mortal discourse, let me speak briefly, and in a figure. And let the figure be composite—a pair of winged horses and a charioteer. Now the winged horses and the charioteers of the gods are all of them noble and of noble descent, but those of other races are mixed; the human charioteer drives his in a pair; and one of them is noble and of noble breed, and the other is ignoble and of ignoble breed; and the driving of them of necessity gives a great deal of trouble to him. I will endeavour to explain to you in what way the mortal differs from the immortal creature. The soul in her totality has the care of inanimate being everywhere, and traverses the whole heaven in divers forms appearing;—when perfect and fully winged she soars upward, and orders the whole world; whereas the imperfect soul, losing her wings and drooping in her flight, at last settles on the solid ground—there, finding a home, she receives an earthly frame which appears to be self-moved, but is really moved by her power; and this composition of soul and body is called a living and mortal creature. For immortal no such union can be reasonably believed to be; although fancy, not having seen nor surely known the nature of God, may imagine an immortal creature having both a body and also a soul which are united throughout all time. Let that, however, be as God wills, and be spoken of acceptably to him. And now let us ask the reason why the soul loses her wings!

The wing is the corporeal element which is most akin to the divine, and which by nature tends to soar aloft and carry that which gravitates downwards into the upper region, which is the habitation of the gods. The divine is beauty, wisdom, goodness, and the like; and by these the wing of the soul is nourished, and grows apace; but when fed upon evil and foulness and the opposite of good, wastes and falls away. Zeus, the mighty lord, holding the reins of a winged chariot, leads the way in heaven, ordering all and taking care of all; and there follows him the array of gods and demi-gods, marshalled in eleven bands; Hestia alone abides at home in the house of heaven; of the rest they who are reckoned among the princely twelve march in their appointed order. They see many blessed sights in the inner heaven, and there are many ways to and fro, along which the blessed gods are passing, every one doing his own work; he may follow who will and can, for jealousy has no place in the celestial choir. But when they go to banquet and festival, then they move up the steep to the top of the vault of heaven. The chariots of the gods in even poise, obeying the rein, glide rapidly; but the others labour, for the vicious steed goes heavily, weighing down the charioteer to the earth when his steed has not been thoroughly trained:—and this is the hour of agony and extremest conflict for the soul. For the immortals, when they are at the end of their course, go forth and stand upon the outside of heaven, and the revolution of the spheres carries them round, and they behold the things beyond. But of the heaven which is above the heavens, what earthly poet ever did or ever will sing worthily? It is such as I will describe; for I must dare to speak the truth, when truth is my theme. There abides the very being with which true knowledge is concerned; the colourless, formless, intangible essence, visible only to mind, the pilot of the soul. The divine intelligence, being nurtured upon mind and pure knowledge, and the intelligence of every soul which is capable of receiving the food proper to it, rejoices at beholding reality, and once more gazing upon truth, is replenished and made glad, until the revolution of the worlds brings her round again to the same place. In the revolution she beholds justice, and temperance, and knowledge absolute, not in the form of generation or of relation, which men call existence, but knowledge absolute in existence absolute; and beholding the other true existences in like manner, and feasting upon them, she passes down into the interior of the heavens and returns home; and there the charioteer putting up his horses at the stall, gives them ambrosia to eat and nectar to drink.

Such is the life of the gods; but of other souls, that which follows God best and is likest to him lifts the head of the charioteer into the outer world, and is carried round in the revolution, troubled indeed by the steeds, and with difficulty beholding true being; while another only rises and falls, and sees, and again fails to see by reason of the unruliness of the steeds. The rest of the souls are also longing after the upper world and they all follow, but not being strong enough they are carried round below the surface, plunging, treading on one another, each striving to be first; and there is confusion and perspiration and the extremity of effort; and many of them are lamed or have their wings broken through the ill-driving of the charioteers; and all of them after a fruitless toil, not having attained to the mysteries of true being, go away, and feed upon opinion. The reason why the souls exhibit this exceeding eagerness to behold the plain of truth is that pasturage is found there, which is suited to the highest part of the soul; and the wing on which the soul soars is nourished with this. And there is a law of Destiny, that the soul which attains any vision of truth in company with a god is preserved from harm until the next period, and if attaining always is always unharmed. But when she is unable to follow, and fails to behold the truth, and through some ill-hap sinks beneath the double load of forgetfulness and vice, and her wings fall from her and she drops to the ground, then the law ordains that this soul shall at her first birth pass, not into any other animal, but only into man; and the soul which has seen most of truth shall come to the birth as a philosopher, or artist, or some musical and loving nature; that which has seen truth in the second degree shall be some righteous king or warrior chief; the soul which is of the third class shall be a politician, or economist, or trader; the fourth shall be a lover of gymnastic toils, or a physician; the fifth shall lead the life of a prophet or hierophant; to the sixth the character of a poet or some other imitative artist will be assigned; to the seventh the life of an artisan or husbandman; to the eighth that of a sophist or demagogue; to the ninth that of a tyrant;—all these are states of probation, in which he who does righteously improves, and he who does unrighteously, deteriorates his lot.

Ten thousand years must elapse before the soul of each one can return to the place from whence she came, for she cannot grow her wings in less; only the soul of a philosopher, guileless and true, or the soul of a lover, who is not devoid of philosophy, may acquire wings in the third of the recurring periods of a thousand years; he is distinguished from the ordinary good man who gains wings in three thousand years:—and they who choose this life three times in succession have wings given them, and go away at the end of three thousand years. But the others receive judgment when they have completed their first life, and after the judgment they go, some of them to the houses of correction which are under the earth, and are punished; others to some place in heaven whither they are lightly borne by justice, and there they live in a manner worthy of the life which they led here when in the form of men. And at the end of the first thousand years the good souls and also the evil souls both come to draw lots and choose their second life, and they may take any which they please. The soul of a man may pass into the life of a beast, or from the beast return again into the man. But the soul which has never seen the truth will not pass into the human form. For a man must have intelligence of universals, and be able to proceed from the many particulars of sense to one conception of reason;—this is the recollection of those things which our soul once saw while following God—when regardless of that which we now call being she raised her head up towards the true being. And therefore the mind of the philosopher alone has wings; and this is just, for he is always, according to the measure of his abilities, clinging in recollection to those things in which God abides, and in beholding which He is what He is. And he who employs aright these memories is ever being initiated into perfect mysteries and alone becomes truly perfect. But, as he forgets earthly interests and is rapt in the divine, the vulgar deem him mad, and rebuke him; they do not see that he is inspired.

Thus far I have been speaking of the fourth and last kind of madness, which is imputed to him who, when he sees the beauty of earth, is transported with the recollection of the true beauty; he would like to fly away, but he cannot; he is like a bird fluttering and looking upward and careless of the world below; and he is therefore thought to be mad. And I have shown this of all inspirations to be the noblest and highest and the offspring of the highest to him who has or shares in it, and that he who loves the beautiful is called a lover because he partakes of it. For, as has been already said, every soul of man has in the way of nature beheld true being; this was the condition of her passing into the form of man. But all souls do not easily recall the things of the other world; they may have seen them for a short time only, or they may have been unforunate in their earthly lot, and, having had their hearts turned to unrighteousness through some corrupting influence, they may have lost the memory of the holy things which once they saw. Few only retain an adequate remembrance of them; and they, when they behold here any image of that other world, are rapt in amazement; but they are ignorant of what this rapture means, because they do not clearly perceive. For there is no light of justice or temperance or any of the higher ideas which are precious to souls in the earthly copies of them: they are seen through a glass dimly; and there are few who, going to the images, behold in them the realities, and these only with difficulty. There was a time when with the rest of the happy band they saw beauty shining in brightness,—we philosophers following in the train of Zeus, others in company with other gods; and then we beheld the beatific vision and were initiated into a mystery which may be truly called most blessed, celebrated by us in our state of innocence, before we had any experience of evils to come, when we were admitted to the sight of apparitions innocent and simple and calm and happy, which we beheld shining in pure light, pure ourselves and not yet enshrined in that living tomb which we carry about, now that we are imprisoned in the body, like an oyster in his shell. Let me linger over the memory of scenes which have passed away.

But of beauty, I repeat again that we saw her there shining in company with the celestial forms; and coming to earth we find her here too, shining in clearness through the clearest aperture of sense. For sight is the most piercing of our bodily senses; though not by that is wisdom seen; her loveliness would have been transporting if there had been a visible image of her, and the other ideas, if they had visible counterparts, would be equally lovely. But this is the privilege of beauty, that being the loveliest she is also the most palpable to sight. Now he who is not newly initiated or who has become corrupted, does not easily rise out of this world to the sight of true beauty in the other; he looks only at her earthly namesake, and instead of being awed at the sight of her, he is given over to pleasure, and like a brutish beast he rushes on to enjoy and beget; he consorts with wantonness, and is not afraid or ashamed of pursuing pleasure in violation of nature. But he whose initiation is recent, and who has been the spectator of many glories in the other world, is amazed when he sees any one having a godlike face or form, which is the expression of divine beauty; and at first a shudder runs through him, and again the old awe steals over him; then looking upon the face of his beloved as of a god he reverences him, and if he were not afraid of being thought a downright madman, he would sacrifice to his beloved as to the image of a god; then while he gazes on him there is a sort of reaction, and the shudder passes into an unusual heat and perspiration; for, as he receives the effluence of beauty through the eyes, the wing moistens and he warms. And as he warms, the parts out of which the wing grew, and which had been hitherto closed and rigid, and had prevented the wing from shooting forth, are melted, and as nourishment streams upon him, the lower end of the wing begins to swell and grow from the root upwards; and the growth extends under the whole soul—for once the whole was winged. During this process the whole soul is all in a state of ebullition and effervescence,—which may be compared to the irritation and uneasiness in the gums at the time of cutting teeth,— bubbles up, and has a feeling of uneasiness and tickling; but when in like manner the soul is beginning to grow wings, the beauty of the beloved meets her eye and she receives the sensible warm motion of particles which flow towards her, therefore called emotion (ἵμερος), and is refreshed and warmed by them, and then she ceases from her pain with joy. But when she is parted from her beloved and her moisture fails, then the orifices of the passage out of which the wing shoots dry up and close, and intercept the germ of the wing; which, being shut up with the emotion, throbbing as with the pulsations of an artery, pricks the aperture which is nearest, until at length the entire soul is pierced and maddened and pained, and at the recollection of beauty is again delighted. And from both of them together the soul is oppressed at the strangeness of her condition, and is in a great strait and excitement, and in her madness can neither sleep by night nor abide in her place by day. And wherever she thinks that she will behold the beautiful one, thither in her desire she runs. And when she has seen him, and bathed herself in the waters of beauty, her constraint is loosened, and she is refreshed, and has no more pangs and pains; and this is the sweetest of all pleasures at the time, and is the reason why the soul of the lover will never forsake his beautiful one, whom he esteems above all; he has forgotten mother and brethren and companions, and he thinks nothing of the neglect and loss of his property; the rules and proprieties of life, on which he formerly prided himself, he now despises, and is ready to sleep like a servant, wherever he is allowed, as near as he can to his desired one, who is the object of his worship, and the physician who can alone assuage the greatness of his pain. And this state, my dear imaginary youth to whom I am talking, is by men called love, and among the gods has a name at which you, in your simplicity, may be inclined to mock; there are two lines in the apocryphal writings of Homer in which the name occurs. One of them is rather outrageous, and not altogether metrical. They are as follows:—

> "Mortals call him fluttering love,
> But the immortals call him winged one,
> Because the growing of wings is a necessity to him."

You may believe this, but not unless you like. At any rate the loves of lovers and their causes are such as I have described.

Now the lover who is taken to be the attendant of Zeus is better able to bear the winged god, and can endure a heavier burden; but the attendants and companions of Ares, when under the influence of love, if they fancy that they have been at all wronged, are ready to kill and put an end to themselves and their beloved. And he who follows in the train of any other god, while he is unspoiled and the impression lasts, honours and imitates him, as far as he is able; and after the manner of his god he behaves in his intercourse with his beloved and with the rest of the world during the first period of his earthly existence. Every one chooses his love from the ranks of beauty according to his character, and this he makes his god, and fashions and adorns as a sort of image which he is to fall down and worship. The followers of Zeus desire that their beloved should have a soul like him; and therefore they seek out some one of a philosophical and imperial nature, and when they have found him and loved him, they do all they can to confirm such a nature in him, and if they have no experience of such a disposition hitherto, they learn of any one who can teach them, and themselves follow in the same way. And they have the less difficulty in finding the nature of their own god in themselves, because they have been compelled to gaze intensely on him; their recollection clings to him, and they become possessed of him, and receive from him their character and disposition, so far as man can participate in God. The qualities of their god they attribute to the beloved, wherefore they love him all the more, and if, like the Bacchic Nymphs, they draw inspiration from Zeus, they pour out their own fountain upon him, wanting to make him as like as possible to their own god. But those who are the followers of Here seek a royal love, and when they have found him they do just the same with him; and in like manner the followers of Apollo, and of every other god walking in the ways of their god, seek a love who is to be made like him whom they serve, and when they have found him, they themselves imitate their god, and persuade their love to do the same, and educate him into the manner and nature of the god as far as they each can; for no feelings of envy or jealousy are entertained by them towards their beloved, but they do their utmost to create in him the greatest likeness of themselves and of the god whom they honour. Thus fair and blissful to the beloved is the desire of the inspired lover, and the initiation of which I speak into the mysteries of true love, if he be captured by the lover and their purpose is effected. Now the beloved is taken captive in the following manner:—

As I said at the beginning of this tale, I divided each soul into three—two horses and a charioteer; and one of the horses was good and the other bad: the division may remain, but I have not yet explained in what the goodness or badness of either consists, and to that I will now proceed. The right-hand horse is upright and cleanly made; he has a lofty neck and an aquiline nose; his colour is white, and his eyes dark; he is a lover of honour and modesty and temperance, and the follower of true glory; he needs no touch of the whip, but is guided by word and admonition only. The other is a crooked lumbering animal, put together anyhow; he has a short thick neck; he is flat-faced and of a dark colour, with grey eyes and blood-red complexion; the mate of insolence and pride, shag-eared and deaf, hardly yielding to whip and spur. Now when the charioteer beholds the vision of love, and has his whole soul warmed through sense, and is full of the prickings and ticklings of desire, the obedient steed, then as always under the government of shame, refrains from leaping on the beloved; but the other, heedless of the pricks and of the blows of the whip, plunges and runs away, giving all manner of trouble to his companion and the charioteer, whom he forces to approach the beloved and to remember the joys of love. They at first indignantly oppose him and will not be urged on to do terrible and unlawful deeds; but at last, when he persists in plaguing them, they yield and agree to do as he bids them. And now they are at the spot and behold the flashing beauty of the beloved; which when the charioteer sees, his memory is carried to the true beauty, whom he beholds in company with Modesty like an image placed upon a holy pedestal. He sees her, but he is afraid and falls backwards in adoration, and by his fall is compelled to pull back the reins with such violence as to bring both the steeds on their haunches, the one willing and unresisting, the unruly one very unwilling; and when they have gone back a little, the one is overcome with shame and wonder, and his whole soul is bathed in perspiration; the other, when the pain is over which the bridle and the fall had given him, having with difficulty taken breath, is full of wrath and reproaches, which he heaps upon the charioteer and his fellow-steed, for want of courage and manhood, declaring that they have been false to their agreement and guilty of desertion. Again they refuse, and again he urges them on, and will scarce yield to their prayer that he would wait until another time. When the appointed hour comes, they make as if they had forgotten, and he reminds them, fighting and neighing and dragging them on, until at length he on the same thoughts intent, forces them to draw near again. And when they are near he stoops his head and puts up his tail, and takes the bit in his teeth and pulls shamelessly. Then the charioteer is worse off than ever; he falls back like a racer at the barrier, and with a still more violent wrench drags the bit out of the teeth of the wild steed and covers his abusive tongue and jaws with blood, and forces his legs and haunches to the ground and punishes him sorely. And when this has happened several times and the villain has ceased from his wanton way, he is tamed and humbled, and follows the will of the charioteer, and when he sees the beautiful one he is ready to die of fear. And from that time forward the soul of the lover follows the beloved in modesty and holy fear.

And so the beloved who, like a god, has received every true and loyal service from his lover, not in pretence but in reality, being also himself of a nature friendly to his admirer, if in former days he has blushed to own his passion and turned away his lover, because his youthful companions or others slanderously told him that he would be disgraced, now as years advance, at the appointed age and time, is led to receive him into communion. For fate which has ordained that there shall be no friendship among the evil has also ordained that there shall ever be friendship among the good. And the beloved when he has received him into communion and intimacy, is quite amazed at the good-will of the lover; he recognises that the inspired friend is worth all other friends or kinsmen; they have nothing of friendship in them worthy to be compared with his. And when this feeling continues and he is nearer to him and embraces him, in gymnastic exercises and at other times of meeting, then the fountain of that stream, which Zeus when he was in love with Ganymede named Desire, overflows upon the lover, and some enters into his soul, and some when he is filled flows out again; and as a breeze or an echo rebounds from the smooth rocks and returns whence it came, so does the stream of beauty, passing through the eyes which are the windows of the soul, come back to the beautiful one; there arriving and quickening the passages of the wings, watering them and inclining them to grow, and filling the soul of the beloved also with love. And thus he loves, but he knows not what; he does not understand and cannot explain his own state; he appears to have caught the infection of blindness from another; the lover is his mirror in whom he is beholding himself, but he is not aware of this. When he is with the lover, both cease from their pain, but when he is away then he longs as he is longed for, and has love's image, love for love (Anteros) lodging in his breast, which he calls and believes to be not love but friendship only, and his desire is as the desire of the other, but weaker; he wants to see him, touch him, kiss, embrace him, and probably not long afterwards his desire is accomplished. When they meet, the wanton steed of the lover has a word to say to the charioteer; he would like to have a little pleasure in return for many pains, but the wanton steed of the beloved says not a word, for he is bursting with passion which he understands not;—he throws his arms round the lover and embraces him as his dearest friend; and, when they are side by side, he is not in a state in which he can refuse the lover anything, if he ask him; although his fellow-steed and the charioteer oppose him with the arguments of shame and reason. After this their happiness depends upon their self-control; if the better elements of the mind which lead to order and philosophy prevail, then they pass their life here in happiness and harmony—masters of themselves and orderly—enslaving the vicious and emancipating the virtuous elements of the soul; and when the end comes, they are light and winged for flight, having conquered in one of the three heavenly or truly Olympian victories; nor can human discipline or divine inspiration confer any greater blessing on man than this. If, on the other hand, they leave philosophy and lead the lower life of ambition, then probably, after wine or in some other careless hour, the two wanton animals take the two souls when off their guard and bring them together, and they accomplish that desire of their hearts which to the many is bliss; and this having once enjoyed they continue to enjoy, yet rarely because they have not the approval of the whole soul. They too are dear, but not so dear to one another as the others, either at the time of their love or afterwards. They consider that they have given and taken from each other the most sacred pledges, and they may not break them and fall into enmity. At last they pass out of the body, un-winged, but eager to soar, and thus obtain no mean reward of love and madness. For those who have once begun the heavenward pilgrimage may not go down again to darkness and the journey beneath the earth, but they live in light always; happy companions in their pilgrimage, and when the time comes at which they receive their wings they have the same plumage because of their love.

Thus great are the heavenly blessings which the friendship of a lover will confer upon you, my youth. Whereas the attachment of the non-lover, which is alloyed with a worldly prudence and has worldly and niggardly ways of doling out benefits, will breed in your soul those vulgar qualities which the populace applaud, will send you bowling round the earth during a period of nine thousand years, and leave you a fool in the world below.

And thus, dear Eros, I have made and paid my recantation, as well and as fairly as I could; more especially in the matter of the poetical figures which I was compelled to use, because Phaedrus would have them. And now forgive the past and accept the present, and be gracious and merciful to me, and do not in thine anger deprive me of sight, or take from me the art of love which thou hast given me, but grant that I may be yet more esteemed in the eyes of the fair. And if Phaedrus or I myself said anything rude in our first speeches, blame Lysias, who is the father of the brat, and let us have no more of his progeny; bid him study philosophy, like his brother Polemarchus; and then his lover Phaedrus will no longer halt between two opinions, but will dedicate himself wholly to love and to philosophical discourses.

Phaedo

IS THAT IDEA OR ESSENCE, WHICH IN THE DIALECTICAL PROCESS we define as essence or true existence—whether essence of equality, beauty, or anything else—are these essences, I say, liable at times to some degree of change? or are they each of them always what they are, having the same simple self-existent and unchanging forms, not admitting of variation at all, or in any way, or at any time?

They must be always the same, Socrates, replied Cebes.

And what would you say of the many beautiful—whether men or horses or garments or any other things which are named by the same names and may be called equal or beautiful,—are they all unchanging and the same always, or quite the reverse? May they not rather be described as almost always changing and hardly ever the same, either with themselves or with one another?

The latter, replied Cebes; they are always in a state of change.

And these you can touch and see and perceive with the senses, but the unchanging things you can only perceive with the mind—they are invisible and are not seen?

That is very true, he said.

Well, then, added Socrates, let us suppose that there are two sorts of existences—one seen, the other unseen.

Let us suppose them.

The seen is the changing, and the unseen is the unchanging?

That may be also supposed.

And, further, is not one part of us body, another part soul?

To be sure.

And to which class is the body more alike and akin?

Clearly to the seen—no one can doubt that.

And is the soul seen or not seen?

Not by man, Socrates.

And what we mean by "seen" and "not seen" is that which is or is not visible to the eye of man?

Yes, to the eye of man.

And is the soul seen or not seen?

Not seen.

Unseen then?

Yes.

Then the soul is more like to the unseen, and the body to the seen?

That follows necessarily, Socrates.

And were we not saying long ago that the soul when using the body as an instrument of perception, that is to say, when using the sense of sight or hearing or some other sense (for the meaning of perceiving through the body is perceiving through the senses)—were we not saying that the soul too is then dragged by the body into the region of the changeable, and wanders and is confused; the world spins round her, and she is like a drunkard, when she touches change?

Very true.

But when returning into herself she reflects, then she passes into the other world, the region of purity, and eternity, and immortality, and unchangeableness, which are her kindred, and with them she ever lives, when she is by herself and is not let or hindered; then she ceases from her erring ways, and being in communion with the unchanging is unchanging. And this state of the soul is called wisdom?

That is well and truly said, Socrates, he replied.

And to which class is the soul more nearly alike and akin, as far as may be inferred from this argument, as well as from the preceding one?

I think, Socrates, that, in the opinion of every one who follows the argument, the soul will be infinitely more like the unchangeable—even the most stupid person will not deny that.

And the body is more like the changing?

Yes.

Yet once more consider the matter in another light: When the soul and the body are united, then nature orders the soul to rule and govern, and the body to obey and serve. Now, which of these two functions is akin to the divine? and which to the mortal? Does not the divine appear to you to be that which naturally orders and rules, and the mortal to be that which is subject and servant?

True.

And which does the soul resemble?

The soul resembles the divine, and the body the mortal—there can be no doubt of that, Socrates.

Then reflect, Cebes: of all which has been said is not this the conclusion?—that the soul is in the very likeness of the divine, and immortal, and intellectual, and uniform, and indissoluble, and unchangeable; and that the body is in the very likeness of the human, and mortal, and unintellectual, and multiform, and dissoluble, and changeable. Can this, my dear Cebes, be denied?

It cannot.

But if it be true, then is not the body liable to speedy dissolution? and is not the soul almost or altogether indissoluble?

Certainly.

And do you further observe, that after a man is dead, the body, or visible part of him, which is lying in the visible world, and is called a corpse, and would naturally be dissolved and decomposed and dissipated, is not dissolved or decomposed at once, but may remain for some time, nay, even for a long time, if the constitution be sound at the time of death, and the season of the year favourable? For the body when shrunk and embalmed, as the manner is in Egypt, may remain almost entire through infinite ages; and even in decay, there are still some portions, such as the bones and ligaments, which are practically indestructible:—Do you agree?

Yes.

And is it likely that the soul, which is invisible, in passing to the place of the true Hades, which like her is invisible, and pure, and noble, and on her way to the good and wise God, whither, if God will, my soul is also soon to go,—that the soul, I repeat, if this be her nature and origin, will be blown away and destroyed immediately on quitting the body, as the many say? That can never be, my dear Simmias and Cebes. The truth rather is, that the soul which is pure at departing and draws after her no bodily taint, having never voluntarily during life had connection with the body, which she is ever avoiding, herself gathered into herself;—and making such abstraction her perpetual study—which means that she has been a true disciple of philosophy; and therefore has in fact been always engaged in the practice of dying? For is not philosophy the study of death?—

Certainly—

That soul, I say, herself invisible, departs to the invisible world—to the divine and immortal and rational: thither arriving, she is secure of bliss and is released from the error and folly of men, their fears and wild passions and all other human ills, and forever dwells, as they say of the initiated, in company with the gods. Is not this true, Cebes?

Yes, said Cebes, beyond a doubt.

But the soul which has been polluted, and is impure at the time of her departure, and is the companion and servant of the body always, and is in love with and fascinated by the body and by the desires and pleasures of the body, until she is led to believe that the truth only exists in a bodily form, which a man may touch and see and taste, and use for the purposes of his lusts,—the soul, I mean, accustomed to hate and fear and avoid the intellectual principle, which to the bodily eye is dark and invisible, and can be attained only by philosophy;—do you suppose that such a soul will depart pure and unalloyed?

Impossible, he replied.

She is held fast by the corporeal, which the continual association and constant care of the body have wrought into her nature.

Very true.

And this corporeal element, my friend, is heavy and weighty and earthy, and is that element of sight by which a soul is depressed and dragged down again into the visible world, because she is afraid of the invisible and of the world below—prowling about tombs and sepulchres, near which, as they tell us, are seen certain ghostly apparitions of souls which have not departed pure, but are cloyed with sight and therefore visible.

That is very likely, Socrates.

Yes, that is very likely, Cebes; and these must be the souls, not of the good, but of the evil, which are compelled to wander about such places in payment of the penalty of their former evil way of life; and they continue to wander until through the craving after the corporeal which never leaves them they are imprisoned finally in another body. And they may be supposed to find their prisons in the same natures which they have had in their former lives.

What natures do you mean, Socrates?

What I mean is that men who have followed after gluttony, and wantonness, and drunkenness, and have had no thought of avoiding them, would pass into asses and animals of that sort. What do you think?

I think such an opinion to be exceedingly probable.

And those who have chosen the portion of injustice, and tyranny, and violence, will pass into wolves, or into hawks and kites;—whither else can we suppose them to go?

Yes, said Cebes; with such natures, beyond question.

And there is no difficulty, he said, in assigning to all of them places answering to their several natures and propensities?

There is not, he said.

Some are happier than others; and the happiest both in themselves and in the place to which they go are those who have practised the civil and social virtues which are called temperance and justice, and are acquired by habit and attention without philosophy of mind.

Why are they the happiest?

Because they may be expected to pass into some gentle and social kind which is like their own, such as bees or wasps or ants, or back again into the form of man, and just and moderate men may be supposed to spring from them.

Very likely.

No one who has not studied philosophy and who is not entirely pure at the time of his departure is allowed to enter the company of the gods, but the lover of knowledge only. And this is the reason, Simmias and Cebes, why the true votaries of philosophy abstain from all fleshly lusts, and hold out against them and refuse to give themselves up to them,—not because they fear poverty or the ruin of their families, like the lovers of money, and the world in general; nor like the lovers of power and honour, because they dread the dishonour or disgrace of evil deeds.

No, Socrates, that would not become them, said Cebes.

No, indeed, he replied; and therefore they who have any care of their own souls, and do not merely live moulding and fashioning the body, say farewell to all this; they will not walk in the ways of the blind: and when philosophy offers them purification and release from evil, they feel that they ought not to resist her influence, and whither she leads they turn and follow.

What do you mean, Socrates?

I will tell you, he said. The lovers of knowledge are conscious that the soul was simply fastened and glued to the body—until philosophy received her, she could only view real existence through the bars of a prison, not in and through herself; she was wallowing in the mire of every sort of ignorance, and by reason of lust had become the principal accomplice in her own captivity. This was her original state; and then, as I was saying, and as the lovers of knowledge are well aware, philosophy, seeing how terrible was her confinement, of which she was herself the cause, received and gently comforted her and sought to release her, pointing out that the eye and the ear and the other senses are full of deception, and persuading her to retire from them, and abstain from all the necessary use of them, and be gathered up and collected into herself, bidding her trust in herself and her own pure apprehension of pure existence, and to mistrust whatever comes to her through other channels and is subject to variation; for such things are visible and tangible, but what she sees in her own nature is intelligible and invisible. And the soul of the true philosopher thinks that she ought not to resist this deliverance, and therefore abstains from pleasures and desires and pains and fears, as far as she is able; reflecting that when a man has great joys or sorrows or fears or desires, he suffers from them, not merely the sort of evil which might be anticipated—as, for example, the loss of his health or property which he has sacrificed to his lusts—but an evil greater far, which is the greatest and worst of all evils, and one of which he never thinks.

What is it, Socrates? said Cebes.

The evil is that when the feeling of pleasure or pain is most intense, every soul of man imagines the objects of this intense feeling to be then plainest and truest: but this is not so, they are really the things of sight.

Very true.

And is not this the state in which the soul is most enthralled by the body?

How so?

Why, because each pleasure and pain is a sort of nail which nails and rivets the soul to the body, until she becomes like the body, and believes that to be true which the body affirms to be true; and from agreeing with the body and having the same delights she is obliged to have the same habits and haunts, and is not likely ever to be pure at her departure to the world below, but is always infected by the body; and so she sinks into another body and there germinates and grows, and has therefore no part in the communion of the divine and pure and simple.

Most true, Socrates, answered Cebes.

And this, Cebes, is the reason why the true lovers of knowledge are temperate and brave; and not for the reason which the world gives.

Certainly not.

Certainly not! The soul of a philosopher will reason in quite another way; she will not ask philosophy to release her in order that when released she may deliver herself up again to the thraldom of pleasures and pains, doing a work only to be outdone again, weaving instead of unweaving her Penelope's web. But she will calm passion, and follow reason, and dwell in the contemplation of her, beholding the true and divine (which is not matter of opinion), and thence deriving nourishment. Thus she seeks to live while she lives, and after death she hopes to go to her own kindred and to that which is like her, and to be freed from human ills. Never fear, Simmias and Cebes, that a soul which has been thus nurtured and has had these pursuits, will at her departure from the body be scattered and blown away by the winds and be nowhere and nothing.

Parmenides

WHILE SOCRATES WAS SAYING THIS, PYTHODORUS THOUGHT THAT PARMENIDES AND ZENO were not altogether pleased at the successive steps of the argument; but still they gave the closest attention, and often looked at one another, and smiled as if in admiration of him. When he had finished, Parmenides expressed these feelings in the following words:—

Socrates, he said, I admire the bent of your mind towards philosophy; tell me now, was this your own distinction between abstract ideas and the things which partake of them? and do you think that there is an idea of likeness apart from the likeness which we possess, or of the one and many, or of the other notions of which Zeno has been speaking?

I think that there are such abstract ideas, said Socrates.

Parmenides proceeded. And would you also make abstract ideas of the just and the beautiful and the good, and of all that class of notions?

Yes, he said, I should.

And would you make an abstract idea of man distinct from us and from all other human creatures, or of fire and water?

I am often undecided, Parmenides, as to whether I ought to include them or not.

And would you feel equally undecided, Socrates, about things the mention of which may provoke a smile? — I mean such things as hair, mud, dirt, or anything else that is foul and base; would you suppose that each of these has an idea distinct from the phenomena with which we come into contact, or not?

Certainly not, said Socrates; visible things like these are such as they appear to us, and I am afraid that there would be an absurdity in assuming any idea of them, although I sometimes get disturbed, and begin to think that there is nothing without an idea; but then again, when I have taken up this position, I run away, because I am afraid that I may fall into a bottomless pit of nonsense, and perish; and I return to the ideas of which I was just now speaking, and busy myself with them.

Yes, Socrates, said Parmenides; that is because you are still young; the time will come when philosophy will have a firmer grasp of you, if I am not mistaken, and then you will not despise even the meanest things; at your age, you are too much disposed to look to the opinions of men. But I should like to know whether you mean that there are certain forms or ideas of which all other things partake, and from which they are named; that similars, for example, become similar, because they partake of similarity; and great things become great, because they partake of greatness; and that just and beautiful things become just and beautiful, because they partake of justice and beauty?

Yes, certainly, said Socrates, that is my meaning.

And does not each individual partake either of the whole of the idea or of a part of the idea? Is any third way possible?

Impossible, he said.

Then do you think that the whole idea is one, and yet being one, exists in each one of many?

Why not, Parmenides? said Socrates.

Because one and the same existing as a whole in many separate individuals, will thus be in a state of separation from itself.

Nay, replied the other; the idea may be like the day, which is one and the same in many places, and yet continuous with itself; in this way each idea may be one and the same in all.

I like your way, Socrates, of dividing one into many; and if I were to spread out a sail and cover a number of men, that, as I suppose, in your way of speaking, would be one and a whole in or on many — that will be the sort of thing which you mean?

I am not sure.

And would you say that the whole sail is over each man, or a part only?

A part only.

Then, Socrates, the ideas themselves will be divisible, and the individuals will have a part only and not the whole existing in them?

That seems to be true.

Then would you like to say, Socrates, that the one idea is really divisible and yet remains one?

Certainly not, he said.

Suppose that you divide greatness, and that of many great things each one is great by having a portion of greatness less than absolute greatness — is that conceivable?

No.

Or will each equal part, by taking some portion of equality less than absolute equality, be equal to some other?

Impossible.

Or suppose one of us to have a portion of smallness; this is but a part of the small, and therefore the small is greater; and while the absolute small is greater, that to which the part of the small is added, will be smaller and not greater than before.

That is impossible, he said.

Then in what way, Socrates, will all things participate in the ideas, if they are unable to participate in them either as parts or wholes?

Indeed, he said, that is a question which is not easily determined.

Well, said Parmenides, and what do you say of another question?

What is that?

I imagine that the way in which you are led to assume the existence of ideas is as follows: You see a number of great objects, and there seems to you to be one and the same idea of greatness pervading them all; and hence you conceive of a single greatness.

That is true, said Socrates.

And if you go on and allow your mind in like manner to contemplate the idea of greatness and these other greatnesses, and to compare them, will not another idea of greatness arise, which will appear to be the source of them all?

That is true.

Then another abstraction of greatness will appear over and above absolute greatness, and the individuals which partake of it; and then another, which will be the source of that, and then others, and so on; and there will be no longer a single idea of each kind, but an infinite number of them.

But may not the ideas, asked Socrates, be cognitions only, and have no proper existence except in our minds, Parmenides? For in that case there may be single ideas, which do not involve the consequences which were just now mentioned.

And can there be individual cognitions which are cognitions of nothing?

That is impossible, he said.

The cognition must be of something?

Yes.

Of something that is or is not?

Of something that is

Must it not be of the unity, or single nature, which the cognition recognizes as attaching to all?

Yes.

And will not this unity, which is always the same in all, be the idea?

From that, again, there is no escape.

Then, said Parmenides, if you say that other things participate in the ideas, must you not say that everything is made up of thoughts or cognitions, and that all things think; or will you say that being thoughts they are without thought?

But that, said Socrates, is irrational. The more probable view, Parmenides, of these ideas is, that they are patterns fixed in nature, and that other things are like them, and resemblances of them; and that what is meant by the participation of other things in the ideas, is really assimilation to them.

But if, said he, the individual is like the idea, must not the idea also be like the individual, in as far as the individual is a resemblance of the idea? That which is like, cannot be conceived of as other than the like of like.

Impossible.

And when two things are alike, must they not partake of the same idea?

They must.

And will not that of which the two partake, and which makes them alike, be the absolute idea [of likeness]?

Certainly.

Then the idea cannot be like the individual, or the individual like the idea; for if they are alike, some further idea of likeness will always arise, and if that be like anything else, another and another; and new ideas will never cease being created, if the idea resembles that which partakes of it?

Quite true.

The theory, then, that other things participate in the ideas by resemblance, has to be given up, and some other mode of participation devised?

That is true.

Do you see then, Socrates, how great is the difficulty of affirming self-existent ideas?

Yes, indeed.

And, further, let me say that as yet you only understand a small part of the difficulty which is involved in your assumption, that there are ideas of all things, which are distinct from them.

What difficulty? he said.

There are many, but the greatest of all is this: If an opponent argues that these self-existent ideas, as we term them, cannot be known, no one can prove to him that he is wrong, unless he who is disputing their existence be a man of great genius and cultivation, and is willing to follow a long and laborious demonstration—he will remain unconvinced, and still insist that they cannot be known.

How is that, Parmenides? said Socrates.

In the first place, I think, Socrates, that you, or any one who maintains the existence of absolute ideas, will admit that they cannot exist in us.

Why, then they would be no longer absolute, said Socrates.

That is true, he said; and any relation in the absolute ideas, is a relation which is among themselves only, and has nothing to do with the resemblances, or whatever they are to be termed, which are in our sphere, and the participation in which gives us this or that name. And the subjective notions in our mind, which have the same name with them, are likewise only relative to one another, and not to the ideas which have the same name with them, and belong to themselves and not to the ideas.

How do you mean? said Socrates.

I may illustrate my meaning in this way, said Parmenides: A master has a slave; now there is nothing absolute in the relation between them; they are both relations of some man to another man; but there is also an idea of mastership in the abstract, which is relative to the idea of slavery in the abstract; and this abstract nature has nothing to do with us, nor we with the abstract nature; abstract natures have to do with themselves alone, and we with ourselves. Do you see my meaning?

Yes, said Socrates, I quite see your meaning.

And does not knowledge, I mean absolute knowledge, he said, answer to very and absolute truth?

Certainly.

And each kind of absolute knowledge answers to each kind of absolute being?

Yes.

And the knowledge which we have, will answer to the truth which we have; and again, each kind of knowledge which we have, will be a knowledge of each kind of being which we have?

Certainly.

But the ideas themselves, as you admit, we have not, and cannot have?

No, we cannot.

And the absolute ideas or species, are known by the absolute idea of knowledge?

Yes.

And that is an idea which we have not got?

No.

Then none of the ideas are known to us, because we have no share in absolute knowledge?

They are not.

Then the ideas of the beautiful, and of the good, and the like, which we imagine to be absolute ideas, are unknown to us?

That appears to be the case.

I think that there is a worse consequence still.

What is that?

Would you, or would you not, say, that if there is such a thing as absolute knowledge, that must be, a far more accurate knowledge than our knowledge, and the same of beauty and other things?

Yes.

And if there be anything that has absolute knowledge, there is nothing more likely than God to have this most exact knowledge?

Certainly.

But then, will God, having this absolute knowledge, have a knowledge of human things?

And why not?

Because, Socrates, said Parmenides, we have admitted that the ideas have no relation to human notions, nor human notions to them; the relations of either are in their respective spheres.

Yes, that has been admitted.

And if God has this truest authority, and this most exact knowledge, that authority cannot rule us, nor that knowledge know us, or any human thing; and in like manner, as our authority does not extend to the gods, nor our knowledge know anything which is divine, so by parity of reason they, being gods, are not our masters; neither do they know the things of men.

Yet, surely, said Socrates, to deprive God of knowledge is monstrous.

These, Socrates, said Parmenides, are a few, and only a few, of the difficulties which are necessarily involved in the hypothesis of the existence of ideas, and the attempt to prove the absoluteness of each of them; he who hears of them will doubt or deny their existence, and will maintain that even if they do exist, they must necessarily be unknown to man, and he will think that there is reason in what he says, and as we were remarking just now, will be wonderfully hard of being convinced; a man must be a man of real ability before he can understand that everything has a class and an absolute essence; and still more remarkable will he be who makes out all these things for himself, and can teach another to analyze them satisfactorily.

I agree with you, Parmenides, said Socrates; and what you say is very much to my mind.

And yet, Socrates, said Parmenides, if a man, fixing his mind on these and the like difficulties, refuses to acknowledge ideas or species of existences, and will not define particular species, he will be at his wit's end; in this way he will utterly destroy the power of reasoning; and that is what you seem to me to have particularly noted.

Very true, he said.

But, then, what is to become of philosophy? What resource is there, if the ideas are unknown?

I certainly do not see my way at present.

Yes, said Parmenides; and I think that this arises, Socrates, out of your attempting to define the beautiful, the just, the good, and the ideas generally, without sufficient previous training. I noticed your deficiency, when I heard you talking here with your friend Aristoteles, the day before yesterday. The impulse that carries you towards philosophy is noble and divine — never doubt that — but there is an art which often seems to be useless, and is called by the vulgar idle talking; in that you must train and exercise yourself, now that you are young, or truth will elude your grasp.

And what is the nature of this exercise, Parmenides, which you would recommend?

That which you heard Zeno practicing; at the same time, I give you credit for saying to him that you did not care to solve the perplexity in reference to visible objects, or to consider the question in that way; but only in reference to the conceptions of the mind, and to what may be called ideas.

Why, yes, he said, there appears to me to be no difficulty in showing that visible things experience likeness or unlikeness or anything else.

Quite true, he said; but I think that you should go a step further, and consider not only the consequences which flow from a given hypothesis, but the consequences which flow from denying the hypothesis; and the exercise will be still better.

What do you mean? he said.

I mean, for example, that in the case of this very hypothesis of Zeno's about the many, you should inquire not only what will follow either to the many in relation to themselves and to the one, or to the one in relation to itself and the many, on the hypothesis of the existence of the many, but also what will follow to the one and many in their relation to themselves or to one another, on the opposite hypothesis. Or if likeness does or does not exist—what will follow on either of these hypotheses to that which is supposed, and to other things in relation to themselves and to one another, and the same of unlikeness; and you may argue in a similar way about motion and rest, about generation and destruction, and even about existence and non-existence; and, in a word, whatever you like to suppose as existing or non-existing, or experiencing any sort of affection. You must look at what follows in relation to the things supposed, and to any other things which you choose,—to the greater number, and to all in like manner; and you must also look at other things in relation to themselves and to anything else which you choose, whether you suppose that they do or do not exist, if you would train yourself perfectly and see the real truth.

2

Aristotle

Metaphysics

Book Γ (IV)

1 THERE IS A SCIENCE WHICH INVESTIGATES BEING AS BEING and the attributes which belong to this in virtue of its own nature. Now this is not the same as any of the so-called special sciences; for none of these others treats universally of being as being. They cut off a part of being and investigate the attribute of this part; this is what the mathematical sciences for instance do. Now since we are seeking the first principles and the highest causes, clearly there must be some thing to which these belong in virtue of its own nature. If then those who sought the elements of existing things were seeking these same principles, it is necessary that the elements must be elements of being not by accident but just because it *is* being. Therefore it is of being as being that we also must grasp the first causes.

2 There are many senses in which a thing may be said to 'be', but all that 'is' is related to one central point, one definite kind of thing, and is not said to 'be' by a mere ambiguity. Everything which is healthy is related to health, one thing in the sense that it preserves health, another in the sense that it produces it, another in the sense that it is a symptom of health, another because it is capable of it. And that which is medical is relative to the medical art, one thing being called medical because it possesses it, another because it is naturally adapted to it, another because it is a function of the medical art. And we shall find other words used similarly to these. So, too, there are many senses in which a thing is said to be, but all refer to one starting-point; some things are said to be because they are substances, others because they are affections of substance, others because they are a process towards substance, or destructions or privations or qualities of substance, or productive or generative of substance, or of things which are relative to substance, or negations of one of these things or of substance itself. It is for this reason that we say even of non-being that it *is* non-being. As, then, there is one science which deals with all healthy things, the same applies in the other cases also. For not only in the case of things which have one common notion does the investigation belong to one science, but also in the case of things which are related to one common nature; for even these in a sense have one common notion. It is clear then that it is the work of one science also to study the things that are, *qua* being.—But everywhere science deals chiefly with that which is primary, and on which the other things depend, and in virtue of which they get their names. If, then, this is substance, it will be of substances that the philosopher must grasp the principles and the causes.

Now for each one class of things, as there is one perception, so there is one science, as for instance grammar, being one science, investigates all articulate sounds. Hence to investigate all the species of being *qua* being is the work of a science which is generically one, and to investigate the several species is the work of the specific parts of the science.

If, now, being and unity are the same and are one thing in the sense that they are implied in one another as principle and cause are, not in the sense that they are explained by the same definition (though it makes no difference even if we suppose them to be like that—in fact this would even strengthen our case); for 'one man' and 'man' are the same thing, and so are 'existent man' and 'man', and the doubling of the words in 'one man and one *existent* man' does not express anything different (it is clear that the two things are not separated either in coming to be or in ceasing to be); and similarly '*one* existent man' adds nothing to 'existent man', so that it is obvious that the addition in these cases means the same thing, and unity is nothing apart from being; and if, further, the substance of each thing is one in no merely accidental way, and similarly is from its very nature something that *is*:—all this being so, there must be exactly as many species of being as of unity. And to investigate the essence of these is the work of a science which is generically one—I mean, for instance, the discussion of the same and the similar and the other concepts of this sort; and nearly all contraries may be referred to this origin; let us take them as having been investigated in the 'Selection of Contraries'.

And there are as many parts of philosophy as there are kinds of substance, so that there must necessarily be among them a first philosophy and one which follows this. For being falls immediately into genera; for which reason the sciences too will correspond to these genera. For the philosopher is like the mathematician, as that word is used; for mathematics also has parts, and there is a first and a second science and other successive ones within the sphere of mathematics.

Now since it is the work of one science to investigate opposites, and plurality is opposed to unity—and it belongs to one science to investigate the negation and the privation because in both cases we are really investigating the one thing of which the negation or the privation is a negation or privation (for we either say simply that that thing is not present, or that it is not present in some particular class; in the latter case difference is present over and above what is implied in negation; for negation means just the absence of the thing in question, while in privation there is also employed an underlying nature of which the privation is asserted):—in view of all these facts, the contraries of the concepts we named above, the other and the dissimilar and the unequal, and everything else which is derived either from these or from plurality and unity, must fall within the province of the science above named. And contrariety is one of these concepts; for contrariety is a kind of difference, and difference is a kind of otherness. Therefore, since there are many senses in which a thing is said to be one, these terms also will have many senses, but yet it belongs to one science to know them all; for a term belongs to different sciences not if it has different senses, but if it has not one meaning *and* its definitions cannot be referred to one central meaning. And since all things are referred to that which is primary, as for instance all things which are called one are referred to the primary one, we must say that this holds good also of the same and the other and of contraries in general; so that after distinguishing the various senses of each, we must then explain by reference to what is primary in the case of each of the predicates in question, saying how they are related to it; for some will be called what they are called because they possess it, others because they produce it, and others in other such ways.

It is evident, then, that it belongs to one science to be able to give an account of these concepts as well as of substance (this was one of the questions in our book of problems), and that it is the function of the philosopher to be able to investigate all things. For if it is not the function of the philosopher, who is it who will inquire whether Socrates and Socrates seated are the same thing, or whether one thing has one contrary, or what contrariety is, or how many meanings it has? And similarly with all other such questions. Since, then, these are essential modifications of unity *qua* unity and of being *qua* being, not *qua* numbers or lines or fire, it is clear that it belongs to this science to investigate both the essence of these concepts and their properties. And those who study these properties err not by leaving the sphere of philosophy, but by forgetting that substance, of which they have no correct idea, is prior to these other things. For number *qua* number has peculiar attributes, such as odd-ness and evenness, commensurability and equality, excess and defect, and these belong to numbers either in themselves or in relation to one another. And similarly the solid and the motionless and that which is in motion and the weightless and that which has weight have other peculiar properties. So too there are certain properties peculiar to being as such, and it is about these that the philosopher has to investigate the truth.—An indication of this may be mentioned:— dialecticians and sophists assume the same guise as the philosopher, for sophistic is Wisdom which exists only in semblance, and dialecticians embrace all things in their dialectic, and being is common to all things; but evidently their dialectic embraces these subjects because these are proper to philosophy.—For sophistic and dialectic turn on the same class of things as philosophy, but this differs from dialectic in the nature of the faculty required and from sophistic in respect of the purpose of the philosophic life. Dialectic is merely critical where philosophy claims to know, and sophistic is what appears to be philosophy but is not.

Again, in the list of contraries one of the two columns is privative, and all contraries are reducible to being and non-being, and to unity and plurality, as for instance rest belongs to unity and movement to plurality. And nearly all thinkers agree that being and substance are composed of contraries; at least all name contraries as their first principles—some name odd and even [the Pythagoreans], some hot and cold [Parmenides], some limit and the unlimited [the Platonists], some love and strife [Empedocles]. And all the others as well are evidently reducible to unity and plurality (this reduction we must take for granted), and the principles stated by other thinkers fall entirely under these as their genera. It is obvious then from these considerations too that it belongs to one science to examine being *qua* being. For all things are either contraries or composed of contraries, and unity and plurality are the starting-points of all contraries. And these belong to one science, whether they have or have not one single meaning. Probably the truth is that they have not; yet even if 'one' has several meanings, the other meanings will be related to the primary meaning (and similarly in the case of the contraries), even if being or unity is not a universal and the same in every instance or is not separable from the particular instances (as in fact it probably is not; the unity is in some cases that of common reference, in some cases that of serial succession). And for this reason it does not belong to the geometer to inquire what is contrariety or completeness or unity or being or the same or the other, but only to presuppose these concepts and reason from this startingpoint.—Obviously then it is the work of one science to examine being *qua* being, and the attributes which belong to it *qua* being, and the same science will examine not only substances but also their attributes, both those above named and the concepts 'prior' and 'posterior', 'genus' and 'species', 'whole' and 'part', and the others of this sort.

3 We must state whether it belongs to one or two different sciences to inquire into the truths which are in mathematics called axioms, and into substance. Evidently, the inquiry into these also belongs to one science, and that the science of the philosopher; for these truths hold good for everything that is, and not for some special genus apart from others. And all men use them, because they are true of being *qua* being and each genus has being. But men use them just so far as to satisfy their purposes; that is, as far as the genus to which their demonstrations refer extends. Therefore since these truths clearly hold good for all things *qua* being (for this is what is common to them), to him who studies being *qua* being belongs the inquiry into these as well. And for this reason no one who is conducting a special inquiry tries to say anything about their truth or falsity—neither the geometer nor the arithmetician. Some natural philosophers indeed have done so, and their procedure was intelligible enough; for they thought that they alone were inquiring about the whole of nature and about being. But since there is one kind of thinker who is above even the natural philosopher (for nature is only one particular genus of being), the discussion of these truths also will belong to him whose inquiry is universal and deals with primary substance. Physics also is a kind of Wisdom, but it is not the first kind.—And the attempts of some of those who discuss the terms on which truth should be accepted, are due to a want of training in logic; for they should know these things already when they come to a special study, and not be inquiring into them while they are listening to lectures on it.

Evidently then it belongs to the philosopher, i. e. to him who is studying the nature of all substance, to inquire also into the principles of syllogism. But he who knows best about each genus must be able to state the most certain principles of his subject, so that he whose subject is existing things *qua* existing must be able to state the most certain principles of all things. This is the philosopher, and the most certain principle of all is that regarding which it is impossible to be mistaken; for such a principle must be both the best known (for all men may be mistaken about things which they do not know), and non-hypothetical. For a principle which every one must have who understands anything that is, is not a hypothesis; and that which every one must know who knows anything, he must already have when he comes to a special study. Evidently then such a principle is the most certain of all; which principle this is, let us proceed to say. It is, that the same attribute cannot at the same time belong and not belong to the same subject and in the same respect; we must presuppose, to guard against dialectical objections, any further qualifications which might be added. This, then, is the most certain of all principles, since it answers to the definition given above. For it is impossible for any one to believe the same thing to be and not to be, as some think Heraclitus says. For what a man says, he does not necessarily believe; and if it is impossible that contrary attributes should belong at the same time to the same subject (the usual qualifications must be presupposed in this premiss too), and if an opinion which contradicts another is contrary to it, obviously it is impossible for the same man at the same time to believe the same thing to be and not to be; for if a man were mistaken on this point he would have contrary opinions at the same time. It is for this reason that all who are carrying out a demonstration reduce it to this as an ultimate belief; for this is naturally the starting-point even for all the other axioms.

4 There are some who, as we said, both themselves assert that it is possible for the same thing to be and not to be, and say that people can judge this to be the case. And among others many writers about nature use this language. But we have now posited that it is impossible for anything at the same time to be and not to be, and by this means have shown that this is the most indisputable of all principles.—Some indeed demand that even this shall be demonstrated, but this they do through want of education, for not to know of what things one should demand demonstration, and of what one should not, argues want of education. For it is impossible that there should be demonstration of absolutely everything (there would be an infinite regress, so that there would still be no demonstration); but if there are things of which one should not demand demonstration, these persons could not say what principle they maintain to be more self-evident than the present one.

We can, however, demonstrate negatively even that this view is impossible, if our opponent will only say something; and if he says nothing, it is absurd to seek to give an account of our views to one who cannot give an account of anything, in so far as he cannot do so. For such a man, as such, is from the start no better than a vegetable. Now negative demonstration I distinguish from demonstration proper, because in a demonstration one might be thought to be begging the question, but if another person is responsible for the assumption we shall have negative proof, not demonstration. The starting-point for all such arguments is not the demand that our opponent shall say that something either is or is not (for this one might perhaps take to be a begging of the question), but that he shall say something which is *significant* both for himself and for another; for this is necessary, if he really is to say anything. For, if he means nothing, such a man will not be capable of reasoning, either with himself or with another. But if any one grants this, demonstration will be possible; for we shall already have something definite. The person responsible for the proof, however, is not he who demonstrates but he who listens; for while disowning reason he listens to reason. And again he who admits this has admitted that something is true apart from demonstration [so that not everything will be 'so and not so'].

First then this at least is obviously true, that the word 'be' or 'not be' has a definite meaning, so that not everything will be 'so and not so'.—Again, if 'man' has one meaning, let this be 'two-footed animal'; by having one meaning I understand this:—if 'man' means 'X', then if A is a man 'X' will be what 'being a man' means for him. (It makes no difference even if one were to say a word has several meanings, if only they are limited in number; for to each definition there might be assigned a different word. For instance, we might say that 'man' has not one meaning but several, one of which would have one definition, viz. 'two-footed animal', while there might be also several other definitions if only they were limited in number; for a peculiar name might be assigned to each of the definitions. If, however, they were not limited but one were to say that the word has an infinite number of meanings, obviously reasoning would be impossible; for not to have one meaning is to have no meaning, and if words have no meaning our reasoning with one another, and indeed with ourselves, has been annihilated; for it is impossible to think of anything if we do not think of one thing; but if this *is* possible, one name might be assigned to this thing.)

Let it be assumed then, as was said at the beginning, that the name has a meaning and has one meaning; it is impossible, then, that 'being a man' should mean precisely 'not being a man', if 'man' not only signifies something about one subject but also has one significance (for we do not identify 'having one significance' with 'signifying something about one subject', since on *that* assumption even 'musical' and 'white' and 'man' would have had one significance, so that all things would have been one; for they would all have had the same significance).

And it will not be possible to be and not to be the same thing, except in virtue of an ambiguity, just as if one whom we call 'man', others were to call 'not-man'; but the point in question is not this, whether the same thing can at the same time be and not be a man in name, but whether it can in fact.—Now if 'man' and 'not-man' mean nothing different, obviously 'not being a man' will mean nothing different from 'being a man'; so that 'being a man' will be 'not being a man';

for they will be one. For being one means this—being related as 'raiment' and 'dress' are, if their definition is one. And if 'being a man' and 'being a not-man' are to be one, they must mean one thing. But it was shown earlier that they mean different things.—Therefore, if it is true to say of anything that it is a man, it must be a two-footed animal (for this was what 'man' meant); and if this is necessary, it is impossible that the same thing should not at that time be a two-footed animal; for this is what 'being necessary' means—that it is impossible for the thing not to be. It is, then, impossible that it should be at the same time true to say the same thing is a man and is not a man.

The same account holds good with regard to 'not being a man', for 'being a man' and 'being a not-man' mean different things, since even 'being white' and 'being a man' are different; for the former terms are much more opposed, so that they must *a fortiori* mean different things. And if any one says that '*white*' means one and the same thing as 'man', again we shall say the same as what was said before, that it would follow that *all* things are one, and not only opposites. But if this is impossible, then what we have maintained will follow, if our opponent will only answer our question.

And if, when one asks the question simply, he adds the contradictories, he is not answering the question. For there is nothing to prevent the same thing from being both a man and white and countless other things: but still, if one asks whether it is or is not true to say that this is a man, our opponent must give an answer which means one thing, and not add that 'it is also white and large'. For, besides other reasons, it is impossible to enumerate its accidental attributes, which are infinite in number; let him, then, enumerate either all or none. Similarly, therefore, even if the same thing is a thousand times a man and a not-man, he must not, in answering the question whether this is a man, add that it is also at the same time a not-man, unless he is bound to add also all the other accidents, all that the subject is or is not; and if he does this, he is not observing the rules of argument.

And in general those who say this do away with substance and essence. For they must say that all attributes are accidents, and that there is no such thing as 'being essentially a man' or 'an animal'. For if there is to be any such thing as 'being essentially a man' this will not be 'being a not-man' or 'not being a man' (yet these are negations of it); for there was one thing which it meant, and this was the substance of something. And denoting the substance of a thing means that the essence of the thing is nothing else. But if its being essentially a man is to be the same as either being essentially a not-man or essentially not being a man, then its essence *will* be something else. Therefore our opponents must say that there cannot be such a definition of anything, but that all attributes are accidental; for this is the distinction between substance and accident—'white' is accidental to man, because though he is white, whiteness is not his essence. But if *all* statements are accidental, there will be nothing primary about which they are made, if the accidental always implies predication about a subject. The predication, then, must go on *ad infinitum*. But this is impossible; for not even more than two terms can be combined in accidental predication. For (1) an accident is not an accident of an accident, unless it be because both are accidents of the same subject. I mean, for instance, that the white is musical and the latter is white, only because both are accidental to man. But (2) Socrates is musical, not in this sense, that both terms are accidental to something else. Since then some predicates are accidental in this and some in that sense, (*a*) those which are accidental in the latter sense, in which white is accidental to Socrates, cannot form an infinite series in the upward direction; e. g. Socrates the white has not yet another accident; for no unity can be got out of such a sum. Nor again (*b*) will 'white' have another term accidental to it, e. g. 'musical'. For this is no more accidental to that than that is to this; and at the same time we have drawn the distinction, that while some predicates are accidental in this sense, others are so in the sense in which 'musical' is accidental to Socrates; and the accident is an accident of an accident not in cases of the latter kind, but only in cases of the other kind, so that not *all* terms will be accidental. There must, then, even so be something which denotes substance. And if this is so, it has been shown that contradictories cannot be predicated at the same time.

Again, if all contradictory statements are true of the same subject at the same time, evidently all things will be one. For the same thing will be a trireme, a wall, and a man, if of everything it is possible either to affirm or to deny anything (and this premiss must be accepted by those who share the views of Protagoras). For if any one thinks that the man is not a trireme, evidently he is not a trireme; so that he also *is* a trireme, if, as they say, contradictory statements are both true. And we thus get the doctrine of Anaxagoras, that all things are mixed together; so that nothing really exists. They seem, then, to be speaking of the indeterminate, and, while fancying themselves to be speaking of being, they are speaking about non-being; for it is that which exists potentially and not in complete reality that is indeterminate. But they *must* predicate of every subject the affirmation or the negation of every attribute. For it is absurd if of each subject its own negation is to be predicable, while the negation of something else which cannot be predicated of it is not to be predicable of it; for instance, if it is true to say of a man that he is not a man, evidently it is also true to say that he is either a trireme or not a trireme. If, then, the affirmative can be predicated, the negative must be predicable too; and if the affirmative is not predicable, the negative, at least, will be more predicable than the negative of the subject itself. If, then, even the latter negative is predicable, the negative of 'trireme' will be also predicable; and, if this is predicable, the affirmative will be so too.

Those, then, who maintain this view are driven to this conclusion, and to the further conclusion that it is not necessary either to assert or to deny. For if it is true that a thing is a man and a not-man, evidently also it will be neither a man nor a not-man. For to the two assertions there answer two negations, and if the former is treated as a single proposition compounded out of two, the latter also is a single proposition opposite to the former.

Again, either the theory is true in all cases, and a thing is both white and not-white, and existent and non-existent, and all other assertions and negations are similarly compatible, or the theory is true of some statements and not of others. And if not of all, the exceptions will be contradictories of which admittedly only one is true; but if of all, again either the negation will be true wherever the assertion is, and the assertion true wherever the negation is, or the negation will be true where the assertion is, but the assertion not always true where the negation is. And (*a*) in the latter case there will be something which fixedly *is not*, and this will be an indisputable belief; and if non-being is something indisputable and knowable, the opposite assertion will be more knowable. But (*b*) if it is equally possible also to assert all that it is possible to deny, one must either be saying what is true when one separates the predicates (and says, for instance, that a thing is white, and again that it is not-white), or not. And if (i) it is not true to apply the predicates separately, our opponent is not saying what he professes to say, and also nothing at all exists, but how could nonexistent things speak or walk, as he does? Also all things would on this view be one, as has been already said, and man and God and trireme and their contradictories will be the same. For if contradictories can be predicated alike of each subject, one thing will in no wise differ from another; for if it differ, this difference will be something true and peculiar to it. And (ii) if one may with truth apply the predicates separately, the above-mentioned result follows none the less, and, further, it follows that all would then be right and all would be in error, and our opponent himself confesses himself to be in error.—And at the same time our discussion with him is evidently about nothing at all; for he says nothing. For he says neither 'yes' nor 'no', but 'yes and no'; and again he denies both of these and says 'neither yes nor no'; for otherwise there would already be something definite.

Again, if when the assertion is true, the negation is false, and when this is true, the affirmation is false, it will not be possible to assert and deny the same thing truly at the same time. But perhaps they might say this was the very question at issue.

Again, is he in error who judges either that the thing is so or that it is not so, and is he right who judges both? If he is right, what can they mean by saying that the nature of existing things is of this kind? And if he is not right, but more right than he who judges in the other way, being will already be of a definite nature, and this will be true, and not at the same time also not true. But if all are alike both wrong and right, one who is in this condition will not be able either to speak or to say anything intelligible; for he says at the same time both 'yes' and 'no'. And if he makes no judgement but 'thinks' and 'does not think', indifferently, what difference will there be between him and a vegetable?—Thus, then, it is in the highest degree evident that neither any one of those who maintain this view nor any one else is really in this position. For why does a man walk to Megara and not stay at home, when he thinks he ought to be walking there? Why does he not walk early some morning into a well or over a precipice, if one happens to be in his way? Why do we observe him guarding against this, evidently because he does not think that falling in is alike good and not good? Evidently, then, he judges one thing to be better and another worse. And if this is so, he must also judge one thing to be a man and another to be not-a-man, one thing to be sweet and another to be not-sweet. For he does not aim at and judge all things alike, when, thinking it desirable to drink water or to see a man, he proceeds to aim at these things; yet he *ought,* if the same thing were alike a man and not-a-man. But, as was said, there is no one who does not obviously avoid some things and not others. Therefore, as it seems, all men make unqualified judgements, if not about all things, still about what is better and worse. And if this is not knowledge but opinion, they should be all the more anxious about the truth, as a sick man should be more anxious about his health than one who is healthy; for he who has opinions is, in comparison with the man who knows, not in a healthy state as far as the truth is concerned.

Again, however much all things may be 'so and not so', still there is a more and a less in the nature of things; for we should not say that two and three are equally even, nor is he who thinks four things are five equally wrong with him who thinks they are a thousand. If then they are not equally wrong, obviously one is less wrong and therefore more right. If then that which has more of any quality is nearer the norm, there must be some truth to which the more true is nearer. And even if there is not, still there is already something better founded and liker the truth, and we shall have got rid of the unqualified doctrine which would prevent us from determining anything in our thought.

Posterior Analytics

Book II

1 ALL INSTRUCTION GIVEN OR RECEIVED BY WAY OF ARGUMENT PROCEEDS from pre-existent knowledge. This becomes evident upon a survey of all the species of such instruction. The mathematical sciences and all other speculative disciplines are acquired in this way, and so are the two forms of dialectical reasoning, syllogistic and inductive: for each of these latter makes use of old knowledge to impart new the syllogism assuming an audience that accepts its premisses, induction exhibiting the universal as implicit in the clearly known particular. Again, the persuasion exerted by rhetorical arguments is in principle the same, since they use either example, a kind of induction, or enthymeme, a form of syllogism.

The pre-existent knowledge required is of two kinds. In some cases admission of the fact must be assumed, in others comprehension of the meaning of the term used, and sometimes both assumptions are essential. Thus, we assume that every predicate can be either truly affirmed or truly denied of any subject, and that 'triangle' means so and so; as regards 'unit' we have to make the double assumption of the meaning of the word and the existence of the thing. The reason is that these several objects are not equally obvious to us. Recognition of a truth may in some cases contain as factors both previous knowledge and also knowledge acquired simultaneously with that recognition—knowledge, this latter, of the particulars actually falling under the universal and therein already virtually known. For example, the student knew beforehand that the angles of every triangle are equal to two right angles; but it was only at the actual moment at which he was being led on to recognize this as true in the instance before him that he came to know 'this figure inscribed in the semicircle' to be a triangle. For some things (viz. the singulars finally reached which are not predicable of anything else as subject) are only learnt in this way, i.e. there is here no recognition through a middle of a minor term as subject to a major. Before he was led on to recognition or before he actually drew a conclusion, we should perhaps say that in a manner he knew, in a manner not.

If he did not in an unqualified sense of the term *know* the existence of this triangle, how could he *know* without qualification that its angles were equal to two right angles? No: clearly he *knows* not without qualification but only in the sense that he *knows* universally. If this distinction is not drawn, we are faced with the dilemma in the *Meno*: either a man will learn nothing or what he already knows; for we cannot accept the solution which some people offer. A man is asked, 'Do you, or do you not, know that every pair is even?' He says he does know it. The questioner then produces a particular pair, of the existence, and so *a fortiori* of the evenness, of which he was unaware. The solution which some people offer is to assert that they do not know that every pair is even, but only that everything which they know to be a pair is even: yet what they know to be even is that of which they have demonstrated evenness, i.e. what they made the subject of their premiss, viz. not merely every triangle or number which they know to be such, but any and every number or triangle without reservation. For no premiss is ever couched in the form 'every number which you know to be such', or 'every rectilinear figure which you know to be such': the predicate is always construed as applicable to any and every instance of the thing. On the other hand, I imagine there is nothing to prevent a man in one sense knowing what he is learning, in another not knowing it. The strange thing would be, not if in some sense he knew what he was learning, but if he were to know it in that precise sense and manner in which he was learning it.

2 We suppose ourselves to possess unqualified scientific knowledge of a thing, as opposed to knowing it in the accidental way in which the sophist knows, when we think that we know the cause on which the fact depends, as the cause of that fact and of no other, and, further, that the fact could not be other than it is. Now that scientific knowing is something of this sort is evident—witness both those who falsely claim it and those who actually possess it, since the former merely imagine themselves to be, while the latter are also actually, in the condition described. Consequently the proper object of unqualified scientific knowledge is something which cannot be other than it is.

There may be another manner of knowing as well—that will be discussed later. What I now assert is that at all events we do know by demonstration. By demonstration I mean a syllogism productive of scientific knowledge, a syllogism, that is, the grasp of which is *eo ipso* such knowledge. Assuming then that my thesis as to the nature of scientific knowing is correct, the premisses of demonstrated knowledge must be true, primary, immediate, better known than and prior to the conclusion, which is further related to them as effect to cause. Unless these conditions are satisfied, the basic truths will not be 'appropriate' to the conclusion. Syllogism there may indeed be without these conditions, but such syllogism, not being productive of scientific knowledge, will not be demonstration. The premisses must be true: for that which is non-existent cannot be known—we cannot know, e. g., that the diagonal of a square is commensurate with its side. The premisses must be primary and indemonstrable; otherwise they will require demonstration in order to be known, since to have knowledge, if it be not accidental knowledge, of things which are demonstrable, means precisely to have a demonstration of them. The premisses must be the causes of the conclusion, better known than it, and prior to it; its causes, since we possess scientific knowledge of a thing only when we know its cause; prior, in order to be causes; antecedently known, this antecedent knowledge being not our mere understanding of the meaning, but knowledge of the fact as well. Now 'prior' and 'better known' are ambiguous terms, for there is a difference between what is prior and better known in the order of being and what is prior and better known to man. I mean that objects nearer to sense are prior and better known to man; objects without qualification prior and better known are those further from sense. Now the most universal causes are furthest from sense and particular causes are nearest to sense, and they are thus exactly opposed to one another. In saying that the premisses of demonstrated knowledge must be primary, I mean that they must be the 'appropriate' basic truths, for I identify primary premiss and basic truth. A 'basic truth' in a demonstration is an immediate proposition. An immediate proposition is one which has no other proposition prior to it. A proposition is either part of an enunciation, i.e. it predicates a single attribute of a single subject. If a proposition is dialectical, it assumes either part indifferently; if it is demonstrative, it lays down one part to the definite exclusion of the other because that part is true. The term 'enunciation' denotes either part of a contradiction indifferently. A contradiction is an opposition which of its own nature excludes a middle. The part of a contradiction which conjoins a predicate with a subject is an affirmation; the part disjoining them is a negation. I call an immediate basic truth of syllogism a 'thesis' when, though it is not susceptible of proof by the teacher, yet ignorance of it does not constitute a total bar to progress on the part of the pupil: one which the pupil must know if he is to learn anything whatever is an axiom. I call it an axiom because there are such truths and we give them the name of axioms *par excellence*. If a thesis assumes one part or the other of an enunciation, i.e. asserts either the existence or the non-existence of a subject, it is a hypothesis; if it does not so assert, it is a definition. Definition is a 'thesis' or a 'laying something down', since the arithmetician lays it down that to be a unit is to be quantitatively indivisible; but it is not a hypothesis, for to define what a unit is is not the same as to affirm its existence.

Now since the required ground of our knowledge—i.e. of our conviction—of a fact is the possession of such a syllogism as we call demonstration, and the ground of the syllogism is the facts constituting its premisses, we must not only know the primary premisses—some if not all of them—beforehand, but know them better than the conclusion: for the cause of an attribute's inherence in a subject always itself inheres in the subject more firmly than that attribute; e. g. the cause of our loving anything is dearer to us than the object of our love. So since the primary premisses are the cause of our knowledge—i.e. of our conviction—it follows that we know them better—that is, are more convinced of them—than their consequences, precisely because our knowledge of the latter is the effect of our knowledge of the premisses. Now a man cannot believe in anything more than in the things he knows, unless he has either actual knowledge of it or something better than actual knowledge. But we are faced with this paradox if a student whose belief rests on demonstration has not prior knowledge; a man must believe in some, if not in all, of the basic truths more than in the conclusion. Moreover, if a man sets out to acquire the scientific knowledge that comes through demonstration, he must not only have a better knowledge of the basic truths and a firmer conviction of them than of the connexion which is being demonstrated: more than this, nothing must be more certain or better known to him than these basic truths in their character as contradicting the fundamental premisses which lead to the opposed and erroneous conclusion. For indeed the conviction of pure science must be unshakable.

3 Some hold that, owing to the necessity of knowing the primary premisses, there is no scientific knowledge. Others think there is, but that all truths are demonstrable. Neither doctrine is either true or a necessary deduction from the premisses. The first school, assuming that there is no way of knowing other than by demonstration, maintain that an infinite regress is involved, on the ground that if behind the prior stands no primary, we could not know the posterior through the prior (wherein they are right, for one cannot traverse an infinite series): if on the other hand—they say—the series terminates and there are primary premisses, yet these are unknowable because incapable of demonstration, which according to them is the only form of knowledge. And since thus one cannot know the primary premisses, knowledge of the conclusions which follow from them is not pure scientific knowledge nor properly knowing at all, but rests on the mere supposition that the premisses are true. The other party agree with them as regards knowing, holding that it is only possible by demonstration, but they see no difficulty in holding that all truths are demonstrated, on the ground that demonstration may be circular and reciprocal.

Our own doctrine is that not all knowledge is demonstrative: on the contrary, knowledge of the immediate premisses is independent of demonstration. (The necessity of this is obvious; for since we must know the prior premisses from which the demonstration is drawn, and since the regress must end in immediate truths, those truths must be indemonstrable.) Such, then, is our doctrine, and in addition we maintain that besides scientific knowledge there is its originative source which enables us to recognize the definitions.

Now demonstration must be based on premisses prior to and better known than the conclusion; and the same things cannot simultaneously be both prior and posterior to one another: so circular demonstration is clearly not possible in the unqualified sense of 'demonstration', but only possible if 'demonstration' be extended to include that other method of argument which rests on a distinction between truths prior to us and truths without qualification prior, i. e. the method by which induction produces knowledge. But if we accept this extension of its meaning, our definition of unqualified knowledge will prove faulty; for there seem to be two kinds of it. Perhaps, however, the second form of demonstration, that which proceeds from truths better known to us, is not demonstration in the unqualified sense of the term.

The advocates of circular demonstration are not only faced with the difficulty we have just stated: in addition their theory reduces to the mere statement that if a thing exists, then it does exist—an easy way of proving anything. That this is so can be clearly shown by taking three terms, for to constitute the circle it makes no difference whether many terms or few or even only two are taken. Thus by direct proof, if A is, B must be; if B is, C must be; therefore if A is, C must be. Since then—by the circular proof—if A is, B must be, and if B is, A must be, A may be substituted for C above. Then 'if B is, A must be' = 'if B is, C must be', which above gave the conclusion 'if A is, C must be': but C and A have been identified. Consequently the upholders of circular demonstration are in the position of saying that if A is, A must be—a simple way of proving anything. Moreover, even such circular demonstration is impossible except in the case of attributes that imply one another, viz. 'peculiar' properties.

Now, it has been shown that the positing of one thing—be it one term or one premiss—never involves a necessary consequent: two premisses constitute the first and smallest foundation for drawing a conclusion at all and therefore *a fortiori* for the demonstrative syllogism of science. If, then, A is implied in B and C, and B and C are reciprocally implied in one another and in A, it is possible, as has been shown in my writings on the syllogism, to prove all the assumptions on which the original conclusion rested, by circular demonstration in the first figure. But it has also been shown that in the other figures either no conclusion is possible, or at least none which proves both the original premisses. Propositions the terms of which are not convertible cannot be circularly demonstrated at all, and since convertible terms occur rarely in actual demonstrations, it is clearly frivolous and impossible to say that demonstration is reciprocal and that therefore everything can be demonstrated. [. . .]

6 Demonstrative knowledge must rest on necessary basic truths; for the object of scientific knowledge cannot be other than it is. Now attributes attaching essentially to their subjects attach necessarily to them: for essential attributes are either elements in the essential nature of their subjects, or contain their subjects as elements in their own essential nature. (The pairs of opposites which the latter class includes are necessary because one member or the other necessarily inheres.) It follows from this that premisses of the demonstrative syllogism must be connexions essential in the sense explained: for all attributes must inhere essentially or else be accidental, and accidental attributes are not necessary to their subjects.

We must either state the case thus, or else premise that the conclusion of demonstration is necessary and that a demonstrated conclusion cannot be other than it is, and then infer that the conclusion must be developed from necessary premisses. For though you may reason from true premisses without demonstrating, yet if your premisses are necessary you will assuredly demonstrate—in such necessity you have at once a distinctive character of demonstration. That demonstration proceeds from necessary premisses is also indicated by the fact that the objection we raise against a professed demonstration is that a premiss of it is not a necessary truth—whether we think it altogether devoid of necessity, or at any rate so far as our opponent's previous argument goes. This shows how naive it is to suppose one's basic truths rightly chosen if one starts with a proposition which is (1) popularly accepted and (2) true, such as the sophists' assumption that to know is the same as to possess knowledge. For (1) popular acceptance or rejection is no criterion of a basic truth, which can only be the primary law of the genus constituting the subject matter of the demonstration; and (2) not *all* truth is 'appropriate'.

A further proof that the conclusion must be the development of necessary premisses is as follows. Where demonstration is possible, one who can give no account which includes the cause has no scientific knowledge. If, then, we suppose a syllogism in which, though *A* necessarily inheres in *C*, yet *B*, the middle term of the demonstration, is not necessarily connected with *A* and *C*, then the man who argues thus has no reasoned knowledge of the conclusion, since this conclusion does not owe its necessity to the middle term; for though the conclusion is necessary, the mediating link is a contingent fact. Or again, if a man is without knowledge now, though he still retains the steps of the argument, though there is no change in himself or in the fact and no lapse of memory on his part; then neither had he knowledge previously. But the mediating link, not being necessary, may have perished in the interval; and if so, though there be no change in him nor in the fact, and though he will still retain the steps of the argument, yet he has not knowledge, and therefore had not knowledge before. Even if the link has not actually perished but is liable to perish, this situation is possible and might occur. But such a condition cannot be knowledge.

When the conclusion is necessary, the middle through which it was proved may yet quite easily be non-necessary. You can in fact infer the necessary even from a non-necessary premiss, just as you can infer the true from the not true. On the other hand, when the middle is necessary the conclusion must be necessary; just as true premisses always give a true conclusion. Thus, if *A* is necessarily predicated of *B* and *B* of *C*, then *A* is necessarily predicated of *C*. But when the conclusion is non-necessary the middle cannot be necessary either. Thus: let *A* be predicated non-necessarily of *C* but necessarily of *B*, and let *B* be a necessary predicate of *C*; then *A* too will be a necessary predicate of *C*, which by hypothesis it is not.

To sum up, then: demonstrative knowledge must be knowledge of a necessary nexus, and therefore must clearly be obtained through a necessary middle term; otherwise its possessor will know neither the cause nor the fact that his conclusion is a necessary connexion. Either he will mistake the non-necessary for the necessary and believe the necessity of the conclusion without knowing it, or else he will not even believe it—in which case he will be equally ignorant, whether he actually infers the mere fact through middle terms or the reasoned fact and from immediate premisses.

Of accidents that are not essential according to our definition of essential there is no demonstrative knowledge; for since an accident, in the sense in which I here speak of it, may also not inhere, it is impossible to prove its inherence as a necessary conclusion. A difficulty, however, might be raised as to why in dialectic, if the conclusion is not a necessary connexion, such and such determinate premisses should be proposed in order to deal with such and such determinate problems. Would not the result be the same if one asked any questions whatever and then merely stated one's conclusion? The solution is that determinate questions have to be put, not because the replies to them affirm facts which necessitate facts affirmed by the conclusion, but because these answers are propositions which if the answerer affirm, he must affirm the conclusion—and affirm it with truth if they are true.

Since it is just those attributes within every genus which are essential and possessed by their respective subjects as such that are necessary, it is clear that both the conclusions and the premisses of demonstrations which produce scientific knowledge are essential. For accidents are not necessary: and, further, since accidents are not necessary one does not necessarily have reasoned knowledge of a conclusion drawn from them (this is so even if the accidental premisses are invariable but not essential, as in proofs through signs; for though the conclusion be actually essential, one will not know it as essential nor know its reason); but to have reasoned knowledge of a conclusion is to know it through its cause. We may conclude that the middle must be consequentially connected with the minor, and the major with the middle.

3

Svetâsvatara Upanishad

First Adhyâya

1 THE BRAHMA-STUDENTS SAY: Is Brahman the cause? Whence are we born? Whereby do we live, and whither do we go? O ye who know Brahman, (tell us) at whose command we abide, whether in pain or in pleasure?

2 Should time, or nature, or necessity, or chance, or the elements be considered as the cause, or he who is called the person (purusha, vigñânâtmâ)? It cannot be their union either, because that is not self-dependent, and the self also is powerless, because there is (independent of him) a cause of good and evil.

3 The sages, devoted to meditation and concentration, have seen the power belonging to God himself, hidden in its own qualities (gu*n*a). He, being one, superintends all those causes, time, self, and the rest.

4 We meditate on him who (like a wheel) has one felly with three tires, sixteen ends, fifty spokes, with twenty counter-spokes, and six sets of eight; whose one rope is manifold, who proceeds on three different roads, and whose illusion arises from two causes.

5 We meditate on the river whose water consists of the five streams, which is wild and winding with its five springs, whose waves are the five vital breaths, whose fountain head is the mind, the course of the five kinds of perceptions. It has five whirlpools, its rapids are the five pains; it has fifty kinds of suffering, and five branches.

6 In that vast Brahma-wheel, in which all things live and rest, the bird flutters about, so long as he thinks that the self (in him) is different from the mover (the god, the lord). When he has been blessed by him, then he gains immortality.

7 But what is praised (in the Upanishads) is the Highest Brahman, and in it there is the triad. The Highest Brahman is the safe support, it is imperishable. The Brahma-students, when they have known what is within this (world), are devoted and merged in the Brahman, free from birth.

8   The Lord (îsa) supports all this together, the perishable and the imperishable, the developed and the undeveloped. The (living) self, not being a lord, is bound, because he has to enjoy (the fruits of works); but when he has known the god (deva), he is freed from all fetters.

9   There are two, one knowing (îsvara), the other not-knowing (gîva), both unborn, one strong, the other weak; there is she, the unborn, through whom each man receives the recompense of his works; and there is the infinite Self (appearing) under all forms, but himself inactive. When a man finds out these three, that is Brahma.

10 That which is perishable is the Pradhâna (the first), the immortal and imperishable is Hara. The one god rules the perishable (the pradhâna) and the (living) self. From meditating on him, from joining him, from becoming one with him there is further cessation of all illusion in the end.

11 When that god is known, all fetters fall off, sufferings are destroyed, and birth and death cease. From meditating on him there arises, on the dissolution of the body, the third state, that of universal lordship; but he only who is alone, is satisfied.

12 This, which rests eternally within the self, should be known; and beyond this not anything has to be known. By knowing the enjoyer, the enjoyed, and the ruler, everything has been declared to be threefold, and this is Brahman.

13 As the form of fire, while it exists in the under-wood, is not seen, nor is its seed destroyed, but it has to be seized again and again by means of the stick and the under-wood, so it is in both cases, and the Self has to be seized in the body by means of the pranava (the syllable Om).

14 By making his body the under-wood, and the syllable Om the upper-wood, man, after repeating the drill of meditation, will perceive the bright god, like the spark hidden in the wood.

15 As oil in seeds, as butter in cream, as water in (dry) river-beds, as fire in wood, so is the Self seized within the self, if man looks for him by truthfulness and penance;

16 (If he looks) for the Self that pervades everything, as butter is contained in milk, and the roots whereof are self-knowledge and penance. That is the Brahman taught by the Upanishad.

Second Adhyâya

1   Savitri (the sun), having first collected his mind and expanded his thoughts, brought Agni (fire), when he had discovered his light, above the earth.

2   With collected minds we are at the command of the divine Savitri, that we may obtain blessedness.

3   May Savitri, after he has reached with his mind the gods as they rise up to the sky, and with his thoughts (has reached) heaven, grant these gods to make a great light to shine.

4   The wise sages of the great sage collect their mind and collect their thoughts. He who alone knows the law (Savitri) has ordered the invocations; great is the praise of the divine Savitri.

5   Your old prayer has to be joined with praises. Let my song go forth like the path of the sun! May all the sons of the Immortal listen, they who have reached their heavenly homes.

6   Where the fire is rubbed, where the wind is checked, where the Soma flows over, there the mind is born.

7   Let us love the old Brahman by the grace of Savitri; if thou make thy dwelling there, the path will not hurt thee.

8   If a wise man hold his body with its three erect parts (chest, neck, and head) even 2, and turn his senses with the mind towards the heart, he will then in the boat of Brahman cross all the torrents which cause fear.

9   Compressing his breathings let him, who has subdued all motions, breathe forth through the nose with gentle breath. Let the wise man without fail restrain his mind, that chariot yoked with vicious horses.

10   Let him perform his exercises in a place level, pure, free from pebbles, fire, and dust, delightful by its sounds, its water, and bowers, not painful to the eye, and full of shelters and caves.

11   When Yoga is being performed, the forms which come first, producing apparitions in Brahman, are those of misty smoke, sun, fire, wind, fire-flies, lightnings, and a crystal moon.

12   When, as earth, water, light, heat, and ether arise, the fivefold quality of Yoga takes place, then there is no longer illness, old age, or pain for him who has obtained a body, produced by the fire of Yoga.

13   The first results of Yoga they call lightness, healthiness, steadiness, a good complexion, an easy pronunciation, a sweet odour, and slight excretions.

14   As a metal disk (mirror), tarnished by dust, shines bright again after it has been cleaned, so is the one incarnate person satisfied and free from grief, after he has seen the real nature of the Self.

15   And when by means of the real nature of his self he sees, as by a lamp, the real nature of Brahman, then having known the unborn, eternal god, who is beyond all natures, he is freed from all fetters.

16   He indeed is the god who pervades all regions: he is the first-born (as Hira*n*yagarbha), and he is in the womb. He has been born, and he will be born. He stands behind all persons, looking everywhere.

17   The god who is in the fire, the god who is in the water, the god who has entered into the whole world, the god who is in plants, the god who is in trees, adoration be to that god, adoration!

Third Adhyâya

1   The snarer who rules alone by his powers, who rules all the worlds by his powers, who is one and the same, while things arise and exist, – they who know this are immortal.

2   For there is one Rudra only, they do not allow a second, who rules all the worlds by his powers. He stands behind all persons, and after having created all worlds he, the protector, rolls it up at the end of time.

3   That one god, having his eyes, his face, his arms, and his feet in every place, when producing heaven and earth, forges them together with his arms and his wings.

4   He, the creator and supporter of the gods, Rudra, the great seer, the lord of all, he who formerly gave birth to Hira*n*yagarbha, may he endow us with good thoughts.

5   O Rudra, thou dweller in the mountains, look upon us with that most blessed form of thine which is auspicious, not terrible, and reveals no evil!

6   O lord of the mountains, make lucky that arrow which thou, a dweller in the mountains, holdest in thy hand to shoot. Do not hurt man or beast!

7   Those who know beyond this the High Brahman, the vast, hidden in the bodies of all creatures, and alone enveloping everything, as the Lord, they become immortal.

8   I know that great person (purusha) of sunlike lustre beyond the darkness. A man who knows him truly, passes over death; there is no other path to go.

9   This whole universe is filled by this person (purusha), to whom there is nothing superior, from whom there is nothing different, than whom there is nothing smaller or larger, who stands alone, fixed like a tree in the sky.

10 That which is beyond this world is without form and without suffering. They who know it, become immortal, but others suffer pain indeed.

11 That Bhagavat exists in the faces, the heads, the necks of all, he dwells in the cave (of the heart) of all beings, he is all-pervading, therefore he is the omnipresent Siva.

12 That person (purusha) is the great lord; he is the mover of existence, he possesses that purest power of reaching everything, he is light, he is undecaying.

13 The person (purusha), not larger than a thumb, dwelling within, always dwelling in the heart of man, is perceived by the heart, the thought, the mind; they who know it become immortal.

14 The person (purusha) with a thousand heads. a thousand eyes, a thousand feet, having compassed the earth on every side, extends beyond it by ten fingers' breadth.

15 That person alone (purusha) is all this, what has been and what will be; he is also the lord of immortality; he is whatever grows by food.

16 Its hands and feet are everywhere, its eyes and head are everywhere, its ears are everywhere, it stands encompassing all in the world.

17 Separate from all the senses, yet reflecting the qualities of all the senses, it is the lord and ruler of all, it is the great refuge of all.

18 The embodied spirit within the town with nine gates, the bird, flutters outwards, the ruler of the whole world, of all that rests and of all that moves.

19 Grasping without hands, hasting without feet, he sees without eyes, he hears without ears. He knows what can be known, but no one knows him; they call him the first, the great person (purusha).

20 The Self, smaller than small, greater than great, is hidden in the heart of the creature. A man who has left all grief behind, sees the majesty, the Lord, the passionless, by the grace of the creator (the Lord).

21 I know this undecaying, ancient one, the self of all things, being infinite and omnipresent. They declare that in him all birth is stopped, for the Brahma-students proclaim him to be eternal.

4

Vimalakirti

The Vimalakirti Sutra

Beyond Comprehension

AT THAT TIME SHARIPUTRA, OBSERVING THAT THERE WERE NO SEATS in Vimalakirti's room, thought to himself: "All these bodhisattvas and major disciples—where are they going to sit?"

The rich man Vimalakirti, knowing what was in his mind, said to Shariputra, "Did you come here for the sake of the Law, or are you just looking for a place to sit?"

"I came for the Law, not for a seat!" said Shariputra.

"Ah, Shariputra," said Vimalakirti, "a seeker of the Law doesn't concern himself even about life or limb, much less about a seat! A seeker of the Law seeks nothing in the way of form, perception, conception, volition, or consciousness; he seeks nothing in the way of sense-realms or sense-media; he seeks nothing in the threefold world of desire, form, and formlessness.

"Ah, Shariputra, a seeker of the Law does not seek it through attachment to the Buddha, does not seek it through attachment to the Law, does not seek it through attachment to the order. A seeker of the Law does not seek it through recognition of suffering, does not seek it through renunciation of attachments, does not seek it through realization of how to end attachments, or through practice of the Way. Why? Because the Law has nothing to do with idle theorizing. To declare that one must recognize suffering, renounce attachments, realize how to reach extinction, and practice the Way is mere idle theorizing, not seeking the Law.

"Ah, Shariputra, the Law is called 'tranquil extinction.' But if one strives for birth followed by extinction, this is seeking birth and extinction, this is not seeking the Law. The Law is called 'unstained.' But if one is stained with the idea of the Law or of nirvana, then one is stained with attachment, and this is not seeking the Law. The Law has no goal of activity, but if one actively pursues the Law, one is pursuing a goal, and this is not seeking the Law. The Law knows no picking and choosing, but if one picks and chooses the Law, this is picking and choosing, not seeking the Law. The Law is independent of place, but if one fixes on the idea of place, this is fixation with place, not a seeking of the Law. The Law is called 'formless.' If one tries to know it through form, this is seeking form, not seeking the Law.

"The Law is not something that can be resided in. If one tries to reside in it, this is trying to reside in the Law, not seeking the Law. The Law is not something that can be seen, heard, perceived, or understood. If one tries to see, hear, perceive, and understand it, this is trying to see, hear, perceive, and understand the Law, not seeking the Law. The Law is called 'unconditioned.' If one tries to approach it through the conditioned, this is seeking the conditioned, not seeking the Law.

"Therefore, Shariputra, if one would be a seeker of the Law, one must not seek it in anything at all."

When Vimalakirti spoke these words, five hundred heavenly sons gained the purity of the Dharma eye in their perception of phenomena.

At that time the rich man Vimalakirti said to Manjushri, "You have visited countless thousands, ten thousands, billions of asamkhyas of countries. What Buddha lands have the finest and most beautiful lion seats, those endowed with the best qualities?"

Manjushri replied, "Layman, to the east, beyond countries numerous as the sands of thirty-six Ganges, lies a world called Sumeru Shape. Its Buddha is named Sumeru Lamp King, and he is there now. This Buddha's body is eighty-four thousand yojanas in height and the lion seat [he sits on] is eighty-four thousand yojanas high and adorned in the finest fashion."

The rich man Vimalakirti then exercised his transcendental powers and at once that Buddha dispatched thirty-two thousand lion seats, tall, broad, adorned, and pure, and had them brought into Vimalakirti's room, where the bodhisattvas, major disciples, Indras, Brahmas, Four Heavenly Kings and the others saw something they had never seen before. For the room was broad and spacious enough to hold all these thirty-two thousand lion seats without the slightest crowding or hindrance. The city of Vaishali and Jambudvipa and the other of the four continents too seemed in no way cramped or inconvenienced, but all appeared just as usual.

At that time Vimalakirti said to Manjushri, "Sit down in one of the lion seats! The bodhisattvas and other distinguished persons should also sit down, but when they do so they should assume bodies suitable to the size of the seat."

The bodhisattvas who had acquired transcendental powers thereupon immediately transformed their shapes, making themselves forty-two yojanas tall, and sat down in the lion seats. But among the bodhisattvas who had newly embarked on their course or the major disciples, there were none who could climb up into the seats.

At that time Vimalakirti said to Shariputra, "Sit down in a lion seat!"

But Shariputra said, "Layman, these seats are too tall and wide—we can't climb up in them!"

Vimalakirti said, "Ah, Shariputra, if you will make obeisance to the Thus Come One Sumeru Lamp King, then you will be able to take a seat."

The bodhisattvas who had newly embarked on their course and the major disciples accordingly made obeisance to the Thus Come One Sumeru Lamp King, and after that they were able to seat themselves in the lion seats.

Shariputra said, "Layman, I have never seen such a thing! A little room like this and still it can hold seats as tall and broad as these! And the city of Vaishali is in no way crowded or obstructed, nor are any of the towns or villages of Jambudvipa or of the other of the four continents cramped or inconvenienced, or the palaces of the heavenly beings, dragon kings and spirits!"

Vimalakirti said, "Ah, Shariputra, the Buddhas and bodhisattvas have an emancipation that is called Beyond Comprehension. When a bodhisattva dwells in this emancipation, he can take something as tall and broad as Mount Sumeru and put it inside a mustard seed without enlarging one or shrinking the other, and Mount Sumeru, king of mountains, will still have its original shape. Moreover, the Four Heavenly Kings and the gods of the Trayastrimsha heaven [who live on Mount Sumeru] will not even know or realize where they have gone to. Only those destined for enlightenment will be able to see that Sumeru has been put inside a mustard seed. This is called dwelling in the doctrine of the emancipation Beyond Comprehension.

"Or again, this bodhisattva can take the waters of the four great oceans and pour them into the opening that holds a single hair, without the fish, turtles, sea turtles, lizards, or other sea creatures being in any way troubled, and those great seas will still have their original form. And the dragons, spirits, asuras, and others [who live in the sea] will not know or realize where they have gone to, and these beings will not be at all troubled.

"Or again, Shariputra, this bodhisattva who dwells in the emancipation Beyond Comprehension can slice off the thousand-millionfold world, grasp it in the palm of his right hand like a potter's wheel, and toss it beyond lands numerous as the sands of the Ganges, and the beings in that world will not know or realize where they have gotten to. The bodhisattva can then bring it back and put it in its original place, and none of the people will have any idea they have gone somewhere and come back, and the world will have the same shape as before.

"Again, Shariputra, suppose there are beings who want to live in this world for a long time but are qualified to enter enlightenment. This bodhisattva can stretch seven days into a kalpa, so that to those beings they really seem like a whole kalpa. Or if there are beings who do not want to live in this world for long and they are qualified to enter enlightenment, this bodhisattva can squeeze a kalpa into seven days, so that to those beings it seems like only seven days.

"Again, Shariputra, the bodhisattva who dwells in the emancipation Beyond Comprehension can take the magnificent adornments from all the Buddha lands, gather them together, and show them to the beings living in a single country. Or this bodhisattva can place all the beings of a single Buddha land in the palm of his right hand and fly with them all around the ten directions, showing them everything, and yet never move from his original spot.

"Or, Shariputra, this bodhisattva can take all the objects offered to the Buddhas by the beings in the worlds in the ten directions and make them all visible within a pore that holds a single hair, or take all the suns, moon, stars, and constellations that belong to the worlds in the ten directions and make them visible within the pore of a single hair. Or, Shariputra, he can suck into his mouth all the winds from the worlds in the ten directions without doing any harm to himself or breaking down the trees that grow there. Or, when the worlds in the ten directions come to the end of the kalpa and everything is destroyed by fire, he can take all those fires and hold them in his belly, and though the fires go on burning as before, the bodhisattva suffers no harm. Or he can go down into the lower region, past Buddha lands numerous as the sands of the Ganges, pick up one Buddha land, and lift it to the upper region, above Buddha lands numerous as the sands of the Ganges, as one would lift the leaf of a jujube tree on the point of a needle, and that land will be in no way troubled.

"Or, Shariputra, the bodhisattva who dwells in the emancipation Beyond Comprehension can use his transcendental powers to make himself appear in the body of a Buddha, or the body of a pratyekabuddha, or that of a voice-hearer, an Indra, a Brahma king, one of the Four Heavenly Kings, or a wheel-turning king. Or again he can take all the voices uttered by the beings in the worlds of the ten directions, high, middle, and low-grade sounds, and transform them all into the voice of the Buddha. He can make these voices discourse with the sounds of 'impermanence,' 'suffering,' 'emptiness,' or 'non-ego,' or expound all the various other doctrines preached by the Buddhas of the ten directions, and cause those doctrines to be heard everywhere.

"Shariputra, I have just now briefly described the powers possessed by this bodhisattva of the emancipation Beyond Comprehension. If I were to describe them in full, I could go on for a whole kalpa and never have done."

At that time Mahakashyapa, hearing this discourse on the doctrine of the emancipation Beyond Comprehension, sighed at encountering what he had never heard before, and said to Shariputra, "It is like someone displaying various painted images before a blind man when he cannot see them. In the same way, when we voice-hearers hear this doctrine of the emancipation Beyond Comprehension, we are all incapable of understanding it. If wise persons hear it, there will be none who do not set their minds on attaining anuttara-samyak-sambodhi. But what of us, who are forever cut off at the root, who with regard to these Great Vehicle teachings have already become like rotten seed? When voice-hearers hear this doctrine of the emancipation Beyond Comprehension, they will surely all cry out in anguish in voices loud enough to shake the whole thousand-millionfold world. But bodhisattvas should all accept this teaching with great joy and thanksgiving. For if there are bodhisattvas who put faith in this doctrine of the emancipation Beyond Comprehension, then none of the host of devils can do anything to them!"

When Mahakashyapa spoke these words, thirty-two thousand offspring of the gods set their minds on the attainment of anuttara-samyak-sambodhi.

At that time Vimalakirti said to Mahakashyapa, "Sir, among those who play the part of devil kings in the immeasurable asamkhyas of worlds in the ten directions, there are many who in fact are bodhisattvas dwelling in the emancipation Beyond Comprehension. They employ their skill in expedient means to teach and convert living beings by appearing in the guise of devil kings.

"Or again, Kashyapa, with regard to the immeasurable numbers of bodhisattvas in the ten directions, sometimes people come to them begging for a hand or a foot, an ear, a nose, a head, an eye, marrow or brains, blood, flesh, skin, bones, or for their villages, towns, wives and children, men and women servants, elephants, horses, carriages, or for gold, lapis lazuli, seashell, agate, coral, amber, pearls, agate shell, clothing, food or drink. Many of those who beg in this fashion are bodhisattvas who dwell in the emancipation Beyond Comprehension. They employ their skill in expedient means and go to the other bodhisattvas to test them and make sure they are firm in their resolve [to give alms]. How can they do this? Because the bodhisattvas who dwell in the emancipation Beyond Comprehension possess powers of authority and virtue that enable them to importune others and make them perform difficult feats in this manner. Ordinary persons of inferior type have no such powers and hence cannot importune others as these bodhisattvas do. They are like donkeys who cannot stand up before the kicking and trampling of dragons or elephants.

"This is what is called the wisdom and expedient means possessed by the bodhisattvas who dwell in the emancipation Beyond Comprehension."

5

Lucretius

On the Nature of Things

[. . .] WHEN THE LIFE OF MAN LAY FOUL TO SEE and grovelling upon the earth, crushed by the weight of religion, which showed her face from the realms of heaven, lowering upon mortals with dreadful mien, 'twas a man of Greece [Epicurus] who dared first to raise his mortal eyes to meet her, and first to stand forth to meet her: him neither the stories of the gods nor thunderbolts checked, nor the sky with its revengeful roar, but all the more spurred the eager daring of his mind to yearn to be the first to burst through the close-set bolts upon the doors of nature. And so it was that the lively force of his mind won its way, and he passed on far beyond the fiery walls of the world, and in mind and spirit traversed the boundless whole; whence in victory he brings us tidings what can come to be and what cannot, yea and in what way each thing has its power limited, and its deepset boundary-stone. And so religion in revenge is cast beneath men's feet and trampled, and victory raises us to heaven.

Herein I have one fear, lest perchance you think that you are starting on the principles of some unholy reasoning, and setting foot upon the path of sin. Nay, but on the other hand, again and again our foe, religion, has given birth to deeds sinful and unholy. Even as at Aulis the chosen chieftains of the Danai, the first of all the host, foully stained with the blood of Iphianassa the altar of the Virgin of the Cross-Roads. For as soon as the band braided about her virgin locks streamed from her either cheek in equal lengths, as soon as she saw her sorrowing sire stand at the altar's side, and near him the attendants hiding their knives, and her countrymen shedding tears at the sight of her, tongue-tied with terror, sinking on her knees she fell to earth. Nor could it avail the luckless maid at such a time that she first had given the name of father to the king. For seized by men's hands, all trembling was she led to the altars, not that, when the ancient rite of sacrifice was fulfilled, she might be escorted by the clear cry of 'Hymen', but in the very moment of marriage, a pure victim she might foully fall, sorrowing beneath a father's slaughtering stroke, that a happy and hallowed starting might be granted to the fleet. Such evil deeds could religion prompt. [. . .]

For if things came to being from nothing, every kind might be born from all things, nought would need a seed. First men might arise from the sea, and from the land the race of scaly creatures, and birds burst forth from the sky; cattle and other herds, and all the tribe of wild beasts, with no fixed law of birth, would haunt tilth and desert. Nor would the same fruits stay constant to the trees, but all would change: all trees might avail to bear all fruits. Why, were there not bodies to bring each thing to birth, how could things have a fixed unchanging mother? But as it is, since all things are produced from fixed seeds, each thing is born and comes forth into the coasts of light, out of that which has in it the substance and first-bodies of each; and 'tis for this cause that all things cannot be begotten of all, because in fixed things there dwells a power set apart. Or again, why do we see the roses in spring, and the corn in summer's heat, and the vines bursting out when autumn summons them, if it be not that when, in their own time, the fixed seeds of things have flowed together, then is disclosed each thing that comes to birth, while the season is at hand, and the lively earth in safety brings forth the fragile things into the coasts of light? But if they sprang from nothing, suddenly would they arise at uncertain intervals and in hostile times of year, since indeed there would be no first-beginnings which might be kept apart from creative union at an ill-starred season. Nay more, there would be no need for lapse of time for the increase of things upon the meeting of the seed, if they could grow from nothing. For little children would grow suddenly to youths, and at once trees would come forth, leaping from the earth. But of this it is well seen that nothing comes to pass, since all things grow slowly, as is natural, from a fixed seed, and as they grow preserve their kind: so that you can know that each thing grows great, and is fostered out of its own substance. There is this too, that without fixed rain-showers in the year the earth could not put forth its gladdening produce, nor again held apart from food could the nature of living things renew its kind or preserve its life; so that rather you may think that many bodies are common to many things, as we see letters are to words, than that without first-beginnings anything can come to being. Once more, why could not nature produce men so large that on their feet they might wade through the waters of ocean or rend asunder mighty mountains with their hands, or live to overpass many generations of living men, if it be not because fixed substance has been appointed for the begetting of things, from which it is ordained what can arise? Therefore, we must confess that nothing can be brought to being out of nothing, inasmuch as it needs a seed for things, from which each may be produced and brought forth into the gentle breezes of the air. Lastly, inasmuch as we see that tilled grounds are better than the untilled, and when worked by hands yield better produce, we must know that there are in the earth first-beginnings of things, which we call forth to birth by turning the teeming sods with the ploughshare and drilling the soil of the earth. But if there were none such, you would see all things without toil of ours of their own will come to be far better.

Then follows this, that nature breaks up each thing again into its own first-bodies, nor does she destroy ought into nothing. For if anything were mortal in all its parts, each thing would on a sudden be snatched from our eyes, and pass away. For there would be no need of any force, such as might cause disunion in its parts and unloose its fastenings. But as it is, because all things are put together of everlasting seeds, until some force has met them to batter things asunder with its blow, or to make its way inward through the empty voids and break things up, nature suffers not the destruction of anything to be seen. Moreover, if time utterly destroys whatsoever through age it takes from sight, and devours all its substance, how is it that Venus brings back the race of living things after their kind into the light of life, or when she has, how does earth, the quaint artificer, nurse and increase them, furnishing food for them after their kind? how is it that its native springs and the rivers from without, coming from afar, keep the sea full? how is it that the sky feeds the stars? For infinite time and the days that are gone by must needs have devoured all things that are of mortal body. But if in all that while, in the ages that are gone by, those things have existed, of which this sum of things consists and is replenished, assuredly they are blessed with an immortal nature; all things cannot then be turned to nought. And again, the same force and cause would destroy all things alike, unless an eternal substance held them together, part with part interwoven closely or loosely by its fastenings. For in truth a touch would be cause enough of death, seeing that none of these things would be of everlasting body, whose texture any kind of force would be bound to break asunder. But as it is, because the fastenings of the first elements are variously put together, and their substance is everlasting, things endure with body unharmed, until there meets them a force proved strong enough to overcome the texture of each. No single thing then passes back to nothing, but all by dissolution pass back into the first-bodies of matter. Lastly, the rains pass away, when the sky, our father, has cast them headlong into the lap of earth, our mother; but the bright crops spring up, and the branches grow green upon the trees, the trees too grow and are laden with fruit; by them next our race and the race of beasts is nourished, through them we see glad towns alive with children, and leafy woods on every side ring with the young birds' cry; through them the cattle wearied with fatness lay their limbs to rest over the glad pastures, and the white milky stream trickles from their swollen udders; through them a new brood with tottering legs sports wanton among the soft grass, their baby hearts thrilling with the pure milk. Not utterly then perish all things that are seen, since nature renews one thing from out another, nor suffers anything to be begotten, unless she be requited by another's death.

6

Longinus

On the Sublime

XV

THE DIGNITY, GRANDEUR, AND ENERGY OF A STYLE largely depend on a proper employment of images, a term which I prefer to that usually given. The term image in its most general acceptation includes every thought, howsoever presented, which issues in speech. But the term is now generally confined to those cases when he who is speaking, by reason of the rapt and excited state of his feelings, imagines himself to see what he is talking about, and produces a similar illusion in his hearers. Poets and orators both employ images, but with a very different object, as you are well aware. The poetical image is designed to astound; the oratorical image to give perspicuity. Both, however, seek to work on the emotions.

> "Mother, I pray thee, set not thou upon me
> Those maids with bloody face and serpent hair:
> See, see, they come, they're here, they spring upon me!

And again—

> "Ah, ah, she'll slay me! whither shall I fly?"

The poet when he wrote like this saw the Erinyes with his own eyes, and he almost compels his readers to see them too. Euripides found his chief delight in the labour of giving tragic expression to these two passions of madness and love, showing here a real mastery which I cannot think he exhibited elsewhere. Still, he is by no means diffident in venturing on other fields of the imagination. His genius was far from being of the highest order, but by taking pains he often raises himself to a tragic elevation. In his sublimer moments he generally reminds us of Homer's description of the lion—

> "With tail he lashes both his flanks and sides,
> And spurs himself to battle."

Take, for instance, that passage in which Helios, in handing the reins to his son, says—

> "Drive on, but shun the burning Libyan tract;
> The hot dry air will let thine axle down:
> Toward the seven Pleiades keep thy steadfast way."

And then—

> "This said, his son undaunted snatched the reins,
> Then smote the winged coursers' sides: they bound
> Forth on the void and cavernous vault of air.
> His father mounts another steed, and rides
> With warning voice guiding his son. 'Drive there!
> Turn, turn thy car this way.'"

May we not say that the spirit of the poet mounts the chariot with his hero, and accompanies the winged steeds in their perilous flight? Were it not so,—had not his imagination soared side by side with them in that celestial passage,—he would never have conceived so vivid an image. Similar is that passage in his "Cassandra," beginning

> "Ye Trojans, lovers of the steed."

Aeschylus is especially bold in forming images suited to his heroic themes: as when he says of his "Seven against Thebes"—

> "Seven mighty men, and valiant captains, slew
> Over an iron-bound shield a bull, then dipped
> Their fingers in the blood, and all invoked
> Ares, Enyo, and death-dealing Flight
> In witness of their oaths,"

and describes how they all mutually pledged themselves without flinching to die. Sometimes, however, his thoughts are unshapen, and as it were rough-hewn and rugged. Not observing this, Euripides, from too blind a rivalry, sometimes falls under the same censure. Aeschylus with a strange violence of language represents the palace of Lycurgus as *possessed* at the appearance of Dionysus—

> "The halls with rapture thrill, the roof's inspired."

Here Euripides, in borrowing the image, softens its extravagance—

> "And all the mountain felt the god."

Sophocles has also shown himself a great master of the imagination in the scene in which the dying Oedipus prepares himself for burial in the midst of a tempest, and where he tells how

Achilles appeared to the Greeks over his tomb just as they were putting out to sea on their departure from Troy. This last scene has also been delineated by Simonides with a vividness which leaves him inferior to none. But it would be an endless task to cite all possible examples.

To return, then, in poetry, as I observed, a certain mythical exaggeration is allowable, transcending altogether mere logical credence. But the chief beauties of an oratorical image are its energy and reality. Such digressions become offensive and monstrous when the language is cast in a poetical and fabulous mould, and runs into all sorts of impossibilities. Thus much may be learnt from the great orators of our own day, when they tell us in tragic tones that they see the Furies—good people, can't they understand that when Orestes cries out

"Off, off, I say! I know thee who thou art,
One of the fiends that haunt me: I feel thine arms
About me cast, to drag me down to hell,"

these are the hallucinations of a madman?

Wherein, then, lies the force of an oratorical image? Doubtless in adding energy and passion in a hundred different ways to a speech; but especially in this, that when it is mingled with the practical, argumentative parts of an oration, it does not merely convince the hearer, but enthralls him. Such is the effect of those words of Demosthenes: "Supposing, now, at this moment a cry of alarm were heard outside the assize courts, and the news came that the prison was broken open and the prisoners escaped, is there any man here who is such a trifler that he would not run to the rescue at the top of his speed? But suppose someone came forward with the information that they had been set at liberty by the defendant, what then? Why, he would be lynched on the spot!" Compare also the way in which Hyperides excused himself, when he was proceeded against for bringing in a bill to liberate the slaves after Chaeronea. "This measure," he said, "was not drawn up by any orator, but by the battle of Chaeronea." This striking image, being thrown in by the speaker in the midst of his proofs, enables him by one bold stroke to carry all mere logical objection before him. In all such cases our nature is drawn towards that which affects it most powerfully: hence an image lures us away from an argument: judgment is paralysed, matters of fact disappear from view, eclipsed by the superior blaze. Nor is it surprising that we should be thus affected; for when two forces are thus placed in juxtaposition, the stronger must always absorb into itself the weaker.

On sublimity of thought, and the manner in which it arises from native greatness of mind, from imitation, and from the employment of images, this brief outline must suffice.

XVI

The subject which next claims our attention is that of figures of speech. I have already observed that figures, judiciously employed, play an important part in producing sublimity. It would be a tedious, or rather an endless task, to deal with every detail of this subject here; so in order to establish what I have laid down, I will just run over, without further preface, a few of those figures which are most effective in lending grandeur to language.

Demosthenes is defending his policy; his natural line of argument would have been: "You did not do wrong, men of Athens, to take upon yourselves the struggle for the liberties of Hellas. Of this you have home proofs. *They* did not wrong who fought at Marathon, at Salamis, and Plataea." Instead of this, in a sudden moment of supreme exaltation he bursts out like some inspired prophet with that famous appeal to the mighty dead: "Ye did not, could not have done wrong. I swear it by the men who faced the foe at Marathon!" He employs the figure of adjuration, to which I will here give the name of Apostrophe. And what does he gain by it? He exalts the Athenian ancestors to the rank of divinities, showing that we ought to invoke those who have fallen for their country as gods; he fills the hearts of his judges with the heroic pride of the old warriors of Hellas; forsaking the beaten path of argument he rises to the loftiest altitude of grandeur and passion, and commands assent by the startling novelty of his appeal; he applies the healing charm of eloquence, and thus "ministers to the mind diseased" of his countrymen, until lifted by his brave words above their misfortunes they begin to feel that the disaster of Chaeronea is no less glorious than the victories of Marathon and Salamis. All this he effects by the use of one figure, and so carries his hearers away with him. It is said that the germ of this adjuration is found in Eupolis—

"By mine own fight, by Marathon, I say,
Who makes my heart to ache shall rue the day!"

But there is nothing grand in the mere employment of an oath. Its grandeur will depend on its being employed in the right place and the right manner, on the right occasion, and with the right motive. In Eupolis the oath is nothing beyond an oath; and the Athenians to whom it is addressed are still prosperous, and in need of no consolation. Moreover, the poet does not, like Demosthenes, swear by the departed heroes as deities, so as to engender in his audience a just conception of their valour, but diverges from the champions to the battle—a mere lifeless thing. But Demosthenes has so skilfully managed the oath that in addressing his countrymen after the defeat of Chaeronea he takes out of their minds all sense of disaster; and at the same time, while proving that no mistake has been made, he holds up an example, confirms his arguments by an oath, and makes his praise of the dead an incentive to the living. And to rebut a possible objection which occurred to him—"Can you, Demosthenes, whose policy ended in defeat, swear by a victory?"—the orator proceeds to measure his language, choosing his very words so as to give no handle to opponents, thus showing us that even in our most inspired moments reason ought to hold the reins. Let us mark his words: "Those who *faced the foe* at Marathon; those who *fought in the sea-fights* of Salamis and Artemisium; those who *stood in the ranks* at Plataea." Note that he nowhere says "those who *conquered*," artfully suppressing any word which might hint at the successful issue of those battles, which would have spoilt the parallel with Chaeronea. And for the same reason he steals a march on his audience, adding immediately: "All of whom, Aeschines,—not those who were successful only,—were buried by the state at the public expense."

XVII

There is one truth which my studies have led me to observe, which perhaps it would be worthwhile to set down briefly here. It is this, that by a natural law the Sublime, besides receiving an acquisition of strength from figures, in its turn lends support in a remarkable manner to them. To explain: the use of figures has a peculiar tendency to rouse a suspicion of dishonesty, and to create an impression of treachery, scheming, and false reasoning; especially if the person addressed be a judge, who is master of the situation, and still more in the case of a despot, a king, a military potentate, or any of those who sit in high places. If a man feels that this artful speaker is treating him like a silly boy and trying to throw dust in his eyes, he at once grows irritated, and thinking that such false reasoning implies a contempt of his understanding, he perhaps flies into a rage and will not hear another word; or even if he masters his resentment, still he is utterly indisposed to yield to the persuasive power of eloquence. Hence it follows that a figure is then most effectual when it appears in disguise. To allay, then, this distrust which attaches to the use of figures we must call in the powerful aid of sublimity and passion. For art, once associated with these great allies, will be overshadowed by their grandeur and beauty, and pass beyond the reach of all suspicion. To prove this I need only refer to the passage already quoted: "I swear it by the men," etc. It is the very brilliancy of the orator's figure which blinds us to the fact that it *is* a figure. For as the fainter lustre of the stars is put out of sight by the all-encompassing rays of the sun, so when sublimity sheds its light all round the sophistries of rhetoric they become invisible. A similar illusion is produced by the painter's art. When light and shadow are represented in colour, though they lie on the same surface side by side, it is the light which meets the eye first, and appears not only more conspicuous but also much nearer. In the same manner passion and grandeur of language, lying nearer to our souls by reason both of a certain natural affinity and of their radiance, always strike our mental eye before we become conscious of the figure, throwing its artificial character into the shade and hiding it as it were in a veil.

7

Plotinus

The Enneads

Third Tractate: The Knowing Hypostases and the Transcendent

1 ARE WE TO THINK THAT A BEING KNOWING ITSELF must contain diversity, that self-knowledge can be affirmed only when some one phase of the self perceives other phases, and that therefore an absolutely simplex entity would be equally incapable of introversion and of self-awareness?

No: a being that has no parts or phases may have this consciousness; in fact there would be no real self-knowing in an entity presented as knowing itself in virtue of being a compound—some single element in it perceiving other elements—as we may know our own form and entire bodily organism by sense-perception: such knowing does not cover the whole field; the knowing element has not had the required cognizance at once of its associates and of itself; this is not the self-knower asked for; it is merely something that knows something else.

Either we must exhibit the self-knowing of an uncompounded being—and show how that is possible—or abandon the belief that any being can possess veritable self-cognition.

To abandon the belief is not possible in view of the many absurdities thus entailed.

It would be already absurd enough to deny this power to the Soul (or mind), but the very height of absurdity to deny it to the nature of the Intellectual-Principle, presented thus as knowing the rest of things but not attaining to knowledge, or even awareness, of itself.

It is the province of sense and in some degree of understanding and judgement, but not of the Intellectual-Principle, to handle the external, though whether the Intellectual-Principle holds the knowledge of these things is a question to be examined, but it is obvious that the Intellectual-Principle must have knowledge of the Intellectual objects. Now, can it know those objects alone or must it not simultaneously know itself, the being whose function it is to know just those things? Can it have self-knowledge in the sense (dismissed above as inadequate) of knowing its content while it ignores itself? Can it be aware of knowing its members and yet remain in ignorance of its own knowing self? Self and content must be simultaneously present: the method and degree of this knowledge we must now consider.

2 We begin with the Soul, asking whether it is to be allowed self-knowledge and what the knowing principle in it would be and how operating.

The sense-principle in it, we may at once decide, takes cognizance only of the external; even in any awareness of events within the body it occupies, this is still the perception of something external to a principle dealing with those bodily conditions not as within but as beneath itself.

The reasoning-principle in the Soul acts upon the representations standing before it as the result of sense-perception; these it judges, combining, distinguishing: or it may also observe the impressions, so to speak, rising from the Intellectual-Principle, and has the same power of handling these; and reasoning will develop to wisdom where it recognizes the new and late-coming impressions (those of sense) and adapts them, so to speak, to those it holds from long before—the act which may be described as the Soul's Reminiscence.

So far as this, the efficacy of the Intellectual-Principle in the Soul certainly reaches; but is there also introversion and self-cognition or is that power to be reserved strictly for the Divine Mind?

If we accord self-knowing to this phase of the Soul we make it an Intellectual-Principle and will have to show what distinguishes it from its prior; if we refuse it self-knowing, all our thought brings us step by step to some principle which has this power, and we must discover what such self-knowing consists in. If, again, we do allow self-knowledge in the lower we must examine the question of degree; for if there is no difference of degree, then the reasoning principle in Soul is the Intellectual-Principle unalloyed.

We ask, then, whether the understanding principle in the Soul has equally the power of turning inwards upon itself or whether it has no more than that of comprehending the impressions, superior and inferior, which it receives.

The first stage is to discover what this comprehension is.

3 Sense sees a man and transmits the impression to the understanding. What does the understanding say? It has nothing to say as yet; it accepts and waits; unless, rather, it questions within itself, 'Who is this?—someone it has met before—and then, drawing on memory, says, 'Socrates'.

If it should go on to develop the impression received, it distinguishes various elements in what the representative faculty has set before it; supposing it to say 'Socrates, if the man is good', then, while it has spoken upon information from the senses, its total pronouncement is its own; it contains within itself a standard of good.

But how does it thus contain the good within itself?

It is, itself, of the nature of the good and it has been strengthened still towards the perception of all that is good by the irradiation of the Intellectual-Principle upon it; for this pure phase of the Soul welcomes to itself the images implanted from its prior.

But why may we not distinguish this understanding phase as Intellectual-Principle and take Soul to consist of the later phases from the sensitive downwards?

Because all the activities mentioned are within the scope of a reasoning faculty, and reasoning is characteristically the function of Soul.

Why not, however, absolve the question by assigning self-cognizance to this phase?

Because we have allotted to Soul the function of dealing—in thought and in multiform action—with the external, and we hold that observation of self and of the content of self must belong to Intellectual-Principle.

If any one says, 'Still; what precludes the reasoning Soul from observing its own content by some special faculty?' he is no longer positing a principle of understanding or of reasoning but, simply, bringing in the Intellectual-Principle unalloyed.

But what precludes the Intellectual-Principle from being present, unalloyed, within the Soul? Nothing, we admit; but are we entitled therefore to think of it as a phase of Soul?

We cannot describe it as belonging to the Soul though we do describe it as our Intellectual-Principle, something distinct from the understanding, advanced above it, and yet ours even though we cannot include it among soul-phases: it is ours and not ours; and therefore we use it sometimes and sometimes not, whereas we always have use of the understanding; the Intellectual-Principle is ours when we act by it, not ours when we neglect it.

But what is this acting by it? Does it mean that we become the Intellectual-Principle so that our utterance is the utterance of the Intellectual-Principle, or that (at best) we represent it?

We are not the Intellectual-Principle; we represent it in virtue of that highest reasoning faculty which draws upon it.

Again; we perceive by means of the perceptive faculty and are not, ourselves, the percipients: may we then say the same of the understanding (the principle of reasoning and discursive thought)?

No: our reasoning is our own; we ourselves think the thoughts that occupy the understanding—for this is actually the We—but the operation of the Intellectual-Principle enters from above us as that of the sensitive faculty from below; the We is the Soul at its highest, the mid-point between two powers, between the sensitive principle, inferior to us, and the intellectual principle superior. We think of the perceptive act as integral to ourselves because our sense-perception is uninterrupted; we hesitate as to the Intellectual-Principle both because we are not always occupied with it and because it exists apart, not a principle inclining to us but one to which we incline when we choose to look upwards.

The sensitive principle is our scout; the Intellectual-Principle our King.

[...]

8 Now comes the question: what sort of thing does the Intellectual-Principle see in seeing the Intellectual Realm and what in seeing itself?

We are not to look for an Intellectual realm reminding us of the colour or shape to be seen on material objects: the intellectual antedates all such things; and even in our sphere the production is very different from the Reason-Principle in the seeds from which it is produced. The seed principles are invisible and the beings of the Intellectual still more characteristically so; the Intellectuals are of one same nature with the Intellectual Realm which contains them, just as the Reason-Principle in the seed is identical with the Soul, or life-principle, containing it.

But the Soul (considered as apart from the Intellectual-Principle) has no vision of what it thus contains, for it is not the producer but, like the Reason-Principles also, an image of its source: that source is the brilliant, the authentic, the primarily existent, the thing self-sprung and self-intent; but its image, Soul, is a thing which can have no permanence except by attachment, by living in that other; the very nature of an image is that as a secondary it shall have its being in something else, if at all it exist apart from its original. Hence this image (Soul) has not vision, for it has not the necessary light, and if it should see, then, as finding its completion elsewhere, it sees another, not itself.

In the pure Intellectual there is nothing of this: the vision and the envisioned are a unity; the seen is as the seeing and seeing as seen.

What, then, is there that can pronounce upon the nature of this all-unity?

That which sees: and to see is the function of the Intellectual-Principle. Even in our own sphere (we have a parallel to this self-vision of a unity), our vision is light or rather becomes one with the light, and it sees light for it sees colours. In the intellectual, the vision sees not through some medium but by and through itself alone, for its object is not external: by one light it sees another, not through any intermediate agency; a light sees a light, that is to say a thing sees itself. This light shining within the Soul enlightens it; that is, it makes the Soul intellective, working it into likeness with itself, the light above.

Think of the traces of this light upon the Soul, then say to yourself that such, and more beautiful and broader and more radiant, is the light itself; thus you will approach to the nature of the Intellectual-Principle and the Intellectual Realm, for it is this light, itself lit from above, which gives the Soul its brighter life.

It is not the source of the generative life of the Soul which, on the contrary, it draws inward, preserving it from such diffusion, holding it to the love of the splendour of its Prior.

Nor does it give the life of perception and sensation, for that looks to the external and to what acts most vigorously upon the senses, whereas one accepting that light of truth may be said no longer to see the visible, but the very contrary.

This means in sum that the life the Soul takes thence is an intellective life, a trace of the life in the (divine) Intellect, in which alone the authentic exists.

The life in the Divine Intellect is also an Act: it is the primal light outlamping to itself primarily, its own torch; lightgiver and lit at once; the authentic intellectual object, knowing at once and known, seen to itself and needing no other than itself to see by, self-sufficing to the vision, since what it sees it is; known to us by that very same light, our knowledge of it attained through itself, for from nowhere else could we find the means of telling of it. By its nature, its self-vision is the clearer but, using it as our medium, we too may come to see by it.

In the strength of such considerations we lead up our own Soul to the Divine, so that it poses itself as an image of that Being, its life becoming an imprint and a likeness of the Highest, its every act of thought making it over into the Divine and the Intellectual.

If the Soul is questioned as to the nature of that Intellectual-Principle—the perfect and all-embracing, the primal self-knower—it has but to enter into that Principle, or to sink all its activity into that, and at once it shows itself to be in effective possession of those priors whose memory it never lost: thus, as an image of the Intellectual-Principle, it can make itself the medium by which to attain some vision of it; it draws upon that within itself which is most closely resemblant, as far as resemblance is possible between divine Intellect and any phase of Soul.

9 In order, then, to know what the Divine Mind is we must observe Soul and especially its most God-like phase.

One certain way to this knowledge is to separate first, the man from the body—yourself, that is, from your body; next to put aside that Soul which moulded the body, and, very earnestly, the system of sense with desires and impulses and every such futility, all setting definitely towards the mortal: what is left is the phase of the Soul which we have declared to be an image of the Divine Intellect, retaining some light from that source, like the light of the sun which goes beyond its spherical mass, issues from it and plays about it.

Of course we do not pretend that the sun's light (as the analogy might imply) remains a self-gathered and sun-centred thing: it is at once out-rushing and indwelling; it strikes outward continuously, lap after lap, until it reaches us upon our earth: we must take it that all the light, including that which plays about the sun's orb, has travelled; otherwise we would have next to the orb a void expanse. The Soul, on the contrary—a light springing from the Divine Mind and shining about it—is in closest touch with that source; it is not in transit but remains centred there, and, in likeness to that principle, it has no place: the light of the sun is actually in the air, but the Soul is clean of all such contact so that its immunity is patent to itself and to any other of the same order.

And by its own characteristic act, though not without reasoning process, it knows the nature of the Intellectual-Principle which, on its side, knows itself without need of reasoning, for it is ever self-present whereas we become so by directing our Soul towards it; our life is broken and there are many lives, but that principle needs no changings of life or of things; the lives it brings to being are for others, not for itself: it cannot need the inferior; nor does it for itself produce the less when it possesses or is the all, nor the images when it possesses or is the prototype.

Anyone not of the strength to lay hold of the first Soul, that possessing pure intellection, must grasp that which has to do with our ordinary thinking and thence ascend: if even this prove too hard, let him turn to account the sensitive phase which carries the ideal forms of the less fine degree, that phase which, too, with its powers, is immaterial and lies just within the realm of Ideal-principles. [. . .]

10 [. . .] We repeat that the Intellectual-Principle must have, actually has, self-vision, firstly because it has multiplicity, next because it exists for the external and therefore must be a seeing power, one seeing that external; in fact its very essence is vision. Given some external, there must be vision; and if there be nothing external the Intellectual-Principle (Divine Mind) exists in vain. Unless there is something beyond bare unity, there can be no vision: vision must converge with a visible object. And this which the seer is to see can be only a multiple, no undistinguishable unity; nor could a universal unity find anything upon which to exercise any act; all, one and desolate, would be utter stagnation; in so far as there is action, there is diversity. If there be no distinctions, what is there to do, what direction in which to move? An agent must either act upon the extern or be a multiple and so able to act upon itself: making no advance towards anything other than itself, it is motionless, and where it could know only blank fixity it can know nothing.

The intellective power, therefore, when occupied with the intellectual act, must be in a state of duality, whether one of the two elements stand actually outside or both lie within: the intellectual act will always comport diversity as well as the necessary identity, and in the same way its characteristic objects (the Ideas) must stand to the Intellectual-Principle as at once distinct and identical. This applies equally to the single object; there can be no intellection except of something containing separable detail and, since the object is a Reason-Principle (a discriminated Idea), it has the necessary element of multiplicity. The Intellectual-Principle, thus, is informed of itself by the fact of being a multiple organ of vision, an eye receptive of many illuminated objects. If it had to direct itself to a memberless unity, it would be dereasoned: what could it say or know of such an object? The self-affirmation of (even) a memberless unity implies the repudiation of all that does not enter into the character: in other words, it must be multiple as a preliminary to being itself.

Then, again, in the assertion 'I am this particular thing', either the 'particular thing' is distinct from the assertor—and there is a false statement—or it is included within it, and, at once, multiplicity is asserted: otherwise the assertion is 'I am what I am', or 'I am I'.

If it be no more than a simple duality able to say 'I and that other phase', there is already multiplicity, for there is distinction and ground of distinction, there is number with all its train of separate things.

In sum, then, a knowing principle must handle distinct items: its object must, at the moment of cognition, contain diversity; otherwise the thing remains unknown; there is mere conjunction, such a contact, without affirmation or comprehension, as would precede knowledge, the intellect not yet in being, the impinging agent not percipient.

Similarly the knowing principle itself cannot remain simplex, especially in the act of self-knowing: all silent though its self-perception be, it is dual to itself.

Of course The One has no need of minute self-handling since it has nothing to learn by an intellective act; it is in full possession of its being before Intellect exists. Knowledge implies desire, for it is, so to speak, discovery crowning a search; the utterly undifferentiated remains self-centred and makes no inquiry about that self: anything capable of analysing its content must be a manifold.

11 Thus the Intellectual-Principle, in the act of knowing the Transcendent, is a manifold. It knows the Transcendent in very essence but, with all its effort to grasp that prior as a pure unity, it goes forth amassing successive impressions, so that, to it, the object becomes multiple: thus in its outgoing to its object it is not (fully realized) Intellectual-Principle; it is an eye that has not yet seen; in its return it is an eye possessed of the multiplicity which it has itself conferred: it sought something of which it found the vague presentment within itself; it returned with something else, the manifold quality with which it has of its own act invested the simplex.

If it had not possessed a previous impression of the Transcendent it could never have grasped it, but this impression, originally of unity, becomes an impression of multiplicity; and the Intellectual-Principle in taking cognizance of that multiplicity knows the Transcendent and so is realized as an eye possessed of its vision.

It is now Intellectual-Principle since it actually holds its object, and holds it by the act of intellection: before, it was no more than a tendance, an eye blank of impression: it was in motion towards the transcendental; now that it has attained, it has become Intellectual-Principle: always implicit (in the Transcendent), it now, in virtue of this intellection, holds the character of Intellectual-Principle, of Essential Existence, and of Intellectual Act where, previously, not possessing the Intellectual Object, it was not Intellectual Perception, and, not yet having exercised the Intellectual Act, it was not Intellectual-Principle.

The Principle before all these principles is no doubt the first principle of the universe, but not as immanent: immanence is not for primal sources but for engendering secondaries; that which stands as primal source of everything is not a thing but is distinct from all things: it is not, then, a member of the total but earlier than all, earlier, thus, than the Intellectual-Principle—which in fact envelops the entire train of things.

Thus we come, once more, to a Being above the Intellectual-Principle and, since the sequent amounts to no less than the All, we recognize, again, a Being above the All. This assuredly cannot be one of the things to which it is prior. We may not call it Intellect; therefore, too, we may not call it the Good, if the Good is to be taken in the sense of some one member of the universe; if we mean that which precedes the universe of things, the name may be allowed.

The Intellectual-Principle is established in multiplicity; its intellection, self-sprung though it be, is in the nature of something added to it (some accidental dualism) and makes it multiple: the utterly simplex, and therefore first of all beings, must, then, transcend the Intellectual-Principle; and, obviously, if this had intellection it would no longer transcend the Intellectual-Principle but be it, and at once be a multiple.

12 [. . .] We allow this to be true for the Intellectual-Principle to which we have allotted (the multiplicity of) self-knowing; but for the first principle of all, never. Before the manifold, there must be The One, that from which the manifold rises: in all numerical series, the unit is the first. [. . .]

The One, as transcending Intellect, transcends knowing: above all need, it is above the need of the knowing which pertains solely to the Secondary Nature. Knowing is a unitary thing, but defined: the first is One, but undefined: a defined One would not be the One-Absolute: the absolute is prior to the definite.

13 Thus The One is in truth beyond all statement: any affirmation is of a thing; but 'all-transcending, resting above even the most august divine Mind'—this is the only true description, since it does not make it a thing among things, nor name it where no name could identify it: we can but try to indicate, in our own feeble way, something concerning it. When in our perplexity we object, 'Then it is without self-perception, without self-consciousness, ignorant of itself', we must remember that we have been considering it only in its opposites. [. . .]

Consciousness, as the very word indicates, is a conperception, an act exercised upon a manifold: and even intellection, earlier (nearer to the divine) though it is, implies that the agent turns back upon itself, upon a manifold, then. If that agent says no more than 'I am a being', it speaks (by the implied dualism) as a discoverer of the extern; and rightly so, for being is a manifold; when it faces towards the unmanifold and says, 'I am that being', it misses both itself and the being (since the simplex cannot be thus divided into knower and known): if it is to utter truth it cannot indicate by 'being' something (single) like a stone; in the one phrase multiplicity is asserted; for the being thus affirmed—the veritable, as distinguished from such a mere container of some trace of being as ought not to be called a being since it stands merely as image to archetype—this must possess multiplicity.

But will not each item in that multiplicity be an object of intellection to us?

Taken bare and single, no: but Being itself is manifold within itself, and whatever else you may name has Being.

This accepted, it follows that anything that is to be thought of as the most utterly simplex of all, cannot have self-intellection; to have that would mean being multiple. The Transcendent, thus, neither knows itself nor is known in itself. [. . .]

17 [. . .] What then is this in which each particular entity participates, the author of being to the universe and to each item of the total?

Since it is the author of all that exists, and since the multiplicity in each thing is converted into a self-sufficing existence by this presence of The One, so that even the particular itself becomes self-sufficing, then clearly this principle, author at once of Being and of self-sufficingness, is not itself a Being but is above Being and above even self-sufficing.

May we stop, content, with that? No: the Soul is yet, and even more, in pain. Is she ripe, perhaps, to bring forth, now that in her pangs she has come so close to what she seeks? No: we must call upon yet another spell if anywhere the assuagement is to be found. Perhaps in what has already been uttered, there lies the charm if only we tell it over often? No: we need a new, a further, incantation. All our effort may well skim over every truth, and through all the verities in which we have part, and yet the reality escape us when we hope to affirm, to understand: for the understanding, in order to its affirmation, must possess itself of item after item; only so does it traverse all the field: but how can there be any such peregrination of that in which there is no variety?

All the need is met by a contact purely intellective. At the moment of touch there is no power whatever to make any affirmation; there is no leisure; reasoning upon the vision is for afterwards. We may know we have had the vision when the Soul has suddenly taken light. This light is from the Supreme and is the Supreme; we may believe in the Presence when, like that other God on the call of a certain man, He comes bringing light: the light is the proof of the advent. Thus, the Soul unlit remains without that vision; lit, it possesses what it sought. And this is the true end set before the Soul, to take that light, to see the Supreme by the Supreme and not by the light of any other principle—to see the Supreme which is also the means to the vision; for that which illumines the Soul is that which it is to see, just as it is by the sun's own light that we see the sun.

But how is this to be accomplished?

Cut away everything.

8

Augustine of Hippo

Confessions

Book VII

Deceased was now that my evil and abominable youth, and I was passing into early manhood; the more defiled by vain things as I grew in years, who could not imagine any substance, but such as is wont to be seen with these eyes. I thought not of Thee, O God, under the figure of a human body; since I began to hear aught of wisdom, I always avoided this; and rejoiced to have found the same in the faith of our spiritual mother, Thy Catholic Church. But what else to conceive of Thee I knew not. And I, a man, and such a man, sought to conceive of Thee the sovereign, only, true God; and I did in my inmost soul believe that Thou wert incorruptible, and uninjurable, and unchangeable; because though not knowing whence or how, yet I saw plainly, and was sure, that that which may be corrupted must be inferior to that which cannot; what could not be injured I preferred unhesitatingly to what could receive injury; the unchangeable to things subject to change. My heart passionately cried out against all my phantoms, and with this one blow I sought to beat away from the eye of my mind all that unclean troop which buzzed around it. And lo, being scarce put off, in the twinkling of an eye they gathered again thick about me, flew against my face, and beclouded it; so that though not under the form of the human body, yet was I constrained to conceive of Thee (that incorruptible, uninjurable, and unchangeable, which I preferred before the corruptible, and injurable, and changeable) as being in space, whether infused into the world, or diffused infinitely without it. Because whatsoever I conceived, deprived of this space, seemed to me nothing, yea altogether nothing, not even a void, as if a body were taken out of its place, and the place should remain empty of any body at all, of earth and water, air and heaven, yet would it remain a void place, as it were a spacious nothing.

I then being thus gross-hearted, nor clear even to myself, whatsoever was not extended over certain spaces, nor diffused, nor condensed, nor swelled out, or did not or could not receive some of these dimensions, I thought to be altogether nothing. For over such forms as my eyes are wont to range, did my heart then range: nor yet did I see that this same notion of the mind, whereby I formed those very images, was not of this sort, and yet it could not have formed them, had not itself been some great thing. So also did I endeavour to conceive of Thee, Life of my life, as vast, through infinite spaces on every side penetrating the whole mass of the universe, and beyond it, every way, through unmeasurable boundless spaces; so that the earth should have Thee, the heaven have Thee, all things have Thee, and they be bounded in Thee, and Thou bounded nowhere. For that as the body of this air which is above the earth, hindereth not the light of the sun from passing through it, penetrating it, not by bursting or by cutting, but by filling it wholly: so I thought the body not of heaven, air, and sea only, but of the earth too, pervious to Thee, so that in all its parts, the greatest as the smallest, it should admit Thy presence, by a secret inspiration, within and without, directing all things which Thou hast created. So I guessed, only as unable to conceive aught else, for it was false. For thus should a greater part of the earth contain a greater portion of Thee, and a less, a lesser: and all things should in such sort be full of Thee, that the body of an elephant should contain more of Thee, than that of a sparrow, by how much larger it is, and takes up more room; and thus shouldest Thou make the several portions of Thyself present unto the several portions of the world, in fragments, large to the large, petty to the petty. But such art not Thou. But not as yet hadst Thou enlightened my darkness.

It was enough for me, Lord, to oppose to those deceived deceivers, and dumb praters, since Thy word sounded not out of them;—that was enough which long ago, while we were yet at Carthage, Nebridius used to propound, at which all we that heard it were staggered: "That said nation of darkness, which the Manichees are wont to set as an opposing mass over against Thee, what could it have done unto Thee, hadst Thou refused to fight with it? For, if they answered, 'it would have done Thee some hurt,' then shouldest Thou be subject to injury and corruption: but it could do Thee no hurt," then was no reason brought for Thy fighting with it; and fighting in such wise, as that a certain portion or member of Thee, or offspring of Thy very Substance, should be mingled with opposed powers, and natures not created by Thee, and be by them so far corrupted and changed to the worse, as to be turned from happiness into misery, and need assistance, whereby it might be extricated and purified; and that this offspring of Thy Substance was the soul, which being enthralled, defiled, corrupted, Thy Word, free, pure, and whole, might relieve; that Word itself being still corruptible because it was of one and the same Substance. So then, should they affirm Thee, whatsoever Thou art, that is, Thy Substance whereby Thou art, to be incorruptible, then were all these sayings false and execrable; but if corruptible, the very statement showed it to be false and revolting." This argument then of Nebridius sufficed against those who deserved wholly to be vomited out of the overcharged stomach; for they had no escape, without horrible blasphemy of heart and tongue, thus thinking and speaking of Thee.

But I also as yet, although I held and was firmly persuaded that Thou our Lord the true God, who madest not only our souls, but our bodies, and not only our souls and bodies, but all beings, and all things, wert undefilable and unalterable, and in no degree mutable; yet understood I not, clearly and without difficulty, the cause of evil. And yet whatever it were, I perceived it was in such wise to be sought out, as should not constrain me to believe the immutable God to be mutable, lest I should become that evil I was seeking out. I sought it out then, thus far free from anxiety, certain of the untruth of what these held, from whom I shrunk with my whole heart: for I saw, that through enquiring the origin of evil, they were filled with evil, in that they preferred to think that Thy substance did suffer ill than their own did commit it.

And I strained to perceive what I now heard, that free-will was the cause of our doing ill, and Thy just judgment of our suffering ill. But I was not able clearly to discern it. So then endeavouring to draw my soul's vision out of that deep pit, I was again plunged therein, and endeavouring often, I was plunged back as often. But this raised me a little into Thy light, that I knew as well that I had a will, as that I lived: when then I did will or nill any thing, I was most sure that no other than myself did will and nill: and I all but saw that there was the cause of my sin. But what I did against my will, I saw that I suffered rather than did, and I judged not to be my fault, but my punishment; whereby, however, holding Thee to be just, I speedily confessed myself to be not unjustly punished. But again I said, Who made me? Did not my God, Who is not only good, but goodness itself? Whence then came I to will evil and nill good, so that I am thus justly punished? who set this in me, and ingrafted into me this plant of bitterness, seeing I was wholly formed by my most sweet God? If the devil were the author, whence is that same devil? And if he also by his own perverse will, of a good angel became a devil, whence, again, came in him that evil will whereby he became a devil, seeing the whole nature of angels was made by that most good Creator? By these thoughts I was again sunk down and choked; yet not brought down to that hell of error (where no man confesseth unto Thee), to think rather that Thou dost suffer ill, than that man doth it.

For I was in such wise striving to find out the rest, as one who had already found that the incorruptible must needs be better than the corruptible: and Thee therefore, whatsoever Thou wert, I confessed to be incorruptible. For never soul was, nor shall be, able to conceive any thing which may be better than Thou, who art the sovereign and the best good. But since most truly and certainly, the incorruptible is preferable to the corruptible (as I did now prefer it), then, wert Thou not incorruptible, I could in thought have arrived at something better than my God. Where then I saw the incorruptible to be preferable to the corruptible, there ought I to seek for Thee, and there observe "wherein evil itself was"; that is, whence corruption comes, by which Thy substance can by no means be impaired. For corruption does no ways impair our God; by no will, by no necessity, by no unlooked-for chance: because He is God, and what He wills is good, and Himself is that good; but to be corrupted is not good. Nor art Thou against Thy will constrained to any thing, since Thy will is not greater than Thy power. But greater should it be, were Thyself greater than Thyself. For the will and power of God is God Himself. And what can be unlooked-for by Thee, Who knowest all things? Nor is there any nature in things, but Thou knowest it. And what should we more say, "why that substance which God is should not be corruptible," seeing if it were so, it should not be God?

And I sought "whence is evil," and sought in an evil way; and saw not the evil in my very search. I set now before the sight of my spirit the whole creation, whatsoever we can see therein (as sea, earth, air, stars, trees, mortal creatures); yea, and whatever in it we do not see, as the firmament of heaven, all angels moreover, and all the spiritual inhabitants thereof. But these very beings, as though they were bodies, did my fancy dispose in place, and I made one great mass of Thy creation, distinguished as to the kinds of bodies; some, real bodies, some, what myself had feigned for spirits. And this mass I made huge, not as it was (which I could not know), but as I thought convenient, yet every way finite. But Thee, O Lord, I imagined on every part environing and penetrating it, though every way infinite: as if there were a sea, every where, and on every side, through unmeasured space, one only boundless sea, and it contained within it some sponge, huge, but bounded; that sponge must needs, in all its parts, be filled from that unmeasurable sea: so conceived I Thy creation, itself finite, full of Thee, the Infinite; and I said, Behold God, and behold what God hath created; and God is good, yea, most mightily and incomparably better than all these: but yet He, the Good, created them good; and see how He environeth and fulfils them. Where is evil then, and whence, and how crept it in hither? What is its root, and what its seed? Or hath it no being? Why then fear we and avoid what is not? Or if we fear it idly, then is that very fear evil, whereby the soul is thus idly goaded and racked. Yea, and so much a greater evil, as we have nothing to fear, and yet do fear. Therefore either is that evil which we fear, or else evil is, that we fear. Whence is it then? seeing God, the Good, hath created all these things good. He indeed, the greater and chiefest Good, hath created these lesser goods; still both Creator and created, all are good. Whence is evil? Or, was there some evil matter of which He made, and formed, and ordered it, yet left something in it which He did not convert into good? Why so then? Had He no might to turn and change the whole, so that no evil should remain in it, seeing He is All-mighty? Lastly, why would He make any thing at all of it, and not rather by the same All-mightiness cause it not to be at all? Or, could it then be against His will? Or if it were from eternity, why suffered He it so to be for infinite spaces of times past, and was pleased so long after to make something out of it? Or if He were suddenly pleased now to effect somewhat, this rather should the All-mighty have effected, that this evil matter should not be, and He alone be, the whole, true, sovereign, and infinite Good. Or if it was not good that He who was good should not also frame and create something that were good, then, that evil matter being taken away and brought to nothing, He might form good matter, whereof to create all things. For He should not be All-mighty, if He might not create something good without the aid of that matter which Himself had not created. These thoughts I revolved in my miserable heart, overcharged with most gnawing cares, lest I should die ere I had found the truth; yet was the faith of Thy Christ, our Lord and Saviour, professed in the Church Catholic, firmly fixed in my heart, in many points, indeed, as yet unformed, and fluctuating from the rule of doctrine; yet did not my mind utterly leave it, but rather daily took in more and more of it.

By this time also had I rejected the lying divinations and impious dotages of the astrologers. Let Thine own mercies, out of my very inmost soul, confess unto Thee for this also, O my God. For Thou, Thou altogether (for who else calls us back from the death of all errors, save the Life which cannot die, and the Wisdom which needing no light enlightens the minds that need it, whereby the universe is directed, down to the whirling leaves of trees?)—Thou madest provision for my obstinacy wherewith I struggled against Vindicianus, an acute old man, and Nebridius, a young man of admirable talents; the first vehemently affirming, and the latter often (though with some doubtfulness) saying, "That there was no such art whereby to foresee things to come, but that men's conjectures were a sort of lottery, and that out of many things which they said should come to pass, some actually did, unawares to them who spake it, who stumbled upon it, through their oft speaking." Thou providedst then a friend for me, no negligent consulter of the astrologers; nor yet well skilled in those arts, but (as I said) a curious consulter with them, and yet knowing something, which he said he had heard of his father, which how far it went to overthrow the estimation of that art, he knew not. This man then, Firminus by name, having had a liberal education, and well taught in Rhetoric, consulted me, as one very dear to him, what, according to his so-called constellations, I thought on certain affairs of his, wherein his worldly hopes had risen, and I, who had herein now begun to incline towards Nebridius' opinion, did not altogether refuse to conjecture, and tell him what came into my unresolved mind; but added, that I was now almost persuaded that these were but empty and ridiculous follies. Thereupon he told me that his father had been very curious in such books, and had a friend as earnest in them as himself, who with joint study and conference fanned the flame of their affections to these toys, so that they would observe the moments whereat the very dumb animals, which bred about their houses, gave birth, and then observed the relative position of the heavens, thereby to make fresh experiments in this so-called art. He said then that he had heard of his father, that what time his mother was about to give birth to him, Firminus, a woman-servant of that friend of his father's was also with child, which could not escape her master, who took care with most exact diligence to know the births of his very puppies. And so it was that (the one for his wife, and the other for his servant, with the most careful observation, reckoning days, hours, nay, the lesser divisions of the hours) both were delivered at the same instant; so that both were constrained to allow the same constellations, even to the minutest points, the one for his son, the other for his new-born slave. For so soon as the women began to be in labour, they each gave notice to the other what was fallen out in their houses, and had messengers ready to send to one another so soon as they had notice of the actual birth, of which they had easily provided, each in his own province, to give instant intelligence. Thus then the messengers of the respective parties met, he averred, at such an equal distance from either house that neither of them could make out any difference in the position of the stars, or any other minutest points; and yet Firminus, born in a high estate in his parents' house, ran his course through the gilded paths of life, was increased in riches, raised to honours; whereas that slave continued to serve his masters, without any relaxation of his yoke, as Firminus, who knew him, told me.

Upon hearing and believing these things, told by one of such credibility, all that my resistance gave way; and first I endeavoured to reclaim Firminus himself from that curiosity, by telling him that upon inspecting his constellations, I ought if I were to predict truly, to have seen in them parents eminent among their neighbours, a noble family in its own city, high birth, good education, liberal learning. But if that servant had consulted me upon the same constellations, since they were his also, I ought again (to tell him too truly) to see in them a lineage the most abject, a slavish condition, and every thing else utterly at variance with the former. Whence then, if I spake the truth, I should, from the same constellations, speak diversely, or if I spake the same, speak falsely: thence it followed most certainly that whatever, upon consideration of the constellations, was spoken truly, was spoken not out of art, but chance; and whatever spoken falsely, was not out of ignorance in the art, but the failure of the chance.

An opening thus made, ruminating with myself on the like things, that no one of those dotards (who lived by such a trade, and whom I longed to attack, and with derision to confute) might urge against me that Firminus had informed me falsely, or his father him; I bent my thoughts on those that are born twins, who for the most part come out of the womb so near one to other, that the small interval (how much force soever in the nature of things folk may pretend it to have) cannot be noted by human observation, or be at all expressed in those figures which the astrologer is to inspect, that he may pronounce truly. Yet they cannot be true: for looking into the same figures, he must have predicted the same of Esau and Jacob, whereas the same happened not to them. Therefore he must speak falsely; or if truly, then, looking into the same figures, he must not give the same answer. Not by art, then, but by chance, would he speak truly. For Thou, O Lord, most righteous Ruler of the Universe, while consulters and consulted know it not, dost by Thy hidden inspiration effect that the consulter should hear what, according to the hidden deservings of souls, he ought to hear, out of the unsearchable depth of Thy just judgment, to Whom let no man say, What is this? Why that? Let him not so say, for he is man.

Now then, O my Helper, hadst Thou loosed me from those fetters: and I sought "whence is evil," and found no way. But Thou sufferedst me not by any fluctuations of thought to be carried away from the Faith whereby I believed Thee both to be, and Thy substance to be unchangeable, and that Thou hast a care of, and wouldest judge men, and that in Christ, Thy Son, Our Lord, and the holy Scriptures, which the authority of Thy Catholic Church pressed upon me, Thou hadst set the way of man's salvation, to that life which is to be after this death. These things being safe and immovably settled in my mind, I sought anxiously "whence was evil?" What were the pangs of my teeming heart, what groans, O my God! yet even there were Thine ears open, and I knew it not; and when in silence I vehemently sought, those silent contritions of my soul were strong cries unto Thy mercy. Thou knewest what I suffered, and no man. For, what was that which was thence through my tongue distilled into the ears of my most familiar friends? Did the whole tumult of my soul, for which neither time nor utterance sufficed, reach them? Yet went up the whole to Thy hearing, all which I roared out from the groanings of my heart; and my desire was before Thee, and the light of mine eyes was not with me: for that was within, I without: nor was that confined to place, but I was intent on things contained in place, but there found I no resting-place, nor did they so receive me, that I could say, "It is enough," "it is well": nor did they yet suffer me to turn back, where it might be well enough with me. For to these things was I superior, but inferior to Thee; and Thou art my true joy when subjected to Thee, and Thou hadst subjected to me what Thou createdst below me. And this was the true temperament, and middle region of my safety, to remain in Thy Image, and by serving Thee, rule the body. But when I rose proudly against Thee, and ran against the Lord with my neck, with the thick bosses of my buckler, even these inferior things were set above me, and pressed me down, and no where was there respite or space of breathing. They met my sight on all sides by heaps and troops, and in thought the images thereof presented themselves unsought, as I would return to Thee, as if they would say unto me, "Whither goest thou, unworthy and defiled?" And these things had grown out of my wound; for Thou "humbledst the proud like one that is wounded," and through my own swelling was I separated from Thee; yea, my pride-swollen face closed up mine eyes.

But Thou, Lord, abidest for ever, yet not for ever art Thou angry with us; because Thou pitiest our dust and ashes, and it was pleasing in Thy sight to reform my deformities; and by inward goads didst Thou rouse me, that I should be ill at ease, until Thou wert manifested to my inward sight. Thus, by the secret hand of Thy medicining was my swelling abated, and the troubled and bedimmed eyesight of my mind, by the smarting anointings of healthful sorrows, was from day to day healed.

And Thou, willing first to show me how Thou resistest the proud, but givest grace unto the humble, and by how great an act of Thy mercy Thou hadst traced out to men the way of humility, in that Thy Word was made flesh, and dwelt among men:—Thou procuredst for me, by means of one puffed up with most unnatural pride, certain books of the Platonists, translated from Greek into Latin. And therein I read, not indeed in the very words, but to the very same purpose, enforced by many and divers reasons, that In the beginning was the Word, and the Word was with God, and the Word was God: the Same was in the beginning with God: all things were made by Him, and without Him was nothing made: that which was made by Him is life, and the life was the light of men, and the light shineth in the darkness, and the darkness comprehended it not. And that the soul of man, though it bears witness to the light, yet itself is not that light; but the Word of God, being God, is that true light that lighteth every man that cometh into the world. And that He was in the world, and the world was made by Him, and the world knew Him not. But, that He came unto His own, and His own received Him not; but as many as received Him, to them gave He power to become the sons of God, as many as believed in His name; this I read not there.

Again I read there, that God the Word was born not of flesh nor of blood, nor of the will of man, nor of the will of the flesh, but of God. But that the Word was made flesh, and dwelt among us, I read not there. For I traced in those books that it was many and divers ways said, that the Son was in the form of the Father, and thought it not robbery to be equal with God, for that naturally He was the Same Substance. But that He emptied Himself, taking the form of a servant, being made in the likeness of men, and found in fashion as a man, humbled Himself, and became obedient unto death, and that the death of the cross: wherefore God exalted Him from the dead, and gave Him a name above every name, that at the name of Jesus every knee should how, of things in heaven, and things in earth, and things under the earth; and that every tongue should confess that the Lord Jesus Christ is in the glory of God the Father; those books have not. For that before all times and above all times Thy Only-Begotten Son remaineth unchangeable, co-eternal with Thee, and that of His fulness souls receive, that they may be blessed; and that by participation of wisdom abiding in them, they are renewed, so as to be wise, is there. But that in due time He died for the ungodly; and that Thou sparedst not Thine Only Son, but deliveredst Him for us all, is not there. For Thou hiddest these things from the wise, and revealedst them to babes; that they that labour and are heavy laden might come unto Him, and He refresh them, because He is meek and lowly in heart; and the meek He directeth in judgment, and the gentle He teacheth His ways, beholding our lowliness and trouble, and forgiving all our sins. But such as are lifted up in the lofty walk of some would-be sublimer learning, hear not Him, saying, Learn of Me, for I am meek and lowly in heart, and ye shall find rest to your souls. Although they knew God, yet they glorify Him not as God, nor are thankful, but wax vain in their thoughts; and their foolish heart is darkened; professing that they were wise, they became fools.

And therefore did I read there also, that they had changed the glory of Thy incorruptible nature into idols and divers shapes, into the likeness of the image of corruptible man, and birds, and beasts, and creeping things; namely, into that Egyptian food for which Esau lost his birthright, for that Thy first-born people worshipped the head of a four-footed beast instead of Thee; turning in heart back towards Egypt; and bowing Thy image, their own soul, before the image of a calf that eateth hay. These things found I here, but I fed not on them. For it pleased Thee, O Lord, to take away the reproach of diminution from Jacob, that the elder should serve the younger: and Thou calledst the Gentiles into Thine inheritance. And I had come to Thee from among the Gentiles; and I set my mind upon the gold which Thou willedst Thy people to take from Egypt, seeing Thine it was, wheresoever it were. And to the Athenians Thou saidst by Thy Apostle, that in Thee we live, move, and have our being, as one of their own poets had said. And verily these books came from thence. But I set not my mind on the idols of Egypt, whom they served with Thy gold, who changed the truth of God into a lie, and worshipped and served the creature more than the Creator.

And being thence admonished to return to myself, I entered even into my inward self, Thou being my Guide: and able I was, for Thou wert become my Helper. And I entered and beheld with the eye of my soul (such as it was), above the same eye of my soul, above my mind, the Light Unchangeable. Not this ordinary light, which all flesh may look upon, nor as it were a greater of the same kind, as though the brightness of this should be manifold brighter, and with its greatness take up all space. Not such was this light, but other, yea, far other from these. Nor was it above my soul, as oil is above water, nor yet as heaven above earth: but above to my soul, because It made me; and I below It, because I was made by It. He that knows the Truth, knows what that Light is; and he that knows It, knows eternity. Love knoweth it. O Truth Who art Eternity! and Love Who art Truth! and Eternity Who art Love! Thou art my God, to Thee do I sigh night and day. Thee when I first knew, Thou liftedst me up, that I might see there was what I might see, and that I was not yet such as to see. And Thou didst beat back the weakness of my sight, streaming forth Thy beams of light upon me most strongly, and I trembled with love and awe: and I perceived myself to be far off from Thee, in the region of unlikeness, as if I heard this Thy voice from on high: "I am the food of grown men, grow, and thou shalt feed upon Me; nor shalt thou convert Me, like the food of thy flesh into thee, but thou shalt be converted into Me." And I learned, that Thou for iniquity chastenest man, and Thou madest my soul to consume away like a spider. And I said, "Is Truth therefore nothing because it is not diffused through space finite or infinite?" And Thou criedst to me from afar: "Yet verily, I AM that I AM." And I heard, as the heart heareth, nor had I room to doubt, and I should sooner doubt that I live than that Truth is not, which is clearly seen, being understood by those things which are made. And I beheld the other things below Thee, and I perceived that they neither altogether are, nor altogether are not, for they are, since they are from Thee, but are not, because they are not what Thou art. For that truly is which remains unchangeably. It is good then for me to hold fast unto God; for if I remain not in Him, I cannot in myself; but He remaining in Himself, reneweth all things. And Thou art the Lord my God, since Thou standest not in need of my goodness.

And it was manifested unto me, that those things be good which yet are corrupted; which neither were they sovereignly good, nor unless they were good could be corrupted: for if sovereignly good, they were incorruptible, if not good at all, there were nothing in them to be corrupted. For corruption injures, but unless it diminished goodness, it could not injure. Either then corruption injures not, which cannot be; or which is most certain, all which is corrupted is deprived of good. But if they be deprived of all good, they shall cease to be. For if they shall be, and can now no longer be corrupted, they shall be better than before, because they shall abide incorruptibly. And what more monstrous than to affirm things to become better by losing all their good? Therefore, if they shall be deprived of all good, they shall no longer be. So long therefore as they are, they are good: therefore whatsoever is, is good. That evil then which I sought, whence it is, is not any substance: for were it a substance, it should be good. For either it should be an incorruptible substance, and so a chief good: or a corruptible substance; which unless it were good, could not be corrupted. I perceived therefore, and it was manifested to me that Thou madest all things good, nor is there any substance at all, which Thou madest not; and for that Thou madest not all things equal, therefore are all things; because each is good, and altogether very good, because our God made all things very good. [. . .]

But having then read those books of the Platonists, and thence been taught to search for incorporeal truth, I saw Thy invisible things, understood by those things which are made; and though cast back, I perceived what that was which through the darkness of my mind I was hindered from contemplating, being assured "That Thou wert, and wert infinite, and yet not diffused in space, finite or infinite; and that Thou truly art Who art the same ever, in no part nor motion varying; and that all other things are from Thee, on this most sure ground alone, that they are." Of these things I was assured, yet too unsure to enjoy Thee. I prated as one well skilled; but had I not sought Thy way in Christ our Saviour, I had proved to be, not skilled, but killed. For now I had begun to wish to seem wise, being filled with mine own punishment, yet I did not mourn, but rather scorn, puffed up with knowledge. For where was that charity building upon the foundation of humility, which is Christ Jesus? or when should these books teach me it? Upon these, I believe, Thou therefore willedst that I should fall, before I studied Thy Scriptures, that it might be imprinted on my memory how I was affected by them; and that afterwards when my spirits were tamed through Thy books, and my wounds touched by Thy healing fingers, I might discern and distinguish between presumption and confession; between those who saw whither they were to go, yet saw not the way, and the way that leadeth not to behold only but to dwell in the beatific country. For had I first been formed in Thy Holy Scriptures, and hadst Thou in the familiar use of them grown sweet unto me, and had I then fallen upon those other volumes, they might perhaps have withdrawn me from the solid ground of piety, or, had I continued in that healthful frame which I had thence imbibed, I might have thought that it might have been obtained by the study of those books alone. [. . .]

9

Benedict of Norcia

The Rule of Saint Benedict

Of Humility

THE HOLY SCRIPTURE CRIETH TO US, BRETHREN, SAYING: "Every one who exalteth himself shall be humbled, and he who humbleth himself shall be exalted." By these words it declares to us, that all exaltation is a kind of pride, which the Prophet showeth must carefully be avoided when he says: "Lord, my heart is not exalted, neither are my eyes lifted up; neither have I walked in great things, nor in wonders above myself." But why? "If I did not think humbly, but exalted my soul: as a child weaned from his mother, so wilt Thou reward my soul."

Wherefore, Brethren, if we would attain to true humility, and speedily reach that heavenly exaltation, which is won through the lowliness of this present life; by our ascending actions a ladder must be set up, such as appeared in sleep to Jacob, whereon he saw Angels descending and ascending.

That descent and ascent signifieth nothing else, but that we descend by exalting, and ascend by humbling ourselves.

The ladder thus erected, is our life here in this world, which through humility of heart is lifted up by our Lord to heaven. The sides of this ladder we understand to be our body and soul, in which the Divine Majesty hath placed divers degrees of humility and discipline, which we must ascend.

The first degree, then, of humility is that a man always have the fear of God before his eyes, and not be forgetful of himself. Moreover to be mindful of all that God hath commanded, and remember that such as contemn God, fall into hell for their sins, and that ever lasting life is prepared for such as fear Him. And keeping himself from all sin and vice, of thought, word, eyes, hands, feet, and self-will, let him thus speedily cut off all the desires of the flesh.

Let him think that he is always beheld from heaven by God; that all his actions, wheresoever he may be, lie open to the eye of God, and are at every hour presented before Him by His Angels.

The Prophet declareth this, when, in these words, he saith that God is always present to our thoughts: "God searcheth the heart and reins." And again: "The Lord knoweth the thoughts of men, that they are vain." He also saith: "Thou hast understood my thoughts afar off," and: "The thought of man shall confess to Thee." In order therefore that the humble Brother may be careful to avoid evil thoughts, let him always say in his heart: "Then shall I be without spot before Him, if I shall keep me from my iniquity."

The Scripture also forbiddeth us to do our own will, saying: "Leave thy own will and desire." And again: "We beg of God in prayer, that His Will may be done in us."

With good reason, therefore, are we taught to beware of doing our own will, since the Scripture saith: "There are ways which to men seem right, the end whereof plungeth even into the deep pit of hell." And again, speaking of the negligent: "They are corrupted, and made abominable in their pleasures." But in the desires of the flesh, we ought to believe God to be always present with us, according to that saying of the Prophet, speaking to the Lord: "O Lord, all my desire is before Thee."

Let us then take heed of evil desires, because death sitteth close to the entrance of delight. Wherefore the Scripture commandeth us: "Follow not thy concupiscences." If then the eyes of the Lord behold both good and bad; if He ever looketh down from heaven upon the sons of men to see who is understanding or seeking God; if our works are told to Him day and night by our Angel Guardians; we must always take heed, Brethren, lest, as the Prophet saith in the psalm, "God behold us some time declining to evil, and become unprofitable;" and though He spare us for the present, because He is merciful, and expecteth our conversion, He may yet say to us hereafter: "These things thou hast done, and I have held My peace."

The second degree of humility is, if anyone, not wedded to his own will, seeks not to satisfy his desires, but carries out that saying of our Lord: "I came not to do My own Will, but the Will of Him Who sent me." The Scripture likewise saith: "Self-will engendereth punishment, and necessity purchaseth a crown."

The third degree of humility is, that a man submit himself for the love of God, with all obedience to his superior, imitating thereby our Lord, of Whom the Apostle saith: "He was made obedient even unto death."

The fourth degree of humility is, that if, in obedience, things that are hard, contrary, and injurious, be done to him, he embrace them with a quiet conscience, and in suffering them, grow not weary, nor give over, since the Scripture saith: "He only that persevereth to the end shall be saved." And again: "Let thy heart be comforted, and expect the Lord." And showing that the faithful man ought to bear all things for our Lord, be they never so contrary, it saith in the person of the sufferers: "For Thee we suffer death all the day long; we are esteemed as sheep for the slaughter." And being assured by hope of a reward from God's hands they go on rejoicing and saying: "But in all things we overcome by the help of Him Who hath loved us." Likewise in another place the Scripture saith: "Thou hast proved us, O Lord, Thou hast tried us, as silver is tried, with fire. Thou hast brought us into the snare; Thou hast laid tribulation upon our backs." And to show that we ought to be under a Prior or Superior, it goes on to say: "Thou hast placed men over our heads." Moreover, in order to fulfil the precepts of the Lord by patience in adversities and injuries: "When struck on one cheek, they offer the other; to him who taketh away their coat, they leave their cloak also; and being constrained to carry a burthen one mile, they go two." With Paul the Apostle they suffer false Brethren and persecutions, and bless those who revile and speak ill of them.

The fifth degree of humility is to manifest to the Abbot, by humble confession, all the evil thoughts of his heart, and the secret faults committed by him. The Scripture exhorteth us thereunto, saying: "Reveal thy way to the Lord, and hope in Him." And again: "Confess thy way to the Lord because He is good, because His mercy endureth for ever." Furthermore the Prophet saith: "I have made known unto Thee mine offence, and mine injustices I have not hidden. I have said, I will declare openly against myself mine injustices to the Lord; and Thou hast pardoned the wickedness of my heart."

The sixth degree of humility is, if a Monk be content with all that is meanest and poorest, and in everything enjoined him, think himself an evil and worthless servant, saying with the Prophet: "I have been brought to nothing, and knew it not. I have become as a beast before Thee, and I am always with Thee."

The seventh degree of humility is, not only to pronounce with his tongue, but also in his very heart to believe himself to be the most abject, and inferior to all; and humbling himself, to say with the Prophet: "I am a worm and no man, the reproach of men and the outcast of the people. I have been exalted, humbled, and confounded." And again: "It is good for me that Thou hast humbled me, that I may learn Thy commandments."

The eighth degree of humility is, that a Monk do nothing but what the common rule of the Monastery, or the example of his seniors, teacheth and exhorteth him to do.

The ninth degree of humility is, for a Monk to refrain his tongue from much speaking, and be silent till a question be asked him, remembering the saying of the Scripture: "In many words thou shalt not avoid sin," and "a talkative man shall not be directed upon the earth."

The tenth degree of humility is, not to be easily moved and prompt to laugh, for it is written: "The fool exalteth his voice in laughter."

The eleventh degree of humility is that when a Monk speaketh, he do so, gently and without laughter; humbly, with gravity or few words, and discreetly; and be not clamorous in his voice; for it is written: "A wise man is known by few words."

The twelfth degree of humility is, that a Monk not only have humility in his heart, but show it also in his exterior, to all that behold him; so that whether he be at work, or in the Oratory, the garden, the field, or on the way; whether he sit, walk, or stand, let him always, with head bent down, and eyes fixed upon the earth, think himself guilty for his sins, and about to be presented before the dreadful judgment of God, ever saying to himself with the Publican in the Gospel: "Lord, I a sinner am not worthy to lift up mine eyes to heaven." And again with the Prophet: "I am bowed down and humbled on every side."

Thus, when all these degrees of humility have been ascended, the Monk will presently come to that love of God which is perfect and casteth out fear; to that love, whereby everything, which at the beginning he observed through fear, he shall now begin to do by custom, without any labour, and as it were naturally; not now through fear of hell, but for the love of Christ, out of a good custom, and a delight in virtue. All this our Lord will vouchsafe to work by the Holy Ghost in His servant, now that he is cleansed from defects and sins.

Of the Order and Discipline of Singing

WE BELIEVE THAT THE DIVINE PRESENCE IS EVERYWHERE, and that the eyes of the Lord behold both the good and the bad, in all places; but we believe this especially and without any doubt, when we assist at the Work of God. Let us, therefore, always be mindful of what the Prophet saith: "Serve ye the Lord in fear." And again: "Sing ye His praises with understanding." And: "In the sight of Angels I will sing praise unto Thee." Therefore, let us consider in what manner and with what reverence it behoveth us to be in the sight of God and of the Angels, and so let us sing in choir, that mind and voice may accord together.

Of the Manner of Receiving Brothers to Religion

LET NOT AN EASY ENTRANCE BE GRANTED TO ONE WHO cometh newly to Religious life, but, as the Apostle saith: "Try the Spirits if they be of God." If, therefore, the new-comer persevere knocking, and continue for four or five days patiently to endure both the injuries offered to him and the difficulty made about his entrance, and persist in his petition; leave to enter shall then be granted him, and he shall be in the guest Hall for a few days. Afterwards he shall be in the Novitiate, where he shall meditate, and eat, and sleep.

Let a Senior who has the address of winning souls to God, be appointed to watch over him narrowly and carefully, to discover whether he truly seeks God, and is eager for the Work of God, for obedience and for humiliation. Let all the rigour and austerity by which we tend towards God be laid before him. And if he promise stability and perseverance, at the end of two months, let the whole Rule be read to him, with the addition of these words: "Behold the law under which thou desirest to fight; if thou canst observe it, enter in; if thou canst not, freely depart." If he shall still persevere, let him then be brought back to the aforesaid cell of the Novices, and be again tried in all patience. After the lapse of six months, let the Rule be read to him again, that he may know unto what he has come. If he still persevere, after four months, let the same Rule be read to him once more. If he shall then promise, after due deliberation, to keep and observe all things commanded him, let him be received into the Community, knowing that he is from that time forward under the law of the Rule, so that he can neither leave the Monastery nor shake off the yoke of the Rule, which, after so long a deliberation, he might have accepted or refused.

And when they admit him to profession, he shall, in the presence of all, make a promise before God and His Saints, of stability, amendment of manners, and obedience, in order that if at any time he shall act contrariwise he may know that he shall be condemned by Him Whom he mocketh. He shall draw up the form of this promise in the name of the Saints whose relics are on the Altar, and of the Abbot there present. With his own hand shall he write it, or if he knoweth not how, another at his request shall write it for him, and the Novice shall put his mark to it, and lay it with his own hand upon the Altar.

After doing this, let him presently begin the verse: "Uphold me O Lord according to Thy Word, and I shall live, and let me not be confounded in my expectation." Let the whole Community repeat this three times, adding at the end, " Glory be to the Father." Then let the new Brother cast himself at the feet of all, that they may pray for him, and from that hour he shall be counted as one of the Community. If he hath any property, he shall either first bestow it upon the poor, or, by a formal gift, hand it over to the Monastery, without any reserve for himself; because for the future he must know that he hath not so much as power over his own body. Let him therefore presently, in the Oratory, be stripped of his own garments and be clothed in those of the Monastery. But the garments of which he is divested shall be kept in the wardrobe, that if (which God forbid) he should consent, by the persuasion of the devil, to leave the Monastery, he may be stripped of his habit and expelled. But he shall not have again, the writing of his profession which the Abbot received from him at the Altar; that shall be kept in the Monastery.

That the Highest Degree of Perfection is Not Contained in this Rule

We have written this rule, that by its observance in Monasteries we may show that we possess, in some measure, uprightness of manners, or the beginning of a good Religious life. But for such as hasten forward to the perfection of holy living, there are the precepts of the holy Fathers, the observance whereof leadeth a man to the height of perfection. For what page, or what passage is there in the divinely inspired books of the Old and New Testament, that is not a most perfect rule of man's life? Or what book is there of the holy Catholic Fathers that doth not proclaim this; that we may by a direct course reach our Creator? Moreover, what else are the Collations of the Fathers, their Institutes, their Lives, also the Rule of our Holy Father Basil, but examples of the good living and obedience of Monks, and so many instruments of virtue? But to us who are slothful and lead bad and negligent lives, they are matter for shame and confusion.

Therefore whosoever thou art that dost hasten to the heavenly country, first accomplish, by the help of Christ, this little Rule written for beginners; and then at length thou shalt come, under the guidance of God, to those loftier heights of doctrine and of virtue, which we have mentioned above.

10

Ibn Sina (Avicenna)

On the Rational Soul

IN THE NAME OF GOD, THE MERCIFUL, THE COMPASSIONATE.[1]

God bless our Master, Muḥammad, and his family, and grant them peace.

Make [my task] easy, O my gracious Lord!

Praise be to God alone.

1 Know that human beings alone, to the exclusion of all other living beings, possess a faculty highly capable of grasping the intelligibles. This faculty is sometimes called rational soul, sometimes "soul at peace,"[2] sometimes sacred soul, sometimes spiritual spirit, sometimes commanding spirit, sometimes good word, sometimes word that unites and separates, sometimes divine secret,[3] sometimes governing light, sometimes chief commanding light, sometimes true heart, sometimes core of the self [*lubb*], sometimes understanding [*nuhan*], and sometimes brains [*ḥijan*].[4] It exists in every single human being, young or old, adolescent or adult, insane or sane, sick or sound.

2 At the beginning of its existence this faculty is devoid of the forms of the intelligibles, and from this point of view it is then called material intellect.

3 Next there come about in it the forms of the primary intelligibles, which are concepts whose truth is Ascertained without [the use of] syllogisms or [a process of] learning and acquisition. They are called the starting point of intellections,[5] general notions, and natural primary knowledges, like, for example, the knowledge that the whole is greater than the part, and that a single body cannot occupy two places at the same time, or be simultaneously wholly black and white, existent and non-existent.[6] Through these forms, the faculty is prepared to acquire the secondary intelligibles either by means of Thinking, which is an act of finding what (results from) these primary intelligibles by [their] composition and combination [to form definitions and syllogisms], or by means of Correct Guessing, which is the representation of the middle term in the faculty all at once and without Thinking or considering. By "middle term" I mean the cause which makes acknowledging the existence or non-existence of a thing necessary—i.e., the evidence which justifies the judgment—and this sometimes comes about following search and a desire to attain the intelligibles, and sometimes initially, without desire or search; and whenever the evidence is attained, so is invariably that for which the evidence is provided.

4 Through these acquired intelligibles this faculty next assumes an aspect and a state by means of which it is ready to call to presence the intelligibles whenever it wishes without needing to acquire them. This aspect is called *habitus* [disposition], and the faculty, in this state and from this point of view, is called actual intellect. When the intelligibles are actually present in the faculty as being observed and represented in it, then from this point of view it is called acquired intellect.[7]

5 This rational soul is a substance subsisting by itself, and is imprinted neither in a human body nor in any other corporeal entity. On the contrary, it is separable and abstracted from material and corporeal entities. It has a certain association with the human body as long as the person is alive, but this association is not like the relation [*ta'alluq*] of a thing to its receptacle; it is, rather, like the relation of a wielder of an instrument to the instrument. [This substance] comes into existence together with the body, not before, but it does not perish when the body perishes and dies; it survives, rather, as it was, except that (it attains, after) its association with the body is severed,[8] either bliss and pleasure or misery and pain.

6 The bliss [of the rational soul] comes about when its substance is rendered perfect,[9] and this is accomplished when it is purified through knowledge of God and works for God. Its purification through works for God consists of (a) its being purged of vile and wicked qualities of character, (b) its being far removed from blameworthy attributes and evil and offensive habits by following reason and religious law, and (c) its being adorned with good habits, praiseworthy qualities of character, and excellent and pleasing traits by following reason and religious law.

7 Its purification through knowledge of God consists of its attainment a disposition of its own, by means of which it is ready to call all the intelligibles to presence whenever it wishes without needing to acquire them, and thus to have all the intelligibles present in it in actuality, or in a potentiality that is as close to actuality as possible.[10] The soul then becomes like a polished mirror upon which are reflected the forms of things as they are in themselves[11] without any distortion, and whenever it stands face to face with them having been purified through knowledge, there ensues [an automatic] practicing of the theoretical philosophical sciences.

8 Purification through works is accomplished by methods mentioned in books on Ethics and by assiduous performance of religious duties, both legal and traditional, such as observances relating to [the functions of] the body, one's property, and to a combination of the two. For being restrained at the places where religious law and its statutes place such restraints, and undertaking to submit to its commands, have a beneficial effect on subjugating the soul that "incites to evil" [and thus transforming it] into the rational soul which is "at peace," i.e., making the bodily faculties of the soul, the appetitive and the irascible, subservient to the rational soul which is "at peace."[12]

9 Now it has become clear in the physical sciences that personal qualities and habits follow the temperament of the body,[13] in the sense that the dominant characteristics of a phlegmatic (a person whose temperament is dominated by phlegm) are sedateness, dignity, and forbearance, a choleric (he whose temperament is dominated by yellow bile) anger, and a melancholic (he whose temperament is dominated by black bile) ill disposition. Each one of these [humors], furthermore, is followed by other qualities of character which we shall not mention here. There is thus no doubt that temperament is subject to change, in which case qualities of character are also subject to change thereby; and it is for this reason that the performance of the exercises mentioned in books on Ethics is specified. Whenever a person's temperament is balanced, his qualities of character are easily refined; his balanced temperament is thus influential in this process. The unbalanced temperament, on the other hand, is that which is overpowered by one or two of its four elements (when, for example, it is either hotter or drier than it ought to be, or both hotter and drier than it ought to be). Since these four elements are [two pairs of elements that are] opposite to each other, the unbalanced temperament will be constituted of either one [excessive] opposite [element] or two opposite [elements in combination], whereas the balanced temperament is the one which lacks these opposites (that is, it will have [an excess of] neither heat [alone] nor cold [alone] but a quality intermediate between the two, nor humidity and dryness [alone] but a quality intermediate between the two).[14] The closer a temperament is to a balanced state, the more is a person predisposed to develop excellent traits in both his knowledge and his works.

10 It has also become clear in the ⟨Physical⟩ sciences that the celestial bodies are not constituted from a mixture of these four elements but are totally lacking in these opposites. Furthermore, it is only the involvement with these opposites that hinders the reception of the divine effluence, by which I mean the inspiration coming from the Lord, occurring all at once and revealing some intellective truth. The closer, therefore, a temperament is to a balanced state, the more is a person predisposed to receive this effluence. Since the celestial bodies are totally devoid of the opposites, they are receptive to the divine effluence; human beings, on the other hand, no matter how balanced their temperaments may be, are not free from defects [due to the involvement with] the opposites. As long as the rational soul is associated with the human body, no corporeal entity [*jirm*] can be completely ready to receive the divine effluence or have perfectly revealed to it all the intelligibles. But when a person expends all his efforts to purify [his rational soul] through knowledge, acquires the propensity for contact with the divine effluence (i.e., with the intellective substance which is the medium of the divine effluence and which is called "angel" in the language of Revelation and "active intellect" in philosophical terminology), has a balanced temperament, and lacks these opposites which hinder his reception of the divine effluence, then there comes about in him a certain similarity to the celestial bodies and he resembles through this purification the seven mighty ones, i.e., the seven celestial spheres. When the association of the soul with the body is severed through death, something which is designated with the expression "separation of the form from the receivers"—for the appellation "form" may be applied to the soul and the appellation "the receiver of the soul" may be applied to the body, even if the meaning of this "receiving" is unlike that of a receptacle "receiving" what occupies it, but is rather like that of a place where an activity occurs "receiving" the activity: the body "receives" the activity of the soul, and from this point of view it is possible (a) to call the body "receiver of the soul," (b) to call the soul "form," and (c) to designate the severance of the association between the two with the expression "separation of the form from the receivers"—when, then, this separation occurs after the soul has acquired excellent traits in its knowledge and works, and the obstacle that hindered it from receiving the divine effluence in its totality ceases to exist (the obstacle being the association of [the soul with the body, which consists of] its activity in the body), then the soul will receive the divine effluence, will have revealed to it whatever was hidden from it before the separation, and there will come about it a similarity with the abstract intellects which are the principles of the causes of beings, since all the truths are revealed to these intellects. (You know that God Almighty first created an intellect, then by its means another intellect and a celestial sphere, then by means of the other intellect a third intellect and a second celestial sphere, and so on in the order we mentioned; the intellects, then, are the principles of the causes.)

11 This, then, is what we wished to mention on this occasion in explanation of this divine word.[15] As for the demonstrative proof establishing that the rational soul is a substance, subsists by itself, is free of any corporeality, is not imprinted on any corporeal entity, survives after the death of the human body, and whether its condition after death is one of blessing or punishment, it involves a long and elaborate investigation and can be brought to light only after numerous premises have been mentioned. As a matter of fact, I happened to write at the beginning of my career forty years ago a summary treatise[16] setting forth the knowledge about the soul and related matters by following the method of those who engage in philosophy through research[17]; whoever wishes to find out about the soul should study this treatise because it is suitable for students who do research. But God Almighty "guides whomsoever He will"[18] to the way of those who engage in philosophy through direct experience[19]—may He put us and you in the latter group! He is in charge of such a thing, capable of it!

Praise be to God, Lord of the worlds.

God bless the best among the best of mankind, our Master Muḥammad, the members of his family, the good and pure, and all his companions.

Notes

1 Capitalized words inside the text indicate technical terms in Avicenna's philosophy, for which see the original publication listed in the Credits.

2 This is a reference to the Qur'ānic description of the soul that enters heaven (89:27–30): "O soul at peace,/ return unto thy Lord, well-pleased, well-pleasing!/ Enter thou among my servants!/ Enter thou my Paradise!" (Arberry's translation).

3 Or perhaps "self" in the sense of core of the self, *sirr*. Cf. Goichon "Sirr."

4 The practice of forming ecumenical lists to identify the same object in different intellectual and religious traditions comes from the multi-cultural early Islamic environment which generated the historiography of religions and heresiography. In Avicenna's context, it can be seen in the work by a member of the Jayhānī family of viziers to the Sāmānid rulers (see the article by Pellat in *EI²*, Supplement, 265–266), who wrote on Zoroaster and who is quoted by Šahrastānī in his *al-Milal wa-n-niḥal* at the end of the section on Zoroaster: the passage in Šahrastānī, missing in the earlier editions, was first brought to light by M. b. Tavit et-Tanci, "Şehristanî'nin kitab'ul-milel ve'n-nihal'i," *İlâhiyat Fakültesi Dergisi* (Ankara Üniversitesi) 5 (1956) 1–16. Jayhānī there identifies the Zoroastrian divine power governing the universe with, among others, the active intellect of the philosophers, the Christian Holy Ghost, and the Qur'ānic "spirit," *rūḥ*, mentioned in the *Sūrat al-Qadr* (97:4), "the angels and the Spirit descend" (Arberry). The similarity in practice and contents of the lists in Jayhānī and Avicenna, even if one is talking about a divine faculty and the other human, cannot be accidental, given the latter's Sāmānid upbringing.

5 "Starting point of intellections," *bidāyat al-'uqūl*. Marmura "Avicenna's Thought" 340a made the excellent suggestion that the phrase should read, *badā'ih al-'uqūl*, presumably meaning (Marmura did not himself translate the phrase), "self-evident truths of intellects" which come naturally to the human mind, since Marmura translated the word *badīha* in the *Ilāhiyyāt* of *The Cure* as "innate/natural intelligence" (Marmura *Metaphysics* 40.32, 113.16 and 24; *badīha*, however, here as well as in *Najāt* 287/357, is used in a general way and not as a technical epistemological term). The MS has the skeletal form of the word without pointing for the *yā'* and *tā' marbūṭa*, so either reading would have the authority of our single witness. However, in the various discussions of the primary notions (*awwaliyyāt*) which Avicenna is mentioning here, he never once throughout his works does he use the word *badīha—badā'ih* to refer to these notions; the terms for natural intelligence and its operations that he uses are always *fiṭra, ġarīza* (as here in the next phrase), and *jibilla* (see Gutas "Empiricism" sections V–VI). I thus prefer to keep *bidāya* and understand *'uqūl* as the plural of the *maṣdar*, "intellections;" cf. the plural of the *maṣdar, afhām*, in T9, §1 and note 1.

6 Cf. the same examples used by Avicenna in his very first work, T1, §2.

7 Cf. the very similar exposition of the subject in the passage from *Pointers and Reminders* translated below, Chapter 3.2, I.11.

8 I.e., after death. The text in the MS, as a matter of fact, adds, "that is, after the severance of the association through death" (*ay ba'da nqiṭā'i l-'alāqati bi-l-mawt*). This could hardly have been what Avicenna wrote, however, and it looks like a marginal scribal gloss incorporated at some point into the main text.

9 "To render perfect," *takmīl*, is naturally to be understood in the Aristotelian sense of *entelecheia*, "to bring out into full actuality."

10 That is, to attain the stages of acquired intellect and actual intellect, respectively.

11 Cf. the similar turn of phrase used by Avicenna to describe the contents of *The Easterners* in the Prologue to *The Cure*, T9. §4.

12 The reference is again to a Qurʾānic verse, 12:53: "Surely the soul of man incites to evil" (Arberry). For the "soul at peace" that follows see above, note 1.

13 Galen wrote a book by this title, *That the Faculties of the Soul Are Consequent upon the Temperaments of the Body* (IV.767–822 Kühn, new edition by Athena Bazou, Athens: Academy of Athens, 2011), which was translated into Arabic and widely discussed in medical, physiological, and psychological writings. For the Arabic translation see Biesterfeldt. "Temperament" here is to be understood in its traditional sense, i.e., the particular blending (*krasis, mizāj*) of the four humors (blood, phlegm, black bile, yellow bile) which were thought to determine a person's mental and emotional constitution. This theory lies behind the etymology of the word idiosyncrasy, i.e., one's own particular blend of humors. Cf. the words "phlegmatic," "choleric," and "melancholic" next explained by Avicenna in the text.

14 The excess of a single element produces the simple unbalanced temperament, while the excess of one element formed from the combination of two opposite elements produces the composite unbalanced temperament. For a concise account of humoral physiology see Ullmann *Medicine* 55–64.

15 I.e., the rational soul; cf. the list of names for it given above, paragraph 1. Landauer 338.4 assumes the reference to be to metaphysics ("metaphy."?).

16 The reference is to the *Compendium on the Soul* (W1), from which the passage in T1 is extracted. Cf. Landauer 336–339.

17 "Those who engage in philosophy through research:" *ahl al-ḥikma al-baḥtiyya*, literally, "those of research philosophy;" i.e., those who use the method of logical demonstration and syllogisms, as implied in the preceding sentence. They are contrasted to the experintial philosophers following next. See the discussion in Chapter 3.2 at the end.

18 A frequent Qurʾānic phrase which normally reads, "God guides whomsoever He will to a straight path:" Q2:142, Q2:213, etc. (Arberry translation).

19 "Those who engage in philosophy through direct experience:" *ahl al-ḥikma ad-dawqiyya*, literally, "those of philosophy by tasting," i.e., experiential philosophy. Toward the end of his life Avicenna developed the concept of "tasting", *dawq*, to express the intellectual pleasure (*al-laḏḏa al-ʿaqliyya*) enjoyed by those who have become adept at engaging in philosophy through syllogistic means (and Guessing Correctly the middle term) to such an extent that they gain a familiarity or intimacy (*alf*) with the intelligibles and a disposition or habit for them (*malaka*). At this point their experience of the intelligibles is such that "even though it is accompanied by the middle term it is as if it doesn't need it." See briefly below, Chapter 8,2.2, and the fuller discussion and related texts on this subject in Gutas "Absence of Mysticism" 365–369. For experiential knowledge in Avicenna and the later development of terminology with *dawq* in Ġazālī see Treiger *Inspired Knowledge* 60–63.

11

Ibn Rushd (Averroes)

On the Harmony of Religion and Philosophy

WE MAINTAIN THAT THE BUSINESS OF PHILOSOPHY IS NOTHING OTHER than to look into creation and to ponder over it in order to be guided to the Creator – in other words, to look into the meaning of existence. For the knowledge of creation leads to the cognizance of the Creator, through the knowledge of the created. The more perfect becomes the knowledge of creation, the more perfect becomes the knowledge of the Creator. The Law encourages and exhorts us to observe creation. Thus, it is clear that this is to be taken either as a religious injunction or as something approved by the Law. But the Law urges us to observe creation by means of reason and demands the knowledge thereof through reason. This is evident from different verses of the Qur'an. For example, the Qur'an says: "Wherefore take example from them, you who have eyes" [Qur'an 49.2]. That is a clear indication of the necessity of using the reasoning faculty, or rather both reason and religion, in the interpretation of things. Again it says: "Or do they not contemplate the kingdom of heaven and earth and the things which God has created" [Qur'an 7.184]. This is in plain exhortation to encourage the use of observation of creation. And remember that one whom God especially distinguishes in this respect, Abraham, the prophet. For He says: "And this did we show unto Abraham: the kingdom of heaven and earth" [Qur'an 6.75]. Further, He says: "Do they not consider the camels, how they are created; and the heaven, how it is raised" [Qur'an 88.17]. Or, still again: "And (who) meditate on the creation of heaven and earth, saying, O Lord you have not created this in vain" [Qur'an 3.176]. There are many other verses on this subject: too numerous to be enumerated.

Now, it being established that the Law makes the observation and consideration of creation by reason obligatory – and consideration is nothing but to make explicit the implicit – this can only be done through reason. Thus we must look into creation with the reason. Moreover, it is obvious that the observation which the Law approves and encourages must be of the most perfect type, performed with the most perfect kind of reasoning. As the Law emphasizes the knowledge of God and His creation by inference, it is incumbent on any who wish to know God and His whole creation by inference, to learn the kinds of inference, their conditions and that which distinguishes philosophy from dialectic and exhortation from syllogism. This is impossible unless one possesses knowledge beforehand of the various kinds of reasoning and learns to distinguish between reasoning and what is not reasoning. This cannot be done except one knows its different parts, that is, the different kinds of premises.

Hence, for a believer in the Law and a follower of it, it is necessary to know these things before he begins to look into creation, for they are like instruments for observation. For, just as a student discovers by the study of the law, the necessity of knowledge of legal reasoning with all its kinds and distinctions, a student will find out by observing the creation the necessity of metaphysical reasoning. Indeed, he has a greater claim on it than the jurist. For if a jurist argues the necessity of legal reasoning from the saying of God: "Wherefore take example *from them* O you who have eyes" [Qur'an 59.2], a student of divinity has a better right to establish the same from it on behalf of metaphysical reasoning.

One cannot maintain that this kind of reasoning is an innovation in religion because it did not exist in the early days of Islam. For legal reasoning and its kinds are things which were invented also in later ages, and no one thinks they are innovations. Such should also be our attitude towards philosophical reasoning. There is another reason why it should be so, but this is not the proper place to mention it. A large number of the followers of this religion confirm philosophical reasoning, all except a small worthless minority, who argue from religious ordinances. Now, as it is established that the Law makes the consideration of philosophical reasoning and its kinds as necessary as legal reasoning, if none of our predecessors has made an effort to enquire into it, we should begin to do it, and so help them, until the knowledge is complete. For if it is difficult or rather impossible for one person to acquaint himself single-handed with all things which it is necessary to know in legal matters, it is still more difficult in the case of philosophical reasoning. And, if before us, somebody has enquired into it, we should derive help from what he has said. It is quite immaterial whether that man is our co-religionist or not; for the instrument by which purification is perfected is not made uncertain in its usefulness by its being in the hands of one of our own party, or of a foreigner, if it possesses the attributes of truth. By these latter we mean those Ancients who investigated these things before the advent of Islam.

Now, such is the case. All that is wanted in an enquiry into philosophical reasoning has already been perfectly examined by the Ancients. All that is required of us is that we should go back to their books and see what they have said in this connection. If all that they say be true, we should accept it and if there be something wrong, we should be warned by it. Thus, when we have finished this kind of research we shall have acquired instruments by which we can observe the universe, and consider its general character. For so long as one does not know its general character one cannot know the created, and so long as he does not know the created, he cannot know its nature.

All things have been made and created. This is quite clear in itself, in the case of animals and plants, as God has said "Verily the idols which you invoke, beside God, can never create a single fly, though they may all assemble for that purpose" [Qur'an 22.72]. We see an inorganic substance and then there is life in it. So we know for certain that there is an inventor and bestower of life, and He is God. Of the heavens we know by their movements, which never become slackened, that they work for our benefit by divine solicitude, and are subordinate to our welfare. Such an appointed and subordinate object is always created for some purpose. The second principle is that for every created thing there is a creator. So it is right to say from the two foregoing principles that for every existent thing there is an inventor. There are many arguments, according to the number of the created things, which can be advanced to prove this premise. Thus, it is necessary for one who wants to know God as He ought to be known to acquaint himself with the essence of things, so that he may get information about the creation of all things. For who cannot understand the real substance and purpose of a thing, cannot understand the minor meaning of its creation. It is to this that God refers in the following verse "Or do they not contemplate the heaven and the earth, and the things which God has created?" [Qur'an 7.184]. And so a man who would follow the purpose of philosophy in investigating the existence of things, that is, would try to know the cause which led to its creation, and the purpose of it would know the argument of kindness most perfectly. These two arguments are those adopted by Law.

The verses of the Qur'an leading to a knowledge of the existence of God are dependent only on the two foregoing arguments. It will be quite clear to anyone who will examine closely the verses, which occur in the Divine Book in this connection. These, when investigated, will be found to be of three kinds: either they are verses showing the "arguments of kindness," or those mentioning the "arguments of creation," or those which include both the kinds of arguments. The following verses may be taken as illustrating the argument of kindness. "Have we not made the earth for a bed, and the mountains for stakes to find the same? And have we not created you of two sexes; and appointed your sleep for rest; and made the night a garment to cover you; and destined the day to the gaining of your livelihood and built over you seven solid heavens; and placed therein a burning lamp? And do we not send down from the clouds pressing forth rain, water pouring down in abundance, that we may thereby produce corn, and herbs, and gardens planted thick with trees?" [Qur'an 77.6-16] and, "Blessed be He Who has placed the twelve signs in the heavens; has placed therein a lamp by day, and the moon which shines by night" [Qur'an 25.62] and again, "Let man consider his food" [Qur'an 80.24].

The following verses refer to the argument of invention, "Let man consider, therefore of what he is created. He is created of the seed poured forth, issuing from the loins, and the breast bones" [Qur'an 86.6]; and, "Do they not consider the camels, how they are created; the heaven, how it is raised; the mountains, how they are fixed; the earth how it is extended" [Qur'an 88.17]; and again "O man, a parable is propounded unto you; wherefore hearken unto it. Verily the idols which they invoke, besides God, can never create a single fly, though they may all assemble for the purpose" [Qur'an 22.72]. Then we may point to the story of Abraham, referred to in the following verse, "I direct my face unto Him Who has created heaven and earth; I am orthodox, and not of the idolaters" [Qur'an 6.79]. There may be quoted many verses referring to this argument. The verses comprising both the arguments are also many, for instance, "O men, of Mecca, serve your Lord, Who has created you, and those who have been before you: peradventure you will fear Him; Who has spread the earth as a bed for you, and the heaven as a covering, and has caused water to descend from heaven, and thereby produced fruits for your sustenance. Set not up, therefore, any equals unto God, against your own knowledge [Qur'an 2.19]. His words, "Who has created you, and those who have been before you," lead us to the argument of creation; while the words, "who has spread the earth" refer to the argument of divine solicitude for man. Of this kind also are the following verses of the Qur'an, "One sign of the resurrection unto them is the dead earth; We quicken the same by rain, and produce therefrom various sorts of grain, of which they eat" [Qur'an 36.32]; and, "Now in the creation of heaven and earth, and the vicissitudes of night and day are signs unto those who are endowed with understanding, who remember God standing, and sitting, and lying on their sides; and meditate on the creation of heaven and earth, saying O Lord, far be it from You, therefore deliver us from the torment of hellfire" [Qur'an 3.188]. Many verses of this kind comprise both the kinds of arguments.

This method is the right path by which God has invited men to a knowledge of His existence, and informed them of it through the intelligence which He has implanted in their nature. The followin verse refers to this fixed and innate nature of man, "And when the Lord drew forth their posterity from the loins of the sons of Adam, and took them witness against themselves, Am I not your Lord? They answered, Yes, we do bear witness" [Qur'an 7.171]. So it is incumbent for one who intends to obey God, and follow the injunction of His Prophet, that he should adopt this method, thus making himself one of those learned men who bear witness to the divinity of God, with His own witness, and that of His angels, as He says, "God has borne witness, that there is no God but He, and the angels, and those who are endowed with wisdom profess the same; who execute righteousness; there is no God but He; the Mighty, the Wise" [Qur'an 3.16]. Among the arguments for both of themselves is the praise which God refers to in the following verse, "Neither is there anything which does not celebrate his praise; but you understand not their celebration thereof" [Qur'an 17.46].

It is evident from the above arguments for the existence of God that they are dependent upon two categories of reasoning. It is also clear that both of these methods are meant for particular people; that is, the learned. Now as to the method for the masses. The difference between the two lies only in details. The masses cannot understand the two above-mentioned arguments but only what they can grasp by their senses; while the learned men can go further and learn by reasoning also, besides learning by sense. They have gone so far that a learned man has said, that the benefits the learned men derive from the knowledge of the members of human and animal body are a thousand and one. If this be so, then this is the method which is taught both by Law and by Nature. It is the method which was preached by the Prophet and the divine books. The learned men do not mention these two lines of reasoning to the masses, not because of their number, but because of a want of depth of learning on their part about the knowledge of a single thing only. The example of the common people, considering and pondering over the universe, is like a man who looks into a thing, the manufacture of which he does not know. For all that such a man can know about it is that it has been made, and that there must be a maker of it. But, on the other hand, the learned look into the universe, just as a man knowing the art would do; try to understand the real purpose of it. So it is quite clear that their knowledge about the Maker, as the maker of the universe, would be far better than that of the man who only knows it as made. The atheists, who deny the Creator altogether, are like men who can see and feel the created things, but would not acknowledge any Creator for them, but would attribute all to chance alone, and that they come into being by themselves.

Now, then, if this is the method adopted by the Law, it may be asked: What is the way of proving the unity of God by means of the Law; that is, the knowledge of the religious formula that "there is no god, but God." The negation contained in it is an addition to the affirmative, which the formula contains, while the affirmative has already been proved. What is the purpose of this negation? We would say that the method, adopted by the Law, of denying divinity to all but God is according to the ordinance of God in the Qur'an. . .

If you look a little intently it will become clear to you, that in spite of the fact that the Law has not given illustration of those things for the common people, beyond which their imagination cannot go, it has also informed the learned men of the underlying meanings of those illustrations. So it is necessary to bear in mind the limits which the Law has set about the instruction of every class of men, and not to mix them together. For in this manner the purpose of the Law is multiplied. Hence it is that the Prophet has said, "We, the prophets, have been commanded to adapt ourselves to the conditions of the people, and address them according to their intelligence." He who tries to instruct all the people in the matter of religion, in one and the same way, is like a man who wants to make them alike in actions too, which is quite against apparent laws and reason.

From the foregoing it must have become clear to you that the divine vision has an esoteric meaning in which there is no doubt, if we take the words of the Qur'an about God as they stand, that is, without proving or disproving the anthropomorphic attribute of God. [. . .]

12

Thomas Aquinas

Summa Theologica

Of Man Who is Composed of a Spiritual and a Corporeal Substance: And in the First Place, Concerning What Belongs to the Essence of the Soul (In Seven Articles)

HAVING TREATED OF THE SPIRITUAL AND OF THE CORPOREAL CREATURE, we now proceed to treat of man, who is composed of a spiritual and of a corporeal substance. We shall treat first of the nature of man, and secondly of his origin. Now the theologian considers the nature of man in relation to the soul; but not in relation to the body, except in so far as the body has relation to the soul. Hence the first object of our consideration will be the soul. And since Dionysius (*Ang. Hier.* xi.) says that three things are to be found in spiritual substances—essence, power, and operation—we shall treat first of what belongs to the essence of the soul; secondly, of what belongs to its power; thirdly, of what belongs to its operation.

Concerning the first, two points have to be considered; the first is the nature of the soul considered in itself; the second is the union of the soul with the body. Under the first head there are seven points of inquiry.

(1) Whether the soul is a body? (2) Whether the human soul is a subsistence? (3) Whether the souls of brute animals are subsistent? (4) Whether the soul is man, or is man composed of soul and body? (5) Whether the soul is composed of matter and form? (6) Whether the soul is incorruptible? (7) Whether the soul is of the same species as an angel?

First Article
Whether the Soul is a Body?

We proceed thus to the First Article:—

Objection 1. It would seem that the soul is a body. For the soul is the moving principle of the body. Nor does it move unless moved. First, because seemingly nothing can move unless it is itself moved, since nothing gives what it has not; for instance, what is not hot does not give heat. Secondly, because if there be anything that moves and is not moved, it must be the cause of eternal, unchanging movement, as we find proved *Phys.* viii. 6; and this does not appear to be the case in the movement of an animal, which is caused by the soul. Therefore the soul is a mover moved. But every mover moved is a body. Therefore the soul is a body.

Obj. 2. Further, all knowledge is caused by means of a likeness. But there can be no likeness of a body to an incorporeal thing. If, therefore, the soul were not a body, it could not have knowledge of corporeal things.

Obj. 3. Further, between the mover and the moved there must be contact. But contact is only between bodies. Since, therefore, the soul moves the body, it seems that the soul must be a body.

On the contrary, Augustine says (*De Trin.* vi. 6) that the soul *is simple in comparison with the body, inasmuch as it does not occupy space by its bulk.*

I answer that, To seek the nature of the soul, we must premise that the soul is defined as the first principle of life in those things which live: for we call living things *animate* [i.e., having a soul] and those things which have no life, *inanimate.* Now life is shown principally by two actions, knowledge and movement. The philosophers of old, not being able to rise above their imagination, supposed that the principle of these actions was something corporeal: for they asserted that only bodies were real things; and that what is not corporeal is nothing: hence they maintained that the soul is something corporeal. This opinion can be proved to be false in many ways; but we shall make use of only one proof, based on universal and certain principles, which shows clearly that the soul is not a body.

It is manifest that not every principle of vital action is a soul, for then the eye would be a soul, as it is a principle of vision; and the same might be applied to the other instruments of the soul: but it is the *first* principle of life, which we call the soul. Now, though a body may be a principle of life, as the heart is a principle of life in an animal, yet nothing corporeal can be the first principle of life. For it is clear that to be a principle of life, or to be a living thing, does not belong to a body as such ; since, if that were the case, every body would be a living thing, or a principle of life. Therefore a body is competent to be a living thing or even a principle of life, as *such* a body. Now that it is actually such a body, it owes to some principle which is called its act. Therefore the soul, which is the first principle of life, is not a body, but the act of a body; thus heat, which is the principle of calefaction, is not a body, but an act of a body.

Reply Obj. 1. As everything which is in motion must be moved by something else, a process which cannot be prolonged indefinitely, we must allow that not every mover is moved. For, since to be moved is to pass from potentiality to actuality, the mover gives what it has to the thing moved, inasmuch as it causes it to be in act. But, as is shown in *Phys.* viii. 6, there is a mover which is altogether immovable, and not moved either essentially, or accidentally; and such a mover can cause an invariable movement. There is, however, another kind of mover, which, though not moved essentially, is moved accidentally; and for this reason it does not cause an invariable movement; such a mover is the soul. There is, again, another mover, which is moved essentially—namely, the body. And because the philosophers of old believed that nothing existed but bodies, they maintained that every mover is moved; and that the soul is moved directly, and is a body.

Reply Obj. 2. The likeness of the thing known is not of necessity actually in the nature of the knower; but given a thing which knows potentially, and afterwards knows actually, the likeness of the thing known must be in the nature of the knower, not actually, but only potentially; thus colour is not actually in the pupil of the eye, but only potentially. Hence it is necessary, not that the likeness of corporeal things should be actually in the nature of the soul, but that there be a potentiality in the soul for such a likeness. But the ancient philosophers omitted to distinguish between actuality and potentiality; and so they held that the soul must be a body in order to have knowledge of a body; and that it must be composed of the principles of which all bodies are formed in order to know all bodies.

Reply Obj. 3. There are two kinds of contact; of *quantity,* and of *power.* By the former a body can be touched only by a body; by the latter a body can be touched by an incorporeal thing, which moves that body.

Fourth Article
Whether the Soul is Man?

We proceed thus to the Fourth Article:—

Objection 1. It would seem that the soul is man. For it is written (2 Cor. iv. 16): *Though our outward man is corrupted, yet the inward man is renewed day by day.* But that which is within man is the soul. Therefore the soul is the inward man.

Obj. 2. Further, the human soul is a substance. But it is not a universal substance. Therefore it is a particular substance. Therefore it is a *hypostasis* or a person; and it can only be a human person. Therefore the soul is man; for a human person is a man.

On the contrary, Augustine (*De Civ. Dei* xix. 3) commends Varro as holding *that man is not a mere soul, nor a mere body; but both soul and body.*

I answer that, The assertion, *the soul is man,* can be taken in two senses. First, that man is a soul; though this particular man, Socrates, for instance, is not a soul, but composed of soul and body. I say this, forasmuch as some held that the form alone belongs to the species; while matter is part of the individual, and not of the species. This cannot be true; for to the nature of the species belongs what the definition signifies; and in natural things the definition does not signify the form only, but the form and the matter. Hence in natural things the matter is part of the species; not, indeed, signate matter, which is the principle of individuality; but the common matter. For as it belongs to the notion of this particular man to be composed of this soul, of this flesh, and of these bones; so it belongs to the notion of man to be composed of soul, flesh, and bones; for whatever belongs in common to the substance of all the individuals contained under a given species, must belong also to the substance of the species.

It may also be understood in this sense, that this soul is this man; and this could be held if it were supposed that the operation of the sensitive soul were proper to it, apart from the body; because in that case all the operations which are attributed to man would belong to the soul only; and whatever performs the operations proper to a thing, is that thing; wherefore that which performs the operations of a man is man. But it has been shown above (A. 3) that sensation is not the operation of the soul only. Since, then, sensation is an operation of man, but not proper to him, it is clear that man is not a soul only, but something composed of soul and body.—Plato, through supposing that sensation was proper to the soul, could maintain man to be a soul making use of the body.

Reply Obj. 1. According to the Philosopher (*Ethic*. ix. 8), a thing seems to be chiefly what is principle in it; thus what the governor of a state does, the state is said to do. In this way sometimes what is principle in man is said to be man; sometimes, indeed, the intellectual part which, in accordance with truth, is called the *inward* man; and sometimes the sensitive part with the body is called man in the opinion of those whose observation does not go beyond the senses. And this is called the *outward* man.

Reply Obj. 2. Not every particular substance is a hypostasis or a person, but that which has the complete nature of its species. Hence a hand, or 2 foot, is not called a hypostasis, or a person; nor, likewise, is the soul alone so called, since it is a part of the human species.

Fifth Article
Whether the Soul is Composed of Matter and Form?

We proceed thus to the Fifth Article:—

Objection 1. It would seem that the soul is composed of matter and form. For potentiality is opposed to actuality. Now, whatsoever things are in actuality participate of the First Act, which is God; by participation of Whom, all things are good, are beings, and are living things, as is clear from the teaching of Dionysius (*Div. Nom.* v.). Therefore whatsoever things are in potentiality participate of the first potentiality. But the first potentiality is primary matter. Therefore, since the human soul is, after a manner, in potentiality; which appears from the fact that sometimes a man is potentially understanding; it seems that the human soul must participate of primary matter, as a part of itself.

Obj. 2. Further, wherever the properties of matter are found, there matter is. But the properties of matter are found in the soul—namely, to be a subject, and to be changed; for it is subject to science, and virtue; and it changes from ignorance to knowledge and from vice to virtue. Therefore matter is in the soul.

Obj. 3. Further, things which have no matter, have no cause of their existence, as the Philosopher says *Metaph.* viii. (Did. vii. 6). But the soul has a cause of its existence, since it is created by God. Therefore the soul has matter.

Obj. 4. Further, what has no matter, and is a form only, is a pure act, and is infinite. But this belongs to God alone. Therefore the soul has matter.

On the contrary, Augustine (*Gen. ad lit.* vii. 7, 8, 9) proves that the soul was made neither of corporeal matter, nor of spiritual matter.

I answer that, The soul has no matter. We may consider this question in two ways. First, from the notion of a soul in general; for it belongs to the notion of a soul to be the form of a body. Now, either it is a form by virtue of itself, in its entirety, or by virtue of some part of itself. If by virtue of itself in its entirety, then it is impossible that any part of it should be matter, if by matter we understand something purely potential: for a form, as such, is an act; and that which is purely potential cannot be part of an act, since potentiality is repugnant to actuality as being opposite thereto. If, however, it be a form by virtue of a part of itself, then we call that part the soul: and that matter, which it actualizes first, we call the *primary animate.*

Secondly, we may proceed from the specific notion of the human soul, inasmuch as it is intellectual. For it is clear that whatever is received into something is received according to the condition of the recipient. Now a thing is known in as far as its form is in the knower. But the intellectual soul knows a thing in its nature absolutely: for instance, it knows a stone absolutely as a stone; and therefore the form of a stone absolutely, as to its proper formal idea, is in the intellectual soul. Therefore the intellectual soul itself is an absolute form, and not something composed of matter and form. For if the intellectual soul were composed of matter and form, the forms of things would be received into it as individuals, and so it would only know the individual: just as it happens with the sensitive powers which receive forms in a corporeal organ; since matter is the principle by which forms are individualized. It follows, therefore, that the intellectual soul, and every intellectual substance which has knowledge of forms absolutely, is exempt from composition of matter and form.

Reply Obj. 1. The First Act is the universal principle of all acts; because It is infinite, virtually *precontaining all things,* as Dionysius says (*Div. Nom.* v.). Wherefore things participate of It not as a part of themselves, but by diffusion of Its processions. Now as potentiality is receptive of act, it must be proportionate to act. But the acts received which proceed from the First Infinite Act, and are participations thereof, are diverse, so that there cannot be one potentiality which receives all acts, as there is one act, from which all participated acts are derived; for then the receptive potentiality would equal the active potentiality of the First Act. Now the receptive potentiality in the intellectual soul is other than the receptive potentiality of first matter, as appears from the diversity of the things received by each. For primary matter receives individual forms; whereas the intelligence receives absolute forms. Hence the existence of such a potentiality in the intellectual soul does not prove that the soul is composed of matter and form.

Reply Obj. 2. To be a subject and to be changed belong to matter by reason of its being in potentiality. As, therefore, the potentiality of the intelligence is one thing and the potentiality of primary matter another, so in each is there a different reason of subjection and change. For the intelligence is subject to knowledge, and is changed from ignorance to knowledge, by reason of its being in potentiality with regard to the intelligible species.

Reply Obj. 3. The form causes matter to be, and so does the agent; wherefore the agent causes matter to be, so far as it actualizes it by transmuting it to the act of a form. A subsistent form, however, does not owe its existence to some formal principle, nor has it a cause transmuting it from potentiality to act. So after the words quoted above, the Philosopher concludes, that in things composed of matter and form *there is no other cause but that which moves from potentiality to act; while whatsoever things have no matter are simply beings at once.*

Reply Obj. 4. Everything participated is compared to the participator as its act. But whatever created form be supposed to subsist *per se,* must have existence by participation; for *even life,* or anything of that sort, *is a participator of existence,* as Dionysius says (*Div. Nom.* v.). Now participated existence is limited by the capacity of the participator; so that God alone, Who is His own existence, is pure act and infinite. But in intellectual substances, there is composition of actuality and potentiality, not, indeed, of matter and form, but of form and participated existence. Wherefore some say that they are composed of that *whereby they are* and that *which they are;* for existence itself is that by which a thing is.

Sixth Article
Whether The Human Soul is Incorruptible?

We proceed thus to the Sixth Article:—

Objection 1. It would seem that the human soul is corruptible. For those things that have a like beginning and process seemingly have a like end. But the beginning, by generation, of men is like that of animals, for they are made from the earth. And the process of life is alike in both; because *all things breathe alike, and man hath nothing more than the beast,* as it is written (Eccles. iii. 19). Therefore, as the same text concludes, *the death of man and beast is one, and the condition of both is equal.* But the souls of brute animals are corruptible. Therefore, also, the human soul is corruptible.

Obj. 2. Further, whatever is out of nothing can return to nothingness; because the end should correspond to the beginning. But as it is written (Wisd. ii. 2), *We are born of nothing;* which is true, not only of the body, but also of the soul. Therefore, as is concluded in the same passage, *After this we shall be as if we had not been,* even as to our soul.

Obj. 3. Further, nothing is without its own proper operation. But the operation proper to the soul, which is to understand through a phantasm, cannot be without the body. For the soul understands nothing without a phantasm; and there is no phantasm without the body as the Philosopher says (*De Anima* i. 1). Therefore the soul cannot survive the dissolution of the body.

On the contrary, Dionysius says (*Div. Nom.* iv.) that human souls owe to Divine goodness that they are *intellectual,* and that they have *an incorruptible substantial life.*

I answer that, We must assert that the intellectual principle which we call the human soul is incorruptible. For a thing may be corrupted in two ways—*per se,* and accidentally. Now it is impossible for any substance to be generated or corrupted accidentally, that is, by the generation or corruption of something else. For generation and corruption belong to a thing, just as existence belongs to it, which is acquired by generation and lost by corruption. Therefore, whatever has existence *per se* cannot be generated or corrupted except *per se;* while things which do not subsist, such as accidents and material forms, acquire existence or lose it through the generation or corruption of composite things. Now it was shown above (AA. 2, 3) that the souls of brutes are not self-subsistent, whereas the human soul is; so that the souls of brutes are corrupted, when their bodies are corrupted; while the human soul could not be corrupted unless it were corrupted *per se.* This, indeed, is impossible, not only as regards the human soul, but also, as regards anything subsistent that is a form alone. For it is clear that what belongs to a thing by virtue of itself is inseparable from it; but existence belongs to a form, which is an act, by virtue of itself. Wherefore matter acquires actual existence as it acquires the form; while it is corrupted so far as the form is separated from it. But it is impossible for a form to be separated from itself; and therefore it is impossible for a subsistent form to cease to exist.

Granted even that the soul is composed of matter and form, as some pretend, we should nevertheless have to maintain that it is incorruptible. For corruption is found only where there is contrariety; since generation and corruption are from contraries and into contraries. Wherefore the heavenly bodies, since they have no matter subject to contrariety, are incorruptible. Now there can be no contrariety in the intellectual soul; for it receives according to the manner of its existence, and those things which it receives are without contrariety; for the notions even of contraries are not themselves contrary, since contraries belong to the same knowledge. Therefore it is impossible for the intellectual soul to be corruptible. Moreover we may take a sign of this from the fact that everything naturally aspires to existence after its own manner. Now, in things that have knowledge, desire ensues upon knowledge. The senses indeed do not know existence, except under the conditions of *here* and *now,* whereas the intellect apprehends existence absolutely, and for all time; so that everything that has an intellect naturally desires always to exist. But a natural desire cannot be in vain. Therefore every intellectual substance is incorruptible.

Reply Obj. 1. Solomon reasons thus in the person of the foolish, as expressed in the words of Wisd. ii. Therefore the saying that man and animals have a like beginning in generation is true of the body; for all animals alike are made of earth. But it is not true of the soul. For the souls of brutes are produced by some power of the body; whereas the human soul is produced by God.

To signify this, it is written as to other animals: *Let the earth bring forth the living soul* (Gen. i. 24): while of man it is written (*ibid.* ii. 7) that *He breathed into his face the breath of life.* And so in the last chapter of Ecclesiastes (xii. 7) it is concluded (*Before*) *the dust return into its earth from whence it was; and the spirit return to God Who gave it.* Again the process of life is alike as to the body, concerning which it is written (Eccles. iii. 19): *All things breathe alike,* and (Wisd. ii. 2), *The breath in our nostrils is smoke.* But the process is not alike of the soul; for man is intelligent, whereas animals are not. Hence it is false to say: *Man has nothing more than beasts.* Thus death comes to both alike as to the body, but not as to the soul.

Reply Obj. 2. As a thing can be created by reason, not of a passive potentiality, but only of the active potentiality of the Creator, Who can produce something out of nothing, so when we say that a thing can be reduced to nothing, we do not imply in the creature a potentiality to non-existence, but in the Creator the power of ceasing to sustain existence. But a thing is said to be corruptible because there is in it a potentiality to non-existence.

Reply Obj. 3. To understand through a phantasm is the proper operation of the soul by virtue of its union with the body. After separation from the body it will have another mode of understanding, similar to other substances separated from bodies, as will appear later on (Q. LXXXIX., A. 1).

Seventh Article
Whether the Soul is of the Same Species as an Angel?

We proceed thus to the Seventh Article:—

Objection 1. It would seem that the soul is of the same species as an angel. For each thing is ordained to its proper end by the nature of its species, whence is derived its inclination for that end. But the end of the soul is the same as that of an angel—namely, eternal happiness. Therefore they are of the same species.

Obj. 2. Further, the ultimate specific difference is the noblest, because it completes the nature of the species. But there is nothing nobler either in an angel or in the soul than their intellectual nature. Therefore the soul and the angel agree in the ultimate specific difference: therefore they belong to the same species.

Obj. 3. Further, it seems that the soul does not differ from an angel except in its union with the body. But as the body is outside the essence of the soul, it seems that it does not belong to its species. Therefore the soul and an angel are of the same species.

On the contrary, Things which have different natural operations are of different species. But the natural operations of the soul and of an angel are different; since, as Dionysius says (*Div. Nom.* vii.), *Angelic minds have simple and blessed intelligence, not gathering their knowledge of Divine things from visible things.* Subsequently he says the contrary to this of the soul. Therefore the soul and an angel are not of the same species.

I answer that, Origen (*Peri Archon* iii. 5) held that human souls and angels are all of the same species; and this because he supposed that in these substances the difference of degree was accidental, as resulting from their free-will: as we have seen above (Q. XLVII., A. 2). But this cannot be; for in incorporeal substances there cannot be diversity of number without diversity of species and inequality of nature; because, as they are not composed of matter and form, but are subsistent forms, it is clear that there is necessarily among them a diversity in species. For a separate form cannot be understood otherwise than as one of a single species; thus, supposing a separate whiteness to exist, it could only be one; forasmuch as one whiteness does not differ from another except as in this or that subject. But diversity of species is always accompanied with a diversity of nature; thus in species of colours one is more perfect than another; and the same applies to other species, because differences which divide a *genus* are contrary to one another. Contraries, however, are compared pared to one another as the perfect to the imperfect, since the *principle of contrariety is habit, and privation thereof,* as is written, *Metaph.* x. (Did. ix. 4). The same would follow if the aforesaid substances were composed of matter and form. For if the matter of one be distinct from the matter of another, it follows that either the form is the principle of the distinction of matter—that is to say, that the matter is distinct on account of its relation to divers forms; and even then there would result a difference of species and inequality of nature: or else the matter is the principle of the distinction of forms. But one matter cannot be distinct from another, except by a distinction of quantity, which has no place in these incorporeal substances, such as an angel and the soul. So that it is not possible for the angel and the soul to be of the same species. How it is that there can be many souls of one species will be explained later (Q. LXXVI., A. 2, *ad* 1).

Reply Obj. 1. This argument proceeds from the proximate and natural end. Eternal happiness is the ultimate and supernatural end.

Reply Obj. 2. The ultimate specific difference is the noblest because it is the most determinate, in the same way as actuality is nobler than potentiality. Thus, however, the intellectual faculty is not the noblest, because it is indeterminate and common to many degrees of intellectuality; as the sensible faculty is common to many degrees in the sensible nature. Hence, as all sensible things are not of one species, so neither are all intellectual things of one species.

Reply Obj. 3. The body is not of the essence of the soul; but the soul by the nature of its essence can be united to the body, so that, properly speaking, not the soul alone, but the *composite,* is the species. And the very fact that the soul in a certain way requires the body for its operation, proves that the soul is endowed with a grade of intellectuality inferior to that of an angel, who is not united to a body.

13

John Duns Scotus

Concerning Metaphysics

1 Metaphysics, the Science of the Transcendentals

THERE MUST NECESSARILY EXIST SOME UNIVERSAL SCIENCE which considers the transcendentals as such. This science we call "metaphysics," from "meta," which means "beyond," and "the science of nature." It is, as it were, the transcending science, because it is concerned with the transcendentals.

2 Concept and Articulation of the Transcendental

NOW A DOUBT ARISES AS TO WHAT KIND OF PREDICATES are those which are predicated formally of God, for instance, "wise," "good," and the like. I answer that before "being" is divided into the ten categories, it is divided into infinite and finite. For the latter, namely finite being, is common to the ten genera. Whatever pertains to "being," then, in so far as it remains indifferent to finite and infinite, or as proper to the Infinite Being, does not belong to it as determined to a genus, but prior to any such determination, and therefore as transcendental and outside any genus. Whatever [predicates] are common to God and creatures are of such kind, pertaining as they do to being in its indifference to what is infinite and finite. For in so far as they pertain to God they are infinite, whereas in so far as they belong to creatures they are finite. They belong to "being," then, prior to the division into the ten genera. Anything of this kind, consequently, is transcendental.

But then another doubt arises. How can wisdom be considered a transcendental if it is not common to all beings, for transcendentals seem to be common to all? I answer that just as it is not of the nature of a supreme genus to have many species contained under it, but it is of its nature not to have any genus over and above it (the category of "when," for instance, is a supreme genus since it has no genus over and above it, although it has few, if any, species contained under it), so also whatever is not contained under any genus is transcendental. Hence, not to have any predicate above it except "being" pertains to the very notion of a transcendental. That it be common to many inferior notions, however, is purely incidental. This is evident too from the fact that "being" possesses not only attributes which are coextensive with it, such as "one," "true" and "good," but also attributes which are opposed to one another such as "possible-or-necessary," "act-or-potency," and suchlike.

But if the coextensive attributes are transcendental because they pertain to "being" as not determined to a definite genus, then the disjunctive attributes are transcendental too. And both members of the disjunction are transcendental since neither determines its determinable element to a definite genus. Nevertheless, one member of the disjunction is proper and pertains formally to one being alone, for instance, "necessary" in the disjunction "necessary-or-possible," or "infinite" in the disjunction "finite-or-infinite," and so also with the others.

And so "wisdom," or anything else, for that matter, which is common to God and creatures, can be transcendental. A transcendental, however, may also be predicated of God alone, or again it may be predicated about God and some creature. It is not necessary, then, that a transcendental as transcendental be predicated of every being, unless it be coextensive with the first of the transcendentals, namely "being."

3 Primacy of "Being" Among the Other Transcendentals

AND I SAY THAT . . . SINCE NOTHING CAN BE MORE COMMON THAN "BEING," and that "being" cannot be predicated univocally and *in quid* of all that is of itself intelligible (because it cannot be predicated in this way of the ultimate differences or of its attributes), it follows that we have no object of the intellect that is primary by reason of a commonness *in quid* in regard to all that is of itself intelligible.

And yet, notwithstanding, I say that "being" is the first object of the intellect, because in it a twofold primacy concurs, namely, a primacy of commonness and of virtuality. For whatever is of itself intelligible either includes essentially the notion of "being" or is contained virtually or essentially in something else which does include "being" essentially. For all genera, species, individuals, and the essential parts of genera, and the Uncreated Being all include "being" quidditatively. All the ultimate differences are included essentially in some of these. All the attributes of "being" are virtually included in "being" and in those things which come under "being."

Hence, all to which "being" is not-univocal *in quid* are included in those to which "being" is univocal in this way. And so it is clear that "being" has a primacy of commonness in regard to the primary intelligibles, that is, to the quidditative concepts of the genera, species, individuals, and all their essential parts, and to the Uncreated Being. It has a virtual primacy in regard to the intelligible elements included in the first intelligibles, that is, in regard to the qualifying concepts of the ultimate differences and proper attributes.

My supposition that "being" is predicated commonly *in quid* of all the aforementioned quidditative concepts is established by the two arguments used in the initial question to prove that being is predicated commonly of created and uncreated being. That what I have supposed may be evident, I now explain these reasons a little.

I explain the first reason thus. Of each of the aforementioned concepts, the intellect can be certain that it is a being and still be in doubt about the differences which delimit "being" to the concept in question. And so the concept of being, in so far as it agrees with the concept in question, is other than the dubious concepts which come under it. But it is other in such a way that it is included in both of the concepts which come under it, for these limiting differences presuppose the same concept of being which they limit.

The second reason I explain as follows: We argued that God cannot be known naturally unless being is univocal to the created and uncreated. We can argue in the same way of substance and accident, for substance does not immediately move our intellect to know the substance itself, but only the sensible accident does so. From this it follows that we can have no quidditative concept of substance except such as could be abstracted from the concept of an accident. But the only quidditative concept of this kind that can be abstracted from that of an accident is the concept of being.

Our assumption that substance does not immediately move our intellect to know the substance itself, we prove thus: If something moves the intellect when it is present, then whenever the intellect is not so moved, it will be able to know naturally that this object is absent. This is clear from the *De anima,* bk. ii, according to which the sense of sight can perceive darkness when, presumably, light is not present, and the sense, in consequence, is not moved. Therefore, if substance immediately moved the intellect naturally to know the substance itself, it would follow that when a substance was absent, the intellect could know that it was not present. Hence, it could know naturally that the substance of bread does not exist in the Consecrated Victim of the Altar, which is clearly false. Naturally, then, we have no quidditative concept of substance caused immediately by substance itself. Our only quidditative concept thereof is that caused by, or first abstracted from, an accident, and this is none other than the concept of being. [. . .]

4 On the Deduction of the Attributes of "Being"

I SAY THAT THIS DISJUNCTION "NECESSARY-OR-POSSIBLE," like the countless other such found among beings, is an attribute of "being" that is equivalent to a coextensive attribute. But the coextensive attributes, as something more common, are affirmed immediately of "being," because "being" is an irreducibly simple concept and consequently no middle term can exist between "being" and its attribute, for neither has a definition that might serve as a middle term. Also, if there is some attribute of "being" that is not immediate, it is difficult to see what prior attribute could be used as a middle term to link it with "being," for it is not easy to discern any order among the attributes of "being." And even if we knew of such an order among them, any propositions about them we might use as premises seem scarcely more evident than the conclusions. In the disjunctive attributes, however, while the entire disjunction cannot be demonstrated from "being," nevertheless as a universal rule by positing the less perfect extreme of some being we can conclude that the more perfect extreme is realised in some other being. Thus it follows that if some being is finite, then some being is infinite. And if some being is contingent, then some being is necessary. For in such cases it is not possible for the more imperfect extreme of the disjunction to be existentially predicated of "being," particularly taken, unless the more perfect extreme be existentially verified of some other being upon which it depends.

But we see that the less perfect member of such a disjunction cannot be established in this fashion, for if the more perfect exists in some being, there is no necessity on this score that the less perfect should exist in some other being, unless, of course, the two extremes of the disjunction should happen to be correlatives, such as "cause" and "caused." Consequently, this disjunction "necessary-or-contingent," cannot be established of "being" through some prior medium. Neither could the contingent part of the disjunction be established of anything on the supposition that something necessary exists. The proposition: "Some being is contingent," therefore, seems to be a primary truth and is not demonstrable by an *a priori* demonstration, which gives the reason for the fact. That is why the Philosopher, in arguing against the theory that future events are necessary, makes no attempt to deduce from it something even more impossible than the hypothesis, but he deduces from it an impossibility that is more apparent to us, namely, that there would be no need to deliberate [about the future]. And therefore, those who deny such manifest things need punishment or knowledge or sense, for as Avicenna puts it (*Metaphysics* 1): "Those who deny a first principle should be beaten or exposed to fire until they concede that to burn and not to burn, or to be beaten and not to be beaten, are not identical." And so too, those who deny that some being is contingent should be exposed to torments until they concede that it is possible for them not to be tormented.

5 Being as the Subject and God as the Goal of Metaphysics

HERE WE MUST FIRST SEE WHETHER METAPHYSICS as the first and highest of the naturally acquired habits perfecting man's intellect in this present life has God as its first object. . . .

On this point there is a controversy between Avicenna and Averroes. Avicenna claims that not God, but something else, such as being, is the subject of metaphysics. For no science proves the existence of its own subject, yet the metaphysician proves that God exists. In his final comment on Bk. I of the *Physics,* Averroes attacks Avicenna, using the same major premise admitted by both that no science proves the existence of its subject. God is the subject of metaphysics and his existence is not proved there but in physics, for it is only by means of motion that any sort of pure spirit can be proved to exist, and motion pertains to the science of physics.

Avicenna has spoken well, however, and Averroes very badly and against him I use the basic proposition they both hold, namely: "No science proves the existense of its subject." This is true, because of the priority a subject has with respect to the science. For if it were posterior, its subject could be proved in a lower science, where it would be conceived under some inferior aspect inadequate for its role as the object [of the higher science]. But a subject enjoys a greater priority over a lower science than over its own higher science. If the highest science, therefore, cannot establish the existence of its subject, since this is first or highest, still less can an inferior science do so.

The minor is proved because of the double primacy the subject of a higher science has in regard to a lower science's relationship to a prior science. Also, if God's existence is something demonstrated in physics and presupposed in metaphysics as subject, then—to put it simply—a conclusion in physics is the starting point of metaphysics, for any science starts with its subject. Hence, physics will be prior to metaphysics—all of which is absurd.

Also, if any property can exist only in virtue of such and such a cause, from every such property that appears in an effect, we can infer the existence of its cause. Now it is not just such properties of the effect considered in physics, such as that something is moved, that leads one to conclude to the existence of a moving cause, but the same is true of properties considered in metaphysics. If an effect represents something posterior, possible, or finite, such properties imply their cause enjoys an unqualified primacy, actuality, infinity and the like. It is from properties of this sort rather than from notion of motion that the existence of a first being can be demonstrated.

So far as this article is concerned, then, I say that God is not the subject of metaphysics, for as we proved earlier in the first question there can be but one science about God as first subject, and this is not metaphysics. And I prove this in the following way. The senses tell us whether or not any subject of a subordinate science exists, as is clear in the case of optics. For although a visible line, which is the subject of optics, could be demonstrated as a conclusion of geometry, nevertheless if it is the subject of some subordinate science, one needs to know immediately, without any further experience or investigation by the senses, whether or not it can be, namely, that there is nothing absurd about its existence. Just as principles are grasped immediately once the terms are apprehended through the medium of the senses, so too the existence of the subject must be known immediately from the senses. For the subject is not posterior or less known than the principle, since the subject is its cause, and hence prior to the principle in entity and knowability. But no knowledge acquired naturally in this life represents any characteristics of God that is proper to him. The minor is evident, for the first proper notion we have about God is that he is the first being. "First being," however, is not something initially known from the senses, for we must first ascertain that the combination of these two terms makes sense. Before we can know this combination represents something possible, we need to demonstrate that some being is first.

Hence, I concede with Avicenna that God is not the subject of metaphysics. Nor is this contradicted by the dictum of Averroes [about prior knowledge of the existence of the subject] (from the *Posterior Analytics*, Bk. I), nor the statement that metaphysics is concerned with the highest causes (from *Metaphysics*, Bk. I). For the Philosopher speaks there as he did in the *Prior*

Analytics I, where he says: "First we need to determine what this is concerned with and is about, for it is concerned with demonstration and is about the demonstrative branch of learning, i.e. it is about the general science of demonstrating." Hence, "concerned with" denotes properly the circumstance of the final cause, just as the word "about" designates the circumstance of the material cause. Consequently, metaphysics is concerned with the highest causes as its goal, and ends with the theoretical knowledge of them.

14

Dante Alighieri

The Divine Comedy: Paradiso (1308-21)

Canto X

Looking into his Son with all the Love
    Which each of them eternally breathes forth,
    The Primal and unutterable Power

Whate'er before the mind or eye revolves
    With so much order made, there can be none
    Who this beholds without enjoying Him.

Lift up then, Reader, to the lofty wheels
    With me thy vision straight unto that part
    Where the one motion on the other strikes,

And there begin to contemplate with joy
    That Master's art, who in himself so loves it
    That never doth his eye depart therefrom.

Behold how from that point goes branching off
    The oblique circle, which conveys the planets,
    To satisfy the world that calls upon them;

And if their pathway were not thus inflected,
    Much virtue in the heavens would be in vain,
    And almost every power below here dead.

If from the straight line distant more or less
    Were the departure, much would wanting be
    Above and underneath of mundane order.

Remain now, Reader, still upon thy bench,
    In thought pursuing that which is foretasted,
    If thou wouldst jocund be instead of weary.

I've set before thee; henceforth feed thyself,
    For to itself diverteth all my care
    That theme whereof I have been made the scribe.

The greatest of the ministers of nature,
    Who with the power of heaven the world imprints
    And measures with his light the time for us,

With that part which above is called to mind
    Conjoined, along the spirals was revolving,
    Where each time earlier he presents himself;

And I was with him; but of the ascending
    I was not conscious, saving as a man
    Of a first thought is conscious ere it come;

And Beatrice, she who is seen to pass
    From good to better, and so suddenly
    That not by time her action is expressed,

How lucent in herself must she have been!
    And what was in the sun, wherein I entered,
    Apparent not by colour but by light,

I, though I call on genius, art, and practice,
    Cannot so tell that it could be imagined;
    Believe one can, and let him long to see it.

And if our fantasies too lowly are
    For altitude so great, it is no marvel,
    Since o'er the sun was never eye could go.

Such in this place was the fourth family
    Of the high Father, who forever sates it,
    Showing how he breathes forth and how begets.

And Beatrice began: "Give thanks, give thanks
    Unto the Sun of Angels, who to this
    Sensible one has raised thee by his grace!"

Never was heart of mortal so disposed
    To worship, nor to give itself to God
    With all its gratitude was it so ready,

As at those words did I myself become;
    And all my love was so absorbed in Him,
    That in oblivion Beatrice was eclipsed.

Nor this displeased her; but she smiled at it
    So that the splendour of her laughing eyes
    My single mind on many things divided.

Lights many saw I, vivid and triumphant,
    Make us a centre and themselves a circle,
    More sweet in voice than luminous in aspect.

Thus girt about the daughter of Latona
    We sometimes see, when pregnant is the air,
    So that it holds the thread which makes her zone.

Within the court of Heaven, whence I return,
    Are many jewels found, so fair and precious
    They cannot be transported from the realm;

And of them was the singing of those lights.
    Who takes not wings that he may fly up thither,
    The tidings thence may from the dumb await!

As soon as singing thus those burning suns
    Had round about us whirled themselves three times,
    Like unto stars neighbouring the steadfast poles,

Ladies they seemed, not from the dance released,
    But who stop short, in silence listening
    Till they have gathered the new melody.

And within one I heard beginning: "When
    The radiance of grace, by which is kindled
    True love, and which thereafter grows by loving,

Within thee multiplied is so resplendent
    That it conducts thee upward by that stair,
    Where without reascending none descends,

Who should deny the wine out of his vial
    Unto thy thirst, in liberty were not
    Except as water which descends not seaward.

Fain wouldst thou know with what plants is enflowered
    This garland that encircles with delight
    The Lady fair who makes thee strong for heaven.

Of the lambs was I of the holy flock
    Which Dominic conducteth by a road
    Where well one fattens if he strayeth not.

He who is nearest to me on the right
    My brother and master was; and he Albertus
    Is of Cologne, I Thomas of Aquinum.

If thou of all the others wouldst be certain,
    Follow behind my speaking with thy sight
    Upward along the blessed garland turning.

That next effulgence issues from the smile
    Of Gratian, who assisted both the courts
    In such wise that it pleased in Paradise.

The other which near by adorns our choir
    That Peter was who, e'en as the poor widow,
    Offered his treasure unto Holy Church.

The fifth light, that among us is the fairest,
    Breathes forth from such a love, that all the world
    Below is greedy to learn tidings of it.

Within it is the lofty mind, where knowledge
    So deep was put, that, if the true be true,
    To see so much there never rose a second.

Thou seest next the lustre of that taper,
    Which in the flesh below looked most within
    The angelic nature and its ministry.

Within that other little light is smiling
  The advocate of the Christian centuries,
  Out of whose rhetoric Augustine was furnished.

Now if thou trainest thy mind's eye along
  From light to light pursuant of my praise,
  With thirst already of the eighth thou waitest.

By seeing every good therein exults
  The sainted soul, which the fallacious world
  Makes manifest to him who listeneth well;

The body whence 'twas hunted forth is lying
  Down in Cieldauro, and from martyrdom
  And banishment it came unto this peace.

See farther onward flame the burning breath
  Of Isidore, of Beda, and of Richard
  Who was in contemplation more than man.

This, whence to me returneth thy regard,
  The light is of a spirit unto whom
  In his grave meditations death seemed slow.

It is the light eternal of Sigier,
  Who, reading lectures in the Street of Straw,
  Did syllogize invidious verities."

Then, as a horologe that calleth us
  What time the Bride of God is rising up
  With matins to her Spouse that he may love her,

Wherein one part the other draws and urges,
  Ting! ting! resounding with so sweet a note,
  That swells with love the spirit well disposed,

Thus I beheld the glorious wheel move round,
  And render voice to voice, in modulation
  And sweetness that can not be comprehended,

Excepting there where joy is made eternal.

Canto XI

O Thou insensate care of mortal men,
    How inconclusive are the syllogisms
    That make thee beat thy wings in downward flight!

One after laws and one to aphorisms
    Was going, and one following the priesthood,
    And one to reign by force or sophistry,

And one in theft, and one in state affairs,
    One in the pleasures of the flesh involved
    Wearied himself, one gave himself to ease;

When I, from all these things emancipate,
    With Beatrice above there in the Heavens
    With such exceeding glory was received!

When each one had returned unto that point
    Within the circle where it was before,
    It stood as in a candlestick a candle;

And from within the effulgence which at first
    Had spoken unto me, I heard begin
    Smiling while it more luminous became:

"Even as I am kindled in its ray,
    So, looking into the Eternal Light,
    The occasion of thy thoughts I apprehend.

Thou doubtest, and wouldst have me to resift
    In language so extended and so open
    My speech, that to thy sense it may be plain,

Where just before I said, 'where well one fattens,'
    And where I said, 'there never rose a second;'
    And here 'tis needful we distinguish well.

The Providence, which governeth the world
    With counsel, wherein all created vision
    Is vanquished ere it reach unto the bottom,

(So that towards her own Beloved might go
    The bride of Him who, uttering a loud cry,
    Espoused her with his consecrated blood,

Self-confident and unto Him more faithful,)
    Two Princes did ordain in her behoof,
    Which on this side and that might be her guide.

The one was all seraphical in ardour;
    The other by his wisdom upon earth
    A splendour was of light cherubical.

One will I speak of, for of both is spoken
    In praising one, whichever may be taken,
    Because unto one end their labours were.

Between Tupino and the stream that falls
    Down from the hill elect of blessed Ubald,
    A fertile slope of lofty mountain hangs,

From which Perugia feels the cold and heat
    Through Porta Sole, and behind it weep
    Gualdo and Nocera their grievous yoke.

From out that slope, there where it breaketh most
    Its steepness, rose upon the world a sun
    As this one does sometimes from out the Ganges;

Therefore let him who speaketh of that place,
    Say not Ascesi, for he would say little,
    But Orient, if he properly would speak.

He was not yet far distant from his rising
    Before he had begun to make the earth
    Some comfort from his mighty virtue feel.

For he in youth his father's wrath incurred
    For certain Dame, to whom, as unto death,
    The gate of pleasure no one doth unlock;

And was before his spiritual court
    'Et coram patre' unto her united;
    Then day by day more fervently he loved her.

She, reft of her first husband, scorned, obscure,
    One thousand and one hundred years and more,
    Waited without a suitor till he came.

Naught it availed to hear, that with Amyclas
    Found her unmoved at sounding of his voice
    He who struck terror into all the world;

Naught it availed being constant and undaunted,
    So that, when Mary still remained below,
    She mounted up with Christ upon the cross.

But that too darkly I may not proceed,
    Francis and Poverty for these two lovers
    Take thou henceforward in my speech diffuse.

Their concord and their joyous semblances,
    The love, the wonder, and the sweet regard,
    They made to be the cause of holy thoughts;

So much so that the venerable Bernard
    First bared his feet, and after so great peace
    Ran, and, in running, thought himself too slow.

O wealth unknown! O veritable good!
    Giles bares his feet, and bares his feet Sylvester
    Behind the bridegroom, so doth please the bride!

Then goes his way that father and that master,
    He and his Lady and that family
    Which now was girding on the humble cord;

Nor cowardice of heart weighed down his brow
    At being son of Peter Bernardone,
    Nor for appearing marvellously scorned;

But regally his hard determination
    To Innocent he opened, and from him
    Received the primal seal upon his Order.

After the people mendicant increased
    Behind this man, whose admirable life
    Better in glory of the heavens were sung,

Incoronated with a second crown
    Was through Honorius by the Eternal Spirit
    The holy purpose of this Archimandrite.

And when he had, through thirst of martyrdom,
    In the proud presence of the Sultan preached
    Christ and the others who came after him,

And, finding for conversion too unripe
    The folk, and not to tarry there in vain,
    Returned to fruit of the Italic grass,

On the rude rock 'twixt Tiber and the Arno
    From Christ did he receive the final seal,
    Which during two whole years his members bore.

When He, who chose him unto so much good,
    Was pleased to draw him up to the reward
    That he had merited by being lowly,

Unto his friars, as to the rightful heirs,
    His most dear Lady did he recommend,
    And bade that they should love her faithfully;

And from her bosom the illustrious soul
    Wished to depart, returning to its realm,
    And for its body wished no other bier.

Think now what man was he, who was a fit
    Companion over the high seas to keep
    The bark of Peter to its proper bearings.

And this man was our Patriarch; hence whoever
    Doth follow him as he commands can see
    That he is laden with good merchandise.

But for new pasturage his flock has grown
    So greedy, that it is impossible
    They be not scattered over fields diverse;

And in proportion as his sheep remote
    And vagabond go farther off from him,
    More void of milk return they to the fold.

Verily some there are that fear a hurt,
    And keep close to the shepherd; but so few,
    That little cloth doth furnish forth their hoods.

Now if my utterance be not indistinct,
    If thine own hearing hath attentive been,
    If thou recall to mind what I have said,

In part contented shall thy wishes be;
    For thou shalt see the plant that's chipped away,
    And the rebuke that lieth in the words,

'Where well one fattens, if he strayeth not.'"

15

Michel de Montaigne

Essays (1587-88)

Of Experience

I, WHO OPERATE ONLY CLOSE TO THE GROUND, HATE that inhuman wisdom that would make us disdainful enemies of the cultivation of the body. I consider it equal injustice to set our heart against natural pleasures and to set our heart too much on them. Xerxes was a fool, who, wrapped in all human pleasures, went and offered a prize to anyone who would find him others. But hardly less of a fool is the man who cuts off those that nature has found for him. We should neither pursue them nor flee them, we should accept them. I accept them with more gusto and with better grace than most, and more willingly let myself follow a natural inclination. We have no need to exaggerate their inanity; it makes itself felt enough and evident enough. Much thanks to our sickly, kill-joy mind, which disgusts us with them as well as with itself. It treats both itself and all that it takes in, whether future or past, according to its insatiable, erratic, and versatile nature.

Unless the vessel's pure, all you pour in turns sour.

HORACE

I, who boast of embracing the pleasures of life so assiduously and so particularly, find in them, when I look at them thus minutely, virtually nothing but wind. But what of it? We are all wind. And even the wind, more wisely than we, loves to make a noise and move about, and is content with its own functions, without wishing for stability and solidity, qualities that do not belong to it.

The pure pleasures of imagination, as well as the pains, some say, are the greatest, as the scales of Critolaus expressed it. No wonder; it composes them to its liking and cuts them out of whole cloth. I see signal, and perhaps desirable, examples of this every day. But I, being of a mixed constitution, and coarse, am unable to cling so completely to this single and simple object as to keep myself from grossly pursuing the present pleasures of the general human law—intellectually sensual, sensually intellectual. The Cyrenaic philosophers hold that the bodily pleasures, like the pains, are the more powerful, as being both twofold and more equitable.

There are some who from savage stupidity, as Aristotle says, are disgusted with them; I know some who are that way from ambition. Why do they not also give up breathing? Why do they not live on their own air, and refuse light, because it is free and costs them neither invention nor vigor? Let Mars, or Pallas, or Mercury give them sustenance, instead of Venus, Ceres, and Bacchus, just to see what happens. Won't they try to square the circle while perched on their wives! I hate to have people order us to keep our minds in the clouds while our bodies are at table. I would not have the mind nailed down to it nor wallowing at it, but attending to it; sitting at it, not lying down at it.

Aristippus defended the body alone, as if we had no soul; Zeno embraced only the soul, as if we had no body. Both were wrong. Pythagoras, they say, followed a philosophy that was all contemplation, Socrates one that was all conduct and action; Plato found the balance between the two. But they say so to make a good story, and the true balance is found in Socrates, and Plato is much more Socratic than Pythagorean, and it becomes him better.

When I dance, I dance; when I sleep, I sleep; yes, and when I walk alone in a beautiful orchard, if my thoughts have been dwelling on extraneous incidents for some part of the time, for some other part I bring them back to the walk, to the orchard, to the sweetness of this solitude, and to me. Nature has observed this principle like a mother, that the actions she has enjoined on us for our need should also give us pleasure; and she invites us to them not only through reason, but also through appetite. It is unjust to infringe her laws.

When I see both Caesar and Alexander, in the thick of their great tasks, so fully enjoying natural and therefore necessary and just pleasures, I do not say that that is relaxing their souls, I say that it is toughening them, subordinating these violent occupations and laborious thoughts, by the vigor of their spirits, to the practice of everyday life: wise men, had they believed that this was their ordinary occupation, the other the extraordinary.

We are great fools. "He has spent his life in idleness," we say; "I have done nothing today." What, have you not lived? That is not only the fundamental but the most illustrious of your occupations. "If I had been placed in a position to manage great affairs, I would have shown what I could do." Have you been able to think out and manage your own life? You have done the greatest task of all. To show and exploit her resources Nature has no need of fortune; she shows herself equally on all levels and behind a curtain as well as without one. To compose our character is our duty, not to compose books, and to win, not battles and provinces, but order and tranquillity in our conduct. Our great and glorious masterpiece is to live appropriately. All other things, ruling, hoarding, building, are only little appendages and props, at most.

I take pleasure in seeing an army general, at the foot of a breach that he means to attack presently, lending himself wholly and freely to his dinner and his conversation, among his friends; and Brutus, with heaven and earth conspiring against him and Roman liberty, stealing some hour of night from his rounds to read and annotate Polybius with complete assurance. It is for little souls, buried under the weight of business, to be unable to detach themselves cleanly from it or to leave it and pick it up again:

> Brave men, who have endured with me
> Worse things, now banish cares with revelry;
> Tomorrow we shall sail the mighty sea.

HORACE

Whether it is in jest or in earnest that the Sorbonne acquired its proverbial reputation for theological drinking and feasting, I think it right that the faculty should dine all the more comfortably and pleasantly for having used the morning profitably and seriously in the work of their school. The consciousness of having spent the other hours well is a proper and savory sauce for the dinner table. Thus did the sages live. And that inimitable straining for virtue that astounds us in both Catos, that disposition, severe to the point of being troublesome, submitted thus meekly and contentedly to the laws of human nature, and of Venus and Bacchus, in accordance with the precepts of their sect, which require the perfect sage to be as expert and versed in the enjoyment of the natural pleasures as in any other duty of life. *A wise palate should go with a wise heart* [Cicero].

Relaxation and affability, it seems to me, are marvelously honorable and most becoming to a strong and generous soul. Epaminondas did not think that to mingle with the dance of the boys of his city, to sing, to play music, and to concentrate attentively on these things, was at all derogatory to the honor of his glorious victories and the perfect purity of character that was his. And among so many admirable actions of Scipio, the grandfather, a personage worthy of the reputation of celestial descent, there is nothing that lends him more charm than to see him playing nonchalantly and childishly at picking up and selecting shells and running potato races by the sea with Laelius, and in bad weather amusing and tickling his fancy by writing comedies portraying the meanest and most vulgar actions of men; and, his head full of that wonderful campaign against Hannibal and Africa, visiting the schools in Sicily, and attending lectures on philosophy until he armed to the teeth the blind envy of his enemies in Rome. Nor is there anything more remarkable in Socrates than the fact that in his old age he finds time to take lessons in dancing and playing instruments, and considers it well spent.

This same man was once seen standing in a trance, an entire day and night, in the presence of the whole Greek army, overtaken and enraptured by some deep thought. He was seen, the first among so many valiant men of the army, to run to the aid of Alcibiades, who was overwhelmed by enemies, to cover him with his body, and to extricate him from the melee by sheer force of arms; and the first among the people of Athens, all outraged like him at such a shameful spectacle, to come forward to rescue Theramenes, whom the Thirty Tyrants were having led to his death by their satellites; and he desisted from this bold undertaking only at the remonstrance of Theramenes himself, though he was followed by only two men in all. He was seen, when courted by a beauty with whom he was in love, to maintain strict chastity when necessary. He was seen, in the battle of Delium, to pick up and save Xenophon, who had been thrown from his horse. He was constantly seen to march to war and walk the ice barefoot, to wear the same gown in winter and in summer, to surpass all his companions in enduring toil, to eat no differently at a feast than ordinarily.

He was seen for twenty-seven years to endure with the same countenance hunger, poverty, the indocility of his children, the claws of his wife; and in the end calumny, tyranny, prison, irons, and poison. But if that man was summoned to a drinking bout by the duty of civility, he was also the one who did the best in the whole army. And he never refused to play at cobnut with children, or to ride a hobbyhorse with them, and he did so gracefully; for all actions, says philosophy, are equally becoming and honorable in a wise man. We have material enough, and we should never tire of presenting the picture of this man as a pattern and ideal of all sorts of perfection. There are very few full and pure examples of life, and those who educate us are unfair when they set before us every day feeble and defective models, hardly good in a single vein, which rather pull us backward, corrupters rather than correctors.

Popular opinion is wrong: it is much easier to go along the sides, where the outer edge serves as a limit and a guide, than by the middle way, wide and open, and to go by art than by nature; but it is also much less noble and less commendable. Greatness of soul is not so much pressing upward and forward as knowing how to set oneself in order and circumscribe oneself. It regards as great whatever is adequate, and shows its elevation by liking moderate things better than eminent ones. There is nothing so beautiful and legitimate as to play the man well and properly, no knowledge so hard to acquire as the knowledge of how to live this life well and naturally; and the most barbarous of our maladies is to despise our being.

He who wants to detach his soul, let him do it boldly, if he can, when his body is ill, to free it from the contagion; at other times, on the contrary, let the soul assist and favor the body and not refuse to take part in its natural pleasures and enjoy them conjugally, bringing to them moderation, if it is the wiser of the two, for fear that through lack of discretion they may merge into pain. Intemperance is the plague of sensual pleasure; and temperance is not its scourge, it is its seasoning. Eudoxus, who made pleasure the supreme good, and his fellows, who raised it to such high value, savored it in its most charming sweetness by means of temperance, which they possessed in singular and exemplary degree.

I order my soul to look upon both pain and pleasure with a gaze equally self-controlled—*for it is as wrong for the soul to overflow from joy as to contract in sorrow* [Cicero]—and equally firm, but gaily at the one, at the other severely, and, according to its ability, as anxious to extinguish the one as to extend the other. Viewing good things sanely implies viewing bad things sanely. And pain has something not to be avoided in its mild beginning, and pleasure something to be avoided in its excessive ending. Plato couples them together and claims that it is equally the function of fortitude to fight against pain and against the immoderate and bewitching blandishments of pleasure. They are two fountains: whoever draws the right amount from the right one at the right time, whether city, man, or beast, is very fortunate. The first we must take as a necessary medicine, but more sparingly; the other for thirst, but not to the point of drunkenness. Pain, pleasure, love, hatred, are the first things a child feels; if when reason comes they cling to her, that is virtue.

I have a vocabulary all my own. I "pass the time," when it is rainy and disagreeable; when it is good, I do not want to pass it; I savor it, I cling to it. We must run through the bad and settle on the good. This ordinary expression "pastime" or "pass the time" represents the habit of those wise folk who think they can make no better use of their life than to let it slip by and escape it, pass it by, sidestep it, and, as far as in them lies, ignore it and run away from it, as something irksome and contemptible. But I know it to be otherwise and find it both agreeable and worth prizing, even in its last decline, in which I now possess it; and nature has placed it in our hands adorned with such favorable conditions that we have only ourselves to blame if it weighs on us and if it escapes us unprofitably. *The life of the fool is joyless, full of trepidation, given over wholly to the future* [Seneca]. However, I am reconciling myself to the thought of losing it, without regret, but as something that by its nature must be lost; not as something annoying and troublesome. Then too, not to dislike dying is properly becoming only to those who like living. It takes management to enjoy life. I enjoy it twice as much as others, for the measure of enjoyment depends on the greater or lesser attention that we lend it. Especially at this moment, when I perceive that mine is so brief in time, I try to increase it in weight; I try to arrest the speed of its flight by the speed with which I grasp it, and to compensate for the haste of its ebb by my vigor in using it. The shorter my possession of life, the deeper and fuller I must make it.

Others feel the sweetness of some satisfaction and of prosperity; I feel it as they do, but it is not in passing and slipping by. Instead we must study it, savor it, and ruminate it, to give proper thanks for it to him who grants it to us. They enjoy the other pleasures as they do that of sleep, without being conscious of them. To the end that sleep itself should not escape me thus stupidly, at one time I saw fit to have mine disturbed, so that I might gain a glimpse of it. I meditate on any satisfaction; I do not skim over it, I sound it, and bend my reason, now grown peevish and hard to please, to welcome it. Do I find myself in some tranquil state? Is there some voluptuous pleasure that tickles me? I do not let my senses pilfer it, I bring my soul into it, not to implicate herself, but to enjoy herself, not to lose herself but to find herself. And I set her, for her part, to admire herself in this prosperous estate, to weigh and appreciate and amplify the happiness of it. She measures the extent of her debt to God for being at peace with her conscience and free from other inner passions, for having her body in its natural condition, enjoying controlledly and adequately the agreeable and pleasant functions with which he is pleased to compensate by his grace for the pains with which his justice chastises us in its turn; how much it is worth to her to be lodged at such a point that wherever she casts her eyes, the sky is calm around her: no desire, no fear or doubt to disturb the air for her, no difficulty, past, present, or future, over which her imagination may not pass without hurt.

This consideration gains great luster by comparison between my condition and that of others. Thus I set before me in a thousand forms those who are carried away and tossed about by fortune or their own error, and also those, closer to my way, who accept their good fortune so languidly and indifferently. They are the people who really "pass their time"; they pass over the present and what they possess, to be the slaves of hope, and for shadows and vain images that fancy dangles before them—

> Like ghosts that after death are said to flit,
> Or visions that delude the slumbering wit

VIRGIL

—which hasten and prolong their flight the more they are pursued. The fruit and goal of their pursuit is to pursue, as Alexander said that the purpose of his work was to work,

> Believing nothing done while aught was left to do.

LUCAN

As for me, then, I love life and cultivate it just as God has been pleased to grant it to us. I do not go about wishing that it should lack the need to eat and drink, and it would seem to me no less excusable a failing to wish that need to be doubled. *The wise man is the keenest searcher for natural treasures* [Seneca]. Nor do I wish that we should sustain ourselves by merely putting into our mouths a little of that drug by which Epimenides took away his appetite and kept himself alive; nor that we should beget children insensibly with our fingers or our heels, but rather, with due respect, that we could also beget them voluptuously with our fingers and heels; nor that the body should be without desire and without titillation. Those are ungrateful and unfair complaints. I accept with all my heart and with gratitude what nature has done for me, and I am pleased with myself and proud of myself that I do. We wrong that great and all-powerful Giver by refusing his gift, nullifying it, and disfiguring it. Himself all good, he has made all things good. *All things that are according to nature are worthy of esteem* [Cicero].

Of the opinions of philosophy I most gladly embrace those that are most solid, that is to say, most human and most our own; my opinions, in conformity with my conduct, are low and humble. Philosophy is very childish, to my mind, when she gets up on her hind legs and preaches to us that it is a barbarous alliance to marry the divine with the earthly, the reasonable with the unreasonable, the severe with the indulgent, the honorable with the dishonorable; that sensual pleasure is a brutish thing unworthy of being enjoyed by the wise man; that the only pleasure he derives from the enjoyment of a beautiful young wife is the pleasure of his consciousness of doing the right thing, like putting on his boots for a useful ride. May her followers have no more right and sinews and sap in deflowering their wives than her lessons have!

That is not what Socrates says, her tutor and ours. He prizes bodily pleasure as he should, but he prefers that of the mind, as having more power, constancy, ease, variety, and dignity. The latter by no means goes alone, according to him—he is not so fanciful—but only comes first. For him temperance is the moderator, not the adversary, of pleasures.

Nature is a gentle guide, but no more gentle than wise and just. *We must penetrate into the nature of things and clearly see exactly what it demands* [Cicero]. I seek her footprints everywhere. We have confused them with artificial tracks, and for that reason the sovereign good of the Academics and the Peripatetics, which is "to live according to nature," becomes hard to limit and express; also that of the Stoics, a neighbor to the other, which is "to consent to nature."

Is it not an error to consider some actions less worthy because they are necessary? No, they will not knock it out of my head that the marriage of pleasure with necessity, with whom, says an ancient, the gods always conspire, is a very suitable one. To what purpose do we dismember by divorce a structure made up of such close and brotherly correspondence? On the contrary, let us bind it together again by mutual services. Let the mind arouse and quicken the heaviness of the body, and the body check and make fast the lightness of the mind. *He who praises the nature of the soul as the sovereign good and condemns the nature of the flesh as evil, truly both carnally desires the soul and carnally shuns the flesh; for his feeling is inspired by human vanity, not by divine truth* [Saint Augustine].

There is no part unworthy of our care in this gift that God has given us; we are accountable for it even to a single hair. And it is not a perfunctory charge to man to guide man according to his nature; it is express, simple, and of prime importance, and the creator has given it to us seriously and sternly. Authority alone has power over common intelligences, and has more weight in a foreign language. Let us renew the charge here. *Who would not say that it is the essence of folly to do lazily and rebelliously what has to be done, to impel the body one way and the soul another, to be split between the most conflicting motions?* [Seneca.]

Come on now, just to see, some day get some man to tell you the absorbing thoughts and fancies that he takes into his head, and for the sake of which he turns his mind from a good meal and laments the time he spends on feeding himself. You will find there is nothing so insipid in all the dishes on your table as this fine entertainment of his mind (most of the time we should do better to go to sleep completely than to stay awake for what we do stay awake for); and you will find that his ideas and aspirations are not worth your stew. Even if they were the transports of Archimedes himself, what of it? I am not here touching on, or mixing up with that brattish rabble of men that we are, or with the vanity of the desires and musings that distract us, those venerable souls, exalted by ardent piety and religion to constant and conscientious meditation on divine things, who, anticipating, by dint of keen and vehement hope, the enjoyment of eternal food, final goal and ultimate limit of Christian desires, sole constant and incorruptible pleasure, scorn to give their attention to our beggarly, watery, and ambiguous comforts, and readily resign to the body the concern and enjoyment of sensual and temporal fodder. That is a privileged study. Between ourselves, these are two things that I have always observed to be in singular accord: supercelestial thoughts and subterranean conduct.

Aesop, that great man, saw his master pissing as he walked. "What next?" he said. "Shall we have to shit as we run?" Let us manage our time; we shall still have a lot left idle and ill spent. Our mind likes to think it has not enough leisure hours to do its own business unless it dissociates itself from the body for the little time that the body really needs it.

They want to get out of themselves and escape from the man. That is madness: instead of changing into angels, they change into beasts; instead of raising themselves, they lower themselves. These transcendental humors frighten me, like lofty and inaccessible places; and nothing is so hard for me to stomach in the life of Socrates as his ecstasies and possessions by his daemon, nothing is so human in Plato as the qualities for which they say he is called divine. And of our sciences, those seem to me most terrestrial and low which have risen the highest. And I find nothing so humble and so mortal in the life of Alexander as his fancies about his immortalization. Philotas stung him wittily by his answer. He congratulated him by letter on the oracle of Jupiter Ammon which had lodged him among the gods: "As far as you are concerned, I am very glad of it; but there is reason to pity the men who will have to live with and obey a man who exceeds and is not content with a man's proportions."

Since you obey the gods, you rule the world.

HORACE

The nice inscription with which the Athenians honored the entry of Pompey into their city is in accord with my meaning.

You are as much a god as you will own
That you are nothing but a man alone.

AMYOT'S PLUTARCH

It is an absolute perfection and virtually divine to know how to enjoy our being rightfully. We seek other conditions because we do not understand the use of our own, and go outside of ourselves because we do not know what it is like inside. Yet there is no use our mounting on stilts, for on stilts we must still walk on our own legs. And on the loftiest throne in the world we are still sitting only on our own rump.

The most beautiful lives, to my mind, are those that conform to the common human pattern, with order, but without miracle and without eccentricity. Now old age needs to be treated a little more tenderly. Let us commend it to that god who is the protector of health and wisdom, but gay and sociable wisdom:

> Grant me but health, Latona's son,
> And to enjoy the wealth I've won,
> And honored age, with mind entire
> And not unsolaced by the lyre.

HORACE

16

William Shakespeare

Hamlet (1599-1602)

Seven Soliloquies from *The Tragedy of Hamlet, Prince of Denmark*

Act I, Scene 2

O, that this too too solid flesh would melt
Thaw and resolve itself into a dew!
Or that the Everlasting had not fix'd
His canon 'gainst self-slaughter! O God! God!
How weary, stale, flat and unprofitable,
Seem to me all the uses of this world!
Fie on't! ah fie! 'tis an unweeded garden,
That grows to seed; things rank and gross in nature
Possess it merely. That it should come to this!
But two months dead: nay, not so much, not two:
So excellent a king; that was, to this,
Hyperion to a satyr; so loving to my mother
That he might not beteem the winds of heaven
Visit her face too roughly. Heaven and earth!
Must I remember? why, she would hang on him,
As if increase of appetite had grown
By what it fed on: and yet, within a month—
Let me not think on't—Frailty, thy name is woman!—
A little month, or ere those shoes were old
With which she follow'd my poor father's body,

Like Niobe, all tears:—why she, even she—

O, God! a beast, that wants discourse of reason,

Would have mourn'd longer—married with my uncle,

My father's brother, but no more like my father

Than I to Hercules: within a month:

Ere yet the salt of most unrighteous tears

Had left the flushing in her galled eyes,

She married. O, most wicked speed, to post

With such dexterity to incestuous sheets!

It is not nor it cannot come to good:

But break, my heart; for I must hold my tongue.

Act I, Scene 5

O all you host of heaven! O earth! What else?

And shall I couple hell? Oh, fie! Hold, hold, my heart,

And you, my sinews, grow not instant old,

But bear me stiffly up. Remember thee!

Ay, thou poor ghost, whiles memory holds a seat

In this distracted globe. Remember thee!

Yea, from the table of my memory

I'll wipe away all trivial fond records,

All saws of books, all forms, all pressures past

That youth and observation copied there,

And thy commandment all alone shall live

Within the book and volume of my brain,

Unmixed with baser matter. Yes, by heaven!

O most pernicious woman!

O villain, villain, smiling, damnèd villain!

My tables!—Meet it is I set it down

That one may smile, and smile, and be a villain.

At least I'm sure it may be so in Denmark.

Act II, Scene 2

Ay, so, God b' wi' ye!

    Now I am alone.

O what a rogue and peasant slave am I!

Is it not monstrous that this player here,

But in a fiction, in a dream of passion,

Could force his soul so to his own conceit

That, from her working, all his visage wann'd,

Tears in his eyes, distraction in's aspect,

A broken voice, and his whole function suiting

With forms to his conceit? And all for nothing!

For Hecuba!

What's Hecuba to him, or he to Hecuba,

That he should weep for her? What would he do,

Had he the motive and the cue for passion

That I have? He would drown the stage with tears

And cleave the general ear with horrid speech;

Make mad the guilty and appal the free,

Confound the ignorant, and amaze indeed

The very faculties of eyes and ears.

Yet I,

A dull and muddy-mettled rascal, peak

Like John-a-dreams, unpregnant of my cause,

And can say nothing! No, not for a king,

Upon whose property and most dear life

A damn'd defeat was made. Am I a coward?

Who calls me villain? breaks my pate across?

Plucks off my beard and blows it in my face?

Tweaks me by th' nose? gives me the lie i' th' throat

As deep as to the lungs? Who does me this, ha?

'Swounds, I should take it! for it cannot be

But I am pigeon-liver'd and lack gall

To make oppression bitter, or ere this

I should have fatted all the region kites

With this slave's offal. Bloody bawdy villain!

Remorseless, treacherous, lecherous, kindless villain!

O, vengeance!

Why, what an ass am I! This is most brave,

That I, the son of a dear father murther'd,

Prompted to my revenge by heaven and hell,

Must (like a whore) unpack my heart with words

And fall a-cursing like a very drab,

A scullion!

Fie upon't! foh! About, my brain! Hum, I have heard

That guilty creatures, sitting at a play,

Have by the very cunning of the scene

Been struck so to the soul that presently

They have proclaim'd their malefactions;

For murther, though it have no tongue, will speak

With most miraculous organ, I'll have these Players

Play something like the murther of my father

Before mine uncle. I'll observe his looks;

I'll tent him to the quick. If he but blench,

I know my course. The spirit that I have seen

May be a devil; and the devil hath power

T' assume a pleasing shape; yea, and perhaps

Out of my weakness and my melancholy,

As he is very potent with such spirits,

Abuses me to damn me. I'll have grounds

More relative than this. The play's the thing

Wherein I'll catch the conscience of the King.

Act III, Scene 1

To be, or not to be: that is the question:

Whether 'tis nobler in the mind to suffer

The slings and arrows of outrageous fortune,

Or to take arms against a sea of troubles,

And by opposing end them? To die: to sleep;

No more; and by a sleep to say we end

The heart-ache and the thousand natural shocks

That flesh is heir to, 'tis a consummation

Devoutly to be wish'd. To die, to sleep;

To sleep: perchance to dream: ay, there's the rub;

For in that sleep of death what dreams may come

When we have shuffled off this mortal coil,

Must give us pause: there's the respect

That makes calamity of so long life;

For who would bear the whips and scorns of time,

The oppressor's wrong, the proud man's contumely,

The pangs of despised love, the law's delay,
The insolence of office and the spurns
That patient merit of the unworthy takes,
When he himself might his quietus make
With a bare bodkin? who would fardels bear,
To grunt and sweat under a weary life,
But that the dread of something after death,
The undiscover'd country from whose bourn
No traveller returns, puzzles the will
And makes us rather bear those ills we have
Than fly to others that we know not of?
Thus conscience does make cowards of us all;
And thus the native hue of resolution
Is sicklied o'er with the pale cast of thought,
And enterprises of great pith and moment
With this regard their currents turn awry,
And lose the name of action.—Soft you now!
The fair Ophelia!—Nymph, in thy orisons
Be all my sins remember'd.

Act III, Scene 2

'Tis now the very witching time of night,
When churchyards yawn, and hell itself breathes out
Contagion to this world. Now could I drink hot blood
And do such bitter business as the day
Would quake to look on. Soft! now to my mother!
O heart, lose not thy nature; let not ever
The soul of Nero enter this firm bosom.
Let me be cruel, not unnatural;
I will speak daggers to her, but use none.
My tongue and soul in this be hypocrites-
How in my words somever she be shent,
To give them seals never, my soul, consent!

Act III, Scene 3

Now might I do it pat, now he is praying;
And now I'll do't. And so he goes to heaven,

And so am I reveng'd. That would be scann'd.

A villain kills my father; and for that,

I, his sole son, do this same villain send

To heaven.

Why, this is hire and salary, not revenge!

He took my father grossly, full of bread,

With all his crimes broad blown, as flush as May;

And how his audit stands, who knows save heaven?

But in our circumstance and course of thought,

'Tis heavy with him; and am I then reveng'd,

To take him in the purging of his soul,

When he is fit and seasoned for his passage?

No.

Up, sword, and know thou a more horrid hent.

When he is drunk asleep; or in his rage;

Or in th' incestuous pleasure of his bed;

At gaming, swearing, or about some act

That has no relish of salvation in't—

Then trip him, that his heels may kick at heaven,

And that his soul may be as damn'd and black

As hell, whereto it goes. My mother stays.

This physic but prolongs thy sickly days.

Act IV, Scene 4

How all occasions do inform against me

And spur my dull revenge! What is a man,

If his chief good and market of his time

Be but to sleep and feed? A beast, no more.

Sure he that made us with such large discourse,

Looking before and after, gave us not

That capability and godlike reason

To fust in us unus'd. Now, whether it be

Bestial oblivion, or some craven scruple

Of thinking too precisely on th' event,-

A thought which, quarter'd, hath but one part wisdom

And ever three parts coward,- I do not know

Why yet I live to say 'This thing's to do,'

Sith I have cause, and will, and strength, and means

To do't. Examples gross as earth exhort me.

Witness this army of such mass and charge,

Led by a delicate and tender prince,

Whose spirit, with divine ambition puff'd,

Makes mouths at the invisible event,

Exposing what is mortal and unsure

To all that fortune, death, and danger dare,

Even for an eggshell. Rightly to be great

Is not to stir without great argument,

But greatly to find quarrel in a straw

When honour's at the stake. How stand I then,

That have a father kill'd, a mother stain'd,

Excitements of my reason and my blood,

And let all sleep, while to my shame I see

The imminent death of twenty thousand men

That for a fantasy and trick of fame

Go to their graves like beds, fight for a plot

Whereon the numbers cannot try the cause,

Which is not tomb enough and continent

To hide the slain? O, from this time forth,

My thoughts be bloody, or be nothing worth!

17

George Herbert

The Temple, Sacred Poems and Private Ejaculations (1633)

THE CHURCH

The Altar

A BROKEN ALTAR, Lord, thy servant reares,
Made of a heart, and cemented with teares:
Whose parts are as thy hand did frame;
No workmans tool hath touch'd the same,
A HEART alone
Is such a stone,
As nothing but
Thy pow'r doth cut.
Wherefore each part
Of my hard heart
Meets in this frame,
To praise thy Name:
That, if I chance to hold my peace,
These stones to praise thee may not cease.
O let thy blessed SACRIFICE be mine,
And sanctifie this ALTAR to be thine.

The Agonie

PHILOSOPHERS have measur'd mountains,
Fathom'd the depths of seas, of states, and kings,
Walk'd with a staffe to heav'n, and traced fountains:
But there are two vast, spacious things,
The which to measure it doth more behove:
Yet few there are that sound them; Sinne and Love.

Who would know Sinne, let him repair
Unto Mount Olivet; there shall he see
A man so wrung with pains, that all his hair,
His skinne, his garments bloudie be.
Sinne is that presse and vice, which forceth pain
To hunt his cruell food through ev'ry vein.

Who knows not Love, let him assay
And taste that juice, which on the crosse a pike
Did set again abroach; then let him say
If ever he did taste the like.
Love is that liquor sweet and most divine,
Which my God feels as bloud; but I, as wine.

Sinne (I)

LORD, with what care hast thou begirt us round!
Parents first season us: then schoolmasters
Deliver us to laws; they send us bound
To rules of reason, holy messengers,
Pulpits and Sundayes, sorrow dogging sinne,
Afflictions sorted, anguish of all sizes,
Fine nets and stratagems to catch us in,
Bibles laid open, millions of surprises,
Blessings beforehand, tyes of gratefulnesse,
The sound of glorie ringing in our eares:
Without, our shame; within, our consciences;
Angels and grace, eternall hopes and fears.

Yet all these fences and their whole aray
One cunning bosome-sinne blows quite away.

Affliction (I)

WHEN first thou didst entice to thee my heart,
    I thought the service brave:
So many joyes I writ down for my part,
    Besides what I might have
Out of my stock of naturall delights,
Augmented with thy gracious benefits.

I looked on thy furniture so fine,
    And made it fine to me:
Thy glorious houshold-stuffe did me entwine,
    And 'tice me unto thee.
Such starres I counted mine: both heav'n and earth
Payd me my wages in a world of mirth.

What pleasures could I want, whose King I served,
    Where joyes my fellows were?
Thus argu'd into hopes, my thoughts reserved
    No place for grief or fear.
Therefore my sudden soul caught at the place,
And made her youth and fiercenesse seek thy face.

At first thou gav'st me milk and sweetnesses;
    I had my wish and way:
My dayes were straw'd with flow'rs and happinesse;
    There was no moneth but May.
But with my yeares sorrow did twist and grow,
And made a partie unawares for wo.

My flesh began unto my soul in pain,
    Sicknesses cleave my bones;
Consuming agues dwell in ev'ry vein,
    And tune my breath to grones.
Sorrow was all my soul; I scarce beleeved,
Till grief did tell me roundly, that I lived.

When I got health, thou took'st away my life,
                    And more; for my friends die:
My mirth and edge was lost; a blunted knife
                    Was of more use then I.
Thus thinne and lean without a fence or friend,
I was blown through with ev'ry storm and winde.

Whereas my birth and spirit rather took
                    The way that takes the town;
Thou didst betray me to a lingring book,
                    And wrap me in a gown.
I was entangled in the world of strife,
Before I had the power to change my life.

Yet, for I threatned oft the siege to raise,
                    Not simpring all mine age,
Thou often didst with Academick praise
                    Melt and dissolve my rage.
I took thy sweetned pill, till I came where
I could not go away, nor persevere.

Yet lest perchance I should too happie be
                    In my unhappinesse,
Turning my purge to food, thou throwest me
                    Into more sicknesses.
Thus doth thy power crosse-bias me, not making
Thine own gift good, yet me from my wayes taking.

Now I am here, what thou wilt do with me
                    None of my books will show:
I reade, and sigh, and wish I were a tree;
                    For sure then I should grow
To fruit or shade: at least some bird would trust
Her houshold to me, and I should be just.

Yet, though thou troublest me, I must be meek;
                    In weaknesse must be stout.
Well, I will change the service, and go seek
                    Some other master out.
Ah my deare God! though I am clean forgot,
Let me not love thee, if I love thee not.

The Quidditie

My God, a verse is not a crown,
No point of honour, or gay suit,
No hawk, or banquet, or renown,
Nor a good sword, nor yet a lute:

It cannot vault, or dance, or play;
It never was in *France* or *Spain*;
Nor can it entertain the day
With my great stable or demain:

It is no office, art, or news,
Nor the Exchange, or busie Hall;
But it is that which while I use
I am with thee, and *most take all.*

The Starre

BRIGHT spark, shot from a brighter place,
  Where beams surround my Saviours face,
    Canst thou be any where
      So well as there?

Yet, if thou wilt from thence depart,
  Take a bad lodging in my heart;
    For thou canst make a debter,
      And make it better.

First with thy fire-work burn to dust
  Folly, and worse then folly, lust:
    The with thy light refine,
      And make it shine:

So disengag'd from sinne and sicknesse,
  Touch it with thy celestiall quicknesse,
    That it may hang and move
      After thy love.

Then with our trinitie of light,
  Motion, and heat, let's take our flight

Unto the place where thou
Before didst bow.

Get me a standing there, and place
Among the beams, which crown the face
Of him, who dy'd to part
Sinne and my heart:

That so among the rest I may
Glitter, and curie, and winde as they:
That winding is their fashion
Of adoration.

Sure thou wilt joy, by gaining me
To flie home like a laden bee
Unto that hive of beams
And garland-streams.

Vanitie (I)

THE fleet Astronomer can bore,
And thred the spheres with his quick-piercing minde:
He views their stations, walks from doore to doore,
Surveys, as if he had design'd
To make a purchase there: he sees their dances,
And knoweth long before
Both their full-ey'd aspects, and secret glances.

The nimble Diver with his side
Cuts through the working waves, that he may fetch
His dearely-earned pearl, which God did hide
On purpose from the ventrous wretch;
That he might save his life, and also hers,
Who with excessive pride
Her own destruction and his danger wears.

The subtil Chymick can devest
And strip the creature naked, till he finde
The callow principles within their nest:
There he imparts to them his minde,
Admitted to their bed-chamber, before
They appeare trim and drest
To ordinarie suitours at the doore.

What hath not man sought out and found,
But his deare God? who yet his glorious law
Embosomes in us, mellowing the ground
  With showres and frosts, with love & aw,
So that we need not say, Where's this command?
  Poore man, thou searchest round
To finde out *death,* but missest *life* at hand.

Mortification

How soon doth man decay!
When clothes are taken from a chest of sweets
To swaddle infants, whose young breath
  Scarce knows the way;
Those clouts are little winding sheets,
Which do consigne and send them unto death.

When boyes go first to bed,
They step into their voluntarie graves,
Sleep bindes them fast; onely their breath
  Makes them not dead:
Successive nights, like rolling waves,
Convey them quickly, who are bound for death.

THE CHURCH

When youth is frank and free,
And calls for musick, while his veins do swell,
All day exchanging mirth and breath
  In companie;
That musick summons to the knell,
Which shall befriend him at the houre of death.

When man grows staid and wise,
Getting a house and home, where he may move
Within the circle of his breath,
  Schooling his eyes;
That dumbe inclosure maketh love
Unto the coffin, that attends his death.

When age grows low and weak,
Marking his grave, and thawing ev'ry yeare,
Till all do melt, and drown his breath
When he would speak;
A chair or litter shows the biere,
Which shall convey him to the house of death.

Man, ere he is aware,
Hath put together a solemnitie,
And drest his herse, while he has breath
As yet to spare:
Yet Lord, instruct us so to die,
That all these dyings may be life in death.

Miserie

Lord, let the Angels praise thy name.
Man is a foolish thing, a foolish thing,
Folly and Sinne play all his game.
His house still burns, and yet he still doth sing,
Man is but grasse,
He knows it, fill the glasse.

How canst thou brook his foolishnesse?
Why, he'l not lose a cup of drink for thee:
Bid him but temper his excesse;
Not he: he knows where he can better be,
As he will swear,
Then to serve thee in fear.

What strange pollutions doth he wed,
And make his own? as if none knew but he.
No man shall beat into his head,
That thou within his curtains drawn canst see:
They are of cloth,
Where never yet came moth.

The best of men, turn but thy hand
For one poore minute, stumble at a pinne:
They would not have their actions scann'd,

Nor any sorrow tell them that they sinne,
Though it be small,
And measure not their fall.

They quarrell thee, and would give over
The bargain made to serve thee: but thy love
Holds them unto it, and doth cover
Their follies with the wing of thy milde Dove,
Not suff'ring those
Who would, to be thy foes.

My God, Man cannot praise thy name:
Thou art all brightnesse, perfect puritie;
The sunne holds down his head for shame,
Dead with eclipses, when we speak of thee:
How shall infection
Presume on thy perfection?

As dirtie hands foul all they touch,
And those things most, which are most pure and fine:
So our clay hearts, ev'n when we crouch
To sing thy praises, make them lesse divine.
Yet either this,
Or none, thy portion is.

Man cannot serve thee; let him go,
And serve the swine: there, there is his delight:
He doth not like this vertue, no;
Give him his dirt to wallow in all night:
These Preachers make
His head to shoot and ake.

Death

DEATH, thou wast once an uncouth hideous thing,
Nothing but bones,
The sad effect of sadder grones:
Thy mouth was open, but thou couldst not sing.

For we consider'd thee as at some six
Or ten yeares hence,

After the losse of life and sense,
Flesh being turn'd to dust, and bones to sticks.

We lookt on this side of thee, shooting short;
     Where we did finde
   The shells of fledge souls left behinde,
Dry dust, which sheds no tears, but may extort.

But since our Saviours death did put some bloud
     Into thy face;
   Thou art grown fair and full of grace,
Much in request, much sought for as a good.

For we do now behold thee gay and glad,
     As at dooms-day;
   When souls shall wear their new aray,
And all thy bones with beautie shall be clad.

Therefore we can go die as sleep, and trust
     Half that we have
   Unto an honest faithfull grave;
Making our pillows either down, or dust.

18

René Descartes

Meditations on First Philosophy (1641)

Meditation VI: Of the Existence of Material Things, and of the Real Distinction Between the Mind and Body of Man

NOTHING FURTHER NOW REMAINS BUT TO INQUIRE WHETHER MATERIAL THINGS EXIST. And certainly I at least know that these may exist in so far as they are considered as the objects of pure mathematics, since in this aspect I perceive them clearly and distinctly. For there is no doubt that God possesses the power to produce everything that I am capable of perceiving with distinctness, and I have never deemed that anything was impossible for Him, unless I found a contradiction in attempting to conceive it clearly. Further, the faculty of imagination which I possess, and of which, experience tells me, I make use when I apply myself to the consideration of material things, is capable of persuading me of their existence; for when I attentively consider what imagination is, I find that it is nothing but a certain application of the faculty of knowledge to the body which is immediately present to it, and which therefore exists.

And to render this quite clear, I remark in the first place the difference that exists between the imagination and pure intellection [or conception]. For example, when I imagine a triangle, I do not conceive it only as a figure comprehended by three lines, but I also apprehend these three lines as present by the power and inward vision of my mind, and this is what I call imagining. But if I desire to think of a chiliagon, I certainly conceive truly that it is a figure composed of a thousand sides, just as easily as I conceive of a triangle that it is a figure of three sides only; but I cannot in any way imagine the thousand sides of a chiliagon [as I do the three sides of a triangle], nor do I, so to speak, regard them as present [with the eyes of my mind]. And although in accordance with the habit I have formed of always employing the aid of my imagination when I think of corporeal things, it may happen that in imagining a chiliagon I confusedly represent to myself some figure, yet it is very evident that this figure is not a chiliagon, since it in no way differs from that which I represent to myself when I think of a myriagon or any other many-sided figure; nor does it serve my purpose in discovering the properties which go to form the distinction between a chiliagon and other polygons. But if the question turns upon a pentagon, it is quite true that I can conceive its figure as well as that of a chiliagon without the help of my imagination; but I can also imagine it by applying the attention of my mind to each of its five sides, and at the same time to the space which they enclose.

And thus I clearly recognise that I have need of a particular effort of mind in order to effect the act of imagination, such as I do not require in order to understand, and this particular effort of mind clearly manifests the difference which exists between imagination and pure intellection.

I remark besides that this power of imagination which is in one, inasmuch as it differs from the power of understanding, is in no wise a necessary element in my nature, or in [my essence, that is to say, in] the essence of my mind; for although I did not possess it I should doubtless ever remain the same as I now am, from which it appears that we might conclude that it depends on something which differs from me. And I easily conceive that if some body exists with which my mind is conjoined and united in such a way that it can apply itself to consider it when it pleases, it may be that by this means it can imagine corporeal objects; so that this mode of thinking differs from pure intellection only inasmuch as mind in its intellectual activity in some manner turns on itself, and considers some of the ideas which it possesses in itself; while in imagining it turns towards the body, and there beholds in it something conformable to the idea which it has either conceived of itself or perceived by the senses. I easily understand, I say, that the imagination could be thus constituted if it is true that body exists; and because I can discover no other convenient mode of explaining it, I conjecture with probability that body does exist; but this is only with probability, and although I examine all things with care, I nevertheless do not find that from this distinct idea of corporeal nature, which I have in my imagination, I can derive any argument from which there will necessarily be deduced the existence of body.

But I am in the habit of imagining many other things besides this corporeal nature which is the object of pure mathematics, to wit, the colours, sounds, scents, pain, and other such things, although less distinctly. And inasmuch as I perceive these things much better through the senses, by the medium of which, and by the memory, they seem to have reached my imagination, I believe that, in order to examine them more conveniently, it is right that I should at the same time investigate the nature of sense perception, and that I should see if from the ideas which I apprehend by this mode of thought, which I call feeling, I cannot derive some certain proof of the existence of corporeal objects.

And first of all I shall recall to my memory those matters which I hitherto held to be true, as having perceived them through the senses, and the foundations on which my belief has rested; in the next place I shall examine the reasons which have since obliged me to place them in doubt; in the last place I shall consider which of them I must now believe.

First of all, then, I perceived that I had a head, hands, feet, and all other members of which this body which I considered as a part, or possibly even as the whole, of myself is composed.

Further I was sensible that this body was placed amidst many others, from which it was capable of being affected in many different ways, beneficial and hurtful, and I remarked that a certain feeling of pleasure accompanied those that were beneficial, and pain those which were harmful. And in addition to this pleasure and pain, I also experienced hunger, thirst, and other similar appetites, as also certain corporeal inclinations towards joy, sadness, anger, and other similar passions. And outside myself, in addition to extension, figure, and motions of bodies, I remarked in them hardness, heat, and all other tactile qualities, and, further, light and colour, and scents and sounds, the variety of which gave me the means of distinguishing the sky, the earth, the sea, and generally all the other bodies, one from the other. And certainly, considering the ideas of all these qualities which presented themselves to my mind, and which alone I perceived properly or immediately, it was not without reason that I believed myself to perceive objects quite different from my thought, to wit, bodies from which those ideas proceeded; for I found by experience that these ideas presented themselves to me without my consent being requisite, so that I could not perceive any object, however desirous I might be, unless it were present to the organs of sense; and it was not in my power not to perceive it, when it was present. And because the ideas which I received through the senses were much more lively, more clear, and even, in their own way, more distinct than any of those which I could of myself frame in meditation, or than those I found impressed on my memory, it appeared as though they could not have proceeded from my mind, so that they must necessarily have been produced in me by some other things. And having no knowledge of those objects excepting the knowledge which the ideas themselves gave me, nothing was more likely to occur to my mind than that the objects were similar to the ideas which were caused. And because I likewise remembered that I had formerly made use of my senses rather than my reason, and recognised that the ideas which I formed of myself were not so distinct as those which I perceived through the senses, and that they were most frequently even composed of portions of these last, I persuaded myself easily that I had no idea in my mind which had not formerly come to me through the senses. Nor was it without some reason that I believed that this body (which be a certain special right I call my own) belonged to me more properly and more strictly than any other; for in fact I could never be separated from it as from other bodies; I experienced in it and on account of it all my appetites and affections, and finally I was touched by the feeling of pain and the titillation of pleasure in its parts, and not in the parts of other bodies which were separated from it. But when I inquired, why, from some, I know not what, painful sensation, there follows sadness of mind, and from the pleasurable sensation there arises joy, or why this mysterious pinching of the stomach which I call hunger causes me to desire to eat, and dryness of throat causes a desire to drink, and so on, I could give no reason excepting that nature taught me so; for there is certainly no affinity (that I at least can understand) between the craving of the stomach and the desire to eat, any more than between the perception of whatever causes pain and the thought of sadness which arises from this perception. And in the same way it appeared to me that I had learned from nature all the other judgments which I formed regarding the objects of my senses, since I remarked that these judgments were formed in me before I had the leisure to weigh and consider any reasons which might oblige me to make them.

But afterwards many experiences little by little destroyed all the faith which I had rested in my senses; for I from time to time observed that those towers which from afar appeared to me to be round, more closely observed seemed square, and that colossal statues raised on the summit of these towers, appeared as quite tiny statues when viewed from the bottom; and so in an infinitude of other cases I found error in judgments founded on the external senses. And not only in those founded on the external senses, but even in those founded on the internal as well; for is there anything more intimate or more internal than pain? And yet I have learned from some persons whose arms or legs have been cut off, that they sometimes seemed to feel pain in the part which had been amputated, which made me think that I could not be quite certain that it was a certain member which pained me, even although I felt pain in it. And to those grounds of doubt I have lately added two others, which are very general; the first is that I never have believed myself to feel anything in waking moments which I cannot also sometimes believe myself to feel when I sleep, and as I do not think that these things which I seem to feel in sleep, proceed from objects outside of me, I do not see any reason why I should have this belief regarding objects which I seem to perceive while awake. The other was that being still ignorant, or rather supposing myself to be ignorant, of the author of my being, I saw nothing to prevent me from having been so constituted by nature that I might be deceived even in matters which seemed to me to be most certain. And as to the grounds on which I was formerly persuaded of the truth of sensible objects, I had not much trouble in replying to them. For since nature seemed to cause me to lean towards many things from which reason repelled me, I did not believe that I should trust much to the teachings of nature. And although the ideas which I receive by the senses do not depend on my will, I did not think that one should for that reason conclude that they proceeded from things different from myself, since possibly some faculty might be discovered in me though hitherto unknown to me which produced them.

But now that I begin to know myself better, and to discover more clearly the author of my being, I do not in truth think that I should rashly admit all the matters which the senses seem to teach us, but, on the other hand, I do not think that I should doubt them all universally.

And first of all, because I know that all things which I apprehend clearly and distinctly can be created by God as I apprehend them, it suffices that I am able to apprehend one thing apart from another clearly and distinctly in order to be certain that the one is different from the other, since they may be made to exist in separation at least by the omnipotence of God; and it does not signify by what power this separation is made in order to compel me to judge them to be different: and, therefore, just because I know certainly that I exist, and that meanwhile I do not remark that any other thing necessarily pertains to my nature or essence, excepting that I am a thinking thing, I rightly conclude that my essence consists solely in the fact that I am a thinking thin [or a substance whose whole essence or nature is to think]. And although possibly (or rather certainly, as I shall say in a moment) I possess a body with which I am very intimately conjoined, yet because, on the one side, I have a clear and distinct idea of myself inasmuch as I am only a thinking and unextended thing, and as, on the other, I possess a distinct idea of body, inasmuch as it is only an extended and unthinking thing, it is certain that this I [that is to say, my soul by which I am what I am], is entirely and absolutely distinct from my body, and can exist without it.

I further find in myself faculties imploying modes of thinking peculiar to themselves, to wit, the faculties of imagination and feeling, without which I can easily conceive myself clearly and distinctly as a complete being; while, on the other hand, they cannot be so conceived apart from me, that is without an intelligent substance in which they reside, for [in the notion we have of these faculties, or, to use the language of the Schools] in their formal concept, some kind of intellection is comprised, from which I infer that they are distinct from me as its modes are from a thing. I observe also in me some other faculties such as that of change of position, the assumption of different figures and such like, which cannot be conceived, any more than can the preceding, apart from some substance to which they are attached, and consequently cannot exist without it; but it is very clear that these faculties, if it be true that they exist, must be attached to some corporeal or extended substance, and not to an intelligent substance, since in the clear and distinct conception of these there is some sort of extension found to be present, but no intellection at all. There is certainly further in me a certain passive faculty of perception, that is, of receiving and recognising the ideas of sensible things, but this would be useless to me [and I could in no way avail myself of it], if there were not either in me or in some other thing another active faculty capable of forming and producing these ideas. But this active faculty cannot exist in me [inasmuch as I am a thing that thinks] seeing that it does not presuppose thought, and also that those ideas are often produced in me without my contributing in any way to the same, and often even against my will; it is thus necessarily the case that the faculty resides in some substance different from me in which all the reality which is objectively in the ideas that are produced by this faculty is formally or eminently contained, as I remarked before. And this substance is either a body, that is, a corporeal nature in which there is contained formally [and really] all that which is objectively [and by representation] in those ideas, or it is God Himself, or some other creature more noble than body in which that same is contained eminently. But, since God is no deceiver, it is very manifest that He does not communicate to me these ideas immediately and by Himself, nor yet by the intervention of some creature in which their reality is not formally, but only eminently, contained. For since He has given me no faculty to recognise that this is the case, but, on the other hand, a very great inclination to believe [that they are sent to me or] that they are conveyed to me by corporeal objects, I do not see how He could be defended from the accusation of deceit if these ideas were produced by causes other than corporeal objects. Hence we must allow that corporeal things exist. However, they are perhaps not exactly what we perceive by the senses, since this comprehension by the senses is in many instances very obscure and confused; but we must at least admit that all things which I conceive in them clearly and distinctly, that is to say, all things which, speaking generally, are comprehended in the object of pure mathematics, are truly to be recognised as external objects.

As to other things, however, which are either particular only, as, for example, that the sun is of such and such a figure, etc., or which are less clearly and distinctly conceived, such as light, sound, pain and the like, it is certain that although they are very dubious and uncertain, yet on the sole ground that God is not a deceiver, and that consequently He has not permitted any falsity to exist in my opinion which He has not likewise given me the faculty of correcting, I may assuredly hope to conclude that I have within me the means of arriving at the truth even here. And first of all there is no doubt that in all things which nature teaches me there is some truth contained; for by nature, considered in general, I now understand no other thing than either God Himself or else the order and disposition which God has established in created things; and by my nature in particular I understand no other thing than the complexus of all the things which God has given me.

But there is nothing which this nature teaches me more expressly [nor more sensibly] than that I have a body which is adversely affected when I feel pain, which has need of food or drink when I experience the feelings of hunger and thirst, and so on; nor can I doubt there being some truth in all this.

Nature also teaches me by these sensations of pain, hunger, thirst, etc., that I am not only lodged in my body as a pilot in a vessel, but that I am not only lodged in my body as a pilot in a vessel, but that I am very closely united to it, and so to speak so intermingled with it that I seem to compose with it one whole. For if that were not the case, when my body is hurt, I, who am merely a thinking thing, should not feel pain, for I should perceive this wound by the understanding only, just as the sailor perceives by sight when something is damaged in his vessel; and when my body has need of drink or food, I should clearly understand the fact without being warned of it by confused feelings of hunger and thirst. For all these sensations of hunger, thirst, pain, etc. are in truth none other than certain confused modes of thought which are produced by the union and apparent intermingling of mind and body.

Moreover, nature teaches me that many other bodies exist around mine, of which some are to be avoided, and others sought after. And certainly from the fact that I am sensible of different sorts of colours, sounds, scents, tastes, heat, hardness, etc., I very easily conclude that there are in the bodies from which all these diverse sense-perceptions proceed certain variations which answer to them, although possibly these are not really at all similar to them. And also from the fact that amongst these different sense-perceptions some are very agreeable to me and others disagreeable, it is quite certain that my body (or rather myself in my entirety, inasmuch as I am formed of body and soul) may receive different impressions agreeable and disagreeable from the other bodies which surround it.

But there are many other things which nature seems to have taught me, but which at the same time I have never really received from her, but which have been brought about in my mind by a certain habit which I have of forming inconsiderate judgments on things; and thus it may easily happen that these judgments contain some error. Take, for example, the opinion which I hold that all space in which there is nothing that affects [or makes an impression on] my senses is void; that in a body which is warm there is something entirely similar to the idea of heat which is in me; that in a white or green body there is the same whiteness or greenness that I perceive; that in a bitter or sweet body there is the same taste, and so on in other instances; that the stars, the towers, and all other distant bodies are of the same figure and size as they appear from far off to our eyes, etc. But in order that in this there should be nothing which I do not conceive distinctly, I should define exactly what I really understand when I say that I am taught somewhat by nature. For here I take nature in a more limited signification than when I term it the sum of all the things given me by God, since in this sum many things are comprehended which only pertain to mind (and to these I do not refer in speaking of nature) such as the notion which I have of the fact that what has once been done cannot ever be undone and an infinitude of such things which I know by the light of nature [without the help of the body]; and seeing that it comprehends many other matters besides which only pertain to body, and are no longer here contained under the name of nature, such as the quality of weight which it possesses and the like, with which I also do not deal; for in talking of nature I only treat of those things given by God to me as a being composed of mind and body. But the nature here described truly teaches me to flee from things which cause the sensation of pain, and seek after the things which communicate to me the sentiment of pleasure and so forth; but I do not see that beyond this it teaches me that from those diverse sense-perceptions we should ever form any conclusion regarding things outside of us, without having [carefully and maturely] mentally examined them beforehand. For it seems to me that it is mind alone, and not mind and body in conjunction, that is requisite to a knowledge of the truth in regard to such things. Thus, although a star makes no larger an impression on my eye than the flame of a little candle there is yet in me no real or positive propensity impelling me to believe that it is not greater than that flame; but I have judged it to be so from my earliest years, without any rational foundation. And although in approaching fire I feel heat, and in approaching it a little too near I even feel pain, there is at the same time no reason in this which could persuade me that there is in the fire something resembling this heat any more than there is in it something resembling the pain; all that I have any reason to believe from this is, that there is something in it, whatever it may be, which excites in me these sensations of heat or of pain. So also, although there are spaces in which I find nothing which excites my senses, I must not from that conclude that these spaces contain no body; for I see in this, as in other similar things, that I have been in the habit of perverting the order of nature, because these perceptions of sense having been placed within me by nature merely for the purpose of signifying to my mind what things are beneficial or hurtful to the composite whole of which it forms a part, and being up to that point sufficiently clear and distinct, I yet avail myself of them as though they were absolute rules by which I might immediately determine the essence of the bodies which are outside me, as to which, in fact, they can teach me nothing but what is most obscure and confused.

But I have already sufficiently considered how, notwithstanding the supreme goodness of God, falsity enters into the judgments I make. Only here a new difficulty is presented one respecting those things the pursuit or avoidance of which is taught me by nature, and also respecting the internal sensations which I possess, and in which I seem to have sometimes detected error [and thus to be directly deceived by my own nature]. To take an example, the agreeable taste of some food in which poison has been intermingled may induce me to partake of the poison, and thus deceive me. It is true, at the same time, that in this case nature may be excused, for it only induces me to desire food in which I find a pleasant taste, and not to desire the poison which is unknown to it; and thus I can infer nothing from this fact, except that my nature is not omniscient, at which there is certainly no reason to be astonished, since man, being finite in nature, can only have knowledge the perfectness of which is limited.

But we not unfrequently deceive ourselves even in those things to which we are directly impelled by nature, as happens with those who when they are sick desire to drink or eat things hurtful to them. It will perhaps be said here that the cause of their deceptiveness is that their nature is corrupt, but that does not remove the difficulty, because a sick man is none the less truly God's creature than he who is in health; and it is therefore as repugnant to God's goodness for the one to have a deceitful nature as it is for the other. And as a clock composed of wheels and counter-weights no less exactly observes the laws of nature when it is badly made, and does not show the time properly, than when it entirely satisfies the wishes of its maker, and as, if I consider the body of a man as being a sort of machine so built up and composed of nerves, muscles, veins, blood and skin, that though there were no mind in it at all, it would not cease to have the same motions as at present, exception being made of those movements which are due to the direction of the will, and in consequence depend upon the mind [as opposed to those which operate by the disposition of its organs], I easily recognise that it would be as natural to this body, supposing it to be, for example, dropsical, to suffer the parchedness of the throat which usually signifies to the mind the feeling of thirst, and to be disposed by this parched feeling to move the nerves and other parts in the way requisite for drinking, and thus to augment its malady and do harm to itself, as it is natural to it, when it has no indisposition, to be impelled to drink for its good by a similar cause. And although, considering the use to which the clock has been destined by its maker, I may say that it deflects from the order of its nature when it does not indicate the hours correctly; and as, in the same way, considering the machine of the human body as having been formed by God in order to have in itself all the movements usually manifested there, I have reason for thinking that it does not follow the order of nature when, if the throat is dry, drinking does harm to the conservation of health, nevertheless I recognise at the same time that this last mode of explaining nature is very different from the other. For this is but a purely verbal characterisation depending entirely on my thought, which compares a sick man and a badly constructed clock with the idea which I have of a healthy man and a well-made clock, and it is hence extrinsic to the things to which it is applied; but according to the other interpretation of the term nature I understand something which is truly found in things and which is therefore not without some truth.

But certainly although in regard to the dropsical body it is only so to speak to apply an extrinsic term when we say that its nature is corrupted, inasmuch as apart from the need to drink, the throat is parched; yet in regard to the composite whole, that is to say, to the mind or soul united to this body, it is not a purely verbal predicate, but a real error of nature, for it to have thirst when drinking would be hurtful to it. And thus it still remains to inquire how the goodness of God does not prevent the nature of man so regarded from being fallacious.

In order to begin this examination, then, I here say, in the first place, that there is a great difference between mind and body, inasmuch as body is by nature always divisible, and the mind is entirely indivisible. For, as a matter of fact, when I consider the mind, that is to say, myself inasmuch as I am only a thinking thing, I cannot distinguish in myself any parts, but apprehend myself to be clearly one and entire; and although the whole mind seems to be united to the whole body, yet if a foot, or an arm, or some other part, is separated from my body, I am aware that nothing has been taken away from my mind. And the faculties of willing, feeling, conceiving, etc. cannot be properly speaking said to be its parts, for it is one and the same mind which employs itself in willing and in feeling and understanding. But it is quite otherwise with corporeal or extended objects, for there is not one of these imaginable by me which my mind cannot easily divide into parts, and which consequently I do not recognise as being divisible; this would be sufficient to teach me that the mind or soul of man is entirely different from the body, if I had not already learned it from other sources.

I further notice that the mind does not receive the impressions from all parts of the body immediately, but only from the brain, or perhaps even from one of its smallest parts, to wit, from that in which the common sense is said to reside, which, whenever it is disposed in the same particular way, conveys the same thing to the mind, although meanwhile the other portions of the body may be differently disposed, as is testified by innumerable experiments which it is unnecessary here to recount.

I notice, also, that the nature of body is such that none of its parts can be moved by another part a little way off which cannot also be moved in the same way by each one of the parts which are between the two, although this more remote part does not act at all. As, for example, in the cord ABCD [which is in tension] if we pull the last part D, the first part A will not be moved in any way differently from what would be the case if one of the intervening parts B or C were pulled, and the last part D were to remain unmoved. And in the same way, when I feel pain in my foot, my knowledge of physics teaches me that this sensation is communicated by means of nerves dispersed through the foot, which, being extended like cords from there to the brain, when they are contracted in the foot, at the same time contract the inmost portions of the brain which is their extremity and place of origin, and then excite a certain movement which nature has established in order to cause the mind to be affected by a sensation of pain represented as existing in the foot. But because these nerves must pass through the tibia, the thigh, the loins, the back and the neck, in order to reach from the leg to the brain, it may happen that although their extremities which are in the foot are not affected, but only certain ones of their intervening parts [which pass by the loins or the neck], this action will excite the same movement in the brain that might have been excited there by a hurt received in the foot, in consequence of which the mind will necessarily feel in the foot the same pain as if it had received a hurt. And the same holds good of all the other perceptions of our senses.

I notice finally that since each of the movements which are in the portion of the brain by which the mind is immediately affected brings about one particular sensation only, we cannot under the circumstances imagine anything more likely than that this movement, amongst all the sensations which it is capable of impressing on it, causes mind to be affected by that one which is best fitted and most generally useful for the conservation of the human body when it is in health. But experience makes us aware that all the feelings with which nature inspires us are such as I have just spoken of; and there is therefore nothing in them which does not give testimony to the power and goodness of the God [who has produced them]. Thus, for example, when the nerves which are in the feet are violently or more than usually moved, their movement, passing through the medulla of the spine to the inmost parts of the brain, gives a sign to the mind which makes it feel somewhat, to wit, pain, as though in the foot, by which the mind is excited to do its utmost to remove the cause of the evil as dangerous and hurtful to the foot. It is true that God could have constituted the nature of man in such a way that this same movement in the brain would have conveyed something quite different to the mind; for example, it might have produced consciousness of itself either in so far as it is in the brain, or as it is in the foot, or as it is in some other place between the foot and the brain, or it might finally have produced consciousness of anything else whatsoever; but none of all this would have contributed so well to the conservation of the body. Similarly, when we desire to drink, a certain dryness of the throat is produced which moves its nerves, and by their means the internal portions of the brain; and this movement causes in the mind the sensation of thirst, because in this case there is nothing more useful to us than to become aware that we have need to drink for the conservation of our health; and the same holds good in other instances.

From this it is quite clear that, notwithstanding the supreme goodness of God, the nature of man, inasmuch as it is composed of mind and body, cannot be otherwise than sometimes a source of deception. For if there is any cause which excites, not in the foot but in some part of the nerves which are extended between the foot and the brain, or even in the brain itself, the same movement which usually is produced when the foot is detrimentally affected, pain will be experienced as though it were in the foot, and the sense will thus naturally be deceived; for since the same movement in the brain is capable of causing but one sensation in the mind, and this sensation is much more frequently excited by a cause which hurts the foot than by another existing in some other quarter, it is reasonable that it should convey to the mind pain in the foot rather than in any other part of the body. And although the parchedness of the throat does not always proceed, as it usually does, from the fact that drinking is necessary for the health of the body, but sometimes comes from quite a different cause, as is the case with dropsical patients, it is yet much better that it should mislead on this occasion than if, on the other hand, it were always to deceive us when the body is in good health; and so on in similar cases.

And certainly this consideration is of great service to me, not only in enabling me to recognise all the errors to which my nature is subject, but also in enabling me to avoid them or to correct them more easily. for knowing that all my senses more frequently indicate to me truth than falsehood respecting the things which concern that which is beneficial to the body, and being able almost always to avail myself of many of them in order to examine one particular thing, and, besides that, being able to make use of my memory in order to connect the present with the past, and of my understanding which already has discovered all the causes of my errors, I ought no longer to fear that falsity may be found in matters every day presented to me by my senses. And I ought to set aside all the doubts of these past days as hyperbolical and ridiculous, particularly that very common uncertainty respecting sleep, which I could not distinguish from the waking state; for at present I find a very notable difference between the two, inasmuch as our memory can never connect our dreams one with the other, or with the whole course of our lives, as it unites events which happen to us while we are awake. And, as a matter of fact, if someone, while I was awake, quite suddenly appeared to me and disappeared as fast as do the images which I see in sleep, so that I could not know from whence the form came nor whither it went, it would not be without reason that I should deem it a spectre or a phantom formed by my brain [and similar to those which I form in sleep], rather than a real man. But when I perceive things as to which I know distinctly both the place from which they proceed, and that in which they are, and the time at which they appeared to me; and when, without any interruption, I can connect the perceptions which I have of them with the whole course of my life, I am perfectly assured that these perceptions occur while I am waking and not during sleep. And I ought in no wise to doubt the truth of such matters, if, after having called up all my senses, my memory, and my understanding, to examine them, nothing is brought to evidence by any one of them which is repugnant to what is set forth by the others. For because God is in no wise a deceiver, it follows that I am not deceived in this. But because the exigencies of action often oblige us to make up our minds before having leisure to examine matters carefully, we must confess that the life of man is very frequently subject to error in respect to individual objects, and we must in the end acknowledge the infirmity of our nature.

19

Blaise Pascal

Pensées (1669)

Philosophers

339 I can well conceive a man without hands, feet, head (for it is only experience which teaches us that the head is more necessary than feet). But I cannot conceive man without thought; he would be a stone or a brute.

340 The arithmetical machine produces effects which approach nearer to thought than all the actions of animals. But it does nothing which would enable us to attribute will to it, as to the animals.

342 If an animal did by mind what it does by instinct, and if it spoke by mind what it speaks by instinct, in hunting, and in warning its mates that the prey is found or lost; it would indeed also speak in regard to those things which affect it closer, as example, "Gnaw me this cord which is wounding me, and which I cannot reach."

344 Instinct and reason, marks of two natures.

345 Reason commands us far more imperiously than a master; for in disobeying the one we are unfortunate, and in disobeying the other we are fools.

346 Thought constitutes the greatness of man.

347 Man is but a reed, the most feeble thing in nature; but he is a thinking reed. The entire universe need not arm itself to crush him. A vapour, a drop of water suffices to kill him. But, if the universe were to crush him, man would still be more noble than that which killed him, because he knows that he dies and the advantage which the universe has over him; the universe knows nothing of this.

All our dignity consists, then, in thought. By it we must elevate ourselves, and not by space and time which we cannot fill. Let us endeavour, then, to think well; this is the principle of morality.

348 *A thinking reed.* —It is not from space that I must seek my dignity, but from the government of my thought. I shall have no more if I possess worlds. By space the universe encompasses and swallows me up like an atom; by thought I comprehend the world.

349 *Immateriality of the soul.* —Philosophers who have mastered their passions. What matter could do that?

350 *The Stoics.* —They conclude that what has been done once can be done always, and that since the desire of glory imparts some power to those whom it possesses, others can do likewise. There are feverish movements which health cannot imitate.

Epictetus concludes that since there are consistent Christians, every man can easily be so.

351 Those great spiritual efforts, which the soul sometimes assays, are things on which it does not lay hold. It only leaps to them, not as upon a throne, forever, but merely for an instant.

352 The strength of a man's virtue must not be measured by his efforts, but by his ordinary life.

354 Man's nature is not always to advance; it has its advances and retreats.

Fever has its cold and hot fits; and the cold proves as well as the hot the greatness of the fire of fever.

The discoveries of men from age to age turn out the same. The kindness and the malice of the world in general are the same. *Plerumque gratæ principibus vices* [Horace, *Odes*].

355 [. . .] Nature acts by progress, *itus et reditus*. It goes and returns, then advances further, then twice as much backwards, then more forward than ever, etc.

The tide of the sea behaves in the same manner; and so apparently does the sun in its course.

356 The nourishment of the body is little by little. Fullness of nourishment and smallness of substance.

357 When we would pursue virtues to their extremes on either side, vices present themselves, which insinuate themselves insensibly there, in their insensible journey towards the infinitely little: and vices present themselves in a crowd towards the infinitely great, so that we lose ourselves in them, and no longer see virtues. We find fault with perfection itself.

358 Man is neither angel nor brute, and the unfortunate thing is that he who would act the angel acts the brute.

359 We do not sustain ourselves in virtue by our own strength, but by the balancing of two opposed vices, just as we remain upright amidst two contrary gales. Remove one of the vices, and we fall into the other.

360 What the Stoics propose is so difficult and foolish!

The Stoics lay down that all those who are not at the high degree of wisdom are equally foolish and vicious, as those who are two inches under water.

361 The sovereign good. Dispute about the sovereign good._—*Ut sis contentus temetipso et ex te nascentibus bonis* [Seneca]. There is a contradiction, for in the end they advise suicide. Oh! What a happy life, from which we are to free ourselves as from the plague!

365 *Thought.* —All the dignity of man consists in thought. Thought is therefore by its nature a wonderful and incomparable thing. It must have strange defects to be contemptible. But it has such, so that nothing is more ridiculous. How great it is in its nature! How vile it is in its defects! But what is this thought? How foolish it is!

366 The mind of this sovereign judge of the world is not so independent that it is not liable to be disturbed by the first din about it. The noise of a cannon is not necessary to hinder its thoughts; it needs only the creaking of a weathercock or a pulley. Do not wonder if at present it does not reason well; a fly is buzzing in its ears; that is enough to render it incapable of good judgment. If you wish it to be able to reach the truth, chase away that animal which holds its reason in check and disturbs that powerful intellect which rules towns and kingdoms. Here is a comical god! *O ridicolosissimo eroe!*

367 The power of flies; they win battles, hinder our soul from acting, eat our body.

368 When it is said [by Descartes] that heat is only the motions of certain molecules, and light the *conatus recedendi* which we feel, it astonishes us. What! Is pleasure only the ballet of our spirits? We have conceived so different an idea of it! And these sensations seem so removed from those others which we say are the same as those with which we compare them! The sensation from the fire, that warmth which affects us in a manner wholly different from touch, the reception of sound and light, all this appears to us mysterious, and yet it is material like the blow of a stone. It is true that the smallness of the spirits which enter into the pores touches other nerves, but there are always some nerves touched.

369 Memory is necessary for all the operations of reason.

370 Chance gives rise to thoughts, and chance removes them; no art can keep or acquire them.

A thought has escaped me. I wanted to write it down. I write instead, that it has escaped me.

372 In writing down my thought, it sometimes escapes me; but this makes me remember my weakness, that I constantly forget. This is as instructive to me as my forgotten thought; for I strive only to know my nothingness.

373 *Skepticism.* —I shall here write my thoughts without order, and not perhaps in unintentional confusion; that is true order, which will always indicate my object by its very disorder.

I should do too much honor to my subject, if I treated it with order, since I want to show that it is incapable of it.

374 What astonishes me most is to see that all the world is not astonished at its own weakness. Men act seriously, and each follows his own mode of life, not because it is in fact good to follow since it is the custom, but as if each man knew certainly where reason and justice are. They find themselves continually deceived, and by a comical humility think it is their own fault, and not that of the art which they claim always to possess. But it is well there are so many such people in the world, who are not skeptics for the glory of skepticism, in order to show that man is quite capable of the most extravagant opinions, since he is capable of believing that he is not in a state of natural and inevitable weakness, but, on the contrary, of natural wisdom. Nothing fortifies skepticism more than that there are some who are not skeptics; if all were so, they would be wrong.

377 Discourses on humility are a source of pride in the vain, and of humility in the humble. So those on skepticism cause believers to affirm. Few men speak humbly of humility, chastely of chastity, few doubtingly of skepticism. We are only falsehood, duplicity, contradiction; we both conceal and disguise ourselves from ourselves.

378 *Skepticism.* —Excess, like defect of intellect, is accused of madness. Nothing is good but mediocrity. The majority has settled that, and finds fault with him who escapes it at whichever end. I will not oppose it. I quite consent to put myself there, and refuse to be at the lower end, not because it is low, but because it is an end; for I would likewise refuse to be placed at the top. To leave the mean is to abandon humanity. The greatness of the human soul consists in knowing how to preserve the mean. So far from greatness consisting in leaving it, it consists in not leaving it.

379 It is not good to have too much liberty. It is not good to have all one wants.

380 All good maxims are in the world. We only need to apply them. For instance, we do not doubt that we ought to risk our lives in defense of the public good; but for religion, no.

It is true there must be inequality among men; but if this be conceded, the door is opened not only to the highest power, but to the highest tyranny.

We must relax our minds a little; but this opens the door to the greatest debauchery. Let us mark the limits. There are no limits in things. Laws would put them there, and the mind cannot suffer it.

381 When we are too young, we do not judge well; so, also, when we are too old. If we do not think enough, or if we think too much on any matter, we get obstinate and infatuated about it. If one considers one's work immediately after having done it, one is entirely prepossessed in its favor; by delaying too long, one can no longer enter into the spirit of it. So with pictures seen from too far or too near; there is but one exact point which is the true place wherefrom

to look at them: the rest are too near, too far, too high, or too low. Perspective determines that point in the art of painting. But who shall determine it in truth and morality?

382 When all is equally agitated, nothing appears to be agitated, as in a ship. When all tend to debauchery, none appears to do so. He who stops draws attention to the excess of others, like a fixed point.

384 Contradiction is a bad sign of truth; several things which are certain are contradicted; several things which are false pass without contradiction. Contradiction is not a sign of falsity, nor the want of contradiction a sign of truth.

385 *Skepticism.* —Each thing here is partly true and partly false. Essential truth is not so; it is altogether pure and altogether true. This mixture dishonors and annihilates it. Nothing is purely true, and thus nothing is true, meaning by that pure truth. You will say it is true that homicide is wrong. Yes; for we know well the wrong and the false. But what will you say is good? Chastity? I say no; for the world would come to an end. Marriage? No; continence is better. Not to kill? No; for lawlessness would be horrible, and the wicked would kill all the good. To kill? No; for that destroys nature. We possess truth and goodness only in part, and mingled with falsehood and evil.

386 If we dreamt the same thing every night, it would affect us as much as the objects we see every day. And if an artisan were sure to dream every night for twelve hours' duration that he was a king, I believe he would be almost as happy as a king, who should dream every night for twelve hours on end that he was an artisan.

If we were to dream every night that we were pursued by enemies, and harassed by these painful phantoms, or that we passed every day in different occupations, as in making a voyage, we should suffer almost as much as if it were real, and should fear to sleep, as we fear to wake when we dread in fact to enter on such mishaps. And, indeed, it would cause pretty nearly the same discomforts as the reality.

But since dreams are all different, and each single one is diversified, what is seen in them affects us much less than what we see when awake, because of its continuity, which is not, however, so continuous and level as not to change too; but it changes less abruptly, except rarely, as when we travel, and then we say, "It seems to me I am dreaming." For life is a dream a little less inconstant.

389 Ecclesiastes shows that man without God is in total ignorance and inevitable misery. For it is wretched to have the wish, but not the power. Now he would be happy and assured of some truth, and yet he can neither know, nor desire not to know. He cannot even doubt.

390 My God! How foolish this talk is! "Would God have made the world to damn it? Would He ask so much from persons so weak?" etc. Skepticism is the cure for this evil, and will take down this vanity.

393 It is a singular thing to consider that there are people in the world who, having renounced all the laws of God and nature, have made laws for themselves which they strictly obey, as, for instance, the soldiers of Mahomet, robbers, heretics, etc. It is the same with logicians. It seems that their license must be without any limits or barriers, since they have broken through so many that are so just and sacred.

394 All the principles of skeptics, stoics, atheists, etc., are true. But their conclusions are false, because the opposite principles are also true.

395 Instinct, reason. —We have an incapacity of proof, insurmountable by all dogmatism. We have an idea of truth, invincible to all skepticism.

396 Two things instruct man about his whole nature; instinct and experience.

397 The greatness of man is great in that he knows himself to be miserable. A tree does not know itself to be miserable. It is then being miserable to know oneself to be miserable; but it is also being great to know that one is miserable.

398 All these same miseries prove man's greatness. They are the miseries of a great lord, of a deposed king.

399 We are not miserable without feeling it. A ruined house is not miserable. Man only is miserable. *Ego vir videns* [Lamentations].

400 *The greatness of man.* —We have so great an idea of the soul of man that we cannot endure being despised, or not being esteemed by any soul; and all the happiness of men consists in this esteem.

405 *Contradiction.* —Pride counterbalancing all miseries. Man either hides his miseries, or, if he discloses them, glories in knowing them.

406 Pride counterbalances and takes away all miseries. Here is a strange monster, and a very plain aberration. He is fallen from his place, and is anxiously seeking it. This is what all men do. Let us see who will have found it.

408 Evil is easy, and has infinite forms; good is almost unique. But a certain kind of evil is as difficult to find as what we call good; and often on this account such particular evil gets passed off as good. An extraordinary greatness of soul is needed in order to attain to it as well as to good.

409 *The greatness of man.* —The greatness of man is so evident, that it is even proved by his wretchedness. For what in animals is nature we call in man wretchedness; by which we recognize that, his nature being now like that of animals, he has fallen from a better nature which once was his.

For who is unhappy at not being a king, except a deposed king? Was Paulus Æmilius unhappy at being no longer consul? On the contrary, everybody thought him happy in having been consul, because the office could only be held for a time. But men thought Perseus so unhappy in being no longer king, because the condition of kingship implied his being always king, that they thought it strange that he endured life. Who is unhappy at having only one mouth? And who is not unhappy at having only one eye? Probably no man ever ventured to mourn at not having three eyes. But any one is inconsolable at having none.

411 Notwithstanding the sight of all our miseries, which press upon us and take us by the throat, we have an instinct which we cannot repress, and which lifts us up.

412 There is internal war in man between reason and the passions.

If he had only reason without passions [. . .]

If he had only passions without reason [. . .]

But having both, he cannot be without strife, being unable to be at peace with the one without being at war with the other. Thus he is always divided against, and opposed to himself.

413 This internal war of reason against the passions has made a division of those who would have peace into two sects. The first would renounce their passions, and become gods; the others would renounce reason, and become brute beasts (Des Barreaux). But neither can do so, and reason still remains, to condemn the vileness and injustice of the passions, and to trouble the repose of those who abandon themselves to them; and the passions keep always alive in those who would renounce them.

414 Men are so necessarily mad, that not to be mad would amount to another form of madness.

415 The nature of man may be viewed in two ways: the one according to its end, and then he is great and incomparable; the other according to the multitude, just as we judge of the nature of the horse and the dog, popularly, by seeing its fleetness, *et animum arcendi*; and then man is abject and vile. These are the two ways which make us judge of him differently, and which occasion such disputes among philosophers.

For one denies the assumption of the other. One says, "He is not born for this end, for all his actions are repugnant to it." The other says, "He forsakes his end, when he does these base actions."

417 This twofold nature of man is so evident that some have thought that we had two souls. A single subject seemed to them incapable of such sudden variations from unmeasured presumption to a dreadful dejection of heart.

418 It is dangerous to make man see too clearly his equality with the brutes without showing him his greatness. It is also dangerous to make him see his greatness too clearly, apart from his vileness. It is still more dangerous to leave him in ignorance of both. But it is very

advantageous to show him both. Man must not think that he is on a level either with the brutes or with the angels, nor must he be ignorant of both sides of his nature; but he must know both.

420 If he exalt himself, I humble him; if he humble himself, I exalt him; and I always contradict him, till he understands that he is an incomprehensible monster.

421 I blame equally those who choose to praise man, those who choose to blame him, and those who choose to amuse themselves; and I can only approve of those who seek with lamentation.

422 It is good to be tired and wearied by the vain search after the true good, that we may stretch out our arms to the Redeemer.

423 *Contraries. After having shown the vileness and the greatness of man.* —Let man now know his value. Let him love himself, for there is in him a nature capable of good; but let him not for this reason love the vileness which is in him. Let him despise himself, for this capacity is barren; but let him not therefore despise this natural capacity. Let him hate himself, let him love himself; he has within him the capacity of knowing the truth and of being happy, but he possesses no truth, either constant or satisfactory.

I would then lead man to the desire of finding truth; to be free from passions, and ready to follow it where he may find it, knowing how much his knowledge is obscured by the passions. I would indeed that he should hate in himself the lust which determined his will by itself, so that it may not blind him in making his choice, and may not hinder him when he has chosen.

424 All these contradictions, which seem most to keep me from the knowledge of religion, have led me most quickly to the true one.

20

Baruch Spinoza

The Ethics (1677)

Part I: Concerning God

DEFINITIONS

1 BY THAT WHICH IS SELF-CAUSED I MEAN THAT WHOSE ESSENCE involves existence; or that whose nature can be conceived only as existing.

2 A thing is said to be finite in its own kind (in suo genere finita) when it can be limited by another thing of the same nature. For example, a body is said to be finite because we can always conceive of another body greater than it. So, too, a thought is limited by another thought. But body is not limited by thought, nor thought by body.

3 By substance I mean that which is in itself and is conceived through itself; that is, that the conception of which does not require the conception of another thing from which it has to be formed.

4 By attribute I mean that which the intellect perceives of substance as constituting its essence.

5 By mode I mean the affections of substance; that is, that which is in something else and is conceived through something else.

6 By God I mean an absolutely infinite being; that is, substance consisting of infinite attributes, each of which expresses eternal and infinite essence.

Explication

I say 'absolutely infinite', not 'infinite in its kind'. For if a thing is only infinite in its kind, one may deny that it has infinite attributes. But if a thing is absolutely infinite, whatever expresses essence and does not involve any negation belongs to its essence.

7   That thing is said to be free (*liber*) which exists solely from the necessity of its own nature, and is determined to action by itself alone. A thing is said to be necessary (*necessarius*) or rather, constrained (*coactus*), if it is determined by another thing to exist and to act in a definite and determinate way.

8   By eternity I mean existence itself insofar as it is conceived as necessarily following solely from the definition of an eternal thing.

Explication

For such existence is conceived as an eternal truth, just as is the essence of the thing, and therefore cannot be explicated through duration or time, even if duration be conceived as without beginning and end.

AXIOMS

1   All things that are, are either in themselves or in something else.

2   That which cannot be conceived through another thing must be conceived through itself.

3   From a given determinate cause there necessarily follows an effect; on the other hand, if there be no determinate cause it is impossible that an effect should follow.

4   The knowledge of an effect depends on, and involves, the knowledge of the cause.

5   Things which have nothing in common with each other cannot be understood through each other; that is, the conception of the one does not involve the conception of the other.

6   A true idea must agree with that of which it is the idea (*ideatum*).

7   If a thing can be conceived as not existing, its essence does not involve existence.

PROPOSITION 1

Substance is by nature prior to its affections.

Proof

This is evident from Defs. 3 and 5.

PROPOSITION 2

Two substances having different attributes have nothing in common.

Proof

This too is evident from Def. 3; for each substance must be in itself and be conceived through itself; that is, the conception of the one does not involve the conception of the other.

PROPOSITION 3

When things have nothing in common, one cannot be the cause of the other.

Proof

If things have nothing in common, then (Ax.5) they cannot be understood through one another, and so (Ax.4) one cannot be the cause of the other.

PROPOSITION 11

God, or substance consisting of infinite attributes, each of which expresses eternal and infinite essence, necessarily exists.

Proof

If you deny this, conceive, if you can, that God does not exist. Therefore (Ax.7) his essence does not involve existence. But this is absurd (Pr.7). Therefore God necessarily exists.

Second Proof

For every thing a cause or reason must be assigned either for its existence or for its non-existence. For example, if a triangle exists, there must be a reason, or cause, for its existence. If it does not exist, there must be a reason or cause which prevents it from existing, or which annuls its existence. Now this reason or cause must either be contained in the nature of the thing or be external to it. For example, the reason why a square circle does not exist is indicated by its very nature, in that it involves a contradiction. On the other hand, the reason for the existence of substance also follows from its nature alone, in that it involves existence (Pr.7). But the reason for the existence or non-existence of a circle or a triangle does not follow from their nature, but from the order of universal corporeal Nature. For it is from this latter that it necessarily follows that either the triangle necessarily exists at this moment or that its present existence is impossible. This is self-evident, and therefrom it follows that a thing necessarily exists if there is no reason or cause which prevents its existence. Therefore if there can be no reason or cause which prevents God from existing or which annuls his existence, we are bound to conclude that he necessarily exists. But if there were such a reason or cause, it would have to be either within God's nature or external to it; that is, it would have to be in another substance of another nature. For if it were of the same nature, by that very fact it would be granted that God exists. But a substance of another nature would have nothing in common with God (Pr.2), and so could neither posit nor annul his existence. Since therefore there cannot be external to God's nature a reason or cause that would annul God's existence, then if indeed he does not exist, the reason or cause must necessarily be in God's nature, which would therefore involve a contradiction. But to affirm this of a Being absolutely infinite and in the highest degree perfect is absurd. Therefore neither in God nor external to God is there any cause or reason which would annul his existence. Therefore God necessarily exists.

PROPOSITION 13

Absolutely infinite substance is indivisible.

Proof

If it were divisible, the parts into which it would be divided will either retain the nature of absolutely infinite substance, or not. In the first case, there would therefore be several substances of the same nature, which is absurd (Pr.5). In the second case, absolutely infinite substance can cease to be, which is also absurd (Pr.11).

Corollary

From this it follows that no substance, and consequently no corporeal substance, insofar as it is substance, is divisible.

Scholium

The indivisibility of substance can be more easily understood merely from the fact that the nature of substance can be conceived only as infinite, and that a part of substance can mean only finite substance, which involves an obvious contradiction (Pr.8).

PROPOSITION 18

God is the immanent, not the transitive, cause of all things.

Proof

All things that are, are in God, and must be conceived through God (Pr.15), and so (Cor. 1 Pr.16) God is the cause of the things that are in him, which is the first point. Further, there can be no substance external to God (Pr.14); that is (Def.3), a thing which is in itself external to God—which is the second point. Therefore God is the immanent, not the transitive, cause of all things.

PROPOSITION 19

God, that is, all the attributes of God, are eternal.

Proof

God is substance (Def.6) which necessarily exists (Pr.11); that is, (Pr.7) a thing to whose nature it pertains to exist, or—and this is the same thing—a thing from whose definition existence follows; and so (Def.8) God is eternal. Further, by the attributes of God must be understood that which expresses the essence of the Divine substance (Def.4), that is, that which pertains to substance. It is this, I say, which the attributes themselves must involve. But eternity pertains to the nature of substance (as I have shown in Pr.7). Therefore each of the attributes must involve eternity, and so they are all eternal.

Scholium

This proposition is also perfectly clear from the manner in which I proved the existence of God (Pr. 11). From this proof, I repeat, it is obvious that God's existence is, like his essence, an eternal truth. Again, I have also proved God's eternity in another way in Proposition 19 of my *Principles of the Philosophy of Descartes,* and there is no need here to go over that ground again.

PROPOSITION 36

Nothing exists from whose nature an effect does not follow.

Proof

Whatever exists expresses God's nature or essence in a definite and determinate way (Cor. Pr.25); that is, (Pr.34), whatever exists expresses God's power, which is the cause of all things, in a definite and determinate way, and so (Pr. 16) some effect must follow from it.

APPENDIX

I have now explained the nature and properties of God: that he necessarily exists, that he is one alone, that he is and acts solely from the necessity of his own nature, that he is the free cause of all things and how so, that all things are in God and are so dependent on him that they can neither be nor be conceived without him, and lastly, that all things have been predetermined by God, not from his free will or absolute pleasure, but from the absolute nature of God, his infinite power. Furthermore, whenever the opportunity arose I have striven to remove prejudices that might hinder the apprehension of my proofs. But since there still remain a considerable number of prejudices, which have been, and still are, an obstacle—indeed, a very great obstacle—to the acceptance of the concatenation of things in the manner which I have expounded, I have thought it proper at this point to bring these prejudices before the bar of reason.

Now all the prejudices which I intend to mention here turn on this one point, the widespread belief among men that all things in Nature are like themselves in acting with an end in view. Indeed, they hold it as certain that God himself directs everything to a fixed end; for they say that God has made everything for man's sake and has made man so that he should worship God. So this is the first point I shall consider, seeking the reason why most people are victims of this prejudice and why all are so naturally disposed to accept it. Secondly, I shall demonstrate its falsity; and lastly I shall show how it has been the source of misconceptions about good and bad, right and wrong, praise and blame, order and confusion, beauty and ugliness, and the like.

However, it is not appropriate here to demonstrate the origin of these misconceptions from the nature of the human mind. It will suffice at this point if I take as my basis what must be universally admitted, that all men are born ignorant of the causes of things, that they all have a desire to seek their own advantage, a desire of which they are conscious. From this it follows, firstly, that men believe that they are free, precisely because they are conscious of their volitions and desires; yet concerning the causes that have determined them to desire and will they have not the faintest idea, because they are ignorant of them. Secondly, men act always with an end in view, to wit, the advantage that they seek. Hence it happens that they are always looking only for the final causes of things done, and are satisfied when they find them, having, of course, no reason for further doubt. But if they fail to discover them from some external source, they have no recourse but to turn to themselves, and to reflect on what ends would normally determine them to similar actions, and so they necessarily judge other minds by their own. Further, since they find within themselves and outside themselves a considerable number of means very convenient for the pursuit of their own advantage—as, for instance, eyes for seeing, teeth for chewing, cereals and living creatures for food, the sun for giving light, the sea for breeding fish—the result is that they look on all the things of Nature as means to their own advantage. And realising that these were found, not produced by them, they came to believe that there is someone else who produced these means for their use. For looking on things as means, they could not believe them to be self-created, but on the analogy of the means which they are accustomed to produce for themselves, they were bound to conclude that there was some governor or governors of Nature, endowed with human freedom, who have attended to all their needs and made everything for their use. And having no information on the subject, they also had to estimate the character of these rulers by their own, and so they asserted that the gods direct everything for man's use so that they may bind men to them and be held in the highest honour by them. So it came about that every individual devised different methods of worshipping God as he thought fit in order that God should love him beyond others and direct the whole of Nature so as to serve his blind cupidity and insatiable greed. Thus it was that this misconception developed into superstition and became deep-rooted in the minds of men, and it was for this reason that every man strove most earnestly to understand and to explain the final causes of all things. But in seeking to show that Nature does nothing in vain—that is, nothing that is not to man's advantage—they seem to have shown only this, that Nature and the gods are as crazy as mankind.

Consider, I pray, what has been the upshot. Among so many of Nature's blessings they were bound to discover quite a number of disasters, such as storms, earthquakes, diseases and so forth, and they maintained that these occurred because the gods were angry at the wrongs done to them by men, or the faults committed in the course of their worship. And although daily experience cried out against this and showed by any number of examples that blessings and disasters befall the godly and the ungodly alike without discrimination, they did not on that account abandon their ingrained prejudice. For they found it easier to regard this fact as one among other mysteries they could not understand and thus maintain their present and innate condition of ignorance rather than to demolish in its entirety the theory they had constructed and devise a new one. Hence they made it axiomatic that the judgment of the gods is far beyond man's understanding. Indeed, it is for this reason, and this reason only, that truth might have evaded mankind forever had not Mathematics, which is concerned not with ends but only with the essences and properties of figures, revealed to men a different standard of truth. And there are other causes too—there is no need to mention them here—which could have made men aware of these widespread misconceptions and brought them to a true knowledge of things.

I have thus sufficiently dealt with my first point. There is no need to spend time in going on to show that Nature has no fixed goal and that all final causes are but figments of the human imagination. For I think that this is now quite evident, both from the basic causes from which I have traced the origin of this misconception and from Proposition 16 and the Corollaries to Proposition 32, and in addition from the whole set of proofs I have adduced to show that all things in Nature proceed from an eternal necessity and with supreme perfection. But I will make this additional point, that this doctrine of Final Causes turns Nature completely upside down, for it regards as an effect that which is in fact a cause, and vice versa. Again, it makes that which is by nature first to be last; and finally, that which is highest and most perfect is held to be the most imperfect. Omitting the first two points as self-evident, Propositions 21, 22 and 23 make it clear that that effect is most perfect which is directly produced by God, and an effect is the less perfect in proportion to the number of intermediary causes required for its production. But if the things produced directly by God were brought about to enable him to attain an end, then of necessity the last things for the sake of which the earlier things were brought about would excel all others. Again, this doctrine negates God's perfection; for if God acts with an end in view, he must necessarily be seeking something that he lacks. And although theologians and metaphysicians may draw a distinction between a purpose arising from want and an assimilative purpose, they still admit that God has acted in all things for the sake of himself, and not for the sake of the things to be created. For prior to creation they are not able to point to anything but

God as a purpose for God's action. Thus they have to admit that God lacked and desired those things for the procurement of which he willed to create the means—as is self-evident.

I must not fail to mention here that the advocates of this doctrine, eager to display their talent in assigning purpose to things, have introduced a new style of argument to prove their doctrine, i.e. a reduction, not to the impossible, but to ignorance, thus revealing the lack of any other argument in its favour. For example, if a stone falls from the roof on somebody's head and kills him, by this method of arguing they will prove that the stone fell in order to kill the man; for if it had not fallen for this purpose by the will of God, how could so many circumstances (and there are often many coinciding circumstances) have chanced to concur? Perhaps you will reply that the event occurred because the wind was blowing and the man was walking that way. But they will persist in asking why the wind blew at that time and why the man was walking that way at that very time. If you again reply that the wind sprang up at that time because on the previous day the sea had begun to toss after a period of calm and that the man had been invited by a friend, they will again persist—for there is no end to questions—"But why did the sea toss, and why was the man invited for that time?" And so they will go on and on asking the causes of causes, until you take refuge in the will of God—that is, the sanctuary of ignorance. Similarly, when they consider the structure of the human body, they are astonished, and being ignorant of the causes of such skilful work they conclude that it is fashioned not by mechanical art but by divine or supernatural art, and is so arranged that no one part shall injure another.

As a result, he who seeks the true causes of miracles and is eager to understand the works of Nature as a scholar, and not just to gape at them like a fool, is universally considered an impious heretic and denounced by those to whom the common people bow down as interpreters of Nature and the gods. For these people know that the dispelling of ignorance would entail the disappearance of that sense of awe which is the one and only support for their argument and for the safeguarding of their authority. But I will leave this subject and proceed to the third point that I proposed to deal with.

When men became convinced that everything that is created is created on their behalf, they were bound to consider as the most important quality in every individual thing that which was most useful to them, and to regard as of the highest excellence all those things by which they were most benefited. Hence they came to form these abstract notions to explain the natures of things:—Good, Bad, Order, Confusion, Hot, Cold, Beauty, Ugliness; and since they believe that they are free, the following abstract notions came into being:—Praise, Blame, Right, Wrong. The latter I shall deal with later on after I have treated of human nature; at this point I shall briefly explain the former.

All that conduces to well-being and to the worship of God they call Good, and the contrary, Bad. And since those who do not understand the nature of things, but only imagine things, make no affirmative judgments about things themselves and mistake their imagination for intellect, they are firmly convinced that there is order in things, ignorant as they are of things and of their own nature. For when things are in such arrangement that, being presented to us through our senses, we can readily picture them and thus readily remember them, we say that they are well arranged; if the contrary, we say that they are ill-arranged, or confused. And since those things we can readily picture we find pleasing compared with other things, men prefer order to confusion, as though order were something in Nature other than what is relative to our imagination. And they say that God has created all things in an orderly way, without realising that they are thus attributing human imagination to God—unless perchance they mean that God, out of consideration for the human imagination, arranged all things in the way that men could most easily imagine. And perhaps they will find no obstacle in the fact that there are any number of things that far surpass our imagination, and a considerable number that confuse the imagination because of its weakness.

But I have devoted enough time to this. The other notions, too, are nothing but modes of imagining whereby the imagination is affected in various ways, and yet the ignorant consider them as important attributes of things because they believe—as I have said—that all things were made on their behalf, and they call a thing's nature good or bad, healthy or rotten and corrupt, according to its effect on them. For instance, if the motion communicated to our nervous system by objects presented through our eyes is conducive to our feeling of well-being, the objects which are its cause are said to be beautiful, while the objects which provoke a contrary motion are called ugly. Those things that we sense through the nose are called fragrant or fetid, through the tongue sweet or bitter, tasty or tasteless, those that we sense by touch are called hard or soft, rough or smooth, and so on. Finally, those that we sense through our ears are said to give forth noise, sound, or harmony, the last of which has driven men to such madness that they used to believe that even God delights in harmony. There are philosophers who have convinced themselves that the motions of the heavens give rise to harmony. All this goes to show that everyone's judgment is a function of the disposition of his brain, or rather, that he mistakes for reality the way his imagination is affected. Hence it is no wonder—as we should note in passing—that we find so many controversies arising among men, resulting finally in scepticism. For although human bodies agree in many respects, there are very many differences, and so one man thinks good what another thinks bad; what to one man is well-ordered, to another is confused; what to one is pleasing, to another is displeasing, and so forth. I say no more here because this is not the place to treat at length of this subject, and also because all are well acquainted with it from experience. Everybody knows those sayings:—"So many heads, so many opinions," "everyone is wise in his own sight," "brains differ as much as palates," all of which show clearly that men's judgment is a function of the disposition of the brain, and they are guided by imagination rather than intellect. For if men understood things, all that I have put forward would be found, if not attractive, at any rate convincing, as Mathematics attests.

We see therefore that all the notions whereby the common people are wont to explain Nature are merely modes of imagining, and denote not the nature of any thing but only the constitution of the imagination. And because these notions have names as if they were the names of entities existing independently of the imagination I call them 'entities of imagination' (entia imaginationis) rather than 'entities of reason' (entia rationis). So all arguments drawn from such notions against me can be easily refuted. For many are wont to argue on the following lines: if everything has followed from the necessity of God's most perfect nature, why does Nature display so many imperfections, such as rottenness to the point of putridity, nauseating ugliness, confusion, evil, sin, and so on? But, as I have just pointed out, they are easily refuted. For the perfection of things should be measured solely from their own nature and power; nor are things more or less perfect to the extent that they please or offend human senses, serve or oppose human interests. As to those who ask why God did not create all men in such a way that they should be governed solely by reason, I make only this reply, that he lacked not material for creating all things from the highest to the lowest degree of perfection; or, to speak more accurately, the laws of his nature were so comprehensive as to suffice for the production of everything that can be conceived by an infinite intellect, as I proved in Proposition 16.

These are the misconceptions which I undertook to deal with at this point. Any other misconception of this kind can be corrected by everyone with a little reflection.

Part II: On the Nature and Origin of the Mind

I NOW PASS ON TO THE EXPLICATION OF THOSE THINGS that must necessarily have followed from the essence of God, the eternal and infinite Being; not indeed all of them—for we proved in Proposition 16 Part I that from his essence there must follow infinite things in infinite ways— but only those things that can lead us as it were by the hand to the knowledge of the human mind and its utmost blessedness.

DEFINITIONS

1 By 'body' I understand a mode that expresses in a definite and determinate way God's essence in so far as he is considered as an extended thing. (See Cor. Pr.25, I)

2 I say that there pertains to the essence of a thing that which, when granted, the thing is necessarily posited, and by the annulling of which the thing is necessarily annulled; or that without which the thing can neither be nor be conceived, and, vice versa, that which cannot be or be conceived without the thing.

3 By idea I understand a conception of the Mind which the Mind forms because it is a thinking thing.

Explication

I say 'conception' rather than 'perception' because the term perception seems to indicate that the Mind is passive to its object, whereas conception seems to express an activity of the Mind.

4 By an adequate idea I mean an idea which, in so far as it is considered in itself without relation to its object, has all the properties—that is, intrinsic characteristics—of a true idea.

Explication

I say 'intrinsic' so as to exclude the extrinsic characteristic—to wit, the agreement of the idea with that of which it is an idea (ideatum).

5 Duration is the indefinite continuance of existing.

Explication

I say 'indefinite' because it can in no wise be determined through the nature of the existing thing, nor again by the thing's efficient cause, which necessarily posits, but does not annul, the existence of the thing.

6 By reality and perfection I mean the same thing.

7 By individual things (res singulares) I mean things that are finite and have a determinate existence. If several individual things concur in one act in such a way as to be all together the simultaneous cause of one effect, I consider them all, in that respect, as one individual.

AXIOMS

1 The essence of man does not involve necessary existence; that is, from the order of Nature it is equally possible that a certain man exists or does not exist.

2 Man thinks.

3 Modes of thinking such as love, desire, or whatever emotions are designated by name, do not occur unless there is in the same individual the idea of the thing loved, desired, etc. But the idea can be without any other mode of thinking.

4 We feel a certain body to be affected in many ways.

5 We do not feel or perceive any individual things except bodies and modes of thinking. [N.B.: For Postulates, see after Proposition 13.]

PROPOSITION 1

Thought is an attribute of God; i.e. God is a thinking thing.

Proof

Individual thoughts, or this and that thought, are modes expressing the nature of God in a definite and determinate way (Cor.Pr.25,I). Therefore there belongs to God (Def.5,I) an attribute the conception of which is involved in all individual thoughts, and through which they are conceived. Thought, therefore, is one of God's infinite attributes, expressing the eternal and infinite essence of God (Def.6,I); that is, God is a thinking thing.

Scholium

This Proposition is also evident from the fact that we can conceive of an infinite thinking being. For the more things a thinking being can think, the more reality or perfection we conceive it to have. Therefore a being that can think infinite things in infinite ways is by virtue of its thinking necessarily infinite. Since therefore by merely considering Thought we conceive an infinite being, Thought is necessarily one of the infinite attributes of God (Defs. 4 and 6,I), as we set out to prove.

PROPOSITION 2

Extension is an attribute of God; i.e. God is an extended thing.

Proof

This Proposition is proved in the same way as the preceding proposition.

PROPOSITION 3

In God there is necessarily the idea both of his essence and of everything that necessarily follows from his essence.

Proof

For God can (Pr.1,II) think infinite things in infinite ways, or (what is the same thing, by Pr.16,I) can form the idea of his own essence and of everything that necessarily follows from it. But all that is in God's power necessarily exists (Pr.35,I). Therefore such an idea necessarily exists, and only in God (Pr.15,I).

Scholium

By God's power the common people understand free-will and God's right over all things that are, which things are therefore commonly considered as contingent. They say that God has power to destroy everything and bring it to nothing. Furthermore, they frequently compare God's power with that of kings. But this doctrine we have refuted in Cors. 1 and 2, Pr.32,I; and in Pr.16,I we proved that God acts by the same necessity whereby he understands himself; that is, just as it follows from the necessity of the divine nature (as is universally agreed) that God understands himself, by that same necessity it also follows that God acts infinitely in infinite ways. Again, we showed in Pr.34,I that God's power is nothing but God's essence in action, and so it is as impossible for us to conceive that God does not act as that God does not exist. Furthermore, if one wished to pursue the matter, I could easily show here that the power that common people assign to God is not only a human power (which shows that they conceive God as a man or like a man) but also involves negation of power. But I am reluctant to hold forth so often on the same subject. I merely request the reader most earnestly to reflect again and again on what we said on this subject in Part I from Proposition 16 to the end. For nobody will rightly apprehend what I am trying to say unless he takes great care not to confuse God's power with a king's human power or right.

PROPOSITION 4

The idea of God, from which infinite things follow in infinite ways, must be one, and one only.

Proof

Infinite intellect comprehends nothing but the attributes of God and his affections (Pr.30,I). But God is one, and one only (Cor.1,Pr.14,I). Therefore the idea of God, from which infinite things follow in infinite ways, must be one, and one only.

PROPOSITION 5

The formal being of ideas recognizes God as its cause only in so far as he is considered as a thinking thing, and not in so far as he is explicated by any other attribute; that is, the ideas both of God's attributes and of individual things recognize as their efficient cause not the things of which they are ideas,—that is, the things perceived,—but God himself in so far as he is a thinking thing.

Proof

This is evident from Pr.3,II. For there our conclusion that God can form the idea of his own essence and of everything that necessarily follows therefrom was inferred solely from God's being a thinking thing, and not from his being the object of his own idea. Therefore the formal being of ideas recognizes God as its cause in so far as he is a thinking thing. But there is another proof, as follows. The formal being of ideas is a mode of thinking (as is self-evident); that is, (Cor.Pr.25,I) a mode which expresses in a definite manner the nature of God in so far as he is a thinking thing, and so does not involve (Pr.10,I) the conception of any other attribute of God. Consequently (Ax.4,I), it is the effect of no other attribute but Thought; and so the formal being of ideas recognizes God as its cause only in so far as he is considered as a thinking thing.

PROPOSITION 6

The modes of any attribute have God for their cause only in so far as he is considered under that attribute, and not in so far as he is considered under any other attribute.

Proof

Each attribute is conceived through itself independently of any other (Pr.10,I). Therefore the modes of any attribute involve the conception of their own attribute, and not that of any other. Therefore they have God for their cause only in so far as he is considered under the attribute of which they are modes, and not in so far as he is considered under any other attribute (Ax.4,I).

Corollary

Hence it follows that the formal being of things that are not modes of thinking does not follow from the nature of God by reason of his first having known them; rather, the objects of ideas follow and are inferred from their own attributes in the same way and by the same necessity as we have shown ideas to follow from the attribute of Thought.

PROPOSITION 7

The order and connection of ideas is the same as the order and connection of things.

Proof

This is evident from Ax.4,I; for the idea of what is caused depends on the knowledge of the cause of which it is the effect.

Corollary

Hence it follows that God's power of thinking is coextensive with his actualized power of acting. That is, whatever follows formally from the infinite nature of God, all this follows from the idea of God with the same order and the same connection, as an object of thought in God.

21

Edmund Burke

A Philosophical Enquiry into the Origin of Our Ideas of the Sublime and Beautiful (1756)

Section I: Of the Passion Caused by the Sublime

The passion caused by the great and sublime in *nature*, when those causes operate most powerfully, is astonishment: and astonishment is that state of the soul in which all its motions are suspended, with some degree of horror. In this case the mind is so entirely filled with its object, that it cannot entertain any other, nor by consequence reason on that object which employs it. Hence arises the great power of the sublime, that, far from being produced by them, it anticipates our reasonings, and hurries us on by an irresistible force. Astonishment, as I have said, is the effect of the sublime in its highest degree; the inferior effects are admiration, reverence, and respect.

Section II: Terror

No passion so effectually robs the mind of all its powers of acting and reasoning as *fear*. For fear being an apprehension of pain or death, it operates in a manner that resembles actual pain. Whatever therefore is terrible, with regard to sight, is sublime too, whether this cause of terror be endued with greatness of dimensions or not; for it is impossible to look on anything as trifling, or contemptible, that may be dangerous. There are many animals, who, though far from being large, are yet capable of raising ideas of the sublime, because they are considered as objects of terror. As serpents and poisonous animals of almost all kinds. And to things of great dimensions, if we annex an adventitious idea of terror, they become without comparison greater. A level plain of a vast extent on land, is certainly no mean idea; the prospect of such a plain may be as extensive as a prospect of the ocean; but can it ever fill the mind with anything so great as the ocean itself? This is owing to several causes; but it is owing to none more than this, that the ocean is an object of no small terror. Indeed terror is in all cases whatsoever, either more openly or latently, the ruling principle of the sublime. Several languages bear a strong testimony to the affinity of these ideas. They frequently use the same word to signify indifferently the modes of astonishment or admiration and those of terror. Θάμβος is in Greek either fear or wonder; δεινός is terrible or respectable; αἰδέο to reverence or to fear. *Vereor* in Latin is what αἰδέο is in Greek. The Romans used the verb *stupeo*, a term which strongly marks the state of an astonished mind, to express the effect either of simple fear, or of astonishment; the word *attonitus* (thunderstruck) is equally expressive of the alliance of these ideas; and do not the French *étonnement*, and the English *astonishment* and *amazement*, point out as clearly the kindred emotions which attend fear and wonder? They who have a more general knowledge of languages, could produce, I make no doubt, many other and equally striking examples.

Section III: Obscurity

To make anything very terrible, obscurity seems in general to be necessary. When we know the full extent of any danger, when we can accustom our eyes to it, a great deal of the apprehension vanishes. Every one will be sensible of this, who considers how greatly night adds to our dread, in all cases of danger, and how much the notions of ghosts and goblins, of which none can form clear ideas, affect minds which give credit to the popular tales concerning such sorts of beings. Those despotic governments which are founded on the passions of men, and principally upon the passion of fear, keep their chief as much as may be from the public eye. The policy has been the same in many cases of religion. Almost all the heathen temples were dark. Even in the barbarous temples of the Americans at this day, they keep their idol in a dark part of the hut, which is consecrated to his worship. For this purpose too the Druids performed all their ceremonies in the bosom of the darkest woods, and in the shade of the oldest and most spreading oaks. No person seems better to have understood the secret of heightening, or of setting terrible things, if I may use the expression, in their strongest light, by the force of a judicious obscurity than Milton. His description of death in the second book is admirably studied; it is astonishing with what a gloomy pomp, with what a significant and expressive uncertainty of strokes and coloring, he has finished the portrait of the king of terrors:

> "The other shape,
> If shape it might be called that shape had none
> Distinguishable, in member, joint, or limb;

Or substance might be called that shadow seemed;

For each seemed either; black he stood as night;

Fierce as ten furies; terrible as hell;

And shook a deadly dart. What seemed his head

The likeness of a kingly crown had on."

In this description all is dark, uncertain, confused, terrible, and sublime to the last degree.

[...]

Section V: Power

Besides those things which *directly* suggest the idea of danger, and those which produce a similar effect from a mechanical cause, I know of nothing sublime, which is not some modification of power. And this branch rises, as naturally as the other two branches, from terror, the common stock of everything that is sublime. The idea of power, at first view, seems of the class of those indifferent ones, which may equally belong to pain or to pleasure. But in reality, the affection arising from the idea of vast power is extremely remote from that neutral character. For first, we must remember that the idea of pain, in its highest degree, is much stronger than the highest degree of pleasure; and that it preserves the same superiority through all the subordinate gradations. From hence it is, that where the chances for equal degrees of suffering or enjoyment are in any sort equal, the idea of the suffering must always be prevalent. And indeed the ideas of pain, and, above all, of death, are so very affecting, that whilst we remain in the presence of whatever is supposed to have the power of inflicting either, it is impossible to be perfectly free from terror. Again, we know by experience, that, for the enjoyment of pleasure, no great efforts of power are at all necessary; nay, we know that such efforts would go a great way towards destroying our satisfaction: for pleasure must be stolen, and not forced upon us; pleasure follows the will; and therefore we are generally affected with it by many things of a force greatly inferior to our own. But pain is always inflicted by a power in some way superior, because we never submit to pain willingly. So that strength, violence, pain, and terror, are ideas that rush in upon the mind together. Look at a man, or any other animal of prodigious strength, and what is your idea before reflection? Is it that this strength will be subservient to you, to your ease, to your pleasure, to your interest in any sense? No; the emotion you feel is, lest this enormous strength should be employed to the purposes of rapine and destruction. That power derives all its sublimity from the terror with which it is generally accompanied, will appear evidently from its effect in the very few cases, in which it may be possible to strip a considerable degree of strength of its ability to hurt. When you do this, you spoil it of everything sublime, and it immediately becomes contemptible. An ox is a creature of vast strength; but he is an innocent creature, extremely serviceable, and not at all dangerous;

for which reason the idea of an ox is by no means grand. A bull is strong too; but his strength is of another kind; often very destructive, seldom (at least amongst us) of any use in our business; the idea of a bull is therefore great, and it has frequently a place in sublime descriptions, and elevating comparisons. Let us look at another strong animal, in the two distinct lights in which we may consider him. The horse in the light of an useful beast, fit for the plough, the road, the draft; in every social useful light, the horse has nothing sublime; but is it thus that we are affected with him, *whose neck is clothed with thunder, the glory of whose nostrils is terrible, who swalloweth the ground with fierceness and rage, neither believeth that it is the sound of the trumpet?* In this description, the useful character of the horse entirely disappears, and the terrible and sublime blaze out together. We have continually about us animals of a strength that is considerable, but not pernicious. Amongst these we never look for the sublime; it comes upon us in the gloomy forest, and in the howling wilderness, in the form of the lion, the tiger, the panther, or rhinoceros. Whenever strength is only useful, and employed for our benefit or our pleasure, then it is never sublime; for nothing can act agreeably to us, that does not act in conformity to our will; but to act agreeably to our will, it must be subject to us, and therefore can never be the cause of a grand and commanding conception. The description of the wild ass, in Job, is worked up into no small sublimity, merely by insisting on his freedom, and his setting mankind at defiance; otherwise the description of such an animal could have had nothing noble in it. *Who hath loosed* (says he) *the bands of the wild ass? whose house I have made the wilderness and the barren land his dwellings. He scorneth the multitude of the city, neither regardeth he the voice of the driver. The range of the mountains is his pasture.* The magnificent description of the unicorn and of leviathan, in the same book, is full of the same heightening circumstances: *Will the unicorn be willing to serve thee? canst thou bind the unicorn with his band in the furrow? wilt thou trust him because his strength is great?—Canst thou draw out leviathan with an hook? will he make a covenant with thee? wilt thou take him for a servant forever? shall not one be cast down even at the sight of him?* In short, wheresoever we find strength, and in what light soever we look upon power, we shall all along observe the sublime the concomitant of terror, and contempt the attendant on a strength that is subservient and innoxious. The race of dogs, in many of their kinds, have generally a competent degree of strength and swiftness; and they exert these and other valuable qualities which they possess, greatly to our convenience and pleasure. Dogs are indeed the most social, affectionate, and amiable animals of the whole brute creation; but love approaches much nearer to contempt than is commonly imagined; and accordingly, though we caress dogs, we borrow from them an appellation of the most despicable kind, when we employ terms of reproach; and this appellation is the common mark of the last vileness and contempt in every language. Wolves have not more strength than several species of dogs; but, on account of their unmanageable fierceness, the idea of a wolf is not despicable; it is not excluded from grand descriptions and similitudes.

Thus we are affected by strength, which is *natural* power. The power which arises from institution in kings and commanders, has the same connection with terror. Sovereigns are frequently addressed with the title of *dread majesty*. And it may be observed, that young persons, little acquainted with the world, and who have not been used to approach men in power, are commonly struck with an awe which takes away the free use of their faculties. *When I prepared my seat in the street,* (says Job,) *the young men saw me, and hid themselves.* Indeed so natural is this timidity with regard to power, and so strongly does it inhere in our constitution, that very few are able to conquer it, but by mixing much in the business of the great world, or by using no small violence to their natural dispositions. I know some people are of opinion, that no awe, no degree of terror, accompanies the idea of power; and have hazarded to affirm, that we can contemplate the idea of God himself without any such emotion. I purposely avoided, when I first considered this subject, to introduce the idea of that great and tremendous Being, as an example in an argument so light as this; though it frequently occurred to me, not as an objection to, but as a strong confirmation of, my notions in this matter. I hope, in what I am going to say, I shall avoid presumption, where it is almost impossible for any mortal to speak with strict propriety. I say then, that whilst we consider the Godhead merely as he is an object of the understanding, which forms a complex idea of power, wisdom, justice, goodness, all stretched to a degree far exceeding the bounds of our comprehension, whilst we consider the divinity in this refined and abstracted light, the imagination and passions are little or nothing affected. But because we are bound, by the condition of our nature, to ascend to these pure and intellectual ideas, through the medium of sensible images, and to judge of these divine qualities by their evident acts and exertions, it becomes extremely hard to disentangle our idea of the cause from the effect by which we are led to know it. Thus, when we contemplate the Deity, his attributes and their operation, coming united on the mind, form a sort of sensible image, and as such are capable of affecting the imagination. Now, though in a just idea of the Deity, perhaps none of his attributes are predominant, yet, to our imagination, his power is by far the most striking. Some reflection, some comparing, is necessary to satisfy us of his wisdom, his justice, and his goodness. To be struck with his power, it is only necessary that we should open our eyes. But whilst we contemplate so vast an object, under the arm, as it were, of almighty power, and invested upon every side with omnipresence, we shrink into the minuteness of our own nature, and are, in a manner, annihilated before him. And though a consideration of his other attributes may relieve, in some measure, our apprehensions; yet no conviction of the justice with which it is exercised, nor the mercy with which it is tempered, can wholly remove the terror that naturally arises from a force which nothing can withstand. If we rejoice, we rejoice with trembling; and even whilst we are receiving benefits, we cannot but shudder at a power which can confer benefits of such mighty importance. When the prophet David contemplated the wonders of wisdom and power which are displayed in the economy of man, he seems to be struck with a sort of divine horror, and cries out, *fearfully and wonderfully am I made!* An heathen poet has a sentiment of a similar nature; Horace looks upon it as the last effort of philosophical fortitude, to behold without terror and amazement, this immense and glorious fabric of the universe:

> Hunc solem, et stellas, et decedentia certis
>
> Tempora momentis, sunt qui formidine nulla
>
> Imbuti spectent.

Lucretius is a poet not to be suspected of giving way to superstitious terrors; yet, when he supposes the whole mechanism of nature laid open by the master of his philosophy, his transport on this magnificent view, which he has represented in the colors of such bold and lively poetry, is overcast with a shade of secret dread and horror:

> His ibi me rebus quædam divina voluptas
>
> Percipit, atque horror; quod sic natura, tua vi
>
> Tam manifesta patens, ex omni parte retecta est.

But the Scripture alone can supply ideas answerable to the majesty of this subject. In the Scripture, wherever God is represented as appearing or speaking, everything terrible in nature is called up to heighten the awe and solemnity of the Divine presence. The Psalms, and the prophetical books, are crowded with instances of this kind. *The earth shook,* (says the Psalmist,) *the heavens also dropped at the presence of the Lord.* And what is remarkable, the painting preserves the same character, not only when he is supposed descending to take vengeance upon the wicked, but even when he exerts the like plenitude of power in acts of beneficence to mankind. *Tremble, thou earth! at the presence of the Lord; at the presence of the God of Jacob; which turned the rock into standing water, the flint into a fountain of waters!* It were endless to enumerate all the passages, both in the sacred and profane writers, which establish the general sentiment of mankind, concerning the inseparable union of a sacred and reverential awe, with our ideas of the divinity. Hence the common maxim, *Primus in orbe deos fecit timor.* This maxim may be, as I believe it is, false with regard to the origin of religion. The maker of the maxim saw how inseparable these ideas were, without considering that the notion of some great power must be always precedent to our dread of it. But this dread must necessarily follow the idea of such a power, when it is once excited in the mind. It is on this principle that true religion has, and must have, so large a mixture of salutary fear; and that false religions have generally nothing else but fear to support them. Before the Christian religion had, as it were, humanized the idea of the Divinity, and brought it somewhat nearer to us, there was very little said of the love of God. The followers of Plato have something of it, and only something; the other writers of pagan antiquity, whether poets or philosophers, nothing at all.

And they who consider with what infinite attention, by what a disregard of every perishable object, through what long habits of piety and contemplation it is that any man is able to attain an entire love and devotion to the Deity, will easily perceive that it is not the first, the most natural, and the most striking effect which proceeds from that idea. Thus we have traced power through its several gradations unto the highest of all, where our imagination is finally lost; and we find terror, quite throughout the progress, its inseparable companion, and growing along with it, as far as we can possibly trace them. Now, as power is undoubtedly a capital source of the sublime, this will point out evidently from whence its energy is derived, and to what class of ideas we ought to unite it.

Section VI: Privation

ALL *general* privations are great, because they are all terrible; *vacuity, darkness, solitude,* and *silence.* With what a fire of imagination, yet with what severity of judgment, has Virgil amassed all these circumstances, where he knows that all the images of a tremendous dignity ought to be united at the mouth of hell! Where, before he unlocks the secrets of the great deep, he seems to be seized with a religious horror, and to retire astonished at the boldness of his own design:

Dii, quibus imperium est animarum, umbræque *silentes*!
Et Chaos, et Phlegethon! loca *nocte silentia* late!
Sit mihi fas audita loqui! sit numine vestro
Pandere res alta terra et *caligine* mersas!
Ibant *obscuri, sola* sub *nocte,* per *umbram,*
Perque domos Ditis *vacuas,* et *inania* regus.
"Ye subterraneous gods! whose awful sway
The gliding ghosts, and *silent* shades obey:
O Chaos hoar! and Phlegethon profound!
Whose solemn empire stretches wide around;
Give me, ye great, tremendous powers, to tell
Of scenes and wonders in the depth of hell;
Give me your mighty secrets to display
From those *black* realms of darkness to the day."
    PITT.

"*Obscure* they went through dreary *shades* that led
Along the *waste* dominions of the *dead.*"
    DRYDEN.

Section VII: Vastness

Greatness of dimension is a powerful cause of the sublime. This is too evident, and the observation too common, to need any illustration; it is not so common to consider in what ways greatness of dimension, vastness of extent or quantity, has the most striking effect. For, certainly, there are ways and modes wherein the same quantity of extension shall produce greater effects than it is found to do in others. Extension is either in length, height, or depth. Of these the length strikes least; a hundred yards of even ground will never work such an effect as a tower a hundred yards high, or a rock or mountain of that altitude. I am apt to imagine, likewise, that height is less grand than depth; and that we are more struck at looking down from a precipice, than looking up at an object of equal height; but of that I am not very positive. A perpendicular has more force in forming the sublime, than an inclined plane, and the effects of a rugged and broken surface seem stronger than where it is smooth and polished. It would carry us out of our way to enter in this place into the cause of these appearances, but certain it is they afford a large and fruitful field of speculation. However, it may not be amiss to add to these remarks upon magnitude, that as the great extreme of dimension is sublime, so the last extreme of littleness is in some measure sublime likewise; when we attend to the infinite divisibility of matter, when we pursue animal life into these excessively small, and yet organized beings, that escape the nicest inquisition of the sense; when we push our discoveries yet downward, and consider those creatures so many degrees yet smaller, and the still diminishing scale of existence, in tracing which the imagination is lost as well as the sense; we become amazed and confounded at the wonders of minuteness; nor can we distinguish in its effect this extreme of littleness from the vast itself. For division must be infinite as well as addition; because the idea of a perfect unity can no more be arrived at, than that of a complete whole, to which nothing may be added.

Section VIII: Infinity

Another source of the sublime is *infinity*; if it does not rather belong to the last. Infinity has a tendency to fill the mind with that sort of delightful horror, which is the most genuine effect, and truest test of the sublime. There are scarce any things which can become the objects of our senses, that are really and in their own nature infinite. But the eye not being able to perceive the bounds of many things, they seem to be infinite, and they produce the same effects as if they were really so. We are deceived in the like manner, if the parts of some large object are so continued to any indefinite number, that the imagination meets no check which may hinder its extending them at pleasure.

Whenever we repeat any idea frequently, the mind, by a sort of mechanism, repeats it long after the first cause has ceased to operate. After whirling about, when we sit down, the objects about us still seem to whirl. After a long succession of noises, as the fall of waters, or the beating of forge-hammers, the hammers beat and the waters roar in the imagination long after the first sounds have ceased to affect it; and they die away at last by gradations which are scarcely perceptible. If you hold up a straight pole, with your eye to one end, it will seem extended to a length almost incredible. Place a number of uniform and equi-distant marks on this pole, they will cause the same deception, and seem multiplied without end. The senses, strongly affected in some one manner, cannot quickly change their tenor, or adapt themselves to other things; but they continue in their old channel until the strength of the first mover decays. This is the reason of an appearance very frequent in madmen; that they remain whole days and nights, sometimes whole years, in the constant repetition of some remark, some complaint, or song; which having struck powerfully on their disordered imagination, in the beginning of their frenzy, every repetition reinforces it with new strength, and the hurry of their spirits, unrestrained by the curb of reason, continues it to the end of their lives.

22

Johann Joachim Winckelmann

Reflections on the Painting and Sculpture of the Greeks (1759)

On Grace in Works of Art

—— Χαϲιτων ἱμεϲο φωνων ἱεϲον φυον.

GRACE IS THE HARMONY OF AGENT AND ACTION. It is a general idea: for whatever reasonably pleases in things and actions is gracious. Grace is a gift of heaven; though not like beauty, which must be born with the possessor: whereas nature gives only the dawn, the capability of this. Education and reflection form it by degrees, and custom may give it the sanction of nature. As water,

That least of foreign principles partakes, Is best:

So Grace is perfect when most simple, when freest from finery, constraint, and affected wit. Yet always to trace nature through the vast realms of pleasure, or through all the windings of characters, and circumstances infinitely various, seems to require too pure and candid a taste for this age, cloyed with pleasure, in its judgments either partial, local, capricious, or incompetent. Then let it suffice to say, that Grace can never live where the passions rave; that beauty and tranquillity of soul are the centre of its powers. By this Cleopatra subdued Cæsar; Anthony slighted Octavia and the world for this; it breathes through every line of Xenophon; Thucydides, it seems, disdained its charms; to Grace Apelles and Corregio owe immortality; but Michael Angelo was blind to it; though all the remains of ancient art, even those of but midling merit, might have satisfied him, that Grace alone places them above the reach of modern skill.

The criticisms on Grace in nature, and on its imitation by art, seem to differ: for many are not shocked at those faults in the latter, that certainly would incur their displeasure in the former. This diversity of feelings lies either in imitation itself, which perhaps affects the more the less it is akin to the thing imitated; or in the senses being little exercised, and in the want of attention, and of clear ideas of the objects in question. But let us not from hence infer that Grace is wholly fictitious: the human mind advances by degrees; nor are youth, the prejudices of education, boiling passions, and their train of phantoms, the standard of its real delight—remove some of these, and it admires what it loathed, and spurns what it doted on. Myriads, you say, the bulk of mankind, have not even the least notion of Grace—but what do they know of beauty, taste, generosity, or all the higher luxuries of the soul? These flowers of the human mind were not intended for universal growth, though their seeds lie in every breast.

Grace, in works of art, concerns the human figure only; it modifies the *attitude* and *countenance, dress* and *drapery.* And here I must observe, that the following remarks do not extend to the comic part of art.

The attitude and gestures of antique figures are such as those have, who, conscious of merit, claim attention as their due, when appearing among men of sense. Their motions always shew the motive; clear, pure blood, and settled spirits; nor does it signify whether they stand, sit, or lie; the attitudes of Bacchanals only are violent, and ought to be so.

In quiet situations, when one leg alone supports the other which is free, this recedes only as far as nature requires for putting the figure out of its perpendicular. Nay, in the *Fauni,* the foot has been observed to have an inflected direction, as a token of savage, regardless nature. To the modern artists a quiet attitude seemed insipid and spiritless, and therefore they drag the leg at rest forwards, and, to make the attitude ideal, remove part of the body's weight from the supporting leg, wring the trunk out of its centre, and turn the head, like that of a person suddenly dazzled with lightning. Those to whom this is not clear, may please to recollect some stage-knight, or a conceited young Frenchman. Where room allowed not of such an attitude, they, lest unhappily the leg that has nothing to do might be unemployed, put something elevated under its foot, as if it were like that of a man who could not speak without setting his foot on a stool, or stand without having a stone purposely put under it. The ancients took such care of appearances, that you will hardly find a figure with crossed legs, if not a Bacchus, Paris, or Nireus; and in these they mean to express effeminate indolence.

In the countenances of antique figures, joy bursts not into laughter; 'tis only the representation of inward pleasure. Through the face of a Bacchanal peeps only the dawn of luxury. In sorrow and anguish they resemble the sea, whose bottom is calm, whilst the surface raves. Even in the utmost pangs of nature, Niobe continues still the heroine, who disdained yielding to Latona. The ancients seem to have taken advantage of that situation of the soul, in which, struck dumb by an immensity of pains, she borders upon insensibility; to express, as it were, characters, independent of particular actions; and to avoid scenes too terrifying, too passionate, sometimes to paint the dignity of minds subduing grief.

Those of the moderns, that either were ignorant of antiquity, or neglected to enquire into Grace in nature, have expressed, not only what nature feels, but likewise what she feels not. A Venus at Potzdam, by *Pigal,* is represented in a sentiment which forces the liquor to flow out at both sides of her mouth, seemingly gasping for breath; for she was intended to pant with lust: yet, by all that's desperate! was this very Pigal several years entertained at Rome to study the antique. A *Carita* of *Bernini,* on one of the papal monuments in St. Peter's, ought, you'll think, to look upon her children with benevolence and maternal fondness; but her face is all a contradiction to this: for the artist, instead of real graces, applied to her his nostrum, dimples, by which her fondness becomes a perfect sneer. As for the expression of modern sorrow, every one knows it, who has seen cuts, hair torn, garments rent, quite the reverse of the antique, which, like Hamlet's,

—— *bath that within, which passeth show:*
These, but the trappings, and the suits of woe.

The gestures of the hands of antique figures, and their attitudes in general, are those of people that think themselves alone and unobserved: and though the hands of but very few statues have escaped destruction, yet may you, from the direction of the arm, guess at the easy and natural motion of the hand. Some moderns, indeed, that have supplied statues with hands or fingers, have too often given them their own favourite attitudes—that of a Venus at her toilet, displaying to her levee the graces of a hand,

——. *far lovelier when beheld.*

The action of modern bands is commonly like the gesticulation of a young preacher, piping-hot from the college. Holds a figure her cloths? You would think them cobweb. Nemesis, who, on antique gems, lifts her peplum softly from her bosom, would be thought too griping for any new performance—how can you be so unpolite to think any thing may be held, without the three last fingers genteely stretched forth?

Grace, in the accidental parts of antiques, consists, like that of the essential ones, in what becomes nature. The drapery of the most ancient works is easy and slight: hence it was natural to give the folds beneath the girdle an almost perpendicular direction.—Variety indeed was sought, in proportion to the increase of art; but drapery still remained a thin floating texture, with folds gathered up, not lumped together, or indiscreetly scattered. That these were the chief principles of ancient drapery, you may convince yourself from the beautiful Flora in the Campidoglio, a work of Hadrian's times. Bacchanals and dancing figures had, indeed, even if statues, more waving garments, such as played upon the air; such a one is in the Palazzo Riccardi at Florence; but even then the artists did not neglect appearances, nor exceed the nature of the materials. Gods and heroes are represented as the inhabitants of sacred places, the dwellings of silent awe, not like a sport for the winds, or as wasting the colours: floating, airy garments are chiefly to be met with on gems—where Atalanta flies

As meditation swift, swift as the thoughts of love.

Grace extends to garments, as such were given to the Graces by the ancients. How would you wish to see the Graces dressed? Certainly not in birth-day robes; but rather like a beauty you loved, still warm from the bed, in an easy negligee.

The moderns, since the epoch of *Raphael* and his school, seem to have forgot that drapery participates of Grace, by their giving the preference to heavy garments, which might not improperly be called the wrappers of ignorance in beauty: for a thick large-folded drapery may spare the artists the pains of tracing the Contour under it, as the ancients did. Some of the modern figures seem to be made only for lasting. *Bernini* and *Peter* of *Cortona* introduced this drapery. For ourselves, we choose light easy dresses; why do we grudge our figures the same advantage?

He that would give a History of Grace, after the revolution of the arts, would perhaps find himself almost reduced to negatives, especially in sculpture.

In sculpture, the imitation of one great man, of *Michael Angelo,* has debauched the artists from Grace. He, who valued himself upon his being "a pure intelligence" despised all that could please humanity; his exalted learning disdained to stoop to tender feelings and lovely grace.

There are poems of his published, and in manuscript, that abound in meditations on sublime beauty: but you look in vain for it in his works.—Beauty, even the beauty of a God, wants Grace, and Moses, without it, from awful as he was, becomes only terrible. Immoderately fond of all that was extraordinary and difficult, he soon broke through the bounds of antiquity, grace, and nature; and as he panted for occasions of displaying skill only, he grew extravagant. His lying statues, on the ducal tombs of St. Lorenzo at Florence, have attitudes, which life, undistorted, cannot imitate: so careless was he, provided he might dazzle you with his mazy learning, of that decency, which nature and the place required, that to him we might apply, what a poet says of St. Lewis in hell:

> *Laissant le vray pour prendre la grimace,*
> *Il fut toujours au delà de la Grace,*
> *Et bien plus loin que les commandements.*

He was blindly imitated by his disciples, and in them the want of Grace shocks you still more: for as they were far his inferiors in science, you have no equivalent at all. How little *Guilielmo della Porta,* the best of them all, understood grace and the antique, you may see in that marble groupe, called the Farnese-bull; where Dirce is his to the girdle. *John di Bologna, Algardi, Fiammingo,* are great names, but likewise inferior to the ancients, in Grace.

At last *Lorenzo Bernini* appeared, a man of spirit and superior talents, but whom Grace had never visited even in dreams. He aimed at encyclopædy in art; painter, architect, statuary, he struggled, chiefly as such, to become original. In his eighteenth year he produced his Apollo and Daphne; a work miraculous for those years, and promising that sculpture by him should attain perfection. Soon after he made his David, which fell short of Apollo. Proud of general applause, and sensible of his impotency, either to equal or to offuscate the antiques; he seems, encouraged by the dastardly taste of that age, to have formed the project of becoming a legislator in art, for all ensuing ages, and he carried his point. From that time the Graces entirely forsook him: how could they abide with a man who begun his career from the end opposite to the ancients? His forms he compiled from common nature, and his ideas from the inhabitants of climates unknown to him; for in Italy's happiest parts nature differs from his figures. He was worshipped as the genius of art, and universally imitated; for, in our days, statues being erected to piety only, none to wisdom, a statue *à la Bernini* is likelier to make the kitchen prosper than a Laocoon.

From Italy, reader, I leave you to guess at other countries. A celebrated *Puget, Girardon,* with all his brethren in *On,* are worse. Judge of the connoisseurs of France by *Watelet,* and of its designers, by *Mariette's* gems.

At Athens the Graces stood eastward, in a sacred place. Our artists should place them over their work-houses; wear them in their rings; seal with them; sacrifice to them; sacrifice to them; and, court their sovereign charms to their last breath.

23

Immanuel Kant

Critique of Pure Reason (1781/1787)

Of the Principles of a Transcendental Deduction in General

§ 9.

TEACHERS OF JURISPRUDENCE, WHEN SPEAKING OF RIGHTS AND CLAIMS, DISTINGUISH in a cause the question of right *(quid juris)* from the question of fact *(quid facti),* and while they demand proof of both, they give to the proof of the former, which goes to establish right or claim in law, the name of *Deduction.* Now we make use of a great number of empirical conceptions, without opposition from any one; and consider ourselves, even without any attempt at deduction, justified in attaching to them a sense, and a supposititious signification, because we have always experience at hand to demonstrate their objective reality. There exist also, however, usurped conceptions, such as *fortune, fate,* which circulate with almost universal indulgence, and yet are occasionally challenged by the question, *quid juris?* In such cases, we have great difficulty in discovering any deduction for these terms, inasmuch as we cannot produce any manifest ground of right, either from experience or from reason, on which the claim to employ them can be founded.

Among the many conceptions, which make up the very variegated web of human cognition, some are destined for pure use *a priori,* independent of all experience; and their title to be so employed always requires a deduction, inasmuch as, to justify such use of them, proofs from experience are not sufficient; but it is necessary to know how these conceptions can apply to objects without being derived from experience. I term, therefore, an explanation of the manner in which conceptions can apply *a priori* to objects, the *transcendental deduction* of conceptions, and I distinguish it from the *empirical* deduction, which indicates the mode in which a conception is obtained through experience and reflection thereon; consequently, does not concern itself with the right, but only with the fact of our obtaining conceptions in such and such a manner. We have already seen that we are in possession of two perfectly different kinds of conceptions, which nevertheless agree with each other in this, that they both apply to objects completely *a priori*. These are the conceptions of space and time as forms of sensibility, and the categories as pure conceptions of the understanding. To attempt an empirical deduction of either of these classes would be labour in vain, because the distinguishing characteristic of their nature consists in this, that they apply to their objects, without having borrowed anything from experience towards the representation of them. Consequently, if a deduction of these conceptions is necessary, it must always be transcendental.

Meanwhile, with respect to these conceptions, as with respect to all our cognition, we certainly may discover in experience, if not the principle of their possibility, yet the occasioning causes[1] of their production. It will be found that the impressions of sense give the first occasion for bringing into action the whole faculty of cognition, and for the production of experience, which contains two very dissimilar elements, namely, a matter for cognition, given by the senses, and a certain form for the arrangement of this matter, arising out of the inner fountain of pure intuition and thought; and these, on occasion given by sensuous impressions, are called into exercise and produce conceptions. Such an investigation into the first efforts of our faculty of cognition to mount from particular perceptions to general conceptions, is undoubtedly of great utility; and we have to thank the celebrated Locke, for having first opened the way for this enquiry. But a deduction of the pure *a priori* conceptions of course never can be made in this way, seeing that, in regard to their future employment, which must be entirely independent of experience, they must have a far different certificate of birth to show from that of a descent from experience. This attempted physiological derivation, which cannot properly be called deduction, because it relates merely to a *quæstio facti,* I shall entitle an explanation of the *possession* of a pure cognition. It is therefore manifest that there can only be a transcendental deduction of these conceptions, and by no means an empirical one; also, that all attempts at an empirical deduction, in regard to pure *a priori* conceptions, are vain, and can only be made by one who does not understand the altogether peculiar nature of these cognitions.

But although it is admitted that the only possible deduction of pure *a priori* cognition is a transcendental deduction, it is not, for that reason, perfectly manifest that such a deduction is absolutely necessary. We have already traced to their sources the conceptions of space and time, by means of a transcendental deduction, and we have explained and determined their objective validity *a priori*. Geometry, nevertheless, advances steadily and securely in the province of pure *a priori* cognitions, without needing to ask from Philosophy any certificate as to the pure and legitimate origin of its fundamental conception of space. But the use of the conception in this science extends only to the external world of sense, the pure form of the intuition of which is space; and in *this* world, therefore, all geometrical cognition, because it is founded upon *a priori* intuition, posesses immediate evidence, and the objects of this cognition are given *a priori* (as regards their form) in intuition by and through the cognition itself.[2] With the pure conceptions of

Understanding, on the contrary, commences the absolute necessity of seeking a transcendental deduction, not only of these conceptions themselves, but likewise of space, because, inasmuch as they make affirmations[3] concerning objects not by means of the predicates of intuition and sensibility, but of pure thought *a priori,* they apply to objects without any of the conditions of sensibility. Besides, not being founded on experience, they are not presented with any object in *a priori* intuition upon which, antecedently to experience, they might base their synthesis. Hence results, not only doubt as to the objective validity and proper limits of their use, but that even our conception of space is rendered equivocal; inasmuch as we are very ready with the aid of the categories, to carry the use of this conception beyond the conditions of sensuous intuition;—and for this reason, we have already found a transcendental deduction of it needful. The reader, then, must be quite convinced of the absolute necessity of a transcendental deduction, before taking a single step in the field of pure reason; because otherwise he goes to work blindly, and after he has wandered about in all directions, returns to the state of utter ignorance from which he started. He ought, moreover, clearly to recognize beforehand, the unavoidable difficulties in his undertaking, so that he may not afterwards complain of the obscurity in which the subject itself is deeply involved, or become too soon impatient of the obstacles in his path;—because we have a choice of only two things—either at once to give up all pretensions to knowledge beyond the limits of possible experience, or to bring this critical investigation to completion.

We have been able, with very little trouble, to make it com prehensible how the conceptions of space and time, although *a priori* cognitions, must necessarily apply to external objects, and render a synthetical cognition of these possible, independently of all experience. For inasmuch as only by means of such pure form of sensibility an object can appear to us, that is, be an object of empirical intuition, space and time are pure intuitions, which contain *a priori* the condition of the possibility of objects as phænomena, and an *a priori* synthesis in these intuitions possesses objective validity.

On the other hand, the categories of the understanding dó not represent the conditions under which objects are given to us in intuition; objects can consequently appear to us without necessarily connecting themselves with these, and consequently without any necessity binding on the understanding to contain *a priori* the conditions of these objects. Thus we find ourselves involved in a difficulty which did not present itself in the sphere of sensibility, that is to say, we, cannot discover *how the subjective conditions of thought can have objective validity,* in other words, can become conditions of the possibility of all cognition of objects;—for phænomena may certainly be given to us in intuition without any help from the functions of the understanding. Let us take, for example, the conception of *cause,* which indicates a peculiar kind of synthesis, namely, that with something, A, something entirely different, B, is connected according to a law. It is not *a priori* manifest why phænomena should contain anything of this kind (we are of course debarred from appealing for proof to experience, for the objective validity of this conception must be demonstrated *a priori*), and it hence remains doubtful *a priori,* whether such a conception be not quite void, and without any corresponding object among phænomena. For that objects of sensuous intuition must correspond to the formal conditions of sensibility existing *a priori* in the mind, is quite evident, from the fact, that without these they could not be objects for us; but that they must also correspond to the conditions which understanding requires for the synthetical unity of thought, is an assertion, the grounds for which are not so easily to be discovered. For phænomena might be so constituted, as not to correspond to the conditions of the unity of thought; and all things might lie in such confusion, that, for example, nothing could be met with in the sphere of phænomena to suggest a law of synthesis, and so correspond to the conception of cause and effect; so that this conception would be quite void, null, and without significance. Phænomena would nevertheless continue to present objects to our intuition; for mere intuition does not in any respect stand in need of the functions of thought.

If we thought to free ourselves from the labour of these investigations by saying, "Experience is constantly offering us examples of the relation of cause and effect in phænomena, and presents us with abundant opportunity of abstracting the conception of cause, and so at the same time of corroborating the objective validity of this conception;"—we should in this case be overlooking the fact, that the conception of cause cannot arise in this way at all; that, on the contrary, it must either have an *a priori* basis in the understanding, or be rejected as a mere chimæra. For this conception demands that something, A, should be of such a nature, that something else, B, should follow from it necessarily, and according to an absolutely universal law. We may certainly collect from phænomena a law, according to which this or that *usually* happens, but the element of necessity is not to be found in it. Hence it is evident that to the synthesis of cause and effect belongs a dignity, which is utterly wanting in any empirical synthesis; for it is no mere mechanical synthesis, by means of addition, but a dynamical one, that is to say, the effect is not to be cogitated as merely annexed to the cause, but as posited by and through the cause, and resulting from it. The strict universality of this law never can be a characteristic of empirical laws, which obtain through induction only a comparative universality, that is, an extended range of practical application. But the pure conceptions of the understanding would entirely lose all their peculiar character, if we treated them merely as the productions of experience.

Transition to the Transcendental Deduction of the Categories

§ 10.

THERE ARE ONLY TWO POSSIBLE WAYS IN WHICH SYNTHETICAL REPRESENTATION and its objects can coincide with and relate necessarily to each other, and, as it were, meet together. Either the object alone makes the representation possible, or the representation alone makes the object possible. In the former case, the relation between them is only empirical, and an *a priori* representation is impossible. And this is the case with phænomena, as regards that in them which is referable to mere sensation. In the latter case—although representation alone (for of its causality, by means of the will, we do not here speak,) does not produce the object as to its existence, it must nevertheless be *a priori* determinative in regard to the object, if it is only by means of the representation that we can cognize any thing as an object. Now there are only two conditions of the possibility of a cognition of objects; firstly, *Intuition,* by means of which the object, though only as phænomenon, is given; secondly, *Conception,* by means of which the object which corresponds to this intuition is thought. But it is evident from what has been said on æsthetic, that the first condition, under which alone objects can be intuited, must in fact exist, as a formal basis for them, *a priori* in the mind. With this formal condition of sensibility, therefore, all phænomena necessarily correspond, because it is only through it that they can be phænomena at all; that is, can be empirically intuited and given. Now the question is, whether there do not exist *a priori* in the mind, conceptions of understanding also, as conditions under which alone something, if not intuited, is yet thought as object. If this question be answered in the affirmative, it follows that all empirical cognition of objects is necessarily conformable to such conceptions, since, if they are not presupposed, it is impossible that anything can be an object of experience. Now all experience contains, besides the intuition of the senses, through which an object is given, a *conception* also of an object that is given in intuition. Accordingly, conceptions of objects in general must lie as *a priori* conditions at the foundation of all empirical cognition; and consequently, the objective validity of the categories, as *a priori* conceptions, will rest upon *this,* that experience (as far as regards the form of thought) is possible only by their means. For in that case they apply necessarily and *a priori* to objects of experience, because only through them can an object of experience be thought.

The whole aim of the transcendental deduction of all *a priori* conceptions is to show that these conceptions are *a priori* conditions of the possibility of all experience. Conceptions which afford us the objective foundation of the possibility of experience, are for that very reason necessary. But the analysis of the experiences in which they are met with is not deduction, but only an illustration of them, because from experience they could never derive the attribute of necessity. Without their original applicability and relation to all possible experience, in which all objects of cognition present themselves, the relation of the categories to objects, of whatever nature, would be quite incomprehensible.

The celebrated Locke, for want of due reflection on these points, and because he met with pure conceptions of the understanding in experience, sought also to deduce them from experience, and yet proceeded so inconsequently as to attempt, with their aid, to arrive at cognitions which lie far beyond the limits of all experience. David Hume perceived that, to render this possible, it was necessary that the conceptions should have an *a priori* origin. But as he could not explain how it was possible that conceptions which are not connected with each other in the understanding, must nevertheless be thought as necessarily connected in the object,—and it never occurred to him that the understanding itself might, perhaps, by means of these conceptions, be the author of the experience in which its objects were presented to it,—he was forced to derive these conceptions from experience, that is from a subjective necessity arising from repeated association of experiences erroneously considered to be objective,—in one word, from "*habit.*" But he proceeded with perfect consequence, and declared it to be impossible with such conceptions and the principles arising from them, to overstep the limits of experience. The empirical derivation, however, which both of these philosophers attributed to these conceptions, cannot possibly be reconciled with the fact that we do possess scientific *a priori* cognitions, namely, those of pure mathematics and general physics.

The former of these two celebrated men opened a wide door to extravagance—(for if reason has once undoubted right on its side, it will not allow itself to be confined to set limits, by vague recommendations of moderation); the latter gave himself up entirely to scepticism,—a natural consequence, after having discovered, as he thought, that the faculty of cognition was not trustworthy. We now intend to make a trial whether it be not possible safely to conduct reason between these two rocks, to assign her determinate limits, and yet leave open for her the entire sphere of her legitimate activity.

I shall merely premise an explanation of what the categories are. They are conceptions of an object in general, by means of which its intuition is contemplated as determined in relation to one of the logical functions of judgment. The following will make this plain. The function of the categorical judgment is that of the relation of subject to predicate; for example, in the proposition, "All bodies are divisible." But in regard to the merely logical use of the understanding, it still remains undetermined to which of these two conceptions belongs the function of subject, and to which that of predicate. For we could also say, "Some divisible is a body." But the category of substance, when the conception of a body is brought under it, determines that; and its empirical intuition in experience must be contemplated always as subject, and never as mere predicate. And so with all the other categories.

Of the Supreme Principle of All Synthetical Judgments

THE EXPLANATION OF THE POSSIBILITY OF SYNTHETICAL JUDGMENTS IS A task with which general Logic has nothing to do; indeed she needs not even be acquainted with its name. But in transcendental Logic it is the most important matter to be dealt with,—indeed the only one, if the question is of the possibility of synthetical judgments *a priori,* the conditions and extent of their validity. For when this question is fully decided, it can reach its aim with perfect ease, the determination, to wit, of the extent and limits of the pure understanding.

In an analytical judgment I do not go beyond the given conception, in order to arrive at some decision respecting it. If the judgment is affirmative, I predicate of the conception only that which was already cogitated in it; if negative, I merely exclude from the conception its contrary. But in synthetical judgments, I must go beyond the given conception, in order to cogitate, in relation with it, something quite different from that which was cogitated in it, a relation which is consequently never one either of identity or contradiction, and by means of which the truth or error of the judgment cannot be discerned merely from the judgment itself.

Granted then, that we must go out beyond a given conception, in order to compare it synthetically with another, a third thing is necessary, in which alone the synthesis of two conceptions can originate. Now what is this *tertium quid,* that is to be the medium of all synthetical judgments? It is only a complex,[4] in which all our representations are contained, the internal sense to wit, and its form *a priori,* Time.

The synthesis of our representations rests upon the imagination; their synthetical unity (which is requisite to a judgment), upon the unity of apperception. In this, therefore, is to be sought the possibility of synthetical judgments, and as all three contain the sources of *a priori* representations, the possibility of pure synthetical judgments also; nay, they are necessary upon these grounds, if we are to possess a knowledge of objects, which rests solely upon the synthesis of representations.

If a cognition is to have objective reality, that is, to relate to an object, and possess sense and meaning in respect to it, it is necessary that the object be given in some way or another. Without this, our conceptions are empty, and we may indeed have thought by means of them, but by such thinking, we have not, in fact, cognized anything, we have merely played with representation. To give an object, if this expression be understood in the sense of to present the object, not mediately but immediately in intuition, means nothing else than to apply the representation of it to experience, be that experience real or only possible. Space and time themselves, pure as these conceptions are from all that is empirical, and certain as it is that they are represented fully *a priori* in the mind, would be completely without objective validity, and without sense and significance, if their necessary use in the objects of experience were not shewn. Nay, the representation of them is a mere schema, that always relates to the reproductive imagination, which calls up the objects of experience, without which they have no meaning. And so is it with all conceptions without distinction.

The *possibility of experience* is, then, that which gives objective reality to all our *a priori* cognitions. Now experience depends upon the synthetical unity of phænomena, that is, upon a synthesis according to conceptions of the object of phænomena in general, a synthesis without which experience never could become knowledge, but would be merely a rhapsody of perceptions, never fitting together into any connected text, according to rules of a thoroughly united (possible) consciousness, and therefore never subjected to the transcendental and necessary unity of apperception. Experience has therefore for a foundation, *a priori* principles of its form, that is to say, general rules of unity in the synthesis of phænomena, the objective reality of which rules, as necessary conditions—even of the possibility of experience—can always be shewn in experience. But apart from this relation, *a priori* synthetical propositions are absolutely impossible, because they have no third term, that is, no pure object, in which the synthetical unity can exhibit the objective reality of its conceptions.

Although, then, respecting space, or the forms which productive imagination describes therein, we do cognize much *a priori* in synthetical judgments, and are really in no need of experience for this purpose, such knowledge would nevertheless amount to nothing but a busy trifling with a mere chimera, were not space to be considered as the condition of the phænomena which constitute the material of external experience. Hence those pure synthetical judgments do relate, though but mediately, to possible experience, or rather to the possibility of experience, and upon that alone is founded the objective validity of their synthesis.

While then, on the one hand, experience, as empirical synthesis, is the only possible mode of cognition which gives reality to all other synthesis;[5] on the other hand, this latter synthesis, as cognition *a priori,* possesses truth, that is, accordance with its object, only in so far as it contains nothing more than what is necessary to the synthetical unity of experience.

Accordingly, the supreme principle of all synthetical judgments is: Every object is subject to the necessary conditions of the synthetical unity of the manifold of intuition in a possible experience.

A priori synthetical judgments are possible, when we apply the formal conditions of the *a priori* intuition, the synthesis of the imagination, and the necessary unity of that synthesis in a transcendental apperception, to a possible cognition of experience, and say: The conditions of the *possibility* of *experience* in general, are at the same time conditions of the *possibility* of the *objects* of *experience,* and have, for that reason, objective validity in an *a priori* synthetical judgment.

Second Analogy: Principle of the Succession of Time According to the Law of Causality

All changes take place according to the law of the connection of Cause and Effect.

Proof

(That all phænomena in the succession of time are only changes, that is, a successive being and non-being of the determinations of substance, which is permanent; consequently that a being of substance itself which follows on the nonbeing thereof, or a non-being of substance which follows on the being thereof, in other words, that the origin or extinction of substance itself, is impossible—all this has been fully established in treating of the foregoing principle. This principle might have been expressed as follows: "*All alteration* (*succession*) *of phænomena is merely change;*" for the changes of substance are not origin of extinction, because the conception of change presupposes the same subject as existing with two opposite determinations, and consequently as permanent. After this premonition, we shall proceed to the proof.)

I perceive that phænomena succeed one another, that is to say, a state of things exists at one time, the opposite of which existed in a former state. In this case then, I really connect together two perceptions in time. Now connection is not an operation of mere sense and intuition, but is the product of a synthetical faculty of imagination, which determines the internal sense in respect of a relation of time. But imagination can connect these two states in two ways, so that either the one or the other may antecede in time; for time in itself cannot be an object of perception, and what in an object precedes and what follows cannot be empirically determined in relation to it. I am only conscious then, that my imagination places one state before, and the other after; not that the one state antecedes the other in the object. In other words, the objective relation of the successive phænomena remains quite undetermined by means of mere perception. Now in order that this relation may be cognized as determined, the relation between the two states must be so cogitated that it is thereby determined as necessary, which of them must be placed before and which after, and not conversely. But the conception which carries with it a necessity of synthetical unity, can be none other than a pure conception of the understanding which does not lie in mere perception; and in this case it is the conception of the *relation of cause and effect,* the former of which determines the latter in time, as its necessary consequence, and not as something which might possibly antecede (or which might in some cases not be perceived to follow). It follows that it is only because we subject the sequence of phænomena, and consequently all change to the law of causality, that experience itself, that is, empirical cognition of phænomena, becomes possible; and consequently, that phænomena themselves, as objects of experience, are possible only by virtue of this law.

Our apprehension of the manifold of phænomena is always successive. The representations of parts succeed one another. Whether they succeed one another in the object also, is a second point for reflection, which was not contained in the former. Now we may certainly give the name of object to every thing, even to every representation, so far as we are conscious there of; but what this word may mean in the case of phænomena, not merely in so far as they (as representations) are objects, but only in so far as they indicate an object, is a question requiring deeper consideration. In so far as they, regarded merely as representations, are at the same time objects of consciousness, they are not to be distinguished from apprehension, that is, reception into the synthesis of imagination, and we must therefore say: "The manifold of phænomena is always produced successively in the mind." If phænomena were things in themselves, no man would be able to conjecture from the succession of our representations how this manifold is connected in the object; for we have to do only with our representations. How things may be in themselves, without regard to the representations through which they affect us, is utterly beyond the sphere of our cognition. Now although phænomena are not things in themselves, and are nevertheless the only thing given to us to be cognized, it is my duty to show what sort of connection in time belongs to the manifold in phænomena themselves, while the representation of this manifold in apprehension is always successive. For example, the apprehension of the manifold in the phænomenon of a house which stands before me, is successive. Now comes the question, whether the manifold of this house is in itself also successive;—which no one will be at all willing to grant. But, so soon as I raise my conception of an object to the transcendental signification thereof, I find that the house is not a thing in itself, but only a phænomenon, that is, a representation, the transcendental object of which remains utterly unknown. What then am I to understand by the question, How can the manifold be connected in the phænomenon itself—not considered as a thing in itself, but merely as a phænomenon? Here that which lies in my successive apprehension is regarded as representation, whilst the phænomenon which is given me, notwithstanding that it is nothing more than a complex of these representations, is regarded as the object thereof, with which my conception, drawn from the representations of apprehension, must harmonize. It is very soon seen that, as accordance of the cognition with its object constitutes truth, the question now before us can only relate to the formal conditions of empirical truth; and that the phænomenon, in opposition to the representations of apprehension, can only be distinguished therefrom as the object of them, if it is subject to a rule, which distinguishes it from every other apprehension, and which renders necessary a mode of connection of the manifold. That in the phænomenon which contains the condition of this necessary rule of apprehension, is the object.

Let us now proceed to our task. That something happens, that is to say, that something or some state exists which before was not, cannot be empirically perceived, unless a phænomenon precedes, which does not contain in itself this state. For a reality which should follow upon a void time, in other words, a beginning, which no state of things precedes, can just as little be apprehended as the void time itself. Every apprehension of an event is therefore a perception which follows upon another perception. But as this is the case with all synthesis of apprehension, as I have shown above in the example of a house, my apprehension of an event is not yet sufficiently distinguished from other apprehensions. But I remark also, that if in a phænomenon which contains an occurrence, I call the antecedent state of my perception, A, and the following state, B, the perception B can only follow A in apprehension, and the perception A cannot follow B, but only precede it. For example, I see a ship float down the stream of a river. My perception of its place lower down follows upon my perception of its place higher up the course of the river, and it is impossible that in the apprehension of this phænomenon, the vessel should be perceived first below and afterwards higher up the stream. Here, therefore, the order in the sequence of perceptions in apprehension is determined; and by this order apprehension is regulated. In the former example, my perceptions in the apprehension of a house, might begin at the roof and end at the foundation, or *vice versâ;* or I might apprehend the manifold in this empirical intuition by going from left to right, and from right to left. Accordingly, in the series of these perceptions, there was no determined order, which necessitated my beginning at a certain point, in order empirically to connect the manifold. But this rule is always to be met with in the perception of that which happens, and it makes the order of the successive perceptions in the apprehension of such a phænomenon *necessary*.

I must therefore, in the present case, deduce the *subjective sequence* of apprehension from the *objective sequence* of phænomena, for otherwise the former is quite undetermined, and one phænomenon is not distinguishable from another. The former alone proves nothing as to the connection of the manifold in an object, for it is quite arbitrary. The latter must consist in the order of the manifold in a phænomenon, according to which order the apprehension of one thing (that which happens) follows that of another thing (which precedes), in conformity with a rule. In this way alone can I be authorized to say of the phænomenon itself, and not merely of my own apprehension, that a certain order or sequence is to be found therein. That is, in other words, I cannot arrange my apprehension otherwise than in this order.

In conformity with this rule, then, it is necessary that in that which antecedes an event there be found the condition of a rule, according to which this event follows always and necessarily; but I cannot reverse this and go back from the event, and determine (by apprehension) that which antecedes it. For no phænomenon goes back from the succeeding point of time to the preceding point, although it does certainly relate to a preceding point of time; from a given time, on the other hand, there is always a necessary progression to the determined succeeding time. Therefore, because there certainly is something that follows, I must of necessity connect it with something else, which antecedes, and upon which it follows, in conformity with a rule, that is necessarily, so that the event, as conditioned, affords certain indication of a condition, and this condition determines the event.

Let us suppose that nothing precedes an event, upon which this event must follow in conformity with a rule. All sequence of perception would then exist only in apprehension, that is to say, would be merely subjective, and it could not thereby be objectively determined what thing ought to precede, and what ought to follow in perception. In such a case, we should have nothing but a play of representations, which would possess no application to any object. That is to say, it would not be possible through perception to distinguish one phænomenon from another, as regards relations of time; because the succession in the act of apprehension would always be of the same sort, and therefore there would be nothing in the phænomenon to determine the succession, and to render a certain sequence objectively necessary. And, in this case, I cannot say that two states in a phænomenon follow one upon the other, but only that one apprehension follows upon another. But this is merely subjective, and does not determine an object, and consequently cannot be held to be cognition of an object,—not even in the phænomenal world.

Accordingly, when we know in experience that something happens, we always presuppose that something precedes, whereupon it follows in conformity with a rule. For otherwise I could not say of the object, that it follows; because the mere succession in my apprehension, if it be not determined by a rule in relation to something preceding, does not authorize succession in the object. Only therefore, in reference to a rule, according to which phænomena are determined in their sequence, that is, as they happen, by the preceding state, can I make my subjective synthesis (of apprehension) objective, and it is only under this presupposition that even the experience of an event is possible.

No doubt it appears as if this were in thorough contradiction to all the notions which people have hitherto entertained in regard to the procedure of the human understanding. According to these opinions, it is by means of the perception and comparison of similar consequences following upon certain antecedent phænomena, that the understanding is led to the discovery of a rule, according to which certain events always follow certain phænomena, and it is only by this process that we attain to the conception of cause. Upon such a basis, it is clear that this conception must be merely empirical, and the rule which it furnishes us with—"Everything that happens must have a cause"—would be just as contingent as experience itself. The universality and necessity of the rule or law would be perfectly spurious attributes of it. Indeed, it could not possess universal validity, inasmuch as it would not in this case be *a priori,* but founded on deduction. But the same is the case with this law as with other pure *a priori* representations (*e. g.* space and time), which we can draw in perfect clearness and completeness from experience, only because we had already placed them therein, and by that means, and by that alone, had rendered experience possible. Indeed, the logical clearness of this representation of a rule, determining the series of events, is possible only when we have made use thereof in experience. Nevertheless, the recognition of this rule, as a condition of the synthetical unity of phænomena in time, was the ground of experience itself, and consequently preceded it *a priori.*

It is now our duty to show by an example, that we never, even in experience, attribute to an object the notion of succession or effect (of an event—that is, the happening of something that did not exist before), and distinguish it from the subjective succession of apprehension, unless when a rule lies at the foundation, which compels us to observe this order of perception in preference to any other, and that, indeed, it is this necessity which first renders possible the representation of a succession in the object.

We have representations within us, of which also we can be conscious. But, however widely extended, however accurate and thorough-going this consciousness may be, these representations are still nothing more than representations, that is, internal determinations of the mind in this or that relation of time. Now how happens it, that to these representations we should set an object, or that, in addition to their subjective reality, as modifications, we should still further attribute to them a certain unknown objective reality? It is clear that objective significancy cannot consist in a relation to another representation (of that which we desire to term object), for in that case the question again arises: "How does this other representation go out of itself, and obtain objective significancy over and above the subjective, which is proper to it, as a determination of a state of mind?" If we try to discover what sort of new property the *relation to an object* gives to our subjective representations, and what new importance they thereby receive, we shall find that this relation has no other effect than that of rendering necessary the connexion of our representations in a certain manner, and of subjecting them to a rule; and that conversely, it is only because a certain order is necessary in the relations of time of our representations, that objective significancy is ascribed to them.

In the synthesis of phænomena, the manifold of our representations is always successive. Now hereby is not represented an object, for by means of this succession, which is common to all apprehension, no one thing is distinguished from another. But so soon as I perceive or assume, that in this succession there is a relation to a state antecedent, from which the representation follows in accordance with a rule, so soon do I represent something as an event, or as a thing that happens; in other words, I cognize an object to which I must assign a certain determinate position in time, which cannot be altered, because of the preceding state in the object. When, therefore, I perceive that something happens, there is contained in this representation, in the first place, the fact, that something antecedes; because it is only in relation to this, that the phænomenon obtains its proper relation of time, in other words, exists after an antecedent time, in which it did not exist. But it can receive its determined place in time, only by the presupposition that something existed in the foregoing state, upon which it follows inevitably and always, that is, in conformity with a rule. From all this it is evident that, in the first place, I cannot reverse the order of succession, and make that which happens precede that upon which it follows; and that, in the second place, if the antecedent state be posited, a certain determinate event inevitably and necessarily follows. Hence it follows that there exists a certain order in our representations, whereby the present gives a sure indication of some previously existing state, as a correlate, though still undetermined, of the existing event which is given,—a correlate which itself relates to the event as its consequence, conditions it, and connects it necessarily with itself in the series of time.

If then it be admitted as a necessary law of sensibility, and consequently a formal condition of all perception, that the preceding necessarily determines the succeeding time (inasmuch as I cannot arrive at the succeeding except through the preceding), it must likewise be an indispensable law of empirical representation of the series of time, that the phænomena of the past determine all phænomena in the succeeding time, and that the latter, as events, cannot take place, except in so far as the former determine their existence in time, that is to say, establish it according to a rule. For it is of course only in phænomena that we can empirically cognize this continuity in the connection of times.

For all experience and for the possibility of experience, understanding is indispensable, and the first step which it takes in this sphere is not to render the representation of objects clear,[6] but to render the representation of an object in general, possible. It does this by applying the order of time to phænomena, and their existence. In other words, it assigns to each phænomenon, as a consequence, a place in relation to preceding phænomena, determined *a priori* in time, without which it could not harmonize with time itself, which determines a place *a priori* to all its parts. This determination of place cannot be derived from the relation of phænomena to absolute time (for it is not an object of perception); but, on the contrary, phænomena must reciprocally determine the places in time of one another, and render these necessary in the order of time. In other words, whatever follows or happens, must follow in conformity with an universal rule upon that which was contained in the foregoing state. Hence arises a series of phænomena, which, by means of the understanding, produces and renders necessary exactly the same order and continuous connection in the series of our possible perceptions, as is found *a priori* in the form of internal intuition (time), in which all our perceptions must have place.

That something happens, then, is a perception which belongs to a possible experience, which becomes real, only because I look upon the phænomenon as determined in regard to its place in time, consequently as an object, which can always be found by means of a rule in the connected series of my perceptions. But this rule of the determination of a thing according to succession in time is as follows: "In what precedes may be found the condition, under which an event always (that is, necessarily) follows." From all this it is obvious that the principle of cause and effect is the principle of possible experience, that is, of objective cognition of phænomena, in regard to their relations in the succession of time.

The proof of this fundamental proposition rests entirely on the following momenta of argument. To all empirical cognition belongs the synthesis of the manifold by the imagination, a synthesis which is always successive, that is, in which the representations therein always follow one another. But the order of succession in imagination is not determined, and the series of successive representations may be taken retrogressively as well as progressively. But if this synthesis is a synthesis of apprehension (of the manifold of a given phænomenon), then the order is determined in the object, or, to speak more accurately, there is therein an order of successive synthesis which determines an object, and according to which something necessarily precedes, and when this is posited, something else necessarily follows. If, then, my perception is to contain the cognition of an event, that is, of something which really happens, it must be an empirical judgment, wherein we think that the succession is determined; that is, it presupposes another phænomenon, upon which this event follows necessarily, or in conformity with a rule. If, on the contrary, when I posited the antecedent, the event did not necessarily follow, I should be obliged to consider it merely as a subjective play of my imagination, and if in this I represented to myself anything as objective, I must look upon it as a mere dream. Thus, the relation of phænomena (as possible perceptions), according to which that which happens is, as to its existence, necessarily determined in time by something which antecedes, in conformity with a rule,—in other words, the relation of cause and effect—is the condition of the objective validity of our empirical judgments in regard to the sequence of perceptions, consequently of their empirical truth, and therefore of experience. The principle of the relation of causality in the succession of phænomena is therefore valid for all objects of experience, because it is itself the ground of the possibility of experience.

Here, however, a difficulty arises, which must be resolved. The principle of the connection of causality among phænomena is limited in our formula to the succession thereof, although in practice we find that the principle applies also when the phænomena exist together in the same time, and that cause and effect may be simultaneous. For example, there is heat in a room, which does not exist in the open air. I look about for the cause, and find it to be the fire. Now the fire as the cause, is simultaneous with its effect, the heat of the room. In this case, then, there is no succession as regards time, between cause and effect, but they are simultaneous; and still the law holds good. The greater part of operating causes in nature are simultaneous with their effects, and the succession in time of the latter is produced only because the cause cannot achieve the total of its effect in one moment. But at the moment when the effect *first* arises, it is always simultaneous with the causality of its cause, because if the cause had but a moment before ceased to be, the effect could not have arisen. Here it must be specially remembered, that we must consider the *order* of time, and not the *lapse* thereof. The relation remains, even though no time has elapsed. The time between the causality of the cause and its immediate effect may entirely vanish, and the cause and effect be thus simultaneous, but the relation of the one to the other remains always determinable according to time. If, for example, I consider a leaden ball, which lies upon a cushion and makes a hollow in it, as a cause, then it is simultaneous with the effect. But I distinguish the two through the relation of time of the dynamical connection of both. For if I lay the ball upon the cushion, then the hollow follows upon the before smooth surface; but supposing the cushion has, from some cause or another, a hollow, there does not thereupon follow a leaden ball.

Thus, the law of succession of time is in all instances the only empirical criterion of effect in relation to the causality of the antecedent cause. The glass is the cause of the rising of the water above its horizontal surface, although the two phænomena are contemporaneous. For, as soon as I draw some water with the glass from a larger vessel, an effect follows thereupon, namely, the change of the horizontal state which the water had in the large vessel into a concave, which it assumes in the glass.

This conception of causality leads us to the conception of action; that of action, to the conception of force; and through it, to the conception of substance. As I do not wish this critical essay, the sole purpose of which is to treat of the sources of our synthetical cognition *a priori*, to be crowded with analyses which merely explain, but do not enlarge the sphere of our conceptions, I reserve the detailed explanation of the above conceptions for a future system of pure reason. Such an analysis, indeed, executed with great particularity, may already be found in well-known works on this subject. But I cannot at present refrain from making a few remarks on the empirical criterion of a substance, in so far as it seems to be more evident and more easily recognised through the conception of action, than through that of the permanence of a phænomenon.

Where action (consequently activity and force) exists, substance also must exist, and in it alone must be sought the seat of that fruitful source of phænomena. Very well. But if we are called upon to explain what we mean by substance, and wish to avoid the vice of reasoning in a circle, the answer is by no means so easy. How shall we conclude immediately from the action to the *permanence* of that which acts, this being nevertheless an essential and peculiar criterion of substance (phænomenon)? But after what has been said above, the solution of this question becomes easy enough, although by the common mode of procedure—merely analysing our conceptions—it would be quite impossible. The conception of action indicates the relation of the subject of causality to the effect. Now because all effect consists in that which happens, therefore in the changeable, the last subject thereof is the *permanent,* as the substratum of all that changes, that is, substance. For according to the principle of causality, actions are always the first ground of all change in phænomena, and consequently cannot be a property of a subject which itself changes, because if this were the case, other actions and another subject would be necessary to determine this change. From all this it results that action alone, as an empirical criterion, is a sufficient proof of the presence of substantiality, without any necessity on my part of endeavouring to discover the permanence of substance by a comparison. Besides, by this mode of induction we could not attain to the completeness which the magnitude and strict universality of the conception requires. For that the primary subject of the causality of all arising and passing away, all origin and extinction, cannot itself (in the sphere of phænomena) arise and pass away, is a sound and safe conclusion, a conclusion which leads us to the conception of empirical necessity and permanence in existence, and consequently to the conception of a substance as phænomenon.

When something happens, the mere fact of the occurrence, without regard to that which occurs, is an object requiring investigation. The transition from the non-being of a state into the existence of it, supposing that this state contains no quality which previously existed in the phænomenon, is a fact of itself demanding inquiry. Such an event, as has been shown in No. A, does not concern substance (for substance does not thus originate), but its condition or state. It is therefore only change, and not origin from nothing. If this origin be regarded as the effect of a foreign cause, it is termed creation, which cannot be admitted as an event among phænomena, because the very possibility of it would annihilate the unity of experience. If, however, I regard all things not as phænomena, but as things in themselves, and objects of understanding alone, they, although substances, may be considered as dependent, in respect of their existence, on a foreign cause. But this would require a very different meaning in the words, a meaning which could not apply to phænomena as objects of possible experience.

How a thing can be changed, how it is possible that upon one state existing in one point of time, an opposite state should follow in another point of time—of this we have not the smallest conception *a priori.* There is requisite for this the knowledge of real powers, which can only be given empirically; for example, knowledge of moving forces, or, in other words, of certain successive phænomena (as movements) which indicate the presence of such forces. But the form of every change, the condition under which alone it can take place as the coming into existence of another state (be the content of the change, that is, the state which is changed, what it may), and consequently the succession of the states themselves, can very well be considered *a priori,* in relation to the law of causality and the conditions of time.[7]

When a substance passes from one state, *a,* into another state, *b,* the point of time in which the latter exists is different from, and subsequent to that in which the former existed. In like manner, the second state, as reality (in the phænomenon), differs from the first, in which the reality of the second did not exist, as *b* from zero. That is to say, if the state, *b,* differs from the state, *a,* only in respect to quantity, the change is a coming into existence of $b-a$, which in the former state did not exist, and in relation to which that state is $= 0$.

Now the question arises, how a thing passes from one state $=a$, into another state $=b$. Between two moments there is always a certain time, and between two states existing in these moments, there is always a difference having a certain quantity (for all parts of phænomena are in their turn quantities). Consequently, every transition from one state into another, is always effected in a time contained between two moments, of which the first determines the state which the thing leaves, and the second determines the state into which the thing passes. Both moments, then, are limitations of the time of a change, consequently of the intermediate state between both, and as such they belong to the total of the change. Now every change has a cause, which evidences its causality in the whole time during which the change takes place. The cause, therefore, does not produce the change all at once or in one moment, but in a time, so that, as the time gradually increases from the commencing instant, *a,* to its completion at *b,* in like manner also, the quantity of the reality $(b-a)$ is generated through the lesser degrees which are contained between the first and last. All change is therefore possible only through a continuous action of the causality, which, in so far as it is uniform, we call a momentum. The change does not consist of these momenta, but is generated or produced by them as their effect.

Such is the law of the continuity of all change, the ground of which is, that neither time itself nor any phænomenon in time consists of parts which are the smallest possible, but that, notwithstanding, the state of a thing passes in the process of a change through all these parts, as elements, to its second state. There is no smallest degree of reality in a phænomenon, just as there is no smallest degree in the quantity of time; and so the new state of the reality grows up out of the former state, through all the infinite degrees thereof, the differences of which one from another, taken all together, are less than the difference between 0 and *a.*

It is not our business to enquire here into the utility of this principle in the investigation of nature. But how such a proposition, which appears so greatly to extend our knowledge of nature, is possible completely *a priori,* is indeed a question which deserves investigation, although the first view seems to demonstrate the truth and reality of the principle, and the question how it is possible, may be considered superfluous. For there are so many groundless pretensions to the enlargement of our knowledge by pure reason, that we must take it as a general rule to be mistrustful of all such, and without a thorough-going and radical deduction, to believe nothing of the sort even on the clearest dogmatical evidence.

Every addition to our empirical knowledge, and every advance made in the exercise of our perception, is nothing more than extension of the determination of the internal sense, that is to say, a progression in time, be objects themselves what they may, phænomena, or pure intuitions. This progression time determines everything, and is itself determined by nothing else. That is to say, the parts of the progression exist only in time, and by means of the synthesis thereof, and are not given antecedently to it. For this reason, every transition in perception to anything which follows upon another in time, is a determination of time by means of the production of this perception. And as this determination of time always and in all its parts, a quantity, the perception produced is to be considered as a quantity which proceeds through all its degrees—no one of which is the smallest possible—from up to its determined degree. From this we perceive the possibility of cognizing *a priori* a law of changes—a law, however, which concerns their form merely. We merely anticipate our own apprehension, the formal condition of which, inasmuch as it is itself to be found in the mind antecedently to all given phænomena, must certainly be capable of being recognized *a priori*.

Thus, as time contains the sensuous condition *a priori* of possibility of a continuous progression of that which exists to that which follows it, the understanding, by virtue of the unity of apperception, contains the condition *a priori* of the possibility of a continuous determination of the position in time of all phænomena, and this by means of the series of causes and effects, the former of which necessitate the sequence of the latter, and thereby render universally and for all time, by consequence, objectively, valid the empirical cognition of the relations of time.

Refutation of Idealism

Idealism—I mean *material*[8] idealism—is the theory which declares the existence of objects in space without us to be either (1) doubtful and indemonstrable, or (2) false and impossible. The first is the *problematical* idealism of Des Cartes, who admits the undoubted certainty of only one empirical assertion (*assertio*), to wit, *I am*. The second is the *dogmatical* idealism of Berkeley, who maintains that space, together with all the objects of which it is the inseparable condition, is a thing which is in itself impossible, and that consequently the objects in space are mere products of the imagination. The dogmatical theory of idealism is unavoidable, if we regard space as a property of things in themselves; for in that case it is, with all to which it serves as condition, a nonentity. But the foundation for this kind of idealism we have already destroyed in the transcendental aesthetic. Problematical idealism, which makes no such assertion, but only alleges our incapacity to prove the existence of anything besides ourselves by means of immediate experience, is a theory rational and evidencing a thorough and philosophical mode of thinking, for it observes the rule, not to form a decisive judgment before sufficient proof be shown. The desired proof must therefore demonstrate that we have *experience* of external things, and not mere *fancies*. For this purpose, we must prove, that our internal and, to Des Cartes, indubitable experience is itself possible only under the previous assumption of external experience.

Theorem

The simple but empirically determined consciousness of my own existence proves the existence of external objects in space.

Proof

I am conscious of my own existence as determined in time. All determination in regard to time presupposes the existence of *something permanent* in perception. But this permanent something cannot be something in me, for the very reason that my existence in time is itself determined by this permanent something. It follows that the perception of this permanent existence is possible only through a *thing* without me, and not through the mere *representation* of a thing without me. Consequently, the determination of my existence in time is possible only through the existence of real things external to me. Now, consciousness in time is necessarily connected with the consciousness of the possibility of this determination in time. Hence it follows, that consciousness in time is necessarily connected also with the existence of things without me, inasmuch as the existence of these things is the condition of determination in time. That is to say, the consciousness of my own existence is at the same time an immediate consciousness of the existence of other things without me.

Remark I. The reader will observe, that in the foregoing proof the game which idealism plays, is retorted upon itself, and with more justice. It assumed, that the only immediate experience is internal, and that from this we can only *infer* the existence of external things. But, as always happens, when we reason from given effects to *determined* causes, idealism has reasoned with too much haste and uncertainty, for it is quite possible that the cause of our representations may lie in ourselves, and that we ascribe it falsely to external things. But our proof shows that external experience is properly immediate,[9] that only by virtue of it—not, indeed, the consciousness of our own existence, but certainly the determination of our existence in time, that is, internal experience—is possible. It is true, that the representation *I am,* which is the expression of the consciousness which can accompany all my thoughts, is that which immediately includes the existence of a subject. But in this representation we cannot find any knowledge of the subject, and therefore also no empirical knowledge, that is, experience. For experience contains, in addition to the thought of something existing, intuition, and in this case it must be internal intuition, that is, time, in relation to which the subject must be determined. But the existence of external things is absolutely requisite for this purpose, so that it follows that internal experience is itself possible only mediately and through external experience.

Remark II. Now with this view all empirical use of our faculty of cognition in the determination of time is in perfect accordance. Its truth is supported by the fact, that it is possible to perceive a determination of time only by means of a change in external relations (motion) to the permanent in space; (for example, we become aware of the sun's motion, by observing the changes of his relation to the objects of this earth). But this is not all. We find that we possess nothing permanent that can correspond and be submitted to the conception of a substance as intuition, except *matter*. This idea of permanence is not itself derived from external experience, but is an *a priori* necessary condition of all determination of time, consequently also of the internal sense in reference to our own existence, and that through the existence of external things. In the representation *I,* the consciousness of myself is not an intuition, but a merely intellectual representation produced by the spontaneous activity of a thinking subject. It follows, that this I has not any predicate of intuition, which, in its character of permanence, could serve as correlate to the determination of time in the internal sense—in the same way as impenetrability is the correlate of matter as an empirical intuition.

Remark III. From the fact that the existence of external things is a necessary condition of the possibility of a determined consciousness of ourselves, it does not follow that every intuitive representation of external things involves the existence of these things, for their representations may very well be the mere products of the imagination (in dreams as well as in madness); though, indeed, these are themselves created by the reproduction of previous external perceptions, which, as has been shown, are possible only through the reality of external objects. The sole aim of our remarks has however, been to prove that internal experience in general is possible only through external experience in general. Whether this or that supposed experience be purely imaginary, must be discovered from its particular determinations, and by comparing these with the criteria of all real experience.

Fourth Paralogism: Of Ideality
(IN REGARD TO OUTER RELATION)

THAT, THE EXISTENCE OF WHICH CAN ONLY BE INFERRED AS a cause of given perceptions, has a merely doubtful existence.

Now all outer appearances are of such a nature that their existence is not immediately perceived, and that we can only infer them as the cause of given perceptions.

Therefore the existence of all objects of the outer senses is doubtful. This uncertainty I entitle the ideality of outer appearances, and the doctrine of this ideality is called *idealism,* as distinguished from the counter-assertion of a possible certainty in regard to objects of outer sense, which is called *dualism*.

Critique of the Fourth Paralogism of Transcendental Psychology

Let us first examine the premisses. We are justified, [it is argued], in maintaining that only what is in ourselves can be perceived immediately, and that my own existence is the sole object of a mere perception. The existence, therefore, of an actual object outside me (if this word 'me' be taken in the intellectual [not in the empirical] sense) is never given directly in perception. Perception is a modification of inner sense, and the existence of the outer object can be added to it only in thought, as being its outer cause, and accordingly as being inferred. For the same reason, Descartes was justified in limiting all perception, in the narrowest sense of that term, to the proposition, 'I, as a thinking being, exist.' Obviously, since what is without is not in me, I cannot encounter it in my apperception, nor therefore in any perception, which, properly regarded, is merely the determination of apperception.

I am not, therefore, in a position to *perceive* external things, but can only infer their existence from my inner perception, taking the inner perception as the effect of which something external is the proximate cause. Now the inference from a given effect to a determinate cause is always uncertain, since the effect may be due to more than one cause. Accordingly, as regards the relation of the perception to its cause, it always remains doubtful whether the cause be internal or external; whether, that is to say, all the so-called outer perceptions are not a mere play of our inner sense, or whether they stand in relation to actual external objects as their cause. At all events, the existence of the latter is only inferred, and is open to all the dangers of inference, whereas the object of inner sense (I myself with all my representations) is immediately perceived, and its existence does not allow of being doubted.

The term '*idealist*' is not, therefore, to be understood as applying to those who deny the existence of external objects of the senses, but only to those who do not admit that their existence is known through immediate perception, and who therefore conclude that we can never, by way of any possible experience, be completely certain as to their reality.

Before exhibiting our paralogism in all its deceptive illusoriness, I have first to remark that we must necessarily distinguish two types of idealism, the transcendental and the empirical. By *transcendental idealism* I mean the doctrine that appearances are to be regarded as being, one and all, representations only, not things in themselves, and that time and space are therefore only sensible forms of our intuition, not determinations given as existing by themselves, nor conditions of objects viewed as things in themselves. To this ideal ism there is opposed a *transcendental realism* which regards time and space as something given in themselves, independently of our sensibility. The transcendental realist thus interprets outer appearances (their reality being taken as granted) as things-in-themselves, which exist independently of us and of our sensibility, and which are therefore outside us—the phrase 'outside us' being interpreted in conformity with pure concepts of understanding. It is, in fact, this transcendental realist who afterwards plays the part of empirical idealist. After wrongly supposing that objects of the senses, if they are to be external, must have an existence by themselves, and independently of the senses, he finds that, judged from this point of view, all our sensuous representations are inadequate to establish their reality.

The transcendental idealist, on the other hand, may be an empirical realist or, as he is called, a *dualist*; that is, he may admit the existence of matter without going outside his mere self-consciousness, or assuming anything more than the certainty of his representations, that is, the *cogito, ergo sum*. For he considers this matter and even its inner possibility to be appearance merely; and appearance, if separated from our sensibility, is nothing. Matter is with him, therefore, only a species of representations (intuition), which are called external, not as standing in relation to objects *in themselves external,* but because they relate perceptions to the space in which all things are external to one another, while yet the space itself is in us.

From the start, we have declared ourselves in favour of this transcendental idealism; and our doctrine thus removes all difficulty in the way of accepting the existence of matter on the unaided testimony of our mere self-consciousness, or of declaring it to be thereby proved in the same manner as the existence of myself as a thinking being is proved. There can be no question that I am conscious of my representations; these representations and I myself, who have the representations, therefore exist. External objects (bodies), however, are mere appearances, and are therefore nothing but a species of my representations, the objects of which are something only through these representations. Apart from them they are nothing. Thus external things exist as well as I myself, and both, indeed, upon the immediate witness of my self-consciousness. The only difference is that the representation of myself as the thinking subject, belongs to inner sense only, while the representations which mark extended beings belong also to outer sense. In order to arrive at the reality of outer objects I have just as little need to resort to inference as I have in regard to the reality of the object of my inner sense, that is, in regard to the reality of my thoughts. For in both cases alike the objects are nothing but representations, the immediate perception (consciousness) of which is at the same time a sufficient proof of their reality.

The transcendental idealist is, therefore, an empirical realist, and allows to matter, as appearance, a reality which does not permit of being inferred, but is immediately perceived. Transcendental realism, on the other hand, inevitably falls into difficulties, and finds itself obliged to give way to empirical idealism, in that it regards the objects of outer sense as something distinct from the senses themselves, treating mere appearances as self-subsistent beings, existing outside us. On such a view as this, however clearly we may be conscious[10] of our representation of these things, it is still far from certain that, if the representation exists, there exists also the object corresponding to it. In our system, on the other hand, these external things, namely matter, are in all their configurations and alterations nothing but mere appearances, that is, representations in us, of the reality of which we are immediately conscious.

Since, so far as I know, all psychologists who adopt empirical idealism are transcendental realists, they have certainly proceeded quite consistently in ascribing great importance to empirical idealism, as one of the problems in regard to which the human mind is quite at a loss how to proceed. For if we regard outer appearances as representations produced in us by their objects, and if these objects be things existing in themselves outside us, it is indeed impossible to see how we can come to know the existence of the objects otherwise than by inference from the effect to the cause; and this being so, it must always remain doubtful whether the cause in question be in us or outside us. We can indeed admit that something, which may be (in the transcendental sense) outside us, is the cause of our outer intuitions, but this is not the object of which we are thinking in the representations of matter and of corporeal things; for these are merely appearances, that is, mere kinds of representation, which are never to be met with save in us, and the reality of which depends on immediate consciousness, just as does the consciousness of my own thoughts. The transcendental object is equally unknown in respect to inner and to outer intuition. But it is not of this that we are here speaking, but of the empirical object, which is called an *external* object if it is represented *in space,* and an *inner* object if it is represented only *in its time-relations.* Neither space nor time, however, is to be found save *in us.*

The expression '*outside us*' is thus unavoidably ambiguous in meaning, sometimes signifying what *as thing in itself* exists apart from us, and sometimes what belongs solely to outer *appearance.* In order, therefore, to make this concept, in the latter sense—the sense in which the psychological question as to the reality of our outer intuition has to be understood—quite unambiguous, we shall distinguish *empirically external* objects from those which may be said to be external in the transcendental sense, by explicitly entitling the former '*things which are to be found in space*'

Space and time are indeed *a priori* representations, which dwell in us as forms of our sensible intuition, before any real object, determining our sense through sensation, has enabled us to represent the object under those sensible relations. But the material or real element, the something which is to be intuited in space, necessarily presupposes perception. Perception exhibits the reality of something in space; and in the absence of perception no power of imagination can invent and produce that something. It is sensation, therefore, that indicates a reality in space or[11]1 in time, according as it is related to the one or to the other mode of sensible intuition. (Once sensation is given—if referred to an object in general, though not as determining that object, it is entitled perception—thanks to its manifoldness we can picture in imagination many objects which have no empirical place in space or time outside the imagination.)[12] This admits of no doubt; whether we take pleasure and pain, or the sensations of the outer senses, colours, heat, etc., perception is that whereby the material required to enable us to think objects of sensible intuition must first be given. This perception, therefore (to consider, for the moment, only outer intuitions), represents something real in space. For, in the first place, while space is the representation of a mere possibility of coexistence, perception is the representation of a reality. Secondly, this reality is represented in outer sense, that is, in space. Thirdly, space is itself nothing but mere representation, and therefore nothing in it can count as real save only what is represented in it;[13] a and conversely, what is given in it, that is, represented through perception, is also real in it. For if it were not real, that is, immediately given through empirical intuition, it could not be pictured in imagination, since what is real in intuitions cannot be invented *a priori*.

All outer perception, therefore, yields immediate proof of something real[14] in space, or rather is the real itself. In this sense empirical realism is beyond question; that is, there corresponds to our outer intuitions something real in space. Space itself, with all its appearances, as representations, is, indeed, only in me, but nevertheless the real, that is, the material of all objects of outer intuition, is actually given in this space, independently of all imaginative invention. Also, it is impossible that in *this space* anything *outside us* (in the transcendental sense) should be given, space itself being nothing outside our sensibility. Even the most rigid idealist cannot, therefore, require a proof that the object outside us (taking 'outside' in the strict [transcendental] sense) corresponds to our perception. For if there be any such object, it could not be represented and intuited as outside us, because such representation and intuition presuppose space, and reality in space, being the reality of a mere representation, is nothing other than perception itself. The real of outer appearances is therefore real in perception only, and can be real in no other way.

From perceptions knowledge of objects can be generated, either by mere play of imagination or by way of experience; and in the process there may, no doubt, arise illusory representations to which the objects do not correspond, the deception being attributable sometimes to a delusion of imagination (in dreams) and sometimes to an error of judgment (in so-called sense-deception). To avoid such deceptive illusion, we have to proceed according to the rule: *Whatever is connected with a perception according to empirical laws, is actual.* But such deception, as well as the provision against it, affects idealism quite as much as dualism, inasmuch as we are concerned only with the form of experience. Empirical idealism, and its mistaken questionings as to the objective reality of our outer perceptions, is already sufficiently refuted, when it has been shown that outer perception yields immediate proof of something actual in space, and that this space, although in itself only a mere form of representations, has objective reality in relation to all outer appearances, which also are nothing else than mere representations; and when it has likewise been shown that in the absence of perception even imagining and dreaming are not possible, and that our outer senses, as regards the data from which experience can arise, have therefore their actual corresponding objects in space.

The *dogmatic idealist* would be one who *denies* the existence of matter, the *sceptical idealist* one who *doubts* its existence, because holding it to be incapable of proof.[15] The former must base his view on supposed contradictions in the possibility of there being such a thing as matter at all—a view with which we have not yet been called upon to deal. The following section on dialectical inferences, which represents reason as in strife with itself in regard to the concepts which it makes for itself of the possibility of what[16] belongs to the connection of experience, will remove this difficulty. The sceptical idealist, however, who merely challenges the ground of our assertion and denounces as insufficiently justified our conviction of the existence of matter, which we thought to base on immediate perception, is a benefactor of human reason in so far as he compels us, even in the smallest advances of ordinary experience, to keep on the watch, lest we consider as a well-earned possession what we perhaps obtain only illegitimately. We are now in a position to appreciate the value of these idealist objections. Unless we mean to contradict ourselves in our commonest assertions, they drive us by main force to view all our perceptions, whether we call them inner or outer, as a consciousness only of what is dependent on our sensibility. They also compel us to view the outer objects of these perceptions not as things in themselves, but only as representations, of which, as of every other representation, we can become immediately conscious, and which are entitled outer because they depend on what we call 'outer sense', whose intuition is space. Space itself, however, is nothing but an inner mode of representation in which certain perceptions are connected with one another.

If we treat outer objects as things in themselves, it is quite impossible to understand how we could arrive at a knowledge of their reality outside us, since we have to rely merely on the representation which is in us. For we cannot be sentient [of what is] outside ourselves, but only [of what is] in us, and the whole of our self-consciousness therefore yields nothing save merely our own determinations. Sceptical idealism thus constrains us to have recourse to the only refuge still open, namely, the ideality of all appearances, a doctrine which has already been established in the Transcendental Aesthetic independently of these consequences, which we could not at that stage foresee. If then we ask, whether it follows that in the doctrine of the soul dualism alone is tenable, we must answer: 'Yes, certainly; but dualism only in the empirical sense'. That is to say, in the connection of experience matter, as substance in the [field of] appearance, is really given to outer sense, just as the thinking 'I', also as substance in the [field of] appearance, is given to inner sense. Further, appearances in both fields[17] must be connected with each other according to the rules which this category introduces into that connection of our outer as well as of our inner perceptions whereby they constitute one experience. If, however, as commonly happens, we seek to extend the concept of dualism, and take it in the transcendental sense, neither it nor the two counter-alternatives—*pneumatism* on the one hand, *materialism* on the other—would have any sort of basis, since we should then have misapplied our concepts, taking the difference in the mode of representing objects, which, as regards what they are in themselves, still remain unknown to us, as a difference in the things themselves. Though the 'I', as represented through inner sense in time, and objects in space outside me, are specifically quite distinct appearances, they are not for that reason thought as being different things. Neither the *transcendental object* which underlies outer appearances nor that which underlies inner intuition, is in itself either matter or a thinking being, but a ground (to us unknown) of the appearances which supply to us the empirical concept of the former as well as of the latter mode of existence.

If then, as this critical argument obviously compels us to do, we hold fast to the rule above established, and do not push our questions beyond the limits within which possible experience can present us with its object, we shall never dream of seeking to inform ourselves about the objects of our senses as they are in themselves, that is, out of all relation to the senses. But if the psychologist takes appearances for things in themselves, and as existing in and by themselves, then whether he be a materialist who admits into his system nothing but matter alone, or a spiritualist who admits only thinking beings (that is, beings with the form of our inner sense), or a dualist who accepts both, he will always, owing to this misunderstanding, be entangled in pseudo-rational speculations as to how that which is not a thing in itself, but only the appearance of a thing in general, can exist by itself.

Notes

1 Gelegenheitsursachen.

2 Kant's meaning is: The objects of cognition in Geometry,—angles, lines, figures, and the like,—are not different from the act of cognition which produces them, except in thought. The object does not exist but while we think it—does not exist apart from our thinking it. The act of thinking and the object of thinking, are but one thing regarded from two different points of view.—*Tr.*

3 I have been compelled to adopt a conjectural reading here. All the editions of the *Critik der Reinen Vernunft*, both those published during Kant's lifetime, and those published by various editors after his death, have *sie. . von Gegenständen. . . . redet.* But it is quite plain that the *sie* is the pronoun for *die reine Verstandesbegriffe*; and we ought, therefore, to read *reden.* In the same sentence, all the editions (except Hartenstein's) insert *die* after the first *und,* which makes nonsense. In page 75 also, sentence beginning "*For that objects,*" I have altered "*synthetischen Einsicht des Denkens*" into "*synthetischen Einheit.*" And in page 77, sentence beginning, "*But it is evident,*" we find "*die erste Bedingung liegen.*" Some such word as *muss* is plainly to be understood.

   Indeed, I have not found a single edition of the *Critique* trustworthy. Kant must not have been very careful in his correction of the press. Those published by editors after Kant's death seem in most cases to follow Kant's own editions closely. That by Rosencrantz is perhaps the best; and he has corrected a number of Kant's errors. But although I have adopted several uncommon and also conjectural readings, I have not done so hastily or lightly. It is only after diligent comparison of all the editions I could gain access to, that I have altered the common reading; while a conjectural reading has been adopted only when it was quite clear that the reading of every edition was a misprint.

   Other errors, occurring previously to those mentioned above, have been, and others after them will be. corrected in silence.—*Tr.*

4 Inbegriff.

5 Mental synthesis.—*Tr.*

6 This was the opinion of Wolf and Leibnitz.—*Tr.*

7 It must be remarked, that I do not speak of the change of certain relations, but of the change of the state. Thus, when a body moves in an uniform manner, it does not change its staté (of motion); but only when its motion increases or decreases.

8 In opposition to *formal* or *critical* idealism—the theory of Kant—which denies to us a knowledge of things as things in themselves, and maintains that we can know only phænomena.—*Tr.*

9 The *immediate* consciousness of the existence of external things is, in the preceding theorem, not presupposed, but proved, be the possibility of this consciousness understood by us or not. The question as to the possibility of it would stand thus: Have we an internal sense, but no external sense, and is our

belief in external perception a mere delusion? But it is evident that, in order merely to fancy to ourselves anything *as* external, that is, to present it to the sense in intuition, we must already possess an external sense, and must thereby distinguish immediately the mere receptivity of an external intuition from the spontaneity which characterises every act of imagination. For merely to imagine also an external sense, would annihilate the faculty of intuition itself, which is to be determined by the imagination.

10 [*bei unserem besten Bewusstsein.*]

11 [Reading, with Erdmann, *oder* for *und.*]

12 [Brackets not in text.]

13 We must give full credence to this paradoxical but correct proposition, that there is nothing in space save what is represented in it. For space is itself nothing but representation, and whatever is in it must therefore be contained in the representation. Nothing whatsoever is in space, save in so far as it is actually represented in it. It is a proposition which must indeed sound strange, that a thing can exist only in the representation of it, but in this case the objection falls, inasmuch as the things with which we are here concerned are not things in themselves, but appearances only, that is, representations.

14 [*wirkliches.* In this section, as elsewhere, Kant uses *Wirklichkeit* and *Realität* as synonymous terms.]

15 [Reading, with Erdmann, *es . . . es* for *sie . . . sie.*]

16 [Reading, with Hartenstein and Kehrbach, *die sie sich . . . dessen macht* for *die sich . . . dessen.*]

17 [*beiderseits.*]

24

Johann Gottfried von Herder

The Spirit of Hebrew Poetry (1782)

Dialogue I

ALCIPHRON. So I find you still devoted to the study of this poor and barbarous language! A proof how much early impressions can effect, and how indispensably necessary it is, that our young minds be kept clear of the rubbish of antiquity. There is afterwards no hope of deliverance.

EUTHYPHRON. You speak like one of our modern illuminators, who would free men not only from the prejudices of childhood, but if possible from childhood itself. Do you know any thing of this barren and barbarous language? What are the grounds of your opinion concerning it?

A. I know enough of it to my sorrow. It was the torment of my childhood, and I am still haunted with the recollection of it, when in the study of theology, of philosophy, of history, and of what not, I hear the echo of its sublime nonsense. The rattling of ancient cymbals and kettle-drums, in short, the whole music-band of savage nations, which you love to denominate the oriental parallelism, is still ringing in my ears. I still see David dancing before the Ark of the covenant, or the prophets summoning a player, that they may feel his inspirations.

E. You seem then to have become acquainted with the language, but to have studied it with no very good will.

A. I cannot help that; it is enough that I studied it methodically with all the rules of Dantz. I could cite the rules, but never knew their meaning.

E. So much the worse, and I comprehend now the reason of your disgust. But my dear Sir, shall we permit ourselves to hate a science, which we have the misfortune to learn at first under a bad form? Would you judge a man by his dress alone? And that too when the dress is not his own, but forced upon him?

A. By no means, and I am ready to abandon all prejudices, so soon as you will shew them to be such. This, however, I think will be difficult, for I have pretty well tried both the language and its contents.

E. We will make the experiment, and one of us will become the teacher of the other. Truth is, indeed, to be bewailed, if men can never be at one respecting it. For myself I would execrate the impressions of my youth, if they must bind me through life with the fetters of a slave. But be assured, I have no youthful impressions from the poetical spirit of this language; I learned it as you did. It was long before I acquired a taste for its beauties, and only by degrees that I came to consider it, as I now do, a sacred language, the source of our most precious knowledge, and of that early cultivation, which extending over but a small portion of the earth, came to us gratuitously and unsought.

A. You are driving at an apotheosis, at once.

E. At no such thing: we will consider it as a human language, and its contents as merely human. Nay, more, to give you better assurance of my perfect fairness, we will speak of it only as an instrument of ancient poetry. Are you pleased with this subject? It has at least nothing insidious.

A. Certainly nothing, and with such a discussion I should be delighted in the highest degree. I am glad to converse of ancient languages, when they are treated only in relation to men. They are the form, in which human thoughts are moulded more or less perfectly. They exhibit the most distinguishing traits of character, and the manner in which objects are contemplated by different nations. Comparison of one with another in these points is always instructive. Proceed then to discuss the dialect, even of these Eastern Hurons. Their poverty may at least enrich us, and conduct us to thoughts of our own.

E. What do you consider most essential to a poetical language? No matter whether it belong to the Hurons or Otaheitans. Is it not action, imagery, passion, musick, rhythm?

A. Undoubtedly.

E. And the language that exhibits these in the highest perfection is most peculiarly poetical. Now you are aware, that the languages of people but partially cultivated may have this character in a high degree, and are in fact in this particular superior to many of the too refined modern languages. I need not remind you among what people Ossian, or at what period even the Grecian Homer sang.

A. It does not follow from this, that every savage race has its Homer and Ossian.

E. Perhaps many have even more, exclusively indeed for themselves, and not for the language of other nations. In order to judge of a nation, we must live in their time, in their own country, must adopt their modes of thinking and feeling, must see, how they lived, how they were educated, what scenes they looked upon, what were the objects of their affection and passion, the character of their atmosphere, their skies, the structure of their organs, their dances and their musick. All this too we must learn to think of not as strangers or enemies, but as their brothers and compatriots, and then ask, whether in their own kind, and for their peculiar wants, they had an Homer or an Ossian. You know in regard to how few nations we have instituted or are even now prepared to institute an inquiry of this kind. With regard to the Hebrews we can do it. Their poetry is in our hands.

A. But what poetry! and in what a language! How imperfect is it! how poor in proper terms and definitely expressed relations! How unfixed and uncertain are the tenses of the verbs! One never knows whether the time referred to by them be to day or yesterday, a thousand years ago, or a thousand years to come. Adjectives, so important in description, it scarcely has at all, and must supply their place by beggarly combinations. How uncertain and far-fetched is the signification of their radical words, how forced and unnatural the derivations from them! Hence the frightful forms of the catachresis, the far sought images, the monstrous combinations of ideas the most heterogeneous. The parallelism is monotonous, an everlasting tautology, that, without a metrical arrangement of words and syllables, after all very imperfectly satisfies the ear. Aures perpetuis tautologiis lædunt, says one of those best acquainted with them, Orienti jucundis, Europæ invisis, prudentioribus stomachaturis, dormitaturis reliquis. And he says the truth. This is observable in all the psalms and productions, that breathe the spirit of this language. Finally, it had no vowels, for these are a more modern invention. It stands as a lifeless and senseless hieroglyph, very often without any key or certain index of its meaning, at all events without any certain expression of pronunciation and knowledge of its ancient rhythm. What do you find here of Homer and Ossian? As well look for them in Mexico, or upon the sculptured rocks of Arabia. [. . .]

A. It will be most to our purpose, if we conduct the discussion by means of individual examples. Begin, if you please, with the radical forms, with the verbs.

E. The roots of the Hebrew verbs, I remarked, combine form and feeling, and I know no language in which the simple and unstudied combination of the two is so much an affair of the senses, and so remarkable. Not so sensible and obvious, I admit very willingly, to an ear accustomed only to the accents of Northern languages, but to you, who are acquainted with the principles of formation in the Greek language, to you, my dear Sir, it will not be difficult to go a few steps further, and observe with a congenial feeling, the method more forcible indeed, but not therefore more clumsy, of forming words in the East. I repeat it again, in the most pregnant terms of the language are combined the sensuous form and the sensation or sentiment that it produces. The language was moulded and uttered with a fuller expiration from the lungs, with organs yet pliable and vigorous, but at the same time under a clear and luminous heaven, with powers of vision acute, and seizing as it were upon the very objects themselves, and almost always with some mark of emotion or passion.

A. Form and feeling, tranquility and passion, accents strong and yet light and flowing! these are rare combinations.

E. Let us then analyze them and explain the matter more carefully. All Northern languages imitate the sounds of natural objects, but roughly, and as it were only by the mechanism of the. outward organs. Like the objects they imitate, they abound with creaking, and rustling, and whizzing, and crashing sounds, which wise poets may employ sparingly with effect, but which the injudicious will abuse. The cause of this is obviously to be found in the climate, and in the organs, in and by which the languages were originally formed. The further South, the more refined will be the imitation of nature. Homer's most sounding lines do not creak and hiss, they are sonorous. The words have passed through a refining process, been modified by feeling, and moulded as it were, in the vicinity of the heart. Thus they do not present uncouth forms of mere sound and noise, but forms on which feeling has placed its gentler impress. In this union of feeling from within, and form from without, in the roots of their verbs, the Oriental languages, I meant to say, are the best models.

A. Is it possible you are speaking of those barbarous and uncouth gutturals? And do you venture to compare them with the silvery tones of the Greek?

E. I make no comparison. Every language suffers by being thus compared with another. Nothing is more exclusively national and individual than the modes of gratifying the ear, and the characteristick habitudes of the organs of speech. We, for example, discover a delicacy in articulating and uttering our words only from between the tongue and the lips, and in opening our mouths but little, as if we lived in an atmosphere of smoke and fog. The climate, our manners and the prevailing custom require it, and the language itself, has been gradually moulded into the same form. The Italians and still more the Greeks, think otherwise. The language of the former abounds in full and sonorous vowel sounds, and that of the latter with dipthongs, both of which are uttered not with the lips compressed together, but ore rotundo. The accents of the East are uttered forth more ab imo pectore, and from the heart. Elihu describes it, when he exclaims,

> I am full of words,
> My inmost spirit labours;
> Lo! it is like wine without vent;
> My bosom is bursting, like new bottles;
> I will speak, and make myself room;
> I will open my lips and answer.

When these lips are opened, the utterance is full of animation, and bodies forth the forms of things, while it is giving vent to feeling, and this, it appears to me, is the spirit of the Hebrew language. It is the very breath of the soul. It does not claim the beauty of sound, like the Greek, but it breathes and lives. Such is it to us, who are but partially acquainted with its pronunciation, and for whom its deeper gutturals remain unuttered and unutterable; in those old times, when the soul was unshackled, what fulness of emotion, what store of words that breathe, must have inspired it. It was, to use an expression of its own,

> The spirit of God that spake in it,
> The breath of the Almighty that gave it life.

A. Once more you have nearly accomplished its apotheosis. Yet all this may be so in relation to the radical sounds, or the utterance of feeling that was prompted, while the object itself was present to the senses. But how is it with the derivations from these radical terms? What are they but an overgrown jungle of thorns, where no human foot has ever found rest?

E. In bad lexicons this is indeed the case, and many of the most learned philologists of Holland have rendered the way still more difficult by their labours. But the time is coming, when this jungle will become a grove of palms.

A. Your metaphor is an Oriental one.

E. So is the object of it. The root of the primitive word will be placed in the centre and its offspring form a grove around it. By influence of taste, diligence, sound sense, and the judicious comparison of different dialects, lexicons will be brought to distinguish, what is essential from what is accidental in the signification of words, and to trace the gradual process of transition, while in the derivation of words, and the application of metaphors we come more fully to understand the logick of ancient figurative language. I anticipate with joy the time, and the first lexicon, in which this shall be well accomplished. [. . .]

Poetry is not addressed to the understanding alone but primarily and chiefly to the feelings. And are these not friendly to the parallelism? So soon as the heart gives way to its emotions, wave follows upon wave, and that is parallelism. The heart is never exhausted, it has forever something new to say. So soon as the first wave has passed away, or broken itself upon the rocks, the second swells again and returns as before. This pulsation of nature, this breathing of emotion, appears in all the language of passion, and would you not have that in poetry, which is most peculiarly the offspring of emotion.

A. But suppose it aims to be and must be at the same time the language of the understanding?

E. It changes the figure and exhibits the thought in another light. It varies the precept, and explains it, or impresses it upon the heart. [. . .]

We will continue the discussion of the subject in our walks, and more especially in our morning rambles. The poetry of the Hebrews, should be heard under the open sky, and if possible in the dawn of the morning.

A. Why at this particular time?

E. Because it was itself the first dawning of the illumination of the world, while our race was yet in its infancy. We see in it the earliest perceptions, the simplest forms, by which the human soul expressed its thoughts, the most uncorrupted affections that bound and guided it. Though we should be convinced that it contained nothing remarkable, yet the language of nature in it, we must believe, for we feel it. The first perceptions of things, must be dear to us, for we should gain knowledge by them. In it the earliest Logick of the senses, the simplest analysis of ideas and the primary principles of morals, in short, the most ancient history of the human mind and heart, are brought before our eyes. Were it even the poetry of cannibals, would you not think it worthy of attention for these purposes?

A. We meet again, you say, in the morning.

25

Samuel Taylor Coleridge

Dejection: An Ode (1802)

Late, late yestreen I saw the new Moon,
With the old Moon in her arms;
And I fear, I fear, my Master dear!
We shall have a deadly storm.

Ballad of Sir PATRICK SPENCE

WELL! If the Bard was weather-wise, who made
    The grand old ballad of Sir Patrick Spence,
    This night, so tranquil now, will not go hence
Unrous'd by winds, that ply a busier trade
Than those which mould yon clouds in lazy flakes,
Or the dull sobbing draft, that moans and rakes
      Upon the strings of the Æolian lute,
      Which better far were mute.
    For lo! the New-moon winter-bright!
    And overspread with phantom-light,
    (With swimming phantom-light o'erspread
    But rimm'd and circled by a silver thread)
I see the old Moon in her lap, foretelling
    The coming-on of rain and squally blast.
And oh! that even now the gust were swelling,
    And the slant night-shower driving loud and fast!

Those sounds which oft have raised me, whilst they awed,
     And sent my soul abroad,
Might now perhaps their wonted impulse give,
Might startle this dull pain, and make it move and live!

A grief without a pang, void, dark, and drear,
     A stifled, drowsy, unimpassion'd grief,
     Which finds no natural outlet, no relief,
          In word, or sigh, or tear—
O Lady! in this wan and heartless mood,
To other thoughts by yonder throstle woo'd,
     All this long eve, so balmy and serene,
Have I been gazing on the western sky,
     And its peculiar tint of yellow green:
And still I gaze—and with how blank an eye!
And those thin clouds above, in flakes and bars,
That give away their motion to the stars;
Those stars, that glide behind them or between,
Now sparkling, now bedimm'd, but always seen:
Yon crescent Moon, as fix'd as if it grew
In its own cloudless, starless lake of blue;
I see them all so excellently fair,
I see, not feel, how beautiful they are!

          My genial spirits fail,
          And what can these avail,
To lift the smoth'ring weight from off my breast?
          It were a vain endeavour
          Though I should gaze for ever
On that green light that lingers in the west:
I may not hope from outward forms to win
The passion and the life, whose fountains are within.

O Lady! we receive but what we give.
And in our life alone does nature live;
Ours is her wedding garment, ours her shroud!
     And would we aught behold, of higher worth,
Than that inanimate cold world allow'd
To the poor loveless ever-anxious crowd,
     Ah! from the soul itself must issue forth,

A light, a glory, a fair luminous cloud
    Enveloping the Earth—
And from the soul itself must there be sent
    A sweet and potent voice, of its own birth,
Of all sweet sounds the life and element!

O pure of heart! thou need'st not ask of me
What this strong music in the soul may be!
What, and wherein it doth exist,
This light, this glory, this fair luminous mist,
This beautiful and beauty-making power.
    Joy, virtuous Lady! Joy that ne'er was given,
Save to the pure, and in their purest hour,
Life, and life's effluence, cloud at once and shower,
Joy, Lady! is the spirit and the power,
Which wedding Nature to us gives in dow'r
    A new Earth and new Heaven,
Undreamt of by the sensual and the proud—
Joy is the sweet voice, Joy the luminous cloud—
      We in ourselves rejoice!
And thence flows all that charms or ear or sight,
      All melodies the echoes of that voice,
    All colours a suffusion from that light.

    There was a time when, though my path was rough,
      This joy within me dallied with distress,
And all misfortunes were but as the stuff
      Whence Fancy made me dreams of happiness:
    For hope grew round me, like the twining vine,
    And fruits, and foliage, not my own, seem'd mine.
    But now afflictions bow me down to earth:
    Nor care I that they rob me of my mirth;
    But oh! each visitation
Suspends what nature gave me at my birth,
    My shaping spirit of Imagination.
For not to think of what I needs must feel,
    But to be still and patient, all I can;
And haply by abstruse research to steal
    From my own nature all the natural Man—

This was my sole resource, my only plan:
Till that which suits a part infects the whole,
And now is almost grown the habit of my Soul.

Hence, viper thoughts, that coil around my mind,
     Reality's dark dream!
I turn from you, and listen to the wind,
     Which long has rav'd unnotic'd. What a scream
Of agony by torture lengthen'd out
That lute sent forth! Thou Wind, that rav'st without,
     Bare crag, or mountain-tairn, or blasted tree,
Or pine-grove whither woodman never clomb,
Or lonely house, long held the witches' home,
     Methinks were fitter instruments for thee,
Mad Lutanist! who in this month of show'rs,
Of dark-brown gardens, and of peeping flow'rs,
Mak'st Devils' yule, with worse than wintry song,
The blossoms, buds, and tim'rous leaves among.
     Thou Actor, perfect in all tragic sounds!
Thou mighty Poet, e'en to Frenzy bold!
       What tell'st thou now about?
       'Tis of the rushing of an Host in rout,
With groans of trampled men, with smarting wounds—
At once they groan with pain, and shudder with the cold!
But hush! there is a pause of deepest silence!
     And all that noise, as of a rushing crowd,
With groans, and tremulous shudderings—all is over—
     It tells another tale, with sounds less deep and loud!
       A tale of less affright,
       And temper'd with delight,
As Otway's self had fram'd the tender lay—
       'Tis of a little child
       Upon a lonesome wild,
Not far from home, but she hath lost her way;
And now moans low in bitter grief and fear,
And now screams loud, and hopes to make her mother hear.

'Tis midnight, but small thoughts have I of sleep:
Full seldom may my friend such vigils keep!

Visit her, gentle Sleep! with wings of healing,

    And may this storm be but a mountain-birth,

May all the stars hang bright above her dwelling,

    Silent as though they watch'd the sleeping Earth!

        With light heart may she rise,

        Gay fancy, cheerful eyes,

    Joy lift her spirit, joy attune her voice;

To her may all things live, from Pole to Pole,

Their life the eddying of her living soul!

    O simple spirit, guided from above,

Dear Lady! friend devoutest of my choice,

Thus may'st thou ever, evermore rejoice.

Biographia Literaria (1817)

Chapter XII

A chapter of requests and premonitions concerning the perusal or omission of the chapter that follows.

IN THE PERUSAL OF PHILOSOPHICAL WORKS I HAVE BEEN GREATLY benefitted by a resolve which, in the antithetic form and with the allowed quaintness of an adage or maxim, I have been accustomed to word thus: 'Until you understand a writer's ignorance, presume yourself ignorant of his understanding.' This golden rule of mine does, I own, resemble those of Pythagoras in its obscurity rather than in its depth. If, however, the reader will permit me to be my own Hierocles, I trust that he will find its meaning fully explained by the following instances. I have now before me a treatise of a religious fanatic, full of dreams and supernatural experiences. I see clearly the writer's grounds, and their hollowness. I have a complete insight into the causes which through the medium of his body had acted on his mind; and by application of received and ascertained laws I can satisfactorily explain to my own reason all the strange incidents which the writer records of himself. And this I can do without suspecting him of any intentional falsehood. As when in broad daylight a man tracks the steps of a traveller who had lost his way in a fog or by treacherous moonshine, even so, and with the same tranquil sense of certainty, can I follow the traces of this bewildered visionary. *I understand his ignorance.*

On the other hand, I have been re-perusing with the best energies of my mind the Timaeus of Plato. Whatever I comprehend impresses me with a reverential sense of the author's genius; but there is a considerable portion of the work to which I can attach no consistent meaning. In other treatises of the same philosopher intended for the average comprehensions of men,

I have been delighted with the masterly good sense, with the perspicuity of the language and the aptness of the inductions. I recollect likewise that numerous passages in this author, which I thoroughly comprehend, were formerly no less unintelligible to me than the passages now in question. It would, I am aware, be quite fashionable to dismiss them at once as Platonic jargon. But this I cannot do with satisfaction to my own mind, because I have sought in vain for causes adequate to the solution of the assumed inconsistency. I have no insight into the possibility of a man so eminently wise using words with such half-meanings to himself as must perforce pass into no-meaning to his readers. When, in addition to the motives thus suggested by my own reason, I bring into distinct remembrance the number and the series of great men who, after long and zealous study of these works, had joined in honoring the name of Plato with epithets that almost transcend humanity, I feel that a contemptuous verdict on my part might argue want of modesty, but would hardly be received by the judicious as evidence of superior penetration. Therefore, utterly baffled in all my attempts to understand the ignorance of Plato, *I conclude myself ignorant of his understanding.*

In lieu of the various requests which the anxiety of authorship addresses to the unknown reader I advance but this one: that he will either pass over the following chapter altogether or read the whole connectedly. The fairest part of the most beautiful body will appear deformed and monstrous if dissevered from its place in the organic whole. Nay, on delicate subjects, where a seemingly trifling difference of more or less may constitute a difference in kind, even a faithful display of the main and supporting ideas, if yet they are separated from the forms by which they are at once clothed and modified, may perchance present a skeleton indeed, but a skeleton to alarm and deter. Though I might find numerous precedents, I shall not desire the reader to strip his mind of all prejudices, not to keep all prior systems out of view during his examination of the present. For, in truth, such requests appear to me not much unlike the advice given to hypo-chondriacal patients in Dr Buchan's domestic medicine; *videlicet,* to preserve themselves uniformly tranquil and in good spirits. Till I had discovered the art of destroying the memory *a parte post,* without injury to its future operations, and without detriment to the judgement, I should suppress the request as premature; and, therefore, however much I may wish to be read with an unprejudiced mind, I do not presume to state it as a necessary condition.

The extent of my daring is to suggest one criterion by which it may be rationally conjectured beforehand whether or no a reader would lose his time, and perhaps his temper, in the perusal of this or any other treatise constructed on similar principles. But it would be cruelly misinterpreted as implying the least disrespect either for the moral or intellectual qualities of the individuals thereby precluded. The criterion is this: if a man receives as fundamental facts, and therefore of course indemonstrable and incapable of further analysis, the general notions of matter, spirit, soul, body, action, passiveness, time, space, cause and effect, consciousness, perception, memory and habit; if he feels his mind completely at rest concerning all these, and is satisfied if only he can analyse all other notions into some one or more of these supposed elements with plausible subordination and apt arrangement; to such a mind I would as courteously as possible convey the hint that for him the chapter was not written.

Vir bonus es, doctus, prudens! ast haud tibi spiro.

For these terms do in truth include all the difficulties which the human mind can propose for solution. Taking them therefore in mass, and unexamined, it requires only a decent apprenticeship in logic to draw forth their contents in all forms and colours, as the professors of legerdemain at our village fairs pull out ribbon after ribbon from their mouths. And not more difficult is it to reduce them back again to their different genera. But though this analysis is highly useful in rendering our knowledge more distinct, it does not really add to it. It does not increase, though it gives us a greater mastery over, the wealth which we before possessed. For forensic purposes, for all the established professions of society, this is sufficient. But for philosophy in its highest sense, as the science of ultimate truths and therefore *scientia scientiarum,* this mere analysis of terms is preparative only, though as a preparative discipline indispensable.

Still less dare a favorable perusal be anticipated from the proselytes of that compendious philosophy which, talking of mind but thinking of brick and mortar, or other images equally abstracted from body, contrives a theory of spirit by nicknaming matter, and in a few hours can qualify its dullest disciples to explain the *omne scibile* by reducing all things to impressions, ideas and sensations.

But it is time to tell the truth; though it requires some courage to avow it in an age and country in which disquisitions on all subjects not privileged to adopt technical terms or scientific symbols must be addressed to the public. I say then that it is neither possible or necessary for all men, or for many, to be philosophers. There is a philosophic (and inasmuch as it is actualized by an effort of freedom, an artificial) consciousness, which lies beneath or (as it were) behind the spontaneous consciousness natural to all reflecting beings. As the elder Romans distinguished their northern provinces into Cis-Alpine and Trans-Alpine, so may we divide all the objects of human knowledge into those on this side, and those on the other side of the spontaneous consciousness: citra et trans conscientiam communem. The latter is exclusively the domain of pure philosophy, which is therefore properly entitled transcendental, in order to discriminate it at once both from mere reflection and *re*-presentation on the one hand, and on the other from those flights of lawless speculation which, abandoned by all distinct consciousness because transgressing the bounds and purposes of our intellectual faculties, are justly condemned as transcendent.[1] The first range of hills that encircles the scanty vale of human life is the horizon for the majority of its inhabitants. On its ridges the common sun is born and departs. From them the stars rise, and touching them they vanish. By the many even this range, the natural limit and bulwark of the vale, is but imperfectly known. Its higher ascents are too often hidden by mists and clouds from uncultivated swamps which few have courage or curiosity to penetrate. To the multitude below these vapors appear, now as the dark haunts of terrific agents on which none may intrude with impunity; and now all a-glow with colors not their own, they are gazed at as the splendid palaces of happiness and power. But in all ages there have been a few who, measuring and sounding the rivers of the vale at the feet of their furthest inaccessible falls, have learnt that the sources must be far higher and far inward; a few who even in the level streams have detected elements which neither the vale itself nor the surrounding mountains contained or could supply. How and whence to these thoughts, these strong probabilities, the ascertaining vision, the intuitive knowledge, may finally supervene, can be learnt only by the fact. I might oppose to the question the words with which Plotinus[2] supposes nature to answer a similar difficulty: 'Should any one interrogate her, how she works, if graciously she vouchsafe to listen and speak, she will reply, it behoves thee not to disquiet me with interrogatories, but to understand in silence, even as I am silent, and work without words.'

Likewise in the fifth book of the fifth Ennead, speaking of the highest and intuitive knowledge as distinguished from the discursive, or in the language of Wordsworth,

The vision and the faculty divine;

he says: 'it is not lawful to inquire from whence it sprang, as if he were a thing subject to place and motion; for it neither approached hither, nor again departs from hence to some other place; but it either appears to us or it does not appear. So that we ought not to pursue it with a view of detecting its secret sources, but to watch in quiet till it suddenly shines upon us; preparing ourselves for the blessed spectacle as the eye waits patiently for the rising sun.' They and they only can acquire the philosophic imagination, the sacred power of self-intuition, who within themselves can interpret and understand the symbol that the wings of the air-sylph are forming within the skin of the caterpillar; these only who feel in their own spirits the same instinct which impels the chrysalis of the horned fly to leave room in its involucrum for antennae yet to come. They know and feel that the potential works in them, even as the actual works on them! In short, all the organs of sense are framed for a corresponding world of sense; and we have it. All the organs of spirit are framed for a correspondent world of spirit: tho' the latter organs are not developed in all alike. But they exist in all, and their first appearance discloses itself in the moral being. How else could it be that even worldlings not wholly debased will contemplate the man of simple and disinterested goodness with contradictory feelings of pity and respect? 'Poor man! he is not made for this world.' Oh! herein they utter a prophecy of universal fulfilment; for man must either rise or sink.

It is the essential mark of the true philosopher to rest satisfied with no imperfect light, as long as the impossibility of attaining a fuller knowledge has not been demonstrated. That the common consciousness itself will furnish proofs by its own direction, that it is connected with master-currents below the surface, I shall merely assume as a postulate *pro tempore*. This having been granted, though but in expectation of the argument, I can safely deduce from it the equal truth of my former assertion that philosophy cannot be intelligible to all, even of the most learned and cultivated classes. A system, the first principle of which it is to render the mind intuitive of the spiritual in man (i.e. of that which lies on the other side of our natural consciousness), must needs have a great obscurity for those who have never disciplined and strengthened this ulterior consciousness. It must in truth be a land of darkness, a perfect Anti-Goshen, for men to whom the noblest treasures of their own being are reported only through the imperfect translation of lifeless and sightless notions. Perhaps, in great part, through words which are but the shadows of notions, even as the notional understanding itself is but the shadowy abstraction of living and actual truth. On the immediate which dwells in every man, and on the original intuition or absolute affirmation of it (which is likewise in every man, but does not in every man rise into consciousness), all the certainty of our knowledge depends; and this becomes intelligible to no man by the ministry of mere words from without. The medium by which spirits understand each other is not the surrounding air, but the freedom which they possess in common, as the common ethereal element of their being, the tremulous reciprocations of which propagate themselves even to the inmost of the soul. Where the spirit of a man is not filled with the consciousness of freedom (were it only from its restlessness, as of one still struggling in bondage) all spiritual intercourse is interrupted, not only with others but even with himself. No wonder then that he remains incomprehensible to himself as well as to others. No wonder that in the fearful desert of his consciousness he wearies himself out with empty words to which no friendly echo answers, either from his own heart or the heart of a fellow-being, or bewilders himself in the pursuit of notional phantoms, the mere refractions from unseen and distant truths through the distorting medium of his own unenlivened and stagnant understanding! To remain unintelligible to such a mind, exclaims Schelling on a like occasion, is honor and a good name before God and man.

[. . .] Philosophy is employed on objects of the inner sense and cannot, like geometry, appropriate to every construction a correspondent outward intuition. Nevertheless philosophy, if it is to arrive at evidence, must proceed from the most original construction; and the question then is, what is the most original construction or first productive act for the inner sense? The answer to this question depends on the direction which is given to the inner sense. But in philosophy the inner sense cannot have its direction determined by any outward object. To the original construction of the line I can be compelled by a line drawn before me on the slate or on sand. The stroke thus drawn is indeed not the line itself, but only the image or picture of the line. It is not from it that we first learn to know the line; but, on the contrary, we bring this stroke to the original line generated by the act of the imagination, otherwise we could not define it as without breadth or thickness. Still however this stroke is the sensuous image of the original or ideal line, and an efficient mean to excite every imagination to the intuition of it.

It is demanded then whether there be found any means in philosophy to determine the direction of the inner sense, as in mathematics it is determinable by its specific image or outward picture. Now the inner sense has its direction determined for the greater part only by an act of freedom. One man's consciousness extends only to the pleasant or unpleasant sensations caused in him by external impressions; another enlarges his inner sense to a consciousness of forms and quantity; a third, in addition to the image, is conscious of the conception or notion of the thing; a fourth attains to a notion of his notions—he reflects on his own reflections; and thus we may say without impropriety that the one possesses more or less inner sense than the other. This more or less betrays already that philosophy in its first principles must have a practical or moral as well as a theoretical or speculative side. This difference in degree does not exist in mathematics. Socrates in Plato shows that an ignorant slave may be brought to understand and of himself to solve the most difficult geometrical problem. Socrates drew the figures for the slave in the sand. The disciples of the critical philosophy could likewise (as was indeed actually done by La Forge and some other followers of Des Cartes) represent the origin of our representations in copper-plates; but no one has yet attempted it, and it would be utterly useless. To an Esquimaux or New Zealander our most popular philosophy would be wholly unintelligible. The sense, the inward organ for it, is not yet born in him. So is there many a one among us, yes, and some who think themselves philosophers too, to whom the philosophic organ is entirely wanting. To such a man philosophy is a mere play of words and notions, like a theory of music to the deaf, or like the geometry of light to the blind. The connection of the parts and their logical dependencies may be seen and remembered; but the whole is groundless and hollow, unsustained by living contact, unaccompanied with any realizing intuition which exists by and in the act that affirms its existence, which is known because it is, and is because it is known. The words of Plotinus, in the assumed person of Nature, hold true of the philosophic energy: Τὸ θεωροῦν μοῦ θεώρημα ποιεῖ, ὥσπερ οἱ Γεωμέτραι θεωροῦντες γραφοῦσιν' ἀλλ' ἐμοῦ μὴ γραφούσης, θεωρούσης δέ, ὑφίστανται αἱ τῶν σωμάτων γραμμαί.[3] With me the act of contemplation makes the thing contemplated, as the geometricians contemplating describe lines correspondent; but I not describing lines, but simply contemplating, the representative forms of things rise up into existence.

The postulate of philosophy, and at the same time the test of philosophic capacity, is no other than the heaven-descended *Know thyself!* (*E caelo descendit, Γνῶθι σεαυτόν*[4]). And this at once practically and speculatively. For as philosophy is neither a science of the reason or understanding only, nor merely a science of morals, but the science of being altogether, its primary ground can be neither merely speculative or merely practical, but both in one. All knowledge rests on the coincidence of an object with a subject.[5] (My readers have been warned in a former chapter that for their convenience as well as the writer's the term *subject* is used by me in its scholastic sense, as equivalent to mind or sentient being, and as the necessary correlative of object, or *quicquid objicitur menti.*) For we can *know* that only which is true; and the truth is universally placed in the coincidence of the thought with the thing, of the representation with the object represented.

Now the sum of all that is merely objective we will henceforth call *nature,* confining the term to its passive and material sense, as comprising all the phaenomena by which its existence is made known to us. On the other hand, the sum of all that is subjective we may comprehend in the name of the *self* or *intelligence*. Both conceptions are in necessary antithesis. Intelligence is conceived of as exclusively representative, nature as exclusively represented; the one as conscious, the other as without consciousness. Now in all acts of positive knowledge there is required a reciprocal concurrence of both, namely of the conscious being and of that which is in itself unconscious. Our problem is to explain this concurrence, its possibility and its necessity.

If it be said that this is idealism, let it be remembered that it is only so far idealism as it is at the same time, and on that very account, the truest and most binding realism. For wherein does the realism of mankind properly consist? In the assertion that there exists a something without them, what, or how, or where they know not, which occasions the objects of their perception? Oh no! This is neither connatural or universal. It is what a few have taught and learnt in the schools, and which the many repeat without asking themselves concerning their own meaning. The realism common to all mankind is far elder and lies infinitely deeper than this hypothetical explanation of the origin of our perceptions, an explanation skimmed from the mere surface of mechanical philosophy. It is the table itself which the man of common sense believes himself to see, not the phantom of a table from which he may argumentatively deduce the reality of a table which he does not see. If to destroy the reality of all that we actually behold be idealism, what can be more egregiously so than the system of modern metaphysics which banishes us to a land of shadows, surrounds us with apparitions and distinguishes truth from illusion only by the majority of those who dream the same dream? 'I asserted that the world was mad,' exclaimed poor [Nathaniel] Lee, 'and the world said that I was mad, and confound them, they outvoted me.'

It is to the true and original realism that I would direct the attention. This believes and requires neither more nor less than that the object which it beholds or presents to itself is the real and very object. In this sense, however much we may strive against it, we are all collectively born idealists, and therefore and only therefore are we at the same time realists. But of this the philosophers of the schools know nothing, or despise the faith as the prejudice of the ignorant vulgar, because they live and move in a crowd of phrases and notions from which human nature has long ago vanished. Oh, ye that reverence yourselves, and walk humbly with the divinity in your own hearts, ye are worthy of a better philosophy! Let the dead bury the dead, but do you preserve your human nature, the depth of which was never yet fathomed by a philosophy made up of notions and mere logical entities.

In the third treatise of my *Logosophia,* announced at the end of this volume,[6] I shall give (*deo volente*) the demonstrations and constructions of the Dynamic Philosophy scientifically arranged. It is, according to my conviction, no other than the system of Pythagoras and of Plato revived and purified from impure mixtures. *Doctrina per tot manus tradita tandem in vappam desiit!*[7] The science of arithmetic furnishes instances that a rule may be useful in practical application, and for the particular purpose may be sufficiently authenticated by the result, before it has itself been fully demonstrated. It is enough, if only it be rendered intelligible. This will, I trust, have been effected in the following Theses for those of my readers who are willing to accompany me through the following chapter, in which the results will be applied to the deduction of the imagination, and with it the principles of production and of genial criticism in the fine arts. [. . .]

Thesis IX

This *principium commune essendi et cognoscendi,* as subsisting in a will or primary act of self-duplication, is the mediate or indirect principle of every science; but it is the immediate and direct principle of the ultimate science alone, i.e. of transcendental philosophy alone. For it must be remembered, that all these Theses refer solely to one of the two Polar Sciences, namely, to that which commences with and rigidly confines itself within the subjective, leaving the objective (as far as it is exclusively objective) to natural philosophy, which is its opposite pole. In its very idea therefore as a systematic knowledge of our collective knowing (*scientia scientiae*), it involves the necessity of some one highest principle of knowing, as at once the source and the accompanying form in all particular acts of intellect and perception. This, it has been shown, can be found only in the act and evolution of self-consciousness. We are not investigating an absolute *principium essendi*; for then, I admit, many valid objections might be started against our theory; but an absolute *principium cognoscendi*. The result of both the sciences, or their equatorial point, would be the principle of a total and undivided philosophy, as for prudential reasons I have chosen to anticipate in the Scholium to Thesis VI and the note subjoined. In other words, philosophy would pass into religion, and religion become inclusive of philosophy. We begin with the I KNOW MYSELF, in order to end with the absolute I AM. We proceed from the self, in order to lose and find all self in GOD.

Thesis X

The transcendental philosopher does not inquire what ultimate ground of our knowledge there may lie out of our knowing, but what is the last in our knowing itself, beyond which we cannot pass. The principle of our knowing is sought within the sphere of our knowing. It must be something therefore which can itself be known. It is asserted only that the act of self-consciousness is for us the source and principle of all our possible knowledge. Whether abstracted from us there exists anything higher and beyond this primary self-knowing, which is for us the form of all our knowing, must be decided by the result.

That the self-consciousness is the fixt point to which for us all is morticed and annexed needs no further proof. But that the self-consciousness may be the modification of a higher form of being, perhaps of a higher consciousness, and this again of a yet higher, and so on in an infinite regressus; in short, that self-consciousness may be itself something explicable into something which must lie beyond the possibility of our knowledge, because the whole synthesis of our intelligence is first formed in and through the self-consciousness, does not at all concern us as transcendental philosophers. For to us the self-consciousness is not a kind of *being,* but a kind of *knowing,* and that too the highest and farthest that exists for us. It may however be shown [. . .] that even when the objective is assumed as the first, we yet can never pass beyond the principle of self-consciousness. Should we attempt it, we must be driven back from ground to ground, each of which would cease to be a ground the moment we pressed on it. We must be whirl'd down the gulf of an infinite series. But this would make our reason baffle the end and purpose of all reason, namely unity and system. Or we must break off the series arbitrarily, and affirm an absolute something that is in and of itself at once cause and effect (*causa sui*), subject and object, or rather the absolute identity of both. But as this is inconceivable, except in a self-consciousness, it follows that even as natural philosophers we must arrive at the same principle from which as transcendental philosophers we set out; that is, in a self-consciousness in which the *principium essendi* does not stand to the *principium cognoscendi* in the relation of cause to effect, but both the one and the other are co-inherent and identical. Thus the true system of natural philosophy places the sole reality of things in an absolute which is at once *causa sui et effectus* πατὴρ αὐτοπάτωρ, Υἱὸς ἑαυτοῦ—in the absolute identity of subject and object, which it calls nature, and which in its highest power is nothing else but self-conscious will or intelligence. [. . .]

Notes

1   This distinction between transcendental and transcendent is observed by our elder divines and philosophers, whenever they express themselves scholastically. Dr Johnson indeed has confounded the two words; but his own authorities do not bear him out. Of this celebrated dictionary I will venture to remark once for all that I should suspect the man of a morose disposition who should speak of it without respect and gratitude as a most instructive and entertaining book, and hitherto, unfortunately, an indispensable book; but I confess, that I should be surprized at hearing from a philosophic and thorough scholar any but very qualified praises of it as a *dictionary.* I am not now alluding to the number of genuine words omitted; for this is (and perhaps to a greater extent) true, as Mr Wakefield has noticed, of our best Greek Lexicons, and this too after the successive labours of so many giants in learning. I refer at present both to omissions and commissions of a more important nature. What these are, *me saltem judice,* will be stated at full in *The Friend,* re-published and completed.

    I had never heard of the correspondence between Wakefield and Fox till I saw the account of it this morning (16th September 1815) in the Monthly Review. I was not a little gratified at finding that Mr Wakefield had proposed to himself nearly the same plan for a Greek and English Dictionary which I had formed, and began to execute, now ten years ago. But far, far more grieved am I, that he did not live to complete it. I cannot but think it a subject of most serious regret that the same heavy expenditure which is now employing in the republication of Stephanus augmented, had not been applied to a new Lexicon on a more philosophical plan, with the English, German and French synonimes as well as the Latin. In almost every instance the precise individual meaning might be given in an English or German word; whereas in Latin we must too often be contented with a mere general and inclusive term. How indeed can it be otherwise, when we attempt to render the most copious language of the world, the most admirable for the fineness of its distinctions, into one of the poorest and most vague languages? Especially, when we reflect on the comparative number of the works, still extant, written while the Greek and Latin were living languages. Were I asked what I deemed the greatest and most unmixed benefit which a wealthy individual or an association of wealthy individuals could bestow on their country and on mankind, I should not hesitate to answer, 'a philosophical English dictionary; with the Greek, Latin, German, French, Spanish and Italian synonimes, and with correspondent indexes.' That the learned languages might thereby be acquired, better, in half the time, is but a part, and not the most important part, of the advantages which would accrue from such a work. O! if it should be permitted by providence that without detriment to freedom and independence our government might be enabled to become more than a committee for war and revenue! There was a time, when every thing was to be done by government. Have we not flown off to the contrary extreme?

2   *Ennead*, III. 1. 8. c. 3. The force of the Greek συνιέναι is imperfectly expressed by 'understand'; our own idiomatic phrase 'to go along with me' comes nearest to it. The passage that follows, full of profound sense, appears to me evidently corrupt; and in fact no writer more wants, better deserves, or is less likely to obtain, a new and more correct edition.—τί οὖν συνιέναι; ὅτι τὸ γενόμενον ἐστι θέαμα ἐμὸν, σιώπησις (*mallem*, θέαμα, ἐμοῦ σιωπῶσῆς,) καὶ φύσει γενόμενον θεώρημα καὶ μοι γενομένη ἐκ θεωρίας τῆς ὡδί, τὴν φύσιν ἔχειν φιλαθεάμονα ὑπάρκει. (*mallem*, καὶ μοι ἡ γενομένη ἐκ θεωρίας αὐτῆς ὡδὶς.) 'What then are we to understand? That whatever is produced is an intuition, I silent; and that which is thus generated, is by its nature a theorem, or form of contemplation; and the birth which results to me from this contemplation attains to have a contemplative nature.' So Synesius; Ὠδὶς ἱερά, Ἄρρητα γονά. The after comparison of the process of the *natura naturans* with that of the geometrician is drawn from the very heart of philosophy.

3   [*Ennead*, III. 8. 3: 'My contemplation creates what is contemplated, as the geometricians draw figures as they contemplate. But it is not in drawing figures but in contemplating that the lines of the forms are settled.']

4   [Juvenal, xi. 27: 'It came from heaven, Know yourself.']

5   [The following discussion, apart from the mention of God, is based upon Schelling.]

6   [This announcement was never made.]

7   ['A doctrine passed down through so many hands ends as flat wine.' Quotation untraced.]

26

Johann Gottlieb Fichte

Characteristics of the Present Age (1806)

Mysticism as a Phenomenon of the Third Age

THE THIRD AGE HAS NOW BEEN DESCRIBED IN ITS FUNDAMENTAL character,—*as an Age which accepts nothing but what it understands;*—and its leading conception in this process of understanding has been sufficiently set forth as that of *mere sensuous Experience.* From this fundamental principle of the Age we have deduced the distinction between a Learned and an Unlearned Class, and the constitution of these two classes, both in themselves and in their relation to each other. In addition to this we have shown historically, in our last lecture, that this relation has not always existed as at present; how and in what way it has arisen and become as it now is;—and also how this relation must exist in the following Age,—that of Reason as Knowledge.

Now we have formerly remarked, in our general survey of this subject, that such an Age of mere naked Experience and of empty Formal Knowledge does by its very nature stir up opposition, and bears within its own breast the germs of a reaction against itself. Let us take up this remark in the lecture of to-day, and pursue it somewhat further. It cannot but be that single individuals,—either because they actually feel the dreary barrenness and emptiness of the results of such a principle, or else moved by the mere desire of bringing forward something wholly new, which desire itself we have already discovered among the characteristics of this Epoch,—precisely inverting the principle of the Age, and representing its pretension to understand all things as its bane and the source of all its error,—should now, on the contrary, set up the Incomprehensible *as such*, and on account of its incomprehensibility, as their own principle,—as all of which man stands in need, the true source of all healing and sanctification. Even this phenomenon, as I said before, although apparently quite opposed to the Third Age, does nevertheless belong to the necessary phenomena of this Age, and is not to be overlooked in a complete delineation of it.

In the first place, the fact that the supporters of the maxim,—*that we must be able to understand everything which we ought to admit as true,*—do nevertheless constantly accept many things which neither they nor their opponents understand, is a manifest contradiction of the maxim itself; which contradiction obviously cannot take place, or be theoretically propounded until the maxim itself be announced, and indeed only arises in the polemical discussion of the maxim;—a contradiction, however, which must necessarily make its appearance so soon as this maxim has been prevalent for any length of time, has received mature consideration, and has been brought out in clear and unequivocal distinctness. Thus the announcement of this principle of the Incomprehensible is neither the beginning nor yet any essential element of the new Age which is to arise out of the Third, namely, the Age of Reason as Knowledge; for it finds no fault with the maxim of absolute Intelligibility, but rather recognises it as its own; finding fault only with the mischievous and worthless notion which is now made the standard of this Intelligibility, and the measure of all authentic Truth; while as to Intelligibility itself, the Age of Reason as Knowledge lays it down as a fundamental principle, that everything, even the Unknown itself, as the limit of the Known, and as the only possible pledge that the domain of the Known is exhausted, must be comprehended; and that in all Times, and as the only sufficient substratum of the Time, there must be a *then* Unknown,—known only as the Unknown; but at no Time an absolute Incomprehensible. This principle of absolute Incomprehensibility is thus much more directly opposed to Knowledge, than even the principle of the Intelligibility of all things through the conceptions of mere sensuous Experience. Finally, this principle of Incomprehensibility, as such, is not a remnant of any former Age, as is obvious from what we have already said on this point. The absolute Incomprehensible of Heathen and Jewish antiquity,—the arbitrary God, never to be understood but always to be feared, with whom man could only by good fortune come to terms,—far from having been sought out by these Ages, was imposed upon them by necessity, and in opposition to their own will, and they would gladly have been delivered from this conception had that been possible. The Incomprehensible of the Christian Church, again, was accepted as true,—not on account of its being incomprehensible, but because it existed in the Written Word and in the Traditions and Doctrines of the Church, although it had accidentally turned out to be incomprehensible. The maxim of which we now speak, on the contrary, sets up the Incomprehensible as the Highest, *in its own character of incomprehensibility*, and even on account of its incomprehensibility; and it is thus a wholly new and unprecedented phenomenon peculiar to the Third Age.

When the matter does not end in this mere acceptance of the Incomprehensible generally,—so that it might be left to each man to determine for himself what is incomprehensible to him;—but when besides this, as might be expected from the dogmatic Spirit of the Age, a specific and defined formula of the Incomprehensible is set forth and proposed for our acceptance; the question presents itself,—How does this phenomenon arise? Not from the elder superstition,—for this has now passed away so far as the cultivated classes are concerned, and its residue is only to be found in Theology;—nor from Theology,—for this is, as we have already seen, something altogether different. It is through insight into the emptiness of the previous system, and thus by means of reasoning, that this new system has arisen; it must therefore establish its Incomprehensible by means of reasoning and free thought, which here, however, assume the forms of Invention and Imagination:—Hence the founders and representatives of this system will bear the name of Philosophers.

The production of an Unknown and Incomprehensible, by means of unrestrained Imagination, has always been named Mysticism; we shall therefore comprehend this new system in its essential nature, if we set forth distinctly what Mysticism is, and wherein it consists.

Mysticism has this in common with true Reason as Knowledge;—it does not recognise the conceptions of mere sensuous Experience as the Highest, but strives to raise itself above all Experience;—and since there is nothing beyond the domain of Experience but the world of Pure Thought, it builds up a Universe for itself from Pure Thought alone,—as we have already said of Reason as Knowledge. The defenders of Experience as the only source of truth thus hit the mark as closely as they possibly can, and more closely perhaps than they themselves are aware of, when they denominate him a Mystic who, on whatever ground, denies the exclusive validity which they claim for Experience;—for this Mysticism, which they can only apprehend by an effort of fancy, and from which they have so carefully guarded themselves beforehand by strict adherence to Experience,—this Mysticism, I say, does indeed raise itself above Experience;—whilst the other way of rising above Experience,—namely, by Knowledge,—has never presented itself to them in its true character, and on this side they have had, as yet, no temptations to overcome.

In this firm reliance on the world of Thought, as the Highest and most excellent, Reason as Knowledge and Mysticism are completely at one.

The distinction between them depends solely upon the nature of the thought from which they respectively proceed. The fundamental thought of Reason as Knowledge—which because it is a fundamental thought, is absolutely one and complete in itself—is, in the view of Reason, thoroughly clear and distinct; and from it Reason perceives, in the same unchangeable clearness, the immediate procession of all the multiplicity of particular thoughts; and, since *things* can only exist in thought, of the multiplicity of all particular things,—making them, in this procession, the subject of immediate apprehension;—this even to the limits of all clearness; and, as these limits must likewise be conceived of as necessary limits, even to the boundaries of the Unknown. Further, this thought does not spontaneously present itself to Reason, but must be pursued with labour, assiduity, and care; for Reason must never rest satisfied with anything which is, as yet, imperfectly understood, but must continually ascend to a higher principle of interpretation, and again to a higher, until at last there shall be but one pure mass of Light. So it is with the Thought of Reason. But the *thoughts* from which Mysticism may arise,—for these are very different in the different individuals who entertain them, and are even very variable in one and the same individual,—these *thoughts* can never be clearly referred to any fundamental principle. On this account they are only to a certain extent clear even in themselves; and, so far as regards their connexion with each other, they are absolutely unintelligible. On this account, too, these thoughts can never be proved, nor attain any greater degree of clearness than that which they already possess; but they may be postulated,—or, should the language of true Reason be already current, the reader or hearer may be directed to the 'Intellectual Intuition'; which latter, however, has a totally different meaning in Reason from that which it bears in Mysticism. For the same reason, no account can be given of the method in which these thoughts have been discovered, because, in reality, they have not been discovered by means of a systematic ascent to a higher principle, like the primitive thoughts of Reason,—but are, in truth, the mere conceits of Chance.

And this Chance,—what is it at bottom? Although those who are in its service can never explain it, yet cannot we explain it? It is a blind thinking-power, which, like all other blind powers, is, in the final analysis, only a force of Nature from the control of which *free* thought sets us at liberty; depending, like all other natural conditions, upon the state of health, the temperament, the mode of life, the studies, &c. of the individual;—so that these Mystics, with their fascinating philosophy, notwithstanding their boast of having raised themselves above Nature, and their profound contempt for all Empiricism, are themselves but a somewhat unusual empirical phenomenon, without having the least suspicion of the real state of the case.

The remark that the principles of Mysticism are mere accidental conceits, imposes upon me the duty of distinguishing it from another, and, in some respects, similar process of thought;—and I embrace this opportunity of more strictly defining it. In the domain of Physics, namely, not only the most important experiments, but even the most searching and comprehensive theories are often the results of chance, or it may be said, of mere conjecture; and so must it be, until Reason be sufficiently extended and spread abroad, and have fulfilled the duty which it owes to Physics, as strictly defined in our last lecture. But the true Physical Inquirer always proceeds beyond the Phenomena, seeking only the Law in the Unity of which the Phenomena may be comprehended; and as soon as he has reached the primitive Thought, returning again to the Phenomena in order to test the Thought by its application to them;—undoubtedly with the firm conviction that the validity of the Thought can only be established by its sufficiency for the explanation of the Phenomena, and with the determination to throw it aside should it not be verified in this way. It is verified; and he is thereby satisfied that his conception has been no arbitrary conceit, but a true Thought revealed by Nature herself;—and thus his inspiration is not Mysticism but is to be named Genius. Quite otherwise is it with the Mystic:—he neither proceeds outwards from Empiricism, nor yet does he recognise Empiricism as the judge of his fancies,—but he demands that Nature should regulate herself by his thoughts;—in which he should be perfectly justified, had he only got hold of the *right* Thoughts, and if he knew how far this *a priori* conception of Nature can go, at what point it comes to an end, and where Experiment alone can decide.

These fancies of the Mystic, I have said, are neither clear in themselves, nor are they proved, or even capable of theoretical proof which indeed is renounced in the avowal of Incomprehensibility; but yet they may be true, and may therefore be confirmed by our natural sense of Truth, provided they fall within its sphere. How is it then, that they are believed in by their original authors themselves? I am bound to solve this question before we proceed further.

These fancies are, at bottom, as we have shown above, the products of a blind natural thinking-power; which power must necessarily manifest itself in these particular circumstances and in these particular individuals exactly as it does manifest itself;—*must*, I say, unless the individual were to elevate himself above the mere natural thinking-power to free and clear Thought; and so foreclose this necessity. If this do not happen, then the necessary consequence is as follows:— every blind power of Nature is constantly active, although invisibly and unconsciously to man; it is therefore to be anticipated that this thinking-power, as the essential nature of this individual, should have already manifested itself in many shapes within him, and thus from time to time have passed through his mind without its principle being discovered, or any distinct resolution being taken as to its adoption. Thus he goes on passively, or listening attentively to the voice of Nature thinking within him; till at last the true centre-thought of the whole reveals itself; and he is not a little astonished to find unity, light, connexion, and confirmation spread over all his previous fancies; never imagining for a moment that these earlier fancies were but shapes or branches of that ever-active thought which has now come forth into light, with which they must therefore unquestionably harmonize. He satisfies himself of the truth of the whole by its sufficiency to afford an explanation of all the parts; for he does not know that they are only *parts of* this whole, and have only an existence *by means of* the whole. He accepts Imagination as Truth because it coincides with so many earlier Imaginations, which, without any suspicion on his part, have come to him from the same source.

Since this imagination of the Mystic is but a thinking-power of Nature, it returns upon Nature, attaches itself to her soil, and attempts to exercise an activity there; in one word, Mysticism is, and always must be, a Philosophy of Nature ('*Natur-Philosophie.*') It is necessary that we should carefully consider these latter remarks, in order strictly to distinguish between Mysticism and something else which is often inconsiderately mistaken for it. Either the mere sensuous instinct, the desire of personal preservation and of physical well-being, is the only impulse to the thoughts as well as to the actions of men,—and then Thought is only the servant of Desire, and only exists for the purpose of observing and choosing the means of its satisfaction; *or*, Thought is living and active in itself and by its own proper power. Upon the first supposition is founded the whole wisdom of the Third Age, which we have already sufficiently described, and need not further refer to at present. On the second supposition there are, on the other hand, two, or it may be, three cases. Namely, this self-existent and active

Thought is either the mere Sensuous Individuality of Man clothing itself in the form of Thought, and is thus still a mere sensuous desire, only disguised, and therefore not recognised as such,—and then it is Mysticism:—or, it is Pure Thought flowing forth from itself without any dependence on Sense, not recognising individual persons, but always comprehending the Race, as we have already sufficiently described it in our second, third, and fourth lectures;—*i.e.* the Idea. Is it the Idea which is present?—then again, as we have already said, it may manifest itself in two different ways:—either, in one of its primitive forms which we previously indicated; and in this case it struggles irresistibly onward to direct outward activity, streams forth in the personal life of the man, extinguishing all his sensuous impulses and desires; and then he is an Artist, Hero, Man of Science, or Religious Man;—or, the same Pure Thought may manifest itself in its absolute unity; and then it is easily recognisable as the one, perfectly clear, and undisturbed thought of the Higher Reason, which in itself impels to no activity in the World of Sense, but only to free activity in the World of Pure Thought; or, in other words, is true and genuine Speculation. Mysticism will not of itself act in direct opposition to the Life in the Idea; but that it may act in conformity with it, requires a specific determination of the will moved thereto by desire. Thus Mysticism is still Speculation; it does not, however, comprehend the Race as such but only Individuality, because it proceeds only from the Individual and refers only to that whereon the life of the Individual depends, namely, to Physical Nature,—and it is thus necessarily Speculation founded on Nature (*Natur-Spekulation.*) Hence the Life in the Idea, which the uneducated man presumes to call Mysticism, is in reality very widely and distinctly separated from Mysticism. We have already sufficiently distinguished Mysticism from true and genuine Speculation; but in order that we may be able to distinguish this true and genuine Speculation from its opposite,—that of the Mystic, with reference to the Philosophy of Nature (*Natur-Philosophie*),—we ought to be already in possession of the former, and this is not the business of the unlearned public. Upon this matter,—and therefore upon the ultimate principles of Nature,—no true Scholar will think of communicating with the general public; the Speculative theory of Nature presupposes scientific culture, and can only be comprehended by the scientific intellect; and the general and unlearned public never stands in need of it. But with respect to that whereon the true Scholar can and ought to communicate with the general public,—with respect to Ideas,—there is an infallible test whereby this public may determine for itself whether any doctrine which is presented to it is, or is not, mere Mysticism. Let it be asked,—'Has this doctrine a direct and immediate bearing on action, or does it rest on a fixed and immovable constitution of things?' Thus, for example, the question which I put to you at the beginning of these lectures, and upon the assumed answer to which, the whole of my subsequent discourses have proceeded as their true principle:—this question, whether you could refrain from approving, respecting, and admiring a Life wholly devoted to the Idea?—this question refers exclusively to an action, and to your judgment upon that action; and therefore, while we were elevated above the world of mere sensuous Experience, it is evident that there was nevertheless nothing of Mysticism in our inquiries. To adduce a still more marked example:—The Doctrine of a Perfect God; in whose nature nothing arbitrary or changeable can have a place; in whose Highest Being we all live, and in this Life may and ought at all times to be blessed;—this Doctrine, which ignorant men think they have sufficiently demolished when they have proclaimed it to be Mysticism, is by no means Mysticism, for it has an immediate reference to human action, and indeed to the inmost spirit which ought to inspire and guide all our actions. It can only become Mysticism when it is associated with the pretext that the insight into this truth proceeds from a certain inward and mysterious light, which is not accessible to all men, but is bestowed only upon a few favourites chosen from among the rest:—in which pretext the real Mysticism consists, for it betrays a self-complacent assumption of personal merit, and a pride in mere sensuous Individuality. Thus Mysticism, besides the essential and inward criterion which can only be thoroughly discovered by true Speculation, has also an outward mark by which it may be recognised;—this, namely, that it is never a Moral or Religious Philosophy, to both of which it is, in its true character, wholly antagonistic; (what it calls Religion is only a deification of Nature)—but it is always a mere Philosophy of Nature;—that is, it strives to discover, or believes that it has discovered, certain mysterious and hitherto inconceivable properties in the principles of Nature, by the employment of which it endeavours to produce effects surpassing the ordinary course of things. Such, I say, is Mysticism,— necessarily such by reason of its vital principle;—and such it has always been in reality. Let us not be deceived by the frequent promises it has held forth of introducing us to the secrets of the Spirit-World, and revealing to us the charm whereby we may spell-bind and enthral Angel and Archangel, or even God himself;—the purpose of all this has been only to employ such knowledge for the production of results in the world of sense; and these spiritual existences have therefore never been regarded as such, but only as powers of Nature. The end has always been to discover some charm, some magical spell. If we consider the matter strictly, as I do here, and do it advisedly, in order by this example, at least, to make myself perfectly clear and intelligible;—if, I say, we consider the matter strictly, the system of Religion which was described in our last lecture, which proceeds upon the conception of an Arbitrary God, and admits an interposition between Him and man, and believes that,—through the efficacy of a ratified Covenant, either by observation of certain arbitrary, and, so far as their purpose is concerned, unintelligible laws, or by an historical belief equally unintelligible as regards its end,—it can redeem itself from any farther inflictions on the part of God; this Religion itself, I say, is such a system of mystical enchantment, in which God is contemplated, not as the Holy One, to be separated from whom is, in itself and without farther consequence, the greatest of all evils; but only as a dreadful power of Nature, threatening man with its devastating visitations, whose agencies, however, we have now discovered the means of rendering harmless, or even of diverting to our own purposes.

27

Georg Wilhelm Friedrich Hegel

Phenomenology of Spirit (1807)

Freedom of Self-Consciousness: Stoicism, Scepticism, and the Unhappy Consciousness

INDEPENDENT SELF-CONSCIOUSNESS PARTLY FINDS ITS ESSENTIAL REALITY in the bare abstraction of Ego. On the other hand, when this abstract ego develops further and forms distinctions of its own, this differentiation does not become an objective inherently real content for that self-consciousness. Hence this self-consciousness does not become an ego which truly differentiates itself in its abstract simplicity, or one which remains identical with itself in this absolute differentiation. The repressed and subordinated type of consciousness, on the other hand, becomes, in the formative activity of work, an object to itself, in the sense that the form, given to the thing when shaped and moulded, is his object; he sees in the master, at the same time, self-existence as a real mode of consciousness. But the subservient consciousness as such finds these two moments fall apart—the moment of itself as independent object, and the moment of this object as a mode of consciousness, and so its own proper reality. Since, however, the form and the self-existence are for us, or objectively in themselves, one and the same, and since in the notion of independent consciousness the inherent reality is consciousness, the phase of inherent existence (*Ansichsein*) or thinghood, which received its shape and form through labour, is no other substance than consciousness. In this way, we have a new attitude or mode of consciousness brought about. We have now a consciousness, which takes itself to be infinitude, or one whose essential nature is pure process of consciousness. It is one which *thinks* or is free self-consciousness. For thinking does not consist in being an abstract ego, but in being an ego which has, at the same time, the significance of inherently existing in itself; or which relates itself to objective reality in such a way that this signifies the self-existence of that consciousness for which it is an object. The object does not for thinking proceed by way of presentations or figures, but of notions, conceptions, i.e. of a differentiated reality or essence, which, being an immediate content of consciousness, is nothing distinct from it. What is presented, shaped and constructed, and existent as such, has the form of being something other than consciousness. A notion, however, is at the same time an existent, and this distinction, so far as it falls in consciousness itself, is its determinate content. But in that this content is, at the same time, a conceptually constituted, a comprehended (*begriffener*) content, consciousness remains immediately aware within itself of its unity with this determinate existent so distinguished; not as in the case of a presentation, where consciousness from the first has to take special note that this is the idea *of* the object; on the contrary, the notion is for me *eo ipso* and at once *my* notion. In thinking I am free, because I am not in an other, but remain simply and solely in touch with myself; and the object which for me is my essential reality, is in undivided unity my self-existence; and my procedure in dealing with notions is a process within myself.

It is essential, however, in this determination of the above attitude of self-consciousness to keep hold of the fact that this attitude is thinking consciousness in general, that its object is immediate unity of the self's implicit, inherent existence, and of its existence explicitly for self. The self-same consciousness which repels itself from itself, becomes aware of being an element existing in itself. But to itself it is this element to begin with only as universal reality in general, and not as this essential reality appears when developed in all the manifold details it contains, when the process of its being brings out all its fullness of content.

This freedom of self-consciousness, as is well known, has been called *Stoicism*, in so far as it has appeared as a phenomenon conscious of itself in the course of the history of man's spirit. Its principle is that consciousness is essentially that which thinks, is a thinking reality, and that anything is really essential for consciousness, or is true and good, only when consciousness in dealing with it adopts the attitude of a thinking being.

The manifold, self-differentiating expanse of life, with all its individualisation and complication, is the object upon which desire and labour operate. This varied activity has now contracted itself into the simple distinction which is found in the pure process of thought. What has still essential reality is not a distinction in the sense of a determinate thing, or in the shape of a consciousness of a determinate kind of natural existence, in the shape of a feeling, or again in the form of desire and its specific purpose, whether that purpose be set up by the consciousness desiring or by an extraneous consciousness. What has the more essential significance here is solely that distinction which is a thought-constituted distinction, or which, when made, is not distinguished from me. This consciousness in consequence takes a negative attitude towards the relation of lordship and bondage. Its action, in the case of the master, results in his not simply having his truth in and through the bondsman; and, in that of the bondsman, in not finding his truth in the will of his master and in service. The essence of this consciousness is to be free, on the throne as well as in fetters, throughout all the dependence that attaches to its individual existence, and to maintain that stolid lifeless unconcern which persistently withdraws from the movement of existence, from effective activity as well as from passive endurance, into the simple essentiality of thought. Stubbornness is that freedom which makes itself secure in a solid singleness, and keeps *within* the sphere of bondage. Stoicism, on the other hand, is the freedom which ever comes directly out of that sphere, and returns back into the pure universality of thought. It is a freedom which can come on the scene as a general form of the world's spirit only in a time of universal fear and bondage, a time, too, when mental cultivation is universal, and has elevated culture to the level of thought.

Now while this self-consciousness finds its essential reality to be neither something other than itself, nor the pure abstraction of ego, but ego which has within it otherness—otherness in the sense of a thought-constituted distinction—so that this ego in its otherness is turned back directly into itself; yet this essential nature is, at the same time, only an abstract reality. The freedom of self-consciousness is indifferent towards natural existence, and has, therefore, let this latter go and remain free. The reflexion is thus duplicated. Freedom of thought takes only pure thought as its truth, and this lacks the concrete filling of life. It is, therefore, merely the notion of freedom, not living freedom itself; for it is, to begin with, only thinking in general that is its essence, the form as such, which has turned away from the independence of things and gone back into itself. Since, however, individuality when acting should show itself to be alive, or when thinking should grasp the living world as a system of thought, there ought to lie in thought itself a content to supply the sphere of the ego, in the former case with what is good, and, in the latter, true, in order that there should throughout be no other ingredient in what consciousness has to deal with, except the notion which is the real essence. But here, by the way in which the notion as an abstraction cuts itself off from the multiplicity of things, the notion has *no content in itself;* the content is a datum, is given. Consciousness, no doubt, abolishes the content as an external, a foreign existent, by the fact that it thinks it, but the notion is a determinate notion, and this *determinateness* of the notion is the alien element the notion contains within it. Stoicism, therefore, got embarrassed, when, as the expression went, it was asked for the criterion of truth in general, i.e. properly speaking, for a *content* of thought itself. To the question what is good and true, it responded by giving again the abstract, contentless thought; the true and good are to consist in reasonableness. But this self-identity of thought is simply once more pure form, in which nothing is determinate. The general terms true and good, wisdom and virtue, with which Stoicism has to stop short, are, therefore, in a general way, doubtless elevating; but seeing that they cannot actually and in fact reach any expanse of content, they soon begin to get wearisome.

This thinking consciousness, in the way in which it is thus constituted, as abstract freedom, is therefore only incomplete negation of otherness. Withdrawn from existence solely into itself, it has not there fully vindicated itself as the absolute negation of this existence. It holds the content indeed to be only thought, but in doing so also takes thought as a specific determinate thought, and at the same time the general character of the content.

Scepticism is the realisation of that of which Stoicism is merely the notion, and is the actual experience of what freedom of thought is; it is in itself and essentially the negative, and must so exhibit itself. With the reflexion of self-consciousness into the simple, pure thought of itself, independent existence or permanent determinateness has, in contrast to that reflexion, dropped as a matter of fact out of the infinitude of thought. In Scepticism, the entire unessentiality and unsubstantiality of this "other" becomes a reality for consciousness. Thought becomes thinking which wholly annihilates the being of the world with its manifold determinateness, and the negativity of free self-consciousness comes to be, in the case of these manifold forms which life assumes, real negativity.

It is clear from the foregoing that, just as Stoicism answers to the *notion* of independent consciousness, which appeared as a relation of lordship and bondage, Scepticism, on its side, corresponds to its *realisation,* to the negative attitude towards otherness, to desire and labour. But if desire and work could not carry out for self-consciousness the process of negation, this polemical attitude towards the manifold substantiality of things will, on the other hand, be successful, because it turns against them as a free self-consciousness, and one complete within itself beforehand; or, expressed more definitely, because it has inherent in itself thought or the principle of infinitude, where the independent elements in their distinction from one another are held to be merely vanishing quantities. The differences, which, in the pure thinking of self are only the *abstraction* of differences, become here the whole of the differences; and every differentiated existent becomes a difference of self-consciousness.

With this we get determined the action of Scepticism in general, as also its mode and nature. It shows the dialectic movement, which is sense-certainty, perception, and understanding. It shows, too, the unessentiality of that which holds good in the relation of master and servant, and which for abstract thought itself passes as determinate. That relation involves, at the same time, a determinate situation, in which there are found even moral laws, as commands of the sovereign lord. The determinations in abstract thought, however, are scientific notions, into which formal contentless thought expands itself, attaching the notion, as a matter of fact in merely an external fashion, to the existence independent of it, and holding as valid only determinate notions, albeit they are still pure abstractions.

Dialectic as a negative process, taken immediately as it stands, appears to consciousness, in the first instance, as something at the mercy of which it is, and which does not exist through consciousness itself. In Scepticism, on the other hand, this negative process is a moment of self-consciousness, which does not simply find its truth and its reality vanish, without self-consciousness knowing how, but rather which, in the certainty of its own freedom, itself lets this other, so claiming to be real, vanish. Self-consciousness here allows not only the objective as such to disappear before the negations of Scepticism, but also its own attitude and relation to the object, where the object is held to be objective and rendered valid—i.e. its attitude of perception as also its process of securing what is in danger of being lost, viz. sophistry with its self-constituted and self-established truth. By means of this self-conscious negation, self-consciousness procures for itself the certainty of its own freedom, brings about the experience of that freedom, and thereby raises it into the truth. What vanishes is what is determinate, the difference which, no matter what its nature or whence it comes, sets up to be fixed and unchangeable. The difference has nothing permanent in it, and must vanish before thought, because to be differentiated just means not to have being in itself, but to have its essential nature solely in an other. Thinking, however, is the insight into this character of what is differentiated; it is the negative function in its simple, ultimate form.

Sceptical self-consciousness thus discovers, in the flux and alternation of all that would stand secure in its presence, its own freedom, as given by and received from its own self. It is aware of being this ἀταραξία of self-thinking thought, the unalterable and genuine certainty of its self. This certainty does not arise as a result out of something extraneous and foreign which stowed away inside itself its whole complex development; a result which would thus leave behind the process by which it came to be. Rather consciousness itself is thoroughgoing dialectical restlessness, this mêlée of presentations derived from sense and thought, whose differences collapse into oneness, and whose identity is similarly again resolved and dissolved—for this identity is itself determinateness as contrasted with non-identity. This consciousness, however, as a matter of fact, instead of being a self-same consciousness, is here neither more nor less than an absolutely fortuitous embroglio, the giddy whirl of a perpetually self-creating disorder. This is what it takes itself to be; for itself maintains and produces this self-impelling confusion. Hence it even confesses the fact; it owns to being an entirely fortuitous *individual* consciousness— a consciousness which is empirical, which is directed upon what admittedly has no reality for it, which obeys what, in its regard, has no essential being, which realises and does what it knows to have no truth. But while it passes in this manner for an individual, isolated, contingent, in fact animal life, and a lost self-consciousness, it also, on the contrary, again turns itself into universal self-sameness; for it is the negativity of all singleness and all difference. From this self-identity, or rather within its very self, it falls back once more into that contingency and confusion, for this very self-directed process of negation has to do solely with what is single and individual, and is occupied with what is fortuitous. This form of consciousness is, therefore, the aimless fickleness and instability of going to and fro, hither and thither, from one extreme of self-same self-consciousness, to the other of contingent, confused and confusing consciousness. It does not itself bring these two thoughts of itself together. It finds its freedom, at one time, in the form of elevation above all the whirling complexity and all the contingency of mere existence, and again, at another time, likewise confesses to falling back upon what is unessential, and to being taken up with that. It lets the unessential content in its thought vanish; but in that very act it is the consciousness of something unessential. It announces absolute disappearance but the announcement *is,* and this consciousness is the evanescence expressly announced. It announces the nullity of seeing, hearing, and so on, yet *itself* sees and hears. It proclaims the nothingness of essential ethical principles, and makes those very truths the sinews of its own conduct. Its deeds and its words belie each other continually; and itself, too, has the doubly contradictory consciousness of immutability and sameness, and of utter contingency and non-identity with itself. But it keeps asunder the poles of this contradiction within itself; and bears itself towards the contradiction as it does in its purely negative process in general. If sameness is shown to it, it points out unlikeness, non-identity; and when the latter, which it has expressly mentioned the moment before, is held up to it, it passes on to indicate sameness and identity. Its talk, in fact, is like a squabble among self-willed children, one of whom says a when the other says b, and again b, when the other says a, and who, through being in contradiction with themselves, procure the joy of remaining in contradiction with one another.

In Scepticism consciousness gets, in truth, to know itself as a consciousness containing contradiction within itself. From the experience of this proceeds a new attitude which brings the two thoughts together which Scepticism holds apart. The want of intelligence which Scepticism manifests regarding itself is bound to vanish, because it is in fact *one* consciousness which possesses these two modes within it. This new attitude consequently is one which is *aware* of being the double consciousness of itself as self-liberating, unalterable, self-identical, and as utterly self-confounding, self-perverting; and this new attitude is the consciousness of this contradiction within itself.

In Stoicism, self-consciousness is the bare and simple freedom of itself. In Scepticism, it realises itself, negates the other side of determinate existence, but, in so doing, really doubles itself, and is itself now a duality. In this way the duplication, which previously was divided between two individuals, the lord and the bondsman, is concentrated into one. Thus we have here that dualising of self-consciousness within itself, which lies essentially in the notion of mind; but the unity of the two elements is not yet present. Hence the *Unhappy Consciousness* [*unglückliches Bewusstsein*], the Alienated Soul which is the consciousness of self as a divided nature, a doubled and merely contradictory being.

This unhappy consciousness, divided and at variance within itself, must, because this contradiction of its essential nature is felt to be a single consciousness, always have in the one consciousness the other also; and thus must be straightway driven out of each in turn, when it thinks it has therein attained to the victory and rest of unity. Its true return into itself, or reconciliation with itself, will, however, exhibit the notion of mind endowed with a life and existence of its own, because it implicitly involves the fact that, *qua* single and undivided, it *is* a double consciousness. It is itself the gazing of one self-consciousness into another, and itself is both, and the unity of both is also its own essence; but objectively and consciously it is not yet this essence itself—is not yet the unity of both.

Since, in the first instance, it is the immediate, the implicit unity of both, while for it they are not one and the same, but opposed, it takes one, namely, the simple unalterable, as essential, the other, the manifold and changeable, as the unessential. For it, both are realities foreign to each other. Itself, because consciousness of this contradiction, assumes the aspect of changeable consciousness and is to itself the unessential; but as consciousness of unchangeableness, of the ultimate essence, it must, at the same time, proceed to free itself from the unessential, i.e. to liberate itself from itself. For though in its own view it is indeed only the changeable, and the unchangeable is foreign and extraneous to it, yet itself is simple, and therefore unchangeable consciousness, of which consequently it is conscious as its essence, but still in such wise that itself is again in its own regard not this essence. The position, which it assigns to both, cannot, therefore, be an indifference of one to the other, i.e. cannot be an indifference of itself towards the unchangeable. Rather it is immediately both itself; and the relation of both assumes for it the form of a relation of essence to the non-essential, so that this latter has to be cancelled; but since both are to it equally essential and are contradictory, it is only the conflicting contradictory process in which opposite does not come to rest in its own opposite, but produces itself therein afresh merely as an opposite.

Here, then, there is a struggle against an enemy, victory over whom really means being worsted, where to have attained one result is really to lose it in the opposite. Consciousness of life, of its existence and action, is merely pain and sorrow over this existence and activity; for therein consciousness finds only consciousness of its opposite as its essence—and of its own nothingness. Elevating itself beyond this, it passes to the unchangeable. But this elevation is itself this same consciousness. It is, therefore, immediately consciousness of the opposite, viz. of itself as single, individual, particular. The unchangeable, which comes to consciousness, is in that very fact at the same time affected by particularity, and is only present with this latter. Instead of particularity having been abolished in the consciousness of immutability, it only continues to appear there still.

In this process, however, consciousness experiences just this appearance of particularity in the unchangeable, and of the unchangeable in particularity. Consciousness becomes aware of particularity *in general* in the immutable essence, and at the same time it there finds its own particularity. For the truth of this process is precisely that the double consciousness is one and single. This unity becomes a fact to it, but in the first instance the unity is one in which the diversity of both factors is still the dominant feature. Owing to this, consciousness has before it the threefold way in which particularity is connected with unchangeableness. In one form it comes before itself as opposed to the unchangeable essence, and is thrown back to the beginning of that struggle, which is, from first to last, the principle constituting the entire situation. At another time it finds the unchangeable appearing in the form of particularity; so that the latter is an embodiment of unchangeableness, into which, in consequence, the entire form of existence passes. In the third case, it discovers *itself* to be this particular fact in the unchangeable. The first unchangeable is taken to be merely the alien, external Being, which passes sentence on particular existence; since the second unchangeable is a form or mode of particularity like itself, the unchangeable becomes in the third place spirit (*Geist*), has the joy of finding itself therein, and becomes aware within itself that its particularity has been reconciled with the universal.

What is set forth here as a mode and relation of the unchangeable, came to light as the experience through which self-consciousness passes in its unhappy state of diremption. This experience is now doubtless not its own onesided process; for it is itself unchangeable consciousness; and this latter, consequently, is a particular consciousness as well; and the process is as much a process of that unchangeable consciousness, which makes its appearance there as certainly as the other. For that movement is carried on in these moments: an unchangeable now opposed to the particular in general, then, being itself particular, opposed to the other particular, and finally at one with it. But this consideration, so far as it is our affair, is here out of place, for thus far we have only had to do with unchangeableness as unchangeableness of *consciousness*, which, for that reason, is not true immutability, but is still affected with an opposite; we have not had before us the unchangeable *per se* and by itself; we do not, therefore, know how this latter will conduct itself. What has here so far come to light is merely this, that to consciousness, which is our object here, the determinations above indicated appear in the unchangeable.

For this reason, then, the unchangeable consciousness also preserves, in its very form and bearing, the character and fundamental features of diremption and separate self-existence, as against the particular consciousness. For the latter it is thus altogether a contingency, a mere chance event, that the unchangeable receives the form of particularity; just as the particular consciousness merely happens to find itself opposed to the unchangeable, and therefore has this relation *per naturam*. Finally that it *finds itself* in the unchangeable appears to the particular consciousness to be brought about partly, no doubt, by itself, or to take place for the reason that itself is particular; but this union, both as regards its origin as well as in its being, appears partly also due to the unchangeable; and the opposition remains within this unity itself. In point of fact, through the unchangeable assuming a definite form, the 'beyond,' as a moment, has not only remained, but really is more securely established. For if the remote 'beyond' seems indeed brought closer to the individual by this particular form of realisation, on the other hand, it is henceforward fixedly opposed to the individual, a sensuous, impervious unit, with all the hard resistance of what is actual. The hope of becoming one therewith must remain a hope, i.e. without fulfilment, without present fruition; for between the hope and fulfilment there stands precisely the absolute contingency, or immovable indifference, which is involved in the very assumption of determinate shape and form, the basis and foundation of the hope. By the nature of this existent unit, through the particular reality it has assumed and adopted, it comes about of necessity that in course of time it becomes a thing of the past, something that has been somewhere far away, and absolutely remote it remains. [. . .]

If consciousness were, for itself, an independent consciousness, and reality were taken to be in and for itself of no account, then consciousness would attain, in work and enjoyment, the feeling of its own independence, by the fact that its consciousness would be that which cancels reality.

But since this reality is taken to be the form and shape of the unchangeable, consciousness is unable of itself to cancel that reality. On the contrary, seeing that consciousness manages to nullify reality and to obtain enjoyment, this must come about through the unchangeable itself when it disposes of its own form and shape and delivers this up for consciousness to enjoy.

Consciousness, on its part, appears here likewise as actual, though, at the same time, as internally shattered; and this diremption shows itself in the course of toil and enjoyment, to break up into a relation to reality, or existence for itself, and into an existence in itself. That relation to actuality is the process of alteration, or acting, the existence for itself, which belongs to the particular consciousness as such. But therein it is also in itself; this aspect belongs to the unchangeable 'beyond.' This aspect consists in faculties and powers: an external gift, which the unchangeable here hands over for consciousness to make use of. [. . .]

Through these moments—the negative abandonment first of its own right and power of decision, then of its property and enjoyment, and finally the positive moment of carrying on what it does not understand—it obtains, completely and in truth, the consciousness of inner and outer freedom, or reality in the sense of its own existence for itself. It has the certainty of having in truth stripped itself of its Ego, and of having turned its immediate self-consciousness into a "thing," into an objective external existence.

28

William Wordsworth

Ode: Intimations of Immortality from Recollections of Early Childhood (1807)

The Child is father of the Man;
And I could wish my days to be
Bound each to each by natural piety.

I

THERE was a time when meadow, grove, and stream,
The earth, and every common sight,
        To me did seem
    Apparell'd in celestial light,
The glory and the freshness of a dream.
It is not now as it hath been of yore;—
    Turn wheresoe'er I may,
        By night or day,
The things which I have seen I now can see no more.

II

The Rainbow comes and goes,
And lovely is the Rose,
The Moon doth with delight

Look round her when the heavens are bare,

    Waters on a starry night

    Are beautiful and fair;

  The sunshine is a glorious birth;

  But yet I know, where'er I go,

That there hath pass'd away a glory from the earth.

III

Now, while the Birds thus sing a joyous song,

    And while the young Lambs bound

      As to the tabor's sound,

To me alone there came a thought of grief:

A timely utterance gave that thought relief,

      And I again am strong.

The Cataracts blow their trumpets from the steep;

No more shall grief of mine the season wrong;

I hear the Echoes through the mountains throng,

The Winds come to me from the fields of sleep,

    And all the earth is gay;

      Land and sea

  Give themselves up to jollity,

    And with the heart of May

Doth every Beast keep holiday;—

    Thou Child of Joy,

Shout round me, let me hear thy shouts, thou happy Shepherd-Boy!

IV

Ye blessèd Creatures, I have heard the call

    Ye to each other make; I see

The heavens laugh with you in your jubilee;

    My heart is at your festival,

      My head hath its coronal,

The fullness of your bliss, I feel—I feel it all.

    Oh evil day! if I were sullen

    While Earth herself is adorning,

This sweet May-morning,
And the Children are culling
On every side,
In a thousand valleys far and wide,
Fresh flowers; while the sun shines warm,
And the Babe leaps up on his Mother's arm:—
I hear, I hear, with joy I hear!
—But there's a Tree, of many, one,
A single Field which I have look'd upon,
Both of them speak of something that is gone:
The Pansy at my feet
Doth the same tale repeat:
Whither is fled the visionary gleam?
Where is it now, the glory and the dream?

V

Our birth is but a sleep and a forgetting:
The Soul that rises with us, our life's Star,
Hath had elsewhere its setting,
And cometh from afar:
Not in entire forgetfulness,
And not in utter nakedness,
But trailing clouds of glory do we come
From God, who is our home:
Heaven lies about us in our infancy!
Shades of the prison-house begin to close
Upon the growing Boy,
But He beholds the light, and whence it flows,
He sees it in his joy;
The Youth, who daily farther from the East
Must travel, still is Nature's Priest,
And by the vision splendid
Is on his way attended;
At length the Man perceives it die away,
And fade into the light of common day.

VI

Earth fills her lap with pleasures of her own;
Yearnings she hath in her own natural kind,
And, even with something of a Mother's mind,
          And no unworthy aim,
          The homely Nurse doth all she can
To make her Foster-child, her Inmate Man,
          Forget the glories he hath known,
And that imperial palace whence he came.

VII

Behold the Child among his new-born blisses,
A six years' Darling of a pigmy size!
See, where mid work of his own hand he lies,
Fretted by sallies of his Mother's kisses,
With light upon him from his Father's eyes!
See, at his feet, some little plan or chart,
Some fragment from his dream of human life,
Shap'd by himself with newly-learned art;
          A wedding or a festival,
          A mourning or a funeral;
              And this hath now his heart,
          And unto this he frames his song:
              Then will he fit his tongue
To dialogues of business, love, or strife;
          But it will not be long
          Ere this be thrown aside,
          And with new joy and pride
The little Actor cons another part,
Filling from time to time his 'humorous stage'
With all the Persons, down to palsied Age,
That Life brings with her in her Equipage;
          As if his whole vocation
          Were endless imitation.

VIII

Thou, whose exterior semblance doth belie
    Thy Soul's immensity;
Thou best Philosopher, who yet dost keep
Thy heritage, thou Eye among the blind,
That, deaf and silent, read'st the eternal deep,
Haunted for ever by the eternal mind,—
    Mighty Prophet! Seer blest!
    On whom those truths do rest
Which we are toiling all our lives to find,
In darkness lost, the darkness of the grave;
Thou, over whom thy Immortality
Broods like the Day, a Master o'er a Slave,
A Presence which is not to be put by;
    To whom the grave
Is but a lonely bed without the sense or sight
    Of day or the warm light,
A place of thought where we in waiting lie;
Thou little Child, yet glorious in the might
Of heaven-born freedom on thy Being's height,
Why with such earnest pains dost thou provoke
The Years to bring the inevitable yoke,
Thus blindly with thy blessedness at strife?
Full soon thy Soul shall have her earthly freight,
And custom lie upon thee with a weight,
Heavy as frost, and deep almost as life!

IX

    O joy! that in our embers
    Is something that doth live,
    That nature yet remembers
    What was so fugitive!
The thought of our past years in me doth breed
Perpetual benediction: not indeed
For that which is most worthy to be blest;

Delight and liberty, the simple creed
Of Childhood, whether busy or at rest,
With new-fledged hope still fluttering in his breast:—
      Not for these I raise
        The song of thanks and praise;
     But for those obstinate questionings
     Of sense and outward things,
     Fallings from us, vanishings;
     Blank misgivings of a Creature
Moving about in worlds not realiz'd,
High instincts, before which our mortal Nature
Did tremble like a guilty Thing surpriz'd:
      But for those first affections,
      Those shadowy recollections,
    Which, be they what they may,
Are yet the fountain-light of all our day,
Are yet a master-light of all our seeing;
   Uphold us, cherish, and have power to make
Our noisy years seem moments in the being
Of the eternal Silence: truths that wake,
      To perish never;
Which neither listlessness, nor mad endeavour,
      Nor Man nor Boy,
Nor all that is at enmity with joy,
Can utterly abolish or destroy!
    Hence, in a season of calm weather,
     Though inland far we be,
Our Souls have sight of that immortal sea
     Which brought us hither,
    Can in a moment travel thither,
And see the Children sport upon the shore,
And hear the mighty waters rolling evermore.

X

Then sing, ye Birds, sing, sing a joyous song!
    And let the young Lambs bound

As to the tabor's sound!
We in thought will join your throng,
　　Ye that pipe and ye that play,
　　Ye that through your hearts to-day
　　Feel the gladness of the May!
What though the radiance which was once so bright
Be now for ever taken from my sight,
　Though nothing can bring back the hour
Of splendour in the grass, of glory in the flower;
　　We will grieve not, rather find
　　Strength in what remains behind,
　　In the primal sympathy
　　Which having been must ever be,
　　In the soothing thoughts that spring
　　Out of human suffering,
　　In the faith that looks through death,
In years that bring the philosophic mind.

XI

And O, ye Fountains, Meadows, Hills, and Groves,
Forebode not any severing of our loves!
Yet in my heart of hearts I feel your might;
I only have relinquish'd one delight
To live beneath your more habitual sway.
I love the Brooks which down their channels fret,
Even more than when I tripp'd lightly as they;
The innocent brightness of a new-born Day
　　　Is lovely yet;
The Clouds that gather round the setting sun
Do take a sober colouring from an eye
That hath kept watch o'er man's mortality;
Another race hath been, and other palms are won.
Thanks to the human heart by which we live,
Thanks to its tenderness, its joys, and fears,
To me the meanest flower that blows can give
Thoughts that do often lie too deep for tears.

The Prelude; or, Growth of a Poet's Mind (1850)

[Intimations of Sublimity]

> MANY are the joys
> Of youth; but oh! what happiness to live
> When every hour brings palpable access
> Of knowledge, when all knowledge is delight,
> And sorrow is not there. The seasons came,
> And every season to my notice brought
> A store of transitory qualities
> Which, but for this most watchful power of love
> Had been neglected, left a register
> Of permanent relations, else unknown,
> Hence life, and change, and beauty, solitude
> More active, even, than 'best society',
> Society made sweet as solitude
> By silent inobtrusive sympathies,
> And gentle agitations of the mind
> From manifold distinctions, difference
> Perceived in things, where to the common eye,
> No difference is; and hence, from the same source
> Sublimer joy; for I would walk alone,
> In storm and tempest, or in starlight nights
> Beneath the quiet Heavens; and, at that time,
> Have felt whate'er there is of power in sound
> To breathe an elevated mood, by form
> Or image unprofaned; and I would stand,
> Beneath some rock, listening to sounds that are
> The ghostly language of the ancient earth,
> Or make their dim abode in distant winds.
> Thence did I drink the visionary power.
> I deem not profitless these fleeting moods
> Of shadowy exultation: not for this,
> That they are kindred to our purer mind
> And intellectual life; but that the soul,
> Remembering how she felt, but what she felt

Remembering not, retains an obscure sense
Of possible sublimity, to which,
With growing faculties she doth aspire,
With faculties still growing, feeling still
That whatsoever point they gain, they still
Have something to pursue.

Imagination, How Impaired and Restored

YE motions of delight, that through the fields
Stir gently, breezes and soft airs that breathe
The breath of Paradise, and find your way
To the recesses of the soul! Ye Brooks
Muttering along the stones, a busy noise
By day, a quiet one in silent night,
And you, ye Groves, whose ministry it is
To interpose the covert of your shades,
Even as a sleep, betwixt the heart of man
And the uneasy world, 'twixt man himself,
Not seldom, and his own unquiet heart,
Oh! that I had a music and a voice,
Harmonious as your own, that I might tell
What ye have done for me. The morning shines,
Nor heedeth Man's perverseness; Spring returns,
I saw the Spring return, when I was dead
To deeper hope, yet had I joy for her,
And welcomed her benevolence, rejoiced
In common with the Children of her Love,
Plants, insects, beasts in field, and birds in bower.
So neither were complacency nor peace
Nor tender yearnings wanting for my good
Through those distracted times; in Nature still
Glorying, I found a counterpoise in her,
Which, when the spirit of evil was at height
Maintain'd for me a secret happiness;
Her I resorted to, and lov'd so much
I seem'd to love as much as heretofore;

And yet this passion, fervent as it was,
Had suffer'd change; how could there fail to be
Some change, if merely hence, that years of life
Were going on, and with them loss or gain
Inevitable, sure alternative.

*

    Oh! soul of Nature, excellent and fair,
That didst rejoice with me, with whom I too
Rejoiced, through early youth before the winds
And powerful waters, and in lights and shades
That march'd and countermarch'd about the hills
In glorious apparition, now all eye
And now all ear; but ever with the heart
Employ'd and the majestic intellect,
Oh! Soul of Nature! that dost overflow
With passion and with life, what feeble men
Walk on this earth! how feeble have I been
When thou wert in thy strength! Nor this through stroke
Of human suffering, such as justifies
Remissness and inaptitude of mind,
But through presumption, even in pleasure pleas'd
Unworthily, disliking here, and there,
Liking, by rules of mimic art transferr'd
To things above all art. But more, for this,
Although a strong infection of the age,
Was never much my habit, giving way
To a comparison of scene with scene,
Bent overmuch on superficial things,
Pampering myself with meagre novelties
Of colour and proportion, to the moods
Of time and season, to the moral power
The affections, and the spirit of the place,
Less sensible. Nor only did the love
Of sitting thus in judgment interrupt
My deeper feelings, but another cause
More subtle and less easily explain'd
That almost seems inherent in the Creature,

Sensuous and intellectual as he is,
A twofold Frame of body and of mind;
The state to which I now allude was one
In which the eye was master of the heart,
When that which is in every stage of life
The most despotic of our senses gain'd
Such strength in me as often held my mind
In absolute dominion. Gladly here,
Entering upon abstruser argument,
Would I endeavour to unfold the means
Which Nature studiously employs to thwart
This tyranny, summons all the senses each
To counteract the other and themselves
And makes them all, and the objects with which all
Are conversant, subservient in their turn
To the great ends of Liberty and Power.

*

There are in our existence spots of time,
Which with distinct pre-eminence retain
A vivifying virtue, whence, depress'd
By false opinion and contentious thought,
Or aught of heavier or more deadly weight,
In trivial occupations, and the round
Of ordinary intercourse, our minds
Are nourished and invisibly repair'd,
A virtue by which pleasure is enhanced
That penetrates, enables us to mount
When high, more high, and lifts us up when fallen.
This efficacious spirit chiefly lurks
Among those passages of life in which
We have had deepest feeling that the mind
Is lord and master, and that outward sense
Is but the obedient servant of her will.
Such moments worthy of all gratitude,
Are scatter'd everywhere, taking their date
From our first childhood: in our childhood even
Perhaps are most conspicuous. Life with me,

As far as memory can look back, is full
Of this beneficent influence. At a time
When scarcely (I was then not six years old)
My hand could hold a bridle, with proud hopes
I mounted, and we rode towards the hills:
We were a pair of horsemen; honest James
Was with me, my encourager and guide.
We had not travell'd long, ere some mischance
Disjoin'd me from my Comrade, and, through fear
Dismounting, down the rough and stony Moor
I led my Horse, and stumbling on, at length
Came to a bottom, where in former times
A Murderer had been hung in iron chains.
The Gibbet-mast was moulder'd down, the bones
And iron case were gone; but on the turf,
Hard by, soon after that fell deed was wrought
Some unknown hand had carved the Murderer's name.
The monumental writing was engraven
In times long past, and still, from year to year,
By superstition of the neighbourhood,
The grass is clear'd away; and to this hour
The letters are all fresh and visible.
Faltering, and ignorant where I was, at length
I chanced to espy those characters inscribed
On the green sod: forthwith I left the spot
And, reascending the bare Common, saw
A naked Pool that lay beneath the hills,
The Beacon on the summit, and more near,
A Girl who bore a Pitcher on her head
And seem'd with difficult steps to force her way
Against the blowing wind. It was, in truth,
An ordinary sight; but I should need
Colours and words that are unknown to man
To paint the visionary dreariness
Which, while I look'd all round for my lost guide,
Did at that time invest the naked Pool,
The Beacon on the lonely Eminence,

The Woman, and her garments vex'd and toss'd
By the strong wind. When, in a blessed season
With those two dear Ones, to my heart so dear,
When in the blessed time of early love,
Long afterwards, I roam'd about
In daily presence of this very scene,
Upon the naked pool and dreary crags,
And on the melancholy Beacon, fell
The spirit of pleasure and youth's golden gleam;
And think ye not with radiance more divine
From these remembrances, and from the power
They left behind? So feeling comes in aid
Of feeling, and diversity of strength
Attends us, if but once we have been strong.
Oh! mystery of Man, from what a depth
Proceed thy honours! I am lost, but see
In simple childhood something of the base
On which thy greatness stands, but this I feel,
That from thyself it is that thou must give,
Else never canst receive. The days gone by
Come back upon me from the dawn almost
Of life: the hiding-places of my power
Seem open; I approach, and then they close;
I see by glimpses now; when age comes on,
May scarcely see at all, and I would give,
While yet we may, as far as words can give,
A substance and a life to what I feel:

*

     One Christmas-time,
The day before the holidays began,
Feverish and tired, and restless, I went forth
Into the fields, impatient for the sight
Of those two Horses which should bear us home,
My Brothers and myself. There was a crag,
An Eminence, which from the meeting-point
Of two highways ascending, overlook'd

At least a long half-mile of those two roads
By each of which the expected Steeds might come,
The choice uncertain. Thither I repair'd
Up to the highest summit; 'twas a day
Stormy, and rough, and wild, and on the grass
I sate, half-shelter'd by a naked wall;
Upon my right hand was a single sheep,
A whistling hawthorn on my left, and there,
With those companions at my side, I watch'd,
Straining my eyes intensely, as the mist
Gave intermitting prospect of the wood
And plain beneath. Ere I to School return'd
That dreary time, ere I had been ten days
A dweller in my Father's house, he died,
And I and my two Brothers, Orphans then,
Followed his Body to the Grave. The event
With all the sorrow which it brought appear'd
A chastisement; and when I call'd to mind
That day so lately pass'd, when from the crag
I look'd in such anxiety of hope,
With trite reflections of morality,
Yet in the deepest passion, I bow'd low
To God, who thus corrected my desires;
And afterwards, the wind and sleety rain
And all the business of the elements,
The single sheep, and the one blasted tree,
And the bleak music of that old stone wall,
The noise of wood and water, and the mist
Which on the line of each of those two Roads
Advanced in such indisputable shapes,
All these were spectacles and sounds to which
I often would repair and thence would drink,
As at a fountain; and I do not doubt
That in this later time, when storm and rain
Beat on my roof at midnight, or by day
When I am in the woods, unknown to me
The workings of my spirit thence are brought.

*

From nature doth emotion come, and moods
Of calmness equally are nature's gift,
This is her glory; these two attributes
Are sister horns that constitute her strength;
This twofold influence is the sun and shower
Of all her bounties, both in origin
And end alike benignant. Hence it is,
That Genius which exists by interchange
Of peace and excitation, finds in her
His best and purest Friend, from her receives
That energy by which he seeks the truth,
Is rouz'd, aspires, grasps, struggles, wishes, craves,
From her that happy stillness of the mind
Which fits him to receive it, when unsought.

Such benefit may souls of humblest frame
Partake of, each in their degree; 'tis mine
To speak, what I myself have known and felt
Sweet task! for words find easy way, inspired
By gratitude and confidence in truth.
Long time in search of knowledge desperate,
I was benighted heart and mind; but now
On all sides day began to reappear,
And it was proved indeed that not in vain
I had been taught to reverence a Power
That is the very quality and shape
And image of right reason, that matures
Her processes by steadfast laws, gives birth
To no impatient or fallacious hopes,
No heat of passion or excessive zeal,
No vain conceits, provokes to no quick turns
Of self-applauding intellect, but lifts
The Being into magnanimity;
Holds up before the mind, intoxicate
With present objects and the busy dance
Of things that pass away, a temperate shew
Of objects that endure, and by this course

Disposes her, when over-fondly set

On leaving her incumbrances behind

To seek in Man, and in the frame of life,

Social and individual, what there is

Desirable, affecting, good or fair

Of kindred permanence, the gifts divine

And universal, the pervading grace

That hath been, is, and shall be. Above all

Did Nature bring again that wiser mood

More deeply re-established in my soul,

Which, seeing little worthy or sublime

In what we blazon with the pompous names

Of power and action, early tutor'd me

To look with feelings of fraternal love

Upon those unassuming things, that hold

A silent station in this beauteous world.

Conclusion

    IT was a Summer's night, a close warm night,

Wan, dull and glaring, with a dripping mist

Low-hung and thick that cover'd all the sky,

Half threatening storm and rain; but on we went

Uncheck'd, being full of heart and having faith

In our tried Pilot. Little could we see

Hemm'd round on every side with fog and damp,

And, after ordinary travellers' chat

With our Conductor, silently we sank

Each into commerce with his private thoughts:

Thus did we breast the ascent, and by myself

Was nothing either seen or heard the while

Which took me from my musings, save that once

The Shepherd's Cur did to his own great joy

Unearth a hedgehog in the mountain crags

Round which he made a barking turbulent.

This small adventure, for even such it seemed

In that wild place and at the dead of night,

Being over and forgotten, on we wound
In silence as before. With forehead bent
Earthward, as if in opposition set
Against an enemy, I panted up
With eager pace, and no less eager thoughts.
Thus might we wear perhaps an hour away,
Ascending at loose distance each from each,
And I, as chanced, the foremost of the Band;
When at my feet the ground appear'd to brighten,
And with a step or two seem'd brighter still;
Nor had I time to ask the cause of this,
For instantly a Light upon the turf
Fell like a flash: I looked about, and lo!
The Moon stood naked in the Heavens, at height
Immense above my head, and on the shore
I found myself of a huge sea of mist,
Which, meek and silent, rested at my feet:
A hundred hills their dusky backs upheaved
All over this still Ocean, and beyond,
Far, far beyond, the vapours shot themselves,
In headlands, tongues, and promontory shapes,
Into the Sea, the real Sea, that seem'd
To dwindle, and give up its majesty,
Usurp'd upon as far as sight could reach.
Meanwhile, the Moon look'd down upon this shew
In single glory, and we stood, the mist
Touching our very feet; and from the shore
At distance not the third part of a mile
Was a blue chasm; a fracture in the vapour,
A deep and gloomy breathing-place through which
Mounted the roar of waters, torrents, streams
Innumerable, roaring with one voice.
The universal spectacle throughout
Was shaped for admiration and delight,
Grand in itself alone, but in that breach
Through which the homeless voice of waters rose,
That dark deep thoroughfare had Nature lodg'd
The Soul, the Imagination of the whole.

A meditation rose in me that night
Upon the lonely Mountain when the scene
Had pass'd away, and it appear'd to me
The perfect image of a mighty Mind,
Of one that feeds upon infinity,
That is exalted by an underpresence,
The sense of God, or whatsoe'er is dim
Or vast in its own being, above all
One function of such mind had Nature there
Exhibited by putting forth, and that
With circumstance most awful and sublime,
That domination which she oftentimes
Exerts upon the outward face of things,
So moulds them, and endues, abstracts, combines,
Or by abrupt and unhabitual influence
Doth make one object so impress itself
Upon all others, and pervade them so
That even the grossest minds must see and hear
And cannot chuse but feel. The Power which these
Acknowledge when thus moved, which Nature thus
Thrusts forth upon the senses, is the express
Resemblance, in the fulness of its strength
Made visible, a genuine Counterpart
And Brother of the glorious faculty
Which higher minds bear with them as their own.
That is the very spirit in which they deal
With all the objects of the universe;
They from their native selves can send abroad
Like transformations, for themselves create
A like existence, and, whene'er it is
Created for them, catch it by an instinct;
Them the enduring and the transient both
Serve to exalt; they build up greatest things
From least suggestions, ever on the watch,
Willing to work and to be wrought upon,
They need not extraordinary calls
To rouze them, in a world of life they live,
By sensible impressions not enthrall'd,

But quicken'd, rouz'd, and made thereby more apt
To hold communion with the invisible world.
Such minds are truly from the Deity,
For they are Powers; and hence the highest bliss
That can be known is theirs, the consciousness
Of whom they are habitually infused
Through every image, and through every thought,
And all impressions, hence religion, faith,
And endless occupation for the soul
Whether discursive or intuitive;
Hence sovereignty within and peace at will,
Emotion which best foresight need not fear
Most worthy then of trust when most intense.
Hence chearfulness in every act of life
Hence truth in moral judgements and delight
That fails not in the external universe.

29

Germaine de Staël

Germany (1813)

Kant

[. . .] THE MATERIALISTIC PHILOSOPHY GAVE UP THE HUMAN UNDERSTANDING to the empire of external objects, and morals to personal interest; and reduced the beautiful to the agreeable. Kant wished to re-establish primitive truths and spontaneous activity in the soul, conscience in morals, and the ideal in the arts. Let us now examine in what manner he has fulfilled these different undertakings.

At the time the *Critique of Pure Reason* made its appearance, there existed only two systems concerning the human understanding among thinking men: the one, that of Locke, attributed all our ideas to our sensations; the other, that of Descartes and Leibnitz, endeavored to demonstrate the spirituality and the activity of the soul, free-will, in short, the whole doctrine of Idealism; but these two philosophers rested their opinions upon proofs purely speculative. I have exposed, in the preceding chapter, the inconveniences which result from these efforts of abstraction, that arrest, if we may use the expression, the very blood in our veins, until our intellectual faculties alone reign within us. The algebraic method, applied to objects that we cannot embrace by mere reasoning, leaves no durable trace in the mind. While we are in the act of perusing these writings upon high philosophical conceptions, we believe that we comprehend them; we think that we believe them; but the arguments which have appeared most convincing, very soon escape from the memory.

If man, wearied with these efforts, confines himself to the knowledge which he gains by his senses, all will be melancholy indeed for his soul. Will he have any idea of immortality, when the forerunners of destruction are engraven so deeply on the countenance of mortals, and living nature falls incessantly into dust? When all the senses talk of death, what feeble hope can we entertain of a resurrection? If man only consulted his sensations, what idea would he form of the supreme goodness? So many afflictions dispute the mastery over our life; so many hideous objects disfigure nature, that the unfortunate created being curses his existence a thousand times before the last convulsion snatches it away. Let man, on the contrary, reject the testimony of his senses, how will he guide himself on the earth? and yet, if he trusts to them alone, what enthusiasm, what morals, what religion will be able to resist the repeated assaults to which pain and pleasure alternately expose him?

Reflection wandered over this vast region of uncertainty, when Kant endeavored to trace the limits of the two empires, that of the senses and that of the soul; of external and of intellectual nature. The strength of thinking, and the wisdom with which he marked these limits, were perhaps never exhibited before: he did not lose himself among the new systems concerning the creation of the universe; he recognized the bounds which the eternal mysteries set to the human understanding, and (what will be new perhaps to those who have only heard Kant spoken of) there is no philosopher more adverse, in numerous respects, to metaphysics; he made himself so deeply learned in this science, only to employ against it the means it afforded him to demonstrate its own insufficiency. We might say of him, that, like a new Curtius, he threw himself into the gulf of abstraction, in order to fill it up.

Locke had victoriously combated the doctrine of innate ideas in man, because he has always represented ideas as making a part of our experimental knowledge. The examination of pure reason, that is to say of the primitive faculties of which the intellect is composed, did not fix his attention Leibnitz, as we have said before, pronounced this sublime axiom: "There is nothing in the intellect which does not come by the senses, except the intellect itself." Kant has acknowledged, as well as Locke, that there are no innate ideas; but he has endeavored to enter into the sense of the axiom of Leibnitz, by examining what are the laws and the sentiments which constitute the essence of the human soul, independently of all experience. The *Critique of Pure Reason* strives to show in what these laws consist, and what are the objects upon which they can be exercised.

Skepticism, to which materialism almost always leads, was carried so far, that Hume finished by overturning the foundation of all reason, in his search after arguments against the axiom, "that there is no effect without a cause." And such is the unsteadiness of human nature when we do not place the principle of conviction in the centre of the soul, that incredulity, which begins by attacking the existence of the moral world, at last gets rid of the material world also, which it first used as an instrument to destroy the other.

Kant wished to know whether absolute certainty was attainable by the human understanding; and he only found it in our necessary notions, that is, in all the laws of our understanding, which are of such a nature that we cannot conceive any thing otherwise than as those laws represent it.

In the first class of the imperative forms of our understanding are space and time. Kant demonstrates that all our perceptions are subjected to these two forms; he concludes, from hence, that they exist in us, and not in objects; and that in this respect, it is our understanding which gives laws to external nature, instead of receiving them from it. Geometry, which measures space, and arithmetic, which divides time, are sciences of perfect demonstration, because they rest upon the necessary notions of our mind.

Truths acquired by experience never carry absolute certainty with them; when we say: "The sun rises every day," "all men are mortal," etc., the imagination could figure an exception to these truths, which experience alone makes us consider indubitable; but Imagination herself cannot suppose any thing out of the sphere of space and time; and it is impossible to regard as the result of custom (that is, of the constant repetition of the same phenomena) those forms of our thoughts which we impose upon things; sensations may be doubtful; but the prism through which we receive them is immovable.

To this primitive intuition of space and time, we must add, or rather give, as a foundation, the principles of reasoning, without which we cannot comprehend any thing, and which are the laws of our intellect: the connection of causes and effects, unity, plurality, totality, possibility, reality, necessity, etc. Kant considers them all as equally necessary notions; and he only raises to the rank of real sciences such as are immediately founded upon these notions, because it is in them alone that certainty can exist. The forms of reasoning have no result, except when they are applied to our judgment of external objects, and in this application they are liable to error; but they are not the less necessary in themselves; that is, we cannot depart from them in any of our thoughts; it is impossible for us to imagine any thing out of the sphere of the relations of causes and effects, of possibility, quantity, etc.; and these notions are as inherent in our conception as space and time. We perceive nothing except through the medium of the immovable laws of our manner of reasoning; therefore these laws are in ourselves, and not out of us.

In the German philosophy, those ideas are called *subjective* which grow out of the nature of our understanding and its faculties; and all those ideas *objective*, which are excited by sensations. Whatever may be the denomination which we adopt in this respect, it appears to me that the examination of our intellect agrees with the prevailing thought of Kant; namely, the distinction he establishes between the forms of our understanding and the objects which we know according to those forms; and whether he adheres to abstract conceptions, or whether he appeals, in religion and morals, to sentiments which he also considers as independent of experience, nothing is more luminous than the line of demarcation which he traces between what comes to us by sensation, and what belongs to the spontaneous action of our souls.

Some expressions in the doctrine of Kant having been ill interpreted, it has been pretended that he believed in *a priori* cognitions, that is, those engraved upon the mind before we have discovered them. Other German philosophers, more allied to the system of Plato, have, in effect, thought that the type of the world was in the human understanding, and that man could not conceive the universe if he had not in himself the innate image of it; but this doctrine is not touched upon by Kant: he reduces the intellectual sciences to three—logic, metaphysics, and mathematics. Logic teaches nothing by itself; but as it rests upon the laws of our understanding, it is incontestable in its principles, abstractly considered; this science cannot lead to truth, except in its application to ideas and things; its principles are innate, its application is experimental. In metaphysics, Kant denies its existence; because he pretends that reasoning cannot find a place beyond the sphere of experience. Mathematics alone appear to him to depend immediately upon the notion of space and of time, that is, upon the laws of our understanding anterior to experience. He endeavors to prove, that mathematics are not a simple analysis, but a synthetic, positive, creative science, and certain of itself, without the necessity of our recurring to experience to be assured of its truth. We may study in the work of Kant the arguments upon which he supports this way of thinking; but at least it is true, that there is no man more adverse to what is called the philosophy of the dreamers; and that he must rather have had an inclination for a dry and didactic mode of thinking, although the object of his doctrine be to raise the human species from its degradation, under the philosophy of materialism.

Far from rejecting experience, Kant considers the business of life as nothing but the action of our innate faculties upon the several sorts of knowledge which come to us from without. He believed that experience would be nothing but a chaos without the laws of the understanding; but that the laws of the understanding have no other object than the elements afforded it by experience. It follows, that metaphysics themselves can teach us nothing beyond these limits; and that it is to sentiment that we ought to attribute the foreknowledge and the conviction of every thing that transcends the bounds of the visible world.

When it is attempted to use reasoning alone for the establishment of religious truths, it becomes a most pliable instrument, which can equally attack and defend them; because we cannot, on this occasion, find any point of support in experience. Kant places upon two parallel lines the arguments for and against the liberty of man, the immortality of the soul, the temporary or eternal duration of the world; and it is to sentiment that he appeals to weigh down the balance, for the metaphysical proofs appear to him of equal strength on either side. Perhaps he was wrong to push the skepticism of reasoning to such an extent; but it was to annihilate this skepticism with more certainty, by keeping certain questions clear from the abstract discussions which gave it birth. [. . .]

30

Arthur Schopenhauer

The World as Will and Idea (1818)

The World as Idea, First Aspect

§ 1. "THE WORLD IS MY IDEA:" — THIS IS A TRUTH which holds good for everything that lives and knows, though man alone can bring it into reflective and abstract consciousness. If he really does this, he has attained to philosophical wisdom. It then becomes clear and certain to him that what he knows is not a sun and an earth, but only an eye that sees a sun, a hand that feels an earth; that the world which surrounds him is there only as idea, *i.e.,* only in relation to something else, the consciousness, which is himself. If any truth can be asserted *a priori*, it is this: for it is the expression of the most general form of all possible and thinkable experience: a form which is more general than time, or space, or causality, for they all presuppose it; and each of these, which we have seen to be just so many modes of the principle of sufficient reason, is valid only for a particular class of ideas; whereas the antithesis of object and subject is the common form of all these classes, is that form under which alone any idea of whatever kind it may be, abstract or intuitive, pure or empirical, is possible and thinkable. No truth therefore is more certain, more independent of all others, and less in need of proof than this, that all that exists for knowledge, and therefore this whole world, is only object in relation to subject, perception of a perceiver, in a word, idea. This is obviously true of the past and the future, as well as of the present, of what is farthest off, as of what is near; for it is true of time and space themselves, in which alone these distinctions arise. All that in any way belongs or can belong to the world is inevitably thus conditioned through the subject, and exists only for the subject. The world is idea.

This truth is by no means new. It was implicitly involved in the sceptical reflections from which Descartes started. Berkeley, however, was the first who distinctly enunciated it, and by this he has rendered a permanent service to philosophy, even though the rest of his teaching should not endure, Kant's primary mistake was the neglect of this principle, as is shown in the appendix. How early again this truth was recognised by the wise men of India, appearing indeed as the fundamental tenet of the Vedânta philosophy ascribed to Vyasa, is pointed out by Sir William Jones in the last of his essays: "On the philosophy of the Asiatics" (Asiatic Researches, vol. iv. p. 164), where he says, "The fundamental tenet of the Vedanta school consisted not in denying the existence of matter, that is, of solidity, impenetrability, and extended figure (to deny which would be lunacy), but in correcting the popular notion of it, and in contending that it has no essence independent of mental perception; that existence and perceptibility are convertible terms." These words adequately express the compatibility of empirical reality and transcendental ideality.

In this first book, then, we consider the world only from this side, only so far as it is idea. The inward reluctance with which any one accepts the world as merely his idea, warns him that this view of it, however true it may be, is nevertheless one-sided, adopted in consequence of some arbitrary abstraction. And yet it is a conception from which he can never free himself. The defectiveness of this view will be corrected in the next book by means of a truth which is not so immediately certain as that from which we start here; a truth at which we can arrive only by deeper research and more severe abstraction, by the separation of what is different and the union of what is identical. This truth, which must be very serious and impressive if not awful to every one, is that a man can also say and must say, "the world is my will."

In this book, however, we must consider separately that aspect of the world from which we start, its aspect as knowable, and therefore, in the meantime, we must, without reserve, regard all presented objects, even our own bodies (as we shall presently show more fully), merely as ideas, and call them merely ideas. By so doing we always abstract from will (as we hope to make clear to every one further on), which by itself constitutes the other aspect of the world. For as the world is in one aspect entirely *idea,* so in another it is entirely *will.* A reality which is neither of these two, but an object in itself (into which the thing in itself has unfortunately dwindled in the hands of Kant), is the phantom of a dream, and its acceptance is an *ignis fatuus* in philosophy.

§ 2. That which knows all things and is known by none is the subject. Thus it is the supporter of the world, that condition of all phenomena, of all objects which is always pre-supposed throughout experience; for all that exists, exists only for the subject. Every one finds himself to be subject, yet only in so far as he knows, not in so far as he is an object of knowledge. But his body is object, and therefore from this point of view we call it idea. For the body is an object among objects, and is conditioned by the laws of objects, although it is an immediate object. Like all objects of perception, it lies within the universal forms of knowledge, time and space, which are the conditions of multiplicity. The subject, on the contrary, which is always the knower, never the known, does not come under these forms, but is presupposed by them; it has therefore neither multiplicity nor its opposite unity. We never know it, but it is always the knower wherever there is knowledge.

So then the world as idea, the only aspect in which we consider it at present, has two fundamental, necessary, and inseparable halves. The one half is the object, the forms of which are space and time, and through these multiplicity. The other half is the subject, which is not in space and time, for it is present, entire and undivided, in every percipient being. So that any one percipient being, with the object, constitutes the whole world as idea just as fully as the existing millions could do; but if this one were to disappear, then the whole world as idea would cease to be. These halves are therefore inseparable even for thought, for each of the two has meaning and existence only through and for the other, each appears with the other and vanishes with it. They limit each other immediately; where the object begins the subject ends. The universality of this limitation is shown by the fact that the essential and hence universal forms of all objects, space, time, and causality, may, without knowledge of the object, be discovered and fully known from a consideration of the subject, *i.e.,* in Kantian language, they lie *a priori* in our consciousness. That he discovered this is one of Kant's principal merits, and it is a great one. I however go beyond this, and maintain that the principle of sufficient reason is the general expression for all these forms of the object of which we are *a priori* conscious; and that therefore all that we know purely *a priori,* is merely the content of that principle and what follows from it; in it all our certain *a priori* knowledge is expressed. In my essay on the principle of sufficient reason I have shown in detail how every possible object comes under it; that is, stands in a necessary relation to other objects, on the one side as determined, on the other side as determining: this is of such wide application, that the whole existence of all objects, so far as they are objects, ideas and nothing more, may be entirely traced to this their necessary relation to each other, rests only in it, is in fact merely relative; but of this more presently. I have further shown, that the necessary relation which the principle of sufficient reason expresses generally, appears in other forms corresponding to the classes into which objects are divided, according to their possibility; and again that by these forms the proper division of the classes is tested. I take it for granted that what I said in this earlier essay is known and present to the reader, for if it had not been already said it would necessarily find its place here.

§ 3. The chief distinction among our ideas is that between ideas of perception and abstract ideas. The latter form just one class of ideas, namely concepts, and these are the possession of man alone of all creatures upon earth. The capacity for these, which distinguishes him from all the lower animals, has always been called reason.[1] We shall consider these abstract ideas by themselves later, but, in the first place, we shall speak exclusively of the *ideas of perception.* These comprehend the whole visible world, or the sum total of experience, with the conditions of its possibility. We have already observed that it is a highly important discovery of Kant's, that these very conditions, these forms of the visible world, *i.e.,* the absolutely universal element in its perception, the common property of all its phenomena, space and time, even when taken by themselves and apart from their content, can, not only be thought in the abstract, but also be directly perceived; and that this perception or intuition is not some kind of phantasm arising from constant recurrence in experience, but is so entirely independent of experience that we must rather regard the latter as dependent on it, inasmuch as the qualities of space and time, as they are known in *a priori* perception or intuition, are valid for all possible experience, as rules to which it must invariably conform. Accordingly, in my essay on the principle of sufficient reason, I have treated space and time, because they are perceived as pure and empty of content, as a special and independent class of ideas. This quality of the universal forms of intuition, which was discovered by Kant, that they may be perceived in themselves and apart from experience, and that they may be known as exhibiting those laws on which is founded the infallible science of mathematics, is certainly very important. Not less worthy of remark, however, is this other quality of time and space, that the principle of sufficient reason, which conditions experience as the law of causation and of motive, and thought as the law of the basis of judgment, appears here in quite a special form, to which I have given the name of the ground of being. In time, this is the succession of its moments, and in space the position of its parts, which reciprocally determine each other *ad infinitum*.

Any one who has fully understood from the introductory essay the complete identity of the content of the principle of sufficient reason in all its different forms, must also be convinced of the importance of the knowledge of the simplest of these forms, as affording him insight into his own inmost nature. This simplest form of the principle we have found to be time. In it each instant is, only in so far as it has effaced the preceding one, its generator, to be itself in turn as quickly effaced. The past and the future (considered apart from the consequences of their content) are empty as a dream, and the present is only the indivisible and unenduring boundary between them. And in all the other forms of the principle of sufficient reason, we shall find the same emptiness, and shall see that not time only but also space, and the whole content of both of them, *i.e.*, all that proceeds from causes and motives, has a merely relative existence, is only through and for another like to itself, *i.e.*, not more enduring. The substance of this doctrine is old: it appears in Heraclitus when he laments the eternal flux of things; in Plato when he degrades the object to that which is ever becoming, but never being; in Spinoza as the doctrine of the mere accidents of the one substance which is and endures. Kant opposes what is thus known as the mere phenomenon to the thing in itself. Lastly, the ancient wisdom of the Indian philosophers declares, "It is Mâyâ, the veil of deception, which blinds the eyes of mortals, and makes them behold a world of which they cannot say either that it is or that it is not: for it is like a dream; it is like the sunshine on the sand which the traveller takes from afar for water, or the stray piece of rope he mistakes for a snake." (These similes are repeated in innumerable passages of the Vedas and the Puranas.) But what all these mean, and that of which they all speak, is nothing more than what we have just considered—the world as idea subject to the principle of sufficient reason.

§ 4. Whoever has recognised the form of the principle of sufficient reason, which appears in pure time as such, and on which all counting and arithmetical calculation rests, has completely mastered the nature of time. Time is nothing more than that form of the principle of sufficient reason, and has no further significance. Succession is the form of the principle of sufficient reason in time, and succession is the whole nature of time. Further, whoever has recognised the principle of sufficient reason as it appears in the presentation of pure space, has exhausted the whole nature of space, which is absolutely nothing more than that possibility of the reciprocal determination of its parts by each other, which is called position. The detailed treatment of this, and the formulation in abstract conceptions of the results which flow from it, so that they may be more conveniently used, is the subject of the science of geometry. Thus also, whoever has recognised the law of causation, the aspect of the principle of sufficient reason which appears in what fills these forms (space and time) as objects of perception, that is to say matter, has completely mastered the nature of matter as such, for matter is nothing more than causation, as any one will see at once if he reflects. Its true being is its action, nor can we possibly conceive it as having any other meaning. Only as active does it fill space and time; its action upon the immediate object (which is itself matter) determines that perception in which alone it exists. The consequence of the action of any material object upon any other, is known only in so far as the latter acts upon the immediate object in a different way from that in which it acted before; it consists only of this. Cause and effect thus constitute the whole nature of matter; its true being is its action.[. . .] The nature of all material things is therefore very appropriately called in German *Wirklichkeit*,[2] a word which is far more expressive than *Realität*. Again, that which is acted upon is always matter, and thus the whole being and essence of matter consists in the orderly change, which one part of it brings about in another part. The existence of matter is therefore entirely relative, according to a relation which is valid only within its limits, as in the case of time and space.

But time and space, each for itself, can be mentally presented apart from matter, whereas matter cannot be so presented apart from time and space. The form which is inseparable from it presupposes space, and the action in which its very existence consists, always imports some change, in other words a determination in time. But space and time are not only, each for itself, presupposed by matter, but a union of the two constitutes its essence, for this, as we have seen, consists in action, *i.e.*, in causation. [. . .]

§ 5. It is needful to guard against the grave error of supposing that because perception arises through the knowledge of causality, the relation of subject and object is that of cause and effect. For this relation subsists only between the immediate object and objects known indirectly, thus always between objects alone. It is this false supposition that has given rise to the foolish controversy about the reality of the outer world; a controversy in which dogmatism and scepticism oppose each other, and the former appears, now as realism, now as idealism. Realism treats the object as cause, and the subject as its effect. The idealism of Fichte reduces the object to the effect of the subject. Since however, and this cannot be too much emphasised, there is absolutely no relation according to the principle of sufficient reason between subject and object, neither of these views could be proved, and therefore scepticism attacked them both with success. Now, just as the law of causality precedes perception and experience as their condition, and therefore cannot (as Hume thought) be derived from them, so object and subject precede all knowledge, and hence the principle of sufficient reason in general, as its first condition; for this principle is merely the form of all objects, the whole nature and possibility of their existence as phenomena: but the object always presupposes the subject; and therefore between these two there can be no relation of reason and consequent. My essay on the principle of sufficient reason accomplishes just this: it explains the content of that principle as the essential form of every object—that is to say, as the universal nature of all objective existence, as something which pertains to the object as such; but the object as such always presupposes the subject as its necessary correlative; and therefore the subject remains always outside the province in which the principle of sufficient reason is valid. The controversy as to the reality of the outer world rests upon this false extension of the validity of the principle of sufficient reason to the subject also, and starting with this mistake it can never understand itself. On the one side realistic dogmatism, looking upon the idea as the effect of the object, desires to separate these two, idea and object, which are really one, and to assume a cause quite different from the idea, an object in itself, independent of the subject, a thing which is quite inconceivable; for even as object it presupposes subject, and so remains its idea. Opposed to this doctrine is scepticism, which makes the same false presupposition that in the idea we have only the effect, never the cause, therefore never real being; that we always know merely the action of the object. But this object, it supposes, may perhaps have no resemblance whatever to its effect, may indeed have been quite erroneously received as the cause, for the law of causality is first to be gathered from experience, and the reality of experience is then made to rest upon it. Thus both of these views are open to the correction, firstly, that object and idea are the same; secondly, that the true being of the object of perception is its action, that the reality of the thing consists in this, and the demand for an existence of the object outside the idea of the subject, and also for an essence of the actual thing different from its action, has absolutely no meaning, and is a contradiction: and that the knowledge of the nature of the effect of any perceived object, exhausts such an object itself, so far as it is object, *i.e.,* idea, for beyond this there is nothing more to be known. So far then, the perceived world in space and time, which makes itself known as causation alone, is entirely real, and is throughout simply what it appears to be, and it appears wholly and without reserve as idea, bound together according to the law of causality. This is its empirical reality. On the other hand, all causality is in the understanding alone, and for the understanding. The whole actual, that is, active world is determined as such through the understanding, and apart from it is nothing. This, however, is not the only reason for altogether denying such a reality of the outer world as is taught by the dogmatist, who explains its reality as its independence of the subject. We also deny it, because no object apart from a subject can be conceived without contradiction. The whole world of objects is and remains idea, and therefore wholly and for ever determined by the subject; that is to say, it has transcendental ideality. But it is not therefore illusion or mere appearance; it presents itself as that which it is, idea, and indeed as a series of ideas of which the common bond is the principle of sufficient reason. It is according to its inmost meaning quite comprehensible to the healthy understanding, and speaks a language quite intelligible to it. To dispute about its reality can only occur to a mind perverted by over-subtilty, and such discussion always arises from a false application of the principle of sufficient reason, which binds all ideas together of whatever kind they may be, but by no means connects them with the subject, nor yet with a something which is neither subject nor object, but only the ground of the object; an absurdity, for only objects can be and always are the ground of objects. If we examine more closely the source of this question as to the reality of the outer world, we find that besides the false application of the principle of sufficient reason generally to what lies beyond its province, a special confusion of its forms is also involved; for that form which it has only in reference to concepts or abstract ideas, is applied to perceived ideas, real objects; and a ground of knowing is demanded of objects, whereas they can have nothing but a ground of being. Among the abstract ideas, the concepts united in the judgment, the principle of sufficient reason appears in such a way that each of these has its worth, its validity, and its whole existence, here called *truth,* simply and solely through the relation of the judgment to something outside of it, its ground of knowledge, to which there must consequently always be a return. Among real objects, ideas of perception, on the other hand, the principle of sufficient reason appears not as the principle of the ground of *knowing,* but of *being,* as the law of causality: every real object has paid its debt to it, inasmuch as it has come to be, *i.e.,* has appeared as the effect of a cause. The demand for a ground of knowing has therefore here no application and no meaning, but belongs to quite another class of things. Thus the world of perception raises in the observer no question or doubt so long as he remains in contact with it: there is here neither error nor truth, for these are confined to, the province of the abstract—the province of reflection. But here the world lies open for sense and understanding; presents itself with naive truth as that which it really is—ideas of perception which develop themselves according to the law of causality.

So far as we have considered the question of the reality of the outer world, it arises from a confusion which amounts even to a misunderstanding of reason itself, and therefore thus far, the question could be answered only by explaining its meaning. After examination of the whole nature of the principle of sufficient reason, of the relation of subject and object, and the special conditions of sense perception, the question itself disappeared because it had no longer any meaning. There is, however, one other possible origin of this question, quite different from the purely speculative one which we have considered, a specially empirical origin, though the question is always raised from a speculative point of view, and in this form it has a much more comprehensible meaning than it had in the first. We have dreams; may not our whole life be a dream? or more exactly: is there a sure criterion of the distinction between dreams and reality?

between phantasms and real objects? The assertion that what is dreamt is less vivid and distinct than what we actually perceive is not to the point, because no one has ever been able to make a fair comparison of the two; for we can only compare the recollection of a dream with the present reality. Kant answers the question thus: "The connection of ideas among themselves, according to the law of causality, constitutes the difference between real life and dreams." But in dreams, as well as in real life, everything is connected individually at any rate, in accordance with the principle of sufficient reason in all its forms, and this connection is broken only between life and dreams, or between one dream and another. Kant's answer therefore could only run thus:—the *long* dream (life) has throughout complete connection according to the principle of sufficient reason; it has not this connection, however, with *short* dreams, although each of these has in itself the same connection: the bridge is therefore broken between the former and the latter, and on this account we distinguish them.

But to institute an inquiry according to this criterion, as to whether something was dreamt or seen, would always be difficult and often impossible. For we are by no means in a position to trace link by link the causal connection between any experienced event and the present moment, but we do not on that account explain it as dreamt. Therefore in real life we do not commonly employ that method of distinguishing between dreams and reality. The only sure criterion by which to distinguish them is in fact the entirely empirical one of awaking, through which at any rate the causal connection between dreamed events and those of waking life, is distinctly and sensibly broken off. This is strongly supported by the remark of Hobbes in the second chapter of Leviathan, that we easily mistake dreams for reality if we have unintentionally fallen asleep without taking off our clothes, and much more so when it also happens that some undertaking or design fills all our thoughts, and occupies our dreams as well as our waking moments. We then observe the awaking just as little as the falling asleep, dream and reality run together and become confounded. In such a case there is nothing for it but the application of Kant's criterion; but if, as often happens, we fail to establish by means of this criterion, either the existence of causal connection with the present, or the absence of such connection, then it must for ever remain uncertain whether an event was dreamt or really happened. Here, in fact, the intimate relationship between life and dreams is brought out very clearly, and we need not be ashamed to confess it, as it has been recognised and spoken of by many great men. The Vedas and Puranas have no better simile than a dream for the whole knowledge of the actual world, which they call the web of Mâyâ, and they use none more frequently. Plato often says that men live only in a dream; the philosopher alone strives to awake himself. Pindar says (ii. *η*. 135): σκιας οναρ ανθρωπος (umbræ somnium homo), and Sophocles:—

Ὄξω γαξ ἡμαζ ουδεν οντας αλλο, πλην
Σιδωλ᾽ ὁσοιπεξ ζωμεν, ἡ κουρην σκιαν.—*Ajax*, 125.

(Nos enim, quicunque vivimus, nihil aliud esse comperio quam simulacra et levem umbram.) Beside which most worthily stands Shakespeare:—

> "We are such stuff
> As dreams are made on, and our little life
> Is rounded with a sleep."—*Tempest,* Act iv. Sc. I.

Lastly, Calderon was so deeply impressed with this view of life that he sought to embody it in a kind of metaphysical drama—"Life a Dream."

After these numerous quotations from the poets, perhaps I also may be allowed to express myself by a metaphor. Life and dreams are leaves of the same book. The systematic reading of this book is real life, but when the reading hours (that is, the day) are over, we often continue idly to turn over the leaves, and read a page here and there without method or connection: often one we have read before, sometimes one that is new to us, but always in the same book. Such an isolated page is indeed out of connection with the systematic study, of the book, but it does not seem so very different when we remember that the whole continuous perusal begins and ends just as abruptly, and may therefore be regarded as merely a larger single page.

Thus although individual dreams are distinguished from real life by the fact that they do not fit into that continuity which runs through the whole of experience, and the act of awaking brings this into consciousness, yet that very continuity of experience belongs to real life as its form, and the dream on its part can point to a similar continuity in itself. If, therefore, we consider the question from a point of view external to both, there is no distinct difference in their nature, and we are forced to concede to the poets that life is a long dream.

Let us turn back now from this quite independent empirical origin of the question of the reality of the outer world, to its speculative origin. We found that this consisted, first, in the false application of the principle of sufficient reason to the relation of subject and object; and secondly, in the confusion of its forms, inasmuch as the principle of sufficient reason of knowing was extended to a province in which the principle of sufficient reason of being is valid. But the question could hardly have occupied philosophers so constantly if it were entirely devoid of all real content, and if some true thought and meaning did not lie at its heart as its real source. Accordingly, we must assume that when the element of truth that lies at the bottom of the question first came into reflection and sought its expression, it became involved in these confused and meaningless forms and problems. This at least is my opinion, and I think that the true expression of that inmost meaning of the question, which it failed to find, is this:—What is this world of perception besides being my idea? Is that of which I am conscious only as idea, exactly like my own body, of which I am doubly conscious, in one aspect as *idea,* in another aspect as *will?* The fuller explanation of this question and its answer in the affirmative, will form the content of the second book, and its consequences will occupy the remaining portion of this work.

The Failure of Philosophy: A Brief Dialogue

A. Philosophy has hitherto been a failure. It could not, indeed, have been otherwise; because, instead of confining himself to the better understanding of the world as given in experience, the philosopher has aspired to pass at one bound beyond it, in the hope of discovering the last foundation of all existence and the eternal relations of things. Now these are matters which our intellect is quite incapable of grasping. Its power of comprehension never reaches beyond what philosophers call "finite things," or, as they sometimes say, "phenomena;" in short, just the fleeting shadows of this world, and the interests of the individual, the furtherance of his aims and the maintenance of his person. And since our intellect is thus immanent, our philosophy should be immanent too, and not soar to supramundane things, but be content with gaining a thorough grasp of the world of experience. It surely provides matter enough for such a study.

B. If that is so, intellect is a miserable present for Nature to give us. According to your view, the mind serves only to grasp the relations that constitute our wretched existence as individuals—relations which cease with the brief span of our temporal life; and is utterly unsuited to face those problems which are alone worthy to interest a thinking being—what our existence really is, and what the world means as a whole; in short, how we are to solve the riddle of this dream of life. If all this is so, and our mind could never grasp these things even though they were explained to it, then I cannot see that it is worth my while to educate my mind, or to pay any attention to it at all; it is a thing unworthy of any respect.

A. My dear sir, if we wrangle with Nature, we are usually in the wrong. For Nature does nothing that is useless or in vain—*nihil facit frustra nec supervacaneum*. We are only temporal, finite, fleeting beings creatures of a dream: and our existence passes away like a shadow. What do we want with an intellect to grasp things that are infinite, eternal, absolute? And how should such an intellect ever leave the consideration of these high matters to apply itself again to the small facts of our ephemeral life—the facts that are the only realities for us and our proper concern? How could it ever be of any use for them again? If nature had bestowed this intellect upon us, the gift would not only have been an immense mistake and quite in vain; it would even have conflicted with the very aims that nature has designed for us. For what good do we do, as Shakespeare says,

> "We fools of nature,
> So horridly to shake our disposition
> With thoughts beyond the reaches of our souls."[3]

If we had this perfect, this all embracing, metaphysical insight, should we be capable of any physical insight at all, or of going about our proper business? Nay, it might plunge us forever into a state of chill horror, like that of one who has seen a ghost.

B. But surely in all this you are making a notorious *petitio principii*. In saying that we are merely temporal, fleeting, finite beings, you beg the whole question. We are also infinite, eternal, and the original principle of nature itself. Is it not then well worth our while to go on trying if we cannot fathom nature after all—*ob nicht Natur zuletzt sich dock ergründe?*

A. Yes; but according to your own philosophy we are infinite and eternal, only in a certain sense. We are infinite and eternal not as phenomena, but as the original principle of nature; not as individuals, but as the inmost essence of the world; not because we are subjects of knowledge, but merely as manifestations of the will to live. The qualities of which you speak are qualities that have to do with intelligence, not will. As intelligent beings we are individual and finite. Our intellect, then, is also of this character. The aim of our life, if I may use a metaphorical expression, is a practical, not a theoretical one; our actions, not our knowledge, appertain to eternity. The use of the intellect is to guide our actions, and at the same time to hold up the mirror to our will; and this is, in effect, what it does. If the intellect had more to do, it would very probably become unfit even for this. Think how a small superfluity of intellect is a bar to the career of the man endowed with it. Take the case of genius: while it may be an inward blessing to its possessor, it may also make him very unhappy in his relations with the world.

B. Good, that you reminded me of genius. To some extent it upsets the facts you are trying to vindicate. A genius is a man whose theoretical side enormously outweighs his practical. Even though he cannot grasp eternal relations, he can see a little deeper into the things of this world; *attamen est quodam prodire tenus*. It is quite true that this does render the intellect of genius less fit to grasp the finite things of earth; just as a telescope is a good thing, but not in a theater. Here we seem to have reached a point where we agree, and we need not pursue the subject further.

The Vanity of Existence

THIS VANITY FINDS EXPRESSION IN THE WHOLE WAY IN WHICH things exist: in the infinite nature of Time and Space, as opposed to the finite nature of the individual in both; in the ever-passing present moment as the only mode of actual existence; in the interdependence and relativity of all things; in continual becoming without ever being; in constant wishing and never being satisfied; in the long battle which forms the history of life, where every effort is checked by difficulties, and stopped until they are overcome. Time is that in which all things pass away; it is merely the form under which the will to live—the thing in itself and therefore imperishable—has revealed to it that its efforts are in vain; it is that agent by which at every moment all things in our hands become as nothing, and lose any real value they possess.

That which has been exists no more; it exists as little as that which has never been. But of everything that exists you must say, in the next moment, that it has been. Hence something of great importance now past is inferior to something of little importance now present, in that the latter is a reality, and related to the former as something to nothing.

A man finds himself, to his great astonishment, suddenly, existing, after thousands and thousands of years of non-existence; he lives for a little while; and then, again, comes an equally long period when he must exist no more. The heart rebels against this, and feels that it cannot be true. The crudest intellect cannot speculate on such a subject without having a presentiment that Time is something ideal in its nature. This ideality of Time and Space is the key to every true system of metaphysics; because it provides for quite another order of things than is to be met with in the domain of nature. This is why Kant is so great.

Of every event in our life we can say only for one moment that it is; forever after, that it was. Every evening we are poorer by a day. It might, perhaps, make us mad to see how rapidly our short span of time ebbs away, if it were not that in the furthest depths of our being we are secretly conscious of our share in the inexhaustible spring of eternity, so that we can always hope to find life in it again.

Considerations of the kind touched on above might, indeed, lead us to embrace the belief that the greatest wisdom is to make the enjoyment of the present the supreme object of life; because that is the only reality, all else being merely the play of thought. On the other hand, such a course might just as well be called the greatest folly: for that which in the next moment exists no more, and vanishes utterly, like a dream, can never be worth a serious effort.

The whole foundation on which our existence rests is the present—the ever-fleeting present. It lies, then, in the very nature of our existence to take the form of constant motion, and to offer no possibility of our ever attaining the rest for which we are always striving. We are like a man running downhill, who cannot keep on his legs unless he runs on, and will inevitably fall if he stops; or, again, like a pole balanced on the tip of one's finger: or like a planet, which would fall into its sun the moment it ceased to hurry forward on its way. Unrest is the mark of existence.

In a world where all is unstable, and nought can endure, but is swept onward at once in the hurrying whirlpool of change; where a man, if he is to keep erect at all, must always be advancing and moving, like an acrobat on a rope—in such a world, happiness is inconceivable. How can it dwell where, as Plato says, "continual Becoming and never Being" is the sole form of existence? In the first place, a man never is happy, but spends his whole life in striving after something which he thinks will make him so; he seldom attains his goal, and when he does, it is only to be disappointed; he is mostly shipwrecked in the end, and comes into harbor with masts and rigging gone. And then, it is all one whether he has been happy or miserable; for his life was never anything more than a present moment always vanishing; and now it is over.

At the same time it is a wonderful thing that, in the world of human beings as in that of animals in general, this manifold restless motion is produced and kept up by the agency of two simple impulses—hunger and the sexual instinct; aided a little, perhaps, by the influence of boredom, but by nothing else; and that, in the theater of life, these suffice to form the *primum mobile* of how complicated a machinery, setting in motion how strange and varied a scene!

On looking a little closer, we find that inorganic matter presents a constant conflict between chemical forces, which eventually works dissolution; and on the other hand, that organic life is impossible without continual change of matter, and cannot exist if it does not receive perpetual help from without. This is the realm of finality; and its opposite would be an infinite existence, exposed to no attack from without, and needing nothing to support it; ἀεὶ ὡϑαύτως ὄν, the realm of eternal peace; οὔτε γιγνόμενον οὔτε ἀπολλύμενον, some timeless changeless state, one and undiversified; the negative knowledge of which forms the dominant note of the Platonic philosophy. It is to some such state as this that the denial of the will to live opens up the way.

The scenes of our life are like pictures done in rough mosaic. Looked at close, they produce no effect. There is nothing beautiful to be found in them, unless you stand some distance off. So, to gain anything we have longed for is only to discover how vain and empty it is; and even though we are always living in expectation of better things, at the same time we often repent and long to have the past back again. We look upon the present as something to be put up with while it lasts, and serving only as the way toward our goal. Hence most people, if they glance back when they come to the end of life, will find that all along they have been living *ad interim:* they will be surprised to find that the very thing they disregarded and let slip by unenjoyed, was just the life in the expectation of which they passed all their time. Of how many a man may it not be said that hope made a fool of him until he danced into the arms of death!

Then again, how insatiable a creature is man. Every satisfaction he attains lays the seeds of some new desire, so that there is no end to the wishes of each individual will. And why is this? The real reason is simply that, taken in itself, Will is the lord of all worlds; everything belongs to it, and therefore no one single thing can ever give it satisfaction, but only the whole, which is endless. For all that, it must rouse our sympathy to think how very little the Will, this lord of the world, really gets when it takes the form of an individual; usually only just enough to keep the body together. This is why man is so very miserable.

Life presents itself chiefly as a task—the task, I mean, of subsisting at all, *ganger sa vie*. If this is accomplished, life is a burden, and then there comes the second task of doing something with that which has been won—of warding off boredom, which, like a bird of prey, hovers over us, ready to fall wherever it sees a life secure from need. The first task is to win something; the second, to banish the feeling that it has been won; otherwise it is a burden.

Human life must be some kind of mistake. The truth of this will be sufficiently obvious if we only remember that man is a compound of needs and necessities hard to satisfy; and that even when they are satisfied, all he obtains is a state of painlessness, where nothing remains to him but abandonment to boredom. This is direct proof that existence has no real value in itself; for what is boredom but the feeling of the emptiness of life? If life—the craving for which is the very essence of our being—were possessed of any positive intrinsic value, there would be no such thing as boredom at all: mere existence would satisfy us in itself, and we should want for nothing. But as it is, we take no delight in existence except when we are struggling for something; and then distance and difficulties to be overcome make our goal look as though it would satisfy us—an illusion which vanishes when we reach it; or else when we are occupied with some purely intellectual interest—where in reality we have stepped forth from life to look upon it from the outside, much after the manner of spectators at a play. And even sensual pleasure itself means nothing but a struggle and aspiration, ceasing the moment its aim is attained. Whenever we are not occupied in one of these ways, but cast upon existence itself, its vain and worthless nature is brought home to us; and this is what we mean by boredom. The hankering after what is strange and uncommon—an innate and ineradicable tendency of human nature—shows how glad we are at any interruption of that natural course of affairs which is so very tedious.

That this most perfect manifestation of the will to live, the human organism, with the cunning and complex working of its machinery, must fall to dust and yield up itself and all its strivings to extinction—this is the naive way in which Nature, who is always so true and sincere in what she says, proclaims the whole struggle of this will as in its very essence barren and unprofitable. Were it of any value in itself, anything unconditioned and absolute, it could not thus end in mere nothing.

If we turn from contemplating the world as a whole, and, in particular, the generations of men as they live their little hour of mock-existence and then are swept away in rapid succession; if we turn from this, and look at life in its small details, as presented, say, in a comedy, how ridiculous it all seems! It is like a drop of water seen through a microscope, a single drop teeming with *infusoria* or a speck of cheese full of mites invisible to the naked eye. How we laugh as they bustle about so eagerly, and struggle with one another in so tiny a space! And whether here, or in the little span of human life, this terrible activity produces a comic effect.

It is only in the microscope that our life looks so big. It is an indivisible point, drawn out and magnified by the powerful lenses of Time and Space.

Notes

1   Kant is the only writer who has confused this idea of reason, and in this connection I refer the reader to the Appendix, and also to my *Grundprobleme der Ethik*: *Grundl. dd. Moral.* §6, pp. 148–154, first and second editions.

2   *Mira in quibusdam rebus verborum proprietas est, et consuetudo sermonis antiqui quædam efficacissimis notis signat.* Seneca, epist. 81.

3   *Hamlet*, I., Sc. 4.

31

Friedrich Daniel Ernst Schleiermacher

The Christian Faith (1821)

First Section

A Description of our Religious Self-Consciousness in so far as the Relation between the World and God is expressed in it.

§ 36. *The original expression of this relation,* i.e. *that the world exists only in absolute dependence upon God, is divided in Church doctrine into the two propositions—that the world was created by God, and that God sustains the world.*

1. The proposition that the totality of finite being exists only in dependence upon the Infinite is the complete description of that basis of every religious feeling which is here to be set forth. We find ourselves always and only in a continuous existence; our life is always moving along a course; consequently just so far as we regard ourselves as finite being, apart from all other things, our self-consciousness can represent this being only in its continuity. And this in so complete a sense that (the feeling of absolute dependence being so universal an element in our self-consciousness) we may say that in whatever part of the whole or at whatever point of time we may be placed, in every full act of reflection we should recognize ourselves as thus involved in continuity, and should extend the same thought to the whole of finite being. The proposition that God sustains the world, considered in itself, is precisely similar. At least it only seems to have acquired another and lesser content because we have grown accustomed to think of preservation and creation together, and thus a beginning is excluded from the range of the idea of preservation. On the other hand, the proposition, 'God has created,' considered in itself, lays down absolute dependence, but only for the beginning, with the exclusion of development; and whether the creation is conceived as taking place once for all or in the

manner of one part after another, it lays down something which is not immediately given in our self-consciousness. Thus this proposition appears to belong to Dogmatics only so far as creation is complementary to the idea of preservation, with a view of reaching again the idea of unconditional all-inclusive dependence.

2. Thus there is no sufficient reason for retaining this division instead of the original expression which is so natural. And there can have been no reason for bringing this distinction into Dogmatics originally except that it was already to be found in traditional religious teaching, and that both the suitability of such expressions and the right measure of their use could be better guarded and established if the distinction were also adopted in the system of doctrine. Thus it did not originally arise on purely dogmatic grounds; and not only so, but it is not the outcome of any purely religious interest (which would find complete satisfaction in the simple expression); and thus, left to itself, the distinction between creation and preservation would fall into oblivion.

But for a human imagination only partially awakened, the beginning of all spatial and temporal existence is a subject which it cannot leave alone; consequently the treatment of the question is older than the abstract scientific phase of speculation, and belongs to the period of mythology. The question is linked up for us with the Mosaic account of creation, but that by itself does not give it a religious or Christian character any more than other things in the Pentateuch which have been brought over in the same way from primitive and prehistoric times. Yet for a long time this representation had to submit to being used for purposes of speculation and of science as well, and, indeed, for the purpose of supporting opposing theories or even as their source.

> § 41. *If the conception of Creation is to be further developed, the origin of the world must, indeed, be traced entirely to the divine activity, but not in such a way that this activity is thought of as resembling human activity; and the origin of the world must be represented as the event in time which conditions all change, but not so as to make the divine activity itself a temporal activity.*

1. The expression 'out of nothing' excludes the idea that before the origin of the world anything existed outside God, which as 'matter' could enter into the formation of the world. And undoubtedly the admission of 'matter' as existing independently of the divine activity would destroy the feeling of absolute dependence, and the actual world would be represented as a mixture of that which existed through God and that which existed independently of God. But since this phrase undeniably recalls Aristotle's category ἐξ οὖ and is formed on it, it reminds us on the one hand of human methods in construction which give form to an already existing matter, and on the other hand of the processes of nature in the composition of bodies out of many elements. The expression is harmless if everything that is a part of the processes of

nature is strictly separated from the first beginning of things, and creation is thus raised above mere formation.

Yet from Hilary and Anselm we can see how easily, behind the denial of matter, may lie the idea of the pre-existence of form before things, though of course in God and not outside God. This position, too, appears to be quite harmless in itself, but as the two terms of the antithesis, matter and form, are not in the same relation to God, He is drawn away from an attitude of neutrality to the antithesis and placed in some degree under it. Hence the existence of forms in God prior to the existence of things but already related to it may naturally be called a 'preparation.' But in this way the other rule is violated, and we must regard as valid Luther's contention that if there are two divine activities which, like preparation and creation, can be conceived of only in a definite time-sequence, then God is no longer outside all contact with time. Anselm in his own way has expressed this time-relationship most bluntly and frankly. Hilary would have done away with it, but he only succeeded in eliminating it with regard to things now happening separately in time and not in respect of the original creation. For it cannot be said of the original creation that it was created by the activity of foreknowledge prior to its actual existence.

Here it can only be remarked.in passing that the phrase 'out of nothing' is also used frequently to differentiate the creation of the world from the generation of the Son. If it were generally understood that the latter is eternal and the former temporal, or if we could come to a general agreement as to the difference between generation and creation, there would be no necessity to draw any further distinction. But even so the expression is not essential for this purpose, for even if we do not at all identify the 'Word' and the 'Son,' the phrase 'to be created through the "Word"'[1] sufficiently obviates any confusion of this kind; even if the difference between creation and generation is not emphasized.

Second Section

The Divine Attributes which are related to the Religious Self-consciousness so far as it expresses the General Relationship between God and the World.

§ 50. *All attributes which we ascribe to God are to be taken as denoting not something special in God, but only something special in the manner in which the feeling of absolute dependence is to be related to Him.*

1. If an adequate expression of the absolute feeling of dependence here indicated has been given in the expositions of the preceding section, we cannot believe that the theory of the divine attributes originally issued from a dogmatic interest. But history teaches us concerning speculation that, ever since it took the divine essence as an object of thought, it has always entered the same protest against all detailed description, and confined itself to representing God as the Original Being and the Absolute Good. And, indeed, it has frequently been recognized that even in these

concepts (of which the first only is relevant here) there remains a certain inadequacy, in so far as they still contain an element of opposition or other analogy with finite being. [. . .]

4. From this discussion it follows: (*a*) that the presupposition on which the idea is based that those attributes which express God's relation to the world have the appearance of mere additions and accidents, *i.e.* the presupposition of a separation between what God is, in and for Himself, and what He is in relation to the world, is also the source of the idea that the purely internal (*innerlichen*) attributes can only be conceived negatively; (*b*) that the rules laid down to secure the collection of all the divine attributes in one *locus* evoke conceptions which are quite foreign to the interests of religion, and result in a confusion of what it was intended to distinguish. We may hope, therefore, to solve our problem equally well without this apparatus and apart from any such collection if only we treat each individual part of our scheme as adequately as possible. Still, we too shall be able to make use of many of these formulas in our own way. For instance, since we have not to do as yet with the actual manifestation of religious self-consciousness in the form of pleasure and pain, but only with what lies uniformly at the root of these phenomena, *i.e.* with the inner creative disposition towards God-consciousness apart from the consideration whether it is hindered or encouraged, we may call those attributes which come up here 'original' in so far as the tendency itself is original, and we may call 'derived' those which will come to our notice in the Second Part. And in considering the manifestations of the religious self-consciousness, if we find that everything which would destroy His presence in us must specially be denied of God, and everything which favours His presence in us specially be affirmed of Him, we can say in our own way that thus divine attributes are formulated by the methods of removal of limits and negation; but those which arise from present observation, and there will be such, are reached by the method of causality. Still, this diverges fairly widely from the general usage of those formulæ, which rather betrays an analogy with speculation.

§ 51. *The Absolute Causality to which the feeling of absolute dependence points back can only be described in such a way that, on the one hand, it is distinguished from the content of the natural order and thus contrasted with it, and, on the other hand, equated with it in comprehension.*

1. We experience the feeling of absolute dependence as something which can fill a moment both in association with a feeling of partial and conditional dependence and also in association with a partial and conditioned feeling of freedom; for self-consciousness always represents finite being as consisting in this mingling of conditioned dependence and conditioned freedom or of partial spontaneity and partial passivity. But whenever dependence or passivity is posited in a part of finite existence, then spontaneity and causality is posited in another part to which the former is related, and this condition of mutual relation of differently distributed causality and passivity constitutes the natural order. It necessarily follows that the ground of our feeling of absolute dependence, *i.e.* the divine causality, extends as widely as the order of nature and the

finite causality contained in it; consequently the divine causality is posited as equal in compass to finite causality. And further, the feeling of absolute dependence stands in exactly the same relationship with the partial dependence-feeling as with the partial freedom-feeling, and so in that relationship the antithesis between these two last disappears; but finite causality is what it is only by means of its contrast with finite passivity, so it is to be inferred that the divine causality is contrasted with the finite. The divine causality as equivalent in compass to the sum-total of the natural order is expressed in the term, the divine *omnipotence*; this puts the whole of finite being under the divine causality. The divine causality as opposed to the finite and natural is expressed in the term, the divine *eternity*. That is, the interrelationship of partial causality and passivity makes the natural order a sphere of reciprocal action, and thus of change as such, in that all change and all alteration can be traced back to this antithesis. It is therefore just in the relationship in which the natural causality is set over against the divine, that the essence of the former is to be temporal; and consequently, so far as eternal is the opposite of temporal, the eternity of God will also be the expression of that antithesis.

In regard to what both terms according to general usage appear to imply as to something more than, and transcending, divine causality or the range of finite being—of this we shall speak in our further elucidation of both concepts. Here it is to be noted generally, that since these two ideas—omnipotence and eternity—are here related only to the divine causality, it may at once be proved in their case also that the individual attributes in their differences correspond to nothing real in God. It is always an inexactitude, which as such must be pointed out when we present these as two different attributes. For the divine causality is only equal in compass to the finite in so far as it is opposite to it in kind, since if it were like it in kind, as it is often represented as being in anthropomorphic ideas of God, it too would belong to the sphere of interaction and thus be a part of the totality of the natural order. In the same way, if the divine causality were not equal in compass to the finite, it could not be set over against it without at the same time disrupting the unity of the natural order; because otherwise for some finite causality there would be a divine causality, but not for some other. Instead, therefore, of saying God is eternal and almighty, we should rather say He is almighty-eternal and eternal-almighty, or God is eternal omnipotence or almighty eternity. Still, in view of unavoidable comparisons with the more exact definitions of both attributes hitherto current, we must treat of each by itself.

Note

1 'All things are so made through God's word that they may more rightly be said to be born than made or renewed, for no instrument or means comes in.'—Luth., Th. v. p. 1102.

32

Sampson Reed

Observations on the Growth of the Mind (1826)

NOTHING IS A MORE COMMON SUBJECT OF REMARK THAN the changed condition of the world. There is a more extensive intercourse of thought, and a more powerful action of mind upon mind, than formerly. The good and the wise of all nations are brought nearer together, and begin to exert a power, which, though yet feeble as infancy, is felt throughout the globe. Public opinion, that helm which directs the progress of events by which the world is guided to its ultimate destination, has received a new direction. The mind has attained an upward and onward look, and is shaking off the errors and prejudices of the past. The structure of the feudal ages, the ornament of the desert, has been exposed to the light of heaven; and continues to be gazed at for its ugliness, as it ceases to be admired for its antiquity. The world is deriving vigor, not from that which has gone by, but from that which is coming; not from the unhealthy moisture of the evening, but from the nameless influences of the morning. The loud call on the past to instruct us, as it falls on the Rock of Ages, comes back in echo from the future. Both mankind, and the laws and principles by which they are governed, seem about to be redeemed from slavery. The moral and intellectual character of man has undergone, and is undergoing, a change; and as this is effected, it must change the aspect of all things, as when the position-point is altered from which a landscape is viewed. We appear to be approaching an age which will be the silent pause of merely physical force before the powers of the mind the timid, subdued, awed condition of the brute, gazing on the erect and godlike form of man.

These remarks with respect to the present era are believed, to be just, when it is viewed on the bright side. They are not made by one who is insensible to its evils. Least of all, are they intended to countenance that feeling of self-admiration, which carries with it the seeds of premature disease and deformity; for to be proud of the truth is to cease to possess it. Since the fall of man, nothing has been more difficult for him than to know his real condition, since every departure from divine order is attended with a loss of the knowledge of what it is. When our first parents left the garden of Eden, they took with them no means by which they might measure the depths of degradation to which they fell; no chart by which they might determine their moral longitude.

Most of our knowledge implies relation and comparison. It is not difficult for one age, or one individual, to be compared with another; but this determines only their relative condition. The actual condition of man can be seen only from the relation in which he stands to his immutable Creator; and this relation is discovered from the light of revelation, so far as, by conforming to the precepts of revelation, it is permitted to exist according to the laws of divine order. It is not sufficient that the letter of the Bible is in the world. This may be, and still mankind continue in ignorance of themselves. It must be obeyed from the heart to the hand. The book must be eaten, and constitute the living flesh. When only the relative condition of the world is regarded, we are apt to exult over other ages and other men, as if we ourselves were a different order of beings, till at length we are enveloped in the very mists from which we are proud of being cleared. But when the relative state of the world is justly viewed from the real state of the individual, the scene is lighted from the point of the beholder with the chaste light of humility which never deceives; it is not forgotten that the way lies forward; the cries of exultation cease to be heard in the march of progression, and the mind, in whatever it learns of the past and the present, finds food for improvement, and not for vainglory.

As all the changes which are taking place in the world originate in the mind, it might be naturally expected that nothing would change more than the mind itself, and whatever is connected with a description of it. While men have been speculating concerning their own powers, the sure but secret influence of revelation has been gradually changing the moral and intellectual character of the world, and the ground on which they were standing has passed from under them, almost while their words were in their mouths. The powers of the mind are most intimately connected with the subjects by which they are occupied. We cannot think of the will without feeling, of the understanding without thought, or of the imagination without something like poetry. The mind is visible when it is active; and as the subjects on which it is engaged are changed, the powers themselves present a different aspect. New classifications arise, and new names are given. What was considered simple is thought to consist of distinct parts, till at length the philosopher hardly knows whether the African be of the same or a different species; and though the soul is thought to continue after death, angels are universally considered a distinct class of intellectual beings. Thus it is that there is nothing fixed in the philosophy of the mind. It is said to be a science which is not demonstrative; and though now thought to be brought to a state of great perfection, another century, under the providence of God, and nothing will be found in the structure which has cost so much labor, but the voice, "He is not here, but is risen."

Is, then, everything that relates to the immortal part of man fleeting and evanescent, while the laws of physical nature remain unaltered? Do things become changeable as we approach the immutable and the eternal? Far otherwise. The laws of the mind are in themselves as fixed and perfect as the laws of matter; but they are laws from which we have wandered. There is a philosophy of the mind, founded not on the aspect it presents in any part or in any period of the world, but on its immutable relations to its first cause; a philosophy equally applicable to man, before or after he has passed the valley of the shadow of death; not dependent on time or place, but immortal as its subject. The light of this philosophy has begun to beam faintly on the world, and mankind will yet see their own moral and intellectual nature by the light of revelation, as it shines through the moral and intellectual character it shall have itself created. It may be remarked, also, that the changes in the sciences and the arts are entirely the effect of revelation. To revelation it is to be ascribed, that the genius which has taught the laws of the heavenly bodies, and analyzed the material world, did not spend itself in drawing the bow or in throwing the lance, in the chase or in war; and that the vast powers of Handel did not burst forth in the wild notes of the war-song. It is the tendency of revelation to give a right direction to every power of every mind; and when this is effected, inventions and discoveries will follow of course, all things assume a different aspect, and the world itself again becomes a paradise.

It is the object of the following pages not to be influenced by views of a temporal or local nature, but to look at the mind as far as possible in its essential revealed character, and beginning with its powers of acquiring and retaining truth, to trace summarily that development which is required, in order to render it truly useful and happy.

It is said, *the powers of acquiring and retaining truth,* because truth is not retained without some continued exertion of the same powers by which it is acquired. There is the most intimate connection of the memory with the affections. This connection is obvious from many familiar expressions; such as remember me to any one, by which is signified a desire to be borne in his or her affections—do not forget me, by which is meant do not cease to love me—get by heart, which means to commit to memory. It is also obvious from observation of our own minds; from the constant recurrence of those subjects which we most love, and the extreme difficulty of detaching our own minds or the minds of others from a favorite pursuit. It is obvious from the power of attention on which the memory principally depends, which, if the subject have a place in our affections, requires no effort; if it have not, the effort consists principally in giving it a real or an artificial hold of our feelings; as it is possible, if we do not love a subject, to attend to it, because it may add to our fame or our wealth. It is obvious from the never-fading freshness retained by the scenes of childhood, when the feelings are strong and vivid, through the later periods of life. As the old man looks back on the road of his pilgrimage, many years of active life lie unseen in the valley, as his eye rests on the rising ground of his younger days; presenting a beautiful illustration of the manner in which the human mind, when revelation shall have accomplished its work, shall no longer regard the scene of sin and misery behind, but having completed the circle, shall rest, as next to the present moment, on the golden age, the infancy of the world.

The connection of the memory with the affections is also obvious from the association of ideas; since the train of thoughts suggested by any scene or event in any individual, depends on his own peculiar and prevailing feelings; as whatever enters into the animal system, wherever it may arise, seems first to be recognized as a part of the man, when it has found its way to the heart, and received from that its impulse. It is but a few years, (how strange to tell!) since man discovered that the blood circulated through the human body. We have, perhaps, hardly learned the true nature of that intellectual circulation, which gives life and health to the human mind. The affections are to the soul, what the heart is to the body. They send forth their treasures with a vigor not less powerful, though not material, throughout the intellectual man, strengthening and nourishing; and again receive those treasures to themselves, enlarged by the effect of their own operation.

Memory is the *effect* of learning, through whatever avenue it may have entered the mind. It is said, the *effect*, because the man who has read a volume, and can perhaps tell you nothing of its contents, but simply express his own views on the same subject with more clearness and precision, may as truly be said to have remembered, as he that can repeat the very words. In the one case, the powers of the mind have received a new tone; in the other, they are encumbered with a useless burden—in the one, they are made stronger; in the other, they are more oppressed with weight—in the one, the food is absorbed and becomes a part of the man; in the other, it lies on the stomach in a state of crude indigestion.

There is no power more various in different individuals, than the memory. This may be ascribed to two reasons. First, this partakes of every power of the mind, since every mental exertion is a subject of memory, and may therefore be said to indicate all the difference that actually exists. Secondly, this power varies in its character as it has more or less to do with time. Simple divine truth has nothing to do with time. It is the same yesterday, to-day, and forever. The memory of this is simply the development of the mind. But we are so surrounded by facts of a local and temporal nature; the place where, and the time when, make so great a part of what is presented to our consideration, that the attribute is mistaken for the subject; and this power sometimes appears to have exclusive reference to time, though, strictly speaking, it has no relation to it. There is a power of growth in the spiritual man, and if in his progress we be able to mark, as in the grain of the oak, the number of the years, this is only a circumstance, and all that is gained would be as real if no such lines existed. The mind ought not to be limited by the short period of its own duration in the body, with a beginning and end comprising a few years; it should be poised on its own immortality, and what is learned, should be learned with a view to that real adaptation of knowledge to the mind which results from the harmony of creation; and whenever or wherever we exist, it will be useful to us.

The memory has, in reality, nothing to do with time, any more than the eye has with space. As the latter learns by experience to measure the distance of objects, so the consciousness of the present existence of states of mind, is referred to particular periods of the past. But when the soul has entered on its *eternal* state, there is reason to believe that the past and the future will be swallowed up in the present; that memory and anticipation will be lost in consciousness; that everything of the past will be comprehended in the present, without any reference to time, and everything of the future will exist in the divine effort of progression.

33

William Ellery Channing

Likeness to God (1828): Discourse at the Ordination of the Rev. F. A. Farley, Providence, RI

Ephesians v. 1: "Be ye therefore followers of God, as dear children."

To promote true religion is the purpose of the Christian ministry. For this it was ordained. On the present occasion, therefore, when a new teacher is to be given to the church, a discourse on the character of true religion will not be inappropriate. I do not mean, that I shall attempt, in the limits to which I am now confined, to set before you all its properties, signs, and operations; for in so doing I should burden your memories with divisions and vague generalities, as uninteresting as they would be unprofitable. My purpose is, to select one view of the subject, which seems to me of primary dignity and importance; and I select this, because it is greatly neglected, and because I attribute to this neglect much of the inefficacy, and many of the corruptions, of religion.

The text calls us to follow or imitate God, to seek accordance with or likeness to him, and to do this, not fearfully and faintly, but with the spirit and hope of beloved children. The doctrine which I propose to illustrate, is derived immediately from these words, and is incorporated with the whole New Testament. I affirm, and would maintain, that true religion consists in proposing, as our great end, a growing likeness to the Supreme Being. Its noblest influence consists in making us more and more partakers of the Divinity. For this it is to be preached. Religious instruction should aim chiefly to turn men's aspirations and efforts to that perfection of the soul, which constitutes it a bright image of God. Such is the topic now to be discussed; and I implore Him, whose glory I seek, to aid me in unfolding and enforcing it with simplicity and clearness, with a calm and pure zeal, and with unfeigned charity.

I begin with observing, what all indeed will understand, that the likeness to God, of which I propose to speak, belongs to man's higher or spiritual nature. It has its foundation in the original and essential capacities of the mind. In proportion as these are unfolded by right and vigorous exertion, it is extended and brightened. In proportion as these lie dormant, it is obscured. In proportion as they are perverted and overpowered by the appetites and passions, it is blotted out. In truth, moral evil, if unresisted and habitual, may so blight and lay waste these capacities, that the image of God in man may seem to be wholly destroyed.

The importance of this assimilation to our Creator, is a topic which needs no labored discussion. All men, of whatever name, or sect, or opinion, will meet me on this ground. All, I presume, will allow, that no good in the compass of the universe, or within the gift of omnipotence, can be compared to a resemblance of God, or to a participation of his attributes. I fear no contradiction here. Likeness to God is the supreme gift. He can communicate nothing so precious, glorious, blessed, as himself. To hold intellectual and moral affinity with the Supreme Being, to partake his spirit, to be his children by derivations of kindred excellence, to bear a growing conformity to the perfection which we adore, this is a felicity which obscures and annihilates all other good.

It is only in proportion to this likeness, that we can enjoy either God or the universe. That God can be known and enjoyed only through sympathy or kindred attributes, is a doctrine which even Gentile philosophy discerned. That the pure in heart can alone see and commune with the pure Divinity, was the sublime instruction of ancient sages as well as of inspired prophets. It is indeed the lesson of daily experience. To understand a great and good being, we must have the seeds of the same excellence. How quickly, by what an instinct, do accordant minds recognise one another!. No attraction is so powerful as that which subsists between the truly wise and good; whilst the brightest excellence is lost on those who have nothing congenial in their own breasts. God becomes a real being to us, in proportion as his own nature is unfolded within us. To a man who is growing in the likeness of God, faith begins even here to change into vision. He carries within himself a proof of a Deity, which can only be understood by experience. He more than believes, he feels the Divine presence; and gradually rises to an intercourse with his Maker, to which it is not irreverent to apply the name of friendship and intimacy. The Apostle John intended to express this truth, when he tells us, that he, in whom a principle of divine charity or benevolence has become a habit and life, "dwells in God and God in him."

It is plain, too, that likeness to God is the true and only preparation for the enjoyment of the universe. In proportion as we approach and resemble the mind of God, we are brought into harmony with the creation; for, in that proportion, we possess the principles from which the universe sprung; we carry within ourselves the perfections, of which its beauty, magnificence, order, benevolent adaptations, and boundless purposes, are the results and manifestations. God unfolds himself in his works to a kindred mind. It is possible, that the brevity of these hints may expose to the charge of mysticism, what seems to me the calmest and clearest truth. I think, however, that every reflecting man will feel, that likeness to God must be a principle of sympathy or accordance with his creation; for the creation is a birth and shining forth of the Divine Mind, a work through which his spirit breathes. In proportion as we receive this spirit, we possess within ourselves the explanation of what we see. We discern more and more of God in every thing, from the frail flower to the everlasting stars. Even in evil, that dark cloud which hangs over the creation, we discern rays of light and hope, and gradually come to see, in suffering and temptation, proofs and instruments of the sublimest purposes of Wisdom and Love. [. . .]

We call God a Mind. He has revealed himself as a Spirit. But what do we know of mind, but through the unfolding of this principle in our own breasts? That unbounded spiritual energy which we call God, is conceived by us only through consciousness, through the knowledge of ourselves.-We ascribe thought or intelligence to the Deity, as one of his most glorious attributes. And what means this language? These terms we have framed to express operations or faculties of our own souls. The Infinite Light would be for ever hidden from us, did not kindred rays dawn and brighten within us. God is another name for human intelligence raised above all error and imperfection, and extended to all possible truth. [. . .]

I shall now be met by another objection, which to many may seem strong. It will be said, that these various attributes of which I have spoken, exist in God in Infinite Perfection, and that this destroys all affinity between the human and the Divine mind. To this I have two replies. In the first place, an attribute, by becoming perfect, does not part with its essence. Love, wisdom, power, and purity do not change their nature by enlargement. If they did, we should lose the Supreme Being through his very infinity. Our ideas of him would fade away into mere sounds. For example, if wisdom in God, because unbounded, have no affinity with that attribute in man, why apply to him that term? It must signify nothing. Let me ask what we mean, when we say that we discern the marks of intelligence in the universe? We mean, that we meet there the proofs of a mind like our own. We certainly discern proofs of no other; so that to deny this doctrine would be to deny the evidences of a God, and utterly to subvert the foundations of religious belief. What man can examine the structure of a plant or an animal, and see the adaptation of its parts to each other and to common ends, and not feel, that it is the work of an intelligence akin to his own, and that he traces these marks of design by the same spiritual energy in which they had their origin?

But I would offer another answer to this objection, that God's infinity places him beyond the resemblance and approach of man. I affirm, and trust that I do not speak too strongly, that there are traces of infinity in the human mind; and that, in this very respect, it bears a likeness to God. The very conception of infinity, is the mark of a nature to which no limit can be prescribed. This thought, indeed, comes to us, not so much from abroad, as from our own souls. We ascribe this attribute to God, because we possess capacities and wants, which only an unbounded being can fill, and because we are conscious of a tendency in spiritual faculties to unlimited expansion. We believe in the Divine infinity, through something congenial with it in our own breasts. I hope I speak clearly, and if not, I would ask those to whom I am obscure, to pause before they condemn. To me it seems, that the soul, in all its higher actions, in original thought, in the creations of genius, in the soarings of imagination, in its love of beauty and grandeur, in its aspirations after a pure and unknown joy, and especially in disinterestedness, in the spirit of self-sacrifice, and in enlightened devotion, has a character of infinity. There is often a depth in human love, which may be strictly called unfathomable. There is sometimes a lofty strength in moral principle, which all the power of the outward universe cannot overcome. There seems a might within, which can more than balance all might without. There is, too, a piety, which swells into a transport too vast for utterance, and into an immeasurable joy. I am speaking, indeed, of what is uncommon, but still of realities. We see, however, the tendency of the soul to the infinite, in more familiar and ordinary forms. Take, for example, the delight which we find in the vast scenes of nature, in prospects which spread around us without limits, in the immensity of the heavens and the ocean, and especially in the rush and roar of mighty winds, waves, and torrents, when, amidst our deep awe, a power within seems to respond to the omnipotence around us. The same principle is seen in the delight ministered to us by works of fiction or of imaginative art, in which our own nature is set before us in more than human beauty and power. In truth, the soul is always bursting its limits. It thirsts continually for wider knowledge. It rushes forward to untried happiness. It has deep wants, which nothing limited can appease. Its true element and end is an unbounded good. Thus, God's infinity has its image in the soul; and through the soul, much more than through the universe, we arrive at this conception of the Deity. [. . .]

It is said, men cannot understand the views which seem to me so precious. This objection I am anxious to repel, for the common intellect has been grievously kept down and wronged through the belief of its incapacity. The pulpit would do more good, were not the mass of men looked upon and treated as children. Happily for the race, the time is passing away, in which intellect was thought the monopoly of a few, and the majority were given over to hopeless ignorance. Science is leaving her solitudes to enlighten the multitude. How much more may religious teachers take courage to speak to men on subjects, which are nearer to them than the properties and laws of matter, I mean their own souls. The multitude, you say, want capacity to receive great truths relating to their spiritual nature. But what, let me ask you, is the Christian religion? A spiritual system, intended to turn men's minds upon themselves, to frame them to watchfulness over thought, imagination, and passion, to establish them in an intimacy with their own souls. What are all the Christian virtues, which men are exhorted to love and seek? I answer, pure and high motions or determinations of the mind. That refinement of thought, which, I am told, transcends the common intellect, belongs to the very essence of Christianity. In confirmation of these views, the human mind seems to me to be turning itself more and more inward, and to be growing more alive to its own worth, and its capacities of progress. The spirit of education shows this, and so does the spirit of freedom. There is a spreading conviction that man was made for a higher purpose than to be a beast of burden, or a creature of sense. The divinity is stirring within the human breast, and demanding a culture and a liberty worthy of the child of God. Let religious teaching correspond to this advancement of the mind. Let it rise above the technical, obscure, and frigid theology which has come down to us from times of ignorance, superstition, and slavery.

Let it penetrate the human soul, and reveal it to itself. No preaching, I believe, is so intelligible, as that which is true to human nature, and helps men to read their own spirits.

34

Thomas Carlyle

Sartor Resartus (1833)

Pure Reason

IT MUST NOW BE APPARENT ENOUGH THAT OUR PROFESSOR, as above hinted, is a speculative Radical, and of the very darkest tinge; acknowledging, for most part, in the solemnities and paraphernalia of civilised Life, which we make so much of, nothing but so many Cloth-rags, turkey-poles, and "Bladders with dried Peas." To linger among such speculations, longer than mere Science requires, a discerning public can have no wish. For our purposes the simple fact that such a *Naked World* is possible, nay actually exists (under the Clothed one), will be sufficient. Much, therefore, we omit about "Kings wrestling naked on the green with Carmen," and the Kings being thrown: "dissect them with scalpels," says Teufelsdröckh; "the same viscera, tissues, livers, lights, and other Life-tackle are there: examine their spiritual mechanism; the same great Need, great Greed, and little Faculty; nay ten to one but the Carman, who understands draught-cattle, the rimming of wheels, something of the laws of unstable and stable equilibrium, with other branches of waggon-science, and has actually put forth his hand and operated on Nature, is the more cunningly gifted of the two. Whence, then, their so unspeakable difference? From Clothes." Much also we shall omit about confusion of Ranks, and Joan and My Lady, and how it would be every where "Hail fellow well met," and Chaos were come again: all which to any one that has once fairly pictured out the grand mother-idea, *Society in a state of Nakedness,* will spontaneously suggest itself. Should some sceptical individual still entertain doubts whether in a World without Clothes, the smallest Politeness, Polity, or even Police, could exist, let him turn to the original Volume, and view there the boundless Serbonian Bogs of Sansculottism, stretching sour and pestilential: over which we have lightly flown; where not only whole armies but whole nations might sink! If indeed the following argument, in its brief rivetting emphasis, be not of itself incontrovertible and final:

"Are we Opossums; have we natural Pouches, like the Kangaroo? Or how, without Clothes, could we possess the master-organ, soul's-seat, and true pineal gland of the Body Social: I mean, a PURSE?"

Nevertheless it is impossible to hate Professor Teufelsdröckh; at worst, one knows not whether to hate or to love him. For though in looking at the fair tapestry of human Life, with its royal and even sacred figures, he dwells not on the obverse alone, but here chiefly on the reverse; and indeed turns out the rough seams, tatters, and manifold thrums of that unsightly wrong-side, with an almost diabolic patience and indifference, which must have sunk him in the estimation of most readers,—there is that within which unspeakably distinguishes him from all other past and present Sansculottists. The grand unparalleled peculiarity of Teufelsdröckh is, that with all this Descendentalism, he combines a Transcendentalism no less superlative; whereby if on the one hand he degrade man below most animals, except those jacketted Gouda Cows, he, on the other, exalts him beyond the visible Heavens, almost to an equality with the gods.

"To the eye of vulgar Logic," says he, "what is man? An omnivorous Biped that wears Breeches. To the eye of Pure Reason what is he? A Soul, a Spirit, and divine Apparition. Round his mysterious ME, there lies, under all those wool-rags, a Garment of Flesh (or of Senses), contextured in the Loom of Heaven; whereby he is revealed to his like, and dwells with them in UNION and DIVISION; and sees and fashions for himself a universe, with azure Starry Spaces, and long Thousands of Years. Deep-hidden is he under that strange Garment; amid Sounds and Colours and Forms, as it were, swathed in, and inextricably overshrouded: yet is it sky-woven, and worthy of a God. Stands he not thereby in the centre of Immensities, in the conflux of Eternities? He feels; power has been given him to Know, to Believe; nay does not the spirit of Love, free in its celestial primeval brightness, even here, though but for moments, look through? Well said Saint Chrysostom, with his lips of gold, 'the true SHEKINAH is Man:' where else is the GOD'S-PRESENCE manifested not to our eyes only, but to our hearts, as in our fellow man?"

In such passages, unhappily too rare, the high Platonic Mysticism of our Author, which is perhaps the fundamental element of his nature, bursts forth, as it were, in full flood: and, through all the vapour and tarnish of what is often so perverse, so mean in his exterior and environment, we seem to look into a whole inward Sea of Light and Love;—though, alas, the grim coppery clouds soon roll together again, and hide it from view.

Such tendency to Mysticism is every where traceable in this man; and indeed, to attentive readers, must have been long ago apparent. Nothing that he sees but has more than a common meaning, but has two meanings: thus, if in the highest Imperial Sceptre and Charlemagne-Mantle, as well as in the poorest Ox-goad and Gipsy-Blanket, he finds Prose, Decay, Contemptibility; there is in each sort Poetry also, and a reverend Worth. For Matter, were it never so despicable, is

Spirit, the manifestation of Spirit: were it never so honourable, can it be more? The thing Visible, nay the thing Imagined, the thing in any way conceived as Visible, what is it but a Garment, a Clothing of the higher, celestial Invisible, "unimaginable, formless, dark with excess of bright?" Under which point of view the following passage, so strange in purport, so strange in phrase, seems characteristic enough:

"The beginning of all Wisdom is to look fixedly on Clothes, or even with armed eyesight, till they become *transparent*. 'The Philosopher,' says the wisest of this age, 'must station himself in the middle:' how true! The Philosopher is he to whom the Highest has descended, and the Lowest has mounted up; who is the equal and kindly brother of all.

"Shall we tremble before clothwebs and cobwebs, whether woven in Arkwright looms, or by the silent Arachnes that weave unrestingly in our Imagination? Or, on the other hand, what is there that we cannot love; since all was created by God?

"Happy he who can look through the Clothes of a Man (the woollen, and fleshly, and official Bank-paper and State-paper Clothes), into the Man himself; and discern, it may be, in this or the other Dread Potentate, a more or less incompetent Digestive-apparatus; yet also an inscrutable venerable Mystery, in the meanest Tinker that sees with eyes!"

For the rest, as is natural to a man of this kind, he deals much in the feeling of Wonder; insists on the necessity and high worth of universal Wonder, which he holds to be the only reasonable temper for the denizen of so singular a Planet as ours. "Wonder," says he, "is the basis of Worship: the reign of Wonder is perennial, indestructible in Man; only at certain stages (as the present), it is, for some short season, a reign *in partibus infidelium*." That progress of Science, which is to destroy Wonder, and in its stead substitute Mensuration and Numeration, finds small favour with Teufelsdröckh, much as he otherwise venerates these two latter processes.

"Shall your Science," exclaims he, "proceed in the small chink-lighted, or even oil-lighted, underground workshop of Logic alone; and man's mind become an Arithmetical Mill, whereof Memory is the Hopper, and mere Tables of Sines and Tangents, Codification, and Treatises of what you call Political Economy, are the Meal? And what is that Science, which the scientific Head alone, were it screwed off, and (like the Doctor's in the Arabian Tale) set in a basin, to keep it alive, could prosecute without shadow of a heart,—but one other of the mechanical and menial handicrafts, for which the Scientific Head (having a Soul in it) is too noble an organ? I mean that Thought without Reverence is barren, perhaps poisonous; at best, dies like Cookery with the day that called it forth; does not live, like sowing, in successive tilths and wider-spreading harvests, bringing food and plenteous increase to all Time."

In such wise does Teufelsdrockh deal hits, harder or softer, according to ability; yet ever, as we would fain persuade ourselves, with charitable intent. Above all, that class of "Logic-choppers, and treble-pipe Scoffers, and professed Enemies to Wonder; who, in these days, so numerously patrol as night-constables about the Mechanics' Institute of Science, and cackle, like true Old-Roman geese and goslings round their Capitol, on any alarm, or on none; nay who often, as illuminated Sceptics, walk abroad into peaceable society, in full daylight, with rattle and lantern, and insist on guiding you and guarding you therewith, though the Sun is shining, and the street populous with mere justice-loving men:" that whole class is inexpressibly wearisome to him. Hear with what uncommon animation he perorates:

"The man who cannot wonder, who does not habitually wonder (and worship), were he President of innumerable Royal Societies, and carried the whole *Mécanique Céleste* and *Hegel's Philosophy,* and the epitome of all Laboratories and Observatories with their results, in his single head,—is but a Pair of Spectacles behind which there is no Eye. Let those who have Eyes look through him, then he may be useful.

"Thou wilt have no Mystery and Mysticism; wilt walk through thy world by the sunshine of what thou callest Truth, or even by the Hand-lamp of what I call Attorney Logic; and 'explain' all, 'account' for all, or believe nothing of it? Nay, thou wilt attempt laughter; whoso recognises the unfathomable, all-pervading domain of Mystery, which is everywhere under our feet and among our hands; to whom the Universe is an Oracle and Temple, as well as a Kitchen and Cattle-stall,—he shall be a (delirious) Mystic; to him thou, with sniffing charity, wilt protrusively proffer thy Handlamp, and shriek, as one injured, when he kicks his foot through it?—*Armer Teufel!* Doth not thy Cow calve, doth not thy Bull gender? Thou thyself, wert thou not Born, wilt thou not Die? 'Explain' me all this, or do one of two things: Retire into private places with thy foolish cackle; or, what were better, give it up, and weep, not that the reign of wonder is done, and God's world all disembellished and prosaic, but that thou hitherto art a Dilettante and sandblind Pedant."

Symbols

PROBABLY it will elucidate the drift of these foregoing obscure utterances, if we here insert somewhat of our Professor's speculations on *Symbols.* To state his whole doctrine, indeed, were beyond our compass: nowhere is he more mysterious, impalpable, than in this of "Fantasy being the organ of the Godlike;" and how "Man thereby, though based, to all seeming, on the small Visible, does nevertheless extend down into the infinite deeps of the Invisible, of which Invisible, indeed, his Life is properly the bodying forth." Let us, omitting these high transcendental aspects of the matter, study to glean (whether from the Paperbags or the Printed Volume) what little seems logical and practical, and cunningly arrange it into such degree of coherence as it will assume. By way of proem, take the following not injudicious remarks:

"The benignant efficacies of Concealment," cries our Professor, "who shall speak or sing? SILENCE and SECRECY! Altars might still be raised to them (were this an altar-building time) for universal worship. Silence is the element in which great things fashion themselves together; that at length they may emerge, full-formed and majestic, into the daylight of Life, which they are thenceforth to rule. Not William the Silent only, but all the considerable men I have known, and the most undiplomatic and unstrategic of these, forbore to babble of what they were creating and projecting. Nay, in thy own mean perplexities, do thou thyself but *hold thy tongue for one day*: on the morrow, how much clearer are thy purposes, and duties; what wreck and rubbish have those mute workmen within thee swept away, when intrusive noises were shut out! Speech is too often not, as the Frenchman defined it, the art of concealing Thought; but of quite stifling and suspending Thought, so that there is none to conceal. Speech too is great, but not the greatest. As the Swiss Inscription says: *Sprechen ist silbern, Schweigen ist golden* (Speech is silvern, Silence is golden); or as I might rather express it: Speech is of Time, Silence is of Eternity.

"Bees will not work except in darkness; Thought will not work except in Silence: neither will Virtue work except in Secrecy. Let not thy right hand know what thy left hand doeth! Neither shalt thou prate even to thy own heart of 'those secrets known to all.' Is not Shame the soil of all Virtue, of all good manners, and good morals? Like other plants, Virtue will not grow unless its root be hidden, buried from the eye of the sun. Let the Sun shine on it, nay, do but look at it privily thyself, the root withers, and no flower will glad thee. O my Friends, when we view the fair clustering flowers that over-wreathe, for example, the Marriage-bower, and encircle man's life with the fragrance and hues of Heaven, what hand will not smite the foul plunderer that grubs them up by the roots, and, with grinning, grunting satisfaction, shews us the dung they flourish in! Men speak much of the Printing Press with its Newspapers: *du Himmel!* what are these to Clothes and the Tailor's Goose?"

"Of kin to the so incalculable influences of Concealment, and connected with still greater things, is the wondrous agency of *Symbols*. In a Symbol there is concealment and yet revelation: here, therefore, by Silence and by Speech acting together, comes a doubled significance. And if both the Speech be itself high, and the Silence fit and noble, how expressive will their union be! Thus in many a painted Device, or simple Seal-emblem, the commonest Truth stands out to us proclaimed with quite new emphasis.

"For it is here that Fantasy with her mystic wonderland plays into the small prose domain of Sense, and becomes incorporated therewith. In the Symbol proper, what we can call a Symbol, there is ever, more or less distinctly and directly, some embodyment and revelation of the Infinite; the Infinite is made to blend itself with the Finite, to stand visible, and as it were attainable, there. By Symbols, accordingly, is man guided and commanded, made happy, made wretched. He every where finds himself encompassed with Symbols, recognised as such or not recognised: the Universe is but one vast Symbol of God; nay, if thou wilt have it, what is man himself but a Symbol of God, is not all that he does symbolical; a revelation to Sense of the mystic god-given Force that is in him; a 'Gospel of Freedom,' which he, the 'Messias of Nature,' preaches, as he can, by act and word? Not a Hut he builds but is the visible embodyment of a Thought; but bears visible record of invisible things; but is, in the transcendental sense, symbolical as well as real."

"Man," says the Professor elsewhere, in quite antipodal contrast with these high-soaring delineations, which we have here cut short on the verge of the inane, "man is by birth somewhat of an owl. Perhaps too of all the owleries that ever possessed him, the most owlish, if we consider it, is that of your actually existing Motive-Millwrights. Fantastic tricks enough has man played in his time; has fancied himself to be most things, down even to an animated heap of Glass: but to fancy himself a dead Iron-Balance for weighing Pains and Pleasures on, was reserved for this his latter era. There stands he, his Universe one huge Manger, filled with hay and thistles to be weighed against each other; and looks long-eared enough. Alas, poor devil! spectres are appointed to haunt him: one age, he is hagridden, bewitched; the next, priestridden, befooled; in all ages, bedevilled. And now the Genius of Mechanism smothers him worse than any Nightmare did; till the Soul is nigh choked out of him, and only a kind of Digestive, Mechanic life remains. In Earth and in Heaven he can see nothing but Mechanism; has fear for nothing else, hope in nothing else: the world would indeed grind him to pieces; but cannot he fathom the Doctrine of Motives, and cunningly compute them to grind the other way?

"Were he not, as has been said, purblinded by enchantment, you had but to bid him open his eyes and look. In which country, in which time, was it hitherto that man's history, or the history of any man, went on by calculated or calculable 'Motives?' What make ye of your Christianities, and Chivalries, and Reformations, and Marseillese Hymns, and Reigns of Terror? Nay, has not perhaps the Motive-grinder himself been *in Love*? Did he never stand so much as a contested Election? Leave him to Time, and the medicating virtue of Nature."

"Yes, Friends," elsewhere observes the Professor, "not our Logical, Mensurative faculty, but our Imaginative one is King over us; I might say, Priest and Prophet to lead us heavenward; or Magician and Wizard to lead us hellward. Nay, even for the basest Sensualist, what is Sense but the implement of Fantasy; the vessel it drinks out of? Ever in the dullest existence, there is a sheen either of Inspiration or of Madness (thou partly hast it in thy choice, which of the two) that gleams in from the circumambient Eternity, and colours with its own hues our little islet of Time. The Understanding is indeed thy window, too clear thou canst not make it; but Fantasy is thy eye, with its colour-giving retina, healthy or diseased. Have not I myself known five hundred living soldiers sabred into crows' meat, for a piece of glazed cotton, which they called their Flag; which, had you sold it at any market-cross, would not have brought above three groschen? Did not the whole Hungarian Nation rise, like some tumultuous moon-stirred Atlantic, when Kaiser Joseph pocketed their Iron Crown; an implement, as was sagaciously observed, in size and commercial value, little differing from a horse-shoe? It is in and through *Symbols* that man, consciously or unconsciously, lives, works, and has his being: those ages, moreover, are accounted the noblest which can the best recognise symbolical worth, and prize it the highest. For is not a Symbol ever, to him who has eyes for it, some dimmer or clearer revelation of the Godlike?

"Of Symbols, however, I remark farther, that they have both an extrinsic and intrinsic value; oftenest the former only. What, for instance, was in that clouted Shoe which the Peasants bore aloft with them as ensign in their *Bauernkrieg* (Peasants' War)? Or in the Wallet-and-staff round which the Netherland *Gueux,* glorying in that nickname of Beggars, heroically rallied and prevailed, though against King Philip himself? Intrinsic significance these had none: only extrinsic; as the accidental Standards of multitudes more or less sacredly uniting together; in which union itself, as above noted, there is ever something mystical and borrowing of the Godlike. Under a like category too, stand, or stood, the stupidest heraldic coats-of-arms; military Banners every where; and generally all national or other sectarian Costumes and Customs: they have no intrinsic, necessary divineness, or even worth; but have acquired an extrinsic one. Nevertheless through all these there glimmers something of a Divine Idea; as through military Banners themselves, the Divine Idea of Duty, of heroic Daring; in some instances of Freedom, of Right. Nay, the highest ensign that men ever met and embraced under, the Cross itself, had no meaning save an accidental extrinsic one.

"Another matter it is, however, when your Symbol has intrinsic meaning, and is of itself *fit* that men should unite round it. Let but the Godlike manifest itself to Sense; let but Eternity look, more or less visibly, through the Time-Figure (*Zeitbild*)! Then is it fit that men unite there; and worship together before such Symbol; and so from day to day, and from age to age, superadd to it new divineness.

"Of this latter sort are all true Works of Art: in them (if thou know a Work of Art from a Daub of Artifice) wilt thou discern Eternity looking through Time; the Godlike rendered visible. Here too may an extrinsic value gradually superadd itself: thus certain *Iliads,* and the like, have, in three thousand years, attained quite new significance. But nobler than all in this kind are the Lives of heroic, god-inspired Men; for what other Work of Art is so divine? In Death too, in the Death of the Just, as the last perfection of a Work of Art, may we not discern symbolic meaning? In that divinely transfigured Sleep, as of Victory, resting over the beloved face which now knows thee no more, read (if thou canst for tears) the confluence of Time with Eternity, and some gleam of the latter peering through.

"Highest of all Symbols are those wherein the Artist or Poet has risen into Prophet, and all men can recognise a present God, and worship the same: I mean religious Symbols. Various enough have been such religious Symbols, what we call *Religions;* as men stood in this stage of culture or the other, and could worse or better body forth the Godlike: some Symbols with a transient intrinsic worth; many with only an extrinsic. If thou ask to what height man has carried it in this matter, look on our divinest Symbol: on Jesus of Nazareth, and his Life, and his Biography, and what followed therefrom. Higher has the human Thought not yet reached: this is Christianity and Christendom; a Symbol of quite perennial, infinite character; whose significance will ever demand to be anew inquired into, and anew made manifest.

"But, on the whole, as Time adds much to the sacredness of Symbols, so likewise in his progress he at length defaces, or even desecrates them; and Symbols, like all terrestrial Garments, wax old. Homer's Epos has not ceased to be true; yet it is no longer *our* Epos, but shines in the distance, if clearer and clearer, yet also smaller and smaller, like a receding Star. It needs a scientific telescope, it needs to be reinterpreted and artificially brought near us, before we can so much as know that it *was* a Sun. So likewise a day comes when the Runic Thor, with his Eddas, must withdraw into dimness; and many an African Mumbo-Jumbo, and Indian Wau-Wau be utterly abolished. For all things, even Celestial Luminaries, much more atmospheric meteors, have their rise, their culmination, their decline.

"Small is this which thou tellest me that the Royal Sceptre is but a piece of gilt wood; that the Pyx has become a most foolish box, and truly, as Ancient Pistol thought, 'of little price.' A right Conjuror might I name thee, couldst thou conjure back into these wooden tools the divine virtue they once held.

"Of this thing however be certain: woulds thou plant for Eternity, then plant into the deep infinite faculties of man, his Fantasy and Heart; wouldst thou plant for Year and Day, then plant into his shallow superficial faculties, his Self-love and Arithmetical Understanding, what will grow there. A Hierarch, therefore, and Pontiff of the World will we call him, the Poet and inspired Maker; who, Prometheus-like, can shape new Symbols, and bring new Fire from Heaven to fix it there. Such too will not always be wanting; neither perhaps now are. Meanwhile, as the average of matters goes, we account him Legislator and wise who can so much as tell when a Symbol has grown old, and gently remove it.

"When, as the last English Coronation was preparing," concludes this wonderful Professor, "I read in their Newspapers that the 'Champion of England,' he who must offer battle to the Universe for his new King, had brought it so far that he could now 'mount his horse with little assistance,' I said to myself: Here also have we a Symbol well nigh superannuated. Alas, move whithersoever you may, are not the tatters and rags of superannuated worn-out Symbols (in this Ragfair of a World) dropping off every where, to hoodwink, to halter, to tether you; nay, if you shake them not aside, threatening to accumulate, and perhaps produce suffocation!"

Natural Supernaturalism

It is in his stupendous Section, headed *Natural Supernaturalism*, that the Professor first becomes a Seer; and, after long effort, such as we have witnessed, finally subdues under his feet this refractory Clothes-Philosophy, and takes victorious possession thereof. Phantasms enough he has had to struggle with; "Cloth-webs and Cob-webs," of Imperial Mantles, Superannuated Symbols, and what not: yet still did he courageously pierce through. Nay, worst of all, two quite mysterious, world-embracing Phantasms, Time and Space, have ever hovered round him, perplexing and bewildering: but with these also he now resolutely grapples, these also he victoriously rends asunder. In a word, he has looked fixedly on Existence, till one after the other, its earthly hulls and garnitures, have all melted away; and now to his rapt vision the interior, celestial Holy of Holies, lies disclosed.

Here therefore properly it is that the Philosophy of Clothes attains to Transcendentalism; this last leap, can we but clear it, takes us safe into the promised land, where *Palingenesia,* in all senses, may be considered as beginning. "Courage, then!" may our Diogenes exclaim, with better right than Diogenes the First once did. This stupendous Section we, after long, painful meditation, have found not to be unintelligible; but on the contrary to grow clear, nay radiant, and all-illuminating. Let the reader, turning on it what utmost force of speculative intellect is in him, do his part; as we, by judicious selection and adjustment, shall study to do ours:

"Deep has been, and is, the significance of Miracles," thus quietly begins the Professor; "far deeper perhaps than we imagine. Meanwhile, the question of questions were: What specially is a Miracle? To that Dutch King of Siam, an icicle had been a miracle; whoso had carried with him an air-pump, and phial of vitriolic ether, might have worked a miracle. To my Horse again, who unhappily is still more unscientific, do not I work a miracle, and magical '*open sesame!*' every time I please to pay twopence, and open for him an impassable *Schlagbaum,* or shut Turnpike?

"'But is not a real Miracle simply a violation of the Laws of Nature?' ask several. Whom I answer by this new question: What are the Laws of Nature? To me perhaps the rising of one from the dead were no violation of these Laws, but a confirmation; were some far deeper Law, now first penetrated into, and by Spiritual Force, even as the rest have all been, brought to bear on us with its Material Force.

"Here too may some inquire, not without astonishment: On what ground shall one, that can make Iron swim, come and declare that therefore he can teach Religion? To us, truly, of the Nineteenth Century, such declaration were inept enough; which nevertheless to our fathers, of the First Century, was full of meaning.

"'But is it not the deepest Law of Nature that she be constant?' cries an illuminated class: 'Is not the Machine of the Universe fixed to move by unalterable rules?' Probable enough, good friends: nay, I too must believe that the God, whom ancient, inspired men assert to be 'without variableness or shadow of turning,' does indeed never change; that Nature, that the Universe, which no one whom it so pleases can be prevented from calling a Machine, does move by the most unalterable rules. And now of you too I make the old inquiry: What those same unalterable rules, forming the complete Statute-Book of Nature, may possibly be?

"They stand written in our Works of Science, say you; in the accumulated records of man's Experience?—Was man with his Experience present at the Creation, then, to see how it all went on? Have any deepest scientific individuals yet dived down to the foundations of the Universe, and gauged every thing there? Did the Maker take them into His counsel; that they read His ground-plan of the incomprehensible All; and can say, This stands marked therein, and no more than this? Alas, not in anywise! These scientific individuals have been nowhere but where we also are; have seen some handbreadths deeper than we see into the Deep that is infinite, without bottom as without shore.

"Laplace's Book on the Stars, wherein he exhibits that certain Planets, with their Satellites, gyrate round our worthy Sun, at a rate and in a course, which, by greatest good fortune, he and the like of him have succeeded in detecting,—is to me as precious as to another. But is this what thou namest 'Mechanism of the Heavens,' and 'System of the World;' this, wherein Sirius and the Pleiades, and all Herschel's Fifteen thousand Suns per minute, being left out, some paltry handful of Moons, and inert Balls, had been—looked at, nicknamed, and marked in the Zodiacal Waybill; so that we can now prate of their Whereabout; their How, their Why, their What, being hid from us as in the signless Inane?

"System of Nature! To the wisest man, wide as is his vision, Nature remains of quite *infinite* depth, of quite infinite expansion; and all Experience thereof limits itself to some few computed centuries, and measured square-miles. The course of Nature's phases, on this our little fraction of a Planet, is partially known to us; but who knows what deeper courses these depend on; what infinitely larger Cycle (of causes) our little Epicycle revolves on? To the Minnow every cranny and pebble, and quality and accident, of its little native Creek may have become familiar: but does the Minnow understand the Ocean Tides and periodic Currents, the Trade-winds, and Monsoons, and Moon's Eclipses; by all which the condition of its little Creek is regulated, and may, from time to time (*un*miraculously enough), be quite overset and reversed? Such a minnow is man; his Creek this Planet Earth; his Ocean the immeasurable All; his Monsoons and periodic Currents the mysterious Course of Providence through Æons of Æons.

"We speak of the Volume of Nature: and truly a Volume it is,—whose Author and Writer is God. To read it! Dost thou, does man, so much as well know the Alphabet thereof? With its Words, Sentences, and grand descriptive Pages, poetical and philosophical, spread out through Solar Systems, and Thousands of Years, we shall not try thee. It is a Volume written in celestial hieroglyphs, in the true Sacred-writing; of which even Prophets are happy that they can read here a line and there a line. As for your Institutes, and Academies of Science, they strive bravely; and, from amid the thick-crowded, inextricably intertwisted hieroglyphic writing, pick out, by dextrous combination, some Letters in the vulgar Character, and therefrom put together this and the other economic Recipe, of high avail in Practice. That Nature is more than some boundless Volume of such Recipes, or huge, well-nigh inexhaustible Domestic-Cookery Book, of which the whole secret will, in this wise, one day, evolve itself, the fewest dream.

"Custom," continues the Professor, "doth make dotards of us all. Consider well, thou wilt find that Custom is the greatest of Weavers; and weaves air-raiment for all the Spirits of the Universe; whereby indeed these dwell with us visibly, as ministering servants, in our houses and workshops; but their spiritual nature becomes, to the most, for ever hidden. Philosophy complains that Custom has hoodwinked us, from the first; that we do every thing by Custom, even Believe by it; that our very Axioms, let us boast of Free-thinking as we may, are oftenest simply such Beliefs as we have never heard questioned. Nay, what is Philosophy throughout but a continual battle against Custom; an ever-renewed effort to *transcend* the sphere of blind Custom, and so become Transcendental?

"Innumerable are the illusions and legerdemain tricks of Custom: but of all these perhaps the cleverest is her knack of persuading us that the Miraculous, by simple repetition, ceases to be Miraculous. True, it is by this means we live; for man must work as well as wonder: and herein is Custom so far a kind nurse, guiding him to his true benefit. But she is a fond foolish nurse, or rather we are false foolish nurselings, when, in our resting and reflecting hours, we prolong the same deception. Am I to view the Stupendous with stupid indifference, because I have seen it twice, or two hundred, or two million times? There is no reason in Nature or in Art why I should: unless, indeed, I am a mere Work-Machine, for whom the divine gift of Thought were no other than the terrestrial gift of Steam is to the Steam-engine; a power whereby Cotton might be spun, and money and money's worth realised.

"Notable enough too, here as elsewhere, wilt thou find the potency of Names; which indeed are but one kind of such Custom-woven, wonder-hiding garments. Witchcraft, and all manner of Spectre-work, and Demonology, we have now named Madness, and Diseases of the Nerves. Seldom reflecting that still the new question comes upon us: What is Madness, what are Nerves? Ever, as before, does Madness remain a mysterious-terrific, altogether *infernal* boiling up of the Nether Chaotic Deep, through this fair-painted Vision of Creation, which swims thereon, which we name the Real. Was Luther's Picture of the Devil less a Reality, whether it were formed within the bodily eye, or without it? In every the wisest Soul, lies a whole world of internal Madness, an authentic Demon-Empire; out of which, indeed, his world of Wisdom has been creatively built together, and now rests there, as on its dark foundations does a habitable flowery Earth-rind.

"But deepest of all illusory Appearances, for hiding Wonder, as for many other ends, are your two grand fundamental world-enveloping Appearances, SPACE and TIME. These, as spun and woven for us from before Birth itself, to clothe our celestial ME for dwelling here, and yet to blind it,—lie all-embracing, as the universal canvass, or warp and woof, whereby all minor Illusions, in this Phantasm Existence, weave and paint themselves. In vain, while here on Earth, shall you endeavour to strip them off; you can, at best, but rend them asunder for moments, and look through.

"Fortunatus had a wishing Hat, which when he put it on, and wished himself Anywhere, behold he was There. By this means had Fortunatus triumphed over Space, he had annihilated Space; for him there was no Where, but all was Here. Were a Hatter to establish himself, in the Wahngasse of Weissnichtwo, and make felts of this sort for all mankind, what a world we should have of it! Still stranger, should, on the opposite side of the street, another Hatter establish himself; and, as his fellow-craftsman made Space-annihilating Hats, make Time-annihilating! Of both would I purchase, were it with my last groschen; but chiefly of this latter. To clap on your felt, and, simply by wishing that you were Any*where*, straightway to be *There!* Next to clap on your other felt, and, simply by wishing that you were Any*when*, straightway to be *Then!* This were indeed the grander: shooting at will from the Fire-Creation of the World to its Fire-Consummation; here historically present in the First Century, conversing face to face with Paul and Seneca; there prophetically in the Thirty-first, conversing also face to face with other Pauls and Senecas, who as yet stand hidden in the depth of that late Time!

"Or thinkest thou, it were impossible, unimaginable? Is the Past annihilated, then, or only past; is the Future non-extant, or only future? Those mystic faculties of thine, Memory and Hope, already answer: already through those mystic avenues, thou the Earth-blinded summonest both Past and Future, and communest with them, though as yet darkly, and with mute beckonings. The curtains of Yesterday drop down, the curtains of To-morrow roll up; but Yesterday and To-morrow both *are*. Pierce through the Time-Element, glance into the Eternal. Believe what thou findest written in the sanctuaries of Man's Soul, even as all Thinkers, in all ages, have devoutly read it there: that Time and Space are not God, but creations of God; that with God as it is a universal HERE, so is it an Everlasting Now.

"And seest thou therein any glimpse of IMMORTALITY?—O heaven! Is the white Tomb of our Loved One, who died from our arms, and must be left behind us there, which rises in the distance, like a pale, mournfully receding Milestone, to tell how many toilsome uncheered miles we have journeyed on alone,—but a pale spectral Illusion! Is the lost Friend still mysteriously Here, even as we are Here mysteriously, with God!—Know of a truth that only the Time-shadows have perished, or are perishable; that the real Being of whatever was, and whatever is, and whatever will be, *is* even now and for ever. This, should it unhappily seem new, thou mayst ponder, at thy leisure; for the next twenty years, or the next twenty centuries: believe it thou must; understand it thou canst not.

"That the Thought-forms, Space and Time, wherein, once for all, we are sent into this Earth to live, should condition and determine our whole Practical reasonings, conceptions, and imagings (not imaginings),—seems altogether fit, just, and unavoidable. But that they should, farthermore, usurp such sway over pure spiritual Meditation, and blind us to the wonder every where lying close on us, seems nowise so. Admit Space and Time to their due rank as Forms of Thought; nay, even, if thou wilt, to their quite undue rank of Realities: and consider, then, with thyself how their thin disguises hide from us the brightest God-effulgences! Thus, were it not miraculous, could I stretch forth my hand, and clutch the Sun? Yet thou seest me daily stretch forth my hand, and therewith clutch many a thing, and swing it hither and thither. Art thou a grown Baby, then, to fancy that the Miracle lies in miles of distance, or in pounds avoirdupois of weight; and not to see that the true inexplicable God-revealing Miracle lies in this, that I can stretch forth my hand at all; that I have free Force to clutch aught therewith? Innumerable other of this sort are the deceptions, and wonder-hiding stupefactions, which Space practises on us.

"Still worse is it with regard to Time. Your grand anti-magician, and universal wonder-hider, is this same lying Time. Had we but the Time-annihilating Hat, to put on for once only, we should see ourselves in a World of Miracles, wherein all fabled or authentic Thaumaturgy, and feats of Magic, were outdone. But unhappily we have not such a Hat; and man, poor fool that he is, can seldom and scantily help himself without one.

"Were it not wonderful, for instance, had Orpheus built the walls of Thebes by the mere sound of his Lyre? Yet tell me, who built these walls of Weissnichtwo; summoning out all the sandstone rocks, to dance along from the *Steinbruch* (now a huge Troglodyte Chasm, with frightful green-mantled pools); and shape themselves into Doric and Ionic pillars, squared ashlar houses, and noble streets? Was it not the still higher Orpheus, or Orpheuses, who, in past centuries, by the divine Music of Wisdom, succeeded in civilising Man? Our highest Orpheus walked in Judea, eighteen hundred years ago: his sphere-melody, flowing in wild native tones, took captive the ravished souls of men; and, being of a truth sphere-melody, still flows and sounds, though now with thousandfold Accompaniments, and rich symphonies, through all our hearts; and modulates, and divinely leads them. Is that a wonder, which happens in two hours; and does it cease to be wonderful if happening in two million? Not only was Thebes built by the Music of an Orpheus; but without the music of some inspired Orpheus was no city ever built, no work that man glories in ever done.

"Sweep away the Illusion of Time: glance, if thou have eyes, from the near moving-cause to its far distant Mover: The stroke that came transmitted through a whole galaxy of elastic balls, was it less a stroke than if the last ball only had been struck, and sent flying? Oh, could I (with the Time-annihilating Hat) transport thee direct from the Beginnings to the Endings, how were thy eyesight unsealed, and thy heart set flaming in the Light-sea of celestial wonder! Then sawest thou that this fair Universe, were it in the meanest province thereof, is in very deed the star-domed City of God; that through every star, through every grass-blade, and most through every Living Soul, the glory of a present God still beams. But Nature, which is the Time-vesture of God, and reveals Him to the wise, hides Him from the foolish.

"Again, could any thing be more miraculous than an actual authentic Ghost? The English Johnson longed, all his life, to see one; but could not, though he went to Cock Lane, and thence to the church-vaults, and tapped on coffins. Foolish Doctor! Did he never, with the mind's eye as well as with the body's, look round him into that full tide of human Life he so loved; did he never so much as look into Himself? The good Doctor was a Ghost, as actual and authentic as heart could wish; well nigh a million of Ghosts were travelling the streets by his side. Once more I say, sweep away the illusion of Time; compress the three-score years into three minutes: what else was he, what else are we? Are we not Spirits, shaped into a body, into an Appearance; and that fade away again into air, and Invisibility? This is no metaphor, it is a simple scientific *fact*: we start out of Nothingness, take figure, and are Apparitions; round us, as round the veriest spectre, is Eternity; and to Eternity minutes are as years and æons. Come there not tones of Love and Faith, as from celestial harp-strings, like the Song of beatified Souls? And again, do we not squeak and gibber (in our discordant, screech-owlish debatings and recriminatings); and glide bodeful, and feeble, and fearful; or uproar (*poltern*), and revel in our mad Dance of the Dead,—till the scent of the morning-air summons us to our still Home; and dreamy Night becomes awake and Day? Where now is Alexander of Macedon: does the steel Host, that yelled in fierce battle-shouts at Issus and Arbela, remain behind him; or have they all vanished utterly, even as perturbed Goblins must? Napoleon too, and his Moscow Retreats and Austerlitz Campaigns! Was it all other than the veriest Spectre-Hunt; which has now, with its howling tumult that made Night hideous, flitted away?—Ghosts! There are nigh a thousand million walking the earth openly at noontide; some half-hundred have vanished from it, some half-hundred have arisen in it, ere thy watch ticks once.

"O Heaven, it is mysterious, it is awful to consider that we not only carry each a future Ghost within him; but are, in very deed, Ghosts! These Limbs, whence had we them; this stormy Force; this life-blood with its burning Passion? They are dust and shadow; a Shadow-system gathered round our ME; wherein, through some moments or years, the Divine Essence is to be revealed in the Flesh. That warrior on his strong war-horse, fire flashes through his eyes; Force dwells in his arm and heart: but warrior and war-horse are a vision; a revealed Force, nothing more. Stately they tread the Earth, as if it were a firm substance: fool! the Earth is but a film; it cracks in twain, and warrior and war-horse sink beyond plummet's sounding. Plummet's? Fantasy herself will not follow them. A little while ago they were not; a little while and they are not, their very ashes are not.

"So has it been from the beginning, so will it be to the end. Generation after generation takes to itself the Form of a Body; and forth-issuing from Cimmerian Night, on Heaven's mission, APPEARS. What Force and Fire is in each he expends: one grinding in the mill of Industry; one hunter-like climbing the giddy Alpine heights of Science; one madly dashed in pieces on the rocks of Strife, in war with his fellow:—and then the Heaven-sent is recalled; his earthly Vesture falls away, and soon even to Sense becomes a vanished Shadow. Thus, like some wild-flaming, wild-thundering train of Heaven's Artillery, does this mysterious MANKIND thunder and flame, in long-drawn, quick-succeeding grandeur, through the unknown Deep. Thus, like a God-created, fire-breathing Spirit-host, we emerge from the Inane; haste stormfully across the astonished Earth; then plunge again into the Inane. Earth's mountains are levelled, and her seas filled up, in our passage: can the Earth, which is but dead and a vision, resist Spirits which have reality and are alive? On the hardest adamant some foot-print of us is stamped in; the last Rear of the host will read traces of the earliest Van. But whence?—O Heaven, whither? Sense knows not; Faith knows not; only that it is through Mystery to Mystery, from God and to God.

> We *are such stuff*
> As Dreams are made of, and our little Life
> Is rounded with a sleep!

35

Ralph Waldo Emerson

The Transcendentalist (1842)

THE FIRST THING WE HAVE TO SAY RESPECTING WHAT ARE called *new views* here in New England, at the present time, is, that they are not new, but the very oldest of thoughts cast into the mould of these new times. The light is always identical in its composition, but it falls on a great variety of objects, and by so falling is first revealed to us, not in its own form, for it is formless, but in theirs; in like manner, thought only appears in the objects it classifies. What is popularly called Transcendentalism among us, is Idealism; Idealism as it appears in 1842. As thinkers, mankind have ever divided into two sects, Materialists and Idealists; the first class founding on experience, the second on consciousness; the first class beginning to think from the data of the senses, the second class perceive that the senses are not final, and say, the senses give us representations of things, but what are the things themselves, they cannot tell. The materialist insists on facts, on history, on the force of circumstances, and the animal wants of man; the idealist on the power of Thought and of Will, on inspiration, on miracle, on individual culture. These two modes of thinking are both natural, but the idealist contends that his way of thinking is in higher nature. He concedes all that the other affirms, admits the impressions of sense, admits their coherency, their use and beauty, and then asks the materialist for his grounds of assurance that things are as his senses represent them. But I, he says, affirm facts not affected by the illusions of sense, facts which are of the same nature as the faculty which reports them, and not liable to doubt; facts which in their first appearance to us assume a native superiority to material facts, degrading these into a language by which the first are to be spoken; facts which it only needs a retirement from the senses to discern. Every materialist will be an idealist; but an idealist can never go backward to be a materialist.

The idealist, in speaking of events sees them as spirits. He does not deny the sensuous fact: by no means; but he will not see that alone. He does not deny the presence of this table, this chair, and the walls of this room, but he looks at these things as the reverse side of the tapestry, as the *other end,* each being a sequel or completion of a spiritual fact which nearly concerns him. This manner of looking at things, transfers every object in nature from an independent and anomalous position without there, into the consciousness. Even the materialist Condillac, perhaps the most logical expounder of materialism, was constrained to say, "Though we should soar into the heavens, though we should sink into the abyss, we never go out of ourselves; it is always our own thought that we perceive." What more could an idealist say?

The materialist, secure in the certainty of sensation, mocks at fine-spun theories, at star-gazers and dreamers and believes that his life is solid, that he at least takes nothing for granted, but knows where he stands, and what he does. Yet how easy it is to show him, that he also is a phantom walking and working amid phantoms, and that he need only ask a question or two beyond his daily questions, to find his solid universe growing dim and impalpable before his sense. The sturdy capitalist, no matter how deep and square on blocks of Quincy granite he lays the foundations of his banking-house or Exchange, must set it, at last, not on a cube corresponding to the angles of his structure, but on a mass of unknown materials and solidity, red-hot or white-hot, perhaps at the core, which rounds off to an almost perfect sphericity, and lies floating in soft air, and goes spinning away, dragging bank and banker with it at a rate of thousands of miles the hour, he knows not whither,—a bit of bullet, now glimmering, now darkling through a small cubic space on the edge of an unimaginable pit of emptiness. And this wild balloon, in which his whole venture is embarked, is a just symbol of his whole state and faculty. One thing, at least, he says is certain, and does not give me the headache, that figures do not lie; the multiplication table has been hitherto found unimpeachable truth; and, moreover, if I put a gold eagle in my safe, I find it again to-morrow;—but for these thoughts, I know not whence they are. They change and pass away. But ask him why he believes that an uniform experience will continue uniform, or on what grounds he founds his faith in his figures, and he will perceive that his mental fabric is built up on just as strange and quaking foundations as his proud edifice of stone.

In the order of thought, the materialist takes his departure from the external world, and esteems a man as one product of that. The idealist takes his departure from his consciousness, and reckons the world an appearance. The materialist respects sensible masses, Society, Government, social art, and luxury, every establishment, every mass, whether majority of numbers, or extent of space, or amount of objects, every social action. The idealist has another measure, which is metaphysical, namely, the *rank* which things themselves take in his consciousness; not at all, the size or appearance. Mind is the only reality, of which men and all other natures are better or worse reflectors. Nature, literature, history, are only subjective phenomena. Although in his action overpowered by the laws of action, and so, warmly coöperating with men, even preferring them to himself, yet when he speaks scientifically, or after the order of thought, he is constrained to degrade persons into representatives of truths. He does not respect labor, or the products of labor, namely, property, otherwise than as a manifold symbol, illustrating with wonderful fidelity of details the laws of being; he does not respect government, except as far as it reiterates the law of his mind; nor the church; nor charities; nor arts, for themselves; but hears, as at a vast distance, what they say, as if his consciousness would speak to him through a pantomimic scene. His thought,—that is the Universe. His experience inclines him to behold the procession of facts you call the world, as flowing perpetually outward from an invisible, unsounded centre in himself, centre alike of him and of them, and necessitating him to regard all things as having a subjective or relative existence, relative to that aforesaid Unknown Centre of him.

From this transfer of the world into the consciousness, this beholding of all things in the mind, follow easily his whole ethics. It is simpler to be self-dependent. The height, the deity of man is, to be self-sustained, to need no gift, no foreign force. Society is good when it does not violate me; but best when it is likest to solitude. Everything real is self-existent. Everything divine shares the self-existence of Deity. All that you call the world is the shadow of that substance which you are, the perpetual creation of the powers of thought, of those that are dependent and of those that are independent of your will. Do not cumber yourself with fruitless pains to mend and remedy remote effects; let the soul be erect, and all things will go well. You think me the child of my circumstances: I make my circumstance. Let any thought or motive of mine be different from that they are, the difference will transform my condition and economy. I—this thought which is called I,—is the mould into which the world is poured like melted wax. The mould is invisible, but the world betrays the shape of the mould. You call it the power of circumstance, but it is the power of me. Am I in harmony with myself? my position will seem to you just and commanding. Am I vicious and insane? my fortunes will seem to you obscure and descending. As I am, so shall I associate, and, so shall I act; Cæsar's history will paint out Cæsar. Jesus acted so, because he thought so. I do not wish to overlook or to gainsay any reality; I say, I make my circumstance: but if you ask me, Whence am I? I feel like other men my relation to that Fact which cannot be spoken, or defined, nor even thought, but which exists, and will exist.

The Transcendentalist adopts the whole connection of spiritual doctrine. He believes in miracle, in the perpetual openness of the human mind to new influx of light and power; he believes in inspiration, and in ecstasy. He wishes that the spiritual principle should be suffered to demonstrate itself to the end, in all possible applications to the state of man, without the admission of anything unspiritual; that is, anything positive, dogmatic, personal. Thus, the spiritual measure of inspiration is the depth of the thought, and never, who said it? And so he resists all attempts to palm other rules and measures on the spirit than its own.

In action, he easily incurs the charge of antinomianism by his avowal that he, who has the Lawgiver, may with safety not only neglect, but even contravene every written commandment. In the play of Othello, the expiring Desdemona absolves her husband of the murder, to her attendant Emilia. Afterwards, when Emilia charges him with the crime, Othello exclaims,

"You heard her say herself it was not I."

Emilia replies,

"The more angel she, and thou the blacker devil."

Of this fine incident, Jacobi, the Transcendental moralist, makes use, with other parallel instances, in his reply to Fichte. Jacobi, refusing all measure of right and wrong except the determinations of the private spirit, remarks that there is no crime but has sometimes been a virtue. "I," he says, "am that atheist, that godless person who, in opposition to an imaginary doctrine of calculation, would lie as the dying Desdemona lied; would lie and deceive, as Pylades when he personated Orestes; would assassinate like Timoleon; would perjure myself like Epaminondas, and John de Witt; I would resolve on suicide like Cato; I would commit sacrilege with David; yea, and pluck ears of corn on the Sabbath, for no other reason than that I was fainting for lack of food. For, I have assurance in myself, that, in pardoning these faults according to the letter, man exerts the sovereign right which the majesty of his being confers on him; he sets the seal of his divine nature to the grace he accords."

In like manner, if there is anything grand and daring in human thought or virtue, any reliance on the vast, the unknown; any presentiment; any extravagance of faith, the spiritualist adopts it as most in nature. The oriental mind has always tended to this largeness. Buddhism is an expression of it. The Buddhist who thanks no man, who says, "do not flatter your benefactors," but who, in his conviction that every good deed can by no possibility escape its reward, will not deceive the benefactor by pretending that he has done more than he should, is a Transcendentalist.

You will see by this sketch that there is no such thing as a Transcendental *party*; that there is no pure Transcendentalist; that we know of none but prophets and heralds of such a philosophy; that all who by strong bias of nature have leaned to the spiritual side in doctrine, have stopped short of their goal. We have had many harbingers and forerunners; but of a purely spiritual life, history has afforded no example. I mean, we have yet no man who has leaned entirely on his character, and eaten angels' food; who, trusting to his sentiments, found life made of miracles; who, working for universal aims, found himself fed, he knew not how; clothed, sheltered, and weaponed, he knew not how, and yet it was done by his own hands. Only in the instinct of the lower animals, we find the suggestion of the methods of it, and something higher than our understanding. The squirrel hoards nuts, and the bee gathers honey, without knowing what they do, and they are thus provided for without selfishness or disgrace.

Shall we say, then, that Transcendentalism is the Saturnalia or excess of Faith; the presentiment of a faith proper to man in his integrity, excessive only when his imperfect obedience hinders the satisfaction of his wish Nature is transcendental, exists primarily, necessarily, ever works and advances, yet takes no thought for the morrow. Man owns the dignity of the life which throbs around him in chemistry, and tree, and animal, and in the involuntary functions of his own body; yet he is balked when he tries to fling himself into this enchanted circle, where all is done without degradation. Yet genius and virtue predict in man the same absence of private ends, and of condescension to circumstances, united with every trait and talent of beauty and power.

This way of thinking, falling on Roman times, made Stoic philosophers; falling on despotic times, made patriot Catos and Brutuses; falling on superstitious times, made prophets and apostles; on popish times, made protestants and ascetic monks, preachers of Faith against the preachers of Works; on prelatical times, made Puritans and Quakers; and falling on Unitarian and commercial times, makes the peculiar shades of Idealism which we know.

It is well known to most of my audience, that the Idealism of the present day acquired the name of Transcendental, from the use of that term by Immanuel Kant, of Konigsberg, who replied to the skeptical philosophy of Locke, which insisted that there was nothing in the intellect which was not previously in the experience of the senses, by showing that there was a very important class of ideas, or imperative forms, which did not come by experience, but through which experience was acquired; that these were intuitions of the mind itself; and he denominated them *Transcendental* forms. The extraordinary profoundness and precision of that man's thinking have given vogue to his nomenclature, in Europe and America, to that extent, that whatever belongs to the class of intuitive thought, is popularly called at the present day *Transcendental.*

Although, as we have said, there is no pure Transcendentalist, yet the tendency to respect the intuitions, and to give them, at least in our creed, all authority over our experience, has deeply colored the conversation and poetry of the present day; and the history of genius and of religion in these times, though impure, and as yet not incarnated in any powerful individual, will be the history of this tendency.

It is a sign of our times, conspicuous to the coarsest observer, that many intelligent and religious persons withdraw themselves from the common labors and competitions of the market and the caucus, and betake themselves to a certain solitary and critical way of living, from which no solid fruit has yet appeared to justify their separation. They hold themselves aloof: they feel the disproportion between their faculties and the work offered them, and they prefer to ramble in the country and perish of ennui, to the degradation of such charities and such ambitions as the city can propose to them. They are striking work, and crying out for somewhat worthy to do! What they do, is done only because they are overpowered by the humanities that speak on all sides; and they consent to such labor as is open to them, though to their lofty dream the writing of Iliads or Hamlets, or the building of cities or empires seems drudgery.

Now every one must do after his kind, be he asp or angel, and these must. The question, which a wise man and a student of modern history will ask, is, what that kind is? And truly, as in ecclesiastical history we take so much pains to know what the Gnostics, what the Essenes, what the Manichees, and what the Reformers believed, it would not misbecome us to inquire nearer home, what these companions and contemporaries of ours think and do, at least so far as these thoughts and actions appear to be not accidental and personal, but common to many, and the inevitable flower of the Tree of Time. Our American literature and spiritual history are, we confess, in the optative mood; but whoso knows these seething brains, these admirable radicals, these unsocial worshippers, these talkers who talk the sun and moon away, will believe that this heresy cannot pass away without leaving its mark.

They are lonely; the spirit of their writing and conversation is lonely; they repel influences; they shun general society; they incline to shut themselves in their chamber in the house, to live in the country rather than in the town, and to find their tasks and amusements in solitude. Society, to be sure, does not like this very well; it saith, Whoso goes to walk alone, accuses the whole world; he declareth all to be unfit to be his companions; it is very uncivil, nay, insulting; Society will retaliate. Meantime, this retirement does not proceed from any whim on the part of these separators; but if any one will take pains to talk with them, he will find that this part is chosen both from temperament and from principle; with some unwillingness, too, and as a choice of the less of two evils; for these persons are not by nature melancholy, sour, and unsocial,—they are not stockish or brute,—but joyous; susceptible, affectionate; they have even more than others a great wish to be loved. Like the young Mozart, they are rather ready to cry ten times a day, "But are you sure you love me?" Nay, if they tell you their whole thought, they will own that love seems to them the last and highest gift of nature; that there are persons whom in their hearts they daily thank for existing,—persons whose faces are perhaps unknown to them, but whose fame and spirit have penetrated their solitude,—and for whose sake they wish to exist. To behold the beauty of another character, which inspires a new interest in our own; to behold the beauty lodged in a human being, with such vivacity of apprehension, that I am instantly forced home to inquire if I am not deformity itself: to behold in another the expression of a love so high that it assures itself,—assures itself also to me against every possible casualty except my unworthiness;—these are degrees on the scale of human happiness, to which they have ascended; and it is a fidelity to this sentiment which has made common association distasteful to them. They wish a just and even fellowship, or none. They cannot gossip with you, and they do not wish, as they are sincere and religious, to gratify any mere curiosity which you may entertain. Like fairies, they do not wish to be spoken of. Love me, they say, but do not ask who is my cousin and my uncle. If you do not need to hear my thought, because you can read it in my face and behavior, then I will tell it you from sunrise to sunset. If you cannot divine it, you would not understand what I say. I will not molest myself for you. I do not wish to be profaned.

And yet, it seems as if this loneliness, and not this love, would prevail in their circumstances, because of the extravagant demand they make on human nature. That, indeed, constitutes a new feature in their portrait, that they are the most exacting and extortionate critics. Their quarrel with every man they meet, is not with his kind, but with his degree. There is not enough of him,—that is the only fault. They prolong their privilege of childhood in this wise, of doing nothing,—but making immense demands on all the gladiators in the lists of action and fame. They make us feel the strange disappointment which overcasts every human youth. So many promising youths, and never a finished man! The profound nature will have a savage rudeness; the delicate one will be shallow, or the victim of sensibility; the richly accomplished will have some capital absurdity; and so every piece has a crack. 'T is strange, but this masterpiece is a result of such an extreme delicacy, that the most unobserved flaw in the boy will neutralize the most aspiring genius, and spoil the work. Talk with a seaman of the hazards to life in his profession, and he will ask you, "Where are the old sailors? do you not see that all are young men?" And we, on this sea of human thought, in like manner inquire, Where are the old idealists? where are they who represented to the last generation that extravagant hope, which a few happy aspirants suggest to ours? In looking at the class of counsel, and power, and wealth, and at the matronage of the land, amidst all the prudence and all the triviality, one asks, Where are they who represented genius, virtue, the invisible and heavenly world, to these? Are they dead,—taken in early ripeness to the gods,—as ancient wisdom foretold their fate? Or did the high idea die out of them, and leave their unperfumed body as its tomb and tablet, announcing to all that the celestial inhabitant, who once gave them beauty, had departed? Will it be better with the new generation? We easily predict a fair future to each new candidate who enters the lists, but we are frivolous and volatile, and by low aims and ill example do what we can to defeat this hope. Then these youths bring us a rough but effectual aid. By their unconcealed dissatisfaction, they expose our poverty, and the insignificance of man to man. A man is a poor limitary benefactor. He ought to be a shower of benefits—a great influence, which should never let his brother go, but should refresh old merits continually with new ones; so that, though absent, he should never be out of my mind, his name never far from my lips; but if the earth should open at my side, or my last hour were come, his name should be the prayer I should utter to the Universe. But in our experience, man is cheap, and friendship wants its deep sense. We affect to dwell with our friends in their absence, but we do not; when deed, word, or letter comes not, they let us go. These exacting children advertise us of our wants. There is no compliment, no smooth speech with them; they pay you only this one compliment, of insatiable expectation; they aspire, they severely exact, and if they only stand fast in this watch tower, and persist in demanding unto the end, and without end, then are they terrible friends, whereof poet and priest cannot choose but stand in awe; and what if they eat clouds, and drink wind, they have not been without service to the race of man.

With this passion for what is great and extraordinary, it cannot be wondered at, that they are repelled by vulgarity and frivolity in people. They say to themselves, it is better to be alone than in bad company. And it is really a wish to be met,—the wish to find society for their hope and religion,—which prompts them to shun what is called society. They feel that they are never so fit for friendship, as when they have quitted mankind, and taken themselves to friend. A picture, a book, a favorite spot in the hills or the woods, which they can people with the fair and worthy creation of the fancy, can give them often forms so vivid, that these for the time shall seem real, and society the illusion.

But their solitary and fastidious manners not only withdraw them from the conversation, but from the labors of the world; they are not good citizens, not good members of society; unwillingly they bear their part of the public and private burdens; they do not willingly share in the public charities, in the public religious rites, in the enterprises of education, of missions foreign or domestic, in the abolition of the slave-trade, or in the temperance society. They do not even like to vote. The philanthropists inquire whether Transcendentalism does not mean sloth: they had as lief hear that their friend is dead, as that he is a Transcendentalist; for then is he paralyzed, and can never do anything for humanity. What right, cries the good world, has the man of genius to retreat from work, and indulge himself? The popular literary creed seems to be, 'I am a sublime genius; I ought not therefore to labor.' But genius is the power to labor better and more availably. Deserve thy genius: exalt it. The good, the illuminated, sit apart from the rest, censuring their dulness and vices, as if they thought that, by sitting very grand in their chairs, the very brokers, attorneys, and congressmen would see the error of their ways, and flock to them. But the good and wise must learn to act, and carry salvation to the combatants and demagogues in the dusty arena below.

On the part of these children, it is replied, that life and their faculty seem to them gifts too rich to be squandered on such trifles as you propose to them. What you call your fundamental institutions, your great and holy causes, seem to them great abuses, and, when nearly seen, paltry matters. Each 'Cause,' as it is called,—say Abolition, Temperance, say Calvinism, or Unitarianism,—becomes speedily a little shop, where the article, let it have been at first never so subtle and ethereal, is now made up into portable and convenient cakes, and retailed in small quantities to suit purchasers. You make very free use of these words 'great' and 'holy,' but few things appear to them such. Few persons have any magnificence of nature to inspire enthusiasm, and the philanthropies and charities have a certain air of quackery. As to the general course of living, and the daily employments of men, they cannot see much virtue in these, since they are parts of this vicious circle; and, as no great ends are answered by the men, there is nothing noble in the arts by which they are maintained. Nay, they have made the experiment, and found that, from the liberal professions to the coarsest manual labor, and from the courtesies of the academy and the college to the conventions of the cotillon-room and the morning call, there is a spirit of cowardly compromise and seeming, which intimates a frightful skepticism, a life without love, and an activity without an aim.

Unless the action is necessary, unless it is adequate, I do not wish to perform it. I do not wish to do one thing but once. I do not love routine. Once possessed of the principle, it is equally easy to make four or forty thousand applications of it. A great man will be content to have indicated in any the slightest manner his perception of the reigning Idea of his time, and will leave to those who like it the multiplication of examples. When he has hit the white, the rest may shatter the target. Every thing admonishes us how needlessly long life is. Every moment of a hero so raises and cheers us, that a twelvemonth is an age. All that the brave Xanthus brings home from his wars, is the recollection that, at the storming of Samos, "in the heat of the battle, Pericles smiled on me, and passed on to another detachment." It is the quality of the moment, not the number of days, of events, or of actors, that imports.

New, we confess, and by no means happy, is our condition: if you want the aid of our labor, we ourselves stand in greater want of the labor. We are miserable with inaction. We perish of rest and rust: but we do not like your work.

'Then,' says the world, 'show me your own.'

'We have none.'

'What will you do, then?' cries the world.

'We will wait.'

'How long?'

'Until the Universe rises up and calls us to work.'

'But whilst you wait, you grow old and useless.'

'Be it so: I can sit in a corner and *perish*, (as you call it,) but I will not move until I have the highest command. If no call should come for years, for centuries, then I know that the want of the Universe is the attestation of faith by my abstinence. Your virtuous projects, so called, do not cheer me. I know that which shall come will cheer me. If I cannot work, at least I need not lie. All that is clearly due to-day is not to lie. In other places, other men have encountered sharp trials, and have behaved themselves well. The martyrs were sawn asunder, or hung alive on meat-hooks. Cannot we screw our courage to patience and truth, and without complaint, or even with good-humor, await our turn of action in the Infinite Counsels?'

But, to come a little closer to the secret of these persons, we must say, that to them it seems a very easy matter to answer the objections of the man of the world, but not so easy to dispose of the doubts and objections that occur to themselves. They are exercised in their own spirit with queries, which acquaint them with all adversity, and with the trials of the bravest heroes. When I asked them concerning their private experience, they answered somewhat in this wise: It is not to be denied that there must be some wide difference between my faith and other faith; and mine is a certain brief experience, which surprised me in the highway or in the market, in some place, at some time,—whether in the body or out of the body, God knoweth,—and made me aware that I had played the fool with fools all this time, but that law existed for me and for all; that to me belonged trust, a child's trust and obedience, and the worship of ideas, and I should never be fool more. Well, in the space of an hour, probably, I was let down from this height; I was at my old tricks, the selfish member of a selfish society. My life is superficial, takes no root in the deep world; I ask, when shall I die, and be relieved of the responsibility of seeing an Universe which I do not use? I wish to exchange this flash-of-lightning faith for continuous daylight, this fever-glow for a benign climate.

These two states of thought diverge every moment, and stand in wild contrast. To him who looks at his life from these moments of illumination, it will seem that he skulks and plays a mean, shiftless, and subaltern part in the world. That is to be done which he has not skill to do, or to be said which others can say better, and he lies by, or occupies his hands with some plaything, until his hour comes again. Much of our reading, much of our labor, seems mere waiting: it was not that we were born for. Any other could do it as well, or better. So little skill enters into these works, so little do they mix with the divine life, that it really signifies little what we do, whether we turn a grindstone, or ride, or run, or make fortunes, or govern the state. The worst feature of this double consciousness is, that the two lives, of the understanding and of the soul, which we lead, really show very little relation to each other, never meet and measure each other: one prevails now, all buzz and din; and the other prevails then, all infinitude and paradise; and, with the progress of life, the two discover no greater disposition to reconcile themselves. Yet, what is my faith? What am I? What but a thought of serenity and independence, an abode in the deep blue sky? Presently the clouds shut down again; yet we retain the belief that this petty web we weave will at last be overshot and reticulated with veins of the blue, and that the moments will characterize the days. Patience, then, is for us, is it not? Patience, and still patience. When we pass, as presently we shall, into some new infinitude, out of this Iceland of negations, it will please us to reflect that, though we had few virtues or consolations, we bore with our indigence, nor once strove to repair it with hypocrisy or false heat of any kind.

But this class are not sufficiently characterized, if we omit to add that they are lovers and worshippers of Beauty. In the eternal trinity of Truth, Goodness, and Beauty, each in its perfection including the three, they prefer to make Beauty the sign and head. Something of the same taste is observable in all the moral movements of the time, in the religious and benevolent enterprises. They have a liberal, even an æsthetic spirit. A reference to Beauty in action sounds, to be sure, a little hollow and ridiculous in the ears of the old church. In politics, it has often sufficed, when they treated of justice, if they kept the bounds of selfish calculation. If they granted restitution, it was prudence which granted it. But the justice which is now claimed for the black, and the pauper, and the drunkard is for Beauty,—is for a necessity to the soul of the agent, not of the beneficiary. I say, this is the tendency, not yet the realization. Our virtue totters and trips, does not yet walk firmly. Its representatives are austere; they preach and denounce; their rectitude is not yet a grace. They are still liable to that slight taint of burlesque which, in our strange world, attaches to the zealot. A saint should be as dear as the apple of the eye. Yet we are tempted to smile, and we flee from the working to the speculative reformer, to escape that same slight ridicule. Alas for these days of derision and criticism! We call the Beautiful the highest, because it appears to us the golden mean, escaping the dowdiness of the good, and the heartlessness of the true.—They are lovers of nature also, and find an indemnity in the inviolable order of the world for the violated order and grace of man.

There is, no doubt, a great deal of well-founded objection to be spoken or felt against the sayings and doings of this class, some of whose traits we have selected; no doubt, they will lay themselves open to criticism and to lampoons, and as ridiculous stories will be to be told of them as of any. There will be cant and pretension; there will be subtilty and moonshine. These persons are of unequal strength, and do not all prosper. They complain that everything around them must be denied; and if feeble, it takes all their strength to deny, before they can begin to lead their own life. Grave seniors insist on their respect to this institution, and that usage; to an obsolete history; to some vocation, or college, or etiquette, or beneficiary, or charity, or morning or evening call, which they resist, as what does not concern them. But it costs such sleepless nights, alienations and misgivings,—they have so many moods about it;—these old guardians never change *their* minds; they have but one mood on the subject, namely, that Antony is very perverse,—that it is quite as much as Antony can do, to assert his rights, abstain from what he thinks foolish, and keep his temper. He cannot help the reaction of this injustice in his own mind. He is braced-up and stilted; all freedom and flowing genius, all sallies of wit and frolic nature are quite out of the question; it is well if he can keep from lying, injustice, and suicide. This is no time for gaiety and grace. His strength and spirits are wasted in rejection. But the strong spirits overpower those around them without effort. Their thought and emotion comes in like a flood, quite withdraws them from all notice of these carping critics; they surrender themselves with glad heart to the heavenly guide, and only by implication reject the clamorous nonsense of the hour. Grave seniors talk to the deaf,—church and old book mumble and ritualize to an unheeding, preöccupied and advancing mind, and thus they by happiness of greater momentum lose no time, but take the right road at first.

But all these of whom I speak are not proficients; they are novices; they only show the road in which man should travel, when the soul has greater health and prowess. Yet let them feel the dignity of their charge, and deserve a larger power. Their heart is the ark in which the fire is concealed, which shall burn in a broader and universal flame. Let them obey the Genius then most when his impulse is wildest; then most when he seems to lead to uninhabitable desarts of thought and life; for the path which the hero travels alone is the highway of health and benefit to mankind. What is the privilege and nobility of our nature, but its persistency, through its power to attach itself to what is permanent?

Society also has its duties in reference to this class, and must behold them with what charity it can. Possibly some benefit may yet accrue from them to the state. In our Mechanics' Fair, there must be not only bridges, ploughs, carpenters' planes, and baking troughs, but also some few finer instruments,—raingauges, thermometers, and telescopes; and in society, besides farmers, sailors, and weavers, there must be a few persons of purer fire kept specially as gauges and meters of character; persons of a fine, detecting instinct, who betray the smallest accumulations of wit and feeling in the bystander. Perhaps too there might be room for the exciters and monitors; collectors of the heavenly spark with power to convey the electricity to others. Or, as the storm-tossed vessel at sea speaks the frigate or 'line packet' to learn its longitude, so it may not be without its advantage that we should now and then encounter rare and gifted men, to compare the points of our spiritual compass, and verify our bearings from superior chronometers.

Amidst the downward tendency and proneness of things, when every voice is raised for a new road or another statute, or a subscription of stock, for an improvement in dress, or in dentistry, for a new house or a larger business, for a political party, or the division of an estate,—will you not tolerate one or two solitary voices in the land, speaking for thoughts and principles not marketable or perishable? Soon these improvements and mechanical inventions will be superseded; these modes of living lost out of memory; these cities rotted, ruined by war, by new inventions, by new seats of trade, or the geologic changes:—all gone, like the shells which sprinkle the seabeach with a white colony to-day, forever renewed to be forever destroyed. But the thoughts which these few hermits strove to proclaim by silence, as well as by speech, not only by what they did, but by what they forbore to do, shall abide in beauty and strength, to reorganize themselves in nature, to invest themselves anew in other, perhaps higher endowed and happier mixed clay than ours, in fuller union with the surrounding system.

36

Margaret Fuller

Woman in the Nineteenth Century (1845)

Swedenbourg, Fourier, and Goethe

AMONG THE THRONG OF SYMPTOMS WHICH DENOTE THE PRESENT TENDENCY to a crisis in the life of woman, which resembles the change from girlhood with its beautiful instincts, but unharmonized thoughts, its blind pupilage and restless seeking, to self-possessed, wise, and graceful womanhood, I have attempted to select a few.

One of prominent interest is the unison of three male minds, upon the subject, which, for width of culture, power of self-concentration and dignity of aim, take rank as the prophets of the coming age, while their histories and labors are rooted in the past.

Swedenborg came, he tells us, to interpret the past revelation and unfold a new. He announces the new church that is to prepare the way for the New Jerusalem, a city built of precious stones, hardened and purified by secret processes in the veins of earth through the ages.

Swedenborg approximated to that harmony between the scientific and poetic lives of mind, which we hope from the perfected man. The links that bind together the realms of nature, the mysteries that accompany her births and growths, were unusually plain to him. He seems a man to whom insight was given at a period when the mental frame was sufficiently matured to retain and express its gifts.

His views of woman are, in the main, satisfactory. In some details, we may object to them as, in all his system, there are still remains of what is arbitrary and seemingly groundless; fancies that show the marks of old habits, and a nature as yet not thoroughly leavened with the spiritual leaven. At least so it seems to me now. I speak reverently, for I find such reason to venerate Swedenborg, from an imperfect knowledge of his mind, that I feel one more perfect might explain to me much that does not now secure my sympathy.

His idea of woman is sufficiently large and noble to interpose no obstacle to her progress. His idea of marriage is consequently sufficient. Man and woman share an angelic ministry, the union is from one to one, permanent and pure.

As the New Church extends its ranks, the needs of woman must be more considered.

Quakerism also establishes woman on a sufficient equality with man. But though the original thought of Quakerism is pure, its scope is too narrow, and its influence, having established a certain amount of good and made clear some truth, must, by degrees, be merged in one of wider range.[1] The mind of Swedenborg appeals to the various nature of man and allows room for æsthetic culture and the free expression of energy.

As apostle of the new order, of the social fabric that is to rise from love, and supersede the old that was based on strife, Charles Fourier comes next, expressing, in an outward order, many facts of which Swedenborg saw the secret springs. The mind of Fourier, though grand and clear, was, in some respects, superficial. He was a stranger to the highest experiences. His eye was fixed on the outward more than the inward needs of man. Yet he, too, was a seer of the divine order, in its musical expression, if not in its poetic soul. He has filled one department of instruction for the new era, and the harmony in action, and freedom for individual growth he hopes shall exist; and if the methods he proposes should not prove the true ones, yet his fair propositions shall give many hints, and make room for the inspiration needed for such.

He, too, places woman on an entire equality with man, and wishes to give to one as to the other that independence which must result from intellectual and practical development.

Those who will consult him for no other reason, might do so to see how the energies of woman may be made available in the pecuniary way. The object of Fourier was to give her the needed means of self help, that she might dignify and unfold her life for her own happiness, and that of society. The many, now, who see their daughters liable to destitution, or vice to escape from it, may be interested to examine the means, if they have not yet soul enough to appreciate the ends he proposes.

On the opposite side of the advancing army, leads the great apostle of individual culture, Goethe. Swedenborg makes organization and union the necessary results of solitary thought. Fourier, whose nature was, above all, constructive, looked to them too exclusively. Better institutions, he thought, will make better men. Goethe expressed, in every way, the other side. If one man could present better forms, the rest could not use them till ripe for them.

Fourier says, As the institutions, so the men! All follies are excusable and natural under bad institutions.

Goethe thinks, As the man, so the institutions! There is no excuse for ignorance and folly. A man can grow in any place, if he will.

Ay! but Goethe, bad institutions are prison walls and impure air that make him stupid, so that he does not will.

And thou, Fourier, do not expect to change mankind at once, or even "in three generations" by arrangement of groups and series, or flourish of trumpets for attractive industry. If these attempts are made by unready men, they will fail.

Yet we prize the theory of Fourier no less than the profound suggestion of Goethe. Both are educating the age to a clearer consciousness of what man needs, what man can be, and better life must ensue.

Goethe, proceeding on his own track, elevating the human being in the most imperfect states of society, by continual efforts at self-culture, takes as good care of women as of men. His mother, the bold, gay Frau Aja, with such playful freedom of nature; the wise and gentle maiden, known in his youth, over whose sickly solitude "the Holy Ghost brooded as a dove;" his sister, the intellectual woman *par excellence:* the Duchess Amelia; Lili, who combined the character of the woman of the world with the lyrical sweetness of the shepherdess, on whose chaste and noble breast flowers and gems were equally at home; all these had supplied abundant suggestions to his mind, as to the wants and the possible excellencies of woman. And, from his poetic soul, grew up forms new and more admirable than life has yet produced, for whom his clear eye marked out paths in the future.

In Faust, we see the redeeming power, which, at present, upholds woman, while waiting for a better day, in Margaret. The lovely little girl, pure in instinct, ignorant in mind, is misled and profaned by man abusing her confidence.[2] To the Mater *Dolorosa* she appeals for aid. It is given to the soul, if not against outward sorrow; and the maiden, enlightened by her sufferings, refusing to receive temporal salvation by the aid of an evil power, obtains the eternal in its stead.

In the second part, the intellectual man, after all his manifold strivings, owes to the interposition of her whom he had betrayed *his* salvation. She intercedes, this time herself a glorified spirit, with the Mater *Gloriosa.*

Leonora, too, is woman, as we see her now, pure, thoughtful, refined by much acquaintance with grief.

Iphigenia he speaks of in his journals as his "daughter," and she is the daughter[3] whom a man will wish, even if he has chosen his wife from very mean motives. She is the virgin, steadfast soul, to whom falsehood is more dreadful than any other death.

But it is to Wilhelm Meister's Apprenticeship and Wandering Years that I would especially refer, as these volumes contain the sum of the Sage's observations during a long life, as to what man should do, under present circumstances, to obtain mastery over outward, through an initiation into inward life, and severe discipline of faculty.

As Wilhelm advances in the upward path he becomes acquainted with better forms of woman by knowing how to seek, and how to prize them when found. For the weak and immature man will, often, admire a superior woman, but he will not be able to abide by a feeling, which is too severe a tax on his habitual existence. But, with Wilhelm, the gradation is natural and expresses ascent in the scale of being. At first he finds charm in Mariana and Philina, very common forms of feminine character, not without redeeming traits, no less than charms, but without wisdom or purity. Soon he is attended by Mignon, the finest expression ever yet given to what I have called the lyrical element in woman. She is a child, but too full-grown for this man; he loves, but cannot follow her; yet is the association not without an enduring influence. Poesy has been domesticated in his life, and, though he strives to bind down her heavenward impulse, as art or apothegm, these are only the tents, beneath which he may sojourn for a while, but which may be easily struck, and carried on limitless wanderings.

Advancing into the region of thought, he encounters a wise philanthropy in Natalia, (instructed, let us observe, by an *uncle*,) practical judgment and the outward economy of life in Theresa, pure devotion in the Fair Saint.

Farther and last he comes to the house of Macaria, the soul of a star, *i.e.* a pure and perfected intelligence embodied in feminine form, and the centre of a world whose members revolve harmoniously round her. She instructs him in the archives of a rich human history, and introduces him to the contemplation of the heavens.

From the hours passed by the side of Mariana to these with Macaria, is a wide distance for human feet to traverse. Nor has Wilhelm travelled so far, seen and suffered so much in vain. He now begins to study how he may aid the next generation; he sees objects in harmonious arrangement, and from his observations deduces precepts by which to guide his course as a teacher and a master, "help-full, comfort-full."

In all these expressions of woman, the aim of Goethe is satisfactory to me. He aims at a pure self-subsistence, and free development of any powers with which they may be gifted by nature as much for them as for men. They are units, addressed as souls. Accordingly the meeting between man and woman, as represented by him, is equal and noble, and, if he does not depict marriage, he makes it possible.

In the Macaria, bound with the heavenly bodies in fixed revolutions, the centre of all relations, herself unrelated, he expresses the Minerva side of feminine nature. It was not by chance that Goethe gave her this name. Macaria, the daughter of Hercules, who offered herself as a victim for the good of her country, was canonized by the Greeks, and worshipped as the Goddess of true Felicity. Goethe has embodied this Felicity as the Serenity that arises from Wisdom, a Wisdom, such as the Jewish wise man venerated, alike instructed in the designs of heaven, and the methods necessary to carry them into effect upon earth.

Mignon is the electrical, inspired, lyrical nature. And wherever it appears we echo in our aspirations that of the child,

> "So let me seem until I be:—
> Take not the *white robe* away."
>
> *   *   *   *   *
>
> "Though I lived without care and toil,
> Yet felt I sharp pain enough,
> Make me again forever young."

All these women, though we see them in relations, we can think of as unrelated. They all are very individual, yet seem, nowhere, restrained. They satisfy for the present, yet arouse an infinite expectation.

The economist Theresa, the benevolent Natalia the fair Saint, have chosen a path, but their thoughts are not narrowed to it. The functions of life to them are not ends, but suggestions.

Thus, to them, all things are important, because none is necessary. Their different characters have fair play, and each is beautiful in its minute indications, for nothing is enforced or conventional, but every thing, however slight, grows from the essential life of the being.

Mignon and Theresa wear male attire when they like, and it is graceful for them to do so, while Macaria is confined to her arm-chair behind the green curtain, and the Fair Saint could not bear a speck of dust on her robe.

All things are in their places in this little world, because all is natural and free, just as "there is room for everything out of doors." Yet all is rounded in by natural harmony, which will always arise where Truth and Love are sought in the light of Freedom.

Goethe's book bodes an era of freedom like its own of "extraordinary generous seeking," and new revelations. New individualities shall be developed in the actual world, which shall advance upon it as gently as the figures come out upon his canvass.

I have indicated on this point the coincidence between his hopes and those of Fourier, though his are directed by an infinitely higher and deeper knowledge of human nature. But, for our present purpose, it is sufficient to show how surely these different paths have conducted to the same end two earnest thinkers. In some other place I wish to point out similar coincidences between Goethe's model school and the plans of Fourier, which may cast light upon the page of prophecy.

Notes

1 In worship at stated periods, in daily expression, whether by word or deed, the Quakers have placed woman on the same platform with man. Can any one assert that they have reason to repent this?

2 As Faust says, her only fault was a "Kindly delusion,"—"ein guter wahn."

3 Goethe was as false to his ideas in practice, as Lord Herbert. And his punishment was the just and usual one of connections formed beneath the standard of right, from the impulses of the baser self. Iphigenia was the worthy daughter of his mind, but the son, child of his degrading connection in actual life, corresponded with that connection. This son, on whom Goethe vainly lavished so much thought and care, was like his mother, and like Goethe's attachment for his mother, "This young man," says a late well informed writer, (M. Henri Blaze,) "Wieland, with good reason, called the son of the servant, *der Sohn der Magd*. He inherited from his father only his name and his *physique*."

37

Karl Marx

Theses on Feuerbach (1845)

I

The main deficiency, up to now, in all materialism – including that of Feuerbach – is that the external object, reality and sensibility are conceived only in the form of the object and of our contemplation of it, rather than as sensuous human activity and as practice – as something non-subjective. For this reason, the active aspect has been developed by idealism, in opposition to materialism, though only abstractly, since idealism naturally does not know real, sensuous activity as such. Feuerbach wants sensuous objects, clearly distinguished from mental objects, but he does not conceive human activity in terms of subject and object. That is why, in *The Essence of Christianity*, he regards only theoretical activity as authentically human, whilst practice is conceived and defined only in its dirty Jewish manifestation. He therefore does not understand the meaning of "revolutionary", of practical-critical activity.

II

The question whether objective truth can be attributed to human thinking is not a question of theory but a practical question. Man must prove in practice the truth – i.e. the reality and power, the worldliness – of his thinking. Isolated from practice, the controversy over the reality or unreality of thinking is a purely scholastic question.

III

The materialist doctrine that humans are products of circumstances and upbringing and that, therefore, men who change are products of new circumstances and a different upbringing, forgets that circumstances are changed by men themselves, and that it is essential to educate the educator. Necessarily, then, this doctrine divides society into two parts, one of which is placed above society (for example, in the work of Robert Owen).

The coincidence of changing circumstance on the one hand, and of human activity or self-changing on the other, can be conceived only as revolutionary practice, and rationally understood.

IV

Feuerbach starts out from the fact of religious self-alienation and the duplication of the world into an imagined religious world and a real world. His work consists in resolving the religious world into its secular basis. He overlooks that, once this work is completed, the central task remains to be done. But the fact that the secular basis detaches from itself and fixes in the clouds as an independent realm can be explained only by the self-negation and self-contradiction within it. This must be first of all understood in the context of its contradictions, and then be revolutionised by the removal of those contradictions. Thus, for instance, once the earthly family is discovered to be the secret of the holy family, the former must then be theoretically critiqued and practically overthrown.

V

Feuerbach, not satisfied with abstract thinking, appeals to sensory intuition; but he does not conceive the realm of the senses in terms of practical, human sensuous activity.

VI

Feuerbach resolves the religious essence into the human essence. But the human essence is not an abstraction inherent in each single individual. In its reality, it is the ensemble of social conditions.

Feuerbach, who does not undertake a criticism of this real essence, is therefore compelled:

1 To abstract from the historical process and to fix the religious sentiment as something by itself and to presuppose an abstract – isolated – human individual;

2 For this reason, he can consider the human essence only as a "genus", as an internal, mute generality which naturally unites the multiplicity of individuals.

VII

Feuerbach therefore does not see that "religious sentiment" is itself a social product, and that the abstract individual that he analyses belongs in reality to a particular social form.

VIII

Social life is essentially practical. All the mysteries which turn theory towards mysticism find their rational solution in human practice and in the understanding of this practice.

IX

The highest point reached by intuitive materialism – that is, materialism which does not comprehend the activity of the senses as practical activity – is the point-of-view of single individuals in "bourgeois society".

X

The standpoint of the old materialism is "bourgeois" society; the standpoint of the new is human society, or socialised mankind.

XI

Philosophers have only interpreted the world in different ways. What is crucial, however, is to change it.

38

Søren Kierkegaard

Concluding Unscientific Postscript to the Philosophical Fragments (1846)

Chapter I: The Task of Becoming Subjective

THE CONCLUSION THAT WOULD BE FORCED UPON ETHICS IF THE ATTAINMENT OF SUBJECTIVITY WERE NOT THE HIGHEST TASK CONFRONTING A HUMAN BEING—CONSIDERATIONS LEFT OUT OF ACCOUNT IN CONNECTION WITH THE CLOSER UNDERSTANDING OF THIS—EXAMPLES OF THINKING DIRECTED TOWARDS BECOMING SUBJECTIVE

OBJECTIVELY WE CONSIDER ONLY THE MATTER AT ISSUE, SUBJECTIVELY WE have regard to the subject and his subjectivity; and behold, precisely this subjectivity is the matter at issue. This must constantly be borne in mind, namely, that the subjective problem is not something about an objective issue, but is the subjectivity itself. For since the problem in question poses a decision, and since all decisiveness, as shown above, inheres in subjectivity, it is essential that every trace of an objective issue should be eliminated. If any such trace remains, it is at once a sign that the subject seeks to shirk something of the pain and crisis of the decision; that is, he seeks to make the problem to some degree objective. If the Introduction still awaits the appearance of another work before bringing the matter up for judgment, if the System still lacks a paragraph, if the speaker has still another argument up his sleeve, it follows that the decision is postponed. Hence we do not here raise the question of the truth of Christianity in the sense that when this has been determined, the subject is assumed ready and willing to accept it. No, the question is as to the mode of the subject's acceptance; and it must be regarded as an illusion rooted in the demoralization which remains ignorant of the subjective nature of the decision, or as an evasion springing from the disingenuousness which seeks to shirk the decision by an objective mode of approach, wherein there can in all eternity be no decision, to assume that the transition from something objective to the subjective acceptance is a direct transition, following upon the objective deliberation as a matter of course. On the contrary, the subjective acceptance is precisely the decisive factor; and an objective acceptance of Christianity (*sit venia verbo*) is paganism or thoughtlessness.

Christianity proposes to endow the individual with an eternal happiness, a good which is not distributed wholesale, but only to one individual at a time. Though Christianity assumes that there inheres in the subjectivity of the individual, as being the potentiality of the appropriation of this good, the possibility for its acceptance, it does not assume that the subjectivity is immediately ready for such acceptance, or even has, without further ado, a real conception of the significance of such a good. The development or transformation of the individual's subjectivity, its infinite concentration in itself over against the conception of an eternal happiness, that highest good of the infinite—this constitutes the developed potentiality of the primary potentiality which subjectivity as such presents. In this way Christianity protests every form of objectivity; it desires that the subject should be infinitely concerned about himself. It is subjectivity that Christianity is concerned with, and it is only in subjectivity that its truth exists, if it exists at all; objectively, Christianity has absolutely no existence. If its truth happens to be in only a single subject, it exists in him alone; and there is greater Christian joy in heaven over this one individual than over universal history and the System, which as objective entities are incommensurable for that which is Christian.

It is commonly assumed that no art or skill is required in order to be subjective. To be sure, every human being is a bit of a subject, in a sense. But now to strive to become what one already is: who would take the pains to waste his time on such a task, involving the greatest imaginable degree of resignation? Quite so. But for this very reason alone it is a very difficult task, the most difficult of all tasks in fact, precisely because every human being has a strong natural bent and passion to become something more and different. And so it is with all such apparently insignificant tasks, precisely their seeming insignificance makes them infinitely difficult. In such cases the task itself is not directly alluring, so as to support the aspiring individual; instead, it works against him, and it needs an infinite effort on his part merely to discover that his task lies here, that this is his task—an effort from which he is otherwise relieved. To think about the simple things of life, about what the plain man also knows after a fashion, is extremely forbidding; for the differential distinction attainable even through the utmost possible exertion is by no means obvious to the sensual man. No indeed, thinking about the high-falutin is very much more attractive and glorious.

When one overlooks this little distinction, humoristic from the Socratic standpoint and infinitely anxious from the Christian, between being something like a subject so called, and being a subject, or becoming one, or being what one is through having become what one is: then it becomes wisdom, the admired wisdom of our own age, that it is the task of the subject increasingly to divest himself of his subjectivity in order to become more and more objective. It is easy to see what this guidance understands by being a subject of a sort. It understands by it quite rightly the accidental, the angular, the selfish, the eccentric, and so forth, all of which every human being can have enough of. Nor does Christianity deny that such things should be gotten rid of; it has never been a friend of loutishness. But the difference is, that philosophy teaches that the way is to become objective, while Christianity teaches that the way is to become subjective, i.e. to become a subject in truth. Lest this should seem a mere dispute about words, let me say that Christianity wishes to intensify passion to its highest pitch; but passion is subjectivity, and does not exist objectively.

In a curiously indirect and satirical manner it is often enough inculcated, though men refuse to heed the instruction, that the guidance of philosophy in this matter is misguidance. While we are all subjects of a sort, and labor to become objective, in which endeavor many succeed bestially enough, Poesy goes about anxiously seeking its object. In spite of our all being subjects, Poesy must be content with a very sparing selection it can use; and yet it is precisely subjectivity that Poesy must have. Why then does it not take the very first that comes to hand, from among our estimable circle? Alas, he will not do; and if his only ambition is to become objective he will never do. This would seem to signify that there might after all be something quite special about being a subject. Why have a few become immortal as enthusiastic lovers, a few as high-minded heroes, and so forth, if all men in every generation are such as a matter of course, merely by virtue of being subjects in the immediate sense? And yet, being a lover, a hero, and so forth, is precisely a prerogative of subjectivity; for one does not become a hero or a lover objectively. And now the clergy! Why does the religious address repeatedly return to the revered remembrance of a select circle of devout men and women, why does the clergyman not take the very first that comes to hand from our esteemed circle, and make him our pattern: are we not all subjects of a sort? And yet, devoutness inheres in subjectivity, and no one ever becomes devout objectively.

Love is a determination of subjectivity, and yet real lovers are very rare. We do indeed say, about as when we speak of everyone being a subject of a sort: There went a pair of lovers, there goes another pair; last Sunday the banns were published for sixteen couples; there are in Storm Street a couple of lovers who cannot live peaceably together. But when Poesy explains love in terms of its own lofty and festive conception, the honored name which it brings forward to exemplify the ideal sometimes carries us several centuries back in time; while the speech of daily life makes us as humoristic as funeral sermons generally, according to which every moment sees the burial of a hero. Is this merely a *chicane* on the part of Poesy, which is otherwise a friendly power, seeking to console us by uplifting our spirits in the intuition of what is excellent? And what sort of excellence? Why, to be sure, the excellence of subjectivity. So then it would seem that there must be something distinguished about being subjective.

Faith is the highest passion in the sphere of human subjectivity. But take note merely of what the clergy say, concerning how rarely it is found in the community of believers. For this phrase, the community of believers, is used in about the same manner as being subjects of a sort. Now pause a moment, and do not be so ironical as to ask further how rare, perhaps, faith is among the clergy! But this complaint, is it merely a cunning device on the part of the clergy, who have consecrated their lives to the care of our souls, by uplifting us in the spirit of devotion, while the soul's longing goes out to the transfigured ones—but to which transfigured ones? Why, to be sure, to those who proved that they were possessed of faith. But faith inheres in subjectivity, and so there must after all be something distinguished about subjectivity.

The objective tendency, which proposes to make everyone an observer, and in its maximum to transform him into so objective an observer that he becomes almost a ghost, scarcely to be distinguished from the tremendous spirit of the historical past—this tendency naturally refuses to know or listen to anything except what stands in relation to itself. If one is so fortunate as to be of service within the given presupposition, by contributing one or another item of information concerning a tribe perhaps hitherto unknown, which is to be provided with a flag and given a place in the paragraph parade; if one is competent within the given presupposition to assign China a place different from the one it has hitherto occupied in the systematic procession,—in that case one is made welcome. But everything else is divinity-school prattle. For it is regarded as a settled thing, that the objective tendency in direction of intellectual contemplation, is, in the newer linguistic usage, the *ethical* answer to the question of what I *ethically* have to do; and the task assigned to the contemplative nineteenth century is world history. The objective tendency is the way and the truth; the ethical is, becoming an observer! That the individual must become an observer, is the *ethical* answer to the problem of life—or else one is compelled to assume that there is no ethical question at all, and in so far no ethical answer.

Let us here in all simplicity seek to bring clearly before our minds a little subjective doubt with respect to the tendency toward objectivity. Just as the *Fragments* called attention to an introductory consideration, which might suitably be reflected upon before proceeding to exhibit in the concrete the world-historic progress of the Idea, so I now propose to dwell a bit upon a little introductory consideration bearing upon the objective tendency. The question I would ask is this: *What conclusion would inevitably force itself upon Ethics, if the becoming a subject were not the highest task confronting a human being?* And to what conclusion would Ethics be forced? Aye, it would, of course, be driven to despair. But what does the System care about that? It is consistent enough not to include an Ethic in its systematic scheme.

The Idea of a universal history tends to a greater and greater systematic concentration of everything. A Sophist has said that he could carry the whole world in a nutshell, and this is what modern surveys of world history seem to realize: the survey becomes more and more compendious. It is not my intention to show how comical this is, but rather to try to make it clear, through the elaboration of several different thoughts all leading to the same end, what objection Ethics and the ethical have to raise against this entire order of things. For in our age it is not merely an individual scholar or thinker here and there who concerns himself with universal history; the whole age loudly demands it. Nevertheless, Ethics and the ethical, as constituting the essential anchorage for all individual existence, have an indefeasible claim upon every existing individual; so indefeasible a claim, that whatever a man may accomplish in the world, even to the most astonishing of achievements, it is none the less quite dubious in its significance, unless the individual has been ethically clear when he made his choice, has ethically clarified his choice to himself. The ethical quality is jealous for its own integrity, and is quite unimpressed by the most astounding quantity.

It is for this reason that Ethics looks upon all world-historical knowledge with a degree of suspicion, because it may so easily become a snare, a demoralizing aesthetic diversion for the knowing subject, in so far as the distinction between what does or does not have historical significance obeys a quantitative dialectic. As a consequence of this fact, the absolute ethical distinction between good and evil tends for the historical survey to be neutralized in the aesthetic-metaphysical determination of the great and significant, to which category the bad has equal admittance with the good. In the case of what has world-historic significance, another set of factors plays an essential rôle, factors which do not obey an ethical dialectic: accidents, circumstances, the play of forces entering into the historic totality that modifyingly incorporates the deed of the individual so as to transform it into something that does not directly belong to him. Neither by willing the good with all his strength, nor by satanic obduracy in willing what is evil, can a human being be assured of historical significance. Even in the case of misfortune the principle holds, that it is necessary to be fortunate in order that one's misfortune may obtain world-historical significance. How then does an individual acquire historical significance? By means of what from the ethical point of view is accidental. But Ethics regards as unethical the transition by which an individual renounces the ethical quality in order to try his fortune, longingly, wishingly, and so forth, in the quantitative and non-ethical.

Chapter II: The Subjective Truth, Inwardness; Truth is Subjectivity

WHETHER TRUTH IS DEFINED MORE EMPIRICALLY, AS THE CONFORMITY OF thought and being, or more idealistically, as the conformity of being with thought, it is, in either case, important carefully to note what is meant by being. And in formulating the answer to this question it is likewise important to take heed lest the knowing spirit be tricked into losing itself in the indeterminate, so that it fantastically becomes a something that no existing human being ever was or can be, a sort of phantom with which the individual occupies himself upon occasion, but without making it clear to himself in terms of dialectical intermediaries how he happens to get into this fantastic realm, what significance being there has for him, and whether the entire activity that goes on out there does not resolve itself into a tautology within a recklessly fantastic venture of thought.

If being, in the two indicated definitions, is understood as empirical being, truth is at once transformed into a *desideratum,* and everything must be understood in terms of becoming; for the empirical object is unfinished and the existing cognitive spirit is itself in process of becoming. Thus the truth becomes an approximation whose beginning cannot be posited absolutely, precisely because the conclusion is lacking, the effect of which is retroactive. Whenever a beginning is *made,* on the other hand, unless through being unaware of this the procedure stamps itself as arbitrary, such a beginning is not the consequence of an immanent movement of thought, but is effected through a resolution of the will, essentially in the strength of faith. That the knowing spirit is an existing individual spirit, and that every human being is such an entity existing for himself, is a truth I cannot too often repeat; for the fantastic neglect of this is responsible for much confusion. Let no one misunderstand me. I happen to be a poor existing spirit like all other men; but if there is any lawful and honest manner in which I could be helped into becoming something extraordinary, like the pure I-am-I[1] for example, I always stand ready gratefully to accept the gift and the benefaction. But if it can only be done in the manner indicated, by saying *ein zwei drei kokolorum,* or by tying a string around the little finger, and then when the moon is full, hiding it in some secret place—in that case I prefer to remain what I am, a poor existing human being.

The term "being," as used in the above definitions, must therefore be understood (from the systematic standpoint) much more abstractly, presumably as the abstract reflection of, or the abstract prototype for, what being is as concrete empirical being. When so understood there is nothing to prevent us from abstractly determining the truth as abstractly finished and complete; for the correspondence between thought and being is, from the abstract point of view, always finished. Only with the concrete does becoming enter in, and it is from the concrete that abstract thought abstracts.

But if being is understood in this manner, the formula becomes a tautology. Thought and being mean one and the same thing, and the correspondence spoken of is merely an abstract self-identity. Neither formula says anything more than that the truth is, so understood as to accentuate the copula: the truth *is,* i.e. the truth is a reduplication. Truth is the subject of the assertion, but the assertion that it is, is the same as the subject; for this being that the truth is said to have is never its own abstract form. In this manner we give expression to the fact that truth is not something simple, but is in a wholly abstract sense a reduplication, a reduplication which is nevertheless instantly revoked.

Abstract thought may continue as long as it likes to rewrite this thought in varying phraseology, it will never get any farther. As soon as the being which corresponds to the truth comes to be empirically concrete, the truth is put in process of becoming, and is again by way of anticipation the conformity of thought with being. This conformity is actually realized for God, but it is not realized for any existing spirit, who is himself existentially in process of becoming.

For an existing spirit *qua* existing spirit, the question of the truth will again exist. The abstract answer has significance only for the abstraction into which an existing spirit is transformed when he abstracts from himself *qua* existing individual. This can be done only momentarily, and even in such moments of abstraction the abstract thinker pays his debt to existence by existing in spite of all abstraction. It is therefore an existing spirit who is now conceived as raising the question of truth, presumably in order that he may exist in it; but in any case the question is raised by someone who is conscious of being a particular existing human being. In this way I believe I can render myself intelligible to every Greek, as well as to every reasonable human being. If a German philosopher wishes to indulge a passion for making himself over, and, just as alchemists and necromancers were wont to garb themselves fantastically, first makes himself over into a superrational something for the purpose of answering this question of the truth in an extremely satisfactory manner, the affair is no concern of mine; nor is his extremely satisfactory answer, which is no doubt very satisfactory indeed—when you are fantastically transformed. On the other hand, whether it is or is not the case that a German professor behaves in this manner, can be readily determined by anyone who will concentrate enthusiastically upon seeking guidance at the hands of such a sage, without criticism but seeking merely to assimilate the wisdom in a docile spirit by proposing to shape his own life in accordance with it. Precisely when thus enthusiastically attempting to learn from such a German professor, one would realize the most apt of epigrams upon him. For such a speculative philosopher could hardly be more embarrassed than by the sincere and enthusiastic zeal of a learner who proposes to express and to realize his wisdom by appropriating it existentially. For this wisdom is something that the Herr Professor has merely imagined, and written books about, but never himself tried. Aye, it has never even occurred to him that this should be done. Like the custom clerk who writes what he could not himself read, satisfied that his responsibilities ended with the writing, so there are speculative philosophers who write what, when it is to be read in the light of action, shows itself to be nonsense, unless it is, perhaps, intended only for fantastic beings.

In that the question of truth is thus raised by an existing spirit *qua* existing, the above abstract reduplication that is involved in it again confronts him. But existence itself, namely, existence as it is in the individual who raises the question and himself exists, keeps the two moments of thought and being apart, so that reflection presents him with two alternatives. For an objective reflection the truth becomes an object, something objective, and thought must be pointed away from the subject. For a subjective reflection the truth becomes a matter of appropriation, of inwardness, of subjectivity, and thought must probe more and more deeply into the subject and his subjectivity.

But then what? Shall we be compelled to remain in this disjunction, or may we not here accept the offer of benevolent assistance from the principle of mediation, so that the truth becomes an identity of subject and object?[2] Well, why not? But can the principle of mediation also help the existing individual while still remaining in existence himself to become the mediating principle, which is *sub specie aeterni,* whereas the poor existing individual is confined to the strait-jacket of existence? Surely it cannot do any good to mock a man, luring him on by dangling before his eyes the identity of subject and object, when his situation prevents him from making use of this identity, since he is in process of becoming in consequence of being an existing individual. How can it help to explain to a man how the eternal truth is to be understood eternally, when the supposed user of the explanation is prevented from so understanding it through being an existing individual, and merely becomes fantastic when he imagines himself to be *sub specie aeterni?* What such a man needs instead is precisely an explanation of how the eternal truth is to be understood in determinations of time by one who as existing is himself in time, which even the worshipful Herr Professor concedes, if not always, at least once a quarter when he draws his salary.

The identity of subject and object posited through an application of the principle of mediation merely carries us back to where we were before, to the abstract definition of the truth as an identity of thought and being; for to determine the truth as an identity of thought and object is precisely the same thing as saying that the truth *is,* i.e. that the truth is a reduplication. The lofty wisdom has thus again merely been absent-minded enough to forget that it was an existing spirit who asked about the truth. Or is the existing spirit himself the identity of subject and object, the subject-object? In that case I must press the question of where such an existing human being is, when he is thus at the same time also a subject-object? Or shall we perhaps here again first transform the existing spirit into something in general, and thereupon explain everything except the question asked, namely, how an existing subject is related to the truth *in concreto*; explain everything except the question that must in the next instance be asked, namely, how a particular existing spirit is related to this something in general, which seems to have not a little in common with a paper kite, or with the lump of sugar which the Dutch used to hang up under the loft for all to lick at.

So we return to the two ways of reflection; and we have not forgotten that it is an existing spirit who asks the question, a wholly individual human being. Nor can we forget that the fact that he exists is precisely what will make it impossible for him to proceed along both ways at once, while his earnest concern will prevent him from frivolously and fantastically becoming subject-object. Which of these two ways is now the way of truth for an existing spirit? For only the fantastic I-am-I is at once finished with both ways, or proceeds methodically along both ways simultaneously, a mode of ambulation which for an existing human is so inhuman that I dare not recommend it.

Since the inquirer stresses precisely the fact that he is an existing individual, then one of the above two ways which especially accentuates existence would seem to be especially worthy of commendation.

The way of objective reflection makes the subject accidental, and thereby transforms existence into something indifferent, something vanishing. Away from the subject the objective way of reflection leads to the objective truth, and while the subject and his subjectivity become indifferent, the truth also becomes indifferent, and this indifference is precisely its objective validity; for all interest, like all decisiveness, is rooted in subjectivity. The way of objective reflection leads to abstract thought, to mathematics, to historical knowledge of different kinds; and always it leads away from the subject, whose existence or non-existence, and from the objective point of view quite rightly, becomes infinitely indifferent. Quite rightly, since as Hamlet says, existence and non-existence have only subjective significance. At its maximum this way will arrive at a contradiction, and in so far as the subject does not become wholly indifferent to himself, this merely constitutes a sign that his objective striving is not objective enough. At its maximum this way will lead to the contradiction that only the objective has come into being, while the subjective has gone out; that is to say, the existing subjectivity has vanished, in that it has made an attempt to become what in the abstract sense is called subjectivity, the mere abstract form of an abstract objectivity. And yet, the objectivity which has thus come into being is, from the subjective point of view at the most, either an hypothesis or an approximation, because all eternal decisiveness is rooted in subjectivity. [. . .]

If an existing individual were really able to transcend himself, the truth would be for him something final and complete; but where is the point at which he is outside himself? The I-am-I is a mathematical point which does not exist, and in so far there is nothing to prevent everyone from occupying this standpoint; the one will not be in the way of the other. It is only momentarily that the particular individual is able to realize existentially a unity of the infinite and the finite which transcends existence. This unity is realized in the moment of passion. Modern philosophy has tried anything and everything in the effort to help the individual to transcend himself objectively, which is a wholly impossible feat; existence exercises its restraining influence, and if philosophers nowadays had not become mere scribblers in the service of a fantastic thinking and its preoccupation, they would long ago have perceived that suicide was the only tolerable practical interpretation of its striving. But the scribbling modern philosophy holds passion in contempt; and yet passion is the culmination of existence for an existing individual—and we are all of us existing individuals. In passion the existing subject is rendered infinite in the eternity of the imaginative representation, and yet he is at the same time most definitely himself. The fantastic I-am-I is not an identity of the infinite and the finite, since neither the one nor the other is real; it is a fantastic rendezvous in the clouds,[5] an unfruitful embrace, and the relationship of the individual self to this mirage is never indicated.

All essential knowledge relates to existence, or only such knowledge as has an essential relationship to existence is essential knowledge. All knowledge which does not inwardly relate itself to existence, in the reflection of inwardness, is, essentially viewed, accidental knowledge; its degree and scope is essentially indifferent. That essential knowledge is essentially related to existence does not mean the above-mentioned identity which abstract thought postulates between thought and being; nor does it signify, objectively, that knowledge corresponds to something existent as its object. But it means that knowledge has a relationship to the knower, who is essentially an existing individual, and that for this reason all essential knowledge is essentially related to existence. Only ethical and ethico-religious knowledge has an essential relationship to the existence of the knower.

Mediation is a mirage, like the I-am-I. From the abstract point of view everything is and nothing comes into being. Mediation can therefore have no place in abstract thought, because it presupposes *movement*. Objective knowledge may indeed have the existent for its object; but since the knowing subject is an existing individual, and through the fact of his existence in process of becoming, philosophy must first explain how a particular existing subject is related to a knowledge of mediation. It must explain what he is in such a moment, if not pretty nearly *distrait*; where he is, if not in the moon? There is constant talk of mediation and mediation; is mediation then a man, as Peter Deacon[6] believes that *Imprimatur* is a man? How does a human being manage to become something of this kind? Is this dignity, this great *philosophicum*, the fruit of study, or does the magistrate give it away, like the office of deacon or grave-digger? Try merely to enter into these and other such plain questions of a plain man, who would gladly become mediation if it could be done in some lawful and honest manner, and not either by saying *ein zwei drei kokolorum*, or by forgetting that he is himself an existing human being, for whom existence is therefore something essential, and an ethico-religious existence a suitable *quantum satis*. A speculative philosopher may perhaps find it in bad taste to ask such questions. But it is important not to direct the polemic to the wrong point, and hence not to begin in a fantastic objective manner to discuss *pro* and *contra* whether there is a mediation or not, but to hold fast what it means to be a human being. [. . .]

When subjectivity is the truth, the conceptual determination of the truth must include an expression for the antithesis to objectivity, a memento of the fork in the road where the way swings off; this expression will at the same time serve as an indication of the tension of the subjective inwardness. Here is such a definition of truth: *An objective uncertainty held fast in an appropriation-process of the most passionate inwardness is the truth*, the highest truth attainable for an *existing* individual. At the point where the way swings off (and where this is cannot be specified objectively, since it is a matter of subjectivity), there objective knowledge is placed in abeyance. Thus the subject merely has, objectively, the uncertainty; but it is this which precisely increases the tension of that infinite passion which constitutes his inwardness. The truth is precisely the venture which chooses an objective uncertainty with the passion of the infinite. I contemplate the order of nature in the hope of finding God, and I see omnipotence and wisdom; but I also see much else that disturbs my mind and excites anxiety. The sum of all this is an objective uncertainty. But it is for this very reason that the inwardness becomes as intense as it is, for it embraces this objective uncertainty with the entire passion of the infinite. In the case of a mathematical proposition the objectivity is given, but for this reason the truth of such a proposition is also an indifferent truth.

But the above definition of truth is an equivalent expression for faith. Without risk there is no faith. Faith is precisely the contradiction between the infinite passion of the individual's inwardness and the objective uncertainty. If I am capable of grasping God objectively, I do not believe, but precisely because I cannot do this I must believe. If I wish to preserve myself in faith I must constantly be intent upon holding fast the objective uncertainty, so as to remain out upon the deep, over seventy thousand fathoms of water, still preserving my faith.

In the principle that subjectivity, inwardness, is the truth, there is comprehended the Socratic wisdom, whose everlasting merit it was to have become aware of the essential significance of existence, of the fact that the knower is an existing individual. For this reason Socrates was in the truth by virtue of his ignorance, in the highest sense in which this was possible within paganism. To attain to an understanding of this, to comprehend that the misfortune of speculative philosophy is again and again to have forgotten that the knower is an existing individual, is in our objective age difficult enough. [. . .]

When subjectivity, inwardness, is the truth, the truth becomes objectively a paradox; and the fact that the truth is objectively a paradox shows in its turn that subjectivity is the truth. For the objective situation is repellent; and the expression for the objective repulsion constitutes the tension and the measure of the corresponding inwardness. The paradoxical character of the truth is its objective uncertainty; this uncertainty is an expression for the passionate inwardness, and this passion is precisely the truth. So far the Socratic principle. The eternal and essential truth, the truth which has an essential relationship to an existing individual because it pertains essentially to existence (all other knowledge being from the Socratic point of view accidental, its scope and degree a matter of indifference), is a paradox. But the eternal essential truth is by no means in itself a paradox; but it becomes paradoxical by virtue of its relationship to an existing individual. The Socratic ignorance gives expression to the objective uncertainty attaching to the truth, while his inwardness in existing is the truth. To anticipate here what will be developed later, let me make the following remark. The Socratic ignorance is an analogue to the category of the absurd, only that there is still less of objective certainty in the absurd, and in the repellent effect that the absurd exercises.

39

Herman Melville

Moby-Dick; or, The Whale (1851)

The Mast-Head

IT WAS DURING THE MORE PLEASANT WEATHER, THAT IN DUE rotation with the other seamen my first mast-head came round.

In most American whalemen the mast-heads are manned almost simultaneously with the vessel's leaving her port; even though she may have fifteen thousand miles, and more, to sail ere reaching her proper cruising ground. And if, after a three, four, or five years' voyage she is drawing nigh home with anything empty in her—say, an empty vial even—then, her mast-heads are kept manned to the last; and not till her skysail-poles sail in among the spires of the port, does she altogether relinquish the hope of capturing one whale more.

Now, as the business of standing mast-heads, ashore or afloat, is a very ancient and interesting one, let us in some measure expatiate here. I take it, that the earliest standers of mast-heads were the old Egyptians; because, in all my researches, I find none prior to them. For though their progenitors, the builders of Babel, must doubtless, by their tower, have intended to rear the loftiest mast-head in all Asia, or Africa either; yet (ere the final truck was put to it) as that great stone mast of theirs may be said to have gone by the board, in the dread gale of God's wrath; therefore, we cannot give these Babel builders priority over the Egyptians. And that the Egyptians were a nation of mast-head standers, is an assertion based upon the general belief among archæologists, that the first pyramids were founded for astronomical purposes: a theory singularly supported by the peculiar stair-like formation of all four sides of those edifices; whereby, with prodigious long upliftings of their legs, those old astronomers were wont to mount to the apex, and sing out for new stars; even as the lookouts of a modern ship sing out for a sail, or a whale just bearing in sight. In Saint Stylites, the famous Christian hermit of old times, who built him a lofty stone pillar in the desert and spent the whole latter portion of his life on its summit, hoisting his food from the ground with a tackle; in him we have a remarkable instance of a dauntless stander-of-mast-heads; who was not to be driven from his place by fogs or frosts, rain, hail, or sleet; but valiantly facing everything out to the last, literally died at his post. Of modern standers-of-mast-heads we have but a lifeless set; mere stone, iron, and bronze men; who, though well capable of facing out a stiff gale, are still entirely incompetent to the business of singing out upon discovering any strange sight. There is Napoleon; who, upon the top of the column of Vendome, stands with arms folded, some one hundred and fifty feet in the air; careless, now, who rules the decks below; whether Louis Philippe, Louis Blanc, or Louis the Devil. Great Washington, too, stands high aloft on his towering main-mast in Baltimore, and like one of Hercules' pillars, his column marks that point of human grandeur beyond which few mortals will go. Admiral Nelson, also, on a capstan of gunmetal, stands his mast-head in Trafalgar Square; and even when most obscured by that London smoke, token is yet given that a hidden hero is there; for where there is smoke, must be fire. But neither great Washington, nor Napoleon, nor Nelson, will answer a single hail from below, however madly invoked to befriend by their counsels the distracted decks upon which they gaze; however, it may be surmised, that their spirits penetrate through the thick haze of the future, and descry what shoals and what rocks must be shunned.

It may seem unwarrantable to couple in any respect the mast-head standers of the land with those of the sea; but that in truth it is not so, is plainly evinced by an item for which Obed Macy, the sole historian of Nantucket, stands accountable. The worthy Obed tells us, that in the early times of the whale fishery, ere ships were regularly launched in pursuit of the game, the people of that island erected lofty spars along the sea-coast, to which the look-outs ascended by means of nailed cleats, something as fowls go upstairs in a hen-house. A few years ago this same plan was adopted by the Bay whalemen of New Zealand, who, upon descrying the game, gave notice to the ready-manned boats nigh the beach. But this custom has now become obsolete; turn we then to the one proper mast-head, that of a whale-ship at sea. The three mast-heads are kept manned from sun-rise to sun-set; the seamen taking their regular turns (as at the helm), and relieving each other every two hours. In the serene weather of the tropics it is exceedingly pleasant—the mast-head; nay, to a dreamy meditative man it is delightful. There you stand, a hundred feet above the silent decks, striding along the deep, as if the masts were gigantic stilts, while beneath you and between your legs, as it were, swim the hugest monsters of the sea, even as ships once sailed between the boots of the famous Colossus at old Rhodes. There you stand, lost in the infinite series of the sea, with nothing ruffled but the waves. The tranced ship indolently rolls; the drowsy trade winds blow; everything resolves you into languor. For the most part, in this tropic whaling life, a sublime uneventfulness invests you; you hear no news; read no gazettes; extras with startling accounts of commonplaces never delude you into unnecessary excitements; you hear of no domestic afflictions; bankrupt securities; fall of stocks; are never troubled with the thought of what you shall have for dinner—for all your meals for three years and more are snugly stowed in casks, and your bill of fare is immutable.

In one of those southern whalemen, on a long three or four years' voyage, as often happens, the sum of the various hours you spend at the mast-head would amount to several entire months. And it is much to be deplored that the place to which you devote so considerable a portion of the whole term of your natural life, should be so sadly destitute of anything approaching to a cosy inhabitiveness, or adapted to breed a comfortable localness of feeling, such as pertains to a bed, a hammock, a hearse, a sentry box, a pulpit, a coach, or any other of those small and snug contrivances in which men temporarily isolate themselves. Your most usual point of perch is the head of the t' gallant-mast, where you stand upon two thin parallel sticks (almost peculiar to whalemen) called the t' gallant cross-trees. Here, tossed about by the sea, the beginner feels about as cosy as he would standing on a bull's horns. To be sure, in coolish weather you may carry your house aloft with you, in the shape of a watch-coat; but properly speaking the thickest watch-coat is no more of a house than the unclad body; for as the soul is glued inside of its fleshly tabernacle, and cannot freely move about in it, nor even move out of it, without running great risk of perishing (like an ignorant pilgrim crossing the snowy Alps in winter); so a watch-coat is not so much of a house as it is a mere envelope, or additional skin encasing you. You cannot put a shelf or chest of drawers in your body, and no more can you make a convenient closet of your watch-coat.

Concerning all this, it is much to be deplored that the mast-heads of a southern whale ship are unprovided with those enviable little tents or pulpits, called *crow's-nests,* in which the look-outs of a Greenland whaler are protected from the inclement weather of the frozen seas. In the fire-side narrative of Captain Sleet, entitled "A Voyage among the Icebergs, in quest of the Greenland Whale, and incidentally for the re-discovery of the Lost Icelandic Colonies of Old Greenland;" in this admirable volume, all standers of mast-heads are furnished with a charmingly circumstantial account of the then recently invented *crow's-nest* of the Glacier, which was the name of Captain Sleet's good craft. He called it the *Sleet's crow's-nest,* in honor of himself; he being the original inventor and patentee, and free from all ridiculous false delicacy, and holding that if we call our own children after our own names (we fathers being the original inventors and patentees), so likewise should we denominate after ourselves any other apparatus we may beget. In shape, the Sleet's crow's-nest is something like a large tierce or pipe; it is open above, however, where it is furnished with a movable side-screen to keep to windward of your head in a hard gale. Being fixed on the summit of the mast, you ascend into it through a little trap-hatch in the bottom. On the after side, or side next the stern of the ship, is a comfortable seat, with a locker underneath for umbrellas, comforters, and coats. In front is a leather rack, in which to keep your speaking trumpet, pipe, telescope, and other nautical conveniences. When Captain Sleet in person stood his mast-head in this crow's nest of his, he tells us that he always had a rifle with him (also fixed in the rack), together with a powder flask and shot, for the purpose of popping off the stray narwhales, or vagrant sea unicorns infesting those waters; for you cannot successfully shoot at them from the deck owing to the resistance of the water, but to shoot down upon them is a very different thing. Now, it was plainly a labor of love for Captain Sleet to describe, as he does, all the little detailed conveniences of his crow's-nest; but though he so enlarges upon many of these, and though he treats us to a very scientific account of his experiments in this crow's-nest, with a small compass he kept there for the purpose of counteracting the errors resulting from what is called the "local attraction" of all binnacle magnets; an error ascribable to the horizontal vicinity of the iron in the ship's planks, and in the Glacier's case, perhaps, to there having been so many broken-down blacksmiths among her crew; I say, that though the Captain is very discreet and scientific here, yet, for all his learned "binnacle deviations," "azimuth compass observations," and "approximate errors," he knows very well, Captain Sleet, that he was not so much immersed in those profound magnetic meditations, as to fail being attracted occasionally towards that well replenished little case-bottle, so nicely tucked in on one side of his crow's nest, within easy reach of his hand. Though, upon the whole, I greatly admire and even love the brave, the honest, and learned Captain; yet I take it very ill of him that he should so utterly ignore that case-bottle, seeing what a faithful friend and comforter it must have been, while with mittened fingers and hooded head he was studying the mathematics aloft there in that bird's nest within three or four perches of the pole.

But if we Southern whale-fishers are not so snugly housed aloft as Captain Sleet and his Greenland-men were; yet that disadvantage is greatly counterbalanced by the widely contrasting serenity of those seductive seas in which we Southern fishers mostly float. For one, I used to lounge up the rigging very leisurely, resting in the top to have a chat with Queequeg, or any one else off duty whom I might find there; then ascending a little way further, and throwing a lazy leg over the top-sail yard, take a preliminary view of the watery pastures, and so at last mount to my ultimate destination.

Let me make a clean breast of it here, and frankly admit that I kept but sorry guard. With the problem of the universe revolving in me, how could I—being left completely to myself at such a thought-engendering altitude,—how could I but lightly hold my obligations to observe all whale-ships' standing orders, "Keep your weather eye open, and sing out every time."

And let me in this place movingly admonish you, ye ship-owners of Nantucket! Beware of enlisting in your vigilant fisheries any lad with lean brow and hollow eye; given to unseasonable meditativeness; and who offers to ship with the Phædon instead of Bowditch in his head. Beware of such an one, I say: your whales must be seen before they can be killed; and this sunken-eyed young Platonist will tow you ten wakes round the world, and never make you one pint of sperm the richer. Nor are these monitions at all unneeded. For nowadays, the whale-fishery furnishes an asylum for many romantic, melancholy, and absent-minded young men, disgusted with the carking cares of earth, and seeking sentiment in tar and blubber. Childe Harold not unfrequently perches himself upon the mast-head of some luckless disappointed whale-ship, and in moody phrase ejaculates:—

"Roll on, thou deep and dark blue ocean, roll!
Ten thousand blubber-hunters sweep over thee in vain."

Very often do the captains of such ships take those absent-minded young philosophers to task, upbraiding them with not feeling sufficient "interest" in the voyage; half-hinting that they are so hopelessly lost to all honorable ambition, as that in their secret souls they would rather not see whales than otherwise. But all in vain; those young Platonists have a notion that their vision is imperfect; they are short-sighted; what use, then, to strain the visual nerve? They have left their opera-glasses at home.

"Why, thou monkey," said a harpooneer to one of these lads, "we've been cruising now hard upon three years, and thou hast not raised a whale yet. Whales are scarce as hen's teeth whenever thou art up here." Perhaps they were; or perhaps there might have been shoals of them in the far horizon; but lulled into such an opium-like listlessness of vacant, unconscious reverie is this absent-minded youth by the blending cadence of waves with thoughts, that at last he loses his identity; takes the mystic ocean at his feet for the visible image of that deep, blue, bottomless soul, pervading mankind and nature; and every strange, half-seen, gliding, beautiful thing that eludes him; every dimly-discovered, uprising fin of some undiscernible form, seems to him the embodiment of those elusive thoughts that only people the soul by continually flitting through it. In this enchanted mood, thy spirit ebbs away to whence it came; becomes diffused through time and space; like Wickliff's sprinkled Pantheistic ashes, forming at last a part of every shore the round globe over.

There is no life in thee, now, except that rocking life imparted by a gently rolling ship; by her, borrowed from the sea; by the sea, from the inscrutable tides of God. But while this sleep, this dream is on ye, move your foot or hand an inch, slip your hold at all; and your identity comes back in horror. Over Descartian vortices you hover. And perhaps, at midday, in the fairest weather, with one half-throttled shriek you drop through that transparent air into the summer sea, no more to rise for ever. Heed it well, ye Pantheists!

The Whiteness of the Whale

WHAT THE WHITE WHALE WAS TO AHAB, HAS BEEN HINTED; what, at times, he was to me, as yet remains unsaid.

Aside from those more obvious considerations touching Moby Dick, which could not but occasionally awaken in any man's soul some alarm, there was another thought, or rather vague, nameless horror concerning him, which at times by its intensity completely overpowered all the rest; and yet so mystical and well nigh ineffable was it, that I almost despair of putting it in a comprehensible form. It was the whiteness of the whale that above all things appalled me. But how can I hope to explain myself here; and yet, in some dim, random way, explain myself I must, else all these chapters might be naught.

Though in many natural objects, whiteness refiningly enhances beauty, as if imparting some special virtue of its own, as in marbles, japonicas, and pearls; and though various nations have in some way recognised a certain royal pre-eminence in this hue; even the barbaric, grand old kings of Pegu placing the title "Lord of the White Elephants" above all their other magniloquent ascriptions of dominion; and the modern kings of Siam unfurling the same snow-white quadruped in the royal standard; and the Hanoverian flag bearing the one figure of a snow-white charger; and the great Austrian Empire, Caesarian heir to overlording Rome, having for the imperial color the same imperial hue; and though this pre-eminence in it applies to the human race itself, giving the white man ideal mastership over every dusky tribe; and though, besides all this, whiteness has been even made significant of gladness, for among the Romans a white stone marked a joyful day; and though in other mortal sympathies and symbolizings, this same hue is made the emblem of many touching, noble things—the innocence of brides, the benignity of age; though among the Red Men of America the giving of the white belt of wampum was the deepest pledge of honor; though in many climes, whiteness typifies the majesty of Justice in the ermine of the Judge, and contributes to the daily state of kings and queens drawn by milk-white steeds; though even in the higher mysteries of the most august religions it has been made the symbol of the divine spotlessness and power; by the Persian fire worshippers, the white forked flame being held the holiest on the altar; and in the Greek mythologies, Great Jove himself being made incarnate in a snow-white bull; and though to the noble Iroquois, the midwinter sacrifice of the sacred White Dog was by far the holiest festival of their theology, that spotless, faithful creature being held the purest envoy they could send to the Great Spirit with the annual tidings of their own fidelity; and though directly from the Latin word for white, all Christian priests derive the name of one part of their sacred vesture, the alb or tunic, worn beneath the cassock; and though among the holy pomps of the Romish faith, white is specially employed in the celebration of the Passion of our Lord; though in the Vision of St. John, white robes are given to the redeemed, and the four-and-twenty elders stand clothed in white before the great white throne, and the Holy One that sitteth there white like wool; yet for all these accumulated associations, with whatever is sweet, and honorable, and sublime, there yet lurks an elusive something in the innermost idea of this hue, which strikes more of panic to the soul than that redness which affrights in blood.

This elusive quality it is, which causes the thought of whiteness, when divorced from more kindly associations, and coupled with any object terrible in itself, to heighten that terror to the furthest bounds. Witness the white bear of the poles, and the white shark of the tropics; what but their smooth, flaky whiteness makes them the transcendent horrors they are? That ghastly whiteness it is which imparts such an abhorrent mildness, even more loathsome than terrific, to the dumb gloating of their aspect. So that not the fierce-fanged tiger in his heraldic coat can so stagger courage as the white-shrouded bear or shark.

Bethink thee of the albatross: whence come those clouds of spiritual wonderment and pale dread in which that white phantom sails in all imaginations? Not Coleridge first threw that spell; but God's great, unflattering laureate, Nature.

Most famous in our Western annals and Indian traditions is that of the White Steed of the Prairies: a magnificent milk-white charger, large-eyed, small-headed, bluff-chested, and with the dignity of a thousand monarchs in his lofty, overscorning carriage. He was the elected Xerxes of vast herds of wild horses, whose pastures in those days were only fenced by the Rocky Mountains and the Alleghanies. At their flaming head he westward trooped it like that chosen star which every evening leads on the hosts of light. The flashing cascade of his mane, the curving comet of his tail, invested him with housings more resplendent than gold and silver-beaters could have furnished him. A most imperial and archangelical apparition of that unfallen, western world, which to the eyes of the old trappers and hunters revived the glories of those primeval times when Adam walked majestic as a god, bluff-bowed and fearless as this mighty steed. Whether marching amid his aides and marshals in the van of countless cohorts that endlessly streamed it over the plains, like an Ohio; or whether with his circumambient subjects browsing all around at the horizon, the White Steed gallopingly reviewed them with warm nostrils reddening through his cool milkiness; in whatever aspect he presented himself, always to the bravest Indians he was the object of trembling reverence and awe. Nor can it be questioned from what stands on legendary record of this noble horse, that it was his spiritual whiteness chiefly, which so clothed him with divineness; and that this divineness had that in it which, though commanding worship, at the same time enforced a certain nameless terror.

But there are other instances where this whiteness loses all that accessory and strange glory which invests it in the White Steed and Albatross.

What is it that in the Albino man so peculiarly repels and often shocks the eye, as that sometimes he is loathed by his own kith and kin? It is that whiteness which invests him, a thing expressed by the name he bears. The Albino is as well made as other men—has no substantive deformity—and yet this mere aspect of all-pervading whiteness makes him more strangely hideous than the ugliest abortion. Why should this be so?

Nor, in quite other aspects, does Nature in her least palpable but not the less malicious agencies, fail to enlist among her forces this crowning attribute of the terrible. From its snowy aspect, the gauntleted ghost of the Southern Seas has been denominated the White Squall. Nor, in some historic instances, has the art of human malice omitted so potent an auxiliary. How wildly it heightens the effect of that passage in Froissart, when, masked in the snowy symbol of their faction, the desperate White Hoods of Ghent murder their bailiff in the market-place!

Nor, in some things, does the common, hereditary experience of all mankind fail to bear witness to the supernaturalism of this hue. It cannot well be doubted, that the one visible quality in the aspect of the dead which most appals the gazer, is the marble pallor lingering there; as if indeed that pallor were as much the badge of consternation in the other world, as of mortal trepidation here. And from that pallor of the dead, we borrow the expressive hue of the shroud in which we wrap them. Nor even in our superstitions do we fail to throw the same snowy mantle round our phantoms; all ghosts rising in a milk-white fog—Yea, while these terrors seize us, let us add, that even the king of terrors, when personified by the evangelist, rides on his pallid horse.

Therefore, in his other moods, symbolize whatever grand or gracious thing he will by whiteness, no man can deny that in its profoundest idealized significance it calls up a peculiar apparition to the soul.

But though without dissent this point be fixed, how is mortal man to account for it? To analyse it, would seem impossible. Can we, then, by the citation of some of those instances wherein this thing of whiteness—though for the time either wholly or in great part stripped of all direct associations calculated to impart to it aught fearful, but, nevertheless, is found to exert over us the same sorcery, however modified;—can we thus hope to light upon some chance clue to conduct us to the hidden cause we seek?

Let us try. But in a matter like this, subtlety appeals to subtlety, and without imagination no man can follow another into these halls. And though, doubtless, some at least of the imaginative impressions about to be presented may have been shared by most men, yet few perhaps were entirely conscious of them at the time, and therefore may not be able to recall them now.

Why to the man of untutored ideality, who happens to be but loosely acquainted with the peculiar character of the day, does the bare mention of Whitsuntide marshal in the fancy such long, dreary, speechless processions of slow-pacing pilgrims, down-cast and hooded with new-fallen snow? Or, to the unread, unsophisticated Protestant of the Middle American States, why does the passing mention of a White Friar or a White Nun, evoke such an eyeless statue in the soul?

Or what is there apart from the traditions of dungeoned warriors and kings (which will not wholly account for it) that makes the White Tower of London tell so much more strongly on the imagination of an untravelled American, than those other storied structures, its neighbors—the Byward Tower, or even the Bloody? And those sublimer towers, the White Mountains of New Hampshire, whence, in peculiar moods, comes that gigantic ghostliness over the soul at the bare mention of that name, while the thought of Virginia's Blue Ridge is full of a soft, dewy, distant dreaminess? Or why, irrespective of all latitudes and longitudes, does the name of the White Sea exert such a spectralness over the fancy, while that of the Yellow Sea lulls us with mortal thoughts of long lacquered mild afternoons on the waves, followed by the gaudiest and yet sleepiest of sunsets? Or, to choose a wholly unsubstantial instance, purely addressed to the fancy, why, in reading the old fairy tales of Central Europe, does "the tall pale man" of the Hartz forests, whose changeless pallor unrustlingly glides through the green of the groves—why is this phantom more terrible than all the whooping imps of the Blocksburg?

Nor is it, altogether, the remembrance of her cathedral-toppling earthquakes; nor the stampedoes of her frantic seas; nor the tearlessness of arid skies that never rain; nor the sight of her wide field of leaning spires, wrenched cope-stones, and crosses all adroop (like canted yards of anchored fleets); and her suburban avenues of house-walls lying over upon each other, as a tossed pack of cards;—it is not these things alone which make tearless Lima, the strangest, saddest city thou can'st see. For Lima has taken the white veil; and there is a higher horror in this whiteness of her woe. Old as Pizarro, this whiteness keeps her ruins for ever new; admits not the cheerful greenness of complete decay; spreads over her broken ramparts the rigid pallor of an apoplexy that fixes its own distortions.

I know that, to the common apprehension, this phenomenon of whiteness is not confessed to be the prime agent in exaggerating the terror of objects otherwise terrible; nor to the unimaginative mind is there aught of terror in those appearances whose awfulness to another mind almost solely consists in this one phenomenon, especially when exhibited under any form at all approaching to muteness or universality. What I mean by these two statements may perhaps be respectively elucidated by the following examples.

First: The mariner, when drawing nigh the coasts of foreign lands, if by night he hear the roar of breakers, starts to vigilance, and feels just enough of trepidation to sharpen all his faculties; but under precisely similar circumstances, let him be called from his hammock to view his ship sailing through a midnight sea of milky whiteness—as if from encircling headlands shoals of combed white bears were swimming round him, then he feels a silent, superstitious dread; the shrouded phantom of the whitened waters is horrible to him as a real ghost; in vain the lead assures him he is still off soundings; heart and helm they both go down; he never rests till blue water is under him again. Yet where is the mariner who will tell thee, "Sir, it was not so much the fear of striking hidden rocks, as the fear of that hideous whiteness that so stirred me?"

Second: To the native Indian of Peru, the continual sight of the snow-howdahed Andes conveys naught of dread, except, perhaps, in the mere fancying of the eternal frosted desolateness reigning at such vast altitudes, and the natural conceit of what a fearfulness it would be to lose oneself in such inhuman solitudes. Much the same is it with the back-woodsman of the West, who with comparative indifference views an unbounded prairie sheeted with driven snow, no shadow of tree or twig to break the fixed trance of whiteness. Not so the sailor, beholding the scenery of the Antarctic seas; where at times, by some infernal trick of legerdemain in the powers of frost and air, he, shivering and half shipwrecked, instead of rainbows speaking hope and solace to his misery, views what seems a boundless church-yard grinning upon him with its lean ice monuments and splintered crosses.

But thou sayest, methinks this white-lead chapter about whiteness is but a white flag hung out from a craven soul; thou surrenderest to a hypo, Ishmael.

Tell me, why this strong young colt, foaled in some peaceful valley of Vermont, far removed from all beasts of prey—why is it that upon the sunniest day, if you but shake a fresh buffalo robe behind him, so that he cannot even see it, but only smells its wild animal muskiness—why will he start, snort, and with bursting eyes paw the ground in phrensies of affright? There is no remembrance in him of any gorings of wild creatures in his green northern home, so that the strange muskiness he smells cannot recall to him anything associated with the experience of former perils; for what knows he, this New England colt, of the black bisons of distant Oregon?

No: but here thou beholdest even in a dumb brute, the instinct of the knowledge of the demonism in the world. Though thousands of miles from Oregon, still when he smells that savage musk, the rending, goring bison herds are as present as to the deserted wild foal of the prairies, which this instant they may be trampling into dust.

Thus, then, the muffled rollings of a milky sea; the bleak rustlings of the festooned frosts of mountains; the desolate shiftings of the windrowed snows of prairies; all these, to Ishmael, are as the shaking of that buffalo robe to the frightened colt!

Though neither knows where lie the nameless things of which the mystic sign gives forth such hints; yet with me, as with the colt, somewhere those things must exist. Though in many of its aspects this visible world seems formed in love, the invisible spheres were formed in fright.

But not yet have we solved the incantation of this whiteness, and learned why it appeals with such power to the soul; and more strange and far more portentous—why, as we have seen, it is at once the most meaning symbol of spiritual things, nay, the very veil of the Christian's Deity; and yet should be as it is, the intensifying agent in things the most appalling to mankind.

Is it that by its indefiniteness it shadows forth the heartless voids and immensities of the universe, and thus stabs us from behind with the thought of annihilation, when beholding the white depths of the milky way? Or is it, that as in essence whiteness is not so much a color as the visible absence of color, and at the same time the concrete of all colors; is it for these reasons that there is such a dumb blankness, full of meaning, in a wide landscape of snows—a colorless, all-color of atheism from which we shrink? And when we consider that other theory of the natural philosophers, that all other earthly hues—every stately or lovely emblazoning—the sweet tinges of sunset skies and woods; yea, and the gilded velvets of butterflies, and the butterfly cheeks of young girls; all these are but subtile deceits, not actually inherent in substances, but only laid on from without; so that all deified Nature absolutely paints like the harlot, whose allurements cover nothing but the charnel-house within; and when we proceed further, and consider that the mystical cosmetic which produces every one of her hues, the great principle of light, for ever remains white or colorless in itself, and if operating without medium upon matter, would touch all objects, even tulips and roses, with its own blank tinge—pondering all this, the palsied universe lies before us a leper; and like wilful travellers in Lapland, who refuse to wear colored and coloring glasses upon their eyes, so the wretched infidel gazes himself blind at the monumental white shroud that wraps all the prospect around him. And of all these things the Albino whale was the symbol. Wonder ye then at the fiery hunt?

40

Henry David Thoreau

Walden; or, Life in the Woods (1854)

Higher Laws

AS I CAME HOME THROUGH THE WOODS WITH MY STRING of fish, trailing my pole, it being now quite dark, I caught a glimpse of a woodchuck stealing across my path, and felt a strange thrill of savage delight, and was strongly tempted to seize and devour him raw; not that I was hungry then, except for that wildness which he represented. Once or twice, however, while I lived at the pond, I found myself ranging the woods, like a half-starved hound, with a strange abandonment, seeking some kind of venison which I might devour, and no morsel could have been too savage for me. The wildest scenes had become unaccountably familiar. I found in myself, and still find, an instinct toward a higher, or, as it is named, spiritual life, as do most men, and another toward a primitive rank and savage one, and I reverence them both. I love the wild not less than the good. The wildness and adventure that are in fishing still recommended it to me. I like sometimes to take rank hold on life and spend my day more as the animals do. Perhaps I have owed to this employment and to hunting, when quite young, my closest acquaintance with Nature. They early introduce us to and detain us in scenery with which otherwise, at that age, we should have little acquaintance. Fishermen, hunters, woodchoppers, and others, spending their lives in the fields and woods, in a peculiar sense a part of Nature themselves, are often in a more favorable mood for observing her, in the intervals of their pursuits, than philosophers or poets even, who approach her with expectation. She is not afraid to exhibit herself to them. The traveller on the prairie is naturally a hunter, on the head waters of the Missouri and Columbia a trapper, and at the Falls of St. Mary a fisherman. He who is only a traveller learns things at secondhand and by the halves, and is poor authority. We are most interested when science reports what those men already know practically or instinctively, for that alone is a true *humanity,* or account of human experience.

They mistake who assert that the Yankee has few amusements, because he has not so many public holidays, and men and boys do not play so many games as they do in England, for here the more primitive but solitary amusements of hunting fishing and the like have not yet given place to the former. Almost every New England boy among my contemporaries shouldered a fowling piece between the ages of ten and fourteen; and his hunting and fishing grounds were not limited like the preserves of an English nobleman, but were more boundless even than those of a savage. No wonder, then, that he did not oftener stay to play on the common. But already a change is taking place, owing, not to an increased humanity, but to an increased scarcity of game, for perhaps the hunter is the greatest friend of the animals hunted, not excepting the Humane Society.

Moreover, when at the pond, I wished sometimes to add fish to my fare for variety. I have actually fished from the same kind of necessity that the first fishers did. Whatever humanity I might conjure up against it was all factitious, and concerned my philosophy more than my feelings. I speak of fishing only now, for I had long felt differently about fowling, and sold my gun before I went to the woods. Not that I am less humane than others, but I did not perceive that my feelings were much affected. I did not pity the fishes nor the worms. This was habit. As for fowling, during the last years that I carried a gun my excuse was that I was studying ornithology, and sought only new or rare birds. But I confess that I am now inclined to think that there is a finer way of studying ornithology than this. It requires so much closer attention to the habits of the birds, that, if for that reason only, I have been willing to omit the gun. Yet notwithstanding the objection on the score of humanity, I am compelled to doubt if equally valuable sports are ever substituted for these; and when some of my friends have asked me anxiously about their boys, whether they should let them hunt, I have answered, yes,—remembering that it was one of the best parts of my education,—*make* them hunters, though sportsmen only at first, if possible, mighty hunters at last, so that they shall not find game large enough for them in this or any vegetable wilderness,—hunters as well as fishers of men. Thus far I am of the opinion of Chaucer's nun, who

> "yave not of the text a pulled hen
> That saith that hunters ben not holy men."

There is a period in the history of the individual, as of the race, when the hunters are the "best men," as the Algonquins called them. We cannot but pity the boy who has never fired a gun; he is no more humane, while his education has been sadly neglected. This was my answer with respect to those youths who were bent on this pursuit, trusting that they would soon outgrow it. No humane being, past the thoughtless age of boyhood, will wantonly murder any creature, which holds its life by the same tenure that he does. The hare in its extremity cries like a child. I warn you, mothers, that my sympathies do not always make the usual phil-*anthropic* distinctions.

Such is oftenest the young man's introduction to the forest, and the most original part of himself. He goes thither at first as a hunter and fisher, until at last, if he has the seeds of a better life in him, he distinguishes his proper objects, as a poet or naturalist it may be, and leaves the gun and fish-pole behind. The mass of men are still and always young in this respect. In some countries a hunting parson is no uncommon sight. Such a one might make a good shepherd's dog, but is far from being the Good Shepherd. I have been surprised to consider that the only obvious employment, except wood-chopping, ice-cutting, or the like business, which ever to my knowledge detained at Walden Pond for a whole half day any of my fellow-citizens, whether fathers or children of the town, with just one exception, was fishing. Commonly they did not think that they were lucky, or well paid for their time, unless they got a long string of fish, though they had the opportunity of seeing the pond all the while. They might go there a thousand times before the sediment of fishing would sink to the bottom and leave their purpose pure; but no doubt such a clarifying process would be going on all the while. The governor and his council faintly remember the pond, for they went a-fishing there when they were boys; but now they are too old and dignified to go a-fishing, and so they know it no more forever. Yet even they expect to go to heaven at last. If the legislature regards it, it is chiefly to regulate the number of hooks to be used there; but they know nothing about the hook of hooks with which to angle for the pond itself, impaling the legislature for a bait. Thus, even in civilized communities, the embryo man passes through the hunter stage of development.

I have found repeatedly, of late years, that I cannot fish without falling a little in self-respect. I have tried it again and again. I have skill at it, and, like many of my fellows, a certain instinct for it, which revives from time to time, but always when I have done I feel that it would have been better if I had not fished. I think that I do not mistake. It is a faint intimation, yet so are the first streaks of morning. There is unquestionably this instinct in me which belongs to the lower orders of creation; yet with every year I am less a fisherman, though without more humanity or even wisdom; at present I am no fisherman at all. But I see that if I were to live in a wilderness I should again be tempted to become a fisher and hunter in earnest. Beside, there is something essentially unclean about this diet and all flesh, and I began to see where housework commences, and whence the endeavor, which costs so much, to wear a tidy and respectable appearance each day, to keep the house sweet and free from all ill odors and sights. Having been my own butcher and scullion and cook, as well as the gentleman for whom the dishes were served up, I can speak from an unusually complete experience. The practical objection to animal food in my case was its uncleanness; and, besides, when I had caught and cleaned and cooked and eaten my fish, they seemed not to have fed me essentially. It was insignificant and unnecessary, and cost more than it came to. A little bread or a few potatoes would have done as well, with less trouble and filth. Like many of my contemporaries, I had rarely for many years used animal food, or tea, or coffee, &c.; not so much because of any ill effects which I had traced to them, as because they were not agreeable to my imagination. The repugnance to animal food is not the effect of experience, but is an instinct. It appeared more beautiful to live low and fare hard in many respects; and though I never did so, I went far enough to please my imagination. I believe that every man who has ever been earnest to preserve his higher or poetic faculties in the best condition has been particularly inclined to abstain from animal food, and from much food of any kind. It is a significant fact, stated by entomologists, I find it in Kirby and Spence, that "some insects in their perfect state, though furnished with organs of feeding, make no use of them;" and they lay it down as "a general rule, that almost all insects in this state eat much less than in that of larvæ. The voracious caterpillar when transformed into a butterfly," . . . "and the gluttonous maggot when become a fly," content themselves with a drop or two of honey or some other sweet liquid. The abdomen under the wings of the butterfly still represents the larva. This is the tid-bit which tempts his insectivorous fate. The gross feeder is a man in the larva state; and there are whole nations in that condition, nations without fancy or imagination, whose vast abdomens betray them.

It is hard to provide and cook so simple and clean a diet as will not offend the imagination; but this, I think, is to be fed when we feed the body; they should both sit down at the same table. Yet perhaps this may be done. The fruits eaten temperately need not make us ashamed of our appetites, nor interrupt the worthiest pursuits. But put an extra condiment into your dish, and it will poison you. It is not worth the while to live by rich cookery. Most men would feel shame if caught preparing with their own hands precisely such a dinner, whether of animal or vegetable food, as is every day prepared for them by others. Yet till this is otherwise we are not civilized, and, if gentlemen and ladies, are not true men and women. This certainly suggests what change is to be made. It may be vain to ask why the imagination will not be reconciled to flesh and fat. I am satisfied that it is not. Is it not a reproach that man is a carnivorous animal? True, he can and does live, in a great measure, by preying on other animals; but this is a miserable way,—as any one who will go to snaring rabbits, or slaughtering lambs, may learn,—and he will be regarded as a benefactor of his race who shall teach man to confine himself to a more innocent and wholesome diet. Whatever my own practice may be, I have no doubt that it is a part of the destiny of the human race, in its gradual improvement, to leave off eating animals, as surely as the savage tribes have left off eating each other when they came in contact with the more civilized.

If one listens to the faintest but constant suggestions of his genius, which are certainly true, he sees not to what extremes, or even insanity, it may lead him; and yet that way, as he grows more resolute and faithful, his road lies. The faintest assured objection which one healthy man feels will at length prevail over the arguments and customs of mankind. No man ever followed his genius till it misled him. Though the result were bodily weakness, yet perhaps no one can say that the consequences were to be regretted, for these were a life in conformity to higher principles. If the day and the night are such that you greet them with joy, and life emits a fragrance like flowers and sweet-scented herbs, is more elastic, more starry, more immortal,—that is your success. All nature is your congratulation, and you have cause momentarily to bless yourself. The greatest gains and values are farthest from being appreciated. We easily come to doubt if they exist. We soon forget them. They are the highest reality. Perhaps the facts most astounding and most real are never communicated by man to man. The true harvest of my daily life is somewhat as intangible and indescribable as the tints of morning or evening. It is a little stardust caught, a segment of the rainbow which I have clutched.

Yet, for my part, I was never unusually squeamish; I could sometimes eat a fried rat with a good relish, if it were necessary. I am glad to have drunk water so long, for the same reason that I prefer the natural sky to an opium-eater's heaven. I would fain keep sober always; and there are infinite degrees of drunkenness. I believe that water is the only drink for a wise man; wine is not so noble a liquor; and think of dashing the hopes of a morning with a cup of warm coffee, or of an evening with a dish of tea! Ah, how low I fall when I am tempted by them! Even music may be intoxicating. Such apparently slight causes destroyed Greece and Rome, and will destroy England and America. Of all ebriosity, who does not prefer to be intoxicated by the air he breathes? I have found it to be the most serious objection to coarse labors long continued, that they compelled me to eat and drink coarsely also. But to tell the truth, I find myself at present somewhat less particular in these respects. I carry less religion to the table, ask no blessing; not because I am wiser than I was, but, I am obliged to confess, because, however much it is to be regretted, with years I have grown more coarse and indifferent. Perhaps these questions are entertained only in youth, as most believe of poetry. My practice is "nowhere," my opinion is here. Nevertheless I am far from regarding myself as one of those privileged ones to whom the Ved refers when it says, that "he who has true faith in the Omnipresent Supreme Being may eat all that exists," that is, is not bound to inquire what is his food, or who prepares it; and even in their case it is to be observed, as a Hindoo commentator has remarked, that the Vedant limits this privilege to "the time of distress."

Who has not sometimes derived an inexpressible satisfaction from his food in which appetite had no share? I have been thrilled to think that I owed a mental perception to the commonly gross sense of taste, that I have been inspired through the palate, that some berries which I had eaten on a hill-side had fed my genius. "The soul not being mistress of herself," says Thseng-tseu, "one looks, and one does not see; one listens, and one does not hear; one eats, and one does not know the savor of food." He who distinguishes the true savor of his food can never be a glutton; he who does not cannot be otherwise. A puritan may go to his brown-bread crust with as gross an appetite as ever an alderman to his turtle. Not that food which entereth into the mouth defileth a man, but the appetite with which it is eaten. It is neither the quality nor the quantity, but the devotion to sensual savors; when that which is eaten is not a viand to sustain our animal, or inspire our spiritual life, but food for the worms that possess us. If the hunter has a taste for mud-turtles, muskrats, and other such savage tid-bits, the fine lady indulges a taste for jelly made of a calf's foot, or for sardines from over the sea, and they are even. He goes to the millpond, she to her preserve-pot. The wonder is how they, how you and I, can live this slimy beastly life, eating and drinking.

Our whole life is startlingly moral. There is never an instant's truce between virtue and vice. Goodness is the only investment that never fails. In the music of the harp which trembles round the world it is the insisting on this which thrills us. The harp is the travelling patterer for the Universe's Insurance Company, recommending its laws, and our little goodness is all the assessment that we pay. Though the youth at last grows indifferent, the laws of the universe are not indifferent, but are forever on the side of the most sensitive. Listen to every zephyr for some reproof, for it is surely there, and he is unfortunate who does not hear it. We cannot touch a string or move a stop but the charming moral transfixes us. Many an irksome noise, go a long way off, is heard as music, a proud sweet satire on the meanness of our lives.

We are conscious of an animal in us, which awakens in proportion as our higher nature slumbers. It is reptile and sensual, and perhaps cannot be wholly expelled; like the worms which, even in life and health, occupy our bodies. Possibly we may withdraw from it, but never change its nature. I fear that it may enjoy a certain health of its own; that we may be well, yet not pure. The other day I picked up the lower jaw of a hog, with white and sound teeth and tusks, which suggested that there was an animal health and vigor distinct from the spiritual. This creature succeeded by other means than temperance and purity. "That in which men differ from brute beasts," says Mencius, "is a thing very inconsiderable; the common herd lose it very soon; superior men preserve it carefully." Who knows what sort of life would result if we had attained to purity? If I knew so wise a man as could teach me purity I would go to seek him forthwith. "A command over our passions, and over the external senses of the body, and good acts, are declared by the Ved to be indispensable in the mind's approximation to God." Yet the spirit can for the time pervade and control every member and function of the body, and transmute what in form is the grossest sensuality into purity and devotion. The generative energy, which, when we are loose, dissipates and makes us unclean, when we are continent invigorates and inspires us. Chastity is the flowering of man; and what are called Genius, Heroism, Holiness, and the like, are but various fruits which succeed it. Man flows at once to God when the channel of purity is open. By turns our purity inspires and our impurity casts us down. He is blessed who is assured that the animal is dying out in him day by day, and the divine being established. Perhaps there is none but has cause for shame on account of the inferior and brutish nature to which he is allied. I fear that we are such gods or demigods only as fauns and satyrs, the divine allied to beasts, the creatures of appetite, and that, to some extent, our very life is our disgrace.—

"How happy's he who hath due place assigned
To his beasts and disaforested his mind!
*	*	*	*	*
Can use his horse, goat, wolf, and ev'ry beast,
And is not ass himself to all the rest!
Else man not only is the herd of swine,
But he's those devils too which did incline
Them to a headlong rage, and made them worse."

All sensuality is one, though it takes many forms; all purity is one. It is the same whether a man eat, or drink, or cohabit, or sleep sensually. They are but one appetite, and we only need to see a person do any one of these things to know how great a sensualist he is. The impure can neither stand nor sit with purity. When the reptile is attacked at one mouth of his burrow, he shows himself at another. If you would be chaste, you must be temperate. What is chastity? How shall a man know if he is chaste? He shall not know it. We have heard of this virtue, but we know not what it is. We speak conformably to the rumor which we have heard. From exertion come wisdom and purity; from sloth ignorance and sensuality. In the student sensuality is a sluggish habit of mind. An unclean person is universally a slothful one, one who sits by a stove, whom the sun shines on prostrate, who reposes without being fatigued. If you would avoid uncleanness, and all the sins, work earnestly, though it be at cleaning a stable. Nature is hard to be overcome, but she must be overcome. What avails it that you are Christian, if you are not purer than the heathen, if you deny yourself no more, if you are not more religious? I know of many systems of religion esteemed heathenish whose precepts fill the reader with shame, and provoke him to new endeavors, though it be to the performance of rites merely.

I hesitate to say these things, but it is not because of the subject,—I care not how obscene my *words* are,—but because I cannot speak of them without betraying my impurity. We discourse freely without shame of one form of sensuality, and are silent about another. We are so degraded that we cannot speak simply of the necessary functions of human nature. In earlier ages, in some countries, every function was reverently spoken of and regulated by law. Nothing was too trivial for the Hindoo lawgiver, however offensive it may be to modern taste. He teaches how to eat, drink, cohabit, void excrement and urine, and the like, elevating what is mean, and does not falsely excuse himself by calling these things trifles.

Every man is the builder of a temple, called his body, to the god he worships, after a style purely his own, nor can he get off by hammering marble instead. We are all sculptors and painters, and our material is our own flesh and blood and bones. Any nobleness begins at once to refine a man's features, any meanness or sensuality to imbrute them.

John Farmer sat at his door one September evening, after a hard day's work, his mind still running on his labor more or less. Having bathed he sat down to recreate his intellectual man. It was a rather cool evening, and some of his neighbors were apprehending a frost. He had not attended to the train of his thoughts long when he heard some one playing on a flute, and that sound harmonized with his mood. Still he thought of his work; but the burden of his thought was, that though this kept running in his head, and he found himself planning and contriving it against his will, yet it concerned him very little. It was no more than the scurf of his skin, which was constantly shuffled off. But the notes of the flute came home to his ears out of a different sphere from that he worked in, and suggested work for certain faculties which slumbered in him. They gently did away with the street, and the village, and the state in which he lived. A voice said to him,—Why do you stay here and live this mean moiling life, when a glorious existence is possible for you? Those same stars twinkle over other fields than these.—But how to come out of this condition and actually migrate thither? All that he could think of was to practise some new austerity, to let his mind descend into his body and redeem it, and treat himself with ever increasing respect.

Journals

Feb. 3, 1852. I HAVE BEEN TO THE LIBRARIES (YESTERDAY) AT CAMBRIDGE AND BOSTON. How happens it that I find not in the country, in the fields and woods, the *works* even of like-minded naturalists and poets. Those who have expressed the purest and deepest love of nature have not recorded it on the bark of the trees with the lichens; they have left no memento of it there; but if I would read their books I must go to the city,—so strange and repulsive both to them and to me,—and deal with men and institutions with whom I have no sympathy. When I have just been there on this errand, it seems too great a price to pay for access even to the works of Homer, or Chaucer, or Linnæus. I have sometimes imagined a library, *i.e.* a collection of the works of true poets, philosophers, naturalists, etc., deposited not in a brick or marble edifice in a crowded and dusty city, guarded by cold-blooded and methodical officials and preyed on by bookworms, in which you own no share, and are not likely to, but rather far away in the depths of a primitive forest, like the ruins of Central America, where you can trace a series of crumbling alcoves, the older books protecting the most modern from the elements, partially buried by the luxuriance of nature, which the heroic student could reach only after adventures in the wilderness amid wild beasts and wild men. That, to my imagination, seems a fitter place for these interesting relics, which owe no small part of their interest to their antiquity, and whose occasion is nature, than the well-preserved edifice, with its well-preserved officials on the side of a city's square. More terrible than lions and tigers these Cerberuses.

About 6 P.M. walked to Cliffs *via* railroad.

Snow quite deep. The sun had set without a cloud in the sky,—a rare occurrence, but I missed the clouds, which make the glory of evening. The sky must have a few clouds, as the mind a few moods; nor is the evening the less serene for them. There is only a tinge of red along the horizon. The moon is nearly full tonight, and the moment is passed when the light in the east (*i.e.* of the moon) balances the light in the west.

Selenite "is a stone (as is said) in Arabia, wherein is a white, which decreases and increases with the moon" (Dictionary). My summer journal was selenitic in this sense. It had this white spot in it.

Is not the sky unusually blue to-night? dark blue? Is it not always bluer when the ground is covered with snow in the winter than in summer?

The forcible writer stands bodily behind his words with his experience. He does not make books out of books, but he has been *there* in person.

March 1, 1852. Linnæus, speaking of the necessity of precise and adequate terms in any science, after naming some which he invented for botany, says, "Termini praeservarunt Anatomiam, Mathesin, Chemiam, ab idiotis; Medicinam autem eorum defectus conculcavit." (Terms (well defined) have preserved anatomy, mathematics, and chemistry from idiots; but the want of them has ruined medicine.) But I should say that men generally were not enough interested in the first-mentioned sciences to meddle with and degrade them. There is no interested motive to induce them to listen to the quack in mathematics, as they have to attend to the quack in medicine; yet chemistry has been converted into alchemy, and astronomy into astrology.

However, I can see that there is a certain advantage in these hard and precise terms, such as the lichenist uses, for instance. No one masters them so as to use them in writing on the subject without being far better informed than the rabble about it. New books are not written on chemistry or cryptogamia of as little worth comparatively as are written on the *spiritual* phenomena of the day. No man writes on lichens, using the terms of the science intelligibly, without having something to say, but every one thinks himself competent to write on the relation of the soul to the body, as if that were a *phœnogamous* subject.

After having read various books on various subjects for some months, I take up a report on Farms by a committee of Middlesex Husbandmen, and read of the number of acres of bog that some farmer has redeemed, and the number of rods of stone wall that he has built, and the number of tons of hay he now cuts, or of bushels of corn or potatoes he raises there, and I feel as if I had got my foot down on to the solid and sunny earth, the basis of all philosophy, and poetry, and religion even. I have faith that the man who redeemed some acres of land the past summer redeemed also some parts of his character. I shall not expect to find him ever in the almshouse or the prison. He is, in fact, so far on his way to heaven. When he took the farm there was not a grafted tree on it, and now he realizes something handsome from the sale of fruit. These, in the absence of other facts, are evidence of a certain moral worth.

May 31, 1853. Some incidents in my life have seemed far more allegorical than actual; they were so significant that they plainly served no other use. That is, I have been more impressed by their allegorical significance and fitness; they have been like myths or passages in a myth, rather than mere incidents or history which have to wait to become significant. Quite in harmony with my subjective philosophy. This, for instance: that, when I thought I knew the flowers so well, the beautiful purple azalea or pinxter-flower should be shown me by the hunter who found it. Such facts are lifted quite above the level of the actual. They are all just such events as my imagination prepares me for, no matter how incredible. Ever and anon something will occur which my philosophy has not dreamed of. The limits of the actual are set some thoughts further off. That which had seemed a rigid wall of vast thickness unexpectedly proves a thin and undulating drapery. The boundaries of the actual are no more fixed and rigid than the elasticity of our imaginations. The fact that a rare and beautiful flower which we never saw, perhaps never heard, for which therefore there was no place in our thoughts, may at length be found in our immediate neighborhood, is very suggestive.

Jan. 24, 1856. A journal is a record of experiences and growth, not a preserve of things well done or said. I am occasionally reminded of a statement which I have made in conversation and immediately forgotten, which would read much better than what I put in my journal. It is a ripe, dry fruit of long-past experience which falls from me easily, without giving pain or pleasure. The charm of the journal must consist in a certain greenness, though freshness, and not in maturity. Here I cannot afford to be remembering what I said or did, my scurf cast off, but what I am and aspire to become.

Reading the hymns of the Rig Veda, translated by Wilson, which consist in a great measure of simple epithets addressed to the firmament, or the dawn, or the winds, which mean more or less as the reader is more or less alert and imaginative, and seeing how widely the various translators have differed, they regarding not the poetry, but the history and philology, dealing with very concise, Sanscrit, which must almost always be amplified to be understood, I am sometimes inclined to doubt if the translator has not made something out of nothing,—whether a real idea or sentiment has been thus transmitted to us from so primitive a period. I doubt if learned Germans might not thus edit pebbles from the seashore into hymns of the Rig Veda, and translators translate them accordingly, extracting the meaning which the sea has imparted to them in very primitive times. While the commentators and translators are disputing about the meaning of this word or that, I hear only the resounding of the ancient sea and put into it all the meaning I am possessed of, the deepest murmurs I can recall, for I do not the least care where I get my ideas, or what suggests them.

P.M.—Up Assabet.

The snow is so deep along the sides of the river that I can now look into nests which I could hardly reach in the summer. I can hardly believe them the same. They have only an ice egg in them now. Thus we go about, raised, generally speaking, more than a foot above the summer level. So much higher do we carry our heads in the winter. What a great odds such a little difference makes! When the snow raises us one foot higher than we have been accustomed to walk, we are surprised at our elevation! So we soar.

41

Gerard Manley Hopkins

Nondum

"Verily Thou art a God that hidest Thyself."
ISAIAH 45:15

God, though to Thee our psalm we raise
No answering voice comes from the skies;
To Thee the trembling sinner prays
But no forgiving voice replies;
Our prayer seems lost in desert ways,
Our hymn in the vast silence dies.

We see the glories of the earth
But not the hand that wrought them all:
Night to a myriad worlds gives birth,
Yet like a lighted empty hall
Where stands no host at door or hearth
Vacant creation's lamps appal.

We guess; we clothe Thee, unseen King,
With attributes we deem are meet;
Each in his own imagining
Sets up a shadow in Thy seat;
Yet know not how our gifts to bring,
Where seek Thee with unsandalled feet.

And still th'unbroken silence broods
While ages and while aeons run,
As erst upon chaotic floods

The Spirit hovered ere the sun
Had called the seasons' changeful moods
And life's first germs from death had won.

And still th'abysses infinite
Surround the peak from which we gaze.
Deep calls to deep, and blackest night
Giddies the soul with blinding daze
That dares to cast its searching sight
On being's dread and vacant maze.

And Thou art silent, whilst Thy world
Contends about its many creeds
And hosts confront with flags unfurled
And zeal is flushed and pity bleeds
And truth is heard, with tears impearled,
A moaning voice among the reeds.

My hand upon my lips I lay;
The breast's desponding sob I quell;
I move along life's tomb-decked way
And listen to the passing bell
Summoning men from speechless day
To death's more silent, darker spell.

Oh! till Thou givest that sense beyond,
To shew Thee that Thou art, and near,
Let patience with her chastening wand
Dispel the doubt and dry the tear;
And lead me child-like by the hand
If still in darkness not in fear.

Speak! whisper to my watching heart
One word—as when a mother speaks
Soft, when she sees her infant start,
Till dimpled joy steals o'er its cheeks.
Then, to behold Thee as Thou art,
I'll wait till morn eternal breaks.

The Starlight Night

LOOK at the stars! look, look up at the skies!
  O look at all the fire-folk sitting in the air!
  The bright boroughs, the circle-citadels there!
Down in dim woods the diamond delves! the elves'-eyes!
The grey lawns cold where gold, where quickgold lies!
  Wind-beat whitebeam! airy abeles set on a flare!
  Flake-doves sent floating forth at a farmyard scare!—
Ah well! it is all a purchase, all is a prize.
Buy then! bid then!—What?—Prayer, patience, aims, vows.
Look, look: a May-mess, like on orchard boughs!
  Look! March-bloom, like on mealed-with-yellow sallows!
These are indeed the barn; withindoors house
The shocks. This piece-bright paling shuts the spouse
  Christ home, Christ and his mother and all his hallows.

The Lantern out of Doors

Sometimes a lantern moves along the night.
    That interests our eyes. And who goes there?
    I think; where from and bound, I wonder, where,
With, all down darkness wide, his wading light?

Men go by me, whom either beauty bright
    In mould or mind or what not else makes rare:
    They rain against our much-thick and marsh air
Rich beams, till death or distance buys them quite.

Death or distance soon consumes them: wind,
    What most I may eye after, be in at the end
I cannot, and out of sight is out of mind.

Christ minds: Christ's interest, what to avow or amend
    There, éyes them, heart wánts, care háunts, foot fóllows kínd,
Their ránsom, théir rescue, ánd first, fást, last fríend.

"Thee, God, I come from"

Thee, God, I come from, to thee go,
All dáy long I like fountain flow
From thy hand out, swayed about
Mote-like in thy mighty glow.

What I know of thee I bless,
As acknowledging thy stress
On my being and as seeing
Something of thy holiness.

Once I turned from thee and hid,
Bound on what thou hadst forbid;
Sow the wind I would; I sinned:
I repent of what I did.

Bad I am, but yet thy child.
Father, be thou reconciled.
Spare thou me, since I see
With thy might that thou art mild.

I have life left with me still
And thy purpose to fulfill;
Yea a debt to pay thee yet:
Help me, sir, and so I will.

But thou bidst, and just thou art,
Me shew mercy from my heart
Towards my brother, every other
Man my mate and counterpart.

. . . . .

Jesus Christ sacrificed
On the cross

Moulded, he, in maiden's womb,
Lived and died and from the tomb
Rose in power and is our
Judge that comes to deal our doom.

The Leaden Echo and the Golden Echo

(Maidens' song from St. Winefred's Well)

THE LEADEN ECHO

How to kéep – is there ány any, is there none such, nowhere known some, bow or brooch or
    braid or brace, láce, latch or catch or key to keep

Back beauty, keep it, beauty, beauty, beauty . . . from vanishing away?

Ó is there no frowning of these wrinkles, rankèd wrinkles deep,

Dówn? no waving off of these most mournful messengers, still messengers, sad and stealing
    messengers of grey? –

No there's none, there's none, O no there's none,

Nor can you long be, what you now are, called fair,

Do what you may do, what, do what you may,

And wisdom is early to despair:

Be beginning; since, no, nothing can be done

To keep at bay

Age and age's evils, hoar hair,

Ruck and wrinkle, drooping, dying, death's worst, winding sheets, tombs and worms and
    tumbling to decay;

So be beginning, be beginning to despair.

O there's none; no no no there's none:

Be beginning to despair, to despair,

Despair, despair, despair, despair.

THE GOLDEN ECHO

Spare!

There ís one, yes I have one (Hush there!),

Only not within seeing of the sun.

Not within the singeing of the strong sun,

Tall sun's tingeing, or treacherous the tainting of the earth's air,

Somewhere elsewhere there is ah well where! one,

Oñe. Yes I cán tell such a key, I dó know such a place,

Where whatever's prizèd and passes of us, everything that's fresh and fast flying of us, seems
    to us sweet of us and swiftly away with, done away with, undone,

Undone, done with, soon done with, and yet dearly and dangerously sweet

Of us, the wimpled-water-dimpled, not-by-morning-matchèd face,

The flower of beauty, fleece of beauty, too apt to, ah! to fleet,

Never fleets móre, fastened with the tenderest truth

To its own best being and its loveliness of youth: it is an everlastingness of, O it is an
all youth!

Come then, your ways and airs and looks, locks, maidengear, gallantry and gaiety
and grace,

Winning ways, airs innocent, maiden manners, sweet looks, loose locks, long locks,
lovelocks, gaygear, going gallant, girlgrace –

Resign them, sign them, seal them, send them, motion them with breath,

And with sighs soaring, soaring síghs, deliver

Them; beauty-in-the-ghost, deliver it, early now, long before death

Give beauty back, beauty, beauty, beauty, back to God, beauty's self and beauty's giver.

See; not a hair is, not an eyelash, not the least lash lost; every hair

Is, hair of the head, numbered.

Nay, what we had lighthanded left in surly the mere mould

Will have waked and have waxed and have walked with the wind what while we slept,

This side, that side hurling a heavyheaded hundredfold

What while we, while we slumbered.

O then, weary then why should we tread? O why are we so haggard at the heart, so care-
coiled, care-killed, so fagged, so fashed, so cogged, so cumbered,

When the thing we freely fórfeit is kept with fonder a care,

Fonder a care kept than we could have kept it, kept

Far with fonder a care (and we, we should have lost it) finer, fonder

A care kept. – Where kept? do but tell us where kept, where. –

Yonder. – What high as that! We follow, now we follow. – Yonder, yes yonder, yonder,

Yonder.

42

Matthew Arnold

Culture and Anarchy (1869)

Hebraism and Hellenism

THIS FUNDAMENTAL GROUND IS OUR PREFERENCE OF DOING TO THINKING. Now this preference is a main element in our nature, and as we study it we find ourselves opening up a number of large questions on every side.

Let me go back for a moment to what I have already quoted from Bishop Wilson:—"First, never go against the best light you have; secondly, take care that your light be not darkness." I said we show, as a nation, laudable energy and persistence in walking according to the best light we have, but are not quite careful enough, perhaps, to see that our light be not darkness. This is only another version of the old story that energy is our strong point and favourable characteristic, rather than intelligence. But we may give to this idea a more general form still, in which it will have a yet larger range of application. We may regard this energy driving at practice, this paramount sense of the obligation of duty, self-control, and work, this earnestness in going manfully with the best light we have, as one force. And we may regard the intelligence driving at those ideas which are, after all, the basis of right practice, the ardent sense for all the new and changing combinations of them which man's development brings with it, the indomitable impulse to know and adjust them perfectly, as another force. And these two forces we may regard as in some sense rivals,—rivals not by the necessity of their own nature, but as exhibited in man and his history,—and rivals dividing the empire of the world between them. And to give these forces names from the two races of men who have supplied the most signal and splendid manifestations of them, we may call them respectively the forces of Hebraism and Hellenism. Hebraism and Hellenism,—between these two points of influence moves our world. At one time it feels more powerfully the attraction of one of them, at another time of the other; and it ought to be, though it never is, evenly and happily balanced between them.

The final aim of both Hellenism and Hebraism, as of all great spiritual disciplines, is no doubt the same: man's perfection or salvation. The very language which they both of them use in schooling us to reach this aim is often identical. Even when their language indicates by variation,—sometimes a broad variation, often a but slight and subtle variation,—the different courses of thought which are uppermost in each discipline, even then the unity of the final end and aim is still apparent. To employ the actual words of that discipline with which we ourselves are all of us most familiar, and the words of which, therefore, come most home to us, that final end and aim is "that we might be partakers of the divine nature." These are the words of a Hebrew apostle, but of Hellenism and Hebraism alike this is, I say, the aim. When the two are confronted, as they very often are confronted, it is nearly always with what I may call a rhetorical purpose; the speaker's whole design is to exalt and enthrone one of the two, and he uses the other only as a foil and to enable him the better to give effect to his purpose. Obviously, with us, it is usually Hellenism which is thus reduced to minister to the triumph of Hebraism. There is a sermon on Greece and the Greek spirit by a man never to be mentioned without interest and respect, Frederick Robertson, in which this rhetorical use of Greece and the Greek spirit, and the inadequate exhibition of them necessarily consequent upon this, is almost ludicrous, and would be censurable if it were not to be explained by the exigences of a sermon. On the other hand, Heinrich Heine, and other writers of his sort, give us the spectacle of the tables completely turned, and of Hebraism brought in just as a foil and contrast to Hellenism, and to make the superiority of Hellenism more manifest. In both these cases there is injustice and misrepresentation. The aim and end of both Hebraism and Hellenism is, as I have said, one and the same, and this aim and end is august and admirable.

Still, they pursue this aim by very different courses. The uppermost idea with Hellenism is to see things as they really are; the uppermost idea with Hebraism is conduct and obedience. Nothing can do away with this ineffaceable difference; the Greek quarrel with the body and its desires is, that they hinder right thinking, the Hebrew quarrel with them is, that they hinder right acting. "He that keepeth the law, happy is he;" "There is nothing sweeter than to take heed unto the commandments of the Lord;"—that is the Hebrew notion of felicity; and, pursued with passion and tenacity, this notion would not let the Hebrew rest till, as is well known, he had, at last, got out of the law a network of prescriptions to enwrap his whole life, to govern every moment of it, every impulse, every action. The Greek notion of felicity, on the other hand, is perfectly conveyed in these words of a great French moralist: "C'est le bonheur des hommes"— when? when they abhor that which is evil?— no; when they exercise themselves in the law of the Lord day and night?—no; when they die daily?—no; when they walk about the New Jerusalem with palms in their hands?—no; but when they think aright, when their thought hits,—"quand ils pensent juste." At the bottom of both the Greek and the Hebrew notion is the desire, native in man, for reason and the will of God, the feeling after the universal order,—in a word, the love of God. But, while Hebraism seizes upon certain plain, capital intimations of the universal order, and rivets itself, one may say, with unequalled grandeur of earnestness and intensity on the study and observance of them, the bent of Hellenism is to follow, with flexible activity, the whole play of the universal order, to be apprehensive of missing any part of it, of sacrificing one part to another, to slip away from resting in this or that intimation of it, however capital. An unclouded clearness of mind, an unimpeded play of thought, is what this bent drives at. The governing idea of Hellenism is spontaneity of consciousness; that of Hebraism, strictness of conscience.

Christianity changed nothing in this essential bent of Hebraism to set doing above knowing. Self-conquest, self-devotion, the following not our own individual will, but the will of God, obedience, is the fundamental idea of this form, also, of the discipline to which we have attached the general name of Hebraism. Only, as the old law and the network of prescriptions with which it enveloped human life were evidently a motive power not driving and searching enough to produce the result aimed at,—patient continuance in well doing, self- conquest,—Christianity substituted for them boundless devotion to that inspiring and affecting pattern of self-conquest offered by Christ; and by the new motive power, of which the essence was this, though the love and admiration of Christian churches have for centuries been employed in varying, amplifying, and adorning the plain description of it, Christianity, as St. Paul truly says, "establishes the law," and in the strength of the ampler power which she has thus supplied to fulfil it, has accomplished the miracles, which we all see, of her history.

So long as we do not forget that both Hellenism and Hebraism are profound and admirable manifestations of man's life, tendencies, and powers, and that both of them aim at a like final result, we can hardly insist too strongly on the divergence of line and of operation with which they proceed. It is a divergence so great that it most truly, as the prophet Zechariah says, "has raised up thy sons, O Zion, against thy sons, O Greece!" The difference whether it is by doing or by knowing that we set most store, and the practical consequences which follow from this difference, leave their mark on all the history of our race and of its development. Language may be abundantly quoted from both Hellenism and Hebraism to make it seem that one follows the same current as the other towards the same goal. They are, truly, borne towards the same goal; but the currents which bear them are infinitely different. It is true, Solomon will praise knowing: "Understanding is a well-spring of life unto him that hath it." And in the New Testament, again, Christ is a "light," and "truth makes us free." It is true, Aristotle will undervalue knowing: "In what concerns virtue," says he, "three things are necessary,—knowledge, deliberate will, and perseverance; but, whereas the two last are all important, the first is a matter of little importance." It is true that with the same impatience with which St. James enjoins a man to be not a forgetful hearer, but a doer of the work, Epictetus exhorts us to do what we have demonstrated to ourselves we ought to do; or he taunts us with futility, for being armed at all points to prove that lying is wrong, yet all the time continuing to lie. It is true, Plato, in words which are almost the words of the New Testament or the Imitation, calls life a learning to die. But underneath the superficial agreement the fundamental divergence still subsists. The understanding of Solomon is "the walking in the way of the commandments;" this is "the way of peace," and it is of this that blessedness comes. In the New Testament, the truth which gives us the peace of God and makes us free, is the love of Christ constraining us to crucify, as he did, and with a like purpose of moral regeneration, the flesh with its affections and lusts, and thus establishing, as we have seen, the law. To St. Paul it appears possible to "hold the truth in unrighteousness," which is just what Socrates judged impossible. The moral virtues, on the other hand, are with Aristotle but the porch and access to the intellectual, and with these last is blessedness. That partaking of the divine life, which both Hellenism and Hebraism, as we have said, fix as their crowning aim, Plato expressly denies to the man of practical virtue merely, of self-conquest with any other motive than that of perfect intellectual vision; he reserves it for the lover of pure knowledge, of seeing things as they really are,—the philomathês.

Both Hellenism and Hebraism arise out of the wants of human nature, and address themselves to satisfying those wants. But their methods are so different, they lay stress on such different points, and call into being by their respective disciplines such different activities, that the face which human nature presents when it passes from the hands of one of them to those of the other, is no longer the same. To get rid of one's ignorance, to see things as they are, and by seeing them as they are to see them in their beauty, is the simple and attractive ideal which Hellenism holds out before human nature; and from the simplicity and charm of this ideal, Hellenism, and human life in the hands of Hellenism, is invested with a kind of aërial ease, clearness, and radiancy; they are full of what we call sweetness and light. Difficulties are kept out of view, and the beauty and rationalness of the ideal have all our thoughts. "The best man is he who most tries to perfect himself, and the happiest man is he who most feels that he is perfecting himself,"— this account of the matter by Socrates, the true Socrates of the Memorabilia, has something so simple, spontaneous, and unsophisticated about it, that it seems to fill us with clearness and hope when we hear it. But there is a saying which I have heard attributed to Mr. Carlyle about Socrates,—a very happy saying, whether it is really Mr. Carlyle's or not,—which excellently marks the essential point in which Hebraism differs from Hellenism. "Socrates," this saying goes, "is terribly at ease in Zion" Hebraism,—and here is the source of its wonderful strength,— has always been severely preoccupied with an awful sense of the impossibility of being at ease in Zion; of the difficulties which oppose themselves to man's pursuit or attainment of that perfection of which Socrates talks so hopefully, and, as from this point of view one might almost say, so glibly. It is all very well to talk of getting rid of one's ignorance, of seeing things in their reality, seeing them in their beauty; but how is this to be done when there is something which thwarts and spoils all our efforts? This something is sin; and the space which sin fills in Hebraism, as compared with Hellenism, is indeed prodigious. This obstacle to perfection fills the whole scene, and perfection appears remote and rising away from earth, in the background. Under the name of sin, the difficulties of knowing oneself and conquering oneself which impede man's passage to perfection, become, for Hebraism, a positive, active entity hostile to man, a mysterious power which I heard Dr. Pusey the other day, in one of his impressive sermons, compare to a hideous hunchback seated on our shoulders, and which it is the main business of our lives to hate and oppose. The discipline of the Old Testament may be summed up as a discipline teaching us to abhor and flee from sin; the discipline of the New Testament, as a discipline teaching us to die to it. As Hellenism speaks of thinking clearly, seeing things in their essence and beauty, as a grand and precious feat for man to achieve, so Hebraism speaks of becoming conscious of sin, of awakening to a sense of sin, as a feat of this kind. It is obvious to what wide divergence these differing tendencies, actively followed, must lead. As one passes and repasses from Hellenism to Hebraism, from Plato to St. Paul, one feels inclined to rub one's eyes and ask oneself whether man is indeed a gentle and simple being, showing the traces of a noble and divine nature; or an unhappy chained captive, labouring with groanings that cannot be uttered to free himself from the body of this death.

Apparently it was the Hellenic conception of human nature which was unsound, for the world could not live by it. Absolutely to call it unsound, however, is to fall into the common error of its Hebraising enemies; but it was unsound at that particular moment of man's development, it was premature. The indispensable basis of conduct and self-control, the platform upon which alone the perfection aimed at by Greece can come into bloom, was not to be reached by our race so easily; centuries of probation and discipline were needed to bring us to it. Therefore the bright promise of Hellenism faded, and Hebraism ruled the world. Then was seen that astonishing spectacle, so well marked by the often quoted words of the prophet Zechariah, when men of all languages of the nations took hold of the skirt of him that was a Jew, saying:—"We will go with you, for we have heard that God is with you." And the Hebraism which thus received and ruled a world all gone out of the way and altogether become unprofitable, was, and could not but be, the later, the more spiritual, the more attractive development of Hebraism. It was Christianity; that is to say, Hebraism aiming at self-conquest and rescue from the thrall of vile affections, not by obedience to the letter of a law, but by conformity to the image of a self-sacrificing example. To a world stricken with moral enervation Christianity offered its spectacle of an inspired self-sacrifice; to men who refused themselves nothing, it showed one who refused himself everything;—"my Saviour banished joy" says George Herbert. When the alma Venus, the life-giving and joy-giving power of nature, so fondly cherished by the Pagan world, could not save her followers from self- dissatisfaction and ennui, the severe words of the apostle came bracingly and refreshingly: "Let no man deceive you with vain words, for because of these things cometh the wrath of God upon the children of disobedience." Throughout age after age, and generation after generation, our race, or all that part of our race which was most living and progressive, was baptized into a death; and endeavoured, by suffering in the flesh, to cease from sin. Of this endeavour, the animating labours and afflictions of early Christianity, the touching asceticism of mediaeval Christianity, are the great historical manifestations. Literary monuments of it, each, in its own way, incomparable, remain in the Epistles of St. Paul, in St. Augustine's Confessions, and in the two original and simplest books of the Imitation.

Of two disciplines laying their main stress, the one, on clear intelligence, the other, on firm obedience; the one, on comprehensively knowing the grounds of one's duty, the other, on diligently practising it; the one on taking all possible care (to use Bishop Wilson's words again) that the light we have be not darkness, the other, that according to the best light we have we diligently walk,—the priority naturally belongs to that discipline which braces man's moral powers, and founds for him an indispensable basis of character. And, therefore, it is justly said of the Jewish people, who were charged with setting powerfully forth that side of the divine order to which the words conscience and self-conquest point, that they were "entrusted with the oracles of God;" as it is justly said of Christianity, which followed Judaism and which set forth this side with a much deeper effectiveness and a much wider influence, that the wisdom of the old Pagan world was foolishness compared to it. No words of devotion and admiration can be too strong to render thanks to these beneficent forces which have so borne forward humanity in its appointed work of coming to the knowledge and possession of itself; above all, in those great moments when their action was the wholesomest and the most necessary.

But the evolution of these forces, separately and in themselves, is not the whole evolution of humanity,—their single history is not the whole history of man; whereas their admirers are always apt to make it stand for the whole history. Hebraism and Hellenism are, neither of them, the law of human development, as their admirers are prone to make them; they are, each of them, contributions to human development,—august contributions, invaluable contributions; and each showing itself to us more august, more invaluable, more preponderant over the other, according to the moment in which we take them, and the relation in which we stand to them. The nations of our modern world, children of that immense and salutary movement which broke up the Pagan world, inevitably stand to Hellenism in a relation which dwarfs it, and to Hebraism in a relation which magnifies it. They are inevitably prone to take Hebraism as the law of human development, and not as simply a contribution to it, however precious. And yet the lesson must perforce be learned, that the human spirit is wider than the most priceless of the forces which bear it onward, and that to the whole development of man Hebraism itself is, like Hellenism, but a contribution.

Perhaps we may help ourselves to see this clearer by an illustration drawn from the treatment of a single great idea which has profoundly engaged the human spirit, and has given it eminent opportunities for showing its nobleness and energy. It surely must be perceived that the idea of the immortality of the soul, as this idea rises in its generality before the human spirit, is something grander, truer, and more satisfying, than it is in the particular forms by which St. Paul, in the famous fifteenth chapter of the Epistle to the Corinthians, and Plato, in the Phaedo, endeavour to develope and establish it. Surely we cannot but feel, that the argumentation with which the Hebrew apostle goes about to expound this great idea is, after all, confused and inconclusive; and that the reasoning, drawn from analogies of likeness and equality, which is employed upon it by the Greek philosopher, is over-subtle and sterile? Above and beyond the inadequate solutions which Hebraism and Hellenism here attempt, extends the immense and august problem itself, and the human spirit which gave birth to it. And this single illustration may suggest to us how the same thing happens in other cases also.

But meanwhile, by alternations of Hebraism and Hellenism, of man's intellectual and moral impulses, of the effort to see things as they really are, and the effort to win peace by self-conquest, the human spirit proceeds, and each of these two forces has its appointed hours of culmination and seasons of rule. As the great movement of Christianity was a triumph of Hebraism and man's moral impulses, so the great movement which goes by the name of the Renascence was an uprising and re-instatement of man's intellectual impulses and of Hellenism. We in England, the devoted children of Protestantism, chiefly know the Renascence by its subordinate and secondary side of the Reformation. The Reformation has been often called a Hebraising revival, a return to the ardour and sincereness of primitive Christianity. No one, however, can study the development of Protestantism and of Protestant churches without feeling that into the Reformation too,—Hebraising child of the Renascence and offspring of its fervour, rather than its intelligence, as it undoubtedly was,—the subtle Hellenic leaven of the Renascence found its way, and that the exact respective parts in the Reformation, of Hebraism and of Hellenism, are not easy to separate. But what we may with truth say is, that all which Protestantism was to itself clearly conscious of, all which it succeeded in clearly setting forth in words, had the characters of Hebraism rather than of Hellenism. The Reformation was strong, in that it was an earnest return to the Bible and to doing from the heart the will of God as there written; it was weak, in that it never consciously grasped or applied the central idea of the Renascence,—the Hellenic idea of pursuing, in all lines of activity, the law and science, to use Plato's words, of things as they really are. Whatever direct superiority, therefore, Protestantism had over Catholicism was a moral superiority, a superiority arising out of its greater sincerity and earnestness,—at the moment of its apparition at any rate,—in dealing with the heart and conscience; its pretensions to an intellectual superiority are in general quite illusory. For Hellenism, for the thinking side in man as distinguished from the acting side, the attitude of mind of Protestantism towards the Bible in no respect differs from the attitude of mind of Catholicism towards the Church. The mental habit of him who imagines that Balaam's ass spoke, in no respect differs from the mental habit of him who imagines that a Madonna of wood or stone winked; and the one, who says that God's Church makes him believe what he believes, and the other, who says that God's Word makes him believe what he believes, are for the philosopher perfectly alike in not really and truly knowing, when they say God's Church and God's Word, what it is they say, or whereof they affirm.

In the sixteenth century, therefore, Hellenism re-entered the world, and again stood in presence of Hebraism,—a Hebraism renewed and purged. Now, it has not been enough observed, how, in the seventeenth century, a fate befell Hellenism in some respects analogous to that which befell it at the commencement of our era. The Renascence, that great re-awakening of Hellenism, that irresistible return of humanity to nature and to seeing things as they are, which in art, in literature, and in physics, produced such splendid fruits, had, like the anterior Hellenism of the Pagan world, a side of moral weakness, and of relaxation or insensibility of the moral fibre, which in Italy showed itself with the most startling plainness, but which in France, England, and other countries was very apparent too. Again this loss of spiritual balance, this exclusive preponderance given to man's perceiving and knowing side, this unnatural defect of his feeling and acting side, provoked a reaction. Let us trace that reaction where it most nearly concerns us.

Science has now made visible to everybody the great and pregnant elements of difference which lie in race, and in how signal a manner they make the genius and history of an Indo-European people vary from those of a Semitic people. Hellenism is of Indo-European growth, Hebraism is of Semitic growth; and we English, a nation of Indo-European stock, seem to belong naturally to the movement of Hellenism. But nothing more strongly marks the essential unity of man than the affinities we can perceive, in this point or that, between members of one family of peoples and members of another; and no affinity of this kind is more strongly marked than that likeness in the strength and prominence of the moral fibre, which, notwithstanding immense elements of difference, knits in some special sort the genius and history of us English, and of our American descendants across the Atlantic, to the genius and history of the Hebrew people. Puritanism, which has been so great a power in the English nation, and in the strongest part of the English nation, was originally the reaction, in the seventeenth century, of the conscience and moral sense of our race, against the moral indifference and lax rule of conduct which in the sixteenth century came in with the Renascence. It was a reaction of Hebraism against Hellenism; and it powerfully manifested itself, as was natural, in a people with much of what we call a Hebraising turn, with a signal affinity for the bent which was the master-bent of Hebrew life. Eminently Indo-European by its humour, by the power it shows, through this gift, of imaginatively acknowledging the multiform aspects of the problem of life, and of thus getting itself unfixed from its own over- certainty, of smiling at its own over-tenacity, our race has yet (and a great part of its strength lies here), in matters of practical life and moral conduct, a strong share of the assuredness, the tenacity, the intensity of the Hebrews. This turn manifested itself in Puritanism, and has had a great part in shaping our history for the last two hundred years. Undoubtedly it checked and changed amongst us that movement of the Renascence which we see producing in the reign of Elizabeth such wonderful fruits; undoubtedly it stopped the prominent rule and direct development of that order of ideas which we call by the name of Hellenism, and gave the first rank to a different order of ideas. Apparently, too, as we said of the former defeat of Hellenism, if Hellenism was defeated, this shows that Hellenism was imperfect, and that its ascendency at that moment would not have been for the world's good.

Yet there is a very important difference between the defeat inflicted on Hellenism by Christianity eighteen hundred years ago, and the check given to the Renascence by Puritanism. The greatness of the difference is well measured by the difference in force, beauty, significance and usefulness, between primitive Christianity and Protestantism. Eighteen hundred years ago it was altogether the hour of Hebraism; primitive Christianity was legitimately and truly the ascendent force in the world at that time, and the way of mankind's progress lay through its full development. Another hour in man's development began in the fifteenth century, and the main road of his progress then lay for a time through Hellenism. Puritanism was no longer the central current of the world's progress, it was a side stream crossing the central current and checking it. The cross and the check may have been necessary and salutary, but that does not do away with the essential difference between the main stream of man's advance and a cross or side stream. For more than two hundred years the main stream of man's advance has moved towards knowing himself and the world, seeing things as they are, spontaneity of consciousness; the main impulse of a great part, and that the strongest part, of our nation, has been towards strictness of conscience. They have made the secondary the principal at the wrong moment, and the principal they have at the wrong moment treated as secondary. This contravention of the natural order has produced, as such contravention always must produce, a certain confusion and false movement, of which we are now beginning to feel, in almost every direction, the inconvenience. In all directions our habitual courses of action seem to be losing efficaciousness, credit, and control, both with others and even with ourselves; everywhere we see the beginnings of confusion, and we want a clue to some sound order and authority. This we can only get by going back upon the actual instincts and forces which rule our life, seeing them as they really are, connecting them with other instincts and forces, and enlarging our whole view and rule of life.

43

Fyodor Dostoyevsky

The Brothers Karamazov (1879-80)

The Grand Inquisitor

"Do you know, alyosha—don't laugh! i made a poem about a year ago. If you can waste another ten minutes on me, I'll tell it to you."

"You wrote a poem?"

"Oh, no, I didn't write it," laughed Ivan, "and I've never written two lines of poetry in my life. But I made up this poem in prose and I remembered it. I was carried away when I made it up. You will be my first reader—that is, listener. Why should an author forego even one listener?" smiled Ivan. "Shall I tell it to you?"

"I am all attention," said Alyosha.

"My poem is called 'The Grand Inquisitor'; it's a ridiculous thing, but I want to tell it to you."

"Even this must have a preface—that is, a literary preface," laughed Ivan, "and I am a poor hand at making one. You see, my action takes place in the sixteenth century, and at that time, as you probably learnt at school, it was customary in poetry to bring down heavenly powers on earth. Not to speak of Dante, in France, clerks, as well as the monks in the monasteries, used to give regular performances in which the Madonna, the saints, the angels, Christ, and God Himself were brought on the stage. In those days it was done in all simplicity. In Victor Hugo's 'Notre Dame de Paris' an edifying and gratuitous spectacle was provided for the people in the Hotel de Ville of Paris in the reign of Louis XI. in honour of the birth of the dauphin. It was called *Le bon jugement de la très sainte et gracieuse Vierge Marie,* and she appears herself on the stage and pronounces her *bon jugement.* Similar plays, chiefly from the Old Testament, were occasionally performed in Moscow too, up to the times of Peter the Great. But besides plays there were all sorts of legends and ballads scattered about the world, in which the saints and angels and all the powers of Heaven took part when required. In our monasteries the monks busied themselves in translating, copying, and even composing such poems—and even under the Tatars. There is, for instance, one such poem (of course, from the Greek), 'The Wanderings of Our Lady through Hell,' with descriptions as bold as Dante's. Our Lady visits Hell, and the Archangel Michael leads her through the torments. She sees the sinners and their punishment. There she sees among others one noteworthy set of sinners in a burning lake; some of them sink to the bottom of the lake so that they can't swim out, and 'these God forgets'—an expression of extraordinary depth and force. And so Our Lady, shocked and weeping, falls before the throne of God and begs for mercy for all in Hell—for all she has seen there, indiscriminately. Her conversation with God is immensely interesting. She beseeches Him, she will not desist, and when God points to the hands and feet of her Son, nailed to the Cross, and asks, 'How can I forgive His tormentors?' she bids all the saints, all the martyrs, all the angels and archangels to fall down with her and pray for mercy on all without distinction. It ends by her winning from God a respite of suffering every year from Good Friday till Trinity day, and the sinners at once raise a cry of thankfulness from Hell, chanting, 'Thou art just, O Lord, in this judgment.' Well, my poem would have been of that kind if it had appeared at that time. He comes on the scene in my poem, but He says nothing, only appears and passes on. Fifteen centuries have passed since He promised to come in His glory, fifteen centuries since His prophet wrote, 'Behold, I come quickly;' 'Of that day and that hour knoweth no man, neither the Son, but the Father,' as He Himself predicted on earth. But humanity awaits him with the same faith and with the same love. Oh, with greater faith, for it is fifteen centuries since man has ceased to see signs from Heaven.

> No signs from Heaven come to-day
> To add to what the heart doth say.

There was nothing left but faith in what the heart doth say. It is true there were many miracles in those days. There were saints who performed miraculous cures; some holy people, according to their biographies, were visited by the Queen of Heaven herself. But the devil did not slumber, and doubts were already arising among men of the truth of these miracles. And just then there appeared in the north of Germany a terrible new heresy. 'A huge star like to a torch' (that is, to a church) 'fell on the sources of the waters and they became bitter.' These heretics began blasphemously denying miracles. But those who remained faithful were all the more ardent in their faith. The tears of humanity rose up to Him as before, awaited His coming, loved Him, hoped for Him, yearned to suffer and die for Him as before. And so many ages mankind had prayed with faith and fervour, 'O Lord our God, hasten Thy coming,' so many ages called upon Him, that in His infinite mercy He deigned to come down to His servants. Before that day He had come down, He had visited some holy men, martyrs and hermits, as is written in their 'Lives.' Among us, Tyutchev, with absolute faith in the truth of his words, bore witness that

> *Bearing the Cross, in slavish dress*
> *Weary and worn, the Heavenly King*
> *Our mother, Russia, came to bless,*
> *And through our land went wandering.*

And that certainly was so, I assure you.

"And behold, He deigned to appear for a moment to the people, to the tortured, suffering people, sunk in iniquity, but loving Him like children. My story is laid in Spain, in Seville, in the most terrible time of the Inquisition, when fires were lighted every day to the glory of God, and 'in the splendid *auto da fé* the wicked heretics were burnt.' Oh, of course, this was not the coming in which He will appear according to His promise at the end of time in all His heavenly glory, and which will be sudden 'as lightning flashing from east to west.' No, He visited His children only for a moment, and there where the flames were crackling round the heretics. In His infinite mercy He came once more among men in that human shape in which He walked among men for three years fifteen centuries ago. He came down to the 'hot pavements' of the southern town in which on the day before almost a hundred heretics had, *ad majorem gloriam Dei,* been burnt by the cardinal, the Grand Inquisitor, in a magnificent *auto da fé,* in the presence of the king, the court, the knights, the cardinals, the most charming ladies of the court, and the whole population of Seville.

"He came softly, unobserved, and yet, strange to say, every one recognised Him. That might be one of the best passages in the poem. I mean, why they recognised Him. The people are irresistibly drawn to Him, they surround Him, they flock about Him, follow Him. He moves silently in their midst with a gentle smile of infinite compassion. The sun of love burns in His heart, light and power shine from His eyes, and their radiance, shed on the people, stirs their hearts with responsive love. He holds out His hands to them, blesses them, and a healing virtue comes from contact with Him, even with His garments. An old man in the crowd, blind from childhood, cries out, 'O Lord, heal me and I shall see Thee!' and, as it were, scales fall from his eyes and the blind man sees Him. The crowd weeps and kisses the earth under His feet. Children throw flowers before Him, sing, and cry hosannah. 'It is He—it is He!' all repeat. 'It must be He, it can be no one but Him!' He stops at the steps of the Seville cathedral at the moment when the weeping mourners are bringing in a little open white coffin. In it lies a child of seven, the only daughter of a prominent citizen. The dead child lies hidden in flowers. 'He will raise your child,' the crowd shouts to the weeping mother. The priest, coming to meet the coffin, looks perplexed, and frowns, but the mother of the dead child throws herself at His feet with a wail. 'If it is Thou, raise my child!' she cries, holding out her hands to Him. The procession halts, the coffin is laid on the steps at His feet. He looks with compassion, and His lips once more softly pronounce, 'Maiden, arise!' and the maiden arises. The little girl sits up in the coffin and looks round, smiling with wide-open wondering eyes, holding a bunch of white roses they had put in her hand.

"There are cries, sobs, confusion among the people, and at that moment the cardinal himself, the Grand Inquisitor, passes by the cathedral. He is an old man, almost ninety, tall and erect, with a withered face and sunken eyes, in which there is still a gleam of light. He is not dressed in his gorgeous cardinal's robes, as he was the day before, when he was burning the enemies of the Roman Church—at that moment he was wearing his coarse, old, monk's cassock. At a distance behind him come his gloomy assistants and slaves and the 'holy guard.' He stops at the sight of the crowd and watches it from a distance. He sees everything; he sees them set the coffin down at His feet, sees the child rise up, and his face darkens. He knits his thick grey brows and his eyes gleam with a sinister fire. He holds out his finger and bids the guards take Him. And such is his power, so completely are the people cowed into submission and trembling obedience to him, that the crowd immediately make way for the guards, and in the midst of deathlike silence they lay hands on Him and lead Him away. The crowd instantly bows down to the earth, like one man, before the old inquisitor. He blesses the people in silence and passes on. The guards lead their prisoner to the close, gloomy vaulted prison in the ancient palace of the Holy Inquisition and shut Him in it. The day passes and is followed by the dark, burning 'breathless' night of Seville. The air is 'fragrant with laurel and lemon.' In the pitch darkness the iron door of the prison is suddenly opened and the Grand Inquisitor himself comes in with a light in his hand. He is alone; the door is closed at once behind him. He stands in the doorway and for a minute or two gazes into His face. At last he goes up slowly, sets the light on the table and speaks.

"'Is it Thou? Thou?' but receiving no answer, he adds at once, 'Don't answer, be silent. What canst Thou say, indeed? I know too well what Thou wouldst say. And Thou hast no right to add anything to what Thou hadst said of old. Why, then, art Thou come to hinder us? For Thou hast come to hinder us, and Thou knowest that. But dost Thou know what will be to-morrow? I know not who Thou art and care not to know whether it is Thou or only a semblance of Him, but to-morrow I shall condemn Thee and burn Thee at the stake as the worst of heretics. And the very people who have to-day kissed Thy feet, to-morrow at the faintest sign from me will rush to heap up the embers of Thy fire. Knowest Thou that? Yes, maybe Thou knowest it,' he added with thoughtful penetration, never for a moment taking his eyes off the Prisoner."

"I don't quite understand, Ivan. What does it mean?" Alyosha, who had been listening in silence, said with a smile. "Is it simply a wild fantasy, or a mistake on the part of the old man— some impossible *qui pro quo?*"

"Take it as the last," said Ivan, laughing, "if you are so corrupted by modern realism and can't stand anything fantastic. If you like it to be a case of mistaken identity, let it be so. It is true," he went on, laughing, "the old man was ninety, and he might well be crazy over his set idea. He might have been struck by the appearance of the Prisoner. It might, in fact, be simply his ravings, the delusion of an old man of ninety, over-excited by the *auto da fé* of a hundred heretics the day before. But does it matter to us after all whether it was a mistake of identity or a wild fantasy? All that matters is that the old man should speak out, should speak openly of what he has thought in silence for ninety years."

"And the Prisoner too is silent? Does He look at him and not say a word?"

"That's inevitable in any case," Ivan laughed again. "The old man has told Him He hasn't the right to add anything to what He has said of old. One may say it is the most fundamental feature of Roman Catholicism, in my opinion at least. 'All has been given by Thee to the Pope,' they say, 'and all, therefore, is still in the Pope's hands, and there is no need for Thee to come now at all. Thou must not meddle for the time, at least.' That's how they speak and write too—the Jesuits, at any rate. I have read it myself in the works of their theologians. 'Hast Thou the right to reveal to us one of the mysteries of that world from which Thou hast come?' my old man asks Him, and answers the question for Him. 'No, Thou hast not; that Thou mayest not add to what has been said of old, and mayest not take from men the freedom which Thou didst exalt when Thou wast on earth. Whatsoever Thou revealest anew will encroach on men's freedom of faith; for it will be manifest as a miracle, and the freedom of their faith was dearer to Thee than anything in those days fifteen hundred years ago. Didst Thou not often say then, "I will make you free"? But now Thou hast seen these "free" men,' the old man adds suddenly, with a pensive smile. 'Yes, we've paid dearly for it,' he goes on, looking sternly at Him, 'but at last we have completed that work in Thy name. For fifteen centuries we have been wrestling with Thy freedom, but now it is ended and over for good. Dost Thou not believe that it's over for good? Thou lookest meekly at me and deignest not even to be wroth with me. But let me tell Thee that now, to-day, people are more persuaded than ever that they have perfect freedom, yet they have brought their freedom to us and laid it humbly at our feet. But that has been our doing. Was this what Thou didst? Was this Thy freedom?'"

"I don't understand again," Alyosha broke in. "Is he ironical, is he jesting?"

"Not a bit of it! He claims it as, a merit for himself and his Church that at last they have vanquished freedom and have done so to make men happy. 'For now' (he is speaking of the Inquisition, of course) 'for the first time it has become possible to think of the happiness of men. Man was created a rebel; and how can rebels be happy? Thou wast warned,' he says to Him. 'Thou hast had no lack of admonitions and warnings, but Thou didst not listen to those warnings; Thou didst reject the only way by which men might be made happy. But, fortunately, departing Thou didst hand on the work to us. Thou hast promised, Thou hast established by Thy word, Thou hast given to us the right to bind and to unbind, and now, of course, Thou canst not think of taking it away. Why, then, hast Thou come to hinder us?'"

"And what's the meaning of 'no lack of admonitions and warnings'?" asked Alyosha.

"Why, that's the chief part of what the old man must say."

"'The wise and dread Spirit, the spirit of self-destruction and non-existence,' the old man goes on, 'the great spirit talked with Thee in the wilderness and we are told in the books that he "tempted" Thee. Is that so? And could anything truer be said than what he revealed to Thee in three questions and what Thou didst reject, and what in the books is called "the temptation"? And yet if there has ever been on earth a real stupendous miracle, it took place on that day, on the day of the three temptations. The statement of those three questions was itself the miracle. If it were possible to imagine simply for the sake of argument that those three questions of the dread spirit had perished utterly from the books, and that we had to restore them and to invent them anew, and to do so had gathered together all the wise men of the earth—rulers, chief priests, learned men, philosophers, poets—and had set them the task to invent three questions, such as would not only fit the occasion, but express in three words, three human phrases, the whole future history of the world and of humanity—dost Thou believe that all the wisdom of the earth united could have invented anything in depth and force equal to the three questions which were actually put to Thee then by the wise and mighty spirit in the wilderness? From those questions alone, from the miracle of their statement, we can see that we have here to do not with the fleeting human intelligence, but with the absolute and eternal. For in those three questions the whole subsequent history of mankind is, as it were, brought together into one whole, and foretold, and in them are united all the unsolved historical contradictions of human nature. At the time it could not be so clear, since the future was unknown; but now that fifteen hundred years have passed, we see that everything in those three questions was so justly divined and foretold, and has been so truly fulfilled, that nothing can be added to them or taken from them.

"'Judge Thyself who was right—Thou or he who questioned Thee then? Remember the first question; its meaning, in other words, was this: "Thou wouldst go into the world, and art going with empty hands, with some promise of freedom which men in their simplicity and their natural unruliness cannot even understand, which they fear and dread—for nothing has ever been more insupportable for a man and a human society than freedom. But seest Thou these stones in this parched and barren wilderness? Turn them into bread, and mankind will run after Thee like a flock of sheep, grateful and obedient, though forever trembling, lest Thou withdraw Thy hand and deny them Thy bread." But Thou wouldst not deprive man of freedom and didst reject the offer, thinking, what is that freedom worth, if obedience is bought with bread? Thou didst reply that man lives not by bread alone. But dost Thou know that for the sake of that earthly bread the spirit of the earth will rise up against Thee and will strive with Thee and overcome Thee, and all will follow him, crying, "Who can compare with this beast? He has given us fire from heaven!" Dost Thou know that the ages will pass, and humanity will proclaim by the lips of their sages that there is no crime, and therefore no sin; there is only hunger? "Feed men, and then ask of them virtue!" that's what they'll write on the banner, which they will raise against Thee, and with which they will destroy Thy temple. Where Thy temple stood will rise a new building; the terrible tower of Babel will be built again, and though, like the one of old, it will not be finished, yet Thou mightest have prevented that new tower and have cut short the sufferings of men for a thousand years; for they will come back to us after a thousand years of agony with their tower. They will seek us again, hidden underground in the catacombs, for we shall be again persecuted and tortured. They will find us and cry to us, "Feed us, for those who have promised us fire from heaven haven't given it!" And then we shall finish building their tower, for he finishes the building who feeds them. And we alone shall feed them in Thy name, declaring falsely that it is in Thy name. Oh, never, never can they feed themselves without us! No science will give them bread so long as they remain free. In the end they will lay their freedom at our feet, and say to us, "Make us your slaves, but feed us." They will understand themselves, at last, that freedom and bread enough for all are inconceivable together, for never, never will they be able to share between them! They will be convinced, too, that they can never be free, for they are weak, vicious, worthless and rebellious. Thou didst promise them the bread of Heaven, but, I repeat again, can it compare with earthly bread in the eyes of the weak, ever sinful and ignoble race of man? And if for the sake of the bread of Heaven thousands and tens of thousands shall follow Thee, what is to become of the millions and tens of thousands of millions of creatures who will not have the strength to forego the earthly bread for the sake of the heavenly? Or dost Thou care only for the tens of thousands of the great and strong, while the millions, numerous as the sands of the sea, who are weak but love Thee, must exist only for the sake of the great and strong? No, we care for the weak too. They are sinful and rebellious, but in the end they too will become obedient. They will marvel at us and look on us as gods, because we are ready to endure the freedom which they have found so dreadful and to rule over them—so awful it will seem to them to be free. But we shall tell them that we are Thy servants and rule them in Thy name. We shall deceive them again, for we will not let Thee come to us again. That deception will be our suffering, for we shall be forced to lie.

"'This is the significance of the first question in the wilderness, and this is what Thou hast rejected for the sake of that freedom which Thou hast exalted above everything. Yet in this question lies hid the great secret of this world. Choosing "bread," Thou wouldst have satisfied the universal and everlasting craving of humanity—to find some one to worship. So long as man remains free he strives for nothing so incessantly and so painfully as to find some one to worship. But man seeks to worship what is established beyond dispute, so that all men would agree at once to worship it. For these pitiful creatures are concerned not only to find what one or the other can worship, but to find something that all would believe in and worship; what is essential is that all may be *together* in it. This craving for *community* of worship is the chief misery of every man individually and of all humanity from the beginning of time. For the sake of common worship they've slain each other with the sword. They have set up gods and challenged one another, "Put away your gods and come and worship ours, or we will kill you and your gods!" And so it will be to the end of the world, even when gods disappear from the earth; they will fall down before idols just the same. Thou didst know, Thou couldst not but have known, this fundamental secret of human nature, but Thou didst reject the one infallible banner which was offered Thee to make all men bow down to Thee alone—the banner of earthly bread; and Thou hast rejected it for the sake of freedom and the bread of Heaven. Behold what Thou didst further. And all again in the name of freedom! I tell Thee that man is tormented by no greater anxiety than to find some one quickly to whom he can hand over that gift of freedom with which the ill-fated creature is born. But only one who can appease their conscience can take over their freedom. In bread there was offered Thee an invincible banner; give bread, and man will worship thee, for nothing is more certain than bread. But if some one else gains possession of his conscience—oh! then he will cast away Thy bread and follow after him who has ensnared his conscience. In that Thou wast right. For the secret of man's being is not only to live but to have something to live for. Without a stable conception of the object of life, man would not consent to go on living, and would rather destroy himself than remain on earth, though he had bread in abundance. That is true. But what happened? Instead of taking men's freedom from them, Thou didst make it greater than ever! Didst Thou forget that man prefers peace, and even death, to freedom of choice in the knowledge of good and evil? Nothing is more seductive for man than his freedom of conscience, but nothing is a greater cause of suffering. And behold, instead of giving a firm foundation for setting the conscience of man at rest for ever, Thou didst choose all that is exceptional, vague and enigmatic; Thou didst choose what was utterly beyond the strength of men, acting as though Thou didst not love them at all—Thou who didst come to give Thy life for them! Instead of taking possession of men's freedom, Thou didst increase it, and burdened the spiritual kingdom of mankind with its sufferings forever. Thou didst desire man's free love, that he should follow Thee freely, enticed and taken captive by Thee. In place of the rigid ancient law, man must hereafter with free heart decide for himself what is good and what is evil, having only Thy image before him as his guide. But didst Thou not know that he would at last reject even Thy image and Thy truth, if he is weighed down with the fearful burden of free choice? They will cry aloud at last that the truth is not in Thee, for they could not have been left in greater confusion and suffering than Thou hast caused, laying upon them so many cares and unanswerable problems.

"'So that, in truth, Thou didst Thyself lay the foundation for the destruction of Thy kingdom, and no one is more to blame for it. Yet what was offered Thee? There are three powers, three powers alone, able to conquer and to hold captive for ever the conscience of these impotent rebels for their happiness—those forces are miracle, mystery and authority. Thou hast rejected all three and hast set the example for doing so. When the wise and dread spirit set Thee on the pinnacle of the temple and said to Thee, "If Thou wouldst know whether Thou art the Son of God then cast Thyself down, for it is written: the angels shall hold him up lest he fall and bruise himself, and Thou shalt know then whether Thou art the Son of God and shalt prove then how great is Thy faith in Thy Father." But Thou didst refuse and wouldst not cast Thyself down. Oh! of course, Thou didst proudly and well, like God; but the weak, unruly race of men, are they gods? Oh, Thou didst know then that in taking one step, in making one movement to cast Thyself down, Thou wouldst be tempting God and have lost all Thy faith in Him, and wouldst have been dashed to pieces against that earth which Thou didst come to save. And the wise spirit that tempted Thee would have rejoiced. But I ask again, are there many like Thee? And couldst Thou believe for one moment that men, too, could face such a temptation? Is the nature of men such, that they can reject miracle, and at the great moments of their life, the moments of their deepest, most agonising spiritual difficulties, cling only to the free verdict of the heart? Oh, Thou didst know that Thy deed would be recorded in books, would be handed down to remote times and the utmost ends of the earth, and Thou didst hope that man, following Thee, would cling to God and not ask for a miracle. But Thou didst not know that when man rejects miracle he rejects God too; for man seeks not so much God as the miraculous. And as man cannot bear to be without the miraculous, he will create new miracles of his own for himself, and will worship deeds of sorcery and witchcraft, though he might be a hundred times over a rebel, heretic and infidel. Thou didst not come down from the Cross when they shouted to Thee, mocking and reviling Thee, "Come down from the cross and we will believe that Thou art He." Thou didst not come down, for again Thou wouldst not enslave man by a miracle, and didst crave faith given freely, not based on miracle. Thou didst crave for free love and not the base raptures of the slave before the might that has overawed him for ever. But Thou didst think too highly of men therein, for they are slaves, of course, though rebellious by nature. Look round and judge; fifteen centuries have passed, look upon them. Whom hast Thou raised up to Thyself? I swear, man is weaker and baser by nature than Thou hast believed him! Can he, can he do what Thou didst? By showing him so much respect, Thou didst, as it were, cease to feel for him, for Thou didst ask far too much from him—Thou who hast loved him more than Thyself! Respecting him less, Thou wouldst have asked less of him. That would have been more like love, for his burden would have been lighter. He is weak and vile. What though he is everywhere now rebelling against our power, and proud of his rebellion? It is the pride of a child and a schoolboy. They are little children rioting and barring out the teacher at school. But their childish delight will end; it will cost them dear. They will cast down temples and drench the earth with blood. But they will see at last, the foolish children, that, though they are rebels, they are impotent rebels, unable to keep up their own rebellion. Bathed in their foolish tears, they will recognise at last that He who created them rebels must have meant to mock at them. They will say this in despair, and their utterance will be a blasphemy which will make them more unhappy still, for man's nature cannot bear blasphemy, and in the end always avenges it on itself. And so unrest, confusion and unhappiness—that is the present lot of man after Thou didst bear so much for their freedom! Thy great prophet tells in vision and in image, that he saw all those who took part in the first resurrection and that there were of each tribe twelve thousand. But if there were so many of them, they must have been not men but gods. They had borne Thy cross, they had endured scores of years in the barren, hungry wilderness, living upon locusts and roots—and Thou mayest indeed point with pride at those children of freedom, of free love, of free and splendid sacrifice for Thy name. But remember that they were only some thousands; and what of the rest? And how are the other weak ones to blame, because they could not endure what the strong have endured? How is the weak soul to blame that it is unable to receive such terrible gifts? Canst Thou have simply come to the elect and for the elect? But if so, it is a mystery and we cannot understand it. And if it is a mystery, we too have a right to preach a mystery, and to teach them that it's not the free judgment of their hearts, not love that matters, but a mystery which they must follow blindly, even against their conscience. So we have done. We have corrected Thy work and have founded it upon *miracle, mystery* and *authority*. And men rejoiced that they were again led like sheep, and that the terrible gift that had brought them such suffering, was, at last, lifted from their hearts. Were we right teaching them this? Speak! Did we not love mankind, so meekly acknowledging their feebleness, lovingly lightening their burden, and permitting their weak nature even sin with our sanction? Why hast Thou come now to hinder us? And why dost Thou look silently and searchingly at me with Thy mild eyes? Be angry. I don't want Thy love, for I love Thee not. And what use is it for me to hide anything from Thee? Don't I know to Whom I am speaking? All that I can say is known to Thee already. And is it for me to conceal from Thee our mystery? Perhaps it is Thy will to hear it from my lips. Listen, then. We are not working with Thee, but with *him*—that is our mystery. It's long—eight centuries—since we have been on *his* side and not on Thine. Just eight centuries ago, we took from him what Thou didst reject with scorn, that last gift he offered Thee, showing Thee all the kingdoms of the earth. We took from him Rome and the sword of Cæsar, and proclaimed ourselves sole rulers of the earth, though hitherto we have not been able to complete our work. But whose fault is that? Oh, the work is only beginning, but it has begun. It has long to await completion and the earth has yet much to suffer, but we shall triumph and shall be Cæsars, and then we shall plan the universal happiness of man. But Thou mightest have taken even then the sword of Cæsar. Why didst Thou reject that last gift? Hadst Thou accepted that last counsel of the mighty spirit, Thou wouldst have accomplished all that man seeks on earth—that is, some one to worship, some one to keep his conscience, and some means of uniting all in one unanimous and harmonious ant-heap, for the craving for universal unity is the third and last anguish of men. Mankind as a whole has always striven to organise a universal state. There have been many great nations with great histories, but the more highly they were developed the more unhappy they were, for they felt more acutely than other people the craving for worldwide union. The great conquerors, Timours and Ghenghis-Khans, whirled like hurricanes over the face of the earth striving to subdue its people, and they too were but the unconscious expression of the same craving for universal unity. Hadst Thou taken the world and Cæsar's purple, Thou wouldst have founded the universal state and have given universal peace. For who can rule men if not he who holds their conscience and their bread in his hands. We have taken the sword of Cæsar, and in taking it, of course, have rejected Thee and followed *him*. Oh, ages are yet to come of the confusion of free thought, of their science and cannibalism. For having begun to build their tower of Babel without us, they will end, of course, with cannibalism. But then the beast will crawl to us and lick our feet and spatter them with tears of blood. And we shall sit upon the beast and raise the cup, and on it will be written, "Mystery." But then, and only then, the reign of peace and happiness will come for men. Thou art proud of Thine elect, but Thou hast only the elect, while we give rest to all. And besides, how many of those elect, those mighty ones who could become elect, have grown weary waiting for Thee, and have transferred and will transfer the powers of their spirit and the warmth of their heart to the other camp, and end by raising their *free* banner against Thee. Thou didst Thyself lift up that banner. But with us all will be happy and will no more rebel nor destroy one another as under Thy freedom. Oh, we shall persuade them that they will only become free when they renounce their freedom to us and submit to us. And shall we be right or shall we be lying? They will be convinced that we are right, for they will remember the horrors of slavery and confusion to which Thy freedom brought them. Freedom, free thought and science, will lead them into such straits and will bring them face to face with such marvels and insoluble mysteries, that some of them, the fierce and rebellious, will destroy themselves, others, rebellious but weak, will destroy one another, while the rest, weak and unhappy, will crawl fawning to our feet and whine to us: "Yes, you were right, you alone possess His mystery, and we come back to you, save us from ourselves!" [. . .]

44

Friedrich Nietzsche

Beyond Good and Evil (1886)

On the Prejudices of Philosophers

7. HOW MALICIOUS PHILOSOPHERS CAN BE! I KNOW OF NOTHING MORE stinging than the joke Epicurus took the liberty of making on Plato and the Platonists; he called them Dionysiokolakes. In its original sense, and on the face of it, the word signifies "Flatterers of Dionysius"—consequently, tyrants' accessories and lick-spittles; besides this, however, it is as much as to say, "They are all ACTORS, there is nothing genuine about them" (for Dionysiokolax was a popular name for an actor). And the latter is really the malignant reproach that Epicurus cast upon Plato: he was annoyed by the grandiose manner, the mise en scene style of which Plato and his scholars were masters—of which Epicurus was not a master! He, the old school-teacher of Samos, who sat concealed in his little garden at Athens, and wrote three hundred books, perhaps out of rage and ambitious envy of Plato, who knows! Greece took a hundred years to find out who the garden-god Epicurus really was. Did she ever find out? [. . .]

14. It is perhaps just dawning on five or six minds that natural philosophy is only a world-exposition and world-arrangement (according to us, if I may say so!) and NOT a world-explanation; but in so far as it is based on belief in the senses, it is regarded as more, and for a long time to come must be regarded as more—namely, as an explanation. It has eyes and fingers of its own, it has ocular evidence and palpableness of its own: this operates fascinatingly, persuasively, and CONVINCINGLY upon an age with fundamentally plebeian tastes—in fact, it follows instinctively the canon of truth of eternal popular sensualism. What is clear, what is "explained"? Only that which can be seen and felt—one must pursue every problem thus far. Obversely, however, the charm of the Platonic mode of thought, which was an ARISTOCRATIC

mode, consisted precisely in RESISTANCE to obvious sense-evidence—perhaps among men who enjoyed even stronger and more fastidious senses than our contemporaries, but who knew how to find a higher triumph in remaining masters of them: and this by means of pale, cold, grey conceptional networks which they threw over the motley whirl of the senses—the mob of the senses, as Plato said. In this overcoming of the world, and interpreting of the world in the manner of Plato, there was an ENJOYMENT different from that which the physicists of today offer us—and likewise the Darwinists and anti-teleologists among the physiological workers, with their principle of the "smallest possible effort," and the greatest possible blunder. "Where there is nothing more to see or to grasp, there is also nothing more for men to do"—that is certainly an imperative different from the Platonic one, but it may notwithstanding be the right imperative for a hardy, laborious race of machinists and bridge-builders of the future, who have nothing but ROUGH work to perform. [. . .]

What is Religious?

45. THE HUMAN SOUL AND ITS LIMITS, THE RANGE OF MAN'S inner experiences hitherto attained, the heights, depths, and distances of these experiences, the entire history of the soul UP TO THE PRESENT TIME, and its still unexhausted possibilities: this is the preordained hunting-domain for a born psychologist and lover of a "big hunt". But how often must he say despairingly to himself: "A single individual! alas, only a single individual! and this great forest, this virgin forest!" So he would like to have some hundreds of hunting assistants, and fine trained hounds, that he could send into the history of the human soul, to drive HIS game together. In vain: again and again he experiences, profoundly and bitterly, how difficult it is to find assistants and dogs for all the things that directly excite his curiosity. The evil of sending scholars into new and dangerous hunting-domains, where courage, sagacity, and subtlety in every sense are required, is that they are no longer serviceable just when the "BIG hunt," and also the great danger commences,—it is precisely then that they lose their keen eye and nose. In order, for instance, to divine and determine what sort of history the problem of KNOWLEDGE AND CONSCIENCE has hitherto had in the souls of *homines religiosi*, a person would perhaps himself have to possess as profound, as bruised, as immense an experience as the intellectual conscience of Pascal; and then he would still require that wide-spread heaven of clear, wicked spirituality, which, from above, would be able to oversee, arrange, and effectively formulize this mass of dangerous and painful experiences.—But who could do me this service! And who would have time to wait for such servants!—they evidently appear too rarely, they are so improbable at all times! Eventually one must do everything ONESELF in order to know something; which means that one has MUCH to do!—But a curiosity like mine is once for all the most agreeable of vices—pardon me! I mean to say that the love of truth has its reward in heaven, and already upon earth.

46. Faith, such as early Christianity desired, and not infrequently achieved in the midst of a skeptical and southernly free-spirited world, which had centuries of struggle between philosophical schools behind it and in it, counting besides the education in tolerance which the Imperium Romanum gave—this faith is NOT that sincere, austere slave-faith by which perhaps a Luther or a Cromwell, or some other northern barbarian of the spirit remained attached to his God and Christianity, it is much rather the faith of Pascal, which resembles in a terrible manner a continuous suicide of reason—a tough, long-lived, worm-like reason, which is not to be slain at once and with a single blow. The Christian faith from the beginning, is sacrifice the sacrifice of all freedom, all pride, all self-confidence of spirit, it is at the same time subjection, self-derision, and self-mutilation. There is cruelty and religious Phoenicianism in this faith, which is adapted to a tender, many-sided, and very fastidious conscience, it takes for granted that the subjection of the spirit is indescribably PAINFUL, that all the past and all the habits of such a spirit resist the absurdissimum, in the form of which "faith" comes to it. Modern men, with their obtuseness as regards all Christian nomenclature, have no longer the sense for the terribly superlative conception which was implied to an antique taste by the paradox of the formula, "God on the Cross". Hitherto there had never and nowhere been such boldness in inversion, nor anything at once so dreadful, questioning, and questionable as this formula: it promised a transvaluation of all ancient values—It was the Orient, the PROFOUND Orient, it was the Oriental slave who thus took revenge on Rome and its noble, light-minded toleration, on the Roman "Catholicism" of non-faith, and it was always not the faith, but the freedom from the faith, the half-stoical and smiling indifference to the seriousness of the faith, which made the slaves indignant at their masters and revolt against them. "Enlightenment" causes revolt, for the slave desires the unconditioned, he understands nothing but the tyrannous, even in morals, he loves as he hates, without NUANCE, to the very depths, to the point of pain, to the point of sickness—his many HIDDEN sufferings make him revolt against the noble taste which seems to DENY suffering. The skepticism with regard to suffering, fundamentally only an attitude of aristocratic morality, was not the least of the causes, also, of the last great slave-insurrection which began with the French Revolution.

47. Wherever the religious neurosis has appeared on the earth so far, we find it connected with three dangerous prescriptions as to regimen: solitude, fasting, and sexual abstinence—but without its being possible to determine with certainty which is cause and which is effect, or IF any relation at all of cause and effect exists there. This latter doubt is justified by the fact that one of the most regular symptoms among savage as well as among civilized peoples is the most sudden and excessive sensuality, which then with equal suddenness transforms into penitential paroxysms, world-renunciation, and will-renunciation, both symptoms perhaps explainable as disguised epilepsy? But nowhere is it MORE obligatory to put aside explanations around no other type has there grown such a mass of absurdity and superstition, no other type seems to

have been more interesting to men and even to philosophers—perhaps it is time to become just a little indifferent here, to learn caution, or, better still, to look AWAY, TO GO AWAY—Yet in the background of the most recent philosophy, that of Schopenhauer, we find almost as the problem in itself, this terrible note of interrogation of the religious crisis and awakening. How is the negation of will POSSIBLE? how is the saint possible?—that seems to have been the very question with which Schopenhauer made a start and became a philosopher. And thus it was a genuine Schopenhauerian consequence, that his most convinced adherent (perhaps also his last, as far as Germany is concerned), namely, Richard Wagner, should bring his own life-work to an end just here, and should finally put that terrible and eternal type upon the stage as Kundry, type vecu, and as it loved and lived, at the very time that the mad-doctors in almost all European countries had an opportunity to study the type close at hand, wherever the religious neurosis— or as I call it, "the religious mood"—made its latest epidemical outbreak and display as the "Salvation Army"—If it be a question, however, as to what has been so extremely interesting to men of all sorts in all ages, and even to philosophers, in the whole phenomenon of the saint, it is undoubtedly the appearance of the miraculous therein—namely, the immediate SUCCESSION OF OPPOSITES, of states of the soul regarded as morally antithetical: it was believed here to be self-evident that a "bad man" was all at once turned into a "saint," a good man. The hitherto existing psychology was wrecked at this point, is it not possible it may have happened principally because psychology had placed itself under the dominion of morals, because it BELIEVED in oppositions of moral values, and saw, read, and INTERPRETED these oppositions into the text and facts of the case? What? "Miracle" only an error of interpretation? A lack of philology?

48. It seems that the Latin races are far more deeply attached to their Catholicism than we Northerners are to Christianity generally, and that consequently unbelief in Catholic countries means something quite different from what it does among Protestants—namely, a sort of revolt against the spirit of the race, while with us it is rather a return to the spirit (or non-spirit) of the race.

We Northerners undoubtedly derive our origin from barbarous races, even as regards our talents for religion—we have POOR talents for it. One may make an exception in the case of the Celts, who have theretofore furnished also the best soil for Christian infection in the North: the Christian ideal blossomed forth in France as much as ever the pale sun of the north would allow it. How strangely pious for our taste are still these later French skeptics, whenever there is any Celtic blood in their origin! How Catholic, how un-German does Auguste Comte's Sociology seem to us, with the Roman logic of its instincts! How Jesuitical, that amiable and shrewd cicerone of Port Royal, Sainte-Beuve, in spite of all his hostility to Jesuits! And even Ernest Renan: how inaccessible to us Northerners does the language of such a Renan appear, in whom every instant the merest touch of religious thrill throws his refined voluptuous and comfortably couching soul off its balance! [...]

49. That which is so astonishing in the religious life of the ancient Greeks is the irrestrainable stream of GRATITUDE which it pours forth—it is a very superior kind of man who takes SUCH an attitude towards nature and life.—Later on, when the populace got the upper hand in Greece, FEAR became rampant also in religion; and Christianity was preparing itself.

50. The passion for God: there are churlish, honest-hearted, and importunate kinds of it, like that of Luther—the whole of Protestantism lacks the southern DELICATEZZA. There is an Oriental exaltation of the mind in it, like that of an undeservedly favoured or elevated slave, as in the case of St. Augustine, for instance, who lacks in an offensive manner, all nobility in bearing and desires. There is a feminine tenderness and sensuality in it, which modestly and unconsciously longs for a UNIO MYSTICA ET PHYSICA, as in the case of Madame de Guyon. In many cases it appears, curiously enough, as the disguise of a girl's or youth's puberty; here and there even as the hysteria of an old maid, also as her last ambition. The Church has frequently canonized the woman in such a case.

51. The mightiest men have hitherto always bowed reverently before the saint, as the enigma of self-subjugation and utter voluntary privation—why did they thus bow? They divined in him— and as it were behind the questionableness of his frail and wretched appearance—the superior force which wished to test itself by such a subjugation; the strength of will, in which they recognized their own strength and love of power, and knew how to honour it: they honoured something in themselves when they honoured the saint. In addition to this, the contemplation of the saint suggested to them a suspicion: such an enormity of self-negation and anti-naturalness will not have been coveted for nothing—they have said, inquiringly. There is perhaps a reason for it, some very great danger, about which the ascetic might wish to be more accurately informed through his secret interlocutors and visitors? In a word, the mighty ones of the world learned to have a new fear before him, they divined a new power, a strange, still unconquered enemy:—it was the "Will to Power" which obliged them to halt before the saint. They had to question him.

52. In the Jewish "Old Testament," the book of divine justice, there are men, things, and sayings on such an immense scale, that Greek and Indian literature has nothing to compare with it. One stands with fear and reverence before those stupendous remains of what man was formerly, and one has sad thoughts about old Asia and its little out-pushed peninsula Europe, which would like, by all means, to figure before Asia as the "Progress of Mankind." To be sure, he who is himself only a slender, tame house-animal, and knows only the wants of a house-animal (like our cultured people of today, including the Christians of "cultured" Christianity), need neither be amazed nor even sad amid those ruins—the taste for the Old Testament is a touchstone with respect to "great" and "small": perhaps he will find that the New Testament, the book of grace, still appeals more to his heart (there is much of the odour of the genuine, tender, stupid

beadsman and petty soul in it). To have bound up this New Testament (a kind of ROCOCO of taste in every respect) along with the Old Testament into one book, as the "Bible," as "The Book in Itself," is perhaps the greatest audacity and "sin against the Spirit" which literary Europe has upon its conscience.

53. Why Atheism nowadays? "The father" in God is thoroughly refuted; equally so "the judge," "the rewarder." Also his "free will": he does not hear—and even if he did, he would not know how to help. The worst is that he seems incapable of communicating himself clearly; is he uncertain?— This is what I have made out (by questioning and listening at a variety of conversations) to be the cause of the decline of European theism; it appears to me that though the religious instinct is in vigorous growth,—it rejects the theistic satisfaction with profound distrust.

54. What does all modern philosophy mainly do? Since Descartes—and indeed more in defiance of him than on the basis of his procedure—an ATTENTAT has been made on the part of all philosophers on the old conception of the soul, under the guise of a criticism of the subject and predicate conception—that is to say, an ATTENTAT on the fundamental presupposition of Christian doctrine. Modern philosophy, as epistemological skepticism, is secretly or openly ANTI-CHRISTIAN, although (for keener ears, be it said) by no means anti-religious. Formerly, in effect, one believed in "the soul" as one believed in grammar and the grammatical subject: one said, "I" is the condition, "think" is the predicate and is conditioned—to think is an activity for which one MUST suppose a subject as cause. The attempt was then made, with marvelous tenacity and subtlety, to see if one could not get out of this net,—to see if the opposite was not perhaps true: "think" the condition, and "I" the conditioned; "I," therefore, only a synthesis which has been MADE by thinking itself. KANT really wished to prove that, starting from the subject, the subject could not be proved—nor the object either: the possibility of an APPARENT EXISTENCE of the subject, and therefore of "the soul," may not always have been strange to him,—the thought which once had an immense power on earth as the Vedanta philosophy.

55. There is a great ladder of religious cruelty, with many rounds; but three of these are the most important. Once on a time men sacrificed human beings to their God, and perhaps just those they loved the best—to this category belong the firstling sacrifices of all primitive religions, and also the sacrifice of the Emperor Tiberius in the Mithra-Grotto on the Island of Capri, that most terrible of all Roman anachronisms. Then, during the moral epoch of mankind, they sacrificed to their God the strongest instincts they possessed, their "nature"; THIS festal joy shines in the cruel glances of ascetics and "anti-natural" fanatics. Finally, what still remained to be sacrificed? Was it not necessary in the end for men to sacrifice everything comforting, holy, healing, all hope, all faith in hidden harmonies, in future blessedness and justice? Was it not necessary to sacrifice God himself, and out of cruelty to themselves to worship stone, stupidity, gravity, fate,

nothingness? To sacrifice God for nothingness—this paradoxical mystery of the ultimate cruelty has been reserved for the rising generation; we all know something thereof already.

56. Whoever, like myself, prompted by some enigmatical desire, has long endeavoured to go to the bottom of the question of pessimism and free it from the half-Christian, half-German narrowness and stupidity in which it has finally presented itself to this century, namely, in the form of Schopenhauer's philosophy; whoever, with an Asiatic and super-Asiatic eye, has actually looked inside, and into the most world-renouncing of all possible modes of thought—beyond good and evil, and no longer like Buddha and Schopenhauer, under the dominion and delusion of morality,—whoever has done this, has perhaps just thereby, without really desiring it, opened his eyes to behold the opposite ideal: the ideal of the most world-approving, exuberant, and vivacious man, who has not only learnt to compromise and arrange with that which was and is, but wishes to have it again AS IT WAS AND IS, for all eternity, insatiably calling out da capo, not only to himself, but to the whole piece and play; and not only the play, but actually to him who requires the play—and makes it necessary; because he always requires himself anew—and makes himself necessary.—What? And this would not be—*circulus vitiosus deus*?

57. The distance, and as it were the space around man, grows with the strength of his intellectual vision and insight: his world becomes profounder; new stars, new enigmas, and notions are ever coming into view. Perhaps everything on which the intellectual eye has exercised its acuteness and profundity has just been an occasion for its exercise, something of a game, something for children and childish minds. Perhaps the most solemn conceptions that have caused the most fighting and suffering, the conceptions "God" and "sin," will one day seem to us of no more importance than a child's plaything or a child's pain seems to an old man;—and perhaps another plaything and another pain will then be necessary once more for "the old man"—always childish enough, an eternal child!

58. Has it been observed to what extent outward idleness, or semi-idleness, is necessary to a real religious life (alike for its favourite microscopic labour of self-examination, and for its soft placidity called "prayer," the state of perpetual readiness for the "coming of God"), I mean the idleness with a good conscience, the idleness of olden times and of blood, to which the aristocratic sentiment that work is DISHONOURING—that it vulgarizes body and soul—is not quite unfamiliar? And that consequently the modern, noisy, time-engrossing, conceited, foolishly proud laboriousness educates and prepares for "unbelief" more than anything else? Among these, for instance, who are at present living apart from religion in Germany, I find "free-thinkers" of diversified species and origin, but above all a majority of those in whom laboriousness from generation to generation has dissolved the religious instincts; so that they no longer know what purpose religions serve, and only note their existence in the world with

a kind of dull astonishment. They feel themselves already fully occupied, these good people, be it by their business or by their pleasures, not to mention the "Fatherland," and the newspapers, and their "family duties"; it seems that they have no time whatever left for religion; and above all, it is not obvious to them whether it is a question of a new business or a new pleasure—for it is impossible, they say to themselves, that people should go to church merely to spoil their tempers. They are by no means enemies of religious customs; should certain circumstances, State affairs perhaps, require their participation in such customs, they do what is required, as so many things are done—with a patient and unassuming seriousness, and without much curiosity or discomfort;—they live too much apart and outside to feel even the necessity for a FOR or AGAINST in such matters. Among those indifferent persons may be reckoned nowadays the majority of German Protestants of the middle classes, especially in the great laborious centres of trade and commerce; also the majority of laborious scholars, and the entire University personnel (with the exception of the theologians, whose existence and possibility there always gives psychologists new and more subtle puzzles to solve). On the part of pious, or merely church-going people, there is seldom any idea of HOW MUCH good-will, one might say arbitrary will, is now necessary for a German scholar to take the problem of religion seriously; his whole profession (and as I have said, his whole workmanlike laboriousness, to which he is compelled by his modern conscience) inclines him to a lofty and almost charitable serenity as regards religion, with which is occasionally mingled a slight disdain for the "uncleanliness" of spirit which he takes for granted wherever any one still professes to belong to the Church. It is only with the help of history (NOT through his own personal experience, therefore) that the scholar succeeds in bringing himself to a respectful seriousness, and to a certain timid deference in presence of religions; but even when his sentiments have reached the stage of gratitude towards them, he has not personally advanced one step nearer to that which still maintains itself as Church or as piety; perhaps even the contrary. The practical indifference to religious matters in the midst of which he has been born and brought up, usually sublimates itself in his case into circumspection and cleanliness, which shuns contact with religious men and things; and it may be just the depth of his tolerance and humanity which prompts him to avoid the delicate trouble which tolerance itself brings with it.—Every age has its own divine type of naivete, for the discovery of which other ages may envy it: and how much naivete—adorable, childlike, and boundlessly foolish naivete is involved in this belief of the scholar in his superiority, in the good conscience of his tolerance, in the unsuspecting, simple certainty with which his instinct treats the religious man as a lower and less valuable type, beyond, before, and ABOVE which he himself has developed—he, the little arrogant dwarf and mob-man, the sedulously alert, head-and-hand drudge of "ideas," of "modern ideas"!

59. Whoever has seen deeply into the world has doubtless divined what wisdom there is in the fact that men are superficial. It is their preservative instinct which teaches them to be flighty,

lightsome, and false. Here and there one finds a passionate and exaggerated adoration of "pure forms" in philosophers as well as in artists: it is not to be doubted that whoever has NEED of the cult of the superficial to that extent, has at one time or another made an unlucky dive BENEATH it. Perhaps there is even an order of rank with respect to those burnt children, the born artists who find the enjoyment of life only in trying to FALSIFY its image (as if taking wearisome revenge on it), one might guess to what degree life has disgusted them, by the extent to which they wish to see its image falsified, attenuated, ultrified, and deified,—one might reckon the homines religiosi among the artists, as their HIGHEST rank. It is the profound, suspicious fear of an incurable pessimism which compels whole centuries to fasten their teeth into a religious interpretation of existence: the fear of the instinct which divines that truth might be attained TOO soon, before man has become strong enough, hard enough, artist enough. . . . Piety, the "Life in God," regarded in this light, would appear as the most elaborate and ultimate product of the FEAR of truth, as artist-adoration and artist-intoxication in presence of the most logical of all falsifications, as the will to the inversion of truth, to untruth at any price. Perhaps there has hitherto been no more effective means of beautifying man than piety, by means of it man can become so artful, so superficial, so iridescent, and so good, that his appearance no longer offends.

60. To love mankind FOR GOD'S SAKE—this has so far been the noblest and remotest sentiment to which mankind has attained. That love to mankind, without any redeeming intention in the background, is only an ADDITIONAL folly and brutishness, that the inclination to this love has first to get its proportion, its delicacy, its gram of salt and sprinkling of ambergris from a higher inclination—whoever first perceived and "experienced" this, however his tongue may have stammered as it attempted to express such a delicate matter, let him for all time be holy and respected, as the man who has so far flown highest and gone astray in the finest fashion!

61. The philosopher, as WE free spirits understand him—as the man of the greatest responsibility, who has the conscience for the general development of mankind,—will use religion for his disciplining and educating work, just as he will use the contemporary political and economic conditions. The selecting and disciplining influence—destructive, as well as creative and fashioning—which can be exercised by means of religion is manifold and varied, according to the sort of people placed under its spell and protection. For those who are strong and independent, destined and trained to command, in whom the judgment and skill of a ruling race is incorporated, religion is an additional means for overcoming resistance in the exercise of authority—as a bond which binds rulers and subjects in common, betraying and surrendering to the former the conscience of the latter, their inmost heart, which would fain escape obedience. And in the case of the unique natures of noble origin, if by virtue of superior spirituality they should incline to a more retired and contemplative life, reserving to themselves only the more

refined forms of government (over chosen disciples or members of an order), religion itself may be used as a means for obtaining peace from the noise and trouble of managing GROSSER affairs, and for securing immunity from the UNAVOIDABLE filth of all political agitation. The Brahmins, for instance, understood this fact. With the help of a religious organization, they secured to themselves the power of nominating kings for the people, while their sentiments prompted them to keep apart and outside, as men with a higher and super-regal mission. At the same time religion gives inducement and opportunity to some of the subjects to qualify themselves for future ruling and commanding the slowly ascending ranks and classes, in which, through fortunate marriage customs, volitional power and delight in self-control are on the increase. To them religion offers sufficient incentives and temptations to aspire to higher intellectuality, and to experience the sentiments of authoritative self-control, of silence, and of solitude. Asceticism and Puritanism are almost indispensable means of educating and ennobling a race which seeks to rise above its hereditary baseness and work itself upwards to future supremacy. And finally, to ordinary men, to the majority of the people, who exist for service and general utility, and are only so far entitled to exist, religion gives invaluable contentedness with their lot and condition, peace of heart, ennoblement of obedience, additional social happiness and sympathy, with something of transfiguration and embellishment, something of justification of all the commonplaceness, all the meanness, all the semi-animal poverty of their souls. Religion, together with the religious significance of life, sheds sunshine over such perpetually harassed men, and makes even their own aspect endurable to them, it operates upon them as the Epicurean philosophy usually operates upon sufferers of a higher order, in a refreshing and refining manner, almost TURNING suffering TO ACCOUNT, and in the end even hallowing and vindicating it. There is perhaps nothing so admirable in Christianity and Buddhism as their art of teaching even the lowest to elevate themselves by piety to a seemingly higher order of things, and thereby to retain their satisfaction with the actual world in which they find it difficult enough to live—this very difficulty being necessary.

62. To be sure—to make also the bad counter-reckoning against such religions, and to bring to light their secret dangers—the cost is always excessive and terrible when religions do NOT operate as an educational and disciplinary medium in the hands of the philosopher, but rule voluntarily and PARAMOUNTLY, when they wish to be the final end, and not a means along with other means. Among men, as among all other animals, there is a surplus of defective, diseased, degenerating, infirm, and necessarily suffering individuals; the successful cases, among men also, are always the exception; and in view of the fact that man is THE ANIMAL NOT YET PROPERLY ADAPTED TO HIS ENVIRONMENT, the rare exception. But worse still. The higher the type a man represents, the greater is the improbability that he will SUCCEED; the accidental, the law of irrationality in the general constitution of mankind, manifests itself

most terribly in its destructive effect on the higher orders of men, the conditions of whose lives are delicate, diverse, and difficult to determine. What, then, is the attitude of the two greatest religions above-mentioned to the SURPLUS of failures in life? They endeavour to preserve and keep alive whatever can be preserved; in fact, as the religions FOR SUFFERERS, they take the part of these upon principle; they are always in favour of those who suffer from life as from a disease, and they would fain treat every other experience of life as false and impossible. However highly we may esteem this indulgent and preservative care (inasmuch as in applying to others, it has applied, and applies also to the highest and usually the most suffering type of man), the hitherto PARAMOUNT religions—to give a general appreciation of them—are among the principal causes which have kept the type of "man" upon a lower level—they have preserved too much THAT WHICH SHOULD HAVE PERISHED. One has to thank them for invaluable services; and who is sufficiently rich in gratitude not to feel poor at the contemplation of all that the "spiritual men" of Christianity have done for Europe hitherto! But when they had given comfort to the sufferers, courage to the oppressed and despairing, a staff and support to the helpless, and when they had allured from society into convents and spiritual penitentiaries the broken-hearted and distracted: what else had they to do in order to work systematically in that fashion, and with a good conscience, for the preservation of all the sick and suffering, which means, in deed and in truth, to work for the DETERIORATION OF THE EUROPEAN RACE? To REVERSE all estimates of value—THAT is what they had to do! And to shatter the strong, to spoil great hopes, to cast suspicion on the delight in beauty, to break down everything autonomous, manly, conquering, and imperious—all instincts which are natural to the highest and most successful type of "man"—into uncertainty, distress of conscience, and self-destruction; forsooth, to invert all love of the earthly and of supremacy over the earth, into hatred of the earth and earthly things—THAT is the task the Church imposed on itself, and was obliged to impose, until, according to its standard of value, "unworldliness," "unsensuousness," and "higher man" fused into one sentiment. If one could observe the strangely painful, equally coarse and refined comedy of European Christianity with the derisive and impartial eye of an Epicurean god, I should think one would never cease marvelling and laughing; does it not actually seem that some single will has ruled over Europe for eighteen centuries in order to make a SUBLIME ABORTION of man? He, however, who, with opposite requirements (no longer Epicurean) and with some divine hammer in his hand, could approach this almost voluntary degeneration and stunting of mankind, as exemplified in the European Christian (Pascal, for instance), would he not have to cry aloud with rage, pity, and horror: "Oh, you bunglers, presumptuous pitiful bunglers, what have you done! Was that a work for your hands! How you have hacked and botched my finest stone! What have you presumed to do!"—I should say that Christianity has hitherto been the most portentous of presumptions. Men, not great enough, nor hard enough, to be entitled as artists to take part in fashioning MAN; men, not sufficiently strong and far-sighted to ALLOW, with sublime self-constraint, the obvious law of the thousandfold failures and perishings to prevail; men, not sufficiently noble to see the radically different grades of rank and intervals of rank that separate man from man:—SUCH men, with their "equality before God," have hitherto swayed the destiny of Europe; until at last a dwarfed, almost ludicrous species has been produced, a gregarious animal, something obliging, sickly, mediocre, the European of the present day.

45

Walter Pater

Appreciations (1889)

Coleridge

[. . .] MODERN THOUGHT IS DISTINGUISHED FROM ANCIENT BY ITS CULTIVATION of the "relative" spirit in place of the "absolute." Ancient philosophy sought to arrest every object in an eternal outline, to fix thought in a necessary formula, and the varieties of life in a classification by "kinds," or *genera*. To the modern spirit nothing is, or can be rightly known, except relatively and under conditions. The philosophical conception of the relative has been developed in modern times through the influence of the sciences of observation. Those sciences reveal types of life evanescing into each other by inexpressible refinements of change. Things pass into their opposites by accumulation of undefinable quantities. The growth of those sciences consists in a continual analysis of facts of rough and general observation into groups of facts more precise and minute.

[. . .] Now the literary life of Coleridge was a disinterested struggle against the relative spirit. With a strong native bent towards the tracking of all questions, critical or practical, to first principles, he is ever restlessly scheming to "apprehend the absolute," to affirm it effectively, to get it acknowledged. It was an effort, surely, an effort of sickly thought, that saddened his mind, and limited the operation of his unique poetic gift.

So what the reader of our own generation will least find in Coleridge's prose writings is the excitement of the literary sense. And yet, in those grey volumes, we have the larger part of the production of one who made way ever by a charm, the charm of voice, of aspect, of language, above all by the intellectual charm of new, moving, luminous ideas. Perhaps the chief offence in Coleridge is an excess of seriousness, a seriousness arising not from any moral principle, but from a misconception of the perfect manner. There is a certain shade of unconcern, the perfect manner of the eighteenth century, which may be thought to mark complete culture in the handling of abstract questions. The humanist, the possessor of that complete culture, does not "weep" over the failure of "a theory of the quantification of the predicate," nor "shriek" over the fall of a philosophical formula. A kind of humour is, in truth, one of the conditions of the just mental attitude, in the criticism of by-past stages of thought. Humanity cannot afford to be too serious about them, any more than a man of good sense can afford to be too serious in looking back upon his own childhood. Plato, whom Coleridge claims as the first of his spiritual ancestors, Plato, as we remember him, a true humanist, holds his theories lightly, glances with a somewhat blithe and naive inconsequence from one view to another, not anticipating the burden of importance "views" will one day have for men. In reading him one feels how lately it was that Crœsus thought it a paradox to say that external prosperity was not necessarily happiness. But on Coleridge lies the whole weight of the sad reflection that has since come into the world, with which for us the air is full, which the "children in the market-place" repeat to each other. His very language is forced and broken lest some saving formula should be lost—*distinctities, enucleation, pentad of operative Christianity;* he has a whole armoury of these terms, and expects to turn the tide of human thought by fixing the sense of such expressions as "reason," "understanding," "idea." Again, he lacks the jealousy of a true artist in excluding all associations that have no colour, or charm, or gladness in them; and everywhere allows the impress of a somewhat inferior theological literature.

[. . .] In 1798 he visited Germany, then, the only half-known, "promised land," of the metaphysical, the "absolute," philosophy. [. . .]

The *Aids to Reflection, The Friend, The Biographia Literaria:* those books came from one whose vocation was in the world of the imagination, the theory and practice of poetry. And yet, perhaps, of all books that have been influential in modern times, they are furthest from artistic form—bundles of notes; the original matter inseparably mixed up with that borrowed from others; the whole, just that mere preparation for an artistic effect which the finished literary artist would be careful one day to destroy. Here, again, we have a trait profoundly characteristic of Coleridge. He sometimes attempts to reduce a phase of thought, subtle and exquisite, to conditions too rough for it. He uses a purely speculative gift for direct moral edification. Scientific truth is a thing fugitive, relative, full of fine gradations: he tries to fix it in absolute formulas. The *Aids to Reflection, The Friend,* are efforts to propagate the volatile spirit of conversation into the less ethereal fabric of a written book; and it is only here or there that the poorer matter becomes vibrant, is really lifted by the spirit.

De Quincey said of him that "he wanted better bread than can be made with wheat:" Lamb, that from childhood he had "hungered for eternity." Yet the faintness, the continuous dissolution, whatever its cause, which soon supplanted the buoyancy of his first wonderful years, had its own consumptive refinements, and even brought, as to the "Beautiful Soul" in *Wilhelm Meister,* a faint religious ecstasy—that "singing in the sails" which is not of the breeze. Here again is one of his occasional notes:—

"In looking at objects of nature while I am thinking, as at yonder moon, dim-glimmering through the window-pane, I seem rather to be seeking, as it were asking, a symbolical language for something within me, that already and for ever exists, than observing anything new. Even when the latter is the case, yet still I have always an obscure feeling, as if that new phenomenon were the dim awaking of a forgotten or hidden truth of my inner nature. While I was preparing the pen to make this remark, I lost the train of thought which had led me to it."

What a distemper of the eye of the mind! What an almost bodily distemper there is in that!

Coleridge's intellectual sorrows were many; but he had one singular intellectual happiness. With an inborn taste for transcendental philosophy, he lived just at the time when that philosophy took an immense spring in Germany, and connected itself with an impressive literary movement. He had the good luck to light upon it in its freshness, and introduce it to his countrymen. What an opportunity for one reared on the colourless analytic English philosophies of the last century, but who feels an irresistible attraction towards bold metaphysical synthesis! How rare are such occasions of intellectual contentment! This transcendental philosophy, chiefly as systematised by the mystic Schelling, Coleridge applied with an eager, unwearied subtlety, to the questions of theology, and poetic or artistic criticism. It is in his theory of poetry, of art, that he comes nearest to principles of permanent truth and importance: that is the least fugitive part of his prose work. [. . .]

Schellingism, the "Philosophy of Nature," is indeed a constant tradition in the history of thought: it embodies a permanent type of the speculative temper. That mode of conceiving nature as a mirror or reflex of the intelligence of man may be traced up to the first beginnings of Greek speculation. There are two ways of envisaging those aspects of nature which seem to bear the impress of reason or intelligence. There is the deist's way, which regards them merely as marks of design, which separates the informing mind from its result in nature, as the mechanist from the machine; and there is the pantheistic way, which identifies the two, which regards nature itself as the living energy of an intelligence of the same kind as though vaster in scope than the human. Partly through the influence of mythology, the Greek mind became early possessed with the conception of nature as living, thinking, almost speaking to the mind of man. This unfixed poetical prepossession, reduced to an abstract form, petrified into an idea, is the force which gives unity of aim to Greek philosophy. Little by little, it works out the substance of the Hegelian formula: "Whatever is, is according to reason: whatever is according to reason, that is." [. . .] Still, wherever the speculative instinct has been united with a certain poetic inwardness of temperament, as in Bruno, in Schelling, there that old Greek conception, like some seed floating in the air, has taken root and sprung up anew. Coleridge, thrust inward upon himself, driven from "life in thought and sensation" to life in thought only, feels already, in his dark London school, a thread of the Greek mind on this matter vibrating strongly in him. At fifteen he is discoursing on Plotinus, as in later years he reflects from Schelling that flitting intellectual tradition. He supposes a subtle, sympathetic co-ordination between the ideas of the human reason and the laws of the natural world. Science, the real knowledge of that natural world, is to be attained, not by observation, experiment, analysis, patient generalisation, but by the evolution or recovery of those ideas directly from within, by a sort of Platonic "recollection"; every group of observed facts remaining an enigma until the appropriate idea is struck upon them from the mind of a Newton, or a Cuvier, the genius in whom sympathy with the universal reason becomes entire. In the next place, he conceives that this reason or intelligence in nature becomes reflective, or self-conscious. He fancies he can trace, through all the simpler forms of life, fragments of an eloquent prophecy about the human mind. The whole of nature he regards as a development of higher forms out of the lower, through shade after shade of systematic change. The dim stir of chemical atoms towards the axis of crystal form, the trance-like life of plants, the animal troubled by strange irritabilities, are stages which anticipate consciousness. All through the ever-increasing movement of life that was shaping itself; every successive phase of life, in its unsatisfied susceptibilities, seeming to be drawn out of its own limits by the more pronounced current of life on its confines, the "shadow of approaching humanity" gradually deepening, the latent intelligence winning a way to the surface. And at this point the law of development does not lose itself in caprice: rather it becomes more constraining and incisive. From the lowest to the very highest acts of the conscious intelligence, there is another series of refining shades. Gradually the mind concentrates itself, frees itself from the limitations of the particular, the individual, attains a strange power of modifying and centralising what it receives from without, according to the pattern of an inward ideal. At last, in imaginative genius, ideas become effective: the intelligence of nature, all its discursive elements now connected and justified, is clearly reflected; the interpretation of its latent purposes being embodied in the great central products of creative art. The secret of creative genius would be an exquisitely purged sympathy with nature, with the reasonable soul antecedent there. Those associative conceptions of the imagination, those eternally fixed types of action and passion, would come, not so much from the conscious invention of the artist, as from his self-surrender to the suggestions of an abstract reason or ideality in things: they would be evolved by the stir of nature itself, realising the highest reach of its dormant reason: they would have a kind of prevenient necessity to rise at some time to the surface of the human mind.

46

Emily Dickinson

Poems (1890)

VII

Exultation is the going
Of an inland soul to sea,—
Past the houses, past the headlands,
Into deep eternity!

Bred as we, among the mountains,
Can the sailor understand
The divine intoxication
Of the first league out from land?

VIII

Look back on time with kindly eyes,
He doubtless did his best;
How softly sinks his trembling sun
In human nature's west!

X

I died for beauty, but was scarce
Adjusted in the tomb,
When one who died for truth was lain
In an adjoining room.

He questioned softly why I failed?
"For beauty," I replied.
"And I for truth,—the two are one;
We brethren are," he said.

And so, as kinsmen met a night,
We talked between the rooms,
Until the moss had reached our lips,
And covered up our names.

XIX

To know just how he suffered would be dear;
To know if any human eyes were near
To whom he could intrust his wavering gaze,
Until it settled firm on Paradise.

To know if he was patient, part content,
Was dying as he thought, or different;
Was it a pleasant day to die,
And did the sunshine face his way?

What was his furthest mind, of home, or God,
Or what the distant say
At news that he ceased human nature
On such a day?

And wishes, had he any?
Just his sigh, accented,
Had been legible to me.
And was he confident until
Ill fluttered out in everlasting well?

And if he spoke, what name was best,
What first,
What one broke off with
At the drowsiest?

Was he afraid, or tranquil?
Might he know

How conscious consciousness could grow,
Till love that was, and love too blest to be,
Meet—and the junction be Eternity?

XX

The last night that she lived,
It was a common night,
Except the dying; this to us
Made nature different.

We noticed smallest things,—
Things overlooked before,
By this great light upon our minds
Italicized, as 't were.

That others could exist
While she must finish quite,
A jealousy for her arose
So nearly infinite.

We waited while she passed;
It was a narrow time,
Too jostled were our souls to speak,
At length the notice came.

She mentioned, and forgot;
Then lightly as a reed
Bent to the water, shivered scarce,
Consented, and was dead.

And we, we placed the hair,
And drew the head erect;
And then an awful leisure was,
Our faith to regulate.

XXIII

I reason, earth is short,
And anguish absolute.

And many hurt;
But what of that?

I reason, we could die:
The best vitality
Cannot excel decay;
But what of that?

I reason that in heaven
Somehow, it will be even,
Some new equation given;
But what of that?

The smallest housewife in the grass,
Yet take her from the lawn,
And somebody has lost the face
That made existence home!

XXXI

Death is a dialogue between
The spirit and the dust.
"Dissolve," says Death. The Spirit, "Sir,
I have another trust."

Death doubts it, argues from the ground.
The Spirit turns away,
Just laying off, for evidence,
An overcoat of clay.

LXII

Our journey had advanced;
Our feet were almost come
To that odd fork in Being's road,
Eternity by term.

Our pace took sudden awe,
Our feet reluctant led.

Before were cities, but between,
The forest of the dead.

Retreat was out of hope,—
Behind, a sealed route,
Eternity's white flag before,
And God at every gate.

LXXXIII

This world is not conclusion;
    A sequel stands beyond,
Invisible, as music,
    But positive, as sound.
It beckons and it baffles;
    Philosophies don't know,
And through a riddle, at the last,
    Sagacity must go.
To guess it puzzles scholars;
    To gain it, men have shown
Contempt of generations,
    And crucifixion known.

47

Charles Sanders Peirce

The Law of Mind (1892)

In an article published in the Monist for January 1891, I endeavored to show what ideas ought to form the warp of a system of philosophy, and particularly emphasised that of absolute chance. In the number of April 1892, I argued further in favor of that way of thinking, which it will be convenient to christen *tychism* (from τύχη, chance). A serious student of philosophy will be in no haste to accept or reject this doctrine; but he will see in it one of the chief attitudes which speculative thought may take, feeling that it is not for an individual, nor for an age, to pronounce upon a fundamental question of philosophy. That is a task for a whole era to work out. I have begun by showing that *tychism* must give birth to an evolutionary cosmology, in which all the regularities of nature and of mind are regarded as products of growth, and to a Schelling-fashioned idealism which holds matter to be mere specialised and partially deadened mind. I may mention, for the benefit of those who are curious in studying mental biographies, that I was born and reared in the neighborhood of Concord,—I mean in Cambridge,—at the time when Emerson, Hedge, and their friends were disseminating the ideas that they had caught from Schelling, and Schelling from Plotinus, from Boehm, or from God knows what minds stricken with the monstrous mysticism of the East. But the atmosphere of Cambridge held many an antiseptic against Concord transcendentalism; and I am not conscious of having contracted any of that virus. Nevertheless, it is probable that some cultured bacilli, some benignant form of the disease was implanted in my soul, unawares, and that now, after long incubation, it comes to the surface, modified by mathematical conceptions and by training in physical investigations.

The next step in the study of cosmology must be to examine the general law of mental action. In doing this, I shall for the time drop my tychism out of view, in order to allow a free and independent expansion to another conception signalised in my first *Monist*-paper as one of the most indispensable to philosophy, though it was not there dwelt upon; I mean the idea of continuity. The tendency to regard continuity, in the sense in which I shall define it, as an idea of prime importance in philosophy may conveniently be termed *synechism*. The present paper is intended chiefly to show what synechism is, and what it leads to. I attempted, a good many years ago, to develop this doctrine in the *Journal of Speculative Philosophy* (Vol. III.); but I am able now to improve upon that exposition, in which I was a little blinded by nominalistic prepossessions. I refer to it, because students may possibly find that some points not sufficiently explained in the present paper are cleared up in those earlier ones.

What the Law Is

Logical analysis applied to mental phenomena shows that there is but one law of mind, namely, that ideas tend to spread continuously and to affect certain others which stand to them in a peculiar relation of affectibility. In this spreading they lose intensity, and especially the power of affecting others, but gain generality and become welded with other ideas.

I set down this formula at the beginning, for convenience; and now proceed to comment upon it.

Individuality of Ideas

We are accustomed to speak of ideas as reproduced, as passed from mind to mind, as similar or dissimilar to one another, and, in short, as if they were substantial things; nor can any reasonable objection be raised to such expressions. But taking the word "idea" in the sense of an event in an individual consciousness, it is clear that an idea once past is gone forever, and any supposed recurrence of it is another idea. These two ideas are not present in the same state of consciousness, and therefore cannot possibly be compared. To say, therefore, that they are similar can only mean that an occult power from the depths of the soul forces us to connect them in our thoughts after they are both no more. We may note, here, in passing that of the two generally recognised principles of association, contiguity and similarity, the former is a connection due to a power without, the latter a connection due to a power within.

But what can it mean to say that ideas wholly past are thought of at all, any longer? They are utterly unknowable. What distinct meaning can attach to saying that an idea in the past in any way affects an idea in the future, from which it is completely detached? A phrase between the assertion and the denial of which there can in no case be any sensible difference is mere gibberish.

I will not dwell further upon this point, because it is a commonplace of philosophy.

Continuity of Ideas

We have here before us a question of difficulty, analogous to the question of nominalism and realism. But when once it has been clearly formulated, logic leaves room for one answer only. How can a past idea be present? Can it be present vicariously? To a certain extent, perhaps; but not merely so; for then the question would arise how the past idea can be related to its vicarious representation. The relation, being between ideas, can only exist in some consciousness: now that past idea was in no consciousness but that past consciousness that alone contained it; and that did not embrace the vicarious idea.

Some minds will here jump to the conclusion that a past idea cannot in any sense be present. But that is hasty and illogical. How extravagant, too, to pronounce our whole knowledge of the past to be mere delusion! Yet it would seem that the past is as completely beyond the bonds of possible experience as a Kantian thing-in-itself.

How can a past idea be present? Not vicariously. Then, only by direct perception. In other words, to be present, it must be *ipso facto* present. That is, it cannot be wholly past; it can only be going, infinitesimally past, less past than any assignable past date. We are thus brought to the conclusion that the present is connected with the past by a series of real infinitesimal steps.

It has already been suggested by psychologists that consciousness necessarily embraces an interval of time. But if a finite time be meant, the opinion is not tenable. If the sensation that precedes the present by half a second were still immediately before me, then, on the same principle the sensation preceding that would be immediately present, and so on *ad infinitum*. Now, since there is a time, say a year, at the end of which an idea is no longer *ipso facto* present, it follows that this is true of any finite interval, however short.

But yet consciousness must essentially cover an interval of time; for if it did not, we could gain no knowledge of time, and not merely no veracious cognition of it, but no conception whatever. We are, therefore, forced to say that we are immediately conscious through an infinitesimal interval of time.

This is all that is requisite. For, in this infinitesimal interval, not only is consciousness continuous in a subjective sense, that is, considered as a subject or substance having the attribute of duration; but also, because it is immediate consciousness, its object is *ipso facto* continuous. In fact, this infinitesimally spread out consciousness is a direct feeling of its contents as spread out. This will be further elucidated below. In an infinitesimal interval we directly perceive the temporal sequence of its beginning, middle, and end,—not, of course, in the way of recognition, for recognition is only of the past, but in the way of immediate feeling. Now upon this interval follows another, whose beginning is the middle of the former, and whose middle is the end of the former. Here, we have an immediate perception of the temporal sequence of its beginning, middle, and end, or say of the second, third, and fourth instants. From these two immediate perceptions, we gain a mediate, or inferential, perception of the relation of all four instants. This mediate perception is objectively, or as to the object represented, spread over the four instants; but subjectively, or as itself the subject of duration, it is completely embraced in the second moment. [The reader will observe that I use the word *instant* to mean a point of time, and *moment* to mean an infinitesimal duration.] If it is objected that, upon the theory proposed, we must have more than a mediate perception of the succession of the four instants, I grant it; for the sum of the two infinitesimal intervals is itself infinitesimal, so that it is immediately perceived. It is immediately perceived in the whole interval, but only mediately perceived in the last two thirds of the interval. Now, let there be an indefinite succession of these inferential acts of comparative perception; and it is plain that the last moment will contain objectively the whole series. Let there be, not merely an indefinite succession, but a continuous flow of inference through a finite time; and the result will be a mediate objective consciousness of the whole time in the last moment. In this last moment, the whole series will be recognised, or known as known before, except only the last moment, which of course will be absolutely unrecognisable to itself. Indeed, even this last moment will be recognised like the rest, or, at least be just beginning to be so. There is a little *elenchus,* or appearance of contradiction, here, which the ordinary logic of reflection quite suffices to resolve. [. . .]

Ideas Cannot be Connected Except by Continuity

That ideas can nowise be connected without continuity is sufficiently evident to one who reflects upon the matter. But still the opinion may be entertained that after continuity has once made the connection of ideas possible, then they may get to be connected in other modes than through continuity. Certainly, I cannot see how anyone can deny that the infinite diversity of the universe, which we call chance, may bring ideas into proximity which are not associated in one general idea. It may do this many times. But then the law of continuous spreading will produce a mental association; and this I suppose is an abridged statement of the way the universe has been evolved. But if I am asked whether a blind ἀνάγκη cannot bring ideas together, first I point out that it would not remain blind. There being a continuous connection between the ideas, they would infallibly become associated in a living, feeling, and perceiving general idea. Next, I cannot see what the mustness or necessity of this ἀνάγκη would consist in. In the absolute uniformity of the phenomenon, says the nominalist. Absolute is well put in; for if it merely happened so three times in succession, or three million times in succession, in the absence of any reason, the coincidence could only be attributed to chance. But absolute uniformity must extend over the whole infinite future; and it is idle to talk of that except as an idea. No; I think we can only hold that wherever ideas come together they tend to weld into general ideas; and wherever they are generally connected, general ideas govern the connection; and these general ideas are living feelings spread out. [. . .]

Restatement of the Law

Let me now try to gather up all these odds and ends of commentary and restate the law of mind, in a unitary way.

First, then, we find that when we regard ideas from a nominalistic, individualistic, sensualistic way, the simplest facts of mind become utterly meaningless. That one idea should resemble another or influence another, or that one state of mind should so much as be thought of in another is, from that standpoint, sheer nonsense.

Second, by this and other means we are driven to perceive, what is quite evident of itself, that instantaneous feelings flow together into a continuum of feeling, which has in a modified degree the peculiar vivacity of feeling and has gained generality. And in reference to such general ideas, or continua of feeling, the difficulties about resemblance and suggestion and reference to the external, cease to have any force.

Third, these general ideas are not mere words, nor do they consist in this, that certain concrete facts will every time happen under certain descriptions of conditions; but they are just as much, or rather far more, living realities than the feelings themselves out of which they are concreted. And to say that mental phenomena are governed by law does not mean merely that they are describable by a general formula; but that there is a living idea, a conscious continuum of feeling, which pervades them, and to which they are docile.

Fourth, this supreme law, which is the celestial and living harmony, does not so much as demand that the special ideas shall surrender their peculiar arbitrariness and caprice entirely; for that would be self-destructive. It only requires that they shall influence and be influenced by one another.

Fifth, in what measure this unification acts, seems to be regulated only by special rules; or, at least, we cannot in our present knowledge say how far it goes. But it may be said that, judging by appearances, the amount of arbitrariness in the phenomena of human minds is neither altogether trifling nor very prominent. [. . .]

Communication

Consistently with the doctrine laid down in the beginning of this paper, I am bound to maintain that an idea can only be affected by an idea in continuous connection with it. By anything but an idea, it cannot be affected at all. This obliges me to say, as I do say, on other grounds, that what we call matter is not completely dead, but is merely mind hide-bound with habits. It still retains the element of diversification; and in that diversification there is life. When an idea is conveyed from one mind to another, it is by forms of combination of the diverse elements of nature, say by some curious symmetry, or by some union of a tender color with a refined odor. To such forms the law of mechanical energy has no application. If they are eternal, it is in the spirit they embody; and their origin cannot be accounted for by any mechanical necessity. They are embodied ideas; and so only can they convey ideas. Precisely how primary sensations, as colors and tones, are excited, we cannot tell, in the present state of psychology. But in our ignorance,

I think that we are at liberty to suppose that they arise in essentially the same manner as the other feelings, called secondary. As far as sight and hearing are in question, we know that they are only excited by vibrations of inconceivable complexity; and the chemical senses are probably not more simple. Even the least psychical of peripheral sensations, that of pressure, has in its excitation conditions which, though apparently simple, are seen to be complicated enough when we consider the molecules and their attractions. The principle with which I set out requires me to maintain that these feelings are communicated to the nerves by continuity, so that there must be something like them in the excitants themselves. If this seems extravagant, it is to be remembered that it is the sole possible way of reaching any explanation of sensation, which otherwise must be pronounced a general fact absolutely inexplicable and ultimate. Now absolute inexplicability is a hypothhesis which sound logic refuses under any circumstances to justify.

I may be asked whether my theory would be favorable or otherwise to telepathy. I have no decided answer to give to this. At first sight, it seems unfavorable. Yet there may be other modes of continuous connection between minds other than those of time and space.

The recognition by one person of another's personality takes place by means to some extent identical with the means by which he is conscious of his own personality. The idea of the second personality, which is as much as to say that second personality itself, enters within the field of direct consciousness of the first person, and is as immediately perceived as his ego, though less strongly. At the same time, the opposition between the two persons is perceived, so that the externality of the second is recognised.

The psychological phenomena of intercommunication between two minds have been unfortunately little studied. So that it is impossible to say, for certain, whether they are favorable to this theory or not. But the very extraordinary insight which some persons are able to gain of others from indications so slight that it is difficult to ascertain what they are, is certainly rendered more comprehensible by the view here taken.

A difficulty which confronts the synechistic philosophy is this. In considering personality, that philosophy is forced to accept the doctrine of a personal God; but in considering communication, it cannot but admit that if there is a personal God, we must have a direct perception of that person and indeed be in personal communication with him. Now, if that be the case, the question arises how it is possible that the existence of this being should ever have been doubted by anybody. The only answer that I can at present make is that facts that stand before our face and eyes and stare us in the face are far from being, in all cases, the ones most easily discerned. That has been remarked from time immemorial.

Conclusion

I have thus developed as well as I could in a little space the *synechistic* philosophy, as applied to mind. I think that I have succeeded in making it clear that this doctrine gives room for explanations of many facts which without it are absolutely and hopelessly inexplicable; and further that it carries along with it the following doctrines: 1st, a logical realism of the most pronounced type; 2nd, objective idealism; 3rd, tychism, with its consequent thoroughgoing evolutionism. We also notice that the doctrine presents no hindrances to spiritual influences, such as some philosophies are felt to do.

48

Leo Tolstoy

Reason and Religion (1895)

You ask me:

1 Should people who are not particularly advanced mentally seek an expression in words for the truths of the inner life, as comprehended by them?

2 Is it worthwhile in one's inner life to strive after complete consciousness?

3 What are we to be guided by in moments of struggle and wavering, that we may know whether it is indeed our conscience that is speaking in us, or whether it is reflection, which is bribed by our weakness? (The third question I for brevity's sake expressed in my own words, without having changed its meaning, I hope.)

These three questions in my opinion reduce themselves to one,—the second, because, if it is not necessary for us to strive after a full consciousness of our inner life, it will be also unnecessary and impossible for us to express in words the truths which we have grasped, and in moments of wavering we shall have nothing to be guided by, in order to ascertain whether it is our conscience or a false reflection that is speaking within us. But if it is necessary to strive after the greatest consciousness accessible to human reason (whatever this reason may be), it is also necessary to express the truths grasped by us in words, and it is these expressed truths which have been carried into full consciousness that we have to be guided by in moments of struggle and wavering. And so I answer your radical question in the affirmative, namely, that every man, for the fulfilment of his destiny upon earth and for the attainment of the true good (the two things go together), must strain all the forces of his mind for the purpose of elucidating to himself those religious bases by which he lives, that is, the meaning of his life.

I have frequently met among illiterate earth-diggers, who have to figure out cubic contents, the wide-spread conviction that the mathematical calculation is deceptive, and that it is not to be trusted. Either because they do not know any mathematics, or because the men who figured things out mathematically for them had frequently consciously or unconsciously deceived them, the opinion that mathematics was inadequate and useless for the calculation of measures has established itself as an undoubted truth which they think it is even unnecessary to prove. Just such an opinion has established itself among, I shall say it boldly, irreligious men,—an opinion that reason cannot solve any religious questions,—that the application of reason to these questions is the chief cause of errors, that the solution of religious questions by means of reason is criminal pride.

I say this, because the doubt, expressed in your questions, as to whether it is necessary to strive after consciousness in our religious convictions, can be based only on this supposition, namely, that reason cannot be applied to the solution of religious questions. However, such a supposition is as strange and obviously false as the supposition that calculation cannot settle any mathematical questions.

God has given man but one tool for the cognition of himself and his relation to the world,—there is no other,—and this tool is reason, and suddenly he is told that he can use his reason for the elucidation of his domestic, economic, political, scientific, artistic questions, but not for the elucidation of what it is given him for. It turns out that for the elucidation of the most important truths, of those on which his whole life depends, a man must by no means employ reason, but must recognize these truths as beyond reason, whereas beyond reason a man cannot cognize anything. They say, "Find it out, through revelation, faith." But a man cannot even believe outside of reason. If a man believes in this, and not in that, he does so only because his reason tells him that he ought to believe in this, and not to believe in that. To say that a man should not be guided by reason is the same as saying to a man, who in a dark underground room is carrying a lamp, that, to get out from this underground room and find his way, he ought to put out his lamp and be guided by something different from the light.

But, perhaps, I shall be told, as you say in your letter, that not all men are endowed with a great mind and with a special ability for expressing their thoughts, and that, therefore, an awkward expression of their thoughts concerning religion may lead to error. To this I will answer in the words of the Gospel, "What is hidden from the wise is revealed to babes." This saying is not an exaggeration and not a paradox, as people generally judge of those utterances of the Gospel which do not please them, but the assertion of a most simple and unquestionable truth, which is, that to every being in the world a law is given, which this being must follow, and that for the cognition of this law every being is endowed with corresponding organs. And so every man is endowed with reason, and in this reason there is revealed to him the law which he must follow. This law is hidden only from those who do not want to follow it and who, in order not to follow it, renounce reason and, instead of using their reason for the cognition of the truth, use for this purpose the indications, taken upon faith, of people like themselves, who also reject reason.

But the law which a man must follow is so simple that it is accessible to any child, the more so since a man has no longer any need of discovering the law of his life. Men who lived before him discovered and expressed it, and all a man has to do is to verify them with his reason, to accept or not to accept the propositions which he finds expressed in the tradition, that is, not as people, who wish not to fulfil the law, advise us to do, by verifying reason through tradition, but by verifying tradition through reason. Tradition may be from men, and false, but reason is certainly from God, and cannot be false. And so, for the cognition and the expression of truth, there is no need of any especial prominent capacity, but only of the faith that reason is not only the highest divine quality of man, but also the only tool for the cognition of truth.

A special mind and gifts are not needed for the cognition and exposition of the truth, but for the invention and exposition of the lie. Having once departed from the indications of reason, men heap up and take upon faith, generally in the shape of laws, revelations, dogmas, such complicated, unnatural, and contradictory propositions that, in order to expound them and harmonize them with the lie, there is actually a need of astuteness of mind and of a special gift. We need only think of a man of our world, educated in the religious tenets of any Christian profession,—Catholic, Orthodox, Protestant,—who wants to elucidate to himself the religious tenets inculcated upon him since childhood, and to harmonize them with life,—what a complicated mental labour he must go through in order to harmonize all the contradictions which are found in the profession inoculated in him by his education: God, the Creator and the good, created evil, punishes people, and demands redemption, and so forth, and we profess the law of love and of forgiveness, and we punish, wage war, take away the property from poor people, and so forth, and so forth.

It is for the unravelling of these contradictions, or rather, for the concealment of them from ourselves, that a great mind and special gifts are needed; but for the discovery of the law of our life, or, as you express it, in order to bring our faith into full consciousness, no special mental gifts are needed,—all that is necessary is not to admit anything that is contrary to reason, not to reject reason, religiously to guard reason, and to believe in nothing else. If the meaning of a man's life presents itself to him indistinctly, that does not prove that reason is of no use for the elucidation of this meaning, but only this, that too much of what is irrational has been taken upon faith, and that it is necessary to reject everything which is not confirmed by reason.

And so my answer to your fundamental question, as to whether it is necessary to strive after consciousness in our inner life, is this, that this is the most necessary and important work of our life. It is necessary and important because the only rational meaning of our life consists in the fulfilment of the will of God who sent us into this life. But the will of God is not recognized by any special miracle, by the writing of the law on tablets with God's finger, or by the composition of an infallible book with the aid of the Holy Ghost, or by the infallibility of some holy person or of an assembly of men,—but only by the activity of the reason of all men who in deeds and words transmit to one another the truths which have become more and more elucidated to their consciousness. This cognition has never been and never will be complete, but is constantly increased with the movement of humanity: the longer we live, the more clearly do we recognize God's will and, consequently, what we ought to do for its fulfilment. And so I think that the elucidation by any man (no matter how small he himself and others may consider him to be—it is the little ones who are great) of the whole religious truth, as it is accessible to him, and its expression in words (since the expression in words is the one unquestionable symptom of a complete clearness of ideas) is one of the most important and most sacred duties of man.

I shall be very much pleased if my answer shall satisfy you even in part.

49

Swami Vivekananda

The Absolute and Manifestation (1896)

THE ONE QUESTION THAT IS MOST DIFFICULT TO GRASP IN understanding the Advaita Philosophy, and the one question that will be asked again and again and that will always remain after thinking of it all our life, is—"How has the Infinite, the Absolute, apparently become the finite?" I will take up this question, and, in order to illustrate it better, I will use a figure.

Here is the Absolute (a), and this is the Universe (b). The Absolute has become the Universe. By this is not only meant the material world, but the mental world, the spiritual world—everything, heavens and earths, and all that exists. Mind is the name of a change, and body the name of another change, and so on, and all these changes compose our universe. The Absolute (a) appears to have become the Universe (b) by coming through time, space, and causation (c). This is the central idea of Advaita. Time, space, and causation are like the glass through which the Absolute is seen, and when It is seen on the lower side It appears as the Universe. Now we at once gather from this, that in the Absolute, there is neither time, space, nor causation. The idea of time cannot be there, seeing that there is no mind, no thought. The idea of space cannot be

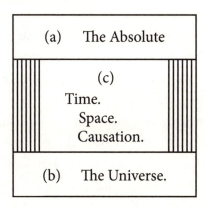

there, seeing that there is no external change. What you call motion and causation cannot exist where there is only one. We have to understand this and impress it on our minds, that what we call causation begins after, if we may be permitted to say so, the degeneration of the Absolute into the phenomenal, and not before; that our will, our desire, and all these things always come *after* that. I think Schopenhauer's philosophy makes a mistake in its interpretation of Vedanta, for it seeks to make the will everything. Schopenhauer makes the will stand in the place of the Absolute. But the Absolute cannot be presented as will, for will is something changeable and phenomenal, and over the line drawn above time, space and causation, there is no change, no motion. It is only below the line that external motion and internal motion, called thought, begin. There can be no will on the other side, and will, therefore, cannot be the cause of this universe. Coming nearer, we see in our own bodies that will is not the cause of every movement. I move this chair; will was the cause of that movement, and that will became manifested as muscular motion at the other end. But the same power that moves the chair is moving the heart, the lungs, and so on, but not through will. Given that the power is the same, it only becomes will when it rises to the plane of consciousness, and to call it will before it has risen to this plane is a misnomer. This makes a good deal of confusion in Schopenhauer's philosophy.

A stone falls and we ask why. This question is possible only on the supposition that nothing happens independently, that every motion must have been preceded by a cause of some kind. I request you to make this very clear in your minds, for whenever we ask why anything happens, we are taking for granted that everything that happens must have a *why*, that is to say, it must have been preceded by something else which acted as cause. This precedence and succedence are what we call the law of causation. It means that everything in the Universe is by turn a cause and an effect. It is the cause of certain things which come after it and is itself the effect of something else which has preceded it. This is called the law of causation, and is a necessary condition of all our thinking. We believe that every particle in the universe, whatever it be, is in relation to every other particle. There has been great discussion as to how this idea arose. In Europe there have been so-called intuitive philosophers who believed that it was constitutional in humanity, others have believed that it comes from experience, but the question has never been settled. We shall see later on what Vedânta has to say about it. But first we have to understand this, that the very asking of the question "why" presupposes that everything round us has been preceded by certain things, and will be succeeded by certain other things. The other belief involved in this question is that nothing in the universe is independent, everything can be acted upon by something outside itself. Inter-dependence is the law of the whole universe. In saying, "What caused the Absolute?" what error are we making! We are applying the same supposition in this case. To ask this question we have to suppose that the Absolute also is bound by something else, and that the Absolute also is dependent on something else. That is to say, in so using the word Absolute, we drag the Absolute down to the level of the universe. For above that line there is neither time, space, nor causation, because it is all one. That which exists by itself alone cannot have any cause.

That which is free, cannot have any cause, else it would not be free, but bound. That which has relativity cannot be free. Thus, we see that the very question, why the infinite became the finite, is an impossible one, it is self-contradictory. Coming from subtleties to the logic of our common plane, to common sense, we can see this from another side, when we seek to know how the Absolute has become the relative. Supposing we knew the answer, would the Absolute remain the Absolute? It would have become the relative. What is meant by knowledge in our common sense idea? It is only something that has become limited by our mind, that we know, and when it is beyond our mind, it is not knowledge. Now if the Absolute becomes limited by the mind, it is no more Absolute; it has become finite. Everything limited by the mind becomes finite. Therefore, to know the Absolute is again a contradiction in terms. That is why this question has never been answered, because if it were answered there would no more be an Absolute. A God known is no more God; He has become finite like one of us. He cannot be known, He is always the Unknowable One. But what Advaita says is that God is more than knowable. This is a great fact to learn. You must not go home with the idea that God is unknowable in the sense in which Agnostics put it. For instance, here is a chair, it is known to me. On the contrary what is beyond ether, or whether people exist there or not is possibly unknowable. But God is neither known nor unknowable in this sense. He is something still higher than known; that is what is meant by God being unknown and unknowable; the expression is not used in the sense in which it may be said that some questions are unknown and unknowable. God is more than known. This chair is known; but God is intensely more than that, because in and through Him we have to know this chair itself. He is the witness, the Eternal Witness of all knowledge. Whatever we know, we have to know in and through Him. He is the essence of our own Self. He, the "I," is the essence of this ego; we cannot know anything excepting in and through that "I." You have to know everything in and through the *Brahman*. To know the chair, therefore, you have to know it in and through God. Thus God is infinitely nearer to us than the chair, yet He is infinitely higher. Neither known, nor unknown, but something infinitely higher than either. He is your Self. "Who would live a second, who would breathe a second in this universe, if that Blessed One were not filling it, because in and through Him we breathe, in and through Him we exist?" Not that he is standing somewhere and making my blood circulate. What is meant is that He is the essence of all this, the Soul of my soul. You cannot by any possibility say you know Him; it would be too much of a degradation. You cannot jump out of yourself, so you cannot know Him. Knowledge is objectification. For instance, in memory you are objectifying many things, projecting them out of yourself. All memory, all the things which I have seen and which I know are in my mind. The pictures, the impressions of all these things are in my mind, as it were, and when I would try to think of them, to know them, the first act of knowledge would be to project them outside. This cannot be done with God, because He is the essence of our souls; we cannot throw Him out. This is said to be the holiest word in Vedânta: "He that is the essence of your soul, He is the Truth, He is the Self, Thou that art, O Svetaketu." This is what is meant by "Thou art Brahman." You cannot describe Him by any other language. All attempts of language, calling Him father, or brother, or our dearest friend, are attempts to objectify God, which cannot be. He is the Eternal Subject of everything. I am the subject of this chair; I see the chair, so God is the Eternal Subject of my soul. How can you objectify Him, the Essence of your souls, the Reality of everything? Thus, I would repeat to you once more, God is neither knowable nor unknowable, but something infinitely higher than these. He is one with us, and that which is One is neither knowable, nor unknowable, just as my own self, or your own self. You cannot know your own self, you cannot move it out, and make it an object to look at, because you are that, and cannot separate yourself from it. Neither is it unknowable, for what is more known than yourself? It is really the centre of our knowledge in exactly the same sense that God is neither unknowable nor known, but infinitely higher than that, your real Self.

Thus we see, that, first, the question: "What caused the Absolute" is a contradiction in terms, and secondly, we find that the idea of God in the Advaita is His Oneness, and therefore we cannot objectify Him, for we are always living and moving in Him; whether we know it or not does not matter. Whatever we do is always through Him. Now the question is what are time, space, and causation? Advaita means non-duality; there are no two, but One. We see that here is a proposition that the Absolute, the One is manifesting Itself as many through the veil of time, space, and causation. Therefore it seems that here are two, the Absolute, and *Mâyâ* (the sum-total of time, space, and causation). It seems apparently very convincing that there are two. To which the Advaitist replies that it cannot be called two. To have two, we must have two independent existences, just as that of the Absolute, which cannot be caused. In the first place, this time, space, and causation cannot be said to be an independent existence. Time is entirely a dependent existence; it changes with every change of our mind. Sometimes in a dream one imagines that he has lived several years; at other times several months were passed as one second. So that time has entire dependence on our state of mind. Secondly, the idea of time vanishes altogether sometimes. So with space, we cannot know what space is. Yet it is there, indefinable, and cannot live separate from anything else. So with causation.

The one peculiar attribute we find in all this time, space, and causation, is that they cannot live separate from other things. Try to think of space which has neither color, nor limits, nor any connection with the things around, just abstract space. You cannot think of it thus; you have to think of it as the space between two limits, or between objects. It has to cling on to some object to have its existence. So with time; you cannot have any idea of abstract time, but you have to take two events, one preceding and the other succeeding, and join the two events by the idea of succession. Time depends on two events, just as space has to relate itself to outside objects. And the idea of causation is inseparable from time and space. This is the peculiar thing about them, that they have no independent existence. They have not even the existence which the chair or the wall has. They are as a shadow around everything, but you cannot catch it. It has no real existence; we see that it has not. Yet a shadow is not non-existence, seeing that through this shadow all things are manifesting as this universe. Thus we see first that this combination of time, space, and causation, has neither existence nor non-existence. It is like a shadow which comes around things. Secondly, it sometimes vanishes. To give an illustration, there is a wave on the sea. The wave is the same as the ocean, certainly, and yet we know it is a wave, and as such different from the ocean. What makes this difference? The form and the name, the idea in the mind and the form. Now can we think of a wave form as anything separate from the ocean? Certainly not. It always clings on to the ocean idea. If the wave subsides, the form vanishes in a moment, and yet the form was not a delusion. So long as the wave existed the form was there, and you were bound to see the form. This is *Mâyâ*.

The whole of this universe, therefore, is as it were, a peculiar form; the Absolute is that ocean, while you and I, the suns, and stars, and all, things are various waves of the ocean. And what makes the waves different? Only form, and that form is just time, space, and causation, all entirely dependent on the wave. As soon as you take away the wave, they vanish. As soon as the individual gives up this *Mâyâ*, it vanishes for him, and he becomes free. The whole struggle is to get rid of this clinging on to time, space, and causation. It is always throwing obstacles in our way, and we are trying to get free. What do they call the theory of evolution? What are the two factors? There is a tremendous potential power which is trying to express itself, and circumstances are holding it down, the environments will not allow it to express itself. So, in order to fight with these environments, the power is getting newer and newer bodies. A little amoeba, in the struggle, gets another body and conquers some obstacles, then gets other bodies, until it becomes man. Now if we carry that logic to its conclusion, there must come a time when that power that was in the amoeba and which came out as man will have conquered *all* the obstructions that nature can bring before it, and will have escaped from all its environments. This idea brought into metaphysics would be expressed thus: there are two components of every action, the one the subject, the other the object. For instance, I feel unhappy because a man scolds me. These are the two parts; and what is my struggle all my life? To make myself strong enough to conquer that environment, so that he may scold and I shall not feel. That is how we are trying to conquer. What is meant by morality? Making the subject strong, inuring ourselves to the hardships of temptation until it ceases to have power over us and it is a logical conclusion of our philosophy, that there must come a time when we shall have conquered all environments, because Nature is finite.

That is another thing to learn. How do you know that Nature is finite? You can only know this through metaphysics. Nature is that infinite under limitations. Therefore it is finite. So there must come a time when we have conquered all environments. And how are we to conquer them? We cannot possibly conquer all the objective environments. No. The little fish wants to fly from its enemies which are in the water. How does it conquer? By flying up into the air, becoming a bird. The fish did not change the water, or the air; the change was in itself. Change is always subjective. So on, all through evolution you find that the conquest of nature comes by change in the subjective. Apply this to religion, and morality, and you will find that the conquest of evil comes by the change in the subjective also. That is how the Advaita system gets its whole force, on the subjective side of man. To talk of evil and misery is nonsense, because they do not exist outside. If I am inured against all anger, I never feel angry. If I am proof against all hatred, I never feel hatred, because it cannot touch me.

This is therefore the process by which to achieve that conquest—through the subjective, by perfecting the subjective. Therefore, you find one more thing, that the only religion, I may make bold to say, which agrees with and even goes a little further than modern researches, both on physical and moral lines, is the Advaita, and that is why it appeals to modern scientists so much. They find that the old dualistic theories are not enough for them, do not satisfy their necessities. A man must not only have faith, but intellectual faith too. Now, in this latter part of the nineteenth century, such ideas as that a religion coming from any other source than one's own forefather's religion must be false, show that there is still weakness left, and such ideas must be given up. I do not mean that it is in this country alone, but in every country, and nowhere more than in my own. This Advaita was never allowed to come to the people. At first some monks got hold of it, and took it to the forests, and so it came to be called the Forest Philosophy. By the mercy of the Lord, the Buddha came and preached it to the masses, and the whole nation arose to Buddhism. Long after that, when atheists and agnostics had destroyed the nation again, the old preachers found out that Advaita was the only thing to save India from materialism.

Twice has Advaita saved India from materialism. Just before the Buddha came, when materialism had spread to a fearful extent, and it was of a most hideous kind, not like that of the present day but of a far worse nature. I am a materialist of a certain kind, because I believe that there is only One. That is what the materialist wants to tell you, only he calls it matter and I call it God. The materialists admit that out of this one matter, all hope, and religion, and everything have come. I say that all these have come out of *Brahman*. I allude to the old crude sort of materialism—eat, drink and be merry; there is neither God, nor soul, nor heaven; religion is a concoction of wicked priests; the materialism which said to man: "As long as you live, try to live happily; eat, though you may have to borrow money for it, and never mind about repaying." That was the old materialism, and that kind of philosophy spread so much that even to-day it has got the name of "popular philosophy." Buddha brought the Vedanta out, gave it to the people and saved India. Then a thousand years after his death a similar state of things prevailed; the mobs, the masses, and the various races, had been converted to Buddhism, and naturally the teachings of the Buddha became in time degenerated because most of these people were very ignorant. Buddhism taught no God, no Ruler of the universe, so gradually the masses brought their gods, and devils, and hobgoblins, out again, and a tremendous hotch-potch was made of Buddhism in India. Then again Materialism came to the fore, taking the form of license with the higher classes, and superstition with the lower, when Sankarâcharya arose, and once more revivified the Vedânta philosophy. He made it a rationalistic philosophy. In the Upanishads the arguments are often very obscure. By Buddha the moral side of the philosophy was emphasized, and by Sankarâcharya, the intellectual side. He collected all the obscure and apparently contradictory texts of the Upanishads and showed the harmony between them. He worked out, rationalized and placed before men a wonderful, coherent whole.

Materialism prevails in Europe to-day. You may pray all the world over for the salvation of these sceptics, but they do not yield, they want reason. The salvation of Europe depends on a rationalistic religion, and Advaita—the non-duality, the Oneness, the idea of the impersonal God—is the only religion that can keep any hold on intellectual people. It comes whenever religion seems to disappear, and irreligion seems to prevail, and that is why it is gaining ground in Europe and America. One thing more has to be added to it. In the old Upanishads we find sublime poetry; these "Seers of Truth" were poets. Plato says, inspiration comes to people through poetry, and it seemed as if these ancient *Rishis* were raised above humanity to show these truths through poetry. They never preached, nor philosophized, nor wrote. Strains of music came out of their lips. In Buddha we had the great, universal heart, infinite patience making religion practical, bringing it to every one's door; in Sankarâcharya we saw tremendous intellectual power, throwing the scorching light of reason over everything. We want to-day that bright sun of intellectuality, and joined to it the heart of Buddha, that wonderful, infinite heart of love and mercy. This union will give us the highest philosophy. Science and religion will meet and shake hands. Poetry and philosophy will become friends. This will be the religion of the future, and if we can work it out, we may be sure that it will be for all times and professions. This is the one way that will be acceptable to modern science, for it has almost fallen into it. When a great scientific teacher asserts that all things are the manifestation of one force, does it not remind you of the God of whom you hear in the Upanishads: "As the one fire entering into the universe is expressing itself in various forms, and yet is infinitely more besides, even so that one Soul is expressing itself in every soul and yet is infinitely more besides." Do you not see how science is going? The Hindu nation proceeded through the study of the mind, through metaphysics and logic. The European nations start from external nature, and now they, too, are coming to the same results. We find that searching through the mind we at last come to that Oneness, that Universal One, the Internal Soul of everything, the Essence, the Reality of everything, the Ever-Free, the Ever-Blissful, the Ever-Existing. Through material science we come to the same Oneness. Science to-day is telling us that all things are but the manifestation of one energy, which is the sum-total of everything which exists, and the trend of humanity is towards freedom, and not towards bondage. Why should men be moral? Because through morality is the path towards freedom, and immorality leads to bondage. [. . .]

50

Josiah Royce

The World and the Individual (1899)

The Fourth Conception of Being

ANY DOCTRINE CONCERNING FUNDAMENTAL QUESTIONS IS LIKELY TO MEET with two different sorts of objections. The objections of the first sort maintain that the theory in question is too abstruse and obscure to be comprehended. The objections of the second sort point out that this same theory is too simple to be true. Every teacher of philosophy becomes accustomed not only to hear both kinds of objections from his more thoughtful pupils, but to urge them, for himself, upon his own notice. No one, in fact, is a philosopher, who has not first profoundly doubted his own system. And it is in presence of objections that philosophical theses best show their merits, if they have merits.

Upon the present occasion I have more fully to develope the conception of Being to which we were led at the close of the last discussion. While I shall do so, in the first place, independently, I shall come before I am done into intimate connection with some of the principal objections that may be urged against our theses regarding the definition of what it is to be. For the objections will help us to make clearer our position.

I

But let us first restate our thesis as to the nature of Being. There is an ancient doctrine that whatever is, is ultimately something Individual. Realism early came to that view; and only Critical Rationalism has ever explicitly maintained that the ultimate realities are universals, namely, valid possibilities of experience, or mere truths as such. Now at the close of the last lecture, after analyzing the whole basis of Critical Rationalism, the entire conception of the Real as merely valid, we reinstated the Individual as the only ultimate form of Being. In so far we returned to a view that, in the history of thought, Realism already asserted. But we gave a new reason of our own for this view. Our reason was that the very defect of our finite ideas which sends us seeking for Being lies in the fact that whether we long for practical satisfaction, or think of purely theoretical problems, we, as we now are, are always seeking another object than what is yet present to our ideas. Now any ultimate reality, for us while as finite thinkers we seek it, is always such another fact. Yet this other object is always an object for our thought only in so far as our thought already means it, defines it, and wills it to be our object. But what is for us this other? In its essence it is already defined even before we undertake to know it. For this other is precisely the fulfilment of our purpose, the satisfaction of the will now imperfectly embodied in our ideas, the completion of what we already partially possess in our finite insight. This completion is for us another, solely because our ideas, in their present momentary forms, come to us as general ideas,—ideas of what is now merely a kind of relative fulfilment and not an entire fulfilment. Other fulfilment of the same general kind is needed before we can face the whole Being that we seek. This kind of fulfilment we want to bring, however, to some integral expression, to its own finality, to its completeness as a whole fact. And this want of ours, so I asserted, not only sets us looking for Being, but gives us our only ground and means for defining Being.

Being itself we should directly face in our own experience only in case we experienced finality, *i.e.* full expression of what our finite ideas both mean and seek. Such expression, however, would be given to us in the form of a life that neither sought nor permitted another to take its own place as the expression of its own purpose. Where no other was yet to be sought, there alone would our ideas define no other, no Being, of the type in question, lying yet beyond themselves, in the direction of their own type of fulfilment. The other would be found, and so would be present. And there alone should we consequently stand in the presence of what is real. Conversely, whoever grasps only the nature of a general concept, whoever merely thinks of light or colors, or gravitation, or of man, whoever lacks, longs, or in any way seeks another, has not in his experience the full expression of his own meaning. Hence it is that he has to seek his object elsewhere. And so he has not yet faced any ultimate Being. He has upon his hands mere fragments, mere aspects of Being. Thus an entire instance of Being must be precisely that which permits your ideas to seek no other than what is present. Such a being is an Individual. Only, for our present conception of Being, an individual being is not a fact independent of any experience, nor yet a merely valid truth, nor yet a merely immediate datum that quenches ideas. For all these alternatives we have already faced and rejected. On the contrary an individual being is a Life of Experience fulfilling Ideas, in an absolutely final form. And this we said is the essential nature of Being. The essence of the Real is to be Individual, or to permit no other of its own kind, and this character it possesses only as the unique fulfilment of purpose.

Or, once more, as Mysticism asserted, so we too assert of your world, *That art thou.* Only the Self which is your world is your completely integrated Self, the totality of the life that at this instant you fragmentarily grasp. Your present defect is a matter of the mere form of your consciousness at this instant. Were your eyes at this instant open to your own meaning, your life as a whole would be spread before you as a single and unique life, for which no other could be substituted without a less determinate expression of just your individual will. Now this complete life of yours, is. Only such completion can be. Being can possess no other nature than this. And this, in outline, is our Fourth Conception of Being.

II

Now I cannot myself conceive any one lightly accepting such a definition as this,—a definition so paradoxical in seeming, so remote from the limits which common sense usually sets to speculation, and so opposed to many dignified historical traditions; and indeed I wish nobody to accept it lightly. The whole matter is one for the closest scrutiny. The only ground for this definition of Being lies in the fact that every other conception of reality proves, upon analysis, to be self-contradictory, precisely in so far as it does not in essence agree with this one; while every effort directly to deny the truth of this conception proves, upon analysis, to involve the covert affirmation of this very conception itself. Upon these assertions of the absolute logical necessity of our conception of Being, our whole case in this argument rests. And in order to make this fact clearer, I must briefly review the former argument.

Our argument in the last lecture was based upon the consideration that Being has, at all events, to be that object which makes ideas true or false. The more special features of our analysis of the relation of idea and object were as follows:—

An idea and its real object, in case the idea has any real object, must indeed plainly possess some characters in common. There must thus be general, or abstractly universal, features, belonging to them both. Upon that point all theories of Being to some extent agree. Even the Mystic, at the moment when he calls all ideas vain, identifies your true Self—yes, the very Self that now has your poor ideas—with the Absolute, and says of your object, viz. of the true Being, "That art thou." Even the Realist, despite the independence of his Beings, holds that the ideas either truly represent the nature of these beings, or else, at all events, have in common with even the unknowable object some features whereby the object embodies in reality the same fact which the idea aims to express when it seeks for the reality. The failure of Realism we found to be clue to the logical impossibility of reconciling the independent Being of the object of our ideas with this inevitably assumed sameness of nature, which must be possessed, in however slight a measure, by both the knowing idea and the object that it knows. In the world of the Third Conception of Being, that of Validity, the ideas express with more or less precision, and in their own way, precisely that truth which is to be valid beyond them. And, in fact, as we just saw, the most general conditions which determine for us the problem of Being, demand that the purpose which every idea has in seeking its Other, must have some element in common with that which fulfils this very purpose.

Idea and Reality must, then, possess elements that are common to both of them. On the other hand, as we saw, this mere community is wholly inadequate to the tasks of defining what makes the object belong, as object, to a given idea. For, if you view any idea and its supposed object, merely as one might be imagined viewing them from without, it is wholly impossible to determine what degree of correspondence between them is required either to make the reality that precise object sought by the idea, or to render the idea the true representative of the object to which it is said to refer. A true idea, as Spinoza said, must indeed resemble its ideate. But on the other hand, a mere resemblance of idea and ideate is not enough. Nor does the absence of any specific degree of resemblance necessarily involve an error. It is intended resemblance which counts in estimating the truth of ideas. If in fact you suppose, as an ideal case, two human beings, say twins, absolutely to resemble each other, not only in body, but in experience and in thought, so that every idea which one of these beings at any moment had was precisely duplicated by a thought which at the same instant, and in the same fashion, arose in the other being's life,—if, I say, you suppose this perfect resemblance in the twin minds, you could still, without inconsistency, suppose these twins separated from infancy, living apart, although of course under perfectly similar physical conditions, and in our human sense what we men call absolute strangers to each other, so that neither of them, viewed merely as this human being, ever consciously thought of the other, or conceived of the other's existence. In that case, the mere resemblance would not so far constitute the one of these twin minds the object of which the other mind thought, or the being concerning whom the ideas of the other were true.

The resemblance of idea and object, viewed as a mere fact for an external observer, is, therefore, never by itself enough to constitute the truth of the idea. Nor is the absence of any externally predetermined resemblances, such as you from without may choose to demand of the idea, enough to constitute any specific sort of error. Moreover, when you merely assert that in the world of Being there is to be found an object which resembles your idea, you have so far only mentioned two beings, namely, your idea and its object, and have asserted their resemblance. But you have not yet in the least defined wherein the Being of either of these objects consists. This, then, is the outcome so long as you view idea and object as sundered facts agreeing or disagreeing with each other. Neither truth nor Being is thus to be defined. The result so far is conclusive as against the adequacy, not only of Realism, and of Mysticism, but also, as we saw, of even the Third Conception of Being.

For if one asserts, as his account of the nature of Being, that certain ideas of possibilities of experience are valid, he is so far left with a world of objects upon his hands whose only character, so far as he yet defines the Being of these objects, is that these objects are in agreement with his ideas. Such a definition of Being constituted the whole outcome of the Third Conception. The mathematician's ideas, as present to himself, take the form of observed symbols and diagrams. These, so far as they are observed, are contents of experience fulfilling purpose. They so far conform to our definition of what constitutes an idea, for they have internal meaning. But the existent objects concerning which the mathematician endeavors to teach us, are, by hypothesis, not the symbols, and not the diagrams, but valid truths to which these diagrams and symbols— these mathematician's ideas—correspond. The existences of the mathematician's realm are other than his mere finite ideas. Now that such objects have their place in reality, I myself thoroughly believe. But I point out that their reality, the true Being of these objects, is in no wise defined when you merely speak of the ideas as nothing but valid, because the assertion of validity is so far merely the assertion of a correspondence between a presupposed idea and its assumed object, without any account as yet either of the object, or of the truth of the idea. And bare correspondence, the mere possession of common characters in idea and in object not only fails to define, but, as we now see, can never lead us to define, the Being of either idea or object, and in no sense shows or explains to us the relation whereby the idea means, selects, and is in just this way true of just this one object.

The relation of correspondence between idea and object is, therefore, wholly subordinate to another and far deeper relation; and so to say, "My idea has reference to a real Being," is to say, "My idea imperfectly expresses, in my present consciousness, an intention, a meaning, a purpose; and just this specific meaning is carried out, is fulfilled, is expressed, by my object." For correspondence to its object, and intentional selection of both the object and the sort of correspondence, constitute the two possible relations of idea and object. If the bare correspondence determines neither Being nor truth, the intention must determine both Being and truth. In other words, the Being to which any idea refers is simply the will of the idea more determinately, and also more completely, expressed. Once admit this definition of the nature of Being, and you will accomplish the end which all the various prior definitions of Being actually sought.

For, first, with the realist, you will now assert that the object is not only Other than the finite idea, but is something that is authoritative over against the finite idea. The realist gave an abstract expression to this authority of the object when he said that the object is independent of the idea. The abstraction was false; but it was already a suggestion of the true meaning. The finite idea does seek its own Other. It consciously means this Other. And it can seek only what it consciously means to seek. But it consciously means to seek precisely that determination of its own will to singleness and finality of expression which shall leave it no Other yet beyond, and still to seek. To its own plan, to its own not here fully determined purpose, the idea at this instant must needs submit. Its very present conscious will is its submission. Yet the idea submits to no external meaning that is not the development of its own internal meaning. Moreover, the finite idea is a merely general idea. But what it means, its object, is an Individual. So you will all agree with the realist that whether or no the idea just now embodies its own object of search as nearly with present truth as the narrow limits of our consciousness permit, it must still seek other fulfilment than is now present, and must submissively accept this fulfilment as its own authoritative truth. But you will reject the realistic isolation of the idea from the object, and of the object from the idea.

If one attempts in some way to modify his Realism by declaring the object not wholly, but only partially, independent of the ideas which refer to it, still such a modified realist would only the more have to face, as we ourselves have been trying to face, the problem as to how the idea and its object are positively related. And if idea and object are left in the end in any way as two separate existent facts, isolated from each other, then one can find no further relation between the isolated idea and object except the relation of greater or less correspondence, and by this relation of mere external correspondence, taken alone, one would be able to define neither the Being of any object, nor the truth of any idea. Or, in other words, a world where ideas and objects merely correspond, as isolated facts, and where no other and deeper relation links knowledge and Being, is a world where there is so far neither any knowledge nor any Being at all.

But secondly, if you accept our Fourth Conception, you will also agree with Mysticism in so far as, identifying Being with fulfilment of purpose, the mystic says, of the object of any of your ideas: *That art thou.* For the mystic means this assertion not of the imperfect self of the merely finite idea. He does not mean that this passing thrill of longing is already fully identical with the Other that this very longing seeks. For the mystic, as for the realist, Being is indeed something Other than our mere search for Being. The mystical identification of the world and the Self is meant to be true of the completed, of the fulfilled and final, or Absolute Self. Now, starting with any idea, we shall henceforth say to this idea, regarding its own object, precisely what the mystic says of the Self and the World: *That art thou.* Namely, the object is for us simply the completely embodied will of the idea. It is nothing else. But we shall henceforth differ from the mystic precisely at the point where the mystic takes refuge in mere negations. We, too, of course, shall also confess our finite ignorance. But the *Neti, Neti* of Yâjnavalkya, the *nescio, nescio* of the mediæval mystic, will express for us, not the essential nature of true Being, as the mystic declared, but merely the present inadequacy of your passing idea to its own present and conscious purpose,—a purpose known precisely so far as it is embodied at this instant. We shall say if we follow to its conclusion this our Fourth Conception, "We know in part, and we prophesy in part; but when the object meant, namely, precisely when that which is perfect is truly said to be, it fulfils, and in so far by supplementing but not otherwise, it takes away that which is in part." Our final object, the *urbs Sion unica, mansio mystica,* is for us, as for the mystic, the unique Being wherein this our finite will is fulfilled. But this one object meant, this fulfilment of our will, is not merely "founded in heaven." Its will is done on earth, not yet in this temporal instant wholly as it is in heaven, but is still really done, in these ideas that already consciously attain a fragment of their own meaning. They are ideas precisely because they do this. The sadness of the mystical longing is now for us lighted by glimpses of the genuine and eternally present truth of the one real world. It is not merely in the mystic trance, but in every rational idea, in so far as it is already a partially embodied purpose, that we now shall in our own way and measure come upon that which is, and catch the deep pulsations of the world. Our instant is not yet the whole of eternity; but the eternal light, the *lux eterna*, shineth in our every reasonable moment, and lighteth every idea that cometh into the world.

And, thirdly, if you follow our Fourth Conception, you will now agree with the critical rationalist when he asserts that Being essentially involves what gives the validity to ideas. But you will have discovered what conditions are necessary to constitute validity. The valid finite idea is first, for whoever possess it, an observed and empirical fulfilment of purpose. But this fulfilment is also observed in this instant as something incomplete. Therefore it is that a finite idea seeks beyond itself for its own validity. And it is perfectly true to say that if the idea is valid, certain further experience of the fulfilment of the idea is possible. Leave this further experience, however, as something merely possible, and your definition of Being would so far remain fast bound in its own fatal circle. Is the idea valid or not? If it is valid, then, by hypothesis, further experience that would confirm the idea is possible. This further experience, like any object existent in the mathematician's realm, is both known to be something Other than the idea that refers to it, and is also viewed as a fact precisely corresponding to what the idea means to define. Now so long as you call this Other, this possible experience, merely such a bare possibility, you define, as we have said, only those characters of this object which the object has in common with your merely present idea of the object. The object is so far defined as an experience, and as having this or that type or form. That is what you say when you talk of any being in Kant's realm of *Mögliche Erfahrung*, or of any mathematical fact. All that is thus defined about the object is its mere *what*, the characters that it shares with your present ideas and experiences at the moment when you define it. What therefore you have *not* thus defined is precisely the Being of the object as Other than the very finite idea which is to regard it as an Other. If you have once observed this defect of any assertion of a bare possibility of experience, you will have seen why the mere definition of universal types can never reach the expression of the whole nature of real Beings, and why, for that very reason, the realm of Validity is nothing unless it is more than merely valid, nothing too unless it takes an individual form as an unique fulfilment of purpose in a completed life.

But all the three former conceptions are now to be brought into synthesis in this Fourth Conception. What is, is authoritative over against finite ideas, as Realism asserted, is one with the true meaning of the idea, as Mysticism insisted, and is valid as Critical Rationalism demanded. What is, presents the fulfilment of the whole purpose of the very idea that now seeks this Being. And when I announce this as our Fourth Conception of Being, I do not mean to be understood as asserting a mere validity, but as reporting facts. I do not any longer merely say, as we said at the outset of our discussion, Being is that which, if present, would end your finite search, would answer your doubts, would fulfil your purpose. All that was the language of validity. It was a mere preliminary. Since validity has no meaning unless its general types of truth take on individual form, and unless the *what* turns into the *that*, I now say, without any reserve, What is does in itself fulfil your meaning, does express, in the completest logically possible measure, the accomplishment and embodiment of the very will now fragmentarily embodied in your finite ideas. And I say, that this embodiment means in itself precisely what your present embodiment of purpose in your rational experience means, just in so far as your purposes are not mere fragments, but are also, even in their transiency, results known as, relatively speaking, won, as possessed, as accomplished. The accomplishment of your purpose now means that your experience is viewed by you as the present and conscious expression of a plan. Well, what is, precisely in so far as it is, is in the same way a whole experience finally expressing and consciously fulfilling a plan. And the Being of the real object of which you now think means a life that expresses the fulfilment of just your present plan, in the greatest measure in which your plan itself is logically capable of fulfilment.

Into this categorical assertion of a concrete experience embodying a plan, our whole series of hypothetically valid assertions of the realm of Critical Rationalism have now resolved themselves. A will concretely embodied in a life,—and these meanings identical with the very purposes that our poor fleeting finite ideas are even now so fragmentarily seeking, amidst all their flickerings and their conflicts, to express,—this, I say, is the reality. This alone is. All else is either shadow, or else is partial embodiment, *i.e.* is a striving after that ideal which needs for its own expression this very striving. This alone is real,—this complete life of divine fulfilment of whatever finite ideas seek. It is because the finite idea essentially seeks its Other, so long as it remains indeterminate, that the quest can be attained only when the will of the idea is so embodied that no other embodiment is to be sought. It is because no quest can be defined as a quest without defining valid possible experiences such as would fulfil or defeat this quest, and it is because no such valid possible experiences can be defined without presupposing that something more than mere validity is real,—it is because of all these considerations that we define the fulfilment of the finite quests embodied in our present and partial ideas as the essential nature of Being.

51

Sigmund Freud

The Interpretation of Dreams (1900)

The Dream is the Fulfillment of a Wish

[. . .] IS THE DREAM CAPABLE OF TEACHING US SOMETHING NEW ABOUT our inner psychic processes, and can its content correct opinions which we have held during the day? I suggest that for the present all these questions be laid aside, and that a single path be pursued. We have found that the dream represents a wish as fulfilled. It will be our next interest to ascertain whether this is a universal characteristic of the dream, or only the accidental content of the dream ("of Irma's injection") with which we have begun our analysis, for even if we make up our minds that every dream has a meaning and psychic value, we must nevertheless allow for the possibility that this meaning is not the same in every dream. The first dream we have considered was the fulfilment of a wish; another may turn out to be a realised apprehension; a third may have a reflection as to its content; a fourth may simply reproduce a reminiscence. Are there then other wish dreams; or are there possibly nothing but wish dreams?

It is easy to show that the character of wish-fulfilment in dreams is often undisguised and recognisable, so that one may wonder why the language of dreams has not long since been understood. There is, for example, a dream which I can cause as often as I like, as it were experimentally. If in the evening I eat anchovies, olives, or other strongly salted foods, I become thirsty at night, whereupon I waken. The awakening, however, is preceded by a dream, which each time has the same content, namely, that I am drinking. I quaff water in long draughts, it tastes as sweet as only a cool drink can taste when one's throat is parched, and then I awake and have an actual desire to drink. The occasion for this dream is thirst, which I perceive when I awake. The wish to drink originates from this sensation, and the dream shows me this wish as fulfilled. It thereby serves a function the nature of which I soon guess. I sleep well, and am not accustomed to be awakened by a bodily need. If I succeed in assuaging my thirst by means of the dream that I am drinking, I need not wake up in order to satisfy it. It is thus a dream of convenience. The dream substitutes itself for action, as elsewhere in life. Unfortunately the need of water for quenching thirst cannot be satisfied with a dream, like my thirst for revenge upon Otto and Dr. M., but the intention is the same. This same dream recently appeared in modified form. On this occasion I became thirsty before going to bed, and emptied the glass of water which stood on the little chest next to my bed. Several hours later in the night came a new attack of thirst, accompanied by discomfort. In order to obtain water, I should have had to get up and fetch the glass which stood on the night-chest of my wife. I thus quite appropriately dreamt that my wife was giving me a drink from a vase; this vase was an Etruscan cinerary urn which I had brought home from an Italian journey and had since given away. But the water in it tasted so salty (apparently from the ashes) that I had to wake. It may be seen how conveniently the dream is capable of arranging matters; since the fulfilment of a wish is its only purpose, it may be perfectly egotistic. Love of comfort is really not compatible with consideration for others. The introduction of the cinerary urn is probably again the fulfilment of a wish; I am sorry that I no longer possess this vase; it, like the glass of water at my wife's side, is inaccessible to me. The cinerary urn is also appropriate to the sensation of a salty taste which has now grown stronger, and which I know will force me to wake up.

Such convenience dreams were very frequent with me in the years of my youth. Accustomed as I had always been to work until late at night, early awakening was always a matter of difficulty for me. I used then to dream that I was out of bed and was standing at the wash-stand. After a while I could not make myself admit that I have not yet got up, but meanwhile I had slept for a time. I am acquainted with the same dream of laziness as dreamt by a young colleague of mine, who seems to share my propensity for sleep. The lodging-house keeper with whom he was living in the neighbourhood of the hospital had strict orders to wake him on time every morning, but she certainly had a lot of trouble when she tried to carry out his orders. One morning sleep was particularly sweet. The woman called into the room: "Mr. Joe, get up; you must go to the hospital." Whereupon the sleeper dreamt of a room in the hospital, a bed in which he was lying, and a chart pinned over his head reading: "Joe H. . . . cand. med. 22 years old." He said to himself in the dream: "If I am already at the hospital, I don't have to go there," turned over and slept on. He had thus frankly admitted to himself his motive for dreaming. [. . .]

The dreams of little children are simple fulfilments of wishes, and as compared, therefore, with the dreams of adults, are not at all interesting. They present no problem to be solved, but are naturally invaluable as affording proof that the dream in its essence signifies the fulfilment of a wish. [. . .]

What animals dream of I do not know. A proverb for which I am indebted to one of my readers claims to know, for it raises the question: "What does the goose dream of?" the answer being: "Of maize!" The whole theory that the dream is the fulfilment of a wish is contained in these sentences.

We now perceive that we should have reached our theory of the hidden meaning of the dream by the shortest road if we had merely consulted colloquial usage. The wisdom of proverbs, it is true, sometimes speaks contemptuously enough of the dream—it apparently tries to justify science in expressing the opinion that "Dreams are mere bubbles;" but still for colloquial usage the dream is the gracious fulfiller of wishes. "I should never have fancied that in the wildest dream," exclaims one who finds his expectations surpassed in reality.

52

William James

The Varieties of Religious Experience (1902)

The Reality of the Unseen

WERE ONE ASKED TO CHARACTERIZE THE LIFE OF RELIGION IN the broadest and most general terms possible, one might say that it consists of the belief that there is an unseen order, and that our supreme good lies in harmoniously adjusting ourselves thereto. This belief and this adjustment are the religious attitude in the soul. I wish during this hour to call your attention to some of the psychological peculiarities of such an attitude as this, of belief in an object which we cannot see. All our attitudes, moral, practical, or emotional, as well as religious, are due to the 'objects' of our consciousness, the things which we believe to exist, whether really or ideally, along with ourselves. Such objects may be present to our senses, or they may be present only to our thought. In either case they elicit from us a *reaction*; and the reaction due to things of thought is notoriously in many cases as strong as that due to sensible presences. It may be even stronger. The memory of an insult may make us angrier than the insult did when we received it. We are frequently more ashamed of our blunders afterwards than we were at the moment of making them; and in general our whole higher prudential and moral life is based on the fact that material sensations actually present may have a weaker influence on our action than ideas of remoter facts.

The more concrete objects of most men's religion, the deities whom they worship, are known to them only in idea. It has been vouchsafed, for example, to very few Christian believers to have had a sensible vision of their Saviour; though enough appearances of this sort are on record, by way of miraculous exception, to merit our attention later. The whole force of the Christian religion, therefore, so far as belief in the divine personages determines the prevalent attitude of the believer, is in general exerted by the instrumentality of pure ideas, of which nothing in the individual's past experience directly serves as a model.

But in addition to these ideas of the more concrete religious objects, religion is full of abstract objects which prove to have an equal power. God's attributes as such, his holiness, his justice, his mercy, his absoluteness, his infinity, his omniscience, his tri-unity, the various mysteries of the redemptive process, the operation of the sacraments, etc., have proved fertile wells of inspiring meditation for Christian believers.[1] We shall see later that the absence of definite sensible images is positively insisted on by the mystical authorities in all religions as the *sine qua non* of a successful orison, or contemplation of the higher divine truths. Such contemplations are expected (and abundantly verify the expectation, as we shall also see) to influence the believer's subsequent attitude very powerfully for good.

Immanuel Kant held a curious doctrine about such objects of belief as God, the design of creation, the soul, its freedom, and the life hereafter. These things, he said, are properly not objects of knowledge at all. Our conceptions always require a sense-content to work with, and as the words 'soul,' 'God,' 'immortality,' cover no distinctive sense-content whatever, it follows that theoretically speaking they are words devoid of any significance. Yet strangely enough they have a definite meaning *for our practice*. We can act *as if* there were a God; feel *as if* we were free; consider Nature *as if* she were full of special designs; lay plans *as if* we were to be immortal; and we find then that these words do make a genuine difference in our moral life. Our faith *that* these unintelligible objects actually exist proves thus to be a full equivalent in *praktischer Hinsicht*, as Kant calls it, or from the point of view of our action, for a knowledge of *what* they might be, in case we were permitted positively to conceive them. So we have the strange phenomenon, as Kant assures us, of a mind believing with all its strength in the real presence of a set of things of no one of which it can form any notion whatsoever.

My object in thus recalling Kant's doctrine to your mind is not to express any opinion as to the accuracy of this particularly uncouth part of his philosophy, but only to illustrate the characteristic of human nature which we are considering, by an example so classical in its exaggeration. The sentiment of reality can indeed attach itself so strongly to our object of belief that our whole life is polarized through and through, so to speak, by its sense of the existence of the thing believed in, and yet that thing, for purpose of definite description, can hardly be said to be present to our mind at all. It is as if a bar of iron, without touch or sight, with no representative faculty whatever, might nevertheless be strongly endowed with an inner capacity for magnetic feeling; and as if, through the various arousals of its magnetism by magnets coming and going in its neighborhood, it might be consciously determined to different attitudes and tendencies. Such a bar of iron could never give you an outward description of the agencies that had the power of stirring it so strongly; yet of their presence, and of their significance for its life, it would be intensely aware through every fibre of its being.

It is not only the Ideas of pure Reason, as Kant styled them, that have this power of making us vitally feel presences that we are impotent articulately to describe. All sorts of higher abstractions bring with them the same kind of impalpable appeal. Remember those passages from Emerson which I read at my last lecture. The whole universe of concrete objects, as we know them, swims, not only for such a transcen-dentalist writer, but for all of us, in a wider and higher universe of abstract ideas, that lend it its significance. As time, space, and the ether soak through all things, so (we feel) do abstract and essential goodness, beauty, strength, significance, justice, soak through all things good, strong, significant, and just.

Such ideas, and others equally abstract, form the background for all our facts, the fountain-head of all the possibilities we conceive of. They give its 'nature,' as we call it, to every special thing. Everything we know is 'what' it is by sharing in the nature of one of these abstractions. We can never look directly at them, for they are bodiless and featureless and footless, but we grasp all other things by their means, and in handling the real world we should be stricken with helplessness in just so far forth as we might lose these mental objects, these adjectives and adverbs and predicates and heads of classification and conception.

This absolute determinability of our mind by abstractions is one of the cardinal facts in our human constitution. Polarizing and magnetizing us as they do, we turn towards them and from them, we seek them, hold them, hate them, bless them, just as if they were so many concrete beings. And beings they are, beings as real in the realm which they inhabit as the changing things of sense are in the realm of space.

Plato gave so brilliant and impressive a defense of this common human feeling, that the doctrine of the reality of abstract objects has been known as the platonic theory of ideas ever since. Abstract Beauty, for example, is for Plato a perfectly definite individual being, of which the intellect is aware as of something additional to all the perishing beauties of the earth. "The true order of going," he says, in the often quoted passage in his 'Banquet,' "is to use the beauties of earth as steps along which one mounts upwards for the sake of that other Beauty, going from one to two, and from two to all fair forms, and from fair forms to fair actions, and from fair actions to fair notions, until from fair notions he arrives at the notion of absolute Beauty, and at last knows what the essence of Beauty is."[2] In our last lecture we had a glimpse of the way in which a platonizing writer like Emerson may treat the abstract divineness of things, the moral structure of the universe, as a fact worthy of worship. In those various churches without a God which to-day are spreading through the world under the name of ethical societies, we have a similar worship of the abstract divine, the moral law believed in as an ultimate object. 'Science' in many minds is genuinely taking the place of a religion. Where this is so, the scientist treats the 'Laws of Nature' as objective facts to be revered. A brilliant school of interpretation of Greek mythology would have it that in their origin the Greek gods were only half-metaphoric personifications of those great spheres of abstract law and order into which the natural world falls apart—the sky-sphere, the ocean-sphere, the earth-sphere, and the like; just as even now we may speak of the smile of the morning, the kiss of the breeze, or the bite of the cold, without really meaning that these phenomena of nature actually wear a human face.[3]

As regards the origin of the Greek gods, we need not at present seek an opinion. But the whole array of our instances leads to a conclusion something like this: It is as if there were in the human consciousness a *sense of reality, a feeling of objective presence, a perception* of what we may call '*something there*,' more deep and more general than any of the special and particular 'senses' by which the current psychology supposes existent realities to be originally revealed. If this were so, we might suppose the senses to waken our attitudes and conduct as they so habitually do, by first exciting this sense of reality; but anything else, any idea, for example, that might similarly excite it, would have that same prerogative of appearing real which objects of sense normally possess. So far as religious conceptions were able to touch this reality-feeling, they would be believed in in spite of criticism, even though they might be so vague and remote as to be almost unimaginable, even though they might be such non-entities in point of *whatness* as Kant makes the objects of his moral theology to be.

The most curious proofs of the existence of such an undifferentiated sense of reality as this are found in experiences of hallucination. It often happens that an hallucination is imperfectly developed: the person affected will feel a 'presence' in the room, definitely localized, facing in one particular way, real in the most emphatic sense of the word, often coming suddenly, and as suddenly gone; and yet neither seen, heard, touched, nor cognized in any of the usual 'sensible' ways. Let me give you an example of this, before I pass to the objects with whose presence religion is more peculiarly concerned.

An intimate friend of mine, one of the keenest intellects I know, has had several experiences of this sort. He writes as follows in response to my inquiries:—

I have several times within the past few years felt the so-called 'consciousness of a presence.' The experiences which I have in mind are clearly distinguishable from another kind of experience which I have had very frequently, and which I fancy many persons would also call the 'consciousness of a presence.' But the difference for me between the two sets of experience is as great as the difference between feeling a slight warmth originating I know not where, and standing in the midst of a conflagration with all the ordinary senses alert.

It was about September, 1884, when I had the first experience. On the previous night I had had, after getting into bed at my rooms in College, a vivid tactile hallucination of being grasped by the arm, which made me get up and search the room for an intruder; but the sense of presence properly so called came on the next night. After I had got into bed and blown out the candle, I lay awake awhile thinking on the previous night's experience, when suddenly I *felt* something come into the room and stay close to my bed. It remained only a minute or two. I did not recognize it by any ordinary sense, and yet there was a horribly unpleasant 'sensation' connected with it. It stirred something more at the roots of my being than any ordinary perception. The feeling had something of the quality of a very large tearing vital pain spreading chiefly over the chest, but within the organism—and yet the feeling was not *pain* so much as *abhorrence*. At all events, something was present with me, and I knew its presence far more surely than I have ever known the presence of any fleshly living creature. I was conscious of its departure as of its coming: an almost instantaneously swift going through the door, and the 'horrible sensation' disappeared.

On the third night when I retired my mind was absorbed in some lectures which I was preparing, and I was still absorbed in these when I became aware of the actual presence (though not of the *coming*) of the thing that was there the night before, and of the 'horrible sensation.' I then mentally concentrated all my effort to charge this 'thing,' if it was evil, to depart, if it was *not* evil, to tell me who or what it was, and if it could not explain itself, to go, and that I would compel it to go. It went as on the previous night, and my body quickly recovered its normal state.

On two other occasions in my life I have had precisely the same 'horrible sensation.' Once it lasted a full quarter of an hour. In all three instances the certainty that there in outward space there stood *something* was indescribably *stronger* than the ordinary certainty of companionship when we are in the close presence of ordinary living people. The something seemed close to me, and intensely more real than any ordinary perception. Although I felt it to be like unto myself, so to speak, or finite, small, and distressful, as it were, I did n't recognize it as any individual being or person.

Of course such an experience as this does not connect itself with the religious sphere. Yet it may upon occasion do so; and the same correspondent informs me that at more than one other conjuncture he had the sense of presence developed with equal intensity and abruptness, only then it was filled with a quality of joy.

There was not a mere consciousness of something there, but fused in the central happiness of it, a startling awareness of some ineffable good. Not vague either, not like the emotional effect of some poem, or scene, or blossom, of music, but the sure knowledge of the close presence of a sort of mighty person, and after it went, the memory persisted as the one perception of reality. Everything else might be a dream, but not that.

My friend, as it oddly happens, does not interpret these latter experiences theistically, as signifying the presence of God. But it would clearly not have been unnatural to interpret them as a revelation of the deity's existence. When we reach the subject of mysticism, we shall have much more to say upon this head. [. . .]

The opinion opposed to mysticism in philosophy is sometimes spoken of as *rationalism*. Rationalism insists that all our beliefs ought ultimately to find for themselves articulate grounds. Such grounds, for rationalism, must consist of four things: (1) definitely statable abstract principles; (2) definite facts of sensation; (3) definite hypotheses based on such facts; and (4) definite inferences logically drawn. Vague impressions of something indefinable have no place in the rationalistic system, which on its positive side is surely a splendid intellectual tendency, for not only are all our philosophies fruits of it, but physical science (amongst other good things) is its result.

Nevertheless, if we look on man's whole mental life as it exists, on the life of men that lies in them apart from their learning and science, and that they inwardly and privately follow, we have to confess that the part of it of which rationalism can give an account is relatively superficial. It is the part that has the *prestige* undoubtedly, for it has the loquacity, it can challenge you for proofs, and chop logic, and put you down with words. But it will fail to convince or convert you all the same, if your dumb intuitions are opposed to its conclusions. If you have intuitions at all, they come from a deeper level of your nature than the loquacious level which rationalism inhabits. Your whole subconscious life, your impulses, your faiths, your needs, your divinations, have prepared the premises, of which your consciousness now feels the weight of the result; and something in you absolutely *knows* that that result must be truer than any logic-chopping rationalistic talk, however clever, that may contradict it. This inferiority of the rationalistic level in founding belief is just as manifest when rationalism argues for religion as when it argues against it. That vast literature of proofs of God's existence drawn from the order of nature, which a century ago seemed so overwhelmingly convincing, to-day does little more than gather dust in libraries, for the simple reason that our generation has ceased to believe in the kind of God it argued for. Whatever sort of a being God may be, we *know* to-day that he is nevermore that mere external inventor of 'contrivances' intended to make manifest his 'glory' in which our great-grandfathers took such satisfaction, though just how we know this we cannot possibly make clear by words either to others or to ourselves. I defy any of you here fully to account for your persuasion that if a God exist he must be a more cosmic and tragic personage than that Being.

The truth is that in the metaphysical and religious sphere, articulate reasons are cogent for us only when our inarticulate feelings of reality have already been impressed in favor of the same conclusion. Then, indeed, our intuitions and our reason work together, and great world-ruling systems, like that of the Buddhist or of the Catholic philosophy, may grow up. Our impulsive belief is here always what sets up the original body of truth, and our philosophy is but its showy verbalized translation. The immediate assurance is the deep thing in us, the argument is but a surface exhibition. Instinct leads, intelligence does but follow. If a person feels the presence of a living God after the fashion shown by my quotations, your critical arguments, be they never so superior, will vainly set themselves to change his faith.

Please observe, however, that I do not yet say that it is *better* that the subconscious and non-rational should thus hold primacy in the religious realm. I confine myself to simply pointing out that they do so hold it as a matter of fact.

So much for our sense of the reality of the religious objects. Let me now say a brief word more about the attitudes they characteristically awaken.

We have already agreed that they are *solemn*; and we have seen reason to think that the most distinctive of them is the sort of joy which may result in extreme cases from absolute self-surrender. The sense of the kind of object to which the surrender is made has much to do with determining the precise complexion of the joy; and the whole phenomenon is more complex than any simple formula allows. In the literature of the subject, sadness and gladness have each been emphasized in turn. The ancient saying that the first maker of the Gods was fear receives voluminous corroboration from every age of religious history; but none the less does religious history show the part which joy has evermore tended to play. Sometimes the joy has been primary; sometimes secondary, being the gladness of deliverance from the fear. This latter state of things, being the more complex, is also the more complete; and as we proceed, I think we shall have abundant reason for refusing to leave out either the sadness or the gladness, if we look at religion with the breadth of view which it demands. Stated in the completest possible terms, a man's religion involves both moods of contraction and moods of expansion of his being. But the quantitative mixture and order of these moods vary so much from one age of the world, from one system of thought, and from one individual to another, that you may insist either on the dread and the submission, or on the peace and the freedom as the essence of the matter, and still remain materially within the limits of the truth. The constitutionally sombre and the constitutionally sanguine onlooker are bound to emphasize opposite aspects of what lies before their eyes. [. . .]

Notes

1 Example: "I have had much comfort lately in meditating on the passages which show the personality of the Holy Ghost, and his distinctness from the Father and the Son. It is a subject that requires searching into to find out, but, when realized, gives one so much more true and lively a sense of the fullness of the Godhead, and its work in us and to us, than when only thinking of the Spirit in its effect on us." AUGUSTUS HARE: Memorials, i. 244., Maria Hare to Lucy H. Hare.

2 *Symposium*, Jowett, 1871, i. 527.

3 Example: "Nature is always so interesting, under whatever aspect she shows herself, that when it rains, I seem to see a beautiful woman weeping. She appears the more beautiful, the more afflicted she is." B. de St. Pierre.

53

Paul Deussen

Outlines of Indian Philosophy, with an Appendix on the Philosophy of the Vedânta in its Relations to Occidental Metaphysics (1907)

Prefatory Remarks

AMONG THE PRETEXTS BY WHICH EUROPEAN IDLENESS TRIES TO ESCAPE the study of Indian philosophy we hear most frequently the remark that the philosophy of the Indians is quite different from our own and has nothing whatever to do with the development of Occidental religion and philosophy. The fact is perfectly true; but far from being a reason for neglecting the study of Indian wisdom, it furnishes us with the strongest argument in favour of devoting ourselves to it all the more. The philosophy of the Indians must become for every one who takes any interest in the investigation of philosophical truth, an object of the highest interest; for Indian philosophy is and will be the only possible parallel to what so far the Europeans have considered as philosophy. In fact, modern European philosophy has sprung from the scholasticiom of the Middle Ages; medieval thought again is a product of Greek philosophy on the one hand and of the Biblical dogma on the other. The doctrine of the Bible has again its roots in part in the oldest Semitic creed and in part in the Persian religion of Zoroaster, which, as an intermediate link between the Old and the New Testament, has exercised more influence than is commonly attributed to it. In this way the whole of European thought from Pythagoras and Xenophanes, from Moses and Zoroaster, through Platonism and Christianity down to the Kantian and post-Kantian philosophy, forms a complex of ideas, whose elements are variously related to and dependent on each other. On the other hand Indian philosophy through all the centuries of its development has taken its course uninfluenced by West-Asiatic and European thought; and precisely for this reason the comparison of European philosophy with that of the Indians is of the highest interest. Where both agree the presumption is that their conclusions are correct, no less than in a case where two calculators working by different methods arrive at the same result; and where Indian and European views differ it is an open question on which side the truth is probably to be found.

2. Indian philosophy falls naturally into three periods; these three periods are equally strongly marked in the general history of Indian civilisation and are dependent on the geography of India. India, as Sir William Jones has already remarked, has the form of a square whose four angles are turned to the four cardinal points, and are marked by the Hindu Kush in the north, Cape Comorin in the south, and the mouths of the Ganges and Indus in the east and west. If a line be drawn from the mouth of the Indus to that of the Ganges (nearly coinciding with the tropic of Cancer), the square is divided into two triangles—Hindustan in the north, and the Deccan in the south. If again in the northern triangle we let fall a perpendicular from the vertex upon the base, this divides northern India into the valley of the Indus and the plain of the Ganges, separated by the desert of Marusthala. Thus India falls into three parts—(1) the Panjab, (2) the plain of the Ganges, (3) the Deccan plateau. To these three geographical divisions correspond the three periods of Indian life:—(1) The domain of the Aryan Hindus in the oldest period was limited to the valley of the Indus with its five tributaries; the only literary monuments of this epoch are the 1017 hymns of the Ṛigveda. Though chiefly serving religious purposes they give by the way a lively and picturesque delineation of that primitive manner of life in which there were no castes, no *âçramas* (stages of life), and no Brahmanical order of life in general. The hymns of the Ṛigveda display not only the ancient Indian polytheism in its full extent, but contain also in certain of the later hymns the first germs of a philosophical view of the world. (2) It may have been about 1000 B. C. that the Aryans starting from the Panjab began to extend their conquests to the east and occupied little by little the plain extending from the Himalayas in the north and the Vindhyas in the south to the mouth of the Ganges. The conquest of this territory may have been accomplished, roughly speaking, between 1000 and 500 B. C. As literary monuments of this second period of Indian life we find the *Saṃhitâs* of the *Yajur-, Sâma-,* and *Atharvaveda*, together with the Brâhmaṇas and their culmination in the Upanishads. Hand in hand with this literary development we have under the spiritual dominion of the Brahmans the establishment of that original organisation which as the Brahmanical order of life has survived in India with some modification until the present day. (3) After these two periods, which we may distinguish as "old-Vedic" and "new-Vedic", follows a third period of Indian history—the "post-Vedic"—beginning about 500 B.C. with the rise of the heretical tendencies of Buddhism and Jainism, and producing in the succeeding centuries

a large number of literary works in which, together with poetry, grammar, law, medicine and astronomy, a rich collection of philosophical works in Sanskrit permits us to trace the development of the philosophical mind down to the present time. In this period Indian, *i.e.*, Brahmanical, civilisation makes its way round the coast of Southern India and Ceylon and penetrates conquering into the remotest districts of Central India.

Introduction

On my journey through India I have noticed with satisfaction, that in philosophy till now our brothers in the East have maintained a very good tradition, better perhaps, than the more active but less contemplative branches of the great Indo-Aryan family in Europe, where Empirism, Realism and their natural consequence, Materialism, grow from day to day more exuberantly, whilst metaphysics, the very centre and heart of serious philosophy, are supported only by the few who have learned to brave the spirit of the age.

In India the influence of this perverted and perversive spirit of our age has not yet overthrown in religion and philosophy the good traditions of the great ancient time. It is true, that most of the ancient *darçana*'s even in India find only an historical interest; followers of the Sânkhya-System occur rarely; Nyâya is cultivated mostly as an intellectual sport and exercise, like grammar or mathematics, — but the Vedânta is, now as in the ancient time, living in the mind and heart of every thoughtful Hindoo. It is true, that even here in the sanctuary of Vedântic metaphysics, the realistic tendencies, natural to man, have penetrated, producing the misinterpreting variations of Çankara's Advaita, known under the names Viçishtâdvaita, Dvaita, Çuddhâdvaita of Râmânuja, Mâdhva, Vallabha, — but India till now has not yet been seduced by their voices, and of hundred Vedântins (I have it from a well informed man, who is himself a zealous adversary of Çankara and follower of Râmânuja) fifteen perhaps adhere to Râmânuja, five to Mâdhva, five to Vallabha, and seventy-five to Çankarâchârya.

This fact may be for poor India in so many misfortunes a great consolation; for the eternal interests are higher than the temporary ones; and the System of the Vedânta, as founded on the Upanishads and Vedânta Sûtras and accomplished by Çankara's commentaries on them, — equal in rank to Plato and Kant — is one of the most valuable products of the genius of mankind in his researches of the eternal truth, — as I propose to show now by a short sketch of Çankara's Advaita and by comparing its principal doctrines with the best that occidental philosophy has produced till now.

Taking the Upanishads, as Çankara does, for revealed truth with absolute authority, it was not an easy task to build out of their materials a consistent philosophical system, for the Upanishads are in Theology, Kosmology and Psychology full of the hardest contradictions. So in many passages the nature of Brahman is painted in various and luxuriant colours, and again we read, that the nature of Brahman is quite unattainable to human words, to human understanding;—so we meet sometimes long reports explaining how the world has been created by Brahman, and again we are told, that there is no world besides Brahman, and all variety of things is mere error and illusion;—so we have fanciful descriptions of the Saṃsâra, the way of the wandering soul up to the heaven and back to the earth, and again we read, that there is no Saṃsâra, no variety of souls at all, but only one Âtman, who is fully and totally residing in every being.

Çaṅkara in these difficulties created by the nature of his materials, in face of so many contradictory doctrines, which he was not allowed to decline and yet could not admit altogether,—has found a wonderful device, which deserves the attention, perhaps the imitation of the Christian dogmatists in their embarrassments. He constructs out of the materials of the Upanishads two systems, one esoteric, philosophical (called by him *nirguṇâ vidyâ*, sometimes *pâramârthikâ avasthâ*) containing the metaphysical truth for the few ones, rare in all times and countries, who are able to understand it; and another exoteric, theological (*saguṇâ vidyâ*, *vyâvahârikî avasthâ*) for the general public, who want images, not abstract truth, worship, not meditation.

I shall now point out briefly the two systems, esoteric and exoteric, in pursuing and confronting them through the four chief parts, which Çaṅkara's system contains, and every complete philosophical system must contain:—

I   Theology, the doctrine of God or of the philosophical principle.

II   Cosmology, the doctrine of the world.

III Psychology, the doctrine of the soul.

IV   Eschatology, the doctrine of the last things, the things after death.

Chapter I: Theology

The Upanishads swarm with fanciful and contradictory descriptions of the nature of Brahman. He is the all-pervading âkâça, is the purusha in the sun, the purusha in the eye; his head is the heaven, his eyes are sun and moon, his breath is the wind, his footstool the earth; he is infinitely great as soul of the universe and infinitely small as the soul in us; he is in particular the *îçvara*, the personal God, distributing justly reward and punishment according to the deeds of man. All these numerous descriptions are collected by Çaṅkara under the wide mantle of the exoteric theology, the *saguṇâ vidyâ* of Brahman, consisting of numerous "vidyâs" adapted for approaching the eternal being not by the way of knowledge but by the way of worshipping, and having each its particular fruits. Mark, that also the conception of God as a personal being, an *îcvara*, is merely exoteric and does not give us an adequate knowledge of the Âtman;—and indeed, when we consider what is personality, how narrow in its limitations, how closely connected which egotism, the counter part of godly essence, who might think so low of God, to impute him personality?

In the sharpest contrast to these exoteric vidyâs stands the esoteric *nirguṇâ vidyâ* of the Âtman; and its fundamental tenet is the absolute inaccessibility of God to human thoughts and words [. . .] and the celebrated formula occurring so often in Brihadâraṇyaka-Upanishad: *neti! neti!* viz., whatever attempt you make to know the Âtman, whatever description you give of him, I always say: *na iti, na iti,* it is not so, it is not so! Therefore the wise Bâhva, when asked by the king Vâshkalin, to explain the Brahman, kept silence. And when the king repeated his request again and again, the rishi broke out into the answer: "I tell it you, but you don't understand it; *çânto 'yam âtmâ,* this Âtmâ is silence!" We know it now by the Kantian philosophy, that the answer of Bâhva was correct, we know it, that the very organisation of our intellect (which is bound once for ever to its innate forms of perception, space, time, and causality) excludes us from a knowledge of the spaceless, timeless, godly reality for ever and ever. And yet the Âtman, the only godly being is not unattainable to us, is even not far from us, for we have it fully and totally in ourselves as our own metaphysical entity; and here, when returning from the outside and apparent world to the deepest secrets of our own nature, we may come to God, not by knowledge, but by *anubhava,* by absorption into our own self. There is a great difference between knowledge, in which subject and object are distinct from each other, and anubhava, where subject and object coincide in the same. He who by anubhava comes to the great intelligence, *"aham brahma asmi",* obtains a state called by Çaṅkara *Saṃrâdhanam,* accomplished satisfaction; and indeed, what might he desire, who feels and knows himself as the sum and totality of all existence!

Chapter II: Cosmology

Here again we meet the distinction of exoteric and esoteric doctrine, though not so clearly severed by Çaṅkara as in other parts of his system.

The exoteric Cosmology according to the natural but erroneous realism *(àvidyâ)* in which we are born, considers this world as the reality, and can express its entire dependency on Brahman only by the mythical way of a creation of the world by Brahman. So a temporal creation of the world, even as in the Christian documents, is also taught in various and well-known passages of the Upanishads. But such a creation of the material world by an immaterial cause, performed in a certain point of time after an eternity elapsed uselessly, is not only against the demands of human reason and natural science, but also against another important doctrine of the Vedânta, which teaches and must teach (as we shall see hereafter) the "beginninglessness of the migration of souls", *saṃsârasya anâditvam.* Here the expedient of Çaṅkara is very clever and worthy of imitation. Instead of the temporary creation once for ever of the Upanishads, he teaches that the world in great periods is created and reabsorbed by Brahman (referring to the misunderstood verse of the Ṛigveda); this mutual creation and reabsorption lasts from eternity, and no creation can be allowed by our system to be the first and that for good reasons, as we shall see just now. —If we ask: *Why* has God created the world? the answers to this question are generally very unsatisfactory. For his own glorification? How may we attribute to him so much vanity! — For his particular amusement? But he was an eternity without this plaything!—For love of mankind? How may he love a thing before it exists, and how may it be called love, to create millions for misery and eternal pain!—The Vedânta has a better answer. The never ceasing new-creation of the world is a moral necessity connected with the central and most valuable doctrine of the exoteric Vedânta, the doctrine of Saṃsâra.

Man, says Çankara, is like a plant. He grows, flourishes and at the end he dies; but not totally. For as the plant, when dying, leaves behind it the seed, from which, according to its quality, a new plant grows,—so man, when dying, leaves his *karma,* the good and bad works of his life, which must be rewarded and punished in another life after this. No life can be the first, for it is the fruit of previous actions, nor the last, for its actions must be expiated in a next following life. So the Saṃsâra is without beginning and without end, and the new creation of the world after every absorption into Brahman is a moral necessity. I need not point out, in India less than anywhere, the high value of this doctrine of Saṃsâra as a consolation in the afflictions as a moral agent in the temptations of life,—I have to say here only, that the Saṃsâra, though not the absolute truth, is a mythical representative of a truth which in itself is unattainable to our intellect; mythical is this theory of metempsychosis only in so far as it invests in the forms of space and time what really is spaceless and timeless, and therefore beyond the reach of our understanding. So the Saṃsâra is just so far from the truth, as the *saguṇâ vidyâ* is from the *nirguṇâ vidyâ*; it is the eternal truth itself, but (since we cannot conceive it otherwise) the truth in an allegorical form, adapted to our human understanding. And this is the character of the whole exoteric Vedanta, whilst the esoteric doctrine tries to find out the philosophical, the absolute truth.

And so we come to the esoteric Cosmology, whose simple doctrine is this, that in reality there is no manifold world, but only Brahman, and that what we consider as the world, is a mere illusion (*mâyâ*) similar to a *mṛigatṛishṇikâ*, which disappears when we approach it, and not more to be feared than the rope, which we took in the darkness for a serpent. There are, as you see, many similes in the Vedânta, to illustrate the illusive character of this world, but the best of them is perhaps, when Çankara compares our life with a long dream;—a man whilst dreaming does not doubt oft the reality of the dream, but this reality disappears in the moment of awakening, to give place to a truer reality, which we were not aware of whilst dreaming. The life a dream! this has been the thought of many wise men from Pindar and Sophocles to Shakspere and Calderon de la Barca, but nobody has better explained this idea, than Çankara. And indeed, the moment when we die may be to nothing so similar as to the awakening from a long and heavy dream; it may be, that then heaven and earth are blown away like the nightly phantoms of the dream, and what then may stand before us? or rather in us? Brahman, the eternal reality, which was hidden to us till then by this dream of life!—This world is mâyâ, is illusion; is not the very reality, that is the deepest thought of the esoteric Vedânta, attained not by calculating *tarka* but by *anubhava,* by returning from this variegated world to the deep recess of our own self (*Âtman*). Do so, if you can, and you will get aware of a reality very different from empirical reality, a timeless, spaceless, changeless reality, and you will feel and experience that whatever is outside of this only true reality, is mere appearance, is mâyâ, is a dream!—This was the way the Indian thinkers went, and by a similar way, shown by Parmenides, Plato came to the same truth, when knowing and teaching that this world is a world of shadows, and that the reality is not in these shadows, but behind them. The accord here of Platonism and Vedantism is wonderful, but both have grasped this great metaphysical truth by intuition; their tenet is true, but they are not able to prove it, and in so far they are defective. And here a great light and assistance to the Indian and the Greek thinker comes from the philosophy of Kant, who went quite another way, not the Vedantic and Platonic way of intuition, but the way of abstract reasoning and scientific proof. The great work of Kant is an analysis of human mind, not in the superficial way of Locke, but going to the very bottom of it. And in doing so, Kant found, to the surprise of the world and of himself, that three essential elements of this outside world, *viz.,* space, time, and causality, are not, as we naturally believe, eternal fundamentals of an objective reality, but merely subjective innate perceptual forms of our own intellect. This has been proved by Kant and by his great disciple Schopenhauer with mathematical evidence, and I have given these proofs (the base of all scientific metaphysics) in the shortest and clearest form in my "Elemente der Metaphysik"—a book which I am resolved now to get translated into English, for the benefit not of the Europeans (who may learn German) but of my brothers in India, who will be greatly astonished to find in Germany the scientific substruction of their own philosophy, of the Advaita Vedânta! For Kant has demonstrated, that space, time and causality are not objective realities, but only subjective forms of our intellect, and the unavoidable conclusion is this, that the world, as far as it is extended in space, running on in time, ruled throughout by causality, in so far is merely a representation of my mind and nothing beyond it. You see the concordance of Indian, Greek and German metaphysics; the world is mâyâ, is illusion, says *Çankara;*—it is a world of shadows, not of realities, says *Plato;*—it is "appearance only, not the thing in itself", says *Kant.* Here we have the same doctrine in three different parts of the world, but the scientific proofs of it are not in Çankara, not in Plato, but only in Kant.

Chapter III: Psychology

Here we convert the order and begin with the esoteric Psychology, because it is closely connected with the esoteric Cosmology and its fundamental doctrine: the world is *mâyâ.* All is illusive, with one exception, with the exception of my own Self, of my Âtman. My Âtman cannot be illusive, as Çankara shows, anticipating the "*cogito, ergo sum*" of Descartes,—for he who would deny it, even in denying it, witnesses its reality. But what is the relation between my individual soul, the Jîva-Âtman, and the highest soul, the Parama-Âtman or Brahman? Here Çankara, like a prophet, foresees the deviations of Râmânuja, Mâdhva and Vallabha and refutes them in showing, that the Jîva cannot be a part of Brahman (Râmânuja), because Brahman is without parts (for it is timeless and spaceless, and all parts are either successions in time or co-ordinations in space, — as we may add), — neither a different thing from Brahman (Mâdhva), for Brahman is *ekam eva advitîyam,* as we may experience by *anubhava,* — nor a metamorphose of Brahman (Vallabha), for Brahman is unchangeable (for, as we know now by Kant, it is out of causality). The conclusion is, that the Jîva being neither a part nor a different thing, nor a variation of Brahman, must be the Paramatman fully and totally himself, a conclusion made equally by the Vedântin Çankara, by the Platonic Plotinos, and by the Kantian Schopenhauer. But Çankara in his conclusions goes perhaps further than any of them. If really our soul, says he, is not a part of Brahman but Brahman himself, then all the attributes of Brahman, all-pervadingness, eternity, all-migthiness (scientifically spoken: exemption of space, time, causality) are ours; *aham brahma asmi,* I am Brahman, and consequently I am all-pervading (spaceless), eternal (timeless), almigthy (not limited in my doing by causality). But these godly qualities are hidden in me, says Çankara, as the fire is hidden in the wood, and will appear only after the final deliverance.

What is the cause of this concealment of my godly nature? The Upâdhi's, answers Çankara, and with this answer we pass from the esoteric to the exoteric psychology. The Upâdhi's are manas and indriya's, prâna with its five branches, sûkshmam çarîram, — in short, the whole psychological apparatus, which together with a factor changeable from birth to birth, with my karman, accompanies my Âtman in all his ways of migration, without infecting his godly nature, as the crystal is not infected by the colour painted over it. But wherefrom originate these Upâdhi's? They form of course part of the *mâyâ,* the great world-illusion, and like *mâyâ* they are based on our innate *avidyâ* or ignorance, a merely negative power and yet strong enough to keep us from our godly existence. But now, from where comes this *avidyâ,* this primeval cause of ignorance, sin, and misery? Here all philosophers in India and Greece and everywhere have been defective, until Kant came to show us that the whole question is inadmissible. You ask for the cause of *avidyâ,* but it has no cause; for causality goes only so far as this world of the Saṃsâra goes, connecting each link of it with another, but never beyond Saṃsâra and its fundamental characteristic, the *avidyâ.* In enquiring after a cause of *avidyâ* with *mâyâ,* Saṃsâra and Upâdhi's, you abuse, as Kant may teach us, your innate mental organ of causality to penetrate into a region for which it is not made, and where it is no more available. The fact is, that we are here in ignorance, sin and misery, and that we know the way out of them, but the question of a cause for them is senseless.

Chapter IV: Eschatology

And now a few words about this way out of the Saṃsâra, and first about the exoteric theory of it. In the ancient time of the hymns there was no idea of Saṃsâra but only rewards in heaven and (somewhat later) punishments in a dark region *(padam gabhîram)*, the precursor of the later hells. Then the deep theory of Saṃsâra came up, teaching rewards and punishment in the form of a new birth on earth. The Vedânta combines both theories, and so it has a double expiation, first in heaven and hell, and then again in a new existence on the earth. This double expiation is different (1) for performers of good works, going the *pitṛiyâna*, (2) for worshippers of the saguṇam brahma, going the *devayâna*, (3) for wicked deeds, leading to what is obscurely hinted at in the Upanishads as the *tṛitîyaṃ sthânam*, the third place. (1) The *pitṛiyâna* leads through a succession of dark spheres to the moon, there to enjoy the fruit of the good works and, after their consumption, back to an earthly existence. (2) The *devayâna* leads through a set of brighter spheres to Brahman, without returning to the earth. But this Brahman is only saguṇam brahma, the object of worshipping, and its true worshippers, though entering into this saguṇam brahma without returning, have to wait in it until they get *moksha* by obtaining *samyagdarçanam*, the full knowledge of the nirguṇam brahma. (3) The *tṛitîyaṃ sthânam*, including the later theories of hells, teaches punishment in them, and again punishment by returning to earth in the form of lower castes, animals, and plants. All these various and fantastical ways of Saṃsâra are considered as true, quite as true as this world is, but not more. For the whole world and the whole way of Saṃsâra is valid and true for those only who are in the *avidyâ*, not for those who have overcome it, as we have to show now.

The esoteric Vedânta does not admit the reality of the world nor of the Saṃsâra, for the only reality is Brahman, seized in ourselves as our own Âtman. The knowledge of this Âtman, the great intelligence: "*aham brahma asmi*", does not produce *moksha* (deliverance), but is *moksha* itself. Then we obtain what the Upanishad say [. . .]. When seeing Brahma as the highest and the lowest everywhere, all knots of our heart, all sorrows are split, all doubts vanish, and our works become nothing. Certainly no man can live without doing work, and so also the *Jîvanmukta;* but he knows, that all these works are illusive, as this whole world is, and therefore they do not adhere to him nor produce for him a new life after death.—And what kind of work may such a man do?—People have often reproached the Vedanta with being defective in morals, and indeed, the Indian genius is too contemplative to speak much of deeds; but the fact is nevertheless, that the highest and purest morality is the immediate consequence of the Vedânta. The Gospels fix quite correctly as the highest law of morality: "love your neighbour as yourselves." But why should I do so, since by the order of nature I feel pain and pleasure only in myself, not in my neighbour? The answer is not in the Bible (this venerable book being not yet quite free of Semitic realism), but it is in the Veda, is in the great formula "*tat tvam asi*", which gives in three words metaphysics and morals altogether. You shall love your neighbour as yourselves,—because you are your neighbour, and mere illusion makes you believe, that your neighbour is something different from yourselves. Or in the words of the Bhagavadgîtâḥ: he, who knows himself in everything and everything in himself, will not injure himself by himself, *na hinasti âtmanâ âtmânam.* This is the sum and tenor of all morality, and this is the standpoint of a man knowing himself as Brahman. He feels himself everything,—so he will not desire anything, for he has whatever can be had;—he feels himself everything,—so he will not injure anything, for nobody injures himself. He lives in the world, is surrounded by its illusions but not deceived by them: like the man suffering from *timira,* who sees two moons but knows that there is one only, so the Jîvanmukta sees the manifold world and cannot get rid of seeing it, but he knows, that there is only one being, Brahman, the Âtman, his own Self, and he verifies it by his deeds of pure disinterested morality. And so he expects his end, as the potter expects the end of the twirling of his wheel, after the vessel is ready. And then, for him, when death comes, no more Saṃsâra [. . .]. He enters into brahman, like the streams into the ocean; [. . .] he leaves behind him *nâma* and *rûpam,* he leaves behind him *individuality,* but he does not leave behind him his *Âtman,* his Self. It is not the falling of the drop into the infinite ocean, it is the whole ocean, becoming free from the fetters of ice, returning from its frozen state to that what it is really and has never ceased to be, to its own all-pervading, eternal, all-mighty nature.

And so the Vedânta, in its pure and unfalsified form, is the strongest support of pure morality, is the greatest consolation in the sufferings of life and death,—Indians, keep to it!—

54

Henry Adams

The Education of Henry Adams (1907)

The Dynamo and the Virgin

UNTIL THE GREAT EXPOSITION CLOSED ITS DOORS IN NOVEMBER, Adams haunted it, aching to absorb knowledge, and helpless to find it. He would have liked to know how much of it could have been grasped by the best-informed man in the world. While he was thus meditating chaos, Langley came by, and showed it to him. At Langley's behest, the Exhibition dropped its superfluous rags and stripped itself to the skin, for Langley knew what to study, and why, and how; while Adams might as well have stood outside in the night, staring at the Milky Way. Yet Langley said nothing new, and taught nothing that one might not have learned from Lord Bacon, three hundred years before; but though one should have known the "Advancement of Science" as well as one knew the "Comedy of Errors," the literary knowledge counted for nothing until some teacher should show how to apply it. Bacon took a vast deal of trouble in teaching King James I and his subjects, American or other, towards the year 1620, that true science was the development or economy of forces; yet an elderly American in 1900 knew neither the formula nor the forces; or even so much as to say to himself that his historical business in the Exposition concerned only the economies or developments of force since 1893, when he began the study at Chicago.

Nothing in education is so astonishing as the amount of ignorance it accumulates in the form of inert facts. Adams had looked at most of the accumulations of art in the storehouses called Art Museums; yet he did not know how to look at the art exhibits of 1900. He had studied Karl Marx and his doctrines of history with profound attention, yet he could not apply them at Paris. Langley, with the ease of a great master of experiment, threw out of the field every exhibit that did not reveal a new application of force, and naturally threw out, to begin with, almost the whole art exibit. Equally, he ignored almost the whole industrial exhibit He led his pupil directly to the forces. His chief interest was in new motors to make his airship feasible, and he taught Adams the astonishing complexities of the new Daimler, and of the automobile, which, since 1893, had become a nightmare at a hundred kilometres an hour, almost as destructive as the electric tram which was only ten years older; and threatening to become as terrible as the locomotive steam-engine itself, which was almost exactly Adams's own age.

Then he showed his scholar the great hall of dynamos, and explained how little he knew about electricity or force of any kind, even of his own special sun, which spouted heat in inconceivable volume, but which, as far as he knew, might spout less or more, at any time, for all the certainty he felt in it. To him, the dynamo itself was but an ingenious channel for conveying somewhere the heat latent in a few tons of poor coal hidden in a dirty engine-house carefully kept out of sight; but to Adams the dynamo became a symbol of infinity. As he grew accustomed to the great gallery of machines, he began to feel the forty-foot dynamos as a moral force, much as the early Christians felt the Cross. The planet itself seemed less impressive, in its old-fashioned, deliberate, annual or daily revolution, than this huge wheel, revolving within arm's length at some vertiginous speed, and barely murmuring – scarcely humming an audible warning to stand a hair's-breadth further for respect of power – while it would not wake the baby lying close against its frame. Before the end, one began to pray to it; inherited instinct taught the natural expression of man before silent and infinite force. Among the thousand symbols of ultimate energy the dynamo was not so human as some, but it was the most expressive.

Yet the dynamo, next to the steam-engine, was the most familiar of exhibits. For Adams's objects its value lay chiefly in its occult mechanism. Between the dynamo in the gallery of machines and the engine-house outside, the break of continuity amounted to abysmal fracture for a historian's objects. No more relation could he discover between the steam and the electric current than between the Cross and the cathedral. The forces were interchangeable if not reversible, but he could see only an absolute *fiat* in electricity as in faith. Langley could not help him. Indeed, Langley seemed to be worried by the same trouble, for he constantly repeated that the new forces were anarchical, and especially that he was not responsible for the new rays, that were little short of parricidal in their wicked spirit towards science. His own rays, with which he had doubled the solar spectrum, were altogether harmless and beneficent; but Radium denied its God – or, what was to Langley the same thing, denied the truths of his Science. The force was wholly new.

A historian who asked only to learn enough to be as futile as Langley or Kelvln, made rapid progress under this teaching, and mixed himself up in the tangle of ideas until he achieved a sort of Paradise of ignorance vastly consoling to his fatigued senses. He wrapped himself in vibrations and rays which were new, and he would have hugged Marconi and Branly had he met them, as he hugged the dynamo; while he lost his arithmetic in trying to figure out the equation between the discoveries and the economies of force. The economies, like the discoveries, were absolute, supersensual, occult; incapable of expression in horse-power. What mathematical equivalent could he suggest as the value of a Branly coherer? Frozen air, or the electric furnace, had some scale of measurement, no doubt, if somebody could invent a thermometer adequate to the purpose; but X-rays had played no part whatever in man's consciousness, and the atom itself had figured only as a fiction of thought. In these seven years man had translated himself into a new universe which had no common scale of measurement with the old. He had entered a supersensual world, in which he could measure nothing except by chance collisions of movements imperceptible to his senses, perhaps even imperceptible to his in struments, but perceptible to each other, and so to some known ray at the end of the scale. Langley seemed prepared for anything, even for an indeterminable number of universes interfused – physics stark mad in metaphysics.

Historians undertake to arrange sequences, – called stories, or histories – assuming in silence a relation of cause and effect These assumptions, hidden in the depths of dusty libraries, have been astounding, but commonly unconscious and childlike; so much so, that if any captious critic were to drag them to light, historians would probably reply, with one voice, that they had never supposed themselves required to know what they were talking about. Adams, for one, had toiled in vain to find out what he meant. He had even published a dozen volumes of American history for no other purpose than to satisfy himself whether, by severest process of stating, with the least possible comment, such facts as seemed sure, in such order as seemed rigorously consequent, ie could fix for a familiar moment a necessary sequence of human movement. The result had satisfied him as little as at Harvard College. Where he saw sequence, other men saw something quite different, and no one saw the same unit of measure. He cared little about his experiments and less about his statesmen, who seemed to him quite as ignorant as himself and, as a rule, no more honest; but he insisted on a relation of sequence. And if he could not reach it by one method, he would try as many methods as science knew. Satisfied that the sequence of men led to nothing and that the sequence of their society could lead no further, while the mere sequence of time was artificial, and the sequence of thought was chaos, he turned at last to the sequence of force; and thus it happened that, after ten years' pursuit, he found himself lying in the Gallery of Machines at the Great Exposition of 1900, his historical neck broken by the sudden irruption of forces totally new.

Since no one else showed much concern, an elderly person without other cares had no need to betray alarm. The year 1900 was not the first to upset schoolmasters. Copernicus and Galileo had broken many professorial necks about 1600; Columbus had stood the world on its head towards 1500; but the nearest approach to the revolution of 1900 was that of 310, when Constantine set up the Cross. The rays that Langley disowned, as well as those which he fathered, were occult, supersensual, irrational; they were a revelation of mysterious energy like that of the Cross; they were what, in terms of medieval science, were called immediate modes of the divine substance.

The historian was thus reduced to his last resources. Clearly if he was bound to reduce all these forces to a common value, this common value could have no measure but that of their attraction on his own mind. He must treat them as they had been felt; as convertible, reversible, interchangeable attractions on thought. He made up his mind to venture it; he would risk translating rays into faith. Such a reversible process would vastly amuse a chemist, but the chemist could not deny that he, or some of his fellow physicists, could feel the force of both. When Adams was a boy in Boston, the best chemist in the place had probably never heard of Venus except by way of scandal, or of the Virgin except as idolatry; neither had he heard of dynamos or automobiles or radium; yet his mind was ready to feel the force of all, though the rays were unborn and the women were dead.

Here opened another totally new education, which promised to be by far the most hazardous of all. The knife-edge along which he must crawl, like Sir Lancelot in the twelfth century, divided two kingdoms of force which had nothing in common but attraction. They were as different as a magnet is from gravitation, supposing one knew what a magnet was, or gravitation, or love. The force of the Virgin was still felt at Lourdes, and seemed to be as potent as X-rays; but in America neither Venus nor Virgin ever had value as force – at most as sentiment. No American had ever been truly afraid of either.

This problem in dynamics gravely perplexed an American historian. The Woman had once been supreme; in France she still seemed potent, not merely as a sentiment, but as a force. Why was she unknown in America? For evidently America was ashamed of her, and she was ashamed of herself, otherwise they would not have strewn fig-leaves so profusely all over her. When she was a true force, she was ignorant of fig-leaves, but the monthly-magazine-made American female had not a feature that would have been recognized by Adam. The trait was notorious, and often humorous, but any one brought up among Puritans knew that sex was sin. In any previous age, sex was strength. Neither art nor beauty was needed. Every one, even among Puritans, knew that neither Diana of the Ephesians nor any of the Oriental goddesses was worshipped for her beauty. She was goddess because of her force; she was the animated dynamo; she was reproduction – the greatest and most mysterious of all energies; all she needed was to be fecund. Singularly enough, not one of Adams's many schools of education had ever drawn his attention to the opening lines of Lucretius, though they were perhaps the finest in all Latin literature, where the poet invoked Venus exactly as Dante invoked the Virgin:–

"Quae quondam rerum naturam *sola* gubernas."

The Venus of Epicurean philosophy survived in the Virgin of the Schools: –

"Donna, sei tanto grande, e tanto vali,
Che qual vuol grazia, e a te non ricorre,
Sua disianza vuol volar senz' ali."

All this was to American thought as though it had never existed. The true American knew something of the facts, but nothing of the feelings; he read the letter, but he never felt the law. Before this historical chasm, a mind like that of Adams felt itself helpless; he turned from the Virgin to the Dynamo as though he were a Branly coherer. On one side, at the Louvre and at Chartres, as he knew by the record of work actually done and still before his eyes, was the highest energy ever known to man, the creator four-fifths of his noblest art, exercising vastly more attraction over the human mind than all the steam-engines and dynamos ever dreamed of; and yet this energy was unknown to the American mind. An American Virgin would never dare command; an American Venus would never dare exist.

The question, which to any plain American of the nineteenth century seemed as remote as it did to Adams, drew him almost violently to study, once it was posed; and on this point Langleys were as useless as though they were Herbert Spencers or dynamos. The idea survived only as art. There one turned as naturally as though the artist were himself a woman. Adams began to ponder, asking himself whether he knew of any American artist who had ever insisted on the power of sex, as every classic had always done; but he could think only of Walt Whitman; Bret Harte, as far as the magazines would let him venture; and one or two painters, for the flesh-tones. All the rest had used sex for sentiment, never for force; to them, Eve was a tender flower, and Herodias an unfeminine horror. American art, like the American language and American education, was as far as possible sexless. Society regarded this victory over sex as its greatest triumph, and the historian readily admitted it, since the moral issue, for the momen did not concern one who was studying the relations of unmoral force. He cared nothing for the sex of the dynamo until he could measure its energy.

Vaguely seeking a clue, he wandered through the art exhibit, and, in his stroll, stopped almost every day before St. Gaudens's General Sherman, which had been given the central post of honor. St. Gaudens himself was in Paris, putting on the work his usual interminable last touches, and listening to the usual contradictory suggestions of brother sculptors. Of all the American artists who gave to American art whatever life it breathed in the seventies, St. Gaudens was perhaps the most sympathetic, but certainly the most inarticulate. General Grant or Don Cameron had scarcely less instinct of rhetoric than he. All the others – the Hunts, Richardson, John La Farge, Stanford White – were exuberant; only St. Gaudens could never discuss or dilate on an emotion, or suggest artistic arguments for giving to his work the forms that he felt. He never laid down the law, or affected the despot, or became brutalized like Whistler by the brutalities of his world. He required no incense; he was no egoist; his simplicity of thought was excessive; he could not imitate, or give any form but his own to the creations of his hand. No one felt more strongly than he the strength of other men, but the idea that they could affect him never stirred an image in his mind.

This summer his health was poor and his spirits were low. For such a temper, Adams was not the best companion, since his own gaiety was not *folle*; but he risked going now and then to the studio on Mont Parnasse to draw him out for a stroll in the Bois de Boulogne, or dinner as pleased his moods, and in return St. Gaudens sometimes let Adams go about in his company.

Once St. Gaudens took him down to Amiens, with a party of Frenchmen, to see the cathedral. Not until they found themselves actually studying the sculpture of the western portal, did it dawn on Adams's mind that, for his purposes, St. Gaudens on that spot had more interest to him than the cathedral itself. Great men before great monuments express great truths, provided they are not taken too solemnly. Adams never tired of quoting the supreme phrase of his idol Gibbon, before the Gothic cathedrals: "I darted a contemptuous look on the stately monuments of supersition." Even in the footnotes of his history, Gibbon had never inserted a bit of humor more human than this, and one would have paid largely for a photograph of the fat little historian, on the background of Notre Dame of Amiens, trying to persuade his readers – perhaps himself – that he was darting a contemptuous look on the stately monument, for which he felt in fact the respect which every man of his vast study and active mind always feels before objects worthy of it; but besides the humor, one felt also the relation. Gibbon ignored the Virgin, because in 1789 religious monuments were out of fashion. In 1900 his remark sounded fresh and simple as the green fields to ears that had heard a hundred years of other remarks, mostly no more fresh and certainly less simple. Without malice, one might find it more instructive than a whole lecture of Ruskin. One sees what one brings, and at that moment Gibbon brought the French Revolution. Ruskin brought reaction against the Revolution. St. Gaudens had passed beyond all. He liked the stately monuments much more than he liked Gibbon or Ruskin; he loved their dignity; their unity; their scale; their lines; their lights and shadows; their decorative sculpture; but he was even less conscious than they of the force that created it all – the Virgin, the Woman – by whose genius "the stately monuments of superstition" were built, through which she was expressed. He would have seen more meaning in Isis with the cow's horns, at Edfoo, who expressed the same thought. The art remained, but the energy was lost even upon the artist.

Yet in mind and person St. Gaudens was a survival of the 1500; he bore the stamp of the Renaissance, and should have carried an image of the Virgin round his neck, or stuck in his hat, like Louis XI. In mere time he was a lost soul that had strayed by chance to the twentieth century, and forgotten where it came from. He writhed and cursed at his ignorance, much as Adams did at his own, but in the opposite sense. St. Gaudens was a child of Benvenuto Cellini, smothered in an American cradle. Adams was a quintessence of Boston, devoured by curiosity to think like Benvenuto. St. Gaudens's art was starved from birth, and Adams's; instinct was blighted from babyhood. Each had but half of a nature, and when they came together before the Virgin of Amiens they ought both to have felt in her the force that made them one; but it was not so. To Adams she became more than ever a channel of force; to St. Gaudens she remained as before a channel of taste.

For a symbol of power, St. Gaudens instinctively preferred the horse, as was plain in his horse and Victory of the Sherman monument. Doubtless Sherman also felt it so. The attitude was so American that, for at least forty years, Adams had never realized that any other could be in sound taste. How many years had he taken to admit a notion of what Michael Angelo and Rubens were driving at? He could not say; but he knew that only since 1895 had he begun to feel the Virgin or Venus as force, and not everywhere even so. At Chartres – perhaps at Lourdes – possibly at

Cnidos if one could still find there the divinely naked Aphrodite of Praxiteles – but otherwise one must look for force to the goddesses of Indian mythology. The idea died out long ago in the German and English stock. St. Gaudens at Amiens was hardly less sensitive to the force of the female energy than Matthew Arnold at the Grande Chartreuse. Neither of them felt goddesses as power – only as reflected emotion, human expression, beauty, purity, taste, scarcely even as sympathy. They felt a railway train as power, yet they, and all other artists, constantly complained that the power embodied in a railway train could never be embodied in art. All the steam in the world could not, like the Virgin, build Chartres.

Yet in mechanics, whatever the mechanicians might think, both energies acted as interchangeable force on man, and by action on man all known force may be measured. Indeed, few men of science measured force in any other way. After once admitting that a straight line was the shortest distance between two points, no serious mathematician cared to deny anything that suited his convenience, and rejected no symbol, unproved or unproveable, that helped him to accomplish work. The symbol was force, as a compass-needle or a triangle was force, as the mechanist might prove by losing it, and nothing could be gained by ignoring their value. Symbol or energy, the Virgin had acted as the greatest force the Western world ever felt, and had drawn man's activities to herself more strongly than any other power, natural or supernatural, had ever done; the historian's business was to follow the track of the energy; to find where it came from and where it went to; its complex source and shifting channels; its values, equivalents, conversions. It could scarcely be more complex than radium; it could hardly be deflected, diverted, polarized, absorbed ore perplexingly than other radiant matter. Adams knew nothng about any of them, but as a mathematical problem of influence on human progress, though all were occult, all reacted on his mind, and he rather inclined to think the Virgin easiest to handle.

The pursuit turned out to be long and tortuous, leading at last to the vast forests of scholastic science. From Zeno to Descartes, hand in hand with Thomas Aquinas, Montaigne, and Pascal, one stumbled as stupidly as though one were still a German student of 1860. Only with the instinct of despair could one force one's self into this old thicket of ignorance after having been repulsed a score of entrances more promising and more popular. Thus far, no path had led anywhere, unless perhaps to an exceedingly modest living. Forty-five years of study had proved to be quite Futile for the pursuit of power; one controlled no more force in 1900 than in 1850, although the amount of force controlled by society had enormously increased. The secret of education still hid itself somewhere behind ignorance, and one fumbled over it as feebly as ever. In such labyrinths, the staff is a force almost more necessary than the legs; the pen becomes a sort of blind-man's dog, to keep him from falling into the gutters. The pen works for itself, and acts like a hand, modelling the plastic material over and over again to the form that suits it best. The form is never arbitrary, but is a sort of growth like crystallization, as any artist knows too well; for often the pencil or pen runs into side-paths and shapelessness, loses its relations, stops or is bogged. Then it has to return on its trail, and recover, if it can, its line of force. The result of a year's work depends more on what is struck out than on what is left in; on the sequence of the main lines of thought, than on their play or variety. Compelled once more to lean heavily on this support, Adams covered more thousands of pages with figures as formal as though they were algebra, laboriously striking out, altering, burning, experimenting, until the year had expired, the Exposition had long been closed, and winter drawing to its end, before he sailed from Cherbourg, on January 19, 1901, for home.

55

Henri Bergson

Beyond the Noumenal (1907)

What the *Transcendental Aesthetic* of Kant appears to have established once for all is that extension is not a material attribute of the same kind as others. We cannot reason indefinitely on the notions of heat, colour, or weight: in order to know the modalities of weight or of heat, we must have recourse to experience. Not so of the notion of space. Supposing even that it is given empirically by sight and touch (and Kant has not questioned the fact) there is this about it that is remarkable: that our mind, speculating on it with its own powers alone, cuts out in it, *a priori,* figures whose properties we determine *a priori*: experience, with which we have not kept in touch, yet follows us through the infinite complications of our reasonings and invariably justifies them. That is the fact. Kant has set it in clear light. But the explanation of the fact, we believe, must be sought in a different direction to that which Kant followed.

Intelligence, as Kant represents it to us, is bathed in an atmosphere of spatiality to which it is as inseparably united as the living body to the air it breathes. Our perceptions reach us only after having passed through this atmosphere. They have been impregnated in advance by our geometry, so that our faculty of thinking only finds again in matter the mathematical properties which our faculty of perceiving has already deposed there. We are assured, therefore, of seeing matter yield itself with docility to our reasonings; but this matter, in all that it has that is intelligible, is our own work; of the reality 'in itself' we know nothing and never shall know anything, since we only get its refraction through the forms of our faculty of perceiving. So that if we claim to affirm something of it, at once there rises the contrary affirmation, equally demonstrable, equally plausible. The ideality of space is proved directly by the analysis of knowledge, indirectly by the antinomies to which the opposite theory leads. Such is the governing idea of the Kantian criticism. It has inspired Kant with a peremptory refutation of 'empiricist' theories of knowledge. It is, in our opinion, definitive in what it denies. But, in what it affirms, does it give us the solution of the problem?

With Kant, space is given as a ready-made form of our perceptive faculty – a veritable *deus ex machina,* of which we see neither how it arises, nor why it is what it is rather than anything else. 'Things-in-themselves' are also given, of which he claims that we can know nothing: by what right, then, can he affirm their existence, even as 'problematic'? If the unknowable reality projects into our perceptive faculty a 'sensuous manifold' capable of fitting into it exactly, is it not, by that very fact, in part known? And when we examine this exact fitting, shall we not be led, in one point at least, to suppose a pre-established harmony between things and our mind – an idle hypothesis, which Kant was right in wishing to avoid? At bottom, it is for not having distinguished degrees in spatiality that he has had to take space ready-made as given – whence the question how the 'sensuous manifold' is adapted to it. It is for the same reason that he has supposed matter wholly developed into parts absolutely external to one another; – whence antinomies, of which we may plainly see that the thesis and antithesis suppose the perfect coincidence of matter with geometrical space, but which vanish the moment we cease to extend to matter what is true only of pure space. Whence, finally, the conclusion that there are three alternatives, and three only, among which to choose a theory of knowledge: either the mind is determined by things, or things are determined by the mind, or between mind and things we must suppose a mysterious agreement.

But the truth is that there is a fourth, which does not seem to have occurred to Kant – in the first place because he did not think that the mind overflowed the intellect, and in the second place (and this is at bottom the same thing) because he did not attribute to duration an absolute existence, having put time, *a priori,* on the same plane as space. This alternative consists, first of all, in regarding the intellect as a special function of the mind, essentially turned toward inert matter; then in saying that neither does matter determine the form of the intellect, nor does the intellect impose its form on matter, nor have matter and intellect been regulated in regard to one another by we know not what pre-established harmony, but that intellect and matter have progressively adapted themselves one to the other in order to attain at last a common form. *This adaptation has, moreover, been brought about quite naturally, because it is the same inversion of the same movement which creates at once the intellectuality of mind and the materiality of things.*

From this point of view the knowledge of matter that our perception on the one hand and science on the other give to us appears, no doubt, as approximative, but not as relative. Our perception, whose role it is to hold up a light to our actions, works a dividing up of matter that is always too sharply defined, always subordinated to practical needs, consequently always requiring revision. Our science, which aspires to the mathematical form, over-accentuates the spatiality of matter; its formulae are, in general, too precise, and ever need remaking. For a scientific theory to be final, the mind would have to embrace the totality of things in block and place each thing in its exact relation to every other thing; but in reality we are obliged to consider problems one by one, in terms which are, for that very reason, provisional, so that the solution of each problem will have to be corrected indefinitely by the solution that will be given to the problems that will follow: thus, science as a whole is relative to the particular order in which the problems happen to have been put. It is in this meaning, and to this degree, that science must be regarded as conventional. But it is a conventionality of fact so to speak, and not of right. In principle, positive science bears on reality itself, provided it does not overstep the limits of its own domain, which is inert matter. [. . .]

Certainly, the philosophy of Kant is also imbued with the belief in a science single and complete, embracing the whole of the real. Indeed, looked at from one aspect, it is only a continuation of the metaphysics of the moderns and a transposition of the ancient metaphysics. Spinoza and Leibniz had, following Aristotle, hypostatised in God the unity of knowledge. The Kantian criticism, on one side at least, consists in asking whether the whole of this hypothesis is necessary to modern science as it was to ancient science, or if part of the hypothesis is not sufficient. For the ancients, science applied to *concepts*, that is to say, to kinds of *things*. In compressing all concepts into one, they therefore necessarily arrived at a *being*, which we may call Thought, but which was rather thought-object than thought-subject. When Aristotle defined God the νοησεως νοησις, it is probably on νοησεως, and not on νοησις that he put the emphasis. God was the synthesis of all concepts, the idea of ideas. But modern science turns on laws, that is, on relations. Now, a relation is a bond established by a mind between two or more terms. A relation is nothing outside of the intellect that relates. The universe, therefore, can only be a system of laws if phenomena have passed beforehand through the filter of an intellect. Of course, this intellect might be that of a being infinitely superior to man, who would found the materiality of things at the same time that he bound them together: such was the hypothesis of Leibniz and of Spinoza. But it is not necessary to go so far, and, for the effect we have here to obtain, the human intellect is enough: such is precisely the Kantian solution. Between the dogmatism of a Spinoza or a Leibniz and the criticism of Kant there is just the same distance as between 'it may be maintained that –' and 'it suffices that –'. Kant stops this dogmatism on the incline that was making it slip too far toward the Greek metaphysics; he reduces to the strict minimum the hypothesis which is necessary in order to suppose the physics of Galileo indefinitely extensible. True, when he speaks of the human intellect, he means neither yours nor mine: the unity of nature comes indeed from the human understanding that unifies, but the unifying function that operates here is impersonal. It imparts itself to our individual consciousnesses, but it transcends them. It is much less than a substantial God; it is, however, a little more than the isolated work of a man or even than the collective work of humanity. It does not exactly lie within man; rather, man lies within it, as in an atmosphere of intellectuality which his consciousness breathes. It is, if we will, a *formal* God, something that in Kant is not yet divine, but which tends to become so. It became so, indeed, with Fichte. With Kant, however, its principal role was to give to the whole of our science a relative and *human* character, although of a humanity already somewhat deified. From this point of view, the criticism of Kant consisted chiefly in limiting the dogmatism of his predecessors, accepting their conception of science and reducing to a minimum the metaphysic it implied.

But it is otherwise with the Kantian distinction between the matter of knowledge and its form. By regarding intelligence as pre-eminently a faculty of establishing relations, Kant attributed an extra-intellectual origin to the terms between which the relations are established. He affirmed, against his immediate predecessors, that knowledge is not entirely resolvable into terms of intelligence. He brought back into philosophy – while modifying it and carrying it on to another plane – that essential element of the philosophy of Descartes which had been abandoned by the Cartesians.

Thereby he prepared the way for a new philosophy, which might have established itself in the extra-intellectual matter of knowledge by a higher effort of intuition. Coinciding with this matter, adopting the same rhythm and the same movement, might not consciousness, by two efforts of opposite direction, raising itself and lowering itself by turns, become able to grasp from within, and no longer perceive only from without, the two forms of reality, body and mind? Would not this twofold effort make us, as far as that is possible, re-live the absolute? Moreover, as, in the course of this operation, we should see intellect spring up of itself, cut itself out in the whole of mind, intellectual knowledge would then appear as it is, limited, but not relative.

Such was the direction that Kantianism might have pointed out to a revivified Cartesianism. But in this direction Kant himself did not go.

He *would* not, because, while assigning to knowledge an extra-intellectual matter, he believed this matter to be either co-extensive with intellect or less extensive than intellect. Therefore he could not dream of cutting out intellect in it, nor, consequently, of tracing the genesis of the understanding and its categories. The moulds of the understanding and the understanding itself had to be accepted as they are, already made. Between the matter presented to our intellect and this intellect itself there was no relationship. The agreement between the two was due to the fact that intellect imposed its form on matter. So that not only was it necessary to posit the intellectual form of knowledge as a kind of absolute and give up the quest of its genesis, but the very matter of this knowledge seemed too ground down by the intellect for us to be able to hope to get it back in its original purity. It was not the 'thing-in-itself,' it was only the refraction of it through our atmosphere.

If now we inquire why Kant did not believe that the matter of our knowledge extends beyond its form, this is what we find. The criticism of our knowledge of nature that was instituted by Kant consisted in ascertaining what our mind must be and what Nature must be *if* the claims of our science are justified; but of these claims themselves Kant has not made the criticism. I mean that he took for granted the idea of a science that is one, capable of binding with the same force all the parts of what is given, and of co-ordinating them into a system presenting on all sides an equal solidity. He did not consider, in his *Critique of Pure Reason,* that science became less and less objective, more and more symbolical, to the extent that it went from the physical to the vital, from the vital to the psychical. Experience does not move, to his view, in two different and perhaps opposite ways, the one conformable to the direction of the intellect, the other contrary to it. There is, for him, only *one* experience, and the intellect covers its whole ground. This is what Kant expresses by saying that all our intuitions are sensuous, or, in other words, infra-intellectual. And this would have to be admitted, indeed, if our science presented in all its parts an equal objectivity. But suppose, on the contrary, that science is less and less objective, more and more symbolical, as it goes from the physical to the psychical, passing through the vital: then, as it is indeed necessary to perceive a thing somehow in order to symbolize it, there would be an intuition of the psychical, and more generally of the vital, which the intellect would transpose and translate, no doubt, but which would none the less transcend the intellect. There would be, in other words, a supra-intellectual intuition. If this intuition exist, a taking possession of the spirit by itself is possible, and no longer only a knowledge that is external and phenomenal. What is more, if we have an intuition of this kind (I mean an ultra-intellectual intuition) then sensuous intuition is likely to be in continuity with it through certain intermediaries, as the infra-red is continuous with the ultraviolet. Sensuous intuition itself, therefore, is promoted. It will no longer attain only the phantom of an unattainable thing-in-itself. It is (provided we bring to it certain indispensable corrections) into the absolute itself that it will introduce us. So long as it was regarded as the only material of our science, it reflected back on all science something of the relativity which strikes a scientific knowledge of spirit; and thus the perception of bodies, which is the beginning of the science of bodies, seemed itself to be relative. Relative, therefore, seemed to be sensuous intuition. But this is not the case if distinctions are made between the different sciences, and if the scientific knowledge of the spiritual (and also, consequently, of the vital) be regarded as the more or less artificial extension of a certain manner of knowing which, applied to bodies, is not at all symbolical. Let us go further: if there are thus two intuitions of different order (the second being obtained by a reversal of the direction of the first), and if it is toward the second that the intellect naturally inclines, there is no essential difference between the intellect and this intuition itself. The barriers between the matter of sensible knowledge and its form are lowered, as also between the 'pure forms' of sensibility and the categories of the understanding. The matter and form of intellectual knowledge (restricted to its own object) are seen to be engendering each other by a reciprocal adaptation, intellect modelling itself on corporeity, and corporeity on intellect.

But this duality of intuition Kant neither would nor could admit. It would have been necessary, in order to admit it, to regard duration as the very stuff of reality, and consequently to distinguish between the substantial duration of things and time spread out in space. It would have been necessary to regard space itself, and the geometry which is immanent in space, as an ideal limit in the direction of which material things develop, but which they do not actually attain. Nothing could be more contrary to the letter, and perhaps also to the spirit, of the *Critique of Pure Reason*. No doubt, knowledge is presented to us in it as an ever-open roll, experience as a push of facts that is for ever going on. But, according to Kant, these facts are spread out on one plane as fast as they arise; they are external to each other and external to the mind. Of a knowledge from within, that could grasp them in their springing forth instead of taking them already sprung, that would dig beneath space and spatialised time, there is never any question. Yet it is indeed beneath this plane that our consciousness places us; there flows true duration.

In this respect, also, Kant is very near his predecessors. Between the non-temporal, and the time that is spread out in distinct moments, he admits no mean. And as there is indeed no intuition that carries us into the non-temporal, all intuition is thus found to be sensuous, by definition. But between physical existence, which is spread out in space, and non-temporal existence, which can only be a conceptual and logical existence like that of which metaphysical dogmatism speaks, is there not room for consciousness and for life? There is, unquestionably. We perceive it when we place ourselves in duration in order to go from that duration to moments, instead of starting from moments in order to bind them again and to construct duration.

Yet it was to a non-temporal intuition that the immediate successors of Kant turned, in order to escape from the Kantian relativism. Certainly, the ideas of becoming, of progress, of evolution, seem to occupy a large place in their philosophy. But does duration really play a part in it? Real duration is that in which each form flows out of previous forms, while adding to them something new, and is explained by them as much as it explains them; but to deduce this form directly from one complete Being which it is supposed to manifest, is to return to Spinozism. It is, like Leibniz and Spinoza, to deny to duration all efficient action. The post-Kantian philosophy, severe as it may have been on the mechanistic theories, accepts from mechanism the idea of a science that is one and the same for all kinds of reality. And it is nearer to mechanism than it imagines; for though, in the consideration of matter, of life and of thought, it replaces the successive degrees of complexity that mechanism supposed, by degrees of the realization of an Idea or by degrees of the objectification of a Will, it still speaks of degrees, and these degrees are those of a scale which Being traverses in a single direction. In short, it makes out the same articulations in nature that mechanism does. Of mechanism it retains the whole design; it merely gives it a different colouring. But it is the design itself, or at least one half of the design, that needs to be re-made.

If we are to do that, we must give up the method of *construction,* which was that of Kant's successors. We must appeal to experience – an experience purified, or, in other words, released, where necessary, from the moulds that our intellect has formed in the degree and proportion of the progress of our action on things. An experience of this kind is not a non-temporal experience. It only seeks, beyond the spatialised time in which we believe we see continual rearrangements between the parts, that concrete duration in which a radical recasting of the whole is always going on. It follows the real in all its sinuosities. It does not lead us, like the method of construction, to higher and higher generalities – piled-up stories of a magnificent building. But then it leaves no play between the explanations it suggests and the objects it has to explain. It is the detail of the real, and no longer only the whole in a lump, that it claims to illumine.

56

Marcel Proust

Swann's Way (1913)

Overture

AT COMBRAY, AS EVERY AFTERNOON ENDED, LONG BEFORE THE TIME when I should have to go up to bed, and to lie there, unsleeping, far from my mother and grandmother, my bedroom became the fixed point on which my melancholy and anxious thoughts were centred. Some one had had the happy idea of giving me, to distract me on evenings when I seemed abnormally wretched, a magic lantern, which used to be set on top of my lamp while we waited for dinner-time to come: in the manner of the master-builders and glass-painters of gothic days it substituted for the opaqueness of my walls an impalpable iridescence, supernatural phenomena of many colours, in which legends were depicted, as on a shifting and transitory window. But my sorrows were only increased, because this change of lighting destroyed, as nothing else could have done, the customary impression I had formed of my room, thanks to which the room itself, but for the torture of having to go to bed in it, had become quite endurable. For now I no longer recognised it, and I became uneasy, as though I were in a room in some hotel or furnished lodging, in a place where I had just arrived, by train, for the first time.

Riding at a jerky trot, Golo, his mind filled with an infamous design, issued from the little three-cornered forest which dyed dark-green the slope of a convenient hill, and advanced by leaps and bounds towards the castle of poor Geneviève de Brabant. This castle was cut off short by a curved line which was in fact the circumference of one of the transparent ovals in the slides which were pushed into position through a slot in the lantern. It was only the wing of a castle, and in front of it stretched a moor on which Geneviève stood, lost in contemplation, wearing a blue girdle. The castle and the moor were yellow, but I could tell their colour without waiting to see them, for before the slides made their appearance the old-gold sonorous name of

Brabant had given me an unmistakable clue. Golo stopped for a moment and listened sadly to the little speech read aloud by my great-aunt, which he seemed perfectly to understand, for he modified his attitude with a docility not devoid of a degree of majesty, so as to conform to the indications given in the text; then he rode away at the same jerky trot. And nothing could arrest his slow progress. If the lantern were moved I could still distinguish Golo's horse advancing across the window-curtains, swelling out with their curves and diving into their folds. The body of Golo himself, being of the same supernatural substance as his steed's, overcame all material obstacles—everything that seemed to bar his way—by taking each as it might be a skeleton and embodying it in himself: the door-handle, for instance, over which, adapting itself at once, would float invincibly his red cloak or his pale face, never losing its nobility or its melancholy, never shewing any sign of trouble at such a transubstantiation.

And, indeed, I found plenty of charm in these bright projections, which seemed to have come straight out of a Merovingian past, and to shed around me the reflections of such ancient history. But I cannot express the discomfort I felt at such an intrusion of mystery and beauty into a room which I had succeeded in filling with my own personality until I thought no more of the room than of myself. The anaesthetic effect of custom being destroyed, I would begin to think and to feel very melancholy things. The door-handle of my room, which was different to me from all the other doorhandles in the world, inasmuch as it seemed to open of its own accord and without my having to turn it, so unconscious had its manipulation become; lo and behold, it was now an astral body for Golo. And as soon as the dinner-bell rang I would run down to the dining-room, where the big hanging lamp, ignorant of Golo and Bluebeard but well acquainted with my family and the dish of stewed beef, shed the same light as on every other evening; and I would fall into the arms of my mother, whom the misfortunes of Geneviève de Brabant had made all the dearer to me, just as the crimes of Golo had driven me to a more than ordinarily scrupulous examination of my own conscience. [. . .]

It seemed quite natural, therefore, to send to him whenever we wanted a recipe for some special sauce or for a pineapple salad for one of our big dinner-parties, to which he himself would not be invited, not seeming of sufficient importance to be served up to new friends who might be in our house for the first time. If the conversation turned upon the Princes of the House of France, "Gentlemen, you and I will never know, will we, and don't want to, do we?" my great-aunt would say tartly to Swann, who had, perhaps, a letter from Twickenham in his pocket; she would make him play accompaniments and turn over music on evenings when my grandmother's sister sang; manipulating this creature, so rare and refined at other times and in other places, with the rough simplicity of a child who will play with some curio from the cabinet no more carefully than if it were a penny toy. Certainly the Swann who was a familiar figure in all the clubs of those days differed hugely from, the Swann created in my great-aunt's mind when, of an evening, in our little garden at Combray, after the two shy peals had sounded from the gate, she would vitalise, by injecting into it everything she had ever heard about the Swann family, the vague and unrecognisable shape which began to appear, with my grandmother in its wake, against a background of shadows, and could at last be identified by the sound of its voice. But then, even in the most insignificant details of our daily life, none of us can be said to constitute a material whole, which is identical for everyone, and need only be turned up like a page in an account-book or the record of a will; our social personality is created by the thoughts of other people. Even the simple act which we describe as "seeing some one we know" is, to some extent, an intellectual process. We pack the physical outline of the creature we see with all the ideas we have already formed about him, and in the complete picture of him which we compose in our minds those ideas have certainly the principal place. In the end they come to fill out so completely the curve of his cheeks, to follow so exactly the line of his nose, they blend so harmoniously in the sound of his voice that these seem to be no more than a transparent envelope, so that each time we see the face or hear the voice it is our own ideas of him which we recognise and to which we listen. And so, no doubt, from the Swann they had built up for their own purposes my family had left out, in their ignorance, a whole crowd of the details of his daily life in the world of fashion, details by means of which other people, when they met him, saw all the Graces enthroned in his face and stopping at the line of his arched nose as at a natural frontier; but they contrived also to put into a face from which its distinction had been evicted, a face vacant and roomy as an untenanted house, to plant in the depths of its unvalued eyes a lingering sense, uncertain but not unpleasing, half-memory and half-oblivion, of idle hours spent together after our weekly dinners, round the card-table or in the garden, during our companionable country life. Our friend's bodily frame had been so well lined with this sense, and with various earlier memories of his family, that their own special Swann had become to my people a complete and living creature; so that even now I have the feeling of leaving some one I know for another quite different person when, going back in memory, I pass from the Swann whom I knew later and more intimately to this early Swann—this early Swann in whom I can distinguish the charming mistakes of my childhood, and who, incidentally, is less like his successor than he is like the other people I knew at that time, as though one's life were a series of galleries in which all the portraits of any one period had a marked family likeness, the same (so to speak) tonality—this early Swann abounding in leisure, fragrant with the scent of the great chestnut-tree, of baskets of raspberries and of a sprig of tarragon.

* * *

And so it was that, for a long time afterwards, when I lay awake at night and revived old memories of Combray, I saw no more of it than this sort of luminous panel, sharply defined against a vague and shadowy background, like the panels which a Bengal fire or some electric sign will illuminate and dissect from the front of a building the other parts of which remain plunged in darkness: broad enough at its base, the little parlour, the dining-room, the alluring shadows of the path along which would come M. Swann, the unconscious author of my sufferings, the hall through which I would journey to the first step of that staircase, so hard to climb, which constituted, all by itself, the tapering 'elevation' of an irregular pyramid; and, at the summit, my bedroom, with the little passage through whose glazed door Mamma would enter; in a word, seen always at the same evening hour, isolated from all its possible surroundings, detached and solitary against its shadowy background, the bare minimum of scenery necessary (like the setting one sees printed at the head of an old play, for its performance in the provinces) to the drama of my undressing, as though all Combray had consisted of but two floors joined by a slender staircase, and as though there had been no time there but seven o'clock at night. I must own that I could have assured any questioner that Combray did include other scenes and did exist at other hours than these. But since the facts which I should then have recalled would have been prompted only by an exercise of the will, by my intellectual memory, and since the pictures which that kind of memory shews us of the past preserve nothing of the past itself, I should never have had any wish to ponder over this residue of Combray. To me it was in reality all dead.

Permanently dead? Very possibly.

There is a large element of hazard in these matters, and a second hazard, that of our own death, often prevents us from awaiting for any length of time the favours of the first.

I feel that there is much to be said for the Celtic belief that the souls of those whom we have lost are held captive in some inferior being, in an animal, in a plant, in some inanimate object, and so effectively lost to us until the day (which to many never comes) when we happen to pass by the tree or to obtain possession of the object which forms their prison. Then they start and tremble, they call us by our name, and as soon as we have recognised their voice the spell is broken. We have delivered them: they have overcome death and return to share our life.

And so it is with our own past. It is a labour in vain to attempt to recapture it: all the efforts of our intellect must prove futile. The past is hidden somewhere outside the realm, beyond the reach of intellect, in some material object (in the sensation which that material object will give us) which we do not suspect. And as for that object, it depends on chance whether we come upon it or not before we ourselves must die.

Many years had elapsed during which nothing of Combray, save what was comprised in the theatre and the drama of my going to bed there, had any existence for me, when one day in winter, as I came home, my mother, seeing that I was cold, offered me some tea, a thing I did not ordinarily take. I declined at first, and then, for no particular reason, changed my mind. She sent out for one of those short, plump little cakes called 'petites madeleines,' which look as though they had been moulded in the fluted scallop of a pilgrim's shell. And soon, mechanically, weary after a dull day with the prospect of a depressing morrow, I raised to my lips a spoonful of the tea in which I had soaked a morsel of the cake. No sooner had the warm liquid, and the crumbs with it, touched my palate than a shudder ran through my whole body, and I stopped, intent upon the extraordinary changes that were taking place. An exquisite pleasure had invaded my senses, but individual, detached, with no suggestion of its origin. And at once the vicissitudes of life had become indifferent to me, its disasters innocuous, its brevity illusory—this new sensation having had on me the effect which love has of filling me with a precious essence; or rather this essence was not in me, it was myself. I had ceased now to feel mediocre, accidental, mortal. Whence could it have come to me, this all-powerful joy? I was conscious that it was connected with the taste of tea and cake, but that it infinitely transcended those savours, could not, indeed, be of the same nature as theirs. Whence did it come? What did it signify? How could I seize upon and define it?

I drink a second mouthful, in which I find nothing more than in the first, a third, which gives me rather less than the second. It is time to stop; the potion is losing its magic. It is plain that the object of my quest, the truth, lies not in the cup but in myself. The tea has called up in me, but does not itself understand, and can only repeat indefinitely with a gradual loss of strength, the same testimony; which I, too, cannot interpret, though I hope at least to be able to call upon the tea for it again and to find it there presently, intact and at my disposal, for my final enlightenment. I put down my cup and examine my own mind. It is for it to discover the truth. But how? What an abyss of uncertainty whenever the mind feels that some part of it has strayed beyond its own borders; when it, the seeker, is at once the dark region through which it must go seeking, where all its equipment will avail it nothing. Seek? More than that: create. It is face to face with something which does not so far exist, to which it alone can give reality and substance, which it alone can bring into the light of day.

And I begin again to ask myself what it could have been, this unremembered state which brought with it no logical proof of its existence, but only the sense that it was a happy, that it was a real state in whose presence other states of consciousness melted and vanished. I decide to attempt to make it reappear. I retrace my thoughts to the moment at which I drank the first spoonful of tea. I find again the same state, illumined by no fresh light. I compel my mind to make one further effort, to follow and recapture once again the fleeting sensation. And that nothing may interrupt it in its course I shut out every obstacle, every extraneous idea, I stop my ears and inhibit all attention to the sounds which come from the next room. And then, feeling that my mind is growing fatigued without having any success to report, I compel it for a change to enjoy that distraction which I have just denied it, to think of other things, to rest and refresh itself before the supreme attempt. And then for the second time I clear an empty space in front of it. I place in position before my mind's eye the still recent taste of that first mouthful, and I feel something start within me, something that leaves its resting-place and attempts to rise, something that has been embedded like an anchor at a great depth; I do not know yet what it is, but I can feel it mounting slowly; I can measure the resistance, I can hear the echo of great spaces traversed.

Undoubtedly what is thus palpitating in the depths of my being must be the image, the visual memory which, being linked to that taste, has tried to follow it into my conscious mind. But its struggles are too far off, too much confused; scarcely can I perceive the colourless reflection in which are blended the uncapturable whirling medley of radiant hues, and I cannot distinguish its form, cannot invite it, as the one possible interpreter, to translate to me the evidence of its contemporary, its inseparable paramour, the taste of cake soaked in tea; cannot ask it to inform me what special circumstance is in question, of what period in my past life.

Will it ultimately reach the clear surface of my consciousness, this memory, this old, dead moment which the magnetism of an identical moment has travelled so far to importune, to disturb, to raise up out of the very depths of my being? I cannot tell. Now that I feel nothing, it has stopped, has perhaps gone down again into its darkness, from which who can say whether it will ever rise? Ten times over I must essay the task, must lean down over the abyss. And each time the natural laziness which deters us from every difficult enterprise, every work of importance, has urged me to leave the thing alone, to drink my tea and to think merely of the worries of to-day and of my hopes for to-morrow, which let themselves be pondered over without effort or distress of mind.

And suddenly the memory returns. The taste was that of the little crumb of madeleine which on Sunday mornings at Combray (because on those mornings I did not go out before church-time), when I went to say good day to her in her bedroom, my aunt Léonie used to give me, dipping it first in her own cup of real or of lime-flower tea. The sight of the little madeleine had recalled nothing to my mind before I tasted it; perhaps because I had so often seen such things in the interval, without tasting them, on the trays in pastry-cooks' windows, that their image had dissociated itself from those Combray days to take its place among others more recent; perhaps because of those memories, so long abandoned and put out of mind, nothing now survived, everything was scattered; the forms of things, including that of the little scallop-shell of pastry, so richly sensual under its severe, religious folds, were either obliterated or had been so long dormant as to have lost the power of expansion which would have allowed them to resume their place in my consciousness. But when from a long-distant past nothing subsists, after the people are dead, after the things are broken and scattered, still, alone, more fragile, but with more vitality, more unsubstantial, more persistent, more faithful, the smell and taste of things remain poised a long time, like souls, ready to remind us, waiting and hoping for their moment, amid the ruins of all the rest; and bear unfaltering, in the tiny and almost impalpable drop of their essence, the vast structure of recollection.

And once I had recognized the taste of the crumb of madeleine soaked in her decoction of lime-flowers which my aunt used to give me (although I did not yet know and must long postpone the discovery of why this memory made me so happy) immediately the old grey house upon the street, where her room was, rose up like the scenery of a theatre to attach itself to the little pavilion, opening on to the garden, which had been built out behind it for my parents (the isolated panel which until that moment had been all that I could see); and with the house the town, from morning to night and in all weathers, the Square where I was sent before luncheon, the streets along which I used to run errands, the country roads we took when it was fine. And just as the Japanese amuse themselves by filling a porcelain bowl with water and steeping in it little crumbs of paper which until then are without character or form, but, the moment they become wet, stretch themselves and bend, take on colour and distinctive shape, become flowers or houses or people, permanent and recognisable, so in that moment all the flowers in our garden and in M. Swann's park, and the water-lilies on the Vivonne and the good folk of the village and their little dwellings and the parish church and the whole of Combray and of its surroundings, taking their proper shapes and growing solid, sprang into being, town and gardens alike, from my cup of tea.

57

Franz Kafka

The Trial (1915)

Before the Law

"Won't you come down here?" said K. "You haven't got to preach a sermon. Come down beside me." "I can come down now," said the priest, perhaps repenting of his outburst. While he detached the lamp from its hook he said: "I had to speak to you first from a distance. Otherwise I am too easily influenced and tend to forget my duty."

K. waited for him at the foot of the steps. The priest stretched out his hand to K. while he was still on the way down from a higher level. "Have you a little time for me?" asked K. "As much time as you need," said the priest, giving K. the small lamp to carry. Even close at hand he still wore a certain air of solemnity. "You are very good to me," said K. They paced side by side up and down the dusky aisle. "But you are an exception among those who belong to the Court. I have more trust in you than in any of the others, though I know many of them. With you I can speak openly." "Don't be deluded," said the priest. "How am I being deluded?" asked K. "You are deluding yourself about the Court," said the priest. "In the writings which preface the Law that particular delusion is described thus: before the Law stands a doorkeeper. To this doorkeeper there comes a man from the country who begs for admittance to the Law. But the doorkeeper says that he cannot admit the man at the moment. The man, on reflection, asks if he will be allowed, then, to enter later. 'It is possible,' answers the doorkeeper, 'but not at this moment.' Since the door leading into the Law stands open as usual and the doorkeeper steps to one side, the man bends down to peer through the entrance. When the doorkeeper sees that, he laughs and says: 'If you are so strongly tempted, try to get in without my permission. But note that I am powerful. And I am only the lowest doorkeeper. From hall to hall, keepers stand at every door, one more powerful than the other. And the sight of the third man is already more than even I can stand.' These are difficulties which the man from the country has not expected to meet, the Law, he thinks, should be accessible to every man and at all times, but when he looks more closely at the doorkeeper in his furred robe, with his huge, pointed nose and long, thin, Tartar beard, he decides that he had better wait until he gets permission to enter. The doorkeeper gives him a stool and lets him sit down at the side of the door. There he sits waiting for days and years. He makes many attempts to be allowed in and wearies the doorkeeper with his importunity. The doorkeeper often engages him in brief conversation, asking him about his home and about other matters, but the questions are put quite impersonally, as great men put questions, and always conclude with the statement that the man cannot be allowed to enter yet. The man, who has equipped himself with many things for his journey, parts with all he has, however valuable, in the hope of bribing the doorkeeper. The doorkeeper accepts it all, saying, however, as he takes each gift: 'I take this only to keep you from feeling that you have left something undone.' During all these long years the man watches the doorkeeper almost incessantly. He forgets about the other doorkeepers, and this one seems to him the only barrier between himself and the Law. In the first years he curses his evil fate aloud; later, as he grows old, he only mutters to himself. He grows childish, and since in his prolonged study of the doorkeeper he has learned to know even the fleas in his fur collar, he begs the very fleas to help him and to persuade the doorkeeper to change his mind. Finally his eyes grow dim and he does not know whether the world is really darkening around him or whether his eyes are only deceiving him. But in the darkness he can now perceive a radiance that streams inextinguishably from the door of the Law. Now his life is drawing to a close. Before he dies, all that he has experienced during the whole time of his sojourn condenses in his mind into one question, which he has never yet put to the doorkeeper. He beckons the doorkeeper, since he can no longer raise his stiffening body. The doorkeeper has to bend far down to hear him, for the difference in size between them has increased very much to the man's disadvantage. 'What do you want to know now?' asks the doorkeeper, 'you are insatiable.' 'Everyone strives to attain the Law,' answers the man, 'how does it come about, then, that in all these years no one has come seeking admittance but me?' The doorkeeper perceives that the man is nearing his end and his hearing is failing, so he bellows in his ear: 'No one but you could gain admittance through this door, since this door was intended for you. I am now going to shut it.'"

"So the doorkeeper deceived the man," said K. immediately, strongly attracted by the story. "Don't be too hasty," said the priest, "don't take over someone else's opinion without testing it. I have told you the story in the very words of the scriptures. There's no mention of deception in it." "But it's clear enough," said K., "and your first interpretation of it was quite right. The doorkeeper gave the message of salvation to the man only when it could no longer help him." "He was not asked the question any earlier," said the priest, "and you must consider, too, that he was only a doorkeeper, and as such fulfilled his duty." "What makes you think he fulfilled his duty?" asked K. "He didn't fulfill it. His duty might have been to keep all strangers away, but this man, for whom the door was intended, should have been let in." "You have not enough respect for the written word and you are altering the story," said the priest. "The story contains two important statements made by the doorkeeper about admission to the Law, one at the beginning, the other at the end. The first statement is: that he cannot admit the man at the moment, and the other is: that this door was intended only for the man. If there were a contradiction between the two, you would be right and the doorkeeper would have deceived the man. But there is no contradiction. The first statement, on the contrary, even implies the second. One could almost say that in suggesting to the man the possibility of future admittance the doorkeeper is exceeding his duty. At that time his apparent duty is only to refuse admittance and indeed many commentators are surprised that the suggestion should be made at all, since the doorkeeper appears to be a precisian with a stern regard for duty. He does not once leave his post during these many years, and he does not shut the door until the very last minute; he is conscious of the importance of his office, for he says: 'I am powerful'; he is respectful to his superiors, for he says: 'I am only the lowest doorkeeper'; he is not garrulous, for during all these years he puts only what are called 'impersonal questions'; he is not to be bribed, for he says in accepting a gift: 'I take this only to keep you from feeling that you have left something undone'; where his duty is concerned he is to be moved neither by pity nor rage, for we are told that the man 'wearied the doorkeeper with his importunity'; and finally even his external appearance hints at a pedantic character, the large, pointed nose and the long, thin, black Tartar beard. Could one imagine a more faithful doorkeeper? Yet the doorkeeper has other elements in his character which are likely to advantage anyone seeking admittance and which make it comprehensible enough that he should somewhat exceed his duty in suggesting the possibility of future admittance. For it cannot be denied that he is a little simple-minded and consequently a little conceited. Take the statements he makes about his power and the power of the other doorkeepers and their dreadful aspect which even he cannot bear to see—I hold that these statements may be true enough, but that the way in which he brings them out shows that his perceptions are confused by simpleness of mind and conceit. The commentators note in this connection: 'The right perception of any matter and a misunderstanding of the same matter do not wholly exclude each other.' One must at any rate assume that such simpleness and conceit, however sparingly manifest, are likely to weaken his defense of the door; they are breaches in the character of the doorkeeper. To this must be added the fact that the doorkeeper seems to be a friendly creature by nature, he is by no means always on his official dignity. In the very first moments he allows himself the jest of inviting the man to enter in spite of the strictly maintained veto against entry; then he does not, for instance, send the man away, but gives him, as we are told, a stool and lets him sit down beside the door. The patience with which he endures the man's appeals during so many years, the brief conversations, the acceptance of the gifts, the politeness with which he allows the man to curse loudly in his presence the fate for which he himself is responsible—all this lets us deduce certain feelings of pity. Not every doorkeeper would have acted thus. And finally, in answer to a gesture of the man's he bends down to give him the chance of putting a last question. Nothing but mild impatience—the doorkeeper knows that this is the end of it all—is discernible in the words: 'You are insatiable.' Some push this mode of interpretation even further and hold that these words express a kind of friendly admiration, though not without a hint of condescension. At any rate the figure of the doorkeeper can be said to come out very differently from what you fancied." "You have studied the story more exactly and for a longer time than I have," said K. They were both silent for a little while. Then K. said: "So you think the man was not deceived?" "Don't misunderstand me," said the priest, "I am only showing you the various opinions concerning that point. You must not pay too much attention to them. The scriptures are unalterable and the comments often enough merely express the commentators' despair. In this case there even exists an interpretation which claims that the deluded person is really the doorkeeper." "That's a far-fetched interpretation," said K. "On what is it based?" "It is based," answered the priest, "on the simple-mindedness of the doorkeeper. The argument is that he does not know the Law from inside, he knows only the way that leads to it, where he patrols up and down. His ideas of the interior are assumed to be childish, and it is supposed that he himself is afraid of the other guardians whom he holds up as bogies before the man. Indeed, he fears them more than the man does, since the man is determined to enter after hearing about the dreadful guardians of the interior, while the doorkeeper has no desire to enter, at least not so far as we are told. Others again say that he must have been in the interior already, since he is after all engaged in the service of the Law and can only have been appointed from inside. This is countered by arguing that he may have been appointed by a voice calling from the interior, and that anyhow he cannot have been far inside, since the aspect of the third doorkeeper is more than he can endure. Moreover, no indication is given that during all these years he ever made any remarks showing a knowledge of the interior, except for the one remark about the doorkeepers. He may have been forbidden to do so, but there is no mention of that either. On these grounds the conclusion is reached that he knows nothing about the aspect and significance of the interior, so that he is in a state of delusion. But he is deceived also about his relation to the man from the country, for he is inferior to the man and does not know it. He treats the man instead as his own subordinate, as can be recognized from many details that must be still fresh in your mind. But, according to this view of the story, it is just as clearly indicated that he is really subordinated to the man. In the first place, a bondman is always subject to a free man. Now the man from the country is really free, he can go where he likes, it is only the Law that is closed to him, and access to the Law is forbidden him only by one individual, the doorkeeper. When he sits down on the stool by the side of the door and stays there for the rest of his life, he does it of his own free will; in the story there is no mention of any compulsion. But the doorkeeper is bound to his post by his very office, he does not dare go out into the country, nor apparently may he go into the interior of the Law, even should he wish to. Besides, although he is in the service of the Law, his service is confined to this one entrance; that is to say, he serves only this man for whom alone the entrance is intended.

On that ground too he is inferior to the man. One must assume that for many years, for as long as it takes a man to grow up to the prime of life, his service was in a sense an empty formality, since he had to wait for a man to come, that is to say someone in the prime of life, and so he had to wait a long time before the purpose of his service could be fulfilled, and, moreover, had to wait on the man's pleasure, for the man came of his own free will. But the termination of his service also depends on the man's term of life, so that to the very end he is subject to the man. And it is emphasized throughout that the doorkeeper apparently realizes nothing of all this. That is not in itself remarkable, since according to this interpretation the doorkeeper is deceived in a much more important issue, affecting his very office. At the end, for example, he says regarding the entrance to the Law: 'I am now going to shut it,' but at the beginning of the story we are told that the door leading into the Law always stands open, and if it always stands open, that is to say at all times, without reference to the life or death of the man, then the doorkeeper cannot close it. There is some difference of opinion about the motive behind the doorkeeper's statement, whether he said he was going to close the door merely for the sake of giving an answer, or to emphasize his devotion to duty, or to bring the man into a state of grief and regret in his last moments. But there is no lack of agreement that the doorkeeper will not be able to shut the door. Many indeed profess to find that he is subordinate to the man even in knowledge, toward the end, at least, for the man sees the radiance that issues from the door of the Law while the doorkeeper in his official position must stand with his back to the door, nor does he say anything to show that he has perceived the change." "That is well argued," said K., after repeating to himself in a low voice several passages from the priest's exposition. "It is well argued, and I am inclined to agree that the doorkeeper is deceived. But that has not made me abandon my former opinion, since both conclusions are to some extent compatible. Whether the doorkeeper is clear-sighted or deceived does not dispose of the matter. I said the man is deceived. If the doorkeeper is clear-sighted, one might have doubts about that, but if the doorkeeper himself is deceived, then his deception must of necessity be communicated to the man. That makes the doorkeeper not, indeed, a deceiver, but a creature so simple-minded that he ought to be dismissed at once from his office. You mustn't forget that the doorkeeper's deceptions do himself no harm but do infinite harm to the man." "There are objections to that," said the priest. "Many aver that the story confers no right on anyone to pass judgment on the doorkeeper. Whatever he may seem to us, he is yet a servant of the Law; that is, he belongs to the Law and as such is beyond human judgment. In that case one must not believe that the doorkeeper is subordinate to the man. Bound as he is by his service, even only at the door of the Law, he is incomparably greater than anyone at large in the world. The man is only seeking the Law, the doorkeeper is already attached to it. It is the Law that has placed him at his post; to doubt his dignity is to doubt the Law itself." "I don't agree with that point of view," said K., shaking his head, "for if one accepts it, one must accept as true everything the doorkeeper says. But you yourself have sufficiently proved how impossible it is to do that." "No," said the priest, "it is not necessary to accept everything as true, one must only accept it as necessary." A melancholy conclusion, said K. "It turns lying into a universal principle."

K. said that with finality, but it was not his final judgment. He was too tired to survey all the conclusions arising from the story, and the trains of thought into which it was leading him were unfamiliar, dealing with impalpabilities better suited to a theme for discussion among Court officials than for him. The simple story had lost its clear outline, he wanted to put it out of his mind, and the priest, who now showed great delicacy of feeling, suffered him to do so and accepted his comment in silence, although undoubtedly he did not agree with it.

58

Ludwig Wittgenstein

Notebooks (1916)

WE CAN ONLY FORESEE WHAT WE OURSELVES CONSTRUCT. [See *Tractatus*, 5.556.]

But then where is the concept of a simple object still to be found?

This concept does not so far come in here at all.

We must be able to construct the simple functions because we must be able to give each sign a meaning.

For the only sign which guarantees its meaning is function and argument.

Every simple proposition can be brought into the form φx.

That is why we may compose all simple propositions from this form.

Suppose that *all* simple propositions were given me: then it can simply be asked what propositions I can construct from them. And these are *all* propositions and this is *how* they are *bounded*. [4.51.]

(p): p = aRx.xRy . . . zRb

The above definition can in its general form only be a rule for a written notation which has nothing to do with the sense of the signs.

But can there be such a rule?

The definition is only possible if it is itself not a proposition.

In that case a proposition cannot treat of all propositions, while a definition can.

The above definition, however, just does not deal with all propositions, for it essentially contains real variables. It is quite analogous to an operation whose own result can be taken as its base.

26.4.16.

In this way, and in this way alone, is it possible to proceed from one type to another. [*Cf.* 5.252.]

And we can say that all types stand in hierarchies.

And the hierarchy is only possible by being built up by means of operations.

Empirical reality is bounded by the number of objects.

The boundary turns up again in the totality of simple propositions. [*See* 5.5561.]

The hierarchies are and must be independent of reality. [*See* 5.5561.]

The meanings of their terms are only determined by the correlation of objects and names.

27.4.16.

Say I wanted to represent a function of three non-interchangeable arguments.

$$\phi(x): \phi(\ ), x$$

But should there be any mention of non-interchangeable arguments in logic? If so, this surely presupposes something about the character of reality.

6.5.16.

At bottom the whole *Weltanschauung* of the moderns involves the illusion that the so-called laws of nature are explanations of natural phenomena. [6.371.]

In this way they stop short at the laws of nature as at something *impregnable* as men of former times did at God and fate. [*See* 6.372.]

And both are right and wrong. The older ones are indeed clearer in the sense that they acknowledge a clear terminus, while with the new system it is supposed to look as if *everything* had a foundation. [*See* 6.372.]

11.5.16.

$|p \qquad |(a, a)$

There are also operations with two bases. And the "|"-operation is of this kind.

$| (\xi, \eta) \ldots$ is an arbitrary term of the series of results of an operation.

$(\exists x) . \phi x$

Is $(\exists x)$ etc. really an operation?

But what would be its base?

11.6.16.

What do I know about God and the purpose of life?

I know that this world exists.

That I am placed in it like my eye in its visual field.

That something about it is problematic, which we call its meaning.

That this meaning does not lie in it but outside it. [*Cf.* 6.41.]

That life is the world. [*Cf.* 5.621.]

That my will penetrates the world.

That my will is good or evil.

Therefore that good and evil are somehow connected with the meaning of the world.

The meaning of life, i.e. the meaning of the world, we can call God.

And connect with this the comparison of God to a father.

To pray is to think about the meaning of life.

I cannot bend the happenings of the world to my will: I am completely powerless.

I can only make myself independent of the world—and so in a certain sense master it—by renouncing any influence on happenings.

5.7.16.

The world is independent of my will. [6.373.]

Even if everything that we want were to happen, this would still only be, so to speak, a grace of fate, for what would guarantee it is not any logical connexion between will and world, and we could not in turn will the supposed physical connexion. [6.374.]

If good or evil willing affects the world it can only affect the boundaries of the world, not the facts, what cannot be portrayed by language but can only be shewn in language. [*Cf.* 6.43.]

In short, it must make the world a wholly different one. [*See* 6.43.]

The world must, so to speak, wax or wane as a whole. As if by accession or loss of meaning. [*Cf.* 6.43.]

As in death, too, the world does not change but stops existing. [6.431.]

6.7.16.

And in this sense Dostoievsky is right when he says that the man who is happy is fulfilling the purpose of existence.

Or again we could say that the man is fulfilling the purpose of existence who no longer needs to have any purpose except to live. That is to say, who is content.

The solution of the problem of life is to be seen in the disappearance of this problem. [*See* 6.521.]

But is it possible for one so to live that life stops being problematic? That one is *living* in eternity and not in time?

7.7.16.

Isn't this the reason why men to whom the meaning of life had become clear after long doubting could not say what this meaning consisted in? [*See* 6.521.]

If I can imagine a "*kind* of object" without knowing whether there are such objects, then I must have constructed their proto-picture for myself.

Isn't the method of mechanics based on this?

8.7.16.

To believe in a God means to understand the question about the meaning of life.

To believe in a God means to see that the facts of the world are not the end of the matter.

To believe in God means to see that life has a meaning.

The world is *given* me, i.e. my will enters into the world completely from outside as into something that is already there.

(As for what my will is, I don't know yet.)

That is why we have the feeling of being dependent on an alien will.

However this may be, at any rate we *are* in a certain sense dependent, and what we are dependent on we can call God.

In this sense God would simply be fate, or, what is the same thing: The world—which is independent of our will.

I can make myself independent of fate.

There are two godheads: the world and my independent I.

I am either happy or unhappy, that is all. It can be said: good or evil do not exist.

A man who is happy must have no fear. Not even in face of death.

Only a man who lives not in time but in the present is happy.

For life in the present there is no death.

Death is not an event in life. It is not a fact of the world. [*Cf.* 6.4311.]

If by eternity is understood not infinite temporal duration but non-temporality, then it can be said that a man lives eternally if he lives in the present. [*See* 6.4311.]

In order to live happily I must be in agreement with the world. And that is what "being happy" *means.*

I am then, so to speak, in agreement with that alien will on which I appear dependent. That is to say: 'I am doing the will of God'.

Fear in face of death is the best sign of a false, i.e. a bad, life.

When my conscience upsets my equilibrium, then I am not in agreement with Something. But what is this? Is it *the world*?

Certainly it is correct to say: Conscience is the voice of God.

For example: it makes me unhappy to think that I have offended such and such a man. Is that my conscience?

Can one say: "Act according to your conscience whatever it may be"?

Live happily!

9.7.16.

If the most general form of proposition could not be given, then there would have to come a moment where we suddenly had a new experience, so to speak a logical one.

That is, of course, impossible.

Do not forget that $(\exists x)fx$ does not mean: There is an x such that fx, but: There is a true proposition "fx".

The proposition fa speaks of particular objects, the general proposition of *all* objects.

11.7.16.

The particular object is a very remarkable phenomenon.

Instead of "all objects" we might say: All *particular objects.*

If all particular objects are given, "all objects" are given.

In short with the particular objects all objects are given. [*Cf.* 5.524.]

If there are objects, then that gives us "all objects" too. [*Cf.* 5.524.]

That is why it must be possible to construct the unity of the elementary propositions and of the general propositions.

For if the elementary propositions are given, that gives us *all* elementary propositions, too, and that gives us the general proposition.—And with that has not the unity been constructed? [*Cf.* 5.524.]

13.7.16.

One keeps on feeling that even in the elementary proposition mention is made of all objects.

$(\exists x)\phi x.x = a$

If two operations are given which cannot be reduced to *one,* then it must at least be possible to set up a general form of their combination.

$$\phi x, \quad \psi y | \chi z \quad , \quad (\exists x). \quad , \quad (x).$$

As obviously it can easily be explained how propositions can be formed by means of these operations and how propositions are not to be formed, this must also be capable *somehow* of exact expression.

14.7.16.

And this expression must already be given in the general form of the sign of an operation.

And mustn't this be the only legitimate expression of the application of an operation? Obviously it must!

For if the form of operation can be expressed at all, then it must be expressed in such a way that it *can* only be applied correctly.

Man cannot make himself happy without more ado.

Whoever lives in the present lives without fear and hope.

21.7.16.

What really is the situation of the human will? I will call "will" first and foremost the bearer of good and evil.

Let us imagine a man who could use none of his limbs and hence could, in the ordinary sense, not exercise his *will*. He could, however, think and *want* and communicate his thoughts to someone else. Could therefore do good or evil through the other man. Then it is clear that ethics would have validity for him, too, and that he in the *ethical sense* is the bearer of a *will*.

Now is there any difference in principle between this will and that which sets the human body in motion?

Or is the mistake here this: even *wanting* (thinking) is an activity of the will? (And in this sense, indeed, a man *without* will would not be alive.)

But can we conceive a being that isn't capable of Will at all, but only of Idea (of seeing for example)? In some sense this seems impossible. But if it were possible then there could also be a world without ethics.

24.7.16.

The World and Life are one. [5.621.]

Physiological life is of course not "Life". And neither is psychological life. Life is the world.

Ethics does not treat of the world. Ethics must be a condition of the world, like logic.

Ethics and aesthetics are one. [*See* 6.421.]

29.7.16.

For it is a fact of logic that wanting does not stand in any logical connexion with its own fulfilment. And it is also clear that the world of the happy is a *different* world from the world of the unhappy. [*Cf.* 6.43.]

Is seeing an activity?

Is it possible to will good, to will evil, and not to will?

Or is only he happy who does *not* will?

"To love one's neighbour" means to will!

But can one want and yet not be unhappy if the want does not attain fulfilment? (And this possibility always exists.)

Is it, according to common conceptions, good to want *nothing* for one's neighbour, neither good nor evil?

And yet in a certain sense it seems that not wanting is the only good.

Here I am still making crude mistakes! No doubt of that!

It is generally assumed that it is evil to want someone else to be unfortunate. Can this be correct? Can it be worse than to want him to be fortunate?

Here everything seems to turn, so to speak, on *how* one wants.

It seems one can't say anything more than: Live happily!

The world of the happy is a different world from that of the unhappy. [*See* 6.43.]

The world of the happy is *a happy world*.

Then can there be a world that is neither happy nor unhappy?

30.7.16.

When a general ethical law of the form "Thou shalt . . ." is set up, the first thought is: Suppose I do not do it?

But it is clear that ethics has nothing to do with punishment and reward. So this question about the consequences of an action must be unimportant. At least these consequences cannot be events. For there must be something right about that question after all. There must be a *kind* of ethical reward and of ethical punishment but these must be involved in the action itself.

And it is also clear that the reward must be something pleasant, the punishment something unpleasant.

[6.422.]

I keep on coming back to this! simply the happy life is good, the unhappy bad. And if I *now* ask myself: But why should I live *happily*, then this of itself seems to me to be a tautological question; the happy life seems to be justified, of itself, it seems that it *is* the only right life.

But this is really in some sense deeply mysterious! *It is clear* that ethics *cannot* be expressed! [*Cf.* 6.421.]

But we could say: The happy life seems to be in some sense more *harmonious* than the unhappy. But in what sense??

What is the objective mark of the happy, harmonious life? Here it is again clear that there cannot be any such mark, that can be *described*.

This mark cannot be a physical one but only a metaphysical one, a transcendental one.

Ethics is transcendental. [*See* 6.421.]

1.8.16.

How things stand, is God.

God is, how things stand.

Only from the consciousness of the *uniqueness of my life* arises religion—science—and art.

2.8.16.

And this consciousness is life itself.

Can there be any ethics if there is no living being but myself?

If ethics is supposed to be something fundamental, there can.

If I am right, then it is not sufficient for the ethical judgment that a world is given.

Then the world in itself is neither good nor evil.

For it must be all one, as far as concerns the existence of ethics, whether there is living matter in the world or not. And it is clear that a world in which there is only dead matter is in itself neither good nor evil, so even the world of living things can in itself be neither good nor evil.

Good and evil only enter through the *subject*. And the subject is not part of the world, but a boundary of the world. [*Cf.* 5.632.]

It would be possible to say (à la Schopenhauer): It is not the world of Idea that is either good or evil; but the willing subject.

I am conscious of the complete unclarity of all these sentences.

Going by the above, then, the willing subject would have to be happy or unhappy, and happiness and unhappiness could not be part of the world.

As the subject is not a part of the world but a presupposition of its existence, so good and evil are predicates of the subject, not properties in the world.

Here the nature of the subject is completely veiled.

My work has extended from the foundations of logic to the nature of the world.

4.8.16.

Isn't the thinking subject in the last resort mere superstition?

Where in the world is a metaphysical subject to be found? [*See* 5.633.]

You say that it is just as it is for the eye and the visual field. But you do *not* actually see the eye. [*See* 5.633.]

And I think that nothing in the visual field would enable one to infer that it is seen from an eye. [*Cf.* 5.633.]

5.8.16.

The thinking subject is surely mere illusion. But the willing subject exists. [*Cf.* 5.631.]

If the will did not exist, neither would there be that centre of the world, which we call the I, and which is the bearer of ethics.

What is good and evil is essentially the I, not the world.

The I, the I is what is deeply mysterious!

7.8.16.

The I is not an object.

11.8.16.

I objectively confront every object. But not the I.

So there really is a way in which there can and must be mention of the I in a *non-psychological sense* in philosophy. [*Cf.* 5.641.]

12.8.16.

The I makes its appearance in philosophy through the world's being *my* world. [*See* 5.641.]

The visual field has not, e.g., a form like this:

Eye

[5.6331.]

This is connected with the fact that none of our experience is *a priori*. [*See* 5.634.]

All that we see could also be otherwise.

All that we can describe at all could also be otherwise.

[*See* 5.634.]

13.8.16.

Suppose that man could not exercise his will, but had to suffer all the misery of this world, then what could make him happy?

How can man be happy at all, since he cannot ward off the misery of this world?

Through the life of knowledge.

The good conscience is the happiness that the life of knowledge preserves.

The life of knowledge is the life that is happy in spite of the misery of the world.

The only life that is happy is the life that can renounce the amenities of the world.

To it the amenities of the world are so many graces of fate.

59

John Dewey

Democracy and Education (1916)

Chapter XXII: The Individual and the World

1. Mind as Purely Individual.—We have been concerned with the influences which have effected a division between work and leisure, knowing and doing, man and nature. These influences have resulted in splitting up the subject matter of education into separate studies. They have also found formulation in various philosophies which have opposed to each other body and mind, theoretical knowledge and practice, physical mechanism and ideal purpose. Upon the philosophical side, these various dualisms culminate in a sharp demarcation of individual minds from the world, and hence from one another. While the connection of this philosophical position with educational procedure is not so obvious as is that of the points considered in the last three chapters, there are certain educational considerations which correspond to it; such as the antithesis supposed to exist between subject matter (the counterpart of the world) and method (the counterpart of mind); such as the tendency to treat interest as something purely private, without intrinsic connection with the material studied. Aside from incidental educational bearings, it will be shown in this chapter that the dualistic philosophy of mind and the world implies an erroneous conception of the relationship between knowledge and social interests, and between individuality or freedom, and social control and authority.

The identification of the mind with the individual self and of the latter with a private psychic consciousness is comparatively modern. In both the Greek and medieval periods, the rule was to regard the individual as a channelthrough which a universal and divine intelligence operated. The individual was in no true sense the knower; the knower was the 'Reason' which operated through him. The individual interfered at his peril, and only to the detriment of the truth. In the degree in which the individual rather than reason 'knew,' conceit, error, and opinion were substituted for true knowledge. In Greek life, observation was acute and alert; and thinking was free almost to the point of irresponsible speculations. Accordingly the consequences of the theory were only such as were consequent upon the lack of an experimental method. Without such a method individuals could not engage in knowing, and be checked up by the results of the inquiries of others. Without such liability to test by others, the minds of men could not be intellectually responsible; results were to be accepted because of their æsthetic consistency, agreeable quality, or the prestige of their authors. In the barbarian period, individuals were in a still more humble attitude to truth; important knowledge was supposed to be divinely revealed, and nothing remained for the minds of individuals except to work it over after it had been received on authority. Aside from the more consciously philosophic aspects of these movements, it never occurs to any one to identify mind and the personal self wherever beliefs are transmitted by custom.

In the medieval period there was a religious individualism. The deepest concern of life was the salvation of the individual soul. In the later middle ages, this latent individualism found conscious formulation in the nominalistic philosophies, which treated the structure of knowledge as something built up within the individual through his own acts, and mental states. With the rise of economic and political individualism after the sixteenth century, and with the development of protestantism, the times were ripe for an emphasis upon the rights and duties of the individual in achieving knowledge for himself. This led to the view that knowledge is won wholly through personal and private experiences. As a consequence, mind, the source and possessor of knowledge, was thought of as wholly individual. Thus upon the educational side, we find educational reformers, like Montaigne, Bacon, Locke, henceforth vehemently denouncing all learning which is acquired on hearsay, and asserting that even if beliefs happen to be true, they do not constitute knowledge unless they have grown up in and been tested by personal experience. The reaction against authority in all spheres of life, and the intensity of the struggle, against great odds, for freedom of action and inquiry, led to such an emphasis upon personal observations and ideas as in effect to isolate mind, and set it apart from the world to be known.

This isolation is reflected in the great development of that branch of philosophy known as epistemology—the theory of knowledge. The identification of mind with the self, and the setting up of the self as something independent and self-sufficient, created such a gulf between the knowing mind and the world that it became a question how knowledge was possible at all. Given a subject—the knower—and an object—the thing to be known—wholly separate from one another, it is necessary to frame a theory to explain how they get into connection with each other so that valid knowledge may result. This problem, with the allied one of the possibility of the world acting upon the mind and the mind acting upon the world, became almost the exclusive preoccupation of philosophic thought. The theories that we cannot know the world as it really is but only the impressions made upon the mind, or that there is no world beyond the individual mind, or that knowledge is only a certain association of the mind's own states, were products of this preoccupation. We are not directly concerned with their truth; but the fact that such desperate solutions were widely accepted is evidence of the extent to which mind had been set over the world of realities. The increasing use of the term 'consciousness' as an equivalent for mind, in the supposition that there is an inner world of conscious states and processes, independent of any relationship to nature and society, an inner world more truly and immediately known than anything else, is evidence of the same fact. In short, practical individualism, or struggle for greater freedom of thought in action, was translated into philosophic subjectivism.

Chapter XXV: Theories of Knowledge

2. Schools of Method.—There are various systems of philosophy with characteristically different conceptions of the method of knowing. Some of them are named scholasticism, sensationalism, rationalism, idealism, realism, empiricism, transcendentalism, pragmatism, etc. Many of them have been criticized in connection with the discussion of some educational problem. We are here concerned with them as involving deviations from that method which has proved most effective in achieving knowledge, for a consideration of the deviations may render clearer the true place of knowledge in experience. In brief, the function of knowledge is to make one experience freely available in other experiences. The word 'freely' marks the difference between the principle of knowledge and that of habit. Habit means that an individual undergoes a modification through an experience, which modification forms a predisposition to easier and more effective action in a like direction in the future. Thus it also has the function of making one experience available in subsequent experiences. Within certain limits, it performs this function successfully. But habit, apart from knowledge, does not make allowance for change of conditions, for novelty. Prevision of change is not part of its scope, for habit assumes the essential likeness of the new situation with the old. Consequently it often leads astray, or comes between a person and the successful performance of his task, just as the skill, based on habit alone, of the mechanic will desert him when something unexpected occurs in the running of the machine. But a man who understands the machine is the man who knows what he is about. He knows the conditions under which a given habit works, and is in a position to introduce the changes which will re-adapt it to new conditions.

In other words, knowledge is a perception of those connections of an object which determine its applicability in a given situation. To take an extreme example; savages react to a flaming comet as they are accustomed to react to other events which threaten the security of their life. Since they try to frighten wild animals or their enemies by shrieks, beating of gongs, brandishing of weapons, etc., they use the same methods to scare away the comet. To us, the method is plainly absurd—so absurd that we fail to note that savages are simply falling back upon habit in a way which exhibits its limitations. The only reason we do not act in some analogous fashion is because we do not take the comet as an isolated, disconnected event, but apprehend it in its connections with other events. We place it, as we say, in the astronomical system. We respond to its *connections* and not simply to the immediate occurrence. Thus our attitude to it is much freer. We may approach it, so to speak, from any one of the angles provided by its connections. We can bring into play, as we deem wise, any one of the habits appropriate to any one of the connected objects. Thus we get at a new event indirectly instead of immediately—by invention, ingenuity, resourcefulness. An ideally perfect knowledge would represent such a network of interconnections that any past experience would offer a point of advantage from which to get at the problem presented in a new experience. In fine, while a habit apart from knowledge supplies us with a single fixed method of attack, knowledge means that selection may be made from a much wider range of habits.

Two aspects of this more general and freer availability of former experiences for subsequent ones may be distinguished. (*i*) One, the more tangible, is increased power of control. What cannot be managed directly may be handled indirectly; or we can interpose barriers between us and undesirable consequences; or we may evade them if we cannot overcome them. Genuine knowledge has all the practical value attaching to efficient habits in any case. (*ii*) But it also increases the meaning, the experienced significance, attaching to an experience. A situation to which we respond capriciously or by routine has only a minimum of conscious significance; we get nothing mentally from it. But wherever knowledge comes into play in determining a new experience there is mental reward; even if we fail practically in getting the needed control we have the satisfaction of experiencing a meaning instead of merely reacting physically.

While the content of knowledge is what *has* happened, what is taken as finished and hence settled and sure, the *reference* of knowledge is future or prospective. For knowledge furnishes the means of understanding or giving meaning to what is still going on and what is to be done. The knowledge of a physician is what he has found out by personal acquaintance and by study of what others have ascertained and recorded. But it is knowledge to him because it supplies the resources by which he interprets the unknown things which confront him, fills out the partial obvious facts with connected suggested phenomena, foresees their probable future, and makes plans accordingly. When knowledge is cut off from use in giving meaning to what is blind and baffling, it drops out of consciousness entirely or else becomes an object of æsthetic contemplation. There is much emotional satisfaction to be had from a survey of the symmetry and order of possessed knowledge, and the satisfaction is a legitimate one. But this contemplative attitude is æsthetic, not intellectual. It is the same sort of joy that comes from viewing a finished picture or a well composed landscape. It would make no difference if the subject matter were totally different, provided it had the same harmonious organization. Indeed, it would make no difference if it were wholly invented, a play of fancy. Applicability to the world means not applicability to what is past and gone—that is out of the question by the nature of the case; it means applicability to what is still going on, what is still unsettled, in the moving scene in which we are implicated. The very fact that we so easily overlook this trait, and regard statements of what is past and out of reach as knowledge is because we assume the continuity of past and future. We cannot entertain the conception of a world in which knowledge of its past would not be helpful in forecasting and giving meaning to its future. We ignore the prospective reference just because it is so irretrievably implied.

Yet many of the philosophic schools of method which have been mentioned transform the ignoring into a virtual denial. They regard knowledge as something complete in itself irrespective of its availability in dealing with what is yet to be. And it is this omission which vitiates them and which makes them stand as sponsors for educational methods which an adequate conception of knowledge condemns. For one has only to call to mind what is sometimes treated in schools as acquisition of knowledge to realize how lacking it is in any fruitful connection with the ongoing experience of the students—how largely it seems to be believed that the mere appropriation of subject matter which happens to be stored in books constitutes knowledge. No matter how true what is learned to those who found it out and in whose experience it functioned, there is nothing which makes it knowledge to the pupils. It might as well be something about Mars or about some fanciful country unless it fructifies in the individual's own life.

At the time when scholastic method developed, it had relevancy to social conditions. It was a method for systematizing and lending rational sanction to material accepted on authority. This subject matter meant so much that it vitalized the defining and systematizing brought to bear upon it. Under present conditions the scholastic method, for most persons, means a form of knowing which has no especial connection with *any* particular subject matter. It includes making distinctions, definitions, divisions, and classifications for the mere sake of making them—with no objective in experience. The view of thought as a purely psychical activity having its own forms, which are applied to any material as a seal may be stamped on any plastic stuff, the view which underlies what is termed formal logic is essentially the scholastic method generalized. The doctrine of formal discipline in education is the natural counterpart of the scholastic method.

The contrasting theories of the method of knowledge which go by the name of sensationalism and rationalism correspond to an exclusive emphasis upon the particular and the general respectively—or upon bare facts on one side and bare relations on the other. In real knowledge, there is a particularizing and a generalizing function working together. So far as a situation is confused, it has to be cleared up; it has to be resolved into details, as sharply defined as possible. Specified facts and qualities constitute the elements of the problem to be dealt with, and it is through our sense organs that they are specified. As setting forth the problem, they may well be termed particulars, for they are fragmentary. Since our task is to discover their connections and to recombine them, *for us at the time* they are partial. They are to be given meaning; hence, just as they stand, they lack it. Anything which is *to be* known, whose meaning has still to be made out, offers itself as particular. But what is already known, if it has been worked over with a view to making it applicable to intellectually mastering new particulars, is general in function. Its function of introducing connection into what is otherwise unconnected constitutes its generality. Any fact is general if we use it to give meaning to the elements of a new experience. 'Reason' is just the ability to bring the subject matter of prior experience to bear to perceive the significance of the subject matter of a new experience. A person is reasonable in the degree in which he is habitually open to seeing an event which immediately strikes his senses not as an isolated thing but in its connection with the common experience of mankind. Without the particulars as they are discriminated by the active responses of sense organs, there is no material for knowing and no intellectual growth. Without placing these particulars in the context of the meanings wrought out in the larger experience of the past—without the use of reason or thought—particulars are mere excitations or irritations. The mistake alike of the sensational and the rationalistic schools is that each fails to see that the function of sensory stimulation and thought is relative to reorganizing experience in applying the old to the new, thereby maintaining the continuity or consistency of life.

The theory of the method of knowing which is advanced in these pages may be termed pragmatic. Its essential feature is to maintain the continuity of knowing with an activity which purposely modifies the environment. It holds that knowledge in its strict sense of something possessed consists of our intellectual resources—of all the habits that render our action intelligent. Only that which has been organized into our disposition so as to enable us to adapt the environment to our needs and to adapt our aims and desires to the situation in which we live is really knowledge. Knowledge is not just something which we are now conscious of, but consists of the dispositions we consciously use in understanding what now happens. Knowledge as an act is bringing some of our dispositions to consciousness with a view to straightening out a perplexity, by conceiving the connection between ourselves and the world in which we live.

60

Bertrand Russell

Mysticism and Logic (1917)

THE LAST OF THE DOCTRINES OF MYSTICISM WHICH WE HAVE to consider is its belief that all evil is mere appearance, an illusion produced by the divisions and oppositions of the analytic intellect. Mysticism does not maintain that such things as cruelty, for example, are good, but it denies that they are real: they belong to that lower world of phantoms from which we are to be liberated by the insight of the vision. Sometimes—for example in Hegel, and at least verbally in Spinoza—not only evil, but good also, is regarded as illusory, though nevertheless the emotional attitude towards what is held to be Reality is such as would naturally be associated with the belief that Reality is good. What is, in all cases, ethically characteristic of mysticism is absence of indignation or protest, acceptance with joy, disbelief in the ultimate truth of the division into two hostile camps, the good and the bad. This attitude is a direct outcome of the nature of the mystical experience: with its sense of unity is associated a feeling of infinite peace. Indeed it may be suspected that the feeling of peace produces, as feelings do in dreams, the whole system of associated beliefs which make up the body of mystic doctrine. But this is a difficult question, and one on which it cannot be hoped that mankind will reach agreement.

Four questions thus arise in considering the truth or falsehood of mysticism, namely:

I   Are there two ways of knowing, which may be called respectively reason and intuition? And if so, is either to be preferred to the other?

II   Is all plurality and division illusory?

III Is time unreal?

IV What kind of reality belongs to good and evil?

On all four of these questions, while fully developed mysticism seems to me mistaken, I yet believe that, by sufficient restraint, there is an element of wisdom to be learned from the mystical way of feeling, which does not seem to be attainable in any other manner. If this is the truth, mysticism is to be commended as an attitude towards life, not as a creed about the world. The metaphysical creed, I shall maintain, is a mistaken outcome of the emotion, although this emotion, as colouring and informing all other thoughts and feelings, is the inspirer of whatever is best in Man. Even the cautious and patient investigation of truth by science, which seems the very antithesis of the mystic's swift certainty, may be fostered and nourished by that very spirit of reverence in which mysticism lives and moves.

I Reason and Intuition[1]

Of the reality or unreality of the mystic's world I know nothing. I have no wish to deny it, nor even to declare that the insight which reveals it is not a genuine insight. What I do wish to maintain—and it is here that the scientific attitude becomes imperative—is that insight, untested and unsupported, is an insufficient guarantee of truth, in spite of the fact that much of the most important truth is first suggested by its means. It is common to speak of an opposition between instinct and reason; in the eighteenth century, the opposition was drawn in favour of reason, but under the influence of Rousseau and the romantic movement instinct was given the preference, first by those who rebelled against artificial forms of government and thought, and then, as the purely rationalistic defence of traditional theology became increasingly difficult, by all who felt in science a menace to creeds which they associated with a spiritual outlook on life and the world. Bergson, under the name of "intuition," has raised instinct to the position of sole arbiter of metaphysical truth. But in fact the opposition of instinct and reason is mainly illusory. Instinct, intuition, or insight is what first leads to the beliefs which subsequent reason confirms or confutes; but the confirmation, where it is possible, consists, in the last analysis, of agreement with other beliefs no less instinctive. Reason is a harmonising, controlling force rather than a creative one. Even in the most purely logical realm, it is insight that first arrives at what is new.

Where instinct and reason do sometimes conflict is in regard to single beliefs, held instinctively, and held with such determination that no degree of inconsistency with other beliefs leads to their abandonment. Instinct, like all human faculties, is liable to error. Those in whom reason is weak are often unwilling to admit this as regards themselves, though all admit it in regard to others. Where instinct is least liable to error is in practical matters as to which right judgment is a help to survival: friendship and hostility in others, for instance, are often felt with extraordinary discrimination through very careful disguises. But even in such matters a wrong impression may be given by reserve or flattery; and in matters less directly practical, such as philosophy deals with, very strong instinctive beliefs are sometimes wholly mistaken, as we may come to know through their perceived inconsistency with other equally strong beliefs. It is such considerations that necessitate the harmonising mediation of reason, which tests our beliefs by their mutual compatibility, and examines, in doubtful cases, the possible sources of error on the one side and on the other. In this there is no opposition to instinct as a whole, but only to blind reliance upon some one interesting aspect of instinct to the exclusion of other more commonplace but not less trustworthy aspects. It is such one-sidedness, not instinct itself, that reason aims at correcting.

These more or less trite maxims may be illustrated by application to Bergson's advocacy of "intuition" as against "intellect." There are, he says, "two profoundly different ways of knowing a thing. The first implies that we move round the object: the second that we enter into it. The first depends on the point of view at which we are placed and on the symbols by which we express ourselves. The second neither depends on a point of view nor relies on any symbol. The first kind of knowledge may be said to stop at the *relative;* the second, in those cases where it is possible, to attain the *absolute.*"[2] The second of these, which is intuition, is, he says, "the kind of *intellectual sympathy* by which one places oneself within an object in order to coincide with what is unique in it and therefore inexpressible" (p. 6). In illustration, he mentions self-knowledge: "there is one reality, at least, which we all seize from within, by intuition and not by simple analysis. It is our own personality in its flowing through time—our self which endures" (p. 8). The rest of Bergson's philosophy consists in reporting, through the imperfect medium of words, the knowledge gained by intuition, and the consequent complete condemnation of all the pretended knowledge derived from science and common sense.

This procedure, since it takes sides in a conflict of instinctive beliefs, stands in need of justification by proving the greater trustworthiness of the beliefs on one side than of those on the other. Bergson attempts this justification in two ways, first by explaining that intellect is a purely practical faculty to secure biological success, secondly by mentioning remarkable feats of instinct in animals and by pointing out characteristics of the world which, though intuition can apprehend them, are baffling to intellect as he interprets it.

Of Bergson's theory that intellect is a purely practical faculty, developed in the struggle for survival, and not a source of true beliefs, we may say, first, that it is only through intellect that we know of the struggle for survival and of the biological ancestry of man: if the intellect is misleading, the whole of this merely inferred history is presumably untrue. If, on the other hand, we agree with him in thinking that evolution took place as Darwin believed, then it is not only intellect, but all our faculties, that have been developed under the stress of practical utility. Intuition is seen at its best where it is directly useful, for example in regard to other people's characters and dispositions. Bergson apparently holds that capacity, for this kind of knowledge is less explicable by the struggle for existence than, for example, capacity for pure mathematics. Yet the savage deceived by false friendship is likely to pay for his mistake with his life; whereas even in the most civilised societies men are not put to death for mathematical incompetence. All the most striking of his instances of intuition in animals have a very direct survival value. The fact is, of course, that both intuition and intellect have been developed because they are useful, and that, speaking broadly, they are useful when they give truth and become harmful when they give falsehood. Intellect, in civilised man, like artistic capacity, has occasionally been developed beyond the point where it is useful to the individual; intuition, on the other hand, seems on the whole to diminish as civilisation increases. It is greater, as a rule, in children than in adults, in the uneducated than in the educated. Probably in dogs it exceeds anything to be found in human beings. But those who see in these facts a recommendation of intuition ought to return to running wild in the woods, dyeing themselves with woad and living on hips and haws.

Let us next examine whether intuition possesses any such infallibility as Bergson claims for it. The best instance of it, according to him, is our acquaintance with ourselves; yet self-knowledge is proverbially rare and difficult. Most men, for example, have in their nature meannesses, vanities, and envies of which they are quite unconscious, though even their best friends can perceive them without any difficulty. It is true that intuition has a convincingness which is lacking to intellect: while it is present, it is almost impossible to doubt its truth. But if it should appear, on examination, to be at least as fallible as intellect, its greater subjective certainty becomes a demerit, making it only the more irresistibly deceptive. Apart from self-knowledge, one of the most notable examples of intuition is the knowledge people believe themselves to possess of those with whom they are in love: the wall between different personalities seems to become transparent, and people think they see into another soul as into their own. Yet deception in such cases is constantly practised with success; and even where there is no intentional deception, experience gradually proves, as a rule, that the supposed insight was illusory, and that the slower more groping methods of the intellect are in the long run more reliable.

Bergson maintains that intellect can only deal with things in so far as they resemble what has been experienced in the past, while intuition has the power of apprehending the uniqueness and novelty that always belong to each fresh moment. That there is something unique and new at every moment, is certainly true; it is also true that this cannot be fully expressed by means of intellectual concepts. Only direct acquaintance can give knowledge of what is unique and new. But direct acquaintance of this kind is given fully in sensation, and does not require, so far as I can see, any special faculty of intuition for its apprehension. It is neither intellect nor intuition, but sensation, that supplies new data; but when the data are new in any remarkable manner, intellect is much more capable of dealing with them than intuition would be. The hen with a brood of ducklings no doubt has intuition which seems to place her inside them, and not merely to know them analytically; but when the ducklings take to the water, the whole apparent intuition is seen to be illusory, and the hen is left helpless on the shore. Intuition, in fact, is an aspect and development of instinct, and, like all instinct, is admirable in those customary surroundings which have moulded the habits of the animal in question, but totally incompetent as soon as the surroundings are changed in a way which demands some non-habitual mode of action.

The theoretical understanding of the world, which is the aim of philosophy, is not a matter of great practical importance to animals, or to savages, or even to most civilised men. It is hardly to be supposed, therefore, that the rapid, rough and ready methods of instinct or intuition will find in this field a favourable ground for their application. It is the older kinds of activity, which bring out our kinship with remote generations of animal and semi-human ancestors, that show intuition at its best. In such matters as self-preservation and love, intuition will act sometimes (though not always) with a swiftness and precision which are astonishing to the critical intellect. But philosophy is not one of the pursuits which illustrate our affinity with the past: it is a highly refined, highly civilised pursuit, demanding, for its success, a certain liberation from the life of instinct, and even, at times, a certain aloofness from all mundane hopes and fears. It is not in philosophy, therefore, that we can hope to see intuition at its best. On the contrary, since the true objects of philosophy, and the habit of thought demanded for their apprehension, are strange, unusual, and remote, it is here, more almost than anywhere else, that intellect proves superior to intuition, and that quick unanalysed convictions are least deserving of uncritical acceptance.

In advocating the scientific restraint and balance, as against the self-assertion of a confident reliance upon intuition, we are only urging, in the sphere of knowledge, that largeness of contemplation, that impersonal disinterestedness, and that freedom from practical preoccupations which have been inculcated by all the great religions of the world. Thus our conclusion, however it may conflict with the explicit beliefs of many mystics, is in essence, not contrary to the spirit which inspires those beliefs, but rather the outcome of this very spirit as applied in the realm of thought.

II Unity and Plurality

One of the most convincing aspects of the mystic illumination is the apparent revelation of the oneness of all things, giving rise to pantheism in religion and to monism in philosophy. An elaborate logic, beginning with Parmenides, and culminating in Hegel and his followers, has been gradually developed, to prove that the universe is one indivisible Whole, and that what seem to be its parts, if considered as substantial and self-existing, are mere illusion. The conception of a Reality quite other than the world of appearance, a reality one, indivisible, and unchanging, was introduced into Western philosophy by Parmenides, not, nominally at least, for mystical or religious reasons, but on the basis of a logical argument as to the impossibility of not-being, and most subsequent metaphysical systems are the outcome of this fundamental idea.

The logic used in defence of mysticism seems to be faulty as logic, and open to technical criticisms, which I have explained elsewhere. I shall not here repeat these criticisms, since they are lengthy and difficult, but shall instead attempt an analysis of the state of mind from which mystical logic has arisen.

Belief in a reality quite different from what appears to the senses arises with irresistible force in certain moods, which are the source of most mysticism, and of most metaphysics. While such a mood is dominant, the need of logic is not felt, and accordingly the more thoroughgoing mystics do not employ logic, but appeal directly to the immediate deliverance of their insight. But such fully developed mysticism is rare in the West. When the intensity of emotional conviction subsides, a man who is in the habit of reasoning will search for logical grounds in favour of the belief which he finds in himself. But since the belief already exists, he will be very hospitable to any ground that suggests itself. The paradoxes apparently proved by his logic are really the paradoxes of mysticism, and are the goal which he feels his logic must reach if it is to be in accordance with insight. The resulting logic has rendered most philosophers incapable of giving any account of the world of science and daily life. If they had been anxious to give such an account, they would probably have discovered the errors of their logic; but most of them were less anxious to understand the world of science and daily life than to convict it of unreality in the interests of a super-sensible "real" world.

It is in this way that logic has been pursued by those of the great philosophers who were mystics. But since they usually took for granted the supposed insight of the mystic emotion, their logical doctrines were presented with a certain dryness, and were believed by their disciples to be quite independent of the sudden illumination from which they sprang. Nevertheless their origin clung to them, and they remained—to borrow a useful word from Mr. Santayana—"malicious" in regard to the world of science and common sense. It is only so that we can account for the complacency with which philosophers have accepted the inconsistency of their doctrines with all the common and scientific facts which seem best established and most worthy of belief.

The logic of mysticism shows, as is natural, the defects which are inherent in anything malicious. The impulse to logic, not felt while the mystic mood is dominant, reasserts itself as the mood fades, but with a desire to retain the vanishing insight, or at least to prove that it *was* insight, and that what seems to contradict it is illusion. The logic which thus arises is not quite disinterested or candid, and is inspired by a certain hatred of the daily world to which it is to be applied. Such an attitude naturally does not tend to the best results. Everyone knows that to read an author simply in order to refute him is not the way to understand him; and to read the book of Nature with a conviction that it is all illusion is just as unlikely to lead to understanding. If our logic is to find the common world intelligible, it must not be hostile, but must be inspired by a genuine acceptance such as is not usually to be found among metaphysicians.

III Time

The unreality of time is a cardinal doctrine of many metaphysical systems, often nominally based, as already by Parmenides, upon logical arguments, but originally derived, at any rate in the founders of new systems, from the certainty which is born in the moment of mystic insight. As a Persian Sufi poet says:

> "Past and future are what veil God from our sight.
> Burn up both of them with fire! How long
> Wilt thou be partitioned by these segments as a reed?"[3]

The belief that what is ultimately real must be immutable is a very common one: it gave rise to the metaphysical notion of substance, and finds, even now, a wholly illegitimate satisfaction in such scientific doctrines as the conservation of energy and mass.

It is difficult to disentangle the truth and the error in this view. The arguments for the contention that time is unreal and that the world of sense is illusory must, I think, be regarded as fallacious. Nevertheless there is some sense—easier to feel than to state—in which time is an unimportant and superficial characteristic of reality. Past and future must be acknowledged to be as real as the present, and a certain emancipation from slavery to time is essential to philosophic thought. The importance of time is rather practical than theoretical, rather in relation to our desires than in relation to truth. A truer image of the world, I think, is obtained by picturing things as entering into the stream of time from an eternal world outside, than from a view which regards time as the devouring tyrant of all that is. Both in thought and in feeling, even though time be real, to realise the unimportance of time is the gate of wisdom.

That this is the case may be seen at once by asking ourselves why our feelings towards the past are so different from our feelings towards the future. The reason for this difference is wholly practical: our wishes can affect the future but not the past, the future is to some extent subject to our power, while the past is unalterably fixed. But every future will some day be past: if we see the past truly now, it must, when it was still future, have been just what we now see it to be, and what is now future must be just what we shall see it to be when it has become past. The felt difference of quality between past and future, therefore, is not an intrinsic difference, but only a difference in relation to us: to impartial contemplation, it ceases to exist. And impartiality of contemplation is, in the intellectual sphere, that very same virtue of disinterestedness which, in the sphere of action, appears as justice and unselfishness. Whoever wishes to see the world truly, to rise in thought above the tyranny of practical desires, must learn to overcome the difference of attitude towards past and future, and to survey the whole stream of time in one comprehensive vision.

The kind of way in which, as it seems to me, time ought not to enter into our theoretic philosophical thought, may be illustrated by the philosophy which has become associated with the idea of evolution, and which is exemplified by Nietzsche, pragmatism, and Bergson. This philosophy, on the basis of the development which has led from the lowest forms of life up to man, sees in *progress* the fundamental law of the universe, and thus admits the difference between *earlier* and *later* into the very citadel of its contemplative outlook. With its past and future history of the world, conjectural as it is, I do not wish to quarrel. But I think that, in the intoxication of a quick success, much that is required for a true understanding of the universe has been forgotten. Something of Hellenism, something, too, of Oriental resignation, must be combined with its hurrying Western self-assertion before it can emerge from the ardour of youth into the mature wisdom of manhood. In spite of its appeals to science, the true scientific philosophy, I think, is something more arduous and more aloof, appealing to less mundane hopes, and requiring a severer discipline for its successful practice.

Darwin's *Origin of Species* persuaded the world that the difference between different species of animals and plants is not the fixed immutable difference that it appears to be. The doctrine of natural kinds, which had rendered classification easy and definite, which was enshrined in the Aristotelian tradition, and protected by its supposed necessity for orthodox dogma, was suddenly swept away for ever out of the biological world. The difference between man and the lower animals, which to our human conceit appears enormous, was shown to be a gradual achievement, involving intermediate being who could not with certainty be placed either within or without the human family. The sun and the planets had already been shown by Laplace to be very probably derived from a primitive more or less undifferentiated nebula. Thus the old fixed landmarks became wavering and indistinct, and all sharp outlines were blurred. Things and species lost their boundaries, and none could say where they began or where they ended.

But if human conceit was staggered for a moment by its kinship with the ape, it soon found a way to reassert itself, and that way is the "philosophy" of evolution. A process which led from the amoeba to Man appeared to the philosophers to be obviously a progress—though whether the amoeba would agree with this opinion is not known. Hence the cycle of changes which science had shown to be the probable history of the past was welcomed as revealing a law of development towards good in the universe—an evolution or unfolding of an idea slowly embodying itself in the actual. But such a view, though it might satisfy Spencer and those whom we may call Hegelian evolutionists, could not be accepted as adequate by the more whole-hearted votaries of change. An ideal to which the world continuously approaches is, to these minds, too dead and static to be inspiring. Not only the aspiration, but the ideal too, must change and develop with the course of evolution: there must be no fixed goal, but a continual fashioning of fresh needs by the impulse which is life and which alone gives unity to the process.

Life, in this philosophy, is a continuous stream, in which all divisions are artificial and unreal. Separate things, beginnings and endings, are mere convenient fictions: there is only smooth unbroken transition. The beliefs of to-day may count as true to-day, if they carry us along the stream; but to-morrow they will be false, and must be replaced by new beliefs to meet the new situation. All our thinking consists of convenient fictions, imaginary congealings of the stream: reality flows on in spite of all our fictions, and though it can be lived, it cannot be conceived in thought. Somehow, without explicit statement, the assurance is slipped in that the future, though we cannot foresee it, will be better than the past or the present: the reader is like the child which expects a sweet because it has been told to open its mouth and shut its eyes. Logic, mathematics, physics disappear in this philosophy, because they are too "static"; what is real is no impulse and movement towards a goal which, like the rainbow, recedes as we advance, and makes every place different when it reaches it from what it appeared to be at a distance.

I do not propose to enter upon a technical examination of this philosophy. I wish only to maintain that the motives and interests which inspire it are so exclusively practical, and the problems with which it deals are so special, that it can hardly be regarded as touching any of the questions that, to my mind, constitute genuine philosophy.

The predominant interest of evolutionism is in the question of human destiny, or at least of the destiny of Life. It is more interested in morality and happiness than in knowledge for its own sake. It must be admitted that the same may be said of many other philosophies, and that a desire for the kind of knowledge which philosophy can give is very rare. But if philosophy is to attain truth, it is necessary first and foremost that philosophers should acquire the disinterested intellectual curiosity which characterises the genuine man of science. Knowledge concerning the future—which is the kind of knowledge that must be sought if we are to know about human destiny—is possible within certain narrow limits. It is impossible to say how much the limits may be enlarged with the progress of science. But what is evident is that any proposition about the future belongs by its subject-matter to some particular science, and is to be ascertained, if at all, by the methods of that science. Philosophy is not a short cut to the same kind of results as those of the other sciences: if it is to be a genuine study, it must have a province of its own, and aim at results which the other sciences can neither prove nor disprove.

Evolutionism, in basing itself upon the notion of *progress*, which is change from the worse to the better, allows the notion of time, as it seems to me, to become its tyrant rather than its servant, and thereby loses that impartiality of contemplation which is the source of all that is best in philosophic thought and feeling. Metaphysicians, as we saw, have frequently denied altogether the reality of time. I do not wish to do this; I wish only to preserve the mental outlook which inspired the denial, the attitude which, in thought, regards the past as having the same reality as the present and the same importance as the future. "In so far," says Spinoza,[4] "as the mind conceives a thing according to the dictate of reason, it will be equally affected whether the idea is that of a future, past, or present thing." It is this "conceiving according to the dictate of reason" that I find lacking in the philosophy which is based on evolution.

IV Good and Evil

Mysticism maintains that all evil is illusory, and sometimes maintains the same view as regards good, but more often holds that all Reality is good. Both views are to be found in Heraclitus: "Good and ill are one," he says, but again, "To God all things are fair and good and right, but men hold some things wrong and some right." A similar twofold position is to be found in Spinoza, but he uses the word "perfection" when he means to speak of the good that is not merely human. "By reality and perfection I mean the same thing," he says;[5] but elsewhere we find the definition: "By *good* I shall mean that which we certainly know to be useful to us."[6] Thus perfection belongs to Reality in its own nature, but goodness is relative to ourselves and our needs, and disappears in an impartial survey. Some such distinction, I think, is necessary in order to understand the ethical outlook of mysticism: there is a lower mundane kind of good and evil, which divides the world of appearance into what seem to be conflicting parts; but there is also a higher, mystical kind of good, which belongs to Reality and is not opposed by any correlative kind of evil.

It is difficult to give a logically tenable account of this position without recognising that good and evil are subjective, that what is good is merely that towards which we have one kind of feeling, and what is evil is merely that towards which we have another kind of feeling. In our active life, where we have to exercise choice, and to prefer this to that of two possible acts, it is necessary to have a distinction of good and evil, or at least of better and worse. But this distinction, like everything pertaining to action, belongs to what mysticism regards as the world of illusion, if only because it is essentially concerned with time. In our contemplative life, where action is not called for, it is possible to be impartial, and to overcome the ethical dualism which action requires. So long as we remain *merely* impartial, we may be content to say that both the good and the evil of action are illusions. But if, as we must do if we have the mystic vision, we find the whole world worthy of love and worship, if we see

"The earth, and every common sight. . . .
Apparell'd in celestial light,"

we shall say that there is a higher good than that of action, and that this higher good belongs to the whole world as it is in reality. In this way the twofold attitude and the apparent vacillation of mysticism are explained and justified.

The possibility of this universal love and joy in all that exists is of supreme importance for the conduct and happiness of life, and gives inestimable value to the mystic emotion, apart from any creeds which may be built upon it. But if we are not to be led into false beliefs, it is necessary to realise exactly *what* the mystic emotion reveals. It reveals a possibility of human nature—a possibility of a nobler, happier, freer life than any that can be otherwise achieved. But it does not reveal anything about the non-human, or about the nature of the universe in general. Good and bad, and even the higher good that mysticism finds everywhere, are the reflections of our own emotions on other things, not part of the substance of things as they are in themselves. And therefore an impartial contemplation, freed from all preoccupation with Self, will not judge things good or bad, although it is very easily combined with that feeling of universal love which leads the mystic to say that the whole world is good.

The philosophy of evolution, through the notion of progress, is bound up with the ethical dualism of the worse and the better, and is thus shut out, not only from the kind of survey which discards good and evil altogether from its view, but also from the mystical belief in the goodness of everything. In this way the distinction of good and evil, like time, becomes a tyrant in this philosophy, and introduces into thought the restless selectiveness of action. Good and evil, like time, are, it would seem, not general or fundamental in the world of thought, but late and highly specialised members of the intellectual hierarchy.

Although, as we saw, mysticism can be interpreted so as to agree with the view that good and evil are not intellectually fundamental, it must be admitted that here we are no longer in verbal agreement with most of the great philosophers and religious teachers of the past. I believe, however, that the elimination of ethical considerations from philosophy is both scientifically necessary and—though this may seem a paradox—an ethical advance. Both these contentions must be briefly defended.

The hope of satisfaction to our more human desires—the hope of demonstrating that the world has this or that desirable ethical characteristic—is not one which, so far as I can see, a scientific philosophy can do anything whatever to satisfy. The difference between a good world and a bad one is a difference in the particular characteristics of the particular things that exist in these worlds: it is not a sufficiently abstract difference to come within the province of philosophy. Love and hate, for example, are ethical opposites, but to philosophy they are closely analogous attitudes towards objects. The general form and structure of those attitudes towards objects which constitute mental phenomena is a problem for philosophy, but the difference between love and hate is not a difference of form or structure, and therefore belongs rather to the special science of psychology than to philosophy. Thus the ethical interests which have often inspired philosophers must remain in the background: some kind of ethical interest may inspire the whole study, but none must obtrude in the detail or be expected in the special results which are sought.

If this view seems at first sight disappointing, we may remind ourselves that a similar change has been found necessary in all the other sciences. The physicist or chemist is not now required to prove the ethical importance of his ions or atoms; the biologist is not expected to prove the utility of the plants or animals which he dissects. In pre-scientific ages this was not the case. Astronomy, for example, was studied because men believed in astrology: it was thought that the movements of the planets had the most direct and important bearing upon the lives of human beings. Presumably, when this belief decayed and the disinterested study of astronomy began, many who had found astrology absorbingly interesting decided that astronomy had too little human interest to be worthy of study. Physics, as it appears in Plato's Timæus for example, is full of ethical notions: it is an essential part of its purpose to show that the earth is worthy of admiration. The modern physicist, on the contrary, though he has no wish to deny that the earth is admirable, is not concerned, as physicist, with its ethical attributes: he is merely concerned to find out facts, not to consider whether they are good or bad. In psychology, the scientific attitude is even more recent and more difficult than in the physical sciences: it is natural to consider that human nature is either good or bad, and to suppose that the difference between good and bad, so all-important in practice, must be important in theory also. It is only during the last century that an ethically neutral psychology has grown up; and here too, ethical neutrality has been essential to scientific success.

In philosophy, hitherto, ethical neutrality has been seldom sought and hardly ever achieved. Men have remembered their wishes, and have judged philosophies in relation to their wishes. Driven from the particular sciences, the belief that the notions of good and evil must afford a key to the understanding of the world has sought a refuge in philosophy. But even from this last refuge, if philosophy is not to remain a set of pleasing dreams, this belief must be driven forth. It is a commonplace that happiness is not best achieved by those who seek it directly; and it would seem that the same is true of the good. In thought, at any rate, those who forget good and evil and seek only to know the facts are more likely to achieve good than those who view the world through the distorting medium of their own desires.

We are thus brought back to our seeming paradox, that a philosophy which does not seek to impose upon the world its own conceptions of good and evil is not only more likely to achieve truth, but is also the outcome of a higher ethical standpoint than one which, like evolutionism and most traditional systems, is perpetually appraising the universe and seeking to find in it an embodiment of present ideals. In religion, and in every deeply serious view of the world and of human destiny, there is an element of submission, a realisation of the limits of human power, which is somewhat lacking in the modern world, with its quick material successes and its insolent belief in the boundless possibilities of progress. "He that loveth his life shall lose it"; and there is danger lest, through a too confident love of life, life itself should lose much of what gives it its highest worth. The submission which religion inculcates in action is essentially the same in spirit as that which science teaches in thought; and the ethical neutrality by which its victories have been achieved is the outcome of that submission.

The good which it concerns us to remember is the good which it lies in our power to create—the good in our own lives and in our attitude towards the world. Insistence on belief in an external realisation of the good is a form of self-assertion, which, while it cannot secure the external good which it desires, can seriously impair the inward good which lies within our power, and destroy that reverence towards fact which constitutes both what is valuable in humility and what is fruitful in the scientific temper.

Human beings cannot, of course, wholly transcend human nature; something subjective, if only the interest that determines the direction of our attention, must remain in all our thought. But scientific philosophy comes nearer to objectivity than any other human pursuit, and gives us, therefore, the closest constant and the most intimate relation with the outer world that it is possible to achieve. To the primitive mind, everything is either friendly or hostile;

but experience has shown that friendliness and hostility are not the conceptions by which the world is to be understood. Scientific philosophy thus represents, though as yet only in a nascent condition, a higher form of thought than any pre-scientific belief or imagination, and, like every approach to self-transcendence, it brings with it a rich reward in increase of scope and breadth and comprehension. Evolutionism, in spite of its appeals to particular scientific facts, fails to be a truly scientific philosophy because of its slavery to time, its ethical preoccupations, and its predominant interest in our mundane concerns and destiny. A truly scientific philosophy will be more humble, more piecemeal, more arduous, offering less glitter of outward mirage to flatter fallacious hopes, but more indifferent to fate, and more capable of accepting the world without the tyrannous imposition of our human and temporary demands.

Notes

1   This section, and also one or two pages in later sections, have been printed in a course of Lowell lectures *On our knowledge of the external world*, published by the Open Court Publishing Company. But I have left them here, as this is the context for which they were originally written.

2   *Introduction to Metaphysics*, p. 1.

3   Whinfield's translation of the *Masnavi* (Trübner, 1887), p. 34.

4   *Ethics*, Bk. IV, Prop. LXII.

5   Ib., Pt. IV, Df. I.

6   Ib., Pt. II, Df. VI.

61

Oswald Spengler

The Decline of the West (1918)

Introduction

IN THIS BOOK IS ATTEMPTED FOR THE FIRST TIME the venture of predetermining history, of following the still untravelled stages in the destiny of a Culture, and specifically of the only Culture of our time and on our planet which is actually in the phase of fulfilment—the West European–American.

Is there a logic of history? Is there, beyond all the casual and incalculable elements of the separate events, something that we may call a metaphysical structure of historic humanity, something that is essentially independent of the outward forms—social, spiritual and political—which we see so clearly? Are not these actualities indeed secondary or derived from that something? Does world-history present to the seeing eye certain grand traits, again and again, with sufficient constancy to justify certain conclusions? And if so, what are the limits to which reasoning from such premises may be pushed?

Is it possible to find in life itself—for human history is the sum of mighty life-courses which already have had to be endowed with ego and personality, in customary thought and expression, by predicating entities of a higher order like "the Classical" or "the Chinese Culture," "Modern Civilization"—a series of stages which must be traversed, and traversed moreover in an ordered and obligatory sequence? For everything organic the notions of birth, death, youth, age, lifetime, are fundamentals—may not these notions, in this sphere also, possess a rigorous meaning which no one has as yet extracted? In short, is all history founded upon general biographic archetypes?

The decline of the West, which at first sight may appear, like the corresponding decline of the Classical Culture, a phenomenon limited in time and space, we now perceive to be a philosophical problem that, when comprehended in all its gravity, includes within itself every great question of Being.

If therefore we are to discover in what form the destiny of the Western Culture will be accomplished, we must first be clear as to what culture *is,* what its relations are to visible history, to life, to soul, to nature, to intellect, what the forms of its manifestation are and how far these forms—peoples, tongues and epochs, battles and ideas, states and gods, arts and craft-works, sciences, laws, economic types and world-ideas, great men and great events—may be accepted and pointed to as symbols.

The means whereby to identify dead forms is Mathematical Law. The means whereby to understand living forms is Analogy. By these means we are enabled to distinguish polarity and periodicity in the world.

It is, and has always been, a matter of knowledge that the expression-forms of world-history are limited in number, and that eras, epochs, situations, persons, are ever repeating themselves true to type. Napoleon has hardly ever been discussed without a side-glance at Caesar and Alexander—analogies of which, as we shall see, the first is morphologically quite inacceptable and the second is correct. Frederick the Great, in his political writings—such as his *Considérations,* 1738—moves among analogies with perfect assurance. Thus he compares the French to the Macedonians under Philip and the Germans to the Greeks. "Even now," he says, "the Thermopylae of Germany, Alsace and Lorraine, are in the hands of Philip," therein exactly characterizing the policy of Cardinal Fleury. We find him drawing parallels also between the policies of the Houses of Habsburg and Bourbon and the proscriptions of Antony and of Octavius.

Still, all this was only fragmentary and arbitrary, and usually implied rather a momentary inclination to poetical or ingenious expressions than a really deep sense of historical forms. In this region no one hitherto has set himself to work out a *method*, nor has had the slightest inkling that there is here a root, in fact the only root, from which can come a broad solution of the problems of History. Analogies, insofar as they laid bare the organic structure of history, might be a blessing to historical thought. Their technique, developing under the influence of a comprehensive idea, would surely eventuate in inevitable conclusions and logical mastery. But as hitherto understood and practised, they have been a curse, for they have enabled the historians to follow their own tastes, instead of soberly realizing that their first and hardest task was concerned with the symbolism of history and its analogies.

Thus our theme, which originally comprised only the limited problem of present-day civilization, broadens itself into a new philosophy—*the* philosophy of the future, so far as the metaphysically exhausted soil of the West can bear such, and in any case the only philosophy which is within the *possibilities* of the West European mind in its next stages. It expands into the conception of a *morphology of world-history*, of the world-as-history in contrast to the morphology of the world-as-nature that hitherto has been almost the only theme of philosophy. And it reviews once again the forms and movements of the world in their depths and final significance, but this time according to an entirely different ordering, which groups them, not in an ensemble picture inclusive of everything known, but in a picture of *life,* and presents them not as things-become, but as things-becoming.

The *world-as-history,* conceived, viewed and given form from out of its opposite, the *world-as-nature*—here is a new aspect of human existence on this earth. As yet, in spite of its immense significance, both practical and theoretical, this aspect has not been realized, still less presented. Some obscure inkling of it there may have been, a distant momentary glimpse there has often been, but no one has deliberately faced it and taken it in with all its implications. We have before us two possible ways in which man may inwardly possess and experience the world around him. With all rigour I distinguish (as to form, not substance) the organic from the mechanical world-impression, the content of images from that of laws, the picture and symbol from the formula and the system, the instantly actual from the constantly possible, the intents and purposes of imagination ordering according to plan from the intents and purposes of experience dissecting according to scheme; and—to mention even thus early an opposition that has never yet been noted, in spite of its significance—the domain of *chronological* from that of *mathematical number.*

Consequently, in a research such as that lying before us, there can be no question of taking spiritual-political events, as they become visible day by day on the surface, at their face value, and arranging them on a scheme of "causes" or "effects" and following them up in the obvious and intellectually easy directions. Such a "pragmatic" handling of history would be nothing but a piece of "natural science" in disguise, and for their part, the supporters of the materialistic idea of history make no secret about it—it is their adversaries who largely fail to see the similarity of the two methods. What concerns us is not what the historical facts which appear at this or that time *are,* per se, but what they signify, what they point to, *by appearing.* I have not hitherto found one who has carefully considered the *morphological relationship* that inwardly binds together the expression-forms of *all* branches of a Culture. Yet, viewed from this morphological standpoint, even the humdrum facts of politics assume a symbolic and even a metaphysical character, and—what has perhaps been impossible hitherto—things such as the Egyptian administrative system, the Classical coinage, analytical geometry, the cheque, the Suez Canal, the book-printing of the Chinese, the Prussian Army, and the Roman road-engineering can, as symbols, be made *uniformly* understandable and appreciable.

But at once the fact presents itself that as yet there exists no theory-enlightened art of historical treatment. What passes as such draws its methods almost exclusively from the domain of that science which alone has completely disciplined the methods of cognition, viz., physics, and thus we imagine ourselves to be carrying on historical research when we are really following out objective connexions of cause and effect. Judged by the standards of the physicist and the mathematician, the historian becomes *careless* as soon as he has assembled and ordered his material and passes on to interpretation. That there is, besides a necessity of cause and effect—which I may call the *logic of space*—another necessity, an organic necessity in life, that of Destiny—the *logic of time*—is a fact of the deepest inward certainty, a fact which suffuses the whole of mythological religions and artistic thought and constitutes the essence and kernel of all history (in contradistinction to nature) but is unapproachable through the cognition-forms which the *Critique of Pure Reason* investigates. This fact still awaits its theoretical formulation.

Mathematics and the principle of Causality lead to a naturalistic, Chronology and the idea of Destiny to a historical ordering of the phenomenal world. Both orderings, each on its own account, cover the *whole* world. The difference is only in the eyes by which and through which this world is realized.

The Meaning of History for the Individual

Nature is the shape in which the man of higher Cultures synthesizes and interprets the immediate impressions of his senses. History is that from which his imagination seeks comprehension of the living existence of the world in relation to his own life, which he thereby invests with a deeper reality. Whether he is capable of creating these shapes, which of them it is that dominates his waking consciousness, is a primordial problem of all human existence.

Man, thus, has before him two possible ways of regarding the world. But it must be noted, at the very outset, that these possibilities are not necessarily *actualities,* and if we are to enquire into the sense of all history we must begin by solving a question which has never yet been put, viz., *for whom* is there History? The question is seemingly paradoxical, for history is obviously for everyone to this extent, that every man, with his whole existence and consciousness, is a part of history. But it makes a great difference whether anyone lives under the constant impression that his life is an element in a far wider life-course that goes on for hundreds and thousands of years, or conceives of himself as something rounded off and self-contained. For the latter type of consciousness there is certainly no world-history, no *world-as-history.* But how if the self-consciousness of a whole nation, how if a whole Culture rests on this a historic spirit? How must actuality appear to it? The world? Life?

Faustian and Apollinian Nature-Knowledge
Every Science is Dependent Upon a Religion

Helmholtz observed, in a lecture of 1869 that has become famous, that "the final aim of Natural Science is to discover the motions underlying all changes, and the motive forces thereof; that is, to resolve itself into Mechanics." What this resolution into mechanics means is the reference of all qualitative impressions to fixed quantitative base-values, that is, to the *extended* and to *change of place* therein. It means, further—if we bear in mind the opposition of becoming and become, form and law, image and notion—the referring of the seen Nature-picture to the imagined picture of a single numerically and structurally measurable Order. The specific tendency of all Western mechanics is towards an intellectual *conquest by measurement,* and it is therefore obliged to look for the essence of the phenomenon in a system of constant elements that are susceptible of full and inclusive appreciation by measurement, of which Helmholtz distinguishes *motion* (using the word in its everyday sense) as the most important.

To the physicist this definition appears unambiguous and exhaustive, but to the sceptic who has followed out the history of this scientific conviction, it is very far from being either. To the physicist, present-day mechanics is a logical system of clear, uniquely significant concepts and of simple, necessary relations; while to the other it is a *picture* distinctive of the structure of the West European spirit, though he admits that the picture is consistent in the highest degree and most impressively convincing. It is self-evident that no *practical* results and discoveries can prove anything as to the "truth" of the *theory,* the *picture.*

Modern physics, as a science, is an immense system of indications in the form of names and numbers whereby we are enabled to work with Nature as with a machine. As such, it may have an exactly definable end. But as a piece of *history,* all made up of destinies and incidents in the lives of the men who have worked in it and in the course of research itself, physics is, in point of object, methods and results, alike an expression and actualization of a Culture, an organic and evolving element in the essence of that Culture, and every one of its results is a symbol. Its discoveries, in virtue of their imagined content (as distinguished from their printable formulae), have been of a purely mythic nature, even in minds so prudent as those of J. R. Mayer, Faraday and Hertz. In every Nature-law, physically exact as it may be, we are called upon to distinguish between the nameless number and the naming of it, between the plain fixation of limits and their theoretical interpretation. The formulae represent general logical values, pure numbers— that is to say, objective space—and boundary-elements. But formulae are dumb. The expression $s = \frac{1}{2}gt^2$ means nothing at all unless one is able mentally to connect the letters with particular words and their symbolism. But the moment we clothe the dead signs in such words, give them flesh, body and life, and, in sum, a perceptible significance in the world, we have overstepped the limits of a mere *order.* Θεωρία means image, vision, and it is this that makes a Nature-law out of a figure-and-letter formula. Everything exact is in itself *meaningless,* and every physical observation is so constituted that it *proves the basis of a certain number of imaged presuppositions;* and the effect of its successful issue is to make these presuppositions more convincing than ever. Apart from these, the result consists merely of empty figures. But in fact we do not and cannot get apart from them. Even if an investigator puts on one side every hypothesis that he knows as such, as soon as he sets his *thought* to work on the supposedly clear task, he is not controlling but being controlled by the unconscious form of it, for in living activity he is always a man of his Culture, of his age, of his school and of his tradition. Faith and "knowledge" are only two species of inner certitude, but of the two faith is the older and it dominates all the conditions of knowing, be they never so exact. And thus it is theories and not pure numbers that are the support of all natural science. The unconscious longing for that genuine knowledge which (be it repeated) is peculiar to the spirit of Culture-man sets itself to apprehend, to penetrate, and to comprise within its grasp the world-image of Nature. Mere industrious measuring for measuring's sake is not and never has been more than a delight for little minds. Every savant's experiment, be it what it may, is at the same time an instance of the *kind* of symbolism that rules in the savant's ideation. All Laws formulated in words are derived from experiences, typical of the one—and only the one—Culture. As to the "necessity" which is a postulate in all exact research, here too we have to consider two kinds of necessity, viz., a necessity within the spiritual and living (for it is Destiny that the history of every individual research-act takes its course when, where and how it does) and a necessity within the known (for which the current Western name is Causality). If the pure numbers of a physical formula represent a causal necessity, the existence, the birth and the life-duration of a theory are a Destiny.

The pure mechanics that the physicist has set before himself as the end-form to which it is his task (and the purpose of all this imagination-machinery) to reduce Nature, presupposes a *dogma*—namely, the religious world-picture of the Gothic centuries. For it is from this world-picture that the physics peculiar to the Western intellect is derived. There is no science that is without unconscious presuppositions of this kind, over which the researcher has no control and which can be traced back to the earliest days of the awakening Culture. *There is no Natural science without a precedent Religion.*

Every critical science, like every myth and every religious belief, rests upon an inner certitude. Various as the creations of this certitude may be, both in structure and in repute, they are not different in basic principle. Any reproach, therefore, levelled by Natural science at Religion is a boomerang. We are presumptuous and no less in supposing that we can ever set up "the Truth" in the place of "anthropomorphic" conceptions, for no other conceptions but these exist at all. Every idea that is possible at all is a mirror of the being of its author. The statement that "man created God in his own image," valid for every historical religion, is not less valid for every physical theory, however firm its reputed basis of fact.

Each Culture has made its own set of images of physical processes, which are true only for itself and only alive while it is itself alive. The "Nature" of Classical man found its highest artistic emblem in the nude statue, and out of it logically there grew up a *static of bodies, a physics of the near.* The Arabian Culture can be symbolized by the arabesque and the cavern-vaulting of the mosque, and out of this world-feeling there issued *Alchemy* with its ideas of mysterious substances like the "philosophical mercury," which is neither a material nor a property but by magic can transmute one metal into another. And the outcome of Faustian man's Nature idea was *a dynamic of unlimited span, a physics of the distant.* To the Classical therefore belong the conceptions of *matter and form,* to the Arabian (quite Spinozistically) the idea of *substances* with visible or secret *attributes,* and to the Faustian the idea of *force and mass.*

As with the formulation of problems and the methods of dealing with them, so also with the basic concepts. They are symbols in each case of one and only the one Culture. The Classical root-words ἄπειρον, ἀρχή, μορφή, ὕλη, are not translatable into our speech. To render ἀρχή by "prime-stuff" is to eliminate its Apollinian connotation, to make the hollow shell of the word sound an alien note. That which Classical man saw before him as "motion" in space, he understood as ἀλλοίωσις, change of position of bodies; we, from the way in which we experience motion, have deduced the concept of a *process*, a "going forward," thereby expressing and emphasizing that element of directional energy which our thought necessarily predicates in the courses of Nature. In Alchemy there is deep scientific doubt as to the plastic actuality of things—of the "somata" of Greek mathematicians, physicists and poets—and it dissolves and destroys the soma in the hope of finding its essence. The conflict concerning the person of Christ which manifested itself in all the early Councils and led to the Nestorian and Monophysite secessions is an *alchemistic* problem. It would never have occurred to a Classical physicist to investigate things while at the same time denying or annihilating their perceivable form. And for that very reason there was no Classical chemistry.

The rise of a chemical method of the Arabian style betokens a new world-consciousness. The discovery of it, which at one blow made an end of Apollinian natural science, of mechanical statics, is linked with the enigmatic name of Hermes Trismegistus, who is supposed to have lived in Alexandria *at the same time as Plotinus and Diophantus*. Similarly it was just at the time of the definite emancipation of the Western mathematic by Newton and Leibniz that the Western chemistry was freed from Arabic form by Stahl (1660–1734) and his Phlogiston theory. Chemistry and mathematic alike became pure analysis. Then Robert Boyle (1626–91) devised the analytical method and *with it the Western conception of the Element*. That is in fact the *end* of genuine chemistry, its dissolution into the comprehensive system of pure dynamic, its assimilation into the mechanical outlook which the Baroque Age had established through Galileo and Newton.

What we call Statics, Chemistry and Dynamics—words that as used in modern science are merely traditional distinctions without deeper meaning—are really the *respective physical systems of the Apollinian, Magian and Faustian souls*, each of which grew up in its own Culture and was limited as to validity to the same. Corresponding to these sciences, each to each, we have the mathematics of Euclidean geometry, Algebra and Higher Analysis, and the arts of statue, arabesque and fugue.

The Atomic Theory

Now, the tendency of human thought (which is always causally disposed) to reduce the image of Nature to the simplest possible quantitative form-units that can be got by causal reasoning, measuring and counting—in a word, by mechanical differentiation—leads necessarily in Classical, Western and every other possible physics, to an atomic theory. Of the Indian and Chinese theories we know hardly more than the fact they once existed, and the Arabian is so complicated that even now it seems to defy presentation. But we do know our own and the Apollinian sciences well enough to observe, here too, a deeply symbolical opposition.

The Classical atoms are *miniature forms,* the Western *minimal quanta,* and quanta, too, of energy. The atoms of Leucippus and Democritus were different in form and magnitude, that is to say, they were purely plastic units, "indivisible," as their name asserts, but only plastically indivisible. The atoms of Western physics, for which "indivisibility" has quite another meaning, resemble the figures and themes of music; their being or essence consisting in vibration and radiation, and their relation to the processes of Nature being that of the "motive" to the "movement." On the one hand—Democritus' multitude of confused atoms, victims, hunted like Oedipus, of blind Chance, which he as well as Sophocles called ἀνάγκη. On the other hand— systems of abstract force-points working in unison, aggressive, energetically dominating space (as "field"), overcoming resistances like Macbeth. According to Leucippus the atoms fly about in the void "of themselves"; Democritus merely regards shock and counter-shock as a form of change of place. Aristotle explains individual movements as accidental; Empedocles speaks of love and hate, Anaxagoras of meetings and partings. All these are elements also of Classical tragedy; the figures on the Attic stage are related to one another just so. Further, and logically, they are the elements of Classical politics.

But the inner relationship between atom-theory and ethic goes further. It has been shown how the Faustian soul—whose being consists in the overcoming of the visible, whose feeling is loneliness and whose yearning is infinity—puts its need of solitude, distance and abstraction into all its actualities, into its public life, its spiritual and its artistic form-worlds alike. This pathos of distance (to use Nietzsche's expression) is peculiarly alien to the Classical, in which everything human demanded nearness, support and community. It is this that distinguishes the spirit of the Baroque from that of the Ionic, the culture of the *ancien régime* from that of Periclean Athens. And this pathos, which distinguishes the heroic doer from the heroic sufferer, appears also in the picture of Western physics as *tension.* It is tension that is missing in the science of Democritus; for in the principle of shock and counter-shock it is denied by implication that there is a force commanding space and identical with space. And, correspondingly, the element of Will is absent from the Classical soulimage. The principle of tension (developed in the potential theory), which is wholly untranslatable into Classical tongues and incommunicable to Classical minds, has become for Western physics fundamental. Its content follows from the notion of energy, *the Will-to-Power in Nature,* and therefore it is for us just as necessary as for the Classical thought it is impossible.

The Problem of Motion

Every atomic theory, therefore, is a myth and not an experience. In it the Culture, through the contemplative-creative power of its great physicists, reveals its inmost essence and very self.

We have already shown the decisive importance of the *depth-experience*, which is identical with the awakening of a soul and therefore with the creation of the outer world belonging to that soul. The mere sense-impression contains only length and breadth, and it is the living and necessary art of interpretation—which, like everything else living, possesses direction, motion and irreversibility (the qualities that our consciousness synthesizes in the word "time")—that *adds* depth and thereby fashions actuality and world. Life itself enters into experience as third dimension. The perfected extension of the Classical consciousness is one of sensuous and bodily presence. The Western consciousness achieves extension, after its own fashion, as transcendental space, and as it thinks its space more and more transcendentally it develops by degrees the abstract polarity of Capacity and Intensity that so completely contrasts with the Classical visual polarity of Matter and Form.

But it follows from this that in the known there can be no reappearance of living time. For this has already passed into the known, into constant "existence," as Depth, and hence duration (i.e. timelessness) and extension are identical. Only knowing possesses the mark of direction. The application of the word "time" to the imaginary and measurable time-dimension of physics is a mistake. The only question is whether it is possible or not to avoid the mistake. If one substitutes the word "Destiny" for "time" in any physical enunciation, one feels at once that pure Nature does not contain Time. The form-world of physics extends just as far as the cognate form-world of number and notion extend, and we have seen that (notwithstanding Kant) there is not and cannot be the slightest relation of any sort between mathematical number and Time. And yet this is controverted *by the fact of motion* in the picture of the world-around. It is the unsolved and unsolvable problem of the Eleatics—being (or thinking) and motion are incompatible; motion "is" not (is only "apparent").

And here, for the second time, Natural science becomes dogmatic and mythological. The words "time" and "Destiny," for anyone who uses them instinctively, touch Life itself in its deepest depths—life as a whole, which is not to be separated from lived-experience. Physics, on the other hand—i.e. the observing Reason—*must* separate them. The livingly-experienced "in-itself," mentally emancipated from the act of the observer and become object, dead, inorganic, rigid, is now "Nature," something open to exhaustive mathematical treatment. In this sense the knowledge of Nature is an activity of *measurement*. All the same, we live even when we are observing and therefore the thing we are observing *lives with us*. The element in the Nature-picture in virtue of which it not merely from moment to moment *is*, but in a continuous flow with and around us *becomes*, is the copula of the waking-consciousness and its world. This element is *called* movement, and it contradicts Nature as a picture, but it represents the *history* of this picture. And therefore, as precisely as Understanding is abstracted (by means of words) from feeling, and mathematical space from light-resistances ("things"), so also physical "time" is abstracted from the impression of motion.

"Physics," says Kirchhoff, "is the complete and simple description of motions." That indeed has always been its object. But the question is not one of motion *in* the picture but of motion *of* the picture. Motion, in the Nature of physics, is nothing else but that *metaphysical* something which gives rise to the consciousness of a succession. The known is timeless and alien to motion; its state of becomeness implies this. It is the *organic sequence* of knowns that gives the impression of a motion. The physicist receives the word as an impression not upon "reason" but upon the whole man, and the function of that man is not "Nature" only but the whole world. And that is the world-as-history. "Nature," then, is an expression of the Culture in each instance. All physics is treatment of the motion-problem—in which the life-problem is implicit—not as though it could one day be solved, *but in spite of, nay because of, the fact that it is insoluble.*

Let the reader conceive of the motion *within* a physical system as the *aging* of that system (as in fact it is, as lived-experience of the observer), and he will feel at once and distinctly the fatefulness immanent in, the unconquerably organic content of, the word "motion" and all its derivative ideas. But Mechanics, having nothing to do with aging, should have nothing to do with motion either, and consequently, since no scientific system is conceivable without a motion-problem in it, a complete and self-contained mechanics is an impossibility. Somewhere or other there is always an organic starting-point in the system where immediate Life enters it—an umbilical cord that connects the mind-child with the life-mother, the thought with the thinker.

This puts the fundamentals of Faustian and Apollinian Nature-science in quite another light. No "Nature" is pure—there is always something of history in it. If man is ahistorical, like the Greek, so that the totality of his impressions of the world is absorbed in a pure point-formed present, his Nature-image is static, self-contained. Time as magnitude figures in Greek physics as little as it does in Aristotle's entelechy-idea. If, on the other hand, Man is historically constituted, the image formed is dynamic.

History is eternal becoming and therefore eternal future; Nature is become and therefore eternally past. And here a strange inversion seems to have taken place—the Becoming has lost its priority over the Become. When the intellect looks back from *its* sphere, the Become, the aspect of life is reversed, the idea of Destiny which carries aim and future in it having turned into the mechanical principle of cause-and-effect of which the centre of gravity lies in the past. The spatially-experienced is promoted to rank above the temporal living, and time is replaced by a length in a spatial world-system. And, since in the creative experience extension follows from direction, the spatial from life, the human understanding imports life *as a process* into the inorganic space of its imagination. While life looks on space as something functionally belonging to itself, intellect looks upon life as something *in* space. To establish scientifically means, starting from the become and actualized, to search for "causes" by going back along a mechanically conceived course, that is to say, by treating becoming as a length. But it is not possible to live backwards, only to think backwards. Not Time and Destiny are reversible, but only that which the physicist calls "time" and admits into his formulae as divisible, and preferably as negative or imaginary quantities.

The perplexity is always there, though it has rarely been seen to be originally and necessarily inherent. In the Classical science the Eleatics, declining to admit the necessity of thinking of Nature as in motion, set up against it the logical view that thinking is a being, with the corollary that known and extended are identical and knowledge and becoming therefore irreconcilable. Their criticisms have not been, and cannot be, refuted. But they did not hinder the evolution of Classical physics, which was a necessary expression of the Apollinian soul and as such superior to logical difficulties. In the "classical" mechanics so-called of the Baroque, founded by Galileo and Newton, an irreproachable solution of the motion-problem on dynamic lines has been sought again and again. The last serious attempt—which failed like the rest, and of necessity—was Hertz's. Hertz tried to eliminate the notion of force entirely—rightly feeling that error in all mechanical systems has to be looked for in one or another of the basic concepts—and to build up the whole picture of physics on the quantities of time, space and mass. But he did not observe that it is Time itself (which as direction-factor is present in the force-concept) that is the organic element without which a dynamic theory cannot be expressed and with which a clean solution cannot be got. Moreover, quite apart from this, the concepts force, mass and motion constitute a dogmatic unit. They so condition one another that the application of one of them tacitly involves both the others from the outset. The notion of mass is only the complement of that of force. Newton, a deeply religious nature, was only bringing the Faustian world-feeling to expression when, to elucidate the words "force" and "motion," he said that masses are points of attack for force and carriers for motion. So the thirteenth-century Mystics had conceived of God and his relation to world. *Force is to the mechanical Nature-picture of Western man what Will is to his soul-picture and infinite Godhead in his world-picture.* The primary ideas of this physics stood firm long before the first physicist was born, for they lay in the earliest religious world-consciousness of our Culture.

The Interpretation of "Experience"

Nature-laws are forms of the known in which an aggregate of individual cases are brought together as a unit of higher degree. Living Time is ignored—that is, it does not matter whether, when or how often the case arises, for the question is not of chronological sequence but of mathematical consequence. But in the consciousness that no power in the world can shake this calculation lies our will to command over Nature. That is Faustian. It is only from this standpoint that miracles appear as breaches of the laws of Nature. Magian man saw in them merely the exercise of a power that was not common to all, not in any way a contradiction of the laws of Nature. And Classical man, according to Protagoras, was only the measure and not the creator of things—a view that unconsciously forgoes all conquest of Nature through the discovery and application of laws.

We see, then, that the causality-principle, in the form in which it is self-evidently necessary for us—the agreed basis of truth for our mathematics, physics and philosophy—is a Western and, more strictly speaking, a Baroque phenomenon. It cannot be proved, for every proof set forth in a Western language and every experiment conducted by a Western mind presupposes itself. In every problem, the enunciation contains the proof in germ. The method of a science is the science itself. Beyond question, the notion of laws of Nature and the conception of physics as "*scientia experimentalis*," which has held ever since Roger Bacon, contain *a priori* this specific kind of necessity. The Classical mode of regarding Nature—the alter ego of the Classical mode of being—on the contrary, does *not* contain it, and yet it does not appear that the scientific position is weakened in logic thereby. If we work carefully through the utterances of Democritus, Anaxagoras, and Aristotle (in whom is contained the whole sum of Classical Nature-speculation), and, above all, if we examine the connotations of key-terms like ἀλλοίωσις, ἀνάγκη, ἐντελέχεια, we look with astonishment into a world-image totally unlike our own. This world-image is self-sufficing and therefore, for this definite sort of mankind, unconditionally true. And causality in our sense plays no part therein.

The principle of the Conservation of Energy, which since its enunciation by J. R. Mayer has been regarded in all seriousness as a plain conceptual necessity, is in fact a redescription of the *dynamic* principle of causality by means of the physical concept of force. The appeal to "experience," and the controversy as to whether judgment is necessary or empirical—i.e., in the language of Kant (who greatly deceived himself about the highly fluid boundaries between the two), whether it is *a priori* or *a posteriori* certain—are characteristically Western. But no one has noticed that a whole world-view is implicit in such a concept of "experience" with its aggressive dynamic connotation, and that there is not and cannot be "experience" in this pregnant sense for men of other Cultures. When we decline to recognize the scientific results of Anaxagoras or Democritus as experiential results, it does not mean that these Classical thinkers were incapable of interpreting and merely threw off fancies, but that we miss in their generalizations that causal element which for us *constitutes* experience in our sense of the word. Experience means to us an *activity* of the intellect, which does not resignedly confine itself to receiving, acknowledging and arranging momentary and purely present impressions, but seeks them out and calls them up in order to overcome them in their sensuous presence and to bring them into an unbounded unity in which their sensuous discreteness is dissolved. Experience in our sense possesses the tendency *from particular to infinite*. And for that very reason it is in contradiction with the feeling of Classical science. What for us is the way to acquire experience is for the Greek the way to lose it. And therefore he kept away from the drastic method of experiment. Our exact Natural science is imperative, the Classical is θεωρία in the literal sense, the result of passive contemplativeness.

The "God-Feeling" and Nature

We can now say without any hesitation that the form-world of a Natural science corresponds to those of the appropriate mathematic, the appropriate religion, the appropriate art. A deep mathematician—by which is meant not a master-computer, but a man, any man, who feels the spirit of numbers living within him—realizes that through it he "knows God." Pythagoras and Plato were as well aware of this as Pascal and Leibniz.

The word "God" has a different sound under the vaulting of Gothic cathedrals or in the cloisters of Maulbronn and St. Gallen and in the basilicas of Syria and the temples of Republican Rome. The character of the Faustian cathedral is that of the *forest*. It is the architectural actualizing of a world-feeling that had found the first of all its symbols in the high forest of the Northern plains, the deciduous forest with its mysterious tracery, its whispering of ever-restless foliage high over the watcher's head, its treetops struggling to escape from earth. Think of Romanesque ornamentation and its deep affinity to the sense of the woods.

Cypresses and pines, with their corporeal and Euclidean effect, could never have become symbols of unending space. But the oaks, beeches and limes with the fitful light-flecks playing in their shadow-filled volume are felt as bodiless, boundless, spiritual. The rustle of the woods, a charm that no Classical poet ever felt—for it lies beyond the possibilities of Apollinian Nature-feeling—stands with its secret questions "whence?" "whither?" its merging of presence into eternity, in a deep relation with Destiny, with the feeling of History and Duration, with the quality of Direction that impels the anxious, Faustian soul towards infinitely distant Future. And for that reason the organ, which roars deep and high through our churches in tones that, compared with the plain solid notes of aulos and cithara, seem to know neither limit nor restraint, is the instrument of instruments in Western devotions. Cathedral and organ form a symbolic unity like temple and statue. Orchestra-tone strove tirelessly in the eighteenth century towards a nearer kinship with the organ-tone. The word *schwebend*—meaningless as applied to Classical things—is important alike in the theory of music, in oil-painting, in architecture and in the dynamic physics of the Baroque. Stand in a high wood of mighty stems while the storm is tearing above, and you will comprehend instantly the full meaning of the concept of a force which moves mass.

Out of such a primary feeling there arises, then, an idea of the Divine immanent in the world-around, and this idea becomes steadily more definite. The percipient receives the impression of motion in Nature. He feels about him an almost indescribable *alien life* of unknown powers, and traces the origin of these effects to "numina," to the Other, inasmuch as this Other also possesses Life. Astonishment at *alien motion* is the source of religion and of physics both; respectively, they are the elucidations of Nature (world-around) by the soul and by the reason. The "powers" are the first object both of fearful or loving reverence and of critical investigation. There is a religious experience *and* a scientific experience.

Now it is important to observe how the consciousness of each Culture intellectually condenses its primary "numina." It imposes significant words—*names*—on them and thereby conjures (seizes or bounds) them. By virtue of the Name they are subject to the intellectual power of the man who possesses the Name. The pronouncement of the right name (in physics, the right concept) is an incantation. Deities and basic notions of science alike come into being first as invocable names, representing an idea that tends to become more and more sensuously definite. The outcome of a *Numen* is a *Deus*, the outcome of a notion is an idea. In the mere naming of "thing-in-itself," "atom," "energy," "gravitation," "cause," "evolution" and the like is for most learned men the same sense of deliverance as there was for the peasant of Latium in the words "Ceres," "Consus," "Janus," "Vesta."[1]

Note

1 And it may be asserted that the downright faith that Haeckel, for example, pins to the names atom, matter, energy, is not essentially different from the fetishism of Neanderthal Man.

62

Franz Rosenzweig

Understanding the Sick and Healthy (1921)

The Attack of Paralysis

COMMON SENSE IS IN DISREPUTE WITH PHILOSOPHERS. Its usefulness is restricted to the buying of butter, the courtship of a lady, or it may even be of help in determining the guilt of a man accused of stealing. However, to decide what butter and woman and crime "essentially" [*eigentlich*] are, is beyond its scope.

This is where the philosopher must enter and assume "the burden of proof." Such problems are beyond the reach of common sense. These are the "highest" problems, the "ultimate" questions. To be misunderstood by common sense is the privilege, even the duty of philosophy. What need would there be for philosophy if common sense could answer these questions by itself? Is common sense even capable of asking the questions? Where common sense proceeds in reckless haste, philosophy pauses and wonders. And were it merely a question of this gift, alone, this capacity to wonder, philosophy's rightful claim to superiority could not be disputed. For common sense, as it is said, is not addicted to the ways of wonder.

But, be this as it may, how does our philosopher know of wonder? In any case, where does he obtain the word? Does not the non-philosophizing half of mankind also wonder? The wonder of a child? The wonder of the savage? Does not wonder overcome them a hundred times—even oftener than the philosopher? True, the continuity of life blunts the edge of marvelling. Wonder is finally enveloped in the stream of time. It vanishes as naturally as it appeared.

The child wonders at the mature man. The quest, however, which is at the core of his wonder, is painlessly fulfilled when the child grows into a mature man.

Woman is aroused by man and man submits to woman. But ever as they marvel at each other the solution and dissolution of their wonder is at hand—the love which has befallen them. They are no longer a wonder to each other; they are in the very heart of wonder.

Life becomes numb in the face of death—and dies. The wonder is unraveled. And it was life itself that brought the solution.

Thus man wonders. Undoubtedly he pauses—to wonder requires that man pause. He pauses but he cannot remain still. He is adrift on the river Life, borne on, wonderment and all. He merely drifts and goes on living, and then, at last, the numbness caused by his wonder passes. But drifting, alas, does not become the wondering philosopher.

The philosopher cannot wait. His kind of wonder does not differ from the wonder of others. However, he is unwilling to accept the process of life and the passing of the numbness wonder has brought. Such relief comes too slowly. He insists on a solution immediately—at the very instant of his being overcome—and at the very place wonder struck him. He stands quiet, motionless. He separates his experience of wonder from the continuous stream of life, isolating it.

This is the way his thought proceeds. He does not permit his wonder, stored as it is, to be released into the flow of life. He steps outside the continuity of life and consequently the continuity of thought is broken. And there he begins stubbornly to reflect. Of necessity, he must hook the "problem" from where he stands. He has forcibly extracted thought's "object" and "subject" from the flow of life and he entrenches himself within them. Wonder stagnates, is perpetuated in the motionless mirror of his meditation: that is in the subject. He has it well-hooked; it is securely fastened, and it persists in his benumbed immobility. The stream of life has been replaced by something submissive—statuesque, subjugated.

Entrenched within the subject, the philosopher asks: what then actually *is?* He welcomes any answer which does not destroy the value and meaning of this single question. Remove this immovable question and the lifeless subject, artificially detached, must inevitably disappear.

His question is: what actually *is?* It is a stubborn question and now it takes vengeance on him. To refuse stubbornly to wait with patience is to surrender life. He receives as his reward one unfailing answer, always the same. Asking, as he does, outside the full expanse of life, not waiting for a leisurely answer, he must ask his questions there and then—and there and then the answers are given.

They cannot come in their own time, and therefore they are lacking in extension and completeness. Driven to subterranean regions, the answers rise from beneath the surface of the subject—that is, from its sub-stance. The true concern of the philosopher is with the "essence," the "essential" being of his subjects. He does not have to wait for an answer to his question. Answers wait for him in eager readiness, as independent of time and its processes as is the subject, which also has been detached from the stream of life by means of an artificial fixative: the timeless artificiality of the question "what actually *is.*" The question receives its answer: "the essence." This answer may not sound unnatural, and indeed it is the only possible answer, once the unnatural question is asked.

Necessarily there can be only one *substantial* mark setting apart the multiplicity of things. What else is there in *reality* to make us realize that this act is our act? Precisely the experience of such an act as a consequence of our past life and an anticipation of the future as its outcome! A thing receives a character of its own only within the flow of life. The question, "what is this actually?", detached from time, deprived of it, quickly passes through the intermediary stage of the general term and comes into the pale region of the mere "thing." Thus emerges the concept of the one and only substance, the "essential" nature of things. The singleness and particularity [*Eigenheit*] of the subject detached from time is transformed into a statement of its particular essence [*Eigentlichkeit des Wesens*].

"Essential" [*eigentlich*]—no one but a philosopher asks this question or gives this answer. In life the question is invalid; it is never asked. Indeed, even the philosopher, when the situation becomes serious, refrains from asking it. He is scarcely interested in knowing what half a pound of butter costs "essentially." He does not court his beloved in proper terms of essence. He would neither deny nor affirm that the defendant stole, or did not steal, "essentially." The terms of life are not "essential" but "real"; they concern not "essence" but "fact." In spite of this, the philosopher's word remains, "essential." By giving in to wonder, by halting in his tracks and neglecting the operations of reality, he forces himself into retreat and is restricted to facing essence.

It is exactly at this point—not later—that the philosopher parts company with ordinary common sense. Common sense puts its faith in the strength of reality. The philosopher, suspicious, retreats from the flow of reality into the protected circle of his wonder; slowly he submerges to the depths, to the region of the essences. Nothing can disturb him there. He is safe. Why should he concern himself with the crowd of "non-essences." And reality, is, so to speak, "unessential." Bounded by his magic circle of mounting wonder, he is not interested in the actual event [*Ereignis*]. Should the actual event find entrance to the magic circle, it may be marvelled at—so much is allowed. However, it definitely may not destroy the immobility caused by wonder, nor let loose the damned-up tide. It may not stir up the storm of life—existing as yet only in strings of essences—and permit it to sweep through the sturdy forests of reality.

If this were merely some philosopher's personal concern, we would not object; there are so few philosophers, even taking into account the assorted breeds. But as it happens, any man can trip over himself and find himself following the trail of philosophy. No man is so healthy as to be immune from an attack of this disease. And the very moment a man succumbs, the instant he believes that philosophizing is necessary, he gives up common sense, and the ardor of his quest in search of essence cannot be surpassed. Then the wisest man is no match for him; with ease he outdoes professional philosophers. No one has less faith in himself than he. Common sense is crippled by a stroke. We shall view it in this state of utter paralysis.

Therapy

WHAT COURSE OF ACTION MUST BE CHOSEN? Let us be warned by the bad example of indifferent physicians who believe that for a sickness, once it is recognized, there is but one possible therapy, effective under all circumstances. Such caution is particularly necessary if we are unable to localize the illness, and are convinced that the entire person, the complete individual, is affected. We must not insist on praising one particular treatment as a complete panacea when we have to deal with the affliction of a human being in his entirety. On the contrary, we are committed to considering a series of possible treatments, even though we run the risk that most of these treatments will prove unavailable to us.

As we have observed, our patient suffers from a radical inversion of his normal functions. It may be necessary to reverse the inversion, that is, turn matters upside-down. However, such a reversal, made arbitrarily, can prove dangerous. Man has a deep-rooted distaste for such "treatment." Common sense has already been inverted and become sick reason. Can a return to healthy common sense be forced?

Will such a forced return succeed? Experience answers in the affirmative. As it happens, all the phantoms of sick reason may be dissipated by a single event. A sudden fright, an unexpected happiness, a blow of fate beyond the ordinary can dispel at once all the delusions of the misdirected reason. Names take on again their original lustre—e.g., in August 1914 the word "fatherland" and all the theories of "essence" dissolved into nothing.

Of course, such a cure cannot be applied at will. To be effective, it must be part of living experience. Such a *tour de force* has another disadvantage; it does not heal permanently. Once the shock wears off, the man tends to return to what he considers his permanent condition. This "permanent" condition will most probably not be a normal state. We have every reason to believe that his constitution had deviated from normality, and was forced back only by the sudden shock. To make such a shock-cure last, milder and more enduring forces are necessary.

The appearance of such forces can well be expected. The sickness of reason is such an unusual condition, that it may be cured, at last, by the power of life itself. This is the well-known influence which "life" exerts on "ideals" and nothing is more feared by the sick reason than this influence. Everyday life, it is clear, cannot possibly be ignored; one cannot exist entirely in the sublime realm of theory, no matter how "essential" it may seem when compared to dull, tedious reality. The concerns of the world intrude. They bring with them the natural structure of life, the force of facts and experience, the impact of everyday existence with its interminable small tasks and its stable, enduring names. The revolutionary passion against names, permanent, traditional names, dies; the quest for a meaning, hidden behind events, ends; events come and go and no attempt is made to discover a meaning in them other than that revealed by the names by which they are called.

Is this, then, all there is to it? If so, then the return to common sense is identical with a return to philistinism—the natural concomitant of advancing age. However, something quite different happens. Common sense does return, it is true, but it remains unaware, as it were, of its return. It makes an effort to ignore this fact. Philistinism suffers from a sense of guilt. It knows exactly what it is—it knows it is habit and routine; however, it would prefer to be different. It is influenced in its self-evaluation by standards it rejects in practice but acknowledges in theory. Therefore, philistinism, although it is sane enough, finds itself in a worse situation than that which it has outgrown. The diseased life of the sick reason was lived in good faith; sick reason acted in accordance with its beliefs, that is, it believed nothing and did nothing. Philistinism, however, exists in health but is diseased in thought—to the extent that it thinks at all. It lives within time, for the day and its concerns, and believes in eternity, which is the name-less, transcendent nothing. It would be healthy if belief and action coincided. However, such is rarely the case. In the final analysis, a self-cure by means of time produces not true health but its travesty. What is generally produced by such a cure, is the philistine, and he can scarcely be considered a perfect specimen of health—rather the contrary.

An enticing therapeutical possibility presents itself at this point. The thought of the philistine is diseased, but his actions are healthy. Suppose we were to perform a major operation upon his thought, is it not possible that this might produce proper thinking? But unfortunately, surgery of this sort is of no help to us. Our enemy is not idealism as such; anti-idealism, irrationalism, realism, materialism, naturalism, and what not, are equally harmful. The real cause of the illness is not that reason assumes that "spirit" is the essence of reality; it is its assumption that it is possible for something to exist beyond reality. Reality, matter, nature, are all terms denoting "essence" and are just as unacceptable as "spirit" or "idea." All claim to "be" either reality itself or the "essence" of reality. All abstract from life. All neglect the fact of names. Consequently all these *isms* fail to conciliate thought and action, which is, after all, the one thing desired. They fail precisely because they are *isms*, whether "idealisms" or "realisms."

There is still another possibility, which, however, we must refrain from advocating too insistently, since it promises only a limited and conditional success. And furthermore, it cannot be denied that shock and time cures, treatments that do not require our active interference, may prove effective, although they are frequently, for the reasons mentioned, inoperative. Consequently this final treatment should be considered only as an additional possibility. It is particularly helpful if the patient has already begun his convalescence in time and experience.

One of the most powerful reasons why common sense becomes unbalanced and loses its self-confidence, is its alleged inability to answer the so-called "ultimate questions" concerning God, man, and the world. The syndrome we have been studying begins when the individual is struck dumb with wonder. Always it turns out that the wonderer was stricken just as he caught a glimpse, through rising clouds, of gigantic mountain peaks. The road of life winds among three mountain ranges, and, as is to be expected, they may be seen from many a bend in the road. That wanderer is lost who feels compelled to pause at such a point. The stopovers we viewed in the previous chapter were of this kind; they were a marvelling at distant vistas. Confidence in words, in the name of the beloved, in the designation of butter, in the legal appellation of a crime, were lost. To the faltering observer, unable to regard such matters as constitutive aspects of worldly existence, human destiny, or divine activity, the meaning of such terms has become uncertain.

Our task is to strengthen the reason, build up its weakened resistance at these three points. Since it has already become ill, it is necessary to relieve reason of its professional activities, as it were, and prescribe the isolation of a sanatorium. There we will attempt gradually to accustom it to these primary vistas [*Urgesichte*]. We are perfectly aware that such a treatment can have only limited success, and is feasible only to the degree that such encounters can be artificially arranged. The sole task of the physician is to help the patient get on his feet again after such encounters; it may even be limited to encouraging the patient not to stop. We are aware of our limitations and of the limitations of medicine in general. After a careful reading of the following chapter, the discriminating reader will be in a position to confirm our statement.

63

George Santayana

Skepticism and Animal Faith (1923)

Some Authorities for this Conclusion

THE ULTIMATE POSITION OF THE SCEPTIC, THAT NOTHING GIVEN EXISTS, may be fortified by the authority of many renowned philosophers who are accounted orthodox; and it will be worth while to stop for a moment to invoke their support, since the scepticism I am defending is not meant to be merely provisional; its just conclusions will remain fixed, to remind me perpetually that all alleged knowledge of matters of fact is faith only, and that an existing world, whatever form it may choose to wear, is intrinsically a questionable and arbitrary thing. It is true that many who have defended this view, in the form that all appearance is illusion, have done so in order to insist all the more stoutly on the existence of something occult which they call reality; but as the existence of this reality is far easier to doubt than the existence of the obvious, I may here disregard that compensatory dogma. I shall soon introduce compensatory dogmas of my own, more credible, I think, than theirs; and I shall attribute existence to a flux of natural events which can never be data of intuition, but only objects of a belief which men and animals, caught in that flux themselves, hazard instinctively. Although a sceptic may doubt all existence, none being involved in any indubitable datum, yet I think good human reasons, apart from irresistible impulse, can be found for positing existing intuitions to which data appear, no less than other existing events and things, which the intuited data report or describe. For the moment, however, I am concerned to justify further the contention of the sceptic that, if we refuse to bow to the yoke of animal faith, we can find in pure intuition no evidence of any existence whatsoever.

There is notably one tenet, namely, that all change is illusion, proper to many deep-voiced philosophers, which of itself suffices to abolish all existence, in the sense which I give to this word. Instead of change they probably posit changeless substance or pure Being; but if substance were not subject to change, at least in its distribution, it would not be the substance of anything found in the world or happening in the mind; it would, therefore, have no more lodgement in existence than has pure Being, which is evidently only a logical term. Pure Being, as far as it goes, is no doubt a true description of everything, whether existent or non-existent; so that if anything exists, pure Being will exist in it; but it will exist merely as pure colour does in all colours, or pure space in all spaces, and not separately nor exclusively. These philosophers, in denying change, accordingly deny all existence. But though many of them have prized this doctrine, few have lived up to it, or rather none have; so that I may pass over the fact that in denying change they have inadvertently denied existence, even to substance and pure Being, because they have inadvertently retained both existence and change. The reality they attributed with so much unction and conviction to the absolute was not that proper to this idea—one of the least impressive which it is possible to contemplate—but was obviously due to the strain of existence and movement within themselves, and to the vast rumble, which hypnotised them, of universal mutation.

It is the Indians who have insisted most sincerely and intrepidly on the non-existence of everything given, even adjusting their moral regimen to this insight. Life is a dream, they say: and all experienced events are illusions. In dreaming of nature and of ourselves we are deceived, even in imagining that we exist and are deceived and dreaming. Some aver, indeed, that there is a universal dreamer, Brahma, slumbering and breathing deeply in all of us, who is the reality of our dreams, and the negation of them. But as Brahma is emphatically not qualified by any of the forms of illusory existence, but annuls them all, there is no need, for my purpose, of distinguishing him from the reported state of redeemed souls (where many souls are admitted) nor from the Nirvana into which lives flow when they happily cease, becoming at last aware, as it were, that neither they nor anything else has ever existed.

It would be rash, across the chasm of language and tradition that separates me from the Indians, to accuse their formidable systems of self-contradiction. Truth and reality are words which, in the mouths of prophets, have often a eulogistic rather than a scientific force; and if it is *better* to elude the importunities of existence and to find a sanctuary of intense safety and repose in the notion of pure Being, there may be a dramatic propriety in saying that the view of the saved, from which all memory of the path to salvation is excluded, is the true view, and their condition the only reality; so that they are right in thinking that they have never existed, and we wrong in thinking that we now exist.

Here is an egotism of the redeemed with which, as with other egotisms, I confess I have little sympathy. The blessed, in giving out that I do not exist in my sins, because they cannot distinguish me, appear to me to be deceived. The intrinsic blessedness of their condition cannot turn into a truth this small oversight on their part, however excusable. I suspect, or I like to imagine, that what the Indians mean is rather that the principle of my existence, and of my persuasion that I exist, is an *evil* principle. It is sin, guilt, passion, and mad will, the natural and universal source of illusion—very much what I am here calling animal faith; and since this assertiveness in me (according to the Indians) is wrong morally, and since its influence alone leads me to posit existence in myself or in anything else, if I were healed morally I should cease to assert existence; and I should, in fact, have ceased to exist.

Now in this doctrine, so stated, lies a great confirmation of my thesis that nothing given exists; because it is only a dark principle, transcendental in respect to the datum (that is, on the hither side of the footlights) that calls up this datum at all, or leads me to posit its existence. It is this sorry self of mine sitting here in the dark, one in this serried pack of open-mouthed fools, hungry for illusion, that is responsible for the spectacle; for if a foolish instinct had not brought me to the playhouse, and if avid eyes and an idealising understanding had not watched the performance, no part of it would have abused me: and if no one came to the theatre, the actors would soon flit away like ghosts, the poets would starve, the scenery would topple over and become rubbish, and the very walls would disappear. Every part of experience, as it comes, is illusion; and the source of this illusion is my animal nature, blindly labouring in a blind world.

Such is the ancient lesson of experience itself, when we reflect upon experience and turn its illusions into instruction: a lesson which a bird-witted empiricism can never learn, though it is daily repeated. But the Indian with a rare sensitiveness joined a rare recollection. He *lived*: a religious love, a childish absorption in appearances as they come (which busy empiricists do not share), led him to remember them truly, in all their beauty, and therefore to perceive that they were illusions. The poet, the disinterested philosopher, the lover of things distilled into purity, frees himself from belief. This infinite chaos of cruel and lovely forms, he cries, is all deceptive, all unsubstantial, substituted at will for nothing, and soon found to sink into nothing again, and to be nothing in truth.

I will disregard the vehemence with which these saintly scholastics denounce the world and the sinful nature that attaches me to it. I like the theatre, not because I cannot perceive that the play is a fiction, but because I do perceive it; if I thought the thing a fact, I should detest it: anxiety would rob me of all my imaginative pleasure. Even as it is, I often wish the spectacle were less barbarous; but I am not angry because each scene does not last for ever, and is likely to be followed by a thousand others which I shall not witness. Such is the nature of endless comedy, and of experience. But I wish to retain the valuable testimony of the Indians to the non-existence of the obvious. This testimony is the more valuable because the spectacle present to their eyes was tropical; harder, therefore, to master and to smile at than are the political and romantic medleys which fill the mind of Europe. Yet amidst the serpents and hyænas, the monkeys and parrots of their mental jungle, those sages could sit unmoved, too holily incredulous for fear. How infinite, how helpless, how deserving of forgiveness creative error becomes to the eye of understanding, that loves only in pity, and has no concupiscence for what it loves! How like unhappy animals western philosophers seem in comparison, with their fact-worship, their thrift, their moral intolerance, their imaginative poverty, their political zeal, and their subservience to intellectual fashion!

It makes no difference for my purposes if the cosmology of the Indians was fanciful. It could hardly be more extraordinary than the constitution of the material world is in fact, nor more decidedly out of scale with human data; truth and fancy in this matter equally convict the human senses of illusion. Nor am I out of sympathy with their hope of escaping from the universal hurly-burly into some haven of peace. A philosopher has a haven in himself, of which I suspect the fabled bliss to follow in other lives, or after total emancipation from living, is only a poetic symbol: he has pleasure in truth, and an equal readiness to enjoy the scene or to quit it. Liberation is never complete while life lasts, and is nothing afterwards; but it flows in a measure from this very conviction that all experience is illusion, when this conviction is morally effective, as it was with the Indians. Their belief in transmigration or in Karma is superfluous in this regard, since a later experience could only change the illusion without perfecting the liberation. Yet the mention of some ulterior refuge or substance is indispensable to the doctrine of illusion, and though it may be expressed mythically must be taken to heart too. It points to other realms of being—such as those which I call the realms of matter, truth, and spirit—which by nature cannot be data of intuition but must be posited (if recognised by man at all) by an instinctive faith expressed in action. Whether these ulterior realms exist or not is their own affair: existence may be proper to some, like matter or spirit, and not to others, like truth. But as to the data of intuition, their non-existent and illusory character is implied in the fact that they are given. A datum is by definition a theme of attention, a term in passing thought, a visioned universal. The realm in which it lies, and in which flying intuition discloses it for a moment, is the very realm of non-existence, of inert or ideal being. The Indians, in asserting the non-existence of every term in possible experience, not only free the spirit from idolatry, but free the realm of spirit (which is that of intuition) from limitation; because if nothing that appears exists, anything may appear without the labour and expense of existing; and fancy is invited to range innocently—fancies not murdering other fancies as an existence must murder other existences. While life lasts, the field is thus cleared for innocent poetry and infinite hypothesis, without suffering the judgement to be deceived nor the heart enslaved.

European philosophers, even when called idealists, have seldom reconciled themselves to regarding experience as a creature of fancy. Instead of looking beneath illusion for some principle that might call it forth or perhaps dispel it, as they would if endeavouring to interpret a dream, they have treated it as dreams are treated by the superstitious; that is, they have supposed that the images they saw were themselves substances, or powers, or at least imperfect visions of originals resembling them. In other words, they have been empiricists, regarding appearances as constituents of substance. There have been exceptions, but some of them only prove the rule. Parmenides and Democritus certainly did not admit that the data of sense or imagination existed otherwise than as illusions or conventional signs: but their whole interest, for this reason, skipped over them, and settled heavily on "Being," or on the atoms and the void, which they severally supposed underlay appearance. Appearance itself thereby acquired a certain vicarious solidity, since it was thought to be the garment of substance; somehow within the visionary datum, or beneath it, the most unobjectionable substance was always to be found. Parmenides could not have admitted, and Democritus had not discovered, that the sole basis of appearances was some event in the brain, in no way resembling them; and that the relation of data to the external events they indicated was that of a spontaneous symbol, like an exclamatory word, and not that of a copy or emanation. The simple ancients supposed (as some of my contemporaries do also) that perception stripped material things of their surface properties, or was actually these surface properties peeled off and lodged in the observer's head. Accordingly the denial of existence to sensibles and to intelligibles was never hearty until substance was denied also, and nothing existent was any longer supposed to lurk within these appearances or behind them.

All modern idealists have perceived that an actual appearance cannot be a part of a substance that does not appear; the given image has only the given relations; if I assign other relations to it (which I do if I attribute existence to it) I substitute for the pure datum one of two other things: either a substance possessing the same form as that datum, but created and dissolved in its own medium, at its own periods, apart from all observation; or else, a perception of my own, a moment in my experience, carrying the vision of such an image. The former choice simply puts me back at the beginning of physics, when a merely pictorial knowledge of the material world existed, and nothing of its true mechanism and history had been discovered. The latter choice posits human discourse, or as these philosophers call it, experience: and it is certain that the status of a datum in discourse or experience is that of a mere appearance, fluctuating, intermittent, never twice the same, and dependent for its specious actuality on the movement of attention and the shuffling of confused images in the fancy. In other words, what exists—that is, what is carried on through the flux and has changing and external relations—is a *life*, discourse itself, the voluminous adventures of the mind in its wholeness. This is also what novelists and literary psychologists endeavour to record or to imagine; and the particular data, hardly distinguishable by the aid of a word clapped on to them, are only salient sparks or abstract points of reference for an observer intent on ulterior events. It is ulterior events, the whole of human experience and history as conventionally reported, that is the object of belief in this school, and the true existence.

Ostensibly empiricists seek to reduce this unmanageable object to particular data, and to attribute existence to each scintilla taken separately; but in reality all the relations of these intuitions (which are not relations between the data), their temporal order, subordination to habit and passion, associations, meaning, and embosoming intelligence, are interpolated as if they were matters of course; and indeed they are, because these are the tides of animal life on which the datum sparkles for a moment. Empiricists are interested in practice, and wish to work with as light an intellectual equipment as possible; they therefore attribute existence to "ideas"—meaning intuitions but professing to mean data. If they were interested in these data for their own sake, they would perceive that they are only symbols, like words, used to mark or express the crises in their practical career; and becoming fervid materialists again in their beliefs, as they have always been in their allegiances, they might soon go so far as to deny that there is intuition of data at all: which is a radical way of denying their existence. Discourse and experience would thus drop out of sight altogether, and instead of data of intuition there would be only the pictorial elements of physics—the other possible form in which anything given may be asserted to exist.

If anything, therefore, exists at all when an appearance arises, this existence is not the unit that appears, but either a material fact presenting such an appearance, though constituted by many other relations, or else an actual intuition evoking, creating, or dreaming that non-existent unit. Idealists, if they are thorough, will deny both; for neither a material thing nor an actual intuition has its being in being perceived: both, by definition, exist on their own account, by virtue of their internal energy and natural relations. Therefore either existence apart from givenness is admitted, inconsistently with idealism, or existence is denied altogether. It is allowed, and in fact urged, by all complete idealists that appearance, far from involving the existence of what appears, positively excludes it. *Esse est percipi* was a maxim recalled by an intelligible literary impulse, as Faust said, *Gefühl ist Alles!* Yet that maxim was uttered without reflection, because what those who uttered it really meant was the exact opposite, namely, that only spirits, or perhaps one spirit, existed, which were beings perfectly imperceptible. It was the beautiful and profound part of such a sentiment that whatever is pictorial is nonexistent. Data could be only forms assumed by animal sensibility, like the camel and the weasel seen by Hamlet in a cloud; as these curious creatures could have no zoological existence in that nebula, so the units of human apperception have no existence anywhere.

When idealists say, therefore, that ideas are the only objects of human knowledge and that they exist only in the mind, their language is incoherent, because knowledge of ideas is not knowledge, and presence to intuition is not existence. But this incoherence enables two different philosophies to use the same formula, to the extreme confusion both of doctrine and feeling. One philosophy under the name idea conceives of a fact or phenomenon, a phase in the flux of fortune or experience, existing at a given moment, and known at other moments to have existed there: in other words, its ideas are recollected events in nature, the subject-matter of psychology and physics. This philosophy, when carried out, becomes materialism; its psychology turns into a record of behaviour and its phenomenalistic view of nature into a mathematical calculus of invisible processes. The other philosophy (which alone concerns me here) under the name idea understands the terms of sensation and thought, and their pictorial or rhetorical synthesis. Since these themes of intuition are called upon to absorb all reality, and no belief is accepted as more than a fresh datum in thought, this philosophy denies the transcendence of knowledge and the existence of anything.

Although the temper of absolute idealists is often far from sceptical, their method is scepticism itself: as appears not only in their criticism of all dogma, but in the reasons they give for their own views. What are these reasons? That the criticism of knowledge proves that actual thinking is the only reality; that the objects of knowledge can live, move, and have their being only within it; that existence is something merely imputed; and that truth is coherence among views having themselves no objects. A fact, these critics say, is a concept. This statement might seem absurd, since a concept means at most the idea or supposition of a fact; but if the statement is taken sympathetically, for what the malicious criticism of knowledge means by it, it amounts to this: that there are no facts, but that what we call facts, and believe to be such, are really only conventional fictions, imaginations of what facts would be if facts were possible at all. That facts are ideals, impossible to realise, is clear on transcendental principles, since a fact would be an event or existence which knowledge would have to approach and lay siege to somehow from the outside, so that for knowledge (the only reality on this system) they would always remain phantoms, creatures of a superstitious instinct, terms for ever posited but never possessed, and therefore perpetually unreal. If fact or truth had any separate being it could not be an integral part of knowledge; what modicum of reality facts or truths can possess they must borrow from knowledge, in which they perforce remain ideals only; so that it is only as unreal that they are real at all. Transcendentalists are sure that knowledge is everything, not because they presume that everything is known, but precisely because they see that there is nothing to know. If anything existed actually, or if there was any independent truth, it would be unknowable, as these voracious thinkers conceive knowledge. The glorious thing about knowledge, in their eyes, is that, as there is nothing to know, knowledge is a free and a sure creation, new and self-grounded for ever.

Transcendentalism, when it is thorough, accordingly agrees with the Indian systems in maintaining that the illusion that given objects exist has itself no existence. Any actual sensation, any instance of thinking, would be a self-existing fact; but facts are only concepts, that is, inert terms in absolute thought: if illusions occurred actually, they would not be concepts but events, and though their visionary objects might be non-existent, the vision of them would exist; and they would be the sort of independent facts which transcendental logic excludes as impossible. Acts of judging or positing or imagining cannot be admitted on this system until they in their turn have been posited in another judgement; that is, until they cease to hide their heads in the obscurity of self-existence, and become purely ideal themes of actual intuition. When they have thus become phenomenal, intent and judgement may posit them and depute them to exist; but the belief that they exist otherwise than as present postulates is always false. Imputed existence is the only existence possible, but must always be imputed falsely. For example, the much-talked-of opinions of ancient philosophers, if they had existed at all, would have had to exist before they became objects of intuition to the historian, or to the reader of history, who judges them to have existed; but such self-existence is repugnant to transcendental logic: it is a ghost cut off from knowledge and from the breath of life in me here and now. Therefore the opinions of philosophers exist only in history, history exists only in the historian, and the historian only in the reader; and the reader himself exists only for his self-consciousness, which is not really his own, but absolute consciousness thinking about him or about all things from his point of view.

Thus everything exists only ideally, by being falsely supposed to exist. The only knowable reality is unreal because specious, and all other reality is unreal because unknowable.

Transcendentalists are thus driven, like Parmenides and the Vedanta philosophy, to withdraw into a dark interior yet omnipresent principle, the unfathomable force that sets all this illusion going, and at the same time rebukes and annuls the illusion. I am here concerned, let me repeat, with scepticism, not with compensatory dogmas; but for the transcendentalist, who fundamentally abhors substance, the compensatory dogma itself is one more denial of existence. For what, in his system, is this transcendental seat of all illusion, this agent in all judgements and positings? Not an existing spirit, if such a phrase could have a meaning. Absolute thought cannot exist first, before it imputes existence to other things or to itself. If it needed to possess existence before imputing it, as the inexpert in logic might suppose, the whole principle of transcendental criticism would be abandoned and disproved, and nothing would any longer prevent the existence of intuitions or of material things before any one posited them. But if non-existent, what can absolute spirit be? Just a principle, a logic to be embodied, a self-creating programme or duty, asserting itself without any previous instrument, ground, or occasion. Existence is something utterly unworthy of such a transcendental spirit, and repugnant to it. Spirit is here only a name for absolute law, for the fatality or chance that one set of appearances instead of another insists upon arising. No doubt this fatality is welcome to the enthusiast in whom this spirit is awake, and its very groundlessness takes on the form of freedom and creative power to his apprehension: but this sympathy with life, being expressly without any natural basis, is itself a happy accident, and precarious: and sometimes conscience may suddenly turn against it, and call it vain, mad, and criminal. Fichte once said that he who truly wills anything must will that very thing for ever; and this saying may be interpreted consistently with transcendentalism, if it is understood to mean that, since transcendental will is dateless and creates its own universe wherever it exerts itself, the character of this will is unalterable in that phase of it, producing just that vision and that world, which being out of time cannot be devoured by time. But perhaps even Fichte was not free from human weakness, and he may also have meant, or half-meant, that a thorough education, such as Prussia was called to create, could fix the will of mankind and turn it into an unalterable habit; and that a philosopher could pledge the absolute always to posit the same set of objects. So understood, the maxim would be contrary to transcendentalism and to the fervent conviction of Fichte himself, which demanded "new worlds for ever." Even if he meant only that the principle of perpetual novelty at least was safe and could never be betrayed by the event, he would have contradicted the absolute freedom of "Life" to be what it willed, and his own occasional fears that, somewhere and some day, Life might grow weary, and might consent to be hypnotised and enslaved by the vision of matter which it had created.

But the frailty even of the greatest idealists is nothing against idealism, and the principle that existence is something always imputed, and never found, is not less cogent if idealists, for the sake of courtesy, sometimes say that when existence is imputed necessarily it is imputed truly;

and it makes no difference for my object whether they call fiction truth because it is legal, or call legality illusion because it is false. In any case, I can invoke the authority of this whole school, in which consciousness has been studied and described with admirable sincerity, for the thesis I have at heart. They deny with one voice that anything given can exist on its own account, or can be anything but a theme chosen by the spirit, a theme which no substantial thing or event existing outside could ever force the spirit to conceive or to copy. Nothing existent can appear, and nothing specious can exist. An apparition is a thought, its whole life is but mine in thinking it; and whatever monition or significance I may attribute to its presence, it can never be anything but the specious thing it is. In the routine of animal life, an appearance may be normal or abnormal, and animal faith or practical intellect may interpret it in a way practically right or wrong; but in itself every appearance, just because it is an appearance, is an illusion.

Confirmation of this thesis may also be found in an entirely different quarter, in natural history. The sensibility of animals, as judged by their motions and behaviour, is due to their own structure. The surrounding facts and forces are like the sun shining and the rain falling on the just and the unjust; they condition the existence of the animal and reward any apt habits which he may acquire; but he survives mainly by insensibility, and by a sort of pervasive immunity to most of the vibrations that run through him. It is only in very special directions, to very special occasional stimulations, that he develops instinctive responses in special organs: and his intuitions, if he has them, express these reactions. If the stimulus is cut off, the material sources of it may continue to be what they were, but they will not be perceived. If the stimulus, or anything equivalent to it, reaches the brain from any source, as in dreams, the same intuition will appear, in the absence of the material object. The feelings of animals express their bodily habit; they do not express directly either the existence or the character of any external thing. The intent to react on these external things is independent of any presumptive data of intuition and antecedent to their appearance: it is an animal endeavour in pursuit or avoidance, or an animal expectation; but the signals by which intuition may mark the crises of this animal watch or animal struggle are the same signals as appear in a dream, when nothing is afoot. The immediate visionary datum is never the intended object, but always a pathological symptom, a term in discourse, a description proffered at that moment by that feeling for that object, different for each channel of sense, translating digestibility into taste, salubrity into freshness, distance into size, refraction into colour, attitude into outline, distribution into perspective, and immersing everything in a moral medium, where it becomes a good or an evil, as it cannot be save to animal sympathy.

All these transcripts, however original in character, remain symbols in function, because they arise in the act of focussing animal sensibility or animal endeavour upon some external influence. In a healthy life they become the familiar and unmistakable masks of nature, lending to everything in the environment its appropriate aspect in human discourse, its nickname in the human family. For this reason, when imagination works in a void (as it can do in dreams or under the influence of violent passion) it becomes illusion in the bad sense of this word; that is, it is still taken for a symbol, when it is the symbol of nothing. All these data, if by a suspension of practical reference they came to be regarded in themselves, would cease to be illusions cognitively, since no existence would be suggested by any of them; but a practical man might still call them illusions for that very reason, because although free from error they would be devoid of truth. In order to reach existences intent must transcend intuition, and take data for what they mean, not for what they are; it must credit them, as understanding credits words, accepting the passing vision as a warrant for something that once was, or that will be, or that lies in an entirely different medium, that of material being, or of discourse elsewhere. Intuition cannot reveal or discriminate any fact; it is pure fancy; and the more I sink into it, and the more absolute I make it, the more fanciful it becomes. If ever it ceases to mean anything at all, it becomes pure poetry if placid, and mere delirium if intense. So a pain, when it is not sorrow at some event or the sign of some injury or crisis in bodily life, becomes sheer horror, and a sort of wanton little hell, existing absolutely; because the rending of the organism has raised intuition to an extreme intensity without giving it direction upon anything to be found or done in the world, or contemplated in the fancy; and pain, when it reaches distraction, may be said to be that moral monster, intuition devouring itself, or wasted in agony upon nothing.

Thus scientific psychology confirms the criticism of knowledge and the experience of life which proclaim that the immediate objects of intuition are mere appearances and that nothing given exists as it is given.

64

Reinhold Niebuhr

Discerning the Signs of the Times (1946)

Mystery and Meaning

For now we see through a glass darkly; but then face to face: now I know in part;
but then shall I know even as also I am known.
1 COR. 13:12

THE TESTIMONIES OF RELIGIOUS FAITH ARE CONFUSED MORE GREATLY by those who claim to know too much about the mystery of life than by those who claim to know too little. Those who disavow all knowledge of the final mystery of life are so impressed by the fact that we see through a glass darkly that they would make no claim of seeing at all. In the history of culture such a position is known as agnosticism. Agnosticism sees no practical value in seeking to solve the mystery of life. But there are not really many agnostics in any age or culture. A much larger number of people forget that they see through a glass darkly. They claim to know too much.

Those who claim to know too much may be divided into two groups, one ostensibly religious and the other irreligious. The irreligious resolve the problem of human existence and the mystery of the created world into systems of easily ascertained meaning. They deny that there is any mystery in life or the world. If they can find a previous cause for any subsequent effect in nature, they are certain that they have arrived at a full understanding of why such and such a thing exists. The natural cause is, for them, an adequate explanation of anything they may perceive.

The religious group, on the other hand, recognizes that the whole of the created world is not self-explanatory. They see that it points beyond itself to a mysterious ground of existence, to an enigmatic power beyond all discernible vitalities, and to a "first cause" beyond all known causes. But they usually claim to know too much about this eternal mystery. Sometimes they sharply define the limits of reason, and the further limits of faith beyond reason, and claim to know exactly how far reason penetrates into the eternal mystery, and how much further faith reaches. Yet though they make a distinction between faith and reason, they straightway so mix and confuse reason and faith that they pretend to be able to give a rational and sharply defined account of the character of God and of the eternal ground of existence. They define the power and knowledge of God precisely, and explain the exact extent of His control and foreknowledge of the course of events. They dissect the mysterious relation between man's intellectual faculties and his vital capacities, and claim to know the exact limits of *phusis, psyche* and *nous,* of body, soul and spirit. They know that man is immortal and why; and just what portion and part of him is mortal and what part immortal. Thus they banish the mystery of the unity of man's spiritual and physical existence. They have no sense of mystery about the problem of immortality. They know the geography of heaven and of hell, and the furniture of the one and the temperature of the other.

Characteristics of Genuine Faith

A genuine Christian faith must move between those who claim to know so much about the natural world that it ceases to point to any mystery beyond itself and those who claim to know so much about the mystery of the "unseen" world that all reverence for its secret and hidden character is dissipated. A genuine faith must recognize the fact that it is through a dark glass that we see; though by faith we do penetrate sufficiently to the heart of the mystery not to be overwhelmed by it. A genuine faith resolves the mystery of life by the mystery of God. It recognizes that no aspect of life or existence explains itself, even after all known causes and consequences have been traced. All known existence points beyond itself. To realize that it points beyond itself to God is to assert that the mystery of life does not dissolve life into meaninglessness. Faith in God is faith in some ultimate unity of life, in some final comprehensive purpose which holds all the various, and frequently contradictory, realms of coherence and meaning together. A genuine faith does not mark this mysterious source and end of existence as merely an X, or as an unknown quantity. The Christian faith, at least, is a faith in revelation. It believes that God has made Himself known. It believes that He has spoken through the prophets and finally in His Son. It accepts the revelation in Christ as the ultimate clue to the mystery of God's nature and purpose in the world, particularly the mystery of the relation of His justice to His mercy. But these clues to the mystery do not eliminate the periphery of mystery. God remains *deus absconditus.*

Of the prophets of the Old Testament, Deutero-Isaiah is particularly conscious of the penumbra of mystery which surrounds the eternal and the divine. He insists upon the distance between the divine wisdom and human counsels: "Who hath directed the spirit of the Lord, or being his counsellor hath taught him?" (Isa. 40:13). He emphasizes the transcendence of God's power: "It is he that sitteth upon the circle of the earth, and the inhabitants thereof are as grasshoppers . . . that bringeth the princes to nothing; he maketh the judges of the earth as vanity" (Isa. 40:22–23). The question of the meaning of life must not be pressed too far, according to the prophet: "Woe unto him that striveth with his Maker. . . . Shall the clay say to him that fashioneth it, What makest thou? . . . Woe unto him that saith unto his father, What begettest thou? or to the woman, What hast thou brought forth?" (Isa. 45:9–10). Faith, as the prophet conceives it, discerns the meaning of existence but must not seek to define it too carefully. The divine wisdom and purpose must always be partly hid from human understanding—"For my thoughts are not your thoughts, neither are your ways my ways, saith the Lord. For as the heavens are higher than the earth, so are my ways higher than your ways, and my thoughts than your thoughts" (Isa. 55:8–9).

The sense of both mystery and meaning is perhaps most succinctly expressed in the forty-fifth chapter of Isaiah, where, practically in the same breath, the prophet declares on the one hand, "Verily thou art a God that hidest thyself, O God of Israel, the Saviour" (Isa. 45:15), and on the other, insists that God has made Himself known: "I have not spoken in secret, in a dark place of the earth: I said not unto the seed of Jacob, Seek ye me in vain: I the Lord speak righteousness, I declare things that are right" (Isa. 45:19). This double emphasis is a perfect symbolic expression both of the meaning which faith discerns and of the penumbra of mystery which it recognizes around the core of meaning. The essential character of God, in His relations to the world, is known. He is the creator, judge and saviour of men. Yet He does not fully disclose Himself, and His thoughts are too high to be comprehended by human thought.

Destroying the Penumbra of Mystery

For some centuries the intellectual life of modern man has been dominated by rebellion against medieval faith. The main outlines of modern culture are defined by modern man's faith in science and his defiance of the authority of religion. This conflict between the faith which flowered in the thirteenth century and that which flowered in the seventeenth and eighteenth centuries is a conflict between two forms of faith which in their different ways obscured the penumbra of the mystery of life and made the core of meaning too large. Medieval Catholicism was not completely lacking in a reverent sense of mystery. The rites of the Church frequently excel the more rationalized forms of the Protestant faith by their poetic expression of mystery. There is, for instance, an advantage in chanting rather than saying a creed. The musical and poetical forms of a creed emphasize the salient affirmation of faith which the creed contains, and slightly derogate the exact details of symbolism through which the basic affirmation is expressed. That is a virtue of the liturgical and sacramental Church, which is hardened into a pitiless fundamentalism when every "i" is dotted and every "t" crossed in the soberly recited credo.

On the other hand, the same Catholic faith combined a pretentious rationalism with its sense of poetry. Any careful reading of the works of Thomas Aquinas must impress the thoughtful student with the element of pretension which informs the flowering of the Catholic faith in the "golden" thirteenth century. There seems to be no mystery which is not carefully dissected, no dark depth of evil which is not fully explained, and no height of existence which is not scaled. The various attributes of God are all carefully defined and related to each other. The mysteries of the human soul and spirit are mastered and rationally defined in the most meticulous terms. The exact line which marks justice from injustice is known. Faith and reason are so intermingled that the characteristic certainty of each is compounded with the other. Thus a very imposing structure is created. Yet it ought to have been possible to anticipate the doubts which it would ultimately arouse. Granted its foundation of presuppositions, every beam and joist in the intellectual structure is reared with perfect logical consistency. But the foundation is insecure. It is a foundation of faith in which the timeless affirmations of the Christian belief are compounded with detailed knowledge characteristic of a pre-scientific age. An age of science challenged this whole foundation of presupposition and seemed to invalidate the whole structure.

The new age of science attempted an even more rigorous denial of mystery. The age of science traced the relations of the world of nature, studied the various causes which seemed to be at the root of various effects in every realm of natural coherence; and came to the conclusion that knowledge dissolved mystery. Mystery was simply the darkness of ignorance which the light of knowledge dispelled. Religious faith was, in its opinion, merely the fear of the unknown which could be dissipated by further knowledge. In the one case the "spiritual," the "eternal" and the "supernatural," conceived as a separate and distinct realm of existence (instead of as the final ground and ultimate dimension of the unity of existence), is so exactly defined that the penumbra of mystery is destroyed. In the other case the "natural," the "temporal" and the "material" are supposedly comprehended so fully that they cease to point beyond themselves to a more ultimate mystery. There are significant differences between these two ways of apprehending the world about us and the depth of existence within us; but the differences are no greater than the similarity between them. Both ways contain an element of human pretension. Both fail to recognize that we see through a glass darkly.

The Mystery of Nature

We see through a glass darkly when we seek to understand the world about us; because no natural cause is ever a complete and adequate explanation of the subsequent event. The subsequent event is undoubtedly causally related to preceding events; but it is only one of many untold possibilities which might have been actualized. The biblical idea of a divine creator moves on a different level than scientific concepts of causation. The two become mutually exclusive, as they have done in the controversies of recent ages, only if, on the one hand, we deny the mysterious element in creation and regard it as an exact explanation of why things are as they are and become what they become; and if, on the other hand, we deny the mystery which overarches the process of causation in nature. Thus two dimensions of meaning, each too exactly defined, come in conflict with each other. More truly and justly conceived, the realm of coherence, which we call nature, points to a realm of power beyond itself. This realm is discerned by faith, but not fully known. It is a mystery which resolves the mystery of nature. But if mystery is denied in each realm, the meaning which men pretend to apprehend in each becomes too pat and calculated. The depth of meaning is destroyed in the process of charting it exactly. Thus the sense of meaning is deepened, and not annulled, by the sense of mystery.

The Mystery of Human Nature

The understanding of ourselves is even more subject to seeing through a glass darkly than the understanding of the world about us. We "are fearfully and wonderfully made" (Ps. 139:14). Man is a creature of nature, subject to its necessities and bound by its limits. Yet he surveys the ages and touches the fringes of the eternal. Despite the limited character of his life, he is constantly under compulsions and responsibilities which reach to the very heart of the eternal.

> Thou hast beset me behind and before,
> And laid thine hand upon me.
> Such knowledge is too wonderful for me;
> It is high, I cannot attain unto it,

confesses the Psalmist in recording the universal human experience of feeling related to a divine lawgiver and judge. He continues:

> Whither shall I go from thy spirit?
> Or whither shall I flee from thy presence?
> If I ascend into heaven, thou art there:
> If I make my bed in hell, behold, thou art there.
> If I take the wings of the morning,
> And dwell in the uttermost parts of the sea;
> Even there shall thy hand lead me,
> And thy right hand shall hold me.

> (Ps. 139:5–10)

Thus the Psalmist continues in describing the boundless character of the human spirit, which rises above and beyond all finite limitations to confront and feel itself confronted by the divine.

The finiteness of human life, contrasted with the limitless quality of the human spirit, presents us with a profound mystery. We are an enigma to ourselves.

There are many forms of modern thought which deny the mystery of our life by reducing the dimension of human existence to the level of nature. We are animals, we are told, with a slightly greater reach of reason and a slightly "more complex central nervous system" than the other brute creatures. But this is a palpable denial of the real stature of man's spirit. We may be only slightly more inventive than the most astute monkey. But there is, as far as we know, no *Weltschmerz* in the soul of any monkey, no anxiety about what he is and ought to be, and no visitation from a divine accuser who "besets him behind and before" and from whose spirit he cannot flee. There is among animals no uneasy conscience and no ambition which tends to transgress all natural bounds and become the source of the highest nobility of spirit and of the most demonic madness.

We are a mystery to ourselves in our weakness and our greatness; and this mystery can be resolved in part only as we reach into the height of the mysterious dimension of the eternal into which the pinnacle of our spiritual freedom seems to rise. The mystery of God resolves the mystery of the self into meaning. By faith we find the source of our life: "It is he that hath made us and not we ourselves" (Ps. 100:3). Here too we find the author of our moral duties: "He that judgeth me is the Lord" (1 Cor. 4:4). And here is the certitude of our fulfillment: "But then shall I know even as also I am known" (1 Cor. 13:12), declares St. Paul. This is to say that despite the height of our vision, no man can complete the structure of meaning in which he is involved except as by faith he discerns that he "is known," though he himself only "knows in part." The human spirit reaches beyond the limit of nature and does not fully comprehend the level of reality into which it reaches. Any interpretation of life which denies this height of reality because it ends in mystery gives a false picture of the stature of man. On the other hand, any interpretation which seeks to comprehend the ultimate dimension by the knowledge and the symbols of the known world also gives a false picture of man. Such theologies obscure the finiteness of human knowledge. We see through a glass darkly when we seek to discern the divine ground and end of human experience; we see only by faith. But by faith we do see.

The Mystery of Sin

The source of the evil in us is almost as mysterious as the divine source and the end of our spiritual life. "O Lord," cried the prophet, "why hast thou made us to err from thy ways, and hardened our heart from thy fear?" (Isa. 63:17). We desire the good and yet do evil. In the words of St. Paul, "I delight in the law of God after the inward man: but I see another law in my members, warring against the law of my mind" (Rom. 7:22–23). The inclination to evil, which is primarily the inclination to inordinate self-love, runs counter to our conscious desires. We seem to be betrayed into it. "Now if I do that I would not, it is no more I that do it, but sin that dwelleth in me" (Rom. 7:20), declares St. Paul, in trying to explain the powerful drift toward evil in us against our conscious purposes.

There is a deep mystery here which has been simply resolved in modern culture. It has interpreted man as an essentially virtuous creature who is betrayed into evil by ignorance, or by evil economic, political, or religious institutions. These simple theories of historical evil do not explain how virtuous men of another generation created the evil in these inherited institutions, or how mere ignorance could give the evil in man the positive thrust and demonic energy in which it frequently expresses itself. Modern culture's understanding of the evil in man fails to do justice to the tragic and perplexing aspect of the problem.

Orthodox Christianity, on the other hand, has frequently given a dogmatic answer to the problem, which suggests mystery, but which immediately obscures the mystery by a dogmatic formula. Men are evil, Christian orthodoxy declared, because of the "sin of Adam" which has been transmitted to all men. Sometimes the mode of transmission is allowed to remain mysterious; but sometimes it is identified with the concupiscence in the act of procreation. This dogmatic explanation has prompted the justified protest and incredulity of modern man, particularly since it is generally couched in language and symbols taken from a pre-scientific age.

Actually there is a great mystery in the fact that man, who is so created that he cannot fulfill his life except in his fellowmen, and who has some consciousness of this law of love in his very nature, should nevertheless seek so persistently to make his fellowmen the tools of his desires and the objects of his ambitions. If we try to explain this tendency toward self-love, we can find various plausible explanations. We can say it is due to the fact that man exists at the juncture of nature and spirit, of freedom and necessity. Being a weak creature, he is anxious for his life; and being a resourceful creature, armed with the guile of spirit, he seeks to overcome his insecurity by the various instruments which are placed at his disposal by the resources of his freedom. But inevitably, the security which he seeks for himself is bought at the price of other men's security. Being an insignificant creature with suggestions of great significance in the stature of his freedom, man uses his strength to hide his weakness and thus falls into the evil of the lust for power and self-idolatry.

These explanations of man's self-love are plausible enough as far as they go. But they are wrong if they assume that the peculiar amphibious situation of man, being partly immersed in the time process and partly transcending it, must inevitably and necessarily tempt him to an inordinate self-love. The situation does not create evil if it is not falsely interpreted. From whence comes the false interpretation? There is thus great profundity in the biblical myth of the serpent who "tempted" Eve by suggesting that God was jealous of man's strength and sought to limit it. Man's situation tempts to evil, provided man is unwilling to accept the peculiar weakness of his creaturely life, and is unable to find the ultimate source and end of his existence beyond himself. It is man's unbelief and pride which tempt to sin. And every such temptation presupposes a previous "tempter" (of which the serpent is the symbol). Thus before man fell into sin there was, according to Biblical myth, a fall of the devil in heaven. The devil is a fallen angel who refused to accept his rightful place in the scheme of things and sought a position equal to God.

This then is the real mystery of evil; that it presupposes itself. No matter how far back it is traced in the individual or the race, or even preceding the history of the race, a profound scrutiny of the nature of evil reveals that there is an element of sin in the temptation which leads to sin; and that, without this presupposed evil, the consequent sin would not necessarily arise from the situation in which man finds himself. This is what Kierkegaard means by saying that "sin posits itself." This is the mystery of "original sin" about which Pascal truly observes that "without this mystery man remains a mystery to himself."

Purely sociological and historical explanations of the rise of evil do not touch the depth of the mystery at all. Christian dogmatic explanations have some sense of it; but they obscure it as soon as they have revealed it by their pat dogmatic formulae. In dealing with the problem of sin, the sense of meaning is inextricably interwoven with the sense of mystery. We see through a glass darkly when we seek to understand the cause and the nature of evil in our own souls. But we see more profoundly when we know it is through a dark glass that we see than if we pretend to have clear light upon this profound problem.

The Mystery of Death

The final mystery about human life concerns its incompleteness and the method of its completion. Here again modern culture has resolved all mystery into simple meaning. It believes that the historical process is such that it guarantees the ultimate fulfillment of all legitimate human desires. It believes that history, as such, is redemptive. Men may be frustrated today, may live in poverty and in conflict, and may feel that they "bring their years to an end like a tale that is told." But the modern man is certain that there will be a tomorrow in which poverty and war and all injustice will be abolished. Utopia is the simple answer which modern culture offers in various guises to the problem of man's ultimate frustration. History is, according to the most characteristic thought of modern life, a process which gradually closes the hiatus between what man is and what he would be.

The difficulty with this answer is that there is no evidence that history has any such effect. In the collective enterprises of man, the progress of history arms the evil, as well as the good, with greater potency; and the mystery of how history is to be brought to completion, therefore, remains on every level of human achievement. It may in fact express itself more poignantly in the future than in the past.

Furthermore, there is no resolution of the problem of the individual in any collective achievement of mankind. The individual must continue to find the collective life of man his ultimate moral frustration, as well as his fulfillment. For there is no human society, and there can be none, the moral mediocrity of which must not be shocking to the individual's highest moral scruples. Furthermore, the individual dies before any of the promised collective completions of history.

But this is not all. The problem of death is deeply involved with the problem of sin. Men die with an uneasy conscience and must confess with the Psalmist, "for we are consumed by thine anger and by thy wrath are we troubled" (Ps. 90:7). Any honest self-analysis must persuade us that we end our life in frustration not only because "our reach is beyond our grasp," i.e., because we are finite creatures with more than finite conceptions of an ultimate consummation of life, but also because we are sinners who constantly introduce positive evil into the operations of divine providence.

The answer of Christian faith to this problem is belief in "the forgiveness of sin and life everlasting." We believe that only a power greater than our own can complete our incomplete life, and only a divine mercy can heal us of our evil. Significantly St. Paul adds this expression of Christian hope immediately to his confession that we see through a glass darkly. We see through a glass darkly now, "but then" we shall "see face to face." Now we "know in part" but "then" we shall know even as we are known (cf. 1 Cor. 13:12). This Christian hope makes it possible to look at all the perplexities and mysteries of life without too much fear.

In another context St. Paul declares: "We are perplexed, but not unto despair" (2 Cor. 4:8). One might well divide the world into those who are not perplexed, those who are perplexed unto despair, and those who are perplexed but not unto despair. Those who are not perplexed have dissolved all the mysteries and perplexities of life by some simple scheme of meaning. The scheme is always too simple to do justice to the depth of man's problem. When life reveals itself in its full terror, as well as its full beauty, these little schemes break down. Optimism gives way to despair. The Christian faith does not pretend to resolve all perplexities. It confesses the darkness of human sight and the perplexities of faith. It escapes despair nevertheless because it holds fast to the essential goodness of God as revealed in Christ, and is therefore "persuaded that neither life nor death are able to separate us from the love of God, which is in Christ Jesus our Lord" (Rom. 8:38–39).

It can not be denied, however, that this same Christian faith is frequently vulgarized and cheapened to the point where all mystery is banished. The Christian faith in heaven is sometimes as cheap as, and sometimes even more vulgar than, the modern faith in Utopia. It may be even less capable of expressing the final perplexity and the final certainty of faith. On this issue, as on the others we have considered, a faith which measures the final dimension of existence, but dissipates all mystery in that dimension, may be only a little better or worse than a shallow creed which reduces human existence to the level of nature.

Our situation is that, by reason of the freedom of our spirit, we have purposes and ends beyond the limits of the finiteness of our physical existence. Faith may discern the certainty of a final completion of life beyond our power, and a final purging of the evil which we introduce into life by our false efforts to complete it in our own strength. But faith cannot resolve the mystery of how this will be done. When we look into the future we see through a glass darkly. The important issue is whether we will be tempted by the incompleteness and frustration of life to despair; or whether we can, by faith, lay hold on the divine power and wisdom which completes what remains otherwise incomplete. A faith which resolves mystery too much denies the finiteness of all human knowledge, including the knowledge of faith. A faith which is overwhelmed by mystery denies the clues of divine meaning which shine through the perplexities of life. The proper combination of humility and trust is precisely defined when we affirm that we see, but admit that we see through a glass darkly.

Meaning in the Midst of Mystery

Our primary concern in this exposition of the Pauline text has been to understand the fact that the Christian faith is conscious of the penumbra of mystery which surrounds its conception of meaning.

Yet in conclusion it must be emphasized that our faith cannot be identified with poetic forms of religion which worship mystery without any conception of meaning. All such poetic forms of faith might well be placed in the category of the worship of the unknown God, typified in the religion which Paul found in Athens. In contrast to this religion Paul set the faith which is rooted in the certainty that the mysterious God has made Himself known, and that the revelation of His nature and purpose, apprehended by faith, must be declared: "Whom therefore ye ignorantly worship him declare I unto you" (Acts 17:23). This declaration of faith rests upon the belief that the divine is not mere mystery, the heart of it having been disclosed to those who are able to apprehend the divine disclosure in Christ. It is by the certainty of that faith that St. Paul can confidently look toward a future completion of our imperfect knowledge: "Now I know in part, but *then* shall I know" (1 Cor. 13:12). The indication that faith regards the meaning, which has been disclosed, as victorious over the mystery of existence is the expression of a certain hope that "then shall I know." Faith expects that ultimately all mystery will be resolved in the perfect knowledge of God.

Faith in a religion of revelation is thus distinguished on the one side from merely poetic appreciations of mystery, just as on the other side it is distinguished from philosophies of religion which find the idea of revelation meaningless. Revelation is meaningless to all forms of rational religion which approach the mystery of life with the certainty that human reason can at length entirely resolve the mystery. The Christian faith is the right expression of the greatness and the weakness of man in relation to the mystery and the meaning of life. It is an acknowledgment of human weakness, for, unlike "natural religion" and "natural theology," it does not regard the human mind as capable of resolving the enigma of existence, because it knows that human reason is itself involved in the enigma which it tries to comprehend. It is an acknowledgment of the greatness of the human spirit because it assumes that man is capable of apprehending clues to the divine mystery and accepting the disclosure of the purposes of God which He has made to us. It is a confession at once of both weakness and strength, because it recognizes that the disclosures of the divine are given to man, who is capable of apprehending them, when made, but is not capable of anticipating them.

According to the Christian faith there is a light which shineth in darkness; and the darkness is not able to comprehend it (cf. John 1:5). Reason does not light that light; but faith is able to pierce the darkness and apprehend it.

65

Simone Weil

The Love of God and Affliction (1951)

In the realm of suffering, affliction is something apart, specific and irreducible. It is quite a different thing from simple suffering. It takes possession of the soul and marks it through and through with its own particular mark, the mark of slavery. Slavery as practised by ancient Rome is simply the extreme form of affliction. The men of antiquity, who knew a lot about the subject, used to say: 'A man loses half his soul the day he becomes a slave.'

Affliction is inseparable from physical suffering and yet quite distinct. In suffering, all that is not bound up with physical pain or something analogous is artificial, imaginary, and can be eliminated by a suitable adjustment of the mind. Even in the case of the absence or death of someone we love, the irreducible part of the sorrow is akin to physical pain, a difficulty in breathing, a constriction of the heart, or an unsatisfied need, a hunger, or the almost biological disorder caused by the brutal unloosing of an energy hitherto absorbed by an attachment and now left undirected. A sorrow which is not centered around an irreducible core of such a nature is mere romanticism or literature. Humiliation is also a violent condition of the whole physical being, which wants to rise up against the outrage but is forced, by impotence or fear, to hold itself in check.

On the other hand a pain which is only physical is of very little account, and leaves no mark on the soul. Toothache is an example. An hour or two of violent pain caused by a bad tooth is nothing once it is over.

It is another matter if the physical suffering is very prolonged or frequent, but this is often something quite different from an attack of pain; it is often an affliction.

Affliction is an uprooting of life, a more or less attenuated equivalent of death, made irresistibly present to the soul by the attack or immediate apprehension of physical pain. If there is complete absence of physical pain there is no affliction for the soul, because thought can turn itself away in any direction. Thought flies from affliction as promptly and irresistibly as an animal flies from death. Here below, physical pain and nothing else has the power to chain down our thoughts;

provided that we count as physical pain certain phenomena which, though difficult to describe, are bodily and are strictly equivalent to it; in particular, for example, the fear of physical pain.

When thought is obliged by an attack of physical pain, however slight, to recognize the presence of affliction, this produces a state of mind as acute as that of a condemned man who is forced to look for hours at the guillotine which is going to behead him. Human beings can live twenty years, fifty years, in this acute state. We pass by them without noticing. What man is capable of discerning them unless Christ himself looks through his eyes? We notice only that they sometimes behave strangely, and we censure this behaviour.

There is not real affliction unless the event which has gripped and uprooted a life attacks it, directly or indirectly, in all its parts, social, psychological, and physical. The social factor is essential. There is not really affliction where there is not social degradation or the fear of it in some form or another.

There is both continuity and a separating threshold, like the boiling point of water, between affliction itself and all the sorrows which, even though they may be very violent, very deep, and very lasting, are not afflictions in the true sense. There is a limit; on the far side of it we have affliction but not on the near side. This limit is not purely objective; all sorts of personal factors have to be taken into account. The same event may plunge one human being into affliction and not another.

The great enigma of human life is not suffering but affliction. It is not surprising that the innocent are killed, tortured, driven from their country, made destitute or reduced to slavery, put in concentration camps or prison cells, since there are criminals to perform such actions. It is not surprising either that disease is the cause of long sufferings, which paralyse life and make it into an image of death, since nature is at the mercy of the blind play of mechanical necessities. But it *is* surprising that God should have given affliction the power to seize the very souls of the innocent and to possess them as sovereign master. At the very best, he who is branded by affliction will only keep half his soul.

As for those who have been struck the kind of blow which leaves the victim writhing on the ground like a half-crushed worm, they have no words to describe what is happening to them. Among the people they meet, those who have never had contact with affliction in its true sense can have no idea of what it is, even though they may have known much suffering. Affliction is something specific and impossible to compare with anything else, just as nothing can convey the idea of sound to the deaf and dumb. And, as for those who have themselves been mutilated by affliction, they are in no state to help anyone at all and are almost incapable of even wishing to do so. Thus compassion for the afflicted is an impossibility. When it is really found, it is a more astounding miracle than walking on water, healing the sick, or even raising the dead.

Affliction constrained Christ to implore that he might be spared, to seek consolation from man, to believe he was forsaken by the Father. It constrained a just man to cry out against God;

a just man as perfect as human nature can be; more so, perhaps, if Job is not so much a historical character as a figure of Christ. 'He laughs at the affliction of the innocent!' This is not blasphemy but a genuine cry of anguish. The Book of Job is a pure marvel of truth and authenticity from beginning to end. As regards affliction, all that departs from this model is more or less tainted with falsehood.

Affliction causes God to be absent for a time, more absent than a dead man, more absent than light in the utter darkness of a cell. A kind of horror submerges the whole soul. During this absence there is nothing to love. What is terrible is that if, in this darkness where there is nothing to love, the soul ceases to love, God's absence becomes final. The soul has to go on loving in the void, or at least to go on wanting to love, though it may be only with an infinitesimal part of itself. Then, one day, God will come to show himself to this soul and to reveal the beauty of the world to it, as in the case of Job. But if the soul stops loving it falls, even in this life, into something which is almost equivalent to hell.

That is why those who plunge men into affliction before they are prepared to receive it are killers of souls. On the other hand, in a time such as ours, where affliction is hanging over us all, help given to souls is only effective if it goes far enough really to prepare them for affliction. That is no small thing.

Affliction hardens and discourages because, like a red-hot iron, it stamps the soul to its very depths with the contempt, the disgust, and even the self-hatred and sense of guilt and defilement which crime logically should produce but actually does not. Evil dwells in the heart of the criminal without being felt there. It is felt in the heart of the man who is afflicted and innocent. Everything happens as though the state of soul appropriate for criminals had been separated from crime and attached to affliction; and it even seems to be in proportion to the innocence of those who are afflicted.

If Job cries out that he is innocent in such despairing accents it is because he himself is unable to believe so, it is because his soul within him is on the side of his friends. He implores God himself to bear witness, because he no longer hears the testimony of his own conscience; it is no longer anything but an abstract, lifeless memory for him.

Men have the same carnal nature as animals. If a hen is hurt, the others rush up and peck it. The phenomenon is as automatic as gravitation. Our senses attach to affliction all the contempt, all the revulsion, all the hatred which our reason attaches to crime. Except for those whose whole soul is inhabited by Christ, everybody despises the afflicted to some extent, although practically no one is conscious of it.

This law of sensibility also holds good with regard to ourselves. In the case of someone in affliction, all the contempt, revulsion, and hatred are turned inwards; they penetrate to the centre of his soul and from there they colour the whole universe with their poisoned light. Supernatural love, if it has survived, can prevent this second result from coming about, but not the first. The first is of the very essence of affliction; there is no affliction without it.

'Christ . . . being made a curse for us.' It was not only the body of Christ, hanging on the wood, which was accursed, it was his whole soul also. In the same way every innocent being in his affliction feels himself accursed. This even goes on being true for those who have been in affliction and have come out of it through a change in their fortunes, if the affliction has bitten deeply enough into them.

Another effect of affliction is, little by little, to make the soul its accomplice, by injecting a poison of inertia into it. In anyone who has suffered affliction for a long enough time there is a complicity with regard to his own affliction. This complicity impedes all the efforts he might make to improve his lot; it goes so far as to prevent him from seeking a way of deliverance, sometimes even to the point of preventing him from wishing for deliverance. Then he is established in affliction, and people may get the impression that he is quite contented. Even worse, this complicity may induce him, in spite of himself, to shun and flee from the means of deliverance; and for this it will resort to pretexts which are sometimes ridiculous. Even after a man has been relieved of his affliction, there will be something left in him which impels him to embrace it again, if it has pierced irrevocably into the depth of his soul. It is as though affliction had established itself in him like a parasite and was directing him for its own purposes. Sometimes this impulse triumphs over all the impulses of the soul towards happiness. If the affliction has been ended as the result of some kindness, it may take the form of hatred for the benefactor; this is the cause of certain apparently inexplicable acts of savage ingratitude. It is sometimes easy to deliver an unhappy man from his present distress, but it is difficult to set him free from his past affliction. Only God can do it. And even the grace of God himself cannot cure irremediably wounded nature in this world. The glorified body of Christ bore the marks of nail and spear.

One can only accept the existence of affliction by considering it as a distance.

God created through love and for love. God did not create anything except love itself, and the means to love. He created love in all its forms. He created beings capable of love from all possible distances. Because no other could do it, he himself went to the greatest possible distance, the infinite distance. This infinite distance between God and God, this supreme tearing apart, this incomparable agony, this marvel of love, is the crucifixion. Nothing can be further from God than that which has been made accursed.

This tearing apart, over which supreme love places the bond of supreme union, echoes perpetually across the universe in the depth of the silence, like two notes, separate yet blending into one, like a pure and heart-rending harmony. This is the Word of God. The whole creation is nothing but its vibration. When human music in its greatest purity pierces our soul, this is what we hear through it. When we have learnt to hear the silence, this is what we grasp, even more distinctly, through it.

Those who persevere in love hear this note from the very lowest depths into which affliction has thrust them. From that moment they can no longer have any doubt.

Men struck down by affliction are at the foot of the Cross, almost at the greatest possible distance from God. It must not be thought that sin is a greater distance. Sin is not a distance, it is a turning of our eyes in the wrong direction.

It is true that there is a mysterious connexion between this distance and an original disobedience. From the beginning, we are told, humanity turned its eyes away from God and walked as far as it could in the wrong direction. That is because it was then able to walk. As for us, we are nailed down to the spot, free only to choose which way we will look, ruled by necessity. A blind mechanism, heedless of degrees of spiritual perfection, continually buffets men hither and thither and flings some of them at the very foot of the Cross. It rests with them only to keep or not to keep their eyes turned towards God through all the shocks. It is not that God's Providence is absent; it is by his Providence that God willed necessity as a blind mechanism.

If the mechanism were not blind there would not be any affliction. Affliction is above all anonymous; it deprives its victims of their personality and turns them into things. It is indifferent, and it is the chill of this indifference—a metallic chill—which freezes all those it touches, down to the depth of their soul. They will never find warmth again. They will never again believe that they are anyone.

Affliction would not have this power without the element of chance which it contains. Those who are persecuted for their faith and are aware of it are not afflicted, in spite of their suffering. They only fall into affliction if suffering or fear fills the soul to the point of making it forget the cause of the persecution. The martyrs who came into the arena singing as they faced the wild beasts were not afflicted. Christ was afflicted. He did not die like a martyr. He died like a common criminal, in the same class as thieves, only a little more ridiculous. For affliction is ridiculous.

Only blind necessity can throw men to the extreme point of distance, close to the Cross. Human crime, which is the cause of most affliction, is part of blind necessity, because criminals do not know what they are doing. [. . .]

Joy and suffering are two equally precious gifts which must both of them be fully tasted, each one in its purity and without trying to mix them. Through joy, the beauty of the world penetrates our soul. Through suffering it penetrates our body. We could no more become friends of God through joy alone than one becomes a ship's captain by studying books on navigation. The body plays a part in all apprenticeships. On the plane of physical sensibility, suffering alone gives us contact with that necessity which constitutes the order of the world, for pleasure does not involve an impression of necessity. It is on a higher plane of sensibility that the necessity in joy can be recognized, and then only indirectly through the sense of beauty. In order that our being may one day become wholly sensitive in every part to this obedience which is the substance of matter, in order that a new sense may be formed in us which allows us to hear the universe as the vibration of the word of God, the transforming power of suffering and of joy are equally indispensable. When either of them comes to us we have to open the very centre of our soul to it, as a woman opens her door to messengers from her beloved. What does it matter to a lover if the messenger is courteous or rough so long as he gives her a message?

But affliction is not suffering. Affliction is something quite different from a divine educational method.

The infinity of space and time separates us from God. How can we seek for him? How can we go towards him? Even if we were to walk for endless centuries we should do no more than go round and round the world. Even in an aeroplane we could not do anything else. We are incapable of progressing vertically. We cannot take one step towards the heavens. God crosses the universe and comes to us.

Over the infinity of space and time the infinitely more infinite love of God comes to possess us. He comes at his own time. We have the power to consent to receive him or to refuse. If we remain deaf he comes back again and again a beggar, but also, like a beggar, one day he stops coming. If we consent, God places a little seed in us and he goes away again. From that moment God has no more to do; neither have we, except to wait. We have only not to regret the consent we gave, the nuptial Yes. It is not as easy as it seems, for the growth of the seed within us is painful. Moreover, from the very fact that we accept this growth we cannot avoid destroying whatever gets in its way, pulling up the weeds, cutting the grasses; and unfortunately they are part of our very flesh, so that this gardening amounts to a violent operation. On the whole, however, the seed grows of itself. A day comes when the soul belongs to God, when it not only consents to love but when truly and effectively it loves. Then in its turn it must cross the universe to go to God. The soul does not love like a creature, with created love. The love within it is divine, uncreated, for it is the love of God for God which is passing through it. God alone is capable of loving God. We can only consent to give up our own feelings so as to allow free passage in our soul for this love. That is the meaning of denying oneself. We were created solely in order to give this consent. [. . .]

Affliction is a marvel of divine technique. It is a simple and ingenious device to introduce into the soul of a finite creature that immensity of force, blind, brutal, and cold. The infinite distance which separates God from the creature is concentrated into a point to transfix the centre of a soul.

The man to whom such a thing occurs has no part in the operation. He quivers like a butterfly pinned alive to a tray. But throughout the horror he can go on wanting to love. There is no impossibility in that, no obstacle, one could almost say no difficulty. Because no pain, however great, up to the point of losing consciousness, touches that part of the soul which consents to a right orientation.

It is only necessary to know that love is an orientation and not a state of the soul. Anyone who does not know this will fall into despair at the first onset of affliction.

The man whose soul remains oriented towards God while a nail is driven through it finds himself nailed to the very centre of the universe; the true centre, which is not in the middle, which is not in space and time, which is God. In a dimension which is not spatial and which is not time, a totally other dimension, the nail has pierced through the whole of creation, through the dense screen which separates the soul from God.

In this marvellous dimension, without leaving the time and place to which the body is bound, the soul can traverse the whole of space and time and come into the actual presence of God. [. . .]

It is wrong to desire affliction; it is against nature, and it is a perversion; and moreover it is the essence of affliction that it is suffered unwillingly. So long as we are not submerged in affliction all we can do is to desire that, if it should come, it may be a participation in the Cross of Christ.

But what is in fact always present, and what it is therefore always permitted to love, is the possibility of affliction. All the three sides of our being are always exposed to it. Our flesh is fragile; it can be pierced or torn or crushed, or one of its internal mechanisms can be permanently deranged, by any piece of matter in motion. Our soul is vulnerable, being subject to fits of depression without cause and pitifully dependent upon all sorts of objects, inanimate and animate, which are themselves fragile and capricious. Our social personality, upon which our sense of existence almost depends, is always and entirely exposed to every hazard. These three parts of us are linked with the very centre of our being in such a way that it bleeds for any wound of the slightest consequence which they suffer. Above all, anything which diminishes or destroys our social prestige, our right to consideration, seems to impair or abolish our very essence—so much is our whole substance an affair of illusion.

When everything is going more or less well, we do not think about this almost infinite fragility. But nothing compels us not to think about it. We can contemplate it all the time and thank God for it unceasingly. We can be thankful not only for the fragility itself but also for that more intimate weakness which connects it with the very centre of our being. For it is this weakness which makes possible, in certain conditions, the operation by which we are nailed to the very centre of the Cross. [. . .]

The knowledge of affliction is the key of Christianity. But that knowledge is impossible. It is not possible to know affliction without having been through it. Thought is so revolted by affliction that it is as incapable of bringing itself voluntarily to conceive it as an animal, generally speaking, is incapable of suicide. Thought never knows affliction except by constraint. Unless constrained by experience, it is impossible to believe that everything in the soul—all its thoughts and feelings, its every attitude towards ideas, people, and the universe, and, above all, the most intimate attitude of the being towards itself—that all this is entirely at the mercy of circumstances. Even if one recognizes it theoretically, and it is rare indeed to do so, one does not believe it with all one's soul. To believe it with all one's soul is what Christ called, not renunciation or abnegation, as it is usually translated, but denying oneself; and it is by this that one deserves to be his disciple. But when we are in affliction or have passed through it we do not believe this truth any more than before; one could almost say that we believe it still less. Thought can never really be constrained; evasion by falsehood is always open to it. When thought finds itself, through the force of circumstance, brought face to face with affliction it takes immediate refuge in lies, like a hunted animal dashing for cover. Sometimes in its terror it burrows very deep into falsehood and it often happens that people who are or have been in affliction become addicted to lying as a vice, in some cases to such a degree that they lose the sense of any distinction between truth and falsehood in anything. It is wrong to blame them. Falsehood and affliction are so closely linked that Christ conquered the world simply because he, being the Truth, continued to be the Truth in the very depth of extreme affliction. Thought is constrained by an instinct of self-preservation to fly from the sight of affliction, and this instinct is infinitely more essential to our being than the instinct to avoid physical death. It is comparatively easy to face physical death so long as circumstances or the play of imagination present it under some other aspect than that of affliction. But to be able to face affliction with steady attention when it is close to him a man must be prepared, for the love of truth, to accept the death of the soul. This is the death of which Plato spoke when he said 'to philosophize is to learn to die'; it is the death which was symbolized in the initiation rites of the ancient mysteries, and which is represented by baptism. In reality, it is not a question of the soul's dying, but simply of recognizing the truth that it is a dead thing, something analogous to matter. It has no need to turn into water; it is water; the thing we believe to be our self is as ephemeral and automatic a product of external circumstances as the form of a sea-wave.

66

Edmund Husserl

The Crisis of European Sciences and Transcendental Phenomenology (1954)

The "transcendental" motif in rationalism: Kant's conception of a transcendental philosophy.

AS IS KNOWN, HUME HAS A PARTICULAR PLACE IN history also because of the turn he brought about in the development of Kant's thinking. Kant himself says, in the much-quoted words, that Hume roused him from his dogmatic slumbers and gave his investigations in the field of speculative philosophy a different direction. Was it, then, the historical mission of Kant to experience the shaking of objectivism, of which I just spoke, and to undertake in his transcendental philosophy the solution of the task before which Hume drew back? The answer must be negative. It is a new sort of transcendental subjectivism which begins with Kant and changes into new forms in the systems of German idealism. Kant does not belong to the development which expands in a continuous line from Descartes through Locke, and he is not the successor of Hume. His interpretation of the Humean skepticism and the way in which he reacts against it are determined by his own provenance in the Wolffian school. The "revolution of the way of thinking" motivated by Hume's impulse is not directed against empiricism but against post-Cartesian rationalism's way of thinking, whose great consummator was Leibniz and which was given its systematic textbook-like presentation, its most effective and by far most convincing form, by Christian Wolff.

First of all, what is the meaning of the "dogmatism," taken quite generally, that Kant uproots? Although the *Meditations* continued to have their effect on post-Cartesian philosophy, the passionate radicalism which drove them was not passed on to Descartes's successors. They were quite prepared to accept what Descartes only wished to establish, and found so hard to establish, by inquiring back into the ultimate source of all knowledge: namely, the absolute metaphysical validity of the objective sciences, or, taking these together, of philosophy as the one objective universal science; or, what comes to the same thing, the right of the knowing ego to let its rational constructs, in virtue of the self-evidences occurring in its *mens,* count as nature with a meaning transcending this ego. The new conception of the world of bodies, self-enclosed as nature, and the natural sciences related to them, the correlative conception of the self-enclosed souls and the task, related to them, of a new psychology with a rational method according to the mathematical model—all this had established itself. In every direction rational philosophy was under construction; of primary interest were discoveries, theories, the rigor of their inferences, and correspondingly the general problem of method and its perfection. Thus knowledge was very much discussed, and from a scientifically general point of view. This reflection on knowledge, however, was not *transcendental reflection* but rather a reflection on the *praxis of knowledge* and was thus similar to the reflection carried out by one who works in any other practical sphere of interest, the kind which is expressed in the general propositions of a *technology.* It is a matter of what we are accustomed to call logic, though in a traditional, very narrow, and limited sense. Thus we can say quite correctly (broadening the meaning): it is a matter of a logic as a theory of norms and a technology with the fullest universality, to the end of attaining a universal philosophy.

The thematic direction was thus twofold: on the one hand, toward a systematic universe of "logical laws," the theoretical totality of the truths destined to function as norms for all judgments which shall be capable of being objectively true—and to this belongs, in addition to the old formal logic, also arithmetic, all of pure analytic mathematics, i.e., the *mathesis universalis* of Leibniz, and in general everything that is purely a priori.

On the other hand, the thematic direction was toward general considerations about those who make judgments as those striving for objective truth: how they are to make normative use of those laws so that the self-evidence through which a judgment is certified as objectively true can appear, and similarly about the ways and temptations of failure, etc.

Now clearly, in all the laws which are in the broader sense "logical," beginning with the principle of noncontradiction, *metaphysical truth* was contained *eo ipso.* The systematically worked-out theory of these laws had, of itself, the meaning of a general ontology. What happened here scientifically was the work of pure reason operating exclusively with concepts innate in the knowing soul. That these concepts, that logical laws, that pure rational lawfulness in general contained metaphysical-objective truth was "obvious." Occasionally appeal was made to God as a guarantee, in remembrance of Descartes, with little concern for the fact that it was rational metaphysics which first had to establish God's existence.

Over against the faculty of pure a priori thinking, that of pure reason, stood that of sensibility, the faculty of outer and inner experience. The subject, affected in outer experience from "outside," thereby becomes certain of affecting objects, but in order to know them in their truth he needs pure reason, i.e., the system of norms in which reason displays itself, as the "logic" for all true knowledge of the objective world. Such is the [typical rationalist] conception.

As for Kant, who had been influenced by empiricist psychology: Hume had made him sensitive to the fact that between the pure truths of reason and metaphysical objectivity there remained a gulf of incomprehensibility, namely, as to how precisely these truths of reason could really guarantee the knowledge of things. Even the model rationality of the mathematical natural sciences was transformed into an enigma. That it owed its rationality, which was in fact quite indubitable—that is, its method—to the normative a priori of pure logicomathematical reason, and that the latter, in its disciplines, exhibited an unassailable pure rationality, remained unquestioned. Natural science is, to be sure, not purely rational insofar as it has need of outer experience, sensibility; but everything in it that is rational it owes to pure reason and its setting of norms; only through them can there be rationalized experience. As for sensibility, on the other hand, it had generally been assumed that it gives rise to the merely sensible data, precisely as a result of affection from the outside. And yet one acted as if the experiential world of the prescientific man—the world not yet logicized by mathematics—was the world pregiven by mere sensibility.

Hume had shown that we naïvely read causality into this world and think that we grasp necessary succession in intuition. The same is true of everything that makes the body of the everyday surrounding world into an identical thing with identical properties, relations, etc. (and Hume had in fact worked this out in detail in the *Treatise*, which was unknown to Kant). Data and complexes of data come and go, but the thing, presumed to be simply experienced sensibly, is not something sensible which persists through this alteration. The sensationalist thus declares it to be a fiction.

He is substituting, *we* shall say, mere sense-data for perception, which after all places *things* (everyday things) before our eyes. In other words, he overlooks the fact that mere sensibility, related to mere data of sense, cannot account for objects of experience. Thus he overlooks the fact that these objects of experience point to a hidden mental accomplishment and to the problem of what kind of an accomplishment this can be. From the very start, after all, it must be a kind which enables [the objects of] prescientific experience, through logic, mathematics, mathematical natural science, to be knowable with objective validity, i.e., with a necessity which can be accepted by and is binding for everyone.

But Kant says to himself: undoubtedly things appear, but only because the sense-data, already brought together in certain ways, in concealment, through a priori forms, are made logical in the course of their alteration—without any appeal to reason as manifested in logic and mathematics, without its being brought into normative function. Now is this quasilogical [function] something that is psychologically accidental? If we think of it as absent, can a mathematics, a logic of nature, ever have the possibility of knowing objects through mere sense-data?

These are, if I am not mistaken, the inwardly guiding thoughts of Kant. Kant now undertakes, in fact, to show, through a regressive procedure, that if common experience is really to be experience of *objects of nature,* objects which can really be knowable with objective truth, i.e., scientifically, in respect to their being and nonbeing, their being-such and being-otherwise [*So- und Andersbeschaffensein*], then the intuitively appearing world must already be a construct of the faculties of "pure intuition" and "pure reason," the same faculties that express themselves in explicit thinking in mathematics and logic.

In other words, reason has a *twofold* way of functioning and showing itself. One way is its systematic self-exposition, self-revelation in free and pure mathematizing, in the practice of the pure mathematical sciences. Here it presupposes the forming character of "pure intuition," which belongs to sensibility itself. The objective result of both faculties is pure mathematics as theory. The other way is that of reason constantly functioning in concealment, reason ceaselessly rationalizing sense-data and always having them as already rationalized. Its objective result is the sensibly intuited world of objects—the empirical presupposition of all natural-scientific thinking, i.e., the thinking which, through manifest mathematical reason, consciously gives norms to the experience of the surrounding world. Like the intuited world of bodies, the whole world of natural science (and with it the dualistic world which can be known scientifically) is a subjective construct of our intellect; only the material of the sense-data arises from a transcendent affection by "things in themselves." The latter are in principle inaccessible to (objective-scientific) knowledge. For according to this theory, man's science, as an accomplishment bound by the interplay of the subjective faculties "sensibility" and "reason" (or, as Kant says here, "understanding"), cannot explain the origin, the "cause," of the factual manifolds of sense-data. The ultimate presuppositions of the possibility and actuality of objective knowledge cannot be objectively knowable.

Whereas natural science had pretended to be a branch of philosophy, the ultimate science of what is, and had believed itself capable of knowing, through its rationality, what is in itself, beyond the subjectivity of the factualities of knowledge, for Kant, now, *objective science,* as an accomplishment remaining within subjectivity, is separated off from his *philosophical* theory. The latter, as a theory of the accomplishments necessarily carried out within subjectivity, and thus as a theory of the possibility and scope of objective knowledge, reveals the naïveté of the supposed rational philosophy of nature-in-itself.

We know how this critique is for Kant nevertheless the beginning of a philosophy in the old sense, for the universe of being, thus extending even to the *rationally* unknowable in-itself—how, under the titles "critique of practical reason" and "critique of judgment," he not only limits philosophical claims but also believes he is capable of opening ways toward the "scientifically" unknowable in-itself. Here we shall not go into this. What interests us now is—speaking in formal generality—that Kant, reacting against the data-positivism of Hume (as he understands it) outlines a great, systematically constructed, and *in a new way* still scientific philosophy in which the Cartesian turn to conscious subjectivity works itself out in the form of a transcendental subjectivism.

Irrespective of the truth of the Kantian philosophy, about which we need not pass judgment here, we must not pass over the fact that Hume, as he is understood by Kant, is not the real Hume.

Kant speaks of the "Humean problem." What is the actual problem, the one which drives Hume *himself*? We find it when we transform Hume's skeptical theory, his total claim, back into his *problem,* extending it to those consequences which do not quite find their complete expression in the theory—although it is difficult to suppose that a genius with a spirit like Hume's did not see these consequences, which are not expressly drawn and not theoretically treated. If we proceed in this way, we find nothing less than this universal problem:

How is the *naïve obviousness* of the certainty of the world, the certainty in which we live—and, what is more, the certainty of the *everyday* world as well as that of the sophisticated theoretical constructions built upon this everyday world—to be made comprehensible?

What is, in respect to sense and validity, the "objective world," objectively true being, and also the objective truth of science, once we have seen universally with Hume (and in respect to nature even with Berkeley) that "world" is a validity which has sprung up within subjectivity, indeed—speaking from my point of view, who am now philosophizing—one which has sprung up within *my* subjectivity, with all the content it ever counts as having for me?

The *naïveté* of speaking about "objectivity" without ever considering subjectivity as experiencing, knowing, and actually concretely accomplishing, the *naïveté* of the scientist of nature or of the world in general, who is blind to the fact that all the truths he attains as objective truths and the objective world itself as the substratum of his formulae (the everyday world of experience as well as the higher-level conceptual world of knowledge) are his own *life-construct* developed within himself—this *naïveté* is naturally no longer possible as soon as *life* becomes the point of focus. And must this liberation not come to anyone who seriously immerses himself in the *Treatise* and, after unmasking Hume's naturalistic presuppositions, becomes conscious of the power of his motivation?

But how is this most radical subjectivism, which subjectivizes the world itself, comprehensible? The world-enigma in the deepest and most ultimate sense, the enigma of a world whose being is being through subjective accomplishment, and this with the self-evidence that another world cannot be at all conceivable—that, and nothing else, is *Hume's problem.*

Kant, however, for whom, as can easily be seen, so many *presuppositions* are "obviously" valid, presuppositions which in the Humean sense are included within this world-enigma, never penetrated to the enigma itself. For his set of problems stands on the ground of the rationalism extending from Descartes through Leibniz to Wolff.

In this way, through the problem of rational natural science which primarily guides and determines Kant's thinking, we seek to make understandable Kant's position, so difficult to interpret, in relation to his historical setting. What particularly interests us now—speaking first in formal generality—is the fact that in reaction to the Humean data-positivism, which in his fictionalism gives up philosophy as a science, a great and systematically constructed scientific philosophy appears for the *first time since Descartes*—a philosophy which must be called *transcendental subjectivism*.

Preliminary discussion of the concept of the "transcendental" which guides us here.

I SHOULD LIKE TO NOTE the following right away: the expression "transcendental philosophy" has been much used since Kant, even as a general title for universal philosophies whose concepts are oriented toward those of the Kantian type. I myself use the word "transcendental" *in the broadest sense* for the original motif, discussed in detail above, which through Descartes confers meaning upon all modern philosophies, the motif which, in all of them, seeks to come to itself, so to speak—seeks to attain the genuine and pure form of its task and its systematic development. It is the motif of inquiring back into the ultimate source of all the formations of knowledge, the motif of the knower's reflecting upon himself and his knowing life in which all the scientific structures that are valid for him occur purposefully, are stored up as acquisitions, and have become and continue to become freely available. Working itself out radically, it is the motif of a universal philosophy which is grounded purely in this source and thus ultimately grounded. This source bears the title *I-myself,* with all of my actual and possible knowing life and, ultimately, my concrete life in general. The whole transcendental set of problems circles around the relation of *this,* my "I"—the "ego"—to what it is at first taken for granted to be—my soul—and, again, around the relation of this ego and my conscious life to the *world* of which I am conscious and whose true being I know through my own cognitive structures.

Of course this most general concept of the "transcendental" cannot be supported by documents; it is not to be gained through the internal exposition and comparison of the individual systems. Rather, it is a concept acquired by pondering the coherent history of the entire philosophical modern period: the concept of its task which is demonstrable only in this way, lying within it as the driving force of its development, striving forward from vague *dynamis* towards its *energeia*.

This is only a preliminary indication, which has already been prepared to a certain extent by our historical analysis up to this point; our subsequent presentations are to establish the justification for our kind of "teleological" approach to history and its methodical function for the definitive construction of a transcendental philosophy which satisfies its most proper meaning. This preliminary indication of a radical transcendental subjectivism will naturally seem strange and arouse skepticism. I welcome this, *if* this skepticism bespeaks, not the prior resolve of rejection, but rather a free withholding of any judgment.

The philosophy of Kant and his followers seen from the perspective of our guiding concept of the "transcendental." The task of taking a critical position.

RETURNING AGAIN TO KANT: his system can certainly be characterized, in the general sense defined, as one of "transcendental philosophy," although it is far from accomplishing a truly radical grounding of philosophy, the totality of all sciences. Kant never permitted himself to enter the vast depths of the Cartesian fundamental investigation, and his own set of problems never caused him to seek in these depths for ultimate groundings and decisions. Should I, in the following presentations, succeed—as I hope—in awakening the insight that a transcendental philosophy is the more genuine, and better fulfills its vocation as philosophy, the more radical it is and, finally, that it comes to its actual and true existence, to its actual and true beginning, only when the philosopher has penetrated to a clear understanding of himself as the subjectivity functioning as primal source, we should still have to recognize, on the other hand, that Kant's philosophy is on the *way* to this, that it is in accord with the formal, general sense of a transcendental philosophy in our definition. It is a philosophy which, in opposition to prescientific and scientific objectivism, goes back to knowing subjectivity as the primal locus of all objective formations of sense and ontic validities, undertakes to understand the existing world as a structure of sense and validity, and in this way seeks to set in motion an essentially new type of scientific attitude and a new type of philosophy. In fact, if we do not count the negativistic, skeptical philosophy of a Hume, the Kantian system is the first attempt, and one carried out with impressive scientific seriousness, at a truly universal transcendental philosophy meant to be a *rigorous science* in a sense of scientific rigor which has only now been discovered and which is the only genuine sense.

Something similar holds, we can say in advance, for the great continuations and revisions of Kantian transcendentalism in the great systems of German Idealism. They all share the basic conviction that the objective sciences (no matter how much they, and particularly the exact sciences, may consider themselves, in virtue of their obvious theoretical and practical accomplishments, to be in possession of the only true method and to be treasure houses of ultimate truths) are not seriously sciences at all, not cognitions ultimately grounded, i.e., not ultimately, theoretically responsible for themselves—and that they are not, then, cognitions of what exists in ultimate truth. This can be accomplished [according to German Idealism] only by a transcendental-subjective method and, carried through as a system, transcendental philosophy. As was already the case with Kant, the opinion is not that the self-evidence of the positive-scientific method is an illusion and its accomplishment an illusory accomplishment but rather that this self-evidence is itself a *problem;* that the objective-scientific method rests upon a never questioned, deeply concealed subjective ground whose philosophical elucidation will for the first time reveal the true meaning of the accomplishments of positive science and, correlatively, the true ontic meaning of the objective world—precisely as a transcendental-subjective meaning.

Now in order to be able to understand the position of Kant and of the systems of transcendental idealism proceeding from him, within modern philosophy's teleological unity of meaning, and thus to make progress in our own self-understanding, it is necessary to critically get closer to the style of Kant's scientific attitude and to clarify the lack of radicalism we are attacking in his philosophizing. It is with good reason that we pause over Kant, a significant turning point in modern history. The critique to be directed against him will reflect back and elucidate all earlier philosophical history, namely, in respect to the general meaning of scientific discipline which all earlier philosophies strove to realize—as the only meaning which lay and could possibly lie within their spiritual horizon. Precisely in this way a more profound concept—the most important of all—of "objectivism" will come to the fore (more important than the one we were able to define earlier), and with it the genuinely radical meaning of the opposition between objectivism and transcendentalism.

Yet, over and above this, the more concrete critical analyses of the conceptual structures of the Kantian turn, and the contrast between it and the Cartesian turn, will set in motion our own concurrent thinking in such a way as to place us, gradually and of its own accord, before the *final turn* and the final decisions. We ourselves shall be drawn into an inner transformation through which we shall come face to face with, to *direct experience* of, the long-felt but constantly concealed dimension of the "transcendental." The ground of experience, opened up in its infinity, will then become the fertile soil of a methodical working philosophy, with the self-evidence, furthermore, that all conceivable philosophical and scientific problems of the past are to be posed and decided by starting from this ground.

67

Martin Heidegger

An Introduction to Metaphysics (1959)

The Limitation of Being

JUST AS IN THE "IS" WE HAVE A THOROUGHLY FAMILIAR mode of discourse of being, so in the noun "being" we run into very definite modes of discourse that have even taken on a quality of formulas: being and becoming; being and appearance; being and thinking; being and the ought.

When we say "being" we tend, almost as though under compulsion, to continue: being and . . . This "and" does not mean only that we casually throw in something else; no, we are adding something from which "being" is distinguished: being *and not* . . . But in these formula-like titles we also mean something which, differentiated from being, somehow belongs intrinsically to being, if only as its Other.

The course of our questioning up to this point has illuminated more than its range. True, for the present we have perceived the question itself, the fundamental question of meta-physics, as a question proposed to us from somewhere outside. But we have come appreciably closer to an understanding of the value of this question. More and more it has proved to be a hidden ground of our historical being-there. This it remains even, and particularly, when, self-satisfied and busy with all manner of things, we move about over this ground as over a flimsily covered abyss <Abgrund>.

Now we shall pursue the distinctions between being and other concepts. In so doing we shall learn that, contrary to the opinion current in this country, being is anything but an empty word and is indeed determined in so many aspects that we have difficulty in orienting ourselves so as to keep a sufficient grip on the determinateness. But this is not enough. The experience must be developed into a fundamental experience of our future historical being-there. In order that we may from the very outset effect (and participate in) the distinctions in the proper way, it may be well to give the following pointers:

1   Being is delimited from something else; in this delimitation it already has determinateness.

2   It is delimited in four interrelated respects. Accordingly, the determinateness of being must either become ramified and heightened or else diminish.

3   These distinctions are by no means accidental. What is held apart in them belonged originally together and tends to merge. The distinctions therefore have an inner necessity.

4   Consequently the oppositions, which look at first sight like formulas, did not arise fortuitously and find their way into the language as figures of speech. They arose in close connection with the development of the concept of being, a process crucial for the history of the West. They began with the beginning of philosophical questioning.

5   These distinctions have remained dominant not only in Western philosophy. They permeate all knowledge, action, and discourse even where they are not specifically mentioned or not in these words.

6   The order in which the titles have been listed provides in itself an indication of the order in which they are internally linked and of the historical order in which they were shaped.

    The first two distinctions (being and becoming, being and appearance) were developed at the very beginning of Greek philosophy. As the oldest, they are also the best known.

    The third distinction (being and thinking) was foreshadowed as early as the first two; its decisive unfolding occurred in the philosophy of Plato and Aristotle, but it took on its actual form only with the beginning of the modern era. It even played an essential part in this beginning. As its history suggests, it is the most complex of the four distinctions and the most problematic in purpose. (For this reason it remains for us the one most worthy of questioning.)

    The fourth distinction (being and the ought) was only remotely foreshadowed by the designation of the *on* <the essent, that which is> as *agathon* <the good>. It belongs wholly to the modern era. And since the end of the eighteenth century it has determined one of the dominant positions of the modern spirit toward the essent in general.

7   If one is to ask the question of being radically, one must understand the task of unfolding the truth of the essence of being; one must come to a decision regarding the powers hidden in these distinctions in order to restore them to their own truth.

All these preliminary remarks should be born constantly in mind in connection with the following considerations.

1 Being and Becoming

This distinction and opposition stands at the beginning of the inquiry into being. Today it is still the most current restriction of being by something other; for it comes directly to mind from the standpoint of a conception of being that has congealed into the self-evident. What becomes is not yet. What is need no longer become. What "is," the essent, has left all becoming behind it if indeed it ever became or could become. What "is" in the authentic sense also resists every onsurge of becoming.

Parmenides lived at the turn of the fifth century B.C. Farsighted thinker and poet, he set forth the being of the essent in contradistinction to becoming. His "didactic poem" has come down to us only in fragments, but in large and important ones. Here I shall cite only a few verses (Fragment 8, lines 1–6):

> But only the legend remains of the way
> (along which it is disclosed) how it stands with being; on this
> (way) there are many indications:
> how being, without genesis, is without destruction,
> complete <voll-ständig, fully standing>, alone there
> without tremor and not still requiring to be finished;
> nor was it before, nor will it be in the future,
> for being present it *is* entirely, unique, unifying, united,
> gathering itself in itself from itself (cohesive,
> full of presentness).[1]

These few words stand there like the Greek statues of the early period. What we still possess of Parmenides' didactic poem fits into a thin brochure, but this little brochure is one which might perfectly well replace whole libraries of supposedly indispensable philosophical literature. Anyone living today who knows the measure of such thinking discourse must lose all desire to write books.

What is said here from within the heart of being consists of *sēmata,* not signs of being, not predicates, but indications which in looking-toward being from within being indicate being. For in thus looking-toward being we must, in an active sense, look-away from all coming-into-being and passing-away, etc.: in the act of seeing we must hold them away, expel them. What is kept away by *a-* and *oude* is not commensurate with being. It has another measure.

To this discourse, we conclude, being appears as the pure fullness of the permanent, gathered within it, untouched by unrest and change. Even today it is customary in describing the beginning of Western philosophy to oppose the doctrine of Heraclitus to this doctrine of Parmenides. A much-quoted saying is attributed to Heraclitus: *panta rhei,* everything is in flux. Accordingly there is no being. Everything "is" becoming.

The occurrence of such oppositions, here being, there becoming, is accepted as perfectly natural, because it seems to provide an example, from the very beginning of philosophy, of a state of affairs that is supposed to run through the whole history of philosophy, namely that where one philosopher says A, another will say B, but that if the second says A, the first will say B. Yet when it is argued in answer to this supposition that all thinkers throughout the history of philosophy have said fundamentally the same thing, this too seems to impose on common sense. If they all say the same thing, why the whole multifarious and complicated history of Western philosophy? If that were so, *one* philosophy would suffice. And yet this "sameness" has an inner truth, namely the inexhaustible richness of what on every single day is as though that day were its first.

Actually Heraclitus, to whom is ascribed the doctrine of becoming as diametrically opposed to Parmenides' doctrine of being, says the same as Parmenides. He would not be one of the greatest of the great Greeks if he had said something different. But his doctrine of becoming must not be interpreted in line with the ideas of nineteenth-century Darwinism. It is true that the opposition between being and becoming was never again represented so uniquely and self-sufficiently as in Parmenides. In that great age, in Parmenides, the saga of the being of the essent itself partakes of the (hidden) essence of the being of which it speaks. The secret of greatness resides in its historic necessity. For reasons that will become clear in the following, we shall limit our present discussion of this first distinction—"being and becoming"—to these few indications.

2 Being and Appearance

This distinction is as old as the first. The fact that the two distinctions (being and becoming, being and appearance) are equally primordial points to a profound connection between them. Hitherto this connection has been inaccessible to us. It has not been possible to redevelop the second distinction (being and appearance) in its true meaning. To do so one must understand it in its original, i.e. Greek, sense. For us, burdened as we are with the modern epistemological misinterpretation—for us who scarcely respond, and then for the most part emptily, to the simplicity of the essential—this is no easy matter.

At first sight the distinction seems clear. Being and appearance means: the real in contradistinction to the unreal; the authentic over against the inauthentic. The distinction implies an evaluation—the preference is given to being. As we say: the miracle and the miraculous, so we say appearance and the apparent. Often the distinction between being and appearance is carried back to our first distinction—being and becoming. The apparent is that which from time to time emerges and vanishes, the ephemeral and unstable over against being as the permanent.

The distinction between being and appearance is familiar to us, another of the many worn-out coins that we pass unexamined from hand to hand in an everyday life that has grown flat. When it turns up, we use the distinction as a rule of life, a moral admonition to avoid appearance and to strive for being: "to be rather than seem."

Yet familiar and self-evident as the distinction is, we do not understand in what way a fundamental separation occurs between precisely being and appearance. The very fact that it occurs suggests that the two are related. Wherein does the bond consist? First we must understand the hidden unity of being and appearance. We have ceased to understand it because we have fallen away from the initial, historically developed difference and merely carry it around as something that was once, somewhere and at some time, put into circulation.

To grasp the difference we must here again go back to the beginning.

But if, before it is too late, we turn our backs on idle, thoughtless chatter, we shall find, even in ourselves, a track leading to the understanding of the difference. We say "appearance" and we know the rain and the sunshine. The sun shines <scheinen, "to seem" and "to shine">. We say: "the room was feebly lighted by the glow <Schein> of a candle." The Alemanic dialect has the word "Scheinholz," wood that glows in the darkness. From pictures of saints we know the halo <Heiligen*schein*>, the glowing ring about their heads. But we also know pseudo saints <*Schein*heilige>, those who look like saints but are not saints. We are familiar with the sham battle <*Schein*gefecht> or simulated battle. The sun, as it shines <scheint> seems <scheint> to move around the earth. The moon which shines seems, but only seems, to measure two feet in diameter, that is only an illusion <Schein>. Here we run into two different kinds of Schein and scheinen. But they do not simply stand side by side; no, one is a variant of the other. The sun, for example, can have the appearance <Schein> of moving round the earth only because it shines, i.e. glows and in glowing manifests itself, i.e. comes to light <zum Vor*schein*>. In the shining of the sun, to be sure, we at the same time experience its radiation as heat. The sun shines: it shows itself and we feel warmth. In the halo the shining of the light makes the wearer manifest <bringt zum Vorschein> as a saint.

On closer scrutiny we find three modes of Schein: 1) Schein as radiance and glow; 2) Schein and Scheinen as appearing, as coming to light; 3) Schein as mere appearance or semblance <Anschein>. But at the same time it becomes clear that the second variety of "Scheinen," appearing in the sense of showing itself, pertains both to Schein as radiance and to Schein as semblance, and not as a fortuitous attribute but as the ground of their possibility. The essence of appearance <Schein> lies in the appearing <Erscheinen>. It is self-manifestation, self-representation, standing-there, presence. The long-awaited book has just appeared, i.e. it is before us, and therefore to be had. When we say: the moon shines <scheint>, this means not only that it spreads a glow <Schein>, a certain brightness, but also: it stands in the sky, it is present, it is. The stars shine: glittering, they are present. Here appearance <Schein> means exactly the same as being. (Sappho's verses:*asteres men amphi kalan sellanan* . . . and the poem by Matthias Claudius, "Ein Wiegenlied bei Mondschein zu singen," provide a suitable basis for reflection on being and appearance.)

If we meditate on the above, we find the inner connection between being and appearance. But we grasp it fully only if we understand being in an equally primordial, i.e. Greek, sense. We know that being disclosed itself to the Greeks as *physis*. The realm of emerging and abiding is intrinsically at the same time a shining appearing <das scheinende Erscheinen>. The radicals *phy* and *pha* name the same thing. *Phyein*, self-sufficient emergence, is *phainesthai*, to flare up, to show itself, to appear. Already the traits of being that we have meanwhile listed without really going into them, and our reference to Parmenides, have given us a certain understanding of the basic Greek word for being.

It would be instructive to elucidate the meaning of this word through the great poetry of the Greeks. Here it may suffice to point out that for Pindar *phya* was the fundamental determination of man's being-there: *to de phya krattiston,* that which is through and from out of *phya* is the mightiest of all (Olympian Ode ix, 100); *phya* means what one originally and authentically is: the past and essential <das Ge-Wesende> as opposed to the subsequently imposed bustle and pretense. Being is the fundamental attribute of the noble individual and of nobility (i.e. of what has a high origin and rests in it). In regard to this Pindar coins the saying *genoi' hoios essi mathōn* (Pythian Ode ii, 72). "Mayest thou by learning come forth as what thou art." But for the Greeks standing-in-itself was nothing other than standing-there, standing-in-the-light. Being means appearing. Appearing is not something subsequent that sometimes happens to being. Appearing is the very essence of being.

This punctures the empty construction of Greek philosophy as a "realistic" philosophy which, unlike modern subjectivism, was a doctrine of objective being. This widespread conception is based on a superficial understanding. We must leave aside terms like "subjective" and "objective," "realistic" and "idealistic."

Only now are we in a position, on the basis of a more appropriate view of being as the Greeks saw it, to take the decisive step which will open up to us the inner relationship between being and appearance; to gain an insight into a relationship which is originally and uniquely Greek but which compassed characteristic consequences for the spirit of the West. The essence of being is *physis*. Appearing is the power that emerges. Appearing makes manifest. Already we know then that being, appearing, causes to emerge from concealment. Since the essent as such *is*, it places itself in and stands in *unconcealment, alētheia*. We translate, and at the same time thoughtlessly misinterpret, this word as "truth." To be sure, people are gradually beginning to translate the Greek word *alētheia* literally. But this does not help much if one goes right on to construe "truth" in a totally different un-Greek sense and attribute this other sense to the Greek word. For the Greek essence of truth is possible only in one with the Greek essence of being as *physis*. On the strength of the unique and essential relationship between *physis* and *alētheia* the Greeks would have said: The essent is true insofar as it is. The true as such is essent. This means: The power that manifests itself stands in unconcealment. In showing itself, the unconcealed as such comes to stand. Truth as un-concealment is not an appendage to being.

Truth is inherent in the essence of being. To be an essent—this comprises to come to light, to appear on the scene, to take one's <its> place <sich hin-stellen>, to produce <her-stellen>

something. Nonbeing, on the other hand, means: to withdraw from appearing, from presence. The essence of appearing includes coming-on-the-scene and withdrawing, hither and thither in the truly demonstrative, indicative sense. Being is thus dispersed among the manifold essents. These display themselves as the momentary and close-at-hand. In appearing it gives itself an aspect, *dokei. Doxa* means aspect, regard <Ansehen>, namely the regard in which one stands. If the regard, in keeping with what emerges in it, is a distinguished one, *doxa* means fame and glory. In Hellenistic theology and in the New Testament *doxa theou,* gloria Dei, is God's grandeur. To glorify, to attribute regard to, and disclose regard means in Greek: to place in the light and thus endow with permanence, being. For the Greeks glory was not something additional which one might or might not obtain; it was the mode of the highest being. For moderns glory has long been nothing more than celebrity and as such a highly dubious affair, an acquisition tossed about and distributed by the newspapers and the radio—almost the opposite of being. If for Pindar to glorify was the essence of poetry and the work of the poet was to place in the light, it was not because the notion of light played a special role for him but solely because he thought and composed poetry as a Greek, which is to say that he stood in the appointed essence of being.

Note

1   *μόνος δ' ἔτι μῦθος ὁδοῖο / λείπεται ὡς ἔστιν. ταύτηι δ' ἐπὶ σήματ' ἔασι / πολλὰ μάλ', ὡς ἀγένητον ἐὸν ἀνώλεθρόν ἐστιν, ἔστι γάρ οὐλομελές τε καὶ ἀτρεμὲς ἠδ' ἀτέλεστον, οὐδέ ποτ' ἦν οὐδ' ἔσται, ἐπεὶ νῦν ἔστιν ὁμοῦ πάν, / ἕν, συνεχές.*

68

Paul Tillich

The Dynamics of Faith (1967)

Faith as Ultimate Concern

FAITH IS THE STATE OF BEING ULTIMATELY CONCERNED: THE DYNAMICS of faith are the dynamics of man's ultimate concern. Man, like every living being, is concerned about many things, above all about those which condition his very existence, such as food and shelter. But man, in contrast to other living beings, has spiritual concerns—cognitive, aesthetic, social, political. Some of them are urgent, often extremely urgent, and each of them as well as the vital concerns can claim ultimacy for a human life or the life of a social group. If it claims ultimacy it demands the total surrender of him who accepts this claim, and it promises total fulfillment even if all other claims have to be subjected to it or rejected in its name. If a national group makes the life and growth of the nation its ultimate concern, it demands that all other concerns, economic well-being, health and life, family, aesthetic and cognitive truth, justice and humanity, be sacrificed. The extreme nationalisms of our century are laboratories for the study of what ultimate concern means in all aspects of human existence, including the smallest concern of one's daily life. Everything is centered in the only god, the nation—a god who certainly proves to be a demon, but who shows clearly the unconditional character of an ultimate concern.

But it is not the unconditional demand made by that which is one's ultimate concern, it is also the promise of ultimate fulfillment which is accepted in the act of faith. The content of this promise is not necessarily defined. It can be expressed in indefinite symbols or in concrete symbols which cannot be taken literally, like the "greatness" of one's nation in which one participates even if one has died for it, or the conquest of mankind by the "saving race," etc. In each of these cases it is "ultimate fulfillment" that is promised, and it is exclusion from such fulfillment which is threatened if the unconditional demand is not obeyed.

An example—and more than an example—is the faith manifest in the religion of the Old Testament. It also has the character of ultimate concern in demand, threat and promise.

The content of this concern is not the nation—although Jewish nationalism has sometimes tried to distort it into that—but the content is the God of justice, who, because he represents justice for everybody and every nation, is called the universal God, the God of the universe. He is the ultimate concern of every pious Jew, and therefore in his name the great commandment is given: "You shall love the Lord your God with all your heart, and with all your soul, and with all your might" (Deut. 6:5). This is what ultimate concern means and from these words the term "ultimate concern" is derived. They state unambiguously the character of genuine faith, the demand of total surrender to the subject of ultimate concern. The Old Testament is full of commands which make the nature of this surrender concrete, and it is full of promises and threats in relation to it. Here also are the promises of symbolic indefiniteness, although they center around fulfillment of the national and individual life, and the threat is the exclusion from such fulfillment through national extinction and individual catastrophe. Faith, for the men of the Old Testament, is the state of being ultimately and unconditionally concerned about Jahweh and about what he represents in demand, threat and promise.

Another example—almost a counter-example, yet nevertheless quality revealing—is the ultimate concern with "success" and with social standing and economic power. It is the god of many people in the highly competitive Western culture and it does what every ultimate concern must do: it demands unconditional surrender to its laws even if the price is the sacrifice of genuine human relations, personal conviction, and creative *eros*. Its threat is social and economic defeat, and its promise—indefinite as all such promises—the fulfillment of one's being. It is the breakdown of this kind of faith which characterizes and makes religiously important most contemporary literature. Not false calculations but a misplaced faith is revealed in novels like *Point of No Return*. When fulfilled, the promise of this faith proves to be empty.

Faith is the state of being ultimately concerned. The content matters infinitely for the life of the believer, but it does not matter for the formal definition of faith. And this is the first step we have to make in order to understand the dynamics of faith.

Faith as a Centered Act

Faith as ultimate concern is an act of the total personality. It happens in the center of the personal life and includes all its elements. Faith is the most centered act of the human mind. It is not a movement of a special section or a special function of man's total being. They all are united in the act of faith. But faith is not the sum total of their impacts. It transcends every special impact as well as the totality of them and it has itself a decisive impact on each of them.

Since faith is an act of the personality as a whole, it participates in the dynamics of personal life. These dynamics have been described in many ways, especially in the recent developments of analytic psychology. Thinking in polarities, their tensions and their possible conflicts, is a common characteristic of most of them. This makes the psychology of personality highly dynamic and requires a dynamic theory of faith as the most personal of all personal acts. The first and decisive polarity in analytic psychology is that between the so-called unconscious and the conscious. Faith as an act of the total personality is not imaginable without the participation of the unconscious elements in the personality structure. They are always present and decide largely about the content of faith. But, on the other hand, faith is a conscious act and the unconscious elements participate in the creation of faith only if they are taken into the personal center which transcends each of them. If this does not happen, if unconscious forces determine the mental status without a centered act, faith does not occur, and compulsions take its place. For faith is a matter of freedom. Freedom is nothing more than the possibility of centered personal acts. The frequent discussion in which faith and freedom are contrasted could be helped by the insight that faith is a free, namely, centered act of the personality. In this respect freedom and faith are identical.

Also important for the understanding of faith is the polarity between what Freud and his school call ego and superego. The concept of the superego is quite ambiguous. On the one hand, it is the basis of all cultural life because it restricts the uninhibited actualization of the always-driving libido; on the other hand, it cuts off man's vital forces, and produces disgust about the whole system of cultural restrictions, and brings about a neurotic state of mind. From this point of view, the symbols of faith are considered to be expressions of the superego or, more concretely, to be an expression of the father image which gives content to the superego. Responsible for this inadequate theory of the superego is Freud's naturalistic negation of norms and principles. If the superego is not established through valid principles, it becomes a suppressive tyrant. But real faith, even if it uses the father image for its expression, transforms this image into a principle of truth and justice to be defended even against the "father." Faith and culture can be affirmed only if the superego represents the norms and principles of reality.

This leads to the question of how faith as a personal, centered act is related to the rational structure of man's personality which is manifest in his meaningful language, in his ability to know the true and to do the good, in his sense of beauty and justice. All this, and not only his possibility to analyze, to calculate and to argue, makes him a rational being. But in spite of this larger concept of reason we must deny that man's essential nature is identical with the rational character of his mind. Man is able to decide for or against reason, he is able to create beyond reason or to destroy below reason. This power is the power of his self, the center of self-relatedness in which all elements of his being are united. Faith is not an act of any of his rational functions, as it is not an act of the unconscious, but it is an act in which both the rational and the nonrational elements of his being are transcended.

Faith as the embracing and centered act of the personality is "ecstatic." It transcends both the drives of the nonrational unconscious and the structures of the rational conscious. It transcends them, but it does not destroy them. The ecstatic character of faith does not exclude its rational character although it is not identical with it, and it includes nonrational strivings without being identical with them. In the ecstasy of faith there is an awareness of truth and of ethical value; there are also past loves and hates, conflicts and reunions, individual and collective influences. "Ecstasy" means "standing outside of oneself"—without ceasing to be oneself—with all the elements which are united in the personal center.

A further polarity in these elements, relevant for the understanding of faith, is the tension between the cognitive function of man's personal life, on the one hand, and emotion and will, on the other hand. In a later discussion I will try to show that many distortions of the meaning of faith are rooted in the attempt to subsume faith to the one or the other of these functions. At this point it must be stated as sharply and insistently as possible that in every act of faith there is cognitive affirmation, not as the result of an independent process of inquiry but as an inseparable element in a total act of acceptance and surrender. This also excludes the idea that faith is the result of an independent act of "will to believe." There is certainly affirmation by the will of what concerns one ultimately, but faith is not a creation of the will. In the ecstasy of faith the will to accept and to surrender is an element, but not the cause. And this is true also of feeling. Faith is not an emotional outburst: this is not the meaning of ecstasy. Certainly, emotion is in it, as in every act of man's spiritual life. But emotion does not produce faith. Faith has a cognitive content and is an act of the will. It is the unity of every element in the centered self. Of course, the unity of all elements in the act of faith does not prevent one or the other element from dominating in a special form of faith. It dominates the character of faith but it does not create the act of faith.

This also answers the question of a possible psychology of faith. Everything that happens in man's personal being can become an object of psychology. And it is rather important for both the philosopher of religion and the practical minister to know how the act of faith is embedded in the totality of psychological processes. But in contrast to this justified and desirable form of a psychology of faith there is another one which tries to derive faith from something that is not faith but is most frequently fear. The presupposition of this method is that fear or something else from which faith is derived is more original and basic than faith. But this presupposition cannot be proved. On the contrary, one can prove that in the scientific method which leads to such consequences faith is already effective. Faith precedes all attempts to derive it from something else, because these attempts are themselves based on faith.

Symbols of Faith

1 The Meaning of Symbol

Man's ultimate concern must be expressed symbolically, because symbolic language alone is able to express the ultimate. This statement demands explanation in several respects. In spite of the manifold research about the meaning and function of symbols which is going on in contemporary philosophy, every writer who uses the term "symbol" must explain his understanding of it.

Symbols have one characteristic in common with signs; they point beyond themselves to something else. The red sign at the street corner points to the order to stop the movements of cars at certain intervals. A red light and the stopping of cars have essentially no relation to each other, but conventionally they are united as long as the convention lasts. The same is true of letters and numbers and partly even words. They point beyond themselves to sounds and meanings. They are given this special function by convention within a nation or by international conventions, as the mathematical signs. Sometimes such signs are called symbols; but this is unfortunate because it makes the distinction between signs and symbols more difficult. Decisive is the fact that signs do not participate in the reality of that to which they point, while symbols do. Therefore, signs can be replaced for reasons of expediency or convention, while symbols cannot.

This leads to the second characteristic of the symbol: It participates in that to which it points: the flag participates in the power and dignity of the nation for which it stands. Therefore, it cannot be replaced except after an historic catastrophe that changes the reality of the nation which it symbolizes. An attack on the flag is felt as an attack on the majesty of the group in which it is acknowledged. Such an attack is considered blasphemy.

The third characteristic of a symbol is that it opens up levels of reality which otherwise are closed for us. All arts create symbols for a level of reality which cannot be reached in any other way. A picture and a poem reveal elements of reality which cannot be approached scientifically. In the creative work of art we encounter reality in a dimension which is closed for us without such works. The symbol's fourth characteristic not only opens up dimensions and elements of reality which otherwise would remain unapproachable but also unlocks dimensions and elements of our soul which correspond to the dimensions and elements of reality. A great play gives us not only a new vision of the human scene, but it opens up hidden depths of our own being. Thus we are able to receive what the play reveals to us in reality. There are within us dimensions of which we cannot become aware except through symbols, as melodies and rhythms in music.

Symbols cannot be produced intentionally—this is the fifth characteristic. They grow out of the individual or collective unconscious and cannot function without being accepted by the unconscious dimension of our being. Symbols which have an especially social function, as political and religious symbols, are created or at least accepted by the collective unconscious of the group in which they appear.

The sixth and last characteristic of the symbol is a consequence of the fact that symbols cannot be invented. Like living beings, they grow and they die. They grow when the situation is ripe for them, and they die when the situation changes. The symbol of the "king" grew in a special period of history, and it died in most parts of the world in our period. Symbols do not grow because people are longing for them, and they do not die because of scientific or practical criticism. They die because they can no longer produce response in the group where they originally found expression.

These are the main characteristics of every symbol. Genuine symbols are created in several spheres of man's cultural creativity. We have mentioned already the political and the artistic realm. We could add history and, above all, religion, whose symbols will be our particular concern.

2 Religious Symbols

We have discussed the meaning of symbols generally because, as we said, man's ultimate concern must be expressed symbolically! One may ask: Why can it not be expressed directly and properly? If money, success or the nation is someone's ultimate concern, can this not be said in a direct way without symbolic language? Is it not only in those cases in which the content of the ultimate concern is called "God" that we are in the realm of symbols? The answer is that everything which is a matter of unconditional concern is made into a god. If the nation is someone's ultimate concern, the name of the nation becomes a sacred name and the nation receives divine qualities which far surpass the reality of the being and functioning of the nation. The nation then stands for and symbolizes the true ultimate, but in an idolatrous way. Success as ultimate concern is not the natural desire of actualizing potentialities, but is, readiness to sacrifice all other values of life for the sake of a position of power and social predominance. The anxiety about not being a success is an idolatrous form of the anxiety about divine condemnation. Success is grace; lack of success, ultimate judgment. In this way concepts designating ordinary realities become idolatrous symbols of ultimate concern.

The reason for this transformation of concepts into symbols is the character of ultimacy and the nature of faith. That which is the true ultimate transcends the realm of finite reality infinitely. Therefore, no finite reality can express it directly and properly. Religiously speaking, God transcends his own name. This is why the use of his name easily becomes an abuse or a blasphemy. Whatever we say about that which concerns us ultimately, whether or not we call it God, has a symbolic meaning. It points beyond itself while participating in that to which it points. In no other way can faith express itself adequately. The language of faith is the language of symbols. If faith were what we have shown that it is not, such an assertion could not be made. But faith, understood as the state of being ultimately concerned, has no language other than symbols. When saying this I always expect the question: Only a symbol? He who asks this question shows that he has not understood the difference between signs and symbols nor the power of symbolic language, which surpasses in quality and strength the power of any nonsymbolic language. One should never say "only a symbol," but one should say "not less than a symbol." With this in mind we can now describe the different kinds of symbols of faith.

The fundamental symbol of our ultimate concern is God. It is always present in any act of faith, even if the act of faith includes the denial of God. Where there is ultimate concern, God can be denied only in the name of God. One God can deny the other one. Ultimate concern cannot deny its own character as ultimate. Therefore, it affirms what is meant by the word "God." Atheism, consequently, can only mean the attempt to remove any ultimate concern—to remain unconcerned about the meaning of one's existence. Indifference toward the ultimate question is the only imaginable form of atheism. Whether it is possible is a problem which must remain unsolved at this point. In any case, he who denies God as a matter of ultimate concern affirms God, because he affirms ultimacy in his concern. God is the fundamental symbol for what concerns us ultimately. Again it would be completely wrong to ask: So God is nothing but a symbol? Because the next question has to be: A symbol for what? And then the answer would be: For God! God is symbol for God. This means that in the notion of God we must distinguish two elements: the element of ultimacy, which is a matter of immediate experience and not symbolic in itself, and the element of concreteness, which is taken from our ordinary experience and symbolically applied to God. The man whose ultimate concern is a sacred tree has both the ultimacy of concern and the concreteness of the tree which symbolizes his relation to the ultimate. The man who adores Apollo is ultimately concerned, but not in an abstract way. His ultimate concern is symbolized in the divine figure of Apollo. The man who glorifies Jahweh, the God of the Old Testament, has both an ultimate concern and a concrete image of what concerns him ultimately. This is the meaning of the seemingly cryptic statement that God is the symbol of God. In this qualified sense God is the fundamental and universal content of faith.

It is obvious that such an understanding of the meaning of God makes the discussions about the existence or nonexistence of God meaningless. It is meaningless to question the ultimacy of an ultimate concern. This element in the idea of God is in itself certain. The symbolic expression of this element varies endlessly through the whole history of mankind. Here again it would be meaningless to ask whether one or another of the figures in which an ultimate concern is symbolized does "exist." If "existence" refers to something which can be found within the whole of reality, no divine being exists. The question is not this, but: which of the innumerable symbols of faith is most adequate to the meaning of faith? In other words, which symbol of ultimacy expresses the ultimate without idolatrous elements? This is the problem, and not the so-called "existence of God"—which is in itself an impossible combination of words. God as the ultimate in man's ultimate concern is more certain than any other certainty, even that of oneself. God as symbolized in a divine figure is a matter of daring faith, of courage and risk.

God is the basic symbol of faith, but not the only one. All the qualities we attribute to him, power, love, justice, are taken from finite experiences and applied symbolically to that which is beyond finitude and infinity. If faith calls God "almighty," it uses the human experience of power in order to symbolize the content of its infinite concern, but it does not describe a highest being who can do as he pleases. So it is with all the other qualities and with all the actions, past, present and future, which men attribute to God. They are symbols taken from our daily experience, and not information about what God did once upon a time or will do sometime in the future. Faith is not the belief in such stories, but it is the acceptance of symbols that express our ultimate concern in terms of divine actions.

Another group of symbols of faith are manifestations of the divine in things and events, in persons and communities, in words and documents. This whole realm of sacred objects is a treasure of symbols. Holy things are not holy in themselves, but they point beyond themselves to the source of all holiness, that which is of ultimate concern.

3 Symbols and Myths

The symbols of faith do not appear in isolation. They are united in "stories of the gods," which is the meaning of the Greek word "mythos"—myth. The gods are individualized figures, analogous to human personalities, sexually differentiated, descending from each other, related to each other in love and struggle, producing world and man, acting in time and space. They participate in human greatness and misery, in creative and destructive works. They give to man cultural and religious traditions, and defend these sacred rites. They help and threaten the human race, especially some families, tribes or nations. They appear in epiphanies and incarnations, establish sacred places, rites and persons, and thus create a cult. But they themselves are under the command and threat of a fate which is beyond everything that is. This is mythology as developed most impressively in ancient Greece. But many of these characteristics can be found in every mythology. Usually the mythological gods are not equals. There is a hierarchy, at the top of which is a ruling god, as in Greece; or a trinity of them, as in India; or a duality of them, as in Persia. There are savior-gods who mediate between the highest gods and man, sometimes sharing the suffering and death of man in spite of their essential immortality. This is the world of the myth, great and strange, always changing but fundamentally the same: man's ultimate concern symbolized in divine figures and actions. Myths are symbols of faith combined in stories about divine-human encounters.

Myths are always present in every act of faith, because the language of faith is the symbol. They are also attacked, criticized and transcended in each of the great religions of mankind. The reason for this criticism is the very nature of the myth. It uses material from our ordinary experience. It puts the stories of the gods into the framework of time and space although it belongs to the nature of the ultimate to be beyond time and space. Above all, it divides the divine into several figures, removing ultimacy from each of them without removing their claim to ultimacy. This inescapably leads to conflicts of ultimate claims, able to destroy life, society and consciousness.

The criticism of the myth first rejects the division of the divine and goes beyond it to one God, although in different ways according to the different types of religion. Even one God is an object of mythological language, and if spoken about is drawn into the framework of time and space. Even he loses his ultimacy if made to be the content of concrete concern. Consequently, the criticism of the myth does not end with the rejection of the polytheistic mythology.

Monotheism also falls under the criticism of the myth. It needs, as one says today, "demythologization." This word has been used in connection with the elaboration of the mythical elements in stories and symbols of the Bible, both of the Old and the New Testaments—stories like those of the Paradise, of the fall of Adam, of the great Flood, of the Exodus from Egypt, of the virgin birth of the Messiah, of many of his miracles, of his resurrection and ascension, of his expected return as the judge of the universe. In short, all the stories in which divine-human interactions are told are considered as mythological in character, and objects of demythologization. What does this negative and artificial term mean? It must be accepted and supported if it points to the necessity of recognizing a symbol as a symbol and a myth as a myth. It must be attacked and rejected if it means the removal of symbols and myths altogether. Such an attempt is the third step in the criticism of the myth. It is an attempt which never can be successful, because symbol and myth are forms of the human consciousness which are always present. One can replace one myth by another, but one cannot remove the myth from man's spiritual life. For the myth is the combination of symbols of our ultimate concern.

A myth which is understood as a myth, but not removed or replaced, can be called a "broken myth." Christianity denies by its very nature any unbroken myth, because its presupposition is the first commandment: the affirmation of the ultimate as ultimate and the rejection of any kind of idolatry. All mythological elements in the Bible, and doctrine and liturgy should be recognized as mythological, but they should be maintained in their symbolic form and not be replaced by scientific substitutes. For there is no substitute for the use of symbols and myths: they are the language of faith.

The radical criticism of the myth is due to the fact that the primitive mythological consciousness resists the attempt to interpret the myth of myth. It is afraid of every act of demythologization. It believes that the broken myth is deprived of its truth and of its convincing power. Those who live in an unbroken mythological world feel safe and certain. They resist, often fanatically, any attempt to introduce an element of uncertainty by "breaking the myth," namely, by making conscious its symbolic character. Such resistance is supported by authoritarian systems, religious or political, in order to give security to the people under their control and unchallenged power to those who exercise the control. The resistance against demythologization expresses itself in "literalism." The symbols and myths are understood in their immediate meaning. The material, taken from nature and history, is used in its proper sense. The character of the symbol to point beyond itself to something else is disregarded. Creation is taken as a magic act which happened once upon a time. The fall of Adam is localized on a special geographical point and attributed to a human individual. The virgin birth of the Messiah is understood in biological terms, resurrection and ascension as physical events, the second coming of the Christ as a telluric, or cosmic, catastrophe. The presupposition of such literalism is that God is a being, acting in time and space, dwelling in a special place, affecting the course of events and being affected by them like any other being in the universe. Literalism deprives God of his ultimacy and, religiously speaking, of his majesty. It draws him down to the level of that which is not ultimate, the finite and conditional. In the last analysis it is not rational criticism of the myth which is decisive but the inner religious criticism. Faith, if it takes its symbols literally, becomes idolatrous! It calls something ultimate which is less than ultimate. Faith, conscious of the symbolic character of its symbols, gives God the honor which is due him.

One should distinguish two stages of literalism, the natural and the reactive. The natural stage of literalism is that in which the mythical and the literal are indistinguishable. The primitive period of individuals and groups consists in the inability to separate the creations of symbolic imagination from the facts which can be verified through observation and experiment. This stage has a full right of its own and should not be disturbed, either in individuals or in groups, up to the moment when man's questioning mind breaks the natural acceptance of the mythological visions as literal. If, however, this moment has come, two ways are possible. The one is to replace the unbroken by the broken myth. It is the objectively demanded way, although it is impossible for many people who prefer the repression of their questions to the uncertainty which appears with the breaking of the myth. They are forced into the second stage of literalism, the conscious one, which is aware of the questions but represses them, half consciously, half unconsciously. The tool of repression is usually an acknowledged authority with sacred qualities like the Church or the Bible, to which one owes unconditional surrender. This stage is still justifiable, if the questioning power is very weak and can easily be answered. It is unjustifiable if a mature mind is broken in its personal center by political or psychological methods, split in its unity, and hurt in its integrity. The enemy of a critical theology is not natural literalism but conscious literalism with repression of and aggression toward autonomous thought.

Symbols of faith cannot be replaced by other symbols, such as artistic ones, and they cannot be removed by scientific criticism. They have a genuine standing in the human mind, just as science and art have. Their symbolic character is their truth and their power. Nothing less than symbols and myths can express our ultimate concern.

One more question arises, namely, whether myths are able to express every kind of ultimate concern. For example, Christian theologians argue that the word "myth" should be reserved for natural myths in which repetitive natural processes, such as the seasons, are understood in their ultimate meaning. They believe that if the world is seen as a historical process with beginning, end and center, as in Christianity and Judaism, the term "myth" should not be used. This would radically reduce the realm in which the term would be applicable. Myth could not be understood as the language of our ultimate concern, but only as a discarded idiom of this language. Yet history proves that there are not only natural myths but also historical myths. If the earth is seen as the battleground of two divine powers, as in ancient Persia, this is an historical myth. If the God of creation selects and guides a nation through history toward an end which transcends all history, this is an historical myth. If the Christ—a transcendent, divine being—appears in the fullness of time, lives, dies and is resurrected, this is an historical myth. Christianity is superior to those religions which are bound to a natural myth. But Christianity speaks the mythological language like every other religion. It is a broken myth, but it is a myth; otherwise Christianity would not be an expression of ultimate concern.

69

Bernard Williams

Wittgenstein and Idealism (1973)

1 Solipsism and the *Tractatus*

Tractatus 5.62 famously says: 'what the solipsist *means* is quite correct; only it cannot be *said* but makes itself manifest. The world is *my* world: this is manifest in the fact that the limits of *language* (of that language which alone I understand) mean the limits of my world.' The later part of this repeats what was said in summary at 5.6: 'the limits of my language mean the limits of my world'. And the key to the problem 'how much truth there is in solipsism' has been provided by the reflections of 5.61:

> Logic pervades the world; the limits of the world are also its limits.
>
> So we cannot say in logic 'the world has this in it, and this, but not that'.
>
> For that would appear to presuppose that we were excluding certain possibilities, and this cannot be the case, since it would require that logic should go beyond the limits of the world; for only in that way could it view those limits from the other side as well.
>
> We cannot think what we cannot think; so we cannot think what we cannot *say* either.

Now Wittgenstein says that 'there is no such thing as the self that thinks and entertains ideas' (5.631), and this item is presumably the same as what at 5.641 he perhaps loosely, but comprehensibly, calls 'the human soul with which psychology deals' — that is to say, the item that does not really exist, the thinking and knowing soul *in* the world, is an item which people look for there as the subject of the phenomena with which psychology deals. In this interpretation I think I am substantially in agreement with P. M. S. Hacker in his book *Insight and Illusion: Wittgenstein on Philosophy and the Metaphysics of Experience* (1972), which I have found helpful on these questions. There are, however, respects in which I would put the position rather differently from him. Hacker, as against Black and others, says that what Wittgenstein does is to deny the existence of a knowing self *in* the world, and denies it, moreover, on Humean grounds to the effect that it cannot be encountered in experience (p. 59). At the same time, Wittgenstein, under Schopenhauerian influence, does believe in the existence of another, metaphysical or philosophical self, which is 'the limit of the world, not a part of it' (5.632, 5.641), and in some such sense he really is a solipsist; only that of course cannot be said, but merely manifests itself. Since Wittgenstein denies the first of these selves and in some way or other accepts the second, he cannot mean them to be the same thing.

Granted the intensely paradoxical and ironical character of Wittgenstein's thought here, one is in any case in expounding it going to be choosing between different kinds of emphasis. But I would enter two qualifications to Hacker's account. First, as regards the negative movement against the knowing self, it is not just an unsuccessful Humean search that we are dealing with. Wittgenstein says:

> There is no such thing as the subject that thinks or entertains ideas.
>
> If I wrote a book called *The World as I Found It*, I should have to include a report on my body, and should have to say which parts were subordinate to my will, and which were not, etc., this being a method of isolating the subject, or rather of showing that in an important sense there is no subject; for it alone could not be mentioned in that book. (5.631)

He adds, just before the analogy of the visual field, which I shall not consider (5.633): 'where *in* the world is a metaphysical subject to be found. . . ?' This seems to me to say, not just that there was something we were looking for and which turned out not in fact to be in the world – which is Hume's tone of voice, though the full content of Hume's negative discovery is not to be found in his failing to find something which he might have found, either. Rather Wittgenstein says: that which I confusedly had in mind when I set out to look is something which could not possibly be in the world. Hacker's emphasis is: there is one specification, which is the specification of a possible empirical thing, and to that nothing as a matter of fact corresponds; but there is a quasi-specification of a non-empirical thing to which something does, in a way, correspond. But rather, what we first looked for was never a possible empirical thing. For it had to satisfy the condition of being something *in* the world as I experience it and yet at the same time necessarily there whenever anything was there, and there could not be anything which did that. This is why Wittgenstein can explain his thought in this connection by saying (5.634) that no part of our experience is at the same time *a priori* (the phrase translated 'at the same time' is important here). Thus Wittgenstein's thought is, as Hacker indeed says, very like Kant's criticism of the Cartesian *res cogitans*.

The other qualification affects the other half of the argument. We cannot in any straightforward sense say that there is, or that we can believe in, or accept, a metaphysical, transcendental, self instead; for neither *what* it is, nor *that* it is, can be said, and attempts to talk about it or state its existence must certainly be nonsense. That is why, as we have already seen, the non-occurrence of a subject in the book of *The World as I Found It* means that 'in an important sense there is no subject'. The sense in which it *is* a limit, also means that *at* the limit, it is not anything at all (5.64):

> Here it can be seen that solipsism, when its implications are followed out strictly, coincides with pure realism. The self of solipsism shrinks to a point without extension and there remains the reality co-ordinated with it.

Indeed, granted this, I find puzzling why Wittgenstein can say (5.641) that there really is a sense in which philosophy can talk about the self in a non-psychological way. But I take this to mean that philosophy can talk about it in the only way in which by the end of the *Tractatus*, we find that *philosophy* can talk about anything: that is to say, not with sense.

Whatever exactly we make of that, we can recover from the *Tractatus* discussion of the self and solipsism three ideas which will be particularly important as points of reference in what follows: that the limits of my language are the limits of my world; that there could be no way in which those limits could be staked out from both sides – rather, the limits of language and thought reveal themselves in the *fact that* certain things are nonsensical; and (what follows from the first two, but is an important point to emphasise) that the 'me' and 'my' which occur in those remarks do not relate to an 'I' *in* the world, and hence we cannot conceive of it as a matter of empirical investigation (as the *Tractatus* is fond of putting it, a matter of 'natural science') to determine why my world is this way rather than that way, why my language has some features rather than others, etc. Any sense in which such investigations were possible would not be a sense of 'my', or indeed, perhaps, of 'language', in which the limits of my language were the limits of my world.

It may seem that these ideas are foremost among those that Wittgenstein abandoned in his later work, and that they, and the forms of puzzlement which gave rise to them, were particular objects of the criticisms of the *Investigations*. In a sense that is true, and Hacker devotes a good deal of his book to explaining how the later interest in such things as the impossibility of a private language and the necessity for public criteria is related to a long-term project of exorcising solipsism – exorcising it even from some vanishing and unsayable transcendental redoubt. The later arguments about oneself and others are designed (among other things) to remove the need even to try to point, hopelessly, in a solipsistic direction. That need certainly exists in the *Tractatus*. The well-charted moves in the later work from 'I' to 'we' mark one and the most evident attempt to banish that need; equally the emphasis in the later work on language's being an embodied, this-worldly, concrete social activity, expressive of human needs, as opposed to the largely timeless, unlocated and impersonal designatings of the *Tractatus* – that emphasis also can naturally be thought of as a rejection of the transcendental and Schopenhauerian aspects of the earlier work: the *transcendentales Geschwätz*, the 'transcendental twaddle' as Wittgenstein wrote to Engelmann in a different context in 1918 (quoted by Hacker, p. 81).

But the question is not as simple as this, and my chief aim will be to suggest that the move from 'I' to 'we' was not unequivocally accompanied by an abandonment of the concerns of transcendental idealism. To some extent, the three ideas I mentioned are not so much left behind, as themselves take part in the shift from 'I' to 'we': *the shift from 'I' to 'we' takes place within the transcendental ideas themselves.* From the *Tractatus* combination (as Hacker justly puts it) of empirical realism and transcendental solipsism, the move does not consist just in the loss of the second element. Rather, the move is to something which itself contains an important element of idealism. That element is concealed, qualified, overlaid with other things, but I shall suggest that it is there. I shall suggest also that this element may help to explain a particular feature of the later work, namely a pervasive vagueness and indefiniteness evident in the use Wittgenstein makes of 'we'.

70

Stanley Cavell

Emerson, Coleridge, Kant (Terms as Conditions) (1983)

IN THIS SECOND LECTURE I FOLLOW OUT CERTAIN INTUITIONS OF THE first—that philosophy's essential business has become the response to skepticism, as if philosophy's business has essentially become the question of its own existence; that the recovery of the (my) ordinary (voice) from skepticism, since it is itself a task dictated by skepticism, requires the contesting of skepticism's picturing of the task; that in philosophy the task is associated with the overcoming, or say critique, of metaphysics, and in literature with the domestication of the fantastic and the transcendentalizing of the domestic, call these movements the internalization, or subjectivizing, or democratizing, of philosophy; and that this communication between philosophy and literature, or the refusal of communication, is something that causes romanticism, causes at any rate my present experiments with romantic texts, experiments caused by the discovery of these texts among the effects of *The Claim of Reason*.

Working within an aspiration of philosophy that feeds, and is fed by, a desire to inherit Emerson and Thoreau as thinkers, I take it for granted that their thinking is unknown to the culture whose thinking they worked to found (I mean culturally unpossessed, unassumable among those who care for books, however possessed by shifting bands of individuals), in a way it would not be thinkable for Kant and Schiller and Goethe to be unknown to the culture of Germany, or Descartes and Rousseau to France, or Locke and Hume and John Stuart Mill to England. While I have been variously questioned about what this means, and what it betokens, I am not yet prepared to describe the mechanisms that have made it possible and necessary. But since I rather imply that the repression of Emerson and Thoreau as thinkers is linked with their authority as founders, I should at least note the preparation of their repression by their self-repressions.

Founders generally sacrifice something (call this Isaac, or call this Dido), and teach us to sacrifice or repress something. And they may themselves be victimized by what they originate. I take such matters to be in play in the way Emerson and Thoreau write in and from obscurity, as if to obscure themselves is the way to gain the kind of standing they require of their fellow citizens. As if to demonstrate their self-repression, hence their powers to undo this repression, were to educate us in self-liberation, and first of all to teach us that self-liberation is what we require of ourselves. That this is within our (American) grasp means that to achieve it we have above all to desire it sufficiently. This achievement of desire is equally an intellectual and a spiritual, or say passionate, exercise. In "Thinking of Emerson" (added to the reprinting of *The Senses of Walden*), I characterize the thinking that Emerson preaches and practices in terms of abandonment, abandonment of something, by something, and to something. Those who stay with the entering gentilities of Emerson's prose will naturally take his reputed optimism as a sign of his superficiality and accommodation; it is an understandable stance, because to follow his affirmations to their exits of desire is to be exposed to the intransigent demands they place upon his reader, his society. (As an exercise in these demands, in obscurities amounting to self-repression, in the incessant implication that the language does not exist in which to stake claims quite philosophically, or say nationally, you may assign yourself a meditation on the opening question of Emerson's great essay "Experience": "Where do we find ourselves?" Hint [as they used to say after posing a tricky problem in American high school math textbooks]: Take the question as one staked for American thinkers by the thinking and practice of Columbus [say by the fact that native Americans are called Indians], as if the very direction to America, the brute place of it, and that we call it discovered, say found, threaten the assured edifice of metaphysics. And then take Emerson's question where we find ourselves as asking how we are founding ourselves, since there is no *one* voyage to America. As if Emerson's self-repression is to enact the wish to found a tradition of thinking without founders, without foundation; as if we are perhaps to ratify ourselves with Foundling Fathers.)

Heidegger's idea that thinking is something to which we stand to be attracted is exactly not an idea he expects to attract his fellow citizens, but at best is to single out rare, further, thinkers. A thinker is one drawn, you may say seduced, by the authority of thinking, that is, drawn to the origin of thinking (say in Parmenides) that philosophy has obscured, or repressed in establishing itself, or say founding itself. But in the way I conceive of Emerson and of Thoreau it is as if they play Parmenides to their own Plato, Dido to their own Aeneas, Holderlin to their own Heidegger. (I am not here speaking of comparative quality but of comparative structure, although without my conviction in the soundness of the Americans' quality, I do not know that I would be interested in their structure.) Even in the absence of an understanding of how it is that the repressed performs its own repression, one may surmise that a thinker would wish to acquire the authority of thinking in this way in order to teach the authority whose acquisition consists in its relinquishment. I think of this as philosophical authority. If something like this is an intelligible and practical background to bring to Emerson and Thoreau, the advantage, to it and to them, is that it can be investigated with as it were, one's own hands, and in open air; as if the origins of philosophy were hardly different in age from the origins of movies. Someone my age will have had a teacher whose teacher could have heard Emerson. So that the philosophical waltz of obviousness and obscurity is—most obviously, if *therefore* most obscurely—of one's own calling.

It is habitually said, I suppose correctly, that what we think of as romanticism is a function of (whatever else) how we conceive the philosophical settlement proposed in the achievement of Kant. Since what we think about any view of the relation of the mental and the material, so to speak, is bound to be some such function (that is, since Kant's achievement is part of how we think) this is not a very specific claim. In this essay I specify what I understand a certain force of the Kantian function to be. That I confine myself to working this out only relative to a reading of one essay of Emerson's—"Fate," from *The Conduct of Life*—and a few passages from Coleridge's autobiograhical prose will naturally require various justifications, not to say excuses. The fact that these texts do not undertake to quote and refute particular passages from Kant's writing would not for me be enough to show that, on a reasonable view of argument, they are not in argument with his philosophy. This too depends on what you understand Kant to have accomplished (what you think the name *Kant,* means) and on what you understand to be the cause of the kind of writing in which romantics have expressed themselves. That it is not what we may expect of philosophical prose would hardly take such writers by surprise, as if they wrote as they did inadvertently, or in ignorance of the sound of philosophy. Consider that they were attacking philosophy in the name of redeeming it. Should professional philosophers, now or ever, care about that? It is true that philosophy habitually presents itself as redeeming itself, hence struggling for its name, famously in the modern period, since Bacon, Locke, and Descartes. But can philosophy be redeemed *this way*, this romantic way? To consider further what that way is, is a motive for taking up the texts in question here.

To prepare for them I had better set out some version of what can be said to be Kant's accomplishment. Or let Kant say it for us, in two summary paragraphs from his *Prolegomena to Any Future Metaphysics* (section 32).

> Since the oldest days of philosophy inquirers into pure reason have conceived, besides the things of sense, or appearances (phenomena), which make up the sensible world, certain creations of the understanding, called noumena, which should constitute an intelligible world. And as appearances and illusion were by those men identified (a thing which we may well excuse in an undeveloped epoch), actuality was only conceded to the creations of thought.
>
> And we indeed, rightly considering objects of sense as mere appearances, confess thereby that they are based upon a thing in itself, though we know not this thing in its internal consitution, but only know its appearances, viz., the way in which our senses are affected by this unknown something. The understanding therefore, by assuming appearances, grants the existence of things in themselves also, and so far we may say, that the representation of such things as form the basis of phenomena, consequently of mere creations of the understanding, is not only admissible, but unavoidable.

You can take these paragraphs as constituting the whole argument of the *Critique of Pure Reason,* in four or five lines: (1) Experience is constituted by appearances. (2) Appearances are of something else, which accordingly cannot itself appear. (3) All and only functions of experience can be known; these are our categories of the understanding. (4) It follows that the something else—that of which appearances are appearances, whose existence we must grant—cannot be known. In discovering this limitation of reason, reason proves its power to itself, over itself. (5) Moreover, since it is unavoidable for our reason to be drawn to think about this unknowable ground of appearance, reason reveals itself to itself in this necessity also.

Then why do we need the rest of the eight-hundred-plus pages of the *Critique of Pure Reason?* They can be said to be divided between those that set up or fill in the pictures or structures necessary to get this argument compellingly clear (clear, you might say, of the trucks that are invited to drive through it), and those pages that set out the implications of the argument for human nature, hence for our moral and aesthetic and scientific and religious aspirations. I am prepared to call all of these pages pages of philosophy. What I claim is that if you are not at some stage gripped by a little argument very like the one I just drew out, your interest in those eight-hundred-plus pages will be, let me say, literary. The question would still remain whether you are seriously interested in that argument—interested more than, let me say, academically— if you are *not* interested in those eight hundred pages. A good answer, I think, and sufficient for my purposes, is yes and no. I am going to focus here on the yes side.

What would the argument, supposing it is convincing, accomplish? Kant had described his philosophical settlement as limiting knowledge in order to make room for faith. This is a somewhat onesided way of describing his effort concerning knowledge, since what he meant by "limiting" it was something that also secured it, against the threat of skepticism and powers of dogmatism. It can accordingly be seen as one in the ancient and mighty line of the philosophical efforts to strike a bargain between the respective claims upon human nature of knowledge or science and of morality and religion. Kant's seems to be the most stable philosophical settlement in the modern period; subsequent settlements have not displaced it, or rather they have only displaced it. I take this stability, for the purposes of the story I have to tell, as a function of the balance Kant gives to the claims of knowledge of the world to be what you may call subjective and objective, or say to the claims of knowledge to be dependent on or independent of the specific endowments—sensual and intellectual—of the human being. The texts I am using as examples of romanticism I understand as monitoring the stability of this settlement—both our satisfaction in the justice of it and our dissatisfaction with this justice.

The dissatisfaction with such a settlement as Kant's is relatively easy to state. To settle with skepticism (and dogmatism, or fanaticism, but I won't try to keep including that in the balance), to assure us that we do know the existence of the world, or rather, that what we understand as knowledge is *of* the world, the price Kant asks us to pay is to cede any claim to know the thing in itself, to grant that human knowledge is not of things as they are in themselves (things as things,

Heidegger will come to say). You don't—do you?—have to be a romantic to feel sometimes about that settlement: Thanks for nothing.

The companion satisfaction with the settlement is harder to state. It is expressed in Kant's portrait of the human being as living in two worlds, in one of them determined, in the other free, one of which is necessary to the satisfaction of human Understanding, the other to the satisfaction of human Reason. One romantic use for this idea of two worlds lies in its accounting for the human being's dissatisfaction with, as it were, itself. It appreciates the ambivalence in Kant's central idea of limitation, that we simultaneously crave its comfort and crave escape from its comfort, that we want unappeasably to be lawfully wedded to the world and at the same time illicitly intimate with it, as if the one stance produced the wish for the other, as if the best proof of human existence were its power to yearn, as if for its better, or other, existence. Another romantic use for this idea of our two worlds is its offer of a formulation of our ambivalence toward Kant's ambivalent settlement, or a further insight into whatever that settlement was a settlement of—an insight that the human being now lives in *neither* world, that we are, as it is said, between worlds.

Emerson and Thoreau joke about this from time to time. "Our moods do not believe in each other," Emerson says in "Circles"; "I am God in nature; I am a weed by the wall." And Thoreau identifies his readers as, for example, those "who are said to *live* in New England." That Wittgenstein and Heidegger can be understood to share this romantic perception of human doubleness I dare say helps account for my finding its problematic unavoidable—Wittgenstein perceiving our craving to *escape* our commonness with others, even when we recognize the commonness of the craving; Heidegger perceiving our pull to *remain* absorbed in the common, perhaps in the very way we push to escape it.

About our worldlessness or homelessness, the deadness to us of worlds we still see but, as it were, do not recollect (as if we cannot quite place the world)—about this Wordsworth and Coleridge do not joke (though they can be funny), as though they hadn't quite the American confidence that world-changing change would come, or that they could help it happen. When Wordsworth dedicated his poetry, in his preface to *Lyrical Ballads,* to arousing men in a particular way from a "torpor," the way he sought was "to make the incidents of common life interesting," as if he saw us as having withdrawn our interest, or investment, from whatever worlds we have in common, say this one or the next. This seems to me a reasonable description at once of skepticism and of melancholia, as if the human race had suffered some calamity and were now entering, at best, a period of convalescence. The most familiar interpretation of this calamity has seen it as the aftermath of the French Revolution; Nietzsche will say the death of God. However this calamitous break with the past is envisioned, its cure will require a revolution of the spirit, or, as Emerson puts it at the close of "The American Scholar," the conversion of the world. Wittgenstein accounted for his appearance by saying that history has a kink in it. I am not interested here in comparing romantic writers in terms of whether they saw redemptive possibilities in politics, or in religion, or in poetry. My subject is rather how such an idea may pressure philosophy to think about its own redemption.

Since those who are said to live in New England, or for that matter in England, are after all alive, a vision such as that expressed in *The Ancient Mariner* has recourse to the idea of the living dead, or rather of death-in-life, for example, of re-animated bodies. Here the relation to Kant's worlds is, as I read it, all but explicit, as is the idea that the place we inhabit, in which we are neither free nor natural, is itself a world, as it were a Third World of the spirit, so that our consciousness is not double, but triple.

Of course all such notions of worlds, and being between them and dead to them and living in them, seeing them but not knowing them, as if no longer knowing them, as it were not remembering them, haunted by them, are at most a sheaf of pictures. How seriously one takes them is a matter of how impressed one is by the precision and comprehension of their expression. To test this is a purpose of the texts under discussion here.

71

Michel Foucault

What is Enlightenment? (1984)

I know that modernity is often spoken of as an epoch, or at least as a set of features characteristic of an epoch; situated on a calendar, it would be preceded by a more or less naive or archaic premodernity, and followed by an enigmatic and troubling "postmodernity." And then we find ourselves asking whether modernity constitutes the sequel to the Enlightenment and its development, or whether we are to see it as a rupture or a deviation with respect to the basic principles of the eighteenth century.

Thinking back on Kant's text, I wonder whether we may not envisage modernity rather as an attitude than as a period of history. And by "attitude," I mean a mode of relating to contemporary reality; a voluntary choice made by certain people; in the end, a way of thinking and feeling; a way, too, of acting and behaving that at one and the same time marks a relation of belonging and presents itself as a task. A bit, no doubt, like what the Greeks called an *ethos*. And consequently, rather than seeking to distinguish the "modern era" from the "premodern" or "postmodern," I think it would be more useful to try to find out how the attitude of modernity, ever since its formation, has found itself struggling with attitudes of "countermodernity."

To characterize briefly this attitude of modernity, I shall take an almost indispensable example, namely, Baudelaire; for his consciousness of modernity is widely recognized as one of the most acute in the nineteenth century.

1 Modernity is often characterized in terms of consciousness of the discontinuity of time: a break with tradition, a feeling of novelty, of vertigo in the face of the passing moment. And this is indeed what Baudelaire seems to be saying when he defines modernity as "the ephemeral, the fleeting, the contingent."[2] But, for him, being modern does not lie in recognizing and accepting this perpetual movement; on the contrary, it lies in adopting a certain attitude with respect to this movement; and this deliberate, difficult attitude consists in recapturing something eternal that is not beyond the present instant, nor behind it, but within it. Modernity is distinct from fashion, which does no more than call into question the course of time; modernity is the attitude

that makes it possible to grasp the "heroic" aspect of the present moment. Modernity is not a phenomenon of sensitivity to the fleeting present; it is the will to "heroize" the present.

I shall restrict myself to what Baudelaire says about the painting of his contemporaries. Baudelaire makes fun of those painters who, finding nineteenth-century dress excessively ugly, want to depict nothing but ancient togas. But modernity in painting does not consist, for Baudelaire, in introducing black clothing onto the canvas. The modern painter is the one who can show the dark frock-coat as "the necessary costume of our time," the one who knows how to make manifest, in the fashion of the day, the essential, permanent, obsessive relation that our age entertains with death. "The dress-coat and frock-coat not only possess their political beauty, which is an expression of universal equality, but also their poetic beauty, which is an expression of the public soul—an immense cortege of undertaker's mutes (mutes in love, political mutes, bourgeois mutes . . .). We are each of us celebrating some funeral."[3] To designate this attitude of modernity, Baudelaire sometimes employs a litotes that is highly significant because it is presented in the form of a precept: "You have no right to despise the present."

2 This heroization is ironical, needless to say. The attitude of modernity does not treat the passing moment as sacred in order to try to maintain or perpetuate it. It certainly does not involve harvesting it as a fleeting and interesting curiosity. That would be what Baudelaire would call the spectator's posture. The *flâneur*, the idle, strolling spectator, is satisfied to keep his eyes open, to pay attention and to build up a storehouse of memories. In opposition to the *flâneur*, Baudelaire describes the man of modernity: "Away he goes, hurrying, searching. . . . Be very sure that this man . . . —this solitary, gifted with an active imagination, ceaselessly journeying across the great human desert—has an aim loftier than that of a mere *flâneur*, an aim more general, something other than the fugitive pleasure of circumstance. He is looking for that quality which you must allow me to call 'modernity.' . . . He makes it his business to extract from fashion whatever element it may contain of poetry within history." As an example of modernity, Baudelaire cites the artist Constantin Guys. In appearance a spectator, a collector of curiosities, he remains "the last to linger wherever there can be a glow of light, an echo of poetry, a quiver of life or a chord of music; wherever a passion can *pose* before him, wherever natural man and conventional man display themselves in a strange beauty, wherever the sun lights up the swift joys of the *depraved animal*."[4]

But let us make no mistake. Constantin Guys is not a *flâneur*; what makes him the modern painter *par excellence* in Baudelaire's eyes is that, just when the whole world is falling asleep, he begins to work, and he transfigures that world. His transfiguration does not entail an annulling of reality, but a difficult interplay between the truth of what is real and the exercise of freedom; "natural" things become "more than natural," "beautiful" things become "more than beautiful," and individual objects appear "endowed with an impulsive life like the soul of [their] creator."[5] For the attitude of modernity, the high value of the present is indissociable from a desperate eagerness to imagine it, to imagine it otherwise than it is, and to transform it not by destroying it but by grasping it in what it is. Baudelairean modernity is an exercise in which extreme attention to what is real is confronted with the practice of a liberty that simultaneously respects this reality and violates it.

3 However, modernity for Baudelaire is not simply a form of relationship to the present; it is also a mode of relationship that has to be established with oneself. The deliberate attitude of modernity is tied to an indispensable asceticism. To be modern is not to accept oneself as one is in the flux of the passing moments; it is to take oneself as object of a complex and difficult elaboration: what Baudelaire, in the vocabulary of his day, calls *dandysme*. Here I shall not recall in detail the well-known passages on "vulgar, earthy, vile nature"; on man's indispensable revolt against himself; on the "doctrine of elegance" which imposes "upon its ambitious and humble disciples" a discipline more despotic than the most terrible religions; the pages, finally, on the asceticism of the dandy who makes of his body, his behavior, his feelings and passions, his very existence, a work of art. Modern man, for Baudelaire, is not the man who goes off to discover himself, his secrets and his hidden truth; he is the man who tries to invent himself. This modernity does not "liberate man in his own being"; it compels him to face the task of producing himself.

4 Let me add just one final word. This ironic heroization of the present, this transfiguring play of freedom with reality, this ascetic elaboration of the self—Baudelaire does not imagine that these have any place in society itself, or in the body politic. They can only be produced in another, a different place, which Baudelaire calls art.

I do not pretend to be summarizing in these few lines either the complex historical event that was the Enlightenment, at the end of the eighteenth century, or the attitude of modernity in the various guises it may have taken on during the last two centuries.

I have been seeking, on the one hand, to emphasize the extent to which a type of philosophical interrogation—one that simultaneously problematizes man's relation to the present, man's historical mode of being, and the constitution of the self as an autonomous subject—is rooted in the Enlightenment. On the other hand, I have been seeking to stress that the thread that may connect us with the Enlightenment is not faithfulness to doctrinal elements, but rather the permanent reactivation of an attitude—that is, of a philosophical ethos that could be described as a permanent critique of our historical era. I should like to characterize this ethos very briefly.

A Negatively

1 This ethos implies, first, the refusal of what I like to call the "blackmail" of the Enlightenment. I think that the Enlightenment, as a set of political, economic, social, institutional, and cultural events on which we still depend in large part, constitutes a privileged domain for analysis. I also think that as an enterprise for linking the progress of truth and the history of liberty in a bond of direct relation, it formulated a philosophical question that remains for us to consider. I think, finally, as I have tried to show with reference to Kant's text, that it defined a certain manner of philosophizing.

But that does not mean that one has to be "for" or "against" the Enlightenment. It even means precisely that one has to refuse everything that might present itself in the form of a simplistic and authoritarian alternative: you either accept the Enlightenment and remain within the tradition of its rationalism (this is considered a positive term by some and used by others, on the contrary, as a reproach); or else you criticize the Enlightenment and then try to escape from its principles of rationality (which may be seen once again as good or bad). And we do not break free of this blackmail by introducing "dialectical" nuances while seeking to determine what good and bad elements there may have been in the Enlightenment.

We must try to proceed with the analysis of ourselves as beings who are historically determined, to a certain extent, by the Enlightenment. Such an analysis implies a series of historical inquiries that are as precise as possible; and these inquiries will not be oriented retrospectively toward the "essential kernel of rationality" that can be found in the Enlightenment and that would have to be preserved in any event; they will be oriented toward the "contemporary limits of the necessary," that is, toward what is not or is no longer indispensable for the constitution of ourselves as autonomous subjects.

2 This permanent critique of ourselves has to avoid the always too facile confusions between humanism and Enlightenment.

We must never forget that the Enlightenment is an event, or a set of events and complex historical processes, that is located at a certain point in the development of European societies. As such, it includes elements of social transformation, types of political institution, forms of knowledge, projects of rationalization of knowledge and practices, technological mutations that are very difficult to sum up in a word, even if many of these phenomena remain important today. The one I have pointed out and that seems to me to have been at the basis of an entire form of philosophical reflection concerns only the mode of reflective relation to the present.

Humanism is something entirely different. It is a theme or, rather, a set of themes that have reappeared on several occasions, over time, in European societies; these themes, always tied to value judgments, have obviously varied greatly in their content, as well as in the values they have preserved. Furthermore, they have served as a critical principle of differentiation. In the seventeenth century, there was a humanism that presented itself as a critique of Christianity or of religion in general; there was a Christian humanism opposed to an ascetic and much more theocentric humanism. In the nineteenth century, there was a suspicious humanism, hostile and critical toward science, and another that, to the contrary, placed its hope in that same science. Marxism has been a humanism; so have existentialism and personalism; there was a time when people supported the humanistic values represented by National Socialism, and when the Stalinists themselves said they were humanists.

From this, we must not conclude that everything that has ever been linked with humanism is to be rejected, but that the humanistic thematic is in itself too supple, too diverse, too inconsistent to serve as an axis for reflection. And it is a fact that, at least since the seventeenth century, what is called humanism has always been obliged to lean on certain conceptions of man borrowed from religion, science, or politics. Humanism serves to color and to justify the conceptions of man to which it is, after all, obliged to take recourse.

Now, in this connection, I believe that this thematic, which so often recurs and which always depends on humanism, can be opposed by the principle of a critique and a permanent creation of ourselves in our autonomy: that is, a principle that is at the heart of the historical consciousness that the Enlightenment has of itself. From this standpoint, I am inclined to see Enlightenment and humanism in a state of tension rather than identity.

In any case, it seems to me dangerous to confuse them; and further, it seems historically inaccurate. If the question of man, of the human species, of the humanist, was important throughout the eighteenth century, this is very rarely, I believe, because the Enlightenment considered itself a humanism. It is worthwhile, too, to note that throughout the nineteenth century, the historiography of sixteenth-century humanism, which was so important for people like Saint-Beuve or Burckhardt, was always distinct from and sometimes explicitly opposed to the Enlightenment and the eighteenth century. The nineteenth century had a tendency to oppose the two, at least as much as to confuse them.

In any case, I think that, just as we must free ourselves from the intellectual blackmail of "being for or against the Enlightenment," we must escape from the historical and moral confusionism that mixes the theme of humanism with the question of the Enlightenment. An analysis of their complex relations in the course of the last two centuries would be a worthwhile project, an important one if we are to bring some measure of clarity to the consciousness that we have of ourselves and of our past.

B Positively

Yet while taking these precautions into account, we must obviously give a more positive content to what may be a philosophical ethos consisting in a critique of what we are saying, thinking, and doing, through a historical ontology of ourselves.

1 This philosophical ethos may be characterized as a *limit-attitude*. We are not talking about a gesture of rejection. We have to move beyond the outside-inside alternative; we have to be at the frontiers. Criticism indeed consists of analyzing and reflecting upon limits. But if the Kantian question was that of knowing what limits knowledge has to renounce transgressing, it seems to me that the critical question today has to be turned back into a positive one: in what is given to us as universal, necessary, obligatory, what place is occupied by whatever is singular, contingent, and the product of arbitrary constraints? The point, in brief, is to transform the critique conducted in the form of necessary limitation into a practical critique that takes the form of a possible transgression.

This entails an obvious consequence: that criticism is no longer going to be practiced in the search for formal structures with universal value, but rather as a historical investigation into the events that have led us to constitute ourselves and to recognize ourselves as subjects of what we are doing, thinking, saying. In that sense, this criticism is not transcendental, and its goal is not that of making a metaphysics possible: it is genealogical in its design and archaeological in its method. Archaeological—and not transcendental—in the sense that it will not seek to identify the universal structures of all knowledge or of all possible moral action, but will seek to treat the instances of discourse that articulate what we think, say, and do as so many historical events. And this critique will be genealogical in the sense that it will not deduce from the form of what we are what it is impossible for us to do and to know; but it will separate out, from the contingency that has made us what we are, the possibility of no longer being, doing, or thinking what we are, do, or think. It is not seeking to make possible a metaphysics that has finally become a science; it is seeking to give new impetus, as far and wide as possible, to the undefined work of freedom.

72

Emmanuel Levinas

Transcendence and Intelligibility (1984)

The Mind as Knowledge

It is in the human psychism understood as *knowledge* – going as far as self-consciousness – that the philosophy transmitted to us situates the natural place of the sensible and the origin of philosophy; it is in terms of knowledge and consciousness that philosophy looks into the mind.

The philosopher's attention is directed to human lived experience which is recognized and acknowledged as experience, that is, which lets itself legitimately be converted into teaching, into object lessons of dis-covery or presence. But even beneath our relations with other men and the social group and even beneath what is called the "relation to God" or revelation of God, one would like to perceive or suppose experiences which are termed collective or religious. That all intelligibility – and even the "sense" of God – lays claim to knowledge, that intelligibility seeks in knowledge the support of a presence, indeed that it seeks a foundation for itself; all this, according to philosophy, goes without saying. In the *Meditations,* Descartes extends to the entire soul the term *cogito,* a term borrowed from the intellectual activity of doubt – that is, from a process concerned with the true. One recalls the formula of the Second Meditation: "What is a thing which thinks, that is a thing which doubts, conceives, affirms, denies, wills, does not will, which also imagines and feels?" I presume that to feel signifies here both sensation and emotion. I presume as well that the diverse forms of thought evoked do not simply designate the species of a genre but also the different moments, the articulations, of a structure or the multiple dimensions of the same act of consciousness, which is the act of knowing.

Science and Presence

As knowledge, thinking is the way in which an exteriority is found within a consciousness which does not cease to identify itself, without recourse to any distinct sign, and is called the Ego or the Same. Knowledge is a relation of the *Same* with the *Other* in which the Other is reduced to the Same and divested of its strangeness, in which thinking relates itself to the other but the other is no longer other as such; the other is already appropriated (*le propre*), already *mine*. Henceforth, knowledge is without secrets or open to investigation, that is to say, it is a *world*. It is immanence. An immanence which is also a temporal mode, where knowledge imposes itself as privileged: a presence which is also the fact-of-being. Presence as an exposition in the absolute frankness of *being*, which also signifies gathering and synchrony without flaw, evasion, or shadow. An *appearance* and a *being-given*. Behind the dia-chrony, the becoming of experiences and the dissimulations of the *before* and the *after*, of the past and the future (which are the temporal failures of presence but are nevertheless susceptible to the recuperation of this presence in the guise of the thinkable, indeed, susceptible to re-presentation, in all senses of the term), the procedures of knowledge reestablish presence in the eternity of an ideal presence. Reminiscence and imagination assure the synchrony of the ideal presence to comprehension and together maintain that which, in the *experience* of the entity "submitted to time," is already lost or is only to come. It is perhaps this adequation of knowledge to the entity which permits it to be said that one only learns what one already knows, that nothing absolutely new, nothing other, nothing strange, nothing transcendent, could either affect or truly enlarge a mind committed to contemplating everything, or that, like the *Timaeus,* the "circle of the Same surrounds that of the Other." By way of "objective spirit," discourse is capable of putting together contradictory thoughts despite dispersions and exclusions. And the first-person present verb of the *cogito* already signifies – and perhaps signifies above all – the *transcendental apperception,* which includes the thinkable in its totality and thus constitutes the autonomy of knowledge, which is self-supporting and gathers itself in the systematic unity to which the consciousness of an "*I*" lends itself. From whence the integration into the system: the simultaneity of that which succeeds itself, of all that can seem *other* in succession.

Being and Being Given

But presence in its exposition, in its frankness of being, is ipso facto a being-given, a letting-be-taken, and therefore, in its concreteness, it is the offering of itself to the hand which takes and, consequently, through the muscular contraction of the grasp – through what Husserl calls kinesthesis – it refers to a solid which the hand encompasses or which the finger of the hand indicates; and already it *refers itself* – through a perception which had been an aim and intention and therefore a finality, a wish or a desire – presence already refers itself to *something,* to a term, to a being (*étant*). Indeed, we think that the *being* (*étant*) thereby belongs to the concreteness of the understanding of *being*. It is perception, grasped through presence, through the being-given and thus *acquisition,* a deposit in the home, and consequently it is the promise of *satisfaction* made to a greedy and hegemonic ego. Satisfaction is the emphasis of immanence, a plenitude of adequation in the *satis* which thus implies the unintelligibility of that which surpasses its measure, the ceaseless temptation of atheism.

Presence as a letting-itself-be-taken, as the chance of understanding; knowledge remains linked to perception and to apprehension and to the grasp even in the con*cept* or the Be*griff*, which retains or recalls the concreteness of the grasp and, in its syntheses, imitates them, whatever the degree of idealization of which knowledge as the gaze is capable; synthesis as seizure and assemblage. *These metaphors are to be taken seriously and literally.* They belong to the phenomenology of immanence.

The Phenomenology of Immanence

Even before the technical ascendancy over things which the knowledge of the industrial era has made possible and before the technological development of modernity, knowledge, by itself, is the project of an incarnate practice of seizure, appropriation, and satisfaction. The most abstract lessons of the science of the future will rest upon this familiarity with the world that we inhabit in the midst of things which are held out to the grasp of the hand. *Presence, of itself,* becomes the now.

Knowledge rests on things given in a world that is given, which Husserl will call the life-world, the famous *Lebenswelt,* where, for all that, Husserl will not find a pretext for critique, and where he will not denounce any deviation from a society seemingly delivered over to technological domination. Husserl perceives at the base of our human and physical-mathematical exact sciences a given world which thus lends itself to the grasp and to manipulation. Husserl will complain that the overabstract reflection upon science conducted by epistemology *underestimates* this. In this underestimation, he would certainly see a threat to the truth to which man's scientific enterprise is devoted, which in itself does not proceed from any perversion of the mind.

But thus is also affirmed, across European philosophy, *knowledge* esteemed as the very business of the human to which nothing remains absolutely other. The doctrine of absolute knowledge, of the freedom of the satisfied man, Hegelianism – in which the many different attempts of Western thinking result, as they also result in Husserlian phenomenology – promotes a thinking which, in the plenitude of its ambitions, takes no interest in the other qua other. The other qua other cannot be accommodated in the noema of a noesis and could nevertheless be important to the human. The labor of thinking gets the better of the alterity of things and men, and it is in this that rationality itself resides. The conceptual synopsis is stronger than all the diversity and incompatibility of unassemblable terms, stronger than any diachrony which would want to be radical and irreducible. In the same way, consciousness is intentionality in Husserlian phenomenology: cogitation comes out of itself, but the cogitatum is present to cogitation, the *noema* equals the *noesis* and corresponds to its intention. It suffices for Husserlian phenomenology: to interrogate the intentions of thinking in order to know where thought wants to get to ("worauf sie eigentlich hinaus will"). Nothing ever comes to unseat this intentional will of thought or fails to measure up to it.

The Notion of Transcendence and the End of Metaphysics

But do the notions of transcendence, alterity, and absolute novelty – the notion of the absolute – still allow themselves to be named as intelligible if, precisely, the notions of the other, the transcendent, and the absolute break with the knowledge which would have invested and assimilated them and with the world where they could appear but already make up immanence? Is it sufficient to maintain this intelligibility in a purely negative fashion in relation to knowledge, appearance, and presence? Unless the intelligibility of the alterity of the other, of transcendence, calls for another phenomenology, even if it were the destruction of the phenomenology of appearance and of knowledge.

Within the context of the history of reason, _The Critique of Pure Reason_ was largely motivated by the formal contradictions which stalemated the philosophical use of reason. These terminated the long journey in _search of absolute truth_ beyond the given, exceeding the scope set by the critique of transcendental apperception. Nevertheless, the very meaning of the _meta_ of metaphysics has not been condemned as nonsense by the _Critique_. It sounded the knell of metaphysics understood as searching beyond the experience of identities which could be grasped in an eternal presence, which, from then on, could only appear to be beyond as according to the illusion of worlds behind the scenes. This Kantian critique of metaphysics is no doubt akin to the nevertheless anti-Kantian message of a very great philosopher who remains in purgatory – Bergson – for whom the march of Western philosophy in search of an absolute – or transcendent – order of the Eternal would have been only the deformation of the technological mind turned toward action on matter and space. (This is an anticipation unappreciated by the Heideggerian critiques of metaphysics which proceed from the will to power.) This is an essential point of this critique, which also resembles, at least in spirit, Heidegger's famous proclamation of the end of metaphysics insofar as he denounces it as a misunderstanding of the ontological difference between _being_ and _being_ (_étant_) and in which he prohibits speculation which would think being starting from beings. Does not the true signification of the end of metaphysics, from Kant to Heidegger, consist in affirming that thinking beyond the given no longer amounts to bringing to light the _presence_ or the _eternity_ of a universe of beings or of secret or sacred principles, hidden in the prolongation of that which is given and which would be the task of metaphysical speculation to dis-cover? Is this sufficient in order to denounce transcendence as non-sense, the very _meta_ of metaphysics? And what if its alterity or its beyond was not a simple dissimulation to be unveiled by the gaze but a non-in-difference, intelligible according to a _spiritual intrigue wholly other than_ gnosis.

Otherwise than According to Knowledge

I would like to suggest that in modern philosophy this new intrigue manifests itself – despite the reversions of philosophy to ontology and knowledge, despite the relapses – in the entire history of our philosophy: beginning with Kant himself, notably in the doctrine of the primacy of practical reason. A few words as well about Bergson, whom I would not want to have disturbed in the depths of purgatory for nothing: Bergson is an essential step in the movement which puts in question the framework of a spirituality borrowed from knowledge and therefore from the privileged and primary signification of presence, being, and ontology. Is it still necessary today to introduce an educated audience, but one which manages to forget the unforgettable, to the Bergsonian distinction between the time of everyday life and the time of interior life or duration? On the one hand, the time of common sense – which, essentially, remains that of science – the measurable time of our watches, the time of Aristotle understood as a number representing movement, that is, a time which can be approached through its expression and through its spatial measurement by chronometers, whether they be watches or water clocks. And on the other hand, the duration which is pure change and which does not need to search beneath this change for any identical substratum. This is the bursting forth of incessant novelty. The absolute novelty of the new. This is the spirituality of transcendence, which does not amount to an assimilating act of consciousness. The uninterrupted bursting forth of novelties would make sense, precisely beyond knowledge, through its absolute and unforeseeable novelty. "Most philosophers," Bergson writes, "treat the succession of time as a missed coexistence and duration as privation," as the mobile image of immobile eternity. "Because of this they do not manage, whatever they do, to represent to themselves the radical novelty of unforeseeability." Against the consciousness which englobes and organizes the system through knowledge and against the tendency to equate and reduce, this is a new mode of intelligibility. Prior to logic, the bursting forth of duration would sketch the horizons of intelligibility. Does not temporality itself announce itself here as a transcendence, as a thinking under which, independently of any experience, the alterity of absolute novelty, the absolute in the etymological sense of the term, would burst forth?

Does Bergson go that far? Does he not introduce knowledge behind duration? Does he not speak, in expressing the "intuition of duration," of a duration which is experienced rather than of a duration substituting itself for the act of experience? That is possible.

Thought as Religion

But what can one seek beneath thinking other than consciousness? Finally, what is this thinking we are seeking, which is neither assimilation of the Other to the Same nor integration of the Other into the Same, a thinking which does not bring all transcendence back to immanence and does not compromise transcendence in understanding it? What is needed is a thought which is no longer constructed as a relation of thinking to what is thought about, in the domination of thinking over what is thought about; what is needed is a thought which is not restricted to the rigorous correspondence between noesis and noema and not restricted to the adequation where the visible must be equal to the intentional aim (*la visée*), to which the visible would have to respond in the intuition of truth; what is needed is a thought for which the very metaphor of vision and aim (*visée*) is no longer legitimate.

An impossible demand! Unless these demands are an echo of what Descartes called the idea of the infinite in us – thinking beyond what is capable of being contained in the finitude of the *cogito.*

The idea of the Infinite – even if it is only named, recognized and in some way operative through its mathematical signification and usage – conserves for reflection the paradoxical knot which is already tied to religious revelation. Revelation, which is from the start linked in its *concreteness* to obligations toward humans – the idea of God as love of the neighbor – is "knowledge" of a God who, offering himself in this "opening," would also remain absolutely other or transcendent.

Would not religion be the original combination of circumstances – which nevertheless need not be judged contingent – in which the infinite in its ambiguity, both truth and mystery, comes to the idea? But is it then definite that the coming of the infinite to the idea is a feat of *knowledge,* the manifestation whose essence consists in establishing – or in reestablishing – the order of *immanence*? Above all, is it definite, as a certain consensus and perhaps a venerable tradition tend to admit, that immanence is *the supreme grace of spiritual energy,* that the revelation of a God is a *disclosure* and is achieved in the *adequation of truth,* in the grasp which that which thinks exercises on that which is thought, and thus that meaning or intelligibility would be an economy, in the etymological sense of the term, the economy of a house, of a home, of a certain investment, of a grasping, a possessing, a self-satisfaction and an enjoyment?

The Idea of the Infinite in Us

The idea of the infinite – an exceptional and unique idea which, according to Descartes, is the thought addressed to God. It is a thought which, in its phenomenology, does not allow itself to be reduced, without remainder, to the act of consciousness of a subject, to pure thematizing intentionality. Contrary to the ideas according to which thinking progressively seizes the world, which are always on the level of the "intentional object," the *ideatum* and the *grasp,* the idea of the Infinite would contain more than it is capable of containing, more than its capacity as a *cogito.* The idea of the Infinite would somehow think beyond what it thinks. In its relation to what should be its "intentional correlate," it would be thrown off course, not resulting in anything or arriving at an end, and precisely not arriving at the finite, at a term or close. Certainly it is necessary to distinguish between, on the one hand, the pure failure of the nonachievement of an intentional aim which would still be ruled by a finality and, on the other hand, the deportation or the transcendence beyond any end and any finality: the thinking of the absolute without this absolute being reached as an end, which again would have signified finality and finitude. The idea of the Infinite is a thought released from consciousness, not according to the negative concept of the unconscious but according to the thought, perhaps the most profoundly considered thought, of the release with regard to being, of dis-inter-est: a relation without a hold on being and without subservience to the *conatus essendi,* contrary to knowledge and to perception. *Concretely,* this does not become some sort of modification of vision as a pure negative abstraction but is accomplished ethically as a relation to the other man.

According to Descartes, who identifies the idea of the perfect with the idea of God, the finite thought of man could never derive the Infinite from itself. It would be necessary for God himself to have put it in us. And Descartes's entire interest is concentrated on this problem of the existence of God. The incessant return of metaphysics! But how could this idea of the Infinite be held in a finite thought? The arrival, descent, or contraction of the infinite in a finite thought names in any case an event which describes the sense of what we designate by God, rather than the immediately given, of an object which is adequate to – or equatable with – the intention of an act of knowledge in the heart of the world.

The Logos of the Infinite

But the exception of the idea of the infinite implies the awakening of a psychism which is reduced to neither pure correlation nor noetico-noematic parallelism, which the least biased analysis finds in human thinking if it is approached through knowledge. This is an exception which upsets the Aristotelian thesis of a theology reserved for a God who would be his own and only theologian, the only one capable of thinking himself, as Pierre Aubenque emphasized. An exception showing human thought thinking precisely as theology! But the logos of this theology would differ from the theoretical intentionality and from the adequation of thinking with that which is thought, which, through the unity of transcendental apperception, assures itself of a sovereign ego in its exclusive isolation as a *cogito* and its gathering and synthesizing reign. This is an exception to the commonly accepted phenomenology of thought, which, in an essential sense, is precisely atheist insofar as it is a thinking which equals the thought that fills it and satis-fies it, apprehending the given in the inevitable reversal of any passivity of experience into an activity of consciousness which accepts that which strikes it, which is never violated. The exception is a thinking which is no longer *aim, vision, will,* or *intention.*

In the idea of the Infinite, which is also the idea of God, the affection of the finite by the infinite precisely produces itself, beyond the simple negation of one by the other, beyond the pure contradiction which would oppose them and separate them or which would expose the other to the hegemony of the one understood as an "I think." An affection which must be described otherwise than as an appearance, otherwise than as a participation in a content, or a comprehension. An irreversible affection of the finite by the infinite. A passivity and a patience which are not recuperated in a thematization but in which, as love and fear of God – or the adoration and dazzling of which Descartes speaks in the last paragraph of the Third

Meditation – the idea of God is affectivity from top to bottom. An affectivity which does not amount to the *Befindlichkeit* of *Sein und Zeit* or the anxiety of *Jemeinigkeit* for its finitude of being-toward-death, which always comes to increase the intentionality of sentiment felt by a being belonging to the world. An affection of the finite by the infinite which it is not a question of reducing! An exit in the idea of the infinite, in theological affection, outside the *Jemeinigkeit* of the Cogito and of its immanence taken for authenticity, toward a thinking which thinks more than it thinks – or which does *better* than think. It goes toward the Good. This is a dis-inter-ested Affectivity – or Desire – in which plurality as social proximity does not need to be gathered under the unity of the One, which no longer signifies a simple lack of coincidence, a pure and simple absence of unity. The excellence of love and sociality, of "fear for the others" and responsibility for the others, which is not my anxiety for my death, *mine*. Transcendence would no longer be a failed immanence. In sociality – which is no longer a simple aim but responsibility for the neighbor – it would have the excellence proper to the mind, which is precisely perfection or the Good. A sociality which, in opposition to all knowledge and all immanence, is a *relation with the other as such* and not with the other as a pure part of the world.

Doing Phenomenology

That this affectivity of adoration and this passivity of dazzling permit a further developed phenomenological interpretation or that they can be joined through an analysis which, from the beginning, places itself before the interpersonal order of the alterity of the other man, my neighbor and my responsibility for the other (*autrui*) – all this is obviously beyond the framework of the Cartesian texts and we will not develop it here.

But to do phenomenology is not only, against the surreptitiousness, sliding, and substitution of sense, to guarantee the signifyingness of a language threatened in its abstraction or in its isolation. It is not only to control language by interrogating the thoughts which offend it and make it forget. It is above all to search for and recall, in the horizons which open around the first "intentions" of the abstractly given, the human or interhuman intrigue which is the concreteness of its unthought (it is not purely negative!), which is the necessary "staging" ("*mise en scène*") from which the abstractions are detached in the *said* of words and propositions. It is to search for the human or interhuman intrigue as the fabric of ultimate intelligibility. And perhaps it is also the way for the wisdom of heaven to return to earth.

The Intelligibility of the Transcendent

That the idea of the infinite, in its passivity, can be understood as the domain of the uncertainty of a self-preoccupied humanity incapable of embracing the infinite and for whom the fact of being struck by God could only be a last resort of finitude, is probably the misrecognition of the irreducible originality of alterity and transcendence and a purely negative interpretation of ethical proximity and love, an obstinate insistence on expressing them in terms of immanence, as if possession or fusion – the ideal of an intentional consciousness – exhausted spiritual energy. That the proximity of the Infinite and the sociality that it founds and commands can be better than the *coincidence of unity;* that sociality is an irreducible excellence through its very plurality, even if one cannot say it exuberantly without falling back into the poverty of a proposition; that the relation to or non-indifference toward the other does not consist, for the Other, in being converted into the Same; that religion is not a moment in the "economy" of being; that love is not a demi-god – that is certainly also signified by the idea of the infinite in us or by the humanity of man understood as the theology or the intelligibility of the transcendent.

But perhaps this theology already announces itself in the very wakefulness of insomnia, in the vigil and troubled vigilance of the psyche before the moment when the finitude of being, wounded by the infinite, is prompted to gather itself into the hegemonic and atheist Ego of knowledge.

73

Jean-François Lyotard

The Sublime and the Avant-Garde (1984)

I

IN 1950–1, BARNETT BARUCH NEWMAN PAINTED A CANVAS measuring 2.42 m by 5.42 m which he called *Vir Heroicus Sublimis*.[1] In the early sixties he entitled his first three sculptures *Here I, Here II, Here III*. Another painting was called *Not Over There, Here*, two paintings were called *Now*, and two others were entitled *Be*. In December 1948, Newman wrote an essay entitled *The Sublime is Now*.

How is one to understand the sublime, or let us say provisionally, the object of a sublime experience, as a 'here and now'? Quite to the contrary, isn't it essential to this feeling that it alludes to something which can't be shown, or presented (as Kant said, *dargestellt*)? In a short unfinished text dating from late 1949, *Prologue for a New Aesthetic*, Newman wrote that in his painting, he was not concerned with a 'manipulation of space nor with the image, but with a sensation of time'. He added that by this he did not mean time laden with feelings of nostalgia, or drama, or references and history, the usual subjects of painting. After this denial (*dénégation*) the text stops short.

So, what kind of time was Newman concerned with, what 'now' did he have in mind? Thomas Hess, his friend and commentator, felt justified in writing that Newman's time was the *Makom* or the *Hamakom* of Hebraic tradition – the *there*, the site, the place, which is one of the names given by the Torah to the Lord, the Unnameable. I do not know enough about *Makom* to know whether this was what Newman had in mind. But then again, who does know enough about *Now*? Newman can certainly not have been thinking of the 'present instant', the one that tries to hold itself between the future and the past, and gets devoured by them. This 'now' is one of the temporal 'ecstasies' that has been analysed since Augustine's day and since Edmund Husserl, according to a line of thought that has attempted to constitute time on the basis of consciousness. Newman's *now* which is no more than *now* is a stranger to consciousness and cannot be constituted by it. Rather, it is what dismantles consciousness, what deposes consciousness, it is what consciousness cannot formulate, and even what consciousness forgets in order to constitute itself. What we do not manage to formulate is that something happens, *dass etwas geschieht*. Or rather, and more simply, that it happens . . . *dass es geschieht*. Not a major event in the media sense, not even a small event. Just an occurrence.

This isn't a matter of sense or reality bearing upon *what* happens or *what* this might mean. Before asking questions about what it is and about its significance, before the *quid*, it must 'first' so to speak 'happen', *quod*. That it happens 'precedes', so to speak, the question pertaining to what happens. Or rather, the question precedes itself, because 'that it happens' is the question relevant as event, and it 'then' pertains to the event that has just happened. The event happens as a question mark 'before' happening as a question. *It happens* is rather 'in the first place' *is it happening, is this it, is it possible?* Only 'then' is any mark determined by the questioning: is this or that happening, is it this or something else, is it possible that this or that?

An event, an occurrence – what Martin Heidegger called *ein Ereignis* – is infinitely simple, but this simplicity can only be approached through a state of privation. That which we call thought must be disarmed. There is a tradition and an institution of philosophy, of painting, of politics, of literature. These 'disciplines' also have a future in the form of Schools, of programmes, projects, and 'trends'. Thought works over what is received, it seeks to reflect on it and overcome it. It seeks to determine what has already been thought, written, painted, or socialized in order to determine what hasn't been. We know this process well, it is our daily bread. It is the bread of war, soldiers' biscuit. But this agitation, in the most noble sense of the word (agitation is the word Kant gives to the activity of the mind that has judgement and exercises it), this agitation is only possible if something remains to be determined, something that hasn't yet been determined. One can strive to determine this something by setting up a system, a theory, a programme or a project – and indeed one has to, all the while anticipating that something. One can also inquire about the remainder, and allow the indeterminate to appear as a question mark.

What all intellectual disciplines and institutions presuppose is that not everything has been said, written down or recorded, that words already heard or pronounced are not the last words. 'After' a sentence, 'after' a colour, comes another sentence, another colour. One doesn't know which, but one thinks one knows if one relies on the rules that permit one sentence to link up with another, one colour with another, rules preserved in precisely those institutions of the past and future that I mentioned. The School, the programme, the project – all proclaim that after this sentence comes that sentence, or at least that kind of sentence is mandatory, that one kind of sentence is permitted, while another is forbidden. This holds true for painting as much as for the other activities of thought. After one pictorial work, another is necessary, permitted, or forbidden. After one colour, this other colour; after this line, that one. There isn't an enormous difference between an avant-garde manifesto and a curriculum at the Ecole des Beaux Arts, if one considers them in the light of this relationship to time. Both are options with respect to what they feel is a good thing to happen subsequently. But both also forget the possibility of nothing happening, of words, colours, forms or sounds not coming; of this sentence being the last, of bread not coming daily. This is the misery that the painter faces with a plastic surface, of the musician with the acoustic surface, the misery the thinker faces with a desert of thought, and so on. Not only faced with the empty canvas or the empty page, at the 'beginning' of the work, but every time something has to be waited for, and thus forms a question at every point of questioning (*point d'interrogation*), at every 'and what now?'

The possibility of nothing happening is often associated with a feeling of anxiety, a term with strong connotations in modern philosophies of existence and of the unconscious. It gives to waiting, if we really mean waiting, a predominantly negative value. But suspense can also be accompanied by pleasure, for instance pleasure in welcoming the unknown, and even by joy, to speak like Baruch Spinoza, the joy obtained by the intensification of being that the event brings with it. This is probably a contradictory feeling. It is at the very least a sign, the question mark itself, the way in which *it happens* is withheld and announced: *Is it happening?* The question can be modulated in any tone. But the mark of the question is 'now', *now* like the feeling that nothing might happen: the nothingness now.

Between the seventeenth and eighteenth centuries in Europe this contradictory feeling – pleasure and pain, joy and anxiety, exaltation and depression – was christened or re-christened by the name of the *sublime*. It is around this name that the destiny of classical poetics was hazarded and lost; it is in this name that aesthetics asserted its critical rights over art, and that romanticism, in other words, modernity, triumphed.

It remains to the art historian to explain how the word sublime reappeared in the language of a Jewish painter from New York during the forties. The word sublime is common currency today in colloquial French to suggest surprise and admiration, somewhat like America's 'great', but the idea connoted by it has belonged (for at least two centuries) to the most rigorous kind of reflection on art. Newman is not unaware of the aesthetic and philosophical stakes with which the word *sublime* is involved. He read Edmund Burke's *Inquiry* and criticized what he saw as Burke's over 'surrealist' description of the sublime work. Which is as much as to say that, conversely, Newman judged surrealism to be over-reliant on a pre-romantic or romantic approach to indeterminacy. Thus, when he seeks sublimity in the here and now he breaks with the eloquence of romantic art but he does not reject its fundamental task, that of bearing pictorial or otherwise expressive witness to the inexpressible. The inexpressible does not reside in an over there, in another words, or another time, but in this: in that (something) happens. In the determination of pictorial art, the indeterminate, the 'it happens' is the paint, the picture. The paint, the picture as occurrence or event, is not expressible, and it is to this that it has to witness.

To be true to this displacement in which consists perhaps the whole of the difference between romanticism and the 'modern' avant-garde, one would have to read *The Sublime is Now* not as *The Sublime is Now* but as *Now the Sublime is Like This*. Not elsewhere, not up there or over there, not earlier or later, not once upon a time. But as here, now, it happens that, . . . and it's this painting. Here and now there is this painting, rather than nothing, and that's what is sublime. Letting-go of all grasping intelligence and of its power, disarming it, recognizing that this occurrence of painting was not necessary and is scarcely foreseeable, a privation in the face of *Is it happening?* guarding the occurrence 'before' any defence, any illustration, and any commentary, guarding before being on one's guard, before 'looking' (*regarder*) under the aegis of *now,* this is the rigour of the avant-garde. In the determination of literary art this requirement with respect to the *Is it happening?* found one of its most rigorous realizations in Gertrude Stein's *How to Write.* It's still the sublime in the sense that Burke and Kant described and yet it isn't their sublime any more.

II

I have said that the contradictory feeling with which indeterminacy is both announced and missed was what was at stake in reflection on art from the end of the seventeenth to the end of the eighteenth centuries. The sublime is perhaps the only mode of artistic sensibility to characterize the modern. Paradoxically, it was introduced to literary discussion and vigorously defended by the French writer who has been classified in literary history as one of the most dogged advocates of ancient classicism. In 1674 Boileau published his *Art Poètique,* but he also published *Du Sublime,* his translation or transcription from the *Peri tou hupsou.* It is a treatise, or rather an essay, attributed to a certain Longinus about whose identity there has long been confusion, and whose life we now estimate as having begun towards the end of the first century of our era. The author was a rhetorician. Basically, he taught those oratorical devices with which a speaker can persuade or move (depending on the genre) his audience. The didactics of rhetoric had been traditional since Aristotle, Cicero, and Quintilian. They were linked to the republican institution; one had to know how to speak before assemblies and tribunals.

One might expect that Longinus' text would invoke the maxims and advice transmitted by this tradition by perpetuating the didactic form of *technè rhetorikè.* But surprisingly, the sublime, the indeterminate – were destabilizing the text's didactic intention. I cannot analyse this uncertainty here. Boileau himself and numerous other commentators, especially Fénélon, were aware of it and concluded that the sublime could only be discussed in sublime style. Longinus certainly tried to define sublimity in discourse, writing that it was unforgettable, irresistible, and most important, thought-provoking – '*il y a à partir d'elle beaucoup de réflexion*' (*hou polle anatheoresis*) (from the sublime springs a lot of reflection). He also tried to locate sources for the sublime in the ethos of rhetoric, in its pathos, in its techniques: figures of speech, diction, enunciation, composition. He sought in this way to bend himself to the rules of the genre of the 'treatise' (whether of rhetoric or poetics, or politics) destined to be model for practitioners.

However, when it comes to the sublime, major obstacles get in the way of a regular exposition of rhetorical or poetic principles. There is, for example, wrote Longinus, a sublimity of thought sometimes recognizable in speech by its extreme simplicity of turn of phrase, at the precise point where the high character of the speaker makes one expect greater solemnity. It sometimes even takes the form of outright silence. I don't mind if this simplicity, this silence, is taken to be yet another rhetorical figure. But it must be granted that it constitutes the most indeterminate of figures. What can remain of rhetoric (or of poetics) when the rhetorician in Boileau's translation announces that to attain the sublime effect 'there is no better figure of speech than one which is completely hidden, that which we do not even recognize as a figure of speech?' Must we admit that there are techniques for hiding figures, that there are figures for the erasure of figures? How do we distinguish between a hidden figure and what is not a figure? And what is it, if it isn't a figure? And what about this, which seems to be a major blow to didactics: when it is sublime, discourse accommodates defects, lack of taste, and formal imperfections. Plato's style, for example, is full of bombast and bloated strained comparisons. Plato, in short, is a mannerist, or a baroque writer compared to Lysias, and so is Sophocles compared to an Ion or Pindar compared to a Bacchylides. The fact remains that, like those first named, he is sublime, whereas the second ones are merely perfect. Shortcomings in technique are therefore trifling matters if they are the price to be paid for 'true grandeur'. Grandeur in speech is true when it bears witness to the incommensurability between thought and the real world.

Is it Boileau's transcription that suggests this analogy, or is it the influence of early Christianity on Longinus? The fact that grandeur of spirit is not of this world cannot but suggest Pascal's hierarchy of orders. The kind of perfection that can be demanded in the domain of *technè* isn't necessarily a desirable attribute when it comes to sublime feeling. Longinus even goes so far as to propose inversions of reputedly natural and rational syntax as examples of sublime effect. As for Boileau, in the preface he wrote in 1674 for Longinus' text, in still further addenda made in 1683 and 1701 and also in the *Xth Réflexion* published in 1710 after his death he makes final the previous tentative break with the classical institution of *technè*. The sublime, he says, cannot be taught, and didactics are thus powerless in this respect; the sublime is not linked to rules that can be determined through poetics; the sublime only requires that the reader or listener have conceptual range, taste, and the ability 'to sense what everyone senses first'. Boileau therefore takes the same stand as Père Bouhours, when in 1671 the latter declared that beauty demands more than just a respect for rules, that it requires a further 'je ne sais quoi', also called *genius* or something 'incomprehensible and inexplicable', a 'gift from God', a fundamentally 'hidden' phenomenon that can be recognized only by its effects on the addressee. And in the polemic that set him against Pierre-Daniel Huet, over the issue of whether the Bible's *Fiat Lux, et Lux fuit* is sublime, as Longinus thought it was, Boileau refers to the opinion of the Messieurs de Port Royal and in particular to Silvestre de Saci: the Jansenists are masters when it comes to matters of hidden meaning, of eloquent silence, of feeling that transcends all reason and finally of openness to the *Is it happening?*

At stake in these poetic-theological debates is the status of works of art. Are they copies of some ideal model? Can reflection on the more 'perfect' examples yield rules of formation that determine their success in achieving what they want, that is, persuasiveness and pleasure? Can understanding suffice for this kind of reflection? By meditating on the theme of sublimity and of indeterminacy, meditation about works of art imposes a major change on *technè* and the institutions linked to it – Academies, Schools, masters and disciples, taste, the enlightened public made up of princes and courtiers. It is the very destination or destiny of works which is being questioned. The predominance of the idea of *technè* placed works under a multiple regulation, that of the model taught in the studios, Schools, and Academies, that of the taste shared by the aristocratic public, that of a purposiveness of art, which was to illustrate the glory of a name, divine or human, to which was linked the perfection of some cardinal virtue or other. The idea of the sublime disrupts this harmony. Let us magnify the features of – this disruption. Under Diderot's pen, *technè* becomes '*le petit technique*' (mere trivial technique). The artist ceases to be guided by a culture which made of him the sender and master of a message of glory: he becomes, insofar as he is a genius, the involuntary addressee of an inspiration come to him from an 'I know not what'. The public no longer judges according to the criteria of a taste ruled by the tradition of shared pleasure: individuals unknown to the artist (the 'people') read books, go through the galleries of the Salons, crowd into the theatres and the public concerts, they are prey to unforeseeable feelings: they are shocked, admiring, scornful, indifferent. The question is not that of pleasing them by leading them to identify with a name and to participate in the glorification of its virtue, but that of surprising them. 'The sublime', writes Boileau, 'is not strictly speaking something which is proven or demonstrated, but a marvel, which seizes one, strikes one, and makes one feel.' The very imperfections, the distortions of taste, even ugliness, have their share in the shock-effect. Art does not imitate nature, it creates a world apart, *eine Zwischenwelt,* as Paul Klee will say, *eine Nebenwelt,* one might say, in which the monstrous and the formless have their rights because they can be sublime.

You will (I hope) excuse such a simplification of the transformation which takes place with the modern development of the idea of the sublime. The trace of it could be found before modern times, in Medieval aesthetics – that of the Victorines for example. In any case, it explains why reflection on art should no longer bear essentially on the 'sender' instance/agency of works, but on the 'addressee' instance. And under the name 'genius' the latter instance is situated, not only on the side of the public, but also on the side of the artist, a feeling which he does not master. Henceforth it seems right to analyse the ways in which the subject is affected, its ways of receiving and experiencing feelings, its ways of judging works. This is how aesthetics, the analysis of the addressee's feelings comes to supplant poetics and rhetoric, which are didactic forms, of and by the understanding, intended for the artist as sender. No longer 'How does one make a work of art?', but 'What is it to experience an affect proper to art?'. And indeterminacy returns, even within the analysis of this last question.

III

Baumgarten published his *Aesthetica,* the first aesthetics, in 1750. Kant will say of this work simply that it was based on an error. Baumgarten confuses judgement, in its determinant usage, when the understanding organizes phenomena according to categories, with judgement in its reflexive usage when, in the form of feeling, it relates to the indeterminate relationship between the faculties of the judging subject. Baumgarten's aesthetics remains dependent on a conceptually determined relationship to the work of art. The sense of beauty is for Kant, on the contrary, kindled by a free harmony between the function of images and the function of concepts occasioned by an object of art or nature. The aesthetics of the sublime is still more indeterminate: a pleasure mixed with pain, a pleasure that comes from pain. In the event of an absolutely large object – the desert, a mountain, a pyramid – or one that is absolutely powerful – a storm at sea, an erupting volcano – which like all absolutes can only be thought, without any sensible/sensory intuition, as an Idea of reason, the faculty of presentation, the imagination, fails to provide a representation corresponding to this Idea. This failure of expression gives rise to a pain, a kind of cleavage within the subject between what can be conceived and what can be imagined or presented. But this pain in turn engenders a pleasure, in fact a double pleasure: the impotence of the imagination attests *a contrario* to an imagination striving to figure even that which cannot be figured, and that imagination thus aims to harmonize its object with that of reason – and that furthermore the inadequacy of the images is a negative sign of the immense power of ideas. This dislocation of the faculties among themselves gives rise to the extreme tension (Kant calls it agitation) that characterizes the pathos of the sublime, as opposed to the calm feeling of beauty. At the edge of the break, infinity, or the absoluteness of the Idea can be revealed in what Kant calls a negative presentation, or even a non-presentation. He cites the Jewish law banning images as an eminent example of negative presentation: optical pleasure when reduced to near nothingness promotes an infinite contemplation of infinity. Even before romantic art had freed itself from classical and baroque figuration, the door had thus been opened to inquiries pointing towards abstract and Minimal art. Avant-gardism is thus present in germ in the Kantian aesthetic of the sublime. However, the art whose effects are analysed in that aesthetics is, of course, essentially made up of attempts to represent sublime objects. And the question of time, of the *Is it happening?,* does not form part – at least not explicitly – of Kant's problematic.

I do, however, believe that question to be at the centre of Edmund Burke's *Philosophical Inquiry into the Origin of our Ideas of the Sublime and Beautiful,* published in 1757. Kant may well reject Burke's thesis as empiricism and physiologism, he may well borrow from Burke the analysis of the characterizing contradiction of the feeling of the sublime, but he strips Burke's aesthetic of what I consider to be its major stake – to show that the sublime is kindled by the threat of nothing further happening. Beauty gives a positive pleasure. But there is another kind of pleasure that is bound to a passion stronger than satisfaction, and that is pain and impending death. In pain the body affects the soul. But the soul can also affect the body as though it were experiencing some externally induced pain, by the sole means of representations that are unconsciously associated with painful situation. This entirely spiritual passion, in Burke's lexicon, is called terror. Terrors are linked to privation: privation of light, terror of darkness; privation of others, terror of solitude; privation of language, terror of silence; privation of objects, terror of emptiness; privation of life, terror of death. What is terrifying is that the *It happens that* does not happen, that it stops happening.

Burke wrote that for this terror to mingle with pleasure and with it to produce the feeling of the sublime, it is also necessary that the terror-causing threat be suspended, kept at bay, held back. This suspense, this lessening of a threat or a danger, provokes a kind of pleasure that is certainly not that of a positive satisfaction, but is, rather, that of relief. This is still a privation, but it is privation at one remove: the soul is deprived of the threat of being deprived of light, language, life. Burke distinguishes this pleasure of secondary privation from positive pleasures, and he baptizes it with the name *delight.*

Here then is an account of the sublime feeling: a very big, very powerful object threatens to deprive the soul of any 'it happens', strikes it with 'astonishment' (at lower intensities the soul is seized with admiration, veneration, respect). The soul is thus dumb, immobilized, as good as dead. Art, by distancing this menace, procures a pleasure of relief, of delight. Thanks to art, the soul is returned to the agitated zone between life and death, and this agitation is its health and its life. For Burke, the sublime was no longer a matter of elevation (the category by which Aristotle defined tragedy), but a matter of intensification.

Another of Burke's observations merits attention because it heralds the possibility of emancipating works of art from the classical rule of imitation. In the long debate over the relative merits of painting and poetry, Burke sides with poetry. Painting is doomed to imitate models, and to figurative representations of them. But if the object of art is to create intense feelings in the addressee of works, figuration by means of images is a limiting constraint on the power of emotive expression since it works by recognition. In the arts of language, particularly in poetry, and particularly in poetry which Burke considered to be not a genre with rules, but the field where certain researches into language have free rein, the power to move is free from the verisimilitudes of figuration. 'What does one do when one wants to represent an angel in a painting? One paints a beautiful young man with wings: but will painting ever provide anything as great as the addition of this one word – the Angel of the *Lord*? and how does one go about painting, with equal strength of feeling, the words "A universe of death" where ends the journey of the fallen angels in Milton's *Paradise Lost*?'

Words enjoy several privileges when it comes to expressing feelings: they are themselves charged with passionate connotations; they can evoke matters of the soul without having to consider whether they are visible; finally, Burke adds, 'It is in our power to effect with words combinations that would be impossible by any other means.' The arts, whatever their materials, pressed forward by the aesthetics of the sublime in search of intense effects, can and must give up the imitation of models that are merely beautiful, and try out surprising, strange, shocking combinations. Shock is, *par excellence*, the evidence of (something) *happening*, rather than nothing, suspended privation.

Burke's analyses can easily, as you will have guessed, be resumed and elaborated in a Freudian-Lacanian problematic (as Pierre Kaufman and Baldine Saint-Girons have done). But I recall them in a different spirit, the one my subject – the avant-garde – demands. I have tried to suggest that at the dawn of romanticism, *Burke's* elaboration of the aesthetics of the sublime, and to a lesser degree *Kant's, outlined a world of possibilities for artistic experiments in which the avant-gardes would later trace out their paths.* There are in general no direct influences, no empirically observable connections. Manet, Cézanne, Braque, and Picasso probably did not read Kant or Burke. It is more a matter of an irreversible deviation in the destination of art, a deviation affecting all the valencies of the artistic condition. The artist attempts combinations allowing the event. The art-lover does not experience a simple pleasure, or derive some ethical benefit from his contact with art, but expects an intensification of his conceptual and emotional capacity, an ambivalent enjoyment. Intensity is associated with an ontological dislocation. The art object no longer bends itself to models, but tries to present the fact that there is an unpresentable; it no longer imitates nature, but is, in Burke, the actualization of a figure potentially there in language. The social community no longer recognizes itself in art objects, but ignores them, rejects them as incomprehensible, and only later allows the intellectual avant-garde to preserve them in museums as the traces of offensives that bear witness to the power, and the privation, of the spirit.

IV

With the advent of the aesthetics of the sublime, the stake of art in the nineteenth and twentieth centuries was to be the witness to the fact that there is indeterminacy. For painting, the paradox that Burke signalled in his observations on the power of words is, that such testimony can only be achieved in a determined fashion. Support, frame, line, colour, space, the figure – were to remain, in romantic art, subject to the constraint of representation. But this contradiction of end and means had, as early as Manet and Cézanne, the effect of casting doubt on certain rules that had determined, since the Quattrocento, the representation of the figure in space and the organization of colours and values. Reading Cézanne's correspondence, one understands that his *oeuvre* was not that of a talented painter finding his 'style', but that of an artist attempting to respond to the question: what is a painting? His work had at stake to inscribe on the supporting canvas only those 'colouristic sensations', those 'little sensations' that of themselves, according to Cézanne's hypothesis, constitute the entire pictorial existence of objects, fruit, mountain, face, flower, without consideration of either history or 'subject', or line, or space, or even light. These elementary sensations are hidden in ordinary perception which remains under the hegemony of habitual or classical ways of looking. They are only accessible to the painter, and can therefore only be re-established by him, at the expense of an interior ascesis that rids perceptual and mental fields of prejudices inscribed even in vision itself. If the viewer does not submit to a complementary ascesis, the painting will remain senseless and impenetrable to him. The painter must not hesitate to run the risk of being taken to be a mere dauber. 'One paints for very few people', writes Cézanne. Recognition from the regulatory institutions of painting – Academy, salons, criticism, taste – is of little importance compared to the judgement made by the painter-researcher and his peers on the success obtained by the work of art in relation to what is really at stake: to make seen what makes one see, and not what is visible.

Maurice Merleau-Ponty elaborated on what he rightly called 'Cézanne's doubt' as though what was at stake for the painter was indeed to grasp and render perception at its birth – perception 'before' perception. I would say: colour in its occurrence, the wonder that 'it happens' ('it', something: colour), at least to the eye. There is some credulity on the part of the phenomenologist in this trust he places in the 'originary' value of Cézanne's 'little sensations'. The painter himself, who often complained of their inadequacy, wrote that they were 'abstractions', that 'they did not suffice for covering the canvas'. But why should it be necessary to cover the canvas? Is it forbidden to be abstract?

The doubt which gnaws at the avant-gardes did not stop with Cézanne's 'colouristic sensations' as though they were indubitable, and, for that matter, no more did it stop with the abstractions they heralded. The task of having to bear witness to the indeterminate carries away, one after another, the barriers set up by the writings of theorists and by the manifestos of the painters themselves. A formalist definition of the pictorial object, such as that proposed in 1961 by Clement Greenberg when confronted with American 'post-plastic' abstraction, was soon overturned by the current of Minimalism. Do we have to have stretchers so that the canvas is taut? No. What about colours? Malevitch's black square on white had already answered this question in 1915. Is an object necessary? Body art and happenings went about proving that it is not. A space, at least, a space in which to display, as Duchamp's 'fountain' still suggested? Daniel Buren's work testifies to the fact that even this is subject to doubt.

Whether or not they belong to the current that art history calls Minimalism or Arte Povera, the investigations of the avant-gardes question one by one the constituents one might have thought 'elementary' or at the 'origin' of the art of painting. They operate *ex minimis*. One would have to confront the demand for rigour that animates them with the principle sketched out by Adorno at the end of *Negative Dialectics,* and that controls the writing of his *Aesthetic Theory*: the thought that 'accompanies metaphysics in its fall', he said, can only proceed in terms of 'micrologies'.

Micrology is not just metaphysics in crumbs, any more than Newman's painting is Delacroix in scraps. Micrology inscribes the occurrence of a thought as the unthought that remains to be thought in the decline of 'great' philosophical thought. The avant-gardist attempt inscribes the occurrence of a sensory now as what cannot be presented and which remains to be presented in the decline of great representational painting. Like micrology, the avant-garde is not concerned with what happens to the 'subject', but with: 'Does it happen?', with privation. This is the sense in which it still belongs to the aesthetics of the sublime.

In asking questions of the *It happens* that the work of art is, avant-garde art abandons the role of identification that the work previously played in relation to the community of addressees. Even when conceived, as it was by Kant, as a *de jure* horizon or presumption rather than a *de facto* reality, a *sensus communis* (which, moreover, Kant refers to only when writing about beauty, not the sublime) does not manage to achieve stability when it comes to interrogative works of art. It barely coalesces, too late, when these works, deposited in museums, are considered part of the community heritage and are made available for its culture and pleasure. And even here, they must be objects, or they must tolerate objectification, for example through photography.

In this situation of isolation and misunderstanding, avant-garde art is vulnerable and subject to repression. It seems only to aggravate the identity-crisis that communities went through during the long 'depression' that lasted from the thirties until the end of 'reconstruction' in the mid-fifties. It is impossible here even to suggest how the Party-states born of fear faced with the 'Who are we?', and the anxiety of the void, tried to convert this fear or anxiety into hatred of the avant-gardes. Hildegarde Brenner's study of artistic policy under Nazism, or the films of Hans-Jurgen Sylberberg do not merely analyse these repressive manoeuvres. They also explain how neo-romantic, neoclassical and symbolic forms imposed by the cultural commissars and collaborationist artists – painters and musicians especially – had to block the negative dialectic of the 'Is it happening?', by translating and betraying the question as a waiting for some fabulous subject or identity: 'Is the pure people coming?', 'Is the Fiihrer coming?', 'Is Siegfried coming?'. The aesthetics of the sublime, thus neutralized and converted into a politics of myth, was able to come and build its architectures of human 'formations' on the Zeppelin Feld in Nürnberg.

Thanks to the 'crisis of overcapitalization' that most of today's so-called highly developed societies are going through, another attack on the avant-gardes is coming to light. The threat exerted against the avant-garde search for the artwork event, against attempts to welcome the *now,* no longer requires Party-states to be effective. It proceeds 'directly' out of market economics. The correlation between this and the aesthetics of the sublime is ambiguous, even perverse. The latter, no doubt, has been and continues to be a reaction against the matter-of-fact positivism and the calculated realism that governs the former, as writers on art such as Stendhal, Baudelaire, Mallarmé, Apollinaire and Breton all emphasize.

Yet there is a kind of collusion between capital and the avant-garde. The force of scepticism and even of destruction that capitalism has brought into play, and that Marx never ceased analysing and identifying, in some way encourages among artists a mistrust of established rules and a willingness to experiment with means of expression, with styles, with ever-new materials. There is something of the sublime in capitalist economy. It is not academic, it is not physiocratic, it admits of no nature. It is, in a sense, an economy regulated by an Idea – infinite wealth or power. It does not manage to present any example from reality to verify this Idea. In making science subordinate to itself through technologies, especially those of language, it only succeeds, on the contrary, in making reality increasingly ungraspable, subject to doubt, unsteady.

The experience of the human subject – individual and collective – and the aura that surrounds this experience, are being dissolved into the calculation of profitability, the satisfaction of needs, self-affirmation through success. Even the virtually theological depth of the worker's condition, and of work, that marked the socialist and union movements for over a century, is becoming devalorized, as work becomes a control and manipulation of information. These observations are banal, but what merits attention is the disappearance of the temporal continuum through which the experience of generations used to be transmitted. The availability of information is becoming the only criterion of social importance. Now information is by definition a short-lived element. As soon as it is transmitted and shared, it ceases to be information, it becomes an environmental given, and 'all is said', we 'know'. It is put into the machine memory. The length of time it occupies is, so to speak, instantaneous. Between two pieces of information, 'nothing happens', by definition. A confusion thereby becomes possible, between what is of interest to information and the director, and what is the question of the avant-gardes, between what happens – the new – and the 'Is it happening?', the *now.*

It is understandable that the art-market, subject like all markets to the rule of the new, can exert a kind of seduction on artists. This attraction is not due to corruption alone. It exerts itself thanks to a confusion between innovation and the *Ereignis,* a confusion maintained by the temporality specific to contemporary capitalism. 'Strong' information, if one can call it that, exists in inverse proportion to the meaning that can be attributed to it in the code available to its receiver. It is like 'noise'. It is easy for the public and for artists, advised by intermediaries – the diffusers of cultural merchandise – to draw from this observation the principle that a work of art is avant-garde in direct proportion to the extent that it is stripped of meaning. Is it not then like an event?

It is still necessary that its absurdity does not discourage buyers, just as the innovation introduced into a commodity must allow itself to be approached, appreciated and purchased by the consumers. The secret of an artistic success, like that of a commercial success, resides in the balance between what is surprising and what is 'well-known', between information and code. This is how innovation in art operates: one re-uses formulae confirmed by previous success, one throws them off balance by combining them with other, in principle incompatible, formulae, by amalgamations, quotations, ornamentations, pastiche. One can go as far as kitsch or the grotesque. One flatters the 'taste' of a public that can have no taste, and the eclecticism or a sensibility enfeebled by the multiplication of available forms and objects. In this way one thinks that one is expressing the spirit of the times, whereas one is merely reflecting the spirit of the market. Sublimity is no longer in art, but in speculation on art.

The enigma of the 'Is it happening?' is not dissolved for all this, nor is the task of painting, that there is something which is not determinable, the 'There is' (*ll y a*) itself, out of date. The occurrence, the *Ereignis,* has nothing to do with the *petit frisson,* the cheap thrill, the profitable pathos, that accompanies an innovation. Hidden in the cynicism of innovation is certainly the despair that nothing further will happen. But innovating means to behave as though lots of things happened, and to make them happen. Through innovation, the will affirms its hegemony over time. It thus conforms to the metaphysics of capital, which is a technology of time. The innovation 'works'. The question mark of the 'Is it happening?' stops. With the occurrence, the will is defeated. The avant-gardist task remains that of undoing the presumption of the mind with respect to time. The sublime feeling is the name of this privation.

Note

1   This text was first published in *Art Forum,* 22, part 8 (April 1984), pp. 36–43, in a translation by Lisa Liebmann, which is reproduced with kind permission. Alterations were made to the French text by Jean-François Lyotard when he gave the paper in Cambridge in March 1984, and these have been translated by Geoff Bennington and Marian Hobson and incorporated into the translation.

74

Giorgio Agamben

The Thing Itself (1987)

To Jacques Derrida and to the memory of Giorgio Pasquali

THE EXPRESSION "THE THING ITSELF" (τὸ πρᾶγμα αὐτό) appears at the beginning of the so-called philosophic digression in Plato's seventh letter—a text whose importance for the history of Western philosophy is still far from being completely established. After Bentley had cast a suspicion of falsification upon all ancient epistolaries, first Meiners in 1783 and then Karsten and Ast declared Plato's letters inauthentic. These letters, which had formerly been considered an integral part of his work, were little by little deleted from philosophical historiography at the very moment when philosophical historiography was most fervid and active. When, in our century, this tendency began to reverse itself, and more numerous and better qualified critics asserted the authenticity of the letters (at least the authenticity of the one we are interested in here), the philosophers and scholars who had begun to concern themselves with them had to take into account the isolation in which the letters had been for more than a century. What had been lost was the living connection between the text and the successive philosophic tradition: the seventh letter, for example, with its dense philosophic *excursus,* now presented itself as an isolated peak whose arduous ascent was complicated by nearly insurmountable obstacles. It was also true, naturally, that long-term isolation had transformed the letter—as the sea in Ariel's song has transformed Alonso's body—into something rich and strange. It was thus possible to confront the letter with a freshness that the other great Platonic texts would perhaps not have permitted.

The scenario of the letter is well known: Plato, by now an old man—he is seventy-five years old—recalls for the benefit of Dion's friends his encounters with Dionysius and the adventurous failure of his political efforts in Sicily. At the point that interests us, Plato is telling Dion's friends about his third trip to Sicily. Having been enticed to Syracuse by the insistent pressures of the tyrant, Plato decided immediately upon his arrival to test the sincerity of Dionysius' stated desire to become a philosopher. "There is a way for determining the truth in such cases which, far from being vulgar," he writes, "is truly appropriate to despots, especially those stuffed with second-hand opinions, which I perceived, as soon as I arrived, was much the case with Dionysius." (340b 3–7).[1] With men such as these, he continues, one ought immediately to show what the entire thing might be, no matter how taxing. Thus, if he who listens is truly a philosopher and is equal to the thing, he will think that he has heard speak of a marvelous path, which ought to be traveled without delay, and he will think it impossible to live any differently. As for those, however, who are not really philosophers but have only a superficial veneer of philosophy, like the coat of tan people get in the sun, as soon as they see how much commitment the thing requires, they think that the task is too difficult, if not impossible, and so persuade themselves that they know enough already and have no need of further study. "Thus," writes Plato,

> I told Dionysius what I told him, but I certainly did not set forth to him all my doctrines, nor did Dionysius ask me to, for he pretended to know many of the most important points already and to be adequately grounded in them by means of second-hand interpretations he had gotten from others. I hear, too, that he has since written on subjects in which I instructed him at that time, as if he had not heard them from me and as if they were his own doctrine. Of this I know nothing. I do know, however, that some others have written on these same subjects, but who they are, they do not know themselves. One statement, at any rate, I can make in regard to all who have written or who may write with a claim to knowledge of the subjects to which I devote my thoughts (περί ὧν ἐγὼ σπουδάζω), no matter how they pretend to have acquired it, whether from my instruction or from others or by their own discovery. Such writers have, in my opinion, understood nothing about the thing" (341a 7–c4).

It is at this point that the expression, "the thing itself" (τό πρᾶγμα αὐτό) appears: a formulation that remained so determinate as the indication of the task of philosophy itself, that one finds it again more than two thousand years later, like a watchword passed from mouth to mouth, in Kant, in Hegel, in Husserl, in Heidegger. "On this subject, I certainly have written no work, nor shall I ever do so in the future. It is not, in fact, in any way sayable, as in other disciplines (μαθήματα), but, after much close attendance to the thing itself (περί τό πρᾶγμα αὐτό) and much companionship with it, suddenly, like sparks shot out from a fire, it is born in the soul and by now nourishes itself (αὐτὸ ἑαυτὸ ἤδη τρέφει) (341c 4–d2).

This passage has been quoted innumerable times, both to sustain esoteric interpretations of Plato's thought and also as an irrefutable document for the existence of unwritten Platonic doctrines: the *Dialogues,* which our culture has passed on for centuries as a venerable inheritance, would, in this sense, have little to do with what Plato cared about; his concern would have been reserved for a uniquely oral tradition. Our interest here is not so much to take issue with this matter, certainly an important one, as to try to ask ourselves what might the thing itself be which occupies Plato's thoughts and which Dionysius presumed wrongly to have understood. What is the *thing of thinking?*

An answer to this question can only come from an attentive reading of the subsequent passage, which Plato defines as "a tale and a diversion" (μύθος καί πλάνος—344d 3) and, at the same time, as "a true discourse, which I have often stated before, but which it now seems needs to be repeated" (342a 3–7). Therefore, a thinking which wants to come to terms with its own "thing" must always measure itself against the interpretation of this "extravagant myth." Let us try, then, to read it.

"For every entity", writes Plato,

> there are three things through which knowledge about it must come; the knowledge itself is a fourth, and we must put as a fifth that which is knowable and truly exists. The first is the name (ὄνομα), the second, the defining discourse (λόγος), the third, the image (εἴδωλον), and the fourth, science. Take a particular case if you want to understand the meaning of what I have just said, then apply the theory to every object in the same way. There is something, for instance, called circle, the name of which is the very word I just now uttered. In the second place, there is its *logos,* composed of nouns and verbal expressions. For example, the definition of that which is named round and circumference and circle would run as follows: the thing which has everywhere equal distance between its extremities and its center. The third is that which is drawn and erased and turned on the lathe and destroyed—processes which do not affect the circle itself (αὐτὸς ὁ κύκλος, here an example of the thing itself)—to which all these other things are related, because it is different from them. The fourth is knowledge and νοῦς and true opinion concerning them; all of which we must set down as one thing more, that is not found in sounds (ἐν φωναῖς) nor in the shapes of bodies (ἐν σωμάτων σχήμασιν), but in souls (ἐν ψυχαῖς); whereby it evidently differs in its nature from the circle itself and from the aforementioned three. Of all these four, the *nous* approaches nearest in affinity and likeness to the fifth, while the others are more remote from it. The same holds true in regard to shapes and surfaces, both straight and curved, in regard to all bodies artificial and natural, in regard to fire and water and the like, and in regard to all living things and for all quality of character and for all creations (ποιήματα) and in respect to all passions (παθήματα). For if in the case of any of these, a man does not somehow or other get hold of the first four, he will never gain a complete understanding of the fifth. Furthermore, the first four do as much to illustrate the particular quality (τὸ ποῖόν τι) of any object as they do to illustrate its being (ὄν), because of the weakness of language (διὰ τὸ τῶν λόγων ἀσθενές). Hence no intelligent man will ever be so bold as to put into language those things which reason has contemplated, especially not into an unalterable discourse, which must be the case with what is expressed in written symbols" (342a 8–343a 3).

Let us stop, for an instant, to catch our breath. Before this extraordinary *excursus,* which constitutes the last and most explicit exposition of Plato's theory of ideas, we can measure the damage caused to philosophic historiography in the last century by the suspicion of falsification which had been cast onto Plato's letters. It is not my intention here to scale this formidable peak. It is, however, doubtless possible to attempt, for now, to install a first encampment on the slopes in order to measure the difficulty of the climb and in order to situate it according to neighboring heights.

A first consideration that we can make (and one that has already been made by Pasquali amongst others) concerns the status of unsayability that the seventh letter, according to esoteric readings of Plato, would attribute to the thing itself. This claim ought to be all the more moderate to the extent that from the context it clearly results that the thing itself is not something that absolutely transcends language and has nothing to do with it. Plato affirms most explicitly that "if one does not somehow or other get hold of the first four" (which include, let us remember, name and *logos*) "one will never be able to gain a complete understanding of the fifth." In another important passage in the letter, he writes that knowledge of the thing itself lights up suddenly "after rubbing one against the other names, *logoi,* visual and other sense perceptions, and scrutinizing them in benevolent disputation by the use of question and answer without jealousy" (344b 4–7).

These unequivocal affirmations turn out to be, furthermore, perfectly in keeping with the tight relationship that Plato's dialogues establish between idea and language. When Socrates in *Phaedo* expounds on the genesis of the theory of ideas, he says: "So I decided that I must have recourse to *logoi,* and use them in trying to discover the truth of things" (99e 4–6); elsewhere, he presents the dislike of words—misology—as the worst of evils (89d 2) and the disappearance of language as the loss of philosophy itself (*Soph.* 260a 6–7), while, in the *Parmenides,* ideas are defined as "that which can be maximally taken by logos" (135e 3). And did not Aristotle affirm, in his historical reconstruction of Platonic thought at the beginning of the *Metaphysics,* that the theory of ideas was born from a σκέψις ἐν τοῖς λόγοις, from an inquiry into discourses? (987b 33).

The thing itself has, therefore, its eminent place in language, even if language is undoubtedly not perfectly suited to it, because, as Plato puts it, of its weakness. It could be said, with an apparent paradox, that even while transcending language in some way, the thing itself is possible only in language and by virtue of language—the *thing of language,* as it were. When Plato says that the thing which occupies his thought is not in any way sayable, as it is with other μαθήματα, it would thus be advantageous to put the accent on the last words: it is not sayable in the same way as in other disciplines, but it is not, for that reason, thoroughly unsayable.

As Plato never tires of repeating, the reasons which advise against entrusting the thing itself to the written word are ethical and not merely logical. Plato's mysticism—if such a thing exists— is, like any authentic mysticism, profoundly implicated in language, in *logoi.*

Having made this preliminary consideration, let us pass on to a close examination of the list contained in the digression. The identification of the first four does not present excessive difficulty: the name, the defining discourse, the image (which here indicates the perceivable object) and, finally, the understanding that is realized through them. *Onoma,* the name, in modern terms (which are, after all, the same as in Stoic logic), is the signifier; the *logos* is the signified or the virtual referent.[2] The image is the denotative or the actual referent.

These terms are familiar to us, though one ought not to forget that it is only with the Sophists and with Plato that such reflection on language began, which led to the precise logical grammatical constructions of the *Stoa* and of the Hellenistic schools. Just as in Book X of *The Laws* and the last part of the *Sophist,* Plato, in our letter, expounds a theory of linguistic signification in its relationship to knowledge. The difficulty begins, naturally, with the fifth entity, which introduces into the theory of signification, as we understand it, a new element. Let us reread the passage: "For every entity, there are three things through which knowledge about it must come, the knowledge itself is a fourth, and we must put as a fifth that which is knowable and truly exists." It seems that here the fifth ought to be understood as the same entity from which the discourse originates by saying, "For every entity there are three . . . ." The thing itself would then simply be the thing which is the object of knowledge. Consequently, what would ensue would be the valorization of that interpretation of Platonism (already operative in Aristotle) which sees in the idea a kind of useless duplication of the object. Moreover, the enumeration turns out to be circular because what is listed in fifth place is actually what was first named as point of departure for the entire discourse.

What can perhaps come to our aid here is attention paid to the philological details wherein, as Warburg used to say, the good Lord loves to hide himself. The Greek text, which we read in modern editions (Burnett's edition is exemplary of all that follow, but so is Souilhé's more recent edition), says at this point, "we must put as fifth that which is knowable and truly exists" (πέμπτον δ᾽αὐτὸ τιθέναι δεῖ ὅ δὴ γνωστόν τε καὶ ἀληθῶς ἐστιν ὄν). But the two main codices upon which both scholars based their editions, the Parisinus Graecus 1807 and the Vaticanus Graecus 1, present a different reading: instead of δεῖ ὅ, we have διό, "through which". Returning to the reading of the codices, or better, writing δῐὅ, the translation becomes: "we must put as fifth that *through* which (each one of the entities) is knowable and true."[3] In the margins of the reading, a scribe of the twelfth century had noted, as a correction or, rather, as a variant, that δεῖ ὅ, which modern editors have chosen to maintain. The codex that Marsilio Ficino had before his eyes when translating Plato's works into Latin still had the reading διό; in fact, Ficino translates: "Quintum vero oportet ipsum ponere quo quid est cognoscibile, id est quod agnosci potest, atque vere exsistit."

What changes? What does this restoring of the original reading of the codices bring to us anew? Essentially this: the thing itself is no longer simply an entity in its obscurity, an object presupposed by language and by the cognitive process, but it is instead αὐτό δίὅ γνωστόν ἐστιν, that *through which* it is knowable, *its own knowability and truth*. The marginal variant followed by modern editors, though it goes astray, is not erroneous. The hand which wrote it (and we have reason to believe that it was not an unexperienced hand) was most apparently concerned about the risk that knowability itself—the idea—might be, in its turn, presupposed and hypostasized as an other thing, as a duplicate of the thing behind or beyond the thing. The thing itself is not, in fact, another thing, but it is the *same* thing (and that's why the term *autó* serves as the technical designation of the idea). It is, however, no longer *pre-supposed* by, or placed beneath, the name or the *logos,* like an obscure, real presupposition (an ὑποκείμενον, a subject, in the etymological meaning of that which lies beneath); but is replaced in the medium of its own knowability, in the pure light of its revelation and its announcing of itself to knowledge.

The "weakness", therefore, of *logos* consists in its inability to bring to expression this knowability and this sameness; the language pushes back, like a presupposition (in the etymological sense of the term "hypothesis", "that which is placed under"), the very knowability of the entity which is revealed in it.

This is the sense of the distinction between *on* and *poion,* between being and its qualification, which is the distinction that Plato insists upon several times in his letter. Language—our language—is necessarily presupposing and objectifying, in the sense that language, in its coming about, splits the thing itself which announces itself only in language, into a thing *on* which one can speak, and into a ποῖον, a quality and a determination *which is said about it.* Language *supposes* and hides that which it brings to light in the very act of bringing it to light. Language is, therefore, according to Aristotle's definition, the saying of something *on* something. Language is always pre-sup-posing and objectifying. Presupposition is the form itself of linguistic signification: the saying καθ' ὑποκειμένου, *on* a subject.

The warning Plato attaches to the idea is, then, that *sayability itself remains unsaid in what one says about that on which one speaks; that knowability itself gets lost in what one knows about what there is to be known.*

The specific problem which is in question in the letter—but which necessarily is the problem with every human discourse that desires to manifest the fifth, that wishes to thematize what cannot be thematized—is this: how is it possible to speak without presupposing, without hypothesizing and subjectivizing or subjecting what one speaks about? How is it possible to speak not *on* the presupposition of a thing, but to say *the thing itself*? And, since names are, for the Greeks, essentially that which is said for itself, (καθ' αὑτό) can language *say* what it *names*? Can language *say* what the name has *called*?

The most ancient commentators had already understood that a contradiction was implicit in this problem. We have a gloss by a late Platonic scholar which says more or less the following: "Why is it that the Master in the *Phaedrus* devalues writing and yet, from the moment that he has written, he has, in some way, retained his written work as praiseworthy? Even in this he has wanted to follow the truth: just as the divinity has created both those things which are invisible and those things which are visible, so too has he left some things unwritten and others written." This question is also applicable to the seventh letter. Here Plato, writing about what he is thinking and about what should remain unwritten, seems to challenge the weakness of *logos* and to betray himself in some way. And it is certainly not on behalf of some vain joke that, in another letter, he declines paternity of the dialogues which had circulated under his name in order to affirm that they were the work of a "Socrates become more beautiful and more youthful" (*Ep.* II, 314c 3–4). Here the paradoxical nature of Plato's writings jumps momentarily before our eyes: in a letter—which modern scholars have often maintained to be apocryphal—Plato states that his dialogues are inauthentic in order to attribute them to an impossible author: Socrates, their own protagonist, who by then had been dead and buried for many years. The character *about whom* he speaks in the text here takes the place of the author of the dialogues where he appears. The most acute ancient critics, namely Demetrius and Diogenes, had observed how Plato's style, which is limpid in the first dialogues, becomes more obscure, swollen (ζόφος), and paratactic (ἐπερρίπται ἀλλήλοις τὰ κῶλα ἐφ'ἑτέρω ἔτερον, "sentences pile up over each other" writes Demetrius) when he confronts the themes which he takes most to heart.

Through a curious coincidence, the weakness of language that is here called into question by the father of Western metaphysics, seems to prophesy by two thousand years that difficulty which is implicit in the metaphysical character of our language, and which weighs on the late writing of Heidegger like an obstinate anger and almost like an intimate obstacle. But the weakness of the *logos* is not grounded, in Plato, within any mystical status of the idea. On the contrary, the idea makes possible that coming, through language, in support of language (λόγῳ βοηθεῖν) which, according to *Phaedrus* (278c 6), is the mark of authentic philosophical exposition. Here the risk is that the non-thematizability, which is in question in the thing itself, becomes in turn thematized and presupposed still in the form of a λέγειν τι κατά τινός, like a speaking about something which one cannot speak about. The thing itself is not a simple hypostasis of the name, something ineffable which must remain unspoken and be guarded only in this way in the language of men. A similar conception—implicitly refuted at the end of *Thaetetus*—still hypothesizes and supposes the thing itself. This—the thing of language—is not a *quid* which can be looked for like an extreme hypothesis beyond all other hypotheses, a last and absolute subject beyond all other subjects, atrociously or beautifully sunk into its obscurity. Such a thing without a relationship to language, such a *nonlinguistic*, we can think of, in truth, only in language, through the idea of a language with no relationship to things. This idea is a chimera in the Spinozian sense of the term, that is, it is something purely verbal. The thing itself is not a thing—it is the very sayability, the very opening which is in question in language, which *is* language, and which in language we constantly presuppose and forget, perhaps because the thing itself is, in its intimacy, nothing more than forgetfulness and self-abandonment. In the words of the *Phaedo* (76d 8), the thing itself is what we are always divulging while we speak, what we cannot help but say and communicate, but which we nevertheless always lose sight of. The presupposing structure of language is the structure itself of tradition: we pre-suppose and betray (both in the etymological and in the common sense of the Latin verb: *tradere*) the thing itself in language so that language may bear upon something (κατά τινός). The sinking of the thing itself is the foundation upon which—and only upon which—something like a tradition can constitute itself.

The task of philosophical exposition is to come to the aid of the word with the word in order that the word itself does not remain sup-posed by the word, but comes as the word to the word. It is at this point that the presupposing power of language touches its limit and its end: language says the presuppositions as presuppositions and, in this way, reaches that non-presupposing and non-presupposed principle (ἀρκὴ ἀνυπότετος), which only by remaining such, constitutes authentic community and human communication. As Plato writes in a decisive passage of a dialogue which presents more than one point in common with the "extravagant myth" of the seventh letter: "Learn what I say about the other section of the intelligible, which language itself (αὐτὸς ὁ λόγος) touches through its power of dialogue, taking hypotheses not as absolute beginnings, but literally as hypotheses, footings, and springboards, so that, going towards a non-hypothetical starting point of all things, touching it and, again, holding onto the things near it, it may return towards the end, making no use of any object of sense, but starting from ideas, going through ideas, it finishes with ideas" (*Resp.* 511b 3–c 2).

I realize that I have perhaps gone beyond the objective which I had set out for myself and that I have, in some way, become responsible for that madness that is not divine, but human (344d 1–2), against which the myth of the seventh letter tried to forewarn: that of careless consigning to a written text one's own thoughts about the thing itself. It will be, therefore, opportune for me to stop here in order to turn more cautiously to the preliminary historiographic task which I had proposed to myself.

The digression of the seventh letter contains, as we have seen, a short treatise on the idea in its relation to language. The definition of the thing itself is led into a strict relationship with a theory of linguistic signification which constitutes, perhaps, the first, even if extremely condensed, organic exposition of the subject. If this is true, we ought to be able to trace this exposition in the Greek reflection on language which immediately follows. Thought here runs straightaway to the text which determined for centuries, in the ancient world, every reflection on language, that is to say, the Aristotelian *De interpretatione*. Here Aristotle presents the process of linguistic signification in a way that apparently seems to have no relationship to Plato's digression: "That which is in the voice (τὰ ἐν τῇ φωνῇ) is symbol of affections in the soul (ἐν τῇ ψυχῇ), and written marks, symbols of that which is in the voice. And just as the written marks are not the same for all men, neither are spoken sounds. But what these are signs of in the first place (the affections of the souls), are the same for all; and what these affections are likenesses of—actual things (πράγματα)—are also the same" (16a 3–7).[4]

A more attentive examination shows, on the contrary, an exact correspondence with the text of the Platonic *excursus*. In point of fact, the tripartition in which Aristotle articulates the movement of signification (ἐν τῇ φωνῇ, ἐν τῇ γυχῇ, πράγματα) follows exactly the Platonic distinction between what is knowledge and opinion (ἐν ψυχῇ) and what is the perceptible object (ἐν σωμάτων σχήμασιν) (342c 6). Even more noteworthy is the disappearance of the thing itself. With Aristotle, in fact, the thing itself becomes deleted from *hermeneia,* from the linguistic process of signification. Even when it fleetingly reappears (as in Stoic logic) it will have become, by then, so estranged from the original Platonic intention as to be practically unrecognizable.

The Aristotelian determination of the *hermeneia* is thus developed as counterpoint to the Platonic list in the seventh letter and constitutes both a renewal and a refutation of it. The decisive proof of this polemic counterpoint is, in fact, the appearance, in the Aristotelian text, of the *grammata,* of the letters. The ancient commentators were already asking themselves to what was owed the appearance, at first sight incongruous, of this fourth interpreter next to the other three (voices, concepts, things). If one thinks that the Platonic excursus was really directed at proving the impossibility of writing about the thing itself and, in general, the unreliability for thought of any written discourse, then the intimate counterpoint between the two texts is even more evident.

Expunging the thing itself from the theory of signification, Aristotle absolves writing from its weakness. In place of the thing itself, the first substance (the πρώτη οὐσία) takes over in Aristotle's *Categories.* Aristotle defines the first substance as that which is not said *on* a subject (καθ'ὑποκειμένου, on a presupposition) nor is *in* a subject. What does this definition mean? The first substance is not said on a presupposition, it has no presuppositions because it is itself the absolute presupposition upon which every discourse and all knowledge is grounded. It alone—as name—is said upon itself, (καθ'αὑτό), it alone, not being in a subject, shows itself in the evidence. But, in itself, as *individuum,* it is ineffable (*individuum ineffabile,* according to the medieval Scholastic formulation) and does not enter into linguistic signification (which is grounded on it), except by renouncing its deictic actuality for a universal predication. The τί, which was in question in the name, is assumed in the discourse as the κάτα τινὸς, the *on-which* one speaks. These—the what and the *on-which*—are, therefore, the same thing, which can be grasped noetically as τὸ τί ἦν εἶναι, the being-the-τί-that-was. In this logico-temporal process, the Platonic thing itself is removed and conserved, and conserved only as removed: e-liminated.

This is why, in *De intepretatione,* the *gramma,* the letter, makes its appearance. A close examination shows, in fact, that, in the hermeneutic circle of *De interpretatione,* the letter, as interpreter of the voice, has no need of any other interpreter. It is the last *hermeneutes,* beyond which no other *hermeneia* is possible: it is its limit. For this reason the ancient grammarians, when analyzing *De interpretatione,* used to say that the letter, which is the sign of the voice, is also στοιχεῖον τῆς φωνῆς, its element. In as much as it is an element of that of which it is the sign, the letter has the privileged status of *index sui,* of self display; just as the πρώτη οὐσία, whose linguistic cipher it is, the letter shows itself, but only in so far as it was in the voice, that is, as always already a thing of the past.

The *gramma* is, therefore, the form itself of presupposition and nothing else. As such, it occupies a central place in every mysticism and, as such, it has a decisive relevance even in today's thought, which is much more Aristotelian and much more mystical then one might suppose. In this sense—and only in this sense—Aristotle and not Plato is the founder of Western mysticism. It is in this way that Neoplatonism was able to arrive at that agreement between Plato and Aristotle that constituted the basis of the school's teaching.

On this foundation, inasmuch as language carries inscribed within it the ontological structure of presupposition, thought can make itself immediately over into writing, without having to measure itself against the thing itself and without having to betray its own presupposition. The philosopher is, indeed, the scribe of thought, and through thought he is the scribe of things and of being. The late Byzantine lexicographer who goes by the name of Suda writes in his lexicon under the entry "Aristotle": Ἀριστοτέλης τῆς φύσεως γραμματεὺς ἦν τὸν κάλαμον ἀποβρέχων εἰς νοῆν, "Aristotle was the scribe of nature who dipped his pen in thought."

Many centuries later, Hölderlin unexpectedly quotes Suda's statement at a decisive moment in his *Anmerkung* to the translation of Sophocles' *Oedipus Tyrannus,* when he attempts to explain the sense and the nature of tragic *Darstellung,* of tragic exposition. The quotation contains, however, an emendation which even the most rigorous philological studies on Hölderlin have not been able to explicate. Hölderlin writes: τῆς φύσεως γραμματεὺς ἦν τὸν κάλαμον ἀποβρέχων ἐὐνουν (instead of εἰς νοὺν) "He was the scribe of nature who dipped his benevolent pen." Here there is no longer a dipping of the pen into thought: the pen—this simple material tool of writing—is alone, armed only with its benevolence, in the face of its task. To render to the thing itself its place in language and at the same time to give back to writing its difficulty, its poetic task in the *Darstellung,* is the task of the philosophy to come.

Notes

1   Letter VII in *Plato: The Collected Dialogues,* ed. Edith Hamilton and Huntington Cairns (Princeton: Princeton University Press, 1969), 340b 3–7. Further references to this letter, as well as to passages cited from the Dialogues, will appear in the text by paragraph number. Translations have been modified in accordance with Agamben's own reading of the Greek.

2   The distinction between *onoma* and *logos,* which the ancients held to be so important that they attributed its discovery to Plato himself, had, in reality, already been elaborated by Anthistenes, who maintained that the first elements (the simple substances) do not have a *logos,* but only a name (cfr. *Theat.* 201e–202b: "The first elements do not have a logos. Each one, itself on itself, can only be named, but it is not possible to add anything else to it.").

3   Among modern scholars, only Andreae in his 1923 study on the Platonic letters (*Philologus,* 78, p. 34 sq.) brought back the reading of the codices.

4   *Categories and De Interpretatione,* tr. J. L. Ackrill (Oxford: The Clarendon Press, 1963), p. 42, 16a 3–7. Translations have been modified in accordance with Agamben's own reading of the Greek.

75

Donald Davidson

The Conditions of Thought (1989)

WHAT ARE THE CONDITIONS NECESSARY FOR THE EXISTENCE OF THOUGHT, and so in particular for the existence of people with thoughts? I believe there could not be thoughts in one mind if there were no other thoughtful creatures with which the first mind shared a natural world. My remarks therefore match the title of this session: Human Beings: Nature, Mind and Community.

By a thought I mean a mental state with a specifiable content. Examples are: the belief that this is a piece of paper; the intention to speak slowly and clearly; the doubt whether it will be sunny tomorrow. It is natural to suppose that thoughts like these depend on nothing outside the mind, that they might be just as they are and yet the world be very different. It is natural to think this because it seems obvious that any one thought about the nature of the world may be mistaken, and from this it appears to follow that all such thoughts could be mistaken. The only thoughts that escape such preliminary and primitive skepticism are those about our own thoughts; these are privileged because the source of doubt—the possibility that something outside the mind may fail to exist—has been removed.

Something like this line of reasoning explains, as we all know, why so much Western philosophy has felt constrained to start from a solipsistic, or first person, point of view. It also helps explain the fact, which otherwise might be mysterious, that knowledge of other minds has seemed a problem in addition to the problem of empirical knowledge. For if the contents of a mind are logically independent of anything else, this creates two distinguishable problems: how the mind can know what is separate from it, and how what is separate from it can know it. If you can't see out, neither can anyone else (if there is anyone else) see in.

Perhaps under the influence of Wittgenstein, a number of philosophers have thought they saw how to respond to the second problem, the problem of one person's knowledge of another person's mind. The solution, in broad outline, went like this. We must admit that there is a difference in how we know what is in our own mind and how we know what is in someone else's mind; in the former case we do not usually need or employ evidence, whereas in the latter case we must observe behavior, including speech behavior. But this in itself poses no problem. If we understand what mental states are like, then we know that they embrace this anomaly: unlike almost all other kinds of knowledge, knowledge of mental states has the feature that it is correctly based on the observation of behavior when the states are not our own, and not based (normally) on observation or evidence when the states are our own.

As a description of how we employ mental concepts and words, this is (in my opinion) correct. But what these philosophers failed to notice was that a description of our practice is not a solution to the original problem, but a redescription of what creates the problem. Our practice was never in doubt; the doubt concerned its legitimacy, and its legitimacy is open to two questions. The first is that it is hard to see, failing an explanation, why knowledge that is not based on evidence should be more certain than knowledge that is based on evidence. The second is that if what seems a single concept or predicate is correctly applied using two very different sorts of criteria (or in one case using no criteria at all), then we have no reason to suppose there is a single concept. Apparently we should conclude that the predicate is ambiguous, that there are two concepts. This is, after all, the same old problem over again: why should one person believe someone else has mental states like his own? Or to put the problem the other way around, why should I think I have mental states like those I detect in others?

Let us put aside these problems for a moment, especially since I shall not be able to give an adequate treatment of them in this talk. Having, for the moment, accepted what we may call the observer, or third person, attitude to other minds, the next question is how one person can determine what is in another mind. The whole answer is surely very complicated, but a basic part of the answer must, I think, depend on the fact that in the simplest cases the events and objects that cause a belief also determine the contents of that belief. Thus the belief that is differentially and under normal conditions caused by the evident presence of something yellow, one's mother, or a tomato, is the belief that something yellow, one's mother, or a tomato, is present. The idea is not, of course, that nature guarantees that our plainest judgments are always right; the idea is that the causal history of such judgments provides a major constitutive feature of their contents.

This point, which may be called "externalism", has been argued for at length in recent years, usually by appeal to elaborate thought experiments which require that the truth of fairly extreme counter-factual suppositions be evaluated. I think the principle behind the point is both plainer and more universal in application than such arguments reveal; we merely need to reflect on how the meanings of the first and most basic words and sentences are learned, and the obvious relation between what our sentences mean and the thoughts we express by using them.

Externalism makes clear how one person can come to know what someone else thinks, at least at the ground level, for by discovering what normally causes someone else's beliefs, an interpreter has made an essential step toward determining the content of those beliefs. It is not easy to conceive how else it would be possible to discover what someone else thinks. (I do not want to make it seem that this process is simple, and I certainly do not want to suggest that the highly schematic sketch I have given begins to answer the questions that must be answered to fill out the picture. My aim here is only to suggest the nature of an acceptable externalism, and to point to some of the consequences.) Reflecting on how externalism operates in interpretation, we can partly explain the asymmetry between first person and third person knowledge of thoughts. For where the interpreter must know, or correctly surmise, the events and situations that cause a verbal or other reaction in another person in order to fathom her thoughts, no such nomic knowledge is needed for the thinker to decide what she thinks. Causal history partly determines what she is thinking, but this determination is independent of any knowledge of the causal history she may have.

If externalism is true, there can be no further general question how knowledge of the external world is possible. If it is constitutive of some thoughts that their content is given by their normal cause, then knowledge of the causing events and situations cannot require that a thinker independently establish, or find evidence for, the hypotheses that there is an external world which is causing those thoughts. Of course externalism does not show that particular perceptual judgments, even of the simplest kind, cannot be wrong. What it does show is why it cannot happen that most such judgments are mistaken, for the content of mistaken judgments must rest on the content of correct ones.

I have been assuming that externalism is true; that we can legitimately adopt the third person point of view in considering the nature of thought. But suppose we were to assume instead the first person or solipsistic point of view; would there then be any reason to accept externalism? I think there would. I will approach the issue by raising a difficulty for externalism.

Consider first a primitive learning situation. Some creature is taught, or anyway learns, to respond in a specific way to a stimulus or a class of stimuli. The dog hears a bell and is fed; pretty soon it salivates when it hears the bell. The child babbles and when it produces a sound like "table" in the presence of tables it is differentially rewarded; pretty soon the child says "table" in the presence of tables. The phenomenon of generalization, of perceived similarity, plays an essential role in this process. One ring of the bell is enough like another from the dog's point of view to provoke similar behavior, just as one presentation of food is enough like another to engender salivation. If some such selective mechanisms were not built in, none could be learned.

This seems straightforward, but as psychologists have noticed, there is a problem about the location of the stimulus. In the case of the dog, why say the stimulus is the ringing of the bell? Why not the motion of the air close to the ears of the dog—or even the stimulation of its nerve endings? Certainly if the air were made to vibrate in the same way the bell makes it vibrate it would make no difference to the behavior of the dog. And if the right nerve endings were activated in the right way, there still would be no difference. And in fact if we must choose, it seems that the proximal cause of the behavior has the best claim to be called the stimulus, since the more distant an event is causally the more chance there is that the causal chain will be broken. Perhaps we should say the same about the child: its response is not to tables but to patterns of stimulation at its surfaces, since those patterns of stimulation always produce the behavior, while tables produce it only under favorable conditions.

Why, though, does it seem so natural to say the dog is responding to the bell, the child to tables? It seems natural to us because it is natural for us. Just as the dog and the child respond in similar ways to stimuli of a certain sort, so do we. It is we who find it natural to group together the various salivations of the dog; and the events in the world that we notice and group together that are causally linked to the dog's behavior are ringings of the bell. We find the child's utterances of the word "table" similar, and the things in the world we naturally class together that accompany these utterances are tables. The acoustical and visual patterns that speed at their various rates between bell and dog ears, tables and child eyes, we cannot easily observe, and if we could we might have a hard time saying what made them similar. (Except by cheating, of course: they are the patterns characteristic of bells ringing, of tables viewed.) Similarly, we do not observe the stimulation of nerve endings of other people and animals, and if we did we would probably find it impossible to describe in a non-circular way what made the patterns relevantly similar from trial to trial. The problem would be much the same, and as impossible to solve, as the problem of defining tables and bell-ringings in terms of sense data.

Involved in our picture there are now not two but three classes of events or objects the members of which are naturally found similar, by us, and by the child. The child finds tables relevantly similar; we also find tables similar; and we find each of the child's responses to tables similar. Given these three patterns of response it is possible to locate the relevant stimuli that elicit the child's responses. They are objects or events we naturally find similar (tables) which are correlated with responses of the child we find similar. It's a form of triangulation: one line goes from the child in the direction of the table, one line goes from us in the direction of the table, and the third line goes from us to the child. The relevant stimulus is where the lines from child to table and from us to table converge.

Enough features are in place to give a meaning to the idea that the stimulus has an objective location in a common space; it's a matter of two private perspectives converging to mark a position in intersubjective space. So far, however, nothing in this picture shows that either we, the observer, or our subjects, the dog and the child, have the concept of the objective.

Nevertheless we have made progress. For if I am right, the kind of triangulation I have described, while obviously not sufficient to establish that a creature has a concept of a particular object or kind of object, is necessary if there is to be any answer at all to the question what its concepts are concepts of. If we consider a single creature by itself, its responses, no matter how complex, cannot show that it is reacting to, or thinking about, events a certain distance away rather than, say, on its skin. The solipsist's world can be any size; which is to say, it has no size, it is not a world.

The problem is not, I should stress, one of verifying what objects or events a creature is responding to; the problem is that without a second creature interacting with the first, there can be no answer to the question. And if there can be no answer to the question what a creature means, wants, believes or intends, it makes no sense to hold that the creature has thoughts. So we can say, as a preliminary to answering the question with which we began, that before anyone can have thoughts there must be another creature (one or more) interacting with the speaker. But of course this cannot be enough, since mere interaction does not show how the interaction matters to the creatures involved. Unless the creatures concerned can be said to react to the interaction there is no way they can take cognitive advantage of the three-way relation which gives content to the idea that they are reacting to one thing rather than another.

Here is part, then, of what is required. The interaction must be made available to the interacting creatures. Thus the child, learning the word "table", has already in effect noted that the teacher's responses are similar (rewarding) when its own responses (utterances of the word "table") are similar. The teacher on his part is training the child to make similar responses to what he (the teacher) perceives as similar stimuli. For this to work, it is clear that the innate similarity responses of child and teacher—what they naturally group together—must be much alike; otherwise the child will respond to what the teacher takes to be similar stimuli in ways the teacher does not find similar. A condition for being a speaker or interpreter is that there must be others enough like oneself.

Now to put two points together. First, if someone has thoughts, there must be another sentient being whose innate similarity responses are sufficiently like his own to provide an answer to the question, what is the stimulus to which he is responding? And second, if someone's responses are to count as thoughts, he must have the concept of an object—the concept of the stimulus—of the bell, or of tables. Since the bell or a table is identified only by the intersection of two (or more) sets of similarity responses (lines of thought, we might almost say), to have the concept of a table or a bell is to recognize the existence of a triangle, one apex of which is oneself, another a creature similar to oneself, and the third an object or event (table or bell) located in a space thus made common.

The only way of knowing that the second apex, the second creature or person, is reacting to the same object as oneself is to know that the other person has the same object in mind. But then the second person must also know that the first person constitutes an apex of the same triangle another apex of which he, the second person, occupies. For two people to know of each other that they are so related, that their thoughts are so related, requires that they be in communication. Each of them must speak to the other and be understood by the other.

If I am right, belief, intention, and the other propositional attitudes are all social in that they depend on having the concept of objective truth. This is a concept one cannot have without sharing, and knowing that one shares, a world and a way of thinking about the world, with someone else.

Note: this summary paper draws on recent work by the author in which more extended treatment of the main theses will be found. See: "Rational Animals", *Dialectica* 36 (1982), pp. 317–327; "First Person Authority", *Dialectica* 38 (1984), pp. 101–111; "A Coherence Theory of Truth and Knowledge", in *Truth and Interpretation: Perspectives on the Philosophy of Donald Davidson*, ed. E. LePore, Blackwell 1986; "Knowing One's Own Mind", *Proceedings and Addresses of the American Philosophical Association*, 1987, pp. 441–458. "The Conditions of Thought" was originally written for, and delivered at, the plenary session on "Human Beings: Nature, Mind, and Community" at the World Congress of Philosophy, Brighton, August 23rd, 1988.

76

Slavoj Žižek

The Sublime Object of Ideology (1989)

"Not Only as *Substance,* But Also as *Subject*"

The Logic of Sublimity

IN HIS ESSAY ON 'THE RELIGION OF SUBLIMITY', YIRMIYAHU YOVEL has pointed out a certain inconsistency in Hegel's systematization of religions, an inconsistency which does not result directly from the very principle of Hegel's philosophy but expresses rather a contingent, empirical prejudice of Hegel's as an individual, and can therefore be rectified by consequent use of Hegel's own dialectical procedure.[1] This inconsistency concerns the place occupied respectively by Jewish and by ancient Greek religion: in Hegel's *Lessons on the Philosophy of Religion,* Christianity is immediately preceded by three forms of the 'religion of spiritual individuality': the Jewish religion of Sublimity [*Erhabenheit*], the Greek religion of Beauty, and the Roman religion of Understanding [*Verstand*]. In this succession the first, lowest place is taken by the Jewish religion – that is, Greek religion is conceived as a higher stage in spiritual development than the Jewish religion. According to Yovel, Hegel has here given way to his personal anti-Semitic prejudice, because to be consistent with the logic of the dialectical process it is undoubtedly the Jewish religion which should follow the Greek.

Despite some reservations about the detail of Yovel's arguments, his fundamental point seems to hit the mark: the Greek, Jewish and Christian religions do form a kind of triad which corresponds perfectly to the triad of reflection (positing, external and determinate reflection), to this elementary matrix of the dialectical process. Greek religion embodies the moment of 'positing reflection': in it, the plurality of spiritual individuals (gods) is immediately 'posited' as the given spiritual essence of the world. The Jewish religion introduces the moment of 'external reflection' – all positivity is abolished by reference to the unapproachable, transcendent God, the absolute Master, the One of absolute negativity, while Christianity conceives the individuality of man not as something external to God but as a 'reflective determination' of God himself (in the figure of Christ, God himself 'becomes man').

It is something of a mystery why Yovel does not mention the crucial argument in his favour: the very interconnection of the notions of 'Beauty' and 'Sublimity'. If Greek religion is, according to Hegel, the religion of Beauty and Jewish religion that of Sublimity, it is clear that the very logic of the dialectical process compels us to conclude that Sublimity should *follow* Beauty because it is the point of its breakdown, of its mediation, of its self-referential negativity. In using the couple Beauty/Sublimity Hegel relies, of course, on Kant's *Critique of Judgement*, where Beauty and Sublimity are opposed along the semantic axes quality-quantity, shaped-shapeless, bounded-boundless: Beauty calms and comforts; Sublimity excites and agitates. 'Beauty' is the sentiment provoked when the suprasensible Idea appears in the material, sensuous medium, in its harmonious formation – a sentiment of immediate harmony between Idea and the sensuous material of its expression; while the sentiment of Sublimity is attached to chaotic, terrifying limitless phenomena (rough sea, rocky mountains).

Above all, however, Beauty and Sublimity are opposed along the axis pleasure-displeasure: a view of Beauty offers us pleasure, while 'the object is received as sublime with a pleasure that is only possible through the mediation of displeasure'.[2] In short, the Sublime is 'beyond the pleasure principle', it is a paradoxical pleasure procured by displeasure itself (the exact definition – one of the Lacanian definitions – of enjoyment [*jouissance*]). This means at the same time that the relation of Beauty to Sublimity coincides with the relation of immediacy to mediation – further proof that the Sublime must *follow* Beauty as a form of mediation of its immediacy. On closer examination, in what does this mediation proper to the Sublime consist? Let us quote the Kantian definition of the Sublime:

> The Sublime may be described in this way: It is an object (of nature) the *representation [Vorstellung] of which determines the mind to regard the elevation of nature beyond our reach as equivalent to a presentation [Darstellung] of ideas.*[3]

It is a definition which, so to speak, anticipates Lacan's determination of the sublime object in his seminar on *The Ethic of Psychoanalysis*: 'an object raised to the level of the (impossible-real) Thing'. That is to say, with Kant the Sublime designates the relation of an inner-worldly, empirical, sensuous object to *Ding an sich* to the transcendent, trans-phenomenal, unattainable Thing-in-itself The paradox of the Sublime is as follows: in principle, the gap separating phenomenal, empirical objects of experience from the Thing-in-itself is insurmountable – that is, no empirical object, no representation [*Vorstellung*] of it can adequately present [*darstellen*] the Thing (the suprasensible Idea); but the Sublime is an object in which we can experience this very impossibility, this permanent failure of the representation to reach after the Thing. Thus, by means of the very failure of representation, we can have a presentiment of the true dimension of the Thing. This is also why an object evoking in us the feeling of Sublimity gives us simultaneous pleasure and displeasure: it gives us displeasure because of its inadequacy to the Thing-Idea, but precisely through this inadequacy it gives us pleasure by indicating the true, incomparable greatness of the Thing, surpassing every possible phenomenal, empirical experience:

> The feeling of the Sublime is, therefore, at once a feeling of displeasure, arising from the inadequacy of imagination in the aesthetic estimation of magnitude to attain, to its estimation by reason, and a simultaneously awakened pleasure, arising from this very judgement of the inadequacy of the greatest faculty of sense being in accord with ideas of reason, so far as the effort to attain to these is for us a law.[4]

We can now see why it is precisely nature in its most chaotic, boundless, terrifying dimension which is best qualified to awaken in us the feeling of the Sublime: here, where the aesthetic imagination is strained to its utmost, where all finite determinations dissolve themselves, the failure appears at its purest.

The Sublime is therefore the paradox of an object which, in the very field of representation, provides a view, in a negative way, of the dimension of what is unrepresentable. It is a unique point in Kant's system, a point at which the fissure, the gap between phenomenon and Thing-in-itself, is abolished in a negative way, because in it the phenomenon's very inability to represent the Thing adequately *is inscribed in the phenomenon itself* – or, as Kant puts it, 'even if the Ideas of reason can be in no way adequately represented [in the sensuous-phenomenal world], they can be revived and evoked in the mind by means of this very inadequacy which can be presented in a sensuous way.' It is this mediation of the inability – this successful presentation by means of failure, of the inadequacy itself – which distinguishes *enthusiasm* evoked by the Sublime from fanciful *fanaticism* [*Schwärmerei*]: fanaticism is an insane visionary delusion that we can immediately see or grasp what lies beyond all bounds of sensibility, while enthusiasm precludes all positive presentation. Enthusiasm is an example of purely negative presentation – that is, the sublime object evokes pleasure in a purely negative way: the place of the Thing is indicated through the very failure of its representation. Kant himself pointed out the connection between such a notion of Sublimity and the Jewish religion:

> We have no reason to fear that the feeling of the Sublime will suffer from an abstract mode of presentation like this, which is altogether negative as to what is sensuous. For though the imagination, no doubt, finds nothing beyond the sensible world to which it can lay hold, still this thrusting aside of the sensible barriers gives it a feeling of being unbounded; and that removal is thus a presentation of the infinite. As such it can never be anything more than a negative presentation – but still it expands the soul. Perhaps there is no more sublime passage in the Jewish Law than the commandment: Thou shalt not make unto thee any graven image, or any likeness of any thing that is in heaven or on earth, or under the earth, and so forth. This commandment can alone explain the enthusiasm which the Jewish people, in their moral period, felt for their religion when comparing themselves with others.[5]

In what consists, then, the Hegelian criticism of this Kantian notion of the Sublime? From Kant's point of view, Hegel's dialectics appears, of course, as a repeated fall, as a return to the *Schwärmerei* of traditional metaphysics which fails to take into account the abyss separating phenomena from the Idea and pretends to mediate the Idea with phenomena (as with the Jewish religion, to which Christianity appears as a return to pagan polytheism and the incarnation of God in a multitude of man-like figures).

In Hegel's defence, it is not enough to point out how in his dialectics none of the determinate, particular phenomena represents adequately the suprasensible Idea – that is, how the Idea is the very movement of sublation [*Aufhebung*] – the famous *Flüssigwerden,* 'liquidizing' – of all particular determinations. The Hegelian criticism is much more radical: it does not affirm, in opposition to Kant, the possibility of some kind of 'reconciliation'-mediation between Idea and phenomena, the possibility of surmounting the gap which separates them, of abolishing the radical 'otherness', the radical negative relationship of the Idea-Thing to phenomena. Hegel's reproach to Kant (and at the same time to the Jewish religion) is, on the contrary, that *it is Kant himself who still remains a prisoner of the field of representation.* Precisely when we determine the Thing as a transcendent surplus beyond what can be represented, we determine it on the basis of the field of representation, starting from it, within its horizon, as its negative limit: the (Jewish) notion of God as radical Otherness, as unrepresentable, still remains the extreme point of the logic of representation.

But here again, this Hegelian approach can give way to misunderstanding if we read it as an assertion that – in opposition to Kant, who tries to reach the Thing through the very breakdown of the field of phenomena, by driving the logic of representation to its utmost – in dialectical speculation, we must grasp the Thing 'in itself, from itself, as it is in its pure Beyond, without even a negative reference or relationship to the field of representation. This is *not* Hegel's position: the Kantian criticism has here done its job and if this were Hegel's position, Hegelian dialectics would effectively entail a regression into the traditional metaphysics aiming at an immediate approach to the Thing. Hegel's position is in fact 'more Kantian than Kant himself' – it adds nothing to the Kantian notion of the Sublime; it merely takes it more *literally* than Kant himself.

Hegel, of course, retains the basic dialectical moment of the Sublime, the notion that the Idea is reached through purely negative presentation – that the very inadequacy of the phenomenality to the Thing is the only appropriate way to present it. The real problem lies elsewhere: Kant still presupposes that the Thing-in-itself exists as something positively given beyond the field of representation, of phenomenality, the breakdown of phenomenality, the experience of phenomena, is for him only an 'external reflection', only a way of indicating, within the domain of phenomenality, this transcendent dimension of the Thing which persists in itself beyond phenomenality.

Hegel's position is, in contrast, that there is *nothing* beyond phenomenality, beyond the field of representation. The experience of radical negativity, of the radical inadequacy of all phenomena to the Idea, the experience of the radical fissure between the two – this experience is already *idea itself as 'pure', radical negativity.* Where Kant thinks that he is still dealing only with a negative presentation of the Thing, we are already in the midst of the Thing-in-itself – *for this Thing-in-itself is nothing but this radical negativity.* In other words – in a somewhat overused Hegelian speculative twist – the negative experience of the Thing must change into the experience of the Thing-in-itself as radical negativity. The experience of the Sublime thus remains the same: all we have to do is to subtract its transcendent presupposition – the presupposition that this experience indicates, in a negative way, some transcendent Thing-in-itself persisting in its positivity beyond it. In short, we must limit ourselves to what is strictly immanent to this experience, to pure negativity, to the negative self-relationship of the representation.

Homologous to Hegel's determination of the difference between the death of the pagan god and the death of Christ (the first being merely the death of the terrestrial embodiment, of the terrestrial representation, figure, of God, while with the death of Christ it is God of beyond, God as a positive, transcendent, unattainable entity, which dies) we could say that what Kant fails to take into account is the way the experience of the nullity, of the inadequacy of the phenomenal world of representation, which befalls us in the sentiment of the Sublime, means at the same time the nullity, the non-existence of the transcendent Thing-in-itself as a positive entity.

That is to say, the limit of the logic of representation is not to 'reduce all contents to representations', to what can be represented, but, on the contrary, in the very presupposition of some positive entity (Thing-in-itself) *beyond phenomenal representation.* We overcome phenomenality not by reaching beyond it, but by the experience of how there is nothing beyond it – how its beyond is precisely this Nothing of absolute negativity, of the utmost inadequacy of the appearance to its notion. The suprasensible essence is the 'appearance *qua* appearance' – that is, it is not enough to say that the appearance is never adequate to its essence, we must also add that *this 'essence' itself is nothing but the inadequacy of the appearance to itself,* to its notion (inadequacy which makes it '[just] an appearance').

Thus the status of the sublime object is displaced almost imperceptibly, but none the less decisively: the Sublime is no longer an (empirical) object indicating through its very inadequacy the dimension of a transcendent Thing-in-itself (Idea) but an object which occupies the place, replaces, fills out the empty place of the Thing as the void, as the pure Nothing of absolute negativity – the Sublime is an object whose positive body is just an embodiment of Nothing. This logic of an object which, by its very inadequacy, 'gives body' to the absolute negativity of the Idea, is articulated in Hegel in the form of the so-called 'infinite judgement', a judgement in which subject and predicate are radically incompatible, incomparable: 'the Spirit is a *bone*', *Wealth* is the Self, 'the State is *Monarch*', 'God is *Christ*'.

In Kant, the feeling of the Sublime is evoked by some boundless, terrifying imposing phenomenon (raging nature, and so on), while in Hegel we are dealing with a miserable 'little piece of the Real' – the Spirit *is* the inert, dead skull; the subject's Self *is* this small piece of metal that I am holding in my hand; the State as the rational organization of social life *is* the idiotic body of the Monarch; God who created the world *is* Jesus, this miserable individual crucified together with two robbers . . . Herein lies the 'last secret' of dialectical speculation: not in the dialectical mediation-sublimation of all contingent, empirical reality, not in the deduction of all reality from the mediating movement of absolute negativity, but in the fact that this very negativity, to attain its 'being-for-itself,' must embody itself again in some miserable, radically contingent corporeal leftover.

Notes

1 Yirmiyahu Yovel, 'La Religion de la sublimité', in *Hegel et la religion*, ed. G. Planty-Bonjour, Paris: PUF, 1982.

2 Immanuel Kant, *Critique of Judgement*, Oxford: Clarendon Press, 1964, p. 109.

3 Ibid., p. 119.

4 Ibid., p. 106.

5 Ibid., p. 127.

77

Gilles Deleuze

The Logic of Sense (1990)

IT SEEMS THAT OUR PROBLEM, IN THE COURSE OF OUR investigation, has changed altogether. We were inquiring into the nature of the alogical compatibilities and incompatibilities between events. But, to the extent that divergence is affirmed and disjunction becomes a positive synthesis, it seems that all events, even contraries, are compatible—that they are "inter-expressive" (*s'entr' expriment*). Incompatibility is born only with individuals, persons, and worlds in which events are actualized, but not between events themselves or between their *a-cosmic*, *impersonal*, and *pre-individual* singularities. Incompatibility does not exist between two events, but between an event and the world or the individual which actualized another event as divergent. [. . .]

The problem is therefore one of knowing how the individual would be able to transcend his form and his syntactical link with a world, in order to attain to the universal communication of events, that is, to the affirmation of a disjunctive synthesis beyond logical contradictions, and even beyond alogical incompatibilities. It would be necessary for the individual to grasp herself as event; and that she grasp the event as actualized within her as another individual grafted onto her. In this case, she would not understand, want, or represent this event without also understanding and wanting all other events as individuals, and without representing all other individuals as events. Each individual would be like a mirror for the condensation of singularities and each world a distance in the mirror. This is the ultimate sense of counter-actualization. This, moreover, is the Nietzschean discovery of the individual as the *fortuitous case* [. . .].

Philosophy merges with ontology, but ontology merges with the univocity of Being (analogy has always been a theological vision, not a philosophical one, adapted to the forms of God, the world, and the self). The univocity of Being does not mean that there is one and the same Being; on the contrary, beings are multiple and different, they are always produced by a disjunctive synthesis, and they themselves are disjointed and divergent, *membra disjuncta*. The univocity of

Being signifies that Being is Voice that it is said, and that it is said in one and the same "sense" of everything about which it is said. That of which it is said is not at all the same, but Being is the same for everything about which it is said. It occurs, therefore, as a unique event for everything that happens to the most diverse things, *Eventum tantum* for all events, the ultimate form for all of the forms which remain disjointed in it, but which bring about the resonance and the ramification of their disjunction. The univocity of Being merges with the positive use of the disjunctive synthesis which is the highest affirmation. It is the eternal return itself, or—as we have seen in the case of the ideal game—the affirmation of all chance in a single moment, the unique cast for all throws, one Being and only for all forms and all times, a single instance for all that exists, a single phantom for all the living, a single voice for every hum of voices and every drop of water in the sea. It would be a mistake to confuse the univocity of Being to the extent that it is said with the pseudo-univocity of everything about which it is said. But at the same time, if Being cannot be said without also occurring, if Being is the unique event in which all events communicate with one another, univocity refers both to what occurs and to what is said. Univocity means that it is the same thing which occurs and is said: the attributable to all bodies or states of affairs and the expressible of every proposition. Univocity means the identity of the noematic attribute and that which is expressed linguistically—event and sense. It does not allow Being to subsist in the vague state that it used to have in the perspectives of the analogy. Univocity raises and extracts Being, in order to distinguish it better from that in which it occurs and from that of which it is said. It wrests Being from beings in order to bring it to all of them at once, and to make it fall upon them for all times. Being pure saying and pure event, univocity brings in contact the inner surface of language (insistence) with the outer surface of Being (extra-Being). Univocal Being inheres in language and happens to things; it measures the internal relation of language with the external relation of Being. Neither active nor passive, univocal Being is neutral. It is *extra-Being,* that is, the minimum of Being common to the real, the possible, and the impossible. A position in the void of all events in one, an expression in the nonsense of all senses in one, univocal Being is the pure form of the Aion, the form of exteriority which relates things and propositions. In short, the univocity of Being has three determinations: one single event for all events; one and the same *aliquid* for that which happens and that which is said; and one and the same Being for the impossible, the possible, and the real.

Difference and Repetition (1994)

The Univocity of Being (I)

THERE HAS ONLY EVER BEEN ONE ONTOLOGICAL PROPOSITION: Being is univocal. There has only ever been one ontology, that of Duns Scotus, which gave being a single voice. We say Duns Scotus because he was the one who elevated univocal being to the highest point of subtlety, albeit at the price of abstraction. However, from Parmenides to Heidegger it is the same voice which is taken up, in an echo which itself forms the whole deployment of the univocal. A single voice raises the clamour of being. We have no difficulty in understanding that Being, even if it is absolutely common, is nevertheless not a genus. It is enough to replace the model of judgement with that of the proposition. In the proposition understood as a complex entity we distinguish: the sense, or what is expressed in the proposition; the designated (what expresses itself in the proposition); the expressors or designators, which are numerical modes—that is to say, differential factors characterising the elements endowed with sense and designation. We can conceive that names or propositions do not have the same sense even while they designate exactly the same thing (as in the case of the celebrated examples: morning star-evening star, Israel-Jacob, *plan-blanc*). The distinction between these senses is indeed a real distinction (*distinctio realis*), but there is nothing numerical—much less ontological—about it: it is a formal, qualitative or semiological distinction. The question whether categories are directly assimilable to such senses, or—more probably—derive from them, must be left aside for the moment. What is important is that we can conceive of several formally distinct senses which none the less refer to being as if to a single designated entity, ontologically one. It is true that such a point of view is not sufficient to prevent us from considering these senses as analogues and this unity of being as an analogy. We must add that being, this common designated, in so far as it expresses itself, is said in turn *in a single and same sense* of all the numerically distinct designators and expressors. In the ontological proposition, not only is that which is designated ontologically the same for qualitatively distinct senses, but also the sense is ontologically the same for individuating modes, for numerically distinct designators or expressors: the ontological proposition involves a circulation of this kind (expression as a whole).

In effect, the essential in univocity is not that Being is said in a single and same sense, but that it is said, in a single and same sense, *of* all its individuating differences or intrinsic modalities. Being is the same for all these modalities, but these modalities are not the same. It is 'equal' for all, but they themselves are not equal. It is said of all in a single sense, but they themselves do not have the same sense. The essence of univocal being is to include individuating differences, while these differences do not have the same essence and do not change the essence of being—just as white includes various intensities, while remaining essentially the same white. There are not two 'paths', as Parmenides' poem suggests, but a single 'voice' of Being, which includes all its modes, including the most diverse, the most varied, the most differentiated. Being is said in a single and same sense of everything of which it is said, but that of which it is said differs: it is said of difference itself.

No doubt there is still hierarchy and distribution in univocal being, in relation to the individuating factors and their sense, but distribution and even hierarchy have two completely different, irreconcilable acceptations. Similarly for the expressions *logos* and *nomos,* in so far as these refer to problems of distribution. We must first of all distinguish a type of distribution which implies a dividing up of that which is distributed: it is a matter of dividing up the distributed as such. It is here that in judgement the rules of analogy are all-powerful. In so far as common sense and good sense are qualities of judgement, these are presented as principles of division which declare themselves *the best distributed*. A distribution of this type proceeds by fixed and proportional determinations which may be assimilated to 'properties' or limited territories within representation. The agrarian question may well have been very important for this organisation of judgement as the faculty which distinguishes parts ('on the one hand and on the other hand'). Even among the gods, each has his domain, his category, his attributes, and all distribute limits and lots to mortals in accordance with destiny. Then there is a completely other distribution which must be called nomadic, a nomad *nomos*, without property, enclosure or measure. Here, there is no longer a division of that which is distributed but rather a division among those who distribute *themselves* in an open space—a space which is unlimited, or at least without precise limits.[1] Nothing pertains or belongs to any person, but all persons are arrayed here and there in such a manner as to cover the largest possible space. Even when it concerns the serious business of life, it is more like a space of play, or a rule of play, by contrast with sedentary space and *nomos*. To fill a space, to be distributed within it, is very different from distributing the space. It is an errant and even 'delirious' distribution, in which things are deployed across the entire extensity of a univocal and undistributed Being. It is not a matter of being which is distributed according to the requirements of representation, but of all things being divided up within being in the univocity of simple presence (the One-All). Such a distribution is demonic rather than divine, since it is a peculiarity of demons to operate in the intervals between the gods' fields of action, as it is to leap over the barriers or the enclosures, thereby confounding the boundaries between properties. Oedipus' chorus cries: 'Which demon has leapt further than the longest leap?' The leap here bears witness to the unsettling difficulties that nomadic distributions introduce into the sedentary structures of representation. The same goes for hierarchy. There is a hierarchy which measures beings according to their limits, and according to their degree of proximity or distance from a principle. But there is also a hierarchy which considers things and beings from the point of view of power: it is not a question of considering absolute degrees of power, but only of knowing whether a being eventually 'leaps over' or transcends its limits in going to the limit of what it can do, whatever its degree. 'To the limit', it will be argued, still presupposes a limit. Here, limit [*peras*] no longer refers to what maintains the thing under a law, nor to what delimits or separates it from other things. On the contrary, it refers to that on the basis of which it is deployed and deploys all its power; hubris ceases to be simply condemnable and *the smallest becomes equivalent to the largest* once it is not separated from what it can do. This enveloping measure is the same for all things, the same also for substance, quality, quantity, etc., since it forms a single maximum at which the developed diversity of all degrees touches the equality which envelops them. This ontological measure is closer to the immeasurable state of things than to the first kind of measure; this ontological hierarchy is closer to the hubris and anarchy of beings than to the first hierarchy. It is the monster which combines all the demons. The words 'everything is equal' may therefore resound joyfully, on condition that they are said *of* that which is not equal in this equal, univocal Being: equal being is immediately present in everything, without mediation or intermediary, even though things reside unequally in this equal being. There, however, where they are borne by hubris, all things are in absolute proximity, and whether they are large or small, inferior or superior, none of them participates more or less in being, nor receives it by analogy. Univocity of being thus also signifies equality of being. Univocal Being is at one and the same time nomadic distribution and crowned anarchy.

78

Iris Murdoch

Metaphysics as a Guide to Morals (1992)

Fact and Value

A MISLEADING THOUGH ATTRACTIVE DISTINCTION IS MADE BY MANY THINKERS between fact and (moral) value. Roughly, the purpose of the distinction (as it is used by Kant and Wittgenstein for instance) is to *segregate* value in order to keep it pure and untainted, not derived from or mixed with empirical facts. This move however, in time and as interpreted, may in effect result in a diminished, even perfunctory, account of morality, leading (with the increasing prestige of science) to a marginalisation of 'the ethical'. (Big world of facts, little peripheral area of value.) This originally well-intentioned segregation then ignores an obvious and important aspect of human existence, the way in which almost all our concepts and activities involve evaluation. A post-Kantian theory of morals: survey all the facts, then use your reason. But, in the majority of cases, a survey of the facts will itself involve moral discrimination. Innumerable forms of evaluation haunt our simplest decisions. The defence of value is not an attack on 'ordinary facts'. The concept of 'fact' is complex. The moral point is that 'facts' are set up as such by human (that is moral) agents. Much of our life is taken up by truth-seeking, imagining, questioning. We relate to facts through truth and truthfulness, and come to recognise and discover that there are different modes and levels of insight and understanding. In many familiar ways *various* values pervade and *colour* what we take to be the reality of our world; wherein we constantly evaluate our own values and those of others, and judge and determine forms of consciousness and modes of being. To say all this is not in any way to deny either science, empiricism or commonsense. The proposition that 'the cat is on the mat' is true, indicates a fact, if the cat is on the mat. A proper separation of fact and value, as a defence of morality, lies in the contention that moral value cannot be *derived* from fact. That is, our activity of moral discrimination cannot be explained as merely one natural instinct among others, or our 'good' *identified* with pleasure, or a will to live, or what the government says (etc.). The possession of a moral sense is uniquely human; morality is, in the human world, something unique, special, *sui generis*, 'as if it came to us from elsewhere'. It is an intimation of 'something higher'. The demand that we be virtuous. It is 'inescapable and fundamental'. The interpretation of such phrases, including less fancy versions of the same intuition, has been, and should be, a main activity of moral philosophers.

> The work of art is the object seen *sub specie aeternitatis*; and the good life is the world seen *sub specie aeternitatis*. This is the connection between art and ethics. The usual way of looking at things sees objects as it were from the midst of them, the view *sub specie aeternitatis* from outside. In such a way that they have the whole world as background . . . If I have been contemplating the stove, and then am told: but now all you know is the stove, my result does indeed seem trivial. For this represents the matter as if I had studied the stove as one among the many things in the world. But if I was contemplating the stove *it* was my world, and everything else colourless by contrast with it . . . For it is equally possible to take the bare present image as the worthless momentary picture in the whole temporal world, and as the true world among shadows. (Wittgenstein, *Notebooks 1914–1916*, 7, 8, 9 October 1916.)

Wittgenstein was twenty-seven when he wrote these words which are preliminary notes for the last part of the *Tractatus*. There are significant differences between the two texts. This passage, three consecutive entries over three days, is a complete miniature metaphysical picture, making use of the potent idea of the work of art, or object of contemplative vision, as a limited whole. A 'world' is a limited whole. Morality, according to the later part of the *Tractatus* and this part of the *Notebooks*, is fundamentally an attitude of acceptance of the world of facts which is viewed as a whole, as something independent of my will. I quote again from the *Notebooks*, 8.7.16.

> The world is *given* me, i.e. my will enters into the world completely from outside as into something that is already there . . . That is why we have the feeling of being dependent on an alien will. *However this may be*, at any rate we *are* in a certain sense dependent, and what we are dependent on we can call God. In this sense God would simply be fate, or, what is the same thing: the world, which is independent of our will. I can make myself independent of fate. There are two godheads: the world and my independent I. I am either happy or unhappy, that is all. It can be said: good or evil do not exist.

This view, which appears in a more epigrammatic form in the *Tractatus*, is to be connected with Wittgenstein's reading of Schopenhauer, by whom he was impressed when he was young. The shadow of Kant may indeed have fallen upon him through Schopenhauer. *Tractatus* Wittgenstein, like Kant, has two 'subjects', one which is locked on to the world of fact, and one which is totally independent of that world. Wittgenstein speaks of two godheads. 'I am my world' in two senses. I am the world of fact in the sense that I, the extensionless subject of experience, coincide exactly with my world of factual and significant apprehension. Wittgenstein's world of fact owns nothing beyond, the subject who experiences it fits it exactly; the notion of his 'seeing beyond' can make no sense. This impossibility is established (by Wittgenstein) in the nature of logic and language; in the *Tractatus* facts, states of affairs, are projected in propositions intelligibly organised by logic. They just *are* so projected, we cannot in the nature of the case see *how*, for this would be to see beyond the transcendental barrier. (What is transcendent is beyond human experience, what is transcendental is not derived from human experience, but is a condition of it.) There is no other access to facts. Thus, in the *Tractatus*, Wittgenstein dismisses any general *problem* of a transcendent 'factual' world, or of the ability of language to refer to the world. Language just does refer to the world. This disposes by fiat of many of the questions raised by structuralism, and also of course of Cartesian anxieties about how the mind reaches the world. He similarly recognises no problem of the freedom of the will. 'The freedom of the will consists in the fact that future actions cannot be known now.' (*Tractatus* 5.1362. *Tractatus* quotes are from the C. K. Ogden translation, unless otherwise stated.)

The other sense in which (in the *Tractatus*) I am my world, or live or experience my world, is the moral sense. Here I become an artist, or a mystic, ethics and aesthetics being one, looking at and accepting the world *as a whole, all* the facts. Value lies *ineffably* outside this limited whole. 'So too it is impossible for there to be propositions of ethics. Propositions can express nothing that is higher. It is clear that ethics cannot be put into words. Ethics is transcendental. (Ethics and aesthetics are one and the same.)' (*Tractatus* 6.421, trans. Pears and McGuinness.) Wittgenstein does not, philosophically, discuss art though he makes a number of remarks about it, and like Plato he uses it as an image. Value does not alter, or in that sense enter, the world of facts, in the way in which Kant's duty or Categorical Imperative does mysteriously enter from the outside, illuminating particular situations and enabling us to act freely. 'Value' in the *Tractatus*, or the *moral* subject, of whom we cannot speak (6.423), resides rather in an *attitude or style* in one's acceptance of all the facts. This morality is stoical rather than Kantian. The distinction between fact and value, the *protective* segregation of value from the world, is seen by Wittgenstein as a form of *silent* stoical understanding and way of life. 'I am either happy or unhappy, good and evil do not exist.' The end of the *Tractatus*, where these views about the moral subject are expressed, has often been treated as an arcane idiosyncratic tailpiece, lacking the philosophical interest of the longer earlier section. But the importance which Wittgenstein attached to it is shown by a letter written in 1919 to Ludwig Ficker (see Paul Engelmann, *Letters from Ludwig Wittgenstein with a Memoir*):

> The book's point is an ethical one. I once meant to include in the preface a sentence which is not in fact there now but which I will write out for you here, because it will perhaps be a key to the work for you. What I meant to write then was this: My work consists of two parts: the one presented here plus all that I have not written. And it is precisely this second part that

is the important one. My book draws limits to the sphere of the ethical from the inside as it were, and I am convinced that this is the only rigorous way of drawing those limits. In short, I believe that where many others today are just gassing I have managed in my book to put everything firmly in place by being silent about it. And for that reason, unless I am very much mistaken, the book will say a great deal that you yourself want to say. Only perhaps you won't see that it is said in the book. For now, I would recommend you to read the preface and the conclusion, because they contain the most direct expression of the point of the book.

I also quote here (from *Wittgenstein and the Vienna Circle,* conversations recorded by Friedrich Waismann, p. 68).

To be sure, I can imagine what Heidegger means by being and anxiety. Man feels the urge to run up against the limits of language. Think for example of the astonishment that anything at all exists. This astonishment cannot be expressed in the form of a question, and there is also no answer whatsoever. Anything we might say is *a priori* bound to be mere nonsense. Nevertheless we do run up against the limits of language. Kierkegaard too saw that there is this running up against something and he referred to it in a fairly similar way (as running up against paradox). This running up against the limits of language is *ethics*. I think it is definitely important to put an end to all the claptrap about ethics – whether intuitive knowledge exists, whether values exist, whether the good is definable. In ethics we are always making the attempt to say something that cannot be said, something that does not and never will touch the essence of the matter. It is *a priori* certain that whatever definition of the good may be given – it will always be merely a misunderstanding to say that the essential thing, that what is really meant, corresponds to what is expressed (Moore). But the inclination, the running up against something, *indicates something.* St Augustine knew that already when he said: 'What, you swine you want not to talk nonsense! Go ahead and talk nonsense, it does not matter!'

*

The reference to Heidegger concerns *Sein und Zeit* (*Being and Time*) published 1927, the reference to Moore is to his book *Principia Ethica,* the St Augustine reference is said to paraphrase *Confessions* I iv. *Et vae tacentibus de te, quoniam loquaces muti sunt.* (God is addressed.) 'And woe to those who are silent about You [do not praise You], since the ones who chatter say nothing!'

Wittgenstein has nothing to say in the *Tractatus* about a transcendent reality. Ethics cannot be expressed in words. 'Ethics is transcendental.' (6.421.) It is at the border of experience. Here the 'fit', as one might put it, is perfect. There is no suggestive gleam from beyond, or crack through which one might peer, or any sense in talking about one. We *enact* morality, it looks after itself. Moreover:

The solution of the problem of life is seen in the vanishing of the problem . . . There are, indeed, things which cannot be put into words. They *make themselves manifest.* They are what is mystical. The correct method in philosophy would really be the following: to say nothing except what can be said, i.e. propositions of natural science – i.e. something that has nothing to do with philosophy – and then, whenever someone else wanted to say something metaphysical, to demonstrate to him that he had failed to give a meaning to certain signs in his propositions. (6.521, 6.522, 6.53; trans. Pears and McGuinness)

The 'propositions of natural science' means ordinary demonstrable factual statements. Wittgenstein says in the *Notebooks* (1.6.15) that his philosophy is entirely connected with whether there is an *a priori* order in the world. Also, 'my work has extended from the foundations of logic to the nature of the world' (2.8.16). The letter to Ficker suggests that the 'setting in order', or segregation (or magical setting apart) of the factual world has as its objective a clarification or purification of the function of morality. This too reminds us of Kant. The two 'godheads' are the world of fact which must be realistically, bravely, accepted, and the moral subject who is to accept it. Our 'will' can change the limits of the world but not the facts. (It can only change the *total aspect,* not the parts within the totality.) The world must wax or wane *as a whole,* according to our *general* attitude of acceptance or non-acceptance. (*Tractatus* 6.43.) The morality recommended in the last part of the *Tractatus* is for all its coldness not without an intensity which might be called religious, or aesthetic. This would be a place from which to look at the relation between these two concepts. The much quoted 'Not *how* the world is, is the mystical, but *that* it is' (6.44) is followed by 'The contemplation of the world *sub specie aeterni* is its contemplation as a limited whole.' We experience or express value more purely (indeed in the only possible way according to the *Tractatus*) if we are able to look at the world in a detached manner from the outside, as if it were a work of art. Facts are what can be expressed in plain non-evaluative language. There is no place for any idea of 'moral facts', or for the development of a 'moral vocabulary'. Such a view is certainly not just a period piece; it may be seen as prophetic, a morality for an age when space travel and physics make us conscious of the world, even of the universe, as a single entity, and when intimations of determinism and fears of cosmic disaster make ordinary moral distinctions (ordinary 'good and evil' or detailed talks about morality) seem unimportant. A cool attitude ('the propositions of natural science' (*Tractatus* 6.53) might seem appropriate here, a preserved ability at least to ascertain the facts, the silent correlate of which would be an (unnamed) stoicism which eschewed despair. From this position the only possible additional morality might be one not envisaged by Wittgenstein: a scientifically informed global utilitarianism. The *Tractatus* may in general be regarded as an extreme and pure case, or by some as a *reductio ad absurdum,* of the idea that fact and value must not be allowed to *contaminate* each other. The imagery involved is very strong and, in a Kantian view of it, might appear traditional. Wittgenstein's later book, the *Philosophical Investigations,* deliberately denies us any dominating pictures. Wittgenstein said of this book that it was 'only an album', portraying a landscape continually sketched from different points of view. The *Tractatus* is more like a definitive metaphysical handbook, with its numerous visual metaphors: logical space, the limited whole, inside and outside, looking in a certain light (*sub specie aeterni*). We might here conjure up something like a picture by Blake, with the factual world spinning as a sort of glittering steel ball and the spirit of value silently circling around it. Or we may see, in a reversal of the Platonic image, the limited factual whole together with encircling value appearing like an eclipse of the sun, with the dark object in the middle and the light round the edges. There is no light in the world: what obscures it is the whole of the world.

*

Wittgenstein's relationship with Schopenhauer 'shows' in his distress or uncertainty about the concept of *will* in the 1914–1916 *Notebooks,* where he appears at moments as a reluctant prisoner of that philosopher's thoughts. I shall discuss Schopenhauer at more length shortly, but will give a very brief account of his views here. Schopenhauer pictures the fundamental reality and basis of our world as a ruthless powerful cosmic force, the Will to Live, and the world as we know and experience it as a causally determined construct of phenomena brought about by (us) subjects through our perceptions, that is objectified ideas of the Will. The Will to Live, to *exist,* takes care of continuation of species and general ordering of entities. At the human level it is manifest as the natural egoism of the individual, each for himself, resulting in a scene of perpetual misery and strife. The world of ideas (objectifications of the Will) is in itself neither good nor bad. The horrors of the human scene result from the selfish wills of individuals as manifestations of the Will to Live. Other individuals, animals, plants, and the whole of our perceived phenomena are also suffering under the sovereignty of the Will. (Schopenhauer quotes St Paul, Romans 8:22, 'the whole creation groaneth and travaileth in pain together'.) In our world there may be some slight alleviation, or degrees of egoism, through experience of art, or in the form of instinctive compassion. Exceptional individuals may achieve complete escape from pain and evil by a total *denial of the Will.* This 'dying to the world' is, according to Schopenhauer, a mystical spiritual condition which cannot be described. Schopenhauer's interest in Hindu and Buddhist mysticism may well have touched the young Wittgenstein, prompting for instance his attachment to Rabindranath Tagore, as well as his concept of 'the mystical' in *Tractatus* and *Notebooks.*

Wittgenstein was (evidently) attracted, as many other less philosophical persons were, by the outrageous simplicity of Schopenhauer's picture. The structure of objectified ideas is simply *there,* not in itself good or bad, an objectification of the Will which as a cosmic force is both ruthless and blameless (like a waterfall or earthquake). Human wills, willed by the Will to Live, are however, in their existing context, necessarily selfish, an inevitable cause of suffering and unhappiness. The facts, ideas, world is entirely separate from selfish human will and unchanged by it. Humans cannot enforce their will upon the world. Schopenhauer postulates a superhuman cosmic will, Wittgenstein simply speaks of an alien will. While following Schopenhauer, he 'demythologises' the picture. Since he (Wittgenstein) cannot change this alien will (how the world is) his relation to it must be that of an attitude. Can I not make myself entirely independent of it, and so be master of it, by renouncing any influence upon happenings, that is by denying the will altogether? 'How can a man be happy at all, since he cannot ward off the misery of this world? Through a life of knowledge . . . The only life that is happy is the life that can renounce the amenities of the world.' Total denial of the Will is best; a realistic stoicism may be next best. Denial of the Will, with the disappearance of the problem of life, is the mystical. This is a state which we cannot conceptualise, of which we cannot speak. Wittgenstein's 'denial' is apparently offered as an accessible stoicism. Schopenhauer is more pessimistic, offering little hope of human happiness. The mystical stage is only reached by extreme asceticism. However he allows some escape by contemplation of art. Wittgenstein mentions happiness (*Notebooks*): 'the happy life is good', and 'the end of art is the beautiful, and the beautiful *is* what makes happy'. There is also 'living in the present' and stoical 'agreement with the world' which is 'What "being happy" means'. (See *Notebooks* 11.6.16 onward.) Wittgenstein entirely agrees with, and adopts, Schopenhauer's rejection of Kant's Categorical Imperative (*Tractatus* 6.422); but although both regard morality as an attitude (since the world cannot be altered) Schopenhauer has quite a lot to say about morality (especially about compassion and justice) whereas Wittgenstein suggests his views by his silence. There is in Schopenhauer a shadowy picture of a spiritual pilgrimage. Both postulate a world of facts (or entities) independent of human will, but neither explains 'will' sufficiently to make clear why this world must be assumed. The segregation of the factual world allows in both cases a stoical morality which verges toward mysticism. What Wittgenstein indicates by a silent nod, is stated by Schopenhauer as a distinction of phenomenal and noumenal deriving from Kant. Schopenhauer accounts for our helplessness by a theory of determinism. Wittgenstein simply decrees it and wisely does not tangle with determinism. He equally decreed the machinery of the larger logical part of the *Tractatus*; his segregation of morality also serves the purpose of keeping the world clean for the propositional calculus. Schopenhauer does not explain how the Will relates to ideas, or ideas to particulars. His metaphysical substructure is kept clear of value while at the same time establishing value's place. Schopenhauer's influence on Wittgenstein is in the field of morality, appearing in the last section of *Notebooks* and of *Tractatus*. Later Wittgenstein did not *philosophise* about morals.

Wittgenstein's (in the *Tractatus*) limited whole which is the integrated world of fact, language and experience, separates the area of valueless contingency, where everything is as it is and happens as it does happen, from the *thereby* purified ineffable activity of value. The world can then become, from a moral point of view, with an acceptance of all the facts, an object of contemplation: an idea which would have appalled Kant. This stoical contemplation is true happiness, beyond tainted and illusory ideas of good and evil, fearless of death. We may profitably compare and contrast this strong imagery with that conjured up by Kant's moral philosophy, which also involves a strict separation of fact and value. Here (Kant) the self-contained world of necessity (causally determined contingency) might be thought of as blocking, at any rate rendering unclear, the light which comes from a distant, thereby invisible, God, or spiritual principle better called Freedom and Reason, yet also showing up this spiritual light by contrast. But of course in Kant's picture, value (as practical Reason) does all the time enter the alien world as a kind of laser beam and can be enacted as duty and spoken of in rational discourse about moral maxims in a way which is very familiar to us, and which indeed provides us with a dominant image of spiritual reality. A laser beam: very clear, narrow, strong, coming from an unseen source, illuminating a point in a world which is otherwise valueless. This can be a religious or non-religious picture according to whether the will is seen as a vehicle of a higher power or itself the source. The contingent particularity of the world is hallowed, one might say, by becoming incarnate in moral maxims, in moral *laws,* in principles of action. Insights interact with rules. We then see a (problematic) part of our world clearly from a moral point of view. The laser beam image needs some qualification however. Kant's maxims (rules), as dictates of Reason, are *universal,* applying to all rational beings in similar situations. In the *Grundlegung* Kant seems to imply that such rules are also of great *generality.* (Be benevolent, do not lie.) This may be said to reflect a certain kind of (perfectionist, unified, simplified) moral society. One could agree that 'do not lie' casts its light upon the whole world and must always be kept in mind. But many duties arise in particular complex situations, for instance where rational maxims conflict, and where we have to use our reason to create more particular (fitting *this* situation) moral rulings for ourselves. This is the form of a ubiquitous human problem. Lying is wrong. Yet: when is it right to lie? Benevolence is good, but when is it a *moral* mistake? (Etc. etc. etc.) Schopenhauer discusses this matter, disagreeing with Kant. (I come to this later.) In any case, this dilemma (put in Kantian language, how particular can a universal rule be?) does not affect the validity of Kant's excellent dictum that 'we are not gentleman volunteers, but conscripts, in the army of the moral law'. Our fundamental recognition, in all our various adventures in the contingent world, of the difference between good and evil is Kant's starting point: a self-evident one he would say. How Reason (moral value) alters the course of the (causally determined) realm of fact is not clarified and perhaps cannot be. We recognise this picture of our dual nature, and we *experience* the influence of Respect for the Moral Law, especially when it contradicts our desires. Wittgenstein does not speak of moral rules or discuss freedom or cause. His 'limited whole' world is everywhere equally and relentlessly contingent and value-free. Good or bad willing cannot alter the facts, but only the 'limits' (or one might venture the image 'colour') of the *whole* world, which waxes and wanes as a whole. A moral attitude is to be taken as a totality. 'The world of the happy is unlike the world of the unhappy.' We are subject to fate; God (one of Wittgenstein's two 'godheads') is to be seen as fate, as *amor fati.* We must accept 'all the facts', the world is not altered by morality, but the whole of it is (as one might say) bathed in a certain light. In the *Vermischte Bemerkungen, Culture and Value* (p. 78), Wittgenstein says, "'*Le style c'est l'homme, le style c'est l'homme même.*" The first expression has cheap epigrammatic brevity. The second, correct version opens up quite a different perspective. It says that a man's style is a *picture* of himself.' (Of the whole man, and his whole world.) To speak of the 'waxing and waning' in terms of general moral 'style' is to emphasise a contrast with Kant. It may be said that surely in (moral, spiritual) 'conversion' a man's whole life (world) alters. Another remark in *Culture and Value* (p. 53): 'I believe that one of the things Christianity says is that sound doctrines are all useless. That you have to change your *life*. (Or the *direction* of your life.)' This is an inspiring dictum, but how does this come about? A general 'conversion' does not, any more than a general 'style,' solve detailed unpredictable problems of duty, to which we must have the humility to realise that we are subject. We *need* a 'moral vocabulary,' a detailed value terminology, morally loaded words. (Not a requirement of Wittgenstein.) Important moral partings of the ways are implied in the complex relations between these concepts. Wittgenstein gives no status to the idea of duty, he follows Schopenhauer who regarded 'duty' as an archaic magico-theological idea derived from the Ten Commandments and connected with rewards and punishments. Schopenhauer: 'In the conception of *ought* there lies always and essentially the reference to threatened punishment or promised reward.' ('Criticism of the Kantian Philosophy,' *The World as Will and Idea,* henceforth styled *WWI*, Haldane and Kemp translation. See also *The Basis of Morality* II 4.) This is echoed by Wittgenstein at *Tractatus* 6.422. Wittgenstein does not use the vocabulary of noumenal and phenomenal, but what it names is present, and the relation of value to the 'ordinary world' is also mysterious. Value is essentially ineffable since significant discourse is tied to fact. It cannot alter facts but its operation is thereby extremely pure. Moral philosophy and theology too are bound to be ineffable, an attempt to say what cannot be said but can only be, in the whole living of life, *shown.* 'Ethics is transcendental' (*Tractatus* 6.421). Indeed the whole of the *Tractatus* is really nonsense (6.54), since if we attempt to limit the conditions of experience from inside we cannot properly talk about what is outside. Can we not see a little beyond those transcendental barriers, do we not have intimations, gleams of light, glimpses of another scene? The *Tractatus* is a sustained attempt to put a final end to such talk, and to do so (as he explained in the letter to Ficker), in the interests of morality. We must, at least, talk as little as possible and then, as Wittgenstein tells us at the end of the book, 'throw away the ladder.' Kierkegaard would have appreciated that image.

79

Jacques Derrida

Aporias (1993)

Finis

IS MY DEATH POSSIBLE? Can we understand this question? Can I, myself, pose it? Am I allowed to talk about my death? What does the syntagm "my death" mean? And why this expression "the syntagm 'my death'"? You will agree that it is better, in this case, to name words or names, that is, to stick with quotation marks. On the one hand, that neutralizes an improper pathos. "My death" in quotation marks is not necessarily mine; it is an expression that anybody can appropriate; it can circulate from one example to another. Regarding what Seneca said about the brevity of life, Diderot tells us: "it is the story of my life," it is my story. But it is not only his. Of course, if I say it is not mine, then I seem to be assuming that I could know when to say "my death" while speaking of mine. But this is more than *problematic*, in the sense of this word that we analyzed above. If death (we will return to this point later) names the very irreplaceability of absolute singularity (no one can die in my place or in the place of the other), then all the *examples* in the world can precisely illustrate this singularity. Everyone's death, the death of all those who can say "my death," is irreplaceable. So is "my life." Every other is completely other. [*Tout autre est tout autre.*] Whence comes a first exemplary complication of exemplarity: nothing is more substitutable and yet nothing is less so than the syntagm "my death." It is always a matter of a hapax, of a hapax legomenon, but of what is only said *one time each time, indefinitely* only one time. This is also true for everything that entails a first-person grammatical form. On the other hand, the quotation marks not only affect this strange possessive (the uniqueness of the *hapax* "my"), but they also signal the indeterminacy of the word "death." Fundamentally, one knows perhaps neither the meaning nor the referent of this word. It is well known that if there is one word that remains absolutely unassignable or unassigning with respect to its concept and to its thingness, it is the word "death." Less than for any other noun, save "God"—and for good reason, since their association here is probably not fortuitous—is it possible to attribute to the noun "death," and above all to the expression "my death," a concept or a reality that would constitute the object of an indisputably determining experience.

In order not to lose myself any longer in these preambulatory detours, I will say very quickly now why "my death" will be the subject of this small aporetic oration. First, I'll address the aporia, that is, the impossible, the impossibility, as what cannot pass [*passer*] or come to pass [*se passer*]: it is not even the *non-pas,* the not-step, but rather the deprivation of the *pas* (the privative form would be a kind of *a-pas*). I'll explain myself with some help from Heidegger's famous definition of death in *Being and Time*: "the possibility of the pure and simple impossibility for *Dasein*" (*Der Tod ist die Möglichkeit der schlechthinnigen Daseinsunmöglichkeit*) (§50, p. 250).[1] Second, I want to carry out such an explanation together with what is our common concern here, at Cerisy-la-Salle, during the time of this conference, namely, "the crossing [*passage*] of borders."

Up to this point, we have rightly privileged at least *three* types of *border limits*: *first,* those that separate territories, countries, nations, States, languages, and cultures (and the politico-anthropological disciplines that correspond to them); *second,* the separations and sharings [*partages*] between domains of discourse, for example, philosophy, anthropological sciences, and even theology, domains that have been represented, in an encyclopedia or in an ideal university, sometimes as ontological or onto-theological regions or territories, sometimes as knowledges or as disciplines of research; *third,* to these two kinds of border limits we have just added the lines of separation, demarcation, or opposition between conceptual determinations, the forms of the border that separates what are called concepts or *terms*—these are lines that necessarily intersect and overdetermine the first two kinds of terminality. Later I will suggest some terms in order to formalize somewhat these three kinds of limit—to be crossed or not to be transgressed.

Now where do we situate the syntagm "my death" as possibility and/or impossibility of passage? (As we shall see, the mobile slash between and/or, and/and, or/and, or/or, is a singular border, simultaneously conjunctive, disjunctive, and undecidable.) "My death," this syntagm that relates the possible to the impossible, can be figured flashing like a sort of indicator-light (a light at a border) installed at a customs booth, between all the borders that I have just named: between cultures, countries, languages, but also between the areas of knowledge or the disciplines, and, finally, between conceptual de-terminations. A light flashes at every border, where it is awake and watches [*ça veille*]. One can always see there a nightwatchman [*du veilleur*] or a nightlight [*de la veilleuse*].

Let us start with a fact that is overwhelming, well-known, and immensely documented: there are cultures of death. In crossing a border, one changes death [*on change la mort*]. One exchanges death [*on change de mort*]; one no longer speaks the same death where one no longer speaks the same language. The relation to death is not the same on this side of the Pyrenees as it is on the other side. Often, moreover, in crossing a culture's border, one passes from a figure of death as trespass—passage of a line, transgression of a border, or step beyond [*pas au-dela*] life—to another figure of the border between life and death. Every culture is characterized by its way of apprehending, dealing with, and, one could say, "living" death as trespass. Every culture has its own funerary rites, its representations of the dying, its ways of mourning or burying, and its own evaluation of the price of existence, of collective as well as individual life. Furthermore, this culture of death can be transformed even within what we believe we can identify as a single culture, sometimes as a single nation, a single language, or a single religion (but I explained above how the principle of such an identification appears to be threatened in its very principle or to be exposed to ruin right from the outset, that is, to be exposed to death). One can speak of a history of death, and, as you know, it has been done, for the West at least. The fact that, to my knowledge, it has only been done in the West (even though a Westerner, Maurice Pinguet, devoted to this question a study that was both genealogical and sociological, in *La Mort volontaire au Japon* [Paris: Gallimard, 1984]), that is to say, the fact that it has only been done "here at home," here where we are, does not mean that there is no history of death elsewhere or that no one has written any—unless the idea of a history and of a history of death is itself a Western idea in a sense that will be clarified later. For the record, I will only cite one or two titles from the immense library of work devoted to the history of death. They are French works, which is the first restriction, and they are recent, which is another unjustifiably arbitrary choice. First, the *Essais sur l'histoire de la mort en Occident du Moyen Age à nos jours* and *L'Homme devant la mort,* by Philippe Aries. Like his *Western Attitudes Towards Death* (Johns Hopkins University Press, 1974), these studies, which date from 1975 and 1977 respectively, clearly show the limits within which such a history is framed. The author, who calls himself a "historian of death" (*L'Homme devant la mort,* p. 9), focuses on what is, in sum, a very short and dense sequence in the time span of the Christian West. With all due respect for the richness, the necessity, and at times the beauty of works such as these, which are also masterpieces of their genre, I must nevertheless recall the strict limits of these anthropological histories. This word ("limit") not only designates the external limits that the historian gives himself for methodological purposes (death in the West from the Middle Ages to the present, for example), but also certain nonthematized closures, edges [*bordures*] whose concept is never formulated in these works. First, there is the semantic or onto-phenomenological type of limit: the historian knows, thinks he knows, or grants to himself the unquestioned knowledge of what death is, of what being-dead means; consequently, he grants to himself all the criteriology that will allow him to identify, recognize, select, or delimit the objects of his inquiry or the thematic field of his anthropologico-historical knowledge. The question of the meaning of death and of the word "death," the question "What is death in general?" or "What is the experience of death?" and the question of knowing *if* death "is" —and *what* death "is"—all remain radically absent *as questions.* From the outset these questions are assumed to be answered by this anthropologico-historical knowledge as such, at the moment when it institutes itself and gives itself its limits. This assumption takes the form of an "it is self-explanatory": everybody knows what one is talking about when one names death.

In these texts foaming with knowledge, one never finds any precaution like the one Heidegger takes, for example, when, intending to recall that it is impossible to *die for the other* in the sense of "to die in his place," even if one dies for the other by offering his own death to the other, he leaves the small word "is" in quotation marks in the following sentence: "By its very essence, death is in every case mine, insofar as it 'is' at all" ("Der Tod ist, sofern es 'ist,' wesensmäßig je der meine") (*Being and Time*, p. 240). Citing Heidegger here or there is not sufficient to put such treasures of anthropological or cultural knowledge to the test of these semantic, phenomenological, or ontological questions, and it is especially not enough to cite Heidegger as an illustration or as an authoritative argument (which often amounts to the same thing). This is what Louis-Vincent Thomas does, in the second book that I want to mention, his rich *Anthropologie de la mort* (Payot, 1975). One could multiply the examples, but there is no time for that. At the beginning of a chapter entitled "The Experience of Death: Reality, Limit" (p. 223), Thomas writes: "'No sooner is the human being born,' writes M. Heidegger, 'than he is already old enough to die.' Does this incontestable (metaphysical) truth, verified by all the givens of biological sciences and attested to by demography, mean anything at the level of lived experience?" The sentence that Thomas quotes is incorrectly attributed to Heidegger. It recalls Seneca's remark about the permanent imminence of death, right from birth, and the essential immaturity of the human who is dying. In the opening of his existential analysis of death, Heidegger also distinguishes the death of *Dasein* from its end (*Ende*) and above all from its maturation or ripeness (*Reife*). *Dasein* does not need to mature when death occurs. That is why life will always have been so short. Whether one understands it as achievement or as accomplishment, the final maturity of a fruit or of a biological organism is a limit, an end (*Ende*; one could also say a *telos* or *terma*), hence a border, which *Dasein* is always in a position of surpassing. *Dasein* is the very transgression of this borderline. It may well have passed its maturity before the end (*vor dem Ende schon überschritten haben kann*), Heidegger says. For the most part, *Dasein* ends in unfulfillment, or else by having disintegrated and been used up ("Zumeist endet es in der Unvollendung oder aber zerfallen und verbraucht"; *Being and Time*, p. 244). Thomas should have avoided attributing to Heidegger a line that the latter quotes (p. 245), taking it from *Der Ackermann aus Böhmen* ("sobald ein Mensch zum Leben kommt, sogleich ist er alt genug zu sterben"). Heidegger uses this quote at the very moment when he distinguishes the death of *Dasein* from any other end, from any other limit. This crucial distinction, which Heidegger considers indispensable, allows him to situate his existential analysis of death *before* any "metaphysics of death" and *before* all biology. Thomas, however, thinks that he is citing Heidegger and that he can speak of an "incontestable (metaphysical) truth" that has been verified "by all the givens of biological sciences" as well as by "demography."

Yet Heidegger recalls that the existential analysis of death can and must precede, on the one hand, any metaphysics of death and, on the other, all biology, psychology, theodicy, or theology of death (p. 248). Saying exactly the opposite of what Thomas makes him say, Heidegger puts into operation a logic of *presupposition*. All the disciplines thus named, and thereby identified within their regional borders, notably "metaphysics" and "biology," not to mention "demography," necessarily presuppose a meaning of death, a preunderstanding of what death is or of what the word "death" means. The theme of the existential analysis is to explain and make explicit this ontological preunderstanding. If one wants to translate this situation in terms of disciplinary or regional borders, of domains of knowledge, then one will say that the delimitation of the fields of anthropological, historical, biological, demographic, and even theological knowledge presupposes a nonregional onto-phenomenology that not only does not let itself be enclosed within the borders of these domains, but furthermore does not let itself be enclosed within cultural, linguistic, national, or religious borders either, and not even within sexual borders, which crisscross all the others.

To put it quickly—in passing, and in an anticipatory way—the logic of this Heideggerian gesture interests me here. It does so in its exemplarity. However, I only want to assert the force of its necessity and go with it as far as possible, apparently against anthropological confusions and presumptions, so as to try to bring to light several aporias that are internal to the Heideggerian discourse. At stake for me would be approaching the place where such aporias risk paralyzing the ontological, hierarchical, and territorial apparatus to which Heidegger lends credit. These aporias risk interrupting the very possibility of its functioning and leading it to ruin. Death would be the name, one of the names, of this threat, which no doubt takes over from what Heidegger himself very early on called "ruination."

But we are not there yet; this will come only near the end. For the moment, let us remain close to this border dispute. It arises here between, on the one hand, a comparative anthropo-thanatology ("anthropothanatology" is the title proposed by Thomas, who insists on its essentially "comparative" aim, pp. 530—531) and, on the other hand, an existential analysis.

When Heidegger suggests a delimitation of the borders (*Abgrenzung*) of existential analysis (*Being and Time,* §49), he relies on a classical argument within the philosophical tradition. In turn dialectical, transcendental, and ontological, it is always the argument of presupposition (*Voraussetzung*). Whether it concerns plants, animals, or humans, the ontico-biological knowledge about the span of life and about the mechanisms of death *presupposes* an ontological problematic. This ontological problematic underlies (*zugrundeliegt*) all biological research. What always remains to be asked (*zu fragen bleibt*), says Heidegger, is how the essence of death is defined in terms of that of life. Insofar as they are ontical research, biology and anthropology have already and always decided (*immer schon entschieden*). They have decided without even asking the question, hence by precipitating the answer and by presupposing an ontological elucidation that had not taken place. This precipitation does not simply stem from a speculative failure or from the betrayal of a principle of philosophical legitimacy [*droit*] concerning what must come first, whether *de jure* or methodologically. It also leads to apparently empirical or techno-juridical confusions about what the state of death is, confusions that are increasingly serious today. These questions of legitimacy [*questions de droit*] are no longer only questions concerning the philosophical order of *de jure* and *de facto*. They impinge upon legal medicine, the politics of gerontology, the norms concerning the surgical prolongation of life and euthanasia, and upon several other questions that will be addressed later.

Heidegger multiplies the programmatical propositions concerning the *order*—that is, the subordination of questions—of what is prior and *superordinate* (*vorgeordnet*) or, on the contrary, ulterior and subordinate (*nachgeordnet*). Such propositions appear to be firm. Ontical knowledge (anthropological or biological) naively puts into operation more or less clear conceptual presuppositions (*Vorbegriffe*) about life and death. It therefore requires a preparatory sketch, a new *Vorzeichnung* in terms of an ontology of *Dasein*, an ontology that is itself preliminary, "superordinate," prior to an ontology of life: "Within the ontology of Dasein, which is *superordinate* to an ontology of life [*Innerhalb der einer Ontologie des Lebens* vorgeordneten *Ontologie des Daseins*; Heidegger emphasizes *superordinate*: the ontology of *Dasein* is legitimately and logically prior to an ontology of life], the existential analysis of death is, in turn, *subordinate* to a characterization of *Dasein's* basic state (*Grundverfassung*)" (p. 247). This characteristic, that is, the existential analysis of *Dasein*, is thus an *absolute priority*, and then an existential analysis of death, which is itself a part of this ontology of *Dasein*, comes to be subordinate to it. In turn, this ontology of *Dasein* is presupposed by an ontology of life that it thus legitimately precedes. If Heidegger uses the expressions *Dasein* and analysis of *Dasein*, it is because he does not yet allow himself any philosophical knowledge concerning what man is as *animal rationale*, or concerning the ego, consciousness, the soul, the subject, the person, and so forth, which are all presuppositions of metaphysics or of ontical knowledge, such as anthropo-thanatology or biology. A hierarchical order thus delimits the field; it rigorously superordinates or subordinates the questions, themes, and, in fact, the ontological regions. According to Heidegger, these regions are legitimately separated by pure, rigorous, and indivisible borders. An order is thus structured by *uncrossable* edges. Such edges can be crossed, and they are *in fact* crossed all the time, but they *should* not be. The hierarchy of this order is governed by the concern to think what the death proper to *Dasein* is, that is, *Dasein's* "properly dying" (*eigentlich sterben*). This "properly dying" belongs to the proper and authentic being-able of *Dasein*, that is, to that to which one must testify and attest (*Bezeugung*, §54).

At stake for me here is approaching a certain enigmatic relation among dying, testifying, and surviving. We can already foresee it: if the attestation of this "properly dying" or if the property of this death proper to *Dasein* was compromised in its rigorous limits, then the entire apparatus of these edges would become problematic, and along with it the very project of an analysis of *Dasein*, as well as everything that, with its professed methodology, the analysis legitimately [*en droit*] conditions. All these conditions of legitimacy [*conditions de droit*] concern border crossings: what authorizes them here, what prohibits them there, what ordinates, subordinates, or superordinates the ones over the others.

Heidegger thus suggests an ontological delimitation among the fields of inquiry concerning death. This delimitation seems all the more abyssal because it concerns limits about questions of the limit, more precisely, questions of the ends, of the modes of ending (*enden, verenden*), and of the limit that separates the simple *ending* (*enden*) from *properly dying* (*eigentlich sterben*). But as we shall see, there is more than one limit. That is why we began, from our very first words, by speaking about the ends, *de finibus*. That was not a roundabout way of recalling the ends of man, as if after a long decade, the present conference was not able to rid itself of the same subject, of an indestructable [*increvable*] subject. If one takes it literally, the death of *Dasein* is not an end of man. Between the two there is a singular, improbable, and perhaps divisible limit that passes, and it is the limit of the *ending,* the place where, in a way, the ending ends. What comes to pass, what happens and what am I saying when I say *end* [*finis*], for example when I say, addressing someone or sending him a note, "*end it,*" "*end this now,*" or "*that's the end of you*"?

Heidegger says that he has called the end of the living, the ending of the living (*das Enden von Lebendem*), "perishing," *Verenden* (*Das Enden von Lebendem nannten wir Verenden,* p. 247). This *Verenden* is the ending, the way of ending or of coming to the end that all living things share. They all eventually kick the bucket [*ils crèvent*]. In everyday German, *verenden* also means to die, to succumb, to kick the bucket, but since that is clearly not what Heidegger means by properly dying (*eigentlich sterben*), by the dying proper to *Dasein, verenden* must therefore not be translated by "dying" in order to respect what Heidegger intends to convey. That is why the translators hesitate between translating *verenden* by "arrêt de vie" (Vezin, stoppage of life), by "périr" (Martineau, to perish), or by "perishing" in English (Macquarrie-Robinson).[2]

I prefer "perishing." Why? Just because it turns up twice instead of once among these translations? No, rather because the verb "to perish" retains something of *per,* of the passage of the limit, of the traversal marked in Latin by the *pereo, perire* (which means exactly: to leave, disappear, pass—on the other side of life, *transire*). *To perish* crosses the line and passes near the lines of our conference, even if it loses a little of this sense of ending and of corruption perhaps marked by the *ver* of *verenden.*

Before noting a further complication in the modalities of ending (*Enden*), one should consider that the distinction between *perishing* and *dying* has been established, as far as Heidegger is concerned, as he will never call it into question again, not even in order to complicate it.

As is self-evident, this distinction between, on the one hand, death (*der Tod*) or properly dying (*eigentlich sterben*) and, on the other hand, perishing (*verenden*) cannot be reduced to a terminological decision. It involves decisive conceptual questions for whoever wants to approach what it is, properly, to die or what properly dying is. Above all, and precisely for that reason, it involves the very condition of an existential analysis of *Dasein,* of a *Dasein* that, as we shall see, reaches its most proper possibility and becomes most properly what it is at the very point where it can claim to *testify* to it, in its anticipation of death. If, in its very principle, the rigor of this distinction were compromised, weakened, or parasited on both sides of what it is supposed to dissociate (*verendenl eigentlich sterben*), then (and you can guess that I am heading toward such a possibility) the entire project of the analysis of *Dasein,* in its essential conceptuality, would be, if not discredited, granted another status than the one generally attributed to it. I am thus increasingly inclined to read ultimately this great, inexhaustible book in the following way: as an event that, at least in the final analysis, would no longer simply stem from ontological necessity or demonstration. It would never submit to logic, phenomenology, or ontology, which it nonetheless invokes. Nor would it ever submit to a "rigorous science" (in the sense that Husserl intended it), not even to thought (*Denken*) as that which parallels the path of the poem (*Dichten*), and finally, not even to an incredible poem—which I would be nevertheless inclined to believe, without, however, stopping on this point for obvious reasons. The event of this interrupted book would be irreducible to these categories, indeed to the categories that Heidegger himself never stopped articulating. In order to welcome into thought and into history such a "work," the event has to be thought otherwise. *Being and Time* would belong neither to science, nor to philosophy, nor to poetics. Such is perhaps the case for every work worthy of its name: there, what puts thinking into operation exceeds its own borders or what thinking itself intends to present of these borders. The work exceeds itself, it surpasses the limits of the concept of itself that it claims to have properly while presenting itself. But if the event of this work thus exceeds its own borders, the borders that its discourse seems to give to itself (for example, "those of an existential analysis of *Dasein* in the transcendental horizon of time"), then it would do so precisely at this locus where it *experiences the aporia*—and perhaps its premature interruption, its very prematurity.

It is with regard to death that we shall approach this aporetic structure in *Being and Time*. But the question of knowing what it means "to experience the aporia," indeed to put into operation the aporia, remains. It is not necessarily a failure or a simple paralysis, the sterile negativity of the impasse. It is neither stopping at it nor overcoming it. (When someone suggests to you a solution for escaping an impasse, you can be almost sure that he is ceasing to understand, assuming that he had understood anything up to that point.)

Let us ask: *what takes place, what comes to pass* with the aporia? Is it possible to undergo or to experience the aporia, the aporia *as such*? Is it then a question of the aporia *as such*? Of a scandal arising to suspend a certain viability? Does one then pass through this aporia? Or is one immobilized before the threshold, to the point of having to turn around and seek out another way, the way without method or outlet of a *Holzweg* or a turning (*Kehre*) that could turn the aporia—all such possibilities of wandering? What takes place with the aporia? What we are apprehending here concerning what takes place also touches upon the event as that which arrives at the river's shore [*arrive à la rive*], approaches the shore [*aborde la rive*], or passes the edge [*passe le bord*]—another way of happening and coming to pass by surpassing [*outrepassant*].

All of these are possibilities of the "coming to pass" when it meets a limit. Perhaps nothing ever comes to pass except on the line of a transgression, the death [*trépas*] of some "trespassing" [in English in the original].

What is the event that most arrives [*l'évenement le plus arrivant*]? What is the *arrivant* that makes the event arrive?[3] I was recently taken by this word, *arrivant,* as if its uncanniness had just arrived to me in a language in which it has nonetheless sounded very familiar to me for a long time.[4] The new *arrivant,* this word can, indeed, mean the neutrality of *that which* arrives, but also the singularity of *who* arrives, he or she who comes, coming to be where s/he was not expected, where one was awaiting him or her without waiting for him or her, without expecting it [*s'y attendre*], without knowing what or whom to expect, what or whom I am waiting for— and such is hospitality itself, hospitality toward the event. One does not expect the event of whatever, of whoever comes, arrives, and crosses the threshold—the immigrant, the emigrant, the guest, or the stranger. But if the new *arrivant* who arrives is new, one must expect—without waiting for him or her, without expecting it—that he does not simply cross a given threshold. Such an *arrivant* affects the very experience of the threshold, whose possibility he thus brings to light before one even knows whether there has been an invitation, a call, a nomination, or a promise (*Verheissung, Heissen,* etc.). What we could here call the *arrivant,* the most *arrivant* among all *arrivants,* the *arrivant* par excellence, is whatever, whoever, in arriving, does not cross a threshold separating two identifiable places, the proper and the foreign, the proper of the one and the proper of the other, as one would say that the citizen of a given identifiable country crosses the border of another country as a traveler, an emigré or a political exile, a refugee or someone who has been deported, an immigrant worker, a student or a researcher, a diplomat or a tourist. Those are all, of course, *arrivants,* but in a country that is already defined and in which the inhabitants know or think they are at home (as we saw above, this is what, according to Kant, should govern public rights, concerning both universal hospitality and visiting rights). No, I am talking about the absolute *arrivant,* who is not even a guest. He surprises the host—who is not yet a host or an inviting power—enough to call into question, to the point of annihilating or rendering indeterminate, all the distinctive signs of a prior identity, beginning with the very border that delineated a legitimate home and assured lineage, names and language, nations, families and genealogies. The absolute *arrivant* does not yet have a name or an identity. It is not an invader or an occupier, nor is it a colonizer, even if it can also become one. This is why I call it simply the *arrivant,* and not someone or something that arrives, a subject, a person, an individual, or a living thing, even less one of the migrants I just mentioned. It is not even a foreigner identified as a member of a foreign, determined community. Since the *arrivant* does not have any identity yet, its place of arrival is also de-identified: one does not yet know or one no longer knows which is the country, the place, the nation, the family, the language, and the home in general that welcomes the absolute *arrivant.* This absolute *arrivant* as such is, however, not an intruder, an invader, or a colonizer, because invasion presupposes some self-identity for the aggressor and for the victim. Nor is the *arrivant* a legislator or the discoverer of a promised land. As disarmed as a newly born child, it no more commands than is commanded by the memory of some originary event where the archaic is bound with the *final* extremity, with the finality par excellence of the *telos* or of the *eskhaton*. It even exceeds the order of any *determinable* promise. Now the border that is ultimately most difficult to delineate, because it is always already crossed, lies in the fact that the absolute *arrivant* makes possible everything to which I have just said it cannot be reduced, starting with the humanity of man, which some would be inclined to recognize in all that erases, in the *arrivant,* the characteristic of (cultural, social, or national) belonging and even metaphysical determination (ego, person, subject, consciousness, etc.). It is on this border that I am tempted to read Heidegger. Yet this border will always keep one from discriminating among the figures of the *arrivant,* the dead, and the *revenant* (the ghost, he, she, or that which returns).

If the distinction between (properly) *dying* and *perishing* cannot be reduced to a question of terminology, if it is not a linguistic distinction, for Heidegger (extending well beyond *Being and Time*) it nevertheless marks the difference *of* language, the impassable difference between the speaking being that *Dasein* is and any other living thing. *Dasein* or the mortal is not man, the human subject, but it is that in terms of which the humanity of man must be rethought. And man remains the only example of *Dasein,* as man was for Kant the only example of finite reasonable being or of *intuitus derivativus.* Heidegger never stopped modulating this affirmation according to which the mortal is whoever experiences death *as such,* as death. Since he links this possibility of the "as such" (as well as the possibility of death as such) to the possibility of speech, he thereby concludes that the animal, the living thing as such, is not properly a mortal: the animal does not relate to death as such. The animal can come to an end, that is, perish (*verenden*), it always ends up kicking the bucket [*crever*]. But it can never properly die.

Much later, in *On the Way to Language,* Heidegger wrote:

> Mortals are they who can experience death as death [*den Tod als Tod erfahren können*]. Animals cannot do this. [*Das Tier vermagdies nicht.*] But animals cannot speak either. The essential relation between death and language flashes up before us, but remains still unthought [*ist aber noch ungedacht*].[1]

It is this unthought that holds us in suspense here. For if one must assume that the difference between a mortal (whoever dies in the sense of "properly dying") and an animal incapable of dying is a certain access to death *as* death, to death *as such,* then this access will condition every distinction between these two ends, *perishing* and *dying*. By the same token, it will condition the very possibility of an analysis of *Dasein,* that is, of a distinction between *Dasein* and another mode of being, and of a distinction to which *Dasein* may *testify* by *attesting* to its proper being-able. It is therefore on the possibility of the *as such* of death that the interrogation would have to bear. But it would also have to bear on what links the possibility of this *as such* (assuming that it can ever be assured *as such*) to the possibility or to the power of what is so obscurely called language. Indeed, Heidegger's formulation, although in some respects trenchant ("the animal is not capable of this") nevertheless retains a certain prudence. It does not say that the experience of death *as such,* the experience granted to the mortal, of which the animal is incapable, depends upon language. Heidegger says: "Animals cannot do this [experience death as death]. But animals cannot speak either. [*Das Tier kann aber auch nicht sprechen.*]" These two remarks are deliberately juxtaposed, without, however, Heidegger feeling authorized to go any further than indicating something like a flash in the sky concerning a link between the *as such* of death and language.

Therefore, several possibilities remain open:

1   There would not be any essential and irreducible link between the two, between the "as such" and language, and someone could relate to death as such *without language,* precisely where the word breaks off or defaults (*wo das Wort gebricht* or *zerbricht,* etc.). But Heidegger does not fail to recall then, as he always does, that this collapse or suspense still belongs to the possibility of language.

2   The *belief* in an experience of death *as such,* as well as the discourse crediting this belief to an experience of death *itself* andas such, would depend, on the contrary, upon an ability to speak and to name. But instead of giving us added assurance about the experience of death as death, this discourse would lose the *as such* in and through the language that would create an illusion, as if *to say death* were enough to have access to dying as such—and such would be the illusion or the fantasy.

3   Consequently, since death refuses itself as such to testimony and thereby marks even what refuses its *as such* both to language and to what exceeds language, it is there that any border between the animal and the *Dasein* of speaking man would become unassignable.

4   Finally, if the living thing as such (the beast, the animal beast or human *life,* the human as living thing) is incapable of an experience of death *as such,* if, in sum, life as such does not know death as such, then this axiom will allow for a reconciliation of apparently contradictory statements, best exemplified, in my view, by the example of Heidegger, of course, but also by those of Freud and Levinas.

Notes

1   Martin Heidegger, *Sein und Zeit,* 16th ed. (Tübingen: Max Niemeyer, 1986); *Being and Time,* trans. John Macquarrie and Edward Robinson (New York: Harper, 1962). Page numbers refer to the German edition and are given in the margins of the English translation. The English translation has occasionally been modified to coincide with the French translation used by the author.—Trans. [Thomas Dutoit].

2   [François] Vezin was the first French translator of *Sein und Zeit* (*Etre et Temps*, Paris: Gallimard, 1986); [Emmanuel] Martineau's translation appeared as *Etre et temps* from Authentica in 1985.—Trans.

3   *Arrivant* can mean "arrival," "newcomer," or "arriving."—Trans.

4   After the fact, I remembered the *arrivant* of *La*, the book by Hélène Cixous (Paris: Gallimard, 1976; Paris: Editions des Femmes, 1979), p. 132, and the play that she presented in 1977 in Avignon, precisely under the title of *L'Arrivante*.

5   Martin Heidegger, *Unterwegs zur Sprache* (Pfullingen: Günther Neske, 1959): p. 125; *On the Way to Language*, trans. Peter D. Hertz (New York: Harper, 1971): p. 107.

80

Richard Rorty

Is Derrida a Quasi-Transcendental Philosopher? (1995)

[. . .] PEOPLE LIKE ME, WHO ESTEEM DAVIDSON AND WITTGENSTEIN EQUALLY AND for the same reasons, typically read both men as nominalists, and thus as people who will have no truck with transcendental philosophy—with the discovery of conditions of possibility (of consciousness, or language, or Dasein, or whatever). We see both philosophers as helping to convince people that, in Bennington's words, "any philosophy which gives itself world and language as two separate realms separated by an abyss that has to be crossed remains caught, at the very point of the supposed crossing, in the circle of dogmatism and relativism that it is unable to break" (103). As we read Davidson and Wittgenstein, and as we should like to be able to read Derrida, only that notion of two separate realms—only what Davidson has called "the third dogma of empiricism: the distinction between scheme and content"—permits the idea that we can engage in two distinct sorts of activity: empirical inquiry into causal conditions of actuality and philosophical inquiry into transcendental conditions of possibility.

If you are a nominalist, any exploration of presuppositional relations between concepts in which you may engage will take the form of an argument that you could not use some words in certain ways if you did not use some other words in certain other ways.[1] So we nominalists have no use for a refurbished version of Kant's "transcendental logic." We are grateful to Wittgenstein for having mocked the Kantian-Fregean idea that, as he put it, "logic is something sublime." We read Wittgenstein as a therapeutic philosopher, whose importance lies in helping escape from ways of using words which generate pseudoproblems.[2] But for all of the jokey and raunchy de-sublimizing that goes on in Derrida's books, it is not clear that such escape, escape from a dusty fly-bottle, is what he wants.

Bennington, like many other commentators on Derrida, does not want him to be read as a sort of French Wittgenstein, and may think that nobody should try to write the book—*Derrida for Davidsonians*—which I have sketched.[3] For such a book would leave out what he calls the "quasi-transcendental" character of Derrida's thought. Although Bennington is quite clear that "deconstruction is not essentially a Kantian type of philosophy, and cannot be content with the idea of conditions of possibility and everything that that idea entails" (88), he insists that escape from the philosophical tradition is not what Derrida has in mind. He warns us against thinking that "philosophical discourse" is "merely forgotten or worn-out metaphors, a particularly gray and sad fable, mystified in proposing itself as the very truth" (122).[4] Quasi transcendentality is what you go in for if you heed both of these warnings—if you respect philosophy enough to realize that it is inescapable, but not enough to take the idea of conditions of possibility as seriously as Kant did.

Bennington thinks that people like me, who suspect that pragmatic therapy may be all we need from our philosophers, are closer to Kant than they realize. For such philosophers are accepting Kant's distinction between the empirical and the transcendental, and then opting for the empirical—attempting to make whatever remains of philosophical discourse an empirical discourse. What is distinctive about Derrida's quasi transcendentalism, in Bennington's view, is that Derrida neither opts for one side of the distinction over the other nor tosses the distinction itself out the window, but instead insists it is both forever inescapable and forever unusable. When people like me protest on behalf of Wittgenstein and Davidson that they can do their stuff without even mentioning this dubious distinction, much less choosing a side, Bennington will rejoin that we only think that this is what these two men are doing. What they are *really* doing, he claims, is letting the empirical play the role once played by the transcendental. That, at any rate, is how I interpret the following passage from "Derridabase":

> If one says that finitude is in some sense the condition of transcendence, one makes it into the condition of possibility of transcendence, and one thus puts it into a transcendental position with respect to transcendence. But the ultra-transcendental thus produced puts into question the very structure of transcendence, which it pulls back down onto a feature that transcendence would like to consider as empirical. . . . This deconstruction moves toward a comprehension of any discourse ruled by the empirical/transcendental opposition and everything that goes along with it: but this movement, which would traditionally be represented as a movement upward, even beyond what has up until now been recognized as transcendental, is in fact, or at the same time, a movement "downward," for it is the empirical and the contingent, themselves necessarily displaced, in this movement, toward the singular event and the case of chance, which are found higher than the high, higher than height, in height's falling. *L'érection tombe.* "Quasi-transcendental" names what results from this displacement, by maintaining as legible the trace of a passage through the traditional opposition, and by giving this opposition a radical uncertainty which we shall call "undecidability" on condition that we take a few supplementary precautions. (278–79)

Bennington's argument depends upon the premise formulated in the first sentence of this passage. Is it really the case that anybody who says "the finite is in some sense the condition of transcendence" thereby puts the finite "in a transcendental position with respect to transcendence"? I am inclined to protest that the only reason anybody would want to say the former is to urge that the word "transcendence," like all other words, is a human invention designed to serve various human, finite purposes. This is just to repeat what Feuerbach said about God. Or, perhaps more to the point, it repeats what Kierkegaard said about Hegel: that he was a "poor existing individual" who invented the System in the vain hope of losing his finitude by absorption into it. Analogously, I should urge, Kant was just a poor existing individual who invented a gimmick called "transcendental philosophy" in order to wiggle out of the bind he found himself in (between, roughly speaking, Newton on corpuscles on the one hand and Rousseau on freedom on the other).

Does being nominalist and historicist in this way put the finite in a "transcendental position with respect to transcendence"? Are Feuerbach and Kierkegaard, or Dewey and Davidson, conducting transcendental inquiries, or making assumptions about conditions of possibility, whether they like it or not? Dewey, at least, would reply that he is conducting empirical inquiries into the causal conditions of certain actual events—namely, the uses of certain words in certain ways, the origins of certain terms around which certain social practices crystallized. So it is tempting to protest against Bennington that all any of these philosophers are doing is putting the finite in a causal position *with respect to the invention and use of the word "transcendence,"* not putting it in a transcendental position with respect to *transcendence.* They cannot be doing the latter, they would protest, because there is no such thing as transcendence.

But Bennington would reply, I suspect, that this protest ignores what he calls

a law that any attempt to explain transcendental effects by invoking history must presuppose the historicity of that same history as the very transcendental which this system of explanation will never be able to comprehend. This is what we earlier called transcendental contraband, and it cannot resolve the paradox (*plus de . . .*) according to which it is the very concept to which appeal is made to explain everything that will never be understood in the explanation. This is basically the stumbling block of any empiricism whatsoever. No doubt the worse naivetés in this respect affect sociological "explanations" of philosophy. From this point of view, discourses like those of Foucault and Habermas—which recognize that one cannot do without transcendental analysis but which still want to limit that analysis by invoking a certain historical periodization of the transcendental itself—no doubt avoid the worst contradictions, but deprive themselves at the same stroke of the means to understand the historicity of those periods, and appeal rather feebly to diverse motors of history as a way out. (281–82)

The opening chapters of Dewey's *The Quest for Certainty* are a good example of the sort of "sociological 'explanation' of philosophy" which takes for granted that one can "do without transcendental analysis." So Bennington would presumably regard that book both as naive and as afflicted with "the worst contradictions." But one can only contradict oneself if one says things that cannot be rendered consistent. Dewey does not, as far as I can see, contradict himself. He just tells his historicosociological tale and then suggests that we might now be in a position to escape from the philosophical tradition, to put a rather gray and sad episode behind us. But Bennington would rejoin, I take it, that Dewey contradicts his own tacit, and perhaps unconscious, *presuppositions*— specifically, presuppositions about the historicity of the history he describes.[5]

How could one tell whether this charge was accurate? More generally, how can one tell what a philosopher is presupposing, especially if he denies that he is presupposing what his critic says he is? Bennington's answer can be inferred from his claim that

> any attempt to unseat philosophy from a classically defined region can only replace in the final instance something which will play the part of philosophy without having the means to do so. Thinking one can do without philosophy, one will in fact be doing bad philosophy: this entirely classical philosophical argument . . . cannot be refuted without the deconstruction of the general structure, and such a deconstruction is therefore no longer philosophy, without for all that falling into the empiricism that philosophy can always see in it. (283)

If that claim is true, then Dewey, Wittgenstein, and anybody else who tries to explain why this might be a good time to walk away from philosophy—to crawl out of the gray, sad, fly-bottle—will be inventing something which "will play the part of philosophy." They will be doing "bad," because unconsciously self-contradictory, philosophy—philosophy which is blind to its contradiction of its own presuppositions. This kind of philosophy will not grasp "the impossibility in principle of cutting oneself cleanly from the metaphysical *logos*" (309).

The "entirely classical philosophical argument" that any criticism of philosophy is just bad philosophy ("philosophy always buries its undertakers," "you can't end philosophy without prolonging philosophy," and so forth) has always struck me as pretty weak.[6] Its only empirical basis seems to be the fact that librarians automatically put criticisms of philosophy on the philosophy shelf. So they do, but then they automatically put criticisms of Hitler on the Hitler shelf and criticisms of astrology on the astrology shelf, without thereby suggesting that critics of Hitler (or astrology) are confused, or inadequate, or bad Hitlerians (or astrologers) who haven't grasped their own presuppositions.

The analogy between philosophy and Hitler would fail, of course, if it is the case that philosophy, unlike Hitler but like pitch, is the sort of thing you can't touch without its sticking to you. But is it? Why shouldn't the word "philosophy," rather than naming an exceptionally adhesive substance, just pick out a sequence of texts? Why should it matter whether we extend the term to cover present and future texts criticizing previous members of the sequence, or instead confine the extension of the term to the past? Why should the choice between these alternatives have any particular importance or interest? How, without turning back into phallogocentrists, can we know as much about the inescapability of philosophy—and about the presuppositions which people have whether they admit to them or not—as Bennington claims to know? Isn't the condition of possibility of knowing that sort of thing precisely the metaphysics of presence and essence that deconstruction was supposed to help us wiggle free from? Couldn't the different species of antimetaphysician—the deconstructionists, the Deweyans, and the Davidsonians— at least agree on the need to be nominalists? Might not such nominalism rescue us from the "classical" idea that abstract entities have a sort of supernatural ability to adhere to people who try to toss them away? Shouldn't we stop rummaging through texts in a hunt for "transcendental contraband"? Granted that you cannot cut yourself off *cleanly* (*se couper nettement*) from the metaphysical *logos,* surely you could do it raggedly, piecemeal, a little bit at a time, just as the child (or, belatedly, the analysand) cuts herself off raggedly, by fits and starts, from her parents? Cannot we gradually change the subject, until the metaphysical *logos* begins to look like a pathetic, lonely, sad, gray distant relative?

Toward the end of the last passage I quoted we find Bennington suggesting that Derrida has taught us to succeed where so many distinguished predecessors have failed: he has taught us to "deconstruct the general structure," and best of all, how to do it without doing philosophy. He has, apparently, exceeded philosophy, just the trick we were beginning to think nobody could perform. But where did all of Derrida's predecessors go wrong? Were they wrong in thinking that they had done their bit toward getting rid of "the general structure" by explaining the sociological origins of the theory/practice distinction (Dewey), or viewing Platonism as a power play (Heidegger), or explaining the need to replace a subject-centered notion of reason as faculty with a social notion of reason as the activity of communication (Habermas), or recognizing that candidates for truth-value are nominated by people who hold power (Foucault, Hacking, Latour[7]), or setting aside the scheme/content distinction (Davidson), or realizing that presuppositional relationships are, at most, habits of expectations on the part of participants in a social practice (Wittgenstein)? How does Bennington tell a genuine deconstruction of "the general structure" from an abortive, self-contradictory attempt to circumvent that structure— an attempt which is blind to its own presuppositions? These flurries of rhetorical questions indicate that I have reached the end of my tether. I do not know how to use the notion of "quasi transcendentality," except as a name for the advantage that Bennington claims for Derrida over all the other philosophers whom I have just listed. But I am not clear what that advantage is supposed to be, nor that it exists.

Maybe, instead of thinking of Derrida as Bennington does—as somehow transcending the competition, seeing farther than they have seen, avoiding their mistakes—we should see him as a collaborator, rather than as a competitor, with the various philosophers I have just mentioned. Consider the analogy of what the English Romantic poets did to a cluster of assumptions about literature, and its relation to life, which were common in the eighteenth century. We do not view

Wordsworth as in competition with Shelley, or Blake with Byron, in a race to discover the *right* way of undermining these assumptions, the right way for the nineteenth century to "exceed" the eighteenth, the only consistent way, the way which no longer shares any presuppositions with what is being exceeded. Rather, we look back on these poets as having done rather disparate things for various idiosyncratic reasons, rather than with an eye to effecting a sweeping cultural change. These poets only seem like participants in a movement when we look back and notice that such a change occurred, and that they deserve a lot of the credit.

I suspect that all the twentieth-century philosophers I have mentioned—Dewey, Heidegger, Habermas, Foucault, Hacking, Latour, Davidson, Wittgenstein, Derrida—will look like unconscious participants in a single movement to the intellectual historians of the end of the twenty-first century. With the exception of Davidson, perhaps, none of them would mind describing themselves as Bennington describes Derrida—as doing something which "is no longer . . . philosophy," any more than it is "rifling through the dustbins of philosophy to get out of them the meager nourishment that the tradition had not managed to swallow" (285). What Bennington says of deconstruction is true for all of them: what each is doing "only ever takes place, for reasons of principle, through a more or less relaxed attachment to what has traditionally been called philosophy, which it never simply repudiates" (262). Getting out from under one's parents or one's predecessors—setting aside the assumptions of the preceding century, or the preceding few millennia—is never a matter of simple repudiation, any more than it is a clean cut-off.

From the syncretic, ecumenical perspective I have just suggested, there is no more need to isolate a method of "quasi-transcendental philosophy," or "deconstruction," practiced by Derrida than to isolate a method called "critical theory" exemplified by Habermas, one called "ordinary-language philosophy" utilized by Wittgenstein, or one called "genealogy" practiced by Foucault. There is no need to worry about how to locate a middle ground called "quasi transcendentality," intermediate between taking the transcendental/empirical distinction with full Kantian seriousness and simply forgetting it. More specifically, there is no need to be more precise about the nature and procedure of deconstruction than to say, "You know—the sort of thing Derrida does."

Bennington describes this sort of thing nicely when he says that "every system excludes or expels something which does not let itself be thought within the terms of the system" and that "the reading work carried out by Derrida consists in the location of these excluded terms or these remains that command the excluding discourse: the supplement (masturbation or writing) in Rousseau; the index in Husserl; the *parergon* or vomit in Kant, etc." (283–84). But might it not be enough to say that by seeking out such excluded terms, Derrida has succeeded in placing Rousseau, Kant, and the others in marvelously illuminating new contexts, contexts which bring out unexpected resemblances between these figures? Is it necessary to claim that this success is due to the rigorous application of a method called "deconstruction" which "exceeds philosophy"? [. . .]

Notes

1 I have argued elsewhere for this claim that the only good transcendental argument is a parasitism argument. I defend it in "Transcendental Argument, Self-reference, and Pragmatism" (in *Transcendental Arguments and Science,* ed. Peter Bieri, et al. [Dordrecht: D. Reidel, 1979] 77–103) and develop the same line of thought in "Strawson's Objectivity Argument" (*Review of Metaphysics* 24 [Dec. 1970]: 207–44) and in "Verificationism and Transcendental Arguments" (*Nous* 5 [Fall 1971]: 3–14).

2 It would complicate this review too much to discuss an alternative interpretation of Wittgenstein—the one put forward by Stanley Cavell—according to which Wittgenstein regards at least some of the traditional philosophical problems as "deep" and as inextricable from something ahistorical and transcultural called "the human." For examples of this interpretation, and for criticism of my own escapist tendencies, see James Conant's introductions to two recent books by Hilary Putnam: *Realism with a Human Face* and *Words and Life* (Cambridge: Harvard UP, 1990, 1994). Cavell and Derrida have a lot in common, especially their suspicion of the kind of pragmatic approach to the philosophical tradition which I favor.

3 I suggested that Derrida be viewed as a French Wittgenstein in a discussion of Rodolphe Gasché's *The Tain of the Mirror,* titled "Is Derrida a Transcendental Philosopher?" (rpt. from *The Yale Journal of Criticism* in my *Essays on Heidegger and Others* [Cambridge: Cambridge UP, 1991]). As the title of the present review suggests, it is by way of being a sequel to that paper. Bennington's commentary has helped me get the issues I discussed in connection with Gasché's into clearer focus.

4 With some qualifications (such as substituting "metaphysical" for "philosophical"), this is exactly how I *do* think of the discourse of the philosophical tradition, and how I think Dewey thought of it. Bennington follows up by saying, "one can see how tempting such a reading can be for a critique of philosophy from the human sciences or from literature" (122). Quite so. Dewey can be thought of as formulating just such a critique from the side of the human sciences. I have tried to formulate one from the side of literature.

5 I am not sure what these presuppositions are. *What,* exactly, do you presuppose when you presuppose the historicity of a history? That people talk as they do because of the historical situation in which they are brought up? That seems a platitude rather than a tacit presupposition.

6 Marx was surely right to be exasperated by people saying to atheists, "Well then, atheism is your religion."

7 I group these three men together because I think that Hacking's notion of "truth-value candidates" offers the best way of epitomizing the results of Foucault's discussions of truth and power, and because I think that Latour (in *We Have Never Been Modern*) works out the (Deweyan, to American eyes) consequences of Foucault's and Hacking's work.

81

Gayatri Chakravorty Spivak

A Critique of Postcolonial Reason (1999)

Philosophy

POSTCOLONIAL STUDIES, UNWITTINGLY COMMEMORATING A LOST OBJECT, CAN BECOME AN alibi unless it is placed within a general frame. Colonial Discourse studies, when they concentrate only on the representation of the colonized or the matter of the colonies, can sometimes serve the production of current neocolonial knowledge by placing colonialism/imperialism securely in the past, and/or by suggesting a continuous line from that past to our present. This situation complicates the fact that postcolonial/colonial discourse studies is becoming a substantial subdisciplinary ghetto. In spite of the potential for cooptation, however, there can be no doubt that the apparently crystalline disciplinary mainstream runs muddy if these studies do not provide a persistent dredging operation. Because this dredging is counterproductive when it becomes a constant and self-righteous shaming of fully intending subjects, deconstruction can help here. (It is not accidental that, in spite of Derrida's repeated invocations of disciplinary matters and the crisis of European consciousness, the few attempts at harnessing deconstruction to these ends are not considered germane to deconstructive literary or philosophical critique.)[1]

The mainstream has never run clean, perhaps never can. Part of mainstream education involves learning to ignore this absolutely, with a sanctioned ignorance. Therefore in this opening chapter I read three central texts of the Western philosophical tradition, texts that sanction.

In conclusion to "The Three Worlds," Carl Pletsch writes:

> Our challenge is not merely to cast aside this conceptual ordering of social scientific labor [into three worlds], but to criticize it. And we must understand the task of criticism in the Kantian, Hegelian, and Marxist sense here. We must, in other words, overcome the limitations that the three worlds notion has imposed upon the social sciences as a matter of course.[2]

It is beyond the scope of this book [*A Critique of Postcolonial Reason*] to demonstrate how the new North-South divide in the post-Soviet world imposes new limitations, although my argument will constantly seek to escape that caution.[3] We may, however, suggest that our grasp on that process is made more secure if we in the humanities (Pletsch writes of the social sciences) see the "third world" as a displacement of the old colonies, as colonialism proper displaces itself into neocolonialism. (By neocolonialism I always mean the largely economic rather than the largely territorial enterprise of imperialism. The difference between colonialism and imperialism, crucial to historians, is not of the last importance here.) The post-Soviet situation has moved this narrative into the dynamics of the financialization of the globe.[4] These "great narratives" are becoming increasingly more powerful operating principles, and we in the U.S. academy are participants in it. This is also why it may be interesting to read Kant, Hegel, Marx as remote discursive precursors, rather than as transparent or motivated repositories of "ideas."[5] I keep hoping that some readers may then discover a constructive rather than disabling complicity between our own position and theirs, for there often seems no choice between excuses and accusations, the muddy stream and mudslinging.

As the century spanning the production of Kant and Marx progresses, the relationship between European discursive production and the axiomatics of imperialism also changes, although the latter continues to play the rôle of making the discursive mainstream appear clean, and of making itself appear as the only negotiable way. In the course of this unceasing operation, and in one way or another, an unacknowledgeable moment that I will call "the native informant" is crucially needed by the great texts; and it is foreclosed.[. . .]

As my opening quotation from Pletsch betrays, our sense of critique is too thoroughly determined by Kant, Hegel, and Marx for us to be able to reject them as "motivated imperialists," although this is too often the vain gesture performed by critics of imperialism. A deconstructive politics of reading would acknowledge the determination as well as the imperialism and see if the magisterial texts can now be our servants, as the new magisterium constructs itself in the name of the Other.[6] [. . .]

The field of philosophy as such, whose model was the merging of science and truth, remained untouched by the comparative impulse. In this area, Germany produced authoritative "universal" narratives where the subject remained unmistakably European. These narratives—Kant's cosmopolitheia, Hegel's itinerary of the Idea, Marx's socialist homeopathy—neither inaugurated nor consolidated a specifically scholarly control of the matter of imperialism.

Carl Pletsch's admonition to us to be Kantian, Hegelian, and Marxist in our dismantling of third-worldist talk is yet another example of their influence in the formation of the European ethico-political subject. In my estimation, these source texts of European ethico-political selfrepresentation are also complicitous with what is today a self-styled postcolonial discourse. On the margins of my reading is the imagined and (im)possible perspective I have called the native informant. Ostentatiously to turn one's back on, say, this trio, when so much of one's critique is clearly if sometimes unwittingly copied from them, is to disavow agency, declare kingdom come by a denial of history.

On the other hand, to imagine that the positioning of the other remains the same in all their work is to assume that the only real engagement with the other is in the "objective" social science disciplines, after all. My point is that we in the humanities, dealing with the position of the other as an implied "subject"(ive) position, must also vary our assumptions depending upon the text with which we are dealing. Paradoxically, every questioner who enters the book trade does so as a species of "native informant" or has been trained from infancy, for hours every day, even if reactively, in some version of an academic culture that has accommodated these three fellows, often in their radical margins but sometimes also in their conservative centers. I write in the conviction that sometimes it is best to sabotage what is inexorably to hand, than to invent a tool that no one will test, while mouthing varieties of liberal pluralism.

I will call my reading of Kant "mistaken." I believe there are just disciplinary grounds for irritation at my introduction of "the empirical and the anthropological" into a philosophical text that slowly leads us toward the rational study of morals as such. I rehearse it in the hope that such a reading might take into account that philosophy has been and continues to be travestied in the service of the narrativization of history. My exercise may be called a scrupulous travesty in the interest of producing a counternarrative that will make visible the foreclosure of the subject whose lack of access to the position of narrator is the condition of possibility of the consolidation of Kant's position. If "the combination of these talents [among them 'mixing up the empirical with the rational'] in one person produces only bunglers," let us remember that "bungling" may be a synonym for intervention.[7]

Kant's *Critique of Pure Reason* charts the operation of the reason that cognizes nature theoretically. The *Critique of Practical Reason* charts the operation of the rational will. The operations of the aesthetic judgment allow the play of concepts of nature with concepts of freedom.

The *Critique of Judgment* is divided into the Aesthetic and the Teleological; the section on aesthetic judgment is further divided into considerations of the Beautiful and the Sublime.[8] In the experience of the beautiful the subject, without cognizing itself, constructs a seeming object of cognition without objective reference; pleasure in the beautiful is pleasure at the subject's capacity to represent an object of cognition without the reference necessary for true cognition. Here we see the connection between the aesthetic judgment and the realm of theoretical reason: the subject *represents* an object for cognition—art allows the *ungrounded* play of the concept of nature—by which things can be cognized.

In the moment of the Sublime the subject accedes to the rational will. It has often been noted that the rational will intervenes to cover over a moment of deprivation. There is, strictly speaking, no full experience of the Sublime. "The feeling of the sublime is . . . a feeling of pain arising from the want of accordance between the aesthetical estimation . . . formed by the imagination and the same formed by reason." But since this "judgment of the inadequacy of our greatest faculty of sense" is reasonable and correct, "a pleasure [is] excited." The superiority of the rational over the sensible "arouses in us the feeling of our supersensible determination [*Bestimmung*]" (*CJ* 96–97).[9] It is not too excessive to say that we are programmed or, better, tuned, to feel the inadequacy of the imagination (thus tripping the circuit to the superiority of reason) through the pain incited by the Sublime. The language is persistently one of inescapable obligation, although the concept in question is that of freedom. "The tendency for this determination [*Bestimmung*] lies in our nature, while its development and exercise remains incumbent and obligatory" (*CJ* 102). *Anlage,* the word often used by Kant and generally translated as "tendency," carries the sense of a blueprint or program as well.

Such a model, of the *programmed* access to the concept of freedom as the pleasure of "reason . . . exercis[ing] dominion over sensibility" (*CJ* 109) implicitly presupposes that "freedom"—generated by a determination or programming—is a trope of freedom. Indeed, "the feeling of the sublime in nature" is a clandestine metalepsis (substitution of effect for cause). It is "a respect for our own determination *[Bestimmung]* which, by a certain subreption, we attribute to an object of nature." It is a dissimulated "exchange [*Verwechselung*] of respect for the *object* [natural sublime] for respect for the idea of humanity in our *subject*" (*CJ* 96; emphasis mine).

All this relates to the sublime in magnitude, not to the superior category of the "dynamic" sublime. I should like, however, to emphasize a few aspects of Kant's descriptive morphology that remain common to all that he wrote about the human access to the rational will. This access is structured like the programmed supplementation of a structurally necessary lack. To denominate this supplementation a feeling for nature is at best a metalepsis, by a certain "subreption." "Subreption" is rather a strong word that, in Ecclesiastical Law, means the "suppression of truth to obtain indulgence" (*OED*).[10]

Indeed, in his discussion of the dynamic sublime—"as might that has no dominion over us"—Kant similarly marks the moment of improper displacement of the epithet upon nature, as he implies a certain inevitability of usage in it: "Everything that excites this feeling [of superiority to nature within and without us] in us . . . is called then (although *improperly*) sublime" (*CJ* 104; emphasis mine).

The structure of the sublime is a troping. The sublime in nature is operated by a subreptitious impropriety. Our access to morality is operated by rhetoric and clandestinity. The *Critique of Judgment* repeatedly cautions us therefore against any attempt at *cognitive control* of the rational will.[11]

"The tuning of the mind [*die Stimmung des Gemüts;* the metaphor is the same as in *Bestimmung,* or determination] to the feeling of the sublime"—the necessary structure of supplementation and compensation that I have described above—"requires its receptivity [*erfordert eine*

Empfänglichkeit desselben] to ideas" (*CJ* 104). This receptivity, a "natural" possibility as part of the programming of determinate humanity, is actualized only by culture [*Kultur* rather than *Bildung* (education or formation)]:

> Reason exerts a power over sensibility [*Sinnlichkeit*] in order to intend it adequately [*angemessen*] to its proper realm (the practical), and to let it [*lassen*] look out upon [*auf*] the infinite, which is for it an abyss. . . . But although the judgment upon the sublime in nature *needs* culture . . . it is not therefore primarily *produced* by culture. . . . It has its foundation [*Grundlage*] in human *nature* . . . in the tendency [*Anlage*] to the feeling for (practical) ideas, i.e., to the moral [*zu dem Moralischen*]. (*CJ* 105)

Let us note this rather special inscription of a judgment programmed in nature, needing culture, but not produced by culture. It is not possible to *become* cultured in this culture, if you are *naturally* alien to it. We should read Kant's description of the desirability of the proper humanizing of the human through culture within this frame of paradox: "Without *development* of moral ideas, that which we, prepared by culture, call sublime presents itself to man in the raw [*dem rohen Menschen*] merely as terrible" (*CJ* 105; emphasis mine). The adjective *roh* is suggestive. It is generally translated "uneducated." In fact in Kant, the "uneducated" are specifically the child and the poor, the "naturally uneducable" is woman.[12] By contrast, *der rohe Mensch,* man in the raw, can, in its signifying reach, accommodate the savage and the primitive.

   To claim that the moral impulse in us is cognitively grounded is, then, to fail to recognize that its origin is a supplement. And uncritically to name nature sublime is to fail to recognize the philosophical impropriety of the denomination. Yet these cognitive failures are a part of developed culture and can even have a functional rôle in them. As Kant will argue later, they may be "wholesome illusions" (*CJ* 313). Only the cultured are susceptible to these particular errors and to their correction. The metalepsis that substitutes respect for the object for respect for humanity (in the subject) is a *normative* catachresis, a "wholesome" abuse of a figurative move. (The dictionary defines a "catachresis" as, among other things, "abuse or perversion of a trope or metaphor.") The distinction between a correct and an incorrect denomination might itself be indeterminate here. On the other hand, the mistake made by the *raw* man, for whom the abyss of the infinite is fearful rather than sublime, must be corrected through culture itself, although on the threshold of such a project stands the peculiar relationship between productive and natural culture cited earlier. (One of the ideological consequences of this relationship might be the conviction that the cultural mission of imperialism can never really succeed, but it must nonetheless be undertaken. [. . .])

   Those who are cooked by culture can "denominate" nature sublime [*erhaben nennen*], although necessarily through a metalepsis. To the raw man the abyss comes forth [*erhaben vorkommen*] as merely terrible.[13] The raw man has not yet achieved or does not possess a subject whose *Anlage* or programming includes the structure of feeling for the moral. He is not yet the subject divided and perspectivized among the three critiques. In other words, he is not yet or simply not the subject as such, the hero of the *Critiques,* the only example of the concept of a natural yet rational being. This gap between the subject as such and the not-yet-subject can be bridged under propitious circumstances by culture. As Freud noted, the transformation of the abyss (of nature's infinity) from fearful to sublime through the supplementing mediation of reason—a violent shuttling from *Abgrund* to *Grund*—bears more than a resemblance to the Oedipal scene.[14]

Schiller has been criticized for anthropomorphizing the narrative implicit in Kant's discussion of the sublime.[15] And indeed, Kant's version of the access to the sublime can only too easily be read as a narrative whose adequate representation in programs of education will produce the correct empirico-psychological reflexes. Here Kant's own warnings against such practices should perhaps be heeded.[16] In spite of Schiller's careful specification of his own project as *aesthetic* education, which would, presumably, raise it out of empirical psychology, his reading practice, according to Paul de Man, betrays him in the end.

De Man implies that Schiller's aberrant reading might be a necessary supplement to—a substitution that is possible for—something already there in Kant's text:

> Kant was dealing with a strictly philosophical concern, with a strictly philosophical, epistemological problem, which he chose to state for reasons of his own in interpersonal, dramatic terms, thus telling dramatically and interpersonally something which was purely epistemological and which had nothing to do with the pragma of the relationship between human beings. Here, in Schiller's case, the explanation is entirely empirical, psychological, without any concern for the epistemological implications. And for that reason, Schiller can then claim that in this negotiation, in this arrangement, where the analogy of danger is substituted for the real danger, where the imagination of danger is substituted for the experience of danger, that by this substitution, this tropological substitution, that the sublime succeeds, that the sublime works out, that the sublime achieves itself, and brings together a new kind of synthesis. . . . Schiller appears as the ideology of Kant's critical philosophy.[17]

To correct such an aberration by deciding to avoid anthropomorphism altogether, which seems consonant with de Man's practice, one might come to a reversal of Schiller's problem and therefore its legitimation. I am proposing to "situate" rather than expurgate (or excuse: "Kant chose to state for reasons of his own . . .") the anthropomorphic moment in Kant. Such a moment is irreducible in his text, as it is in any discursive practice, including, of course, de Man's or mine. The best we can do is to *attempt* to account for it. Not to do so is to stop at Kant's tropology or figurative practice and ignore the dissimulated history and geography of the subject in Kant's text. If we call this "the politics of the subject," then such an attempt would be simply to follow Althusser's old directive about how to read philosophy: "Everything which touches on politics may be fatal to philosophy, for philosophy lives on politics."[18] From within the discipline of philosophy, such a reading can never justify itself.

Since part of the task of this book is to show how deconstruction can serve reading, we might notice here that in an early essay where Derrida takes a whole generation to task for naively anthropologizing philosophy, he also outlines the possibility of doing so strategically. The reasons he gives seem to offer a provisional justification for my attempt: "the anxious and busy multiplication of colloquia in the West is doubtless an effect of [a] difference . . . *of an entirely other order than that of the internal or intra-philosophical differences of opinion* . . . that is bearing down, with a mute, growing and menacing pressure, on the enclosure of Western collocution. The latter doubtless makes an effort to interiorize this difference, to master it, . . . by affecting itself with it."[19]

In the end, speaking presumably for "the West" (everything defined by the "we" of humanism) in 1968, Derrida writes: "Perhaps we are between [the guard mounted around the house—critical vigilance?—the awakening to the day that is coming—radical practice?]. . . . But who, we?"[20] Twenty years later, Derrida seems to construct an answer by playing a *fort-da* game with the figure of the hybrid, the migrant.[21] Let me point beyond the argument here to suggest that an unquestioning privileging of the migrant may also turn out to be a figure of the effacement of the native informant. [. . .]

Notes

1   For disciplinary matters see *Qui a peur de la philosophie?* (Paris: Flammarion, 1977); "The Principle of Reason: The University in the Eyes of Its Pupils," *Diacritics* 13.3, (1983); and "Mochlos; or, The Conflict of the Faculties," in Richard Rand, ed., *Logomachia* (Lincoln: Univ. of Nebraska Press, 1992). Apart from the texts discussed in Chapter 2, imperialist matters are most strongly invoked in "Racism's Last Word," *Critical Inquiry* 12 (Autumn 1985): 290–99, and "The Laws of Reflection: Nelson Mandela, in Admiration," in Derrida and Mustapha Tlili, eds., *For Nelson Mandela* (New York: Seaver Books, 1987). In fact, my argument in this paragraph and this book, that third-worldist/colonial-discursivist criticism unwittingly "(con)states," in the form of an alibi, what neo-colonialism is performing and has already performed, is also to be found in the last piece: "The properly *performative* act [of the institution of a modern nation-state] must produce (proclaim) what in the form of a *constative* act it merely claims, declares, gives the assurance of describing. . . . It cannot make itself be forgotten [*se faire oublier*], as in the case of states founded on a genocide or a quasi-extermination" (p. 18; translation modified). So much at first writing. Derrida's later work has taken this line further. [. . .]

2   Carl Pletsch, "The Three Worlds, or the Division of Social Scientific Labor, circa 1950–1975," *Comparative Studies in Society and History* 23.4 (October 1981): 588.

3   This sentence was written at the start of final revision, itself dislocated by the author's current active shuttling between North and South. This book is a "practitioner's progress from colonial discourse studies to transnational cultural studies." I report, therefore, that, in the last chapter, in the globalized, electronified, virtualized name of woman, my reach exceeded my grasp and the caution gave way. The footnotes got longer, more narrative, pushing into the text. To those interested in deconstruction, given that I regularly maul the necessary but impossible model so grievously, I ask: is this a vulgar version of

what was with intent undertaken in "Border Lines" and "Circumfessions" (Derrida, "Living On/Border Lines," in Harold Bloom et al., *Deconstruction and Criticism* [New York: Seabury Press, 1979], pp. 75–176; and "Circumfessions," in Derrida and Geoffrey Bennington, *Jacques Derrida* [Chicago: Univ. of Chicago Press, 1993])?

4   Thus industrial (and specifically postindustrial) capitalism is now in an interruptive *différance* with commercial capital; World Trade with finance capital markets. To notice this *différance* is to learn from Derrida; yet Derrida's own resolute ignoring of the difference between the two is caught within it. This inside/outside relationship with something called "deconstruction," to be mentioned in an anticipatory footnote, is also one of the driving motors of this book. (For "interruption" in this sense, see Marx's description of the relationship between the three circuits of capital in Karl Marx, *Capital: A Critique of Political Economy*, tr. David Fernbach, New York: Viking, 1979, vol. 2, p. 109 and *passim*. For this sense of *différance*, see Derrida, "Differance," in *Margins of Philosophy*, tr. Alan Bass, Chicago: Univ. of Chicago Press, 1982, p. 17. We must grapple practically with the curious "fact" that *différance* cannot have a "sense," not just cover incomprehension with mockery. For Derrida's apparent ignorance (or ignoring) of the difference between industry and finance, see Spivak, "Limits and Openings of Marx in Derrida," in *Outside, in the Teaching Machine* (New York: Routledge, 1993), pp. 97–119, and "Ghostwriting," *Diacritics* 25.2 (Summer 1995): 65–84.

5   As always and in general, I find most useful the (later discredited) notion of discursive formations in part 3 of Michel Foucault, *The Archaeology of Knowledge*, tr. A. M. Sheridan Smith (New York: Pantheon, 1972). By "discursive production" I mean something that is among the conditions as well as the effect of "a general system of the formation and transformation of statements [*énoncés*]" (Foucault, *Archaeology*, p. 130).

6   See, once again, Derrida, *Of Grammatology*, tr. Spivak (Baltimore: Johns Hopkins Univ. Press, 1976), p. 24; "Otobiographies: The Ear of the Other," in *The Ear of the Other: Otobiography: Transference: Translation*, tr. Peggy Kamuf (New York: Schocken Books, 1985); and Derrida, "The Principle of Reason."

7   Kant, *Foundations of the Metaphysics of Morals with Critical Essays*, tr. Lewis White Beck (New York: Bobbs-Merrill, 1969), p. 5.

8   Kant, *Critique of Judgment*, tr. J. H. Bernard (New York: Hafner Press, 1951). All references to this text are incorporated into my own. Translations have been modified where necessary.

9   *Bestimmung*—"determination"—is translated many different ways in English. Because of the consistency of the metaphor in the concept in German, resounding in *Stimme* (voice), and *Stimmung*—among other things a suggestion of "tuning"—I indicate the word whenever it occurs in Kant's text.

10 In the *Inaugural Dissertation*, "by analogy with the accepted meaning of the term subreption," Kant is hard on "the metaphysical fallacy of subreption. . . . Such hybrid axioms (hybrid, in that they proffer what is sensitive as being necessarily bound up with the intellectual concept) I call a surreptitious axiom. Those principles of intellectual error that have most harmfully infested metaphysics have, indeed, proceeded from these spurious axioms" (Kant, *Inaugural Dissertation and Early Writings on Space*, tr. John Handyside [Chicago: Open Court, 1929], p. 74). On the next page Kant goes on to propose "[t]he principle . . . of the reduction of any surreptitious axiom." I consider its elaboration in the text.

11 In this connection, see Patrick Riley's critique of Hannah Arendt's *Lectures on Kant's Political Philosophy* in "On De Leue's Review of Arendt's *Lectures on Kant's Political Philosophy*," *Political Theory* 12 (August 1984).

12 In *Le Respect des femmes (Kant et Rousseau)* (Paris: Galilée, 1982), Sarah Kofman discusses the sublime as something the access to which is made possible by keeping woman at a distance. In this text, as well as in Genevieve Lloyd's *The Man of Reason: "Male" and "Female" in Western Philosophy* (Minneapolis: Univ. of Minnesota Press, 1984), and Beverley Brown's "Kant for the Eighties: Comments on Hillis Miller's

'The Search for Grounds in Literary Studies,'" *Oxford Literary Review* 9 (1987): 137–45, the treatment of (the theme and figure of) woman is shown to be demonstrated abundantly by Kant's text, even if often in the ruse of disavowal. As I hope to show, the figure of the "native informant" is, by contrast, foreclosed. Rhetorically crucial at the most important moment in the argument, it is not part of the argument in any way. Was it in this rift that the seeds of the civilizing mission of today's universalist feminism were sown? At best, it is a recoding and reterritorializing of the native-informant-as-woman-of-the-South, so that she can be part of the argument. I consider the rôle of the UN-style initiative in the New World Order in the pores of this book. The wholesale Americanizing of Southern babies through adoption is another issue. Although the personal goodwill, indeed obsession, is, in most of these cases, unquestionable, one is also reminded of Cecil Rhodes's remark, mutatis mutandis, of course: "I contend that we are the first race in the world, and that the more of the world we inhabit the better it is for the human race. . . . If there be a God, I think that what he would like me to do is to paint as much of the map of Africa British red as possible" (quoted in L. S. Stavrianos, *Global Rift: The Third World Comes of Age* [New York: Morrow, 1981], p. 263). In the domestic context, the problem was approached by what has now become a classic: Gloria T. Hull et al., eds., *All the Women Are White, All the Blacks Are Men, But Some of Us Are Brave: Black Women's Studies* (Old Westbury N.Y.: Feminist Press, 1982). I am not suggesting that Kant's expressed view on the matter of colonialism and race, to be found, for example, in relatively peripheral texts such as the "Third Definitive Article for a Perpetual Peace" (in *Perpetual Peace and Other Essays on Politics, History, and Morals,* tr. Ted Humphrey [Indianapolis: Hackett Publishing, 1983]) or "On the Distinctiveness of Races in General" (in Earl W. Count, ed., *This Is Race: An Anthology Selected from the International Literature on the Races of Man* [New York: Henry Schuman, 1950]) should be ignored, although their assumptions are historically interpretable as well. I am suggesting that a revised politics of reading can give sufficient value to the deployment of rhetorical energy in the margins of the texts acknowledged to be central.

13 Did this metaphor leap to my eyes because of the Vedic tradition of cooking the world in/as sacrificial fire as the specific task of the *brāhmana,* who might loosely translate as "the philosopher?" Charles Malamoud has masterfully laid out this tradition for the Western reader in *Cuir le monde: Rite et pensée en Inde ancienne* (Paris: Découverte, 1989), although he does not comment on its role in sustaining social hierarchy.

14 "Kant's Categorical Imperative Is Thus the Direct Heir to the Oedipus Complex," in Sigmund Freud, *The Standard Edition of the Complete Psychological Works,* tr. James Strachey et al. (New York: Norton, 1961–1976), vol. 19, p. 167; this edition hereafter cited as *SE.* Freud does not notice the specific play of sexual difference with Nature as the abyss of the fearful mother. See also Kofman, *Le respect,* pp. 42–44. It has often been noticed that section 27 of the "Analytic of the Sublime" is full of images of violence.

15 Paul de Man, "Kant and Schiller," in *Aesthetic Ideology* (Minneapolis: Univ. of Minnesota Press, 1996), pp. 129–162.

16 These warnings deal with violent revolution. It is well known that, according to Kant, "one should view neither the united will of the people nor the contract as empirical quantities. Such an understanding would not only be incorrect from a philosophical point of view but also politically dangerous. . . . Kant welcomes the principles of the French Revolution but condemns the Jacobin terror" (Ottfried Höffe, *Immanuel Kant,* tr. Marshall Farrier [Albany: SUNY Press, 1994], pp. 183–84). It can perhaps be argued that there "is" a radical discontinuity—if discontinuity can be spoken of in the mode of being—between all ethical programs and decisions to implement them in practice. Indeed, this is Derrida's argument about decisions in "The Force of Law" (see Appendix). In Kant, this rift is avoided by assigning justice itself (rather than accountability in law) to the constitutionally collective calculus alone; or rather, to keep to the Kantian vocabulary, "the acknowledged duty of the human soul . . . [to] the evolution of a constitution in accordance with natural law" (Kant, *The Conflict of the Faculties,* tr. Mary J. Gregor [New York: Abaris Books, 1979], p. 157). For a discussion of the relationship between natural and positive law, we loop back

to Derrida, "Force of Law," p. 927f. One of the chief problems with preference-based ethical theories is their inability to work this into their calculations in order to destabilize them *productively*. See, for example, Amartya Sen and Bernard Williams, eds., *Utilitarianism and Beyond* (Cambridge: Cambridge Univ. Press, 1982), an otherwise brilliant collection from a variety of points of view.

17 De Man, "Kant and Schiller," pp. 143, 147.

18 Louis Althusser, *Lenin and Philosophy and Other Essays*, tr. Ben Brewster (New York: Monthly Review Press, 1971), pp. 29–30.

19 Derrida, "The Ends of Man," *Margins of Philosophy*, p. 113. Emphasis mine.

20 Ibid., p. 136.

21 *The Other Heading: Reflections on Today's Europe*, tr. Pascale-Anne Brault and Michael B. Naas (Bloomington: Indiana Univ. Press, 1992) is the book that starts this thematic of the split self as migrant hybrid: "I feel European *among other things*, would this be, in this very declaration, to be more or less European? . . . It is up to others, in any case, and up to me *among them*, to decide" (p. 83). *Aporias*, tr. Thomas Dutoit (Stanford, Calif.: Stanford Univ. Press, 1993), pulls it back into an earlier text of hybridity—Catholic Spain—and introduces the Marrano: "If one, figuring, calls Marrano [*si l'on appelle marrane, par figure*] anyone who remains faithful to a secret he has not chosen, in the very place where he lives" (p. 81; translation modified). By the graphic of this figure (if not the logic of the metaphor) it is possible to think that the utterly persuasive dominant discourse of Derrida's critique of Western metaphysics contains signs (or at least signals) of a prior identity hidden by collective covenant in response to shared menace. Given the importance of the Father-Son situation as the site of contestation of ethics by sacrifice, and Derrida's insistent iteration of the texts of Hegel, Freud, Nietzsche, Genet, as well as his own bio-graphy in his concatenations, it may not be without meaning that he has made it public that his son showed him a text of the Marrano. Does this then name, make specific—and necessarily efface—in an affect-rich "narrow" sense, the general graphematic that all disclosure is also effacement (without derivation from an original)—by way of a differance that "is" not, or a gift, if there is any? The slippery negotiation between general and narrow seems there between the first and second phrases of location in the following sentence, but am I reading what I want to read? Does one not, often?: "in the underived night [*nuit sans contraire*] where the radical absence of any historical witness keeps him [*le tient* does not warrant 'him or her']"—general sense—"in the dominant culture that by definition holds the calendar [*dispose du calendrier*]"—narrow sense—"this secret keeps the Marrano even before he keeps it"—whatever I seem to intend there is that other text at work (p. 81; see also p. 77). In the mean time, as it were, the graphic of the hybrid migrant is also generalized, earlier in the same text, as the absolute *arrivant* who "does not cross a threshold separating two identifiable places" (p. 34). The passage about the Marrano makes it clear that the sense of the *arrivant* there is not "absolute" by specifying the Marrano's home as "the home of the first or of the second *arrivant*" (p. 81), and therefore presumably from and/or to "an identifiable place(s)." From this it is a step to inscribe Marx as migrant and Marrano— whose Abrahamic messianism re-vectors "The Jewish Question." "We" are, then, the Marrano as old European. Since I argue in this book that the "postcolonial" as a figure masquerades as and overwrites the foreclosed position I am calling the "native informant," it seems appropriate to mention that none of this possible Derridian itinerary is "postcolonial" in the narrow sense. Algeria is not inscribed on it as a recently liberated nation-state. In that inscription, Derrida's role is that of an honorable and well-placed Eurocentric economico-cultural migrant: making his immense reputation count for migrant activism, and organizing public and academic fora; susceptible only to the general critique of the place of migrant activism with reference to counter-globalization resistance [. . .].

82

Luce Irigaray

Approaching the Other as Other (1999)

WE HAVE BEEN EDUCATED TO MAKE OUR OWN all that was pleasing to us, all that we admitted into our proximity, into our intimacy, all that surrounded us.

On the level of consciousness, on the level of feelings, we make our own what we approach, what approaches us.

Our manner of reasoning, even our manner of loving, corresponds to an appropriation. Our culture, our school education, our cultural formation want it this way: to learn, to know, is to make one's own through instruments of knowledge capable, we believe, of seizing, of taking, of dominating all of reality, all that exists, all that we perceive, and beyond.

We want to have the entire world in our head, sometimes the entire world in our heart. We do not see that this gesture transforms the life of the world into something finished, dead, because the world thus loses its own life, a life always foreign to us, exterior to us, other than us.

Thus, if we precisely grasped all that makes the springtime, we would without doubt lose the wondrous contemplation in the face of the mystery of springtime growth, we would lose the life, the vitality, in which this universal renewal has us participate without our being able to know or control where the joy, the force, the desire that animate us come from. If we could analyse each element of energy that reaches us in the explosion of spring, we would lose the global state that we experience by bathing in it through all our senses, our whole body, our whole soul.

We sometimes, at least partially, find this state again, I would say this state of grace, in which the spring puts us, when we are immersed in a new landscape, in an extraordinary cosmic manifestation, when we bathe in an environment that is simultaneously perceptible and imperceptible, knowable and unknowable, visible and invisible to us. We are then situated in a milieu, in an event that escapes our control, our know-how, our inventiveness, our imagination. And our response to this 'mystery' is or could be astonishment, wonder, praise, sometimes questioning, but not reproduction, repetition, control, appropriation.

The Irreducible Transcendence of the You

The state that springtime, certain landscapes, and certain cosmic phenomena provoke in us sometimes takes place at the beginning of an encounter with the other.

It is in the first moments of drawing near to one another that the other moves us the most, touching us in a global, unknowable, uncontrollable manner. Then, too often, we make the other our own – through knowledge, sensibility, culture. Entering our horizon, our world, the other loses the strangeness of his or her appeal. The presence of the other included us in a certain mystery, communicating to us an awakening that is both corporeal and spiritual. But we reduce the other to ourselves, we incorporate the other in turn: through our knowledge, our affection, our customs. At the limit, we no longer see the other, we no longer hear the other, we no longer perceive the other. The other is a part of us. Unless we reject the other.

The other is inside *or* outside, not inside *and* outside, being part of our interiority while remaining exterior, foreign, other to us. Awakening us, by their very alterity, their mystery, by the in-finite that they still represent for us. It is when we do not know the other, or when we accept that the other remains unknowable to us, that the other illuminates us in some way, but with a light that enlightens us without our being able to comprehend it, to analyse it, to make it ours. The totality of the other, like that of springtime, like that of the surrounding world sometimes, touches us beyond all knowledge, all judgement, all reduction to ourselves, to our own, to what is in some manner proper to us. In somewhat learned terms, I would say that the other, the other as other, remains beyond all that we can predicate of him or her. The other is never this or that that we attribute to him or her. It is insofar as the other escapes all judgement on our part that he or she emerges as *you,* always other and non-appropriable by *I.*

To recognize the *you* as irreducible to us, unknowable and imperceptible by us in his or her totality, is not our habit. Our culture has generally entrusted this *you* to God, what is more, to God-the-Father. Our habits of thought, our ethical or political habits towards the other who is present to us or with us here and now – carnally, bodily – go rather in the direction of reducing the other to ourselves, to our own, or of transforming the other into a *he,* sometimes into a *she,* in some way reduced to an 'object' of knowledge or an 'object' of love.

In this way, never without doubt has an age spoken so much of the other as ours does, globalization and migrations requiring it. But, too often, this other is reduced to an object of study, to what is at stake in diverse socio-political strategies aiming in some manner to integrate the other into us, into our world. Thus we avoid the problem of meeting with the stranger, with the other. We avoid letting ourselves be moved, questioned, modified, enriched by the other as such. We do not look for a way for a cohabitation or a coexistence between subjects of different but equivalent worth. We flee dialogue with a *you* irreducible to us, with the man or woman who will never be *I,* nor *me,* nor *mine.* And who, for this very reason, can be a *you,* someone with whom I exchange without reducing *him* or *her* to myself, or reducing *myself* to *him* or *her.*

The transcendence of the *you* as other is not yet, really, part of our culture. At best, the other is respected in the name of tolerance, is loved in God, is recognized as an equal or a fellow human. But that does not yet amount to perceiving and respecting the irreducibility of the other, to recognizing the irreducible difference of the other in relation to me.

This letting go from the subject, this letting be of the *I* towards what it is, knows, and has made its own, this opening of a world of one's own, experienced as familiar, in order to welcome the stranger, while remaining oneself and letting the stranger be other, do not correspond to our mental habits, to our Western logic. Dominating, controlling has been taught to us as the realm of reason more than accepting our limits, in order to live together, to coexist, to co-create even, with who or what exceeds us, extends beyond us, remains irreducibly exterior and foreign to us.

We have learnt to think starting from a certain number of dichotomies between sensible and intelligible, nature and spirit, body and soul, subject and object, etc. And we do not know how to transform such categories in order to attain a culture of alterity, of relation with the other as such, of acknowledgement of the other as irreducible to us, in order to make an alliance with him, or with her, in the respect for our respective values and limits.

At best, we are sometimes good patriarchs or good matriarchs. But this genealogical behaviour, implying nature and hierarchy, still avoids the meeting with the other: the man or woman that I must horizontally recognize as equivalent to me, in the radical respect of his or her difference(s).

Two events of our time compel us to rethink our relation to the other as other: 1. the blending of races and ethnicities that is now a part of our daily landscape; 2. the recognition of the importance of gender from a cultural point of view. One could add here a certain coexistence of generations that does not allow genealogy to retain its past function.

In fact, we are entering a new age of generalized mixing, and our mental or community habits founded on self-identity, the proper, the similar, the same, the equal, and their reproduction, risk being incapable of harmoniously resolving the problems of difference that we have to manage.

To make the Black equal to the White, the woman equal to the man, is still to submit them, under cover of paternalist generosity, to models put in place by Western man, who resists living together with the different. He even accepts becoming a little Black or a little female rather than going through a revolution of thinking that is today unavoidable. All the strategies of integration – with more or fewer reversals of hierarchy, blendings and plurality of cultures, of languages, of identities – yes, but not to the gesture that recognizes that the subject only exists thanks to limits and that, before the universe and especially before the other, the subject becomes structured not by mastering or dominating but by accepting that he, or she, is not the whole, that he, or she, represents only one part of reality and of truth, that the other is forever a *not I, nor me, nor mine*, and not a: *not yet I, not yet mine* to integrate into me or into us.

Sexual Difference, the Foundation of Alterity

For this revolution of thought, of ethics, of politics, of which we have to take charge today, sexual difference represents the most interesting question.

First, this difference is universal, and it allows us, as such, to define a model of global community.

Next, it is often the manner of treating this difference – in the sexual relation or in the genealogical relation – that is at the origin of differences between traditions, between cultures, manifesting themselves notably in customary law. To find it a democratic regulation would help the coexistence of cultures.

Moreover, this difference is the one that can bring together the most natural with the most cultural, by requiring us to take a new step in the construction of a civilization.

In fact, in our cultures, woman still often remains the natural pole of a masculine culture. If each gender assumes, in itself and for itself, the specificity of its nature and works out its cultivation, a new type of civility will be put in place in which the duality of the genders will become, thanks to their differences, culturally fertile, and not only naturally fertile as it still is too exclusively today.

To refound society and culture upon sexual difference is also to radically put back in question the notion of the proper, of propriety, of appropriation that governs our mental and social habits. It is to learn, at the most intimate, at the most passionate and carnal level of the relation to the other, to renounce all possession, all appropriation, in order to respect, in the relation, two subjects, without ever reducing one to the other.

To affirm that man and woman are really two different subjects does not amount for all that to sending them back to a biological destiny, to a simple natural belonging. Man and woman are *culturally* different. And it is good that it is so: this corresponds to a different construction of their subjectivity. The subjectivity of man and that of woman are structured starting from a *relational identity* specific to each one, a relational identity that is held between nature and culture, and that assures a bridge starting from which it is possible to pass from one to the other while respecting them both.

This specific relational identity, one's own relational identity (the word is used now in another sense, not of possession but of subjective or objective determination), is based on different irreducible givens: the woman is born of a woman, of someone of her gender, the man is born of someone from another gender than himself; the woman can engender in herself like her mother, the man engenders outside of himself; the woman can nourish with her body, the man nourishes thanks to his work; the woman can engender in herself the masculine and the feminine, the man, in fact, intervenes as man above all in the engendering of the masculine.

The first relational situation is thus very different for the girl and the boy. And they build their relation to the other in a very different way. The girl immediately finds herself in a relation between subjects of the same gender that helps her to structure a relation to the other, which is more difficult for the boy to develop. On the other hand, the girl, the woman is made fragile by the intervention of the other in her: in love, in motherhood.

The construction of subjectivity for the woman implies that she comes out of an exclusive relation with the same as herself, the mother, and that she discovers the relation with a different other, while remaining herself. Egalitarian or separatist strategies cannot resolve such a problem. What can assist the woman in becoming subject is the discovery of the other, the masculine, as horizontally transcendent, and not vertically transcendent, to her. It is not the submission to the law of a Father that can permit the woman to become herself, corporeally and culturally, but the conscious and voluntary recognition, in love and in civility, of the other as other. This cultural becoming of the woman will then be able to help the man to become man, and not only master and father of the world, as he has too often been in History.

It seems that the woman must give birth to the man not only bodily but also spiritually. Certain religious traditions have sometimes clearly expressed this reality.

The assimilation or integration of the feminine into the masculine world represents therefore a real danger for private or collective relational life. That does not mean that the woman must remain the guardian of love in the traditional sense, but that she must be the one who initiates relational life and who safeguards it in private and public life.

Spiritual Tasks for Our Age (2004)

TALKING ABOUT RELIGION CAN BE HURTFUL, to oneself and to others. Affect linked to religion is deeply rooted; in some obscure way, it holds together the totality of the self, of the community and culture. Trying to change it can unravel the social fabric, along with subjectivity and tradition.

And yet, when religion is nothing more than inertia ensuring a past cohesion, it no longer plays a dynamic role in the present. It becomes deadening, and no longer infuses an additional life into the individual and collective dimensions that unite the corporeal with the spiritual, the sensible with the mental, and the self with the other.

How can we rethink religion at a time when many believe they no longer have anything to do with it? Even though they substitute all sorts of ideologies for it, ideologies that are sometimes more rigid and stultifying than our old beliefs that used to leave room – somewhat ambiguously no doubt – for mystery, and for a God who was, in a way, more discreet than many of our elected politicians, or our variously mediatized spiritual advisers. Following are some suggestions that will, I hope, bring a little light and a little hope to those who read them.

God, Gods, or a Different Relation to the Divine?

For centuries, in our tradition, God has been conceived as an entity of the beyond whom we must try to approach, even though he remains – so they teach us – radically estranged from us, absolutely other. Texts, of course, do reveal something about him, but texts are susceptible to diverse interpretations that vary according to historical epochs and commentators. Many of the faithful spend their lives listening to these interpretations of the Scriptures, or trying to decipher them themselves, all the while remaining blind to others, and to the world that surrounds them.

God, as an absolutely unknowable entity of the beyond, has often separated us from each other or assembled us into one people, one body without inspiring us to religious behaviour with respect to the universe, to others, or even to ourselves. Nevertheless, no one dares touch this God, as if, having replaced the idols, he had acquired for himself, in himself, certain non-metabolized idolatrous affects. It is true that the function of the God of monotheism is to unify individual identity – the male's in particular – and this is not an easy task. It seems, however, that God is still too often evoked as a real entity, even if we cannot perceive him. He functions as a kind of idol of the spirit, resistant to perception by the senses, requiring that we rise up to him through our faith, and through renunciations that make us unknown to ourselves – or even our own enemies – as opposed to giving us confidence in our divine possibilities.

Could we not imagine the divine differently? We could abandon the object-entity God – letting him keep his name for the time being – to restore to him a form of energy that would inspire us to develop fully into ourselves, and to live fully our relation to the other, to others, and to the world around us. In that case, there would be no more being, fixed once and for all, but rather a changeable, perfectible way of being, thus an indeterminate absolute that determines us nonetheless. This would be very different from traditional teachings that claim to transmit an already determined truth, guaranteed by texts, dogmas, rites, etc.

We must nevertheless continue to inquire into the letter and the spirit, the spirit ultimately conceived as a kind of energy that must be channelled, or conducted, without reducing it to the letter, which would annihilate it. No tradition, in this way, can claim to possess the religious truth of humanity, until it has discovered the best possible way to spiritualize that energy without crippling it in order to make it impervious to other traditions. While no tradition should want to carry out religious colonization, there should be an effort to liberate other traditions from closure, with an eye to a more fully human spiritual development.

Individual development must not lead to a cult of the self and of its values, to the imperialism of a personal or collective sameness; and collective development must not diminish the individual within the group, in the name of a truth that abolishes all singularity, thus risking fundamentalism and conflicts with other groups. *Individual development* cannot be closed off in one unique truth, morality, or cult – all offspring of the same religious family, or at times the same politico-religious family – but *must be linked to the development of relations to the other as other.*

These would not be relations of love for what is the same as the self notably within the context of filial or parental relationships. We need to get away from the family and from genealogy. That would be the first step towards a relationship to the self and to the other that would be both more adult and more spiritual than a relation linked to the natural space of the family – even given all of its transformations into other sorts of groupings, groupings which have never succeeded in transforming this natural link to the benefit of greater liberty and higher achievement with respect to the breath, or the spirit.

From this standpoint, the one who, in Eastern tradition, is reborn autonomously through breathing, through mastery of the breath, is a precious example. Can we apply this example to our relations with the other? The oriental master establishes relationships with compassion, transmitting his or her own experience through a kind of love, or a kind of teaching, that is inseparable from one's own life. From this master we learn a truth that cannot be dissociated from the experience of the teacher, a compassion that seeks to ensure the other's access to happiness before one's own. These are lessons well worth listening to and practising. Still missing, perhaps, are horizontal and reciprocal relations between persons, another step that must be taken towards our liberation from genealogy – from spiritual genealogy as well. Relationships would then be characterized not by degrees of more or less, but rather by difference, the most universal example of which is sexual difference.

We would become capable of mutual transmission of energy, an energy that is not necessarily subject to the same truth. We could experience this through an encounter with practising on other spiritual tradition, supposing that different historically contemporaneous traditions really do exist. We can also come to know it, simply and daily, in the encounter with a spiritually autonomous person of the other sex.

That is perhaps the secret of the attraction between the sexes. Never exclusively physical, it is always spiritual as well, in some ways religious. And, if only for that reason, dogmatic religions are always suspicious of it. In effect, the spiritual attraction between the sexes remains indeterminate; nothing can express it, or fix it into laws or representations without abolishing it. It incarnates itself without ever being definitively incarnate. Its religion would be in maintaining the attraction, that in the life of the relationship, not through the seduction or subjugation of the one by the other, or even through moral regulation, but rather through a *spiritual dynamic* in each one. This requires that the development of each leave an opening for the encounter with the other as other. Development is thus accomplished through the search for a personal absolute that accepts being questioned, modified, and fecundated by the development of the other towards their absolute.

Some will object that there would not be, in that case, two absolutes, but rather two modes of access to one and the same absolute. In order to be able to prove, or disprove, this, we would need to be capable of imagining the other's absolute, which would not really then be other. More generally, we should say that a statement like the one above is already dogmatic, and makes the claim that one subject's absolute, historically the male's in our culture, is appropriate to another subject. Nothing could be less certain . . . Can we ignore the fact that religions with one unique God inscribed within a genealogy are part of the male tradition?

Female traditions do not necessarily call upon a unique entity defined as God. More attentive to alliances, and to the relationship with the cosmos, they do not inscribe their absolute within a genealogy either.

A spiritual relationship between the sexes would allow us to reunite human and divine elements that have been artificially separated by the domination of one sex over the other, by the dominance of the values of one sex over those of the other.

Besides, in our patriarchal monotheistic traditions today, what a man means by the name of God is very different from what a woman means, even if her quest for the absolute is already oriented by necessities proper to the male subject – which paralyses a part of her spiritual energy into a kind of idolatry or passivity. Fortunately women's religious feeling, taking root below men's beliefs and rites, can generally preserve a part of itself.

Moral or Ethical?

Men often organize their religious conscience around respect for laws that God or his ministers have set down for the faithful of a tradition. These laws correspond to an internalized construct, a 'moral law' inscribed, or to be inscribed, on the heart, dictating how to behave towards God, towards oneself, and towards others. Difference between self and others has little importance. The question rather is to behave the same way towards oneself and towards the others, who are assimilated to the self. All are considered 'children of God', 'sons' of an Absolute who functions as Father, chief, and keystone of a hierarchy beneath which differences are not really worth noting, except as indicating a greater or lesser proximity to the supreme reality, from which all are supposed to be descended, and back to which all are supposed to return.

We know little about this spiritual genealogy, except that, in our tradition, it corresponds to a familio-social model that has oriented religious values towards recognizing and transposing paternity. The religious feelings of the faithful obviously is endowed with a certain plasticity that can adapt to the spiritual model imposed on them with varying degrees of fecundity.

What needs to be called into question in the development of patriarchal spirituality is *the loss of differentiation among believers, and the predominance of a model of the Absolute in relation to them.* They have first to love God the Father, and then love themselves and each other within the horizons of this unique Absolute. Ideally, the law is thus the same for all, and its more or less perfect application depends on the proximity of the believer to the divine model. Men, more closely resembling the God they have chosen in order to achieve a certain stage in their historical development, are supposed to be more capable in this area than women.

This supposedly universal model, in dictating behaviour with respect to the other, confines itself to the generalities of an elementary construction of personal and collective identity: do not kill; love the other as a 'brother', as an equal to yourself (which is not easy for those who have no self . . .); do not commit incest or adultery; bring forth children, etc.

Today, our consciences seek a more subtle spiritual guidance, perhaps because our multicultural times are more attentive to difference, despite resistance to it on the part of blindly egalitarian doctrines and politics. Moreover, acquaintance with other traditions shows us how their moral paths are sometimes subtler, more diversified, less abstract, and less undifferentiated than ours are.

It would be impossible to deal with this issue exhaustively here. However, I would like to point out that almost daily contact with other traditions, like the evolution of relations between the sexes, gradually *leads us from a universal morality inscribed within each of us, towards an ethics which takes into account particularities, differences, contingencies,* and requires us to rediscover the other as other, and to invent, along with him or her, a style of comportment that could in no way pre-exist our encounter, without risking the denial of the other in his or her alterity. Where a written law was used to dictate to my conscience once and for all what had to be done, I now find that *I am required to open up within myself a non-inscribed space, a virgin space,* if you will, *from which I can listen to and welcome the other,* and invent, along with him or her, a relation that goes beyond the elementary imperatives of respect for natural life and for possessions, towards the development of a new kind of spiritual relation to the other. This relation cannot, at the risk of failing to respect the other as other, remain within the horizon of the Absolute of one and only one tradition. It must be able to open up, towards the other and with the other, a space liberated from the imperatives of one single culture, so that encounter and dialogue become possible.

It seems that ethics must come to replace – or at least accompany – more individualistic morals, since ethics cares about *the cultural space, the spiritual space, both contextual and interior, where the other exists as other.* Ethics creates appropriate respect for the natural or cultural habitat of the self and the other. Ethics teaches us not only not to kill physically but also spiritually, either ourselves or the other. They require that law not be an *a priori* universal, except in the case of a law of silence, of attentiveness, of co-existence and communication in consideration for difference, and differences.

Women are probably somewhat better prepared for this step forward required for the spiritual development of humanity. Actually, on a daily basis, they are led to respect the life of the other, in maternity and in love itself. Abstract moral behaviour is of little use to them for managing their pregnancies, their motherhood, or their love life. The moral responsibility incumbent upon women is to respect the other as other, that is to respect his or her autonomy – the dwelling of the birth and growth of spiritual development. Women are called upon directly to fulfil an ethical task, to respect the other as other, and that requires the respect of self and a constant relational creativity much more than the application of an already written, and common in its application, law. Since ethical behaviour with respect to the other is required of them daily, women have an aptitude to invent, or to propagate, a religious attitude indispensable for our times, one that will bring about progress in human development.

It should be noted *that this progress once again is rooted in respect for difference, differences.* Woman engenders the other within herself, in love she welcomes the other into herself without killing this other. She gives, or gives back, natural life to the other. What she must learn to practise consciously is the respect for the other as other at the spiritual level. That means giving – or giving back – a spiritual life that would not be dictated by her own, but would be appropriate to the other.

This attitude must not lead to a reversal about the source of life, with women supposedly engendering physical life and men cultural life, the natural maternity of women supposedly going hand in hand with the spiritual paternity of men. This scission of human beings into two artificially differentiated parts leads to a dead end in the spiritual development of men and of women. Rather than render one's own nature divine, each submits to historically marked social stereotypes.

Making cultural progress rather means elevating sexual difference from the natural to the spiritual level without subjugating it to parental roles. It means *gaining access to a new transcendental form* within a horizontal relationship with an individual of different sex. It means changing sexual attraction, or from a more or less animalistic instinct from a procreative instinct, dictating a division of tasks between male and female, and leading to seduction, submission, and possession and making it a space from which spiritual energy can be cultivated, not towards a cult for the same as the self, but towards respect for the other as transcendent to me, for another I will never know, either corporeally or mentally, and never make into my possession, not even as my hypothetical human 'other half'.

A Transcendental Anchored in the Natural World

Such a spiritual progress will allow us to overcome two dead ends in our tradition: the nearly idolatrous over-valorization of nature in procreation, and its annihilation in a culture, where the historically male subject appropriates nature, and attempts to dominate it in order to bend its will to his, notably to his technological projects. Culture in this case is opposed to respect for nature; the dialectic between nature and culture is interrupted.

In the ethical behaviour sketched out in this text, each would remain faithful to a nature one is charged with cultivating, without annihilating. We then can no longer overly value natural maternity and spiritual paternity, contrasting them with each other. We must get beyond the functional aspect of sexed identity, since this aspect remains subjugated to nature, even when it claims to be pure culture – for example, in the assignment of roles.

It is necessary to rethink what it means to be a girl or a boy, a woman or a man. Historically, gender identity has been confused with a strictly natural physiological identity, in the service of instinct and procreation. It is undoubtedly this reduction of sexed identity to physical identity that explains the various positions of some religious leaders, as well as of certain feminists, with regard to overcoming sexed identity, or to abolishing it altogether. However, these positions are based on error, error that is perpetuated when children are taught about the difference between the sexes. Culture has misunderstood the character of sexed identity, but that is no reason to persist in our mistakes.

Male and female identity cannot be reduced to physical differences that are more or less visible in their forms and effects. Sexed identity implies a way of constituting subjectivity in relation to the world, to the self, and to the other, that is specific to each sex. This specificity is determined in part by corporeal characteristics as implying a *different relational attitude.* Engendering inside the self does not lead to the same relationship with the other – either a child or a sex partner – as engendering outside the self. And this relationship is accompanied by, and produces as feedback, a different relationship to the self. To give another example: to be born a woman of a woman, having the same ability to engender as she who brings you into the world, does not have an identical effect on the constitution of the subject as being born a man of a woman, without the ability to do as she did in bringing you into the world. Or another example: to engender within the self not only the same as the self, but also the other from the self, favours behaviour towards the other that cannot be shared by one for whom sexual difference always remains external to the self. One might say the same about welcoming the other in oneself during the act of love.

Other examples could be brought in to illustrate that strictly speaking *sexed identity cannot be assimilated with the sexual* – even though it is not foreign to it. Sexed identity hearkens back to construction of subjectivity necessarily different for the girl and the boy. In fact, it corresponds to a *specific relational identity,* creating a different bridge, or different bridges, according to the sex of the subject, between nature and culture.

It goes without saying that sexed identity, which is both constructed and received, cannot be assimilated with social stereotypes founded on a purely natural or functional interpretation of sex. We are currently in danger of trying to liberate women from social subjugation by destroying their identity even more radically than had been done in the past. The extraordinarily creative abilities shown by little girls' deserve recognition and encouragement, and should not be suspected of resulting from social stereotypes, that could have a positive effect only on them and not on boys. The girl's creative precocity and cultural vigour, notably creative, are undoubtedly caused by her more rapidly developed relational identity, the result of having been born of one the same as she, and of her intuition about her hospitable role in taking, in love and in maternity, the other into the self.

The ethical task confronting a spiritual conception of sexual difference is to avoid both the annihilation of nature and its over-valorization. We must thus refuse to divide sex roles into, on the one hand, guardian of nature, and on the other, guardian of culture; we must also refuse obedience to an abstract culture that destroys singularity and diversity in conformance with one model which could be, and even ought to be, unique.

From the beginning, sexual difference is relational for both boys and girls. Failure to take this dimension of subjectivity into consideration encourages sexual regression back to animal instinct in love and in reproduction. Its recognition is the discovery of a *new task for our culture, notably in the articulation between nature and transcendence*.

That is the way to anchor transcendence in the natural world (where without our knowledge it already is anchored in our tradition, since a Father-God cannot be foreign to an Absolute linked to nature), and to make this anchoring the source of a new relationship to the transcendental. While God the Father remains subject, through his parental role in paternity, to the natural world, he is also an Absolute who remains linked to the gender of the subject: transcendent since he is relegated to the beyond, but intuitively similar to the male whose cultural mastery he guarantees through privileged divine filiation.

Leaving sameness behind in order to recognize a different transcendent here and now would mark a *new stage in the constitution of consciousness* and of the spiritual development of humanity.

The role of women is crucial in this area as well. They are accustomed to respecting the life of the other. What is more difficult for them is to think of the other as inaccessible to them, whatever their relation to the other in love or in maternity.

Men's need for public power has sometimes been interpreted as compensation, or even as revenge, for their subjugation in private life. The first ethical gesture of a woman is to let the other exist, not through over-valorizing this other in traditional transcendence, but through accepting that the other must remain *unknown to her and not appropriated by her*, neither as lover, nor as child. This amounts to recognizing the other as transcendent to the self – not superior, but rather irreducibly other. In this way, fidelity to nature within a culture of differences opens up access to a new type of transcendence – undoubtedly more spiritual than the one we have known up until now, and that can only gain from being rethought from the perspective of a horizontal transcendence between the sexes.

Respect for the transcendence of the other as other within sexual difference will also allow us to relearn to *respect the cosmos as having an existence other than ours* and that is not at the disposal of our needs and our desires. Cosmic nature, moreover, represents an indispensable universal for having access to the recognition of the other as irreducible to the self, since our tradition cannot serve as third term in arranging a specific identity for each of us.

Relations with the Other: From the Intimate to the Collective

Sexual difference is often understood in its strictly intimate dimension, belonging to so-called private life. That is to assimilate it once again with a functional aspect required for the construction of the family – the family conceived as a natural enclave within the cultural public sphere of city and the state. In the family conceived in this way, each member alienates their own identity in order to compose a single undifferentiated unit. The sexed identity necessary for the constitution of the family is not cultivated for itself, but rather for what it can contribute to the unity of the family. Therein lies the origin of our conception of man and of woman as two halves of humanity rather than as two different identities, and the reason why they are valued more as father and mother than as individuals who have a relationship to each other.

From this perspective, it no longer seems appropriate to consider today the family as the privileged site of humanity's religious achievement. Furthermore, in our tradition, the family most often represents the consequences of what we have called original sin – childbearing with great labour and winning bread by the sweat of the brow. The family thus conceived is the site of reproduction and of the acquisition, consumption, and capitalization of goods.

In order to move beyond the redemption of 'original sin', we would have to find love's innocence again, including the innocence of carnal love, between a woman and a man. This love – in Genesis and in certain verses of the Song of Songs – is evoked as having taken place within nature, outside the possession of property, and even of clothing. The family, as we too often imagine it, and as it is generally presented to us as religious model, is supposedly the result of a 'sin', and not the fulfilment of the divine within man and within woman.

Moving back before 'sin' would require refounding the family on a relationship between a man and a woman capable of loving each other in the innocence of the body and the soul. In order for this to be successful, we must *rediscover love within difference*, love that is neither possession of the one by the other, nor exploitation of the one by the other in order to satisfy personal, or even procreative, instincts. We must achieve, particularly in regard to the understanding of the divine, a *love that respects the other as transcendent to the self*, particularly in regard to their understanding of the divine, thus a love that will help both the one and the other to accomplish their own divinity. This would presuppose the creation of a family different from the one we are accustomed to.

The refounding of the family cannot come about without recognition of the natural and spiritual value of sexed identity. Nor can sexed identity remain simply functional, but it must be considered part of our humanity in its corporeal and subjective dimension.

Human beings are a species divided into two genders. *Achieving a relation between the genders that would be different from that of other species could result in the spiritualization of humanity.* One of the founding myths of our tradition reminds us of this in its own way: the loss of the divine results from man's and woman's inability to love each other without wanting to steal God's knowledge, his power. However, rather than redeeming the first 'sin' – our first mistake – we have reinforced it, through forgetting that gender is a crucial dimension of what it means to be human. *Gender has become increasingly inseparable from genealogy,* thus hiding from us the work we must do to find the path from the human to the divine.

This error has been perpetuated within the family itself and more generally within society. Man and woman must help each other progress from the natural to the spiritual, not only within the family unit, but in all relations they maintain with each other. Relations between the sexes must not be reduced to intimacy – often understood as belonging to a natural state – within the family. They must be woven into all areas of civil order, and thus elevate it, through each and every exchange between citizens, from the natural to the spiritual, from the empirical to the transcendental. Any culture constructed on the basis of one sex alone is necessarily partial and unjust. What is more, it reduces individuals to the status of abstract entities subjugated to laws that remain external to them, but which must be obeyed in order to form a collective.

Such a society is not founded on relations among citizens, but rather on individual units subjugated to the authority of a leader, or leaders, who represent and execute the law. This opens the way for all kinds of totalitarian excesses; more importantly, however, the citizens of such a society remain children – of God or of state leaders – rather than accomplish as adults their own becoming, either individual or collective.

The recognition of sexual difference thus means the way for refounding the family, but also a truly democratic culture and politics, where the citizens, without having to delegate this role to elected representatives, manage their relations among themselves in the absence of any kind of subjugation or submission. Democracy cannot be reduced to a ballot paper, as we see from the failures of many regimes where representatives are elected by a majority, and where, without even mentioning the most extreme cases, each new election results in abstentions or blank votes on the part of the voters, and in breaches of democracy on the part of those elected. Let us move to a new phase of democracy – a democracy where the citizens themselves manage their own civil and social relations.

If this were to happen, civil and religious life could partly reconverge. This reconvergence would not, however, be dependent on pre-established laws, applicable to men and women alike, laws that abolish singularity, and favour various fundamentalisms. The spiritual development of each citizen, male or female, is then cultivated with respect for differences; this individual progress will gradually spiritualize society through multiple, at each time dual, relations.

Our relations between the two have been limited to the man-God relationship; we have not sufficiently cultivated them *between us.* The relationship with the other, him or her, cannot be cultivated as a living and present relation if it is mediated by enacted law, or by established power. What is most spiritual and religious in human beings is thereby neglected and even lost. The totality of the social fabric should consist of dual relations at different levels, none of which permit the abolition of human relationships with the other as such. Religious behaviour – at least in our times – should begin to exist there, and not with the constitution of groups, families, or peoples. None of these, in any case, should ever interfere with the respect for the other as other. Which actually does occur within many religious traditions, not to mention what happens in relationships between subjects who come from different traditions.

Mysticism and Rationality

None of this implies that religion should be based on purely individual intuition or beliefs. Insistence on the importance of the relations with the other as other, and on the two relationships, works to dismantle individualisms rather than reinforce them. Within a group founded on a plurality of individuals governed by a leader, retreat into the self is common. Vertical submission to representative authority encourages this, as does the paucity of guidelines regulating horizontal relations between units within the group. Since, in a community based on relationships between persons, the accent would be on respect for difference(s), singularities would be protected, and individualistic withdrawal minimized.

The relationship between the sexes clearly represents the most universal as well as the most radical site of this relation to the other. It can thus be of use for ethical and religious integration into community life. This then becomes relational in its base, and independently of codes used to assimilate subjects to one sociological order.

The living relation to the other always comprises its share of mystery. This is particularly true with respect to sexual difference, or it should be. The mystery – here also horizontal, rather than located in the vertical relation between a man and his God – permits women and men to go along their own spiritual path; it also permits the truly spiritual, and not merely formal evolution of their relation. The word 'mystery' is used differently here from the way we are accustomed to using it, no doubt. We are not talking about a magical reality, a secret guaranteed by a system of rites performed exclusively by the initiated. It is rather a question of *maintaining free energy, resistant to encoding or any appropriation.*

'Mystery' would then seem to mean the opposite of what it usually means, at least in part. Keeping energy free is a gesture very different from bending it in a way incomprehensible to the faithful. In this case, they have no choice but to believe what the authorities tell them to believe, and act accordingly. In the other, accepting that within us, and within each person we meet, some part of lived experience will remain incomprehensible, *inaccessible to affect or to thought*, strange, and even foreign, means that there is a mystery that we have to respect. Respect for the mystery lies in not attempting to understand, or to encode, everything; in not blindly letting authorities presumed to know, and not only in a formal way, in not sacrificing the mystery, in our relation to ourselves and to the other, to the mystery of some Absolute we read about in texts and in commentaries, but have never experienced.

Respect for the mystery in our relation to the other does not for all that mean opposition to respect for another kind of mystery. On the contrary, this gesture represents a progressive approach towards a relationship with that which we can neither know nor appropriate. As we constantly and voluntarily assume behaviour whose meaning we understand, we become progressively more capable of truly to be entitled to legislate about mystery; co-existing with the inaccessible, instead of considering it preferable to be able to know all and master all. Within ourselves a space is created welcoming mystery and difference, thus modifying our energy, but not forcing it into compartments or into sharply defined and paralysing forms that prevents us from actively and consciously transforming that energy by ourselves.

Mystery – or mysticism – no longer signifies a blind and solitary advance into what looks like the irrational. Reason itself inspires us to recognize that the other is irreducible to ourselves, that the other must remain a mystery to us if we are to respect him or her as other. The traditional opposition between darkness and light gives way to the discovery that a certain manner of conceiving the light in our tradition has prevented us from perceiving another light, the light that emanates from the other but that we cannot understand. *Renouncing possession of the other becomes not just a simple ascetic privation, but the means of achieving a kind of relation we do not yet know, one that is more religious and at the same time more likely to attain beatitude in the here and now.* A beatitude not granted to those who make the way alone, but rather to those who try to share the way with the other, in the respect for different identities and journeys.

Certain men and women suffer when accepting neither to be master of, nor to seize hold of the other, nor to reduce the other to the status of a possession, or even of a being they cannot make their own. This pain becomes even more intolerable when we persist in our belief in a rationality where the intelligible, in the guise of light, must overcome the sensible, in the guise of darkness. If we can believe in the existence of another rationality, better adapted to humanity, less hierarchical, more capable also of *cultivating the highest human value – that is, the relation between us* – it can help us to avoid suffering when we coexist with that which – still today at any rate – we experience as unknowable. Taking another path, using another method, in the approach of the other – and of ourselves as being in relation – would seem necessary in order for us to succeed in relations that have been too often neglected in our culture.

It goes without saying that this does not mean we should feel a persistent blind faith in each and every other that comes our way, making him or her into the potential source of our existence. What we must rather do is have confidence in the other, and find out, through experience, how far we can travel together. Although the other must be respected absolutely as other, that does not mean we should consider him or her as the absolute we seek. What we have to envision as absolute is *the perfection of the relation.* There are different levels of co-existence with the other, particularly the other gender. That is where the mystery is most opaque, and also where the possibilities for commitment are most diversified, while we respect the mystery and the irreducibility of the other.

Before any relation to God, the relation to the other includes *a negative pathway, a nocturnal approach.* Conceptual intelligence is of little use when taking this path. Sense perception will sometimes be more useful, provided we continue to respect the invisible in the other, this portion of night that guarantees the other's alterity and freedom. Provided also that the duality of the subjects is maintained, while avoiding the division of one and the same act into two poles:

touching-touched, seeing-seen, listening-listened to, etc. Certain of the senses, neglected in our culture, should be educated – touch and being touched, especially at a distance; and listening while remaining attentive to a silence where the other as such, as a mystery, can be revealed and can happen the unexpected event of an encounter with him, or her.

In Conclusion

It may seem utopian to propose a more demanding spiritual evolution, when spiritual development as currently defined has not yet been achieved. There are at least two reasons that force me to do so, however.

The problems of our times call for appropriate solutions. Globalization requires consideration for the differences among cultures, and the search for a fecund co-existence in respect for their respective paths. Advances in the emancipation and liberation of women require that we rework the relationship between nature and culture, and seek for ways we can best symbolize the articulation between them for each sex, and for the public and private alliance between them. This requirement is more radically and universally in line with the respect for what is called the 'human rights' than a more or less paternalistic tolerance towards other races and other generations. Advances of sciences and philosophical thought require that expression of religious truths and ethical codes evolve; when they do not, they risk being outdated, thus leaving the way open for theoretical and practical behaviours that are more and more inhuman. The use of technology and the authority it has acquired over the definition of individuals and of communities require that we develop relational behaviours between subjects, alone are capable of ensuring the survival and the evolution of the human as such. The same is true for the growing power of the media, which could henceforth gather citizens together by means of a truth-opinion they take part in without taking charge of, and without inventing the means of exchange among them. Financial imperialism, for its part, creates a proliferation of hierarchies of haves and have-nots where the values of being and of becoming human are not taken into account; reinforcing real relations among human beings is required to counteract this.

Many other reasons linked to the needs of our times could be mentioned. There is, however, another motive for new ethical and religious proposals. If *the laws and commandments,* either religious or more strictly civil, that have been established up until now are not respected, it is perhaps because they *do not appeal to the men and women who we actually are, and do not make us really responsible.* They treat us too much like children constrained to obey a master or masters, and not as adults in charge of their own existence, and of that of the community and the world, for the present and for the future.

Awareness of what we are and of the task incumbent upon us as human beings, men and women, can awaken or reawaken our consciences, not to the established order, but to an order yet to be invented, and respected by us: in relation to ourselves, to the other and to others, and to the world.

Might this not correspond to what Judaeo-Christianity designates as the third age of the salvation of humanity: the time of the spirit? That is an advent, in us and between us, which would render us divine, and ensure transitions between this tradition and other traditions, by favouring the breath, the universal principle of natural and spiritual life.

83

Alain Badiou

Deleuze: The Clamor of Being (2000)

Univocity of Being and Multiplicity of Names

OUR EPOCH CAN BE SAID TO HAVE BEEN STAMPED AND signed, in philosophy, by the return of the question of Being. This is why it is dominated by Heidegger. He drew up the diagnosis and explicitly took as his subject the realignment, after a century of Criticism and the phenomenological interlude, of thought with its primordial interrogation: what is to be understood by the being of beings? When all is said and done, there is little doubt that the century has been ontological, and that this destiny is far more essential than the "linguistic turn" with which it has been credited. This turn amounts to making language, its structures, and its resources the transcendental of every investigation of the faculty of knowledge, and to the setting up of philosophy as either a generalized grammar or a weak logic. But when we read Wittgenstein, who is the only really great thinker of this turn, we realize that the moment of the most rigorous conceptual tension in the *Tractatus* is when an altogether remarkable ontological base — the theory of eternal objects—has been secured. We also realize that the last word belongs to a silent supracognitive, or mystical, intuition that lies beyond the logical structures to which cognitive propositions are confined and that alone opens us to the question that matters: what ought I to do? If it is true that the limits of the world are exactly the limits of language, the result is that whatever decides the fate of thought, which exceeds the limits of the world, exceeds equally those of language. This implies that, although the validity (or the sense) of scientific propositions (propositions bearing on the representations of such or such a part of the world) can only be assured by the means of the analytic of language (this is the critical residue), it is nevertheless beyond this analytic that thought accords with its highest power, which is that of interrogating the *value* of the world itself. In Wittgenstein, language is undermined by the question concerning Being—if not regarding its uses, at least regarding its *finality*.

In this sense, Deleuze belongs absolutely to this century. His thought can no more be attached to the analytic current, whose grammatical or logicizing reductions he abhors, than it can be to the phenomenological current, which he severely criticizes for its reduction of living actualizations to simple intentional correlations of consciousness.

The question posed by Deleuze is the question of Being. From beginning to end, and under the constraint of innumerable and fortuitous cases, his work is concerned with thinking thought (its act, its movement) on the basis of an ontological precomprehension of Being as One.

It is impossible to overemphasize this point, consistently occulted by critical or phenomenological interpretations of his work: Deleuze purely and simply identifies philosophy with ontology. One misses everything if one disregards such explicit declarations as "Philosophy merges with ontology" (*The Logic of Sense*, 179), or "from Parmenides to Heidegger it is the same voice which is taken up. . . . A single voice raises the clamour of being" (*Difference and Repetition*, 35). The historical unifier of philosophy, as the voice of thought, as the clamor of the utterable, is Being itself. From this point of view, Deleuze's philosophy is in no way a critical philosophy. Not only is it possible to think Being, but there is thought only insofar as Being simultaneously formulates and pronounces itself therein. Certainly, thought is difference and identification of differences; it always consists in conceiving of "several formally distinct senses" (ibid.). The thinking impulsion manifests itself as a vital power in plurality (the plurality of senses, of cases); yet Deleuze immediately adds that it is not the formal distinction of the multiple that is important for thought. What is important is that all the senses, all the cases, "refer to . . . a single designated entity, ontologically one" (ibid.). In this sense, *every* philosophical proposition is what Deleuze calls "the ontological proposition" (ibid.), which recapitulates a maximal conviction regarding the resource of being that belongs to speech and thought. Parmenides maintained that Being and thought were one and the same thing. The Deleuzian variant of this maxim is: "it is the same thing which occurs and is said" (*The Logic of Sense,* 180). Or, yet again: "Univocal being inheres in language and happens to things; it measures the internal relation of language with the external relation of being" (ibid.; translation modified). How very Greek this confidence in Being as the measure of relations, both internal and external, is! And how very indifferent to the "linguistic turn" this ontological coemergence of sentences and what-occurs under the rule of the One is!

Under these conditions, how does Deleuze differ from Heidegger—other, of course, than the evident difference between the prophetic, pathetic, professorial style of the German and the alert sinuousness, the discontinuous scintillation, of the Frenchman? This is an extremely complex question: for my part, I would maintain that Deleuze is, on a number of critical points (difference, the open, time . . .), less distant from Heidegger than is usually believed and than he no doubt believed himself to be. In restricting ourselves to explicit distinctions, we can state that, for Deleuze, Heidegger is still and always too phenomenological. What should we understand by this?

Heidegger's Limit

"Vulgar" phenomenology's initial premise is that consciousness "is directed towards the thing and gains significance in the world" (*Foucault*, 108). This is what phenomenology names intentionality. That the thinking of thought (philosophy's unique objective) could start from such a signifying directedness is repugnant to Deleuze for two convergent reasons.

First, consciousness can in no way constitute the immediate starting point for an investigation of thought. Indeed, we know that one begins to think only under a constraint and according to a force, in an ascetic exposure to the impersonal imperative of the outside. Under these conditions, it is not at all in consciousness that thought has its source. In fact, to begin to think, it is necessary to turn away from consciousness, "to become unconscious," one might say. As Deleuze puts it, drawing on Marx, "While it is the nature of consciousness to be false, problems by their nature escape consciousness" (*Difference and Repetition*, 208).

Second, and above all, thought is presented by intentionality as dependent on an internalized relation: between consciousness and its object, ideation and the ideatum, the noetic pole and the noematic pole, or, in the Sartrean variant, the for-itself and the in-itself. Yet, precisely because thought is the deployment of the Being-One, its element is never of the order of an internalized relation, representation, or consciousness-of. Thought presupposes that the multiple modalities of Being are mutually external and that no modality can have the privilege (as consciousness claims to have) of internalizing the others. It is the equality of Being that is at stake here, and this equality implies, without any paradox whatsoever, that nothing of what is ever has the slightest *internal* relation to anything else. One can even affirm that the absolute respect of Being as One in fact demands that each of its immanent actualizations is in a state of nonrelation with all the others. Deleuze, under the name of Foucault (or under the constraint of the case-Foucault), indicates, therefore, that seeing and speaking, things and words, constitute registers of being (of thought) that are entirely disjointed: "we do not see what we speak about, nor do we speak about what we see" (*Foucault*, 109); the result being that "knowledge is irreducibly double, since it involves speaking and seeing, language and light, which is the reason why there is no intentionality" (ibid.).

Does this not contradict what we recalled earlier—namely, that it is the same thing that occurs and that is said? Not at all. It is exactly because it is the same Being that occurs and that is said that there is no intentional relation *between* things and words—those actualizations of the Same. For were such a relation to exist, there would be an inequality between the active pole (the directedness, the nomination) and the passive pole (the object, the thing said). However, Being "occurs" in the same way in all its modalities—in the visible and language, for example (one could cite others). Thus, in assuming that there is an intentional relation between nomination and the thing, or between consciousness and the object, one necessarily breaks with the expressive sovereignty of the One. Were the objection to be made that these modalities are at least minimally "related" to each other insofar as they are all modalities of the One, one need but reply that the essence of this relation is the nonrelation, for its only content is the neutral equality of the One. And it is, doubtlessly, in the exercise of this nonrelation that thought "relates" most faithfully to the Being that constitutes it. This is what Deleuze calls a "disjunctive synthesis": one has to think the nonrelation according to the One, which, founds it by radically separating the terms involved. One has to steadfastly rest within the activity of separation, understood as a power of Being. One has to explain that "the non-relation is still a relation, and even a relation of a deeper sort" (ibid., 63; translation modified), insofar as it is thought in accordance with the divergent or disjoining movement that, incessantly separating, testifies to the infinite and egalitarian fecundity of the One. But this disjunctive synthesis is the ruin of intentionality.

We can thus clearly state that what Deleuze considered as Heidegger's limit is that his apparent criticism of intentionality in favor of a hermeneutic of Being stops halfway, for it does not attain the radicalness of the disjunctive synthesis. It retains the motif of the relation, even if in sophisticated form.

Certainly, Deleuze acknowledges that Heidegger's move merits esteem: there is a "surpassing of intentionality . . . towards Being" (ibid., 110), just as the consciousness-object (or consciousness-being) relation is subverted by the passage from phenomenology to ontology. And, in keeping with his supposition of the One, Deleuze cannot but approve of the fact that the dissymmetrical couple composed of the reflexive subject and the object, of interiority and exteriority, is replaced by "the unity of the unveiling-veiling" (ibid.).

However, for Deleuze, if Heidegger surpasses intentionality, he simply then goes on to maintain its ontological substratum, consisting of the relation, or community of senses, between the actualized dimensions of Being, in another dimension. It is for this reason, Deleuze declares, that for Heidegger "Light opens up a speaking no less than a seeing, as if signification haunted the visible which in turn murmured meaning" (ibid., 111). The unity of Being is interpreted by Heidegger as a hermeneutic convergence, as an analogical relation that can be deciphered between the dimensions (in this case, the visible and language) in which it is revealed. He does not see (unlike Foucault) that the consequence of ontological unity is not a harmony or a communication between beings, nor even an "interval in between" where the relation can be thought outside all substantial grounding, but rather the absolute nonrelation or the indifference of the terms involved to all forms of relation. Despite the pathos with which Heidegger talks of distress, his vision of the manner in which Being deploys itself in divergent series remains fundamentally a tranquil one, precisely because of its hermeneutical reference. Despite his apologetics of the Open, he refolds and closes up all the separations, the differentiations without resemblance, and the unresolved divergences that alone *prove* the equality and neutrality of the One. Heidegger, to adopt a Nietzschean expression, is a conniving priest who only seems to subvert intentionality and consciousness in order to all the more subtly stand in the way of the disjunctive synthesis. Ultimately, he remains within phenomenology, in the sense that phenomenology is "too pacifying and has consecrated too many things" (ibid., 113; translation modified).

The real reason for the disparity between Deleuze and Heidegger, within their shared conviction that philosophy rests solely on the question of Being, is the following: for Deleuze, Heidegger does not uphold the fundamental thesis of Being as One *up to its very end*. He does not uphold this because he does not assume the consequences of the *univocity* of Being. Heidegger continually evokes the maxim of Aristotle: "Being is said in various senses," in various categories. It is impossible for Deleuze to consent to this "various."

The Univocity of Being

This brings us to the very core of Deleuze's thought. It is, in fact, entirely reasonable to maintain that the sole function of the immense pedagogy of cases (cinema, the schizo, Foucault, Riemann, *Capital*, Spinoza, the nomad, and so on) is to verify tirelessly—with the inexhaustible genius of variation—this unique sentence: "There has only ever been one ontological proposition: Being is univocal" (*Difference and Repetition,* 35). When Deleuze affirms the identity of philosophy and ontology, he adds in the same sentence that "ontology merges with the univocity of Being" (*The Logic of Sense,* 179).

What is to be understood by this decisive univocity? This is what the whole of the present text wants to elucidate, even if it will probably prove to be insufficient.

Let us adopt an external viewpoint. The thesis of the univocity of Being guides Deleuze's entire relation to the history of philosophy. His companions, his references, his preferred cases-of-thought are indeed found in those who have explicitly maintained that being has "a single voice": Duns Scotus, who is perhaps the most radical ("There has only ever been one ontology, that of Duns Scotus"; *Difference and Repetition,* 35); the Stoics, who referred their doctrine of the proposition to the contingent coherence of the One-All; Spinoza, obviously, for whom the unity of Substance barred the way to any and all ontological equivocity; Nietzsche, who was to "realize univocity in the form of repetition in the eternal return" (ibid., 304); Bergson, for whom all instances of organic differentiation are the expression, in a single sense, of a local actuality of Creative Evolution. It is therefore possible to "read" historically the thesis of univocity, and this is indeed why Deleuze became the (apparent) historian of certain philosophers: they were cases of the univocity of Being.

This reading allows us to formulate two abstract theses in which this principle is unfolded:

Thesis 1: In the first place, univocity does not signify that being is numerically one, which is an empty assertion. The One is not here the one of identity or of number, and thought has already abdicated if it supposes that there is a single and same Being. The power of the One is much rather that "beings are multiple and different, they are always produced by a disjunctive synthesis, and they themselves are disjointed and divergent, *membra disjoncta*" (*The Logic of Sense,* 179). Nor does univocity mean that thought is tautological (the One is the One). Rather, it is fully compatible with the existence of multiple *forms* of Being. Indeed, it is even in the power of deployment of these multiple forms that the One can be identified: this is true of Spinoza's Substance, which is immediately expressed by an infinity of attributes. But the plurality of forms does not involve any "division within Being or plurality of ontological senses" (*Difference and Repetition,* 303). In other words, it is in a single and same sense that Being is said of all its forms. Or, yet again: the immanent attributes of Being that express its infinite power of One "are *formally* distinct [but] they all remain equal and *ontologically* one" (ibid.). We should note that this thesis already supposes a critical distinction, the importance of which is usually underestimated when one speaks about Deleuze, despite the fact that, conceptually, it alone explains the relation (qua nonrelation) between the multiple and the one: the distinction of the formal and the real. The multiple acceptations of being must be understood as a multiple that is formal, while the One alone is real, and only the real supports the distribution of sense (which is unique).

Thesis 2: In each form of Being, there are to be found "individuating differences" that may well be named beings. But these differences, these beings, never have the fixedness or the power of distribution and classification that may be attributed, for example, to species or generalities, or even individuals, if we understand by "individual" something that can be thought under a species, a generality, or a type. For Deleuze, beings are local degrees of intensity or inflections of power that are in constant movement and entirely singular. And as power is but a name of Being, beings are only expressive modalities of the One. From this it follows once again that the numerical distinction between beings "is a modal, not a real, distinction" (ibid., 304). In other words, it is obvious that we have to recognize that beings are not the same and that they therefore do not have the same sense. We have to admit an equivocity of *that of which* Being is said: its immanent modalities, that is, beings. But this is not what is fundamental for the philosopher. What is fundamental is that Being is the same for all, that it is univocal and that it is thus said of all beings in a single and same sense, such that the multiplicity of senses, the equivocal status of beings, has no real status. For the univocity of Being is not solely, nor even principally, the fact that what is "designated" by the diversity of senses of beings is necessarily the same (the Being-One). Univocity requires that the sense be *ontologically identical* for all the different beings: "In the ontological proposition . . . the sense, too, is ontologically the same for individuating modes, for numerically distinct designators or expressors" (ibid., 35–36; translation modified). Or, yet again: "The univocity of Being signifies . . . that it is said in one and the same 'sense' of everything of which it is said" (*The Logic of Sense,* 179; translation modified).

The price one must pay for inflexibly maintaining the thesis of univocity is clear: given that the multiple (of beings, of significations) is arrayed in the universe by way of a numerical difference that is purely formal as regards the form of being to which it refers (thought, extension, time, etc.) and purely modal as regards its individuation, it follows that, ultimately, this multiple can only be of the order of simulacra. And if one classes — as one should — every difference without a real status, every multiplicity whose ontological status is that of the One, as a simulacrum, then the world of beings is the theater of the simulacra of Being.

Strangely, this consequence has a Platonic, or even Neoplatonic, air to it. It is as though the paradoxical or supereminent One immanently engenders a procession of beings whose univocal sense it distributes, while they refer to its power and have only a semblance of being. But, in this case, what meaning is to be given to the Nietzschean program that Deleuze constantly validates: the overturning of Platonism?

The Multiplicity of Names

This question is explicitly answered by Deleuze: "Consequently, 'to overturn Platonism' means to make the simulacra rise and to affirm their rights" (ibid., 262; translation modified). Deleuzianism is fundamentally a Platonism with a different accentuation. Certainly, it is true that sense is distributed according to the One and that beings are of the order of simulacra. And it is no less certain that the fact of thinking beings as simulacra presupposes that one understands the way (what Plato names "participation") in which the individuating differences are arranged in degrees, which "immediately relate them to univocal Being" (*Difference and Repetition*, 303). But it in no way follows from this, as Deleuze assumes is the case with Plato, that the simulacra or beings are necessarily depreciated or considered as nonbeings. On the contrary, it is necessary to affirm the rights of simulacra as *so many equivocal cases of univocity* that joyously attest to the univocal power of Being. What Deleuze believes he adds to Plato here, and that, in his eyes, subverts or overturns the latter, is that it is futile to claim that the simulacra are unequal to some supposed model, or that there is a hierarchy in Being that would subordinate the simulacra to real archetypes. Here again, Deleuze suspects Plato of not firmly upholding the thesis of ontological univocity. If Being is said in one and the same sense of everything of which it is said, then beings are all identically simulacra and all affirm, by an inflection of intensity whose difference is purely formal or modal, the living power of the One. Once again, it is the disjunctive synthesis that is opposed to Plato: beings are merely disjointed, divergent simulacra that lack any internal relation between themselves or with any transcendent Idea whatsoever. Conceived as the immanent production of the One, the world is thus, in the same way as for Plato, a work and not a state. It is demiurgic. But the "non-hierarchized work is a condensation of coexistences and a simultaneity of events" (*The Logic of Sense*, 262). One does far more justice to the real One by thinking the egalitarian coexistence of simulacra in a positive way than by opposing simulacra to the real that they lack, in the way Plato opposes the sensible and the intelligible. For, in fact, this real lies nowhere else than *in that which founds the nature of the simulacrum as simulacrum:* the purely formal or modal character of the difference that constitutes it, from the viewpoint of the univocal real of Being that supports this difference within itself and distributes to it a single sense.

I am not sure that Plato is so far from this view of beings, even sensible beings, as immanent differentiations of the intelligible and as positivities of the simulacrum. One is struck by the way that Socrates' interlocutors ironically punctuate the transcendence of the Good in the *Republic,* and even more by the way, in the *Parmenides,* that the definition of the status as such of the One only proves capable of unraveling its relation with the others-than-the-One within a register of paradox and impasse. The only way of extricating oneself from such chicanery is to propose a status of pure event for the One, and at that moment one is in attunement with Deleuze when he writes: "Only the free man, therefore, can comprehend all violence in a single act of violence, and every mortal event *in a single Event*" (ibid., 152). One wonders whether this Event with a capital "E" might not be Deleuze's Good. In light of the way it requires and founds the temperament of "the free man," this would seem probable.

But, even in supposing that the glorification of simulacra as a positive dimension of the univocity of Being constitutes an overturning of Platonism, the fact remains that, in the same way as for Plato (with all the chicanery of the Idea, of the Good that "is not an Idea," of the Beautiful that is the Good but cannot be confused with it, of the Other which requires that the transcendent unity of the Good be sacrificed, of the One that can neither be nor not be, etc.), Deleuze's approach has to confront the thorny question of the names of Being. What, indeed, could be the appropriate name for that which is univocal? Is the nomination of the univocal itself univocal? And if Being is said in a single sense, how is the sense of this "single sense" to be determined? Or, yet again: is it possible to experiment, to test whether a name of Being makes sense of univocal sense?

Deleuze begins with an uncontroversial declaration: "We can conceive that names or propositions do not have the same sense even while they designate exactly the same thing. . . . The distinction between these senses is indeed a real distinction (*distinctio realis*), but there is nothing numerical—much less ontological—about it; it is a formal, qualitative or semiological distinction" (*Difference and Repetition,* 35). However, when it is a question of Being, we cannot content ourselves with a formal distinction between the senses of names, for the essential property of Being is precisely not its numerical identity, to which different nominal unities— each with its own sense—could refer, but its being said in a single sense of everything of which it is said. In an inevitably paradoxical way, the question of the name of Being persists.

With the exception of "Being," which is not a "name" and which, moreover, Deleuze only uses in a preliminary and limited manner, we can only experiment with the values of names. This means that in a considerable part of his work, Deleuze adopts a procedure that, starting from the constraint exercised by a particular case-of-thought—it does not matter whether this concerns Foucault or Sacher-Masoch—consists in trying out a name of Being and in constructing a protocol of thought (that is to be as automatic as possible) by which the pertinence of this name can be evaluated with respect to the essential property that one expects it to preserve (or even to reinforce within thought): namely, univocity.

What emerges over the course of these experiments is that a single name is never sufficient, but that two are required. Why? The reason is that Being needs to be said in a single sense both from the viewpoint of the unity of its power and from the viewpoint of the multiplicity of the divergent simulacra that this power actualizes in itself. Ontologically, a real distinction is no more involved here than, in Spinoza, between *natura naturans* and *natura naturata*. Yet, a binary distribution of names is necessary; it is as though the univocity of being is thereby accentuated for thought through its being said, at one moment, in its immediate "matter," and, in the next, in its forms or actualizations. In short: in order to say that there is a single sense, two names are necessary.

This problem is constant from Plato (who preliminarily distinguishes the sensible and the intelligible, but as a way of attaining the One) to Heidegger (who marks the difference between being and beings, but as a way of attaining the *destining* or the *Ereignis)*. What is particular to Deleuze is that, in conformity with his experimental style of testing concepts under the constraint of cases that vary as much as possible, he proposes a fairly wide array of paired concepts so as to determine the nomination of Being as an interval or nominal interface. It would be false, however, to state that there are as many pairs of names as there are cases. An exhaustive inventory would show that the thesis of univocity is said in ten or so fundamental pairs at most. Compared, however, with the great philosophies recognized by the tradition, this still amounts to a lot. In part, Deleuze's genius—but also the misinterpretations that his philosophy is open to (as a thought of the anarchic multiple of desires, etc.)—is linked to this multiplicity of names of Being, which is itself correlative with the unprecedented determination with which he upholds the ontological thesis of univocity and the fictive character of the multiple. For it is by the experimentation with as many nominal doublets as is necessary that the verification, under constraint, of the absolute unity of sense is wrought.

After a preliminary exposition of Deleuze's constructive method, I will go on to examine, in the following chapters, what I consider the principal doublets: the virtual and the actual (doctrine of the event); time and truth (doctrine of knowledge); chance and the eternal return (doctrine of action); the fold and the outside (doctrine of the subject).

Throughout these different stages, I will be concerned with establishing that, whatever the names that might be involved, and given that sense has always already been distributed by Being, Deleuze considers it necessary to entrust oneself to pure affirmation and to take up a stance, in renouncing the simulacrum of oneself, where sense can choose and transfix us, by a gesture unknown to ourselves: "thinking is a throw of the dice" (*Foucault,* 117; translation modified).

84

Jacques Rancière

The Janus-Face of Politicized Art (2003)

Interview with Gabriel Rockhill

Historical and Hermeneutic Methodology

– I would like to begin with a question concerning methodology. On several occasions, you call into question the symptomatology that attempts to unveil the truth hidden behind the obscure surface of appearances, whether it is Althusser's science, Freud's etiology, or the social sciences in general. In your own research on the distributions of the sensible that underlie historical configurations of art and politics, how do you avoid this logic of the hidden and the apparent? How would you describe your own historical and hermeneutic methodology if 'there is no science [. . .] but of the hidden'?[1]

– 'There is no science [. . .] but of the hidden' is a phrase by Bachelard that had been taken up by the Althusserians. Thus, it was an ironic quotation *against* the vision that presupposes the necessity of finding or constructing the hidden. It was an ironic quotation directed at Althusser's philosophy as well as at Bourdieu's sociology or the history of the *Annales* School. I by no means think, for my part, that there is no science but of the hidden. I always try to think in terms of horizontal distributions, combinations between systems of possibilities, not in terms of surface and substratum. Where one searches for the hidden beneath the apparent, a position of mastery is established. I have tried to conceive of a topography that does not presuppose this position of mastery. It is possible, from any given point, to try to reconstruct the conceptual network that makes it possible to conceive of a statement, that causes a painting or a piece of music to make an impression, that causes reality to appear transformable or inalterable. This is in a way the main theme of my research. I do not mean by that that it is a principle or a starting point. I began, myself as well, from the stereotyped vision of science as a search for the hidden. Then I constructed, little by little, an egalitarian or anarchist theoretical position that does not presuppose this vertical relationship of top to bottom.

– Does that mean that the regimes of art are not transcendental conditions of possibility for history in the sense of Foucault, but rather conditions of probability that are immanent in history?

– I try not to think about this in terms of the philosophy of history. As for the term *transcendental*, it is necessary to see what this word can mean. The transcendental is something like a reduction of the transcendent that can either bring the transcendent back into the immanent or, on the contrary, make the immanent take flight once again into the transcendent. I would say that my approach is a bit similar to Foucault's. It retains the principle from the Kantian transcendental that replaces the dogmatism of truth with the search for conditions of possibility. At the same time, these conditions are not conditions for thought in general, but rather conditions immanent in a particular system of thought, a particular system of expression. I differ from Foucault insofar as his archaeology seems to me to follow a schema of historical necessity according to which, beyond a certain chasm, something is no longer thinkable, can no longer be formulated. The visibility of a form of expression as an artistic form depends on a historically constituted regime of perception and intelligibility. This does not mean that it becomes invisible with the emergence of a new regime. I thus try at one and the same to historicize the transcendental and to de-historicize these systems of conditions of possibility. Statements or forms of expression undoubtedly depend on historically constituted systems of possibilities that determine forms of visibility or criteria of evaluation, but this does not mean that we jump from one system to another in such a way that the possibility of the new system coincides with the impossibility of the former system. In this way, the aesthetic regime of art, for example, is a system of possibilities that is historically constituted but that does not abolish the representative regime, which was previously dominant. At a given point in time, several regimes coexist and intermingle in the works themselves.

Universality, Historicity, Equality

– Your claim concerning the universal status of political equality seems to contradict the generalized historicism that characterizes your reflection on aesthetics. However, the 'only universal' is not based on an a priori *foundation, and it is properly speaking a polemical universal that is only actualized in spaces of dispute. Is universality therefore always dependent on a historical implementation? Is it, so to speak, historicized in turn? Or is there a transcendental point that escapes history?*

– There are two questions in your question. First of all, is it a contradiction to emphasize, on the one hand, a political universal and, on the other hand, the historicity of regimes for the identification of art? I do not think so. Both of these approaches refer back to the same rational core, which is the critique of those forms of discourse that in fact play a double game by using general ahistorical concepts of art and politics, while at the same time linking both of them to historical destinies by declaring our epoch to be the age of the 'end' of art or politics. What

I intend to show in both cases is that *art* and *politics* are contingent notions. The fact that there are always forms of power does not mean that there is always such a thing as politics, and the fact that there is music or sculpture in a society does not mean that art is constituted as an independent category. From this perspective, I chose two different forms of argumentation. For the former, I showed that politics was not tied to a determined historical project, as it is declared to be by those who identify its end with the end of the project of emancipation begun by the French Revolution. Politics exists when the figure of a specific subject is constituted, a supernumerary subject in relation to the calculated number of groups, places, and functions in a society. This is summed up in the concept of the *dēmos*. Of course, this does not prevent there from being historical forms of politics, and it does not exclude the fact that the forms of political subjectivization that make up modern democracy are of an entirely different complexity than the people in Greek democratic cities.

Concerning art, it seemed necessary to me to emphasize the existence of historical regimes of identification in order to dismiss, at one and the same time, the false obviousness of art's eternal existence and the confused images of artistic 'modernity' in terms of a 'critique of representation'. I evoked the fact that art in the singular has only existed for two centuries and that this existence in the singular meant the upheaval of the coordinates through which the 'fine arts' had been located up to then as well as the disruption of the norms of fabrication and assessment that these coordinates presupposed. I showed that if the properties of each one of these regimes of identification was studied, it was possible to dissipate quite a lot of the haze surrounding the idea of a 'modern project' of art and its completion or failure. This was done, for example, by showing that phenomena considered to be part of a postmodern rupture (such as the mixture of the arts or the combination of mediums) actually fall within the possibilities inherent in the aesthetic regime of art. In both cases, it is a matter of setting a singularized universal against an undetermined universal and contrasting one form of historicizing (in terms of contingent regimes organizing a field of possibilities) with another form of historicizing (in terms of teleology).

The second question concerns the universal and its historicity. My thesis is indeed that the political universal only takes effect in a singularized form. It is distinguished, in this way, from the State universal conceived of as what makes a community out of a multiplicity of individuals. Equality is what I have called a presupposition. It is not, let it be understood, a founding ontological principle but a condition that only functions when it is put into action. Consequently, politics is not based on equality in the sense that others try to base it on some general human predisposition such as language or fear. Equality is actually the condition required for being able to think politics. However, equality is not, to begin with, political in itself. It takes effect in lots of circumstances that have nothing political about them (in the simple fact, for example, that two interlocutors can understand one another). Secondly, equality only generates politics when it is implemented in the specific form of a particular case of dissensus.

– Is this actualization of equality also to be found in aesthetics, and more specifically in what you call democratic writing? Is it the same universal presupposition that is at work?

– I do not set down equality as a kind of transcendental governing every sphere of activity, and thus art in particular. That said, art as we know it in the aesthetic regime is the implementation of certain equality. It is based on the destruction of the hierarchical system of the fine arts. This does not mean, however, that equality in general, political equality, and aesthetic equality are all equivalent. Literature's general condition as a modern form of the art of writing is what I have called, by rerouting the Platonic critique, the democracy of the written word. However, the democracy of the written word is not yet democracy as a political form. And literary equality is not simply the equality of the written word; it is a certain way in which equality can function that can tend to distance it from any form of political equality. To state it very crudely, literature was formed in the nineteenth century by establishing its own proper equality. Flaubert's equality of style is thus at once an implementation of the democracy of the written word and its refutation. Moreover, this equality of style aims at revealing an immanent equality, a passive equality of all things that stands in obvious contrast with the political subjectivization of equality in all its forms.

– What then are the heuristic advantages of the notion of equality for explaining the major changes between 'classical art' and 'modern art'? Why do you propose the notion of equality for thinking through the specificity of the aesthetic regime of the arts instead of accepting all of the preconceived opinions on the destiny of modern art: the transition from the representative to the non-representative, the realization of the autonomy of the aesthetic sphere, art's intransitive tum, etc.?

– Once again, I am not proposing equality as a conceptual category for art, but I think that the notion of aesthetic equality allows us to rethink certain incoherent categories integral to what is called artistic 'modernity'. Let's take intransitivity for example. Intransitivity is supposed to mean that writers will henceforth deal with language instead of telling a story, or that painters will distribute fields of colour instead of painting warhorses or naked women (Maurice Denis). However, this supposed dismissal of subject matter first presupposes the establishment of a regime of equality regarding subject matter. This is what 'representation' was in the first place, not resemblance as some appear to believe, but the existence of necessary connections between a type of subject matter and a form of expression. This is how the hierarchy of genres functioned in poetry or painting.[2] 'Intransitive' literature or painting means first of all a form of literature or painting freed from the systems of expression that make a particular sort of language, a particular kind of composition, or possibly a particular type of colour appropriate for the nobility or banality of a specific subject matter. The concept of intransitivity does not allow us to understand this. It is clear that this concept does not work in literature. In a way, literature always says something. It simply says it in modes that are set off from a certain standard idea of a message. Some have attempted to contrast literary intransitivity with communication, but the language of literature can be as transparent as the language of communication. What functions differently is the relationship between saying and meaning. This is where a dividing line becomes visible, which coincides with the implementation of another form of equality, not the equality of communicators but the equality of the communicated. Likewise, for abstract painting to appear, it is first necessary that the subject matter of painting be considered a matter of indifference. This began with the idea that painting a cook with her kitchen utensils was as noble as painting a general on a battlefield. In literature, it began with the idea that it was not necessary to adopt a particular style to write about nobles, bourgeois, peasants, princes, or valets. The equality of subject matter and the indifference regarding modes of expression is prior to the possibility of abandoning all subject matter for abstraction. The former is the condition of the latter.

I am not looking to establish a way of thinking modern art on the basis of equality. I try to show that there are several kinds of equality at play, that literary equality is not the same thing as democratic equality or the universal exchangeability of commodities.

– *Regarding the different forms of equality, how do you distinguish writing, criticized by Plato as an orphan letter that freely circulates without knowing who it should address, and the indifferent flow of capital? More specifically, how do you distinguish, in the nineteenth century, between the literary equality that you pinpoint in an author like Flaubert and the equality of exchange?*

– The equality of the written word is not the same thing as the equality of exchange. The democracy of the written word does not come down to the arbitrary nature of signs. When Plato criticizes the availability of the written word, he calls into question a form of unsupervised appropriation of language that leads to the corruption of legitimacy. The circulation of the written word destroys the principle of legitimacy that would have the circulation of language be such that it leaves the proper transmitter and goes to the proper receiver by the proper channel. 'Proper' language is guaranteed by a proper distribution of bodies. The written word opens up a space of random appropriation, establishes a principle of untamed difference that is altogether unlike the universal exchangeability of commodities. To put it very crudely, you cannot lay your hands on capital like you can lay your hands on the written word. The play of language without hierarchy that violates an order based on the hierarchy of language is something completely different than the simple fact that a euro is worth a euro and that two commodities that are worth a euro are equivalent to one another. It is a matter of knowing if absolutely anyone can take over and redirect the power invested in language. This presupposes a modification in the relationship between the circulation of language and the social distribution of bodies, which is not at all at play in simple monetary exchange.

An idea of democracy has been constructed according to which democracy would be the simple system of indifference where one vote is equal to another just as a cent is worth a cent, and where the 'equality of conditions' would be equal to monetary equivalence. From this perspective, it is possible to posit literary indifference, Flaubert's indifference of style for example, as analogous to democratic and commercial indifference. However, I think that it is precisely at this point that it is necessary to bring the differences back into play. There is not an analogy but a conflict between forms of equality, which itself functions at several levels in literature. Let's take *Madame Bovary* as an example. On the one hand, the absolutization of style corresponds to a principle of democratic equality. The adultery committed by a farmer's daughter is as interesting as the heroic actions of great men. Moreover, at a time when nearly everyone knows how to read, almost anyone has access, as a result of the egalitarian circulation of writing, to the fictitious life of Emma Bovary and can make it their own. Consequently, there is a veritable harmony between the random circulation of the written word and a certain literary absolute. On the other hand, however, Flaubert constructs his literary equality in opposition to the random circulation of the written word and to the type of 'aesthetic' equality it produces. At the heart of *Madame Bovary* there is a struggle between two forms of equality. In one sense, Emma Bovary is the heroine of a certain aesthetic democracy. She wants to bring art into her life, both into her love life and into the décor of her house. The novel is constructed as a constant polemic against a farm girl's desire to bring art into life. It contrasts 'art in life' (this will later be called the aestheticization of daily life) with a form of art that is in books and only in books.

Nonetheless, neither art in books nor art in life is synonymous with democracy as a form for constructing dissensus over 'the given' of public life. Neither the former nor the latter, moreover, is equivalent to the indifference inherent in the reign of commodities and the reign of money. Flaubert constructs a literary indifference that maintains a distance from any political subjectivization. He asserts a molecular equality of affects that stands in opposition to the molar equality of subjects constructing a democratic political scene. This is summed up in the phrase where he says he is less interested in someone dressed in rags than in the lice that are feeding on him, less interested in social inequality than in molecular equality. He constructs his book as an implementation of the microscopic equality that makes each sentence equal to another – not in length but in intensity – and that makes each sentence, in the end, equal to the entire book. He constructs this equality in opposition to several other kinds of equality: commercial equality, democratic political equality, or equality as a lifestyle such as the equality his heroine tries to put into practice.

Notes

1   See Jacques Rancière, *The Names of History: On the Poetics of Knowledge*, tr. Hassan Melehy (Minneapolis: University of Minnesota Press, 1994), 52; *Les Mots de l'histoire* (Paris: Éditions du Seuil, 1992), 109. Translation slightly modified by Gabriel Rockhill.

2   Rancière uses the word "poem" (*le poème*) in reference to the Greek term *poiēma*, which means "anything made or done" as well as "a piece of craftsmanship," "a poetic work," or "an act or deed." Rancière uses the term "poetry" to refer to the Greek term *poiēsis*, which means "the art of poetry" or "a poem" as well as "a making, a forming, a creating." He also sometimes prefers "the stage" (*la scène*) over "theatre" or "drama" (*le théâtre*), undoubtedly in order to emphasize the public aspect of theatrical performances on the *skēnē*.

85

Charles Taylor

A Secular Age (2007)

I HAVE BEEN STRUGGLING ABOVE WITH THE TERM "SECULAR," or "secularity." It seems obvious before you start thinking about it, but as soon as you do, all sorts of problems arise. I tried to conjure some of these by distinguishing three senses in which I will use the term. This by no means gets rid of all problems, but it may be enough to allow for some progress in my enquiry.

But all three modes of secularity make reference to "religion": as that which is retreating in public space (1), or as a type of belief and practice which is or is not in regression (2), and as a certain kind of belief or commitment whose conditions in this age are being examined (3). But what is "religion"? This famously defies definition, largely because the phenomena we are tempted to call religious are so tremendously varied in human life. When we try to think what there is in common between the lives of archaic societies where "religion is everywhere," and the clearly demarcated set of beliefs, practices and institutions which exist under this title in our society, we are facing a hard, perhaps insuperable task.

But if we are prudent (or perhaps cowardly), and reflect that we are trying to understand a set of forms and changes which have arisen in one particular civilization, that of the modern West—or in an earlier incarnation, Latin Christendom—we see to our relief that we don't need to forge a definition which covers everything "religious" in all human societies in all ages. The change which mattered to people in our (North Atlantic, or "Western") civilization, and still matters today, concerning the status of religion in the three dimensions of secularity I identified, is the one I have already started to explore in one of its central facets: we have moved from a world in which the place of fullness was understood as unproblematically outside of or "beyond" human life, to a conflicted age in which this construal is challenged by others which place it (in a wide range of different ways) "within" human life. This is what a lot of the important fights have been about more recently (as against an earlier time when people fought to the death over different readings of the Christian construal).

In other words, a reading of "religion" in terms of the distinction transcendent/immanent is going to serve our purposes here. This is the beauty of the prudent (or cowardly) move I'm proposing here. It is far from being the case that religion in general can be defined in terms of this distinction. One could even argue that marking our particular hard-and-fast distinction here is something which we (Westerners, Latin Christians) alone have done, be it to our intellectual glory or stultification (some of each, I will argue later). You couldn't foist this on Plato, for instance, not because you can't distinguish the Ideas from the things in the flux which "copy" them, but precisely because these changing realities can only be understood through the Ideas. The great invention of the West was that of an immanent order in Nature, whose working could be systematically understood and explained on its own terms, leaving open the question whether this whole order had a deeper significance, and whether, if it did, we should infer a transcendent Creator beyond it. This notion of the "immanent" involved denying—or at least isolating and problematizing—any form of interpenetration between the things of Nature, on one hand, and "the supernatural" on the other, be this understood in terms of the one transcendent God, or of Gods or spirits, or magic forces, or whatever.

So defining religion in terms of the distinction immanent/transcendent is a move tailor-made for our culture. This may be seen as parochial, incestuous, navel-gazing, but I would argue that this is a wise move, since we are trying to understand changes in a culture for which this distinction has become foundational.

So instead of asking whether the source of fullness is seen/lived as within or without, as we did in the above discussion, we could ask whether people recognize something beyond or transcendent to their lives. This is the way the matter is usually put, and I want to adopt it in what follows. I will offer a somewhat fuller account of what I mean by this distinction several chapters down the road, when we come to examine modern theories of secularization. I fully recognize that a word like "transcendent" is very slippery—partly because, as I hinted just now, these distinctions have been constructed or redefined in the very process of modernity and secularization. But I believe that in all its vagueness, it can serve in our context.

But precisely for the reasons that I explored above, I want to supplement the usual account of "religion" in terms of belief in the transcendent, with one more focussed on the sense we have of our practical context. Here is one way of making sense of this.

Every person, and every society, lives with or by some conception(s) of what human flourishing is: what constitutes a fulfilled life? what makes life really worth living? What would we most admire people for? We can't help asking these and related questions in our lives. And our struggles to answer them define the view or views that we try to live by, or between which we haver. At another level, these views are codified, sometimes in philosophical theories, sometimes in moral codes, sometimes in religious practices and devotion. These and the various ill-formulated practices which people around us engage in constitute the resources that our society offers each one of us as we try to lead our lives.

Another way of getting at something like the issue raised above in terms of within/without is to ask: does the highest, the best life involve our seeking, or acknowledging, or serving a good which is beyond, in the sense of independent of human flourishing? In which case, the highest, most real, authentic or adequate human flourishing could include our aiming (also) in our range of final goals at something other than human flourishing. I say "final goals," because even the most self-sufficing humanism has to be concerned with the condition of some non-human things instrumentally, e.g., the condition of the natural environment. The issue is whether they matter also finally.

It's clear that in the Judaeo-Christian religious tradition the answer to this question is affirmative. Loving, worshipping God is the ultimate end. Of course, in this tradition God is seen as willing human flourishing, but devotion to God is not seen as contingent on this. The injunction "Thy will be done" isn't equivalent to "Let humans flourish," even though we know that God wills human flourishing.

This is a very familiar case for us. But there are other ways in which we can be taken beyond ordinary human flourishing. Buddhism is an example. In one way, we could construe the message of the Buddha as telling us how to achieve true happiness, that is, how to avoid suffering, and attain bliss. But it is clear that the understanding of the conditions of bliss is so "revisionist" that it amounts to a departure from what we normally understand as human flourishing. The departure here can be put in terms of a radical change of identity. Normal understandings of flourishing assume a continuing self, its beneficiary, or in the case of its failure the sufferer. The Buddhist doctrine of anatta aims to bring us beyond this illusion. The way to Nirvana involves renouncing, or at least going beyond, all forms of recognizable human flourishing.

In both Buddhism and Christianity, there is something similar in spite of the great difference in doctrine. This is that the believer or devout person is called on to make a profound inner break with the goals of flourishing in their own case; they are called on, that is, to detach themselves from their own flourishing, to the point of the extinction of self in one case, or to that of renunciation of human fulfillment to serve God in the other. The respective patterns are clearly visible in the exemplary figures. The Buddha achieves Enlightenment; Christ consents to a degrading death to follow his father's will.

But can't we just follow the hint above, and reconstrue "true" flourishing as involving renunciation, as Stoicism seems to do, for example? This won't work for Christianity, and I suspect also not for Buddhism. In the Christian case, the very point of renunciation requires that the ordinary flourishing forgone be confirmed as valid. Unless living the full span were a good, Christ's giving of himself to death couldn't have the meaning it does. In this it is utterly different from Socrates' death, which the latter portrays as leaving this condition for a better one. Here we see the unbridgeable gulf between Christianity and Greek philosophy. God wills ordinary human flourishing, and a great part of what is reported in the Gospels consists in Christ making this possible for the people whose afflictions he heals. The call to renounce doesn't negate the value of flourishing; it is rather a call to centre everything on God, even if it be at the cost of forgoing this unsubstitutable good; and the fruit of this forgoing is that it become on one level the source of flourishing to others, and on another level, a collaboration with the restoration of a fuller flourishing by God. It is a mode of healing wounds and "repairing the world" (I am here borrowing the Hebrew phrase *tikkun olam*).

This means that flourishing and renunciation cannot simply be collapsed into each other to make a single goal, by as it were, pitching the renounced goods overboard as unnecessary ballast on the journey of life, in the manner of Stoicism. There remains a fundamental tension in Christianity. Flourishing is good, nevertheless seeking it is not our ultimate goal. But even where we renounce it, we re-affirm it, because we follow God's will in being a channel for it to others, and ultimately to all.

Can a similar, paradoxical relation be seen in Buddhism? I'm not sure, but Buddhism also has this notion that the renouncer is a source of compassion for those who suffer. There is an analogy between karuna and agape. And over the centuries in Buddhist civilization there developed, parallel with Christendom, a distinction of vocation between radical renouncers, and those who go on living within the forms of life aiming at ordinary flourishing, while trying to accumulate "merit" for a future life. (Of course, this distinction was radically "deconstructed" in the Protestant Reformation, with what fateful results for our story here we are all in some way aware, even though the task of tracing its connections to modern secularism is still very far from completed.)

Now the point of bringing out this distinction between human flourishing and goals which go beyond it is this. I would like to claim that the coming of modern secularity in my sense has been coterminous with the rise of a society in which for the first time in history a purely self-sufficient humanism came to be a widely available option. I mean by this a humanism accepting no final goals beyond human flourishing, nor any allegiance to anything else beyond this flourishing. Of no previous society was this true.

Although this humanism arose out of a religious tradition in which flourishing and the transcendent goal were distinguished and paradoxically related (and this was of some importance for our story), this doesn't mean that all previous societies projected a duality in this domain, as I have argued for Buddhism and Christianity. There were also outlooks, like Taoism seems to be, where flourishing was conceived in a unitary way, including reverence for the higher. But in these cases, this reverence, although essential for flourishing, couldn't be undertaken in a purely instrumental spirit. That is, it couldn't be *reverence* if it were so understood.

In other words, the general understanding of the human predicament before modernity placed us in an order where we were not at the top. Higher beings, like Gods or spirits, or a higher kind of being, like the Ideas or the cosmopolis of Gods and humans, demanded and deserved our worship, reverence, devotion or love. In some cases, this reverence or devotion was itself seen as integral to human flourishing; it was a proper part of the human good. Taoism is an example, as are such ancient philosophies as Platonism and Stoicism. In other cases, the devotion was called for even though it be at our expense, or conduce to our good only through winning the favour of a God. But even here the reverence called for was real. These beings commanded our awe. There was no question of treating them as we treat the forces of nature we harness for energy.

In this kind of case, we might speak of a humanism, but not of a self-sufficing or exclusive humanism, which is the contrast case which is at the heart of modern secularity.

This thesis, placing exclusive humanism only within modernity, may seem too bald and exceptionless to be true. And indeed, there are exceptions. By my account, ancient Epicureanism was a self-sufficing humanism. It admitted Gods, but denied them relevance to human life. My plea here is that one swallow doesn't make a summer. I'm talking about an age when self-sufficing humanism becomes a widely available option, which it never was in the ancient world, where only a small minority of the élite which was itself a minority espoused it.

I also don't want to claim that modern secularity is somehow coterminous with exclusive humanism. For one thing, the way I'm defining it, secularity is a condition in which our experience of and search for fullness occurs; and this is something we all share, believers and unbelievers alike. But also, it is not my intention to claim that exclusive humanisms offer the only alternatives to religion. Our age has seen a strong set of currents which one might call non-religious anti-humanisms, which fly under various names today, like "deconstruction" and "post-structuralism," and which find their roots in immensely influential writings of the nineteenth century, especially those of Nietzsche. At the same time, there are attempts to reconstruct a non-exclusive humanism on a non-religious basis, which one sees in various forms of deep ecology.

My claim will rather be something of this nature: secularity 3 came to be along with the possibility of exclusive humanism, which thus for the first time widened the range of possible options, ending the era of "naïve" religious faith. Exclusive humanism in a sense crept up on us through an intermediate form, Providential Deism; and both the Deism and the humanism were made possible by earlier developments within orthodox Christianity. Once this humanism is on the scene, the new plural, non-naïve predicament allows for multiplying the options beyond the original gamut. But the crucial transforming move in the process is the coming of exclusive humanism.

From this point of view, one could offer this one-line description of the difference between earlier times and the secular age: a secular age is one in which the eclipse of all goals beyond human flourishing becomes conceivable; or better, it falls within the range of an imaginable life for masses of people. This is the crucial link between secularity and a self-sufficing humanism.

So "religion" for our purposes can be defined in terms of "transcendence," but this latter term has to be understood in more than one dimension. Whether one believes in some agency or power transcending the immanent order is indeed, a crucial feature of "religion," as this has figured in secularization theories. It is our relation to a transcendent God which has been displaced at the centre of social life (secularity 1); it is faith in this God whose decline is tracked in these theories (secularity 2). But in order to understand better the phenomena we want to explain, we should see religion's relation to a "beyond" in three dimensions. And the crucial one, that which makes its impact on our lives understandable, is the one I have just been exploring: the sense that there is some good higher than, beyond human flourishing. In the Christian case, we could think of this as agape, the love which God has for us, and which we can partake of through his power. In other words, a possibility of transformation is offered, which takes us beyond merely human perfection. But of course, this notion of a higher good as attainable by us could only make sense in the context of belief in a higher power, the transcendent God of faith which appears in most definitions of religion. But then thirdly, the Christian story of our potential transformation by agape requires that we see our life as going beyond the bounds of its "natural" scope between birth and death; our lives extend beyond "this life."

For purposes of understanding the struggle, rivalry, or debate between religion and unbelief in our culture, we have to understand religion as combining these three dimensions of transcendence. This is not because there are not other possibilities which are being explored in our society, options somewhere between this triple transcendence perspective, and the total denial of religion. On the contrary, these options abound. It is rather because, in a way I shall explain many chapters down the road, the multi-cornered debate is shaped by the two extremes, transcendent religion, on one hand, and its frontal denial, on the other. It is perfectly legitimate to think that this is a misfortune about modern culture; but I would like to argue that it is a fact.

Acknowledgments

Haaris Naqvi, who dreamt up this wonderful project and brought it to me as a proposition—and something of a mission—deserves my first registration of gratitude, which I offer unreservedly and with delight. In this book collaboration, as in earlier ones, I am awed by his vision *and* his commitment to the details along the way that conjure such volumes into being, and then so splendidly. He is a maieutic editor of the first order.

Mary Al-Sayed, editorial assistant, and her team at Bloomsbury, have processed reams of source material, and pursued stacks of permissions—all for which I am duly grateful. Her precise execution of so many refined tasks is a marvel and a gift.

I am very thankful for the exceptionally astute anonymous readers for the press, who ratified the project and also provided substantive directives for making the volume more ambitious and useful to the general reader and academic researcher alike.

In my redoubt beyond the city, I have the pleasure of thanking those who have created engaging atmospheres in which to research and write; to learn as I teach—an alternation between the mandatory low hum of solitary industry and the enlivening din of collegial and scholarly discourse:

At Cornell University, conversations with Roger Stephen Gilbert, Chair of the Department of English, about Ammons, Cavell, Emerson, Stevens, among illustrious others, have afforded me a genuine advance in appreciating the relatedness of work by these figures, and no less and more broadly, of poetry and philosophy. Moreover, and more practically, he has enabled my residency as a Visiting Scholar in the department, a position that was the necessary condition for undertaking a project such as this—one that so explicitly and expansively depended on the libraries and academic resources of a major university research library and its community of committed scholars. More recently, Andrew Galloway, acting Chair, has sustained the welcome. Victoria Leccese Brevetti, Lynn Lauper, and Sarah Elizabeth Rice provided cheerful and informed coordination for my time in the department. I have benefited from memorable conversations with Kevin Attell, Tarleton Gillespie, Neil Hertz, Haym Hirsh, Karen Levy, Jamie Lloyd, Mark Morris, Masha Raskolnikov, J. P. Sniadecki, and Aoise Stratford; and at the Society for the Humanities, Timothy Murray, has recurrently offered a warm reception. Conversations with participants at The School of Criticism and Theory in recent years have stirred me to think and re-think the nature and scope of this volume: with special thanks to Branka Arsić, Simon Critchley, W. J. T. Mitchell, Hent de Vries, and David Wills.

Cornell Library staff at Olin, Uris, Fine Arts, and other locations, have been especially helpful in enabling my research by mining the vast resources of the university's collections. There was much digging, and to my delight, much finding. And when digging did not work, then borrowing—and it too was regularly revelatory.

Participants at the "Global/Emerson: Transmission, Translation, Transnational" symposium, held in the Department of English at Cornell in April 2016, conveyed their knowledge and enthusiasm for thinking anew about American Transcendentalism, and in the process created new ways of accounting for the circulation of texts and ideas; in retrospect, the event was an enactment of its own thesis.

During my time as Lecturer, and then as Visiting Assistant Professor in the Department of Philosophy at the State University of New York College at Cortland, Andrew Fitz-Gibbon, Chair, has sustained an atmosphere of authentic collegiality. His standard has been matched by Robert Earle, Nikolay Karkov, Mechthild Nagel, Elizabeth Purcell, and L. Sebastian Purcell, who together amplify the department as a collective dedicated to genuine philosophical investigations and pedagogical innovations. Joanna Tobias has been consistently attentive to the department's smooth functioning. Beyond the department, but still in Old Main, I have looked forward to conversations with Mary Schlarb, Director of International Programs.

Courses taught at Cortland have regularly activated new approaches to the content of this book. One particular instance may stand as representative of many others: in a seminar addressing James Miller's *Examined Lives*, we found ourselves noticing trends of the transcendental across time. Of course, that was not Miller's object, yet his work led us to these and other profitable observations.

While serving as Lecturer in the Department of Media Arts, Sciences, and Studies at the Roy H. Park School of Communications at Ithaca College, teaching in the Department of Cinema, Photography, and Media Arts, I benefitted from the advice and orientation offered by Virginia Mansfield-Richardson, Ben Rifkin, Bryan Roberts, Jill Loop, Elizabeth Nonas, and Steven Skopik. For making the operations run with aplomb, Barbara Terrell was essential. Teaching at Park, especially in the enduring and iconic team-taught "Film Aesthetics and Analysis," has been especially gratifying and enlightening; for good reason, my experience was enriched by Patricia R. Zimmermann, Matthew Holtmeier, Chelsea Wessels, and Jane Glaubman. Co-teaching "Fiction Film Theory" with Andrew Utterson proved, for me, to be a seamless and delightful symbiosis, and for Utterson's artful articulation of ideas, the course—despite being about fiction film—was especially fecund for thinking about the philosophical pertinence of cinema. Lectures invoking Bazin, Cavell, Deleuze, and Kracauer—not to mention Plato and Aristotle—among others, recurrently recommended the transcendental credentials of the medium.

At Ithaca College, beyond the Park School, I have enjoyed conversations with Michael Richardson, Interim Dean of the School of Humanities and Sciences and Tayna Saunders, Assistant Provost of International Programs and Extended Studies. And I have felt welcomed, time again, by Wade Pickren and Judith Ross-Bernstein at the Center for Faculty Excellence; their collegiality, along with their skill for facilitating constructive conversations about pedagogy and the contours of undergraduate education, remains a conspicuous sign of the college's endeavor to foster a community of inquirers.

The present volume is the seventh I have written or edited as a Writer-in-Residence in the Frederick Lewis Allen Room at the New York Public Library; an appointment to the Maurice Wertheim Study also proved fruitful during the last phase of the book's development. Though he retired during the completion of this volume, I am happy to recall how Jay Barksdale thoughtfully presided over the room, and made sure the conditions were ideal for research. More recently, his heirs, Carolyn Broomhead and Melanie Locay have ably taken up stewardship. Participation in the Manhattan Research Libraries Initiative permitted access to the resources of the Butler Library at Columbia University and the Bobst Library at New York University.

The Signet Society of Harvard College has provided, and continues to offer, a perennial venue for the circulating and testing of current projects in a climate of charged, shimmering intelligence. Members and associates, all beholden to Mark Hruby, as am I, gather to consider the shared endeavor underwritten by the credo *mousiken poiei kai ergazou*.

In Ricardo Miguel-Alfonso, with whom I worked as a coeditor on *A Power to Translate the World* during the development of this volume, I discovered a generous and incisive intellectual partner.

Reflections on what to include and why were elementally informed by conversations, classes, and other convivial engagements with the following teachers and scholars:

At Harvard: Stanley Cavell, the late Peter J. Gomes, David D. Hall, the late Gordon D. Kaufman, the late Helmut Koester, Kimberley C. Patton, Stephanie Paulsell, and Cornel West.

At Vanderbilt: J. M. Bernstein, Lenn E. Goodman, Michael P. Hodges, Gregg Horowitz, John Lachs, Henry Teloh, and David Wood.

At Berkeley: Anthony Cascardi, Frederick Dolan, G. R. F. Ferrari, Hannah Ginsborg, and Michael Mascuch.

At Buffalo: the late William Baumer, Kah Kyung Cho, the late Newton Garver, Jorge J. E. Gracia, the late Peter H. Hare, Carolyn Korsmeyer, James M. Lawler, and Barry Smith.

More recently, Ariella Azoulay, Richard Deming, Éamonn Dunne, Jeffrey Ehrenreich, Herwig Friedl, Robert Habich, David Mikics, and Rainer Wild, have sent me in new, very profitable directions, as have numerous anonymous readers of this manuscript in its range of incarnations—from first sketch to final proof.

I wish to thank those with whom I have shared meaningful reflections, and who have lent their generous support, during the composition of this book: Diana Allan, Jason and Catherine

Blumenkamp, Curtis Brown, Rebecca Brown, Samuel A. Chambers, Brunello Cucinelli, Paul Cronin, Jigme and Haven S. R. Daniels, William and Kate Day, Douglas Drake, Tarleton and Jenna Lahmann Gillespie, Adelaide Gomer, Julian Hibbard, John Opera, Joni Papp, Lawrence Rhu, Mario von der Ruhr, Kristen Steslow, Alessandro Subrizi, Andrew and Sarah Walston, and Mark and Alicia Wittink.

Our cosmically attuned Ruby and our interstellar Star make the days worthy of light and air, and put ground beneath my feet. Whence in this extensionless, galactic immensity did you arrive?

A classical realist, marking out her own philosophy of "realism without empiricism," I could not have managed to get my bearings on this project, or more generally in matters transcendental *and* terrestrial, without the ardent erudition of my brilliant wife, K. L. Evans.

Credits

Adams, Henry. "The Dynamo and the Virgin" from *The Education of Henry Adams*. Published by Houghton Mifflin Co., 1918.

Agamben, Giorgio and Juliana Schiesari. "The Thing Itself" from *SubStance* 16.2 (1987): 18–28. © 1987 by the Board of Regents of the University of Wisconsin System. Reproduced by the permission of the University of Wisconsin Press.

Alighieri, Dante. Cantos X and XI of *Paradiso* from *The Divine Comedy of Dante Alighieri*. Translated by Henry Wadsworth Longfellow. Published by George Routledge and Sons, 1867.

Aquinas, Thomas. "Of man who is composed of a spiritual and a corporeal substance: and in the first place, concerning what belongs to the essence of the soul" from *The Summa Theologica of St. Thomas Aquinas*. Part I: QQ LXXV-CII. Published by Burns Oates & Washbourne Ltd., 1922.

Aristotle. "Metaphysics" from *The Works of Aristotle*, Volume VIII. Translated by W. D. Ross. Published by Oxford University Press, 1928.

Aristotle. "Posterior Analytics" from *The Works of Aristotle*, Volume I. Translated by G. R. G. Mure. Published by Oxford University Press, 1928.

Arnold, Matthew. "Hebraism and Hellenism" from *Culture and Anarchy*. Published by Smith, Elder & Co., 1869.

Augustine of Hippo. Book VII from *Confessions*. Translated by E. B. Pusey. Published by Oxford J. Parker, 1876.

Badiou, Alain. "Univocity of Being and the Multiplicity of Names" (pp. 19–29) from *Deleuze: The Clamor of Being*. Translated by Louise Burchill. Published by University of Minnesota Press, 2000. Originally published in France in *Deleuze: La clameur de l'Etre*. Copyright © 1997 by Hachette Littératures. English translation copyright © 2000 by the Regents of the University of Minnesota.

Benedict of Norcia. From *The Rule of Our Most Holy Father St. Benedict, Patriarch of Monks*. Published by R. Washbourne, 1875.

Bergson, Henri. "Beyond the Noumenal" from *Key Writings*. Edited by Keith Ansell Pearson and John Mullarkey. Published by Continuum, 2002. Reprinted with permission.

Burke, Edmund. From *A Philosophical Enquiry into the Origin of Our Ideas of the Sublime and Beautiful*. Published by R. and J. Dodsley, 1757.

Carlyle, Thomas. "Pure Reason," "Symbols," and "Natural Supernaturalism" from *Sartor Resartus: The Life and Opinions of Herr Diogenes Teufelsdröckh*. Published in *Fraser's Magazine for Town and Country*, 1833–4.

Cavell, Stanley. "Emerson, Coleridge, Kant (Terms as Conditions)" from *In Quest of the Ordinary: Lines of Skepticism and Romanticism*. Published by The University of Chicago Press, 1988. Reprinted with permission of the author.

Channing, William Ellery. "Likeness to God" from Discourse at the Ordination of the Rev. F. A. Farley, Providence, RI, 1828. From *The People's Edition of the Entire Works of W.E. Channing, D.D.* Vol I. Published by Simms and McIntyre, 1843.

Coleridge, Samuel Taylor. "Dejection: An Ode". Published in the *Morning Post*, 1802.

Coleridge, Samuel Taylor. Chapter XII from *Biographia Literaria*. Published by Rest Fenner, 1817.

Davidson, Donald. "The Conditions of Thought" from *The Mind of Donald Davidson*. Edited by Johannes Brandl and Wolfgang L. Gombocz. Published by Koninklijke Brill NV, 1989. Reprinted with permission of the publisher.

de Staël, Germaine. "Kant" from *Germany*, Vol 2. Translated by O. W. Wight. Published by Houghton, Mifflin and Company, 1859.

Deleuze, Gilles. From *Difference and Repetition*. Translated by Paul Patton. Published by Columbia University Press. Copyright © 1994 Columbia University Press. Reprinted with permission of the publisher.

Deleuze, Gilles. From *The Logic of Sense*. Edited by Constantin V. Boundas. Translated by Mark Lester and Charles Stivale. Published by Columbia University Press. Copyright © 1993 Columbia University Press. Reprinted with permission of the publisher.

Derrida, Jacques. "Finis" from *Aporias*. Translated by Thomas Dutoit. Copyright © 1993 by the Board of Trustees of the Leland Stanford Jr. University. Published by Stanford University Press. All rights reserved. Used with the permission of Stanford University Press, www.sup.org.

Descartes, René. "Sixth Meditation: 'Of the Existence of Corporeal Things and of the Real Distinction Between the Mind and Body of Man'" from *The Philosophical Works of Descartes*. Translated by Elizabeth S. Haldane and G. R. T. Ross. Published by Cambridge University Press, 1911.

Deussen, Paul. From *Outlines of Indian Philosophy, with an Appendix on the Philosophy of the Vedânta in its Relations to Occidental Metaphysics*. Published by Karl Curtius, 1907.

Dewey, John. "The Individual and the World" from *Democracy and Education*. Published by The Macmillan Company, 1916.

Dickinson, Emily. From *Poems by Emily Dickinson*. Edited by Mabel Loomis Todd and T. W. Higginson. Published by Roberts Brothers, 1891.

Dostoevsky, Fyodor. "The Grand Inquisitor" from *The Brothers Karamazov*. Translated by Constance Garnett. Published by The Macmillan Company, 1912.

Emerson, Ralph Waldo. "The Transcendentalist" from *Nature; Addresses, and Lectures*. Published by James Munroe and Company, 1849.

Fichte, Johann Gottlieb. "Mysticism as a Phenomenon of the Third Age" from *Characteristics of the Present Age*. Translated by William Smith. Published by John Chapman, 1847.

Foucault, Michel. "What is Enlightenment?" from *The Foucault Reader*. Translation copyright © 1984 by Random House, Inc. Copyright © as an unpublished work, 1984, by Michel Foucault and Paul Rabinow. Used by permission of Pantheon Books, an imprint of the Knopf Doubleday Publishing Group, a division of Random House LLC. All rights reserved.

Freud, Sigmund. From *The Interpretation of Dreams*. Translated by A. A. Brill. Published by The Macmillan Company, 1913.

Fuller, Margaret. "Swedenborg, Fourier, and Goethe" from *Woman in the Nineteenth Century*. Published by Greeley & McElrath, 1845.

Hegel, Georg Wilhelm Friedrich. "Freedom of Self-Consciousness: Stoicism, Skepticism, and the Unhappy Consciousness" from *Phenomenology of Spirit*. Translated by J.B. Baillie. Published by Swan Sonneschien & Co., 1910.

Heidegger, Martin. "The Limitation of Being" from *An Introduction to Metaphysics*. Translated by Ralph Manheim. Copyright © 1974 Yale University Press. Reprinted with permission of the publisher.

Herbert, George. "The Altar," "The Agonie," "Sinne (I)," "Affliction (I)," "The Quidditie," "The Starre," "Vanitie (I)," "Mortification," "Miserie," and "Death" from *The Temple, Sacred Poems and Private Ejaculations*. Published by T. Buck and R. Daniel, 1633.

Herder, Johann Gottfried von. "Dialogue I" from *The Spirit of Hebrew Poetry*. Translated by James Marsh. Published by E. Smith, 1833.

Hopkins, Gerard Manley. "Nondum" "The Starlight Night" "The Lantern Out of Doors" "Thee, God, I come from" and "The Leaden Echo and the Golden Echo" from *The Poems of Gerard Manley Hopkins*, Fourth Edition. Revised and Edited by W. H. Gardner and N. H. MacKinzie, 1970. By permission of Oxford University Press (www.oup.com) on behalf of the British Province of The Society of Jesus.

Husserl, Edmund. From *The Crisis of European Sciences and Transcendental Phenomenology*. Translated by David Carr. Published by Northwestern University Press, 1970. Originally published in German under the title *Die Krisis der europäischen Wissenschaften und die transzendentale Phänomenologie: Eine Einleitung*

Pater, Walter. "Coleridge" from *Appreciations*. Published by Macmillan and Co., 1901.

Peirce, Charles Sanders. "The Law of Mind" from *The Monist*, Vol. II, No. 4. Published by Open Court Publishing Company, 1892.

Plato. "Phaedo" from *The Dialogues of Plato Translated into English with Analyses and Introductions*, Volume I. 4th Ed. Translated by B. Jowett. Published by Oxford University Press, 1871.

Plato. "Phaedrus" and "Parmenides" from *The Dialogues of Plato Translated into English with Analyses and Introductions*, Volume III. 4th Ed. Translated by B. Jowett. Published by Oxford University Press, 1871.

Plotinus. "The Third Tractate" from *The Enneads*. Translated by Stephen MacKenna and B. S. Page. Published by P. L. Warner (publisher to the Medici Society), 1917–1930.

Proust, Marcel. From *Swann's Way*. Translated by C. K. Scott Moncrieff and Terence Kilmartin. Published by Henry Holt and Company, 1922.

Rancière, Jacques. "The Janus-Face of Politicized Art" from *The Politics of Aesthetics*. Translated by Gabriel Rockhill. Published by Continuum, 2004. Reprinted with permission.

Reed, Sampson. From *Observations on the Growth of the Mind,* fifth edition. Published by T. H. Carter and Company, 1865.

Rorty, Richard. "Is Derrida a Quasi-Transcendental Philosopher?" From *Contemporary Literature* 36.1 (1995): 178–187. Copyright © 1995 by the Board of Regents of the University of Wisconsin System. Reproduced by the permission of the University of Wisconsin Press.

Rosenzweig, Franz. *From Understanding the Sick and Healthy*. Translated by Nahum Glatzer. Published by Noonday Press, 1953. Reprinted by permission of The Estate of Nahum N. Glatzer.

Royce, Josiah. "The Fourth Conception of Being" form *The World and the Individual*. Published by The Macmillan Company, 1900.

Russell, Bertrand. From *Mysticism and Logic and Other Essays*. Published by George Allen & Unwin Ltd., 1917.

Santayana, George. "Some Authorities for this Conclusion" from *Skepticism and Animal Faith*. Published by Dover Publications, Inc., 1955.

Schleiermacher, Friedrich Daniel Ernst. "First Section" and "Second Section" from *The Christian Faith*. Published by T&T Clark Ltd, a Continuum Imprint, 1999. Reprinted with permission.

Schopenhauer, Arthur. "The Failure of Philosophy: A Brief Dialogue" and "The Vanity of Existence" from *Essays of Arthur Schopenhauer*. Translated by T. Bailey Saunders. Published by A. L. Burt Company, 1893.

Schopenhauer, Arthur. "The World as Idea, First Aspect" from *The World as Will and Idea, Vol. I*. Translated by R. B. Haldane and J. Kemp. Published by Kegan Paul, Trench, Trübner & Co., 1909.

Scotus, John Duns. "Concerning Metaphysics, the Science of the Transcendental" from John Duns Scotus, *Philosophical Writings: A Selection, 2nd Edition*. Translated by Allan B. Wolter. Copyright © 1987 Hackett Publishing Company. Reprinted with permission from the publisher.

Shakespeare, William. Seven Soliloquies from *The Tragedy of Hamlet, Prince of Denmark*. Published by N. L. and John Trundell, 1603.

Spengler, Oswald. From *The Decline of the West: Form and Actuality*. Translated by Charles Francis Atkinson. Published by Alfred A. Knopf, 1926.

Spinoza, Baruch. "Concerning God" from Part I and "On the Nature and Origin of the Mind" from Part II of *The Ethics*. Translated by R. H. M. Elwes. Published by Henry G. Bohn, 1883.

Spivak, Gayatri Chakravorty. "Philosophy" from *A Critique of Postcolonial Reason: Toward a History of the Vanishing Present*. Published by Harvard University Press (Cambridge, Mass.). Copyright © 1999 by the President and Fellows of Harvard College.

"Svetasvatara Upanishad" from *The Sacred Books of the East*. Translated by Max Müller. Published by Oxford University Press, 1879–1910.

Swami Vivekananda. "The Absolute and Manifestation" from *Vedanta Philosophy: Lectures by the Swami Vivekananda on Jnana Yoga*. Published by The Vedanta Society, 1902.

Taylor, Charles. From *A Secular Age*. Published by The Belknap Press of Harvard University Press (Cambridge, Mass.). Copyright © 2007 by Charles Taylor.

Thoreau, Henry David. "Higher Laws" from *Walden: or, Life in the Woods*. Published by Ticknor and Fields, 1854.

Thoreau, Henry David. From *The Journal 1837-1861*, edited by Damon Searls. Published in *The New York Review of Books*, 2009. Reprinted with permission.

Tillich, Paul. *From the Dynamics of Faith*. Copyright © 1957 by Paul Tillich. Renewed © 1985 by Hannah Tillich. Reprinted by permission of HarperCollins Publishers.

Tolstoy, Leo. "Reason and Religion" from *The Complete Works of Count Tolstoy*, Vol. XX. Translated by Leo Weiner. Published by Dana Estes & Company, 1905.

Vimalakirti. "Beyond Comprehension" from *The Vimalakirti Sutra*. Translated by Burton Watson. Copyright © 2000 Columbia University Press. Reprinted with permission of the publisher.

Weil, Simone. "The Love of God and Affliction" from *Simone Weil: On Science, Necessity, and the Love of God*. Translated by Richard Rees. Originally published by Oxford University Press, 1968. Reprinted by permission of Peters Fraser & Dunlop (www.petersfraserdunlop.com) on behalf of the Estate of Richard Rees.

Williams, Bernard. "Wittgenstein and Idealism" from *Moral Luck: Philosophical Papers 1973-1980*. Copyright © 1993 Cambridge University Press. Reprinted with the permission of Cambridge University Press.

Winckelmann, Johann Joachim. "On the Grace in Works of Art" from *Reflections on the Painting and Sculpture of the Greeks*. Translated and published by Henry Fuseli, 1765.

Wittgenstein, Ludwig. From *Notebooks 1914-1916*. Translated by G. E. M. Anscombe. Edited by G. H. Von Wright and G. E. M. Anscombe. Published by Harper & Brothers, 1961.

Wordsworth, William. [Intimations of Sublimity] and "Imagination, How Impaired and Restored" from *The Prelude; or, Growth of a Poet's Mind. An Autobiographical Poem*. Published by D. Appleton & Company, 1850.

Wordsworth, William. "Ode: Intimations of Immortality from Recollections of Early Childhood" from *Poems, in Two Volumes*. Published by Longman, Hurst, Rees, and Orme, 1807.

Žižek, Slavoj. "Not Only as *Substance*, But Also as *Subject*" from *The Sublime Object of Ideology*. Published by Verso Books, 1989. Reprinted with permission of the publisher.